P9-BJM-702

DP
203
C3
1982

Date Due

OXFORD HISTORY OF
MODERN EUROPE

General Editors
ALAN BULLOCK *and* F. W. D. DEAKIN

Oxford History of Modern Europe

THE STRUGGLE FOR MASTERY IN EUROPE, 1848–1918
BY A. J. P. TAYLOR

THE RUSSIAN EMPIRE, 1801–1917
BY HUGH SETON-WATSON

FRANCE, 1848–1945
BY THEODORE ZELDIN *Available in paperback in five volumes*:
AMBITION AND LOVE
POLITICS AND ANGER
INTELLECT AND PRIDE
TASTE AND CORRUPTION
ANXIETY AND HYPOCRISY

GERMANY 1866–1945
BY GORDON A. CRAIG *Available in paperback*

THE LOW COUNTRIES 1780–1940
BY E. H. KOSSMANN

SPAIN

1808–1975

BY

RAYMOND CARR
WARDEN OF ST. ANTONY'S COLLEGE,
OXFORD

SECOND EDITION

CLARENDON PRESS · OXFORD
1982

Oxford University Press, Walton Street, Oxford OX2 6DP

London Glasgow New York Toronto
Delhi Bombay Calcutta Madras Karachi
Kuala Lumpur Singapore Hong Kong Tokyo
Nairobi Dar es Salaam Cape Town
Melbourne Auckland

and associate companies in
Beirut Berlin Ibadan Mexico City

Published in the United States by
Oxford University Press, New York

© *Oxford University Press 1966, 1982*

All rights reserved. No part of this publication may be reproduced, stored in a retrieval system, or transmitted, in any form or by any means, electronic, mechanical, photocopying, recording, or otherwise, without the prior permission of Oxford University Press

First published 1966
Reprinted (with corrections) 1970, 1975
Second Edition 1982

British Library Cataloguing in Publication Data
Carr, Raymond
Spain 1808–1975.—2nd ed.—(Oxford history of modern Europe)
1. Spain—History—19th century 2. Spain—History—20th century
1. Title
946'.07 DP203

ISBN 0-19-822127-4
ISBN 0-19-822128-2 paperback

Library of Congress Cataloging in Publication Data
Carr, Raymond.
Spain, 1808–1975.
(Oxford History of modern Europe)
Rev. ed. of: Spain, 1808–1939. 1966.
Bibliography: p.
Includes index.
1. Spain—History—19th century. 2. Spain—History—20th century. 1. Title. II. Series.
DP203.C3 1982 946.08 81-21708
ISBN 0-19-822128-2 (pbk.) AACR2
ISBN 0-19-822127-4

Printed in Great Britain
at the University Press, Oxford
by Eric Buckley
Printer to the University

PREFACE TO THE SECOND EDITION

SINCE this book was written in 1966 there has been a revolution in Spanish historiography. Once regarded as an ill-conceived essay in liberalism the more modern history of Spain was a neglected, even dangerous field, unexplored except by a handful of brave men of whom my lamented friend Jaime Vicens Vives was one. It has now come into its own. The title of Professor Artola's book *Orígenes de la España contemporánea*, published in 1959, now reflects a central concern that has sustained a growth industry.

The contributions of Spanish scholars to the history of modern Spain has been outstanding and has enriched my own understanding of Spanish history. I would like to acknowledge my own debt to their achievements. Since I have not altered the main text, this acknowledgement can only take the form of an expanded bibliography. A comparison with the original bibliography highlights the progress that has been made, particularly in the field of economic history.

In this edition I have added chapters that bring the story up to the death of General Franco. They owe much to the collaboration of Professor J. P. Fusi contained in our *España: De la dictadura a la democrácia* (Editorial Planeta, Barcelona, 1979).

The bibliographical references in these new chapters are not incorporated in the bibliographical index, but full details are contained in the footnotes.

R. C.

PREFACE TO THE FIRST EDITION

In venturing into what is, in terms of modern historical scholarship, largely an unmapped region, the author is very conscious both of his great debt to those few great scholars who have depicted some features of the landscape and of the immensity of the unexplored. The economy of Spanish historiography of the modern period is in an acute state of imbalance which is, no doubt, reflected in this book. Thus, if the author has exaggerated the role of Catalonia, this is partly because Catalan historians have examined their past with greater care than the historians of some other regions. Much fundamental work remains to be done and ignorance has sometimes encouraged a surrogate for scholarship—large-scale generalizations on the nature of Spain and Spanishness. More would be achieved by patient investigation of those features of Spain's political and economic underdevelopment which she shares with other societies. Thus there was nothing unique, for example, in the gap between improvers' schemes and farming practices in the later eighteenth century. What was unusual was the relative failure of the land in the nineteenth century outside the productive periphery. Yet even this regional contrast of prosperity and stagnation, which provides a key to the modern history of Spain, is a characteristic shared by other developing countries.

Any historian who endeavours to write on a long period of time must be aware of imperfections and inequalities of treatment, of departures from an ideal balance. No doubt many will find the general proportions eccentric and ill conceived; these inevitably depend on the author's own knowledge and interests however much he may have strived to treat what is important in its own right.

An attempt has been made to combine social history and political history—often at the cost of coherent narrative and to the almost complete exclusion of foreign affairs. The heart of the book is in the middle and it is weak at both extremities where the reader will find less evidence of what is often called original research. As it approaches modern times, politics are treated in greater detail and have tended to oust the description of society;

this in part derives from the peculiar nature of the sources, in part from the conjecture that the fundamental failure was a political failure. Some day I hope that I may be able to construct a more rounded picture of this later period, full of problems as it is.

To ease the understanding of the narrative a chronological table has been added. The bibliography is highly selective and the true bibliography is in the footnotes, since much is mined from sources which the author of a general history might have hoped to find exploited by his predecessors. Where it is appropriate brief biographical details are included in the index.

The Spanish edition of this work contains certain additions, many of them for the period after 1898. For much of this supplementary material I am indebted to Joaquín Romero Maura.

I must express gratitude not only to those Spanish scholars who have guided me (in particular to the late Jaime Vicens Vives from whose investigations much of the statistical appendices are derived) but for the help unstintingly given by Dr. Alistair Hennessy, Dr. Eric Christiansen, Dr. J. M. Houston, Mr. Burnett Bolloten, Señor Juan Martínez Alier, Mr. Richard Robinson, Mr. Hugh Thomas, and Mr. Malcolm Deas. Both the Master of St. Catherine's College and Mr. F. W. D. Deakin have given me invaluable editorial counsel, and Professor Robin Humphreys read some of the sections on Latin America. Acknowledgement of aid is accompanied by the customary disclaimer of any responsibility, on the part of those who gave it, for faults in the present text.

My deepest debt is to St. Antony's College. For many years, long before it honoured me with a Fellowship, both its Warden and its members supported and encouraged my work. On a long haul such support was a necessity and it was given without the asking.

R. C.

CONTENTS

ABBREVIATIONS

A.E.	*Anuario estadístico.*
A.N.	Archives nationaux: French Foreign Office Archives. *Correspondance politique, Espagne.*
B.A.E.	*Biblioteca de autores españoles* (Rivadeneira collection and its continuation by the Spanish Royal Academy).
D. Ec.	*De economía.*
D.S.C.	*Diario de las sesiones del Congreso de Diputados.*
E.H.M.	*Estudios de historia moderna.*
E.G.	*Estudios geográficos.*
Es. In.	*Escritos inéditos* of author concerned.
F.O.	Public Record Office, Foreign Office Papers.
H.A.H.R.	*Hispanic American Historical Review.*
I.R.S.	The reports and statistics published by the Instituto de Reformas Sociales.
O.C.	*Obras completas* of the author concerned.
O.S.	*Obras selectas* of the author concerned.
P.P.	*Parliamentary Papers* (Commercial and Consular Reports).
R.C.	*Rapports consulaires* (printed reports of the French Consuls in Spain).
R.E.P.	*Revista de estudios políticos.*
R. Ec. P.	*Revista de economía política.*
R. Est. Ec.	*Revista de estudios económicos.*
R.H.	*Révue hispanique.*
St. Antony's MSS.	Reports of Seminar on the Spanish Civil War, St. Antony's College, Oxford.
Vaughan MSS.	Vaughan Manuscripts, All Souls College, Oxford.

Periodicals and manuscript sources cited rarely are given in full.

The first reference to other works gives the author, full title, and place and date of publication. Thereafter reference is made to the author and a short title, except in the case of newspapers. First citations can be discovered by reference to the Index.

NOTE ON PLACE NAMES AND PROPER NAMES

1. *Place names.* Some Spanish place names have been anglicized, e.g.:

Andalucía	—	Andalusia
Cataluña	—	Catalonia
Castilla	—	Castile
La Coruña	—	Corunna
Extremadura	—	Estremadura
Mallorca	—	Majorca
Navarra	—	Navarre
Sevilla	—	Seville
Vizcaya	—	Biscay
Zaragoza	—	Saragossa

Accents have been omitted in the text where English usage demands, e.g. Cádiz, Córdoba, León, Málaga, San Sebastián.

2. *Proper names.* The Spanish usage is clearly explained in S. de Madariaga, *Spain* (1942 ed.), Appendix V. The maternal name has been usually omitted, except where necessary to avoid confusion. Those forms of name are used which are customary in historical literature, e.g. Marcelino Domingo and Santiago Alba but not Miguel Azaña or Antonio Cánovas del Castillo, Ortega y Gasset but not Unamuno Jugo.

CHRONOLOGICAL TABLE

THE COLLAPSE OF THE *ANCIEN RÉGIME*, THE FRENCH INVASION, AND THE CORTES OF CADIZ 1808–1814

1807	
December	Napoleon gives orders for the military occupation of Spain.
1808	
18–19 March	*Motín de la Granja*: abdication of Charles IV, fall of Godoy, accession of Ferdinand VII.
10 April	Ferdinand VII leaves Madrid to meet Napoleon.
2 May	Popular rising at Madrid against Murat.
5 May	Charles IV and Ferdinand VII resign the Crown to Napoleon at Bayonne; insurrection spreads in Spain.
21 July	Castaños captures Dupont's Army at Bailén.
1 August	Joseph I leaves Madrid.
4 December	Madrid surrenders to French.
1809	
22 May	Central Junta proposes a Cortes.
27–28 July	Battle of Talavera.
19 November	Soult defeats the Junta's army at Ocaña.
1810	
January–February	Joseph I conquers Andalusia. Central Junta flees from Seville to Cadiz.
19 April	The *cabildo abierto* of Caracas deposes the captain-general and establishes a Provisional Junta on behalf of Ferdinand VII.
25 May	Establishment of the Provisional Junta of the Provinces of the River Plate.
16 September	Hidalgo's revolt in Mexico: defines his aim 'The proclamation of the liberty and independence of the Mexican nation'. Defeated January 1811.
24 September	Cortes meets at la Isla de Léon.
1811	
5 July	Congress of delegates from captaincy general of Venezuela declares independence from Spain.

1812	
19 March	Constitution of Cadiz issued: the 'liberal codex'.
22 July	Wellington defeats Marmont at Salamanca. Joseph retires from Madrid.
1813	
21 June	Vitoria. The French withdraw from Spain.

ABSOLUTISM RESTORED: FERDINAND VII 1814–1820

1814	
24 March	Ferdinand VII, *El Deseado*, returns to Spain.
22 April	Address of the sixty-nine 'Persian' deputies against the Constitution of 1812 proposing a return to the 'traditional' Cortes.
4 May	Ferdinand VII repudiates the Constitution of 1812.
10 May	Arrest of the liberal leaders in Madrid.
1815	
11 May	General Morillo enters Caracas and by 1816 has re-established Spanish authority in Venezuela and New Granada.
September	Porlier's unsuccessful pronunciamiento at Corunna.
1817	
January	San Martín starts the invasion of Chile.
April	General Lacy's conspiracy broken.
1818	
April	Battle of Maipú and defeat of the Spanish royalist forces in Chile.
1819	
July	La Bisbal and Sarsfield break the first Cadiz conspiracy.

THE REVOLUTION AND THE 'THREE YEARS' OF THE CONSTITUTION. 1820–1823

1820	
1 January	Riego and Quintana pronounce for the Constitution of 1812.
7 March	Ferdinand accepts the Constitution and appoints the ministry of the 'jail birds'.
9 July	Cortes assemble.
31 August	Riego's 'triumphal' entry to Madrid.

1821

24 February	Iturbide's 'Plan of Iguala' for an independent, monarchical Mexico.
March	Bardaxí ministry.
September	Provincial revolt against the ministry and the 'Battle of Las Platerías' in Madrid (18 September).
8 September	San Martín lands at Pisco, Peru, and declares against Spain and the 1820 constitution as 'a fraudulent attempt to conserve a colonial system'.

1822

28 February	Martínez de la Rosa's ministry of conservative liberals; its programme of constitutional reform defeated by Guards Rebellion of 7 July.
August	Ministry of Evaristo San Miguel (i.e. military radicals).
November	Establishment of royalist Regency at Seo de Urgel; driven into France by Mina.

1823

7 April	French invasion. 'The hundred thousand sons of St. Louis' under Angoulême.
1 October	Ferdinand restored to full power: all legislation 1820–3 annulled.

THE OMINOUS DECADE. 1823–1833

1823

December	Caso Irujo ministry with de la Cruz (War) and Ballesteros (Finance).

1827

September	'Revolt of the Aggrieved' in Catalonia.

1829

December	Marriage of Ferdinand VII and María Cristina of Naples.

1830

July	Revolution in France and the abortive pronunciamientos of Mina and Torrijos (October 1830 and January 1831).
10 October	Birth of the Infanta Isabella (later Isabella II).

1832

September	'The Events of La Granja': revocation of the Pragmatic Sanction. Temporary victory of Don Carlos.

1 October	Victory of the *cristino* party and appointment of Cea Bermúdez's ministry.

1833

29 September	Death of Ferdinand VII.

THE CIVIL WAR: CARLISM AND LIBERALISM 1833–1840

1833

October	Carlist rebellion against Isabella II begins in north.

1834

15 January	Martínez de la Rosa takes office.
10 April	Royal Statute issued; an essay in a non-radical constitutional settlement.
22 April	Quadruple alliance signed at London.
11 July	Don Carlos appoints Zumalacárregui as C.-in-C. of Carlist forces in north.
16–18 July	Cholera riots and monk murders at Madrid.
25 December	All liberals amnestied, i.e. return of *exaltado* radicals.

1835

9 June	Toreno succeeds Martínez de la Rosa as Prime Minister.
June	First siege of Bilbao and death of Zumalacárregui.
3 July	Córdova appointed C.-in-C. Army of the North and wins the victory of Mendigorría (15 July).
25–27 July	Riots in Barcelona: General Bassa murdered.
August	Wave of radical pronunciamientos in the south.
14 September	Mendízabal called to power: in October orders a quinta of 100,000 men.

1836

15 May	Istúriz succeeds Mendízabal.
July–August	Series of provincial rebellions against Istúriz.
13 August	Sergeants' Mutiny of La Granja: Regent decrees Constitution of 1812, i.e. a return to radical constitutionalism.
15 August	Quesada murdered at Madrid: Calatrava and Mendizábal (Finance) succeed Istúriz.

1837

28 June	Constitution of 1837 promulgated; a modified radical constitutional settlement.

June–August	Series of mutinies on the northern front; murders of Generals Escalera and Sarsfield.
14–17 August	Strike of Espartero's Guards Officers at Aravaca; Calartava government resigns.
May–September	Don Carlos's Royal Expedition; the last great Carlist effort (reaches Madrid 12 September).

1838

January	Cabrera takes Morella.
November	Generals Córdova and Narváez involved in Seville pronunciamiento: Muñagorri active in north for a 'moderate' peace settlement.

1839

17 February	Maroto shoots his enemies at Estella; Carlism disintegrates.
April	Espartero and Maroto begin negotiations.
31 August	Treaty of Vergara: end of war in the north.
2 September	Progressive Cortes opened: dissolved 31 October: Alaix (Espartero's representative) leaves the government.

1840

May–July	Espartero defeats Cabrera; end of Eastern Carlism.
4 June	Moderate Cortes passes the Municipal Law (i.e. challenges Progressive radicals).
July	Espartero and queen regent meet in Barcelona (i.e. Radicals challenged Moderates and Court).
1 Sepember	Madrid pronounces against María Cristina; Espartero takes office and queen regent abdicates 12 October.

THE REGENCY OF ESPARTERO. 1841–1843

1841

9 May	Espartero proclaimed Sole Regent and appoints the González ministry.
2–7 October	'Moderate' revolt against Espartero; O'Donnell pronounces against Espartero at Pamplona; Léon and Concha's attempt on the Palace at Madrid.
26 October	Basque *Fueros* suppressed.

1842

May	Anti-government coalition of Progressives formed.
20 June	General Rodil takes office.
15 November	Barcelona pronounces against Espartero; bombarded on 3 December.

1843	
10 May	López takes office with General Serrano as War Minister, quarrels with Espartero and resigns.
27 May	Colonels Prim and Milans del Bosch pronounce at Reus.
11–12 June	Pronunciamientos of Moderates and anti-Espartero Progressives at Seville, Valencia, and Barcelona.
27 June	Narváez and his allies land at Valencia and set up a provisional government under López and Serrano.
22 July	Seoane's army joins Narváez at Torrejón de Ardoz.
30 July	Espartero embarks on H.M.S. *Malabar* at Cadiz.
2 September	The Centralists gain control of Barcelona, which surrenders to Prim after bombardment (13 November).

THE COLLAPSE OF THE PROGRESSIVES AND THE HEGEMONY OF THE MODERATES. 1843–1854

1843	
25–28 November	Olózaga's Progressive coalition ministry; followed by González Bravo, i.e. elimination of Progressives by the Court.
1844	
January–March	Centralist pronunciamientos at Alicante, Valencia, and Cartagena.
4 May–13 February 1846	Narváez appointed Premier and War Minister with Mon at the Treasury.
November	Zurbano's abortive pronunciamiento.
1845	
24 May	The Moderate's Constitution issued.
19–20 August	Tax riots at Madrid.
1846	
2 April	Galician pronunciamiento at Lugo.
17 March–4 April	Narváez second ministry; followed by a period of acute ministerial instability during marriage negotiations.
18 October	Isabella II marries Francisco de Asis, Duke of Cadiz, and the Infanta Luisa marries the Duke of Montpensier.
1847	
4 October	Narváez returns to power, with Sartorius as Minister of the Interior.

1848	
1 March	Narváez voted emergency powers by Cortes.
26 March	Abortive civilian rising in Madrid.
7 May	Mutiny of España Regiment in Madrid.
23 June	Cabrera re-enters Spain; recrudescence of Carlism in Catalonia: expelled by Concha April–May 1849.
1851	
14 January	Bravo Murillo takes office.
16 March	Concordat with Rome signed.
1852	
May	League of generals and politicians formed against Bravo Murillo's proposed 'authoritarian' constitutional reform.
1853	
March	Government attacked for railway concessions to Salamanca.
19 September	Count of San Luis takes office.
9 December	Government Railway Bill defeated in the Senate.
1854	
13 January	Opposition generals protest against the Government and are exiled.

THE REVOLUTION OF 1854 AND THE 'BIENIO' 1854–1856

1854	
28 June	Generals Dulce and O'Donnell pronounce: indecisive engagement with government forces at Vicálvaro (30 June) O'Donnell appeals to the country with Manzanares proclamation (6 July).
17–19 July	Madrid rises: San Luis succeeded by the Duke of Rivas, who is followed by his War Minister F. Fernández de Córdova: General San Miguel takes control and revolution in hands of Progressives. Espartero accepted as Prime Minister by the Queen.
29 July	Espartero and O'Donnell enter Madrid: O'Donnell succeeds San Miguel as War Minister, i.e. coalition of Progressives and moderate Liberals and the exclusion of Democrats.
17 September	Manifesto of the Liberal Union issued.
8 November	Constituent Cortes opened.

1855	
28 April	The Queen refuses consent to the bill for ecclesiastical disentailment.
1856	
June	Bread riots in Old Castile.
13 July	Cabinet crisis; O'Donnell succeeds Espartero, and (15–17 July) wins Madrid from the National Guards with Regulars. Defeat of Progressives and Democrats.
15 August	National Militia dissolved.

THE ERA OF THE LIBERAL UNION AND THE FALL OF THE BOURBON MONARCHY. 1856–1868

1858	
30 June	O'Donnell's long ministry with Posada Herrera as Minister of Interior.
1 October	Progressives split over whether to support O'Donnell.
1859	
28 November	O'Donnell lands at Ceuta: Moroccan war.
1860	
1 April	Ortega's Carlist pronunciamiento at San Carlos de la Rápita.
1861	
28 June	Pérez de Alamo's rural rising at La Loja.
1862	
9 April	Conference of Orizava: end of Spanish intervention in Mexico.
1863	
2 March	Miraflores ministry; attempt to bring Progressives into politics fails with *retraimiento* (8 September); Miraflores resigns January 1864.
1865	
10 April	Night of St. Daniel: student demonstration suppressed.
June	Prim's pronunciamiento; first of a series of revolts against the Government.
11 June	O'Donnell's last ministry.
24 July	Recognition of Kingdom of Italy agreed to by Cabinet.

1866	
22 June	Mutiny of San Gil suppressed in Madrid.
10 July	O'Donnell succeeded by Narváez with González Bravo. Return to 'strong' government.
16 August	Congress at Ostend; negotiations for revolutionary alliance between the Progressives and the Democrats.
1868	
20 April	Death of Narváez: second ministry of González Bravo.
7 July	Generals Serrano, Zavala, Córdova arrested and exiled: Unionist–Progressive alliance against government sealed, i.e. the exclusion of the Democrats.
18 September	Admiral Topete pronounces at Cadiz; joined by Prim and Serrano.
30 September	Isabella II leaves Spain.
1868	
October	Beginning of the Cuban insurrection: formation of Republican party; local risings on dissolution of Juntas.
1869	
June	Constitution of 1869; Serrano Regent with Prim as Prime Minister; Republican revolts.
1870	
16 November	Amadeo of Savoy elected King of Spain: 'Constitutional monarchy' with ministries of O'Donnell's Unionists, Sagasta's Progressives, or Ruiz Zorilla's Radicals.
27 December	Assassination of General Prim.
1872	
2 May	Don Carlos crosses frontier. Fails to start Carlist war.
1873	Resignation of Serrano leaves dynasty 'captive' to Radicals whose demands in army issue lead to abdication of Amadeo (11 February 1873).
	THE REPUBLIC OF 1873
	Presidents: Figueras (February–24 April); Pi y Margall (24 April–July); Salmerón (18 July–6 September); Castelar (6 September–December).
	Revival of Carlism and military successes in north: 27 June, General Concha killed at Abarzuza.
July	Cantonalist (i.e. extremist Federal Republican) risings in Alcoy, Cartegena, and Andalusia.

1874	
January	General Pavía's pronunciamiento against a left Republic; Conservative government under Serrano.
29 December	Pronunciamiento of General Martínez Campos proclaiming Alfonso XII as King of Spain.

RESTORATION MONARCHY. 1875–1923

(i) ALFONSO XII (January 1875–November 1885)

(The main ministries are given in footnote, pp. 356–7. Until 1897 most Conservative ministries were headed by Cánovas and the Liberal ministries by Sagasta.)

1876	
30 June	Promulgation of the Constitution of 1876 (remained in force until September 1923).
1878	
10 February	Peace of Zanjón; end of Cuban war.
1880	
23 May	Foundation of Fusionist party which became Sagasta's Liberal party: it assumes office 10 February 1881.
1885	
25 November	Death of Alfonso XII.

(ii) REGENCY OF MARÍA CRISTINA

1885	
27 November	Sagasta invited to form a government: the 'long ministry' enacts the 'liberal conquests' and the Law of Universal Suffrage (5 May 1890).
1890	Return of Cánovas; the Liberal–Conservative party begins to split; Romero Robledo's feud with Silvela; Silvela's 'dissidence' (6 December 1892).
1893	
3 June	Maura's projected reform of the Cuban administration.
September	Terrorist bomb throwings in Barcelona.
1895	
24 February	Martí lands in Cuba; beginning of the War of Secession.
1896	
10 February	Weyler succeeds Martínez Campos as Captain-General of Cuba; drastic military measures against rebels.

1897	
8 August	Assassination of Cánovas.
4 October	Sagasta's government; concedes autonomy to Cuba but fails to prevent U.S. intervention.
1898	
April	U.S. declares war on Spain; destruction of Spanish fleet in Santiago (3 July).
10 December	Treaty of Paris by which Spain lost Cuba, Puerto Rica, and the Philippines.
1899	
3 March	Silvela's first ministry including Polavieja and Durán y Bas as ministers. First attempt at Conservative 'regeneration'.

(iii) Alfonso XIII

December 1902 to June 1905	Conservative ministries of Silvela, Villaverde, and Maura.
June 1905 to December 1906	Liberal governments of Montero Ríos and Moret. Law of Jurisdictions provokes conflict with Catalonia; formation of *Solidaridad Catalana* which defeats traditional parties in elections of 1907.
25 January 1907 to 21 October 1909	Maura's long government; attempt at settlement of the Catalan question with Cambó and *Solidaridad Catalana* fails.
1909	
26 July	Tragic week in Barcelona.
20 October	Execution of Ferrer results in Maura's resignation; Moret ministry. Maura moves into 'implacable hostility' to Liberals.
1910	
9 February	Canalejas (radical Liberal) forms government.
1910	
23 December	Settlement of status of Orders by *Ley del Candado*.
1912	
12 November	Assassination of Canalejas.
1913	
27 October	Dato's government of orthodox Conservatives; Maura abandons leadership of the Conservative party and becomes the Chief of 'Maurismo'.

1914

6 April	Establishment of the Mancommunidad of Catalonia (i.e. local self-government for certain purposes).

1917

1 June	Manifesto of *Juntas Militares de Defensa.*
11 June	Dato's government; the Assembly movement (i.e. coalition of Catalans, Republicans, and Socialists against traditional parties) gathers strength.
10 August	Wave of strikes begins.
3 November	García Prieto's ministry brings the Assembly Movement to an end.

1918

22 March to 9 November	Maura's National Government.
1919–1923	Conservative government until García Prieto's government of 7 December 1922; strike waves and assassinations, particularly in Catalonia (C.N.T. strike at *La Canadiense* 21 February 1919). Failure in Moroccan War (Disaster at Annual on 21 July 1921).

THE DICTATORSHIP OF PRIMO DE RIVERA AND THE FALL OF THE MONARCHY

September 1923–April 1931

1923

13 September	*Coup d'état* of General Primo de Rivera.

1924

8 March	Municipal Statute.
14 April	Formation of the Dictator's party—the Patriotic Union.
1925	Franco-Spanish co-operation in Moroccan war allows the landing at Alhucemas in September; leads to defeat of Abd el krim (May 1926).
December	Civil government formed.

1926

27 November	Co-operative organization of Labour movement.

1927

11 October	Opening of the National Assembly.

1929

January	Rebellion of Sánchez Guerra in Valencia.
18 February	Dissolution of the Artillery Corps; breach in the 'harmony of the military family'; student strikes.

1930

28 January	Resignation of Primo de Rivera.
30 January	Berenguer government—'the bland dictatorship'.
17 August	The Republicans, Socialists, and Catalans agree on revolution with the Pact of San Sebastian; rising at Jaca (12 December).

1931

31 January	Berenguer announces elections to Cortes; abstention of Communists, Republicans, and Socialists forces his resignation on 13 February.
18 February	Aznar government; student riots.
12 April	Municipal elections reveal the large cities to be Republican.
14 April	Negotiations of Romanones and the Republican leaders lead to the proclamation of the Provisional government; Alfonso XIII leaves Spain.

THE SECOND REPUBLIC

1931

18 April	Formation of the Generalidad of Catalonia.
11 May	The burning of the Madrid convents.
13 October	Alcalá Zamora and Miguel Maura resign over religious issue; Azaña's government, relying on Socialist support, i.e. end of co-operation with Radicals.

1932

January	C.N.T. revolts.
10 August	General Sanjurjo rises in Seville.

1933

12 January	The shootings at Casas Viejas. Attacks on Azaña government.
19 November	Triumph of the right in the elections; Lerroux forms a government with the 'benevolence' of Gil Robles and the CEDA.

1934

13 February	Fusion of the Falange with J.O.N.S.

4 October	Lerroux invites CEDA ministers into his government; signal for the Socialist rising in the Asturias and the Catalan separatist revolt in Barcelona.
1935	
April	Beginning of a period of ministerial instability which ends with the victory of the Popular Front in February 1936.
1936	
10 May	Azaña becomes President of the Republic and Casares Quiroga Prime Minister.
June	Widening of breach between Prieto and Largo Caballero; increasing violence in streets; clashes of the Falange and Socialists.
13 July	Assassination of Calvo Sotelo.

THE CIVIL WAR

17–18 July	Rising of the garrison at Melilla in Morocco; military rising spreads to Spain.
	Resignation of Casares Quiroga; failure of Martínez Barrios to negotiate settlement with the military rising; formation of the Giral government (Republican); 'arms to the people'.
4 September	Formation of Largo Caballero's government which the C.N.T. joins on 5 November.
November	Advance of the Nationalist Army on Madrid (8 November—first of the International Brigade appears on the Madrid front).
1937	
February	Increasing military failure of militia system; 8 February fall of Málaga.
8 March	Italian attack on Guadalajara front; successful Republican counter-offensive 15 March.
18 April	The unification of the Nationalist movement with the fusion of the Falange and the Traditionalist Communion.
3 May	The Barcelona troubles between the POUM–CNT and the Republican–Communists results in the overthrow of the Largo Caballero government; formation of the Negrín Ministry (17 May).
18 June	The fall of Bilbao; the actions at Brunete (6 July) and Belchite (6 September) fail to save the Republican position in the north.
1937	
15 December	Capture of Teruel by the Republicans; General Franco drawn from Madrid.

1938		
23 February		Reconquest of Teruel by the Nationalists and Nationalist offensive on the Aragõn front.
July		The last Republican offensive on the Ebro.
December		Nationalist offensive in Catalonia.
1939		
15 March		The Council of Defence set up in Madrid against the Communists; failure of peace negotiations with the Nationalists.
1 April		General Franco announces the end of the Civil War.
1939	4 September	Spain declares its neutrality.
1940	13 June	Declaration of non-belligerency.
	16 October	Serrano Suñer appointed Foreign Minister.
	23 October	Hendaye meeting between Hitler and Franco.
1941	June	Blue Division recruited.
1942	16 August	Begoña incident.
	3 September	Dismissal of Serrano Suñer and General Varela.
1945	19 March	Don Juan's Lausanne Manifesto against Franco.
	17 July	Spaniards' Charter promulgated (*Fuero de los Españoles*).
1946	12 December	U.N. recommends diplomatic boycott of Spain.
1951	1 March	Barcelona tramway strike.
1953	27 August	Concordat with Vatican signed.
	20 September	Base Agreement between U.S.A. and Spain signed.
1955	14 December	Spain admitted to U.N.
1956	February	Student troubles; dismissal of Ruiz Giménez and Fernández Cuesta.
1957	25 February	Franco forms sixth government, including the technocrats of Opus Dei.
1959	22 July	Stabilization Plan announced.
1962	9 February	Spain requests negotiations with E.E.C.
	May	Strikes in Asturias and elsewhere, first appearance of Workers' Commissions.
	5–6 June	Spanish opposition participates in Munich meeting.
1963	20 April	Execution of Grimau.
	28 December	First Development Plan.
1964	30 October	Protest of intellectuals against repression in the Asturian mining strikes.
1966	18 March	Fraga Iribarne's Press Law.
	22 November	Organic Law of State presented to Cortes.
1967	21 September	Admiral Carrero Blanco appointed Deputy Head of Government.

1969	22 July	Franco presents Juan Carlos as his successor.
1970	3–28 December	Burgos Trials of ETA.
1972	10 March	Serious strike in El Ferrol, Galicia.
1973	8 June	Carrero Blanco appointed Prime Minister.
	20 December	Carrero Blanco assassinated.
	29 December	Arias Navarro appointed Prime Minister.
1974	29 July	Opposition forms Democratic Junta.
		XIII Congress of P.S.O.E. Felipe González representing the 'interior' elected Secretary-General.
	29 October	Dismissal of 'liberal' Minister of Information, Pío Cabanillas.
	23 December	New Law of Political Associations.
1975	February	Wave of strikes.
	June	Moderate opposition forms the Platform of Democratic Convergence.
	21 September	Five ETA and F.R.A.P. members executed. Protests all over Western Europe.
	20 November	Franco dies.
	22 November	Juan Carlos crowned King.

I

THE ECONOMIC STRUCTURE OF THE *ANCIEN RÉGIME*

THE most reassuring explanation for the failure of liberal revolution in Spain is that political change was unaccompanied by those social and economic changes that give to political revolution its substance. The black legend of a closed society, proud in its resistance to modern ideas, is transposed from the spheres of intellectual intractability into the lower regions of economic necessity; lack of capital, the persistence of artisan attitudes in industry, and routine in agriculture become the causes of liberal failure; the wooden plough, the sickle, the earth threshing floor, and the wood-fired blast furnace become its symbols. It would nevertheless be misleading to take a vision of an unchanging Spain, foisted on Europe by the literary travellers of the Romantic movement, as the key to her history. The social and economic changes of the nineteenth century were often dramatic and far reaching; but they were sporadic in incidence, a characteristic that was to produce economic imbalance and to underly civil war. Thus by 1930, when a Roman would still have felt at home on an Andalusian estate, Catalonia contained some of the largest textile concerns in Europe and the immigrant labour, which poured into the Catalan towns in order to escape the wretchedness of rural life, brought into the labour movements of a modern industrial civilization the millenarian tradition of peasants and landless labourers.

Sharp contrast between regions of movement and regions of quiescence is not peculiar to Spain: in Italy the problem of the static south, ill-united with the progressive north, was as distressing as the comparable tensions in Spain between the unmoving centre and the developing periphery. Even within one region economic and social change was not uniform but a fugue in which old voices do not cease to sound when new voices enter. A conservative peasantry worked within sight of the mines and blast furnaces of the north and the textile mills of Catalonia; a primitive society, local markets and local customs persisted, emphasized by the size of the country and the inadequacies of road and railway. Probably not until the 1920's were the old ways challenged all over Spain; then local tools vanish before factory products; local dresses and dances become conscious folk-lore; doctors begin to win the battle against village quacks; the lorry—vehicle of progress, especially to remote regions—replaces the donkey and the mule.

This coexistence of change and resistance owes something to the limits set by nature. In an agricultural society poor soil conditions, often the consequence of centuries of abusive cultivation, together with the amount and nature of the rainfall, set bounds to the possibilities of progress. Throughout the eighteenth and most of the nineteenth centuries the myth of a decline from former prosperity tended to conceal these limits and it was not until the 1890's that a first and very approximate calculation of her agricultural potential radically reversed the notion of a nation richly endowed by nature.[1] As it happened, these estimates were unduly pessimistic. Nevertheless they made plain the painful contrast between the limited 'privileged' areas—the deep black soils of the Guadalquivir or the market gardens and orange groves of Valencia—and the parched, thin limestone and granite soils of the central tableland.

The crucial division is that which separates wet and dry Spain.[2] Except where aridity can be countered by irrigation, low rainfall tends to monoculture and social instability or to the poorest type of cereal farming. Where rainfall is adequate soil is frequently bad: hence the rain-soaked, acid fields in parts of Galicia. In those areas where rain falls seldom, it

[1] Cf. M. Gutiérrez Barquin, 'La agricultura como factor de la decadencia económica española' (in *De Ec.* iv. 10 (1956), 625 ff.). The first pessimistic view of Spain's agricultural potential was derived from Mallada's rough calculations contained in *Los males de la patria* published in 1890. Mallada's calculations were largely guesswork: he put 10 per cent. barren soil; 35 per cent. very poor (drought, &c.); 45 per cent. medium but lacking water; 10 per cent. only he considered 'privileged'.

[2] The division between wet and dry Spain was first made by J. Brunhes in *L'Irrigation dans la Peninsule ibérique et l'Afrique du Nord* (Paris, 1902). It was based on a precipitation of 600 mm. German geographers later refined this division by evaporation rates, number of days per year, &c. This drew attention to the contrast between *immerfeuchtes* and *sommertrockenes Iberien*, i.e. areas of summer drought as opposed to areas of even rainfall (see F. Fernández Alonso, 'Ensayo de revisión de los conceptos "Iberia húmeda", "Iberia secá" ', *E.G.* xviii (1957).

falls in torrents, rarely in the summer months, on skeletal, degenerate soils poor in humus; they can retain no moisture and the thin covering of earth is readily swept away. Possibly more than half the soils in the semi-arid regions are subject to severe erosion. Once the vegetational cover of the hard schists was destroyed they could not easily be restored to cultivation. The mixed forest and holm oaks which, it has been assumed, once covered much of the peninsula have gone. Around the semi-arid core lie the green belt of the Cantabrian west and the favoured irrigated regions of the Mediterranean littoral. In a few miles the traveller passes from the summer droughts and deserts of Africa to the climate of northern Europe. 'The north western provinces', observed Richard Ford, 'are more rainy than Devonshire, while the centre plains are more calcined than those of the deserts of Arabia, and the littoral south or eastern coasts altogether Algerian'.[1]

The main characteristic, therefore, of Spanish agriculture is its startling diversity: it ranges from wheat lands with the lowest yields in Europe to the richest of irrigated gardens. Galicia is an area of minute holdings; from Santander, through the Basque provinces, Navarre, and Pyrenean Aragon to Catalonia stretches a band of small proprietors enjoying relatively secure tenures; to the south lie the medium and small cereal farms of Castile and Léon and the remnants of a once great sheep economy; in the deep south, reaching into Estremadura and New Castile, stretch the latifundia worked by day labourers; along the Levante coast small proprietors or tenants produce from carefully irrigated *huertas* specialized export crops. In the mid nineteenth century, Fermín Caballero attempted to divide agricultural Spain into three parts: the Cantabrian regions, where the hard-working race of 'gothic' small farmers had survived to create a stable peasant economy; the basins of the Guadiana, the Guadalquivir, and Aragon, where the economic legacy of the Arab conquest was the latifundia; the centre, where the two races had mingled and left an intermediary, medium-sized farm. Such divisions exclude striking exceptions and no 'region' is homogeneous; thus water will produce a *huerta* in a predominantly dry cereal region. Estremadura, often considered as one vast scrub pasture, has

[1] *Gatherings from Spain* (Everyman, London), 10.

always contained valuable irrigated regions now devoted to market gardening, cotton, and tobacco.[1] The 'bizarre confusions' of the regions of Spain were the delight of nineteenth-century novelists and the despair of reformers in search of 'general legislation which can apply to all the provinces of the monarchy.'[2]

1. *The Land*

Travellers, taking the main road from Paris to Madrid, entered Spain through the steep green hills of the Basque Provinces; returning thither from the burnt highlands of Castile they were 'revived by the sight of a rich studied culture, a clean-looking smiling people, good furniture, neat houses, fine woods, good roads and safe bridges'.[3] It is an indication of the slow decline of central Spain that these provinces, once dismissed as a poor region, were now considered as a fortunate Spanish Switzerland where Homeric simplicity was relieved by a certain luxury in eating and drinking.[4] All agreed in attributing this prosperity to the family farm: the homestead *caserío* was praised by every agricultural reformer in contrast to the settlement more typical of Spain—the agrarian village or small town in which the cultivator lived far from his fields. In Guipúzcoa, Biscay, and northern Navarre these scattered homesteads gave the countryside the appearance of one vast village.

[1] Fermín Caballero, *Fomento de la población rural* (1863), 105 *et passim.*

[2] Cf. the verdict of the mission of the International Bank for Reconstruction and Development (*The Economic Development of Spain*, 1962). The report divides agricultural Spain thus: Galicia (medium soil, adequate rainfall but heavy population density); East Cantabria (from the Asturias to the Basque Provinces, with favourable climatic and soil conditions and a diversified agriculture); the North Meseta (high land with extreme temperatures, once devoted to forests and grazing, now a poor cereal economy); the South Meseta (milder temperatures with wheat, vineyards, and grazing); Andalusia (mild climate, with cereal monocultures *and* varied crops, especially olives and citrus fruits); Levante (barren inland with a 'garden' coastal strip); Catalonia (often an advanced, diversified agriculture). It would be easy to criticize this, as with every other division.

[3] H. Swinburne, *Travels through Spain . . . 1775 and 1776* (London, 1779), 424. The Basque Provinces are Guipúzcoa, Vizcaya, and Alava; Alava has the climate and appearance of the *meseta* and though almost equal in area to the other two provinces combined contains only a seventh of their population.

[4] G. Bowles believed that the whole iron production of the provinces was expended on imported wine; before this cider had been the regional drink as it still was in the poorer provinces of Asturias: *Introducción a la historia natural . . . de España* (1782), 309.

This disseminated type of settlement, in hamlets and isolated farms, had as its foundation the ten-acre holding preserved by inheritance laws that kept the farm, with its distinctive name, as a unit within the family. In Basque law the farm could be left to any child—even a daughter—while co-heirs were bought out: this encouraged emigration of younger sons (the rich returned 'Indian' was a feature of Basque life) and thus mitigated some of the evils of rural over-population.[1] Not until the twentieth century did the increase in population force an uneconomic division of farms and seriously threaten Basque rural prosperity. Beggars, the mark of over-populated under-employed Spain, were rare in an egalitarian society where the peasant held his land on a secure tenure and at a low rent; where the hold of the anarchic nobility had long been destroyed; where it was socially impossible to evict; and where women were the social and legal equals of men.[2] Such a society could work the traditional institutions of local government enshrined in the fiercely defended regional laws—the *fueros*.[3] There were few conflicts within this rural society: the conflict lay between the towns and the country. The foral institutions, which preserved the status of the peasant, degraded merchants and lawyers into second-class citizens: seen from the towns, rustic democracy appeared an oligarchy rigged by rural notables.

The agricultural system was stable but not stagnant: it had come to depend on the cow, maize, and wheat, sensible rotations and no fallow. The Basque was a careful farmer: forests, destroyed elsewhere in Spain without thought, were preserved by complicated methods of replanting that made good the losses to forges and shipyards. In many ways farming techniques appeared archaic: the main cultivating tool, the *laya* (a two-pronged fork), seemed a primitive survival to enthusiasts for the plough.[4] Like many so-called archaic methods it was the

[1] The contrast between Castilian law and Basque law is described formally in S. Moret y Prendergast, *La familia foral y la familia Castellana* (1863). The Basque family was an ideal example of Le Play's *famille souche ou stable*; cf. L. Levillain, *Les caractères de la famille stable* (Paris, 1910).

[2] Basque women work in the fields. It has been asserted, with some exaggeration, that in those regions of Spain where women do not do outdoor work, their position is inferior and 'Moorish'.

[3] For a description of the foral régime see below, pp. 63–64.

[4] In fact *layas* have often ousted the plough because of their superiority on hilly slopes. They demand, of course, an incredible amount of labour. Where ploughs

result of long adaption of means to ends; like many supposed pockets of peasant routine the Basque system could adapt itself to new demands. Thus in the eighteenth and nineteenth centuries wheat expanded, rye was replaced by maize and potatoes. Without any alteration of techniques, the *caserío* could become, in the twentieth century, a commercialized concern with off-the-farm sales to the towns. The social and political conservatism of a stable community—reflected in the harsh punishments for illegitimate children and the cows at funerals, which survived until the twenties of this century—does not imply economic inadaptability.[1] It was on the marginal farms of Castile, without capital and without markets, that change proved so difficult of achievement.

What the homestead enthusiasts regarded as the typical virtues of the Basque countryside were more particularly confined to the predominantly Basque-speaking districts in Guipúzcoa and Biscay where rainfall favours an intensive agriculture. Towards the limits of the pluviose zone, in Alava and southern Navarre, the village begins to replace the homestead and the aristocratic element in society is stronger.[2] The crops become the typical crops of Spain—wheat and vines. Castilian speech, Castilian ploughs, Castilian fallows, and the Castilian attitude to economic activity go together. Thus it was the area where the archaic Basque language survived that was most progressive. The Basques went into fishing, navigation, and finally into iron; the Caracas Company that developed Venezuela in the eighteenth century was a Basque concern, the Economic Societies were a Basque invention and it would seem that the Basques were the best-read Spaniards of the late eighteenth century.[3] Beside the mercantile society of San Sebastian and Bilbao, the capital of Navarre—Pamplona—appeared a somnolent ecclesiastical and administrative centre. Thus the tension between town and country, which divided the liberalism of towns like Bilbao and San Sebastian from the

were used they still varied from valley to valley in the nineteenth century (cf. Castile, where they were uniform); modern times have seen the advance of 'standard' ploughs from Vitoria and Pamplona.

[1] Cf. J. Caro Baroja, *Los Vascos* (1949), 326 ff., for a description of these survivals.

[2] There were vestigial feudal dues in twentieth-century Navarre. Ibid. 288.

[3] Cf. L. M. Enciso Real, *Cuentas del 'Mercurio' y la 'Gaceta'* (Valladolid, 1957), 137 ff.

fierce catholic conservatism of Carlism in the countryside, was less evident in Alava and Navarre.[1] Navarre was a conservative, stable agrarian society in which Catholic Credit societies flourished in the late nineteenth century. In 1936 Pamplona was the capital of militant Carlism and Navarre the only province that rose for Franco.

Towards the west the peasant society of the wet zone decreases in stability and prosperity until, in the extreme north-west, over-population and its consequence, the minute holding (*minifundium*), have reduced Galicia to a depressed region. Around Santander share-croppers and peasant proprietors enjoyed a less solid and secure prosperity than their neighbours to the east, the Basques. The well-being of the community—largely composed of dairy-farmers—as a whole was bound up in the extensive municipal common lands, the existence of which not merely helped the poor but put a limit on the land hunger of the richer peasants.[2] Thus two developments could threaten this society of thrifty peasants, most of whom could read and write: the division of holdings—a process that custom prevented in the Basque Provinces—and an assault on the commons that created and sustained the municipal community and the egalitarian society.[3] By the 1830's the richer proprietors were pressing for the alienation of the commons.

Further west lies the rain-clouded Asturias, where the green fields around Oviedo reminded an English clergyman of the 'richer parishes in England'.[4] But behind the coastal belt

[1] For an examination of Carlism see below Chap. V, section 3.

[2] Le Play, *Les Ouvriers européens* (Paris, 1877), iv. 288–90. Le Play believed the role of commons in Santander more important 'than anywhere else in Western Europe'.

[3] A curious characteristic of these northern settled, peasant societies, from the Basque Provinces to the Asturias, is their exclusion of certain pastoral groups of the population as pariahs, an exclusion maintained in the rest of Spain against gipsies: in the Basque Provinces the *agotes* (reputed to have tails), in the *montaña* of Santander the *pasiegos* (who were considered to eat disgustingly), in the Asturias the *vaquieros*. These exclusions were the result of endogamy and fixed occupation (cattle husbandry) rather than of racial origins. For a description of the fiercely endogamous pastoral *brañas* of the Asturias, see under *brañas* in S. de Miñano, *Diccionario geográfico-estadístico de España y Portugal* (1826), ii. 158.

[4] J. Townshend, *A Journey Through Spain in the Years 1786 and 1787* (London, 1791), i. 400. There can be as little as sixteen sunny days per year. For an excellent description of the Asturias see A. Fugier, *La Junte Supérieure des Asturies et l'invasion française* (Paris, 1930).

stretches a poor region of upland and mountain pasture. It was an unspectacular, stable society, like the Basque Provinces enjoying a large degree of local autonomy. There were few peasant proprietors (perhaps six per cent.) but tenant farmers enjoyed the best customary tenure outside Catalonia and the Basque Provinces; if rents were higher, the tenant could not be evicted; he was compensated for improvement and his rents settled by arbitration. Thus until the rise of the coal industry there was little social conflict. Even the large landowners living in Madrid prided themselves on their interest in their tenantry. The smaller resident landowners lived a simple life and were, like the Basque nobility, interested in the reform movement of the late eighteenth century and supplied many of its leaders. The nobility were a real force; they played an important part in local government and took a lead in the resistance to Napoleon. Like the Basque Provinces, Asturias exhibited a 'progressive' element centred in Gijón and Oviedo, side by side with a conservative, settled peasantry.

The general quality of life nevertheless was poor, especially in the less-favoured inland regions. Asturias was a cereal-importing province, essentially bound to the wheat lands of Léon. Excessive subdivision of holdings, at its worst on the borders of Galicia, revealed the pressure on the land.[1] As yet Asturian industry could not absorb the surplus population: hazel nuts were a more important export than coal.

Galicia, in the far western corner, was the Ireland of Spain, a land of granite and gorse: its landscape was created by an extreme subdivision of holdings, which produced the 'handkerchief plots' of an acre and under.[2] These minute holdings, the consequence of a growing population in combination with a form of gavelkind, were the Galician problem.[3]

Thus the whole of Galician life and politics came to centre round the *foros*, the quasi-emphyteutic tenure on which these

[1] For this subdivision see the report of the 1887 Commission, *La crisis agrícola y pecuaria* (1887), iv. 45, 52. As in Ireland tenants subdivided with their married children and property rights became extremely confused.

[2] The disseminated settlement of Galicia was not as uniform as is sometimes supposed. In the south-east there are largish villages and the areas of great dispersion are the centre and the north. For types of settlement see *Ibero-Amerikanisches Archiv*, viii (Berlin, 1934), 1.

[3] To take an extreme contemporary instance: an area of 117 hectares is divided among 263 owners and broken into 2,486 plots.

minute plots were held.[1] The tenants (*foreros*) paid a customary quit rent to the owner of the *dominium eminens* or *forista*; as in most parts of the world where such tenures obtained, tenants came to look on themselves as outright owners. Thus when population and prices rose in the eighteenth century the tenant *foreros* sublet at great profits to themselves since their payments to the *foristas* had long ceased to represent an economic rent. It was now that the true landlords, the Church and the nobility, sought to assert their half-forgotten rights of eviction and rent-raising in order to trap some of the profits from rising land values.[2] A bitter and complex dispute was decided by the crown jurists in the interests of the *foreros* (1763), and when the entailed lands of the nobility and the church estates were put on the market by the liberal legislation of the nineteenth century they purchased their *foros* and became the outright owners of land they had rented; they became *foristas*. These two measures, one the work of paternalistic Bourbon civil servants and the other of *laissez-faire* liberals, combined to create the rural bourgeoisie of Galicia:[3] the merchants of Pontevedra, Vigo, and Corunna, the returned 'Indians' and lawyers who invested in the purchase of *foros*.

The dispute now lay between the new class of *foristas* and their sub-tenants who cultivated the land. It was in this social struggle that the typical alliance of lawyers and small land-owners that was to control Galician local politics developed; the lawyers prospered in the complicated disputes and as Morillo, Galicia's most distinguished Captain General noted, 'had absolute domination over the countryside'.[4] Their manipulation of parliamentary elections made the Galician constituencies among the most easily manageable in liberal Spain.

Galicia's economy of rye, maize, potatoes, chestnuts, cattle, and pigs was poor, despised by other Spaniards as a region

[1] The nearest English equivalent to the *foro* is, perhaps, copyhold tenure. There is an excellent description of Galician *foros* in G. Brenan, *The Spanish Labyrinth* (Cambridge, 1936), 92–94.

[2] The Monastery of San Salvador received 3,715 *reales* from its *foreros*; these sublet at 923,116.

[3] For the connexion between anti-aristocratic Bourbon reformism and liberal legislation see below, esp. p. 98.

[4] A. Rodríguez Villa, *Don Pablo Morillo* (1908), i. 565. They were natural election agents because the disputes over the proportions of a single *foro* to be paid by a number of sub-tenants put the latter under the thumb of the lawyers.

where women worked as farm-labourers, as railway porters, and road menders.[1] This poverty was supposedly reflected in the highest illegitimacy rate in the country. As in all areas of mainly disseminated settlement and self-sufficient farms—woollen garments, kitchen utensils, even ploughs were home-made—misery was concealed by its dispersion. Subsistence economies sometimes achieve a low-grade stability by the very poverty of the general standard of living.[2]

Nevertheless, as was inevitable with a rising population, favoured as in Ireland by ease of settlement in a society of early marriage, conditions deteriorated in the nineteenth century. There was an 'Irish famine' in 1853–4. The agricultural future lay with cattle-raising (the cow or the pig was the only cash product of the small farmer and was sold, to pay his taxes, in the markets that were the centre of Galician social intercourse), and this could not develop until railways brought the market centre of Lugo into contact with the mass consumption of Madrid and Barcelona. Otherwise the only internal development that could relieve the pressure of men on land was a fishing industry, developed by Catalans in the late eighteenth century and given wide markets by the railways and, much later, the invention of the sardine tin.[3]

The real outlet for the misery of the north and north-west could only be emigration. Export of superfluous man-power from the poorer inland farms was an established tradition by the eighteenth century. It was the seasonal migrants who impressed the rest of Spain with Galician poverty; under their 'kings' perhaps 30,000 labourers went south for the harvest in

[1] Hence, as in other northern provinces of disseminated settlement women enjoyed a relatively high status; cf. the number of nineteenth-century women writers who were Galicians: Concepción Arenal, the social and penal reformer; Rosalía Castro, the poetess; Emilia Pardo Bazán, the novelist.

[2] For a vivid contemporary account of Galician misery see P. Rovira, *El campesino gallego* (1904). Wages were so low in Galicia in the 1920's that hand-made lace could successfully compete with factory products.

[3] The best description of agricultural conditions in Galicia is contained in E. G. H. Dobbie, 'Galicia', *Geographical Review*, xxvi (New York, 1936), 555–80. For the importance of fishing, which experienced a boom after the 1936–9 war when wheat was scarce, see J. M. Casas Torres, 'Sobre la geografía humana de la ria de Muros', *E.G.* iv (1943), 559 ff. Mussels, for instance, became an important industry in the Vigo estuary after the war. For fishing in the later nineteenth century cf. *P.P.* 1908, cxvi. 455. Women often worked the land while the men fished.

the 1890's. Besides seasonal migration there was the semi-permanent emigration to other parts of Spain and to America. Galicians and Asturians and *montañeses* from the province of Santander were the waiters, water carriers, wet-nurses, and porters of the Spanish towns, and the Galician domestic servant was a stock theatre character. In Asturias there was a strong tradition of early migration in the poor mountain villages.[1] Only industry could absorb locally this surplus the land would not support, and in the early half of the nineteenth century there was none.

Compared to these regions the mountains and plains of central Spain were the despair of the traveller: 'the barest and most melancholy I ever beheld'.[2] Apart from regions of mountain pasture and forest, the plains of Castile afforded a bare landscape occasionally interrupted by nondescript villages, the colour of the soil from which they arose. Only monotony granted a certain grandeur. Neither geography nor history had been kind to the centre of the Spanish empire: rainfall was erratic with summer droughts, the soil poorish. In Madrid, intolerable in the heats of summer, sentries froze at their posts in the winter.[3] A stable and balanced agrarian economy had degenerated into precarious monocultures and backwater towns. From the seventeenth century a whole school of economic pessimists, unable to analyse the causes, described the symptoms of this degeneration: depopulation, 'luxury', monks, sheep, obsession with aristocratic values, too many schoolboys learning Latin, absenteeism. They were no doubt correct in believing that the financial burdens of Empire fell heavily on the two Castiles: heavy taxation drove industry and population to the peripheral regions and emphasized the decline

[1] Clarín has a true story of these emigrants in *Adios Cordera*; even Palacio Valdés, whose novels idealized the Asturian village, gave poor children 'the mark of the vagabond'. The economic effects of these migrations have not been studied. They must have meant an import of capital from the rest of Spain and the outer world and no doubt played havoc with land values. For eighteenth-century internal emigration see A. Meijide Pardo, 'La emigración gallega intrapeninsular en el siglo XVIII', *Estudios de historia social de España*, IV. ii (1960), 463 ff.

[2] Swinburne, *Travels*, 326. Cf. D. Ramos, 'El problema de las comarcas de la Bureba', *Boletín de la R.S. Geográfica*, lxxxiii (1947), 651–75; and I. Escagues de Javierre, *La estructura del valle del Duero* (1959): 'In Castile any region of rural life lacks an authentic singularity.'

[3] Nearly all agricultural land of the central tableland is above 600 metres: Avila, Segovia, and Soria are above 1,000 m.

of agriculture. The generation of 1898 redressed in literature the balance that had been upset in the economic development of Spain: with some exaggeration the rediscovery of the desolate attractions of Castile by poets and essayists, many of whom came from peripheral regions, can be seen as a repentant gesture to the centre, devastated for the greater glory of Spain.

The agricultural history of Castile had been a battle between sheep-owners and agriculturists. Sheep-owners were few, rich, and organized in a powerful corporation, the *Mesta*.[1] Because of the loans it could provide, its demands for prohibition of enclosure, extensive pastures, and rights of way were backed by the crown. The agriculturists, on the other hand, had been poor and numerous, supported only by pamphleteers. But, in the later eighteenth century, the pamphleteers became government servants at a time when rising wheat and oil prices brought the graziers' privileges and the accepted primacy of wool within the economy into question. Complaints from Estremadura, where scrub pasture (*dehesas*) covered much of the province, started a movement for agricultural reform that involved an attack on the *Mesta*. Saved by the financial straits of the crown from effective attack by the reforming bureaucrats of the later eighteenth century, the sheep-owners could not hope to defeat the pressure of the municipalities and local courts, when supported by opinion increasingly hostile to corporate privilege, which was seen as an impediment to economic development. In 1839 the *Mesta*, the greatest economic corporation in Spain, was finally destroyed; in the name of *laissez-faire* the liberals completed the task of the civil servants of the *ancien régime*.

This did not mean the end of large-scale sheep-farming, which was still the basis of large fortunes in the nineteenth century: migrant merino flocks still passed from summer pastures in the Sierras along the sheep roads to Estremadura and the south; but with the destruction of animal stock in the War of Independence, the disruption of the sheep routes, and the general decline of wool the great transhumant flocks persisted only in those regions where no other method of feeding was possible—in the more remote parts of the bleak province of

[1] The history of this great corporation of sheep-owners, which protected the rights of the transhumant flocks that crossed Spain from summer to winter pasture, is set out in J. Klein, *The Mesta* (Cambridge, Mass., 1920).

Soria for example.[1] The battle between graziers and agriculturists continued up to modern times, but in less dramatic wrangles between village councils, which preferred cultivators, and the larger owners who favoured the more reliable rents of the cattle and sheep men. Nevertheless in most regions sheep and wheat complemented each other: commons were auctioned to sheep-owners by municipalities, and fallows by peasants, from the harvest until September.[2] In the smaller villages of the Sierras life was isolated and stagnant, a degraded survival, semi-pastoral, semi-agricultural, with timber as an important source of income. It was there that Carlism found its supporters in Old Castile.

Outside the pastoral regions lay the classic cultures of the central tableland—cereals, olives, and vines; its agrarian history is the history of shifts from one of these crops to another where local needs for food permitted a response to market conditions. In the eighteenth and nineteenth centuries the 'thirst for new land', as in the past, resulted in the breaking up of marginal scrub for wheat. This meant that some of the old *despoblados*, the deserted towns that had been the despair of the economists for two hundred years, came back under cultivation, just as in the town of Salamanca, centre of a great wheat region, the empty houses left untenanted by the recession of the seventeenth century were occupied once more.[3] But these were risky gains: with little animal manure and no capital, the peasant broke up more land than he could use, only to abandon it in a drought or when prices fell.

In much of Castile harassed tenants and peasantry were driven by short, often verbal leases, high rents and bad years

[1] R. Miralbes Bedera, 'La transhumancia soriana', *E.G.* xv (1954), 337 ff. In some of the 'reception areas' the establishment in the nineteenth century of flocks of 'stationary' sheep (*estantes*) excluded *transhumantes*; thus the Soria flocks found new pastures in Aragon. Casual labourers for olives, &c., used the old routes, after the sheep they had once followed had abandoned them.

[2] In many parts of Spain farmers were both agriculturists and owners of flocks: thus the battle was against the flocks of *other* peasant pastoralists. Litigation over straying animals in the north corresponds with litigation over 'water theft' in the south. Cf. M. Kenny, *Spanish Tapestry* (London, 1961), 28. In Estremadura there were complex feuds between pig-owners and wheat-growers who used the same land, at different times of the year, for different purposes.

[3] Cf. A. Cabo Alonso, 'La Armuña y su evolución económica', *E.G.* lix (1959), 367 ff. Cf. the repopulation of a large estate: mid-eighteenth century: 189 inhabitants; 1787: 393; 1825 (estimate): 436; 1887: 861.

into the clutches of village usurers and corn merchants.[1] Increasingly in the late eighteenth and nineteenth centuries landlords sought to raise rents with prices and to avoid secure customary tenures, a practice by no means confined to absentee landlords; most landowners were local nobles and bourgeois, though the great aristocratic houses had large 'states' scattered over both Castiles. The eighteenth-century administration sought to protect those whom the intendant of Burgos called the 'wretched slaves' of the landlords: there were proposals to freeze rents at the 1770 level, to set up arbitration boards of peasants and landlords. Such paternalism was impossible in the War of Independence against Napoleon (1808–14) and out of fashion after it. The plight of the poor cultivator, in provinces like Avila with its stony fields, constituted the most intractable problem of the agrarian world. Rack renting combined with taxes and tithes—according to the abolitionists of the thirties these alone consumed a quarter of the peasants' net income—drove out the enterprising and condemned those who remained to one of the most hopeless forms of subsistence farming.

There were striking exceptions to this pattern of poverty, from the irrigated land round Valladolid—'a perfect garden'—to the timber villages in the mountains of old Castile. Even cereal Castile was not uniform: the proprietors of Salamanca or Valladolid were independent men of substance, very different from the subsistence farmers of Avila. Nowhere north of the Tagus was there a class like the landless rural proletariat of Andalusia and Estremadura, and this may account for the relative political stability of Castile: only one nineteenth-century revolt started in the classic wheat lands.

To the south of New Castile lay Andalusia; to the west, Estremadura. It was in these arid regions, where twenty per cent. of the total population lived, that agrarian reformers, from the eighteenth century to the second Republic, found the agrarian problem of Spain *par excellence*, tending to neglect, by comparison, the plight of the marginal farmer in central Spain.[2]

[1] Castilian tenures were highly diverse, varying from emphyteutic tenures to *precaria*: crop sharing, money rents, customary tenures (the classic *censo* for instance), 'Lawyer's tenures', peasant proprietorships. Landlords were as diverse as their rents.

[2] This very concentration of effort, together with the romantic travellers' obsessions with 'flamenco Spain', has over-emphasized the role of Andalusia in

Not all of Andalusia and Estremadura was a kingdom of vast entailed latifundia peopled by overseers and landless labourers, given over to huge fields of wheat, barley, and fallows, to olive monocultures (as in Jaén), or to the scrub pastures and the bull ranches of the great houses. These gave Andalusia its reputation: to Bourgoing it was a desert. 'The great landowner seems to reign there like the lion in his forest, driving from him by his roars all who seek to approach his presence.'[1] In the *serranía* (the mountain districts) there were large areas of poor pasture or small holdings and it was in these regions rather than on the great estates that Anarchism was later to find its most fanatical adherents. The irrigated, fertile *vega* of Granada was an area of intense farming; round Cordoba, the clay soil was fertile and deep ploughing could resist the droughts that desolated the dry plains; Jerez was the centre of a sophisticated wine industry. There were pockets where reasonable crop-sharing leases produced stable communities. There were areas where sheep-farming or cattle-breeding was still the most important economic activity.[2]

Nevertheless it was the great estates of absentee landowners that gave Andalusia its reputation. The latifundia had persisted since Roman times: the descendant of the Roman *villicus*, the bailiff of the absentee landlord, still exploited the *instrumentum vocale*—the day labourer. The white buildings of the *cortijo*, with its great gate and tower, still dominated the yellow landscape.[3] The *cortijo* was 'a unit of exploitation, not a centre of population'; around it was a relatively small area, well culti-

Spanish economic life. 'Central Spain' (i.e. both Castiles and Leon) contained 29·2 per cent. of the population in 1797 and 24·9 per cent. in 1940. For Andalusia the figures are 18·06 and 20·17. Estremadura, the other 'difficult' region, contained always between 4 and 5 per cent. of the total population. Ford's *Handbook to Spain*, written in 1844–5, and issued in revised editions, did much to mould the Anglo-Saxon attitude to Spain.

[1] J. F. Bourgoing, *Voyage en Espagne* (Paris, 1793), i. 219.

[2] For a contemporary description of the varied crops round Granada see W. Jacob, *Travels in the South of Spain* (London, 1811). In the *vega* (irrigated but not capable of the intensive cropping of the *huerta*) wheat was an important *irrigated* crop but fruits, hemp, mulberries, &c., were grown; cf. P. Madoz, *Diccionario geográfico-estadístico-histórico de España* (3rd edition, 1848–50), viii. 470, 482–3. For Cordoba see J. Díaz del Moral, *Historia de las agitaciones campesinas andaluces* (Córdoba–Madrid, 1929), 6–10, 20.

[3] J. Caro Baroja, *Los Pueblos de España* (Barcelona, 1946), 396–400, for origins of *latifundia*.

vated and manured, given over to barley and chick peas; the rest of a great estate was usually divided between fallows, grazed stubble, and wheat. Only a small staff of permanent employees lived in the *cortijo*; for the harvest the bailiff hired day labourers from the emigrant provinces and the local towns.[1] Huddled together in the barns of the *cortijo* and fed on doles of garlic soup when they were employed, half starved at home during the slack seasons that are the concomitant of extensive monocultures, the Andalusian *braceros* were a primitive revolutionary class, unique in Europe, alternating between waves of exaltation and fatalistic 'Moorish' resignation to misery. In such a society, as in southern Italy, the stronger spirits took to brigandage or smuggling and became the epic heroes of a depressed race.

In the later eighteenth century the economy of the entailed latifundia began to be considered as an intolerable abuse. Spectacular rises in corn prices encouraged landlords to evict in order to farm themselves, a process which led to the creation of *despoblados*; middling tenants refused to sublet and a wave of rent rises seems to have started in the 1760's.[2] At the same time a group of agrarian reformers came to have influence with the crown. In 1766 Charles III appointed Aranda, perhaps the most radical of the group, as his minister. To the reformers the solution was simple. 'Why in our villages are there men without land and in our countryside land without men? Bring them together and all will be served.'[3] Thus started a movement for some redistribution of land to small cultivators as a solution to the problems of Andalusia and Estremadura.

It can be argued that the *individual* peasant proprietorship envisaged by reformers was not a practical solution to the agrarian problems of the southern *secano*. Both the incidence of

[1] See the description in G. Martínez y González (one of the *Memorias* submitted for the Royal Essay Prize of 1903). He calculated that fixed labour was paid 1·75 pesetas a day; seasonal labour 4·50 pesetas.

[2] Leases were between one and six years and thus rents could be pushed up easily. M. Defourneaux (*Revue Historique*, clxviii. 48) says rents rose much faster than prices. Some of the complaints seem fantastic: e.g. near Ronda a sixfold rise in under thirty years. For the deliberate creation of *despoblados* cf. the Intendant of Cordoba: 'A great part of the *despoblados* can be blamed on the lord's desire to exploit the land himself.' Similar accusations were made in the 1914–18 war. Perhaps, both in the late eighteenth century and in the twentieth, they preferred *despoblados* to controlled rents.

[3] G. de Jovellanos, *Diarios*, ii. 101.

bad years and the type of settlement were against it.[1] 'How can the *cortijos*', Aranda's reforming government asked its intendants in vain, 'be turned into villages?' It was the economic fragility of peasant proprietorship in areas of monoculture and drought, where two bad years drove the small man to sell his lands, that led more far-sighted reformers to argue against outright peasant proprietorship and in favour of a state-controlled and state-aided colonization with the family as the settled unit. Technically admirable, in that it saved the peasant from himself as well as from his oppressors, colonization demanded great expenditure to bring the land above the level of subsistence farming—an expenditure the liberal state of the nineteenth century could neither approve in principle nor afford in practice. Nor could colonization and controlled tenures satisfy the deep-rooted popular desire for outright ownership. A *reparto*, the division of the great estates among the agrarian poor, was the recurring demand of the endemic *jacqueries* of Andalusia as a once and for all cure for chronic underemployment.

The great estates were not always farmed directly by their owners. The general practice of letting a *cortijo* as a unit to one substantial tenant created a powerful class, the *labradores*, who, as tenants-in-chief, controlled all rentable land, letting out only the distant or poorer parts of the estates to the small men—the *peletrines*. Rack renting of this marginal land, bitterly attacked by reformers but never remedied, was the greatest single cause of hardship to those who had not sunk or been born into the vast reservoir of casual labour. The control of the landlords and the *labradores* over municipal government completed their monopoly by giving into their hands the only other surplus land—the municipal commons—which became, according to reforming bureaucrats, 'the private patrimony of the town counsellors'.[2]

Thus the real struggle in Andalusia was between the alliance of landlord or his agents and the *labrador*, and the rest. The former constituted the local oligarchy of the *poderosos*, the powerful ones, who, from the days of Aranda to the debates of 1934, resisted any reforms intended to relieve the poor. The only reforms this group could admit were reforms that benefited

[1] For the problems of settlement see below.

[2] J. Costa, *Colectivismo agrario en España* (1898), 129.

its members: the sale of the common lands and the entailed estates of the Church, an operation that they could dominate and from which they could draw profit.

The old kingdom of Valencia contained within its borders the contrasts typical of Spain. The northern and western fringes were 'all mountains, deserts and gullies. The soil is unkind and denies to the cultivator the means of life: the heights are, in general, bare rocks with little water and bitterly cold.'[1] With weed-choked crops, badly pruned mulberries, olives killed off by frost, mean strips of wheat on terraces maintained at vast expense of labour, only the extension of the domestic wool industry could save this region from decline and depopulation. As in Galicia, the lowness of the general standards concealed a hopeless poverty. The continued existence of these mountain peasants, surviving on bread, oil, and beans, 'proves how little the human race needs in order to exist and to propagate'.

How different was the rich, irrigated coastal plain! Prosperity began at Vinaroz, with wells and easy access to the coast, the latter important because much produce was exported to northern Europe and America. These regions, tedious to the eye, were a continuous marke tgarden with five crops every two years. 'The soil never rests in these *huertas*, crops succeed each other without interruption. . . . Night does not end work: each field is irrigated in its turn at the appointed hour, even in the middle of the night.' Outside market-garden plots, vines and carobs flourished.[2] Prosperity and rising prices were reflected in new building in the towns and in a rapidly rising population—only in the rice regions did public prosperity impair public health.[3] Thus the Valencian *huerta* came to have the highest rural density in Europe: similar conditions produced an equal density in irrigated Murcia. Yet this great growth and the consequent diminution of the size of holdings until a 'large' farm was two acres, meant that labour was getting less pro-

[1] A. J. Cavanilles, *Observaciones sobre la historia natural . . . de Valencia* (1797), i. 17.

[2] The one difficulty was manure. This was obtained from the streets of the towns by the *fermaters* (Cavanilles, op. cit. 107). Carobs are the locusts, which, together with wild honey, constituted a Biblical diet.

[3] To take one example, Vinaroz had 2,904 inhabitants in 1714 and in the 1770's 9,075. Prices for most agricultural products, according to Cavanilles, had doubled in twenty years (op. cit. i. 105). For building, ibid. 134.

ductive—a phenomenon reflected in the huge difference in price between land with and land without vacant possession. It was not land that was bought but the prospect of self-employment.[1]

This intense cultivation of varied crops, so sharp a contrast to the monocultures of the centre, was dependent on irrigation. The small-scale irrigation systems of the Levante present a combination of great technical and juridical sophistication. Though they were attributed to the Moors, the Moors themselves regarded the irrigation works themselves as an inheritance from a previous Christian civilization; age-old, they represent a degree of social organization and co-operation that compels admiration.[2] Water belonged to the community and was sold with the land. The constant disputes as to its use in time of scarcity were regulated by a communal organization; the most famous was the Water Tribunal of Valencia, which gave its verbal judgements, never contested, in an open-air court outside the cathedral. In later irrigation schemes water belonged to the capitalists who had built the system and was auctioned to the cultivators: hence the conflict, inconceivable in the older systems, between water-owners and cultivators that was typical of the nineteenth century.

In Aragon, as in Valencia, there were great agrarian contrasts, emphasizing the historic contrast between the mountain core of the old kingdom and the reconquered territories where Arab influence, even today, is apparent to the architectural eye. High Aragon was a region of poor crops and migrant flocks—some of the biggest *transhumante* flocks of the nineteenth century belonged to Aragonese magnates and villages. An extreme climate and thin, stony soils made the windy plateaux (the *páramos*) of Teruel and Huesca the most sparsely populated parts of Spain.[3] In the upland region an old-established pastoral economy and the local industry that supported it was in sharp

[1] These changes are called by René Dumont, *Types of Rural Economy* (London, 1957), 'unequivocally retrogressive' (223–4); in the Murcian huerta 7 acres were worked in 1890 with 2 horses and 1 man; fifty years later 2 acres of the same land were worked by 1 mule and 2 men. There was thus concealed under-employment. Vacant possession was worth ten times as much as land with a sitting tenant.

[2] Cf. J. Caro Baroja, *Razas, pueblos y linajes* (1957), 77 ff.

[3] In the winter of 1937–8 the battle of Teruel was fought in a temperature of −19°.

decline. Thus the Carlism of the Maestrazgo—the mountain region of Lower Aragon—can be seen as a revolution of desperation in the creeping misery of a contracting economy.[1]

Against these regions of contraction stood the prosperous *secanos* of the centre and the irrigated lands of the Ebro valley. Towns like Daroca combined highly productive wheat-lands and vineyards with *huertas*, but it was the Ebro that created a green line of prosperity through the barest country imaginable. The older areas of irrigation were extended and intensified by the Imperial Canal; begun under Charles V, its completion was the greatest public work of the eighteenth century. More water and, later in the nineteenth century, artificial manure brought flexibility and variety, enabling rapid adjustment to market conditions. In the eighteenth century the old irrigated lands were still largely devoted to wheat with yearly fallows: in the 1890's sugar-beet became the most profitable crop, later supplemented by lucerne and potatoes.[2] What Aragon could be like without water appears in the Monegros: a complete desert in a dry year, it could, with winter rains, give the heaviest yields in Spain. These climatic contrasts were marked by sharp social-tenurial contrasts. Thus in Jaca there were allotments for the poor labourers and no agrarian destitute class; around Saragossa the labourers had enforced a customary eight-hour day and worked in their free hours on their own plots; but on the great estates of dry Aragon labour conditions could only be matched in Andalusia.[3]

Catalonia, like Valencia, showed contrasts of progress and stagnation; as in the Basque country an industrial civilization grew up surrounded by a conservative peasantry, a division that was to determine political alignments in Catalonia. The

[1] I. de Asso, *Historia de la economía política de Aragón* (Saragossa, 1798), attributes the decline to the Pragmatic of 1773, which favoured corn at the expense of pasture: in fact the whole industry was in a process of slow decline (180–3). For the remarkable decline of Cantavieja, ibid. 177. Cantavieja was one of the two strongholds of Cabrera, the Carlist guerilla leader.

[2] The farmers of the *vega* were, relatively speaking, technically adventurous. They abandoned the 'Roman' plough in the 1880's and took rapidly to artificials after 1875. For an excellent account of a *vega* see J. I. Fernández Marco, *Sobradiel* (Saragossa, 1955).

[3] Costa was an enthusiast for the allotment system he found in parts of Upper Aragon: see J. M. Costa, *La tierra y la cuestión social* (1912), 67 ff., 95 ff. (Jaca), and 17, 26 (Saragossa).

mountainous inland Young found 'all poor and miserable'; bad crops, bad fallows, and wretched towns.[1] It was from these regions that Catalan industry was to draw its cheap labour, while the wild valleys of the Pyrenees were an enclosed world with a tradition of brigandage and family feuds; here Carlism was to take on the violence and cruelty of the local society.

The agricultural riches of Catalonia lay in the wheat plains and vineyards of the centre and the rich cultures of the coastal plain. Agricultural prosperity rested on secure tenures that made the substantial farmers feel themselves to be full proprietors. The symbol of this security was the *masía*—the solidly built farmhouse that dominated the landscape of rural Catalonia and often bore the name of the family that had lived in it for generations. In the strict hierarchy of the Catalan countryside these peasant farmer families almost ranked as a petty nobility.

The typical Mediterranean wine–olive–wheat complex began, in the eighteenth century, an expansion and modification that were to continue, after the shocks of war, into the nineteenth and which were to transform the agricultural potential of Catalonia. It was this drive that led travellers to comment on the Catalans' capacity to make 'soil out of rock'. The transformation was both extensive and intensive. The profits to be made out of wine in the first half of the century encouraged substantial farmers to let out their outlying fields, landowners and municipalities their hitherto unproductive wastes, on *rabassa morta*—a lease of land based on the life of the vine and intended to bring bad land into cultivation. It was thus that the classic wine-growing areas—the *Camp* of Tarragona and the Panadés—were expanded and the western regions re-peopled.

Small-scale irrigation works increased production (wheat yielded three times as much on irrigated land) and diversified it: lucerne, for instance, became a valuable crop. But it was in the market-garden economies of the coast, stimulated by the demands of Barcelona, that the transformation was most intense. 'Every scrap of land', wrote Young, of Mataró, 'is well cultivated.' Such regions, by the late eighteenth century, had a 'modern' population density.

This transformation had important consequences. It emphasized the contrast between the periphery and the centre of

[1] A. Young, *Travels during the Years 1787, 1788 and 1789* (Dublin, 1793), ii. 307.

Spain by the creation of an agrarian economy that fed the towns—Barcelona above all—and was linked to the wider economies of Europe and America. Combined with industrial and commercial developments, it enabled Catalonia to support a population that doubled within the eighteenth century. Large areas of Catalonia became dependent on a single specialized export—wine and cheap brandy were sent in such quantities to America and northern Europe that the world price of brandy was set by the market of Reus.[1]

2. *The Prospects of Progress*

In the late eighteenth century the economy of Spain appeared to be on the move. There were signs that agricultural production was responding to the rise in prices common to Europe and marked after 1760.[2] There was a notable industrial revival in Catalonia. Along the whole Mediterranean coast there was a considerable increase in the volume of trade both in agricultural products sought by northern Europe and in exports to the colonies. In 1785 the directors of the Bank of San Carlos (founded in 1782 as the first national bank of Spain and in itself an indication of a new spirit) could report in glowing terms. They praised 'the progress of our industry, the multiplicity of modern factories in Catalonia, the growth of agriculture, and the increase in demand for its products'.[3] British merchants, who had exploited the incapacity of the old-established monopolists of Cadiz and Seville to supply Spain's American Empire with goods, professed alarm at 'the commercial spirit which is beginning to prevail in the Spanish nation'.[4] How were these advances achieved? What was the balance between stagnation and growth?[5]

[1] Cf. F. Rahola Tremols, *El comercio de Cataluña con América* (Barcelona, 1931), and E. Giralt y Raventós, 'La viticultura y el comercio catalán del siglo XVIII', *E.H.M.* ii (1952), 159–76.

[2] For prices see E. J. Hamilton, *War and Prices in Spain 1651–1800* (Cambridge, Mass., 1947).

[3] For the bank see E. J. Hamilton, 'The Foundation of the Bank of Spain', *Journal of Political Economy*, liii (1945), 97 ff.

[4] A. Christelow, 'Great Britain and the trades from Cadiz and Lisbon 1759–63', *H.A.H.R.* xxviii (1948), 13.

[5] Since the progress of the coastal plains has been briefly described the following pages are primarily devoted to the *secano* as an economic and agrarian problem.

On the development of the productivity of its agriculture depended the whole future of Spain. Only by a greater yield from the land could a growing population be supported, and savings and a market be created for a resumption of 'lost' industrial prosperity.

By 1800 Spain was producing more wheat at steadier prices than at any time since the sixteenth century. Slowly, in spite of lean years, devastating famines were passing away.[1] Since average yields on non-irrigated land could not rise much above fivefold the seed, the increase must have been the result of extending the cultivated area by ploughing marginal land: Jovellanos in the eighteenth century, Fermín Caballero in the 1850's, and the Report on the agricultural crisis of 1887 all accuse the farmer of ploughing up more than he could maintain in cultivation.[2] 'Thirst for new land' set off a continuous process of abandoning and resuming cultivation until, in some districts, erosion took over. The sedentary farmer succeeded the migrant shepherd as the agent by whom the soil of Spain was squandered; by the early nineteenth century cereals occupied perhaps three-quarters of the cultivable land, an imbalance between crop and animal husbandry as pernicious as that which prevailed in the heyday of wool.

Extensive cultivation was the capital vice of the *secano* farming, afflicting alike the great latifundia and the peasant farm. It created the characteristic landscape of the central tableland: a tawny countryside pinned by drought to the classic Mediterranean monocultures—wine, wheat, and olives. They shared the same social defect—seasonal unemployment—and the same natural hazards—extreme variability in yield between bad and normal years. Shifts could be made from one monoculture to another in response to market conditions and were made both in the eighteenth and nineteenth centuries;

[1] A. Domínguez Ortiz, *La sociedad española en el siglo XVIII* (1955), 264 ff. G. Desdevizes du Dezert, *La richesse et la civilisation espagnole au XVIIIe siecle* (Paris, 1928), 38, calculated that wheat production per head exceeded that of France.

[2] Fermín Caballero believed quite small farmers ploughed up as much as ninety hectares when they could cultivate only eight or ten. The Report of 1887 claimed that *half* the land brought under cereal cultivation as a result of sales of church and common land was later abandoned. Of course the eighteenth and nineteenth centuries witnessed merely an *acceleration* of a process that had begun in the sixteenth and seventeenth centuries: cf. J. García Fernández, 'Horche', *E.G.* xiv (1953), 265 ff.

but they were made without any fundamental change in the traditional crop economy or any mitigation of the problems of rural under-employment. The great treeless plains from Salamanca to Valladolid were most economically employed with wheat and grazed fallows, while other poorer provinces—Avila for instance—could grow little else, even if it meant wretched crops and three-year fallows. Wheat was favoured, not merely because of its immediate importance as a basic food, but because it demanded least capital and least care, even where it meant wretched cultivations: only one-tenth of the cereal *secano* was farmed in regular rotations of wheat and legumes; a quarter was cultivated only once every six or ten years.

Much of the contemporary and subsequent criticism of the *secano* farming attributed to peasant routine the inescapable consequences of poor soil, drought, and lack of capital. When the philosopher-agronomists advocated new crops and new methods they were met with the excuse so often given to Cavanilles on his tour of Aragon, 'We do as our fathers do.' Sometimes this obstinacy was the refuge of the poor man who cannot afford change and to whom stagnation has become a habit of mind necessary for survival; at other times it represented a sound rejection of improper techniques culled by 'philosophical' amateurs from the journals of French and English agricultural societies. Peasants often have more practical experience than philosophers and are just as keen to make money out of their produce.[1] The peasants' plough, according to critics, 'scratched the soil' but deep ploughing would have destroyed it. Mules were 'sterile monsters', 'the most fatal vice of our agricultural system', but they work fast, and can stand heat.[2] There was 'too much fallow', but this fallow was an essential process in dry farming on poor land. The worst consequence of extensive cultivation was a radical separation of animal and

[1] The whole of Sarrailh's treatment of Spanish agricultural conditions is vitiated by its insistence on *le poids de la routine*. (J. Sarrailh, *L'Espagne éclairée de la seconde moitié du XVIIIe siècle* (Paris, 1954).)

[2] Anyone who has tried to plough more than an acre with oxen will soon find himself kindly disposed to mules, just as he will abandon trying to feed horses in grassless steppes. For an impassioned attack on mules see Fermín Caballero, *Fomento*, 83 *et passim*. He maintained, in the 1850's, that the number of mules had quintupled since 1750.

crop husbandry. Once wheat had triumphed on poor land, the imbalance between cattle, sheep, and cash crops became incurable.

Three factors, which acted in the regions of dry cereal farming with particular intensity, have been blamed for the low levels of productivity: first, extensive common lands; secondly, a maldistribution of landed property—the twin problem of the latifundia and the minifundia—combined with insecure tenures and high rents; thirdly, a type of settlement where the majority of the agricultural population lived in large villages and towns.

In the favoured regions of the north the common lands gave social strength to the community and were not detrimental to good husbandry. In regions like Estremadura they could be agriculturally pernicious. 'The waste and desert appearance is partly caused by the vast extent of the common lands belonging to the towns and villages, the system of management of which is ruinous in the extreme, and the finest districts, capable of enriching the proprietors and the country at large, are abandoned to, and only serve as pasture for goats, sheep or a few asses.' This was an exaggeration; the desert appearance of poor pasture and dried-out stubble remained after the commons had gone. Nevertheless critics of liberal legislation that 'destroyed' the common lands failed to remember that, although the commons may have contributed to 'the independence and dignity so striking in the demeanour of the Spanish peasant', the price of these social benefits was a level of agricultural production that precluded progress.[1]

The abuses of the latifundia had been recognized before the systematic criticism of the later eighteenth century and the case against the great estate remained as the emotional drive behind all land reform. Indubitably, too much land was concentrated in too few hands though the agricultural reasons for extensive farming were not always appreciated.[2] Many lati-

[1] 'In consequence of this (the division of the commons annually in the pueblo of Logrosan, Estremadura) and their bad management the place is extremely poor.' Logrosan, a town of 4,000 inhabitants, had no shop and no glass windows. (S. E. Widdrington, *Spain and the Spaniards* (London, 1844), i. 117–19; ii. 407.)

[2] Thus La Mancha was often assumed to be a latifundia area; but cf. W. Laver, 'Tipos de cultivo en la España semiárida' in *E.G.* xxi (1960), 519: 'The latifundia in La Mancha, when they exist at all, are confined to marginal and newly cultivated

fundia were, no doubt, 'abusive'; but many were on poor land suited only for extensive and occasional cereal production and ranching. Many reformers were ignorant of farming conditions in Andalusia. Olavide, in the later eighteenth century, dreamed of transforming the whole of lower Andalusia on the model of the English countryside, without seeming to suspect that climatic conditions were radically different and that the creation of artificial meadows was a snare and delusion under the arid sun of southern Spain.

Again reformers were undoubtedly right in pointing to precarious tenures as removable hindrances (*estorbos*): many Castilian and Andalusian tenures made improvement by the tenant equivalent to economic suicide and encouraged short leases and rack renting.[1] What these critics did not see so clearly was that elsewhere customary tenures had so confused conceptions of ownership that a clear, profitable, and workable landlord-tenant relationship was difficult to conceive; while in many regions customary quit rents gave the landlord little surplus to invest, even had he been inclined so to do. Moreover, the whole history of aristocratic landownership showed that socially secure customary tenures, in the long run, had meant a loss of economic control by the landowner. In Galicia a liberal historian of property rights called the 1763 settlement (which gave tenants such security that the landlords could neither evict nor raise rents) 'an act of sheer expropriation against the aristocracy'. Finally, the prevalance of crop-sharing leases was an indication of incapacity or unwillingness to put capital into land, of a preference for social stability at the price of economic improvement.[2]

Travellers' tales of uninhabited wastes are often based on the

land.' The latifundia of Ciudad Real lie outside La Mancha where the average size of a holding is 4 hectares. See Table, Appendix I, for the modern distribution of landed property. The provinces of Badajoz and Cárceres, Cádiz, Seville, and Córdoba are the great centres of the latifundia; cf. M. Defourneaux, *Pablo de Olavide* (Paris, 1959), 71, 161.

[1] For Andalusian rents see above, p. 16. For examples from Aragon see I. Asso, *Aragón*, 126, and Cavanilles, *Valencia*, *passim*.

[2] Crop-sharing (i.e. a proportion of the products paid to the landlord who provides the land and sometimes a portion of the capital) is known as *aparcería*. Not all *aparcería* tenancies were socially stable, entailing a just division between tenant and landlord. For an example of 'confused' tenures cf. the series of rights to use the same piece of land (e.g. for pig-grazing, wheat, cork), which was common practice in Estremadura.

sight of dried-out wheat stubble in areas where agricultural towns and villages (*pueblos*) are spaced ten to twenty miles apart.[1] William Beckford travelled for five hours in Estremadura without seeing 'any animals, bipeds or quadrupeds'. To Fermín Caballero, writing at the turn of the nineteenth century, this pattern of agricultural settlement constituted the chief bar to progress: a more intensive system was the key to higher production but the physical relation of the labourer and farmer to the land, the distance from the house in which he slept to the field he worked, made intense cultivation impossible.[2] The fact that a peasant's farm buildings were in the *pueblo* limited the number of cattle and hens he could keep (it may be quite difficult to buy an egg in a town of 3,000 inhabitants) and was one more factor inhibiting a satisfactory balance between animal and crop husbandry. Yet, outside the areas of dispersed settlement—Galicia, the Basque Provinces, and parts of Catalonia—the large agrarian village or small town was a social heritage it was impossible to destroy in the interests of agricultural efficiency; in arid country the peasant regards the land as the source of a poor livelihood, not as a mystique; he prefers to live away from it; the social satisfactions of the *pueblo* were subsumed in the concept of *animación*, the absence of rural boredom to be found only in an urban or semi-urban community.

It was the combination of this type of settlement with the excessive fragmentation of holdings that was the most generally unperceived but pernicious feature of the traditional system. Handkerchief plots were by no means confined to Galicia. In much of Castile minifundia were created by inheritance laws that divided equally among children, whereas in the Basque Provinces and Catalonia the family farm remained as a unit for generations. As population grew so, in parts of Castile, the farm unit became smaller and the number of strips or fields

[1] Cf. A. de Laborde, *Itinéraire descriptif de l'Espagne* (Paris, 1808), ii. 121: 'The districts devoted to grain and (extensive) pasture are almost entirely uninhabited.' In a sense this was untrue, in that the working population were housed in the towns.

[2] Fermín Caballero's book contains interesting work plans on various types of settlement. To take an extreme modern example: should a farmer wish to change to a row crop on a field six miles from his home—a distance by no means inconceivable in Andalusia—he might have to make two mule journeys a day for one hundred and sixty days of the year.

that comprised the unit minute. The minifundium is frequently to be found side by side with the latifundium; indeed the existence of the great entailed estates increased the pressure of men on the land. Thus within twenty-five miles of Madrid miserable plots exist side by side with ranch estates.[1] Combined with concentrated settlement in *pueblos*, the resultant wastage of labour in cultivation could be enormous; as much as twenty to thirty days a year could be lost on walking to scattered and distant strips. The out-fields were badly cultivated, cattle husbandry almost impossible, trees a luxury on small plots where land could not be 'wasted'; the sheer cadastral complexity of the system was one of the most serious bars to badly needed systems of agricultural credit for the small man.[2] One of the most obvious 'improvements' was a concentration of strip holdings, but to this day little has been accomplished. It was natural that reformers should attack latifundia, where the under-utilization of the land and the pressure of population were obvious, rather than settle down to the complicated legal technicalities involved in the consolidation of vast numbers of dispersed strips.

[1] Statistics of average size of holdings are for technical reasons difficult to interpret. On one twenty-acre farm between the Escorial and Avila I found forty-two 'parcels'. Cf. J. García Fernández, *Horche*, 221 ff. An 'average' farm in this *pueblo* of Guadalajara would seem to be 6–20 hectares, split into 14–20 fields or *parcelas*. The following table shows that in some areas (e.g. Galicia) both farms and fields are small and that in others (e.g. Burgos) sizeable farms are split into minute fields.

Province	*Average size of farm (hectares)*	*Average size of fields (hectares)*
Alava	20·96	0·95
Burgos	20·55	0·51
Coruña	4·31	0·21
Cuenca	26·99	0·98
Guadalajara	33·85	0·66
Jaén	15·20	0·47
Logroño	11·81	0·70
Lugo	9·06	0·50
Orense	6·99	0·24
Oviedo	7·04	0·82
Pontevedra	2·97	0·16
Soria	29·14	0·51

[2] Cf. M. González Moreno y Balda, *Concentración parcelaria y cotos acasarados* (1951). Though an exaggerated attack on the twin evils of fragmentation and concentrated settlement, it contains some useful figures.

The changes in the classic agricultural structure of Spain between 1750 and 1850 were achieved by rearrangement of the traditional economy, by its expansion in space, not by any fundamental change. Most of Spain did not experience the dramatic rise in agricultural production per acre that was achieved elsewhere in Europe by an intensification of cultures and new fodder crops. Drought—Spain is the only major European country where over large areas rainfall is less than fifteen inches a year—precluded such changes on the *secano*. There were no new fodder or root crops, except for the various leguminous plants that did something to improve fallows in the eighteenth century. Lucerne, on which Young set such high hopes, could only be grown on deep soils or on irrigated land, and there it was to produce a minor revolution.[1] Thus great areas of central Spain were condemned to the extensive farming of cereals for low yields at great expense of labour.[2]

In the latter half of the eighteenth century in Spain, as in other countries, an industrial revival and a surge of commercial optimism accompanied a rise in population and in agricultural prices. Striking though the industrial revival was we need not examine it in detail. Industry, outside the domestic crafts, created only a small proportion of the national income and, compared with primary products, of the foreign trade of Spain. Moreover, many of the conquests of the eighteenth century were not to be maintained. Thus the silk industry of Valencia, frequently noted by travellers as one of the most promising features of the economy, apart from a period of prosperity between 1835 and 1852, remained relatively stagnant throughout the nineteenth century; in the late eighteenth century a technically advanced industry, in the nineteenth it could not keep pace with Lyons.[3] The new departure, which became a permanent conquest, though there were hard times to come,

[1] Cattle were kept permanently, in large towns like Barcelona, on lucerne brought in from the country. Lack of water in the subsoil made lucerne cultivation impossible on the *secano*.

[2] In Córdoba wheat gets five to six times the labour it is given in French wheat-growing regions.

[3] The nineteenth-century decline may have been due in part to disease of cocoons. It is hard to judge from P. Madoz (*Diccionario geográfico-estadístico*, xv. 422) the state of the industry; it would not seem technically backward in 1845, for there were four steam factories 'brilliantly installed and equipped'.

was the localization of a cotton industry round Barcelona. This was to be the basis of the first true industrial complex of modern Spain: the Catalan textile industry.

The roots of these developments in Catalonia, where the traditions of a mercantile civilization had long existed, are complex. Intensification and specialization in agriculture, especially in the vineyards, gave rise to commercial exchange and opportunity for profit and saving. There was, in the mid century, a gap between rising wages and even more rapidly rising prices that favoured investment. There was, too, after 1760, the stimulation of the Latin-American market, the investment of American profits, and the effects of a new influx of Mexican silver.[1] There was a prohibition of the import of cotton cloth (1771); the gap between Castilian and Catalan taxation, which favoured Catalonia; the rapid importation of foreign improvements in textile manufacture (especially in the early years of the nineteenth century). Finally—a factor peculiarly stressed by Catalan historians—there was the industrious artisan family's propensity to save, which provided the economic and psychological springs of industrial progress.[2]

The Catalan renaissance was based on cotton and brandy together with the staples of the colonial trade (soap, shoes, paper) and the expansion of the merchant marine. Barcelona became once more a great Mediterranean port—its trade, which had been the pride of medieval Catalonia, had quintupled since the early years of the century—and it now started its career as an industrial city.

Catalonia had possessed only a small section of a textile industry scattered all over Spain but it was round Barcelona that the cotton factory made its appearance.[3] Starting with the printing of imported calicoes in the forties, by the nineties Catalonia held the biggest concentration of dyers and weavers

[1] See below, pp. 34–36.

[2] For the gap between wages and prices see P. Vilar, 'Élan urbain et mouvement des salaires', *Revue d'histoire économique et sociale* (1950), xxvii. The classic description of the Catalan industrial psychology is C. Pi Sunyer, *L'aptitut econòmica de Catalunya* (2 vols., Barcelona, 1927). For a description of the taxational privileges see R. Herr, *The Eighteenth-Century Revolution in Spain* (Princeton, 1958), 128–9.

[3] Catalonia produced only 3 per cent. of the total production of woollen goods. Cf. Salvador Lloret, *E.G.* vii (1946), 729 ff.

outside Lancashire.[1] In the decade after 1770 the industrialized regions became centres of high wages drawing on the surplus labour of the hinterland, setting up a wave of immigration that was to spread outwards until, in the later nineteenth century, it tapped the poverty of the deep south and Murcia. A shortage of domestic servants and farm labourers, noted in the later eighteenth century, is a crude index of economic progress. Already in the late eighteenth century Catalonia exhibited another phenomenon of industrial civilization: unemployment consequent on the collapse of market and the deterioration of general trading conditions.

The prosperity of the Catalan economy had thus come to be at the mercy of events outside Spain. It was jeopardized by the wars of 1779 and 1796, with the consequent loss of the American market, and the entry of French textiles in the War of Independence (1808–14). After the war the industry was too depressed to re-equip itself as it had done in 1804. Thus it could not compete with Lancashire, and rigid protection of the home market became the creed of all Catalan industrialists.[2] One smaller Catalan industry, cork, was more consistent in its growth because it held a monopoly of raw material. From small beginnings in the eighteenth century it prospered in the depression after 1814. In spite of its prosperity, the cork industry was the classic example of the unenterprising side of the Catalan artisanate. With its strong guild, its suspicion of machinery, it remained representative of an older industrial civilization that persisted alongside the drive of the cotton men, and represented an attitude that could delay the modernization of the economy. This was the obverse of the image of the industrious Catalan artisan as the basis of industrial progress.[3]

As a result of her prosperity, uncertain though it often appeared, Catalonia began to appear as the model and exemplar

[1] For a summary of this development see L. Beltrán Flórez, *La industria algondonera española* (Barcelona, 1943). There is a mass of detail in J. Carrera Pujal, *Historia de la economía española* (Barcelona, 1947), vol. iv; and F. Torrella Nubio, *El moderno resurgir textil de Barcelona* (Barcelona, 1961), contains the early history of the calico industry and its struggles against the efforts of the guilds to capture it (34 ff.). Cotton spinning started in 1765.

[2] See below, pp. 278–80.

[3] See R. Medir Jofra, *Historia del gremio corchero* (1953). By the 1840's the cork industry employed 6,000. In the 1850's an attempt to introduce a modification of an English machine of 1812 was successfully resisted by riots.

of mercantile and industrial civilization, a role that was to bring her into sharp conflict with traditional values and interests. Catalan emigrants were taking new attitudes into Spain itself. After restoring their own fishing industry, Catalans re-established that of Galicia. Borrow found Catalans everywhere as innkeepers and carriers. There are signs that their enterprise was resented, a foretaste of the accusations of selfish materialism that were to be pinned on Catalans for a hundred years to come.[1] Already Catalan employers were organized in powerful associations to fight for the maintenance of import prohibitions. Already the enemies were smugglers, the English, free traders, and governments that wished to tax the industrious to support sterile bureaucrats and pensioners. Already there were counter-warnings from Castile of selfish interests, of the dangers of high costs and failure to modernize that would be the consequence of excessive protection.

> If they sleep in the shade of prohibitions for foreign goods, besides harming the Treasury and the Nation, they will harm themselves. When a nation cannot produce as cheaply or as well as foreigners, then no barriers will save it against smugglers, fashion and the consumer's interest. The true method is to adapt foreign machines which will enable national products to be as cheap and good as those of other countries.'[2]

In the expansive atmosphere of the turn of the century Catalan and Valencian manufacturers were doing precisely this: in 1790 the first steam engine came to Barcelona.

The new prosperity of 'industrious' Catalonia and 'opulent' Valencia threw into contrast the industrial decline that had left central Spain a backwater of artisan industry. Almost all the great Castilian wool towns were shadows, 'skeletons of towns once populous and crammed with factories, workshops and stalls, now full of churches, convents and hospitals . . . destitute of commerce, supported by the church'.[3] Valladolid,

[1] 'Those who love laziness and wish to get rich with little work at the expense of their neighbours cannot tolerate Catalans establishing themselves outside their principality. But sensible men appreciate their worth and regard them as brother Spaniards.' Larruga in 1792: quoted J. Vicens Vives, *Historia social y económica de España y América* (Barcelona, 1954), iii 194.

[2] *Correo Mercantil*, 10, i, 1803, quoted in L. M. Enciso Real, *La prensa económica del siglo XVIII* (Valadolid, 1958), 48.

[3] Townsend, *Travels*, i. 378.

Salamanca, Toledo, and Segovia were administrative and ecclesiastical capitals, glorified market towns with hat and soap factories, a hundred or so looms, flour mills, and brickyards. Besides a domestic textile industry scattered through every town and village, certain small towns had specialities that served wider markets; steel knives at Guadix, horse rugs at Morella, textiles and pottery at Puente del Arzobispo, sickles at La Solana, in La Mancha. Much of this small industry was stagnant or declining, especially after the disruption and contraction that accompanied and followed the War of Independence. In the eighteenth century Aragon, where agriculture was prospering and olive groves had doubled in a hundred years, had become an industrially depressed region. Textiles were in full decline; the old metal trades had vanished to the point where no artisan could explain the traditional techniques. Only leather prospered.[1] The wretched towns of lower Aragon, detested by liberal soldiers, became strongholds of Carlism and it was the desolation of decaying artisan towns that set off the polemics on the effectiveness of ecclesiastical charity.

Sometimes decline can be explained as an inevitable concomitant of development; thus the heyday of Valencian prosperity was matched by a dramatic decline in the silk industry of Granada and the smaller industry of the Aragonese valleys may have suffered from Catalan competition. Nevertheless, the most serious limitation on the development of the core of Spain was the shape of the Peninsula itself.

Even with good roads, transport costs, in a large square country where canals are an economic and physical impossibility, must remain high. Napoleon was to find that the best roads in Europe could not create a European market. It was space that lamed the prospects of a truly national economy; it was distance by land that doomed the government's expensive attempt to re-create, in the eighteenth century, a great wool industry in central Spain and hampered the creation of an

[1] 'Never have the manufactures of Aragon been so decayed as at this moment when agriculture is flourishing, and the population increasing', I. Asso, *Aragón*, 207. Asso's testimony cannot be rejected, although he represents the prejudices of his age. The decline is evident from a cessation of building in the late eighteenth century, which can be observed in a derelict *pueblo* like Mirambel.

internal market in the nineteenth.[1] An industrial revival cannot for long remain based on mules and donkeys. Not the least of the advantages enjoyed by the peripheral regions was cheap coastal transport.

It was the possibility of directly profiting from a revival of Spanish overseas trade that brought prosperity to these same regions: to the 'companies' of Catalan, to the merchants of the Levante ports, and to the Basque shippers. Already, in the first half of the century, a Basque concern, the Caracas Company, developed a flourishing trade in cocoa with a hitherto undeveloped region of the American Empire—Venezuela.[2] The trade revival of the later eighteenth century was independent, in its origins, of the gradual process by which Charles III destroyed the long-standing monopoly of Cadiz and Seville in the later eighteenth century. The old colonial system stood in the way of any attempt to replace an empire based on bullion imports by a mercantilist empire à la Colbert, reserved for Spanish products and feeding the prosperity of the mother-country; regimentation had failed when interlopers and smugglers had turned the Castilian monopoly into a fiction, when 'Spain kept the cow, the rest of Europe drank the milk'. Charles III determined to increase the Spanish share of the colonial market by increasing the number of Spanish ports privileged to trade with America and by a sustained effort to diminish the legal and illegal trade in foreign hands—especially British and French. There can be little doubt that liberalization (by which is meant effective restriction of the colonial trade to a larger number of Spanish merchants than under the old system) greatly increased the volume and the proportion of Spanish goods in the legal trade, and therefore acted as a direct stimulant to industrial and commercial revival. From the complaints of British and French merchants it is clear that the colonial trade was ceasing to be a 'device by

[1] The most ambitious attempt was the factory of Guadalajara: at its height it seems to have employed 4,000 hands. For the long struggle to stave off disaster by the injection of governmental subsidies, see J. Vicens Vives, *Historia económica de España* (Barcelona, 1959), 474–5. It was transport costs that ruined the attempt to re-establish a silk industry in Toledo (G. Desdevises du Dezert, *L'Espagne de l'ancien régime* (Paris, 1904), iii. 132) and prevented the revival of the woollen industry of Segovia in spite of its obvious advantages as centre of a wool region.

[2] See R. D. Hussey, *The Caracas Company, 1782–84* (Cambridge, Mass., 1934).

which was canalized, under royal control, the supply of goods from the rest of Europe'.[1] It was this success that made the merchants of England reflect on the desirability of destroying 'despotism' in Spanish America in order to establish direct trade in a market that British goods and British credit terms would dominate.[2]

It was the belief of Chaptal, Napoleon's Minister, that the attempt to create a colonial market came too late. Its continued prosperity depended on three conditions: Spain's control of the seas, her continued political control of a vast empire, and her capacity to supply her colonies with the goods they needed. If she could not, given a venal customs service, smugglers would.[3] War with England (1796–1802) was a sheer disaster, revealing all the inherent weaknesses of Spain's position in the American market; American ports were opened to neutrals when it became evident that Spain herself could no longer supply her colonies. The war of 1808 and the movement for independence in the colonies was to complete the defeat of Spain's effort to create a mercantilist empire. The opportunity vanished. Spain did not become a great mercantile nation because she failed as a naval power to retain political control of her great empire, and as a producer to supply cheap goods. By 1829 her foreign trade was a third of that of 1785. There was a most serious consequence: Spanish trade, throughout the nineteenth century, was unable to conquer the import surplus, which in the eighteenth century had been concealed by the export of American silver. Once wool had declined there was

[1] Cf. J. B. Williams, 'The establishment of British commerce with Argentina', *H.A.H.R.* xv. 193, pp. 44 ff. For reactions to the new restrictions see V. L. Brown, *Smith College Studies in History*, xv (1929). Since 1772 no foreign goods had been allowed on the regular fleets: before this French and British exceeded Spanish goods. In the later eighteenth century the proportion of Spanish and foreign products among the *regular* exports to America was about equal. Cf. M. Peuchet, *État des colonies* (Paris, 1821), 278.

[2] A. Christelow, *Trades*, 19–27. But cf. H. S. Fern, who points out (*Britain and Argentina in the Nineteenth Century* (Oxford, 1960), 10) that by 1763 there was 'evidence that the flow of British goods to Spanish America was in excess of the demand in this market' and that Spanish colonial rule was pernicious to British trade less through laws to keep out foreign goods, which had been evaded for years, than because it prohibited an expansive society.

[3] See D. B. Goebel, 'British trade to Spanish Colonies 1796–1823', *American Historical Review*, xlviii (1930), 298. Humboldt, in his *Essai politique sur l'isle de Cuba* (Paris, 1826), noted the failure of Spain to supply cheap imports.

no staple: brandy, wheat, fruits, oil, wine, and lead for Europe, shoes, textiles, paper, and hats for the colonies could not close the gap. It was not until the Basque iron deposits were exploited by foreign capital, instead of by the archaic techniques of the Basque miners, that Spain was to acquire a substitute for wool.[1]

What is significant for the future of the developments of the later eighteenth century? Evident in all aspects of the economy is the imbalance between the prosperity of the periphery and the stagnation of the centre. Change, in industry, commerce, and agriculture, was most evident and most rapid in the periphery.

In the eighteenth century, particularly after 1770, the population of Spain began to share the general European increase, rising by four million to over ten million.[2] What is noticeable about this rise is its concentration in peripheral Spain: Galicia, Catalonia, the Basque Provinces, Santander, and the Levante. The contrasts between the wheat prices of Catalonia and the Basque Provinces and those of central Spain are another indication of divergence.[3] In Castile violent fluctuations in price were the consequence of continued dependence on the local harvest; Barcelona imported most of her meat and wheat, and imports levelled out prices. These depended, therefore, on the harvests of northern Europe—an indication of the degree to which the more 'modern' economy of the periphery was involved in a wider world and of the perils of specialization: a drop in the European demand for wine meant disaster for the marginal *rabassa morta* cultivators. Perhaps the most dramatic indications of this growing imbalance are the rising wages and population of Barcelona and Valencia, compared with those of Madrid, the centre of Old Spain. 'In the undoubted progress realized in the eighteenth century', writes Vilar, 'was implicit a relationship between the various regions of the Peninsula quite distinct from that of the *siglo de oro*. Demographically and economically the centre of Spain loses its dominating position.

[1] For the old structure of iron-mining see F. Sánchez Ramos, *La economía siderúrgica española* (1945).

[2] The demography of eighteenth-century Spain is examined in Domínguez Ortiz, *Sociedad*, 54–75, and in detail for the small port of Palamos in J. Nadal, 'Demografía y economía', *E.H.M.* vi (1959), 286 ff. Cf. the densities per square kilometre: Valencia 48; Valadolid 27; Avila 22; Estremadura and La Mancha 14.

[3] Cf. esp. P. Vilar, *Catalogne*, ii. 337–44.

There is a return to the balance of antiquity when peripheral Spain—especially Mediterranean Spain—attracted to itself population, activity and production.'[1] This differing developmental rhythm was to have profound social and political consequences.

[1] Vilar has examined wages after 1774: Barcelona wages rose 66–110 per cent.; Madrid 14–30 per cent. The population of Madrid rose from 130,000 (1723) to 167,607 (1797): Barcelona from 37,000 (1714) to 115,000 (1802).

II

TRADITIONAL SOCIETY AND ITS CRITICS

AT the Congress of Vienna the pretensions of Spain were dismissed as those of a *cour secondaire*; at the accession of Charles III, in 1759, such an attitude would have been inconceivable and unrealistic. The Spanish empire, which stretched over the American continent from California to the Straits of Magellan, was the most imposing political structure of the Western world; to Napoleon it was still the greatest supplier of silver and to British merchants the greatest unexploited market. The reign of Charles III was to see an attempt to realize, in terms of prosperity and power, the potentialities of this great empire and of metropolitan Spain.

This essay in governmental reform has parallels in most other European countries. In Spain it was distorted and cut short by the crisis of 1789 and the French invasion of 1808, but not before it had modified, if not the traditional structure of society, at least the traditional attitudes. We must first examine within this society both those elements that resisted change and those that would be considered as instruments of progress. We must then attempt to evaluate governmental reform both in terms of what it set out to achieve and of its legacy to later liberalism. This legacy was a programme for a revolution from above: often incoherent in its premisses, its common criterion was utility: institutions, classes, and laws must be judged in terms of their utility as producers of felicity. Advanced in the interests of increasing the resources and efficiency of the State, the programme of the civil servants of Charles III contained in its armoury weapons that would destroy the complex of values upholding the static society of the old régime. The revolutionary implications of utility were developed by radicals, and it is the interconnexion of governmental and radical reform that we must finally consider.

1. *The Traditional Order*

The secret of Spanish stagnation had long been sought in the excessive size of the 'unproductive classes', from grandees down to vagrant schoolmasters. The census of 1797 still put these classes, slowly diminishing as an element in the State, at 30 per cent. of the active male population. Even worse, it was estimated that two of the unproductive classes, the nobility and the Church, held two-thirds of the land of Spain in entail and mortmain.[1] Much of the criticism of the Church and nobility, dressed out in the commonplaces of the Enlightenment, had its root in the conviction that the 'slavery' of entail was the greatest single obstacle in the way of progress.

The *mayorazgo*, the unbreakable Spanish entail, was the central institution of the old aristocracy.[2] Its declared aim was to preserve a family name by attaching it perpetually to an estate that passed undivided to a single heir. *Mayorazgos* had spread geographically outwards from Castile, socially downwards from the great houses—hence the creation of small 'abusive' entails by non-nobles—and had come to include movables—jewels, relics, and pictures.[3] Among the aristocracy the growth of vast entails was consistently favoured by lawyers' evasions of the 'doctrine of incompatibility', designed to prevent accumulation of entailed estates. Thus intermarriage could bring huge concentrations of titles and entailed property to a few surviving great houses.

The *mayorazgos* had been bitterly criticized since the sixteenth century for encouraging laziness as well as being an injustice to younger children. In the eighteenth century criticism was less moralistic than utilitarian and economic. It came from statesmen and reformers who held that entails, by

[1] A very rough estimate of the distribution of landed property in Spain *c.* 1800 is: Church 9·09 million *fanegas*; Nobility 28·3; Commoners 17·5 (the *fanega* = 0·64 hectares). Certain provinces, for instance Avila, were much more in the hands of the nobility than these figures indicate; others much less, as was the case in the Basque Provinces.

[2] The Orders of Chivalry were of immense importance in maintaining the corporate spirit of the aristocracy, but by the nineteenth century the test of blood had become more of a formality.

[3] Cf. Marqués del Saltillo, *La nobleza en el pasado* (1930), esp. 17 ff. For an old-fashioned treatment see R. Carr, 'Spain', in *The European Nobility in the Eighteenth Century*, ed. A. Goodwin (London, 1953).

precluding a free market in land, artificially raised its value so that investment became unprofitable; it was a hindrance to a wider diffusion of ownership, which was universally held to be a precondition of increased production. It had long been held as a general axiom—quite incorrectly, as Catalonian experience showed—that entail caused a régime of short, unstable leases and once again stood at the head of the *estorbos*, the impediments to progress. Thus the campaign against entail was not a campaign against aristocratic landownership as such, but a crusade for capital investment in land and agricultural efficiency. Most reformers admitted that entail was a social and political necessity if the nobility were to survive with *decoro*. Reforms, therefore, concentrated on the suppression of small entails and the prohibition of future entails.[1] In 1793 the government gave permission to convert entailed property into treasury bonds. This strange conjunction of the fiscal necessities of the crown and the campaign against entail would, if implemented, have converted the landed property of the aristocracy into paper assets.

The social prestige, and much of the income of the aristocracy, derived from their *señorios*. These seigniorial rights were varied and complex: some were disguised rent payments; other residuary feudal dues; others arose from the sale or grant of municipal office. The radical attack on *señorios* came from Aragon and Valencia where the confusion between rent payment and feudal dues was most marked and where the lords had transferred to their Christian subjects the obligations that had once rested on the moriscos.[2] There are a few signs of that fierce screwing up of feudal payments characteristic of the later stages of the *ancien régime* in France; in Catalonia, for instance, a steady increase in the price of the farms of feudal dues overtook the rise in agricultural prices.[3] Many judicial rights were more trouble than they were worth, but, burdensome or trivial, they

[1] For a history of early disentailing legislation see J. Sempere y Guarinos, *Historia de los vínculos y mayorazgos* (1805).

[2] Cavanilles and Asso are full of denunciations of abusive exaction: e.g. Cavanilles, *Valencia*, i. 162; ii. 34. Asso's set-piece is his description of Ribera de Jalón.

[3] Among the resented features were the oil-milling monopolies of the south. The Medinacelis had been in the courts with one of their towns for 149 years on this subject. In Galicia occasional feudal payments fell heavily on a poor peasantry. The problem is local; for instance there were virtually no feudal survivals in the Basque Provinces.

were nevertheless a foundation of aristocratic influence; in half the villages and towns as mayor, councillor, or judge, the lord or his representative stood between the subject and his king.

No doubt the moral and physical absenteeism of the Spanish nobility has been over-emphasized and misunderstood. Nobles were urban, but outside the areas of disseminated settlement the peasants and farmers were likewise town dwellers. There were differing levels of absenteeism at differing levels of the noble's world. The great aristocratic houses were real absentees at court and a visit of a grandee to his estates ranked as a great event in local history. The lesser aristocracy in the south concentrated in 'noble' towns like Ronda or Baeza where their social life could centre on the local horse-breeding club, the *Maestranza*. But in the small towns of Castile and the north the local *hidalgo* was no more an absentee than his peasants. He would have his seat in the parish church, his municipal office. In some regions the lesser nobles, both titled and untitled, were interested in local concerns and in agricultural improvement: thus the Basque and Asturian lesser nobility were admirable local patriots, good landlords, influential in their districts. It was these northern gentry who became the model for those who sought to save the influence of the nobility by involving it in a movement for reform and economic progress. Economic Societies—an invention of the Basques—would allow the provincial nobility to 'contribute to the happiness of the kingdom'.[1] As a whole the nobility failed to respond to this call. The habits of mind that went with the *mayorazgo* were not those of the ideal improving landlord of the Economic Societies, 'always occupied in the felicity of his village'. The noble landowners' outlook was that of passive rentiers who made it a point of pride to be cheated by their bailiffs; even if entail had not put technical difficulties in the way of raising capital it is hard to believe that Spanish aristocrats would have conceived of higher rents as a reward of investment.[2] They survived through the sheer size of their rent rolls.

[1] *Discurso para la abertura de las Juntas Generales que celebró la Sociedad Bascongada en la Villa de Vergara* (1785).

[2] Cf. the typically English viewpoint of Beckford who sees the connexion between high rents and good farming: 'These immense properties (of the Duke of Alba) are underlet and wretchedly cultivated', *Journal of W. Beckford 1787–1788*, ed. Boyd Alexander (London, 1954), 288.

Yet there was no widespread attack on aristocratic landowners by those who suffered directly from their incurable indifference to country life—in spite of royal example they did not hunt, there was little shooting until the late nineteenth century, and they would have found English country-house life inconceivable.[1] In Catalonia there was little criticism of a territorial aristocracy that took little or no interest in its lands: the large farmers were confident and secure in an aristocratic rural society where an early and major defeat of the economic power of the nobility had left the *masovers* a rural bourgeoisie.[2] Together with the prosperous shopkeepers and merchants, rather than seeking to challenge the aristocracy, they found opportunities for investment and perhaps superior status in the farming of feudal dues. They became involved in sustaining the feudal superiorities from which they profited in a small way.[3] It was the marginal cultivators that took land on *rabassa morta*, who found tithes and feudal dues an intolerable burden, and they were not powerful enough to challenge either the large farmers or the aristocrats from whom they held their lands. Only in the War of Independence did they occasionally raise their voices against 'the rich'.[4]

By the end of the eighteenth century in political life, as in economic life, the old aristocracy had lost much of its influence, through incompetence and indifference. Once the days of the great favourites and the aristocratic clique had passed, the higher nobility withdrew. The grandees never recovered the influence lost in the War of Succession, when they proved themselves politically unreliable, incompetent, and excessively tetchy.[5] In their place the crown employed lesser nobles and lawyers who had no awkward pretensions to political influence.

[1] A. Young, *Travels*, ii. 323–5.

[2] The medieval struggle is described in J. Vicens Vives, *Historia de los remensas en el siglo XV* (Barcelona, 1945).

[3] See P. Vilar, *Catalogne*, ii. 482 ff.

[4] J. Vicens Vives, *Els catalans en el segle XIX* (Barcelona, 1958), 121.

[5] The French administrators of Philip V despised them and excluded them from influence by working through the *despacho* (i.e. a modern ministry) rather than through the 'aristocratic' Councils. Philip seems to have acted on Louis XIV's advice: 'Preserve all the external prerogatives of their rank and, at the same time, exclude them from a knowledge of all matters which might add to their credit.' (*Correspondance de Louis XIV avec Amelot*, ed. Baron de Giradot (Nantes, 1804), Letter of 20 August 1705.)

The so-called Aragonese party (led by the strong man of the military aristocracy, Aranda, who came to power in 1766) may, perhaps, be seen as a belated attempt to recover power, at a moment of crisis for the king, from the hands of professional civil servants. The last political triumph of the old aristocracy was the overthrow of Godoy—an obscure, Estremaduran *hidalgo* who, in social origins, was a typical servant of a monarchy whose only test was zeal in its service.[1] Thus the higher aristocracy kept its court positions but lost effective power to 'the aristocracy of *empleados*' (State employees).[2]

Spanish values had been noble. In the later eighteenth century the concept of nobility was subject to an attack that reached surprising verbal violence: the useful bourgeois was set against the useless noble as the pattern of social virtue. Combined with the decline in the political influence of the great aristocracy this has led to the notion of a 'crisis of the nobility'. Such a phrase neglects the fact that the attack on the nobility was a European literary fashion and that the Spanish nobility was undergoing a complex change, which was later to allow it to revive some of its social and political influence.[3]

In Spain the attack on aristocratic values was enhanced by the extent of the nobility: when half a million Spaniards, from the poor *hidalgo* 'eating black bread under the genealogical tree' to the great grandees, claimed noble birth, the economic disadvantages of aristocratic attitudes—for example, contempt for 'vile' trades—were serious. In the eighteenth century this undifferentiated mass nobility had tended to contract, and it was the lower ranges of this class who, as ennobled civil servants, collected to themselves the influence lost by the great court aristocracy. Like the provincial nobility of the northern provinces, this was a working nobility. Thus the anti-aristocratic debate, in so far as it was not a literary fashion, was a polemical weapon in a struggle within the nobility between the

[1] For the 'popular' aristocratic conspiracy against Godoy, see below, pp. 83–84.

[2] The phrase is used by the marqués de Miraflores, a minister of Isabella II.

[3] For diatribes against aristocracy cf. J. Sarrailh, *Espagne éclairée*, 518 ff. This trend is already present in the father of the Enlightenment, Feijóo, and becomes quite bitter in later writers, e.g. Cadalso. Most of the eighteenth-century reformers exhibit traces of this hostility. But since many (e.g. Jovellanos) were provincial nobles, their aim was rather to make the nobility *effective* by pruning away its characteristic vices than to destroy it as a social force.

trained *golillas* (pen-men, usually of modest noble origin) and the 'military' aristocracy, who may have regarded office as the reward of rank. It represented, not the ambitions of an economically powerful bourgeoisie, but the claim of one section of the nobility to replace another as the chosen instrument of the crown.[1] The civil servants of enlightened despotism had little conception of systematically using institutional power against the aristocracy; bureaucrats thought of themselves as government servants, not as combatants in a class struggle. The *golillas*'s conflict with the so-called military aristocracy, if it represents anything, is perhaps best considered as a foretaste of the nineteenth-century conflict between soldiers and civilians.

Like every other class and institution, the nobility was tested in the crisis of 1808 and the French invasion: it does not seem to have failed in this test as completely as has been asserted. Where the local nobility provided leadership in the rising against the French it was accepted, as the composition of the Juntas shows; the role of these local notables has yet to be studied, but they represent a type of 'patriot' in 1808. Nevertheless, the intellectual climate of the Cortes of Cadiz was anti-aristocratic.[2] The notion of a Spanish House of Lords was rejected. Thus the creation by conservative liberals of a semi-hereditary Second Chamber in the constitutions of the nineteenth century represents a recovery of aristocratic influence within liberalism, even though the extent of this influence was incomparably less than that exercised by the English aristocracy.

In modern times the Spanish aristocracy has given little cultural leadership: in the late eighteenth century the few *esprit forts* who corresponded with Voltaire or Rousseau were swamped by the traditional formality and tedium that made Madrid society a nightmare for intelligent ambassadors.[3] The conspicuous waste of the Spanish aristocracy was not the

[1] Cf. below, p. 61. V. Rodríguez Casado ('La revolución burguesa del siglo XVIII' in *Arbor*, no. 61 (1951), pp. 367–74) stipulates a 'bourgeois revolution' in the later eighteenth century and the manning of institutions by bourgeois (i.e. legally-trained less nobles). The evidence that the riots against Esquilache in 1766 were an aristocratic counter-revolution against a bourgeois monarchy is weak. For a penetrating analysis see A. Domínguez Ortiz, *Sociedad*, 176–82.

[2] See below, pp. 94 ff.

[3] See R. Carr, *Spain*, 57–59.

patronage of art or civilized living but the maintenance of hordes of retainers and domestic hangers-on. They thus created a class of semi-employed pensioners, which was the foundation of their social strength in the larger towns.[1]

As a social institution the Church was superior in influence to the nobility. 'The real power in Spain', wrote Wellington, 'is in the clergy. They kept the people right against France.' In 1821 the former guerrilla leader Mina, an advanced liberal, recognized that a canon of Pamplona had more popular power than the provincial parliament of Navarre.[2] This power was in part a consequence of the Church's position as a landlord, as a charitable institution, and as a direct employer of labour in a 'beggar economy'. The great ecclesiastical towns lived on the churches and monasteries—perhaps a twentieth of the population of Valladolid depended on the Church—while soup and bread doles from the episcopal palaces and monasteries were an important element in the budget of the urban poor.[3] An English traveller described Leon as 'kept in existence by The Church'. Like the aristocracy, therefore, the Church could count on its urban mob, and in the riots of 1766 the Orders were accused of releasing this urban clientèle against a reforming administration; Aranda, the most conspicuous of Charles III's anti-clerical ministers, called to power to deal with the rioters, seems to have planned a serious attack on poverty precisely because he feared the influence of a Church with a monopoly of outdoor relief. He set his closest co-operator, Olavide, to reform the Madrid Hospital for poor invalids and attempted to clear all beggars out of Madrid.

More profoundly the influence of the Church depended on its penetration at every level of social life. Catholicism was, and is, not merely a personal faith but the formal sign of belonging

[1] All travellers comment on this host of servants; e.g. W. Jacob, *Travels*, 14. All 'keep a much greater number of domestic servants than families of the same description in England'. Townsend (*Travels*, ii. 155 ff.) gives details of the households of the Dukes of Alba and Medinaceli. There are some few signs of a modern attitude to the economic profitability of the great estates: even so there were too many accountants. The house of Peñafiel employed twenty-nine.

[2] General Francisco Espoz y Mina, *Memorias* (1851–2), ii. 301.

[3] Townsend, *Travels*, 305, 378. The number of churches in Castilian towns is staggering. Burgos (population 9,000, with 14 parish churches and 42 monasteries and convents), Olmedo (2,000, with 7 churches and 7 monasteries). It is said that the Cathedral of Saragossa employed 349 priests.

to Spanish society. Heresy becomes a social solecism, a self-declared exile, as the personal history of Protestant converts amply proves: George Borrow's Bible peddling was regarded as a threat to society itself or an incomprehensible eccentricity. The Church's great feasts, organized by the lay brotherhoods that canalized so much popular piety in Castile, were the expression of the corporate existence of a town. Foreign catholics who saw grandees giving up their carriages to the sacrament, theatre audiences falling to their knees as the viaticum passed in the streets, were astonished by the universal reverence for the outward forms of worship.

The Spanish Church was democratic: one eighteenth-century primate was the son of a charcoal burner, a situation inconceivable in France.[1] Most of the bishops made their way by scholarships to the *colegios mayores* of the great universities from the obscurity of the minor provincial nobility. There were no luxurious princes of the Church: a bishop was expected to give all his surplus income to charity once his simple household needs were satisfied. The average parish priest was poor and remained so throughout the nineteenth and twentieth centuries: he earned less than a well-paid labourer and was often dependent, in rural parishes, on the sale of eggs and on other minor agricultural pursuits. It was this condition that brought him close to his parishioners. Coming almost certainly from a middle-class or working-class home, once his seminary days were over he had little opportunity for further education. Hence the undeniable defect of the lower clergy was its low intellectual standards, especially when, perhaps as a result of liberal meanness in the settlements of the nineteenth century, the seminaries stagnated. In the eighteenth century his simple accomplishments were enough to shine out in a world of darkness. Thus the hold of the parish priest was uncontested in rural Spain especially in the stable peasant societies of the Basque country and Catalonia and where, as in Galicia outside the towns, he sided with his own class in the land war. It was later to be challenged in urban Spain—not merely that of the great city but also the sizeable southern agrarian pueblo—because his parishioners were confronted with rival ideologies

[1] Marquis de Custine, *L'Espagne sous Ferdinand VII* (Paris, 1838), ii. 58: 'La constitution du clergé espagnol est tout à fait républicaine.'

and because the priests tended to side with the notables. Violent anti-clericalism, as in 1835–6 and again in 1936, was an urban phenomenon imposed by the town on the countryside.

The weakness of the Church was the wasteful distribution of its resources relative to its recognized social functions. There were too few parish priests in the countryside, too many canons, vast numbers of unbeneficed priests, and hangers-on in minor orders in the towns.[1] In the later eighteenth century the 'useful' poorly-paid parish priest becomes a reformer's hero; he might be counted on as a leader of the Economic or Patriotic Societies and as a propagandist of improved agricultural methods. Thus the liberalism of 1808 could hope for the support of the intelligent lower clergy. In an age in which social utility was paramount, the Regular Orders, on the other hand, were considered 'useless'; nuns, wrote Jovellanos, should be made to knit. The sheer number of monks became an obsession that bound together reforming bureaucrats and their liberal heirs, showing how both drew on the criticism of the 'sterile' classes, which goes back at least to the sixteenth century. Moreover, the Regular Orders, with some exceptions, were in full organizational and intellectual decadence.[2] Their internal squabbles, a symptom of this decadence, made them peculiarly vulnerable; it was the quarrel between the Augustinians and Jesuits that opened the door to the regalist onslaught of the sixties on the privileges of the Church. The dissolution of the monasteries by the French in 1809 was the violent culmination of a twenty years' campaign.

The liberals of the Cortes of Cadiz accepted this dissolution as a *fait accompli* and it was this that made the Orders the chief enemies of liberalism in Spain. From the interruption of the war years the monasteries never recovered: their buildings had been stripped, their recruitment impeded, their incomes

[1] The census of 1797 gives the following figures for the secular clergy: parish priests 16,481; beneficed priests 17,411; patrimonial priests, 18,669; minor orders 18,669; canons 2,393; regular clergy (including novices, lay brothers, &c.), men 53,098, women 24,471. There was only 1 parish priest per 1,000 inhabitants in Estremadura: cf. the position in the great Castilian towns.

[2] The crushing, if prejudiced, verdict of G. Desdivises du Dezert, *L'Espagne*, ii. 151. The orders admitted novices too freely: itinerant begging of the Mendicant Orders relaxed discipline and prevented serious study.

dilapidated. In financial difficulties, the Jesuits could not re-establish their educational system in 1814.[1] For this blow the Orders never forgave liberalism: they preached against its constitution and its philosophy as the 'ultimate, supreme grade of evil'.[2]

It may be hazarded that it was this inevitable alliance with reaction, especially after 1820, that weakened the popularity of the Regular Orders in Spain and produced the convent burning and assassination that disgraced popular urban liberalism. Given the paucity and poverty of the parish clergy, the Orders were more closely connected with everyday religious life than is imagined.[3] They were popular preachers and evangelists—Diego de Cadiz, a Capuchin revivalist preacher, attracted audiences which fought for scraps of his clothing. They thus found a ready acceptance, in the war against the 'heretic' French in 1793, for their violent Francophobia. In the War of Independence they were the true mass leaders, the prophets of a primitive nationalism. After 1814 this influence, as a matter of survival, could only be directed against liberalism and was therefore committed wherever possible to Carlism. In Carlist territory monasteries were restored: in liberal Spain they became farms, barracks, schools, ministries, or simply fell into ruins.

2. *The Useful Classes*

The reformers of the eighteenth century, like many critics of traditional Spain, looked to the 'useful classes' as the instrument of progress. It has been an axiom of historical interpretation to attribute the failure of reform, in its eighteenth- and nineteenth-century forms, to the absence of a Spanish 'middle class'. Marxist theoreticians argued that without a confident class to support it liberalism failed to complete the bourgeois

[1] Cf. P. Lesmes Frías, *Historia de la Compañía de Jesús en su existencia moderna de España* (1933), i. 300 ff. For Catalonia see P. Aragonés, *Historia de los frailes franciscos de Cataluña*, 247–8.

[2] Quoted P. Sanahuja, *Historia de la seráfica provincia de Cataluña* (Barcelona, 1959), 526. The tone of this work is an astounding revelation of the feelings of the Orders concerning the liberalism that destroyed them.

[3] Especially in the large towns the function of the parish priest was 'a monitory rather than an apostolic one'; thus regular clergy were preferred as confessors: cf. M. Kenny, *Spanish Tapestry* (London, 1961), 146–7.

revolution against feudalism; thus they sought tactical models in Tsarist Russia that represented a stage of development comparable to that of modern Spain.[1] This analysis, which acquired a great vogue in the Civil War of 1936, hid the presence of a middle sector of society that was to divide along classic lines into a grand and petty bourgeoisie, the Moderates and Progressives of the mid-century.[2] Running from army officers to shopkeepers, from the *poderosos* (the 'powerful ones') of rural towns to the cotton magnates of Barcelona, this inchoate conglomerate of the middle sections of society was to dominate the political life of the nineteenth century. Its weakness as a political force lay, not in lack of numbers, but in the disparity and localism of its interests. 'For forty years', claimed a liberal statesman in 1855, 'the middle class has governed the nation; it has lost the New World, compromised the stability of society and has not yet learnt how to form a government.'[3]

In the eighteenth century the professions, which were to be the core of the nineteenth-century middle class, brought some social esteem but little economic power. The persistent characteristic of the Spanish professional class, especially in its lower ranges, is the necessity of double employment. Many university professors were paid less than labourers in the eighteenth century; if not clerics, they were forced, as were academics throughout the nineteenth century, to seek outside work to gain a living.[4] There were more schoolmasters *per capita* in Spain than in any other country in Europe, but they were vilely paid. They became carpenters, gamekeepers, and letter-writers. The universities, using an antiquated syllabus, turned out theologians, doctors, and lawyers and were dominated by the self-

[1] The class analysis of the failure of bourgeois revolution against 'feudalism' was popularized by Joaquín Maurín, a leader of the Marxist revolutionaries of the P.O.U.M.: it first appears in his *Los hombres de la dictadura* (1930).

[2] See below, pp. 158–64.

[3] Ríos Rosas, 17 Mar. 1855, quoted L. Sánchez Agesta, *Historia del constitucionalismo español* (1955), 109.

[4] In Salamanca the traditional chairs were relatively well endowed, the chairs in newer disciplines miserably paid. This created in the 1770's an opposition within the university that welcomed royal reforms of syllabus and methods, especially since the well-paid chairs usually went to members of the exclusive *colegios mayores*. 'The (university) reform movement (of the 1770's) was, in a sense, a social protest of the least privileged section of the academic community against its oppressors, aided by a sympathetic monarch' (G. M. Addy, 'The reform of 1771', *H.A.H.R.* xli (1961), 3 ff.).

recruiting major colleges (*colegios mayores*). These were residential colleges whose members had a virtual monopoly of the best jobs in the university and a privileged start in the civil service and the Church. As centres of culture the decadent universities played little part in national life and the inquiries of a government reform in the 1770's reveal an abysmal indifference to learning.[1]

Doctors hardly counted till after 1850 and no one could have foreseen the later social power of lawyers.[2] There was no *noblesse de robe*, no powerful corporation as in France. Except in Catalonia, the lower ranges of the legal profession were despised—in the Basque Provinces lawyers were debarred from participation in the local assemblies. University-trained lawyers dominated the civil service but only the highest posts gave social prestige.

The nineteenth century saw the transference of social prestige from a minority of lawyers acting as civil servants to a large number of lawyers acting as politicians. Like the great civil servants of the eighteenth century, nearly all the great civilian politicians of liberalism were trained as lawyers and until the emergence of the technicians in the twentieth century—their first rivals were railway engineers—they constituted the professional class *par excellence*. The predominance of lawyers in politics was to become a weapon in the crusade against the 'artificiality' of liberal parliamentarianism: deputies did not represent the 'live forces' (*fuerzas vivas*) of the community but the interests and ambitions of a small class of lawyer politicians. This was a polemical exaggeration: as in the United States today, many lawyers were closely connected with local life and later with business concerns as company lawyers. The position of lawyers is explained by what Spaniards call the 'lack of preparation' of other classes and the predominance of law as a general course of study in the universities. This produced a lawyer intelligentsia to whom politics was one of the subsidiary occupations open to the under-employed professional classes.

[1] For an amusing account of university life by a professor whom Gregorio Marañón calls 'a rogue of the market square' see Torres Villaroel's *Vida* (Valencia, 1743). That Torres Villaroel could become a professor of mathematics at the premier university of Spain is a revelation of the moral and intellectual level of university life.

[2] For the continuing prejudice against doctors see R. Ford, *Gatherings from Spain* (Everyman ed., London, 1906), 230–5. 'This low social position is very classical' (ibid. 234).

A bourgeoisie on the European pattern, distinct in outlook from the oligarchy that controlled the municipal government and the guilds, could only be found in the merchants and shippers of the great ports. A military accident stationed the first liberal parliament (1810) in Cadiz, the only town with a liberal society, a large French colony, a daily performance at the French theatre, a social life devoid of aristocratic prejudice, and where the test of status, even for nobles (who invested in trade), was wealth.[1] The prosperity of Cadiz, based on the American trade, was to decline sharply in the nineteenth century and allow Barcelona to take over its position as the exemplar of middle-class civilization, although it was never to replace the Andalusian towns as nurseries of liberal politicians.

In the early eighteenth century the old-established trading oligarchy of Barcelona and the Catalan towns was conservative: wholesale trade was reputed noble and the merchants of Barcelona wore the sword. This class was badly hit in the crisis of the early years of the century and, with recovery, it was outdistanced by a new and more enterprising group. In the *Junta de Comercio*, founded in 1758 as 'an institution informed with a new spirit, audacious and progressive', these new men fought the 'prejudices' of the guilds and participated in the most diverse enterprises. The customary framework of the 'company' allowed an industrious and enterprising shopkeeper to participate, on a minute scale, in a variety of undertakings: shipbuilding, the fish and wine trade, the farming of royal or seignorial revenues, the new American trade, textiles, the importation of wheat and meat.[2] By such a mechanism, in which family ties played an important part, a relatively rapid ascent was opened up for the younger sons of the prosperous Catalan farmers who must leave the farm to the chosen heir (the *hereu*); within a generation a man could make a modest fortune, exposed to the risk of loss as well as the hope of gain. Connected

[1] Cadiz seems to have invented the public café, which was to supplement the private *tertulia* and to become one of the central social institutions of liberal political life. For a description of Cadiz see R. Solis, *El Cádiz de las Cortes* (1958).

[2] These processes are described with massive detail and authority in vols. ii and iii of P. Vilar's *Catalogne*: see esp. iii. 386. The 'company' was often formed *ad hoc* for each enterprise and allowed the small man to invest in the same concerns with established wholesalers and the few nobles and Castilian officials who took to commerce.

with the markets of Spain, Europe, and, later, America, where Catalan agents gauged the rates of profit and sold the cargoes of Catalan ships, the merchants and shippers of Barcelona suffered directly from the crises of bad trade and war.[1] But even the war of 1808–14 and the French occupation produced its crop of *nouveaux riches*, flourishing on army contracts. Such doubtful activities were the making of one of the most splendid Catalan fortunes—that of Gaspar de Remisa, who prospered while artisans starved and merchants were ruined.[2]

On a smaller scale there was a nucleus of liberal lawyers and merchants in other coastal towns: in Cadiz, with its seventy-nine French exporting houses; in Bilbao and San Sebastian, where the pretensions of the rural oligarchy confronted the interests of an experienced and prosperous community of merchants; in Santander, which was to become a centre of the flour trade with Cuba; in Seville, with its American trade and its tobacco factory; in Valencia, with its silk manufacturers and its fruit trade; in Malaga, with its strong English and German connexions.[3] The urban improvements—town halls, paved streets—of the late eighteenth century reflected prosperity and local patriotism.[4] One inland town, Saragossa, produced in Goicoechea—a rich merchant, an enthusiast for poor-law reform, chairs of political economy, and agricultural progress—one of the best examples of late eighteenth-century enlightened, progressive city patriotism.

Yet these were islands standing out from a motionless sea: ten thousand individuals at the most. Just as Catalan ships were small compared with the merchant marine of France or England, so her 'companies' reveal a concentration of what has been called 'Lilliputian' capital. Predestined heroes of the bourgeois ethic, favoured by the Government in the 1760's,

[1] These came in 1744–8, 1787, 1780, with the war with France which cut short the bright prospects of 1791–3, and again in 1802–5.

[2] For Remisa see below, p. 204.

[3] For Hamburg's trade with Cadiz and Malaga see H. Pohl, *Die Beziehungen Hamburgs zu Spanien* (Wiesbaden, 1963).

[4] Outside the Basque Provinces the initiative for urban improvement tended to come from 'enlightened' Captains General, e.g. in Cadiz, Alicante, Valencia, and Barcelona. Most Castilian towns were too poor to improve, e.g. Zamora, whose municipality was bankrupt. Even small towns in lower Aragon show signs of a wave of municipal improvement, which, as far as I can judge, came to an end in the period 1799–1808.

the Spanish commercial and industrial classes were ill-fitted for leadership; the Economic Societies, centres of diffusion for the new gospel of productive labour, were early dominated by landowners, priests, and civil servants.[1] The 'economic' press of the late eighteenth century represented the 'directed journalism' of an optimistic government rather than the needs of a developed commercial class.[2] Depression in the epoch of the absolutist restoration after 1814 was both to convert the commercial and industrial interests to liberalism and to destroy the confidence of the years of prosperity, cut short by the loss of the American market and the dislocations of the war of 1808–14. It was not until the industrial recovery of the thirties that Barcelona became a force in liberal politics and a significant influence in the political crises of the mid century.

The institutional expression of the traditional, warm, intimate yet formalized urban civilization was the guild system. To the reformers the guilds, like entailed estates, were yet another historical hindrance (*estorbo*) to progress, a consecration of the forces of routine. The liberals, who were to abolish the guild system in 1834, reinforced these views with their doctrinaire belief in the virtues of competition. Yet this final dissolution was the culmination of a long decline. The public functions of the guilds had been increasingly restricted to the organization of religious processions and the distribution of charity. They were part of a society of determined hierarchies, impregnated with religious values and defended by conservatives for their social as distinct from their economic functions.[3] Even if their abolition increased mobility—in Catalonia it allowed the recruitment of entrepreneurs from the ranks of prudent shopkeepers and industrious artisans—the closed life of the family, which the guild had represented, remained the most durable social institution of the urban middle classes.

Beneath the substantial merchants were a numerous class of

[1] For the Patriotic or Economic Societies see below, pp. 70–72.

[2] Cf. L. M. Enciso Real, *Cuentas del 'Mercurio' y 'la Gaceta'* (Valladolid, 1957), esp. 137 ff., and *Prensa económica del siglo XVIII* (Valladolid, 1958). Subscribers to these papers included a large number of priests and the largest subscription was from the Basque Provinces.

[3] Most writers side with the reformers but for a modern defence see A. Romeu de Armas, *Historia de la previsión social en España* (chapters xx–xxii).

artisans, scattered in towns and villages all over Spain. There can be little doubt that, in many large towns from the 1770's on, its fate was becoming less enviable, its living less secure. This deterioration and the progressive proletarianization of the artisanate was to be particularly noticeable in Catalonia, where it represented an inevitable stage in the growth of capitalist industry: hence the outbreaks of Luddism in the 1840's. Some artisans—smiths, carpenters, for instance—maintained their position; but the largest single section in this patchwork of local industries, textiles, was declining as an artisan pursuit throughout the century, though the decline was slow.[1] This contraction was most severely felt by the few employees in the smaller workshops. In the late eighteenth century economic change began the destruction of long-established and comfortable patterns of town life; the intensification of this process in the nineteenth century was one of the psychological preconditions of primitive urban radicalism.

Outside the royal factories and the new concerns of Valencia and Barcelona, there was no proletariat physically and morally isolated from its employers. Throughout most of the towns of Spain, up till about 1850, the employers out-weighed the employees, a relationship that changed slowly in the later nineteenth century with the breakdown of local markets in consumer goods. The failure of democratic radicalism to develop a doctrine of class conflict was a reflection of this situation: master and man wanted the same relief from conscription and food taxes. Every radical revolt of mid-nineteenth-century Spain could unite the artisans and workers in a protest against the *consumos*.[2] Only in Catalonia, where there was a true industrial civilization, could there be a radical proletariat; but the working-class politics of Barcelona remained a world apart until the late nineteenth century.

What struck every sensitive observer was the presence of beggars on the streets of every Spanish town.[3] Long after Bar-

[1] Decline was arrested by the relatively late development of a wool industry in Catalonia.

[2] It was a dogma of popular radicalism that these excise duties levied on prime necessities were mainly responsible for dear foods: in 1820 a radical called their abolition or restoration 'thermometer of revolution'.

[3] In prosperous Valencia, Townsend was 'struck with the sight of poverty, of wretchedness and of rags in every street' (*Journey*, iii. 255).

celona had become an industrial city, the *miserables* invaded the streets on religious festivals to reveal the massive urban poverty that Spain shared with nineteenth-century Europe. These submerged classes survived on the charitable foundations of the past: Madrid convents provided 30,000 bowls of soup daily. It was the danger of these semi-beggar squatters to public order in every urban economy that lead the statesmen of the eighteenth century to favour effective price control, to attempt a state reform of the 'abusive' charitable foundations of the Church, and to preach the chilly gospel of workhouse labour. Nineteenth-century liberalism was to inherit hostility to religious charity without substituting for it the planned charity of the state. The poor, as Catholic conservatives were later to point out, were disinherited by liberal legislation.[1]

In Madrid there was a tradition of mob action by the semi-beggar class, attracted by ecclesiastical charity and by the conspicuous waste of the higher aristocracy; in the seventeenth century the monarchy feared a mob addicted to these great spenders.[2] In the late eighteenth century this symbiosis of peers and paupers is revealed in the fashionable aping of lower-class *mores* and dress, a version of the return to nature that came naturally to an upper class lacking a culture of its own. The mob had shown its power in 1766 when Charles III was driven by a riot to sacrifice his minister, Esquilache, 'out of love for the people of Madrid'. The king never recovered from his fear of street noises. By 1808 there was a developed pattern of street violence and the 'people' of the *barrios bajos*—the poor southern quarter of Madrid—after functioning as the 'blind instruments' of an aristocratic *fronde* against Godoy were to become the heroes of the Second of May, when they rose against the French troops. The pressure of the streets was to be of decisive importance in the liberal revolution of 1820, when it

[1] See below, pp. 272–3, 285. Ecclesiastical charity was impotent to neutralize a general price rise: it did relieve much occasional hardship. State reform of charity produced acute local conflicts between the agents of government reform and ecclesiastics connected with charitable administration: cf. the experiences of the poet Meléndez Valdés as a government emissary in Avila and the attempts of Olavide to break the lay brotherhoods (*cofradías*) of Seville on the grounds that they 'wasted' money on religious processions. These localized conflicts are an interesting indication of the opposition between reform and the Church, as they are of the limits of 'enlightenment' within the clergy itself.

[2] Cf. C. Vinas y Mey, *El problema de la tierra en el siglo XVI* (1941), 124 ff.

was organized by the secret societies. By the mid century respectable citizens were thoroughly alarmed at this revolutionary alliance, by then in the hands of the radical agitators and journalists of the cheap lodging houses rather than the instrument of conspirators in the clubs and lodges.[1]

Three-quarters of the population throughout the eighteenth and most of the nineteenth centuries lived by the land. Everywhere the land and its concerns seeped into town-life: the towns of the south had agricultural suburbs inhabited by day labourers hired in the square by the bailiffs of the great estates. Even large towns like Saragossa were provincial agricultural capitals with a developed artisanate supplying the surrounding countryside. We have already considered the highly diverse structure of this rural society, differing from province to province, from mountain valley to mountain valley. In this diversified structure the self-contained economies moved slowly in response to general movements.[2] It was the 'export' provinces, which supplied a more general market, where economic changes shifted the balance of society.

Apart from the industrialists, merchants, and farmers of peripheral Spain it is probable that the main class that benefited from the rise in agricultural prices was the rural bourgeoisie of south, west, and centre. As in every part of southern Europe, those furthest removed from the subsistence level tended to increase their margin of advantage. A bad year was a disaster to the small peasant while it might well benefit the large farmers or merchants who could store grain for ten years, 'observing this rule so consistently that they would pawn their last jewels or load their lands with mortgages until years of high prices'. This independence and opportunity for large profit must have been the most important distinction between riches and grinding poverty and must have played a greater part in creating the economic hierarchy of rural society than any other factor. It was emphasized by usury. The small tenant and peasant easily fell into debt: in the Levante, *huertas* to the merchants of the ports; in Castile, to the corn merchants;

[1] Cf. the comments on J. M. Jover in *Conciencia obrera en la España contemporánea* (1956).

[2] Nevertheless Galicia proves how a poor economy responds, within its limits, to price changes.

in Galicia, to the lawyers. Yet in all the dramatic descriptions of eighteenth- and nineteenth-century rural Spain these factors are scarcely mentioned.[1]

This rural bourgeoisie was not, as is so often assumed, a 'new feudalism' created by the sales of church and common lands after the 1830's.[2] The *poderosos*, or powerful ones, are already, in the eighteenth century, a formidable force: local landowners, the substantial tenants of the *cortijos*, oil millers, corn dealers, the bailiffs of the large estates, small-town lawyers. The hold of this class on municipal government was central to its power: as municipal oligarchs they controlled wages, prices, and the letting of the municipal commons in their own interests.[3] Thus the effect of the nineteenth-century sales was to turn them from a class of privileged municipal tenants into outright owners of the surplus land of the community.

These small-town bosses, characteristic of Andalusia and Estremadura, were not an attractive class. Ill-educated, with a mixture of lawyer and peasant cunning, they were violent in the defence of their position, if need be in alliance with brigands and town gangs.[4] In the nineteenth century they manned the lower ranges of the political structure by combining with their traditional municipal powers the electoral patronage of parliamentary government. We must, nevertheless, beware of looking at Spain through Andalusian spectacles and generalizing from the violent and precarious structure of the latifundia districts. There were areas of settled peasant proprietorship, of long leases and stable crop-sharing tenures. These weighed as heavily

[1] The only descriptions I have been able to find are in Zabala's *Miscellanea*, written in 1723: odd references in Madoz make clear the economic strength of the corn merchants. For the debt relationship between fruit and wine producers and exporters, cf. the interesting comments in Jacob, *Travels*, 245. In Granada, silk producers were in a continuous debt relationship with the silk manufacturers, and cf. the tantalizing hints in F. Bejerano, *Historia del Consulado y de la Junta de Comercio de Málaga* (Madrid, 1947), 139 *et passim*.

[2] The rise of the *poderosos* is dated by C. Viñas y Mey, *Problema de la tierra* (24 ff.) to the agricultural expansion of the sixteenth century.

[3] These lettings were condemned by a royal official as 'deals between the gang (*entre compadres*) to submit the poor to the rich'. (Cf. J. Costa, *Colectivismo*, 126–8.)

[4] The relationship with brigands is described at great length in J. de Zugasti, *El bandolerismo* (10 vols., 1876, and a shortened version, 1934). For gangs see J. Díaz del Moral, *Agitaciones*, 69. At Montilla the *poderosos* had a gang to fight political opponents and defend property in 1868–73. The classic portrait of a small town boss is Estébanez Calderón's 'Don Opando' in *Escenas andaluzas* (Austral ed., 1941), 41–78.

in the social balance as the areas of social tension like Galicia. Unless they are taken into account the conservatism of rural life in much of Spain is inexplicable: this conservatism was sustained by the intensity of local life.

All interpreters of Spain have insisted on the primacy of local ties and the rule of inverse proportion—the greater the area to which patriotism is applied the less intense it becomes. The imperfect sense of national unity is thus explained, not altogether satisfactorily, in terms of those structures and *mores* that gave Spain social cohesion at a lower level. National unity came late and could not conquer the sense of belonging to pre-national societies. Of these societies (outside those areas of disseminated settlement where the parish tended to become the first unit beyond the family and that of those neighbouring farmers who helped each other out at harvest and ploughing) the most significant was the pueblo. The word *el pueblo* means both town and town-dwellers and by extension 'the people' in general, an indication of the all-embracing nature of this primary concept in Spanish life.

A Spaniard's natural emotional loyalty is to his pueblo, to his province; he identifies himself progressively against those of another village or province, against other Spaniards, and finally against all foreigners. Spanish popular speech is full of contemptuous, even obscene, references to the virility, morality, and poverty of the next-door village or province.[1] 'Rather be a tart than a Gallegan.' This antagonism and rivalry existed between large towns: to take one example, the rivalry of Santiago, the cathedral city, and Corunna, the seaport, was to have a decisive influence on the fate of liberal revolutionary movements in nineteenth-century Galicia. The federal pattern of democratic revolution and the *Centralista* tradition can only be understood in terms of this municipal patriotism.[2] It was a constant in the revolutionary waves that swept across Spain in 1808, 1820, 1835, 1840, 1869–73, and finally in 1936. It both created

[1] A selection of these *apodos* is given in J. Caro Baroja, *Razas pueblos y linajes* (1957), 263 ff., a most suggestive essay. 'The inhabitants of Haro salute bull fighting enthusiasts and all foreigners, except those of Logroño.' Logroño was the neighbouring town.

[2] Centralist democrats argued that a central Junta representing local elected juntas was the only legitimate government until a Constituent Cortes had democratized the constitution.

the revolution and paralysed it. In the Federalist rising of 1873 the canton of Castellón regarded the canton of Valencia as its greatest rival, though both were participating in a common democratic revolution in peril from a 'reactionary' attack.

The pueblo was a moral, economic, and governmental unit: as a centre of government the larger municipalities could rule a surrounding area as large as a small English county.[1] Within the pueblo all are moral equals and this moral equality overlay social distinctions based on wealth; wealth has its social expressions in the creation of bonds of obligation (god-parenthood, for instance) and not in the snobbery of conspicuous waste, absurd in a society where economic status is evaluated exactly by gossip. This network of friendship and patronage became one of the less objectionable instruments of nineteenth-century electoral corruption and the instrument with which the small man met and defended himself against the state. The patron became the *cacique* (electoral boss) who in return for a vote purveyed the benefits or averted the penalties of the national administration.[2] As the national administration made more demands in the form of conscription and taxation, so the recommendation of a patron became more important. The government officials recognized the system since most bureaucrats owed their own position to nepotism and patronage, perpetuating 'a procedure to which they originally resorted and to which they are committed and indebted'.

It is easy to over-estimate the strength and 'Spanishness' of the pueblo. Its social cohesion was no stronger than that of an isolated nineteenth-century English village, and in the long run its solidarity against the outside world could neither defeat class conflict nor evade the power of the centralizing state. Hatred of the absentee landlord, for instance, fitted the moral structure of the pueblo because he could be felt as an intruder from an alien city world: hence the emotional content of Andalusian village anarchism. The persistence of the pueblo

[1] Its mechanism is well explained in J. Pitt-Rivers, *The People of the Sierra* (London, 1954).

[2] For a discussion of the reciprocal nature of patronage see M. Kenny, 'Patterns of patronage in Spain', *Anthropological Quarterly*, Washington, D.C., xxxiii (1960), 14–23.

as a social and economic unit depended on bad roads and bad political education. It is significant because it affected a wide proportion of the inhabitants of Spain and because the preconditions of its strength persisted until very late. Cut off from the outside world, the Spaniard needed an intimate social life and the interest it supplied to conversation. Spaniards did not read books: they talked.[1] The central feature of eighteenth- and nineteenth-century social life was the *tertulia*—the group of relations or friends who gathered regularly to talk in the evenings. The Economic Societies of the eighteenth century started with a *tertulia* of Basque gentry and conversation remained the main focus of intellectual life in the twentieth century.[2] Every splinter group of liberalism was to centre round a café table. Spanish politicians discussed the political crises of the nineteenth century with the intimate precision with which a family discusses its affairs or a village gossips.

3. *Enlightenment and Reform, 1760–1790*

Under Charles III a group of ministers and civil servants, distinguished by their energy and their ability, undertook the task of modernizing the monarchy.[3] This effort, as far as the administrative machinery was concerned, was initiated by the French advisers who came to Spain in the early years of the century with the first Bourbon king, Philip V; later it was encouraged by Choiseul, who saw in the effective mobilization of the resources of his ally the means to defeat England and lay

[1] 'Books are little read' (Townsend, *Travels*, ii. 154). I do not mean to insult Spaniards when I say that the poverty of books in Spanish well-to-do homes is astonishing. On their own standards—and who is to judge?—they have better things to do. Much of Spain may pass from the pre-book age straight to the television age, as have South American countries.

[2] This emphasis on conversational exchange and journalism was one of the main weaknesses of Spanish intellectual life: conversation was the essential foundation of Ortega y Gasset's work.

[3] The most influential figures were: Aranda (1718–99), an Aragonese aristocrat and *esprit fort* called to power in 1766; Campomanes (1723–1802), a scholarly administrator who, as Fiscal of the Council of Castile, provided the official encouragement and central direction of reform; Floridablanca (1728–1808), a cautious, conservative-minded Murcian civil servant who was Charles III's chief minister in the later years of the reign. Jovellanos (1744–1811) and Meléndez Valdés (1754–1817) were humanists who made a career in the public administration. Cabarrús (1752–1810) and Olavide (1725–1803) are best considered as technicians whose knowledge of foreign techniques was useful to the government.

the foundations of a Franco-Spanish world power.[1] In his declared aim of regenerating Spain for his own profit Napoleon was to inherit a portion of these ambitions.

In the overhaul of government that accompanied the War of the Spanish Succession the servants of Philip V rejected the system of the Great Councils, less because it gave the grandees too much political power than because it was incurably inefficient and incapable of organizing the monarchy for the defence of the French dynasty. For the old polycentric system of the Council they sought to substitute departments controlled by ministers. A ministerial system, run by career bureaucrats, was the instrument of Charles III, who had served his apprenticeship as an enlightened ruler in Naples; he did not destroy the great Councils but day-to-day business escaped them. But in the last decades of the century rational administration was no longer an end in itself. It aimed at the release of social energies crippled by outworn institutions and archaic policies in order to strengthen the power of the monarchy. Civil servants accepted 'the truths of political economy'; it was the task of government to remove the obstacles that lay in the path of 'felicity'.

It was as architects rather than as builders that the Caroline bureaucrats bequeathed to liberalism this programme: their concrete achievements remained limited, but there is no practical reform of the nineteenth century, no reforming attitude of mind, that cannot be traced back to one of the servants of Charles III. Thus it was Floridablanca, a stiff bureaucrat, who planned the road system radiating from Madrid, the completion of which was to be the achievement of Isabelline liberalism; indeed, the fate of the Corps of Road Engineers, set up in the eighteenth century, was bound up with the fate of liberalism itself; dismantled by Ferdinand VII it was set up by the Liberal Revolution in 1820; dissolved in the reaction of 1823, it was re-established by liberals in 1834. It was Olavide, a radical *esprit fort* capable of jokes in bad taste about 'superstition', and Aranda, the Aragonese aristocrat and correspondent of the *philosophes*, both zealous proponents of the latest

[1] For French influence on Charles III's imperial reforms see A. S. Aiton, 'Spanish Colonial Reorganization', *H.A.H.R.* xii (1932), 269 ff.; and cf. H. I. Priestley, *José de Gálvez* (Berkeley, 1916), 39–40.

advances from abroad, who put forward in the 1760's radical reforms that remained unfulfilled in 1931.

In order to illustrate the links between the programme of the Caroline bureaucrats and that of the nineteenth-century liberals we may take as examples the reform of the administrative structure (both in Spain and in America), agrarian reform, church reform, and educational reform.

> A body composed of other and smaller bodies, separated and in opposition to one another, which oppress and despise each other and are in a continuous state of war. Each province, each religious house, each profession is separated from the rest of the nation and concentrated in itself. . . . Modern Spain can be considered as a body without energy . . . a monstrous Republic formed of little republics which confront each other because the particular interest of each is in contradiction with the general interest.[1]

Thus an enlightened eighteenth-century Spanish civil servant defined the state he served. Uniform centralization was the administrative pre-condition of all other reform, as the Caroline bureaucrats found when their agrarian programme was blocked by oligarchic municipalities. This centralizing mission the bureaucrats of Charles III found beyond their strength and they bequeathed its fulfilment to their liberal successors. Uniform provinces and municipalities were the programme of radical liberalism in the Cortes of Cadiz; the final redrafting of the political geography of Spain into provinces was the work of Javier de Burgos, admirer alike of Napoleonic administrative techniques and the enlightened servants of Charles III. In the 1830's this moderate liberal finally substituted for the omnicompetent Council of Castille a 'modern' Ministry of the Interior and a Supreme Court. Finally, the uniform taxational system, by which eighteenth-century reformers hoped to replace the fiscal confusions of an historic conglomeration of indirect taxes, was the achievement of a mid-century liberal, Mon.[2]

The centralizing mission of the old monarchy had been

[1] M. Defourneaux, *Olavide*, 84–85.

[2] The only parts of the monarchy with a relatively equitable taxational system were Catalonia, Valencia, and Aragon. For the work of Burgos see below, pp. 115 and 196, and of Mon, pp. 235–6.

limited by provincial privilege. Whereas Philip V succeeded (where two hundred years of Hapsburg effort had failed) in dismantling the political institutions that gave Catalonia, Valencia, and Aragon a quasi-independent status his successors failed to diminish the *fueros* of the Basque Provinces—Guipúzcoa, Vizcaya, Alava—and of Navarre.[1] Thus the *fueros*, which supported the independence of these foral provinces, remained as the main political challenge to nineteenth-century liberalism.

Although the institutions of self-government varied in detail with each of the Basque Provinces, everywhere the sovereign body was a broadly chosen General Assembly with a smaller permanent Deputation.[2] Both were manned by a gentry proud of its local influence, provincial patriots who devoted themselves to improving roads and preserving historical monuments. Royal agents were subject to stringent control as natural enemies of provincial liberties: the Viceroy of Navarre—the only viceroy outside the American Empire—was regarded as a constitutional monarch within his province, and reminded of his status by the meanness of his palace beside that of the Provincial Deputation. Important as was the consciousness of self-government, the *fueros* would not have been defended with such obstinacy had they not conferred substantial economic advantages, designed originally to favour poor frontier provinces. The foral provinces were exempt from Spanish conscription, taxation, and customs duties: thus the national customs frontier ran along the Ebro.

For those who enjoyed them, the preservation of the *fueros* was 'an instinct and a poetry' and the struggle to defend them linked the backward-looking Carlism of the 1830's with the cultural nationalism of the later nineteenth century. To the foral provinces their attachment to Spain was a contract dependent on the maintenance of their liberties and economic

[1] Catalonia kept its own civil law. Catalanism in the later nineteenth century defended this law against the uniform, 'liberal' Castilian code and proceeded to the demand for Home Rule as a resuscitation of the medieval political liberties lost in 1714.

[2] In Guipúzcoa the Junta was composed of municipal delegates: in Vizcaya it was elected by all householders. Navarre was unique in that it allowed no judicial appeal beyond the province. The foral machinery is described in Desdevises du Dezert, 'Le régime foral en Espagne au XVIIIe siècle', *R. Hist.*, 1896; and in H. Baumgarten, *Geschichte Spaniens vom Ausbruch der französischen Revolution* (Leipzig, 1865), ii. 176 ff.

advantages: enlightened despotism and liberalism, refusing to accept the contractual status of the foral provinces, were by definition anti-Basque.[1] Every attempt by the absolute monarchy to raise the taxational quotas was met by the claim that the quota was a contract alterable only by both consenting parties. Every attempt by liberals in the nineteenth century to replace foral liberties by the uniform liberty of a liberal constitution was resisted in the name of provincial liberties. Nevertheless liberalism succeeded in destroying the *fueros* and it was only after its triumph that conservative liberals challenged the maxim that 'centralization is neither more nor less than liberty itself'.

Apart from this tenacious defence of local liberties the Caroline bureaucrats, in common with other administrative technicians of the *ancien régime* in Europe, found that the main obstacle to modernization lay in the inertia of the average Spanish office-holder and the sheer size of the administrative apparatus—the superfluity of posts that nourished what was later to be termed *empleadismo*. Thus reform often petered out in a rearrangement of government offices—a persistent feature of Spanish administrative history—which failed to eradicate the inherited vices of a paper-loving bureaucracy; the navy, for example, remained a ground-based pasture for underpaid civil servants to browse on, a defect that had costly results at Trafalgar.[2] It remains true that, apart from the foral provinces, government became more effective, defined, and concentrated as it approached the subject. The Captain General, a civilian as much as a military administrator, was master of his province, the *corregidor* of his district as the minister was not yet master of his department. Only the *audiencias*, burdened with written procedures in which lawyers were paid by the page, and fulfilling both the functions of an appeal court and a provincial

[1] This is apparent in Llorente's treatment of the *fueros* in his *Noticias históricas*, which was written in order to justify Godoy's attempt to incorporate the provinces into the Spanish administration by dismantling the *fueros* in the interests of uniform government, and as a punishment for 'separatist' negotiations with the French invaders in 1793–5. See M. García Venero, *Historia del nacionalismo vasco* (1945), 46 ff. As an *afrancesado* Llorente combined the traditions of enlightened despotism with 'liberalism'.

[2] There is an excellent, if old-fashioned, description of Spanish government in G. Desdevizes du Dezert, *L'Espagne de l'ancien régime*, ii; *Les Institutions* (Paris, 1899).

administrative council, recalled the polysynodical system of the great councils.[1] The fatal flaw was the last link in the chain of command—municipal government. It was here that the Caroline reformers achieved nothing because the crown could not recapture the powers it had made over to local municipal oligarchs. The impetus of reform and modernization was dissipated in the town hall where the government failed to insert effective instruments of its will.[2] As in the case of the foral provinces, the destruction of these 'little republics' was left to the liberal statesmen of the nineteenth century who added to the notion of rational administration that of civil equality. It was only after the imposition of a system of local government imitated from France that the benefits of uniformity and centralization was questioned.

Paradoxically, it was the relative success of Charles III's reforms in America—the first systematic overhaul of the imperial administration since the sixteenth century—that undermined the foundations of empire. Reform was inspired by the consciousness that ineffective administration produced revenues inadequate for imperial defence and by the desire to strengthen the hold of Spanish commerce in Latin America against competitors. Charles III's minister, Floridablanca, believed good government would solve the colonial problem; this was a profound misconception, inherited by Spanish liberalism, for it was not *mal gobierno* that the creoles rejected but government by *peninsulares* (peninsular Spaniards) as such. The efficiency of government could only be increased at the expense of its popularity; the more corrupt and less efficient the government, the more acceptable it was to creole merchants and

[1] Spanish law was extremely confused given the contradictions of the various *recopilaciones* and the unresolved conflicts between Castilian law and the local codes. For the law's delays, see G. Desdevizes du Dezert, op. cit. 86; and Townshend, *Travels*, i. 363. Of course, these vices of the legal and administrative system were characteristic of the *ancien régime* in Europe—not least in France itself.

[2] For the attempts at municipal reform see M. Defourneaux, *Olavide*, and R. Leonhard, *Agrarpolitik und Agrarreform in Spanien unter Carl III* (Munich, 1909). The municipalities of the large towns were 'aristocratic', those of the smaller municipalities usually controlled by the powerful *vecinos* (i.e. registered inhabitants). The crown, alarmed at the municipal oligarchs' unwillingness to regulate food prices in the interests of public order, unsuccessfully attempted to insert popularly elected syndics on the councils.

landowners.[1] Charles III's reforms improved the quality of the imperial civil service while denying to the creoles a share in the system—perhaps because, as Floridablanca maintained, creoles were too enmeshed in local graft to be trusted. Reform was 'a flash of lightning illuminating us for one moment only, to leave us in greater darkness'. Thus the implantation of the intendant system weakened rather than strengthened the hold of metropolitan Spain, by ending corrupt practices that had allowed creoles control of their own affairs, and by creating bitter rivalries between the new officials and their subordinates.[2] The creoles' desire for office, economic freedom, and free trade could never perhaps have been satisfied within the static Spanish theory of imperialism. In so far as Charles III's reforms encouraged local prosperity—as they did in the newly created Viceroyalty of Buenos Aires—they gave the societies of Latin America a more lively sense of the inconveniences of the Spanish connexion. Where the absolute monarchy sought to solve the colonial problem by an efficient imperial administration, the liberals hoped to satisfy colonists who wanted free trade and home rule by an imperial, liberal constitution. Just as the creoles did not want good government manned by the civil servants of an absolute monarch, so they would not accept rule by a metropolitan parliament, managed by Spanish liberals.

It was the waste of national resources and, to a lesser extent, the amount of human suffering in rural Spain, that in the years 1766–73 set off the most remarkable attempt at agrarian reform that Spain was to know until the days of the Second Republic. Like their Republican successors in the 1930's, the agrarian reformers of Charles III's reign were obsessed by the violent social situation and the agrarian unemployment on the great latifundia and *dehesas* (scrub pasture) of Andalusia and Estremadura. The simple proposition behind all agrarian reform was that surplus land should be distributed to surplus labour. Aranda and Olavide entertained ambitious schemes of state colonization, of which the best known was their partially

[1] This is clearly the case with taxation, smuggling, and enforcement of protective legislation in the interests of Indian subjects. To Gálvez, a great imperial civil servant, reform meant 'an enforcement of a more rigid adherence to the paramount interests of the mother country'.

[2] Cf. L. E. Fisher, *The Intendant System in Spanish America* (1929), 64 ff., and J. Lynch, *Spanish Colonial Administration, 1783–1810* (London, 1958).

successful attempt to settle German immigrants in a model colony of symmetrical plots along the brigand-infested road over the Sierra Morena. It represented all the 'prejudices' of the reformers: neo-classical architecture, a preference for corn as opposed to sheep and goats, the exclusion of the Regular Orders from the settlements.[1]

Such state-directed paternalism could not be the model for liberal land reform. Its bible was the *Informe* of Jovellanos published in 1795, a stylistic masterpiece that applied the commonplaces of economic individualism to the land problem in Spain. Corporate property and entail were sins against the 'natural tendency towards perfection': individual interest, i.e. ownership, was the 'first instrument of prosperity'. Combining these two propositions, it followed that the task of nineteenth-century liberalism was confined to the creation of a free market in land by the abolition of entail, and the sale of the church estates and the common lands.

The sale of these lands on the open market did not solve the social aspects of the agrarian problem—particularly the chronic unemployment and grinding poverty afflicting the *braceros*. Later reformers, therefore, professed to find in the policies of Aranda and Olavide the models of a 'collectivist' solution, which regarded property as a social institution. Land that was not 'used' could be expropriated for the benefit of the industrious poor; rents should be controlled, the needy farmer aided. This 'school' was set against that of Jovellanos whose *laissez-faire* individualism held property to be a natural right with the market as the regulator of the economic relationships between men. Jovellanos regarded rent control as useless and an evil in itself; he considered land as a commodity that must find its natural price in the open market and held that it was 'vanity' to try to protect peasants from the effects of economic laws. 'Interest', complained a reforming chaplain, was the only stimulant in the new philosophy and it was this philosophy that inspired nineteenth-century liberalism.[2]

The most controversial of all the legacies the eighteenth-

[1] For a brilliant description of the colonies see J. Caro Baroja, *Razas*, 205 ff.

[2] In my view the contrast between the two 'schools' has been exaggerated for polemical purposes. The 'radicals' were chary of expropriation and it was Olavide who coined the precept 'He who buys, improves'.

century reformers bequeathed to their successors was the subordination of the Church as a political, economic, educational, and charitable institution to the supremacy of the State. As was the case with their administrative reforms, the liberals of the nineteenth century were to rest their offensive on different ideological foundations; but their practical demands on the Church remained, largely, an extension of the regalism of the late-eighteenth-century civil servants. Regalism can best be defined as Erastianism and it represented little more than the modernization and systematization of the traditional claim of the crown to control what it considered the temporal aspects of church government.

The regalist offensive of Charles III's ministers, in spite of its respectable antecedents, was the most significant domestic issue in eighteenth-century politics. Initially concerned mainly with royal patronage, it broadened until it involved a claim by the state to regulate every aspect of the activities of the Church, from its right as a corporation to hold property to its control over university education and charitable foundations. The traditional arguments of the crown, set out by Macanaz for Philip V, were sharpened by the influence of Italian regalists and connected with what was loosely called Jansenism, by which was meant a Spanish edition of Gallicanism.[1] The crown's case was contested by the 'corrupt and abominable' ultramontane political theory of the Jesuits and the canon lawyers of the universities. The Jesuits were expelled (1767) from both Spain and Spanish America—a measure that gave its author, Aranda, a European reputation as an *esprit fort*—and the reformers attempted to turn the universities into state-controlled educational institutions teaching useful knowledge instead of Aristotelean 'words'. By Charles IV's reign regalism proceeded to an attack on church property, and with Urquijo, most radical of the regalists, it bordered on schism. In 1800, however, the regalists fell from favour and 'Jansenism' was con-

[1] See H. Baumgarten, *Geschichte Spaniens*, i. 36 ff., for an account of regalist doctrine. Campomanes was the theorist of Caroline regalism. His *Tratado de la regalia de amortización* (published 1765), upholding the right of the civil state to control mortmain, became the regalist bible. Of course Charles III, like his servants, was influenced by the regalist arguments of Tanucci and other Italian regalists. For the regalist controversy see the very illuminating treatment in R. Herr, *Eighteenth-century Revolution*, 398–434.

demned. Before the conservative country-offensive had become official policy they had flirted with French supporters of the Civil Constitution of the Clergy (regarded by its Spanish admirers as a piece of thoroughgoing regalism), and had supplied a stock of ideas that were to govern, not only the church settlement made by the liberals in the Cortes of Cadiz, but the programme of liberalism until 1939. Ministers of the Second Republic quoted the ministers of Charles III.

Finally we must examine the intellectual movement that accompanied the reformers and that many of them favoured. It has become the centre of a bitter controversy: Catholic conservative accusations of treason to the national spirit and of religious heterodoxy have obscured the implications of *luces* (Enlightenment), and the intentions of its advocates within the government service. The Spanish Enlightenment, as an intellectual movement, was second-rate and derivative: hence the confusions consequent on combining borrowings from the earlier Spanish diagnosticians of national decadence (Ustáriz, Ulloa, and Ward), from Colbertism, the Physiocrats, and Adam Smith; hence its failure—if we except Goya, who shared the horror of superstition common to the supporters of *luces*—to fling up a European celebrity.[1]

Its interest lies in its function as the creed of a reforming *élite*, confronted with the difficulties of a state-sponsored economic revival in an under-developed economy, a revival that had to contend with the resistances of the traditional structure and the misrepresentations of a peculiarly narrow Catholic conservatism. The watchword 'utility', natural to men of government, produced exaggerations that ill became distinguished humanists: Jovellanos and his school held that poetry should be socially useful, Campomanes that the sewing-needle was 'more profitable' than Aristotle.[2] It led to impossibly

[1] Cf. Goya's *Caprichos* in their treatment of monks: F. D. Klingender, *Goya* (London, 1948), 78 ff. The medical sciences, favoured by royal interest, may constitute another exception. Some Spanish doctors of the late eighteenth century were known outside Spain, e.g. Antonio de Gimbernat, a Catalan surgeon of humble origins who invented a technique for hernia operations adopted by the English surgeon, Hunter, and also gave his name to a ligament of the pubis. (For Gimbernat see *Tres treballs premiats en el concurs d'homenatge a Gimbernat* (Barcelona, 1936).) The Spaniard who has contributed most to modern science was also a doctor—the neurologist Ramón y Cajal.

[2] M. Menéndez y Pelayo, *Ideas estéticas O.C.*, vi. 93–95.

puritan attitudes, a crusade against the enjoyments of the artisan, onslaughts on the bullfight, not because it was cruel, but because it wasted working time; it supported an attack on charity as an anti-social habit, which merged with the bleak belief of later liberals in the virtues of competition.[1] Exaggeration and crudity were pardonable. Jovellanos, in his campaign for technical education and the useful arts as a means of raising living standards, may be forgiven for his attacks on the dead languages. As a reformer confronted with an ignorant and conservative society it is understandable that Olavide saw universities only as 'workshops for the production of an *élite* to serve the state and enlighten the multitude'. Liberalism was to place the centralized university system under state control: the result would be that, while theology could not be studied as a subject, professors could be expelled for their religious opinions.

The success of governmental reform depended on intelligent local co-operation. The creation of an enlightened *élite*, committed to reform, among the provincial notables was the function of the government-sponsored Economic or Patriotic Societies and the 'economic' press which was to diffuse a government-sponsored view of the new gospel of progress.[2] This was part of a general campaign for education; the enemy of progress was ignorance.

The first Economic Society grew up spontaneously from the *tertulia* of a group of Basque gentry: it read foreign periodicals, discussed the useful sciences, set up a school and attacked the Gothic prejudice of aristocratic idleness. By 1800, societies had been founded in provincial capitals all over Spain and the whole movement was centralized in the Madrid Society, 'receiving its impulses from the provinces and reflecting those influences thither strengthened'. The Economic Societies encouraged local industries, set up model farms, and sponsored new crops. Much of the activity was puerile and faded away

[1] 'One of the greatest obstacles to the establishment of factories is the soup of the convents': quoted E. J. Hamilton, *War and Prices*, 93. This criticism affected the Church itself: enlightened bishops set up workhouses and model farms as a more modern way of dealing with distress than indiscriminate charity. Cf. J. Sarrailh, *Espagne éclairée*, 128–9. The Bishop of Sigüenza was a particularly active 'economist' bishop of the late eighteenth century.

[2] For Economic Societies see R. J. Shafer, *The Economic Societies in the Spanish World* (Syracuse, N.Y., 1958).

once the initial pride in seeing the list of names and the hopes of government favour had vanished. It is easy to scoff at the movement—with its prizes for knitting and tafetta umbrellas, its hyperboles about the happy revolution to be accomplished by wheel ploughs, its scientific amateurism—as the naïve posturings of a minority engaged in a self-conscious crusade against the forces of routine and conservatism.[1] Nevertheless the influence of the Societies can be clearly traced in the reform movement of 1808–9 and again, as a remote cause, in the reforms of the 1830's. The significance of the Societies survived their failure; they represented the first attempt to interest public opinion in the reform of the traditional structure of Spanish society.[2]

The Spanish Enlightenment remained a government-sponsored, government-censored movement largely confined to the better spirits of the public administration. Hence it was reduced to relative impotence when the radicalism of the French Revolution strengthened the forces of resistance in the government itself. What we may call 'the generation of 1760' was composed of paternalistic modernizers and enlightened patriots in the eighteenth-century sense of the term. Their neo-classical enthusiasms are an indication of their isolation from what even Jovellanos could term 'the vulgar and idiotic people' who preferred the Spanish drama to the precepts of Boileau. It failed to foster an independent, bourgeois culture. There were exceptional individuals but the intellectuals of the eighteenth and early nineteenth centuries were priests or bureaucrats and it was in this latter capacity that journalists figured in the reign of Charles III. The 'enlightened classes' failed to appear and respond to a creed forged in their supposed

[1] The proceedings of the Societies have often that depressing air of well-intentioned scientific amateurism that so irritated Arthur Young in the agricultural societies in France. For a typical example see the work of the army chaplain Nicolás de Palma: *Memorias de la sociedad económica* (Madrid, 1877). He represents the belief that modern methods, in whatever climate or conditions they have been evolved, are preferable to the peasant inclination 'to follow a custom or a method which they have acquired from their fathers'.

[2] The influence of the Societies persisted longer than has sometimes been supposed: the Madrid Society survived to support the Madrid *Ateneo* (founded in 1835), which became a central literary and political institution of parliamentary liberalism. Cf. R. M. de Labra, *El Ateneo de Madrid* (1878), 64. One of the first lectures was 'On the influence which the eighteenth century has exercised on the intellectual condition of Spain'.

interests: the propaganda of *luces* could no more create in Spain a bourgeoisie in the French image than the propaganda of free trade, half a century later, could create an English middle class.

4. *The Radical Challenge, 1790–1808*

The radicalism which makes its appearance in Spain after 1790, under the influence of events in France, was far removed in tone and purpose from the governmental reformism of the generation of the 1760's. From the first the government made every effort to exclude any knowledge or discussion of the French Revolution; Floridablanca's *cordon sanitaire* was the strictest in Europe; in 1791 he suspended the entire periodical press and kept a careful watch on the large French colony in Spain.[1] To the ministry enlightenment was government property, to be regulated, censored and, if dangerous, rejected: regalism and the campaign against the Inquisition became suspect; the government and the Inquisition now combined in an effort to search out dangerous books. Godoy's modification of these procedures in 1793 and again in 1797 and the renewal of the alliance with intellectuals like Jovellanos and Meléndez Valdés was a temporary affair.[2] In 1798 Caballero, 'the enemy of enlightenment', swept the intellectuals and 'Jansenists' from office and instilled anew a fear of France and progress in the court. Thus a great event like the French Revolution had little resonance in Spanish opinion and the efforts at revolutionary propaganda had little success.[3] The terror and the execution of the king paralysed and disgusted those intellectuals who, formed by French books and sharing the ideologies which had inspired the moderates in 1789, now saw ordered progress drowned in blood. 'What atrocities! What horrors! . . . And we

[1] See R. Herr, *Eighteenth-century Revolution*, 239–68.

[2] Thus in 1793 Meléndez Valdés and his friends proposed to exploit Godoy's sympathies for *luces* by publishing a review that would propagate 'safe' modern ideas. Godoy's interest in the scheme or his power was insufficient to stop the Council from killing the project by insisting on the previous submission of articles *for a whole year* (G. Demerson, *Don Juan Meléndez Valdés* (Paris, 1962)). In his Memoirs Godoy blames the 'reaction' on Caballero: yet cf. his letter of 26 November 1800 in Pereira, *Cartas confidenciales de la reina María Luisa* (1935), 378–9.

[3] For French propaganda efforts see B. F. Hyslop, 'French Jacobin Nationalism and Spain' (in *Essays inscribed to C. J. H. Hayes*, ed. E. M. Earle (New York, 1950), 190–240). M. Santos Oliver in *Los españoles en la revolución francesa* (Madrid, 1914) remarks on the rarity of literary references to the Revolution.

were interested in such people. Let us be ashamed of our involuntary deception and take a lesson for the future.'[1]

The efforts of the government and the reversal of the alliance with the intellectuals failed to keep out a trickle of French newspapers: contraband books were picked up by the Inquisition all over Spain between 1790 and 1792.[2] Thus, on the outbreak of war with France (1793), there was a small band of pro-French democrats in Madrid. According to Godoy, the government decided on peace in 1795 because it was alarmed by Picornell's republican conspiracy in Madrid and rumours of republican, pro-French committees in the north. Godoy himself traced the origins of liberalism to the pro-French peace party who greeted the returning French ambassador with cries of *Vive la Liberté*.[3] With peace and the French alliance, there could be no effective barrier to French influence.[4] With the Consulate France became respectable—the Concordat allowed Napoleon to appear as the protector of Catholicism. Above all she had become powerful. Belief in salvation from France was an essential element in the crisis of the intellectuals in 1808. Though enlightened Spaniards might detest the brutal deceit of Napoleon's seizure of Spain they felt that perhaps he alone could regenerate her.[5] When confronted with the excesses of the anti-French mobs in 1808 it was almost natural that such men, with fear as much as hope in their hearts, should become supporters of French rule.

Clearly radical ideas were the property of a minute minority: in 1793 the people listened, not to French agents, but to friars preaching a crusade against atheism.[6] Yet it is clear that there was a more general temper—among the intellectuals of

[1] Letter of Meléndez Valdés, n.d., G. Demerson, op. cit., Appendix 6.

[2] Cf. C. Corona Baratech, *Revolución y reacción en el reinado de Carlos IV* (1957), 244–5. There were not enough priests to read the tracts for the Inquisition.

[3] Godoy believed that under French influence democrats were discussing the classic issue of future republicanism—the merits of a unitary as opposed to a federal republic.

[4] Cf. the verdict of Muriel, a contemporary, who insisted that French books were both cheap and plentiful ('Historia de Carlos IV', *B.A.E.* cxiv (1958), 269).

[5] 'It is time for the French to come and drive out those who are unfit to rule the country' (Sandoz's dispatch of 6 August 1794, quoted H. Baumgarten, *Geschichte Spaniens*, i. 530.

[6] For the war enthusiasm in Catalonia see A. Ossorio y Gallardo, *Historia del pensamiento político catalán 1793–95* (1931), 7 ff.

Salamanca, Valladolid, and Seville for example—which was bitterly critical of Spanish society. An echo of this criticism survives in Goya's *Caprichos* and in the poetry of Meléndez Valdés, vague but radical in its humanitarianism: one of the Salamantine group, the Abbé Marchena became a French propagandist, appealing to Spain to destroy the Inquisition and imitate the 'sublime' revolution of France.[1]

This Jacobinism was exceptional; more significant was the gradual growth of the idea that the monarch's power, however beneficent it appeared when directed against the strongholds of privilege, must be limited by a constitution in the event of its being exercised by an irresponsible favourite like Godoy. The virtue of the Prince must be 'secured, like Ulysses, to the mast of the law, in order to save it from the seductive voices of flattery and vanity'.[2]

This vague notion of the desirability of a constitution gained the support of a powerful myth when contemporary contractual theory and the ideas of Montesquieu were built into a version of Spanish history. This myth was later popularized by Martínez Mariana's *Teoría de las Cortes*, where it was argued that the destruction of medieval Cortes by the Hapsburgs, a destruction completed by the suppression of the *comunero* rebellion of Padilla (1520), was the necessary prelude to three hundred years of 'slavery and despotism'. To revive liberty was to revive the Cortes. Mariana's critics pointed out that his 'gothic perfections' hid what they considered a crass historical error: liberty was founded not on democratic pressures but on grants from the crown.[3] Nevertheless the Spanish translation of Rousseau's *Social Contract* could appeal to a 'son of Padilla'; it was enthusiasm for the parliamentary institutions of medieval Spain which allowed the Cortes of Cadiz to present a constitution, founded on the constitutions of Revolutionary

[1] For Marchena see R. Herr, *Revolution in Spain*, 272–7, and A. Morel Fatio, 'José Marchena et la propagande révolutionnaire en Espagne' (*Revue historique*, xliv (1890)). The conservative view in M. Menéndez Pelayo, *El abate Marchena* (Buenos Aires, 1946).

[2] For this change of attitude see *Cartas al conde de Lerena* (edited Rodríguez Villa, 1887). Although the author believes the monarchy is the 'nerve of reform' he nevertheless puts forward the standard argument that absolute power demands an impossible absolute of wisdom.

[3] J. H. Maravall, 'El pensamiento político en España a comienzos del siglo XIX' (*R.E.P.* 1955).

France, as the culmination of the 'true' constitutional development of Spain.[1] It was thus that radicalism became, historically speaking, respectable.

Both radicals and the men of government criticized traditional Spain and its values; this criticism opened up the polemics of Europeanization which have lasted until today. Were the old values of a Catholic society sufficient and necessary for a modern state? Was any attack on them to be construed as national treason? To the defenders of tradition there was little difference between the cautious civil servants of the generation of 1760 and the radical intellectuals of the nineties. Both shared the belief of the Enlightenment that legislation could procure felicity; that the evils of society were remediable, not punishments for original sin since 'more than natural causes political errors cause the decadence of peoples'.[2] Both shared the common assumption that Spain was itself decadent and 'behind' Europe: the radicals were pessimists and wholesale Europeanizers like the later Progressive Liberals, while the Caroline bureaucrats were moderate patriots who resented the airs of superiority which the French *philosophes* adopted towards Spain. Finally, in the crisis of 1808 some of the reformists and many of the radical intellectuals deserted the national cause and served 'the intruder', the French king, Joseph I. To traditionalists this treason was inevitable since both derived their ideas from the national enemy.[3]

The conjoint condemnation of enlightened reform from above and a radicalism which derived from doctrines of popular sovereignty was useful because it allowed conservatives to discredit any effort to reform traditional society; it was possible because the generation of 1760 included pious bureaucrats like Floridablanca, *esprits forts* like Aranda, and cosmopolitan experts like Olavide; it was made plausible by the Janus-like

[1] Martínez de la Rosa s play *The Widow of Padilla* was performed in Cadiz when the liberal Cortes was sitting.

[2] This was the creed of Sempere y Guarinos, a believer in the absolute but reforming monarchy and a stout defender of the claims of the crown against the pretensions of the Church. He became an *afrancesado*. For his views see R. Fernández Carvajal, 'La historiografía constitucional de Sempere y Guarinos' (*R.E.P.*, no. 82, 1955), 68 ff.

[3] Dependence on French ideas has been over-stressed by both conservative enemies and French scholars enamoured with the diffusion of French culture; the influence of English and Italian thought has never been studied.

face of reform itself.[1] Regalism was a traditional position of the crown, not an attempt to create a lay state—Charles III, the regalist king, was devoted to the doctrine of the Immaculate Conception. Yet the private language of the regalists was as strong as that of any nineteenth-century anti-clerical: Azara dramatized his struggles with the Jesuits as 'a modern Iliad'. They were enemies of the sovereign, public thieves, full of vice, and atheists whose pernicious doctrine could only be met by illuminating men's minds with geometry, physics, and astronomy.[2] To fight for the crown against the Church and in order to neutralize the influence of canon lawyers, the regalists introduced the teaching of Natural Law, an innovation which was promptly suppressed in 1794 when the revolutionary dangers of secular political thought were made evident in France. Equality before the law, for the reformers the principal condition of the effective exercise of royal power, contained the pattern of a social revolution which must destroy the privileged groups of traditional society. Liberty entered into men's minds in the struggle against the economic prejudices of the *ancien régime*, a struggle waged by servants of the crown. To destroy guilds was to defend 'civil liberty'.[3]

In a sense Spanish clerical conservatives were correct in thinking that there was no such thing as a 'safe' Enlightenment; however respectable the proponents of *luces* appeared, at the root of their creed lay a rationalism that denied Divine Providence and that must lead to an attack on the position of the Church in society, even if they professed to respect dogma. Feijóo, 'father of the Enlightenment', whose encyclopaedic works first popularized ideas of experimental science early in the century, was a monk and devout believer. Yet his

[1] The links between enlightened despotism and democratic radicalism are to be sought in the humanitarianism of men like Meléndez Valdés (a poet who was a civil servant). The key figure who connects governmental reformism and democratic radicalism is perhaps Cabarrús. A servant of Charles IV, he was far more radical in his ideas than Charles III's minister, Floridablanca; a reader of Rousseau he believed (in private) that the monarchy could only preserve itself by bowing to the general will (*B.A.E.* lxii. 552, 554, 568). Cabarrús sided with the 'intruder' King Joseph, whereas Floridablanca took the patriot side.

[2] His letters are full of anti-clerical bite; cf. C. Corona Baratech, *José Nicolás de Azara* (Saragossa, 1948), 86–87, 125.

[3] Jovellanos, *B.A.E.* l. 41–45. (Cf. L. Sánchez Agesta, *El pensamiento político del despotismo ilustrado* (Madrid, 1953), 128–30.)

criticism of false miracles undermined the foundations of popular belief and it was to him that the future heretic Blanco White acknowledged his debt.[1] The outward religious respectability of the leading personalities of the Enlightenment in Spain is not necessarily a proof of their innocence of real hostility to the Church: the Inquisition, weak though it was, combined with stiff royal censorship to make the public expression of heterodox views an impossibility. The trial and disgrace of Olavide by the Inquisition in 1778 was a penalty for the tactless folly of a man who could not resist mocking superstitious priests; its significance is that the Inquisition could still destroy a leading statesman.

Nevertheless the Church could not preserve men's minds from modern heresy; it failed in the campaign to exclude 'dangerous' books nor could it prevent the influence of contacts established by Aranda and others with the French intellectuals.[2] Indeed the Church's counter-offensive made common property the most familiar arguments of deists and natural law philosophers in order to refute them. Thus there was in Spain a minority who, if not free thinkers, were extremely critical of the position and claims of the Spanish Church; in the Salamanca of the seventies, a small group of intellectuals had read books containing rejections of the central beliefs of Catholicism itself. The Inquisition was an ineffective irritant, slow and erratic in its procedures; it merely put up the price of books, forcing readers to all sorts of subterfuges in order to consume often out-dated heresies. Even a pious man like Jovellanos could feel bitterly at the attempts of the Inquisition to sabotage his plans for establishing a modern technical institute at

[1] For an example of Feijóo's method see the demolition of the miraculous flowers of the Hermitage of St. Louis (*B.A.E.* lvi, pp. xiii ff.). The sales of Feijóo were enormous by Spanish standards: 3,000 copies of the fifth and sixth volumes of his *Teatro crítico* were printed. For his influence see G. Delpy, *L'Espagne et l'esprit européen, l'œuvre de Feijóo* (Paris, 1936). He fills the role of a Voltaire in Spain as a *vulgarisateur* of the Enlightenment, and the quality of the Spanish Enlightenment can best be judged by comparing the confusion of his compilations with the clarity of Voltaire's *Lettres philosophiques*.

[2] J. R. Spell, *Rousseau in the Spanish World* (Austin, 1938), asserts with some exaggeration, 'all the leaders of the Reform movement . . . were almost without exception friends and admirers of Rousseau' (49). This was certainly true of Cabarrús, the most ardent of Charles IV's reforming ministers. *Eusebio*, a plagiarism of *Émile*, sold 60,000 copies. Meléndez Valdés was reading a large number of French books in the seventies and eighties.

Gijon.[1] No Spaniard could freely obtain the works of Voltaire, Rousseau, or Buffon. At the beginning of every avenue of progress, intellectual or material, stood the Church with the feeble Inquisition as a symbol of Spain's distance from cultivated Europe.[2]

[1] Again we are confronted with the ambivalence of men like Jovellanos: he had excluded religious instruction from the curriculum (cf. J. Sarrailh, *Espagne éclairée*, 134). For the bitterness of Jovellanos at the refusal of the ecclesiastical authorities to permit the use of modern books in the Institute see his *Diarios 1790–1801* (1915), entries for 6 August 1795 and 5 September 1795.

[2] For an excellent description of the efficacy and influence of the Inquisition see M. Defourneaux, *L'Inquisition espagnole et les livres français au XVIIIe siècle* (Paris, 1903). The author claims that, while it failed to stop the diffusion of French books, it developed in the intellectuals of the Enlightenment 'un sentiment d'infériorité qui put constituer . . . une véritable souffrance' (105).

III

THE CRISIS OF THE *ANCIEN RÉGIME* 1808–1814

CHARLES III, the reformers' king, whose life was a mechanical ritual of hunting and hard work, died in the last month of the last year when reform was still respectable—1788. His son Charles IV was a domesticated, well-intentioned man, soon dominated by his wife María Luisa. During his reign the factions of the court destroyed the stable ministerial tradition which had been the precondition of his father's achievements, substituting for it the rule of a favourite—the queen's supposed lover, Godoy. It was this ministerial system in decline which had to face the strains imposed on the European state system by the ideas and the armies of the French Revolution. The consequent crisis was an imperial crisis loosening the fabric of the absolute monarchy and bringing into question the principles on which it was based from the Basque Provinces and Catalonia to New Granada and the River Plate. It accelerated Spain's descent from great-power status. By 1824 she had lost all her American empire except for Cuba and Puerto Rico, while in metropolitan Spain the struggle waged in the thirties between constitutionalists and traditionalists was to reduce the core of the monarchy to bankruptcy and near anarchy.

This protracted crisis began on 17 March 1808 when a mob of soldiers, peasants, and palace grooms forced Charles IV to dismiss Godoy, found hiding in terror in a rolled-up carpet;[1] two days later another mob forced Charles IV to abdicate in favour of his son, the Prince of Asturias who became Ferdinand VII. In April, at Bayonne, Napoleon, who had already thrown French troops into Spain, compelled Ferdinand to abdicate the throne of Spain in favour of Joseph, the emperor's brother. In the early summer, a national revolution in the name of 'the

[1] For this *émeute*, the Tumult of Aranjuez, see below, pp. 83–84.

Desired One', Ferdinand, now a captive in France, split Spain into a conglomeration of city-states and autonomous provinces ruled by committees (juntas) of local notables. These Provincial Juntas organized resistance to the French occupation authorities and, on 19 July, the army of the Seville Junta defeated Dupont's isolated corps at Bailén. This unexpected victory forced Joseph to withdraw from Madrid and, assured of English help with Moore's army, the patriotic cause appeared about to triumph. With Napoleon's invasion of Spain it collapsed. By 1810 the legal government of independent Spain (which had transformed itself from a Central Junta, composed of delegates from the Provincial Juntas, into a Regency) was cooped up in Cadiz surrounded by a French army; there it sought to find the sinews of war and to regularize the constitutional position by summoning a Cortes which met on 24 September 1810. The subsequent liberation of Spain was largely the work of Wellington's armies; after the battle of Vitoria (June 1813) Joseph left Spain and in the spring of 1814 the Desired One returned to his kingdom.

From these events the monarchy of the *ancien régime* was never to recover. When the Prince of Asturias put a candle in his window to start a riot against his father, he called into existence a process which led through constitutional monarchy to a democratic republic. A king, who came to his throne through 'popular power', it was argued, must submit to limitations.[1] In 1812 the Cortes of Cadiz drew up a constitution which consecrated the dogma of the sovereignty of the nation. This democratic revolution was accepted neither by the king himself nor by conservative-clerical Spain; to them the War of Independence was fought in defence of the 'old constitution', i.e. the absolute monarchy and the Church. When the Cortes returned to liberated Madrid (5 January 1814) and the Desired One to Spain, the Persians, a group of conservative deputies, petitioned the king to denounce the constitution of 1812; this he did in the Manifesto of 4 May 1814. Thus, in the reign of Ferdinand VII, the contest between liberalism and conservatism could not be fought out within a constitutional system; it concerned the existence of a constitution as such.

[1] A. Alcalá Galiano, 'Memorias', *B.A.E.* lxxxiii. 329.

1. *The French Invasion and the Patriot Rebellion, 1808–1809*

The crisis of the *ancien régime* is marked by that interplay between foreign policy and domestic faction which typifies the collapse of enfeebled states. For twenty years Floridablanca's 'system'—the French alliance—had given Spain the appearance of a first-class naval, military, and colonial power. Suddenly the French Revolution destroyed the premise of the system; the war against France (1793–5) exposed the weakness of Spain's position in Europe—incapacity to resist a French invasion. 'How can you want Spain mixed up in such great events', Aranda complained to the Prussian Minister, 'when she lacks all means to wage war.' Given this incapacity Spain could never hope to maintain diplomatic independence against France or to resist French demands for war against Great Britain, in spite of knowledge of the disastrous consequences of such a war to the Spanish colonial empire and its trade. Napoleon, therefore, regarded Spain as a power to whose alliance he possessed a natural right. Hence he never bothered to devote much time to Spanish affairs; wishful thinking and ignorance exposed his views on the value of Spain to a series of disillusionments. She failed him as a great 'silver' power, as a naval power at Trafalgar, and by 1807 her domestic politics were so confused by court intrigue that she appeared scarcely a reliable political ally.

In spite of disappointments, neither Napoleon nor his agents revised their illusions. Spain was potentially a great power, unreliable and ineffective because her resources were badly managed. Towards the end of 1807 Napoleon determined to convert Spain into a satellite state in order to control its foreign policy and to manage its resources; but he was not yet clear how this should be accomplished. In the meantime and, as a first step, under cover of a joint war against Portugal, he secured the partial occupation of Spain by French troops (Treaty of Fontainebleau, 17 October 1807). It was at this point that Napoleon became entangled in the feuds of the court factions; his exploitation of these feuds after the tumult of Aranjuez gave a confused start to a national revolution.

'The Revolution in Spain', prophesied General Augereau to the Directory, 'will be directed, in the first instance, against the Prince of the Peace.'[1] Godoy, Prince of the Peace, was neither a reactionary nor a brutal tyrant; indeed he was a mild progressive who consistently posed as the friend of enlightenment, earning for himself that hatred of priests and monks which contributed to his fall.[2] He attacked intramural burial, the Mendicant Orders, and bullfights—all characteristic policies of enlightened statesmen. The breach with the inherited system lay not in Godoy's policies but in the relegation to impotence of the trained bureaucrats who had been the servants of Charles III; it lay in the scandalous origins and untrammelled nature of his power as the queen's supposed lover and the 'dearest friend' of the complaisant Charles IV. His correspondence with the queen, while it may confute accusations of lasciviousness, reveals the poverty of his courtier mind; his main concern and topic was the health of the royal couple and his bond with María Luisa seems to have been hypochrondriacal rather than sexual in nature.[3] His offence was not flagitiousness but the vulgarity, ostentation, and political inexperience of a parvenu. Godoy was a good-looking Guards officer of twenty-five when he was granted power more absolute than that possessed by any subsequent ruler of Spain until General Franco. When Floridablanca's rigid hostility to Revolutionary France and Aranda's neutralism had both failed it was to such an adviser that the court turned to solve the problem of Franco-Spanish relations. As a courtier, he saw all issues in the light cast by the shifting world of court favour: thus Godoy's support of the French alliance was consistently conditioned by his desire to use it against his enemies at court or his hopes of a safe retreat from these enemies in a Portuguese principality bestowed on him by France. Napoleon despised him and exploited him because he guessed his motives and could not take seriously his defence of Spanish independence.

As in all mild dictatorships, the dictator's control of patron-

[1] Quoted C. Corona Baratech, *Revolución y reacción en el reinado de Carlos IV* (1957), 327.

[2] For his early relationship with the reformers see R. Herr, *Eighteenth-century Revolution*, 348–75; C. Corona Baratech, *Carlos IV*, 274, and S. Serrano Poncela, 'Godoy y los ilustrados', *C.A.* (1960), 180 ff. Cf. his 'advanced' programme in October 1798 (ibid. 289).

[3] This correspondence is printed in C. Pereyra, *Cartas confidenciales de María Luisa y Godoy* (n.d.).

age created an opposition of 'outs'. Thus the poet Quintana's friends, when royal patronage and the censor backed 'Godoy's gang' of literary admirers, set up Voltaire's dramatic theories against those of Batteux, favoured by the régime's dramatist and Godoy's friend, Moratín. Like all such oppositions it was cliquy, largely conversational, expressing itself in 'private grievances, expressive silences, above all in abstention from praise or at the most, timid insinuations'.[1] By 1808 the unpopularity of Godoy had spread beyond these circles to embrace all classes and the revolution prophesied in 1798 was turning against the court that supported his power: a monarchy which could disgrace itself and by its foreign policy plunge Spain into inflation, dear bread, commercial depression, and the loss of the American market must be limited by a constitution.[2]

The Tumult of Aranjuez, which overthrew both Godoy and his king, was not, however, the work of informed 'liberal' opinion. It was engineered by a group of malcontent nobles in alliance with the faction of the Prince of the Asturias, using as their instruments army officers and the mob. The vague reformism of the epoch was, in these circles, channelled into an even vaguer brand of aristocratic constitutionalism which revived the claims of the old 'rich men' (*ricos hombres*) of Castile; grandees could stomach rule by career bureaucrats but the career of court favourite was an aristocratic preserve not to be exercised by the 'sausage maker', Godoy.[3] The Prince of the Asturias was in contact with this aristocratic opposition, publishing caricatures distributed in taverns in order to discredit his father's court and the favourite around which it centred.[4] Ferdinand believed Godoy was scheming for a regency to exclude him from the throne; Godoy knew that Ferdinand was

[1] Cf. A. Alcalá Galiano, *Memorias*, lxxxiii. 314–15. A typical opposition activity was the refusal of an old conservative officer to subscribe to a *fiesta* in Godoy's honour.

[2] Godoy's system was particularly unpopular in Catalonia, where war with Great Britain (1804–8) caused most economic suffering: see J. Mercader, *Els capitans generals* (Barcelona, 1957), 162–4.

[3] The nickname was a reference to Godoy's home province, Estremadura—the centre of extensive pig breeding.

[4] These activities are described in H. Castro Bonez, 'Manejos de Ferdinando VII contra sus padres y contra Godoy' (*Boletín de la Universidad de Madrid*, ii (1930), 397–408, 493–503; ii. 93–102).

intriguing against him with the French ambassador. By 1807 politics had become a fight to the death between the two factions. Godoy struck first hoping, in the Escorial Trial, that Ferdinand might be found guilty of political parricide. The trial only revealed Godoy's political and moral isolation and convinced Napoleon that these 'dirty intrigues' made either faction an impossibly unreliable ally.

As Godoy claimed, the Tumult of Aranjuez was the work of seduced plebeians, a revolution that seeped down from above. Next day the prosperous citizens of Madrid put up their shutters while the mob pillaged the houses of Godoy and his supporters. A court tumult had become 'a formidable national revolution'.[1] As in 1766, the crown surrendered its chosen servant to the only forces it was to respect in the nineteenth century—the mob and the army officers. The accidental factor, that belonged to the past, was the leadership of the aristocracy: in the later nineteenth century the *sans culottes* of Madrid streets could not be brought out by the traditional symbiotic relationship of aristocratic employers and plebeian clientele. Yet it was from the delirious welcome accorded to him by his partisans in the Madrid streets that Ferdinand VII formed his conceptions of political power; in 1814 he was to use the Aranjuez mixture of plebeian loyalty and army support in order to defeat the liberal constitution. What he did not realize was that the same combination of forces could be used against the monarchy. Hence the revolutions that stretch from 1820 to 1931.

It is ironic that Godoy was overthrown and treated with ignominy as a traitor at the moment when he had decided to resist Napoleon: it was his plan to remove the king to Seville, out of the way of the French, which set off the Tumult of Aranjuez. Years later Toreno, the liberal historian, acknowledged the 'correctness' of this policy.[2] When Godoy was contemplating patriotism his enemy Ferdinand, who had been intriguing for French support for some months, put all his faith in Napoleon's endorsement of the revolution of Aranjuez. Rumours of this purpose account for the early popularity of the

[1] The comment of Mesonero Romanos in *Memorias de un setentón* (1881), i. 20. It is clear from his account that, though Godoy was generally hated, the *motín* was 'the work of certain classes'.

[2] 'Historia del levantamiento, guerra y revolución de España' (*B.A.E.* lxiv), 20.

French; they had come to support the 'Desired One'. Aranjuez, however, had clarified Napoleon's muddled thinking on the Spanish question and he had no intention of using the opportunity it presented in order to support a puppet king whose character and intentions he mistrusted. Instead he played off the resentment of the 'old court' at their humiliations and Charles IV's frantic appeals that the French should save Godoy from the vengeance of his enemies against Ferdinand's craving for French backing.[1] Thus the emperor could settle the dynastic question by enticing Ferdinand to Bayonne and there forcing both him and his father to abdicate in favour of his own brother, Joseph (10 May 1808). In their competition for French support Ferdinand and his father became the first *afrancesados* (Frenchifiers).

As long as Napoleon appeared the supporter of Ferdinand against Godoy, Spain 'awaited its fate from the Emperor'. By dethroning Ferdinand Napoleon turned the revolution of Aranjuez against himself: the rising against Napoleon was thus, in part, a revolution of disappointed hopes. Since Ferdinand's instructions to the Junta of Government (which he left in Madrid to govern while he was at Bayonne) were to cultivate French friendship at all costs, and since these counsels were not modified until *after* the outbreak of a popular rising, it meant that official Spain could not take the leadership of the instinctive movement against France. Resistance to the French troops who 'occupied' Spain under cover of the Treaty of Fontainebleau and the national revolution against France which broke out all over unoccupied Spain came, therefore, from those whom the French commanders termed *le petit peuple* and from those local notables who were outside an administration manned by appointees of Godoy.

In the confused situation of March and April 1808 the hesitations of the official classes in occupied Spain are under-

[1] The negotiations with the old court are described in Toreno, *Levantamiento*, 27 ff. Charles IV immediately appealed to Murat, as commander of the French forces in Spain, against his son. Murat obviously had his own private ambitions but was in ignorance of Napoleon's intentions. Napoleon's letter of 27 March is perhaps the decisive turning-point in his confused policy. (Cf. G. de Grandmaison, 'Savary en Espagne', *Revue des questions historiques*, lxviii (Paris, 1909), 188–213.) The French undoubtedly saved Godoy from trial and perhaps from lynching.

standable. Neither the Council of Castile nor the Junta of Government could be expected to lead a hopeless revolt against French garrisons by disobeying Ferdinand's explicit orders.[1] Irritated by the exactions of French quartermasters and suspecting French intentions, the Council, nevertheless, co-operated with Murat, the commander of the French army of occupation. After the abdication of Ferdinand at Bayonne, it refused to recognize the change of dynasty, grounding its refusal on legal formalities. Though Murat considered this niggling opposition an encouragement to disaffection—'the yeast of all this ferment' (25 July)—in the euphoria after the patriot victory of Bailén (19 July 1808) the dignified trimmings of magistrates appeared the feebleness of treason.

The possibility of resistance lay in an appeal to the sovereign nation in the form of the mob. In the May of 1808 the constituted authorities all over Spain were confronted with the dilemma which discredited civil governors on the outbreak of the Civil War in July 1936. Was the defeat of the usurper worth the dangers of an armed mob out of control in the streets? The Council of Castile had refused public recognition of Joseph's title to the Spanish crown on the grounds that such a claim was *ultra vires* without consulting the nation. Hence, in the mouths of conservative lawyers, we catch an appeal to the radical doctrine of the sovereignty of the nation; it alone could provide a theoretical basis for resistance to a French king whose claim was legally established by the formal abdication of both Ferdinand VII and his father. To talk of the rights of the nation was one thing, to descend to the streets and appeal to the mob was unthinkable to magistrates whose obsessive concern was the preservation of order.[2] How could Ezpeleta, a soldier-administrator well on in his seventies and now Captain General in Barcelona, be expected to appeal to the unemployed dockers, artisans, and cotton operatives, called by the French commander *l'immense canaille de Barcelone*, against an overwhelmingly superior French garrison? Ezpeleta and the local administra-

[1] Ferdinand's first instructions for the organization of resistance arrived in Madrid after 9 May. Cf. Azanza y O'Farrill, 'Memoria' (*B.A.E.* xcvii), 296–7.

[2] M. Artola, *Orígenes de la España contemporánea* (1959), 109–21, takes a much sterner view of the weakness of the Council of Castile than does Desdevises du Dezert in his detailed study 'Le Conseil de Castille en 1808', *R.H.* xvii (1907), 66–378.

tion followed events and there is no reason to suppose that judges and municipal officials would have abandoned their ambiguous collaborationism had not St. Cyr, the French commander, later forced on them an oath of loyalty to Joseph—repugnant to the very legalism which, combined with inertia and pay, had kept them at their posts. To the propertied classes in *occupied* Spain, therefore, co-operation with the French authorities was the only reasonable course.

It was the urban mob which ended the hesitations of the official classes wherever resistance was a possibility. The first act of rebellion, and what remained the symbolic centre-piece of revolutionary nationalism—the Madrid rising of 2 May 1808—was the work of 'low people', alarming the Council of Castile as much as Murat. At 1 p.m. it rode round Madrid with the other Councils in full dress to restore order and in the following days it co-operated with the French authorities in the collection of arms.[1] In *unoccupied* Spain the constituted authorities did not have the excuse of overwhelming military force and it was their failure in crisis which condemned the *ancien régime*. Their desire to preserve order (that is, obey instructions from a government in Madrid dominated by Murat) and their shilly-shallying when confronted with a demand to arm and lead a national revolution against the French, were swamped by popular risings. These were set off by news of Bayonne, of Murat's executions of the patriots of the 2nd of May in Madrid, or of the failure of the authorities to celebrate the feast of St. Ferdinand. Cuesta, Captain General of Old Castile, took the patriotic cause 'seriously' when the students of Valladolid erected a gallows in his courtyard and after his colleague in Badajoz had been murdered. In the Asturias a mob of a thousand peasants and university students, after pillaging the arsenal of its rifles, made an end of the hesitations of the *Audiencia* and the constituted authorities, who were afraid to defy Murat; the general assembly of the province, which happened to be holding one of its triennial meetings, took the leadership of the insurrection, and, on 25 May, declared war on Napoleon.[2]

[1] The episodic history of the 2 May rising is set out in J. Pérez de Guzmán, *El 2 de Mayo de 1808* (1908).

[2] The efficacy of mob action was not confined to the city in which it took place: thus the authorities of Seville were alarmed by the bloodshed in Cadiz, those of

In the classic phrase of Toreno, 'the people rose' in 'unanimous, energetic' revolt, in the weeks after 2 May. The true nature of this revolt is still obscure. Was it a political Great Fear, a contagion that spread from city to city, village to village? Was it the last act of a popular drama begun at Aranjuez and thwarted by Napoleon's desertion of Ferdinand and protection of Godoy, a revolution of disappointed vengeance, a revolution directed against Godoy's creatures in the provincial administrations who now followed the French? Was it an outburst of fanatical xenophobia led by monks and friars?[1]

Napoleon and the French in Spain entirely failed to grasp the significance of this popular movement. French officials knew that the patriotism of the official classes was dubious and lukewarm; they calculated that, if the Captains General went over, the people would follow; the people of Spain were vile cowards 'like the Arabs'. Murat and the French Ambassador, La Forest, saw the 2nd of May as the opportunity for one of those severe lessons which had been so effective in Naples. On 1 July La Forest believed the revolution was dying.[2] The sole result of anarchy would be to drive the 'honourable men of property' into the arms of the French.

Of the great fear of the men of property our sources leave us in no doubt. Alcalá Galiano, as an old man, remembered the terror of the middle-class citizens as the ragged 'patriots' of the

Murcia by events in Cartagena. The best description of this chain reaction is still that of Toreno, *Historia del levantamiento*, 56–81. For a summary see M. Artola, *Orígenes*, i. 123–46.

[1] Corona Baratech argues (in *Precedentes ideológicos de la guerra de Independencia*, Saragossa, 1959) that the revolt was *led* by those implicated in the conspiracy against Godoy: hence its simultaneity and the fact that the mobs showed particular violence against 'those who they thought enjoyed most favour in the reign of Charles IV'. Cf. Azanza and O'Farrill, 'Memoria Justificativa' (*B.A.E.* xcvii. 308*b*). In fact, the leaders appear to have been an assortment of local personalities—canons, monks, friars, officers, doctors—and no very clear picture emerges. Monks and friars were regarded by Napier, the English historian, as 'invariably' the leaders, a view shared by Napoleon who wished to present the 'national' revolution as the resistance of blind fanaticism to enlightened reform. The leadership of members of the Regular Orders is established only in the most anarchic period in Valencia and Cadiz: it is merely one more proof of their genuine popularity.

[2] La Forest quoted Lt.-Col. Clerc, *Guerre d'Espagne, Capitulation de Baylen* (Paris, 1903), 135. The French Consul at Cadiz believed that, in spite of anti-French riots, all depended on winning over the Captains General: 'Les dispositions du pays sont bonnes' (ibid. 75). Savary was more realistic. 'L'insurrection s'organize et depuis six semaines nous n'avons pas fait un pas', quoted Desdevises du Dezert, *Conseil de Casteille*, 210.

Valencian army, their hats covered with relics, marched into Madrid; in Cadiz only the Capuchins could disarm the rioters who, after murdering the Governor, had seized the Arsenal. In Oviedo an infuriated mob was only prevented from lynching the distinguished poet Meléndez Valdés by the appearance of priests with the exposed host. Perhaps it is hardly surprising that Meléndez Valdés became an *afrancesado*.[1]

Nevertheless, this panic reaction was neither universal nor permanent; if it had been there could have been no War of Independence. 'The nobles, clergy and soldiers united with the people in the nick of time and calmed the disorders.'[2] A significant proportion of local notables joined the popular revolution in order to master anarchy: this was to be the classic pattern of revolution in the nineteenth century.

Thus in Saragossa, the capital of Aragon, where a mob with red cockades in their hats demanded arms and patriotic resistance, Palafox accepted the leadership by becoming a 'revolutionary' Captain General and regularizing the movement by summoning the Cortes of Aragon. Palafox was a great aristocrat, known to be a friend of the deposed Ferdinand and anything but a democrat; but, as his brother made clear, the future hero of the siege of Saragossa could not master the people on any other terms. In Oviedo the popular revolt was respectably channelled into the Junta of the province and the leadership of the Marqués de Santa Cruz. Elsewhere, the main instrument for this capture of control by the notables—an English diplomat called them the gentry—was the election of Juntas. Once assured of their willingness to adopt the patriot cause the 'people' turned to their natural, local leaders and disappeared from the stage except for a few significant reappearances and a few protests against 'the rich'.[3] Yet it was the people who

[1] For the Oviedo incident see R. Álvarez Valdés, *Memorias del levantamiento de Asturias* (Oviedo, 1889), 79 ff.

[2] 'Memorias del Marqués de Ayerbe', *B.A.E.* xcvii. 245. These disorders were worst in Valencia: W. Napier, *History of the War in the Peninsula* (London, 1886), i. 23, goes too far in saying 'all who opposed the people's will' in Leon were slaughtered: Toreno is probably too optimistic in his estimate that Valencia aside, three hundred were killed.

[3] The Catalan Junta, representing the 'egoism of the rich', was overthrown by Campoverde and an elected congress of 'tribunes of the people'. Cf. the important reference in J. Vicens Vives, *Els Catalans*, 121–2. 'The *somatents* (popular militia) from 1808 to 1814 fought not only against the French but against the *senyors* and

continued to embody what English agents called 'enthusiasm', the xenophobic church and king patriotism which never lost its terrors for the men of property. 'Whatever good will there is,' wrote Moore in December, 'and *among the lower orders* I believe there is a good deal, is taken no advantage of.'[1]

As the French armies advanced, in the contracting area controlled by the patriots effective government and the war effort of the years 1808–14 lay in the hands of the Juntas. Like the committees of July 1936, they issued passports, raised local levies, licensed apothecaries. At the base of the revolutionary pyramid lay the popularly elected town Juntas, sometimes two in the same town. Above the town Juntas, and chosen originally from them, came the Provincial Juntas. These bodies were controlled by the 'men of 1808', local landowners, clergy, officers, and administrators who had taken the patriot side. In the Asturias, the Junta was driven from mountain village to mountain village with a stable as a committee room, without pen or ink. Its members wearied of the task, seeking relief in absence which reduced the Junta to a handful of members. They were feeble in policy, loth to tax the propertied classes and the clergy, paralysed by opposition, yet they remained the centre of the civilian war effort, taxing, organizing guerillas, chasing deserters, and countering defeatist propaganda.

These harassed men were revolutionaries in spite of themselves. When the Juntas were thwarted in their organization of a war effort by the spiky legalism of those local organs of the *ancien régime* which survived in unoccupied Spain, they could defend their authority only be deriving it from the elections of 'a free people who did not wish to perish'. It was this democratic claim that shocked the conservative lawyers of the Council of Castile, and the judges of the *Audiencias*. In the first months the Provincial Juntas acted as independent sovereign states. Delegations were dispatched to London 'as nation to nation', armies were regarded as provincial forces not to be sacrificed either to the needs of neighbouring provinces or to

great landowners as well.' In February 1809 a Cadiz mob, incensed at the prospect of conscription, nearly murdered the Governor and could be brought to heel only by the Capuchins.

[1] Quoted, C. Oman, *A History of the Peninsular War* (Oxford, 1902), i. 506.

those of the nation. The Seville Junta behaved with criminal selfishness and, but for the moderation of its general, it might have declared war on Granada; it refused to send the Andalusian Army to the critical Ebro front where the French, after Joseph had withdrawn from Madrid in the panic caused by the defeat of French corps by the patriots of Bailén, were massing for a reinvasion of Spain.[1] To later Federal Republicans the Spain of the War of Independence was already a federal republic, run by conservatives. The deepest chord in Spanish revolutionary politics is the *centralista* tradition which holds that central government is an emanation from the direct democracy of the popularly elected municipality.

Nevertheless the conservatives who manned the Juntas were not provincial separatists: they were inspired, not merely by a vague programme of reform on a national level, but by a sense of order that forced them to see the necessity of a central government. The Council of Castile, in spite of its repeated claims to be the only legally constituted authority, was discredited by its supposed subservience to Murat; its orders were treated with contempt by the Provincial Juntas. It could not be allowed to represent the nation in arms. A central authority would only be accepted if it represented the Juntas; backed by British agents, who thoroughly disliked the military consequences of federalism, the movement for the creation of a Central Junta triumphed over the jealousies of the important Juntas. The adhesion of Seville, the virtual capital of the early months and now strong in the victory of Bailén, was decisive. In September 1880 the delegates of the Provincial Juntas met at Aranjuez—the jealousy of Seville precluded Madrid—as the Central Junta.

The Central Junta has a bad reputation; a clumsy body of thirty-five presided over by the aged Floridablanca, President of the Junta of Murcia, its pretensions as a sovereign body with the title 'Majesty' were slightly ridiculous. It was opposed by the renascent claims of the Provincial Juntas as direct representa-

[1] See W. R. de Villa-Urrutia, *Relaciones entre España e Inglaterra durante la guerra de la independencia* (1912), i. 164 *et passim*, for the competing activities of these emissaries in London; they formed separate bodies, the Deputies of the North and the South. They went home in driblets in October leaving Admiral Apodaca as representative of the Central Junta; this did not prevent various provincial emissaries turning up later to embarrass Canning.

tives of the sovereign people; by conservatives and malcontent grandees who hoped to put an end to Junta government altogether; by the emergent power of the generals whose incipient Caesarism was represented by Palafox and Cuesta, both of whom were intriguing for political power. Above all its claims were rejected by the Council of Castile as a usurpation of sovereign power which belonged to the king and to his appointed administrators. Overpoweringly jealous of the revolutionary claims of the Provincial Juntas, it could not bring itself to recognize the legality of their offspring.[1]

After the shattering defeat of Ocaña (November 1809—the Central Junta's attempt at decisive defeat of Joseph's armies) the demand for a 'concentration of government' became irresistible. Discredited and abused, the Junta retreated before the French, first to Seville, then to Cadiz: there its members resigned, to be insulted by the 'patriots' of Cadiz who searched their baggage for stolen government funds and finally imprisoned them.[2] Its successor, the conservative Regency of Five (presided over by the Bishop of Orense, later to gain notoriety by his public denunciation of the doctrine of national sovereignty) was caught between, on the one side, the urban democracy of Cadiz, where a 'Junta of merchants', elected by a ballot of householders, had assumed the airs of a sovereign body and, on the other, the antiquated obstructionism of the Councils. Without the support of British troops, the nominal central government of Spain might have collapsed altogether.

2. *The Cortes of Cadiz and the Liberal Settlement in Spain and Latin America, 1810–1813*

Except to hidebound conservatives, it was evident that, whatever body of men governed patriot Spain, it must seek strength and legitimacy by summoning the nation to a Cortes. The debate on the nature and functions of the Cortes brought

[1] The Council's case against the Central Junta was, characteristically, based on deductions from the provisions for a regency for a minor contained in the medieval *Partidas*. Its resentments were gathered together in the Consulta of 19 February 1810. It was against these bitter accusations that Jovellanos published his passionate defence of the Central Junta (printed *B.A.E.* xlvi. 502–621).

[2] The letters of Jovellanos to Lord Holland (*B.A.E.* lxxxvi) give a moving account of the humiliations of the Junta, while Jacob's *Travels* give a vivid description of its opponents (cf. 370 ff.).

into the open the issue which, since May, had divided conservative officials from revolutionary patriots. As representatives of the sovereign nation whose king was a captive in Talleyrand's chateau, the patriots claimed to supplant the structure of the *ancien régime* that had so signally failed in the supreme test of patriotism. The debate, pursued in periodicals and pamphlets, was the first public debate on the fundamental conditions of political life that Spain had known. It concerned the nature of the War of Independence itself.

Was the war, as liberal patriots maintained, a revolution to regenerate Spain by new laws? Had the social contract been broken and the nation, 'which had done all' in the way of resistance to the intruder, resumed its constituent powers? Were, as conservatives replied, the old laws, which they continued to administer, and the old institutions which they still manned, the only valid constitution? Were, therefore, the deputies of the Cortes to limit themselves to the study of the 'means and methods of expelling the French army', or was their sacred task to endow Spain with a constitution that would limit the despotism which had ended in French invasion? The supporters of 'our revolution' believed, like the Prussian patriots of 1806, that men who fought as soldiers must be rewarded as citizens, that 'independence would be accompanied by a reform of abuses'.[1] Conservatives taunted them that they might find themselves, fugitives in Africa, 'drawing from under their arm a very fine plan of a constitution while they had not a foot of land to stand upon', after having opened the doors to 'the revolutionary spirit which had destroyed France'.[2] Between this bald administrative and military conception and the threat of radical constitutionalism stood Jovellanos's Burkean defence of the 'ancient and venerable constitution of Spain'.[3]

The issue between radical patriots and conservatives centred on whether the privileged estates should preserve the separate representation they had enjoyed as 'arms' of the medieval Cortes, or whether all should merge in a general congress.

[1] For the parallel with Prussia see J. M. Jover Zamora, *La guerra de Independencia en el marco de las guerras europeas de liberación* (Saragossa, 1958).

[2] Vaughan MSS., 15 December 1810. A. M. Artola, *Orígenes de la España contemporánea* (1959), i. 279.

[3] The best exposition of Jovellanos's creed of evolution based on 'ancient forms' is in his letter to Lord Holland of 22 May 1809 (in *B.A.E.* lxxxvi. 377).

Jovellanos saw in a House of Lords the only wall that could stem the tide towards democracy that would run in a single chamber. The reactionary Regency, which succeeded the Central Junta as the executive power, abandoned the second chamber before what the liberal Argüelles called 'the irresistible pressure of public opinion' embodied in the deputies from the provinces assembled in Cadiz. Given the political feebleness of the Regency and the imprecise antiquarianism of the conservative programme, there could be no other result once the constituent issue had been raised. The Spanish House of Lords, a product of Jovellanos's correspondence with Lord Holland, seemed an artificial piece of antiquarianism in a country which had enjoyed no constitutional life since the sixteenth century and where the aristocracy were suspect as indifferent patriots. 'Has a grandee ever liberated a village?'

The Cortes of Cadiz, elected in theory by a complicated system of indirect household suffrage, assembled in the besieged Isla de Leon on 24 September 1810. It was to draw up the Constitution of 1812, the 'sacred codex' which defined Spanish liberalism as a political creed. This 'codex' was to become the classical liberal constitution of Latin Europe in the early nineteenth century.

The Constitution of Cadiz was always represented by conservatives as the handwork of a radical minority, divorced from any representative opinion in Spain. In a sense this was false, as recent historians have been at pains to prove. The replies to the *consulta* of 1809 (by which the leading authorities were asked for their views on the task of the Cortes) reveal a widespread, if ill-defined, feeling for a constitution based on a division of powers, for uniform, modern laws, for civil equality, and the curtailment of corporate privilege.[1] The liberals of Cadiz, therefore, did not represent merely a minority group within the political nation in spite of their imperfect election credentials; as far as there was a political nation, it was reformist. What remains true is that the enlightened were a minority within the nation *as a whole*, which neither shared nor understood the patriotism of these 'medieval knights,

[1] The replies are collected in the second volume of M. Artola, *Orígenes*. They are also discussed in J. Jiménez de Gregorio, 'La convocación de las Cortes constituyentes' (*E.H.M.* v. 223 ff.). They correspond to the *cahiers* of 1789.

noble, generous men of the spirit'. It is also true that the Constitution of 1812 went beyond the naïve reformism of liberal priests, lawyers, and local notables who formed the substantial majority of the deputies. When it came to the drafting of the constitution those with clear ideas imposed them: these ideas, disguised by historical arguments, derived from the radicalism of the 1790's and the only principle which underlay 'our Revolution'—the sovereignty of the people. It was outside rather than inside the Cortes that a conservative opposition built up against the liberals and by 1811 the unity of patriotic reformism was broken.

Within the Cortes the strength of the liberals lay in their eloquent leadership—the 'divine' Argüelles; Torrero, the radical priest; Toreno, an Asturian aristocrat and historian of the Revolution—rather than in a party organization. The only bases for such an organization were journalistic cliques and the *tertulia*, evening gatherings of familiar acquaintance.[1] This reliance on the compulsive power of oratory started a rhetorical tradition which in the long run weakened liberalism; rhetoric is unsuitable to the politics of interest and easily becomes the property of extremists. The liberal working majority was based on the votes of the *suplentes* (the substitute deputies for occupied districts and Spanish America, elected under radical pressure at Cadiz). This gave liberalism a southern tinge (many deputies came from Estremadura and Andalusia) and meant that, as 'proprietary' deputies arrived from liberated Spain, so the liberal position weakened. Organized Cadiz radicalism favoured the liberals throughout: from the public galleries the great liberal speeches received what an English observer called the 'loud approbation of the public'.[2] Thus the nature of liberal support, conveniently for conservatives, could be made to rob the work of the Cadiz liberals of any claim to represent the nation: liberalism appeared the vested interest of a ruthless political minority, 'the criminal conspiracy of a handful of *facciosos*'.[3]

The political theory of liberalism was derived from a variety

[1] It is nevertheless clear that the decisive early vote which established the sovereignty of the nation must have been organized beforehand. How, we do not know.

[2] Vaughan MSS., report on Cortes. Solis considers it an exaggeration to talk of 'the pressure of the galleries' (*Cádiz*, 275).

[3] J. Jiménez de Gregorio, *Convocación*, 232. *Facciosos* means factious rebels and was later applied by liberals to Carlists.

of sources: the facts and necessities of the national rising; the commonplaces of the eighteenth-century natural law school and Montesquieu; the historically tinged constitutionalism and the generalized feeling for reform that was characteristic of the Godoy epoch; the more radical brand of constituent reform that found strong press support in 1808; the influence and example of France; the works of Bentham.[1] Thus the central dogma of the constitution—that the sovereign nation could enact the constitution that suited it—could be derived alike from the premisses of the radicals or from the necessity of rebutting Joseph's claim to be legal king of Spain as a result of the abdication of Bayonne: a transfer of the crown by Ferdinand alone was invalid *por falta de consentimiento de la nación*. Jovellanos recognized that such assertions of popular sovereignty 'destroyed our old constitution' by eliminating its monarchical character, yet they were the logical necessities of resistance, practical consequences of the action of a king who, in Torenos's words, had left his nation an orphan.

The strongest ideological current in the Cortes was the historic constitutionalism associated with the works of Martínez Mariana.[2] 'There is nothing in the project of the constitutional committee that cannot be found in the most authentic and solemn fashion in the different codes of Spanish laws.' The deputies were 're-establishing laws which had made our ancestors free men'. Hence debates had an antiquarian tone: little was heard of the rights of man, a great deal about the rights of the crown of Aragon, of the Councils of Toledo and Leon, of the Goths as founders of liberty.[3] Nevertheless, for all their historical theorizing the liberals were concerned with power: they were not restoring a lost medieval constitution but meeting the potential absolutism of a restored monarchy with fundamental laws derived from contractualist political theory. Their historical fictions collapsed in debate. When a

[1] For the interest in constitutional reform see H. Juretschke, *Vida, obra y pensamiento de Alberto Lista* (Madrid, 1951), 53–55. Lista edited a paper in Seville which showed intelligent interest in the theory and practice of representative government. Bentham's influence dated from the translation of his works by Dumont in 1802 but it did not become powerful until 1820 (Bentham's *Works*, ed. J. Bowring (London, 1843), viii. 465–6).

[2] See above, p. 74.

[3] Contractual theories, of course, had respectable antecedents in Suárez and Molina, defenders of the popular *origins* of government. See L. Díez del Corral, *El liberalismo doctrinario* (1945), chap. xxi.

deputy demanded that each medieval law revived should be cited, Calatrava called such conduct worthy of a court of law, not of a constituent assembly. Argüelles was forced to admit that no ancient law could infringe the sovereign rights of the nation: the ancient constitution was kept only because it was supposed to contain the 'first principles of national felicity'.

Respect for medieval precedent was a tactical device, a protective colouring to make the constitution respectable to conservative Spain. 'The spirit and ideas of the liberals were republican although in order not to affront openly the opinions of the masses, they pretended no other aim than a limited monarchy, basing their projects on laws and events in the history of Spain adapted to their purposes.'[1] Their constitution embodied a radical fear of the executive and an extreme division of powers that could have no conceivable medieval precedent.[2] The king kept only those functions which the Cortes could not in practice exercise itself, together with a severely limited suspensive veto. His control over the administration was subjugated, via the responsibility of his secretaries of state, to an automatically elected unicameral assembly. In the intervals between its sessions the king was watched by a Deputation.[3] In the exercise of his remaining prerogatives the king was watched over by a Council of State—a miniature second chamber chosen by the king from a list submitted by the Cortes. In 1820, when the Constitution of 1812 was in force, the king found that he could not change the Captain General of New Castile on his own order. Blanco White, from his London exile, saw the liberals' mistake: their treatment of the king as 'a constitutional wild beast' inevitably condemned the constitution to destruction on the king's return. Like Gustav III of Sweden, he would easily overturn an unreasonable constitution within which no self-respecting monarch could move.[4]

[1] The verdict of Sempere y Guarinos, in his *Histoire des Cortes* (Bordeaux, 1815), 334. He was an *afrancesado*; the *afrancesados* delighted in exposing the sophisms of the liberals in order to work their passage to favour after 1814.

[2] The debt of the constitution of 1812 to the French revolutionary constitutions is much debated but seems, in general terms, sufficiently obvious.

[3] Nevertheless it must be noted that the Cortes assembled for only three or four months during the year. Bentham later considered this the weakest feature of the constitution.

[4] *El Español* (London, 1809), v. 76.

The transcendent importance of this constitution in the subsequent history of Spanish constitutionalism conceals that liberalism was more than a political creed. The men of 1812 meant to create the legal framework of a bourgeois society; they had given political power, by an intricate combination of universal suffrage and indirect election, to the middle classes considered as the 'regulator' of other classes. The details of the liberal programme (attack on regional, ecclesiastical, and aristocratic privilege, guilds, and the *Mesta*) were inherited from regalists and political economists, from the servants of Charles III who had attacked the privileged in the interests of a modernized monarchy unencumbered with private jurisdictions. Now the programme was justified in different terms: civil equality, personal liberty, the rights of property, and freedom of contract. 'Liberty, Equality and property are natural rights, God-given natural rights which men protect when they enter society.'[1] In the name of these principles the Cortes produced on paper (for neither the constitution nor its legislative consequences were ever effective) a Spain that would have delighted the monarchical bureaucrats: a clumsy taxational system, with endless provincial divergencies, was to be replaced by a uniform income tax; the machinery of the *ancien régime* with its characteristic confusion of administrative and judicial function was dismantled. The 'bizarre' quasi-federal structure of local government vanished, to be replaced by a system of uniform municipalities and provinces under a *jefe político*, ancestor of the all-powerful Civil Governor.

Though later liberals were to divide on the issues of the election or selection of local government officials (with radicals in favour of popular election and conservatives for appointment of mayors and councils by the ministry), *all* liberals, in spite of lip-service to the ideal of the medieval municipality, accepted two propositions: that the Cortes, as 'sole representative of the sovereign nation', *must* enforce a uniform and centralized system and that, within this system, the municipalities were 'subaltern corporations'.[2] This conception of the relationship

[1] Canga Argüelles: quoted M. Artola, *B.A.E.* xcviii, Introduction, p. xxxvi. The officer corps was formally opened to non-nobles—an illustration of the convergence of war-time necessity and the principle of equality before the law, characteristic of the work of the constituent Cortes.

[2] For the notion of the medieval municipality see A. Posada, *Evolución legislativa*

between local and central government, derived from the French model, stamped the whole subsequent history of Spain. The destruction of the historic provinces and their replacement by 'artificial' entities—the new provinces—was at the root of the regionalist and nationalist movements of Catalonia and the Basque Provinces; these looked to a revival of medieval institutions, finally destroyed by the legislators of liberalism, as the safeguard of local interests and true liberty alike.[1] The control over local affairs that the new system entrusted to the agent of the central government was held responsible both for the electoral mechanics which distorted parliamentary liberalism and for the decay of local citizenship.[2] Thus when, in the early years of the twentieth century, conservative statesmen wished both to satisfy regionalist demands and make the parliamentary system work as a vehicle for the 'real' demands of the electorate, it was the system of local government, first set up in Cadiz, that they attempted to reform. But after a century this 'artificial' system had created a political life and interests of its own which were strong enough to resist its replacement.

It is in their attitude to agrarian reform that the premisses of liberalism emerge most clearly. The liberals of Cadiz were not primarily concerned with a socially desirable redistribution of landed property but rather with the establishment of clear and absolute property rights—the Roman Law notion of *jus utendi et abutendi* as against the medieval confusions of multiple claims to enjoy the use of the same piece of property. The untramelled right of the individual to dispose of his own property as he saw fit was the essential foundation of a liberal economy and a bourgeois society. Hence the establishment of the right to enclose land, to sell or rent it, subject only to the 'will of the contracting parties': the right to enclose was a blow at the

del régimen local (1910), 19 ff. Toreno, for instance, recognized the 'natural' value of the pueblo but his doctrine of the sovereignty of the nation forbade the granting of any 'independent' powers to the municipality. 'The municipalities are only agents of the executive power for the economic government of the pueblo', i.e. for education, sanitation, food supply, and the distribution of taxation (*D.S.C.* iv. 2590). The functions of local government are set out in the Royal Decree of 23 June 1813.

[1] Catalonia was split into four new Provinces: Lérida, Barcelona, Gerona, and Tarragona.

[2] Some deputies recognized the dangers to political independence and freedom in the powers granted to the *jefe político* (A. Posada, op. cit. 29).

pasturing rights of the *Mesta* which patently infringed the individual's right to dispose of his property. The individual was superior to the corporation.

There can be little doubt that radicals would have liked to have gone beyond the sale of monastic land to a wider offensive against ecclesiastical property. This would have solved the problem of the national debt (the influence of French precedent is revealed by their translation of *biens nationaux* as *bienes nacionales.*)[1] Moreover, they were the heirs of the regalists' campaign against mortmain and the political economists' attacks on the entailed *mayorazgos*. Political prudence and the dangers of a frontal attack on the Church restrained them to the sale of common lands and the abolition of civil entails, 'pulling up by the roots the tree which bears such bitter fruits'.

Most controversial was the abolition of seignorial jurisdictions (*señorios*): this was not a measure to relieve an oppressed peasantry but to establish property rights on an acceptable contractual basis and to abolish enclaves of private jurisdiction in constitutional Spain. Typically enough, the liberals claimed to be re-establishing the early medieval *fuero juzgo*—a claim which caused endless legal confusion—when in fact they were crowning the work of the eighteenth-century civil servants with the economic individualism of the French Revolution.

It has been argued that the liberals' respect for property precluded any satisfaction of land-hungry labourers (some of whom had seized land in the troubles, a process of which we know nothing), and that the abolition of the guilds—again the programme of the eighteenth-century economists—worsened the condition of the small artisan. It is true that liberalism could not back a jacquerie and that it preferred to paternalism the teaching of political economy in schools. Yet the liberals of 1812 were involved in the myth of the people who had risen while the aristocracy had remained inert and they were not unaware of the advantages of creating a class of small peasants devoted to the

[1] Artola maintains (*Orígenes*, i. 506–36) that the purchasers of national debt *vales* of the nineties, now depreciated, constituted an interest group pressing for the recognition of the debt and its security by the sale of church lands, while the conservatives were prepared for the old refuge of absolutism-bankruptcy. Clearly the problem of the national debt affected the problem of land sales and lay at the root of Mendizábal's alienation of church property to debt-holders in the 1830's (see below, pp. 172–3).

liberal revolution—again an implication of their interest in the French Revolution. Hence half of the common lands was to go to war veterans and the propertyless. The conflict between the economic necessity of a free market in land, which must benefit the rich buyer, and the desirability of peasant support was to confuse the liberal tradition until the days of the Second Republic.

The contradictions of liberalism—particularly those involved in the conflict between local liberties and a uniform liberal constitution—were nowhere more disastrous and more evident than in America. It was these contradictions which, in the crisis of 1808–14, combined with inherited grievance to damage the structure of the Spanish Empire beyond repair.

Already, after the American War of Independence, Aranda had argued that to retain any sort of hold in America, Spain must abandon the old theory of Empire and set up local independent Bourbon thrones or even slough off Peru.[1] Nevertheless it is difficult to judge how far a movement for independence in Latin America, inspired by North American example and the ideology of the French Revolution, had advanced beyond the traditional colonial grievances. Republican conspirators had found little support; Picornell, whom we have met as a republican conspirator in Spain, failed to engineer a rebellion, while Miranda's expedition of 1806 was a fiasco. It was the wars of the French Revolution and Napoleon which first drove the colonials to independent action; war exposed the impotence of Spain as an imperial power and revealed her incapacity to supply her colonies with merchandise. With Great Britain, the greatest maritime and trading power, as an enemy the disadvantages of the Spanish connexion and the advantages of independence became clear.[2] In spite of these inconveniences, and their exploitation by British policy, it was the collapse of Spanish authority rather than a creole revolution which began the processes by which the Empire was

[1] For these schemes see R. Konetzke, *Die Politik des Grafen Aranda* (Berlin, 1929). The authenticity of Aranda's memorial of 1783 is discussed in A. R. Wright, 'The Aranda Memorial: Genuine or Forged?' *H.A.H.R.* xviii (1938), 445–60, and in 'The pseudo-Aranda Memoir', ibid. xvii (1937), 287–313.

[2] Cf. the violent fluctuations in the trade of Vera Cruz as a result of European wars (R. S. Smith, 'Shipping in the Port of Vera Cruz', *H.A.H.R.* xxiii (1943), 5–20). As a result of the war of 1796 and the British blockade exports from Buenos Aires fell from 5,470,000 to 350,000 pesos (R. Levene, *A History of Argentina*, trans. W. S. Robertson (Chapel Hill, 1937), 134).

destroyed. In 1806, when British troops captured Buenos Aires, the Spanish authorities retired. It was the creoles themselves who raised a citizen army to defend Spanish sovereignty. By twice defeating the British invaders the creoles discovered their own strength. They also discovered the benefits of free trade; pushing aside the objections of peninsular officials and Spanish merchants, they traded with British merchants who flocked to the River Plate. 'The economic emancipation of Buenos Aires was determined before its political independence began.'[1]

The defeats of the Spanish armies in the Peninsula, the abdication of Ferdinand VII, and the final disgrace of the Central Junta left the Spaniards in America rootless and confused. It was not that the Americans rose against Spain; it was that Spain fell away from America. In the imperial crisis of 1809–14 the local bodies which sprang up, as the Juntas had sprung up in Spain, professed to be preserving the authority of Ferdinand VII against agents of Joseph seeking to capture American allegiance for the French kingship. Nevertheless, local action often entailed the deposition of the existing authorities and their replacement by local notables. Within the framework of a 'loyalist' revolt emerged the idea of 'the liberty of the nation'.[2] On the news of the occupation of Andalusia by the French armies Buenos Aires set up a Junta which deposed the Viceroy in order to 'preserve' the Viceroyalty for Ferdinand VII. Yet this action (25 May 1810), by creating a creole government, is rightly celebrated as the birthday of an independent Argentine Republic, although formal independence was not to be declared until 1816. In what was ultimately to become Venezuela the revolutionary implications of the movement were decisive; a Junta in Caracas swept aside the existing administration and, in the

[1] R. A. Humphreys, *Liberation in South America* (London, 1952), 4 ff. For British trade see J. B. Goebel, 'British Trade in the Spanish Colonies 1796–1823' (*H.A.H.R.* xlviii (1930), 298 ff., esp. 309–11). For the British expedition to Buenos Aires see H. S. Ferns, *Britain and Argentina*, 18–51.

[2] As in Spain, the fact that many of the existing civil servants were creatures of Godoy complicated the situation. The confusions inherent in 'loyalty' are apparent in the American proclamations of 1809–10. Thus in the creole revolt in Quito (the capital of modern Ecuador) the Junta in 1809 claimed that 'Spanish America ought not to follow the fate of Spain but conserve the independence of New Granada so that Ferdinand VII might come to rule it' (R. L. Gilmore, 'The imperial crisis in New Granada', *H.A.H.R.* xl (1960), 2 ff.). In Mexico Hidalgo revolt used similarly ambiguous language. He claimed to be fighting both for Ferdinand VII and 'the liberty of the nation'.

name of preserving America for Ferdinand VII, disowned the authority of the Cadiz Regency, that is of the legal government of Spain. The implications of this action became clear; the Junta declared the ports open to trade from every nation to which the Regency replied by a blockade; in 1811 a Congress declared itself independent and decreed a republican constitution.

Spanish governments between 1809 and 1814 had neither the force to suppress the revolt nor could liberal political thought embrace the notion of colonial autonomy. Liberal premisses produced divergent theories of empire on different sides of the Atlantic. Latin Americans quoted the verse of the Spanish patriots of 1808 in defence of the *patria* against the despotism of the foreigner: but for them the *patria* was 'all the great extent of both Americas' and the oppressor Spain.[1] The solution of the Cadiz liberals for the colonial desire for self-government was the concession of full political rights to American citizens *within* a unified empire; the colonies were an integral part of metropolitan Spain and would be 'freed', with the same constitution that gave Spain herself freedom. The first step therefore was to grant representation to the colonies—though the word was avoided—in the Cortes. This was merely to recast the Hapsburg theory of Empire in liberal terms. 'From this moment, Spanish Americans, you see yourselves free men. . . . Your destiny no longer depends on minister, viceroys or governors; they are in your own hands.' America, like Spain itself, had been ruined by three centuries of theological intolerance and political despotism; if a unitary liberal constitution was the remedy in Spain, it must also be the remedy in America.

Once the boon of common liberal institutions had been granted by a generous metropolis, a refusal to accept the rule of Spain was conceived as 'indecent' ingratitude, as a separatist rebellion.[2] The liberals did little to win colonial opinion; they

[1] Quoted from a Lima newspaper of 1812 in J. Basadre, *La iniciación de la República* (Lima, 1929), i. 11. Quintana's patriotic odes against the French could be used against the Spanish *patria* by the sons of Padilla in Peru where a Spanish review of Martínez de la Rosa's play on Padilla was republished in March 1814. L. Monguío, 'Nacionalismo y protesta social en la literatura española', *Cuadernos* (Paris, 1962), lviii. 42.

[2] Toreno's view. Argüelles (in his *Examen histórico de la reforma que hicieron las Cortes*, London, 1835) likewise argued that *both* Spain and America had been oppressed and that in America, after the decree of 15 Oct. 1810 (extending the right of representation to America), there was no legitimate ground for revolt.

restricted the number of American deputies in the new constitution lest American opinion should 'swamp' the Cortes; they neglected the protests that the 'American' deputies already in Cadiz had no claims to represent American opinion; they refused any substantial concession of freer trade. They resented British pressure for a mediated settlement as the outcome of selfish mercantile designs on the American market.[1] Their insistence on the integrity of the Spanish monarchy and their rooted hostility to any form of autonomy thus allowed those creoles who wished to sever the Spanish connexion to present rebellion as the only course.

This rebellion had two main *foci*: the Viceroyalties of the Rio de la Plata and of New Granada, where resistance was to be symbolized by Bolívar, the greatest of the liberators of Latin America. Independence was the achievement of a heroic minority working with a myth—the 'slavery' of the South American populations to Spanish despotism.[2] The mass of the population (especially the *mestizos* and the coloured and Indian populations who were truly 'slaves') were either indifferent or actively hostile to the political ambitions of the white creoles of the towns and the large estates, who represented a more immediate oppression than that of the Spanish crown.[3] Thus by 1814 Bolívar was driven out of Venezuela by a savage backlands revolt, accidentally royalist, led by Boves, a smuggler and sergeant of the Spanish marines, who established a brutal domination over the mounted herdsmen of the plains. Boves's *mestizos* aimed to exterminate the creoles and to destroy their property.[4]

By 1814, with the war in the Peninsula ended and the

[1] Wellesley reported in July 1812, 'No disposition exists here (at Cadiz) to make any commercial concessions, even for the important object of tranquillizing America' (*Correspondence, Despatches and other Papers of Viscount Castlereagh* (London, 1851), viii. 269).

[2] Cf. Bolívar's proclamation to his army before his forces invaded Peru. 'You are about to complete the greatest undertaking that Heaven has granted to men—that of saving an entire world from slavery', *Proclamas y discursos del Liberator* (ed. V. Lecuna, Caracas 1959), 288–9.

[3] Revolutionaries in Buenos Aires justified terrorism as a measure against 'that sort of neutrality which until then was observed by the bulk of the people' (J. Miller, *Memoirs of General Miller* (London, 1828), 67).

[4] Cf. J. R. Poinsett's remarks about the Mexican royalist troops, *Notes on Mexico* (London 1825), 239, and C. G. Griffin, 'Economic and social aspects of the era of Spanish American independence' in *H.A.H.R.* xxix (1949), 170 ff.

arrival of 10,000 Spanish troops under General Morillo, the prospects for independence were gloomy; Bolívar had been driven out of Venezuela and New Granada was about to be recaptured. Only in the homogeneous white population of the United Provinces of the River Plate did independence seem secure. Ferdinand VII could believe that, as in Spain itself, the years 1808–14 could be treated as if they had not existed and the ancient order could be restored.

3. *The War of Independence and its Legacies, 1808–1814*

If, in perspective, the loss of the American Empire was the greatest single consequence of the crisis of 1808, the legacy of the War of Independence moulded the subsequent history of Spain itself. It gave liberalism its programme and its technique of revolution. It defined Spanish patriotism, endowing it with an enduring myth. It saddled liberalism with the problem of generals in politics and the mystique of the guerilla. Most awkward and indigestible of all it left the problem of the *afrancesados*. Twelve thousand Spanish families who had served the French kingship followed Joseph across the Pyrenees after the battle of Vitoria. For a generation these exiles, who included the ablest men in Spain, were to be distrusted by both liberals and reactionaries.

Modern Spanish nationalism of a type comparable to nascent nationalism in other European countries was created by the fact of resistance to Napoleon. It gave to the administrative unity of Bourbon Spain, 'the supreme creation of the eighteenth century', an emotional content. For a generation of European Romantics it created the image of a nation *sui generis*, a natural force uncontaminated by Europe, an image consecrated by the greatest writer of nineteenth-century Spain, the novelist Galdós. A myth of enormous potency, available to radicals and traditionalists alike, grew out of Spain's unique and proud resistance. Nevertheless, given the strength of local ties, the patriotism that was to mark the great crises remained an abstract emotion, imperfectly felt at the most intimate levels. The patriotism evoked in the *Episodios nacionales* of Galdós's is less deeply felt than that of Hardy's *Dynasts*. For this reason defeat was psychologically disastrous. Exalted patriotism attached itself to victory over the United States in 1898, to conquest in Morocco, even to the success of Peral's submarine. When campaigns ended in disaster and the submarine sank disillusionment and self-criticism set in. Thus the War of Independence remained, if we except O'Donnell's African conquests (1860), the only satisfactory exhibition of nationalism on a large scale.

How far do the realities of Spain's war effort correspond with the patriotic myth of a nation rising and driving out its oppressors? The Spanish victory of Bailén (July 1808) was the inevitable consequence of Napoleon's belief that the conquest of Spain was a police operation that could be entrusted to inferior troops. Dupont was assigned the task of conquering Andalusia with a corps composed mainly of conscripts straight from the depots: half-starved by the rupture of its supply lines, this nondescript force was utterly defeated by the numerically superior levies of the Seville Junta under Castaños, and by what Napoleon termed Dupont's 'horrible generalship'. Madrid was evacuated, the Spaniards believed they had defeated 'the victors of Austerlitz' and victory engendered a mania for pitched battles. They brought, not another Bailén, but defeat after defeat, justifying Napoleon's judgement that the Spanish regular army was the worst in Europe.[1] Wellington's judgement was fixed by the generalship of Cuesta and the flight of the Spanish troops at the battle of Talavera.[2] 'I have never known the Spaniards *do anything*, much less do anything well.' As commander-in-chief—he would not co-operate with Spanish generals on any other terms—Wellington was loth to regard native troops as an instrument that could be used with safety in battle. Nor were such views confined to prejudiced and exasperated Englishmen: performances like Medellín

[1] The only considerable Spanish victory after Bailén was del Parque's defeat of Marchant at Tamames (October 1809). Ocaña was a rout precipitated by Areizaga's astonishing combination of vacillation and timidity; Oman considers Cuesta's determination to fight at Medellín the act of a criminal lunatic (*Peninsular War*, ii. 160).

[2] Wellington *later* believed he had been baulked of a Spanish Waterloo at Talavera by Cuesta's 'madness'. The Spaniards, in turn, bitterly criticized Wellington for his 'desertion' by retreating to Portugal after the battle. Anglo-Spanish relations never recovered from this controversy. Cf. his remarks to his brother: 'I shudder when I reflect upon the enormity of the task I have undertaken . . . without assistance of any kind from the Spaniards' (*Despatches*, ix. 374; *Supplementary Despatches*, vii. 482–3).

(March 1809), Ocaña (September 1809), astonished the French.

Exalted patriotism was generated by the battle of Bailén, by the sieges of Saragossa and Gerona. If Bailén was a fluke, the siege of Saragossa astonished a Europe accustomed to the conventional sieges of the Italian and German campaigns. For two and a half months Saragossa, a poorly fortified town, resisted a good siege train, and when the walls were gone the inhabitants fought in the streets. It was a unique war with a unique morality. Spanish regular officers shamelessly violated the capitulation of Bailén, leaving 10,000 troops to starve on a barren island because they felt under no obligation to obey the rules of war with a 'captain of bandits'. Atrocity stories—the shootings on the night of 2 May, Dupont's sack of Cordoba, the pillage of soldiers in a country where the Napoleonic system of living on the country broke down—fed xenophobic hatred of the French as vandals and heretics. 'They have behaved worse than a horde of Hottentots. They have profaned our temples, insulted our religion and raped our women.'[1] Enthusiasm was fed by falsehoods and exaggeration. 'This race despises foreigners, a contempt explained by the exaggerated opinion it holds of itself. *Miles Gloriosus* is the Spaniard.' Exaltation was subject to evaporation in the squabbles of defeat, and Moore noted with bitterness that 'the enthusiasm of which we heard so much nowhere appears'. After feeding themselves with rumours of Napoleon's defeat, Andalusia and Valencia made no attempt to resist the French. Andalusia's welcome to Joseph in 1810 appeared ecstatic to his courtiers: priests, nobles, and peasants came to greet him in every town. If ever Joseph felt King of Spain it must have been on his triumphal progress in Andalusia.[2]

Wellington's graceless contempt for the Spanish war effort is as unjustifiable as the Spanish claim that the English did little but pillage. The contribution of Spain to her own deliverance was sheer continuity of resistance. No Austerlitz was possible against the amorphous political and military federalism of the Juntas; no king *in situ* could negotiate his kingdom away; the politicians of Cadiz, whatever their failings, never contemplated

[1] Proclamation of the Valencian Junta, 7 June 1809.

[2] For the atmosphere in Andalusia before the French conquest, cf. W. Jacob, *Travels*, 294.

a deal with the usurper. Ill-equipped and deplorably led armies behaved shamingly in action; but resistance continued. 'In any other country', wrote Jourdan after Cuesta had destroyed his army by advancing on a four-mile front, four men deep with no reserves, 'two such successes as Medellín and Ciudad Real would have reduced the countryside to submission.'[1]

It was this continuous resistance, feeble though it often was, which broke Napoleon's doctrine of maximum concentration in the attempt to solve the contradictory demands of operation and occupation in a hostile countryside. 'If I concentrate 20,000 men,' wrote Bessières, worn out in the north by 1811, 'all my communications are lost and the insurgents make great progress. We occupy too much territory.' Jourdan saw the military problem as insoluble without a partial evacuation, an admission of failure that neither Napoleon nor the great military feudatories would accept. Spain would have been cowed without Wellington's field force: Wellington could not have operated with a small army without the diversionary effects of Spanish resistance. It was Spaniards who proved Wellington's own maxim: 'the more ground the French hold, the weaker they will be at any point'.

Since the failures of the regular army were patent, the guerrilla tradition became central to Spanish patriotism. There were, perhaps, 30,000 *guerilleros* ranging from small bands to Mina's organized group of 8,000 men who were scarcely distinguishable from regular troops. It is not in the nature of partisan warfare to produce victory in the field: loth to leave their territories or to receive orders from soldiers, guerrillas were difficult to use in strategical combination. Smaller bands could not hope to act in planned campaigns.[2] Their function was to reoccupy areas evacuated by the French and impose a patriot terror, bullying the population into resistance. They attacked only where they could do so with overwhelmingly superior numbers; in danger they disbanded. El Empecinado's boast that he had never lost a man in action represented sound

[1] J.-B. Jourdan, *Mémoires militaires*, ed. Grouchy (Paris, 1899), 187–8: cf. the comments of J. Gómez de Arteche, *Guerra de la Independencia* (1868–1903), v. 420 ff.

[2] The better organized guerrillas were so used; thus Caffarelli was pinned in the north for the 1812 campaign by Brooke-Popham's joint operations with Porlier and Longa's 'bandits'; this relieved pressure on Wellington and helped him to win the battle of Salamanca (June 1812).

partisan thinking. French commanders were committed to wearying hunting operations, with bad maps and no help from the peasantry; guerrilla screens thickened the fog of war; important dispatches fell into the hands of Wellington's intelligence officers. Above all territory must be effectively occupied or it would fall to the partisans; this kept French troops from the battlefield.

Guerrilla warfare shared many of the characteristics of resistance movements in the Second World War. It was a rural phenomenon, like Carlism an aspect of peasant hatred for urban civilization. This was inevitable: partisan warfare is confined to rough country and the French governed the great towns with little difficulty. It had undertones of social war. 'C'est, à proprement parler, la guerre des pauvres contre les riches.'[1] It frequently approximated to brigandage when large areas were laid under irregular taxation. The ethics of partisan warfare, the cult of the individual leader, patriotic contempt for the law of the foreigner and his collaborators, introduced a new element of instability into society. Guerrilla warfare 'accustomed the Spaniard to live outside the law, to reject the norms of social life and take as his great achievement the maintenance of his own personality'.[2] It romanticized revolution and regularized insubordination, sanctifying that preference for violent individual action that was to bedevil the politics of nineteenth-century Spain. When his political convictions were outraged the Spaniard could 'put on his *alpargatas* [the canvas shoes of the guerrillas] and take up his rifle'. Both the Carlist right and the extremist left could later appeal to this primitive rebellion.

The most lasting legacy of the war was the claim of the army officers to rule the state. In the War of Independence the Central Junta and the Provincial Juntas represented the civilian state; very soon the generals were on bad terms with both and intriguing to replace them. General Cuesta, an old-fashioned soldier and military administrator, hated the revolutionary claims of the Provincial Juntas. He actually arrested two members of a Junta. Commanders resented the Central Junta's

[1] Caffarelli to Berthier, 31 Oct. 1811. Of course it was in French interest to discredit the resistance.

[2] F. Solano Costa, 'Influencia de la Guerra de Independencia' in *J. Zurita, Cuadernos de Historia*, III, 116–17. Cf. the same author's *El guerrillero y su transcendencia* (Saragossa, 1959).

emulation of French revolutionary assemblies with missions of representatives to the Ebro front (August 1808), its interference with promotions, and, in 1809, its readiness to blame defeats on generals who considered themselves ill-supplied by civilian authorities.[1]

This military opposition found its leaders in General Romana and in the staff of Palafox's Army of Aragon.[2] Palafox and Romana are thus the first of a long succession of generals who claimed that the army officers embodied the general will of the nation, perverted by a selfish clique of unpopular politicians. In 1809 these were the harassed members of the Juntas. 'The greater part of the nation detested the [Central] Junta's proceedings, loved its king, desiring his return and the end of the Junta, in such a fashion that the necessity of a counter revolution was already considered.'[3] The malcontent generals saw their role as leaders of this counter revolution which would save the nation and end the war.

Romana believed the Junta of the Asturias to be 'republican' in sympathy, and accused it of starving him of supplies. He became the instrument of the resentment of the shocked conservatism of the *Audiencia* and chapter of Oviedo; in May 1809 he sent fifty grenadiers to dissolve the Junta.[4] This provincial *brumaire* was bitterly criticized by civilians of the Central Junta: Jovellanos could neither forgive nor forget Romana's 'tyranny'. The quarrel spread to Seville and Cadiz, where the friends of Romana and Palafox were the bitterest opponents of the Central Junta's claims and were intriguing for an amenable Regency or a military government based on popular feeling whipped up against the Junta. 'All eyes are fixed on him [Romana] in the hope that he will overturn the present system.' Throughout the war talk of a military take-over from inept civilians never ceased.[5]

It was to resist this wave of caesarism that Jovellanos pressed

[1] For the effect of these feuds on military operations see C. Oman, *Peninsular War*, i. 355 ff.

[2] For a description of the atmosphere among the officers of the army of Aragon see Marqués de Ayerbe, *Memorias*, esp. 258–66.

[3] Ayerbe, op. cit. 264–5.

[4] For Romana's *coup* see A. Fugier, *Asturies*, 12 ff. and 65 ff.

[5] Cf. Vaughan MSS., Correspondence 1811, for talk of O'Donnell putting 'an end both to the government and the Cortes'.

for the summoning of a general Cortes which would represent the nation against the generals. Though the generals were brought to some sort of obedience by the Cortes and the Regency, in the provinces they used the 'egoism' of the Juntas and their endless disputes with the relics of the old administration in order to extend their own power.[1] 'Can one deny', wrote the old Marqués de Santa Cruz, an Asturian conservative patriot, 'that Spain is governed by soldiers? How can you say she is defending her laws when none are respected? How can I avoid seeing that it is this kind of government that threatens my grandchildren?'[2] What he could not foresee was that generals would renew their political role after 1814, not as representatives of the old order, but as liberal paladins. Already in Catalonia, Campoverde, a self-appointed general, had staged a popular *pronunciamiento* in support of the claims of an elected congress against the 'egoism of the rich' represented by the Provincial Junta.

The *afrancesados* were the collaborators of the War of Independence—the timid, the misguided, the conformists by nature who took the French side against the patriots. Before the patriot victory at Bailén, collaboration with the intruder represented the legal hesitations of the constituted authorities, left without instructions by the king and caught between the overwhelming superiority of French garrisons on the one side and the Federal anarchy of the patriot revolution on the other. After Bailén, what divided collaborators from resisters was 'opinion as to the result of the war'. Before the Russian campaign, an event no one could reasonably foresee, those who were to be *afrancesados* held it 'morally impossible' that the French would be defeated. Resistance was not a matter of patriotic feeling but of calculation, of patriotic responsibility. No one had a duty to plunge his country into a hopeless struggle which would, moreover, involve a dangerous appeal to the people against the only legal government that existed. Joseph's *afrancesado* minister, Azanza, held that to encourage resistance was to ensure 'the dissolution of society' by encouraging anarchy feared by all conservatives

[1] This was especially the case in Catalonia where the quarrel between the *Audiencia* and the Junta opened the way for an extension of military justice (G. Desdevizes du Dezert, *La Junte Supérieure de Catalogne*. *Rev. H.* xxii (1910), 119).

[2] A. Fugier, *La Junte Supérieure des Asturies* (Paris, 1930), 77.

in 1808.[1] 'Your Majesty', wrote Llorente, the historian of the Inquisition and a prominent *afrancesado*, 'recognized Joseph as the legal sovereign. . . . I have always been and am a royalist. I believed I was being useful to my country and conserving the monarchical system against republicanism.'

The core of the *afrancesado* position was that collaboration, not resistance, was the best way to protect national independence: allegiance to Joseph at least saved Spain from direct military rule from Paris and the division of the kingdom by right of conquest. The premiss of *afrancesado* policy was, therefore, the cessation of the patriot rebellion which made French military intervention a necessity: they consistently clung to the idea of a negotiated settlement as a way out of their difficulties.[2] Since negotiations failed and the rebellion, once supported by England, could only be defeated by increasing injections of Napoleon's soldiers and money, the ideal of an independent civil government appealing to hearts, in Joseph's phrase, was rejected by the emperor and his generals who knew no law but military necessity.[3] Joseph and his Spanish supporters tried to break the fiefs of the occupying generals by sending out civil commissioners, who soon found that, if they were to get anything done at all, it could only be done as subordinates of the generals on the spot. An impoverished Spanish government, appealing for funds to France, was in no condition to defend Spanish independence. Against the decree of February 1810, which put the Ebro provinces under direct military rule, the *afrancesados* and their king protested violently but in vain: the *raison d'être* of Joseph's monarchy had vanished and the *afrancesado* policy was bankrupt.

Many of the prominent *afrancesados* were cultured bureaucrats who saw in the Napoleonic system a hope of ordered re-

[1] By far the best presentation of the *afrancesado* case is contained in Azanza and O'Farrill's 'Memoria justificativa', *B.A.E.* xcvii. 277–343. Cf. Azanza's appeal to Jovellanos (8 June 1808) which summarizes the whole *afrancesado* dilemma. 'I appeal to you to save our country (*patria*) from the horrors which threaten it if you support the mad idea of resisting the orders of the Emperor of the French which, in my opinion, are directed to the welfare of Spain' (*B.A.E.* lxxxvi. 336).

[2] For La Forest's views on negotiations see G. de Grandmaison, *Napoléon et l'Espagne* (Paris, 1908), ii. 177, 254, 409; iii. 63.

[3] Cf. Savary's strictures on the policy of gaining hearts. 'La Forest veut gagner les cœurs; non, je reponds que je n'en voudrais pas de mille pour le prix de la ration d'un soldat' (quoted G. Desdevizes du Dezert, *Conseil de Castille*, 206).

generation by modern laws and administrative practices. It was this group which brought Murat round to the idea of a new constitution and who co-operated with Napoleon in that masterpiece of enlightened despotism, the Constitution of Bayonne.[1] War allowed little time for reform; the regenerating Constitution of Bayonne was never applied to Spain; ambitious schemes for a new system of education, for a modern code based on the *Code Napoléon* came to nothing. To Napoleon, the reduction of the monasteries and the abolition of the Inquisition were not part of a plan to reform and regenerate Spain but improvised responses to financial necessity and to the French *idée fixe* that rebellion was the work of monks. Yet there can be little doubt that Joseph's reformism was genuine and was combined with an attempt to appeal to the national past; he encouraged the national theatre, set up a commission to exhume Cervantes' remains, patronized a national museum of painting. His street planning was symbolic of his reign; he had no money to build where he had destroyed. Taxation was crippling on the small area of his effective kingdom. The population of Madrid starved on bread substitutes. When Wellington entered Madrid, he was greeted with cries of 'Viva the peseta loaf'.

Laziness, a desire to hold on to salaries and to stay with families, accounts for much *afrancesado* collaboration. As in the Civil War of 1936 loyalty was often geographical: those caught in French areas became *afrancesados*.[2] In Andalusia little was to be gained by resistance at a time when French power looked invincibly stable: the intellectuals of Seville went over *en bloc* and acceptance of the inevitable became active collaboration in those groups where hatred of Godoy's 'tyranny' had been combined with a qualified admiration for the French Revolution and enthusiastic regalism. Thus the poet Lista, a reformist

[1] P. Conard maintains (*La Constitution de Bayonne*, Lyon, 1909) that Napoleon's idea of saving Spain from 'hideous laws' came late and was a reaction to Murat's letter of 16 May 1808, written *after* consultations with O'Farrill and other Spaniards (op. cit. 21).

[2] Cf. the interesting cases of Jovellanos and Meléndez Valdés. There was not much distinction between the two friends on the eve of Joseph's second entry into Madrid—Meléndez Valdés had written two patriotic odes against the French. Whereas Jovellanos got away, Meléndez Valdés's arrangements for flight broke down; he remained in Madrid and wrote enthusiastic odes to Joseph.

priest, became a freemason and a journalist in Marshal Soult's pay.[1]

In Barcelona active resistance ended with the plot of May 1809: when the French Government looked stable, theatres opened, social life picked up, and some of the *émigrés* returned. Each stage of the occupation had its specific brand of collaborator. When the uneasy initial co-operation of the authorities was broken by the oath to Joseph (April 1809) Duhesme's corrupt military government was served by Casanova:[2] a profiteer in identity cards, ransoms, and municipal marketing, an adventurer with a mistress and a mansion, he became one of the richest, as well as the most powerful man, in occupied Barcelona.[3] Less offensive were those who could not face dismissal: 'He who won't swear the oath will lose his job.' Augereau (January–May 1810), advised by sincere *afrancesados*, tried to clear out these time-servers and appeal to enlightened Catalan opinion in order to convince local patriots of the positive advantages of French rule and a modern system of government.[4] This 'moral conquest' could not take root, if only because modern government meant efficient taxation. The new municipal councils worked only where troops were stationed and with military defeat the system collapsed.

Yet despite taxation, starvation, and the paramount claims of the French army in Joseph's kingdom and in the independent feudatories of the generals, a rational, modern administration replaced the confusions of the *ancien régime*. In Aragon and Valencia, General Suchet overhauled the finances, reformed the municipalities, and dissolved the monasteries. Spanish officials were trained by French experts.[5] Some of Joseph's creations—the all-powerful Ministry of the Interior, working through the

[1] Like Llorente, he used his opportunities to examine the papers of the dissolved Inquisition. H. Juretschke, *Lista*, 61–71.

[2] See above, pp. 86–87, for the early reactions of the authorities in Barcelona.

[3] P. Conard, *La Catalogne*, 314 ff. Casanova overstepped the mark by murdering one of his victims and was dismissed; similar to Casanova was Ollivier who 'controlled' the property of emigrants.

[4] Augereau used the Catalan language in official documents (see J. Mercader Riba, *Barcelona durante la occupación francesa* (1949), Appendix xxi). He clearly misunderstood Napoleon's annexationist policy which demanded a government dependent on Paris.

[5] J. Mercader Riba, 'El Mariscal Suchet', in *J. Zurita, Cuadernos de Historia*, ii (1951), 127–42.

prefect—fascinated a generation of bureaucrats: Javier de Burgos, who served Joseph as a sub-prefect, was to make his French experience the basis for the administrative reconstruction of Spain.

It was the enlightened *afrancesados* who were to confuse political issues by their peculiar relation to liberalism. Conservatives maintained that the 'foreign' nature of liberalism was proven by the identity of the laws of the Cortes of Cadiz and the decrees of Josephine Spain. The 'nerve' of the national defence was constituted by the 'popular masses' and the clergy who hated both *afrancesados* and liberals. Thus patriot liberalism and the treason of the *afrancesados* were involved in a common anathema.[1] This conjunction misses an essential distinction. The liberals were democrats, while the *afrancesados* believed in reform from above. Liberalism meant the sovereignty of the nation, not merely a Spain divided into 'rational' provinces and rid of the Inquisition and monks.

4. *The Conservative Opposition and the Return of Ferdinand VII, 1813–1814*

The liberals of Cadiz were well aware of the perils of attacking the position of the Church in an assembly where the largest single group was the clergy; they saw their majorities on church questions sink alarmingly. Whatever their private opinions, the liberals were willing to establish catholicism as the sole religion of Spain, to make heresy a crime, to allow episcopal censorship of religious works; as Larra was to observe, it was a one-legged freedom that permitted only 'political' discussion and it shows the limitations imposed on liberalism by fear of the Church.[2] It was therefore the extreme claims of the clerical right that forced the issue: these claims were incompatible with the minimum demands of the liberal state even when these represented,

[1] For this view see M. Méndez Bejerano in his 'Historia política de los afrancesados' (*Revista de Archivos Bibliotecas y Museos* (1911), xxiv. 339–49, 498–509). Suárez Verdeguer calls liberals and *afrancesados* 'men moved by the same ideology', i.e. an ideology 'opposed to the nation' (F. Suárez Verdeguer, *La crisis política del antiguo régimen* (1950), esp. 41).

[2] These limitations were incomprehensible to English sympathizers with the Spanish Revolution (e.g. Lord Holland). Wellington was one of the few English observers who understood the power of the Church in Spain and Latin America—but then he was an Irish landlord.

as in so much else, the continuation of the work of the monarchy. The liberals hoped that the Inquisition, like the monasteries, would die a natural death as the result of French legislation: the publication of the *Diccionario crítico burlesco*, a crude piece of Voltairean anticlericalism, stung the clericals into a demand for the re-establishment of the Holy Office.

The debate on this issue (November 1813) was a series of oratorical field days lasting seventeen sessions. The regalist commonplaces of Macanaz were supplemented by the historical and legal knowledge of a small group of 'Jansenist' priests who regarded the Inquisition as an ultramontane institution, usurping the powers of the bishops.[1] The Inquisition was declared unconstitutional and the old laws of the *Partidas* a sufficient defence against heresy. 'With this declaration no innovation was made.' The liberals once more hoped to hide their liberalism under the mantle of reverence for the historic constitution. Protective antiquarianism could not conceal the true issues: the rights of the sovereign nation to decide on all matters (liberal regalism, with the Cortes playing the role of the prince) and the contest between traditional and liberal Spain involving the significance of her historical past. The Inquisition 'had suppressed the truths of philosophy, physics and geology'; it had enslaved the Spanish mind and denied progress. Here was the seed of the whole debate of the nineteenth century. The preponderance of the Church was responsible for Spain's decadence, laming her in the race of progress. The Church claimed that lip service to catholic unity, which liberalism still professed, meant nothing without the instruments to enforce it: that the contemplative life of the regular clergy was essential to a catholic country; that liberalism and catholicism were incompatible, in spite of liberal assertions to the contrary.

The strangest feature about the early triumphs of liberalism at Cadiz is the absence of any consistent conservative opposition to the enactments of a political philosophy based on the constituent powers of the sovereign people. After the early but ineffective protest of the Bishop of Orense against the sovereignty of the nation, the most radical clauses of the constitution passed

[1] Cf. M. Menéndez Pelayo, *Historia de los heterodoxos españoles* (Madrid, 1881), iii. 467. Typical of the more serious-minded clergy was Villanueva, whose diary (printed *B.A.E.* xcviii) is a valuable source for the secret sessions of the Cortes.

without effective criticism. It was not until 1811 that the seeming unity of patriotism split, not until 1813 that the privileged orders saw the possibility of a conservative reaction appealing to the 'people' against a radical minority. Wellesley, sensing this swing of opinion, wondered whether the time had not come for 'striking at democracy' by constitutional revision.[1]

The conservative opposition was composed of the privileged orders and institutions whose position had been challenged by liberal legislation. The opposition of the Council of Castile, as long as it existed, was consistent: the old constitution, and with it the powers of the Council, was unalterable without the king's consent.[2] A similar attitude was taken by the provincial *audiencias*, now confined to strictly judicial functions.[3] The nobles protested against the abolition of the *señorios*, the old municipalities against their constitutional successors. Legislation created a host of unemployed bureaucrats, municipal and seignorial officials, who exhibited what liberals called 'passive' opposition to the constitution—the refusal of local authorities to carry out the administrative changes and apply the laws of the Cortes. This opposition became more acute when, in 1813, the liberated areas, where a modern administration was only known as a French imposition, came within the new constitution.

It was the opposition of the clergy that gave this resistance of the privileged orders a country-wide leadership and a cause equal in emotive appeal to the myth of the sovereign people. If the lower clergy had been sympathetic to church reform on 'Jansenist' lines the hierarchy was hostile and, as the liberal attack on church property developed, it was joined by all but a handful of liberal priests. A group of bishops fled to Mallorca. Their pastoral letter of December 1812 condemned the Cortes's attack on the discipline, doctrine, privileges, and property of the Church. It was the church question which gave the opposition an intellectual content beyond the two-hundred-year-old theory of the unbreakable original contract

[1] Cf. Wellington's *Despatches*, x. 473, xi. 188; *Supplementary Despatches* (London, 1865), xi. 199, 216; vii. 635. Wellesley never abandoned the idea of constitutional revision on 'English lines'.

[2] 'Absolute power remains exclusively with the King and in his absence, in the tribunals, that is, the Council, and consequently the Cortes have no authority beyond that of raising men and money for the war' (*D.S.C.*, 15 Oct. 1811).

[3] For the functions of the *audiencias*, see above, p. 64.

with the monarch. Liberalism was heretical: Jansenism and Jacobinism went together. Thus liberals regarded this resistance as part of 'a vast and daring plan', a great clerical conspiracy backed by the Regents and the Papal Nuncio.[1] By 1812 the polemical tone had become bitter: the two conceptions of Spain became the subject of a journalistic war.

The *serviles*, as the conservative opposition was known, had few prospects in the Constituent Cortes: on 23 May 1813 the Cortes summoned its successor, the Ordinary Cortes, which was to meet first in Cadiz and then Madrid. It would seem that the priests fought a hard election campaign for the liberals began to press for the limitation of clerical deputies—a step inconceivable in 1809. Thus conservatives, supported by a violent press, and better represented in the Ordinary Cortes, felt able to challenge 'Jacobinism'. The liberals were equally determined to use their parliamentary power to prevent reaction: in masonic circles there seems even to have been talk of a republican dictatorship.[2] It was at this time that the idea of a citizen militia to defend the constitution against its enemies gathered support.

The political future of Spain now depended on Ferdinand VII. On 24 March 1814, released by the French, the Desired One entered his kingdom, hesitating over what system he should adopt. The liberals, *in extremis*, had made the recognition of the king dependent on his solemn oath to the constitution (2 February) and carefully stipulated his route to Madrid. Two considerations ended Ferdinand's doubts as to the possibility of defying liberalism. General Elio offered the support of his troops to maintain him in the fullness of his rights; at the same time the Manifesto of the Persians, signed by 96 'servile' deputies, reached the king at Valencia. It condemned the 1812 constitution root and branch and suggesting a return to the 'traditional' constitution. Secure in the backing of an army corps and a party in Madrid the king refused to recognize the authority of the Regency; on 4 May he published his first decree declaring the work of the Cortes null and void and adopting a modi-

[1] A. de Argüelles, *Examen*, ii. 247: it is fair to say that Toreno considered this an exaggeration. The Regents were accused of appointing *serviles* to posts in liberated Spain and, by refusing to enforce the reading of liberal legislation against the Inquisition, seemed to condone the resistance of priests and monks.

[2] Cf. Vaughan MSS., 14 Jan. 1814. The liberals were no longer 'reformers'; the party had 'completely become that of the Jacobins of the French Revolution'.

fication of the Persian programme. General Eguía, secretly appointed Captain General of Castile, entered Madrid and imprisoned the liberal leaders (10 May). Next day the 'lowest plebeians' terrorized the 'respectable classes' by sacking the Cortes building and breaking the stone of the constitution. The *coup d'état* of May was a throwback to the Aranjuez coalition: Ferdinand, the army, the mob.

The king's action determined the nature of the political struggle in Spain. It was the first of the total rejections of a previous régime which sent the supporters of that régime into exile, and the exiles of 1814 were the first representatives of a phenomenon typical of Spanish politics throughout the nineteenth century: 'a trans-Pyrenean colony' with no alternative but to plot the overthrow of the government by revolution. It demonstrated, in language of royalist papers, that political opponents were 'bloody dogs' who must be put down. Louis XVIII, another restored monarch, accepted a constitution in 1814 on condition that the constitution was reasonably 'balanced' and was seen as an act of grace by the crown and not as an imposition upon it. Ferdinand refused any form of constitution outright. Ferdinand's rejection of all compromise, as Wellesley saw, was just as alarming as the 'Republican Principles' which had made the constitution of 1812 a political edifice which no king could inhabit with dignity.

IV

REACTION AND REVOLUTION 1814–1833

1. *Absolutism Restored, 1814–1820*

FERDINAND VII was not the dedicated despot of liberal historiography. A martyr to gout, simple to the point of austerity in his personal tastes, and, contrary to liberal assertions, loved by his servants, he was a trimmer by nature, altogether lacking that *fermeté* which French agents found in his younger brother, Don Carlos. Early in his reign he realized that liberalism was unpopular with the masses, and he deliberately scorned the classes: his power, as Lord Liverpool observed from a distance, was based on an alliance of proletariat and priests against 'landlords' and middle classes. For Ferdinand the memories of Aranjuez, the welcome to Madrid, and the popular terror of May 1814 represented the roots of power. Like the Neapolitan Bourbons, he adopted a royal version of lower-class life. One of the main purposes of his low-born *camarilla* was to maintain contact with 'opinion' in order to manipulate it by his agents. As elsewhere in Restoration Europe, the secret police served as a partial and imperfect substitute for parliamentary institutions by informing the ruler of the state of popular feeling.[1] Yet, late in his reign, this complex and careful trimmer was ready to pose as an enlightened despot and woo his educated subjects. A rigid absolutist in political principle, in practice, it was observed, he 'ceded to the exigencies of the moment'. He would have provided an excellent model for Stendhal's portrait of the capricious but timid despot of Parma whose minister warned him that 'to have received power from Providence is no longer enough in these times; it requires brains and a strong character to succeed in being a despot'.

[1] The 'perverted' side of Ferdinand's character is attested by too many sources to be solely a propaganda exaggeration of liberal historiography. For a recent defence of Ferdinand VII see Maria Carmen del Pintos Vieites, *La política de Fernando VII entre 1814 y 1820* (Pamplona, 1958), a product of the Suárez Verdeguer School. (See below.)

Ferdinand's declared programme in May 1814 was based on the programme of the Persians. For one school of modern historians this programme (to which it attributes transcendent importance in the development of Carlism) represents a reversion to a traditional monarchy ruling with the historic Cortes and subject to God and the law, a *via media* between imported liberalism and the equally foreign ministerial despotism of the eighteenth century, a truly Spanish solution of the political problem of modern Spain.[1] Its institutional imprecision and evident anachronism weakened it as the basis for a compromise settlement; whatever its intention, the fate of the Persian Manifesto was to serve as a base from which to sally against liberalism and all its works. The king took from the Persians only their attack on the constitution of 1812; the project for a Cortes was 'lost' in the unsympathetic deliberations of the Council of Castile.[2]

In so far as Ferdinand had a system it was the restoration of the machinery of government and the society that he had known in 1808: ministerial despotism superimposed on the old Councils, the very system the Persians professed to abhor. The novel feature was the incoherence and instability of ministerial government and its rejection of those reforming traditions incompatible with the atmosphere of 1814. Thus the Jesuits were readmitted: as elsewhere in Europe, the appropriation of the Gallican-regalist tradition by revolutionaries made its continuation by the restored monarchies an impossibility. Ministerially the king lived from hand to mouth, on occasions with a double ministry of foreign affairs. Each minister was responsible directly to the monarch, subject to sudden dismissal and disgrace, and kept in total ignorance of his colleagues' policies. Cevallos, as foreign minister, was for four months in ignorance of the fact that Spain had 'joined' the Holy Alliance. The purchase of ships from the Russians was kept from the

[1] This school is represented in the works of F. Suárez Verdeguer. The restoration of the historic Cortes was impossible, but cf. the curious evidence of the Barcelona shopkeeper J. Coroleu (*Memorias de un menestral*, Barcelona (1916), 83). Relying on his father's memories he rejects the view that the Persian programme was a 'trap'; it may perhaps represent the mild constitutionalism evident in the replies to the questionnaire of 1809. (See above, p. 94.)

[2] According to J. C. Comellas, *Los primeros pronunciamientos en España* (1958), 'the shelving of the Cortes project was intimately connected with the fall of Macanáz', drafter of the proclamation of 4 May. Certainly San Carlos talked to Wellesley as if the Cortes were a certainty (*S.D.* xii. 37).

Minister of Marine: when he insisted on the examination of the ships he was dismissed.[1] Between 1814 and 1820 the average life of a minister was six months.

The explanation of this instability lies in bankruptcy, which in turn reflected the post-war depression, deepened by a restrictive monetary policy. Ministerial despotism could not be profitably run by clerical reactionaries ignorant of the financial world. The employment of able servants, particularly in the Treasury, entailed recurrent attempts to conciliate what was usable of the reformist tradition and even to appease the purged remnants of liberalism. In January 1816, Cevallos ended political persecution in the hope that 'the names of *serviles* and liberals will disappear'. Garay, Finance Minister from December 1816 to September 1818, was a friend of Jovellanos. His 'reformist' policy of strict economy and taxation of the privileged orders was strenuously resisted by representatives of the *ancien régime*, lead by Eguía, who wore an eighteenth-century wig. Driven away from conciliation by an obscure masonic conspiracy in 1816, it would appear that, on the verge of the revolution of 1820, the king once again contemplated some form of concession. We lack the knowledge to explain the true meaning of these lurches: the early reign did not lack certain eighteenth-century reformist traits—chairs in political economy, an interest in 'safe' elementary education, the building of the Prado. The king would probably have liked to attract liberals *on his own terms* but all attempts at an amnesty after 1816 came to nothing.[2]

With this unstable machine and the limited resources of post-war Spain, Ferdinand hoped to recover the American Empire; his dilemma was that only American silver could stave off bankruptcy while only a solvent state could reconquer America. The American question was thus of central importance for the success of restored despotism. Few Spanish statesmen could recognize that America was irretrievably lost; it is only after 1820 that a handful of liberals talked of the 'inevitability' of the fruit falling from the tree. Indeed, reconquest did not appear impossible. With the war ended in Spain Ferdinand could send 10,000 men under Morillo, a ranker general of great

[1] H. Baumgarten, *Geschichte Spaniens*, i. 161. For the Russian ships see M. de Saralegui y Medina, *Un negocio escandaloso* (1904).

[2] Cf. M. del Pintos Vieites, *Fernando VII*, 196 ff., 210–11.

courage and ability: relatively easily, he pacified Venezuela and captured Cartagena in New Granada. But in 1816 Bolívar came back to Venezuela, where the horsemen of the plains now joined the Liberator and his small army of creoles and foreign volunteers. In semi-tropical warfare, as the history of Cuba was to show, Spanish regular troops faced almost insuperable difficulties. By 1819 the balance of war had turned against Morillo, first in Venezuela, then in New Granada; with his armies shrunken to 2,500 men, without pay or supplies, bothered by corrupt local officials, only a new expedition could save the situation in the north.[1] In the United Provinces of the River Plate matters were beyond recovery: San Martín, in a beautifully planned campaign, had taken his army across the Andes into Chile and was preparing to move by sea against Peru, the centre of loyalist power in South America.[2]

Ferdinand failed to save what might have been saved from the wreck of the American Empire by his refusal to face realities and his obstinate insistence on reducing America to its traditional obedience to his crown. Some form of local autonomy, some abandonment of the old commercial system might have weakened the revolt; the most Ferdinand would concede (and that as a short-lived experiment) was the appointment of creoles within the old administration. Spain refused to recognize that nothing could be done in America without Britain, the greatest naval power; but Castlereagh considered Spain 'proud and vindictive', while British diplomacy showed little consideration for the susceptibilities of a declining imperialism, recommending an imitation of George III's 'generosity' to America and the British commercial system in India. Britain offered mediation, based on respect for Spanish sovereignty, in return for open markets and concessions to the rebels: since she would neither intervene against the rebels herself nor let others intervene should concession fail, her talk of Spanish sovereignty seemed hypocritical. Unwisely Spain intrigued for an anti-British coalition as she intrigued for an anti-American coalition in 1898; as Wellington observed, Spain acted 'as if Europe were at her feet'.[3]

[1] A. Rodríguez Villa, *Morillo*, i. 332–55.

[2] The royalist forces in Chile were destroyed at the battle of Maipú (April 1818). There were 5,000 men on each side of whom 2,500 were killed.

[3] For British policy see C. K. Webster, *Britain and the Independence of South America* (London, 1938).

The refusal to concede that gives an obstinate glory to Spanish policy, conquered any thought of a negotiated settlement. The last gamble, which would make concession unnecessary, was a new expeditionary force to defeat the rebels. But Ferdinand's bankrupt Spain could not produce the small army that might have postponed defeat. In 1818 the government began to concentrate in Andalusia an expeditionary army to reinforce Morillo: the expeditionary force defeated, not American rebels, but the monarchy itself. In January 1820 two of its junior officers 'pronounced' for the constitution of 1812.

The pronunciamiento was the instrument of liberal revolution in the nineteenth century. It was an officer revolt, justified by a crude political theory which made the officer corps the ultimate repository of a general will. When that will was vitiated either by the monarch's evil counsellors or, as the later theoreticians of military indiscipline were to maintain, by the corrupt operation of Parliamentary institutions run by a clique of 'anti-national' politicians, then it could be salvaged by the heroic gesture of a general or the conspiracy of an officers' mess. The origins of military intervention in politics lay perhaps in the role of generals in the eighteenth-century administration, and in the conflicts of politicians and soldiers during the War of Independence, but it was in Ferdinand's reign that this intervention developed the rigid form of classical drama. First came the preliminary soundings (the *trabajos*) and the winning over of officers and sergeants by a small activist group in touch with civilian conspirators; then the *compromisos* by which accomplices were bound to action; finally the chosen leaders set off the last stage by the cry—the *grito*. It was here, in the traditional speech to the drawn-up troops, that revolutionary formalism was most apparent. As a species of conspiracy it had its persistent weakness: fear of discovery led to revolt before the *compromisos* were firm enough. Most pronunciamientos went off at half-cock.[1]

Throughout the century the relative immunity which an inefficient police gave conspirators, and the idiosyncrasies of the prison system, encouraged conspiracy.[2] Malcontent generals

[1] For a general discussion, see R. Carr in *Soldier and Governments* (ed. M. Howard, London, 1957), 135–48.

[2] Thus the Inquisition, entrusted with breaking the Masonic Conspiracy of 1819–20, got involved in antiquated paper procedure. The liberties of Spanish

could invent excuses of bad health in order to meet fellow conspirators—thus, from Lacy to Prim, mineral spas were favoured plotting places. Quiroga, arrested as a suspect in 1819, was allowed extraordinary liberties: he played billiards with brother officers, walked about the streets on parole, and Alcalá Galiano, agent of the Cadiz masons, actually passed the night in his cell.[1] Scarcely surprisingly, he became one of the figureheads of the revolution of 1820. A ramshackle despotism encourages irresponsibility; there was always a chance of success and it was the weakest of the conspiracies—that of 1820—which defeated the government.

The pronunciamientos of 1814–20 were a combination of officer discontents, thwarted ambition, and liberal principle.[2] Ferdinand was bankrupt. He could not even pay the small army he desperately needed to reconquer America; still less could he pay the inflated army bequeathed by the War of Independence. Economy forced a return to the regular army of the *ancien régime*. This threw into opposition the ablest men in the army—the new officers whose liberal sympathies and patriotic energy had earned them rapid promotion in the War of Independence. Porlier found his career as a guerrilla general rewarded by posting to a provincial garrison. Lacy, a poor professional soldier who was a Captain General at thirty-seven, was banished. Mina, who regarded Navarre as his personal fief, saw his guerrillas dissolved—as they must be for they could not be paid—and his efforts on their behalf cold-shouldered by the new courtiers.[3] Richart, who plotted to assassinate the king in a brothel, was a liberal army paymaster who was passed over for

prisons were in part due to state poverty (prisoners paid for their own food, brought from outside) and to the feeling of gaolers that they were dealing with their masters, should a revolution be successful. (For the Inquisition as a detective force see J. C. Comellas, *Pronunciamientos*, 264–5.)

[1] A. Alcalá Galiano, *Memorias* (*B.A.E.* lxxxiv. 7–8) and *Recuerdos de un anciano* (*B.A.E.* lxxxiii. 114).

[2] The plots and pronunciamientos concerned were: Mina's attempt to seize Pamplona (1814); Porlier who raised Corunna, but whose troops betrayed him when he tried to take Santiago (1815); the Triangulo Conspiracy to murder the king (1816); Lacy's attempt in Catalonia and Vidal's in Valencia (1817); the Cadiz Conspiracy (1819–20).

[3] Girón's letters in F. Arzadún, *Fernando VII y su tiempo* (1942), gives a very clear picture of the 'two castes' in the army (cf. esp. 81, 88). Girón, who was a royalist, complains bitterly of his pay. On 1 July 1814 guerrillas, threatened with dissolution, invaded the palace (Vaughan MSS. Reports).

absorption into the civil service—the only career for superfluous officers. It was neglect which made liberals out of those passed over in promotion.[1]

In spite of the promptings of self-interest these men took great risks and were illuminated by the concept of the romantic hero: failure meant death and entry into the liberal calendar of martyrs. To their opponents they were *oficialillos* deluded by rapid war promotion into posing as cheap, imitation Bonapartes: to themselves they were 'drunk with glory'. At least the pronunciamiento had not become a speculative business enterprise for generals. Riego took real risks in 1820 and, in the end, he was executed. The established military rebels of the mid-century rarely faced such a fate.

The opposition of the civilian liberals to Ferdinand was inevitable after the persecutions of 1814, when the leaders were arrested, imprisoned, or sought safety in exile. It was the opposition of those whose careers were ruined—bankrupt restorations cannot reward the victors and conciliate the vanquished—and of those who, having lived in a free society, could not tolerate the frustrations of an unfree society in which private criticism could not be translated into public action. The 'insipid monotony' of a social life without a press (only two government papers were tolerated), without clubs, without 'respectable cafés', was broken only by religious and court festivals.[2] Only the opera flourished.

Thus the military conspirators could count on a growing area of civilian support. Mina's attempt to sieze Pamplona in 1814 was a purely personal undertaking, but in 1815 Porlier's attempt to raise Corunna was supported by the town's leading liberals and earned enough popular support for 'serenades and a brilliant illumination'.[3] He failed because he could not carry his sergeants with him and because of the jealousy of ecclesiastical Santiago against mercantile Corunna. Lacy and the Valencian conspirators could count on wider support, from merchants

[1] It is obvious from Mina's own account, *Memorias*, ii. 135–69, that he was driven to rebellion not by liberal convictions but by 'slights' against 'his' army. It was his position as a failed conspirator that determined his liberalism.

[2] Cf. Quintana's observations, *B.A.E.* xix. 544, and R. de Mesonero Romanos's descriptions of Restoration Madrid in *Memorias*, chapters x and xi.

[3] According to E. Blaquière, *Historical Review of the Spanish Revolution* (London, 1822), 221.

like Beltrán de Lis—in contact with officers as an army contractor—to shoemakers and farmers.

Civilian revolution was organized in Masonic lodges and it is the undoubted contribution of Freemasonry to the Revolution of 1820 that created the myth of its occult force. According to clerical conservatives, liberalism was nothing but a permanent Masonic conspiracy. Though Masonry was always to be an element in the liberal forces—particularly in later non-socialist brands of Republicanism—it was never again, as it was from 1815 to 1820, its chief framework; even then it was not so much a system of belief as the only clandestine organization available for conspiracy.

As such it had serious defects: like all other Spanish parties, the Masons were distinguished by their domestic divisions. Spanish Masonry had its ultimate origins in the deistic humanitarianism of a few eighteenth-century *esprits forts*. In 1814–20 it was a trifid movement: a conservative-tinged Freemasonry which had been introduced among the official classes by the French during the occupation; a liberal-nationalist group, perhaps influenced by English Masonry, with its first stronghold in Cadiz—the Masonry of Istúriz, Alcalá Galiano, Mendizábal; a purely military Masonry of young officer activists. Civilian 'lodges', widespread by 1817, were driven towards action by military 'trenches'. These conspiracies were broken by the government, inefficient though it was, leaving the initiative in 1820 in the hands of the military Masonry.

Why after the earlier failures did the military rising of 1820, 'risky to the point of being ridiculous' in the opinion of one of the conspirators, nevertheless succeed? Alcalá Galiano's explanation was simple: 'the repugnance of the rank and file against embarking for America' for the first time made soldiers and sergeants receptive to 'the sublime and generous ideas of their officers'.[1] Revolution meant no American campaign. Officer conspirators were working on their sergeants by offers of land and release from the army—a reduction in service was

[1] A. Alcalá Galiano, *Apuntes*, *B.A.E.* lxxxiv. 330. The conspirators *may* have received money from American rebels: the interest of Americans in any revolution that weakened the Spanish monarchy is evident—hence the curious relations between Cubans and a later generation of liberals. There were many liberals—Istúriz among them—whose trading interests were bound up with America and who therefore resisted the American connexion of liberalism.

later to be the standard inducement to mutiny offered by generals to their troops.[1] As the army of America waited month after month, in cantonments round Cadiz, whole regiments became infected—a concentration of malcontents which the war minister warned would destroy the monarchy.

After the failure of a 'respectable' revolution in 1819 the conspiracy fell into the hands of young officers and Masons who used the mysterious procedures of the sect in order to hide the fact that they did not have the 'old gang's' financial backing for the reward of wholesale desertion.[2] In the army no one above the rank of colonel would compromise himself: hence the conspirators 'made' their own general out of Colonel Quiroga, later to be eclipsed by Major Riego. It was Riego who gave the revolution its programme by declaring on 1 January 1820 for the constitution of 1812: thus a single man, acting on impulse and without consulting civilians, committed liberalism to the constitution that was to destroy it. Yet it is not altogether inapt that the Hymn of Riego became the anthem of liberalism. Childishly vain, he was brave, resourceful, and alone had the determination to persist in revolution until the régime collapsed.

In January and February 1820 an extraordinary situation developed. The Masons failed to stage a revolution in Cadiz where rain and inefficiency kept Quiroga inactive; Riego took his men on a round tour of Andalusia where only the mountain pueblo of Grazalema welcomed the liberator.[3] The Revolution remained a military sedition and appeared likely to die a natural death.[4] It was resurrected by the rising of Corunna which, by a reversion to the revolutionary federalism of 1808, claimed to be the capital of all Galicia, and by risings in Barcelona, Saragossa, and Pamplona where officers had been plotting with the

[1] For Quiroga's land offer see Wellesley's dispatch, *F.O.*, 4 Feb. 1820. This was a revival of a piece of popular radicalism current in 1808–12.

[2] The 'respectable' conspiracy was an attempt by General the Conde de la Bisbal to use his army corps to force a constitution out of the king. La Bisbal withdrew at the last moment and arrested the conspirators. For his own account of his 'treason' which lost him a possible role as the first of the nineteenth-century general-politicians, see his letter of 22 Mar. 1820, published in the newspaper *El Despertador Constitucional*.

[3] Riego's Andalusian expedition is described in General Evaristo San Miguel's *Memoria sobre lo acaecido en la columna movil al mando . . . de D. Rafael de Riego* (Barcelona, 1820).

[4] The opinion of the British consul at Seville (see his reports in *F.O.*, 7 Jan. and after). 'I did not observe a single person in the crowd shout with the troops.'

poet Quintana (21 February to 5 March). The success of the Revolution is therefore explicable in terms of the weakness of the king's government. For two months a vastly superior army refused serious action against the rebels and finally backed them.

The triumph of liberalism was therefore the result of the attitude of the army: a minor officers' revolt had been backed by what was later termed a 'negative pronunciamiento'—the refusal of the army to support the government. It was this same denial of support which drove Maria Cristina to abdicate as Regent in 1840 and Alfonso XIII to withdraw from Spain in 1931. To Riego liberalism had been installed solely by officers: civilians had missed any title to glory by failing to raise Cadiz after the army had pronounced. He pushed aside the civilian Junta using it only to give decent sanction to new promotions. In Madrid civilian liberalism had waited on events. 'Nothing is more remarkable', wrote Wellesley, 'than the apathy of the people who have taken neither side of the question but look on the quarrel as to be one between the army and the king.'[1] The crowds who gathered round the palace were respectable citizens cheering a king who had already conceded to the army and to provincial garrisons: they were not an organized pressure group which had forced the crown to become liberal by accepting the constitution of 1812, appointing a liberal municipality, and a Junta to supervise the establishment of the constitution.

2. *The Revolution of 1820, Constitutional Spain, and the Independence of Spanish America, 1820–1823*

1820 set the procedures of liberal revolution: an army revolt, backed by a provincial rising and finally sanctioned by a change of course in Madrid. This was 'the Spanish method of making a revolution' repeated in 1854 and 1868.[2] As a technique it gave the early stages of the Revolution a federalist tinge. Thus until July, Spain was ruled by provincial and town committees or the restored constitutional municipalities of 1814 where they existed. The Madrid Junta created and controlled

[1] *F.O.*, 17 Jan. 1820. Liberal opinion in Madrid mounted between January and March. By the end of February he estimated two-thirds of the population 'sympathized' with the rebels. On the news of the Galician rebellion government bonds sank 10 per cent.

[2] M. J. Quintana, *B.A.E.* xix. 541.

the first ministry of the constitutional monarchy, that of the 'jail-birds' (March 1820), but its powers extended only over Castile; the Junta of Galicia and the southern Juntas abolished taxation, communicating with other Juntas as sovereign states, one to another.[1] Thus the first task of the government of the revolution was to master provincial anarchy—the urban and military radicalism which claimed to have 'made' the Revolution and which took Riego as its figurehead. Its second task was to keep Ferdinand VII faithful to the constitution of 1812 which he had sworn to defend and out of the hands of a royalist reaction. These two necessities dictated the course of events in the 'Constitutional Triennium'. Until July 1822 liberal ministries manœuvred between the king's intrigues and the counter demonstrations of the radicals; from then until the defeat of constitutional Spain by foreign invasion, radicals ruled in face of the open hostility of the constitutional king.

If liberalism had maintained a semblance of unity it would have been better able to resist the royalists' attempts to destroy constitutional government. But by the time the Cortes met (in July 1820) the government's attempt to impose order on liberty had dissipated the 'harmony of the liberal family': liberalism had begun the process which was to divide it into two streams, two traditions—'moderate' liberalism and the radicalism of the *exaltados*. This division, essentially between liberals and democrats, between men of property and position and urban radicals, was common to the European liberalism whence the two schools derived their programmes. Spanish liberalism lacks any originality of thought; there is little that cannot be derived from the French doctrinaires and their democratic opponents, or, more rarely, from English radicalism and from Bentham in particular. What gives Spanish liberalism its characteristic flavour is its use of a unique system of historical reference, while its significance lies in its attempt to apply, by means of military sedition, the politics of interest and the machinery of parliamentary government to an underdeveloped society.

The moderate stream in the liberalism of 1820–3 was repre-

[1] Cf. the reports of the British Consul in Seville in February and of the British Ambassador in Madrid for 4 May and 15 May. The Cartagena Junta threatened to open the port to foreign textiles if the Barcelona Junta refused it funds. All local Juntas abolished the *consumos*.

sented by the liberal exiles and 'jail-birds'—so called by the king because he had imprisoned them in 1814. They were the men of 1812 (*doceañistas*) tempered by exile, for whom politics were no longer an abstract science deducible from self-evident propositions. Most considered the constitution of 1812 an unworkable experiment 'out of touch with the spirit of the age'. The whole problem of moderate liberalism in 1820 and after was to secure a workable 'balanced' constitution which would establish liberty with order by revising the constitution of 1812 without appearing to abandon in public the principles of 1812. Such a moderate constitution, which would establish a second chamber and reasonable liberty of action for the executive, they hoped would secure the co-operation of Ferdinand by respecting the personal prerogatives of the monarch. Once constitutional revision proved unacceptable to the king and to the radical democrats moderate liberalism was doomed. In 1820 the *doceañistas* were the ministers of a revolution they had not made; they became its Girondins, hating and hated by the radical clubs and at the same time disowned by the king. Their moment passed and after the crisis of the July Days (1822) they withdrew from politics.

The political convictions of the *afrancesados* were not far removed from those of the moderate liberals yet, in the constitutional period, they became internal exiles, the 'jews and pariahs' of the revolution. In spite of personal ties and ideological affinities, the liberals could not welcome the return to political life of the 'traitors' of 1808–14. Unable to share the patronage of the liberal triumph, they became its professional critics and, since they were the ablest single group in political life, their journalistic criticism was damaging. Some, like Lista, remained genuine liberals; others, like Hermosilla and Miñano, had come to hate the Revolution as a Jacobin affair and were rewarded for their polemics by the restored monarchy after 1823. Like the moderate liberals, their future allies, they withdrew from political life in disgust after the July days.[1]

[1] M. Lafuente (*Historia de España* (Barcelona, 1889), xviii. 315) believed that the *afrancesados* were working with the king against the liberals as early as September 1820. For Lista see H. Juretschke, *Lista*, 84–120. Quintana was typical of the older generation in that he respected the talents of the *afrancesados* but could not credit them with any good intentions in politics. The *afrancesados* were particular objects of suspicion to the English ambassador.

The *exaltados*, who represented the anarchical stage of the primitive revolution, regarded the preservation of the constitution of 1812 as a democratic duty. By definition they were the 'outs' of politics: having made the Revolution they were treated as 'poor folk', pushed aside by 'a horde of harpies'—the *doceañistas*—whom 'their' revolution had brought to office. Successful revolution implied a new deal in patronage which the older generation of liberals, now in office, could not afford. This left a crowd of discontented radical office-seekers—the *pretendientes*—who were to embarrass every government that issued from a revolution.[1]

The strength of the *exaltados* lay in the provincial capitals and above all in Riego's army, a *cosa de casa* or household property of southern urban radicalism. In the capital, radical power lay in the clubs and the press, which sprang up with the Revolution, and in their Masonic affiliations: these factors allowed the radical leaders to subject the government to a series of street riots.

Neither the clubs nor the streets were always the dark forces of the slum underworld conjured up by the novelist Galdós as 'vulgar, obscene and above all, cowardly'. The clubs aimed at a Jacobin respectability: well lighted, 'a guard of soldiers attends to preserve order and a military band is present which plays patriotic airs before the speeches commence and in the intervals between them'.[2] Many of the street affrays had the air of an unruly *fiesta*, prearranged and watched with interest from balconies. But, as the Revolution ran into foreign and domestic opposition, so the force of *exaltado* liberalism with its cry 'The Constitution or Death' hardened and coarsened into the language of the *sans-culotte* defensive reaction of 1793. The man in the street saw the revolution in the crude terms of broad-

[1] The *Gaceta* (the Government gazette) of 22 Apr. restored the office holders of 1814. Alcalá Galiano became a discontented radical because he was given no promotion in the Foreign Ministry as a reward for his revolutionary services in 1820. There was no conception of professional promotion; Alcalá Galiano had not done a stroke of official work since 1814. The connexion between political opposition and jobs is illustrated by the fact that, when the radicals themselves became ministers, they were confronted by the claims of the jobless *comuneros* who claimed to be more patriotic and exalted than the ministry.

[2] M. Quin, *Visit to Spain* (London, 1823). One of the uses of the band was to stifle 'exaltation'.

sheets and popular prints, whereon patriots bludgeoned priests and *serviles* to death.[1]

The appeal of *exaltado* radicalism to the underprivileged was primitive and direct. 'The poor cannot pay taxes, therefore the rich must.' One of the features of 1820 had been the spontaneous abolition of the *consumos*—indirect taxes levied on prime necessities. When the government tried to reimpose these hated taxes, radicals warned that taxation was the 'thermometer' by which the people judged their institutions and that attempts to restore the old taxes would leave constitutional enthusiasm to 'a few instructed citizens'.[2] Their hostility to constitutional revision and to the conservative liberals was social as well as political: the radicals were anti-aristocratic and detested the idea of the second chamber which figured in the plans of the moderates.[3]

The ministry of the jail-birds was confronted with the task of establishing an ordered government; this left the *exaltados* with the duty of 'enlightening the people as to their duties and censuring the abuses of the ministry'. This meant keeping the revolutionary army in being and coercing the ministry by the streets lest it should sacrifice Liberty to Order. Thus the minister of war's attempt to dissolve the southern army and to post liberal generals to other provinces made the schism in the constitutional forces irreparable. When Riego appeared in Madrid (21 August 1820) posing as a radical hero, the clubs brought out the streets against the government.

Struggling with enthusiasm on the left, the ministry was threatened from the right by royalist plots backed by a king whom his ministers presented in public as Ferdinand the Great, the paragon of constitutional virtue. 'Had the King', wrote the British ambassador, who told Ferdinand to his face that he

[1] Broadsheets traditionally contained accounts of notable murders, robberies, &c. Extreme royalism and extreme liberalism both used popular ballad forms and a study of them reveals the primitive violence of political life. Two such broadsheets are illustrated in F. Soldevila, *Historia de España*, vii. 396–7.

[2] Cf. J. Carrera Pujal, *Historia política de Cataluña* (Barcelona, 1957), ii. 58–114. Hostility to the reimposition of taxes represented the traditional resistance of provincial Catalan authorities (the Provincial Deputations and the Municipalities) to the demands of the agents of the central government (the Intendant).

[3] Cf. their attitude to the abolition of *señorios*. The moderates wished to protect those 'feudal' payments which were really rent payments. The radicals showed no such respect for property rights. In their hostility to a second chamber they were supported by Bentham: *Works*, viii. 465–86.

entertained a very erroneous view of his situation, 'pursued a straightforward line with his ministers, discountenancing all plots against the New System, much progress would have been made in reforming it.'[1] Trained as a despot, Ferdinand could not become a constitutional king overnight; he utterly failed to realize the possibilities that the widespread desire for constitutional revision, which would have been acceptable to his ministers, afforded him for a recovery of royal power.

The king's proposals for constitutional revision were so alarming (they were to be backed by a foreign army) that Wellesley advised him to burn them. In November 1820 he appeared to be contemplating a Spanish 'Flight to Varennes', and it is at this time that the king's unpopularity in radical circles begins, together with the proposals for a regency to replace him. He was regarded as giving covert support to anti-constitutionalist elements in the Guards and to royalist partisans, alleged to get their horses from the royal stables.[2] To bring the king to his senses the ministry allied with the *exaltados*; for three days he was humiliated by the 'pacific disorder' of street demonstrations outside the palace, tolerated by his ministers. After accusing them, not without cause, of failing to protect him from public insult and reducing him, as he complained to sympathetic ambassadors, to the status of a slave, he dismissed them (March 1821).

The appointment of the Bardaxí ministry (March 1821), more acceptable to the king than that of the obnoxious 'jail-birds', was the signal for a revolt of provincial radicalism which threatened to reduce Spain to anarchy.[3] Inspired by the 'persecution of patriots' (i.e. the local distribution of governmental patronage against the radicals), it was fed by unemployment and distress which local authorities tried to meet with doles and public works. In Cadiz extremists proposed blowing up the bridge that connected the town with the mainland and declared for a Hanseatic Republic of Cadiz. For two months the town refused to admit 'any chiefs named by the present ministry even

[1] i.e. in the direction of a stronger executive. Wellesley maintained that 'most opinion' outside the radical clubs favoured constitutional revision. *F.O.*, Wellesley's dispatches of 20 Oct. 1820, 25 Feb., 10 Mar., 18 Apr. 1821.

[2] Ibid., 1, 4, 5 Feb. 1821.

[3] Eusebio Bardaxí (1776–1842) had been secretary of the Cortes of Cadiz; he was a diplomat of moderate political convictions.

after the opinion of the Cortes had been given on the subject'. Thus the Cadiz radicals would not accept a decision of the Cortes, let alone of the legal ministry. In the north Galicia had never been brought securely under central government control. The people of Corunna declared their intention of disobeying the orders of a detested ministry; 'to save public order', the Captain General, Mina, declared for the rebels. This was to be the standard excuse of every general who compromised with radicalism.[1] In September 1821 the Madrid radicals staged a pro-Riego demonstration in Madrid: it was easily mastered by the urban militia and the army in the comic-opera Battle of Las Platerías. This revealed that the strength of radicalism lay, not in the capital, which had been the last great city to pronounce in 1820, but in the independent radicalism of the provinces.

This surge of provincial radicalism which destroyed the Bardaxí ministry was reflected in the *exaltado* majority of the new Cortes. Since, as in the French constitution of 1791 and with the same disastrous results on effective government, ministers could not be chosen from among the deputies, the king appointed a ministry chosen from the moderate liberals of the first Cortes under Martínez de la Rosa (28 February 1822). A *doceañista* for whom liberty was no longer a Furious Bacchante but a Sober Matron, he was a leader of the Romantic movement in Spain and an established playwright, welcome in the 'seat of servile ideas' as the *exaltados* termed the salons of Madrid. He regarded his mission as the mastery of the clubs and the radical press; the ministry would then reform the constitution by means of an 'aristocratic' second chamber, a property qualification for voters and a strengthened executive, a course that was approved by the French ambassador as the best way of saving the monarchy. By May 1822 the ministry had mastered the *exaltados* in the Cortes; this precarious victory for order and the hopes it held out for constitutional revision were destroyed by the intrigues of the king in the July Days.

The July Days were the culmination of the discontents of the Royal Guards. Veteran troops, officered by aristocrats, flattered by the king, the Guards Regiments were the best-dis-

[1] For Mina's tortuous explanation of his conduct see his *Memorias*, ii. 382–467. Mina's radicalism was not as firm as that of his supporters.

ciplined troops in the army;[1] when garrisoned in Madrid they constituted the most important single element in revolutionary politics since they could wrest control of the streets from the militia, formed to defend a constitution which was the symbol of the king's 'slavery'. Brawls between the Guards and the militia culminated in the 'martyrdom' of a liberal officer Landaburu (1 July), one of the set pieces of the broadsheets. The ministry was attempting to force the king to discipline the Guards when four battalions, without orders, withdrew outside Madrid to the Pardo while two other battalions cut the palace off from the town. On 7 July the Pardo battalions marched on Madrid.

The Guards' programme was as confused as their action was hesitant: some were absolutists, others wished to force the pace of the ministry's constitutional revision.[2] From the beginning it was clear that the Permanent Deputation of the Cortes, the municipality and the militia were determined to resist—if necessary by declaring a regency. The Captain General, Morillo, and the ministry, imprisoned in the palace without food, were less resolute and worked for a compromise with the Guards.[3] The king himself lacked the courage to carry through a *coup*. On 8 July he tearfully embraced his partisans in the palace while the Guards were being defeated in the streets by troops and militia loyal to the constitutional authorities.[4] If it was a serious attempt at counter revolution condoned by the king, it was badly planned and worse executed. In the eyes of his supporters Ferdinand's conduct had been disastrous and determined royalists turned towards his brother Don Carlos.[5]

[1] Fernando Fernández de Córdoba's *Mis memorias íntimas* (1886), i, *passim*, gives an excellent picture of the Guards.

[2] The leader of the 'constitutional' conspiracy was Luis Fernández de Córdoba (brother of Fernando), who proposed to Ferdinand that he should leave Madrid and grant a conservative–liberal constitution; when the king refused, his fellow officers acted against Córdoba's advice and faced certain failure (F. Fernández de Cordoba, op. cit. i. 38 ff.).

[3] For Morillo's defence see *Vida*, iv. 402 ff. For a defence of the ministry see J. Sarrailh, *Martínez de la Rosa* (Bordeaux, 1930), 120 ff., and J. Puyol, *Diego de Clemencín* (Madrid, 1929), 41 ff.

[4] J. Arzadún, *Fernando VII*, 154. Amarillas exonerates the king from the liberal accusation that he encouraged with hunting whoops the constitutional soldiers to fire on the Guards. He argues that the king was quite open in his sympathies with the rebels (ibid. 173–4).

[5] 'The most determined royalists are raging at the behaviour of the king.' The

With the lamentable failure of Ferdinand in the Guards' rebellion, palace royalism was bankrupt; the hopes of the royalist cause now lay in the countryside and, by the end of 1822, what has been called the first Spanish Civil War had begun. In large areas of rural Spain the army and the militia were hunting down small groups of royalist partisans—a spontaneous resurgence of the guerrilla tradition. There were royalist Juntas organizing the rebellion in Navarre, Aragon, and Galicia, where priests were stirring the 'superstitious' countryside against the 'enlightened' towns.

Without funds, without arms, royalism could not defeat the regular army, still loyal to the revolution it had made. The sole hope of success lay, therefore, in the French help for which royalist exiles had been angling since 1821. Like all exiles they were split by personal feuds. Eguía, an old-fashioned and ineffective general, entangled with a Bayonne pastrycook, was ready to buy French military aid on French terms: the imposition on the king of a constitution based on the *Charte* of 1814. Thus, paradoxically, the programme of Eguía's royalists was identical with that which his constitutional ministers wished to impose on the king on the eve of the July Days: a French-backed imitation of a French constitution.

Although they might recognize the necessity of apparent concession as an indispensable condition for French money and troops, most royalists preferred to any *afrancesado* charter the revival of the 'ancient constitution'. In practice this was indistinguishable from absolutism. The 'pure' royalists were led by the Marqués de Mataflorida, one of the devisers of the Persian programme and the reaction of 1814. He won over Baron Eroles, the only serving general who fought for a royalist reaction, and set up a royalist Regency in the Pyrenean town of Seo de Urgel.

In my view, the strength of the so-called 'popular royalism', represented by Mataflorida, has been exaggerated by recent historians. Its strongholds were the north and the mountains of Catalonia. In Catalonia the royalist factions were mastered by

Prussian minister, Schepeler (quoted H. Baumgarten, *Geschichte Spaniens*, ii. 475). According to a report in the Vaughan MSS. (5 July) if the king had joined the Guards the best regiments in the army would have supported him; the army, except for the Artillery, was now disillusioned with the *exaltados* (ibid. 11 Apr.) and would have backed the Moderates (i.e. constitutional revision).

Mina's military terrorism; as an ex-guerrilla he knew the key to victory lay in the ruthless destruction of aid from the countryside.[1] Elsewhere the liberals were not wrong in arguing that the factions were 'the lowest orders of society'; both extreme liberalism and extreme royalism were popular in the worse sense of the word. Reduced to its own resources and without French aid, royalism could not have imposed its views on Spain.

The July Days were the watershed of the Revolution for royalists and constitutionalists alike. The fiction of Ferdinand the Great's constitutionalism was finally exploded and it was a fiction without which the constitution itself could not survive. From August 1822 with the eclipse of the moderate liberals, the government was in the hands of those who professed to have 'made' the revolution of 1820—the young Masons and army officers under Colonel Evaristo de San Miguel who had commanded the militia in the July Days. San Miguel's ministry, a dictatorship of the military left, was opposed by moderate liberals and the *sàns-culotte* radicalism of Romero Alpuente's *comuneros*.[2] However far to the left liberal governments moved, they were always to find an opposition of unsatisfied place hunters posing as the depositaries of the true revolution. Romero Alpuente was the type of social misfit—an opponent called him ugly, dirty, and badly dressed—who rationalized his discontents by imitating the language of the Jacobins in the Great Revolution which haunted the imaginations of radicals all over Europe. Against a counter-revolution backed by foreign arms Romero Alpuente recalled the September massacres 'when in one night fourteen-thousand were executed'. Indeed the situation seemed to justify a patriot defensive reaction as it became increasingly clear that the reactionary powers were about to destroy the Spanish constitution by a military invasion.[3]

From its beginnings the existence of liberal, constitutional

[1] The royalists had no real army. In the 'decisive' victory of Pobla de Segur, Mina claimed to have lost only two men (*Memorias*, iii. 98). For his rigour, cf. the destruction of Castellfullit and his proclamation of 22 Oct. 1822 (ibid. 70–74). When he entered Cervera he found it deserted.

[2] The adoption of the name *comuneros* shows how even radicalism imported from France made obeisance to Spanish history—hence the notion that the sixteenth-century defenders of municipal privilege against the crown were ancestors of modern democrats.

[3] There are many parallels with 1936. In Catalonia there was even a battalion of militia women under Lacy's widow.

government in Spain was a European concern, as it was to be in the 1830's and again in 1936–9. The Spanish Revolution of 1820 was significant in Restoration Europe, not through the originality of its ideas, but because it was the first crack in the conservative structure of 1815. The Spanish constitution of 1812 became a rallying cry in Naples and the techniques of Spanish military liberalism were taken as a model by Decembrists in Russia and liberal officers in Piedmont.[1] With the defeat of the revolution in Italy, Spain became, to liberal exiles, 'the last stronghold of liberty'. Only by declaring war on France and joining the 'general cause of liberty' in Europe could constitutional Spain save itself from the wrath of reactionaries who would overcome their dissensions to stamp out liberty where it survived.[2]

Intervention against Naples (agreed on by Prussia, Russia, and Austria in December 1820) implied intervention against the progenitors of the Neapolitan Revolution. Although the French ultras looked on the Spanish absolutist partisans as Vendéens and the liberal Cortes as a Convention, Villèle would have preferred to save monarchical principles by a revision of the Spanish constitution such as had been proposed by the ministry of Martínez de la Rosa. When this was impossible he gave in to *ultra* pressure for a royalist crusade to liberate Ferdinand VII.

Once the threat of French intervention had become serious, liberalism was maintained by a series of myths. Spain would display once more 'the energy and decision that had astonished the world in 1808'. 'Yes, you will conquer them since one free man is worth a thousand slaves. Animated by the spirit of liberty, three hundred Greeks vanquished as many millions

[1] The Decembrists, as a small group in a large inert country, were interested in the Spanish pronunciamients as a means of effecting radical political change without an appeal to the social discontents of the masses. 'Our revolution will be similar to the Spanish Revolution of 1820; it will not cost a single drop of blood, for it *will be executed by the army alone without the assistance of the people*': A. G. Mazour, *The First Russian Revolution 1825* (Stanford, 1961), cf. 151. For Italy see G. Spini, *Mito e realta della Spagna nella rivoluzione italiana del 1820–21* (Rome, 1950).

[2] 'G.G.D.V.', *Letters on the political state of Spain* (London, 1825), 12, 255. By a Piedmontese exile, Vandancourt, this book gives a description of the unhappy plight of the exiles in Spain. Vandancourt bombarded the government with his plan for an invasion of France; when he was cold-shouldered he turned to the 'patriots' of the left.

who sought to oppress them.' Derived from Rousseau's enthusiasm for the military virtues of the independent republic, the myth of the free man's superiority over the trained slave army was to do incalculable damage in 1823 as in 1936. Governments did not believe in it; but it conveniently covered the political, financial, and diplomatic difficulties of preparing for war. As in 1936, Spanish liberals did not dare distinguish between popular demonstrations of left-wing solidarity in other countries and government policy. To the end San Miguel seems to have hoped for active British support, an illusion based on English opinion rather than on Canning's declared policy which was to forestall French intervention by forcing a revised constitution, acceptable to Ferdinand and the French, on San Miguel.[1] Since San Miguel could not modify a constitution declared 'sacred' in an emotional 'Roman' session of the Cortes (9 January 1823), intervention was inevitable.

In the meantime, with the prospect of deliverance by foreign arms, the king's relations with his ministers deteriorated rapidly; he pleaded illness and refused to move to Andalusia out of reach of the French armies. Beneath the formal courtesies, the ministers treated the king as a prisoner in his lugubrious, empty palace. When he dismissed San Miguel's ministry he was forced to recall it by the Regency Riots (19 February 1823).[2] Tolerated, if not inspired by the ministers, a nasty mob gathered before the palace demanding the deposition of the king and the installation of a regency: the authorities made no attempt to control the crowd. The king was forced to retire, against his will, with a new and more radical government to Seville, where the Cortes temporarily deposed the king and set up a regency. This was the most violent official act of the revolution; the king never forgave its authors who remained on the list of proscripts to the end of his reign.[3]

[1] Canning's policy was clearly set out in the dispatch of 31 Mar. 1823 (cf. H. W. V. Temperley, *The Foreign Policy of Canning* (Cambridge, 1923), 81 ff.). Unlike the conservatives in 1936 he did give constitutional government in Spain what Villèle termed an *appui moral*.

[2] For a description of these riots see M. Quin, *Visit*, 227–42. Quin was an eye-witness.

[3] The liberals argued that the deposition of the king (again occasioned by his refusal to accept another translation, this time to Cadiz) was not an act of republicanism but an act of necessity; if the king had not been deposed he would have been outraged by the Seville *exaltado* mob (Alcalá Galiano, *B.A.E.* lxxxiv, pp. iii, 255–8).

On 7 April 1823 the Hundred Thousand Sons of St. Louis had crossed the frontier. Carefully paying for their supplies, the French forces met with no resistance in a country where stragglers from Napoleon's armies had been savagely murdered. The revolution had been made by the army; the generals now deserted the constitution in an attempt to secure their own position by negotiating a compromise settlement. 'They behaved in this fashion so that they might keep their jobs and their honours, remaining at the top in one system as they had been in the other.'[1] Morillo, in Galicia, disliked equally the Constitutional Regency in Cadiz and the Royalist Regency: he sought to impose, through negotiations with the French, a moderate constitutional settlement which would appeal to the 'sensible men of property' against the 'hallucinated minority'.[2] La Bisbal, military dictator of the province of Madrid, put forward a last-minute programme of amnesty and constitutional revision. Without an army to defend them (Riego's old regiment supported Morillo and the town garrison was on the point of mutiny), the civilian government besieged in Cadiz sought to save their persons at the expense of the Sacred Code. On 30 September, in return for the promise of an amnesty, they released Ferdinand who had spent his last days as constitutional king launching paper darts from the roof in full view of the French army. The 'three years of the constitution' were at an end.

'The constitution of 1812', declared a liberal officer on surrendering to the French, 'was made entirely for the people but they hated it.'[3] This unpopularity was, in part, due to factors outside the control of the upholders of the constitution: yellow fever, floods followed by droughts, unemployment. In part it was the consequence of the sudden imposition of freedom in a society accustomed to absolutism; the violence of the press and the clubs created problems of public order which liberals attempted to solve by legislation, only to be driven to *ad hoc* 'despotism' and the rule of the militia. Liberal revolutions throughout Europe were broken by this dilemma. In part the

[1] Quintana, *B.A.E.* xix. 581. Only Mina in Catalonia tried serious resistance.

[2] For Morillo's attempt at the moderate constitution, see A. Rodríguez Villa, *Morillo*, iv. 440–98.

[3] F. Espoz y Mina, *Memorias*, iv. 339.

liberal programme—it was a repetition and amplification of the legislation of the Cortes of Cadiz—had little popular appeal. Above all, hatred of the constitution was a sign that the liberal system had divided Spanish society by attacking the interests of the Church.

Two symbolic figures, frequently portrayed in literature, represented this social schism: the local anti-clerical of the clubs and lodging houses who encouraged popular hatred of priests and monks; the political priest, at home in the *tertulia* of the pious bourgeoisie and aristocracy and at the same time in contact with the underworld of the church and king mob.[1]

The moderate liberals were practising Catholics and aware of the dangers of a conflict with the Church; they detested the extreme anti-clericals among the *exaltados*. In the early months of 1820 patriots gloried in the harmony of the constitution and the Church, enshrined in Article XII which established Catholicism as the sole religion of Spaniards; the constitution, wrote a Catalan poet, was 'the new Gospel, the law of the Creator'. This harmony was disturbed by the legislation of 1820, the work, not of extremists, but of moderate liberals. The expulsion of the Jesuits (July), the abolition of the clerical *fuero* (September), and the regulation of the Regular Orders were not forced on the ministry by pressure from the clubs. They were an inescapable part of the liberal programme.[2] At first the hierarchy had preached acceptance of the constitution. Its neutrality evaporated with the attacks on its property and jurisdiction and with the government's failure to control the press and punish the anti-clerical *meneurs*. The heresies of *Russo* and *Volter*, of Jansen and of the Synod of Pisa, reappeared unpunished by the secular arm and sustained by the greatest heresy of the age—liberalism. 'The pseudo philosophers of our time', declared the Bishop of Barcelona, 'have added nothing to the heresies of the early centuries of the Church.'

[1] The murder of the priest Vinuesa (May 1821), frequently reproduced on broadsheets, was a consequence of the clash of these two forces. Vinuesa was in prison on a charge of conspiracy to restore absolute government; he was assassinated by militiamen and members of *exaltado* clubs. The extreme *exaltados* took the hammer, with which he was done to death, as a badge.

[2] The law of 25 Oct. 1820 put all Orders under the Bishops (i.e. ended the autonomous provinces), suppressed the smaller monasteries, allowed only one house for each order in any one town, and forbade the reception of novices.

For the Regular Orders the overthrow of the constitution was a condition of their continuing existence as religious communities. They therefore became its most violent and outspoken enemies. Some convents—Mora del Ebro, for example—sheltered royalist rebels. Towards the end of 1822 local authorities ruthlessly applied the October laws in areas of dissaffection and, as a consequence, only four of the thirty-two Franciscan convents in Catalonia had any monks left by 1823. By that year the Church could count the first of its political martyrs: the monks of Mora del Ebro were shot for their counter-revolutionary activities, a bishop and fourteen priests massacred by a militia column.[1] The violence of the 'mushroom despots'—soldiers and provincial Jacobins—who presided over the agonies of constitutional Spain in 1823 appalled the respectable classes.

The Revolution of Riego was not merely a *crise de conscience* for Spain and Europe; it was a decisive event across the Atlantic, in that it finally assured the creation of the independent Republics of Latin America.[2]

The American policy of the liberals of 1820 repeated the confusions and misunderstandings of the Cortes of Cadiz: they could neither continue despotism nor evolve a policy to reconcile liberal Spain and her revolted colonies. The government's policy was still conciliation on the basis of recognition of the sovereignty of constitutional Spain; it failed to realize that the constitution of 1812 and representation in the Spanish Cortes might be considered by Americans as no better than despotism. Americans wanted not 'principles so philosophical that they captivate the mind' embodied in a unitary constitution, however liberal, but free trade and complete control of their own affairs. All schemes for autonomy under decentralized Bourbon monarchies in America—a solution which at least recognized the nature of American demands—broke on the rigid view the king took of his constitutional relation with the imperial territories and on the failure of the Cortes to take any serious and consis-

[1] Exhumed in 1823, the bodies of the monks of Mora were found to be 'uncorrupted and with a sweet odour'. For the fate of the Franciscans, see P. Sanahuja, *Seráfica provincia de Cataluña*, 539 ff.

[2] See above, p. 127, note 1. The connexion between liberal revolution in Spain and American freedom is illustrated by the expedition of Mina (a nephew of the radical hero) to Mexico in 1817. He fought for a constitutional, not an independent, Mexico—a clear indication of the difference between creole and peninsular liberals.

tent interest in American affairs.[1] The deputies had no reliable information and assumed that only 'a few disturbances' had troubled the joyful acceptance of the constitution; more could be learned of America, said one deputy, 'in a London Tavern than in Madrid'.[2]

The failure of liberal Spain to evolve a liberal American policy, combined with its military impotence, made American independence a fact. The twin prongs of San Martín's expedition, carried by Admiral Cochrane from Chile to Peru, and Bolívar's advance from the north, where he had finally liberated New Granada (1819) and Venezuela (1821), concentrated the entire forces of the continental independence movement against the last strongholds of royalist resistance in Peru. In July 1822 San Martín and Bolívar met at Guayaquil, in modern Ecuador. In December 1824 Bolívar's lieutenant Sucre defeated the royalists at Ayacucho. Spain was exhausted and her armies no longer had any fight left in them. 'This harrassing war is now over,' the captured Spanish commander told General Miller, 'and, to tell the truth, we were all heartily tired of it.'[3]

At the same time New Spain achieved its independence as Mexico. The movement for independence and the ejection of the *gachupines* (peninsular Spaniards who dominated trade and the administration) came more slowly in Mexico because the *gachupines* had acted with decision in the confusion created by the collapse of Spanish authority in the War of Independence and because the movement for independence had taken some of the forms of a radical social revolution favouring the Indians and the poor against the rich creoles—elsewhere in Latin America, the leaders of liberation. This was the unexpected result of the decision of parish priest, Hidalgo, to appeal to the Indians when the creole conspiracy collapsed in 1810; his successor as leader of the revolt against Spain, Morelos, a *mestizo* and former agricultural labourer, was prepared to set

[1] The various schemes and their fate are outlined in M. J. Van Aken, *Pan-Hispanism* (Berkeley, 1959), 8–14.

[2] See M. Fernández Almagro, *La emancipación de América y su reflejo en la conciencia española* (1944), 61 ff., and J. Delgado, *España y Mexico en el siglo XIX* (1950), 10 ff.

[3] There is an excellent account of the battle in Miller's *Memoirs*, ii. 157–79. For the supposed ambivalent attitude of the 'Masonic' officers, see M. Fernández Almagro, *Emancipación*, Appendixes ii and ix. S. de Madariaga, *Bolívar* (Mexico, 1951, ii. 300–1), argues that the battle was 'fixed'.

off an agrarian revolution.[1] Before the prospect of expropriation or massacre by 'an ignorant and infuriated body of Indians' the wealthy creoles were ready to support the Spanish administration in spite of their own desire for independence.[2] Thus royal authority was maintained in Mexico when it was vanishing elsewhere.

In 1820, however, the prospect of a liberal constitution and anti-clerical legislation imposed by a liberal metropolis flung the conservatives and the Church into the independence movement; now only an independent Mexico, cut off from liberal Spain, could preserve the old order.[3] They found a leader in an ambitious creole officer, Agustín de Iturbide, whose Plan of Iguala was both an instrument of independence and a guarantee of conservative interests. The plan preserved the possibility of a Spanish monarch of an independent state and was accepted by the Spanish local commander; the Cortes, however, rejected a settlement which might have preserved Mexico as a dynastic apanage. Liberal Spain could not contemplate surrender and in May 1822 Iturbide was declared Emperor of an independent state.

For many years official Spain refused to recognize it had lost America: it cherished illusions of a military come-back in Peru, of a 'spontaneous' return of a continent exhausted by the anarchy of independence. Hence the refusal to recognize the new nations: pressure for reconciliation came from a desire to reopen trade (which had ceased since 1824) and to preserve as Spanish possessions the only remnants of the Empire—Cuba and Puerto Rico.[4] Hence the spread of the belief that

[1] Hidalgo saw that lacking an army he must appeal to the masses, if possible without losing the creoles. For some of the difficulties of trying to harness a popular movement to the interests of the creole *élite* see H. M. Hamill, 'Early psychological warfare in the Hidalgo revolt' (*H.A.H.R.* xli). Loyalty to Ferdinand was one of the devices used to hide the cracks (ibid. 211–12).

[2] Calleja, who commanded the Spanish army, believed that the creoles who fought against Hidalgo were nevertheless disloyal to the Spanish connexion: this was revealed when they used the constitution of 1812 to vote into office men 'interested in the ruin of Spain in this hemisphere' (cf. his reports quoted H. G. Ward, *Mexico in 1827* (London, 1828), 509–25).

[3] For the changed attitude of the higher clergy (who were Spanish as opposed to the creole lower clergy) see K. M. Schmitt, 'The Clergy and the Independence of New Spain' (*H.A.H.R.* xxxiv (1954), 289).

[4] The desire by reconciliation to preserve Cuba from attacks by independent unrecognized nations is the main thesis of J. D. Flinter's *Consideraciones sobre España y sus colonias* (1834). According to Van Aken (*Pan-Hispanism*, 18 ff.) this poor tract was very influential in moulding opinion towards reconciliation.

emancipation had been inevitable and that Spain should not nurse her resentment at a 'premature separation'. Recognition, nevertheless, took sixty years in all. To the last the Spanish view of America was befuddled with illusion: there was really little prospect of re-establishing Spanish prosperity on the basis of trade with an independent and grateful America; except for those articles which especially appealed to Spanish tastes among Americans, peninsular goods were not cheap enough, in a régime of freer trade, to compete with imports from England and the United States.[1] Thus all Spanish interests and hopes were centred on the retention of the Puerto Rican and Cuban markets as privileged preserves, closed to non-Spanish merchants. To Flinter the Antilles were 'worth an Empire'. As for Pan-Hispanism, only the Yankee menace and the laments of troubled American conservatives for a vanished and stable past gave it any substance; it came to nothing in practice.

3. *The Ominous Decade, 1823–1833*

Nowhere have the preconceptions of liberals so distorted the history of Spain as in the description and judgement of what they term 'the ominous decade' (1823–33), presented as a period of unrelieved clerical reaction. 'Nothing good can be accomplished here; this country will tear itself to pieces for years to come.' The despair of Angoulême, Commander of the French army of occupation, at his failure to limit reprisals and impose a moderate settlement, hides the fact that the cruel reaction which he castigated was relatively short.[2] Ferdinand would suffer no liberals near the court; neither would he tolerate talk of a constitution or any kind of political discussion whatsoever. He was not, however, a clerical tyrant in the hands of reactionary *apostólico* ministers. Like other rulers of Spain, he found authoritarianism welcomed after revolutionary anarchy. 'The king gave the peace desired by the intelligent and sought

[1] Spanish flour was twice as expensive as American.

[2] G. de Grandmaison, *L'Expédition française en Espagne* (Paris, 1929), 152. Angoulême could not tolerate reprisals by local authorities in breach of capitulations made by French officers with constitutional forces. By the Ordinance of Andujar (8 August 1823) he prohibited any arrest by Spanish authorities in areas occupied by the French. Angoulême's 'jacobinism' was rejected by his own government.

by the prudent.'[1] In the confusions of the thirties the ominous decade appeared almost desirable as an era of social peace and optimistic expansion. A king who travelled across his kingdom in a single carriage without an escort could not be said to have ruled by brute force.

Ferdinand's system was ministerial despotism, adulterated by the presence in ministries of servants like Ugarte and Calomarde whose political philosophy is summed up in the word with which they addressed the king—*amo*, a term used by domestics to their masters. None of the 'respectable' ministers supported a policy of wholesale proscription; to purify by military tribunals all those who had any connexion with the constitutional government was too vast an operation, entailing the persecution of an entire social class. It was consistently opposed by the French ambassador and the French occupying forces. The army was virtually dissolved and a dossier drawn up on every officer. But by 1827 purification had become something of a formality and Llauder, as Inspector of Infantry, gazetted officers before they had been 'purified'. The control of the composition of the officer corps in the 'new' army was in his hands and it came to consist of professional soldiers rather than of professional royalists.[2] After 1825 persecution was practised officially only when the king was frightened into an alliance with the clericals by attempts at liberal revolution. Thus Valdés's landing in Tarifa (August 1824), a liberal pronunciamiento doomed to failure, allowed the clericals to get rid of the war minister, de la Cruz, who had attempted to dissolve the royalist Volunteers, the strongest arm of reaction. It was not the central government but the restored local authorities who were responsible for the White Terror, a reprisal for the radical terror of 1822–3.[3] Thus in Catalonia a policy of concord and oblivion (1824–7) was imposed by officers of the French army of occupation and the Captain General Campo Sagrado who earned the gratitude

[1] The verdict of Donoso Cortés in his conservative liberal period (*O.C.* (1946), i. 816); cf. Javier de Burgos, *Anales del reinado de Isabel II* (Madrid, 1850), ii. 12.

[2] Nevertheless, officers who had joined secret societies (possibly a quarter of the total strength) were not re-employed. They became a destitute class. Lord Carnarvon, *Portugal and Galicia* (London, 1848), describes 'constitutional' officers 'in a state of great destitution . . . some had died of hunger'.

[3] The activities of the Junta of the Faith in Valencia which condemned a schoolmaster to death for heresy earned a sharp rebuke even from Calomarde; see E. R. Eggers, *Zea Bermúdez y su época* (1958), 97.

of liberal academics by allowing the removal of incriminating books from the university library before its inspection by local purifiers.[1]

The whole of Ferdinand's policy was conditioned, as in his early years, by bankruptcy: he devoted an incredible amount of his time to raising small private loans to pay the palace staff and to minor house-keeping economies. Pure royalism had no answer to the financial problem and the king was bound to listen to the suggestions of his more moderate ministers; these recommended either a modernization of the tax system or a foreign loan. Both were incompatible with pure royalism. A modern tax system would infringe the privileged foral provinces while a unified sacrosanct budget was consistently opposed by reactionaries who regarded it as a covert form of constitutionalism, limiting the king's personal action in a system of 'departmental' ministries. Ferdinand had repudiated the foreign loans of the constitutional government and his attempts to raise money on the Paris and London markets were blocked by bankers, a 'liberal league', in that they had invested heavily in constitutional Spain.[2] There was therefore constant financial pressure on Ferdinand to change to a more liberal system and by a generous amnesty to recall the exiles who were 'poisoning the springs of credit'.

For nine years of the ominous decade the finance ministry was in the hands of Ballesteros. A minor Galician landowner, he was a treasury technician, an enthusiast for the industrial revival of Catalonia and double-entry book-keeping. He was not a liberal but he had strong sympathies with the modern outlook of the *afrancesados*, whose abilities he recognized, and he was prepared to overlook a liberal past in treasury appointments. With such men the years after 1826 saw a revival of enlightened despotism run largely by repentant *afrancesado* administrative technicians.[3]

[1] For the reaction in Catalonia see J. Carrera Pujal, *Cataluña*, ii. 180–90, *et passim*.

[2] The only available loan was that originally made by Gebhardt to the royalist Regency. Ferdinand made a disastrous personal attempt to raise the Gebhardt funds via Aguado, a friend of Rossini and a fruit-wholesaler turned banker, who demanded a 73 per cent. commission. (See Ballesteros's protest in Natalio Rívas Santiago, *Luis López Ballesteros* (1945), 129–40.)

[3] His desire for financial regularity brought him up against royalists; cf. his quarrel, as a protectionist, with the privileges of the royalist Volunteers whose

Even more remarkable was the attempt to propagandize enlightened despotism by the employment of *afrancesado* journalists. The penultimate pose of Ferdinand VII was that of an august patron of the arts, defender of the dramatist Moratín, benefactor of the Prado, who could reasonably expect congratulatory odes from the liberal poet, Quintana. It was Lista, a writer with an *afrancesado* past, who set out to publicize the king's efforts to 'capture intelligence' by fostering industry; all those who represented 'enlightenment and social consequence' should support a government which built roads, endowed Madrid with a primitive Stock Exchange, staged an Industrial Exhibition in 1828, and believed in 'progressive education in the natural sciences and useful arts'.[1] Ferdinand encouraged material progress as a surrogate for liberalism; this was possible in a régime of silence where there were no newspapers but official gazettes, where little was published beyond anodyne literature and devotional works. Progress and despotism were ultimately to prove incompatible: it was one of the propagandists for Ferdinand's new course who established as an axiom that 'where there is industry, liberty is easily born'.

The nature of Ferdinand's government is best revealed by the opposition it encountered. Before 1830 the only serious revolts were those of the extreme royalists. The core of their discontent was Ferdinand's refusal to make his government an *apostólico* concern; not to clear liberals out of jobs which royalists might profitably occupy was 'atrocious persecution'. The royalist Volunteers, originating in the partisans of 1821–3, were intended to be a militarized police corps, directly dependent on the king, and which could be used against a revolution. Detested by most regular officers, unsupported by the government which left their pay to the municipalities, the Volunteers became a semi-organized force of a hundred thousand malcontents.[2]

Extreme royalists in Catalonia, where the protection and

houses could not be searched for contraband. His liberal and *afrancesado* affiliations were noted by Mesonero Romanos who called him patron of 'political and literary phalanx, semi-liberal, composed of the notables of the old *afrancesado* party'.

[1] Cf. Juretschke, *Lista*, 132–49.

[2] Cf. 'Los cuerpos de Voluntarios Realistas' (*Annuario de historia del derecho español* (1936), xxvi), esp. 84 ff. The Volunteers had their own Inspector General and thus escaped the orders of the Captains General.

employment of ex-liberals was particularly noticeable, turned in disgust from Ferdinand to his brother Don Carlos. They found in the clergy of Manresa and Vich a band of propagandists to whom a government which refused to restore the Inquisition was indistinguishable from liberalism. The 'Revolt of the Aggrieved' in Catalonia (1827) is the first Carlist revolt, though Don Carlos refused to sanction it. The conditions which the rebels would have imposed on the king are the first draft of the Carlist programme: dissolution of the liberal army and its replacement by a royalist army; the exile of all liberal government servants; the abolition of 'novelties' like education; the impeachment of the ministry and the restoration of the Inquisition.[1]

The fiction which justified revolt was that the king was 'imprisoned by Freemasons'. This fiction was dispersed by the king's journey to Barcelona and the suppression of the revolt. Ferdinand became the hero of the Barcelona middle classes; they granted him a loan, he rewarded them with protectionist duties. But there could be no permanent royal alliance with any genuine form of liberal sentiment and no consistent policy of any kind. España, the new Captain General of Catalonia, was a fitting representative of the mindless absolutism which persisted as a strand in Ferdinand's government. His tyranny, more than any other single factor, converted Barcelona to liberalism. Fearing liberal contagion from France after 1830, España revived the royalist Volunteers; but in Barcelona only seven officers and twenty men reported for service.[2]

The immediate origins of Carlism as a political party and the beginnings of the process which was to substitute constitutional monarchy for the ministerial despotism of Ferdinand are to be sought in the clash of court factions between 1830 and 1832—a prolonged crisis which was to culminate in the 'Events of La Granja', as the theatrical denouement of September 1832 is known. In December 1830 Ferdinand had married María Cristina of Naples. From her arrival in Spain, María Cristina saw that her power depended on the exclusion of Don Carlos

[1] Cf. A. Pirala, *Historia de la guerra civil* (Madrid, 1889 ed.), i. 57.

[2] It is characteristic of the conflicts of 1823–30 that some of the funds of the Volunteers had been diverted to 'progress', i.e. the Urgel Canal (J. Carrera Pujal, *Cataluña*, ii. 254–5). Liberals always dismissed España as a brutal martinet; he was a conscientious soldier who took immense care in the training of his troops.

from political influence at court and from the succession on Ferdinand's death—obviously not far removed—should she produce a daughter instead of a son, since the right of a female to succeed to the throne was not universally accepted.

There is no reason whatever to impute liberal sympathies to the queen—she took what support she could get from the known opponents of the clerical absolutism associated with Don Carlos: from the liberals of Barcelona, outraged by the Conde de España; from grandees who disapproved of Ferdinand's stingy court and his preference for 'lackeys'; from the army officers who disliked the parallel army of the royalist Volunteers. In March 1830 her faction at court persuaded the king to the decisive step: he published the Pragmatic Sanction which would exclude Don Carlos from the succession *even if* the Queen's child was a daughter. With the birth of Isabella, Carlism seemed condemned to political impotence. It was therefore committed to dispute the legality of the Pragmatic Sanction in order to sustain the claims of Don Carlos to the throne.[1]

Until the death of the king the Carlists, with Don Carlos's public approval, never went beyond attempts to impugn the legality of the Sanction and to fight the queen's party at court. His cause was favoured by a new burst of liberal revolutionary activity. Though the miseries of exile in Euston and Jersey exaggerated rather than healed the divisions between activist radicals and moderates (who hoped for a change of system in Spain rather than a rising set off by invading liberals), the July Revolution of 1830 in France opened up prospects that even the moderates could not resist: Mina, who was backed by the

[1] For the legal rights and wrongs of the succession issue see H. Butler Clarke, *Modern Spain* (Cambridge, 1906), 82–84. The original laws of the *Partidas* governing the succession had been in harmony with Spanish law in general, i.e. they preferred females in default of male heirs of equal consanguinity. Philip V in 1713 introduced the Salic Law which preferred males. In 1789 Charles IV revived the original laws in the Pragmatic Sanction, approved by a Cortes but not published. The weaknesses of the Carlist case were: (i) the 1789 Sanction had the consent of the 'nation' in the Cortes, while the 1713 settlement was a royal decree; (ii) it was an odd argument for a traditional party to prefer the Bourbon Family Law to the medieval *Partidas*. The weaknesses of Isabella's claim were: (i) the 1789 Sanction had never been published (except on one occasion in the War of Independence) nor had it been printed in the collection of laws: thus until 1830 it was assumed by everyone that Carlos's rights were valid; (ii) Carlos had been born in 1788, before the Pragmatic Sanction; his claim therefore anteceded it and could not be cancelled by it.

banker Lafitte, hoped for French support. But this was only given by Louis Philippe as a lever to force diplomatic recognition for himself; when Spanish recognition was forthcoming he dropped the liberals, leaving them with the slender resources of admirers—Tennyson's Cambridge Apostles among them. The liberal invasions were total failures; Torrijos was captured and shot in Malaga; Mina, after incredible hardships, escaped back into France. Such undertakings can only be explained by the political *spes phthisis* of exiles and the working philosophy of the pronunciamiento. No general who 'declared' against the régime expected to engage on a military conquest of his own country: the army, undermined by compromises, would support the symbolic gesture of the *grito*, and the government would collapse as it had in 1820. The invasions of 1831 were one of the many miscalculations as to the degree of disaffection in the army and the binding force of vague promises.

The liberal invasions weakened the forces of moderation in Spain as such enterprises always must. The king turned to the absolutists and there was a revival of political purification. 'The king of Spain', wrote Custine who was in Spain at this time, 'becomes a tyrant through fear.'[1] Reaction isolated the queen at court and left her powerless to resist the Carlist *coup d'état* which took its name from the summer palace of La Granja.

It was there, in the September of 1832, that Ferdinand succumbed to what all his medical advisers believed would be a fatal attack of gout. Alone in La Granja, with her political supporters in Madrid, the queen was bullied into revoking the Pragmatic Sanction when Don Carlos threatened civil war if she maintained her daughter's right on the king's death (17–18 September). In the next week her supporters rallied and on 1 October the whole ministry was replaced by one headed by Cea Burmúdez. This change has been described as a liberal revolution, directed behind the scenes by liberal courtiers like Miraflores. This it was not. It was a defensive reaction of the

[1] Marquis de Custine, *L'Espagne*, ii. 326. He believed the king's fears exaggerated. Spain was not 'infected' except in the 'maritime south'. The total lack of response to Torrijo's desperate invasion proves that even there the countryside was firmly loyal to Ferdinand VII.

queen's faction who sought support by opening the monarchy to the declared enemies of Don Carlos. It was the original contract by which the *cristino* party—so called because it supported María Cristina and the claims of her daughter against the Carlists—was founded: 'Support me and I will support you.'

The terms of the contract did not include a constitution, an inconceivable innovation to a career bureaucrat like Cea; it did imply a change of course within the framework of the traditional monarchy and it may be argued that such a change would bring to power and influence those who would not be content with absolutism tempered by administrative reform. This new course was the work of the 'liberal' wing of Cea's ministry: the universities were opened after a two years' closure; a wider amnesty was granted to former liberals, of whom 10,000 could now return to Spain; the army was purged of known Carlists; the royalist Volunteers were broken as an independent financial and military organization.[1] Most important of all, the king, on his recovery, condemned the Carlists' attempts to force themselves on the country at La Granja, commended the queen's actions, and solemnly republished the Pragmatic Sanction.

Thus, when the king died at last in September 1833, the machinery of the state was in the hands of the *cristinos*. The army had been reformed after 1825 to exclude both extreme liberals and extreme royalists; the soldiers were regularly paid, and the officers reliable professionals—a reversal of Ferdinand's 'neglect' after 1814 which probably saved his daughter's throne. The Captains General and the important military commanders could be counted on to resist a Carlist take-over. Don Carlos was in exile in Portugal, his followers out of favour at court. If his cause was to triumph, Carlism must cease to rely on the power of a court faction and become a popular movement which could defeat the *cristinos* in the field.

With his brother's death the pretender's scruples about encouraging armed rebellion vanished. His chances in a civil war

[1] The funds of the Volunteers were cut down, and the corps was opened to all citizens 'without hateful memories of their former opinions', i.e. destroyed as a pure royalist force.

he had rated highly. 'The nation is for me', he told María Cristina; liberalism was an exotic plant, an affair of 'imbecile grandees', army officers, and littérateurs, without roots in Spain. This was a profound miscalculation. Spanish society had changed in such a manner that the triumph of Carlism was a social and economic and intellectual impossibility.[1]

[1] For these changes see below, pp. 196–209.

V

LIBERALISM AND CARLISM
1833–1840

THE death of Ferdinand VII turned the contentions of court factions into a civil war between the supporters of Don Carlos and the defenders of the throne of Queen Isabella. The Seven Years War, starting as a struggle between two versions of absolute monarchy, one represented by Cea's system and the other by Don Carlos, was transformed, by the enforced alliance of María Cristina with the liberals, into a war between the great principles of liberalism and reaction. As in 1936, idealists, journalists, as well as adventurers and soldiers of fortune, descended on Spain because they felt that great issues of European civilization were at stake on her battlefields. The morals of intervention, the military value and pay claims of foreign volunteers, or the smuggling of arms across the French frontiers occupied a place in the European press of the 1830's that was occupied a hundred years later by non-intervention, the International Brigade, and the vicissitudes of the Spanish Revolution and the Civil War. *The Times*, for instance, in the 1830's devoted a twice-weekly column to detailed description of military and political events in Spain.[1] In both cases this projection of the conscience of Europe into Spain distorted and oversimplified the issues at stake.

1. *Liberals and Radicals, and the Royal Statute of 1834*

The pivot of the defence of Isabella's throne against the Carlists was her mother, María Cristina, appointed queen

[1] There was an endless correspondence devoted to the performance and grievances of Evans's troops who were volunteers co-operating with the liberal armies on the Northern Front. As with the International Brigade, conservatives impugned the motives of the volunteers, dismissing them as 'Irish blackguard ruffians' serving for pay. Evans's account of his service is contained in *Memoranda of the Contest in Spain* (London, 1840). The difference between English attitudes in the 1830's and in 1936–9 was that a large number of Englishmen, as a consequence of Wellington's campaigns, knew Spain well.

regent by Ferdinand's will. As long as fear of the anarchy of '23 persisted and the king's life stood between the 'enlightened classes' and Carlism, intelligent men could regard the unreformed monarchy as 'the sole anchor of salvation left to Spain'. With Ferdinand's death, as he himself had prophesied, the cork came out of the beer-bottle. Faced with the Carlist revolt the monarchy was forced to come to terms with what a contemporary called 'the ideas of felicity which abounded in the imagination of the rich and enlightened'; if the queen regent's party was to defeat Carlism in the field it would have to call on the resources and abilities of those who held that the refusal to grant a liberal constitution had kept Spain 'below the level of Europe'.[1]

Cea Bermúdez, inherited as prime minister from Ferdinand, hoped to hold Spain to the only system he knew, the enlightened despotism of which he was a model servant. Working fourteen hours a day, seeing only his immediate family, he had no notion of the growing demand for some form of representative government. To Cea the demand for political reform, as opposed to administrative improvement, was the platform of an ambitious group of politicians with no support outside Madrid; to sacrifice the monarchy to the demands of this group could only drive a conservative country to Carlism and alienate the Eastern courts whose friendship it was Cea's obsession to gain. He would neither modify his support of absolutism in Portugal (liberals regarded Isabella's struggle against Don Carlos as one with Queen María of Portugal's contest with the clericalist conservative pretender, Dom Miguel) nor listen to appeals from the British and French ambassadors to moderate his anti-liberal intransigence. Hence his declaration, in October, that he would maintain the traditional order in Church and state, a declaration which Guizot considered an irretrievable blunder.[2]

The group of courtiers, soldiers, and bureaucrats who, together with their allies in the aristocratic *salons* of Madrid, engineered Cea's fall were fully aware of the dangers of a re-

[1] The best expression of this standpoint is Miguel de Pedro's *Reflexiones políticas* (1834), from which all quotations are taken.

[2] F. P. Guizot, *Mémoires* (Paris, 1858–67), iv. 66, 316. Guizot had a high opinion of Cea. For Palmerston's hostile views see C. Webster, *The Foreign Policy of Palmerston* (London), i. 374.

surgence of the democratic radicalism of the twenties. They wished for a constitutional settlement based on 'prudent liberty' which 'would win over sensible opinion from exaggerated pretensions'. Rather than appeal to what Burgos called 'the licentiousness of popular cliques and the manœuvres of secret societies', the enemies of Cea preferred to destroy his system of political immobility by pressure at court and by accepting the intervention of like-minded generals. Quesada and Llauder, Captains General of Old Castile and Catalonia, presented memorials demanding political reform, the first example of the new forms of military politics systematized after 1837. Llauder disowned any desire to pose as 'interpreter of the national will'. He nevertheless recognized the central axiom of military action: the protest of the generals put Cea in a position 'in which it was impossible to govern'.[1] A conservative constitutional settlement, perhaps going a little further than Ferdinand's promises in 1814, imposed on the monarchy by respectable soldiers, would win liberal enthusiasm for the war against Carlism without admitting the revolution—in Llauder's own words 'the throne of Isabella II without tumults and without violence', that is, without the *exaltados*.[2] This settlement was embodied in a new constitution, the Royal Statute of April 1834, drafted by the ministry of Martínez de la Rosa who succeeded Cea in January.

To the crown, such a respectable brand of liberalism seemed a safe investment; the Royal Statute was based on the *Charte* of 1814—a settlement that had been acceptable to the restored Bourbon monarchy in France. The long-term dangers of the liberal investment appeared when the main clause of the original contract—'the exclusion of the exaggerated pretensions of radicalism'—could not be maintained in the face of military defeat at the hands of the Basque Carlists. The 'safe' constitution of 1834 could not command the loyalty of all liberals; it was a creation of one group of amnestied liberal

[1] For Llauder's own account of his action see *Memorias documentadas del Teniente General Don Manuel Llauder* (1844), 70 ff. Llauder professed to base his action on Ferdinand's decree of 1 May 1814 which promised to restore the traditional Cortes 'anchor of our salvation'.

[2] Cf. the views of Miraflores in *Memorias* (1843), v, i. xv, LXI; J. de Burgos, *Anales*, i. 168–70, 226. Burgos, after first supporting Cea, came to the conclusion that limited concessions were inevitable.

exiles who accepted power on terms that still excluded another—those who were not amnestied until Christmas 1834. Once the *exaltados* were back in politics liberalism divided, as it had during the first constitutional period, into a radical and a conservative stream. These two streams were to flow into the *Progresista* or Progressive and the *Moderado* or Moderate parties.

After 1837 these two groupings, which in differing re-incarnations were to divide power and patronage within the constitutional monarchy until its fall in 1931, appear as two tendencies distinct in constitutional doctrine, in social composition, and in their views on the conduct of the war and the foreign alliances to be favoured. Neither in the formative period, which lasted at least until 1837, nor in their heyday were the two groups disciplined parties, nor did they understand the conventions which govern the alternation of parties in a mature constitutional system. They often behaved like the parties of eighteenth-century England, with government patronage as the glue of politics. It was the fluidity of this system which was to make the crown, as the 'moderating power', the essential pivot of the political mechanism.

The Moderates were the oligarchs of liberalism.[1] There were the landowners of Biscay who feared the intrusion of the lawyers and merchants of San Sebastian and Bilbao into their monopoly of local government. There were aristocrats like the marqués de Miraflores, courted by María Cristina in the difficult days of 1833, and with no taste for the priests and obscure favourites of the impoverished Carlist court. There were career civil servants—their most distinguished representative was perhaps Javier de Burgos—representing 'the aristocracy of public office' which, according to Miraflores, had replaced the old aristocracy as a political force;[2] bureaucrats with no liking for the new political life yet prepared to make the best of a bad job by allying with the most respectable forces within it. Established lawyers, who managed the affairs of aristocratic landowners, and *afrancesado* journalists, who hated the patriotic exclusiveness of radicalism and who could work their passage within conservative liberalism, were likely to belong to the Moderates.

[1] It must be emphasized that the names Moderate and Progressive, until 1840, were not in common use. The social groupings and political doctrines of the two parties are reasonably clear in 1834 and the Revolution of 1836 finally crystallized the two parties.

[2] For Javier de Burgos see p. 196.

After the events of August 1836, which forced a radical ministry on the crown by a sergeants' revolt,[1] conservative liberalism went increasingly in fear of a primitive social revolution using as its instruments democratically elected municipalities and the National Militia—both enshrined in the Progressive constitution of 1837. In 1836 the older Urban Militia became a force open to all householders and tradesmen 'procuring their living in a way satisfactory to the municipal authority', which made out commissions and to whose orders the militia commanders were subject. In combination with municipalities elected on a low property franchise, the militia would become the private army of radical town councils, licensed to terrorize the supporters of a conservative constitution. One of these crude militants described his activities to Borrow: 'If we meet any person who is obnoxious to us, we fall upon him, and with a knife or bayonet generally leave him wallowing in his blood on the pavement; no one but a national would be permitted to do that.'[2] The Moderates regarded the militia with horror; Istúriz was said so to detest militiamen that he refused to walk in a street where they might be seen. Together with the municipal revolution the militia symbolized the end of the notables; they would have to obey their cobblers and tailors in the town hall and their butchers and barbers in the streets.[3]

The social composition of the Moderates dictated the content of their constitutional doctrine. The task of their political thought was to find a defence for a ruling class which should not be based on traditionalist (i.e. Carlist) premises. The Burkean hue of their thought comes from their mixture of the historical conservatism of Jovellanos (the Moderates were known as *Jovellanistas* by radicals) with principles derived from the French *doctrinaires* and the study of the English constitution. Martínez de la Rosa, who had been an exile in Paris, represented French ideas while Alcalá Galiano, who gradually abjured his radical past, came to admire the stable politics of

[1] For the mutiny of La Granja see below pp. 177–8.

[2] G. Borrow, *Bible in Spain* (Everyman edition), 116. For a description of the militia see Duncan, F., *The English in Spain* (London, 1877), 333, appendix.

[3] J. de Burgos, *Anales*, iii. 44 ff.; cf. the reaction of the upper middle classes to the militia in July 1936.

England and the practical utilitarians he had met in London.[1] Between them they founded the Moderate creed and were the nearest approach to original thinkers thrown up by Spanish liberalism. The reconciliation of liberty and order, of progress and tradition was achieved by the rejection of abstract political principle: in its place the Moderates presented what they chose to conceive as the historic constitution of Spain.

Their political theory assumed that the traditional society of simple manners and recognized hierarchies, praised by Catholic apologists like the Catalan priest Balmes, was dead; in a modern society, claims to political power must be based on riches and its product, intelligence.[2] Constitutions could not be based on the sovereignty of the people and to deduce wide suffrage from such an unreal premise would be to prefer ignorance to enlightenment. Political power must follow social power and political principles be subject to 'public utility', by which Martínez de la Rosa meant existing social interests. Like the Girondins, the Moderates talked of Athenian elegance, of the rights of those who dressed well, read intelligent newspapers, knew what was going on in contemporary Europe, and were no longer deceived by Jacobin slogans.[3] They became the outspoken defenders of middle-class rule, by which they meant the rule of all socially significant interests except those committed to Carlism, and it was to defend these interests that the Royal Statute of 1834 was designed.[4] Stripped of historic trappings, the constitution of 1845—the classical constitution of conservative liberalism—was to serve the same purpose.

Like the liberators of 1812, the makers of the constitution of 1834 claimed to have 're-established in full force and vigour the fundamental laws of the monarchy'. Progress and tradition,

[1] Alcalá Galiano believed constitutions must reflect, not abstract theories of sovereignty, but social forces; thus, whatever its constitutions, England would be an aristocratic society. Spain was predominantly a 'plebeian' society (hence the genuine popularity of Ferdinand VII). To avoid plebeian government either in the form of a 'royalist democracy' or of 'mob' liberalism the middle and upper classes must unite against the plebeians and restrict the governing class to themselves.

[2] Cf. Alcalá Galiano's later views in *Lecciónes de derecho* (1843), 48.

[3] Thus Sartorius, a former *exaltado*, felt attracted to the Moderates by 'his social relations and his idealization of all that was elegant' (*Historia del Eczmo. Sr. Don Luis Sartorius* (1850), esp. 9 ff.).

[4] The constitution of 1834 was drawn up before the groups that were to make the Moderate party had properly coalesced: nevertheless it represents the views of those who were to be that party's intellectual leaders.

order and liberty would be reconciled by the rejection of abstract principle in favour of the processes of history which had created the 'internal constitution' of Spain. This constitution, recognized but not created by the Cortes, embodied the independent and parallel sovereignties of *rex* and *regnum*, of the crown and Cortes. This avoided recognition of either the democratic dogma of the constituent powers of the nation or the royalist claim that constitutions were the gracious concessions of a king. Translated into legal terms the fiction of an endeavour to 'save old institutions by rejuvenating them' meant a strong executive as the emanation of the prerogatives of the crown; a Cortes summoned and dismissed by the crown with no right to initiate legislation; a second chamber composed of grandees and ecclesiastical, civil, and military dignitaries nominated by the crown; a high property franchise.

Yet no amount of historical Romanticism could hide the fact that the Procurators and Notables of the new constitution were something other than medieval estates. The 'modern' principles of public debate and a free press would break through the careful limitations of the Statute and establish the responsibility of ministers and the historic constitution would become as uncomfortable for conservatives as the medieval costumes which the deputies were to wear. Thus radical deputies soon embarrassed the ministry of Martínez de la Rosa by exploiting those rights which the constitution could not deny: they sought to expand the right of petition, the right to reply to the address from the throne, the right to hear ministers' reports in order to break down all the carefully drafted limitations on the political initiative and power of the lower house and to demand a new constitution altogether.[1] No ministry could survive against a consistently hostile lower chamber. When the Cortes broke the ministry of Istúriz, a royal nominee, the queen regent appealed by a dissolution (22 May 1836) 'to the nation to judge the differences dividing my ministers and the deputies'. When confronted with a conflict between the twin sovereignties of history—the monarch and the Cortes—Moderate constitutional doctrine collapsed. It could resolve

[1] For an account of radical tactics see H. Baumgarten, *Geschichte Spaniens*, iii. 282 ff.

its contradictions only by an appeal either to military force or to the sovereign nation.

It was the sovereign power of the nation, rejected by the Moderates as the foundation of constitutional law, which was the slogan of the Progressive party and had provided the doctrinal foundations for the constitution of 1812. To the main body of the Progressives, the constitution which had given Spanish liberalism its European reputation was becoming an embarrassing heritage; once in power, they substituted for it the constitution of 1837—to remain until 1869 the classic expression of advanced liberalism. Relatively jejune in the declarations of abstract principle, it was drafted by philosophic radicals who, influenced by English example, admired progress and saw its connexion with stable government. It was an attempt to find a simple, modern, and efficient instrument of parliamentary government; unlike the Moderates, the Progressives made no concessions to historic revivalism and were prepared 'to adopt from foreigners improvements to maintain liberty'.

The constitution of 1837 therefore differed radically from the Codex of 1812. It provided for a second chamber nominated by the crown from lists presented by the electors; ministers were chosen by the crown and could sit in the Cortes (a radical deviation from the dogmas of Cadiz); the crown could dismiss and summon the Cortes and the only remnant of the 1812 determination to imprison the crown was the automatic summoning of the Cortes should the crown attempt to rule without a parliament. The breach with Moderate constitutional thought lay in the sanction of the constitution rather than its content in that it drew its validity from the sovereignty of the nation and was *accepted* by the crown. Only one clause made the constitution a party constitution; the municipalities were to be popularly elected and were to control the National Militia. Otherwise the Moderate leaders recognized it for what it was—a workable constitution, respectable rather than radical in tone.

How, then, were the Progressives distinct from the Moderates? They were more radical Europeanizers than the conservative liberals. Their attack on the Church was more resolute, their economic individualism more radical than that of the

Moderates, but it was calculated neither to capture the loyalty of the poor nor to alienate the sympathies of the rich. Like the Moderates, the Progressives accepted that political and property rights were concomitant and justified the rule of an 'enlightened' middle class; but their criteria of property were more modest while they regarded enlightenment as having spread beyond the upper reaches of the middle class. These differences were matters of emphasis rather than principle. Thus there was always a sense in which liberalism could be defined as merely anti-Carlism and, as a consequence, that the 'harmony of the liberal family' demanded a one-party system. The vision of a re-united liberal party haunted politicians for years to come.[1]

What distinguished the two groups most clearly was the Progressives' theory of the legitimacy of revolution; the Moderates rejected the radical tradition of revolution while the Progressives were its embarrassed dependants.[2] Thus the *exaltado* heritage within the Progressive party lay not in doctrine but in political technique: the sovereign nation could be called to the barricades when no 'legal' means existed by which the Progressives could come to power.

The sovereign nation made, by the instrument of a constituent Cortes, a constitution, a fundamental code; if this constitution was attacked by the conservative parliamentary majority of an Ordinary Cortes, then there was a 'legal right of rebellion'. This was the argument of the Progressives when the Moderates attempted to modify the constitution of 1837, and the issue in the Revolution of 1840.[3] If the crown chose evil counsellors who tampered with the constitution, or when it refused to respect the supposed will of the nation by maintaining power 'illegitimately' in the hands of the political opponents of the

[1] For a short discussion of the persistence of the ideal of a single liberal party see D. Sevilla Andrés, 'Los partidos políticos hasta 1868' (*Revista general de derecho*, 1958), xiv. 682 ff.

[2] Thus a tripartite division was used by *The Times* and by the British ambassador in his reports. *The Times* calls the three parties *moderés*, *tiers parti*, and *exaltés*.

[3] 'When congresses, *without special powers from the people*, infringe the constitution . . . then one of two things follows: either the constitution dies and law is the caprice of a tyrannical congress . . . or the congress dies . . . and its dispositions cannot be sanctioned by the crown or create obligations of obedience in the subjects.' (Address of the Provisional Junta, 4 Sept. 1840, quoted *Reseña histórica del glorioso alzamiento de 1840* (1840), 58–64.)

Progressives, then sovereignty reverted to the nation. Constitutional government, argued Mina, meant that the people could pronounce against ministers without incurring the charge of rebellion against the crown. Nothing could illustrate more clearly the extremist lack of sympathy with the mechanics of liberal parliamentarianism. A 'legitimate' right to revolt distinguished constitutional government from absolutism.[1] When the Moderates wished to rebel in 1843 they could not rest their revolution on their own Burkean premisses and were forced to borrow a theory of constitutional rebellion from their opponents.

It was not consistency of principle that kept the Progressives true to popular revolution, but political necessity: the hostility of the crown and the electoral strength of the Moderates within a restricted franchise left elevation by revolution as the only means to office. Thus in 1835, 1836, and 1840 the radical liberals were swept into power by a provincial urban revolution, aided in 1836 by a sergeant's mutiny and in 1840 by Espartero's army. The Moderates, observed Arrazola one of their leaders, would rule most of the time because they could draw on the strength of generalized conservative feeling alarmed by the excesses of democracy; the Progressives must 'make up for lack of numbers by energy'—in other words, break through the resistance of the court and the countryside by revolution and then *create* from the government what Mendizábal called new interests, that is a stable class basis for Progressive politics.[2]

The course of these revolutions, difficult to map in the sources, would seem to involve three stages. First came the primitive provincial revolution which spread 'like a contagious disease' from town to town. It usually originated in an obscure local incident which released endemic discontents; mobs gathered and the local authorities lost control. In the second stage local Progressive politicians and notables captured the popular revolution, 'restoring social peace' by setting up a Junta of respectable citizens, sometimes afforced by a representative of the people. This may be called the committee stage of revolution in which local excesses were tamed but during

[1] F. Espoz y Mina, *Memorias*, v. 245. No right to revolt existed in an absolute government; it did 'where the people exercised sovereignty in union with the crown'.

[2] See A. Pirala, *Historia de la guerra civil*, iii. 614–15.

which the central government abdicated control of the country to a network of local committees or newly formed municipalities. The final stage, therefore, was the reimposition, by a ministry that 'represented' the revolution, of central government control. In the jargon of the time, the primitive revolution was the work of the *populacho*, the 'plebeian dregs' whose excesses were either deplored or excused as a revolutionary necessity; the second stage was dominated by the *pueblo*, the respectable representatives of the sovereign people: the third stage was the reconciliation of order and liberty by the government carried to power in Madrid by provincial revolutions it must seek to master.[1]

Almost always in the primitive stage of the revolution two conditions are present: some sharpening of the misery of the urban masses and the fear of Carlist plots and government treason. Each outburst corresponds fairly exactly with industrial dislocation or unemployment (especially in Barcelona, rapidly becoming a revolutionary capital) and with high wheat prices. Disturbances nearly always came in 'dear' months and no doubt represent the direct reaction to near starvation and *la vie chère* familiar in the history of the French Revolution. Wheat prices doubled between 1833 and 1835 and the most consistent demand of the primitive revolution was the abolition of the *consumos*, the indirect taxes which kept up the price of food.

As in the Civil War of 1936 the presence in every town of fifth columnists created an atmosphere of tension and suspicion. Surrounded by a Carlist countryside, with no trust in the government's conduct of the war, local radicals easily saw themselves as Jacobins saving the revolution from treason. This mentality accounts for certain characteristic phenomena of

[1] The troubles of Valencia in 1835 can be taken as an illustration of the course of revolution. On 5 August, in a town filled with refugees from the Carlist countryside, the Captain General, Almodóvar, could not prevent an attack on the prison. Next day the town was invaded by peasants demanding the abolition of *consumos* and feudal dues. By means of a Junta of respectable Progressives Almodóvar regained some control; in September news of a Carlist massacre set off a second popular revolution of angry crowds from which Almodóvar fled. The militia was thrown open to all citizens, but these 'scandalous elements' were once more defeated (Vincente Boix, *Historia de la ciudad y reino de Valencia* (1845), iii. 291 ff.). According to Mariano de Caberizo (pamphlet containing unprinted article addressed to *Eco de Comercio*, Cádiz, 1835) the 'scandalous elements' numbered sixty, the only accurate estimate familiar to me of the size of an extremist group sufficiently strong to seize power for a short time.

these primitive waves of 'anarchism': convent-burning, prison massacres, and popular brutality.[1] General Bassa's body was dragged through the streets of Barcelona, General Quesada's severed hand passed round the tables of the *Café Nuevo*. It was the defensive reaction of the Great Revolution, acted out by obscure *meneurs*; waiters, pedlars, carpenters, small shop-keepers, the 'characters' of working-class quarters imagined themselves 'bloody parodies of Robespierre', arresting suspect priests, preaching revolutionary war against the Carlists. Even their language is reminiscent of the Hébertistes: dear bread was the fault of the aristocrats who fattened on the sweat of the people.[2]

The last operation of the revolution was its most hazardous and delicate. How could politicians whose power was based on the 'tremendous rage of the people' tame revolutionary local authorities? The government must master the committee stage in order to re-establish the normal hierarchies of administrative command by dissolving the Juntas and dismissing a portion of patriot officials. The alliance with popular revolution invariably broke on the necessities of ordered government. However tactful the treatment of provincial enthusiasts, a gap developed between the Madrid leaders and the provincial rank and file who saw in the reimposition of central control a betrayal of the revolution.[3] Espartero's rule was a long process of alienation from the revolution that had made him Regent in 1840. By 1843 the gap between leaders and masses had become the central weakness of the Progressive party.

This gap reflected the social heterogeneity of the Progressive party. The Moderates represented a relatively uniform aristocratic, *haut bourgeois*, military and professional grouping. The Progressives counted generals and sergeants, needy jour-

[1] Prison massacres usually correspond either with Carlist raids or Carlist atrocities, e.g. the January massacres of 1836 in Barcelona came after news of a Carlist execution of liberal officers at Hort.

[2] *The Times*, 8 Dec. 1835. These *meneurs* gave a formless outburst revolutionary shape: thus, as in 1936, convent-burning was organized rather than spontaneous, cf. the remarks of J. Coroleu, *Memorias de un menestral* (Barcelona, 1946), 114, 'the perpetrators were acting on a prepared plan'.

[3] Cf. Mina's difficulties as Captain General of Catalonia. As a radical Progressive he paid homage to the 'heroic cry of Catalona': he nevertheless was anxious to absorb and control the spontaneous Barcelona Junta by a governmental creation (*Memorias*, v. 256–70).

nalists and wholesale merchants, respectable lawyers and bull-fighters. Hence the obsession of Progressive leaders with the artificial creation by legislation of 'interests', of a class that represented the Progressive revolution. Yet Progressivism obstinately remained a system of beliefs rather than a coalition of interests. The vaguer these beliefs, the more easily they covered the cracks in the social base. 'We professed an abstract kind of liberalism, not very clear, not always logical, afflicted with a certain mysticism in virtue of which we accepted conventional formulae as sacred axioms, the more respectable in our eyes as they were abstruse and mysterious.' Enthusiasm for a vague ideology was later used by Federal Republicans in order to avoid the dangers of drafting a programme that would drive asunder interests combined by oratorical formulae.

The core of the party were the *pretendientes*, those sections of the underemployed urban middle classes who were dependent on government posts for a livelihood, a class whose miseries and humiliations are a recurring theme in the novels of Galdós.[1] To be an aspirant for a government post was almost an honoured, and certainly a recognized profession, entailing ritual visits to ministries and the cultivation of the *prohombres* of the party. As in modern India or southern Italy they were a class educated (often very crudely) to pretensions and prospects beyond the absorptive capacity of an underdeveloped society. It is impossible to understand the politics of mid-century Spain without bearing constantly in mind how numerous was this class; in 1840 there were 3,636 applicants for thirty-three places in the Post Office.[2] It was the struggle for the town hall's patronage which gave politics their meaning for most Spaniards and made municipal government the central issue between 1838 and 1840. Each party had its 'aristocracy of local mandarins' and its horde of clients. Each wished to control local government in order to maintain them.[3]

This situation created especial difficulties for the Progressive leadership: without enough pasture for the beasts to feed on, those left outside, when patronage was divided out among the

[1] There is a characteristic portrait of a *pretendiente* in the opening chapters of his *Mendizábal*.

[2] A. Pirala, *Guerra civil*, iii. 712.

[3] Pastor Díaz (*O.C.* v. 36–37) maintains that the Progressive 'mandarins' exerted their influence through debts, &c.

pretendientes, went into opposition; the dissident Progressive opposition of 1840–3 was considered as a party of those for whom Espartero's governments could not find jobs. With every Progressive revolution, Juntas showered posts on local supporters, only to find their appointments refused by the government the revolution had brought to power. Once again this inevitable and necessary pruning of the Bohemian world of self-appointed functionaries was regarded as a betrayal of the masses by the leaders.

The incidence of misery and the threats of Carlism gave revolution its geography: in 1835 its centre was Andalusia, where there was an attempt to revert to the 1808 plan of a Central Junta of the southern towns imposed by an 'army' led on Madrid by the Conde de Navas in a Phrygian bonnet. In 1837 the neuralgic points were Saragossa, Barcelona, and Malaga whence the movement spread north. Madrid was thus exposed to a pincer movement of revolution from Aragon–Catalonia and Andalusia–Estremadura.

Madrid was not a revolutionary capital; it had to be captured by the revolution of the provinces. Securely garrisoned by loyal troops, a population of *empleados* and shopkeepers dependent on court and aristocratic custom, it showed little initiative in popular revolution. Radicals cursed the 'artificial' capital and their weakness accounts for the penchant for street *coups* organized by secret societies against weak governments.[1] In November 1834 the command of the streets was entrusted to an officer, whose twenty-four years as a second lieutenant laid him open to the blandishments of the societies. His men seized the Puerta del Sol, the central square of Madrid, but the movement collapsed for want of popular support.

Thus in both 1835 and 1836 Moderate governments held Madrid when the provinces were in open revolt. In 1835 the Urban Militia were successfully disarmed by regular soldiers and General Quesada put down a *coup* planned by the secret societies when boys calling 'The Constitution or Death' got no popular support; in 1836, but for the government's terror at the

[1] The most famous of these societies was the *Isabelina* organized on *carbonari* lines by Aviraneta, the hero of many of Pío Baroja's novels. Its political aims are obscure and in 1834 it plotted for a moderate constitution under the patronage of Don Francisco, the queen's uncle. It included most of the radical firebrands.

sergeants' revolt in La Granja, the 'brute bull' might again have defeated the revolution in Madrid almost single-handed.[1] Madrid was usually the last great town to pronounce.[2]

2. *The Politics of Liberalism, 1835–1840, and the Rise of Espartero*

In the spring and summer of 1835 repeated changes in the army commands had failed to bring decisive victory for the *cristino* army, engaged against the Carlist bands in the north. Martínez de la Rosa, believed that the war would be won by a constitution which would rally what he called 'the great interests of society', experienced generals, and French support under the terms of the Quadruple Alliance.[3] He was exposed, not merely to the opposition in the Cortes, but to a revival of Jacobin patriotism in the towns; radicals believed the war would be won by a *levée en masse* and the elimination of traitors by the people's justice, that is, by a revival of the *exaltado* tradition. In reply to generals and politicians who looked to ordered government and French aid as the recipe for victory, the radicals chanted appeals to the patriotism of 1808. 'Il faudrait faire un appel au peuple.'[4]

When French help did not come to aid the government against reaction in the north and 'anarchy' in liberal Spain, Martínez de la Rosa resigned (7 June 1835). His successor Toreno, in spite of his attack on Church property and the first real victory over the Carlists (in the battle of Mendigorría, 16 July 1835), succeeded no better in disarming the suspicions of the radicals; in July a wave of provincial revolutions reduced his government to impotence. To save what could be saved of the 1834 settlement by shifting its centre of gravity to the left, Toreno had called Mendizábal to the Ministry of Finance from

[1] There is a splendid eyewitness account of the effect of Quesada's bravery on a large mob in Borrow's *Bible in Spain*, 135–40.

[2] An exception to this rule was the 1845 opposition to the new fiscal system. The British minister considered that the August *émeute* 'might have ensured another revolution' had the National Militia still been in existence (*F.O.*, 23 Aug. 1845).

[3] For the course of the war see section 3, pp. 190–4, below. The attractions of the French alliance to Moderates proved permanent and in 1840 María Cristina and the Moderate exiles went to Paris as to a second home. Radicals never wearied of illustrating the personal and intellectual connexions of Moderates with the oppressors of 1808 and 1823, thus equating patriotism and radicalism.

[4] San Miguel's remark to Elliot (who had come out to negotiate an agreement to save the lives of prisoners of war). (*F.O.*, Elliot to Palmerston, 11 May 1835.)

a twelve years' exile in London. On 14 September 1835 Mendizábal became prime minister in the hopes that his revolutionary reputation would contain the radical revolt.

Mendizábal was thus the first statesman called upon to master from Madrid the creeping provincial revolution that had brought him to power; his solution was an endeavour to restore 'harmony' by absorbing the revolutionary Juntas into the legal Provincial Deputations and by distributing jobs to local *pretendientes*. This was the solution essayed by the Republican government in the autumn of 1936; to conservatives this method of swamping revolution was to compromise with anarchy and call it government.

Mendizábal did not come to power as leader of a party. His professed aim was the 'reconciliation of parties', 'the maintenance of the harmony of the liberal family' by a revision of the Royal Statute in order to remove some of the features obnoxious to radicals. It was in the muddled debates on the franchise (for the Cortes which should revise the Statute) that *ad hoc* liberal harmony vanished and that the lineaments of the two parties emerged. When, in the Cortes of 1836, conservative liberals allied with the crown to dismiss Mendizábal, he was forced to move to the left and ally with Calatrava and the *exaltados*. This alliance, based not on liberal reconciliation but on party revenge, was brought to power by the Revolution of 1836 and was the origin of the Progressive party.

Mendizábal is more than the first political hero of the Progressive party; to later generations of Spaniards he was the first modern statesman. A Jew who had made his reputation out of financing Portuguese liberalism, a huge man, impressive even with his gold chain and bedroom slippers, he boasted that he was neither an aristocrat nor a politician but simply a business man.[1] To the radicals he was a revolutionary dictator, the Jupiter of Reform whose system would save the country and whose name would be blessed in the most miserable villages of Spain.[2] To conservative liberals he appeared as a hybrid of Law and Cromwell, Cagliostro and Robespierre. In fact he

[1] Mendizábal's Jewish origins were exploited by his opponents. In caricatures he was portrayed with a tail with the motto 'Come on boys, after the Jew. Pull the tail of Juanillo' (F. Soldevila, *Historia* (1922), vii. 105–6).

[2] Cf. A. García Tejero, *Historia política-administrativa de Mendizábal* (1858), 145–8.

was the first of the iron surgeons who, with foreign nostrums, would save a country that had lost confidence in its capacity to save itself.[1] Hence his virtue was the mystery that surrounded an unknown, untried man who had long lived abroad. When the Cortes in January 1836, by a vote of confidence, gave Mendizábal full powers to implement his system they were surrendering to a wizard. Unfortunately the first modern statesman of Spain turned out to be a second-rate merchant banker to whom energy—to use an emotive term of the mid-century political vocabulary—was a substitute for political talent.

What was Mendizábal's famous system that would win the war against the Carlists?[2] It was what he called 'the astonishing and magic power of credit' which could finance a new conscript army. Where the Moderates put their hopes in a French expeditionary corps, Mendizábal trusted to his twelve years' experience of the London money market. To get an English loan he was prepared to sacrifice the support of Catalan Progressives by the abolition of prohibitions on English cloth (securing the interest on a loan by an import duty of 25 per cent. on admitted textiles) or by the mortgage of the Cuban Customs. Villiers, the English minister, who had advised the queen 'as an English gentleman' to appoint Mendizábal, favoured these schemes; Palmerston rejected them because he rightly feared the loan would fail and would worsen relations with France to whom Mendizábal was little better than a paid English agent. Mendizábal's English loan collapsed when the speculative interest in Spanish bonds evaporated in the crash of 1835. English investors, Ricardo told Palmerston, were more interested in railway stock than Spanish loans.[3]

[1] For the practice and theory of iron surgery see below, pp. 526, 531, 567, 574–81.

[2] Some branches of the system were only added in the Mendizábal–Calatrava ministry of 1836–7 (see below, p. 178). For the sake of analysis these later additions have been included in the description of the system as a whole.

[3] C. Webster, *Palmerston*, i. 451; cf. J. H. Palmer, *Causes and Consequences of the Pressure on the Money Market* (London, 1837). Spanish bonds became 'the football of the stock exchange'. The quotation of 'Active' Spanish Bonds for 1836–7 are as follows (from *The Times*): 1835, April 69*s.*, June 34*s.*, September 41*s.*, November 48*s.*; 1836, January 51*s.*, March 42*s.*, April 49*s.*, May 38*s.* The worst fall comes in September 1836, after the revolution of La Granja, 29*s.* *The Times* calls these movements (26 July 1836) 'the most extraordinary series of fluctuations that has ever occurred'.

Without the money to pay it, the famous levy of 100,000 men remained an affair of ill-equipped and mutinous conscripts.

It was the second limb of Mendizábal's system—the attack on church property and the liberation of the land—that secured his place as a founding father of the Progressive party. This attack was closely connected with his credit schemes; the church lands, converted into *bienes nacionales*, would be used to pay off the National Debt and would restore the government's borrowing power. After 1820 there could be nothing original in an attack on the Church; indeed the offensive was started by Mendizábal's more moderate predecessors, and his attack on church lands was regarded as the continuation of a liberal policy, reversed unjustly by the despotism of Ferdinand VII;[1] he merely extended its scope. In March 1836 he converted *all* monastic property into *bienes nacionales* and, in July 1837, proposed the sale of the landed endowment of the secular church together with the abolition of tithes.[2] The attack proceeded to embrace the jurisdiction of the Church; in a civil war the Carlist sympathies of many local priests led the state to reassert the old regalian claim of civil supremacy, as Charles III had asserted it against the supposed subversive activities of the Jesuits. In its efforts to oust those who were 'disaffected or enemies of the legitimate throne and national liberty', the government withdrew preaching licences from factious priests and imprisoned the Chapter of Oviedo for its refusal to accept a bishop unrecognized by the Pope. It was this concern for the political loyalty of the Church which, later, was to drive the pious Espartero to the brink of schism.[3]

The attack on the landed property of the Church was the work of radicals carried to completion by the Progressive dic-

[1] The Papacy had already broken off diplomatic relations with Spain before Mendizábal's accession to power. For the objections to Ferdinand VII's annulment of sales, see *Representacion dirigida al rey* (Cádiz, 1824). According to the petitioners there had been 30,000 purchasers of the landed property of the regular clergy who lost their money when Ferdinand annulled the sales in 1823. The landed endowment of the Orders was stated to be in excess of their needs. Thus in Jerez, where lands worth 20 million reales were sold, there were only 51 monks (ibid. 19).

[2] For a summary of this legislation, see P. Lesmes Frías, *Historia de la Compañía de Jesus* (1944), vol. ii, pt. i, 6 ff.

[3] Thirty-two of the sixty-two Sees were 'vacant' in Espartero's Regency as a consequence of the suspension of diplomatic relations which made regular appointment impossible.

tatorship of Espartero after 1840. It thus divided the Progressives from the Moderates. The alliance of the persecuted Church and the Moderates was dictated by their fears for property in general, and by their desire to disassociate themselves from the excesses of urban radicalism in order to establish a socially respectable brand of liberalism. Nevertheless, the Moderates could not become clericals and reverse, once they were in power, what they had called 'the spoliations of a violent and domineering minority'. To the despair of their clerical supporters their most emphatic defence of the Church was, therefore, made from the opposition benches; in office, the most they would do was to suspend further sales of the property of the secular clergy, seeking the retrospective approval of the Papacy for sales that had already been made. This policy, if it recognized papal rights by denying the radical doctrine of a *dominium eminens* in the state over ecclesiastical property, at the same time made the re-creation of a property-holding Church impossible by sanctioning the accomplished fact of the revolutionary Church settlement.[1] Papal supremacy was saved at the expense of an economically independent Spanish Church and the Regular orders.

The liberal attack had fallen on a Church that was declining in numbers—though there were more priests per inhabitant in Spain than in any other Catholic country—and in intellectual authority. Thus the Spanish Church could not make use of the Romantic movement as the Catholics did in France.[2] The Regular clergy proved unable to recover from the disruptions of the War of Independence; monasteries were emptying, the Jesuits in severe financial difficulties.[3] The secularizations of liberalism were nevertheless a terrible blow, a physical disaster; in Madrid alone forty-four churches and monasteries vanished.

[1] Pacheco (1808–65), a Moderate dissident with strong Catholic convictions, ran a campaign against Espartero's secularizations but did nothing, during his own brief ministry of 1846, that tampered with the sales. The result of these half-hearted attempts of the Moderates was probably confusion in the laws applied to clerical stipends—to the disadvantage of a meanly maintained clergy.

[2] Cf. M. Meléndez y Pelayo's description of the 'posthumous scholasticism' of Catholic apologetics in the early nineteenth century, J. M. Quadrado, *Ensayos* (1893), Preface, xxxvii.

[3] Lesmes Frías, *Compañia de Jesus*, iii. 300 ff., argues that the Jesuits were in such a sorry state that their expulsion in 1820 can be regarded as 'a Providence of God'.

Nine were sold as building sites, one was converted into a Ministry, another into the Senate chamber, others became variously a riding school, a prison, a theatre, and barracks. In the countryside monasteries often fell into the hands of speculators or degenerated into farm buildings. Yuste, the noble retreat of Charles V, was saved from total ruin only by the piety of the house of Mirabel.

Liberal Spain did not come into conflict with the Papacy because liberalism favoured heresy or a modern, lay tolerant state; the constitution of 1837 preserved the privileged position of the Catholic Church in Spain against all other faiths, as George Borrow found to his cost when he sought to peddle the Bibles of a Protestant missionary society. The claim the Church could not accept nor the liberals abandon was the liberal version of the old claim of the absolute monarchy—the unilateral regulation of the temporal affairs of the Church by the state. Thus the arguments of the Cortes repeated old fashioned Regalist–Jansenist commonplaces: priests must be subject to the civil power as in the days of the Visigothic monarchy; 'legions of monks' upheld the supremacy of Rome, and to spare the missionary orders would leave 'a poisoned seed'.[1] There was nothing in the content of these arguments which would have shocked Campomanes; his generation had argued, as did the orators of 1836, that monks 'were out of harmony with the present epoch'.[2] What distinguished the work of eighteenth-century reformers from that of their liberal successors was the atmosphere of popular anti-clerical violence that accompanied liberal legislation—the monk murders of July 1835, the bullying of priests by local authorities, the desecration of churches by militia men. These activities, strictly comparable with those of their descendants a hundred years later, would have been inconceivable twenty years earlier.[3]

It is most difficult to gauge the consequences of the political and economic offensives on the intimate life of the Church. It has been too easily assumed that, in these years, the Church

[1] *D.S.C.* (1837), 3710, Urquioan's speech, 28 May.

[2] J. M. Antequera, *La desamortación eclesiástica* (1885), 183 ff.

[3] The excesses of local authorities are in part explained by the confusion of the laws they applied, but cf. the desecration of cemeteries, mock parades in ecclesiastical vestments which occurred again in 1936. The use of church towers as sniping posts, stores of arms, &c., was less of a myth in 1835 than it was in 1936.

'lost its hold over the middle classes' and was to spend the rest of the century in an endeavour to re-establish its control over the consciences of the *élite* of the nation at the price of working-class piety. Neither of these propositions bears examination. The aristocracy and the middle classes, imitating the *dévots* of the court, were respectably pious: in spite of the vogue for Eugène Sue, there were fewer *esprits forts* in the salons of the liberal era than in the days of Olavide and Aranda. Once the Carlist confusions had passed, the alliance between the Moderates and the hierarchy was a permanent factor in spite of the recriminations of clericalists at the Moderates' 'desertion' of the Church. Popular piety flourished beside popular anti-clericalism—a phenomenon with parallels in other Catholic countries—even in radical towns like Valencia. Espartero, the low-born radical hero, was devout to the point of superstition; it was his rival, the socially respectable Narváez, who had a reputation for 'Voltaireanism'. Atheism appeared timidly only in Republican, working-class circles in Barcelona in the fifties. It was not heretical inclination but the absence of any form of liberal catholicism that drove some Progressives to a vague Deism. The Church stood against Progress. This was symbolized by the fate of monastic property: the great town monasteries and their walled gardens had to be destroyed before urban improvement was possible; revolutionary juntas destroyed churches both to provide employment in moments of crisis and to widen the streets. In Barcelona old monastic buildings housed the new factories.[1]

The liberation of the land from the 'slavery' of mortmain and entail was likewise an eighteenth-century programme in modern dress. Mendizábal's originality lay in his connexion of a revolution in landownership with the creation of a modern economy 'bringing to Spain *animación*, life and a future'—a vision not entirely absent in the eighteenth-century economists. The largest transfer of landed property since the Reconquest was based on the laws and decrees which put church lands on the market and, quantitatively most important of all, the law of

[1] Travel books contain valuable indications of the fate of monastic buildings, e.g. Widdrington's *Spain*, i. 8–9, 36, 247, 345. For the building boom consequent on the urban dissolutions, cf. his description of Madrid: 'Every plaza, every part of the wider streets was occupied by piles of old material' (ibid. i. 17).

August 1836, which re-enacted the 1820 legislation against civil entail.[1] It was the abolition of entail which allowed a dramatic redistribution of the landed property of the nobility.[2]

It has often been held that this legislation was inspired by the self-interest of a land-hungry middle class. Yet the laws were the work of a radical party whose aim was to create widespread support for a revolutionary war. This is evident in the debate on the *señorios*: when conservatives maintained that the old legislation of 1820 was impractical—as in a legal sense it was—a radical deputy objected that the 'people' must get something in order to create 'new interests'. What radicals, with their knowledge of the great Revolution, desired was a revolutionary peasantry, a left-wing rural bourgeoisie, a 'numerous family of peasant proprietors whose prosperity and existence will depend principally on the complete triumph of the present institutions.'[3] The land settlement of the Progressives was not intended to favour a rural oligarchy of *kulaks*, to strengthen the hold of the larger landowners, or to fling up a race of land speculators. Not selfish intent but dogmatic belief in the virtues of free trade in land, combined with a total ignorance of its consequences, marred liberal land legislation: it was not sufficiently realized that the small men could not compete with *poderosos* in open market transactions where victory went to those already strong. Thus, as Mendizábal's biographer and admirer regretfully admits, the land Mendizábal's legislation put on the market was bought up by caciques and speculators.[4]

By the spring of 1836 the Mendizábal system was bankrupt.[5] While the 'men of energy' in his ministry still appeared capable of mounting the war effort moderate *cristino* notables like General Luis Fernández de Córdoba, commander in the North, were prepared to shut their ears to courtiers who denounced Mendizábal's connexions with revolutionary radicalism; when,

[1] As in the case of his ecclesiastical legislation, all had been previously enacted 1820–3, and the beginnings of the liberation of the land was started by the Moderate's law of March 1834 (sale of certain commons for improvement).

[2] See below, pp. 272–5.

[3] Mendizábal's proposal to abolish tithes were specifically aimed at the *labradores*, i.e. cultivators of the more prosperous kind.

[4] A. García Tejero, *Mendizábal*, i. 189 ff.

[5] Cf. the famous verdict of the poet Larra in his review of Espronceda's *El ministerio Mendizábal* (1836). Larra became a deputy of nine days as a supporter of Istúriz.

after repeated promises, the ministry left the armies starving and unpaid, Córdoba could no longer agree with Villiers that Mendizábal alone could save the country. Increasingly the ministry was driven to rely on the patriotic left and the English minister—neither course calculated to endear its chief to the queen regent who shared the view of the Moderate generals that her daughter's cause could only be saved by 'respectable' governments and French intervention. In May 1836 she felt strong enough to dismiss Mendizábal, forming a new ministry under Istúriz. This was the first decisive instance of the monarch's power within a constitutional system: Istúriz was in a minority in the Cortes, where the radical opposition now wanted a revival of the constitution of 1812. To enable Istúriz to 'make' a less radical Cortes the queen regent granted Istúriz a decree of dissolution. In August 1836 the left were restored to power by revolution before the Istúriz government had met the Cortes.

The Revolution of 1836 was a repetition of the provincial creeping anarchy of 1835, combined with a pronunciamiento of sergeants which forced a government that could control Madrid to follow the lead of the provinces. This mutiny was considered by Cánovas, the great minister of Alfonso XII, as the last of the pronunciamientos inspired by political principle before ambitious generals turned military rebellion into a business enterprise; its uniqueness resided less in the principles which inspired it—the demand for a democratic constitution—than in the fact that it was the only successful revolt of non-commissioned officers. Politics, in 1836, were no longer the monopoly of the officer corps; on the northern front where the Guards' sergeants had learned 'libertarian ideas' from the Progressive press, the troops were unpaid and restive.[1] This combination of economic grievance and the 'liberal spirit' of the sergeants' mess produced a type of military rebellion which died out after 1843 except for a few unsuccessful performances. The sergeant's revolt did not become, as the officers' revolt was to become, a recognized instrument of political change and a step in the military career: Sergeant García, like any successful officer rebel, asked for promotion but was sharply refused.

[1] For an account by one of the sergeants concerned in the revolt, see A. Gómez, *Los sucesos de la Granja en 1836* (1864).

Returning to Madrid from the northern front, the sergeants of the Guards found the 'liberal spirit' frowned on by the government, which announced its intention of dissolving the militia—regarded by radicals as the only safeguard against a conservative reaction and by Istúriz as the vanguard of plebeian dictatorship. On 12 August the sergeants, allegedly drunken and bribed by Mendizábal and Calatrava, burst in on the queen regent at La Granja, forcing her to accept a radical ministry and to restore the constitution of 1812 and the National Militia.[1] Their political ideas were primitive; a sergeant, when asked by María Cristina why he supported the constitution of 1812, replied, 'It was better before. In '22 in Corunna there were no duties on tobacco and salt.' The revolution put into power Calatrava, a patriot radical, who appointed Mendizábal as his finance minister; he summoned a Constituent Cortes for October 1836. It was this body which enacted the classical constitution of democratic liberalism, the Progressives' constitution of 1837.

The constitution of 1837 was an attempt by radical liberals at a compromise which would create the harmony of the liberal family from the left. For the sake of harmony they were willing to abandon the single chamber and impotent royal executive of the 'impossible' constitution of 1812.[2] This compromise was rejected by the *exaltados* and the forces of left-wing liberalism divided. To the *exaltados* the parliamentary Progressives had betrayed democracy by abandoning the Sacred Codex; after an increasingly uncomfortable sojourn with the Progressives they were to find a most congenial home in the crypto-republicanism of the Democratic party of the forties.

Extreme radicalism, especially in Barcelona, was moving not merely beyond the frontiers of the Progressive party but outside the framework of constitutional monarchy. 'Death to tyrants, down with thrones . . . liberty, justice, equality, virtue and the universal republic.'[3] This left the authors of the constitution of 1837 as the only legal representatives of the radical tradition within the monarchy. Whenever, in the future, these

[1] Gómez and the sergeants denied drunkenness: 'the liberal spirit predominated in all that we did'.

[2] See above, p. 162, for the 'conservative' nature of the constitution of 1837.

[3] An acrostic contained in the Barcelona radical paper, *La Bandera*.

legal Progressives appealed to the revolution as a device to unseat their political enemies they would be appealing to forces which included those who no longer accepted the historic connexion between the throne of Isabella and liberty.

It was the rejection of the constitution of 1837 by the men whose political thought was enshrined in the Royal Statute of 1834 that created the Moderate party and proved to the Progressives the sterility of their sacrifice of support on the left in the hope of creating a Liberal Centre party. While admitting the reasonable nature of the constitution the Moderates could not tolerate the methods by which its sponsors had gained power; they therefore rejected 'the testimony of the honesty of the Progressive party'.[1] The Revolution of 1836 not merely used force to persecute political opponents but had encouraged revolutionary threats to the established social order. Thus the Moderates became the beneficiaries of the alarm of the conservative classes and of the utter failure of Mendizábal to supply the armies in the field. The consequence of this failure was a serious outbreak of mutinies by troops who had received little food and no issue of pay or clothing for months. This turned almost the entire officer corps against the Radical government.[2] It was this swing of opinion which, unexpectedly, produced a Moderate majority in the first Cortes elected under the new constitution.[3] To Cánovas, the greatest of the Moderates, this was a proof of the natural conservatism of the Spanish countryside.

During the next three years the attitude of the generals becomes *the* deciding factor in cabinet making as opposed to an influence asserted on occasion. It is the key to the complex politics of 1837–40.[4] Thus the Moderate victory was unstable.

[1] A. Fernández de los Rios, *Estudio histórico de la luchas políticas de la España del siglo XIX* (1879), i. 248.

[2] The officers, as well as the troops, were short of pay. It was a strike of the Guards' officers at Pozuelo de Aravacas which caused the resignation of the Calatrava–Mendizábal government (August 1837). It was army resentment which brought Espartero into politics as an *opponent* of Radical incompetence; like all other commanders he detested the attempts of Radical journalists to undermine discipline for political ends.

[3] 'As a consequence of this event (the mutiny of La Granja) the conservative party attracted all the middle class', *Historia del excmo. Sr. D. Luis José Sartorius*, 9. For the new conservatism of former radical stalwarts like the Commander of the National Militia in Bilbao, see J. M. de Areilza, *Historia de una conspiración romántica* (Bilbao, 1950), 54–55.

[4] For the rise of the army in politics, see below, pp. 214–18.

The queen regent subordinated her sympathies for the Moderates to the necessity of conciliating Espartero, now the most powerful of the generals;[1] prepared to dissolve the conservative Cortes (June 1839), when it became clear that Espartero preferred a non-party government devoted to the needs of his army, it was only with great misgivings that she decided to back the Moderates and dissolve the radical Cortes (November 1839). The conservative majority of the new Cortes determined to force 'exclusiveness' on the ministry and, in the name of order against the 'perpetual revolution of anarchy', to drive the Progressives out of jobs and the radical left out of public life.

With Espartero uncommitted—in spite of the radical noises of his staff the general could still curse the extremist press as 'subversive' and exhibit effusive loyalty to his queen—party conflict centred on the municipal law proposed by the Moderate majority. The Moderates knew that such a step, by destroying an objectionable 'democratic' feature of the constitution of 1837, would put an end to any talk of liberal reconciliation in a constitutional centre party. Both parties regarded the municipal law as central to their political power since it was the municipal authorities which drew up the voting lists and conducted the elections. The Progressives favoured popular election on a wide franchise; the law proposed by the Moderates, besides raising the municipal franchise, gave to provincial governors in the small towns and to the government in the large towns the right to appoint and dismiss mayors.

To the Moderates, French centralization was the recipe for *gobierno fuerte*, the end of the permanent revolution by which the municipalities became 'so many little states, independent of the central government'.[2] In an absolutist government municipal independence might be a bulwark of freedom; with a regular constitution 'the idea that the municipalities represent the people'—combined with popular election on a democratic franchise—consecrated the anarchy of local 'plebeian tyrannies'. From French example the Moderate deduced that 'uniformity and subordination' (i.e. the mayor as a government agent) were essential features of a modern state. This destruction of

[1] See below, p. 183. He had already brought down the ministries of Bardaxí and Ofalia.

[2] J. de Burgos, *Anales*, iv. 12. Cf. A. Posada, *Régimen local*, 119 ff.

municipal independence was, to twentieth-century conservatives, the historic crime of liberalism. Yet in 1840 it was the radical Progressives who defended the municipality's rights against the central government.

Their reasons were clear. The Moderates enjoyed crown favour—whenever possible the regent used the prerogative of appointment of ministers to favour conservative ministries. The Progressives counted on a strong following in the larger towns where the mayors elected under the constitution of 1837 had been Progressives. Thus, if Moderates, granted office by the crown, could obtain a favourable dissolution and eliminate Progressive electoral strength in the towns by partisan application of the proposed municipal law, then power would be a permanent monopoly of the Moderates.[1] Hence it was a matter of political life and death to the Progressives that the 'exclusive' project of 1840 should not become law.

To justify the violent reaction of the Progressives to the municipal law the doctrine of legal revolution was to hand. No Ordinary Cortes could modify the constitution; if it did so, then rebellion became a legal duty.[2] Thus, if the queen regent sanctioned the law, the Progressive municipalities would revolt; like the army, the municipalities claimed a right to 'pronounce', as depositories of the national will, against a 'corrupt' Cortes dominated by their political enemies. The decisive factor would be the attitude of the army and its Commander-in-Chief, Espartero. Acting on what her ministers called an inspiration of Beelzebub, the regent, on the excuse of sea baths for her daughter, went to Espartero's headquarters in Catalonia; the gamble that the general might, at the last moment, be brought to support *gobierno fuerte*, put the regent at his mercy. Espartero made it clear to her that the ministry and the Cortes must go and that she must refuse her sanction to the municipal law. Espartero's slogan, 'The throne of Isabella II, the Queen Regent and the Constitution', now contained an internal contradiction: if the regent defied the constitution, then the throne of her daughter was in peril. His mind was working

[1] For the crown's use of the 'moderating power' and its results, see below, pp. 213–14.

[2] See above, pp. 163–4. The case for legal rebellion was not as clear-cut as Progressives maintained. Borrego, a sensible Moderate, regarded the Moderate's law as 'legal but tactless'.

towards a new catch-phrase, 'Let the will of the people be fulfilled'. Petitions from Progressive municipalities that came to him in June convinced him that the will of the people was identified with the Progressive party line.

The regent's immediate reaction was surrender to Espartero: she offered him the ministry on the terms which the Progressive leaders had set out for him. It was her retraction of these terms which set off the long-drawn Revolution of 1840. The revolution was not an affair of barricades—shops were open throughout—but a series of street demonstrations, first in Barcelona and later in Valencia, rigged by the Progressive municipalities and the National Militia, directed against the regent and acclaiming Espartero. 'A national fiesta with bands and illuminations', it would not have cowed the Moderates into surrender but for the army.[1]

What Progressive rhetoric called the Glorious Revolution was really a 'negative pronunciamiento'. Espartero refused to back the government against 'opinion' and use his troops against the rebellious Progressive municipalities. Therefore all the Progressives had to do was to organize enough 'opinion' to make the country ungovernable for a period of two months. The novelty of the revolution was that the capital, though it revolted late, backed the most radical of the revolutionary projects: the Madrid Junta demanded, not merely the annulment of the new municipal law, but a public recantation by the regent of her constitutional sins and even a new regency. When Espartero, at last prime minister, under pressure from the Madrid radicals, adopted this programme and tried to force a somewhat modified edition of it on María Cristina she abdicated rather than become a Progressive puppet. Cortina, leader and organizer of the Madrid Radical Junta, threatened to reveal her secret marriage. Probably the queen regent was tired of the factions. In 1838 Villiers had observed, 'The Queen has for some time past been sinking in public estimation . . . [she] is occupied solely with one thought which is how to get away.'[2] The government of the country now fell into the hands of Espartero as head of an interim regency (October 1840–

[1] *Reseña histórica*, 52. Cf. Mesonero Romanos's description of the 1843 revolution in Andalusia as 'amiable disorder with guitars and castanets', *Memorias*, ii. 184.

[2] C. Webster, *Palmerston*, i. 462.

May 1841). Radical liberalism had surrendered itself to a general. Conservative liberalism, in order to throw off his hegemony, was to surrender itself to his military rival—Narváez. The militarization of politics, as far-sighted defenders of civilian government now began to realize, had entered a stage beyond the natural predominance of generals in times of civil war.[1]

The new era of military politics was symbolized by the enormous prestige of Espartero, duke of Victory and pacifier of Spain. The northern army had become his private concern. Worshipped by his men because, as an ex-ranker, he understood their needs, and with a group of officers devoted to his interests and recruited in part from his former colleagues in the colonial wars, he had proved the most successful commander of the war by his refusal to commit his armies to action without adequate supplies and the certitude of victory. Both parties hoped to use his prestige and courted his favour; his refusal to commit himself drove ministers to distraction.[2] Even after his protests against the Moderates' dissolution of 1839 the regent hoped that, by presents of cigar-cases, portraits, or a dukedom, he might be induced to see himself as the protector of a widowed mother, ready to fling herself on what she repeatedly called his manly character. The Progressives, on the other hand, hoped to flatter him into the role of the protector of liberty. The initiative thus lay with the politicians who played on the childish vanity of his conception of his own indispensability.

As with so many figures in this period, we can only hazard a guess at Espartero's intentions. A political simpleton with a vulgar mind and a loud voice, devoted to whist, his correspondence reveals a political theory that moved in slogans, difficult to translate into precise political action. Probably his

[1] Cf. the comment of a Progressive leader to Borrego, 'I prefer to see my party succumb than to see it owe, in a purely civil and political issue, its triumph to the intercession of bayonets.'

[2] It is clear from Rumigny's reports (*Archives nationaux: Ministère des Affaires etrangères: Correspondance politique, Espagne*, esp. February, March, April 1840) that though the Moderates regarded him as imbecile and *funeste* they did not regard him as irretrievably committed to the Progressives but as a 'stubborn horse' who might be managed. Some of Espartero's entourage—his secretary Linaje and van Halen above all—were considered a dangerous pressure group in a radical direction; nevertheless Espartero's outbursts against radical journalists allowed the Moderates a hope that he would turn into a respectable man of order.

ambitions were limited to being a permanent hero, above politics and party, provided the politicians did not attack him or his group of officer cronies, elevate his rivals, or dissolve his army. The party struggle of 1839–40 would not let him rest on his laurels as duke of Victory and national hero. He was dragged into politics by the Progressives to stop a process of 'reaction' they were impotent to halt.

3. *The Rise and Decline of the Carlist Cause, 1833–1868*

Spain, which gave liberalism its name, produced in Carlism a classic form of counter-revolution. The battle for survival between parliamentary liberalism and Carlism lasted from 1833 to 1840. The descendants of these original Carlists remained as an active force in Spanish politics to the present day; but after their first failure, even the complete disintegration of the system which had defeated them failed to secure a Carlist restoration. Once more in 1936, the Carlists of Navarre were to train in their villages for the last battle against the revolution; the fruits of victory, however, were to go to more potent forces in the anti-revolutionary coalition.

The Carlism of the thirties was a negative creed, a crusade 'for the elimination of the liberal *canaille*', the battle against 'the Revolution' as the residuary legatee of sixteenth-century heresy and eighteenth-century atheism. The Revolution of Freemasons had twice been beaten, in 1814 and 1823. In the last years of Ferdinand VII's reign, 'those who were defeated in 1823' had begun to come back to power and on his death they controlled the government. Carlists were those who, triumphing in 1823, had set up the royalist Volunteers as an instrument of permanent domination; these men, pushed aside when the royalist Volunteers were dismantled, turned to Carlist conspiracy, finally rising against 'a traitorous crowd of crooks who occupy the best posts in the nation through the weakness of a woman'. They became the politicians of Carlism, the local leaders of organized conspiracy who set up the primitive administration of the Carlist districts, the courtiers of Charles V, as the legitimists termed Don Carlos on the death of his brother.[1] Carlism had its own brand of *empleomanía*, its own

[1] This type of Carlism is represented by the Conde de Villemur: he was relieved

pretendientes waiting for victory.[1] It was a revolution of frustration, a revolution of the inadaptables, from the prince who had been pushed aside by court faction to the violent men who took to the hills in Catalonia and Aragon. Such men became the prisoners of an intransigent ideal: legitimacy and the Catholic unity of Spain. Against the court of Isabella stood the austere court of the true king, Charles V, regular in his habits and punctilious in his devotions, his army under the supreme command of the Virgin of the Sorrows.

To the great mass of Carlists, therefore, devotion to the Church and to the king was the core of their creed. Devotion to the principle of legitimacy gave to Charles V, unsympathetic and ungrateful, a right to command sacrifices which no shortcomings as a leader could diminish. His strength and attraction to the mass of his followers lay in the obstinate anachronism with which he faced the modern world. A Carlist victory would have brought to the throne a man who believed absolute power under God *must* be exercised for the 'Glory of God and the prosperity and splendour of his Sacred Religion'. There is no evidence that Don Carlos sympathized with the renovating royalism and the traditional constitution of the Persian Manifesto: he was never anything but a sixteenth-century theocrat who passed among his followers as a saint.[2] The journalists and the statesmen of France and England could scarcely credit the nakedness of the Carlist creed. Guizot alone sensed the religious nature of the complex of emotional forces that could find no programme that made sense to an outsider: William IV and Palmerston sought to pin down faith to interest. This interest they found in the Basque's defence of their privileges—

by the 'liberals' as military governor of Barcelona and sub-inspector of the royalist Volunteers. Erro, Don Carlos's 'Universal Minister' in 1836, was appointed a counsellor of state and finance minister in the 1823 reaction: he was disgraced in 1830. Cf. the royalist past of the Baron de Hervas, one of the most respectable leaders of Aragonese Carlism ('Aragón en la primera guerra carlista' in *J. Zurita Cuadernos*, vi (Saragossa), 1958).

[1] *Empleomanía* is the mania for jobs. The civilian *empleados* were the core of the 'Castilian party' in Carlism: for its disastrous effects on military strategy, see below, p. 191.

[2] See C. Seco, 'Semblanza de un rey carlista en la paginas de su diario íntimo', *Revista de la Universidad de Madrid*, xix (1956), 339. Seco successfully destroys the claims of Verdeguer and his school who see Carlism in the *thirties* as a middleway of 'Spanish' reform between ministerial despotism and 'foreign' liberalism. Cf. the summary in *B.A.E.* cxxvii, *Estudio Preliminar*, xliii–xlviii.

the *fueros*—against the implications of liberal centralizing constitutionalism.[1]

The *fueros* were a conservative rather than a Carlist concern. The local notables would desert Carlism if the *fueros*, instrument of their ascendancy, could be 'reconciled' with constitutional Spain. Thus the Moderates, uncomfortable with the Jacobin patriotism of total war, found sympathy in the conservative classes of the foral provinces, equally uncomfortable in a war sustained by Carlist fanaticism, for the idea of a negotiated peace which recognized the *fueros* in Biscay and Guipuzcoa.[2] In 1838 an iron manufacturer, Muñagorri, tried to raise an army with the banner '*Peace and Fueros*'; his neutralism failed as a military adventure though, as sceptics admitted, it 'educated' opinion towards a settlement guaranteeing the Basque liberties —a solution which grew in attractiveness as the northern provinces felt the burden of supporting the Carlist army.[3] Once Espartero agreed to guarantee the *fueros*, peace was possible. Neither pure Carlists nor radical liberals accepted the compromise peace of Vergara which ended the civil war in the north. Both argued that Carlism was more than the defence of local self-government. 'Where there are *fueros* and where there are not you will find Carlism . . . consequently the rebellion began irrespective of the *fueros* and will not be ended even if they are confirmed.'[4] The Navarrese, as the core of Carlism, never seem to have displayed great interest in the *fueros*: their creed was throne and altar. To them Vergara was *la grande trahaison*, a contract to preserve local notables in power at the expense of the faith.

The foral issue was, nevertheless, an expression of what was perhaps the deepest current in Carlism: the hatred of the country for the town, the mountain for the plain. The Carlist camp followers came to Bilbao with sacks on their backs to

[1] For a description of the *fueros*, see above, pp. 63–64.

[2] Cf. Marqués de Miraflores: 'The [radical] political revolution was maintained because the Carlist question remained unsolved' (*Memorias*, i. 228).

[3] For a hostile account of Muñagorri's activities, see F. Duncan, *The English in Spain*, chapter xvii.

[4] Memorandum of San Sebastian, May 1834, quoted Múgica, *Carlistas*, 292. The early Carlist proclamations (e.g. Verastegui at Vitoria, 7 Oct. 1833, in A. Pirala, *Guerra civil*, Document 31, i. 1033) contain little mention of *fueros*; Santos Ladrón, the Carlist leader in Navarre, did not mention them at all.

pillage the liberal Gomorrah.[1] The base of Carlism was the countryside of the Basque Provinces and Navarre where its organized rural state remained ringed round by liberal towns: Bilbao, San Sebastian, Pamplona, and Vitoria. The obsession of Carlist strategists was the conquest of these towns: hence the fatal attraction of a siege of Bilbao which wasted the slender chances of a Carlist victory. Outside the north, Carlism only took root in the backward, primitive society of the mountains of Aragon and Catalonia. It was this rural character which made Carlism so difficult to defeat; its strongholds were inaccessible—the foothills of the Pyrenees, the difficult country of the Maestrazgo, through which modern armies found it difficult to operate in 1937. It also made it impossible for Carlism to win: it occupied no great wheat area, no great town. Estella, a sizeable market town, was the largest town held by the Carlists. Cabrera's capital in the Maestrazgo was the second-rate fortress of Morella, a mountain town with a decaying textile industry. The Carlist armies must either exhaust their home base or seek to burst out, inviting defeat in country where their tactics failed and supporters were few.

Because of its rural character Carlism failed to gain any support in the 'enlightened classes' who saw in liberalism a political system better suited to their interests and way of life. This explains the Isabelline sympathies of the higher aristocracy. They would not exchange Madrid for the migrant court of Don Carlos, with its 'brutes' and 'yokels'. Carlism, therefore, was anti-aristocratic in feeling, popular rather than patrician.[2] The hatred of the *urban* middle class and proletariat for Carlism found its most deplorable expression in the prison massacres, its most useful in the Urban Militia which helped to relieve the regular army of garrison duties. More important was the loyalty of bureaucrats and officers, the two

[1] There were, for instance, long-standing disputes over jurisdiction between Bilbao and its surrounding districts; the relationship between these struggles and early Carlism has yet to be studied.

[2] Carlism, of course, did have a handful of aristocratic sympathizers (e.g. in the disastrous Junta of Catalonia) but they were less influential than ecclesiastics, or social nonentities like Tejeiro. The Pretender, on several occasions, was bitter about this failure of the aristocracy. Merino, the guerrilla leader, once said to Don Carlos that the Spanish Debrett contained the sum of Spanish disasters; he replied, 'Yes, in future there will be no nobles but those whom I create.' For Carlist feeling against aristocrats, cf. M. Lassala, *Historia política del partido carlista* (1841), 32.

ruling classes in Spain. No civil servant of note deserted, no regiment staged a Carlist pronunciamiento.[1] The loyalty of the army was decisive: it alone saved liberalism from defeat and it demanded its price in terms of political influence.

Politically, socially, and militarily, Carlism was inelastic. Its only chance of widening its original basis was when the radical sergeants' revolution of La Granja frightened the propertied classes and induced the queen mother to contemplate a peace based on the marriage of Don Carlos's son and Isabella.[2] It could not exploit this political opportunity, which came at the moment when the Carlist armies were in sight of Madrid. Court Carlism could not invent a viable national programme; to the central and southern provinces it remained an elaborate form of brigandage. Like all forms of political brigandage, Castilian Carlism ended by becoming a nuisance rather than a cause: already, in 1834, Merino the priest guerrilla of the War of Independence could not control his men who were 'making him hateful to the people'. In the east, Carlism could always be presented as a continual raid of the poor mountains on the rich plains: Cabrera's men burnt factories and ravaged the *huertas* of the Levante.

Carlism, therefore, remained a romantic epic in which selfless devotion to an ideal was soiled by treason, desertion, and incapacity. It hoped for foreign aid which never came except for a handful of volunteers—they included Henningsen and Prince Lichnowsky, who both left remarkable accounts of the war—and a trickle of money.[3] The liberals were backed by the Quadruple Alliance, which furnished useful British naval aid (important at Bilbao), the volunteer corps of Evans, the French Foreign Legion and supplies of rifles, clothing, and ammunition. Extreme liberalism was very hostile to foreign aid while Moderates believed that Isabella could only be saved by a French army; in fact neither France nor England wished

[1] The absence of a Carlist pronunciamento was due, in part, to the changes of command in the last year of Ferdinand's reign (see above, p. 153). In 1833 no Carlist sympathizer held a command which would have enabled him to stage a successful military rising (cf. M. Ferrer, *Historia del tradicionalismo español*, Seville, 1941-5, iii. 130-5).

[2] See below, p. 193, for the 'fusionist' solution.

[3] Lichnowsky's account is in his *Erinnerungen aus den Jahren 1837-9*, 2 vols. (Frankfurt a. M. 1841); C. F. Henningsen's, in *A Twelve months' campaign with Zumalacárregui* (London, 1836).

to commit themselves deeply in Spain. Nevertheless their sympathy was vital: liberal finances were deplorable but they would have been worse without foreign loans. The Carlists had no finances except what local levies could produce: Tejeiro, greeted as the Carlist Mendizábal who could engineer the victory loan, produced nothing.[1] It was the reversal of this situation which was to help the allies of Carlism to victory in 1936–9, when the Left looked in vain for another Quadruple Alliance.

Had the government been able to send a well-equipped army to the north in October 1833, Carlism would have been snuffed out before it had acquired a military and civil organization; by 1835 it had small munition factories, an officers' academy, even a 'university', and the administrative machinery that made Carlist territory a state within the liberal state. Delay had given Zumalacárregui, a regular soldier who turned himself into a partisan leader of genius, time to build up and train an army of 20,000 to 30,000 troops, hardened and equipped by the spoils of a series of brilliantly conceived minor operations. With the *cristino* army pinned in the north, there were no troops to spare for the prompt eradication of the resurgent bands in Catalonia and Aragon. Cabrera, trained as a priest, a violent and resourceful self-made soldier, disciplined the partisan groups of Aragon where all other local chieftains had failed. The 'Tiger' later became a respectable politician: in the first Carlist war he imposed his authority, both on his own commanders and the localities in which he operated, by terror. This produced a liberal counter-terror and the execution of hostages, including Cabrera's mother. In January 1838 he captured Morella, which he made the capital of his mountainous, roadless base in lower Aragon, but he never succeeded in organizing a Carlist administration in the eastern theatre comparable with that of the north. The Catalan Carlists were half bandits: the regular soldiers sent to command them could neither stomach their cruelty and rapacity nor co-ordinate their movements.[2]

[1] Tejeiro was appointed as 'prime minister' by Don Carlos in 1837. For Carlist finances, see A. Pirala, *Guerra civil*, ii. 928 ff. Occasional gifts came e.g. from Naples and Savoy (ibid. iii. 149–51). For later subsidies, see Lichnowsky, op. cit. ii. 355.

[2] The maximum number of men under arms in Catalonia by 1838 was probably about 10,000, all in small bands of 100 to 500 men.

Against the Carlist forces in the north a succession of *cristino* commanders each favoured a 'system' that would end what one of them called the 'languid war'—the stalemate that comes if regular troops are pitted against guerrillas in difficult country. These systems demanded a large, well-supplied army either to seal off the Basque Provinces behind fortified lines or to provide an operational force to invade them. Quesada, as commander-in-chief of the north, by May 1835 saw that the difficulties of guerrilla war would only be overcome by a numerical superiority which the government would not recognize as necessary. 'My system is based on superiority of numbers. . . . I need 14,000 men *to force them to fight and to take away their resources.*' Since such an army was not forthcoming, the advantages lay with the Carlists; the *cristino* armies, with a third of their strength pinned down in garrison duties in a hostile countryside, were led over hill and dale, worn out by fruitless marches, caught in ambushes, their commanders driven to desperation by their inability to bring Zumalacárregui to an action on equal terms.[1] It was the failure of the government to supply the army which prolonged the partisan era even after the victories of Mendigorría (July 1835) and the relief of Bilbao (December 1836); men would not fight in linen trousers and canvas shoes, and without supplies and pay, operations ground to a standstill for months on end. Oráa's men were forced to abandon the siege of Cabrera's capital, Morella, through starvation. Nevertheless there is a culminating point when attrition is turned against the partisan; when not the opposing army, but the partisan home base, is worn out; when, if victory is to be achieved, large-scale action can no longer be avoided by the partisans. Carlism had probably reached this point by 1836 when the Carlist civil administration found the task of providing rations and pay from a rural population of half a million beyond it; conscription became unpopular and desertion frequent.[2]

[1] The phrase 'languid war' is used by General Luis Fernández de Córdoba in his *Memoria justificativa* (1837), 48. For the refusal of the enemy to fight, ibid. 84 ff. Cf. Oráa's complaints that his Army of the Centre was a 'passive spectator'.

[2] The demands of war alienated local authorities and, as in liberal Spain, these were frequently pushed aside by the generals. Taxation rose by 30 per cent. and there were frequent special levies. From the beginning (cf. the decree of 28 Dec. 1833) there were severe penalties for desertion; as in the liberal armies, there were pay mutinies. The notion of a universally popular crusade needs modification.

It was the desire for total victory which drove the Carlist civilians to support the ambitious plan of the 'Castilian' faction for a grand expedition to break out of the confined base in the north. The more experienced soldiers opposed expeditions into liberal Spain for which the court strategists clamoured: Gómez's expedition reached Andalusia but accomplished nothing.[1] The greatest failure of Carlism was its final gamble, the Royal Expedition of 1837; in 150 days, over appalling country, the Carlist army marched through Catalonia and Valencia to within sight of the walls of Madrid, only to be driven back to its northern base. Retreat proved decisively that Carlism could not expand beyond its homeland; it exposed the myth of a Spain disgusted with liberal excesses, ready to rise for the true king.[2] By 1838 the military balance had swung against the Carlists. By 1839 on the northern front General Espartero had 100,000 men and 700 guns against 32,000 men and 52 guns. His predecessors had been less fortunate. Oráa had tried to take Morella with 7 guns and 17,000 men; Espartero took it with 40 guns and 70,000 men.[3] The Carlist reservoirs of man-power, their improvised munitions factories, their taxes and contributions were incapable of sustaining a war against the resources of nine-tenths of Spain.

Carlism had never been a united cause and its agony was accompanied by the bitter feuds of rival factions. In 1838 Don Carlos appointed Maroto as commander-in-chief of the north. A professional soldier from the American wars, whose strength lay in his power to 'electrify' the troops under his command, Maroto personified the distaste of fighting men and the *gente decente* for the clerical court; he soon became involved in a life and death struggle with the court which was to turn him into the great traitor to whom all the defeats of Carlism could be conveniently attributed. He determined to get rid of Tejeiro, the chief of the clerical absolutists, and the Navarrese generals

[1] Gómez's instructions were to foment a rising amongst the local Carlists in Galicia. His extraordinary career (he occupied Córdoba and the mines of Almadén) hid the fact that he had failed in his task of creating another regional basis for Carlism in Galicia.

[2] M. Lassala (*Historia política*) calls the expeditions 'the destruction of the Carlist party'. For Carlism's lack of programme, ibid. 112.

[3] For the difficulties of the *cristino* forces in Aragon, see Duncan, *English in Spain*, 283 ff.

before they destroyed him. In February 1839 the latent crisis became a blood feud: Maroto shot six of his army enemies, the allies of Tejeiro and the absolutist faction at court. Tejeiro and the *apostólicos* were exiled. Don Carlos had virtually abdicated. The struggle had been so intense that Maroto aged ten years in two days; to save himself from the revenge of the *apostólicos*, backed by Cabrera from Aragon, he resumed peace negotiations with Espartero. Maroto had to choose between being shot by his own side or coming to terms with his enemies.[1]

As Espartero drove into Carlist territory (April–May 1839), devastating as he went, the desire for peace, provided the *fueros* were respected, grew among the Basque contingents.[2] A compromise peace was anathema to both Carlist *apostólicos* and liberal *exaltados*; but in the summer of 1839 Moderate 'trans-actionists' on both sides were temporarily in power. The negotiations were extremely lengthy and complex and had to be carried out in great secrecy. Maroto's position was increasingly difficult: the Fifth Navarese battalion revolted against 'trans-action' and Don Carlos in a new uniform—a characteristic ineptitude—made a last attempt to rally Maroto's war-weary men against their commander. On 29 August Maroto finally abandoned all attempts to save the rights of Don Carlos and signed the Convention of Vergara which recognized Isabella as legitimate queen. The Convention safeguarded both the Carlist officers' pay and promotion and the *fueros* of the provinces. As in 1936, Navarre was the true centre of Catholic resistance in the north: but when the Basques 'sold out' Navarre could not fight alone.

The forlorn hope of Carlism was the eastern theatre: Catalonia and Aragon. In 1839 concentration in the north had allowed Cabrera and España local successes but by 1840 neither could hope to hold out against well-supplied and superior armies. España, whose command had been a wearing struggle against the indiscipline and incompetence of Catalan partisan leaders backed by the 'aristocratic' Junta, was brutally

[1] Cf. J. de Burgos, *Anales*, vi. 197.

[2] The Guipúzcoa regiments came out for a 'foral republic' with Maroto as President. Even if he had been loyal to his king, Maroto could only with difficulty have got the Basques to fight on. He probably made no attempt to halt Espartero: his operations were to Duncan, an English observer, 'altogether inexplicable', cf. Lichnowsky, *Erinnerungen*, ii. 362.

murdered by his own troops. Cabrera's capital, Morella, was taken and, a sick man, he fled to France.

From this defeat Carlism was never to recover. Its strength still lay in the Basque Provinces and especially in Navarre: there it became a family tradition, a piously preserved and persistent enclave in the political map of liberal Spain. In Catalonia residual political brigandage kept the movement in being as a militant concern. It could not hope for victory and suffered the usual fate of such movements when the countryside, wearying of exaction and insecurity, turned against it.

The only real chance for Carlism lay in the internal disintegration of the liberal system. To encourage this collapse Carlists could adopt two courses. They could attempt to win over to the cause of legitimacy those conservative catholics to whom liberalism was an uncomfortable home. This would be engineered by a fusion of the two dynasties which recognized the Carlist claims and a consistent sympathizer with such plans was Isabella's own husband, Franciso de Asis.[1] The 'fusionist' solution had found its greatest advocate in Balmes, a Catalan theologian and apologist, who saw in a dynastic alliance the only solution that would give Spain political peace. On the other hand, those activists who regarded fusionism as betrayal, aimed to destroy the constitutional monarchy by armed rebellion, if necessary in alliance with Republicanism. This unnatural alliance of the extremes of radical democracy and clerical absolutism against the middle way of liberal constitutionalism is one of the strangest features of nineteenth-century political life. No doubt it existed more often in liberal propaganda than in fact.

In 1846–9 Catalonian Carlist brigandage developed into a full-scale partisan war in the name of the new pretender Montemolin, son of Don Carlos. The government doctored newspaper reports to hide the incapacity of the regular troops against guerrillas supported by the countryside. 'They make every effort to avoid an encounter with the army which can only get at them after countless exertions—without decisive

[1] In the early forties the fusionists hoped for a marriage of Don Carlos's son, the count of Montemolin with Isabella. In 1854 they planned for the marriage at some future date of his son and Isabella's daughter.

results because they disperse.' This was the lament of French commanders in the War of Independence, of the French officers in Naples in 1810, of the Italian officers in the brigand war of the 1860's. The support of the Catalan countryside was secured by local grievances: Mon's new taxation, conscription, and the government's free-trade proclivities. Difficult to suppress, the *Montemolinista* revolt could not expand. Cabrera judged it hopeless from the start as a military enterprise; his commanders—the Tristanys, Borges, and Marsal—were brilliant guerrilla commanders who could ransom a village or destroy an isolated detachment, but no more. The revolt was kept in being, not by devotion to the old cause but by loyalty to local leaders. Thus 'Montemolinism' remained unsupported by Basque Carlism and many eastern Carlists detested Cabrera's understandings and joint operations with Republican militants. During the last stages of the war Cabrera was forced to use terrorism against delation and desertion.

The failure of the constitutional monarchy to defend the conservative classes against Radicalism, evident in the Revolution of 1854, gave Carlism its second great opportunity.[1] Once more the movement was split between Carlist moderates, who hoped to force fusion on a terrified court, and the militants among the Paris exiles; once more it failed to capitalize conservative panic or the resentments of the 'poor robbed of their patrimony' by the disentailing legislation; once more it failed to move the old strongholds of the faith; once more Catalan Carlism fizzled out in pointless raids.

Carlism now pinned its hopes on a pronunciamiento, a course which reflects the weakening of Carlism as a local protest;[2] moreover military sedition was a revolutionary mechanism foreign to Carlism because it could not hope for effective officer support. The landing of Montemolin and General Ortega at San Carlos de la Rápita (August 1860) collapsed of its own accord once the officers and the troops learned the purpose of the movement in an harangue from Ortega, rendered less convincing when his hard-mouthed horse ran away with him.

[1] See below, pp. 246–56, for the Revolution of 1854.

[2] A pronunciamiento had been first tried in 1855 with an unsuccessful cavalry pronunciamiento in Saragossa.

Behind the movement lay the habitual intrigues of Isabella's king consort, Francisco de Asis (for he never lost the conviction that he was a usurper), and General Ortega's conversion to democratic Carlism, the emotional root of which was a protest against the 'new feudalism' of the liberal oligarchs.

The miserable fiasco of San Carlos de la Rápita ushered in what, to Carlists, is the most depressing era in the history of the party. It ceases to be recognizable. Montemolin was a weak leader ready to sacrifice his leadership to marry Miss Horsey de Horsey.[1] His successor Don Juan, virtually divorced from his pious wife, jettisoned the principle of legitimacy by subordinating it to the people's choice and endowing it with a liberal programme—a course that made the cause meaningless to its old supporters who considered Don Juan better off in a lunatic asylum.[2] His son the duke of Madrid and the Carlos VII of the Carlist dynasty, was only beginning to reconstruct the party when the Revolution of 1868 gave Carlism the third great chance of its history.

Throughout the years of defeat Carlism had survived, less through its own strength than through the unwillingness of conservative governments to crush a movement whose alliance they might need against the revolution: thus Narváez shot Republicans and amnestied Carlists. Already on the eve of the Revolution of 1868 the Carlist party was being strengthened by the adhesion of neo-catholics who feared the revolution which must follow the collapse of the dynasty. At the same time Carlism was intriguing with the left to precipitate the revolution against the monarchy of Isabella.[3] But, even in an era of political chaos, the Carlist creed failed to impose itself on Spain and by 1875 the constitutional monarchy was more secure than it had ever been.[4]

1 For this episode, see Countess of Cardigan, *My Recollections* (London, 1909), 70–90. She was horrified at 'poor weak Montemolin's' desertion of his supporters in 1849. Carlists regarded Miss Horsey as 'the Delilah who had ruined Carlism'.

2 Conde de Rodezno, *Carlos VII* (1944), 38.

3 The tactical flexibility of Carlism is astonishing: thus in 1867 Carlist leaders were in touch with the Progressives for a joint rebellion that would make Charles VII a democratically elected king. The Progressive revolutionaries, of course, wanted the support of the northern provinces for their pronunciamiento, ibid. 41–45.

4 See below, pp. 337–40, for these later developments.

4. *The Lineaments of Liberal Society, 1830–1850*

In the early 1840's Alcalá Galiano described the Spain which had emerged from the crisis of Carlism as a mercantile and literary society where the material and no small part of the moral force was seated in the enlightened classes.[1] It was the presence of such classes that made the liberalism of the thirties and forties a stable concern compared with that of 1820–3, and which enabled liberal constitutionalism to defeat Carlism. Carlism was always presented by liberals as the revolt of 'monks and low people' against the spirit of the century. It was not that Spain had become, or was to become, a bourgeois capitalist society on advanced Western lines. The enlightened were not a class, but, as the phrase always ran, classes. Against the attempt to force Spain into the past there was an overall identity of interest between aristocrats, landowners, manufacturers, artisans, 'factory' workers, lawyers, soldiers, and journalists. It was this identity of interests between divergent groups against Carlism which explains at the same time the external unity and the internal schisms of liberalism.

The lineaments of what was called a liberal society are evident from 1820. Its development was fostered by enlightened despotism, especially after 1826, in order to gain the alliance of the enlightened classes by the substitution of material progress and efficient administration for liberty. This was the credo of men like Ballesteros and his *afrancesado* circle, of Cea Bermúdez and Javier de Burgos. All these men were hostile to liberalism as a political system. To Cea administrative reforms were 'the *only* reforms which produce immediate prosperity'. Burgos shared this belief in the curative properties of a modern administration—'a fiat of the Ministry will restore the Lower Ebro to prosperity'. As a minister in Cea's government of 1833–4 he patronized a host of reforms from the rational division of Spain into provinces to the castration of merino sheep, chairs of arithmetic, and free soap.[2]

It was not the encouragement of government, however, but the autonomous processes of economic development which had strengthened the enlightened classes, created the elements of a mercantile society and produced the beginnings of a revival

[1] Alcalá Galiano, *Lecciónes de derecho político* (1843), 38.

[2] For these projects see J. de Burgos, *Anales*, II. i. 16–18.

in the economy. After the War of Independence Spain was prostrate: by 1827 recovery was in evidence.

Accompanying economic change was a demographic revolution which had begun in the eighteenth century but which did not assume European proportions till the nineteenth: by the 1860's the population had risen to sixteen million from the ten million of 1800: this growth was above the European average.[1] It became apparent first in regions of economic progress which could afford better sanitation, nutrition, and clothing together with more opportunities for employment. Thus Catalonia increased its share of total population of Spain from 8·1 per cent. (1797) to 10·5 per cent. (1857). Later in the century the central regions recovered, as economic progress and medicine seeped inwards from the periphery.[2]

In general, western Europe met the demands of an increased population by industrial expansion and intensive husbandry. This response, as we have seen, was prohibited in much of Spain by the poverty of her capital resources and of her soil; its place was taken by a surprising increase in the extensive cultivation of cereals. This first expansive impulse of the century took place mainly in the Castilian heartlands, not in the periphery. Moreau de Jonnés in the early thirties considered it the most remarkable growth in Europe: a gain of thousands of hectares from semi-desert lands. He saw Spain as the future granary of the continent.[3]

So uncertain are the statistical foundations of our knowledge

[1]

	Spain	*Europe*	(Base 1800 = 100)
1800 . .	100	100	
1850 . .	149	145	
1900 . .	171	191	

[2] For Catalan population see J. Vicens Vives, *Els catalans en el segle XIX* (Barcelona, 1958), 16 ff. J. Nadal in *E.H.M.* vi (1959), 286 ff., shows that the most dramatic increase in the small Catalan port of Palamós comes with the decline of child mortality in the first years of the nineteenth century, due, perhaps, to the introduction of Jenner's smallpox vaccination in 1800 and to the increased prosperity which came with the development of American trade, merchant shipping, and cork.

[3] Miñano (*Diccionario*, ii. 193) quotes what is obviously a French statistical computation of the income of the province of Burgos: cereals account for over half the total net income, industry, &c., included. Moreau de Jonnés's figures in his *Statistique de l'Espagne* (Paris, 1834) must, in my opinion, be treated with great caution. He came to the improbable conclusion that Spain doubled her cereal production between 1800 and the 1830's.

that it is difficult to say whether this agrarian surge came about before or after 1835. Larraz prefers to place it before the industrial developments of the thirties; Vicens Vives in the forties.[1] In part this expansion was the renewal of eighteenth-century beginnings, interrupted by the wars. The increases of the eighteenth century are explicable in terms of the general price rise: any expansion in the earlier years of the nineteenth century must have taken place against a background of stable or falling agrarian prices—one of the strongest reasons for dating it to the thirties and after. My own guess is that the increase was due less to the necessity of making good the loss of American silver by which Spain's food imports had been financed (as Moreau de Jonnés suggests) than to speculative marginal farming by the new landowners of the thirties and forties. Cereals were the only marketable crop that could be grown quickly on the new lands without heavy capital investment, while the tariff of 1825 forced peripheral Spain to consume Castilian wheat, despite heavy internal transport costs, in preference to cheaper foreign wheat imported by sea. Like most speculative farming it exhausted the soil and yields fell.[2] The barren steppes which Machado and the poets of the nineties found so moving in their desolation were, in part, the creation of these years of cereal mania.

As a result, in these years, with reasonable harvests, Spain was self-supporting in cereals. Bad harvests and bad transport could still cause violent seasonal and local price variations. Wheat prices in 1836 were double those of 1833—the sharpest rise of the century until 1867. Prices rose and fell in different regions at different times and at different rates; thus, in 'dear years', suspension of the prohibition against the importation of foreign wheat and municipal purchase could make prices in the periphery fall below those of the wheat-producing centre, usually areas of low prices.[3] High cereal prices, for a population which,

[1] Cf. the summary of Larraz's arguments in *Un siglo en la vida del Banco de Bilbao* (Bilbao, 1957), 9–10, and cf. J. Vicens Vives in *Historia económica de España* (1958), 578–80.

[2] A crude estimate of wheat yields and cultivated area is:

Area in million hectares		*Annual yield per hectare*	
1800	*1860*	*1800*	*1860*
2,900	5,100	6·31 q.m.	5·8

[3] Because we lack any precise knowledge of the marketing system, stocks, &c., it is difficult to relate prices precisely with harvests, nor can we estimate their more

in most regions, lived on bread and vegetables with little or no meat, meant suffering and urban unrest. Poor peasant farmers could not benefit from high prices, as could the grain dealers and large farmers, nor could they store in years of low prices. The nature of the cereal market therefore sharpened the social struggle in the countryside and provided urban radicalism with its strongest weapons—the abolition of food taxes or *consumos*.

The most striking economic achievement of the first half of the nineteenth century was the consolidation and growth of the industrial complex in Catalonia.[1] Catalan industry was by no means as exclusively textile or as concentrated round Barcelona itself as the phrase 'the Manchester of Spain' implies. There were significant textile and leather concerns in many Catalan towns.[2] There were smallish businesses devoted to the manufacture of paper and soap—important articles in the colonial trade. In the forties various efforts were made to establish large-scale metallurgy. Nevertheless, it was the concentration of a cotton industry—a new pattern for the woollen industry had been widely dispersed—which changed the appearance of Barcelona: the prints of the 1850's show the old port ringed round by factory chimneys.

The first quarter of the century held little promise of such developments. Depression, contracting markets, war, and deflation had ruined the modern cotton concerns built up between 1803 and 1808, leaving the industry to struggling artisans. During the War of Independence a proportion of profits were siphoned off to France as a result of Napoleon's determination to turn the Catalonia economy into a satellite economy.[3] A European recession and the flood of contraband French textiles which swept in the wake of French armies in 1823—as in 1808—killed the revival which marked the era of constitutional government (1820–3). 'Most of the factories have closed', wrote Aribau,

distant effects on the economy and on the propensity to consume of different groups.

[1] See above, pp. 31–32, for the earlier history of Catalan industry.

[2] e.g. Berga, Tarrasa, Sabadell, Igualada.

[3] For the activities of French merchants see Y. Roustit, 'Raymond Durand (1808–14)', *E.H.M.* vi. 311–401. For the deflationary policy of Ferdinand VII see J. Sardá, *La política monetaria y los fluctuaciones de la economía española* (1948). The financial difficulties of liberal governments, both in 1820–3 and after 1833, favoured a policy of foreign loans and devaluation which may have favoured domestic growth.

the Catalan poet and industrial propagandist, in 1824, 'the looms are covered with dust and the artisans begging in the streets.'

Revival was evident in 1827 and it was the subsequent expansion that established the uncontested supremacy of Catalonia in cotton. Catalans visited England and France, modernizing antiquated equipment: between 1830 and 1840 the production of cotton goods almost tripled and in the next five years it doubled once more.[1] Still a horse-and-water industry in 1833, in the subsequent decade began the struggle to set up a steam-powered industry: the Bonaplata's factory *El Vapor* was not merely a steam-powered factory but a machine shop and iron foundry where textile machinery could be made and maintained. This process was delayed by lack of capital and luddism: the Bonaplata factory was burned down by a mob in the troubles of 1836 just as the introduction of the 'devil's invention', self-acting mules, set off strikes in the 1840's.

It was not till the forties that, with increasingly heavy capital investment, the largish cotton factory with modern machinery established itself. Between 1831–41 and 1842–51 the rate of capital investment in cotton increased eightfold and there was a spectacular change to steam power round 1845. These years saw the establishment of the great industrial dynasties: the Güells, champions of protection and first of the new industrialists to take a title; the six Muntada brothers who set up *España Industrial*, the biggest factory in Spain; the Serra brothers. Intermarriage produced some of the richest private textile empires in the world.[2] Industrialists were often connected with the large concerns trading with America—it was in the thirties that Catalan and Levante captains began the triangular Atlantic 'beef run'—and their enterprises financed by profits made in wholesale and retail trade in Cuba—almost exclusively in Spanish hands. Thus Joan Güell invested his Cuban fortune

[1] An example of Catalan imitation was Ferrán Puig Gisbert who perfected the spinning of sewing-thread by visits to France and Scotland. P. Madoz, *Diccionario*, iii. 459 ff., contains invaluable statistical material mostly deriving from Sairó's 1841 report.

[2] Thus the Serra concern remained a private company until 1940: before that date Eusebio Bertrand Serra possessed what was probably the largest individually owned cotton-spinning concern in the world.

in Catalan industry.[1] Yet it must be stressed that the overwhelming majority of Catalan 'factories' employed ten to twenty men and most of the Catalan shippers were small concerns.

To Catalans who regarded Catalonia as constituting a self-contained economic unit this industrial revolution seemed an incomplete, lop-sided achievement. The persistent attempt to create a heavy industry, beginning in these years with the engineering concerns of Bonaplata and others, was an aspiration rather than an achievement. Textiles themselves remain a high-cost industry without an expanding domestic market which could bear the cost of repeated modernization and without cheap coal (the attempt to exploit the Catalan deposits was a failure). Throughout their history Catalan textiles were dependent—apart from later developments in the Antilles—on the purchasing power of the Spanish peasant: even in the twentieth century a bad harvest meant a 30 per cent. drop in textile sales. Hence the determination of the Catalans to secure this market against cheap English textiles. Protectionism became the creed of Catalonia; the price of Catalan political support for Madrid governments was prohibition of textile imports. Organized as a pressure group in the Commission of Factories, Catalans regarded freer trade as a national disaster and the prevalance of smuggling, on a large enough scale to distort the market, a standing reproach to a state run by Madrid politicians indifferent to national prosperity.[2]

Madrid, which liberalism was to make the hub of a centralized governmental machine, remained largely a political capital: where there had been courtiers there were now *pretendientes*, the professional job-seekers of an underpaid civil service. Accusations against the tyranny of Madrid are combined with attacks on its economic 'artificiality'. It was a city of consumers and luxury trades—as were many capitals—and their stimulating effect on an economy was something regional

[1] In Xifré's case (see below, p. 204) there was no direct investment of commercial gains in industrial enterprise: urban real estate was always a safer investment.

[2] Smuggled imports were estimated at anything between 10 per cent. and 40 per cent. of Catalan production, and in 1828 smuggling *tripled* French exports to Spain as a whole; see W. O. Henderson, *The Industrial Revolution on the Continent* (London, 1961), 105. Clearly Gibraltar was a place of entry for English textiles; cf. the figures for the early century: Moreau de Jonnès, *Statistique*, 192, and those for smuggling cases in the courts of Algeciras and Cadiz (*Anuario Estadístico*, 1861).

protectionists did not see. Without cheap transport no large-scale industries could be established in central Spain. Madrid's minor trades included 27 umbrella 'factories', 62 silversmiths, 45 printing works—it was the intellectual capital and it was the descendants of these printers who were to be the first Federal Republicans and Socialists—5 guitar-string makers, and 6 manufacutrers of false teeth.[1]

The developments of the first half of the century foreshadow but feebly the great economic interests of the century: the wheat of Castile, the textiles of Catalonia, the steel and iron of the Basque Provinces, the coal of the Asturias, the varied agricultural and mineral exports of the south.[2] As yet they could not dominate a national market which lacked the connecting tissues of credit and good roads. The Caroline road building, at its height in Charles IV's reign, stopped with the War of Independence which, together with the Carlist War, was responsible for much destruction of the existing system. Coach services, beginning locally in Catalonia and Valencia in the early years of the Restoration, connected Madrid with Barcelona and Valencia; but the journey took eight days and cost a year's wages for a prosperous artisan. Canals Spain could never have —the canal of Castile which would have connected the bread-basket of Spain to the northern ports and cheap transport was projected but never built—and it was only on the threshold of the railway age that Spain got good trunk roads and reasonable inns.[3] Thus the mule trains of Borrow's Spain meant prohibitive transport costs except for the coastal regions served by

[1] Paula Mellado, *Diccionario*, 21–22. Madrid was still physically a small town—perhaps twenty minutes' walk from wall to wall.

[2] All these interests were beginning in the thirties (cf. Ballesteros's interest in Asturian coal; Heredia's blast furnace at Marbella; the Ybarras in Bilbao) but their full development belongs to a later period.

[3] Any guide or travel book is eloquent on Spanish inns. The defect of the road system was its inconsistency: the trunk roads contained some of the best and some of the worst stretches of roads in western Europe, while local roads were tracks. Madoz is full of complaints of bad local roads. To take one example: in Alicante, a relatively developed province, where export products needed to get to ports, there does not appear to have been a single decent road in 1845 (*Diccionario*, i. 626). Many earlier and important roads were now abandoned 'to the prejudice of industry and commerce', e.g. the Córdoba–Málaga road (ibid. vi. 640). Those provinces on the main trunk roads from Madrid were best served, e.g. Ciudad Real (vi. 424). It could thus supply wine to Madrid. The province Avila had only one league of road for wheeled traffic (iii. 123).

a large number of small ships—a fact which helps to account for peripheral progress as against central stagnation. Central Spain was still a congery of local, self-sufficient markets centred on the larger towns. What strikes one, therefore, in the geographical dictionaries (Miñano, 1825; F. de P. Mellado, 1845) is the persistence of the remnants of a decayed industry. Every sizeable pueblo had its looms—especially for linen and in Castile and Aragon wool—serving the needs of the town and its surrounding district, together with a few specialized artisans serving a wider market. Village domestic industry, largely a seasonal secondary occupation, survived into the twentieth century.

Limited and localized though the changes in the infra structure of society may have been, they renewed the eighteenth-century concern with the problem of modernizing a backward state and a backward society on approved foreign precedents. However, the problems of development were now seen in different terms. Whereas the eighteenth century dreamed of a society refashioned by an *élite* using the machinery of the state, now it was considered that society would change of itself and that these autonomous changes would demand modifications of the political structure itself. What a previous generation had called 'illustration' would be the work, not of a dedicated and isolated *élite*, but of the enlightened classes. In the *ancien régime*, urban improvement had been the work of kings and Captains General breaking through the inertia of hereditary municipalities. After 1834 these municipalities were the representatives of citizens concerned with the improvement of their own towns; with the dissolution of the monasteries it became possible to get space for wider streets and for private speculators to buy building plots.[1]

These municipal improvers represented a new force in society and in politics: the alliance of the upper ranges of the bourgeoisie and politically active aristocracy which was to be the foundation of conservative politics for the next hundred years.[2] As the careers of Miraflores, Frías, and Rivas show, aristocrats played an important role in political life, mainly as the leaders

[1] Urban development had revived in the later years of Ferdinand's reign: it was then that Barcelona got paved streets with gutters. Improvement in Madrid dates from the mayoralty of the marqués de Pontejos (1835–7).

[2] For Alcalá Galiano's justification of this alliance see above, p. 160, footnote 1.

of conservative liberalism; the idea of an hereditary or partly hereditary second chamber became politically respectable and a hallmark of conservative liberalism. In Madrid the aristocratic salon set the tone for the social life of the respectable classes; aristocrats and middle class notables served together on committees of subscription balls, savings banks, charity schools, and literary societies, 'initiating a new era of progress in the material and moral interests of society'.[1]

This alliance had as its precondition significant changes both in the world of the aristocrat and of the bourgeois. The old aristocracy of the grandees remained, isolated, proud, and inordinately attached to its honorific court offices, but it was becoming an increasingly rarefied class. Through death and intermarriage, the last duke of Osuna united in his person over fifty titles and enjoyed an income of £60,000—enormous by Spanish standards. Chronic extravagance and the attempt to compete with European aristocrats totally ruined him.[2] Lower down the scale the secure world of the *hidalgo* vanished in the vast transfer of landed property brought about by the disentailing laws of the 1830's.[3] It was the debt-encumbered small noble who sold up. Only the aristocrat who adopted bourgeois virtues could survive.

Increasing prosperity gave the nascent bourgeoisie the confidence and the courage to step outside the confines of the family business. The richest men in Spain were no longer grandees but Catalan business men and bankers. The two great Spanish new fortunes were those of Xifré, made in Cuban trade, and of Remisa, made in army contracts with the French. Xifré, who built a town house on the scale of a grandee's palace, remained a banker and a real property dealer while Remisa went into the borderland of public and private finance as Director of Taxes, farmer of the state-owned Rio Tinto mines, Director of the Canal of Isabella II, and as a banker dealing in government loans.[4]

[1] Mesonero Romanos, *Memorias*, ii. 141.

[2] There is a romanticized account of Osuna's attempt to raise the extravagant gesture into a personal ethic in A. Marchilar, *Duke of Osuna* (London, 1932). The nobility was beginning to imitate English fashion. This imitation was primitive: in the first flat race a gipsy beat all runners.

[3] J. Vicens Vives, *Historia social*, v. 84.

[4] For Remisa and Xifré see the biographies by J. M. Ramón de San Pedro (Barcelona, 1953 and 1956) and pp. 206, 265, 270 below.

The commercial and industrial bourgeoisie of peripheral Spain were *cristino* liberals. Clerical abolutism and bad trade went together,[1] a connexion that was partly an accidental reflection of European fluctuations. Istúriz and Mendizábal in Cadiz, the merchants of San Sebastian and Bilbao, Beltrán de Lis in Valencia, are typical representatives of the commercial liberalism of the thirties and of its connexion with government loans. The negotiation of these loans, which liberal ministries needed to fight Carlism, both brought the commercial classes into political life and bound their interests to a liberal triumph. Although the liberalism of the Barcelona bourgeoisie was conditioned by the dangers of dogmatic liberal free trade, the Catalan industrial class was resolutely liberal; the alternatives were factory-burning Carlists or the erratic favours of an absolute monarchy. The Commission of Spinning Factories supported Ferdinand's enlightened minister, Ballesteros, and in return got protection against English thread; it supported the king against the Catalan Carlists in 1827 and welcomed María Cristina as a protector of the industrial interest.[2] The industrialists backed the new Captain General, Llauder, whom *The Times* called 'the idol of the liberal party', in his struggles against the royalist Volunteers and in his hostility to the guilds which 'had constantly opposed industrial progress'.[3]

It is impossible to understand the structure of liberal politics unless we realize that political initiative lay with the great towns and that it was in the towns the emerging conservative alliance of notables and *haute bourgeoisie* was challenged by the radical alliance of the lesser bourgeoisie and the *menu peuple*.[4] Thus the early radical sympathies of the Barcelona Commission

[1] Cf. the setting up of factories at Berga (P. Madoz, *Diccionario*, iv. 253–5). Very few were set up except in 1820–3 and again in 1830–4.

[2] Thus they appealed to Maria Cristina when, in 1829, they were seriously alarmed by the tariff concessions granted to Dolfuss—the last of many government attempts to create large-scale textile industry near Madrid.

[3] *The Times*, 11 Mar. 1934. For the Comision de Fábricas see G. Graell, *Historia del Fomento del Trabajo Nacional* (Barcelona, n.d.), 29–61. For the crisis of the thirties see R. Ortega Canadell, in *E.H.M.* v. 351–84. The monarchy was always suspicious of the Spinner's Commission and tended to support the guilds for reasons of administrative convenience; for the guilds see Graell, ibid. 72–81. One of the first acts of the liberal ministry was the establishment of freedom of manufacture against the restrictive practices of the guilds.

[4] This latter alliance was unstable. It was the smaller *fabricantes* of Catalonia, struggling with machine competition, who were the worst employers.

of Factories were modified by the labour troubles of the thirties and forties: while demanding state protection for their own interests in the name of infant industry, they resisted, in the name of freedom of contract, all government attempts to save the workers from abusive practices.[1] Labour unrest they dismissed as the work of a 'few discontented spirits', inspired by Carlists who wished to ruin Catalan prosperity by driving the rest of Spain to boycott Catalan textiles. This swing to the right and the alliance with conservative interests which was to underpin the Moderate party is evident in the function of Remisa as a liaison between Catalan industry and conservative liberal politics, in the increasing conservative tone of liberalism of the Basque towns. The *gente decente* went in fear of the 'anarchy' of urban radicalism: hence their willingness to tolerate an army take-over when the traditional 'revolutionary' take-over of the local notables could no longer guarantee social peace.

The revolutionary temper of the urban lower middle class is explained by the precarious nature of its existence. The traditional independent artisans of the Catalan towns, Barcelona in particular, were beginning their descent into the upper regions of employed labour. Those who maintained their independence merged into the shopkeeping class, still politically conservative in 1814 but by the forties and fifties providing many radical leaders; Barcelona radical politics were to centre in gatherings of journalists and artisans such as that which met in Soler's clock shop.[2]

Radical politics could have a working-class following only in Barcelona, the textile towns of Catalonia, and the great ports and cities of the south. In Catalonia grievances were rooted in the unstable conditions of the industry itself: the laying off of hands in times of bad trade, piece-work disputes which were largely the result of mechanization—hence the destruction of machines in 1836 and 1845. The textile operatives became serious radicals through the refusal of conservative governments to remove the legal restrictions on workers' associations; enrolled in the militia they were the radicals' fighting

[1] These practices were mostly piece-work rates connected with the width of cloth to be woven on new and old machines. The workers constantly resisted employers' attempts to widen cloths—the main dispute until 1845.

[2] Soler's *tertulia* belongs to a later period. Its activities are described at length in C. Roure, *Recuerdos de mi vida larga* (Barcelona, 1926).

force. Beneath them were the *miserables*: the dockers, the quasi-mendicant street hawkers, the mass of urban poor, whose presence, in spite of efforts at public assistance, made the streets of Barcelona an unforgettable experience to the sensitive mind even in the late nineteenth century.[1] In every large southern town there was an underworld of desperate poverty and casual labour peopled by the strong characters whom Borrow met on his travels.[2] No one can understand the spontaneous combustion of radical revolution in Spain without visiting the poorer quarters of a Mediterranean port.

The society that emerged after 1833 was a discussing society; if it remained true that religion and orthodox morals remained beyond debate, the atmosphere of absolutism (which has asphyxiated the poet Larra and made the publication of even the most innocuous book a hazardous operation of negotiation and private influence with the censorship authorities) had passed. Discussion was political and literary (serious economic debate belongs to the fifties) and was carried on in the periodical press and in the public debating and literary society—an extension of the intimate, family *tertulia*. It was easy to establish newspapers, and in 1840–3 a well-organized campaign exhibited for the first time the political power of the press.[3] The Athenaeum (*Ateneo*) was founded as a literary club in 1835: it was to possess a unique political and literary influence and was to establish the respectability of the intellectual in social and political life and the primacy of public, informed debate.[4]

The renewal of public debate corresponded with the beginnings of the Romantic movement imported into Spain by the liberal exiles who returned to Spain from France and England

[1] Cf. the terrifying descriptions of the parade of the mutilated *esguerrats* (old soldiers) in J. M. de Sargarra, *Memories* (Barcelona, 1954), 214–18.

[2] For this underworld of *mala gente* in the southern towns see H. D. Inglis, *Spain in 1830* (London, 1831), ii. 50 (Seville), 181 (Malaga), 331 (Valencia). Inglis attributed the existence of the 'idle' poor to low food prices and ecclesiastical charity: 'In Valencia, every idle person is sure of his dinner.'

[3] The connexion between a free press and progressive politics is shown by the newspapers published in Barcelona. 1815: two; 1820–3: twelve; 1823–33: one; 1834: two; 1835: six; 1837: six; 1838: four; 1839: four; 1841: five; 1842: ten (including one republican paper); 1834: eight. The number dropped off sharply in periods of conservative liberal rule.

[4] For the political significance of the *Ateneo* see R. Labra, *El Ateneo de Madrid* (1878). It was most influential as a gathering place of the political opposition—especially for conservative liberals in periods of radical ascendancy.

after 1833. Primarily a movement in the theatre, the Romantic debate 'acted as a link between the most varied classes of cultivated society'. In a sense it was the literary credo of early liberalism. 'This intimate union of the political ideas and our literature explains the ardour', wrote the poet Escosura, 'with which our youth scale the mountains of Navarre in order to drive from them the representatives of ignorance.'[1]

Romanticism could not give the enlightened classes a programme: this derived from the eighteenth-century reformers, from post-revolutionary France and from the English intellectuals whom the exiles had known in the 1820's. Like liberalism Romanticism was, in Valera's phrase, imported ready-made; and, as in liberal constitutions, foreign origin was concealed by an excess of native historical costume. The best spirits hoped for regeneration from a return to the theatre of the *siglo de oro*, much as the intellectuals of 1898 were to connect national and literary revival. These hopes were defeated when Romanticism became an imitation of French models—an almost inevitable decline when translations were paid as highly as original plays. It was Larra's virulent attack on this facile aping of foreigners which made him the hero of the generation of '98. Romanticism was little more than the transient creed of a liberal *élite*: only in Catalonia, where it became connected with the attempt to revive a sense of Catalan nationality, was its influence significant, lasting and wholesome.[2]

Thus Romanticism, after a short period, lost its position as a cohesive force in liberalism. The *Liceo* (the public salon where the 'mingling of classes' was most evident) soon closed. The *Ateneo*, after almost perishing in political squabbles, became a stronghold of conservative liberalism. The poet Espronceda became a Republican, Martínez de la Rosa a respectable conservative. By 1837 the harmony of the liberal family was vanishing in its literary as well as its political manifestations.

In a deeper sense Romanticism was not without a more permanent influence. It is one of the founts of that politico-

[1] Quoted H. Juretschke, *Lista*, 334.

[2] Whereas 'Castilian' Romantics copied French models, Catalan Romantics were influenced by the German and English historical schools, e.g. Scott. For Romanticism in general see E. Allison Peers, *A History of the Romantic Movement in Spain* (Liverpool, 1940).

literary tradition which broods on the problem of Spain. Literate Spaniards saw their own country through the eyes of those French Romantic travellers who sought in Spain the contrasts provided by a civilization 'untouched by Europe'.[1] By making them aware of their idiosyncrasies it encouraged the attribution of the problems of Spain, not to social and economic backwardness, which could be remedied, but to some indefinable, infinitely debatable, and ineradicable 'Spanishness' which would defeat modernization on the European model. Spaniards could either glory in their uniqueness and regional diversities or see in this local colour the symbol of Spain's *atraso*—her time-lag behind Europe. There was, therefore, both an aping of foreign fashion to close the cultural gap and a concern to record the lineaments of traditional Spain before it should succumb to Europeanization. To preserve a record of the Spain that was passing away, albeit slowly and imperceptibly except in the great towns, was the concern of the *costumbrista* school of writers, faithful recorders of strange 'types' and regional oddity. Even this act of literary piety and patriotism was inspired by French models.[2]

[1] The classic of Romantic travel in Spain is Gautier's *Voyage en Espagne* published in 1843; cf. Le Gentil, *Le Poète Bretón de los Herreros* (Paris, 1909), 245. 'From 1830 to 1850 one can say that the Spaniards saw their own country through French reminiscences.'

[2] For an interesting treatment of the *costumbrista* writers see J. F. Montesinos, *Costumbrismo y novela* (Valencia, 1960). The model of the early *costumbristas* was the French writer Jouy, while the literature of types derived from the French literature of 'physiologies'. This later vein was exploited in the most well known of all these productions, *The Spaniards Depicted by Themselves*, published in 1843. There was a periodical devoted to *costumbrismo* called *The Picturesque Weekly* (1836).

VI

PRAETORIAN PARLIAMENTARIANISM
1840–1856

1. *The Army, the Parties, and the Crown*

WITH the peace of Vegara Spain ceased to occupy the concern and conscience of Europe; she reverted to her natural level in the diplomacy of the Great Powers as one of *les cours secondaires*. The Carlist wars left the political development of the country determined by the balance of the three internal forces which accepted the Isabelline constitutional monarchy as a framework of action—the crown, the army, and the dynastic parties—and by the strength and unity they showed against those irreconcilable foes outside the system who rejected it *in toto*. Normally all three forces reacted in union against external threats from the Carlists and the Republicans, while any two forces within the system could, at least for a brief period, counterbalance the third. Thus Espartero and the Progressives could eliminate the crown; the crown and the army could eliminate the politicians, as with Primo de Rivera after 1923; the politicians and the crown together could diminish the influence of the army, for this was the achievement of Cánovas after 1875. When the crown alienated both the support of the army and of the politicians, then the crown must retreat: hence 1854, 1868, and 1931. In 1856 and in 1873–4 it was saved when the revolutionary coalitions disintegrated, and the threat of 'anarchy' drove a section of the politicians and most of the army to order as represented by the crown. In 1936 the crown did not exist and the forces of order were forced to seek a substitute in an *ad hoc* military dictatorship. We must, therefore, examine this triple equation and the relations between its constituent terms in its formative years.

The central factor was the crown's position as 'moderating power', as possessing the two personal prerogatives of appointing and dismissing ministers and granting to a minister a decree of dissolution. It was the constant accusation of the left that these prerogatives were consistently exercised in favour of the right.

There can be little doubt that both María Cristina as regent and Isabella as queen often acted as if the Progressives were scarcely distinguishable from their revolutionary allies: María Cristina never forgot her humiliation at the hands of the sergeants of La Granja nor her interviews with Espartero. Isabella, except for a short period after 1840, was brought up in a conservative court where the Progressive leaders were distrusted. She shared the sentimental piety of her generation which regarded the Progressives as, at the best, indifferent to the position of the Church. The Progressives, in their turn, regarded her attachment to Sor Patrocino, a nun who professed to have received the stigmata and to 'love Your Majesty more truly than anyone else in this miserable world', as a breach of political ethics.[1]

Both mother and daughter weakened their political position by their private behaviour: María Cristina married in secret an ex-sergeant, son of a shopkeeper; the radicals could always threaten to expose this morganatic marriage (she concealed with difficulty her repeated pregnancies) and thus deprive her of her legal title to the regency and its incomes. Isabella was consistently accused of supporting 'favourites' when her own marriage was a failure. María Cristina further weakened her position by an avaricious determination to build up a secure private fortune. She snapped up all available funds abroad (hence her interest in the Cuban revenues) and was accused of replacing the state silver services with substitutes of pewter. She was engaged, as a private person, in the Cuban slave trade and it was her joint speculations with her husband Muñoz (who became duke of Riansares) which made her so unpopular in 1853–4. Isabella was considered a frivolous 'impossible' woman (the Condesa de Espoz y Mina found her a self-willed,

[1] The only exception to conservative court influence was the period 1840–3 when Argüelles was the queen's tutor and the wife of Mina her nanny. For a description of this period see Condesa de Espoz y Mina, *Memorias* (Aguilar edition, Madrid, 1944). The Progressives had a hard tussle against the old grandees and courtiers and were finally defeated by them when Olózaga was forced to resign (see below, p. 227). For Sor Patrocinio see R. Olivar Bertrand, *Así cayó Isabel II* (Barcelona, 1955), appendix ii.

charming, but ill-educated child) whose sexual guilt may have put her at the mercy of her confessor's and her husband's clericalism.

All these failings, whether genuine or based on scandalous rumour, were exploited by the democratic and opposition press. Yet in spite of rumour, ichthyosis, obesity, and what Washington Irving, the American writer, described as her 'rough and somewhat mealy look' the queen retained her popularity till the sixties. Like her father she understood the populace and failed to understand respectable politicians. It was they who dethroned her when she was still only thirty-eight.

The second factor of the equation was the dynastic politicians. Their normal instrument was a parliamentary machine which already ran along lines many were to consider as laid down only by the so-called debased parliamentarianism of the last quarter of the century. All the techniques of local influence and electoral management were well-tried devices by the fifties; they worked more easily because, with a small electorate, the noise of the machine was less audible. How this machine worked under the various liberal constitutions and in the context of provincial life, how candidates were chosen, how they were financed, we do not know.[1] It is sufficiently clear that elections in the smaller constituencies were largely controlled by the Ministry of the Interior whose local agent, the *Jefe Político* and later the provincial governor, could secure election for the official candidate by negotiations with local politicians whose influence he must respect.[2] The secret ballot meant secret scrutiny, while the publication of a mutilated electoral register too late for protest, and brute force, provided emergency devices.[3] But the main resort was to the votes of government servants who constituted a large proportion of the electorate; combined

[1] A prolonged study of the press might reveal how candidates were chosen; cf., as an example, the description of the selection of the deputy for the Andalusian constituency Carmona in *El Heraldo*, 21 September 1844.

[2] Most of the 349 constituencies of the 1845 constitution consisted of 200–500 electors: the smallest constituencies were in Galicia (100–200 electors): Barcelona and Madrid constituencies were roughly between 1,000 and 2,000. Thus O'Donnell's widening of the franchise (see below, p. 297) would have had important results if the Progressives could have been persuaded to accept it.

[3] For a description of these devices see T. M. Hughes, *Revelations of Spain in 1845* (London, 1845), ii. 266.

with the abstention of opposition parties from contests they could not hope to gain, the government had a ready-made majority in most constituencies.[1] Thus, as long as abstention did not become a revolutionary device, it was a condition of the successful functioning of the parliamentary system.

It was the Progressives who turned abstention into a weapon of total protest. They replied to the crown's refusal to call them to office, which alone could allow them to use government machinery to 'make' a majority, by boycotting the 'false' system which excluded them. The systematization of abstention in the *retraimiento* (the complete abstention of opposition parties from the polls) must threaten the existence of the constitutional monarchy. It only seems to have worked effectively in the large urban constituencies which possessed an electorate in some degree independent of the management characteristic of, say, Galician and southern rural constituencies.[2] While the *retraimiento* accentuated the electoral strength of the dominant party, it both exposed the falsity of its claim to represent the electorate and encouraged its internal dissensions: every parliamentary majority, in a Cortes in which there was no serious opposition, showed with time a tendency to fray at the edges and to dissolve into groups. A Democrat described the Moderates as 'divided into half a dozen factions, each with its cabinet and gang of office seekers, many of them common to several factions though they follow the victor for the time being'.[3] In the interests of party discipline and constitutional decency alike it was therefore advisable to encourage an opposition. By the sixties both Miraflores and O'Donnell, confronted by Progressive abstention, were anxious to make deals with the Progressives in order to entice them into the Cortes. The devices

[1] A calculation made from the *Anuario Estadístico* (1865) would seem to indicate that, in some constituencies at least, nearly half the electorate was composed of government and municipal employees or those on government pensions. The conservative Moderates abstained in the elections of 1839 which gave the subsequent Cortes an overwhelming Radical majority; they repeated these tactics in the elections to Espartero's Cortes (see above, p. 180).

[2] Thus in 1858 the national average was an abstention of under one-third of the electorate: in some Barcelona constituencies 50 per cent. abstained and in the Lavapies constituency of Madrid (a Radical–Progressive stronghold) 399 voted as against 744 abstainers. Towns like Málaga, Córdoba, Badajoz had high polls.

[3] Cf. below, p. 222, for the effects of the lack of an opposition on Espartero's parliamentary strength.

of parliamentary government demanded, if not alternative governments, at least the appearance of an opposition party: if a *turno político* did not come naturally into being it must be created by artificial respiration.

The Progressives' objection to the partial use of the 'moderating power' exposes one of the fundamental weaknesses of the constitutional system. The most important consequence of 'made' elections was that it exposed the crown to the charge of party favouritism: any minister called on by the crown could, by a dissolution, gain a majority. Even had the crown been determined to act as a neutral 'moderating power' the prerogative of dissolution would have made its task difficult without a defined party system and an independent electorate which could present the crown with a clear choice, and favour the growth of customs of the constitution to guide that choice. None of these prerequisites for the smooth functioning of a mature constitutional monarchy existed.[1] This is not to excuse the partiality and political narrow-mindedness of both María Cristina as regent and Isabella as queen. They were Moderate monarchs who consistently convinced themselves that the state of opinion in the country did not justify the appointment of a Progressive ministry, equipped with a decree of dissolution to 'make' a Progressive Cortes. It was precisely their failure to call on the Progressives which left the Progressive leaders without a chance of electoral victory and with no alternative but that of forcing the closet by revolutionary procedures from the *retraimiento* to the pronunciamiento. Their constitutional doctrines, like those of the Foxite Whigs, were therefore conditioned by royal exclusion. As in the case of the Whigs these doctrines would have been tempered with office; yet their existence made the crown regard the Progressive ministry as a last resort. This drove the party to the brink of revolution and the threat of revolution was then used to justify the conservatism of the crown.

The third factor was the army. Its function in politics had been transformed by the Carlist wars so that by 1840 it was the

[1] A useful comparison showing the difficulties confronting a conscientious monarch functioning as 'moderating power' with 'false' parties is provided by the experience of Pedro II of Brazil. The difficult dilemmas of constitutional kingship in these conditions are set out in Oliveira Vianna, *O Ocaso do imperio* (S. Paulo, 1933), 12–66. Spanish political history (via Portugal) was not without influence in Brazil.

strongest power in the state. Military politics, in time of war, are always the result of mutual needs; generals want political backing for their particular strategies of victory; politicians want victory in order to strengthen their party position. Thus the ailing Mina was told by his radical friends to win a victory even if he had to be carried to the battlefield on a litter, while the Moderates always hoped for a crowning victory in the north from General Córdoba. In Spain, military intervention became a chronic manifestation because the politicians' desire for military backing expanded beyond this primary war-time need and combined with military ambition to produce a race of soldier politicians. It was not merely that the army was the home of liberalism and its defence against Carlism; it was the only solid institution in the liberal state. The political factions, sensing their weakness and isolation after 1837, appealed to the generals. 'All parties have their eyes fixed on me', wrote Narváez. Thus in November 1838 it was the radical politicians of Seville who appealed to General Córdoba to head their local revolution against the constituted authorities; there is, perhaps, something in Córdoba's case that, in a confused situation, he accepted this political role against his will in order to contain the revolution and save the face of the authorities.[1]

It took the generals some time to adapt themselves to a new role as permanent party leaders rather than as the occasional interpreters of the national will in the mechanism of the pronunciamiento. The initial hesitations of Narváez and Espartero, threatening, courted, but uncommitted, confused party politics.[2] In view of their later roles, it is surprising that Narváez at one time appeared as the rising hope of the Progressives and Espartero was considered as a possible instrument of the queen's friends.

[1] Cf. *Historia militar y política de Don Ramón Nárvaez* (Madrid, 1849), 529 ff. Córdoba appealed to Narváez to help him in the 'absurd and anti-logical position the cursed Junta' had placed him. Narváez professed that he intended to 'calm' the revolution and that his actions were misinterpreted by his superior General Clonard and by a government committed to his military rivals, i.e. Espartero and his staff. Córdoba's explanation cannot be accepted in its entirety: he had curious connexions with the southern radicals and was probably planning to institute a Liberal Union government of which he would be the leading figure.

[2] Cf. the attempts of both parties to attract Narváez in Oct. 1838. To these temptations he opposed 'a series of negatives' (ibid. 501) which led to attempts to malign him (522).

The first stages of the process of involvement came when generals, without funds from the central government, became 'satraps' in their military commands, bludgeoning local authorities into supplying their men, or replacing civilian authority altogether by declarations of a state of siege. O'Donnell, who was ready to mutiny for soap, enforced his I.O.U.s on local authorities and contractors, and the seizure of local government was a particularly striking feature of the military administration of Narváez in the south in 1838. 'We have reached the unhappy situation of seeing ourselves reduced in these provinces to our own authority alone.'[1]

Military rule may be seen as a transference of this local predominance to the sphere of central government. When politicians could not spread limited supplies over the different operational armies, it became a necessity for commanders to have friends in the government in order to secure what supplies there were. 'A cabinet that would help me and give me supplies', wrote Narváez, 'and I would respond with an act worthy of the nation';[2] but to supply Narváez and his Army of the Centre meant neglecting Espartero's Army of the North. The ministry supported Espartero. Where he had been a commander competing for preferential treatment, Narváez now saw himself as a *political* enemy of Espartero and the ministry that had backed his rival. He regarded Espartero's favoured war minister, Alaix, as 'the enemy of my glory', and intrigued with Córdoba for an anti-Espartero government. Espartero's sole test of a government in the critical years of 1838–9 was quite simply its willingness to supply him with the means of victory. Such a government was one which kept Alaix at the Ministry of War; like many soldiers, his personal preference was for non-party governments.

The failure of civilian governments to supply the armies in the field forced generals into politics dramatically in 1837. The government declared officially that the armies were starving because the generals were lining their own pockets.

[1] Narváez to Clonard, 31 Mar. 1838; Clonard MSS. *Archivo Histórico Militar.* For the constant friction between civil and military authorities in Catalonia see J. Carrera Pujal, *Cataluña*, iii. 258. De Meer's 'tyranny' as Captain General of Catalonia was exercised against the municipality of Barcelona and the Provincial Deputations.

[2] Narváez to Córdoba, 12 May 1838.

Soldiers, with government declarations on their bayonets, murdered their officers in a wave of mutinies which swept over the northern armies in the summer. Moreover, the extreme Progressives were trying to win over the sergeants and men to oppose their officers—as they did in the La Granja 'revolution'. Espartero began to talk of politicians with contempt; English admirers saw him as a Cromwell come to end the squabbles of parliamentarians. More significantly, once the 1837–8 crisis had passed, the failure of successive governments to provide the sinews of war made the victories of the generals look like triumphs for private enterprise. In 1835 Spain had turned to a civilian saviour: by 1837 a civilian saviour was inconceivable.

The appeal to generals did not appear as a surrender to a caste apart. Military rule is incomprehensible unless we remember that the division between military and civilian society was indistinct. There was little social difference between an underpaid officer and an underpaid civil servant: both were members of the under-employed middle class which depended on political patronage for promotion. Like the *pretendientes* the officer corps, inflated by war promotions and by the intake of Carlist officers under the terms of the peace of Vergara, had become too numerous for the available posts and saw further promotion in terms of engineering a revolution that would secure it. The officer without promotion, like the *pretendiente*, was seen hob-nobbing with politicians in the cafés of Madrid; while serving officers they could sit as deputies or senators and it became an issue whether their immunity as senators covered their actions as military conspirators. Thus military rule was a symbiotic growth where politicians leant on soldiers and soldiers appeared as working politicians.[1] When Narváez and Espartero were stripped of their civilian character to appear as military dictators, they fell.

Paradoxically, once they had assumed political power, the

[1] Of course the army had its peculiar divisions and factions which derived from the internal politics of the army: thus in 1836 a pamphleteer noted three divisions: Ahumada's party (e.g. Córdoba and Narváez, the 'aristocratic' generals); the generals promoted in 1820 (e.g. Lopez Baños, San Miguel); the soldiers who had fought in America, called *Ayacuchos* (e.g. Espartero, Seoane). These latter were a particularly cohesive group because they shared the guilt of deposing the Captain-General of Peru, Pezuela, and were always suspected of 'selling out' before Ayacucho. *La milicia por de dentro* (Cadiz, 1836), *passim*. For Ayacucho see above, p. 144.

attempt to invest themselves with civilian characteristics inevitably weakened the politician-general's hold on the army by an attack on its interests for the sake of a balanced budget. Thus Espartero, with the best will in the world, could not solve the problem of an inflated war-time army which must be reduced when the state was too poor either to maintain it or pension it off. In August 1841 he reduced the Guards Regiments; by the winter these regiments were the centre of a conspiracy against him. It was arrears of pay that gave the officers' sedition of 1843 its hold among soldiers who had revered Espartero. Thus, if to civilians he appeared a military dictator, to soldiers he tended to appear as a general who had forgotten how to look after the army. The lesson was not lost on his successor, Narváez.

2. *The Regency of Espartero, 1840–1843*

The regency of Espartero—he became sole regent in May 1841—is the most striking example of the new symbiosis of politicians and soldiers. Its impurity, as representative of this system, lay in the popular revolution which made September 1840 something more than a mere military take-over. This 'glorious revolution' was a compound of the 1836 model (the consecration by the army of a civil revolution in the great towns) and the 'negative pronunciamiento' (the refusal of influential soldiers to back the government against a surge of opinion). The mixture proved chronically unstable, and the power given to Espartero by the Revolution of September was subject to a continuous process of erosion until it came to rest, top heavy, on a military clique, detestable alike to disillusioned revolutionaries and defeated conservatives. Espartero was overthrown by an alliance of the architects of the September Revolution (the Barcelona Radicals and the left-wing Progressives) with their bitterest enemies (the Moderate generals and politicians). It was this alliance which confused for a decade the forces of popular revolution. Having helped to destroy the Tyrant, the Progressives could find no figure of comparable stature and influence to represent their aspirations within the military caste. Thus they were condemned to political impotence until 1854.

It is often and wrongly maintained that the army turned

conservative only after 1873. It was staunchly liberal, in the sense that it was opposed to Carlism; but *cristino* officer liberalism could cover either the extension of liberal conquests towards democracy and alliance with the Revolution, or defence of what were known as the acquired interests of liberalism. Most of the generals were men of order, willing to serve the conservative interests of the liberal state. Thus, apart from a group of military friends whose careers depended on his power—Linaje, Espartero's secretary, Van Halen, Seoane, and Zurbano—many officers disliked Espartero's alliance with revolution in 1840, especially as radicals threatened the interests of the army by their cry for economies in the military budget. The ineluctable fate of successful military rebellion was that it set precedents of sedition: when Espartero praised the 'civic bravery' of the Regiment of Cazadores for what was a mutiny against their superior officers in September 1840, he invited similar demonstrations of civic bravery against himself.[1]

Already in 1841 some military authorities were slack in their defence of the new regent; thus O'Donnell, like Mola in 1936, plotted undisturbed in Pamplona in spite of civilian warnings. In the summer of 1843 the desertion of the officers was decisive. Their loyalty had been undermined by the Spanish Military Order, half Order of Chivalry, half secret society based on Masonic techniques, and organized by Narváez with funds supplied by María Cristina from her exile in Paris. The innovation was that the conspiratorial network ran in 'triangles' of three initiates from the *superior officers down*, a Masonic device which made officer compromises secure but kept sergeants and men in their place in the lower ranks of the Order.

Once María Cristina made clear her intentions to plot against Espartero with French support, the alliance of Espartero's military enemies, Narváez and O'Donnell, with the Moderate politicians was inevitable. By October 1841 the generals believed that a pure conservative army revolt, with no compromise to attract Espartero's enemies on the left, would be successful. This calculation was based on the new-found Moderate strength in the north. The rural notables feared that the Progressives,

[1] Cf. the comments of the Moderate journalist Pastor Díaz, *El Conservador*, Jan. 1841, quoted E. Chao Espina, *Pastor Díaz dentro del Romanticismo* (1949), 84–95.

under Espartero, whose government included representatives of the anti-foralist view of the San Sebastian liberals, would destroy the *fueros* on which their local predominance over 'foreigners' was based and which had been guaranteed by the Moderates in November 1839. This destruction was implicit in the Progressive claim that a liberal constitution for *all* Spaniards left foral liberties as an archaic and unnecessary conservative vestige.

The October rising of generals and Moderates was condemned to failure in the north by the denial of the Carlist alliance; Carlism would not support a conservative counter-revolution in the interests of a usurping dynasty. To militant Carlists the foral liberties which the rebels proclaimed were of no interest in themselves: Carlism wished to destroy the parliamentary monarchy, the Moderate oligarchs to exploit it by the exclusion of radicals and democrats. The northern revolt itself was ill-timed and planned—as so often happened, it went off at half-cock because O'Donnell feared discovery. He failed to hold Pamplona; Montes de Oca's foralist Junta at Vitoria, a rebellion in Bilbao, and military sedition in Saragossa soon collapsed. In Madrid, Diego de León and Manuel Concha, both young war-time generals of Romantic dispositions, were forced to act through O'Donnell's precipitation. They attempted to seize the palace and the infant queen but were defeated by the unexpected resistance of a few Halberdiers.[1] It is a curious reflection on the ethics of the pronunciamiento that neither side in the battle on the palace stairs fired to kill and that Espartero's execution of the leading conspirators was regarded as a breach of the military convention that all generals had a right to revolt. Diego de León's noble conduct to the soldiers who shot him entered romantic mythology; the cigars he had distributed to his escort now repose, with his uniforms, in the Madrid Military Museum. His execution left the *Ayacuchos*, as Espartero's friends in the army were called, in moral isolation; the Conchas were already a powerful military clan.

The northern Moderates had gambled with the generals in order to save their predominance within the foral régime.

[1] In spite of the many accounts of this episode the lack of casualties remains inexplicable. It *may* be the consequence of the angle between the stairs and the landing.

Defeat, therefore, enabled radical liberalism to attempt the dismantling of foral independence. Its essential mechanism, the 'foral pass' (the right of local authorities to allow or disallow Spanish laws) was declared invalid against a government order; the powers of the Juntas were handed over to the constitutional Provincial Deputations; the customs line was drawn along the national frontiers, and the provinces subjected to conscription. It seemed almost a complete triumph for centralization and the urban liberalism of San Sebastian in its desire to destroy the privileges of the rural notables and the customs barrier which kept merchandise from Spain. Nevertheless, to postpone the full incorporation of the Provinces into constitutional Spain became the aim of the foralist party in the north which represented the conservatism defeated in '41. The 'rights' lost between 1839 and 1841 became the subject of a romantic historical tradition in which the Basques figured as a free people endowed with an ancient constitution, subject to the rule of Spanish kings only by its own consent.[1] The foralists claimed the restitution of this lost independence and resisted all attempts of the central government to raise taxes and conscripts.

We must now trace the erosion of Espartero's politico-military rule and the formation against him of the monstrous coalition of parliamentary Progressives and Moderate generals which was to drive him into exile. His political vices were hubris and *naïveté*, so that his enemies could claim that he 'pitted the will of one man against that of the nation'. Like all generals he claimed to represent the national will in a higher form than it could be found in an elected Cortes. Thus he saw no necessity to behave as a neutral moderating power, basing his government on parliamentary majorities—a position not surprising in a general who had backed revolution against a parliamentary ministry and who claimed to regard majority rule as a novel convention without sanction in the text of the constitution.

In its origins the left-wing parliamentary opposition represented the constitutional scruples of radical Progressives, with no love for the army, who regarded Espartero's appointment

[1] See M. García Venero, *Nacionalismo Vasco*, 107–81. The beauties of Basque institutions were the subjects of the popular composer and guitarist Iparraguire (b. 1820) who wrote 'The Tree of Gernika'. This tree was the central symbol of foralist romanticism. (See below, pp. 556–8, for the further development of Basque nationalism.)

as *sole* regent as a triumph engineered by the *Ayacuchos* 'against the nation'. It was rapidly augmented by the rage of jobless young *pretendientes* within a large Progressive majority. The very strength of the Progressives in the Cortes encouraged opposition from within the party; without an effective Moderate opposition to strengthen party discipline, the government majority seemed the creation of a Spanish Guizot.[1] Thus, as the opposition grew in numbers, the leaders of Progressive parliamentary opposition, Olózaga and López, could claim they were defending the central principle of liberal parliamentarianism: the responsibility of ministers to the Cortes as an effective control over the prerogative of appointing and dismissing ministers.[2]

The Progressive opposition, therefore, brought against Espartero all the charges of unconstitutional use of prerogatives that had been brought against María Cristina. In May 1841 the groups led by Cortina, López, and Olózaga decisively defeated the ministry in the Cortes. Espartero defied the rebels by the appointment of a general, Rodil—an *Ayacucho* who enjoyed Espartero's confidence but had no Parliamentary support. A dissolution did not save Rodil and the new Cortes forced Espartero to appoint López (9 May 1843) after all his attempts to find an alternative ministry had failed. López demanded the dismissal of Linaje from his post as Espartero's military secretary and an amnesty which would have allowed the Moderate conspirators back to Spain. Espartero rightly regarded the latter as a dangerous concession to his bitterest army enemies and the former as an interference with what was, to him, his court. 'The dismissal of General Linaje', López confessed, 'became the principal and almost exclusive occupation of the Cabinet.' Espartero refused to give in, dismissed López, and dissolved the Cortes. This gave the revolution banner which

[1] Cf. A. Pirala, *Guerra civil*, iii. 707, represents its absence as 'a great inconvenience for the Progressive party' and its parliamentary discipline, cf. above, p. 213.

[2] S. Olózaga (1805–73) and J. M. López (1798–1855) were both lawyers, both had served in the militia, and both had been connected with Calatrava whom López had served as Minister of the Interior. The reputation of both and their claims to the leadership of the left wing of the Progressives were based on their oratorical talents, e.g. Olózaga's famous denunciation of Espartero ('God Save the Queen, God Save the Country'). It was López's eclipse after 1843 that gave Olózaga the leadership of the civilian Progressives.

could unit Moderate and Progressive rebels: the restoration of López and of constitutional normality.

In view of later history, the most significant element of the coalition against Espartero was the hostility of Catalonia, centred on its capital, Barcelona. In 1820–3 and throughout the Carlist wars, a sense of the distinct interests of Catalonia had developed against the exactions of Captain Generals and other representatives of the central government. This 'provincial egoism' had its roots deep in the past. It was as yet incoherent. Though the Catalan bonnet and flag appear, it was far removed from conscious Catalanism or historically tinged regionalism. Rooted in the city patriotism of Barcelona, it represented a provincialist reaction against the inconveniences and injustices of control by Madrid politicians who had no special concern for what was called 'the differential factor' of Catalonia. The centralizing Municipalities law was therefore bitterly opposed in Catalonia and the Revolution of 1840 appeared a triumph for municipalist provincialism as well as for the Progressive programme. In 1840 Barcelona was a centre of Espartero's strength.

Espartero's rule brought no satisfaction to his Catalan supporters. Colonel Prim found the central government uninterested in suppressing smuggling, the bane of Catalan industrialists. 'I only met with vexation, hindrance and opposition of every kind. Everything is rotten, men and institutions. My countrymen [i.e. *the Catalans*] know me well enough not to doubt my words . . . my efforts have been sterile because the government so desired it and does not care if our industry is ruined, our factories abandoned and Catalonia ruined. For this reason commotions are inevitable.' Catalan discontent and the tactics of threatened revolution produced in Espartero and his generals what was to become the conditioned reflex of Castile. Why should Catalonia claim special treatment? 'Rich Barcelona cannot refuse to pay what a miserable village pays: the inhabitants of Barcelona have no natural properties which exempt them from conscription.' Catalonia, concluded General Seoane, was best ruled by the stick.

Espartero's breach with the Barcelona radicalism dated from his determination to cut short any further radical demands once the revolution of September had brought him to power. He had the support of respectable Progressives, both in his hostility to the crypto-republicanism of the Democrats and in his suppression of the workers' associations. The abolition of protected urban leases (a measure which doubled the value of urban property) was likewise as acceptable to Progressives as a piece of doctrinaire economic individualism as it was unpopular in the lower classes. The Progressives detested the anarchy of republican 'gangs' who terrified middle-class families into leaving the city by the language of social revolution. 'When the people wishes to conquer its rights, the masses must seize arms and cry *Viva la República*. It must kill all those who oppose it by force. It must annihilate all those who conserve power against it—that is all those who depend on the present system—Cortes, throne, ministers, law courts, in a word all public functionaries.'[1]

It was Espartero's use of the Castilian stick and, above all, his supposed 'English' free-trade inclinations which re-created the Radical-Progressive coalition against him.[2] Employer and employee combined in a desperate defence of import prohibitions. Thus the Popular Junta of November 1841 added protection for national industry to its programme and the 'dissolved' Workers' Association forbade foreign clothes to union members. In return the Municipality sanctioned the Association, even granting it a loan to set up a producers' co-operative.

Espartero's contest with Barcelona started with the Junta of Vigilance of October 1841. In origins a defensive reaction of the Barcelona Progressive militants against Moderate counter-revolution of October, the movement developed into an anti-Espartero affair when the Junta proceeded to demolish the Citadel, the fortress built by Philip V to dominate a rebel city. Bourgeois desire for urban extension and building sites ran together with municipal patriotism. The government regarded the demolition as treason and punished it accordingly. The movement of November 1842 shows the rapid and independent advance of radicalism. A minor affray between workers

[1] Quoted J. Coroleu, *Memorias*, 216.

[2] The prohibitionist campaign was frenetic in its hatred of England: there were suggestions of raising rebellion in Ireland and for the re-creation of Napoleon's continental system against English smuggling. The connexion between free trade and opposition to Espartero is shown by the belief that the English consul had encouraged Espartero to bombard Barcelona and had supplied shells for that purpose.

returning from a Sunday picnic and customs guards who wished to tax their wine was exploited by republican extremists; the next day 'there was not a street without barricades' and the city was at the mercy of gangs organized by 'pastry cooks and waiters'. Espartero could have saved his political position by an understanding with Progressives who were struggling to recover control of the city from 'anarchists' waving black flags by means of a Conciliatory Junta (28 November 1842). Instead of accepting the terms of the respectable citizens, Espartero besieged and bombarded the city and treated it as collectively guilty, imposing a large fine.[1] Only at the last moment did he attempt to recover popularity by remitting the fine which the city obstinately refused to pay in full.[2]

This mounting hostility was not confined to Barcelona. All over Spain the Juntas de Vigilancia of October 1841 had encouraged anti-Espartero extremists. The government's heavy-handed suppression of a legally free press—one of the conquests of 1840—had produced local coalitions of radical opposition Progressives and Moderates and by 1843 local working alliances between dissident Progressives and Moderate conspirators had become general. In Valencia the Progressive stalwart Beltrán de Lis was imprisoned beside the radical journalist and historian Boix. When Valencia pronounced against Espartero the Captain General surrendered to the 'expression of the sincere opinion of all classes, without distinction'. The only secure supports of Espartero's last government were his personal following among the *Ayacucho* generals, those Progressives who feared his 'tyranny' less than a counter-revolution dominated by Moderates, and the Madrid militia. Since most prosperous citizens had bought themselves out, the militia had become a purely professional body whose existence and pay were bound up with Espartero's power.[3]

On the 23 May pronunciamientos spread throughout Andalusia, culminating in the rebellion of Seville (17 July): in June

[1] The respectable classes wished to disarm the gangs and to come to terms with Van Halen who was besieging the city; he refused reasonable terms and would not admit that the Junta and National Militia had saved 'a blood bath'. Cf. *Reseña histórica de los actos de la Junta Conciliadora* (Barcelona, 1843), especially Documentos 1–11.

[2] For the attempts of Seoane to browbeat the Barcelona authorities see J. Carrera Pujal, *Cataluña*, iii. 310–17.

[3] *Arch. Nat.*, Rumigny's report of 20 June 1843. In the Andalusian towns the National Guard were anti-Espartero.

the movement gained a hold in Catalonia. The Supreme Junta of Barcelona, exercising its sovereign rights, deposed Espartero and appointed General Serrano, who had been López's Minister of War, as Universal Minister (29 June). The Catalan revolution flung into prominence Colonel Prim, a proven Progressive. If the revolution had triumphed through Prim and Barcelona, the Progressives would have been in a strong position, but Espartero's army was defeated in battle by Narváez and Narváez was a Moderate who looked on revolution as a military operation devoid of popular content.[1] Landing in Valencia, he adopted the coalition programme (the Lopéz ministry, the constitution of 1837, and liberal union), put up with Progressives, and marched against Madrid while Espartero was wasting his forces in an attempt to stamp out sedition in Andalusia. Seoane and Zurbano, after failing to preserve Catalonia, were left to defend Madrid with an army that was rotted by desertions at the rate of five hundred a day. As in all mid-century military sedition the predisposing cause was lack of pay: in towns like Oviedo, where the troops had been paid, they remained loyal. At Torrejón de Ardoz (22 July 1843), after a quarter of an hour of desultory firing, the troops embraced. Victory cost Narváez three light casualties. Serious fighting was a rarity in military politics.

The pronunciamiento and the confused civilian rebellion had been directed primarily against the *Ayacuchos*—the military clique of Espartero. From the Progressive point of view the revolutionary coalition was a mistake; as an English sympathizer pointed out, Espartero offered the only hope of 'rational freedom' and to overthrow him was to play the game of the Moderates. In vain the regent's government warned provincial Progressives of the dangers of an alliance with those who 'wished to push Spain into anarchy in order to lay a road for despotism'. In some towns, as news of the Moderates' predominant role in the revolt became known, they sought to 'dispronounce' and started arresting known Moderate conspirators.[2] Too late the

[1] Cf. General Concha's attitude to the Granada Junta: 'I will not interfere with the Junta but I will not permit anyone to mix in military matters and I will shoot any soldier who disobeys', i.e. who put the commands of the Junta above those of the general.

[2] There is an excellent description of the 1843 pronunciamiento in Galicia by S. E. Widdrington, *Spain*, ii. 172 ff. Some of the Progressive rebels seem to have

more radical Progressives realized their blunder. On 30 July Espartero, after failing to hold Seville and Cadiz, embarked on a British man-of-war; on 13 August the victors stripped him of all titles, ranks, and honours, branded him as a peculator deserving the contempt of the heroic people who had rejected his rule. His ultimate successor as 'sword' of the Progressive party, Colonel Prim, was made count of Reus for his part in a rebellion that was to exclude his party from effective power for a decade.

3. *Narváez and the Hegemony of the Moderates, 1843–1854*

The coalition that had overthrown Espartero under the motto of 'reconciliation of parties' could not hold as a ministry against the determination of orthodox Moderates and Progressive purists to secure for themselves what later politicians were to call an 'exclusive situation'. J. M. López, the prime minister whose name symbolized the joint campaign of 1843, could not find parliamentary support for continuing the coalition once he had declared the queen's majority; this step put the political life of Spain in the hands of the advisers of a girl whose occupations were sweet-eating and modelling in paper. Olózaga who succeeded him was more of a party man than López and more keenly aware of the ambitions of the Moderates; he determined to seize power for a pure Progressive ministry. Defeated in the Cortes, he got a decree of dissolution from the queen in circumstances that laid him open to the charge of using physical force against his sovereign. The Moderate leaders and Narváez used their court connexions to incriminate Olózaga who was dismissed, arraigned in the Cortes, and condemned.[1]

been surprised when it was pointed out that the rebellion was aimed at the regent (ibid. 252).

[1] This incident is the delight of Spanish historians. It was alleged that Olózaga locked the queen in her room and forced her to sign an undated decree of dissolution. If Olózaga was to succeed, even if he did not use force, he must keep the decree secret and in believing a child could keep a secret he put himself in the hands of his enemies at court. Pidal was told a cock-and-bull story by the queen and advised the dismissal of the ministry. There can be no possibility that the queen's story that she had been locked in her room was true in its entirety; it carried conviction in the Cortes apparently because the queen's confessor was one of the witnesses to her statement. Olózaga had perhaps shut the door to baffle court eavesdroppers; it had no lock.

Whether Olózaga used force or not, he stands condemned for an effort to gain exclusive power for his party by a ruthless use of the royal prerogative. It was a personal and political blunder which was to rob the Progressive leaders of the key to political power—the royal prerogative to appoint ministers and to grant them a decree of dissolution. After the short ministry of González Brabo (leader of a young conservative grouping called *Joven España*), Narváez, the military leader of the Moderates, became prime minister (May 1844). In 1845 he established Moderate rule by a new constitution.[1]

The Progressives' subsequent weakness cannot be explained entirely in terms of a loss of court favour or the jettisoning of a general who, with all his faults, represented their greatest asset. In aiding the coalition ministry to defeat the *Centralista* rebellion of September 1843 they also cut themselves off from their one other source of strength—provincial radicalism. The *centralistas* had seen in the Revolution against Espartero an opportunity to secure democracy by a central Junta which should keep the revolution in being until a democratic constitution became law; when the coalition ministry robbed them of the fruits of revolution they revolted once more. Saragossa, where Esparterist Progressives were strong, declared on 18 September. In Barcelona the rebellion, which spread throughout Catalonia, was the last surge of working-class discontent. It was suppressed, after nearly three months, by the Progressives' hero, Prim, who referred to the rebels as bandits, *canaille*, rats.[2] In every radical stronghold in Spain the governmental Progressives had joined in defeating their allies on the left and disarming the militia. It was hardly surprising that provincial radicalism could only respond to Olózaga's dismissal with two feeble pronunciamientos.

This disillusioned radicalism strengthened the growing Democratic party which traced its origins to the minority of extremist activists, heirs of the *exaltados*, who appear in every outburst of revolutionary activity of the thirties and forties. The Democrats

[1] See below, p. 237.

[2] For a detailed account see A. Pirala, *Historia contemporánea* (1875–8), i. 31–89, and J. Carrera Pujal, *Cataluña*, iii. 329 ff. Casualties were forty in Saragossa and much heavier in Barcelona. There were isolated movements in Léon, Cadiz, Cordoba, Seville, various southern *pueblos*, and Vigo. For Prim's pathological attitude see R. Olivar Betrand, *Prim* (Barcelona, 1951), ii. 16–24.

were scattered groups of crypto-republicans. They had a following in Barcelona, where a federal republican constitution enjoyed a vogue, and the movement struck deep roots in the Ampurdán and Gerona.[1] Cadiz had republican broadsheets in the thirties and it was here that Fourier's influence entered Spain. Other centres were Galicia, Málaga, and Teruel. Like the Anarchists of the twentieth century, Republican apostles were making propaganda tours in the south where the Andalusian towns had a violent revolutionary tradition.[2] In 1840 'Republicans' had two papers in Madrid: there the movement had its notables and its intellectuals, Espronceda, the greatest of the Romantic poets, among them.

The Democrats did their best to exploit the primitive revolt of the urban poor, which had emerged as a factor in the local revolutions of the thirties, and they were the only party with a serious working-class following. By means of literary clubs and choirs they were endeavouring 'to moralize the character and democratize the ideas' of the working classes. The catechisms distributed outside factories included two of the most popular working-class demands: the abolition of *consumos* and conscription. While the Progressives regarded the function of politics as the reflection of the existing balance of social forces, the Democrats alone professed to regard political power as an instrument for the creation of a just society.[3] Nevertheless their popular support was unstable and fickle: transient waves of popular feeling against an immoral court did not mean, as Espronceda maintained, that 'the people are completely mature, disposed for the most complete liberty, for equality of rights, for power and command'.

The Democratic party, as it emerged in the forties, was vague

[1] One of the Republican leaders, Abdón Terradas, had become mayor of Figueras in 1842. Republicanism was strong enough in the Ampurdán for a revolution to be attempted in 1869 (see below, p. 314).

[2] E. Rodríguez-Solis, *Historia del partido repúblicano* (1892), ii. 406 ff. Astonishingly enough the Empress Eugénie (who was a Spaniard) read the works of Fourier at this time.

[3] Cf. the attitude of the Democrats to the French Revolution which they regarded as 'progressive in politics' but 'retrogade in economics'. 'The political system is not an end in itself but a means of arriving at a good political and *social system*,' wrote Orense, the marqués de Albaida, a Valencian grandee who became one of the most influential Republican leaders, in his pamphlet *Que hará en el poder el partido progresista* (1847).

in ideology and divided in tactics. In 1843 Democrats had split over participation in a revolution with Progressives and Moderates. From then on they divided over the desirability of a working alliance with the Progressives. This division was reflected in the fifties in the debate over what came to be called 'socialism', which was less a debate about socialism than a divergence of tactics. Sixto Cámara, Pi y Margall, and Garrido wanted an independent revolutionary party.[1] Co-operation with the Progressives glued the Democrats to outdated political formulae and rejected their true source of strength—contact with the urban proletariat. Against the 'socialist' revolutionaries stood the established Democrats, Orense and Rivero; Rivero's money, derived from a fortunate bourgeois marriage, financed the Democrat press in Madrid and his influence in Democratic politics was consequently large. They were determined to avoid all deviations from doctrinaire economic individualism which might scare the Progressives. Thus in 1854 the Democrats met revolution divided: the leaders were arrested at a meeting where these differences were being debated.

Like all other Spanish parties which failed to establish themselves in public opinion, the Democrats and their allies amongst the revolutionary Progressives looked to the army. Unlike the established politicians they pinned their faith, not in the ambitions of a general, but in the mutinous spirit of junior officers, sergeants, and men. These had their post-war discontents, as Espartero himself had discovered: irregular pay (nearly all troubles were preceded by pay stoppages); poor promotion for non-commissioned officers; a recruiting system which made every private regard his service as a sort of serfdom from which release might be sought in successful mutiny.[2] Half-pay and poorly pensioned officers were natural conspirators. Even in the service itself no officer, up to and including colonels,

[1] Sixto Cámara (1825–57), Pi y Margall (1824–1901), and Garrido (1821–83) were all journalists active in the Democratic press of the fifties. Garrido was influenced by Fourier and, after a visit to Rochdale, became the foremost Spanish advocate of co-operatives. For the 'socialist' debate see C. A. M. Hennessy, *The Federal Republic in Spain* (Oxford, 1962), 17 ff.

[2] This was the famous *quinta*: selection by lot with the possibility of the rich buying themselves out. The Democrats consistently exploited agitation against this system. It was also criticized by professional soldiers. For Espartero's difficulties see above, p. 218.

could live on his pay—Galdós pictures a colonel starving as a part-time lawyer's copyist. Given the social origins of most professional soldiers—as an Englishman remarked, a Spanish officer was not 'a gentleman of independent means but a member of the salaried classes'—there was much discontent in what was called the *pueblo militar*. The grievances of the lower officers were already serious enough in Espartero's regency to support a periodical, *The Cry of the Army*, with nearly a thousand subscribers.[1] With whole regiments unreliable, radicals could always hope to set off a ranker's pronunciamiento led by a captain, bored with *la vie obscure et monotone* of a garrison town on short pay, dreaming of dramatic promotion as the reward for successful rebellion as the way out of a difficult and tedious life.

The revolution from 1844 to 1848 was therefore based on an attempt to unite the discontents of the poor and the grievances of soldiers and sergeants. In Lugo a Republican, Solis, persuaded the Zamora regiment to pronounce in June 1846; the movement, helped by local Progressives and exploiting resentment against Mon's new taxes, spread in Galicia.[2] In Madrid, in 1848, the Republicans acted alone. They failed in the poorer suburbs in March and with the University students in April. In May the sergeants of the Regiment of Spain, proselytized by an officer on the retired list, rose and occupied the Plaza Mayor. None of these risings came within sight of success and extensive relief measures seem to have damped down the revolution in Catalonia where its connexions with the Carlist revolt made it dangerous. The Carlist alliance, in itself, is an indication of a desperate need for allies against 'what exists'.[3]

[1] 'Nothing is more common than to see Spanish officers . . . begging alms in the streets of Madrid after having in vain tried to earn a livelihood as servants in hotels' (*The Times*, 9 Aug. 1847). *El grito del ejercito* expressed the 'general disgust' at the post-war neglect of the army's 'just demands'. After twenty years' service, the pension was 20 per cent. of the pay; many war-time officers had served only six years and did not qualify for any pension.

[2] For Galicia see F. Tettamancy Gastón, *La revolución Gallega de 1846* (1909). Solis had only part of the Zamora Regiment; since the troops sent against the rebels came from the same regiment an armistice was inevitable. It would seem that the Concha brothers, military rivals of Narváez, had some part in these troubles as long as they were directed against his dictatorship.

[3] For the Madrid troubles, *El Heraldo* for Mar. and May 1848, *The Times*, 15 May. For the relief measures in Catalonia, A. Pirala, *Historia contemporánea*, ii. 13.

As long as the Progressive leaders refused to act there was no hope for an independent Democratic rising. The fundamental flaw of the revolutionary equation was therefore the division of the Progressive party. 'Legal' Progressives hoped power might come from respectability—in a government engineered by the queen's favourite, the 'handsome general' Serrano who had Progressive sympathies, or by the banker Salamanca. It was only the left wing of the party which clung to the doctrine of legal revolution. In these circumstances the perpetual conspiracy of the Democrats and the Progressive left wing was doomed to failure; there was no Spanish 1848. The only result of unsuccessful revolution was to justify the extremities of military dictatorship.[1]

It was these divisions of the Progressive party which had reduced them almost to impotence by 1848 and which facilitated the long hegemony of the Moderates. Apart from the brief hiatus afforded by the revolution of 1854–6 Spain was ruled by conservative groupings from the fall of Olózaga to the revolution of 1868. The revolution of 1843 had created the spectre of anarchy and strengthened conservative sentiments. It made the Progressives appear as inevitable harbingers of what was being called '*The* Revolution', a fear in part justified by the continued addiction of the Progressive left to the dogma of legal revolution. Conservative accounts of the Barcelona revolution of 1843 read like a foretaste of accounts of anarchist 'atrocities' in July 1936: prostitutes dancing in churches; excrement in uncleaned streets; trees destroyed by 'men without faith and without education'; the adoption of working-class clothes; the flight from the city of the well-to-do. The revolution left Barcelona, wrote a clerical journalist, 'a mountain of ruins and a lake of blood'.[2]

The rule of the Moderates after 1844 exploited and represented this fear of revolution. There must be a return to order

[1] The most serious rising was the pronunciamiento of the Esparterist general, Zurbano in Nov. 1844. Through Progressive historians deplored the effect of Democrat infiltration in producing useless revolutions, they would never deny the right of legal revolution. Zurbano's revolution was a legitimate protest 'in favour of the fundamental law', i.e. the constitution of 1837 abrogated by the Moderates. Cf. A. Fernández de los Ríos, *Luchas políticas*, ii. 108.

[2] J. M. Quadrado, *Ensayos* (1893), i. 27. A hat was suspect as a bourgeois adornment in 1843; observers made similar comments in July 1936.

'the foundation without which we cannot conceive material progress. . . . Radical parties are an anachronism in the present state of society.'[1] The Catalan bourgeoisie put up with Moderate centralization, uniform taxes, and the Civil Guard, in return for the Spanish market and no labour problems.[2] The Church, as the guardian of social order, found able secular defenders for the first time in a group of Moderate thinkers—Pacheco, Pastor Díaz, Donoso Cortés who presented the Progressive legislation of the thirties as the great crime of liberalism. Though the attempt to create a clerical party failed in 1843 and though clericals like Quadrado complained bitterly of the lukewarm catholicism of the Moderates, the influence of the Church was felt in party politics for the first time since 1834. It drew the Moderates steadily to the right.

The characteristic achievements of conservative rule were a criminal code, an efficient police force, a modern taxation system, and a settlement of the Church question—achievements of able administrators which were to survive the destruction of the Moderate party and, in some respects, to outlast the monarchy itself.

The Civil Guard, like so much of the Moderate programme, was based on a French model. Its first commander introduced the principles which were to create the strong corporate spirit of 'The Institute'. It was a military *corps d'élite* dependent on the Ministry of War for internal discipline and promotion but on the Home Office for its use.[3] Officers and men could not be natives of the districts in which they served, a disposition which defeated local influence and corruption and prevented a militarized police from degenerating into a party machine, like the militia. Thus, though in its origins it represented the Moderate determination to eliminate the Progressive militia, the Civil Guard became an instrument for law and order above party, and was accepted as such by the Progressives in 1854. The later unpopularity of the Institute was inevitable; it served all governments against all forms of political sedition

[1] Quotations from *El Heraldo*, 27 June, 19 July 1844.

[2] For a short account of these years in Catalonia see J. Vicens Vives, *Els catalans*, 257–61.

[3] For its origins and history see C. Ximénez de Sandoval, *Las instituciones de pública seguridad* (1958), and the summary in E. Iglesia, *Reseña histórica de la Guardia Civil* (1898). The decree of 1844 was a copy of the Napoleonic *gendarmerie* law.

and thus became the great enemy of working-class movements and the 'permanent sedition' of republicanism. After making the rural south safe for travellers by stamping out brigandage, the Civil Guard made it safe for landlords by suppressing every manifestation of primitive social revolt. A hundred years later the rural disinherited took a terrible revenge at Castiblanco, a poverty-stricken village in Estremadura. On 1 January 1932 four Civil Guards were hacked to pieces and the women of the village danced round their bodies.[1] It was the Andalusian poet, Lorca, who reflected the labourer's hatred when he made the Civil Guard a symbol of all that was evil and stupid in Spain; their strange hats, their patrolling in pairs seemed a visual embodiment of the moral atmosphere of conservative Spain.

The Church settlement was achieved in the Concordat of 1851. It recognized, in principle, the injustice of the Erastian liberal claim for a *dominium eminens* in the state and of the unilateral confiscation of the property of the secular clergy. In return for the clear recognition by the state of its duty to pay the secular clergy, the Vatican recognized the validity of past expropriations. The scale of compensation was mean—very few priests in Spain had a decent living wage and in 1931 well over half received under £40 a year. Unsatisfactory and ungenerous though the Concordat was as a compromise, it gave the Church a legal and economic basis for its activities; indeed, one of its by-products was a Church trimmed free of the host of unbeneficed clergy and under-employed canons.[2] As long as liberalism maintained the Catholic unity of Spain and undertook to pay the clergy, the hierachy would grudgingly accept the liberal state. In a Church based on a Concordat it is unlikely that bishops will be subversive.

The Concordat provided no compensation at all for the regular clergy, and it was round the clause which governed

[1] As Brenan points out (*Spanish Labyrinth*, 256–7) the murders were a collective deed for which responsibility could not be pinned on any individual.

[2] Perhaps, as Bravo Murillo suggested, one of the reasons which led the papacy to accept the Concordat was that it clearly recognized the right of the Church to acquire property in the future after robbing it of all its possessions inherited from the past. *Opúsculos* (1863), 181 ff. For an example of reduction of superfluous clerics cf. Oviedo, where the cathedrals' eighty canons and prebends were cut to a mere fifty-one. A. Viñayo, *El seminario de Oviedo* (Oviedo, 1955), 62 ff.

the future existence of the Regular Orders in Spain that the Church question was to revolve until the twentieth century. Article 29 of the Concordat declared that, for 'works of charity and public utility', the government would make arrangements, after consulting the bishops, for the establishment of houses of 'St. Vincent of Paul, St. Philip Neri and *one other order* from among those approved by the Holy See'. The bishops used this clause to establish 'one other' order in each diocese, a reading of a confused and unsatisfactory piece of drafting which would allow the re-establishment of the Regular Orders in Spain; it was contested bitterly by anti-clerical liberals to whom the existence of the Regular Orders was not merely an intolerable anachronism but, since many of them were teaching orders, a source of 'poison' in a liberal state.[1]

The administrative and legal measures of the Moderates during the constructive phase of their rule represented conservatism at its best—putting into legislative shape uncontentious reforms first proposed by radicals. Spanish law was an historical jumble symbolizing the piecemeal achievement of political unity; advanced liberals had long advocated codification but it was conservative reformers who, in 1829, produced a uniform commercial code and, in 1848, a criminal code.[2] The greatest representative of administrative reform was Narváez's finance minister in 1844, Alejandro Mon. An Asturian lawyer, he was the Peel of Spain, and like Peel, he disliked civil-service jobbery and hoped for a permanent civil service. Rather than overhaul the inherited system of multiple and unevenly distributed taxes, the liberals had relied on deficits, expensive short-term loans, and the non-payment of salaries. Mon funded the huge floating debt at 3 per cent. and created a uniform tax system for the whole of Spain based on a graded land tax, a tax on urban rents, on commercial and industrial profits,

[1] The anti-clericals declared that the Concordat permitted one 'other' order in the whole of Spain, not in each diocese. For a statement of the Catholic counter-case see A. Allison Peers, *Spain, the Church and the Orders* (London, 1939), 80–85. The strongest argument of Catholics is based on the full recognition of Canon Law in Articles 4 and 43.

[2] There is no adequate history of Spanish law. There is an historical commentary in D. R. Domingo de Morato, *Estudios de ampliación de la historia de los codigos españoles* (Valladolid, 1856). The driving force behind the codification of the criminal law was Pacheco. See Romero Girón, 'Pacheco y la legislación penal en España' (in *España del siglo XIX*, 1886–7).

stamp duties, and the *consumos*. Mon's system was the basis of the Spanish budget for the whole of the nineteenth century.[1]

The new system was most unpopular. It set off the Galician revolt and goes far to explain the nature of provincial discontent until 1868. In redistributing the burden of taxation more evenly over the whole of Spain, Mon ended the relative privileges enjoyed by Catalonia: hence the feeling of Castilian oppression and the later demand for a Catalan *concierto económico*—a lump-sum settlement negotiated with the Treasury. The *consumos* (excise duties collected on sales of wine, meat, soap, &c.) gave radicalism its most valuable slogan. Since the *consumos* seemed an obvious cause of high food prices their abolition figured in all Democratic programmes, especially as the proportion of indirect to direct taxation mounted with time.[2] Without the *consumos* and conscription it may be doubted whether democratic radicalism could have created a popular following in the fifties and sixties.

Nowhere is the Moderates' conviction that order was the consequence of uniform centralization and firm governmental control more in evidence than in the educational system they created and which remains, in essentials, that of Spain today. The universities—of which the first rectors were the civil governors 'wearing spurs'—and the schools were state controlled; the Central University of Madrid became the sole factory of higher degrees; professors were put on a uniform pay scale, their appointments standardized via the *oposición* (a public competitive performance which was to spread throughout Spanish public life). The Moderates' university legislation was attacked by both clericals as favouring secularism—the Catholic Balmes called professors 'state servants'—and by radical intellectuals as limiting freedom of thought. In fact, the Moderates' ideas were 'neither liberal nor ultra-montane,

[1] It is described in J. Mª. Tallada Pauli, *Historia de las finanzas españolas en el siglo XIX* (1946), 47 ff.

[2] It has been calculated that the *consumos* represented 70 per cent. of the cost of wine, 24 per cent. of oil, and 14 per cent. of meat. Nevertheless the later abolition of *consumos* did not bring down food prices. For a brief history of the *consumos* see A. Dutard, *L'Octroi en Espagne* (Toulouse, 1909). One of the consequences of the tax was that it made municipal budgets dependent on the level fixed by the state for the octroi since municipal duties were calculated as a proportion of the state duties. The tax was usually farmed out locally and became part of the machinery of local electoral politics.

but regalist and civilian'.[1] Thought was an *instrumentum regni.* Thus in the 1850's extreme liberals found the centralized university system a convenient machine to propagate ideas which challenged the Moderate *via media*; once the political implications were apparent the Moderate governments used state control in order to deny 'the freedom of the chair'—the right of professors as civil servants to preach heterodoxy in a catholic state.

Liberals accepted the university system created by the Moderates because the renewed influence of the university after 1850 proved the efficacy of reform, and because there was no acceptable alternative. The lamentable state of the professorate, as Unamuno was to admit in the 1890's, and the indifference of society made the autonomous university of Germany or England an intellectual and administrative impossibility. Without state supervision a private 'free' university system would have been dominated by the strongest force in society—the Church.[2]

Interspersed with reversions to military rule or administrative despotism backed by the court, the Moderates' hegemony was based on the constitution of 1845. It was the purest embodiment of the doctrine of the 'internal constitution', the representative instrument of a new aristocracy which took as its device that 'poverty was a sign of stupidity'.[3] It left Spain a parliamentary state but removed objectionable features imported by the Progressives in 1837 in the name of the sovereignty of the people: these were a weak prerogative, an elective Senate, a national militia, trial by jury for press offences.

Yet, in spite of a constitution which embodied their profoundest political beliefs, an administrative system of their own

[1] Cf. V. Cacho Viu, *La Institución Libre de Enseñanza* (1962), 46. The 1845 decrees were the work of Antonio Gil de Zárate, a civil servant of undoubted liberal sentiments. Gil de Zárate described his work in his history of Spanish education, *De la Instrucción pública en España* (1855).

[2] Cf. the effect of the suppression of the Faculty of Theology in state universities by the Revolution of 1868. 'It was to renounce any intervention or control of the state in the education of the clergy, to whom high social and spiritual functions were still confided.' J. Castillejo, *Wars of Ideas in Spain* (London, 1937), 87. The price of state control was not only occasional onslaughts on intellectual freedom but constant governmental tinkering with the syllabus and internal organization of the university.

[3] *D.S.C.*, 25–26 Nov. 1845. Hence the higher property franchise. For an explanation of the doctrine of the 'internal constitution' see below, p. 349.

devising, and the favour of the crown, the Moderates appear from 1844 to 1854 less as a political party than as a collection of oligarchs held together only by the fear of revolution. When this agglutinate of fear lost its efficacy, the party split into factions and the old idea of a liberal union which would bring rich and respectable Progressives back into government triumphed over Moderate exclusiveness. It was then that the party could reject its strong man, Narváez. Yet since the revolutionary threat was always revived, the politics of conservative rule were dominated by his personality.[1] He was the only politician prepared 'to combat, without truce, moral and material anarchy'.

Narváez, now duke of Valencia, looked what he was: an Andalusian squire, a military politician in the Spanish style, *muy brutal*. He loved power for its own sake and for the rewards it brought: a palace (purchased from a grandee for £20,000) in which he appeared as host 'literally covered with gold and diamonds'; stock exchange tips; ballerinas and fine coaches.[2] The foundation of power he saw in an obedient, contented army. To ensure its political reliability he was prepared to devote 'the whole of the resources of the country to the maintenance of the army alone'; regular pay and 'the stick' would restore discipline, and by 1849 the army was the obedient instrument of the generals, if not of the crown.[3] He was determined that no civilian ministers should interfere in his province. 'It is best', he told his war minister General Cordóba, 'that we don't bother the lawyers with these matters.'[4]

The duke regarded himself as a liberal. The duty of the army was to defend the constitution against court clericalism (which he called 'absolutism'), against the intrigues of the queen

[1] Narváez's two important ministries were those of May 1844 to Feb. 1846 and Oct. 1847 to Jan. 1851. He was in power Mar. to Apr. 1846, and out for a day on 20 Oct. 1849.

[2] *The Times*, 28 Nov. 1844. His most successful stock-exchange deal was his purchase of government bonds (which had fallen on the news of General Zurbano's pro-Espartero rising in Nov. 1844) when he and his cronies alone knew that the rebellion had been defeated.

[3] Ibid., 11 June 1844. Cf. Howden, 20 Apr. 1854, commented on 'the happy and contented state of the army whose comfort and material wants are sedulously attended to'.

[4] F. Fernández de Córdoba, *Memorias*, iii. 150. He forced Bravo Murillo to resign (Nov. 1850) when his economies threatened the army budget.

mother, and, above all, against democratic sedition. His authoritarianism was rooted rather in his character than in his beliefs. His violent temper (which *The Times* called his 'savage bonhomie') could bear no contradiction—whether from the queen mother, the politicians, or even from his fellow generals. It was this violence that lay at the root of his political difficulties: his milder opponents were 'filthy mutineers'. He was dismissed by the queen mother in April 1846 for what may be termed political insolence. In return he was prepared to get rid of her.

His obsession with sedition has been regarded as the occupational disease of a dictator. Yet as long as the army was unreliable and left-wing Progressives were haunted by the dogma of legal revolution, no government could feel secure. Troops left in garrison town soon became absorbed into civilian society and shared civilian discontents—particularly in Galicia and Catalonia.[1] General Fernando de Córdoba, a moderate man, saw 'the Revolution coming at us from all sides'. The Great Fear of the Moderate generals was that their troops would not obey them. Now that he was gone, Espartero, whose portrait appeared on cigar wrappers, was becoming once more a ranker's hero. At any moment an *Ayacucho* general, an officer passed over in promotion, or a group of Progressive sergeants might see in sedition revenge for the 'treason' of 1843.

Confronted by a permanent sedition which imperilled constitutional rule as he understood it, Narváez easily abandoned the liberal promises with which he began his ministries in 1844 and 1847.[2] To 'save the constitution' he had no hesitation in muzzling the press, in employing spies and *agents provocateurs*, in taxing and legislating by decree. 'I have no enemies', he is reputed to have said on his deathbed, 'I have shot them all.'

The crudity of Narváez's conception of order shocked not

[1] Cf. F. de Córdoba's remarks on the garrison of Barcelona as 'rotten' with conspiracy. In Corunna officers were attracted to the Progressive salon of the Condesa de Espoz y Mina, widow of the radical hero (cf. F. Tettamancy Gaston, *Revolución en Galicia*, 32). Regiments were frequently shifted to avoid this contamination: Solis had to rise before his regiment marched to a new posting in the interior.

[2] In 1844 he professed a wish to end González Brabo's persecution of the Progressives. It is clear that the Progressive leadership took Narváez's liberalism seriously for a short time in spite of the difficulties of believing 'those who today preach liberty, but yesterday knew no régime but the sword' (see the Progressive, *Eco de Comerco*, May–July 1844).

only civilians but his rivals among the generals. General Manuel Concha, member of a powerful Moderate military clan, told the British minister Bulwer 'to govern *with* an army is well enough, to be governed *by* an army is intolerable. Civil authority in any hands is to be preferred.'[1] There were other Moderates who, in moments of relative tranquillity, disliked the rule of the sword and who saw that conservative stability could not be maintained by bayonets. The alternatives to military liberalism were either civilian authoritarianism backed by the court, or a broadening and civilianizing of the old Moderate party as the dominant party within the constitutional monarchy. The former was represented by Bravo Murillo, the latter by Pacheco, both distinguished and successful lawyers, the only professional grouping which could hope to provide an *élite* to match that of the generals.

Pacheco's group of opposition conservatives was known as 'the Puritans'. They rejected the duke of Valencia's militaristic edition of Moderate hegemony as brainless and 'sceptical'—the general was somewhat Voltairian and shared none of the average Moderates' belief in the Church as a pillar of order or a 'good' press as an antidote to revolution.[2] They wished to create a modern party, with a programme and an organization in the constituencies, defending conservative interests but by constitutional rule and free discussion. Moderate political thinking would cease to be a mere negation of Progressivism and convert that party's more sensible elements from the sterile dogma of legal revolution. Borrego, the intellectual and journalistic force of the proposed party, regarded the 'exclusivism' which had rejected the constitution of 1837 and driven the Progressives to Espartero and revolution as a political blunder, repeated in 1845.[3] The basis of the new conservatism would be the reconciliation of parties, the 1843 alliance of Progressives and Moderates turned against generals, a new version of that

[1] *F.O.* Bulwer to Aberdeen, 21 Jan. 1844. Concha was prepared to intrigue against Narváez to the point of military sedition.

[2] Cf. the views of Pastor Díaz on the press; he opposed Narváez's continual press prosecutions on the grounds that the press had been a conservative force in politics (cf. *El Heraldo*, 14 Nov. 1844). Narváez's views on the press were simple, 'It is not enough to confiscate papers; to finish with bad newspapers you must kill all the journalists.'

[3] Cf. A. Borrego, *De la situación y los intereses de España* (1848).

'restoring the harmony of the liberal family' which had haunted politicians, in varying forms, since 1833.[1] This alliance of sensible Moderates and cautious Progressives failed as a civilian concern. As the Liberal Union of the sixties it dominated political life—once it was backed by a general, O'Donnell.

The combination of the schisms and discontents within the Moderate ranks and the designs of the court was to produce acute ministerial instability. The queen mother detested the bullying of Narváez and dismissed him (January 1846); with his fall began a lamentable period of cabinet shuffles rendered more confused by the competing influences of the French and British ministers—both of whom backed different ministries and acted at times as if Spanish politicians had ceased to count as governors of an independent nation.[2] These changes make sense only in terms of the queen mother's determination to find a pliable instrument for her marriage schemes, which finally condemned her daughter to a hopeless union with the effeminate Francisco de Asis. This marriage can only be justified by the belief that the dynasty was not secure unless backed unconditionally by Louis Philippe.[3] Her ministerial changes taught her daughter to find compensation for a bankrupt marriage by herself engaging in political intrigue in order to keep the 'handsome general' Serrano at court. When Sotomayor opposed Serrano's presence he was sacked by the young queen.

Four years of social peace had almost detsroyed the old

[1] Cf. the remarks on Mendizábal above, p. 170. González Brabo (an ex-radical who had assumed responsibility for the dismissal of Olózoga in 1843) had attempted a reconstruction of liberal unity from the right during his short ministry. His plans had been defeated by the 'exclusive' Moderates and Narváez, who dropped González Brabo in favour of a pure Moderate ministry (May 1844). For González Brabo see L. de Taxonera, *González Brabo y su tiempo* (1941).

[2] Governments under Miraflores (Jan.–Mar. 1846), Narváez (Apr. 1846) himself now out of court favour (Mar. 1846), Istúritz (Mar. 1846–Jan. 1847), Sotomayor, Pacheco, and Goyena García-Salamanca succeeded each other between Feb. 1846 and Oct. 1847.

[3] The marriage took place on 10 Oct. 1846; for the diplomatic details see E. Jones Parry, *The Spanish Marriages 1841–46* (London, 1936). Francisco de Asis was Isabella's cousin: he was a *dévot* and such a hypochondriac that he refused to give audiences to anyone with a cold. Her sister was to marry the duke of Montpensier and there was thus a sporting chance (which may have been thwarted by one of Isabella's supposed amours) that the grandchild of Louis Philippe would become ruler of Spain as the heir of the childless Isabella and her supposedly impotent husband. Francisco de Asis, as an extreme clerical, was always in danger of coming to terms with the Carlists.

Moderate party: by 1847 the idea of a third party which would gather all but clericals and democrats into a reunited liberal family was gaining ground at the expense of Moderate 'exclusiveness'. Thus the Pacheco–Salamanca ministries were scarcely recognizable as Moderate concerns and appear as dress rehearsals of the tolerant politics and high finance of Liberal Unionism. The Progressives even hoped for a come-back through Serrano's influence with the queen; the Moderate hard core opposed a Serrano ministry, less because they feared for the respectability of the monarchy with the queen in the hands of 'a little Godoy who does not know how to behave like a gentleman', than because they feared that Serrano's Progressive connexions might lead to a ministry under Olózaga, still in exile but their bitterest enemy. At the same time the court was alarmed at the exploitation by radicals of court scandals—the king and the queen were living apart. Thus Narváez was recalled to office.

The duke of Valencia's long ministry (October 1847 to January 1851) enabled him to recover a firm hold on his party. Far from starting as a dictator Narváez hoped to get the Progressives back into politics; it was the revolution of 1848 in Europe, and the revival of conspiracy in Spain, which induced him to seek dictatorial powers and gave him, with Nicholas I, a European reputation as a strong man who had defeated the spirit of '48. In fact the forces of revolution were weak in Spain —the radical *émeutes* of the spring and summer in Madrid were easily suppressed—and the Progressives were looking less to revolution than to an alliance with Moderate malcontents.[1] The most serious threat came, not from the left, but from the extreme right with another Carlist outbreak in Catalonia.[2]

Narváez's *ad hoc* dictatorship was elevated to the realm of principle by the theological extremism of Donoso Cortés, a second-rate thinker whose reputation was based on importations from French clerical conservatives. Just as heresy strengthened faith, so revolution, its secular concomitant, must exalt authority; just as God suspended the workings of natural laws by miracles, so governments must suspend the political order to

[1] As in 1843 this split the Progressives between collaborators and purists: see A. Pirala, *Historia contemporánea* (Madrid, 1875), ii. 91, 128, 130.

[2] For the Carlist rising see above, pp. 193–4.

meet revolution by dictatorship. 'The question lies not between dictatorship and liberty but between the dictatorship of revolution and the dictatorship of government.'[1] Narváez had little sympathy with this hot air. He sought strength in an appeal to 'material interests'. He failed because the politicians persisted obstinately in identifying modernity with parliamentary government. Opposed in Parliament, deserted by his best minister, Mon, who refused to sacrifice his tariff reform to Narváez's determination to avoid trouble in Catalonia—for, as the politicians of interest were to find, to satisfy one interest meant to outrage another—he was exposed to the jealousies of the rival generals of the powerful Concha clan, strong in the Senate, and to the unremitting hostility of the court. The king consort, Francisco de Asis, and his clerical camarilla, who had got rid of him for a day in 1849, now forced his resignation (January 1851). In spite of their discontents, the Moderate party had sacrificed principle and the prospects of a constitutional conservative party to the only man who looked like a leader. Now the man disappeared and nothing was left except a conglomeration of personal groupings which Carlists and Republicans alike could condemn as 'bands of egoists'.[2]

As in 1923, the apparent collapse of the party system was the premise of an attempt to abandon the forms of liberal constitutionalism altogether. The exponent of modernized absolutist revolution was Bravo Murillo, the new prime minister, whose schemes are one more proof of the direct influence of the French models on Spanish political life; whereas the Moderates had looked to the July monarchy, he was impressed by the *coup d'état* of Napoleon III. With no support from the generals, the press, or the parties, he proposed a constitution that would turn the Cortes into an advisory body chosen by 25,000 electors, debating in secret and with no control over the budget.

Bravo Murillo was an honest politician and competent administrator in the *afrancesado* tradition, the last of the civil ser-

[1] Donoso's extremism has appealed to Spanish and German reactionaries. Cf. R. Fernández Carvajal, 'Los constantes de Donoso Cortés' (*R. Est. P.* xcv. 75–109).

[2] Cf. the address of the Carlist leader Masgoret in A. Pirala, *Historia contemporánea*, ii. 15–16. Cf. A. Borrego, *Situación*, 92, 106 ff.

vants of enlightened despotism.[1] He regarded his constitutional reform as a removal of the irritating impediments to efficient administration imposed by a quasi-constitutional system which 'paralysed the action of government'. He scorned the hypocrisies of politicians who went through laborious pretences of elections and dissolutions; it was more honest to draft an authoritarian constitution, which could be applied, than to pervert a liberal constitution in the name of order and administrative convenience.[2] The cries of liberals in distress did not move him. They were defending an illusion. The reality was rule by generals for which Bravo Murillo wished to substitute civilian autocracy. 'They are mad. They imagine themselves to be liberals and let themselves be hypnotized by epaulettes and uniforms. I could call them absolutists with much more justification. They are tyrants who seek to subject their country to men of the sword.'

Bravo Murillo was one of a long line of Spanish statesmen who believed that the task of bringing Spain's material civilization into line with Europe was beyond the machinery of liberal constitutionalism and private enterprise. England was a freak, France the true model. A minor exponent of the techniques of iron surgery, his programme of public works was more ambitious than that of any government since the eighteenth century; under his government the Ministry of Economic Development (*Fomento*) sponsored railways, a national theatre, the canal of Isabella II which gave Madrid a modern water-supply, the canal of Castile which would open the northern markets to the wheat of Castile. He reorganized provincial administration and sought to create an informed public opinion by government periodicals. The Moderates had consistently professed that they were snatching the banner of Progress from their opponents; prosperity would make politics irrelevant and establish the Moderates, in Balmes's phrase, as

[1] For his regulation of the National Debt see G. Hubbard, *Histoire de l'Espagne contemporaine* (Paris, 1869), v. 149–51. It was the emasculation of his project by the Cortes which increased his hostility to hindrances to good government. For a criticism see E. Vera y González, *Pi y Margall y la política contemporánea* (Barcelona, 1886) i. 346–8.

[2] Cf. the comment of Butler Clarke, *Spain*, 224: 'The projected reform of the constitution was, in fact, little more than an attempt to codify and legalize actual practice.'

the 'men of profit'. They were unwilling, however, to have prosperity forced on them at the expense of power. What Bravo Murillo failed to realize was that in the space of ten years bastard constitutionalism had become the instrument of a powerful oligarchy. The chosen instrument of this oligarchy was the Senate; there sat the successful generals whose rights as Senators had become as important as their position in the army in a system where military influence was written into the constitutional structure.[1] They led the fight against Bravo Murillo's projected reforms as champions of the constitution, but in their military capacity they retained the threat of insurrection. Privately they caballed in two committees, and publicly blocked all legislation in the upper house, so that the prime minister had either to appeal to force himself, or abandon his policy. Frightened by the protests of the generals and the politicians, the court dropped him (December 1852), and after two stop-gap ministries turned to the Conde de San Luis, the recently enobled Moderate journalist, Sartorious, now a rich 'capitalist'.

In the constitutional opposition to Bravo Murillo and San Luis, Borrego hoped to find his union of conservative liberals, which would turn Narváez into a liberal hero and the constitution of 1845 into the banner of the sensible Progressives. Although this coalition came into existence to fight the elections of February 1853, effective opposition to the ministry became a Moderate concern, centred in the Senate's opposition to the attempt of San Luis to cover the railway deals of Salamanca and the queen mother. 'Morality' was the chosen slogan of the opposition and hatred of the queen mother its demagogic resource. When the opposition press was silenced, the clandestine 'Bat' exposed the scandals of a family whose members 'like prostitutes sell their honour for money'—even to the extent of stealing pictures from the Escorial.[2] Thus by its congruence with the campaign of the radical left against the court, the oligarchic opposition came to have popular overtones. San Luis

[1] Even under Narváez dissident generals had claimed, as Senators, the right to criticize their military superior, i.e. Narváez himself.

[2] *The Times* was banned in Spain because it revealed the railway scandals. A monarchist suggested the proper course was to bribe *The Times* 'as has been done on other occasions 'with other journals like *Punch* (A. Pirala *Historia contemporánea*, ii. 219).

was insanely confident: a revolution was unlikely with the Moderates divided, the Progressives powerless. He forgot the army. San Luis paid his soldiers regularly, but when he refused to compromise with the opposition generals, they were able to pit their authority among the officers against his. When he ordered the arrest and exile of O'Donnell and his friends, he made an appeal to force inevitable, since the constitutional voice of the army was thereby silenced. By the winter of 1853 malcontent generals were revealing to the British minister that they were prepared to overthrow the dynasty.

4. *The Revolution and the Liberal 'bienio', 1854–1856*

The Revolution of 1854 was a pronunciamiento of conservative generals supported by civilian politicians and accompanied by a popular revolt which gave to the discontents of the oligarchs the appearance of a national democratic revolution. This strange alliance was in part rooted in the economic discontents of both capital and labour. San Luis lost the confidence of those businessmen and financiers who had backed Bravo Murillo.[1] The rebellion in Barcelona, which decided the retreat of the Madrid government, had its origins in a textile workers' strike in which the strikers demanded the recognition of workers' associations for the negotiation of wage agreements and the replacement of self-acting mules. These were demands reflecting wages which had failed to keep up with rising prices and the technological unemployment consequent on the industrial re-equipment of Catalonia in the preceding years.[2] The workers joined the revolution with the cry 'Association of Death! Work and Bread'. Perhaps the setting up of a Revolutionary Junta in Barcelona may be seen as an attempt of the employers to deal with working-class discontent by effective action on the spot, at a moment when the central government represented the feebleness of intransigent politics unsupported by an obedient army. The revolution made Madoz, a left-wing Progressive and foremost political representative of Catalan capitalism, civil

[1] Cf. the comments of the English diplomatists, Howden and Otway, on the discontents of the capitalists. *F.O.*, 22 Mar., 22 May 1854.

[2] J. Carrera Pujal, *Cataluña*, iv. 235. In March the workers were complaining of food prices. Cholera undoubtedly increased the pre-revolutionary tension: the rich left the town and the poor died.

governor of Barcelona.[1] This was a repetition of the take-over of spontaneous revolution by respectable local politicians, the traditional tactic of the Progressives. The programme this process bequeathed was the radical demand for the abolition of the *consumos* and conscription.

We do not know the precise connexion between hardship and revolt: what is certain is that domestic wheat prices were rising as a result of heavy exports to England to make up for the loss of Russian imports during the Crimean war, and that Galicia was experiencing an 'Irish famine'.[2] One of the first demands of the Barcelona Junta was free importation of corn. This discontent was exploited by the Democrats and to a lesser extent by the Progressives. But permanent political co-operation based on support of working-class demands was unthinkable. The Progressives, once in government, went back on their promises to abolish the *consumos* and conscription. Figuerola, to whom the government's attempt to impose minimum wages was 'communism', wrote a passionate defence of the owner's right to install *selfactinas*, the 'devil's machines' of the workers' petition.[3] Thus the alliance of the Progressives and the Barcelona workers was precarious: every food riot was treated by the government as the work of incendiaries or socialists and a threat to its reputation as guardian of the social order. It was more concerned with the confidence of the rich (like every revolutionary government it stood in need of loans) than the sympathy of the poor. In June 1855 General Zapatero determined 'to finish with strikes and settle the social question once and for all'.

Banished or disgraced by San Luis, the opposition generals were politically ruthless and quite undisturbed by notions of loyalty to the crown. If the Bourbons would not get rid of objectionable ministers they were ready to get rid of the

[1] This is a working hypothesis only: Graell and Pujal, for instance, give quite different accounts of the attitude of the Captain General to the workers' strikes. Madoz, as governor, accepted collective agreements. Cf. C. Martí, 'La correspondencia official del consol francés a Barcelona 1854–6' (*Serra d'Or*, Nov. 1960).

[2] I owe this point to Professor Niholás Sánchez Albornoz. Cf. J. Carrera Pujal, *Cataluña*, iii. 252.

[3] Figuerola was a radical Progressive; he went in fear of assassination by working-class militants. There was a section of the Democrat leadership (influenced by Fourier, Cabet, and the French *émigrés* of 1851) ready to think in terms of a working-class programme.

Bourbons. 'We are risking our lives and if need arises won't stop short of a republic.'[1] Nevertheless they wanted a military, not a civilian revolution and they had no thought of using those whom the British minister called the 'energetic *proletarii*'. O'Donnell, who emerged as leader because he was the only general brave enough to stay in hiding for five months, made no serious efforts to get civilian backing and had no programme beyond a change of ministry and, possibly, of dynasty.

On 28 June he pronounced with the few troops he could command; after an indecisive and unenthusiastic action fought with loyal troops at Vicálvaro he retreated south. It was at this point that he was persuaded, as a last chance, to sign a programme that was an open appeal for Progressive support. In the Manzanares letter (6 July) he promised to restore the National Militia. It was a dangerous step. If it did not, as the British minister claimed, 'electrify the lower orders' it must, as Narváez saw, bring the Progressives and Espartero back into power.[2] By 17 July Barcelona, Valencia, St. Sebastian, and Valladolid had declared against the ministry and were controlled by Juntas. It was this provincial revolution that saved O'Donnell from defeat and forced Isabella to dismiss San Luis.

It was a revolution in Madrid which ruined an attempt by the court to come to terms with the generals' revolt. San Luis was succeeded (17 July) by the duke of Rivas; his ministry, reformed under Fernando de Córdoba, included respectable Progressives and Ríos Rosas, a Moderate conspirator. The Madrid rising outran this compromise. Córdoba failed to defeat the rebels with grape-shot, though the army was loyal to the government and held out for four days against barricades and street fighting, the toughest which Madrid was to know until 1936.[3] The protagonists of the July days seem to have

[1] O'Donnell's reply to Fernández de los Ríos (*Luchas políticas*, ii. 361–2). Fernández de los Ríos, in whose house O'Donnell hid, was continually trying to force O'Donnell to a programme that would satisfy the Progressives. O'Donnell was unmoved, but cf. Córdoba's assertions that the generals harboured no designs against the dynasty (*Memorias*, iii. 354).

[2] *F.O.*, Howden's report of 25 Oct. 1854. Marx, like Howden, argued (*Revolution in Spain* (New York, 1939), 97) that 'military insurrection has obtained the support of a popular insurrection only by submitting to the conditions of the latter', and that this meant the end of the army as a revolutionary factor for private ends.

[3] For an account of Córdoba's failure see his *Memorias*, iii. 377–406.

been a relatively small group of obscure *meneurs* who could count on the sympathies of a mob inspired by domestic hatreds and private revenges and given targets by the agitation against the court.[1] Two forces, the Democratic activists and the Progressives, in their different ways, sought to turn the initial chaos of popular revolution to their advantage.

In a confused revolutionary situation a politically sophisticated and determined minority can seize the initiative provided it can exploit mass discontent. The Democrats were not such a minority.[2] Pi y Margall, later to become the intellectual leader of Federal Republicanism, accused the Democrat leaders of failing to consolidate the revolution by a social policy which would bring working-class support for a federal republic—admittedly the programme of a small band of converts. This was to apply the lessons of 1848 in France, where the *foule révolutionnaire* had been educated in the tradition of political action, to the response of a mob to court scandal and local grievance. Such a force was incapable of the consistent defence of a class programme. The enthusiasm of primitive revolt decayed of its own accord once its immediate object was achieved.

The trained revolutionaries who knew how to master primitive protest for their own ends were the Progressive soldiers and politicians, determined to avert any threat to property once they had been brought to power by a popular *journée*. Under General San Miguel, a brave man not frightened by barricades, they set up a Junta in order to bring the court to terms and to contain a revolution which threatened, in San Miguel's words, 'ruin, blood and anarchy'. The 'respectable' Junta absorbed the popular Junta of the southern working-class districts, turning its figurehead, Pucheta, into 'a blind and feeble instrument of reactionaries'; his toughs were soon beating up Republican broadsheet vendors.[3] In the first days of violent confusion diplomats and revolutionaries alike believed that Isabella would

[1] As in Barcelona in 1835, in Madrid the mob was gathered together by a bull-fight. Its characteristic expressions were the sacking of the house of Salamanca and San Luis and the shooting, after a 'popular' trial, of a police chief accused of usury based on funds supplied by protected criminals.

[2] For the divisions of the Democrat party on the eve of 1854 see above, p. 230.

[3] See F. Garrido, *Historia del reinado del último Borbón de España* (Barcelona, 1868–9), iii. 225.

have to abdicate and that the generals would be the unwilling progenitors of a democratic revolution.[1] In fact the revolution was less dangerous than it looked, as revolutions in Spain are wont to be. Throughout the whole nineteenth century the Spanish bourgeoisie went in terror of a social revolution which never materialized.

It was San Miguel's Junta which gave Queen Isabella the chance to save the dynasty by dropping the ministry which had defended her against the streets. On 27 July she called in Espartero. If the Democrats were to force the pace of revolution they must keep Espartero's alliance. This was the aim of the Democrat Garrido's pamphlet, *Espartero and the Revolution*, which contained a clear appeal to Espartero to dethrone the 'hangmen of Spain' and which placed great emphasis on the speech of Espartero's agent, Allendesalazar, to the Patriotic Union of Madrid on the day before the duke's arrival. 'I can assure you he is resolved to consolidate the revolution, to be the Washington of Spain'—a formula that could hide anything from the presidency of a republic to the prime ministership under a democratic constitution. The test of Espartero's revolutionary seriousness would be the fate of the queen mother; Espartero decided to let her leave Madrid without the humiliation of a public trial. After failing to bully Espartero, the Democrats attempted a feeble street protest; easily suppressed, it meant the end of the alliance between Espartero and the Democratic revolutionaries. Their clubs were shut, their papers suppressed. 'On the 28 August the revolution was defeated and crushed.'

The suppression of the revolutionary left meant a loss of primitive enthusiasm; the subsequent schisms in the 'respectable' governmental coalition meant that the Revolution of 1854 was to prove a brief parenthesis in the conservative hegemony of Isabelline Spain. By July 1856 O'Donnell and the conservative wing of the coalition had gained exclusive power as guardians of social order. In October 1856 Narváez was in the saddle once more. The Progressives failed to hold the accidental supremacy which the miscarriage of the original

[1] 'An honest man', reflected Cánovas, who was O'Donnell's civilian adviser, 'can take part in only one revolution and that only because he does not know what revolutions are.'

'limited' revolution of the military oligarchs had placed in their hands.

To the radical left, Espartero was not merely the symbol but the active cause of this failure; he was, in Marx's phrase, a burden on the back of the revolution. Vain, a political innocent though he was, it is scarcely surprising—even creditable—that he resisted the pressure of radicals to become a revolutionary dictator. His 'eternal jingle' that the will of the people must be done was the soft centre of the only political creed he knew and he refused to identify that will with democratic radicalism. The extraordinary popular ovations he received throughout the biennium led him to think of himself as a symbol above party, the ranker who had come to contain within himself the aspirations of a whole nation, a representative of the forgotten masses in whose career the simple found that projection of their own desire to escape poverty which led to the idolization of bull-fighters and bandits. It was this notion of his national indispensability which led him to reject the role of leader of the Progressive party for that of the suffering Christ of Spanish politics.[1] Loyal to the crown, loyal to O'Donnell, he found himself without the support of the only party which could have saved him against both.

Leopold O'Donnell, created count of Lucena for his successful generalship in the Carlist wars, was an ambitious, dour, clear-headed military politician; although the unwanted democratic tinge of his own revolution depressed him, he was not a reactionary. To him the revolution was an opportunity to build up a liberal centre party which, by eschewing the 'exclusiveness' of both Progressives and Moderates, would unite sensible men of both parties who rejected their extremist allies. It was only when the hopes of a Liberal Union that would carry him to power had faded that he consented to become the instrument of a palace *coup*. His rightward course was slow, hidden by concessions to current revolutionary rhetoric which deceived most Progressives until early in 1856. It was sure, because he kept a firm hand on the army. Espartero allowed him to remain

[1] Espartero's extraordinary language would seem to indicate that this identification was real: e.g. his reference to office as a 'bitter cup'. This is scarcely surprising when his picture, surrounded by candles, was substituted for that of the Virgin Mary. Howden gives many portraits of Espartero in his dispatches, cf. *F.O.*, 21 Aug. 1854: 'the vainest man I ever met with'.

war minister throughout the biennium. To radical Progressives this was Espartero's greatest blunder; they forgot that in 1854 Espartero was no longer a serving general with men disciplined to obey him. To reject O'Donnell would have meant a show-down with the generals which Espartero could not have faced with any hope of success.

The unexpected feature of the biennium was the crown's recovery of a position that had appeared forfeit in July. In every Spanish revolution the diplomats and democrats of the capital consistently neglected the latent royalism of the countryside; thus their political prophecies always underrated the forces of conservatism. Moreover in the summer of 1854 the diplomats had been especially impressed by the apparent resolute hatred which the generals expressed for the royal house. Yet, once confronted with democratic sedition, the generals defended the dynasty against which they had conspired as the guarantee of a familiar political order. The miscalculations of optimistic Democrats and pessimistic diplomats were exposed by the vote of the Constituent Cortes, the inevitable constitutional consecration of successful revolution; in a single chamber, elected by universal suffrage, the monarchy was secured by an overwhelming majority. Espartero would have accepted a presidency as a gift of the 'national will'; he lacked either the unscrupulousness—to the end he exhibited with pride the letter in which his queen called on him to save her—or the energy to force it through. Olózaga, a bitter personal enemy of Isabella, would not dethrone her. The abortive constitution of the revolution itself contained no serious limitation on the royal prerogative.

What was astonishing was Isabella's refusal to recognize that the revolution had altered the degree to which she could assert her personal prerogatives for her own ends. In November she asked Howden in a 'pettish manner' whether she could avoid Espartero, still the most popular man in Spain.[1] Tactics, as well as inclination, drove her to pose as the defender of Catholicism against 'revolutionary' attacks on church property. The *camarilla* reappeared and there was a serious danger that the king might force a dynastic alliance with Carlism in order to defend the Church against revolution. At the height of these

[1] Howden, *F.O.*, 28 Nov. 1854.

astonishing intrigues the queen refused to sanction the Progressives' legislation against ecclesiastical property; O'Donnell supported the government and the queen had to submit because she lacked the power to defy the cabinet (May 1855). The Carlists never succeeded in staging a successful rising, and opinion was relatively indifferent to violent propaganda in defence of a mildly persecuted church. Thus the queen failed, if such was her aim, as the leader of a clerical-conservative counter revolution. A surer way of defeating the Progressives and the revolution was to win over O'Donnell to the notion that court favour was preferable to Liberal Union and co-operation with Espartero as a means of political advancement.

Only a united Progressive party might have stopped a drift to the right with O'Donnell as its instrument. Espartero's 'inexplicable conduct' and the pressure of the Democratic radicals split the party and wasted its strength. The *puros*—about fifty deputies—under Olózaga and the Catalan Progressive Madoz, ended by rejecting the alliance with O'Donnell to which Espartero clung. They wanted exclusive power with Espartero as a captive figure-head but their constant pressure on him to cast loose from reactionary colleagues only drove him closer to O'Donnell and those Progressives, who because they disliked and feared the Democrats, were ready for a liberal centre party. Without Espartero's blessing there could be no Mountain.

The Democrats were themselves divided; once the monarchy had been accepted by the Constituent Cortes, the parliamentary party could only seek to amplify the democratic conquests by alliance with the Progressives' *puros*. This alliance was strained to breaking-point when the Progressives accepted the *consumos* (under another name), a large conscript army, and the political bona fides of O'Donnell. The 'Maratist' wing of the Democrats rejected an alliance, and the parliamentary manœuvring it demanded, in favour of extra-parliamentary pressure. This division between 'legalists' and 'activists' was to divide the extreme left for the rest of its history. In 1856, while Rivero's *Discusión* was still angling for the *puros* and talking of the peaceful triumphs of Democracy as the embodiment of 'the sweetest harmonies of the moral world', Sixto Cámara was demanding socialism, terrorism, and a thousand aristocratic heads.

The *puros* alone were unable to prevent the government disarming the 'unreliable' popular elements of the militia—the only force which could defend the revolution against the generals. Espartero and his colleagues dreaded the charge of pandering to 'Socialism' by weak government. In 1856 food riots and incendiarism at Valladolid were presented by the conservative press as 'anarchism' in the hitherto uncontaminated heart-lands of Castile; the doubtful attitude of the militia to the mobs alarmed the government. Espartero and his colleagues took the view that it was better to gain the alliance of the respectable classes by a defence of order than to arm the less respectable classes against counter-revolution.[1] This dilemma broke every revolutionary government in Spain. Too late, Escosura, Espartero's Minister of the Interior, realized the growing perils on the right; his attempt to close up the ranks to the left by holding Carlists, rather than 'socialists', responsible for the Valladolid riots, was opposed by O'Donnell who insisted on Escosura's resignation.

On 14 July the queen and O'Donnell, during a recess in the Cortes, used the Escosura crisis in order to force Espartero's resignation. O'Donnell's appointment was a *coup d'état* against a Parliamentary majority; he took an enormous risk in gambling on Espartero's ineffectiveness and the duke's conviction that his presence in Madrid would be sufficient to save liberty.[2] The democratic revolution would be defeated, as it had been made, in the streets of the capital. Success would depend on the relative strengths of the army, which would follow O'Donnell, and the militia, the only force at the Progressives' disposal.

The Madrid Militia battalions, weak in artillery but numerically superior to the regular troops, had taken up their posts as soon as they heard of Espartero's resignation. Neither Espartero nor the parliamentary Progressives under Madoz, gathered in the Cortes and concerned in posing as martyrs for liberty rather than in organizing resistance, gave the Militia a lead. It was left without munitions or orders. The Militia officers showed

[1] Every local disturbance was used by the government to disarm the militia (e.g. at Saragossa, after a food riot in Nov. 1855).

[2] The last-minute efforts of Calvo Asensio and Fernández de los Ríos to persuade Espartero to support Escosura in his quarrel with O'Donnell are described in Fernández de los Ríos, *Luchas políticas*, ii. 425–9.

no enthusiasm perhaps because they, like the Progressive leaders, were alarmed at the growing radicalism of the ranks. Resistance, left to the working-class districts of the south (where Pucheta, the hero of the barricades, met his death), was defeated.[1] All over Spain the Militia, after varying periods of resistance, abandoned a fight for which they could find no leadership. This failure, particularly Madoz's dispersion of the Militia during a truce with the army, was to be held against the Progressives in Democrat circles for years to come. The Progressives' motives are clear: they were afraid of barricades and a revolution which must destroy the throne. Isabella owed the last twelve years of her reign to the indecision or loyalty of Baldermero Espartero. His reward was political death. 'To the throne I am presented as a demagogue, to the people as a deserter from their sacred cause.'

The Revolution of 1854 was an apparent failure. The democratic constitution of 1856 never came into operation. But to see only this political failure is but to misinterpret the significance of the biennium. The appeal to material interests, which the Moderates had seen as a social necessity or a political device, became a regenerating creed: capitalism, credit, and free trade would destroy the *ancien régime*. Thus the Constituent Cortes concerned themselves with every aspect of the economic life of Spain: afforestation, railways, electric telegraphs, roads, banks. It was the legislation of 1854 (Company, Railway, and Mining Laws) which largely provided the legal structure for the prosperity and expansion which lasted till 1867.[2]

The symbolic act of faith in the benefits of expansion and the characteristic expression of the upsurge of economic confidence which accompanied the Revolution was the codification and extension of the disentailing laws by Madoz. Once again, this legislation professed to encourage the emergence of a new race of peasant proprietors; but without credit facilities, as some Democrats saw, the need for even a small down-payment in cash excluded the poorer peasants from the public

[1] The army lost 38 killed and about 200 wounded. For a military account see *Relación de la sucesos de Madrid* (1856) with a good map. The decisive factor was the artillery superiority (40 guns to 16) of the regular troops.

[2] For an enthusiastic summary of this expansion see F. Garrido, *España contemporánea* (Barcelona, 1865). The Revolution was contemporaneous with the electric telegraph and beginning of a railway boom.

auctions.[1] The extent of sales of ecclesiastical and common lands must rest uncertain;[2] to the Progressives they were more than a mere expedient to stave off state bankruptcy. Ecclesiastical disentailment would regenerate Spain, giving back to production the lands which Visigothic conquerors had donated to the Church. A portion of the profits from sales was to be invested in canals and roads. The Progressives hoped to pay the National Debt, not merely by selling the landed capital of the nation, but by investment which would raise the level of production and the yield of taxation. O'Donnell's faith in expansion made him, in this respect at least, a true representative of the biennium.

[1] Cf. the speeches of Bueno and Madoz (*D.S.C.* (1859), ii. 213). Cf. Garrido, op. cit. i. 423 ff. The law of 1855 covered municipal commons, charitable property, lands of the Orders of Chivalry, i.e. all corporate property. Ten per cent. of total value was demanded at the time of sale and the rest could be paid over a period of fifteen years.

[2] Compared with the period 1836–44 (400 million reales worth of land of the secular clergy; 500 million of the regular clergy) the period 1854–6 shows a sharp decline in sales of monastic land, most of which had already been sold (80 million) and some decline for lands of secular clergy (350 million). The government figures for the sale of communal land are difficult to use for analysis in periods. The legislation provided for monetary compensation on a valuation basis; the profits of the state consisted in the difference between this valuation and the sale price.

VII

PROGRESS AND REVOLUTION 1856–1868

FROM 1856 to the Revolution of 1868 the political history of Spain is dominated by the failure of an attempt to engender a liberal grouping, a potpourri of the historic parties, which would exclude the extremes of revolution and court reaction. As we have seen, temperate minds had been seduced for some time by the notion of a form of constitutional government which would defend social interests and promote prosperity without sacrificing the apparatus and appearances of liberty. The collapse of this attempt left the constitutional monarchy exposed to revolution. Having failed in their historic mission of reconciling liberty and order, the liberals blamed this failure on a dynasty which pushed reaction until it imperilled property and destroyed prosperity. A self-imposed process of political contraction isolated the dynasty from all but a hard core of conservatives and neo-catholics. As in 1854, cautious politicians and generals with no head for popular revolution were forced to risk the expulsion of the dynasty in order to 'save property from the tremendous social revolution which threatened it and which was fomented by reactionary governments'.[1]

1. *The Liberal Union, 1856–1863*

The only successful example of the recurrent essays in reconciling order and liberty took form with O'Donnell's Liberal Union. Its origins go back to the Puritan opposition to the 'exclusive' version of Moderate government and to the constitutional opposition of Progressives and Moderates before the Revolution of 1854 which was symbolized in the 'embrace' of Espartero and O'Donnell in 1854. The old hands of political life abused the Liberal Union as an immoral concern set up to attract office-hungry Progressives and Moderates by a joint

[1] Prim's Lisbon Manifesto of 1865.

sacrifice of political principle, as a governmental contrivance based on an intelligent and discriminating use of electoral management, as an assemblage of the ambitious 'without traditions, without principles, without a future'. They denied it the status of a party. It was a hotch-potch of mere politicians 'which greatly resembles the irregular troops of Turkey'.[1]

Yet the political creed of O'Donnell and of civilian Unionists like Ríos Rosas was as coherent as, and infinitely more realistic than, the outworn dogmas of the historic parties. It can be legitimately considered as a positive contribution towards a stable form of political life. The function of politics, under the Unionist system, was the reconciliation of interests rather than the imposition of dogmatic solutions on defeated opponents. O'Donnell saw doctrinal intransigence and 'exclusive situations' as an impediment to good government. He had broken with Espartero once his Progressive followers sought to turn the *bienio* into a party monopoly. Less obviously, he was determined to remain a liberal of sorts and to save something of the liberal front from the wreck of 1856 and the revenge of conservatives. Hence his reluctance to return to the Moderate conservative constitution of 1845 which he sought to modify by an Additional Act, granting an elective senate and a jury for press offences. Though he was willing to pose as a *dévot* for his queen, he resigned rather than sacrifice the liberal church settlement in its totality to a clerical court. Narváez returned to power in October 1856 and his neo-catholic minister, Nocedal, was responsible for a press law which made any criticism of the government impossible. Nevertheless the Narváez ministry—it lasted a year, falling because the general refused a promotion to a favourite of the queen—and its successors proved that court reaction could not survive even with a doctored Parliamentary system. 'A regular uncompromising absolutist ministry' was no longer possible.[2] Once he returned to power (June 1858), O'Donnell was ready to widen the basis of oligarchical rule by constitutional reform and an extension of the suffrage.

The modernity of the Liberal Union made those Moderates, who kept themselves to themselves and refused to join with

[1] *Las Novedades*, 24 May 1861.

[2] Lord Howden, the British minister, discussing the possibility of a renewed attempt at a reactionary ministry under Bravo Murillo. *F.O.*, 5 Jan. 1858.

O'Donnell in recognizing repentant Progressives as respectable allies in government, appear as reactionaries and court politicians. In the sixties the Moderates found an apologist in the poet Campoamor (1817–1901), author of 'The Express Train'. He presented the party as the mean between neo-catholic reaction and demagogy.[1] But this mean was already outdated. The party split into an opportunist wing and a hard core of doctrinaires scared by 1854 into 'exorcising the revolution'.[2] To Narváez and the soldiers, revolution was a problem of police repression which could be reconciled with attempts to attract liberals; to civilian Moderates of the authentic right, revolution could only be resisted by a rigid high Tory authoritarianism which excluded all compromise with the Progressive tradition. Hence it was these civilian Moderates, sympathizing with the neo-catholic revival, who pinned all their faith in crown favour. Narváez was ready to save the court *in extremis* or to accept neo-catholic ministers, but he was independent of both. Ready to serve his queen in the most unpromising and compromising circumstances, he was too conscientious a policeman to become a courtier.

As was the intention of its creators, the Liberal Union embarrassed and weakened the Progressives—indeed Democrats claimed that the old party had altogether ceased to exist. It was split between *resellados*, who were ready to serve under O'Donnell, and *puros* who rejected him and who were therefore driven closer to the Democrats. Espartero was the titular leader of the *puros* and to him Progressive dogmas were the unchangeable truths of the moral universe, given by God, 'The Great Progressive'. Compromise was neither possible nor profitable since the march of progress, identified with that of the Progressives, could not be permanently resisted.[3] With Espartero posing as Cincinnatus in his 'corner' at Logroño, the real leadership of the Progressive *puros* fell to Olózaga.[4] To the

[1] Campoamor's political writings are contained in *O.C.* ii. For his views see R. Hilton, *Campoamor, Spain and the World* (Stanford).

[2] The phrase comes from Bravo Murillo's speech, *D.S.C.*, 30 Jan. 1858.

[3] R. Olivar Bertrand, *Isabel II*, 46, appendixes 1 and 8.

[4] There was frequent rumour of an opposition coalition of anti-Unionist *puros* and the Moderate malcontents; this proved impossible, if for no other reason because Olózaga detested González Brabo, the Moderate leader (cf. Sir A. Buchanan, *F.O.*, 22 Nov. 1860).

resellados O'Donnell's liberalism would be proved by his appointments of Progressives and his resistance to the 'White League' of the court High Tories.

O'Donnell's Long Ministry (June 1858 to March 1863)—the most stable ministry constitutional Spain had seen—was a foretaste of the so-called artificial stability of Restoration Spain after 1875 and it was as secretary in the Ministry of the Interior that Cánovas del Castillo, the creator of the Restoration settlement, served his political apprenticeship. Unlike Moderate essays in *gobierno fuerte*, it did not outrage liberal sensibilities; the Cortes, prefabricated by Posada Herrero, the Great Elector of the Ministry of the Interior, and prudently equipped with a respectable Progressive and Moderate minority, was in frequent session; budgets were regularly presented and the press relatively unmolested. Only those outside the system, the Carlists and the Republicans, were persecuted and silenced. Within these limits the Liberal Union was an attempt to achieve government by consent.

The most remarkable feature of O'Donnell's government was a series of foreign adventures. There was an expedition to Cochin China, the African war, the temporary resumption of Spanish rule in Santo Domingo, and the Mexican expedition of 1861.[1] The most successful was the Moroccan expedition which ended with the capture of Tetuan (February 1860). Like all subsequent Moroccan expeditions, behind a limited police operation to defend the garrison towns of Melilla and Ceuta from the raids of tribesmen (whom the Sultan could not control but for whose crimes he was held responsible), lay vague notions of an African mission and a new Crusade against the infidel Moors.[2] The war was a hazardous operation, carried out at the height of the rainy season, with an ill-equipped army—two-thirds of the 7,000 deaths were from cholera—badly planned in a roadless country, but it de-

[1] But for Prim, the commander of the Mexican expedition, Spain might have become involved in a discreditable war with the Mexican liberals under Juárez, in order to keep Maximilian on the throne of a Mexican empire. Prim had married a niece of Juárez's Minister of Justice and understood the narrow basis of the demand for a monarchist restoration. Hence his resistance to Serrano's adventurous policy.

[2] Cf. D. Sevilla Andrés, *África en la política española* (1960), 84 ff. For criticism of Spain's supposed African future, ibid. 87.

lighted the Spanish public and restored the confidence of the army.[1]

The capture of Tetuan evoked a nation-wide apotheosis of the army with the queen as the heiress of the Great Isabella. The war brought no territorial gains—these were forbidden by England—but vindicated Spain's mission against the infidel and slaked the thirst for national regeneration. In O'Donnell's words it succeeded in 'raising Spain from her prostration'.[2] It was a classic example of a war of honour unsupported by economic interest, the reflex action of a nation that felt itself growing in prosperity and ripe for colonial responsibility in some abstract, non-materialist sense; hence Spanish resentment at England's carping tutelage. In Catalonia the popularity of the Volunteers and of Prim, the Catalan general, exponent of the 'gesture' at the battle of Castillejos (January 1860) were extraordinary; this was a proof that national patriotism could still subsume regional loyalties in the sixties.[3] The Moroccan war was, like many wars, a unifying political emotion; a link between the jingoism that would later risk war with Germany and face war with the United States and the patriotic myth of 1808. It was the only satisfaction enjoyed by Spanish national pride in modern times and was accompanied, as nationalism is wont to be in Spain, by a mild wave of Anglophobia.

The background to political stability was economic expansion. The best years of the Liberal Union corresponded with the heights of the railway boom. The Moderates had their connexions with bankers and industrialists from Remisa's days while the Progressives of 1854–6 had dreamed of a Spain revivified by capital investment. Individual economic advantage through useful connexions in the ministry now combined with the notion that it was the function of government to

[1] There is an excellent description of the campaign in F. Hardman, *The Spanish Campaign in Morocco* (Edinburgh, 1860). Hardman believed the troops showed great qualities of sobriety and endurance in conditions where an English army would have mutinied. He was convinced that the army merely wanted 'self satisfaction' (255 ff.) and that only civilian politicians dreamed of permanent territorial gains. In the twentieth century this position was reversed.

[2] Cf. speech of Cánovas in 1894, *D.S.C.*, 11 V. (1894), 4107–8.

[3] For an account of Catalan enthusiasm see C. Roure, *Recuerdos de mi vida larga* (Barcelona, 1926–7), i. 143–55. The Bank of Barcelona gave an interest free loan: poems and plays took the Volunteers as their subject. Cf. P. A. de Alarcón, *Diario de un testigo de la guerra de África* (*O.C.* iii).

develop the economy by fostering what were called 'material interests'.[1] Riches, not Civil Guards, were the true cure for social revolution.[2] Prosperity became a political and social mystique. In Galdós's novel *O'Donnell* the courtesan heroine abandons honourable poverty with a Democrat after what can only be called a quasi-religious experience before the house of a banker.

The centre-piece of the Liberal Unionist plan for a new Spain, respected and prosperous, was the budget of 1859. In many ways O'Donnell's rule is a mild foretaste of Primo de Rivera's dictatorship after 1923: no sterile political squabbles, the support of an army satisfied with conquest in Africa and influence in the state, boom prosperity. Thus the Extraordinary Budget of 1859 is a distant antecedent of the dictator's support of public works financed by loans and extraordinary resources. In 1859 these were to be provided by the continuation of disentailing laws and their extension to charitable foundations. The budget was bitterly attacked by conservatives as the continuation of 'evil principles'; it had a Progressive soul.[3] On the other extreme of political life the Democrat Garrido, like the critics of Primo de Rivera, attacked the budget as financing prestige and the armed forces instead of productive investment.[4] Thus stood revealed the 'hollowness in the soul of Liberal Unionism', its

[1] For a panegyric of prosperity see C. M. Navarro y Rodrigo, *O'Donnell y su tiempo* (1869), 158.

[2] It must be noted that the more enlightened Liberal Unionists were capable of more foresight and a deeper interest in the solution of social problems; Borrego, Ríos Rosas, and Pastor Díaz were primitive Christian Democrats. In 1858 Ríos Rosas appealed for social legislation 'to enforce the solution of Jesus Christ'—thus his programme was timid. Borrego was consistently in favour of a 'social' solution to problems left by land sales conducted on strictly individualist premisses. Thus he is a link between early radicals (e.g. Floréz Estrada) and later catholic social reformers. For the anti-individualism of Pastor Díaz see L. Legaz y Lacambra, 'El socialismo visto por Nicomedes Pastor Díaz' in *Estudios de historia social de España*, iii (1955), 125 ff.

[3] The conservative protests are conveniently collected in *Los presupuestos de 1859* (1860).

[4] For Garrido's attacks *La España contemporánea* (Barcelona, 1865, 2 vols.), *passim*. The greatest single item was road building followed, in order, by the fleet, ports, and lighthouses, &c., fortifications, barracks, irrigation. The building of a naval squadron showed O'Donnell's determination that Spain should appear as a great power and a desire to favour the new metallurgical industries as far as this could be done without offending Progressive free-traders. For the war contracts see Alberto del Castillo, *Maquinista*, 108–15.

false liberalism: rather than schools or dams, O'Donnell built barracks and a fleet.

This budget exposed the political weakness of O'Donnell's position. It revealed an irreconcilable conflict between modernity, as the Liberal Union conceived it, and religion as the court conceived it. O'Donnell venerated the queen (with whom his relations remind the English reader of those of Gladstone and Victoria) and wished to remain her prime minister, but the Church stood between them. He compromised over disentailment, but he could not compromise over the recognition of Italy. To Catholics and Liberals alike the recognition of Victor Emanuel's kingdom was the central political test; to recognize 'atheist' Italy was to declare against the pope.

Under stress the 'polyglot party' began to disintegrate. The blistering attacks of Olózaga made the Progressive ministerial *resellados* uncomfortable. Prim, hated by Serrano and the Concha family on account of his influence with the prime minister, abandoned the search for place and power under O'Donnell for the role of Progressive *caudillo*.[1] The argument of the *resellados* had been that O'Donnell would last; that he would succeed in making himself the indispensable architect of a novel quasi-liberal system. Now Madoz and Olózaga's warnings that this belief rested on ignorance of the designs of 'a certain house and certain people'—the High Tories and the court—triumphed. O'Donnell's parliamentary majority of the centre disintegrated: the longevity of the ministry made personal differences a surrogate for political principles in a group of 'dissidents' who had once supported the Liberal Union. Ríos Rosas, one of its founding fathers, deserted in 1860 and was followed by Alonso Martínez and Mon. The minority came to include the most able and—more alarming—the ambitious. In spite of a parliamentary majority and the loyalty of the army O'Donnell's position was weakening in face of a revolt of political notabilities. A reconstruction of the ministry to include the friends of Ríos Rosas and Mon could not make it safe against 'a certain house'.[2] Isabella refused a dissolution and thus forced

[1] For Prim's evolution, clearly revealed in his speeches in the Senate, see R. Olivar Betrand, *Así Cayó*, 163–5.

[2] For the seemingly meaningless cabinet shifts, intended to re-create governmental unity, see *F.O.*, Sir J. Crampton's reports, 29 January to 27 February.

O'Donnell's resignation (27 February 1863); his ministry had lasted four years, seven months, and twenty-eight days.

2. *Economic Expansion, 1856–1867*

The economic optimism of the men of the biennium and the prosperity which supported O'Donnell's Liberal Union are inexplicable without considering the economic growth of Spain in mid-century. Her foreign trade doubled between 1852 and 1862; her agriculture prospered, even if it still could not supply corn at stable prices; her industry was re-equipped and a new industrial complex was beginning its slow growth in the north; her main railways were constructed in the years around 1860. From the France of Napoleon III Spain became mildly infected with a belief in unlimited expansion by means of easy credit, daring investment, and public works.

Much of the expansion of the middle decades was based on an over-optimistic forecast of Spain's future as a modern economy. Throughout the century economists were haunted by the proposition that her people 'were endowed with the inexhaustible sources of prosperity' which awaited only sensible exploitation.[1] Yet no country in nineteenth-century Europe could hope to compete with the advanced industrial economies without *cheap* coal, the capital to create new industry, and the purchasing power to absorb its products. Of the prerequisites of growth Spain possessed only abundant supplies of iron and other metals, and these she lacked the capital to exploit. Spain's mineral deposits were so rich that even under-capitalized and haphazard native exploitation could produce a trickle of exports, but it was only foreign capital and foreign experts which brought them to world significance.

The importance of Spain's zinc deposits was first appreciated by an enterprising Belgian, Jules Hauzeur. He could raise no money from his Spanish associates for their exploitation. Thus the Royal Company of the Asturias (1853) was financed by a Belgian bank and became a Belgian company with a sprinkling of Spanish directors for the sake of appearance and political influence—the finance minister Mon was on the Spanish board.[2]

[1] J. Herrera Davila, *Coleción de tratados breves* (Seville, 1829), 5.
[2] *La Compagnie royale* (Brussels, n.d.), 29 ff.

It was the same with copper: the Rio Tinto mine, the greatest deposit of copper in Europe, was knocked down to a British firm for £3,700,000, not because the government was ignorant of the wealth of the deposits, but because no Spaniard—even a rich capitalist like Remisa who farmed the mine after 1829—could gather together the money and men to exploit them.[1]

Similarly the establishment, in its main lines, of the Spanish railway network in the decade after 1855 was the work of foreign capital.[2] Over half of this capital was French. Thus it was that the capital of the Rothschilds and Pereires centred the control of the Spanish railway system in Paris with boards of straw directors sitting in Madrid. The only exception was Catalan capital which was invested, not merely in Catalan lines, but in northern Spain and Andalusia; but by 1866 the French Norte Company bought out the Saragossa–Barcelona line and the last large Catalan concern was absorbed by the M.Z.A. (Madrid–Zaragoza–Alicante) in 1898. Similarly the Basque bankers who built the Bibao–Tudela line could not hold out against the superior resources of the Norte Company.[3] This process of concentration left three great lines—the M.Z.A., the Norte (Madrid–Irun), and the Andalusian net-work over against eighty small concerns.

Native historians and English railwaymen have combined to make French capital and French engineers the villains of Spanish railway history. English capital demanded a guaranteed interest which Spanish politicians, mistrusting their compatriots' book-keeping, refused. Hence England lost a market for locomotives and rails while Spain was invaded by young graduates of the *École Polytechnique*, French engineers, and an 'exaggerated copy' of French working rules instead of adopting the

[1] See W. G. Nash, *The Rio Tinto Mine* (London, 1904). The main change made by the English concern was the introduction of open-cast mining. According to W. R. Lawson, *Spain of Today* (London, 1890), a London–Bremen syndicate invested £8 million immediately after the purchase.

[2] Only one successful line (Barcelona–Mataró) was in operation in the forties, paying 22 per cent. in its first year. For later construction see Figures 2 and 3.

[3] By 1914 French companies controlled 85 per cent. of the Spanish system. The Norte was originally largely financed by the Pereires, the M.Z.A. by Rothschilds. French capital was calculated at £70 million, the Spanish state subsidies at £24 million; cf. P. E. Cameron, *France and the Economic Development of Europe* (Princeton, 1961), 248 ff.

supposedly more flexible English system.[1] Spaniards believed that the import concessions to French contractors ruined the prospects of a domestic iron industry: in fact no railway system could have been constructed at all by native resources given the production costs of Spanish iron—twice that of the great iron centres. Thus the construction of railways could only invigorate the economy in so far as it endowed it with an adequate communications system and with the wages of those engaged on construction work: the usual 'multiplier' effect of railways was restricted.

Throughout their history Spanish railways were controversial.[2] The original government engineer's report, besides imposing a broad gauge (admired by railwaymen but which isolated Spain from any European through traffic) had insisted on the grant of concessions to bona fide companies, thus eliminating their speculative resale by the original purchaser.[3] This salutary clause was modified in such a way that concession hunting entered politics. First granted by royal decree, the insistent demands of the constitutional opposition of the 1850's was that concessions should be brought under parliamentary control. The victory of the opposition in 1854 meant, therefore, that they became a matter of parliamentary and local pressures rather than of court influence.

The railways, as a whole, were never very profitable. This was only partly a result of linear subventions which encouraged meandering lines. More seriously, as happened elsewhere in Europe, fierce competition in the nineties led the large companies to buy up small lines burdened with debts. The battle between the two giants—M.Z.A. and the Norte—did not end until 1924. The main characteristic of railway finance was thus a heavy proportion of debenture stock: the directors did well, the Parisian waiters who were said to have invested heavily in ordinary stock, in spite of vigorous occasional protest, rarely saw a dividend.[4] Debt charges were so heavy that renewal of

[1] Higgins represents the English view of state railway engineers trained on French lines as 'extremely paternal and exceedingly troublesome and annoying', *Commercial and Industrial Spain* (London, 1886), 63.

[2] To make clear the problems involved, this account exceeds the chronological limits of this chapter.

[3] For this and much valuable detail, see *Cien años de ferrocariles* (1945), i, esp. 67.

[4] The Norte paid 6 per cent. in the first few years: nothing from 1865 to 1873 and from 1891 to 1906; M.Z.A. never passed a dividend while the Estremadura line never

equipment and track was impossible: hence the sorry state of the rolling stock which had become by the end of the century, apart from the main trains, as primitive as that of a Balkan state. The usual accusations that high working costs precluded profit do not bear examination: in spite of formidable engineering difficulties, single lines cut down construction costs and working costs were strikingly low.[1] Those who suffered in this low cost system, with its inflexible determination to make the dead load as near the pay load as possible, were the passengers and consigners; endless waits at junctions, packed and uncomfortable trains, and delayed deliveries were the penalty paid for a railway system constructed on the cheap. The load of debt apart, the economy could not provide the traffic and the profits to finance improvement. Here was an example of the 'vicious circle of poverty' which bedevils developing countries.[2]

The railway system still left great areas of Spain isolated: Galicia was ill-connected with the rest of Spain, the port of Almería was without a railway. It was therefore of great importance that the eighteenth-century concern for road building was revived in the Isabelline period. Half the state road system existing by 1868 had been constructed since 1840. In the Carlist wars of the seventies government troops and artillery penetrated the Maestrazgo which had defied them in the 1830's—an improvement which made the mopping up of the semi-bandit *sequelae* of civil war a less formidable military task.[3] With railways and roads it was easier for the state to act against revolution. Provided the army was loyal, local rebellion could not grow into national revolution as easily as it had done in the first half of the century. The rebels of 1820 could not have been successful in the railway age. Against this, railways facilitated the organization of revolutionary movements: the

paid one. Andalusian lines never really paid. See G. L. Gloag, *Railways of Spain* (London, 1923), for some observations on Spanish railway finance.

[1] Gradients *were* a serious problem, e.g. in coal trains from the Asturias where trains had to be very short. The virtual length of Spanish railways is 2·1 miles and the difficulties created by mountains is sufficiently evident to any observer on the old Norte line.

[2] Even so the régime of competitive bidding caused French companies to underestimate costs and therefore led directly to the financial difficulties which dogged them.

[3] Cf. A. Pirala, *Historia contemporánea*, v. 53. In 1868–73 loyal troops could be easily transferred to troubled districts: order collapsed when there were no loyal troops to move.

Internationalist Federalist Congresses of the 1870's were dependent on cheap railway fares for the delegates.

In the years of the railway boom the twin pillars of the Catalan economy—the textile industry and colonial commerce, together with the industries which supplied it—entered on a period of expansion. After the crisis of the forties came 'Crimean' prosperity, investment, and, in the large cotton mills, extensive modernization with the steam engine as the main source of power. This was accompanied by a process of capital concentration which diminished the number of old mills with written-off machinery, though these were probably sufficient in number to deny adequate profit margins to progressive manufacturers when trade slacked off. The new conquest was wool, never before a Catalan product. Increasingly after 1850 the wool industry came to concentrate round Sabadell and Tarrasa—probably because these towns had lacked water power to drive cotton machinery and could now utilize the resources of steam.[1] The creation and rapid growth of this modern wool industry was a crippling blow to thousands of small looms all over Spain.

Catalan industrialists were conscious of the dangers of a lop-sided industrial structure based exclusively on textiles. They made what have been described as heroic efforts to create new industries. Thus in Catalonia the railway age was marked by an attempt to break beyond textiles into a diversified, modern industrial economy. This attempt was doomed to failure: investment in coal and iron mining could produce little result.[2] The attempt to set up a metallurgical industry which, as we have seen, started in the thirties, resulted in three considerable firms beside sixty or so minor concerns. The metallurgists blamed Madrid tariffs for their relative lack of success: imported machines paid 2 per cent. duty which perhaps reflected a desire to supply the cotton factories with cheap English equipment rather than a determined attempt to destroy an engineering industry in Catalonia by politicians committed to free trade.

[1] Until the fifties steam was only used where an adequate head of water was lacking (e.g. the plain of Barcelona). Both Tarrasa and Sabadell had been second-rate cotton towns. See J. Vilá Valenti, 'El origen de la industria catalana moderna' *E.G.* lxxviii (1960), 5 ff. The first *fabricante* in Tarrasa to go over to wool (in 1838) was the father of the Catalan politician and wool millionaire, Alfonso Sala Argemí.

[2] For this and what follows see J. Vicens Vives, *Els Catalans*, 52 ff., and especially the diagrams 56–58.

La Maquinista terrestre y marítima, the newest and richest of the metallurgical firms, built a modern factory outside the city walls but did not get beyond textile machinery, small ships, and marine engines. It never made a locomotive or a rail in the great period of construction: these came, free of all duty, from France and Great Britain.

Although Catalonia remained the greatest industrial complex in Spain, by 1868 a second centre was slowly beginning to develop in the Basque Provinces. Although, as in the case of Catalonia, there was a long tradition of small industry and American trade, Basque industry can be considered as, in a direct sense, the creation of liberalism. The liberal's abolition of the *fueros* and the consequent removal of the customs barrier to the national frontiers gave ironmasters a wider market in Spain itself.[1] Like the Catalans, the Basques had what a Basque writer, Maeztu, called 'the sense of reverence for money'. The Basque *bourgeoisie* was piously catholic; it was nevertheless 'open' and sensitive to the economic climate of Europe.

The foundation of its wealth in the later nineteenth century was iron. At first it seemed as if Basque iron would be taken to the coal of the Asturias; but, in spite of preferential duties and improved transport to the sea, the difficult seams of the Asturian field failed to provide Spain with cheap coal. The availability of English coal as a return freight for iron-ore was to fix the industry near the iron mines of the north-east.

The industry had been anything but progressive; it resisted all change in the eighteenth century and until the late sixties the largest blast furnace—still using charcoal—was in Heredia's concern at Marbella, between Málaga and Gibraltar. In the north the dispersed family enterprises concentrated slowly and were technically archaic. The origins of the modern industry must nevertheless be sought in the activities of a group of friends, led by the Bilbao banker Avellano, and in the Ybarra family whose firm was the ancestor of the great Basque concern —the Altos Hornos.[2] Their companies, by English standards, were under-capitalized and backward; perhaps because the companies owned woods, they preferred to use charcoal. The consequence of technical backwardness was a high-cost industry

[1] See above, p. 221, for the abolition of the *fueros*.

[2] For these concerns see *Banco de Bilbao*, 156–8.

which demanded protective tariffs—a situation which turned Basque industrialists into the natural allies of the Catalans.[1] The Basques argued that any breach of protection was fatal to an infant industry and contested the import concessions granted to railway constructors, without which railways could not have been built at all. Without the railway market, domestic consumption *per capita* was lower than that of Russia and could not create a demand that might have allowed economies of scale. Thus the expansion and modernization of the iron industry and its localization in the north of Spain was a process financed from abroad: first by France and then by English money which began to buy Biscayan iron ore in the seventies.

Expansion necessitated modern commercial legislation and credit institutions. The company acts of 1848 and 1856 were the foundation of a new business world. Madrid, Barcelona, and to a less extent Bilbao emerge as banking centres, though the massive, neo-classical buildings which were to symbolize this new activity came a generation later. The banker becomes a respected figure in Catalan and Basque society. Manuel Girona (1818–1905) founded the Bank of Barcelona in 1844 and, from 1852, the private bank of Evaristo Arnús became the channel by which Catalan savings went into safe railway shares and into the building development by which Barcelona started its career as a modern city. Both institutions were old-fashioned and paternal, but by prudence avoided the disaster which overtook others in 1866. The Bank of Bilbao, founded in 1855, was likewise conservative: not till 1861 did it reach its maximum permitted note issue.

The contrast is startling between these conservative bankers of peripheral Spain and the group of Madrid financiers and politicians headed by Remisa, Salamanca, and Istúriz, who founded the Bank of Isabella II in 1844 with a capital of 100 million reales compared with the modest 8 million of the Bank of Bilbao. Its adventurous expansion was crippled by the slump of 1847 and it was only the bank's political connexions which allowed it to save itself by amalgamation with the older Bank of San Fernando. This crisis restricted credit very severely after

[1] The first coke furnace, constructed in the Asturias in 1848 in co-operation with an English company, long remained without rivals; the Ybarra furnaces, the largest in Biscay, were constructed to use charcoal as late as 1859. See F. Sánchez Ramos, *La economía siderúrgica española* (1945), i. 121 *et passim.*

the rapid expansion of 1844–7. Throughout the fifties growth was steady, becoming spectacular in the sixties: the Madrid financiers were intoxicated by the productive possibilities of credit and the development of public utilities revealed by the activities of *Crédit Mobilier* in France. The French bank had a Spanish subsidiary and credit companies of various kinds pullulated in the boom atmosphere; but by 1865 the whole credit structure was dangerous. As in 1847 optimism had gone too far.[1]

That so much of the energy for expansion had come from Paris meant that Spain was in danger of becoming an economic dependency of France; the Pereire brothers and the Rothschilds looked as if they might accomplish by their capital what Napoleon I had failed to accomplish by his arms. Both of these financial houses conceived of the Spanish railways system as a tributary feeding their rival lines in France. The Pereires extended their activities from discount banking and insurance to coal-mining, brick manufacturing, sugar refining, and gas-works. Nor were they alone. French nationals—they constituted 90 per cent. of the alien colony—were engaged in major and minor enterprises from dye-works and tanneries to metallurgy and great public utilities. French workers from Decazeville came to supervise the new furnaces at Mieres; French signal-men and accountants ran the new railways. It was only the influx of British capital in the 1870's which diminished this monopoly.

This extensive commitment of France was to have important political consequences which have escaped the diplomatic historians in their probings for the war guilt of 1870. With

[1] Graell's figures give a rough estimate for investment distribution and growth in Catalonia (millions of pesetas). Totals include remaining investments.

Year	*Railways*	*Banks*	*Industry*	*Maritime insurance*	*Steam shipping*	*Total*
1857 . .	30	23	35·5	8	8·5	111·5
1859 . .	77	30	42·5	8	9·5	167·5
1860 . .	116	30	43·5	8	8·5	218·5
1862 . .	160	27	36·5	6	8	260·5
1863 . .	181	27	35	6	8	281·5
1864 . .	194	36	38	6	8	298·5

These represent the nominal capital of companies *registered* under the acts of 1848 and 1856.

35 per cent. of French total foreign investment in Spain the Hohenzollern candidature appeared to Napoleon III as an economic disaster as well as a political threat. Conversely, French influence brought the financial and political *mores* of the French empire to the court of Madrid; Gónzalez Brabo, Isabella II's last minister, swept aside by the Revolution of 1868, had been a director of the Pereire's *Crédito Mobiliario*.[1] His combination of high finance and absolutism was offensive once it ceased to be effective; from 1861 the government was in danger of bankruptcy and could raise no loans in Paris.

The optimism and expansion of the middle decades of the century were reflected in the final stages of the 'liberation' of the land which was the characteristic achievement of Progressive liberalism. Not merely the lands of the Church, the bulk of which was sold before 1850, but a large proportion of the municipal commons became private property as a result of the Progressive disentailing laws. There seems no reason to doubt that the sale of common lands, as elsewhere, *in the long run* increased agricultural efficiency. What we do not know with any certainty is their more immediate effects on production and their role in what came to be called, in these years, the social question, i.e. the harsh conditions of the small peasant proprietor or tenant farmer and of the landless labourer.

It was maintained by catholic conservatives and Republican 'socialists' alike that the sales represented the triumph, over social justice and national interest alike, of the bourgeois speculator and rack-renter who bought 'national lands' at knock-down prices only to re-let or re-sell them at great profit. Nothing effective was done to produce the race of secure and prosperous peasant proprietors, as Flórez Estrada and other agrarian reformers had demanded. This left the state with an obligation to maintain the poor it had created by squandering public land and selling up charitable endowments.[2] Catholic apologists drew pictures of the new destitute classes, victims of liberalism. Among the Republicans Pi y Margall, in the same manner but from different premisses, attributed deepening

[1] P. F. Cameron, *France and the Economic Development of Europe*, contains much interesting detail on these matters, esp. 90–92, 166–8, 275 ff.

[2] Cf. A. Borrego, *Historia . . . de las clases jornaleras*, 1890. Pi's ideas are excellently expounded in C. A. M. Hennessy, *The Federal Republic in Spain* (Oxford, 1962), 20 ff.

agrarian distress to the economics of liberalism. The historical tendency since 1789—he thought in a large Hegelean framework—was the 'generalization of property'. Why should this process stop with the landowners who were the beneficiaries of the 'generalization' made possible by liberal disentailing laws and who were the 'caciques' of a new feudalism? From Proudhon and a long Spanish tradition he advocated peasant proprietors aided by state loans.

Curiously enough, largely because they fit into later socialist polemics, these views have gone unchallenged and the great transfer of land has been made responsible for an exacerbation of the old disease of *latifundismo* and every other evil of the countryside. How far can these criticisms be maintained?

The sale of the municipal commons was a social disaster in that it took away the livelihood of the marginal men and it was the marginal subsistence cultivators who rioted against the 'theft' of the common lands.[1] It was probably a natural disaster in that it speeded up deforestation and erosion, so that, from the mid-century onwards, the forest question begins to be a central theme in regenerationist literature. Sales lamed the small municipality as a natural community. It was the income from common lands—often very extensive in the north—which paid the schoolmaster and doctor and, in many of the *stable* regions, allowed the municipality to exercise 'that tutelary influence which, in other countries, is the finest attribute of the landed proprietors'.[2]

These disturbances of settled social patterns are indisputable although the extent of their incidence has probably been somewhat exaggerated.[3] Where the common lands were an

[1] To take two examples, the muleteers, whose characteristics are a favourite topic with travel writers, kept most of their beasts on common land; village carpenters got their wood from the commons.

[2] P. G. F. Le Play, *Les Ouvriers européens* (Paris, 1877), iv, esp. 285–8. As Le Play noted, with some inaccuracy, game rights, in aristocratic England the privilege of landowners, in Spain belonged to the municipality. His observations were based on N. Castile; cf. above, p. 7.

[3] By the 1860's the largest sales of common land as against 'reserved' commons had taken place in Estremadura and parts of Aragon; in the pastoral districts of the north and in parts of old Castile substantial areas of commons still remained. I base this on the figures, difficult to interpret, of the *Anuario estadístico* for 1860–1, 451 ff. Commons had never been greatly important in Galicia and Catalonia and thus in some of these provinces they constituted, after sales, only ½ per cent. of the land. In Santander and León they still constituted 30 per cent.

integral part of the agricultural system they tended to survive; where they seemed to benefit those outside the pueblo—owners of immigrant flocks, muleteers on their journeys—they were often distributed within the pueblo itself. In some districts there is little evidence for the existence of the speculative purchaser; in Navarre, for example, local Juntas distributed the commons among the local inhabitants. 'There is not a village in Navarre', it was claimed by a speaker in the agrarian reform debate in 1932, 'where all the *vecinos* (i.e. bona fide inhabitants) do not possess a bit of [former] communal lands.'[1] In many parts of Spain the municipalities still possess quite extensive commons.

At the time liberal economists insisted that it was the *medium* peasant proprietor, not the great landlord or the speculator, who was rendered more prosperous and more secure;[2] just as Le Play had noted earlier it was richer *peasants* who pressed for the division of the common lands.[3] Sales inevitably benefited the more prosperous proprietor who could withstand bad years and buy out his less fortunate neighbours. Isolated examples would seem to show that sales, at least in Castile, far from strengthening the large latifundia proprietors, increased, over the century the numbers of the substantial peasantry.[4] The effects of nineteenth-century land transfers near Toledo have been summarized thus: 'a diminution of latifundia, the disappearance of nearly all communal land and rough pasture, an increase in the number of tenant farmers, the creation of a relatively large and prosperous group of small proprietors, a greater area under cultivation, a greater yield and consequently a rise in production which gave a district a more substantial economy, prosperity and a higher standard of living.'[5] This is not at all the picture presented by the opponents of open-

[1] A. Mori, *Crónica de las Cortes Constituyentes* (1932), viii. 240 ff.

[2] Cf. *El Economista*, Jan. 1856, 35–36. The 'crime' of the sales of common lands has entered peasant mythology. Thus a Castilian farmer, farming about 25 acres, once complained to me that 'they' had robbed the poor man by selling the commons. I later discovered that 10 acres of his own farm were former municipal commons.

[3] See above, p. 7.

[4] Jiménez de Gregorio, 'La población en la Jara Toledano' (*E.G.* xiv (1954), 214). A similar reinforcement of medium and small property owners seems to have taken place at Ocaña. The payments demanded in the 1855 legislation were reasonable.

[5] Cf. even in a supposed semi-latifundia district like La Mancha, substantial *small* proprietors were on the increase (see above, p. 25).

market sales and by subsequent historians. The effects of these sales may have been the opposite in the west and south but it would be idle to maintain that latifundia were created by the transfers of the nineteenth century; the effect of free sale, inevitably, was to strengthen what was already the most productive, economically most powerful, type of farming.

Whatever the social merits of small peasant proprietorship as a supposed curative for rural under-employment, *outside* its traditional homes it could not raise output by technical improvement. Savings were invested in animals and the lack of cheap credit (Pi believed 14½ per cent. a usual rate in the forties) precluded improvement by the peasant himself. It was therefore a consistent complaint of those who disapproved of sales that public land ought to have been made the basis of a widespread system of rural banks. Peasant credit to proven farmers would have encouraged increased production and better techniques. In underdeveloped countries where an experienced class of small farmers *already exists* it is better to back these than to create a new race of subsistence farmers doomed to destruction. Some economists were beginning to argue that 'capitalist' farming would cure the ills of Spain; but, where labour is the cheapest factor of production, large farms will neither raise production *per acre* nor cure the evils of rural over-population.[1]

There were signs of a new capitalist agriculture in a small class of landlords, attracted by the profitable exploitation of scientific improvements. Periodicals like *La España Agricultora* publicized, on a surprising scale, machines, modern commercial methods in wine production, and artificial manure.[2] One of the Liberal Unionist grandees, the marqués de Duero, ruined himself by improvements on his estates near Malaga; indeed, in this region, the commercial and industrial fief of the Heredia and Larios families, agricultural investors were particularly active. Another periodical, *El Azucarero*, tried to

[1] Cf. Indian experience excellently described by E. J. Long, 'Economic Basis of Land Reform' in *Land Economics* (Wisconsin), xxxvii. 2.

[2] This periodical was the 'official' organ of the General Association of Farmers (*Labradores*) and ran for a few years after 1863. Its editor was an agent for English and French machinery and artificial manure.

establish a modern industry based on cane sugar.[4] It failed but it was a pointer to the way specialized crops could be industrialized.

With improved communications and perhaps as a result of the interest in scientific agriculture which was manifest in the 1850's, a more balanced agricultural economy, based on the interchange of specialized crops, became a possibility. The critical decade in the history of agriculture is the sixties, as the effects of the great sales were working themselves out, when the abolition of tithes had freed the land of a heavy burden, and when the great agricultural regions, as they exist today, were defining themselves.[1] Wheat begins its slow retreat to the granary of Castile; in León, La Mancha, and the Rioja the more profitable vine advances; new crops were diversifying the agriculture of the Levante, and in the north maize and potato were making it possible to feed an increasing population.

It was the specialized, commercialized cultures which contributed most to Spain's foreign trade: thus wine and olive-oil provided a third of the total exports. Catalan wines went to France as black strap to mix with clarets; Andalusian wine, in the form of sherry, to England and America. The Andalusian wine trade is an early example of economic specialization produced by the combination of foreign capital—mostly British—and native skill. The best sherries were the products of great care on the part of growers and blenders—the latter, usually Asturians, were alleged to make great fortunes. Worth five times as much as wine, sherry had no market in Spain; when the popularity of fine sherry in England waned, this crisis was met by the manufacture of cheap brandies.[3] Elsewhere methods

[1] Cf. *El Azucarero*, November 1846. By March 1847 a factory had been established with Belgian machinery. This group (it included Ramón de la Sagra) apparently hoped for a capital of 260 million reales.

[2] I cannot explain (otherwise than as a statistical error) the diminution of the total cultivated area in these years; statistics are in conflict with other evidence. It *may* be due to the quick exhaustion of land turned over to cereals after the sales; nor can I explain the decline in animal husbandry. The figures are most unreliable but would seem to indicate a decline in the numbers which started in 1860, and lasted till 1890. Cf. A. Cabo Alonso, 'La ganadería española' (*E.G.* lxxix (1960), 128).

[3] For figures of wine trade see tables in Figuerola. There is a description of the sherry trade in R. Ford's *Gatherings from Spain*, 166 ff., and a colourful account of a large sherry firm and the vicissitudes of the trade in the later nineteenth century in Blasco Ibañez's *La bodega* (1919), esp. 25 ff.

were careless and transport costs—always a crucial factor in Spain away from the coast—prohibitive. Thus the excellent wines of Valdepeñas scarcely got beyond Madrid. With more care, Spanish olive-oil might have captured more of the European market; but good oil could scarcely be expected from olives beaten off the tree when green, then piled up in yards to ferment so that, when pressed, they more resembled 'masses of manure than any other substance'.[1]

3. *The Affluent Society, 1856–1866*

Economic advance, even when precarious and quantitatively insignificant, meant that at least a section of society was capable of seeing politics in economic terms and was sensitive to the fluctuations of prosperity; hence the appearance, in the flood of parliamentary rhetoric, of the 'material interests' and of the conflicts between them. From the thirties this economic debate centred on the advantages or disasters of protection. Though its statistical apparatus varied, the terms of this argument remained unchanged for half a century.

To the liberals of Madrid, the benefits of free trade were axiomatic and Bastiat the prophet. In 1856 they founded the *Economist*, a doctrinaire journal of extreme *laissez-faire* views. It objected to subventions to a national theatre (art was an industry which, like other industries, must survive on legitimate profits) and to conscription (troops should be hired at market prices). Any state intervention was a 'communistic' redistribution of riches. Protection was responsible for high and fluctuating wheat prices; public purchase of corn in dear times by state or municipality a palliative that did more harm than good. Espartero's unpopular freeing of urban rents was praised as 'one of the most precious conquests of our political regeneration'.[2] The villains were the Catalan protectionists: they lied about the effects of lowered tariffs in 1849—far from ruining

[1] *P.P.* lxxxiii (1877), 1516.

[2] The 'advance' in economic thinking over the still eighteenth-century *afrancesado* tone of the *Revista Económica de Madrid* (1842) is remarkable. The *Revista* was not dogmatic and did not support the main axiom of the *Economista*—that there were universally applicable truths in political economy. The *Economista* maintained a campaign, very much *de haut en bas*, with the agrarian allies of the Catalans whose mouthpiece was *El Eco de la Ganadería*.

Catalan prosperity, raw cotton imports doubled.[1] They were prepared to sacrifice the prosperity of the nation to their own inability to lower costs. Lack of originality was concealed by violence of tone: protectionism was bastard regionalism, the industrialists 'birds of prey, hungry wolves, bedouins, oppressors of labour'. Nevertheless, by the sixties repetition and the 'absurdities' of a system which solemnly prohibited the entry of trumpets, masks, and paper lanterns, and of Navigation Acts which prevented Spanish ships from picking up profitable cargoes, had won converts for free trade.

It was in Madrid that these free traders could make themselves felt. Catalans therefore attributed the advocacy of free trade to the sensitivity of politicians, living in a community of consumers and shopkeepers, to 'anti-national' pressure groups who put profit above the development of domestic industry. Chief of these were merchants of Cadiz, the railway companies, and the southern landowners, interested in cheap rails and agricultural exports. These were politically powerful in that many liberal politicians—Sagasta and Moret are later examples—were railway directors and in that Andalusia was probably over-represented within the political system. A minor indication of the conflict between the southern export interest and the industry of Catalonia is the struggle of the Catalan cork industry against the export of raw cork. In the thirties the manufacturers' agents had bought at bargain prices from Andalusian landlords. Once the landlords—mostly aristocrats who had used their cork forests only for charcoal—recovered a sense of their own interests, they resisted the cork manufacturers' determination to restrict the export of unmanufactured cork. To the Catalan defenders of 'national industry' the landlords were parasitic profiteers.

Such arguments hid from Catalans that the products of the soil not only provided most Spaniards with a living but the state with most of its income and the economy as a whole with its purchasing power abroad. It is easy to see why most finance ministers were free traders at heart and unresponsive

[1] Mon's proposed tariff in 1849 although based on revenue considerations was modified in a protectionist sense by Catalan pressure. It maintained only fourteen import prohibitions (e.g. cereals, small boats) and the general prohibition for textiles was replaced by prohibition above certain gauges.

to the claims of industry for continued high protection at the expense of export staples. Figuerola defended his revolutionary free-trade budget in 1869 by pointing to the state of foreign trade. 'The nature of Spanish exports has not varied for fifty years. We sell what we sold, though we sell more. Minerals and agriculture earn our purchasing power abroad. The whole of the manufacturing industry does not provide 5 per cent. of our exports.'[1] Madrid was a free-trade city precisely because its 'artificiality', it could be argued, made it a clearer mirror of the Spanish economy as a whole than the factory towns of Catalonia. The free-trade ideas of most Progressive politicians made for great difficulties with the party's Catalan wing. Madoz, though in other respects an advanced liberal, was a committed protectionist. When the Cadiz Progressives announced their support of free trade he protested that he 'would rather break off all relations with his party than abandon the defence of native industry'.[2]

Catalan industrialists and intellectuals, for three generations, were to defend protection by variations on the single theme that it was a *national* necessity, not a Catalan interest. One of the most consistent propaganda points of the protectionists was the 'unselfish' refusal of Catalan industrialists to press for free trade in grain in order to bring cheap food and low wages. Thus in February 1859 the industrialists attacked a lowering of cereal protection 'in the interests of the nation'. To abolish industrial protection would condemn thousands of workers to starvation, agriculture to unsold crops, and the country as a whole to social revolution. A prosperous Catalonia was the indispensable importer of Castilian grain: free trade condemned Spain to the 'slavery' of an archaic agrarian economy. It was not merely that English manufacturers sought, in periods of depression, to murder an infant industry by dumping, smuggling, or extorting tariff concessions for loans. Protection was not a device against the teething troubles of a new departure but a permanent necessity for an industry condemned to inevitable inferiority. The debating weakness of protectionists was precisely this acceptance of their incapacity to produce at competitive costs. Much of their case was therefore dismissed as polemical

[1] For his views, *La Reforma arancelaria* (Madrid, 1879).
[2] *F.O.*, Sir A. Buchanan, 19 Dec. 1860.

exaggeration used in the defence of an interest group which was less enterprising than it claimed to be. The strength of the Catalan case was its down-to-earth refutation of the 'facile truths' of political economy. If the figures used by Catalan protectionists were often contradictory (thus they tried to prove with the same statistics that Catalan industry was making magnificent advances and the proposition that the 1849 duties had ruined Catalonia), as manufacturers they knew that the constant threats of tariff changes made long term planning and expansion hazardous.[1]

The Catalan campaign was marshalled by Juan Güell i Ferrer, a manufacturer who devoted his life to the cause of protection; his allies were Madoz, the intellectual of the Catalan Progressives, Aribau the poet, and Durán y Bas, disciple of Savigny and defender of Catalan law. Organized as a pressure group in the Fomento and its offshoots, they made every effort to establish the argument outside Catalonia, and by deputations and pressure in Madrid to rebutt the charge of 'cotton exclusiveness' and regional interest.[2]

The national campaign was a failure. The natural economic allies of Catalonia—Basque industrialists and the Castilian cerealists—were unorganized and their alliance did not save the protectionist crusade from appearing as a Catalan affair engaged in exploiting its connexions with politicians like Prim and the Conchas in order to discredit 'the triumph of an idea exempt from all egotistical calculation'. The Catalan protest delayed but could not defeat freer trade. More successful was the determination to strengthen in the Antilles the protected market threatened in Metropolitan Spain. It was not till 1864–7 that the Industrial Institute's campaign secured Spanish textiles and flour free entry into Cuba. This combined the wheat interest with the textile and shipping interests in a Cuban lobby; a powerful pressure group, devoted to the defence of imperial protection, its activities in the sixties and seventies have never been studied.[3]

[1] Thus *La España industrial* dropped its plans to set up factories outside Catalonia as a result of the 1849 tariff.

[2] The Society for the Defence of National Labour (1839) and the Industrial Institute (1840) both represent early attempts to create a national movement for protection.

[3] G. Graell, *Fomento*, 278 ff. José Concha, who had defended the tariffs of 1849

It was not the industrialists of Catalonia with their gospel of hard work and common sense who were the characteristic representatives of the society of the fifties and sixties. There was some reason for their distrust of a society where the springs of political power were manipulated by generals, lawyer-politicians, civil servants, and speculators, by the consumers and not by the producers of wealth. In so far as any region symbolized the prevalent conditions of political life it was Andalusia—contemporary commentators speak of an Andalusian invasion of salons and ministries. In so far as any economic activity commanded attention in Madrid, it was what Catalans were apt to call speculation, the attempt to revive and modernize Spain by credit. The fifties was an age of financial scandals of which the most important were those connected with the queen mother's railway speculations and the sale of stone to the Ministry of Development for the construction of a canal.[1]

It was in the full-blooded Balzacian speculative genius of Salamanca that the novelist Galdós was to find the fitting symbol of the age. Salamanca's career as a financier spans the whole period from the thirties until the Revolution of 1868 which ruined him. An Andalusian lawyer, his immense fortune was created by speculation in the borderlands of public and private finance.[2] His political connexions gave him the Salt Monopoly, a vast field of private patronage, which yielded a profit of 300 million reales within five years. By 1845, already an influential politician, he was using his inside knowledge to speculate in government securities. In the fifties he moved into railways and his last great speculations were connected with the beginnings of urban expansion—the construction of the splendid district that still bears his name in Madrid and the development of San Sebastian as a watering place. It was the lack of cheap domestic,

against free traders and whose relations with the Catalan Industrial Institute Graell describes as 'intimate', was the first minister of the newly created Colonial Ministry. For the Institute's defence of Castillian wheat, cf. ibid. 280.

[1] Galdós constantly refers to both the magic of credit and the accompanying financial corruption in his novels describing this period, e.g. in *O'Donnell* and *La familia de Léon Roch* (1878). For the stone scandal see M. Fernández Almagro, *Cánovas del Castillo* (1951), 112 ff. The minister who suffered was the dupe of a corrupt civil servant who escaped, as civil servants often do, the consequences of a 'blunder'.

[2] For Salamanca see Conde de Romanones, *Salamanca* (1940).

institutional credit which ruined Salamanca and in the end he was paralysed by those very difficulties which had enabled him to 'help' a treasury willing to pay 24 per cent. on medium term loans. All his operations were designed to cover borrowings, largely from France, at high rates of interest. Thus he could never overcome the difficulties of raising money cheaply for long term enterprises: this bankrupted him as a railway contractor and prevented him from developing his building projects.[1]

The garniture of his life represented the new age of an *haute bourgeoisie* which had abandoned all connexion with the artisan-merchant tradition.[2] The first man in Spain to have a private bathroom and a private railway coach—equipped with gold plate—a theatrical impresario with his own *corps de ballet* which became an expression of his political rivalry with Narváez, the owner of great palaces with magnificent pictures bought from the bankrupt house of Altamira, the first collector of El Grecos and Goyas, he represented single-handed that importation of the civilization of the Second Empire which characterized the taste of the Spanish new rich. In his great days he lured Napoleon III's chef to Spain by offering higher wages than the emperor could afford to pay. It was as a symbol of the financial politics of liberalism and the railway scandals of María Cristina's court that the mob sacked his house in 1854 and the Carlists burned his private railway coach. By 1867 he was ruined and auctioning his pictures in Paris.[3] His last desperate coup, a bid for the Tobacco Monopoly, was ruined by the advent of the Republic of 1873.

Beside the speculator the most magnificent figures in the society of the fifties and sixties were successful generals. The rewards of the military oligarchs were splendid and the genuine lack of class feeling in most regiments made the army an instru-

[1] There is nothing novel about Salamanca's railway finance. To build railways he had to borrow at high rates, covering his loans either by money raised for further construction or by selling out to foreign backers, as he sold the Aranjuez–Alicante line to the Rothschilds when he could not use his political influence to get the government to shoulder his losses.

[2] As a railwayman Salamanca was a free trader and had he survived as Minister of Finance in 1846 he would have lowered tariffs. His fall was greeted by public rejoicing in Catalonia.

[3] It is of interest that the value of his Goyas quintupled between 1867 and the last sale of 1875.

ment of social mobility without equal in Europe. Espartero's father was a cartwright, Oráa's a peasant. The career of Prim, son of a lawyer-officer, grandson of a chemist, affords the most astonishing example of the military career open to talents. Transferring to the regular army from the Volunteers in 1838, by 1843 he was a general and a count, and by 1847 he was Captain General of Puerto Rico. He neither looked nor behaved like an aristocrat: after marrying a fashionable Mexican heiress for her money—a great deal of which he lost in speculations characteristic of the Salamanca epoch—he enjoyed vulgar ostentation as a fashionable cosmopolitan at Vichy and Paris.[1] His political talents were of the highest order. Apart from bravery he had no great qualifications as a general. Political generals did not waste their time in the duties of a regular soldier; as Prim himself was to conclude, after a visit to the Crimea, the Spanish army was not a modern army capable of waging 'la grande guerre'.

No longer absorbed in its proper professional function as the defence of the state against external aggression, the army's secondary function (the defence of the state against internal enemies) combined with its traditional role in Spain as interpreter of the general will. Thus Serrano in his appeal to the loyal Novaliches before the battle of Acolea, which toppled the monarchy in 1868, represented in its purest form the political theory of the army: loyalty to 'opinion' came before loyalty to the legally established government and the soldier's oath to his queen. The army's rival as a vehicle of opinion, the National Militia, went into eclipse after the revolutions of 1843 when it was replaced as the force of public order by the Civil Guard, a military institution. The army was thus the strongest single organized force in the state, and a force devoted to the defence of interests other than its own professional ones.[2]

Because the generals never represented merely a separate army interest they were characteristic representatives of the

[1] For his speculations see R. Olivar Bertrand, *Prim*, Appendix II, clxx: for his love of money, xcix, ccix: for his snobbery, cxxiv.

[2] The following figures for the Civil Guard make this development clear: (in 1,000's): 1845: 5·9; 1852: 8·1; 1856: 9·4; 1858: 10·9. The militia was abolished in 1844 and after the biennium in 1856.

new society. They gambled on the stock exchange—Narváez at one stage collaborated with Salamanca; they were electoral managers, capitalist farmers, railway directors.[1] Thus, compared with the sudden glory of Riego or the power of Espartero as a popular idol, the political influence of Narváez and O'Donnell was of a different magnitude and exercised in a different fashion. It was a permanent feature of political life because the generals were a social fixture. They were absorbed into the aristocracy by a continuous process of new creation. The peak was reached in the years 1845–50 with ten grandeeships and fifty-three other new titles—a level not surpassed until the 1870's when the river of Isabelline creations became a flood.

The generals infused into the aristocracy a new strength and a new vulgarity. While, as grandees, their lack of manners shocked the court officials, their influence as senators and ministers represented that afforcement of aristocratic influence which we have already noted.[2] Nobility recovered the prestige of military origins when some of the popularity of liberal generals rubbed off on to the aristocracy as a whole. Moreover, new accretions represented superior survival values to the *rentier* habit of mind which distinguished the old families. When the new aristocrats were ruined it was not by indifference to bailiffs' accounts but by rash development schemes and stock exchange crashes.

The amalgam of speculators, industrialists, landowners, together with the prosperous lawyers and ennobled generals who were its political voice *par excellence*, constituted what democrats were beginning to call a ruling oligarchy—estimated at five hundred families. Their way of life was—in its upper reaches—'cosmopolitan' in its imitation of the culture of the French *haute bourgeoisie*. It is to these years that the novelist Valera dated the introduction of imported luxury. The literature read in the Madrid soirée had lost all touch with popular traditions; these were artificially maintained in the *costumbrista* novel describing regional life. The abundant literature of the fifties and sixties—unless we are to take Campoamor's philosophic doubts seriously—moralized in the interests of a

[1] There is a very close parallel with Marshal Saldanha in Portugal.

[2] See above, pp. 203–4.

class.[1] Only in the late sixties does the Spanish novel emerge as an independent form of art and its great flowering belongs to the seventies as a criticism of the philistine and narrow society which had grown up in the preceding two decades.[2]

The mark of this society was its quest for respectability which found expression in a revival of catholic piety. 'Persecution' of the Church was associated with the revolutionary surges of 1840 and 1854. The religious toleration granted in the *biennio* was regarded by the Church as a disaster. But from 1856 it was gaining in social influence and it was the political exploitation of this advance by the neo-catholic party of the sixties backed by the court which destroyed the monarchy.

This party represented an attempt to make the catholic unity of Spain a political and intellectual reality against the tolerant spirit of the *biennio*.[3] As such it was a breeding ground of future Carlists: Candído Nocedal, the architect of the fiercest press law of constitutional Spain, and the political leader of neo-Catholicism, was to become one. Its polemical strength lay in its criticism of the workings of liberal parliamentarianism and its warnings of the social revolution. Aparisi, the ablest of the Traditionalists, could pose as an outraged democrat with a social conscience. 'Be genuine Parliamentarians or finish the farce.' The disentailing laws plundered not only the Church but the poor in the interests of a 'caste of five hundred'. 'Remember', warned Aparisi, 'you have told the people they are sovereign yet you have forgotten the poor in a revolution to enrich a handful.' The consequence—'Proudhon, axe in hand, is waiting to fall on the social edifice'. The remedy—'Religion against the Revolution'.[4] Liberalism inspired by the 'French spirit, sceptic, materialist and revolutionary' had not merely failed to create a just society: it would be incapable of defending the unjust society it had created.[5]

[1] Cf. J. López-Morillas, *El Krausismo español* (Mexico, 1956), 124. Of course there were exceptions, e.g. Pastor Díaz and Becquer.

[2] Galdós wrote *La Fontana de Oro* in 1867.

[3] An indication of this intolerance was the increased molestation of Protestants; in the sixties several cases of imprisonment produced protests from the Protestant powers. English advocacy of Protestant claims to burial, &c., embarrassed diplomatic relations with Spain.

[4] For these views see *D.S.C.*, 1855, 21 Jan. A. Aparisi y Guijarra, *Obras* (1873), 143, and *Los presupuetos de 1859* (1859), 79 ff.

[5] The ultramontane neo-catholics were as dependent on French models as the

The re-catholicization of society, in the narrow sense of the word, was aided by the improved legal position of the Church with the concordat of 1851 and a wave of catholic evangelism.[1] This movement started in Catalonia and is associated with Father Claret, 'Apostle of Spain' and founder of the missionary order of the Sons of the Holy Sacrament. Claret's missionary tours started in the days of Espartero's persecution and were dramatically successful: his Catechism was alleged to have sold over four million copies.[2] In 1857, as confessor to the queen, he came to Madrid, where he inspired the aristocracy to undertake works of piety and charity by warnings of the social revolution—he was deeply shocked by the peasant rebellion at Loja—which must accompany the spread of atheism.[3]

Father Claret became the chosen target of radical-liberal abuse as the fountain-head of political catholicism. The queen considered him a miracle-working saint and under his influence became a *beata*—an excessively pious catholic.[4] Though Claret scrupulously and sensibly refrained from any direct interference in the minutiae of political life he considered it his duty to use his influence at Court in church matters; the queen consulted him over the appointment of bishops and he left the court when his opposition to the recognition of Italy failed to make the queen defy the liberals. As his hagiographer admits he wanted the queen to banish liberal principles from her government in so far as they were incompatible with the teachings and interests of the Church.

The revival of catholicism, however useful as a social cement,

liberals they attacked. The last truly independent mind in Spanish catholicism was Balmes and his originality lies not in the theological apparatus of his works but in the acuteness and penetration of his political and social analyses.

[1] Thus the schools of the Escolapian Order, which had been excepted from the worst persecution, began a period of expansion in 1845 that was to last to the end of the century. P. Calanza Bau, *Historia de la Escuelas Pias* (Barcelona, 1951), cf. the statistics of pupils in appendix x.

[2] The biography of Claret by Mariano Aguilar (1894) gives a most illuminating picture of mid-century piety. Claret's evangelism seems rooted in a childhood vision of hell-fire and in a miraculous escape from drowning, due to the Virgin.

[3] For his sermons, ibid. i. 121, for his aristocratic connexion, ii. 91, 179 ff.

[4] She seems to have had a vision of him surrounded by *resplandores* at Mass (ibid. ii. 223) and to have been impressed by his miracles (ii. 6). His continued influence may have been due to his success in patching up Isabella's marriage with her *dévot* husband. Claret's only criticism of Isabella was directed at her *décolleté* dresses.

embarrassed and divided the liberalism of O'Donnell's centre party. There was a limit beyond which it could not reach in concession to the Church without betraying itself. This limit of concession was twice touched by O'Donnell. Thus the conservative liberals never satisfied the clerical party: liberals were all 'more or less regalists'. When they restored the Escalopian schools it was to subject them to 'the general law of public education and the special orders of the government'. In the debates of the *bienio* the bishop of Barcelona had warned that no amount of prosperity could compensate for the loss of the priceless treasure of religious unity. To O'Donnell no amount of religious unity could compensate for the loss of prosperity.

Spanish speech distinguished between the prosperous upper middle classes and the new aristocracy (*las clases acomodadas*) and the middle class proper (*la clase media*). This middle class was neither socially nor politically coherent. A whole section was dependent on miserably paid official posts: the better salaries ran between 5,000 and 8,000 reales but a village schoolmaster or postman—characteristically listed as postal administrator—was lucky if he was paid, as opposed to promised, the wage of a day labourer. One of the characteristic features of Spain has been the instability of this class in its lower regions: its history in the nineteenth and twentieth centuries was a calvary of keeping up appearances by means of 'double employment'. Civil servants and officers worked as copyists and business agents; journalists wrote for several papers and could only support a family when given political posts by their party—a feature of double employment which prevented the emergence of an independent press.[1]

While the *haute bourgeoisie* was denying any revolutionary origin and becoming steadily conservative, politically and socially, the middle and lower middle classes in the towns, subjected to the strains of the dissolution of an old society, became more revolutionary. The great majority of radical agitators and journalists came from those reaches of society where the poorly paid professional merged with the artisan. Pérez del Álamo, the Republican agitator of Andalusia, was a municipal

[1] The exceptions were Borrego's papers and the *Diario de Barcelona* from 1847. These papers had clearly defined political leanings but were not servile representatives of party interests.

veterinary surgeon. Lerroux, the greatest mob politician of the late nineteenth century, was the son of an army veterinary surgeon. Rather than the industrial workers of Barcelona, it was this class which defeated the generals' attempts at a conservative stabilization of the Revolution of 1868 and provided the leaders of the Republic of 1873.

Catalan historians have drawn a distinction between the respectable Catalan operative and the immigrant revolutionary worker. The *miserables* from the Catalan countryside were successfully absorbed into the respectable classes only to be replaced by a flood of unassimilable 'foreign' labour from the impoverished south. Whether this distinction is significant or not in terms of revolutionary incentive, the conditions of the Catalan workers in the mid-century were those of the English cotton operatives of the 1820's: a thirteen-hour day for a subsistence wage, the threat of unemployment through the laying-off of hands in slumps or the adoption of machinery.[1] In themselves these conditions are sufficient to account for the characteristic labour troubles of Barcelona: luddism followed by the demand for the recognition of workers' associations.[2]

The struggle for the right of association accounts for the occasional political alliance of the Barcelona operatives with the Progressives, their disillusionment with this alliance and their maintenance of clandestine societies in periods of legal suppression. Whenever political conditions were favourable unions revived; until 1854 their main concern was to limit the use of machines and the width of cloths. In 1854 the struggle which started with factory burning and the destruction of self-acting spindles ended with a general strike and banners inscribed 'Association or Death: Work or Bread'.[3] The Progressives in power were generally hostile to the associations but impotent to suppress them; the counter-revolution of 1857 suppressed them completely. Dulce's tolerant rule (1864–6) in

[1] The results of Cerdá's *Monografía estadística de la clase obrera de Barcelona en 1856* are summarized in J. Vicens Vives, *Els Catalans*, 149.

[2] The longevity of the machine controversy is perhaps another indication of the primitive structure and slow development of Spanish industry. In 1877 the *Fomento de los Artes* could still publish a prize essay, prefaced by Moret, in order to convince 'the modest and intelligent worker' of the benefits of mechanization. The essay prize was won by a viscount.

[3] C. Martí, *Correspondencia oficial*, 16 ff.

Catalonia allowed them to spring into existence only to be dissolved once more. In these circumstances the Democratic sympathies of working-class leaders are understandable: even the individualist, anti-socialist Democrats stood for association. The workers' organizations which went underground in 1866 represented, not merely an organization and level of leadership which could stage a Workers' Congress (1865) and support two newspapers, but the beginnings of a distinct and separate working-class culture. Clavés' working-class choirs and the Workmen's Athenaeum, both supported by the Democrats and advanced Progressives, had 'moralized' the more intelligent working-class leaders. Yet though both Progressives and Democrats sought the working-class alliance, neither fully understood its leaders whose creed was an amalgam of the old-fashioned associationism of '48 and the apolitical syndicalism that was to be the distinctive mark of Barcelona labour.[1]

The Catalan employers reacted to this 'respectable' unionism as did their fellow employers throughout Europe. Denying liberal economics when they ran against their own interests, as in the protectionist campaign, they insisted on absolute freedom of contract in labour relations. They argued that unions coerced the employer and non-union labour alike; they blamed the high costs, which made Catalan industry weak in competition with other nations, on high wages 'extorted' by workers' associations. What made the Spanish situation unique was the state's occasional interventions in labour disputes. In 1840–3 and 1854–6 it attempted to negotiate settlements by juries composed of workers and employers under the chairmanship of the local authorities. The employers rejected such settlements whenever they were powerful enough to do so. Patriarchal in their way of life, the Catalan employers opposed the most stubborn resistance to any interference with their business concerns.[2] Denial of legal outlets in association and negotiation

[1] C. Martí, *Orígines del Anarquismo en Barcelona* (Barcelona, 1959), 34 ff. The Progressives used the Athenaeum in order to wean 'socialists' into individualist paths, though it is clear from Madoz's correspondence that they realized its utility only *after* its foundation.

[2] Cf. Figuerola's resistance to the governor's replacement of self-acting by mule jennies at the demand of the workers (1854). 'Interference by the authorities to regulate the conditions of production, the oppression or threatening of one or other of the contracting parties is to alter prices arbitrarily or constitute a communist

produced the beginnings of terrorism: when General Zapatero determined 'to end the social question' by the suppression of workers' associations, the President of the Industrial Institute was assassinated in the street.

In the latter years of the century, migration and the anarchist movement were to connect, in a loose fashion it is true, the discontents of the revolutionary worker of Catalonia with those of the day labourer of the south. In 1868 these regions were distinct and unconnected. Andalusian peasant revolt began to trouble politics in the sixties and is reflected in police precautions: a proposed increase in the Civil Guard to 15,000 and the formation of Rural Guards to protect crops from burning and cattle from maiming.[1] The relationship between the endemic slave rebellion of the latifundia and the professional revolutionaries of the small towns is obscure. If the career of Pérez del Álamo is typical, at least some revolutionaries were seeking to broaden political agitation by an appeal to agrarian discontent; but it would appear that most concentrated on the creation of cells in towns with a long tradition of political revolution.[2] The Spanish Peasants' Revolt never materialized because no one, with the exception of the anarchists, was willing to appeal to the *jacquerie* of Andalusia as an instrument of revolution.

4. *The Coming of the Revolution, 1863–1868*

From the fall of O'Donnell in 1863 until the Revolution of 1868 the revolutionary factor was the Progressives' boycott of political life, the *retraimiento*. The *retraimiento*, in theory a protest against electoral corruption and 'falsifications', was in reality a retort to Isabella's refusals to form a Progressive ministry. Thus the primal political sin of Isabella was that by her refusal to admit the Progressives to power she tested their dynastic loyalty too hard and drove them to revolution. In 1863 and 1864 she dangled office before them and at any time a call from the palace would have turned men like Madoz or Prim into

society.' Propagandists used the word 'communism' as a synonym for state intervention (G. Graell, *Fomento*, 243).

[1] Iglesia, the historian of the Civil Guard, regards these increases as 'a political measure against the coming revolution' but they also reflect the fears of southern landlords.

[2] But cf. p. 294 below.

loyal servants, willing to run considerable risks with their own followers in order to avoid an irretrievable breach with the throne. In 1864 Prim and Madoz resisted Catalan extremists' demands for a *retraimiento*, arguing that if the Progressives won enough seats they could impose themselves on the queen. When the queen refused to modify the electoral law—the technical cause of the *retraimiento*—Prim had no alternative but to give in to the party masses.[1] The Progressive leaders were haunted by the dangers of extremist courses diminishing their chances of 'a jump to the Capitol' rather than by dreams of dethroning the dynasty. They constantly argued the call from the palace must come, restraining impatient followers from outbursts against the 'traditional obstacles'. When the call was denied it was proof that the obstacles existed. Prim was anything but a revolutionary leader and would have formed a very moderate Progressive government; Narváez believed he would do anything for a job. When no jobs came he started the *trabajos* that would lead to rebellion.[2]

Inadvisable and irresponsible though her exclusion of the Progressives was, Isabella's determination to commit political suicide could nevertheless be reconciled with a narrow interpretation of her role as moderating power.[3] She was not confronted with a two-party system and a Progressive majority; she was called on to fabricate both by the exercise of her personal prerogative—that is by calling on Progressive ministers and granting them a decree of dissolution in order to allow them to 'make' their majority. It was her error that she refused to convert bastard parliamentarianism into a politically stable régime, responsive to pressures it could not register by the existing machinery of parliamentary election. To Isabella, the threat of the Progressive leaders that 'revolution' could only be staved off by a truly liberal ministry appeared as an attempt to put the crown in chains. Moreover, once the Progressive leaders had assumed revolutionary attitudes to coerce the crown, the party would not let them lay the pose aside. Thus their refusal to co-operate with O'Donnell in his last-

[1] See *Cartas de conspiradores*, edited R. Llopis (1929), 106–10.

[2] For Narváez's attack, cf. *D.S.C.* 4, v. (1863). Narváez believed Prim would have become a respectable politician had he been made Captain General of Puerto Rico again.

[3] For Isabella's constitutionalism, see Chapter VI, section (1).

minute attempts to liberalize the régime was dictated by the feelings of the mass of the party to whom any compromise with a court was a moral impossibility. It was the tail of the party which forced the *retraimiento* on a hesitant leadership. Moreover, with all their hesitations, these leaders represented something more than a thirst for office on any terms. They wanted a liberal, tolerant, lay state with limited concession to the democratic demands embodied in the constitution of 1837. Isabella sensed this and resisted them. She did not sense what, according to the British minister, was apparent 'even to the most superficial observer': that the excluded Progressives were increasingly coming to represent 'the prevalent opinion in the country'.[1]

Logically, the failure of the *retraimiento* to coerce the crown implied revolution against the crown, just as the failure of the Anarchist 'Don't Vote' campaign implied revolution after the disastrous election of 1933. Once more the mere prospect of revolutionary action split the Progressives. Madoz, Figuerola, and others feared that the systematic use of the *retraimiento* would lead to a revolutionary coalition with the Democrats and through the Democrats with working-class radicalism. Madoz (strengthened in his attitude by the counsel of French radicals) called total abstention 'suicide' since it would swallow up the party's positive programme and would lead to 'the other thing' —revolution.[2] Moreover, the Progressives were divided over the leadership itself. Espartero, its titular head and now in his political dotage, would not move out of the realms of platitude while Olózaga, who had re-created the party after 1846, was determined to push him aside—even if this meant cutting the Progressives off from a fund of ready-made military loyalty. In October 1864 the party patched up its differences only to run into the same difficulties once more over the *retraimiento* against O'Donnell's last attempt to woo the Progressives in 1865. Only the utter refusal of Isabella to consider the Progressives as other than a crypto-revolutionary party drove its divided leadership to 'the other thing', the dangers of which were only too well known.

[1] Cf. *F.O.*, Sir J. Crampton, 27 July 1865.

[2] For the hesitations of Madoz, see Olivar Bertrand, *Prim*, 130, appendixes 62, 74, 76, 77.

These dissensions in the Progressives were fomented by the existence of the Democrat party, which was itself divided. Drawing the Progressives towards anti-dynastic revolution, the Democrats were themselves drawn towards republicanism and away from the Progressive alliance by a new generation of intellectuals who, in the sixties, challenged the old leadership. Orense and Rivero, a marquis and a wealthy man respectively, were disillusioned Progressives, democratic monarchists who saw the future of their movement in a party that would attract other disillusioned Progressives. Any talk of a republic or socialism would not only bring the press and police persecution. It would scare off desirable recruits.

The 'socialism' of Pi y Margall was therefore a sign of his rejection, at the same time, of the Progressive womb and of the tactics of the leadership; the failures in 1854 had exposed the futility of alliance with pseudo-revolutionary Progressives.[1] Pi's 'socialism' did not get beyond wage arbitration, a minimum of state action to improve working conditions, agricultural credit, and 'a generalization of property' which would extend the liberal land revolution beyond the 'new feudalism' to the agrarian poor. Castelar denounced these doctrines as heretical deviations from individualism: liberty of association was a sufficient instrument for the amelioration of social conditions. A professor of history and the mildest of the new generation, yet a power through the humourless vanity which made him the greatest orator of his day, Castelar was an 'attractionist' and a historicist: the Republic was an ineluctable necessity, but it would be best brought forth from history by converted Progressives. He therefore supported Rivero's view that democracy was a political creed without social implications. Beyond Pi lay the carbonari activists of Andalusia to whom revolution was an end in itself, a view never shared by sober and austere Democratic purists of Pi's stamp. All these groups were jockeying for position on committees and editorial boards: when Rivero resigned the leadership of *La Discusión* in which the polemics between individualists and socialists had been conducted, he took the office furniture with him in order to 'ruin' his opponents.

At the last moment the Democrats were to be pushed out of

[1] This was the theme of Pi's *Reacción y revolución* (1854).

the revolutionary conspiracy which overthrew the monarchy by the generals and their most important contribution to its success was passive—the moral isolation of the monarchy by their clandestine press. Yet it was the Democrats who made the Revolution of 1868 more than a pronunciamiento of outraged generals: they gave it its democratic tinge and its cadre of lower middle-class and working-class enthusiasts. Thus the debate between Castelar and Pi was followed by the Barcelona working-class associations, and it is significant that they sided with Castelar and self-improvement by association. In both Madrid and Barcelona there were lecture societies where Democrats could debate 'socialism'. Especially in Catalonia a nucleus of republicans, mostly connected with the nascent popular Catalan theatre, maintained and strengthened the traditions of the revolution.[1]

The most striking conquests were made in the towns of the rural south where the *exaltado* tradition of secret societies had never died out. A society, organized on carbonari lines, successfully fought Narváez's electoral tyranny centred on his home town, Loja, and in 1861 Pérez del Álamo escaped from prison and took the town with a peasant levy.[2] If, for most of the followers, it represented a resurgence of the millennial demands of the poor tenants and labourers for the *reparto*, the leaders were inspired by Democrat newspapers. 'What was my banner? Democracy. What were my aspirations? Of a Republican character. What was my aim? From a hypostatical [*sic*] monarchy to a human republic.' Rightly the Loja revolt has attracted the attention of sociologists searching for the origins of rural anarchism and peasant spartacism; together with its heady enthusiasm (the Loja peasants were led by a brass band), its asceticism (the movement was teetotal), its leaders display the characteristics of the *obrero conciente* of later anarchism.[3]

[1] See above, p. 229. There were other centres at Béjar (a wool town caught in depression), Castellón de la Plana, and Teruel. There is a lively account of the Republicans among the Catalan dramatists who gathered in a *tertulia* in Soler the leading Catalan playwright, in C. Roure, *Memorias de una vida larga*, ii, *passim*.

[2] The Revolution is described by Pérez de Álamo in *Apuntes históricos sobre dos revoluciones* (Seville, 1872), 18–59. The ringleaders, Calvo and Pérez, escaped and were later pardoned. Calvo became a police commissioner for Madrid, through the influence of Marfori, Narváez's member for Loja.

[3] Cf. C. Bernaldo de Quirós, 'El espartaquismo' (*Revista general de jurisprudencia y legislación*, 1919).

By 1868, therefore, there was a nucleus of enthusiasts ready to make a revolution far more radical than the mere substitution of a new dynasty. Where they could, they forced on the Juntas, which sprang up with revolution in 1868, the full Democratic programme. When the generals refused to accept this programme the enthusiasts believed the revolution had been betrayed; they therefore attempted revolution once more in the summer of 1869.

We must now trace the development of the conspiracy which was to engineer the Glorious Revolution of September 1868.

Active leadership of the revolutionary conspiracy of the Progressive party was in the hands of Juan Prim; the Progressives could not afford the civilian leadership of Olózaga in a revolution that could only succeed with army support. Prim himself would have preferred an old-fashioned pronunciamiento, a provincial military rebellion which would force a change of policy on Madrid. 'I am afraid that mixing soldiers and civilians will destroy discipline and fling the throne out of the window. With my method I arrive in the capital, in a state of *moral* insurrection, with forces superior to the garrison. The court surrenders and when the country learns of the rebellion I already have a government which, without bloodshed or troubles, has changed the political course.'[1] Such a revolution, the ideal revolution of all generals, would have left him master of Spain.

Prim's repeated attempts at military rebellion in the sixties failed; divided conspirators lost their nerve setting off premature revolts. In face of these defeats Prim's true greatness as a revolutionary leader appears. He was undaunted by failure and above the bitter recrimination of *émigré* circles; active in building up funds, discovering spies, he carried all the chores of conspiracy. He was a revolutionary realist, not a romantic conspirator; thus when his plans for military sedition failed, he was ready for the only revolutionary alliance open to him—that of the left-wing Progressives and their Democrat allies. Differences were hidden behind the formula of the destruction of the existing régime and the submission of the question of the future form of government to a Constituent Cortes. The Progressives and all except the intransigent Democrats accepted

[1] Quoted, A. Pirala, *Historia contemporánea*, iii. 94.

Prim's leadership of the Revolutionary Committee set up at Ostend (August 1866). Nevertheless, the revolutionary alliance was precarious. Olózaga was intensely jealous of Prim and his 'militarism', while Prim disliked Olózaga's ideas of Iberian Union under a Portuguese king and his insistence on a declaration against the dynasty which might make rebellion difficult for officers. In June 1866 the Democrats had bungled a sergeants' rising in Madrid.[1] Another abortive rising (August 1867) brought recriminations. Prim had been driven to premature revolutions in order to settle the doubts of his allies and to prove his revolutionary bona fides to civilians who risked little. Once the Liberal Unionist generals were willing to conspire, Prim saw that he must cold-shoulder the ineffective conspirators of the left, and work for a traditional pronunciamiento in alliance with officers who would have no time for the Democrat alliance.

Against this mounting revolutionary ferment ministries, after the fall of the Liberal Union, lurched between liberal conciliation to woo the Progressives from the *retraimiento* and relapses into military rule and civilian authoritarianism. Miraflores's attempt to reconstruct artificially a two-party system was defeated when the Progressives refused his offer of a 'sincere' election. With his resignation (15 January 1864) ended the first attempt at conciliation by minor constitutional reform. His successors continued his avoidance of provocation. Even Narváez, who returned again in September 1864, threatened to be 'more liberal than Riego', but, without O'Donnell's support for a policy of liberal reunion, he was forced to rely on the extreme conservatism of men like Cándido Nocedal, a fierce but intelligent reactionary. Narváez fell, in part as a consequence of the first effective student agitation in Spain. When the students demonstrated at the removal of Castelar, who had published a famous article against Isabella, the army was let loose in the

[1] Prim's agent Moriones lost control of the sergeants' conspiracy with the result that the civilians set off revolution before Prim's military plans were complete (cf. E. M. Villarasa and J. I. Gatell, *Historia de la revolución de setiembre* (Barcelona, 1875), i. 21–31). General Pavía, who was Prim's A.D.C., never forgave the civilians and their officer advisers, Hidalgo and Pierrad. In Pavía there was a characteristic conflict between his feelings as a proud artillery officer and as a revolutionary (cf. his conversations with A. Houghton in *Les Origines de la restauration des Bourbons* (Paris, 1890), 11–14.)

streets.[1] When the first of Prim's pronunciamientos proved that Narváez could no longer hold the army and his government was attacked in the Cortes, the queen sacked him and returned to O'Donnell (June 1865).

O'Donnell hoped to reconstruct the bridge to the Progressive *resellados*. His remedy for stability was still the destruction of Progressive discipline by holding out office to its leaders; provided he 'sang the hymn of Riego' and allowed free elections they might once more hope to reach the Capitol. He proved his liberalism by proposing the restoration of the dismissed professors, a liberal press law, an electoral law which halved the property qualification, and the recognition of Italy. Thus O'Donnell offered the Progressives effective constitutional government in return for their re-entry into politics; the resolute militant temper of the Progressive masses made it impossible for the leaders to accept the deal and abandon the *retraimiento* (October 1865). When in January 1866 Prim tried military rebellion once more O'Donnell became a counter-revolutionary with the slogan 'either revolution or dictatorship'. On 22 June the artillery sergeants of San Gil mutinied and shot their officers. The rising was partly caused by the resentment of the artillery sergeants against the aristocratic exclusivism of their officer corps which refused to allow promotion from the ranks, common in the infantry, partly it was the result of Democratic propaganda.[2] For the first time since 1836 the officers had lost control of their men. The generals were shocked and O'Donnell shot sixty sergeants. To avoid unpopularity the queen dismissed him; 'they sacked us like lackeys'. This sheer ingratitude O'Donnell never forgave. The only political force which could have saved the throne was O'Donnell's conservative Liberal Union but 'certain people at court' could never tolerate or understand his concern with converting Progressive quasi-revolutionaries into ministerial liberals.[3]

[1] The student riots exhibited a feature that became a fixed factor in revolutionary dynamics; understandably enough, soldiers posted in the streets lost their tempers, under continuous insults, stone-throwing, &c. This resulted in rough handling of student rioters.

[2] See below, p. 560. Cf. C. Navarro y Rodrigo, *O'Donnell*, 265, note 1. It is curious how O'Donnell's partisans describe the defeat of the rebellion (O'Donnell repeated his tactics of 1856 and cut Madrid in two, separating the rebels) as if it were a national victory over a foreign enemy.

[3] Cf. L. West to Lord Russell, *F.O.*, 27 July and 26 Aug. 1865.

With the collapse of O'Donnell's attempt to contain the left, subsequent governments considered revolution inevitable with the Progressives as the revolutionary force. In these circumstances 'resistance' appeared the sole remedy. Yet resistance, as the Carlist Aparisi pointed out, was impossible once one wing of the conservative oligarchy, the Liberal Unionists, refused to fight.[1] Narváez returned to rule as a military despot with González Brabo as his strong man. From July 1866 until March 1867 he ruled without parliament and after that date with a Cortes of 'third-class passengers' and an opposition of four. He looked more and more like a Spanish foretaste of Porfirio Díaz with his 'herd of tame horses' in the chamber ready to cover the denial of parliamentary government with decent constitutional clothes. On Narváez's death González Brabo, to whom the revolution was a 'raging flood', determined to 'show Spain that a civilian can be a dictator'. In July 1868 he exiled all the military notables of the Liberal Union, Serrano, Dulce, Zabala, Córdoba, and Echagüe, because he was convinced they were plotting with the queen's brother-in-law, the duke of Montpensier. Thus by 1868 the government rested on the slender base of pure Moderates. The Liberal Unionist generals had been treated as if they were vulgar conspirators; González Brabo finally added an element which had never appeared in the revolutionary sodality—the admirals irritated by the reduction of the naval budget by a civilian.[2]

With the death of O'Donnell (November 1867), whose bitterness would not mutate into sedition, and the exile of the generals, the conspiracy entered a new stage. The army was not attached to González Brabo and the Liberal Unionist generals were now willing to pronounce. Relieved of the necessity of Progressive and Democrat civilian support which had produced three crushing defeats in three months and driven him further to the left than he found comfortable, Prim could now revert to his original notion of a military revolt, turning the revolution back into familiar channels. All that divided the Unionist generals and Prim was the Unionists' candidate for the throne—the duke of Montpensier, whom Prim refused to support or be supported by on the grounds that, as a son of Louis Philippe,

[1] Quoted, E. M. Villarasa and J. I. Gatell, *Revolución*, 101.

[2] See below, p. 300.

his candidature would alienate Napoleon III. As with the Democrats in 1866, differences were hidden by the blanket formula of a national decision in a constituent assembly. The Progressive leaders disliked the new course: Olózaga saw the Unionists were necessary but wanted a 'popular rising strong enough to give law to the generals'. A secret committee of Progressives and Unionists was set up in Madrid to act as a liaison body between Prim in London and the Unionist generals now in exile in the Canaries. Democrats were excluded because they were no longer needed: they were to be sleeping partners in a generals' revolution.

This revolution was to start with a naval pronunciamiento in Cadiz to be followed by the traditional declaration of the generals. Prim, warned by his agents that the Unionists would steal a march, arrived from Gibraltar on a boat provided by Mr. Bland the English shipping agent, and succeeded in getting Admiral Topete to declare (18 September 1868). Topete was a committed *Montpensierista* but he accepted Prim's favourite healing formula of a Constituent Cortes 'for the re-establishment of the constitutional monarchy'. Two days later the Unionist generals arrived, got together an army, and marched on Cordoba. The revolution caught the court on holiday at San Sebastian; once the rebels had defeated the loyal army at Alcolea (28 September) neither compromise with nor resistance to the revolution was seriously attempted. Even Cheste, loyalist Captain General of Catalonia, decided it was more vital to preserve order and keep the army intact than to save the dynasty—the standard argument for refusing to fight a revolution.[1] All over southern and eastern Spain the constituted authorities gave way before juntas of the revolutionary coalition. With peculiar delicacy San Sebastian waited till the queen was in the train for exile and France before it pronounced against her.

5. *The Crisis of the Monarchy, 1867–1868*

The Revolution of 1868 was not solely the crisis of a political system which lacked the confidence to suppress or the flexibility to absorb the revolutionary threat. The struggles of 1864–8

[1] Marqués de Rozalejo, *Cheste* (1939), 222: 'the situation in Madrid cannot be maintained and they [the generals] only seek to maintain order in this capital'.

were accompanied by a loss of commercial confidence and a budgetary crisis (which had as its background a European recession and a crack in the railway boom which had supported O'Donnell) and by a cotton crisis, the result of the American Civil War.[1] Exports fell, railway construction dropped dramatically, cotton firms in Catalonia cancelled orders for new looms as trade declined, a decline which industrialists attributed to the government's tariff policy rather than to the European slump. The government of Gónzalez Brabo, at its wits' end when it could raise no loans, attempted to meet the deficit produced by falling tax income, by increasing the land tax by 10 per cent. and cancelling the order for a new fleet.[2] This retrenchment, apart from its consequences for the dynastic loyalty of naval officers, directly threatened the nascent Catalan heavy industry; with blank order-books even the powerful *Maquinista* only saved itself from bankruptcy by selling its urban land and reducing wages.[3] The crash of the *Crédit mobilier* brought a financial crisis to an economy still largely dependent on the French capital market. Finally, in 1867 a contracting economy with much unemployment was confronted with the highest wheat prices of the century.[4]

The boom broke at the moment when the court was attempting to defeat constitutional government as the oligarchy had understood it. Absolutism was, therefore, connected with economic recession. As an Englishman remarked, it was the railways which caused the Revolution of 1868: a railway civilization could not tolerate shrinking profits. Thus the crisis of 1867, when high corn prices added the sufferings of the poor to the discontents of the rich, provides a transition from old to new economic determinants of revolution: a cyclical depression,

[1] Trade statistics in L. Figuerola, *Reforma arancelaria*. Cuban trade, for instance, fell by one-third in 1867. Railway construction eased off after 1864: by 1867 the import of rails, &c., had dropped by five-sixths. Spain's export trade suffered from a catastrophic drop in metal prices and her imports from Europe fell very heavily as a consequence.

[2] The Paris money market had been closed to the Spanish government since 1861 and the financial difficulties of the government were increased by O'Donnell's wars. The war with Chile and Peru, which culminated in the bombardment of Callao (May 1866), was stupid in itself and particularly alienated creditors in London and Paris with interests in the Pacific republics.

[3] A. Castillo, *La Maquinista*, contains an excellent description of the crisis as it affected the metallurgical industry, 126–50.

[4] In Seville wheat was selling at 275 reales a fanega, six times the average price.

European in origins and reflected in a catastrophic drop in export prices, combined with the traditional 'dear times' to produce an explosive situation.

It would be an exaggeration to talk of a spiritual crisis accompanying this loss of economic confidence. Nevertheless, it is to these years that we must date a radical challenge to those accepted values in the realm of thought which the monarchy seemed to symbolize. It was to the fifties that Giner traced the intellectual and moral origins of modern Spain and it is against the members of the 'generation of '68' rather than against the regenerationists of 1898 that the strictures of catholic conservatives are most correctly directed. To arch-conservatives, experts in the paranoid style, it was these intellectual allies of Democrats and Progressive Freemasons who injected into the body of Spain those poisons which were only to be driven out in 1939.[1]

Why did this intellectual movement take the form of the propagation in university circles of the ideas of a minor German philosopher, Krause, whose main work had been written in 1811? This bizarre phenomenon is explicable only in terms of the conditions of the inherited culture. This was either a barren form of catholic traditionalism, of little use to men who wished to find a philosophic basis for a radical reconstruction of Spain, or it was an imitation of French civilization dismissed by moral regenerationists as materialist and facile.[2] The 'superiority' of the French, an assumption of Moderates and Progressives for whom it had provided intellectual capital for a generation, was resented by men who, in their fashion, were cultural chauvinists yet who wanted to 'open' Spain to 'modern' ideas. Thus there was a vacuum which could be filled by nonsense provided it was not French in origin. German Krausism, by what must be considered an intellectual accident, became for an isolated intellectual world a means of reunion with the stream of European thought. Sanz del Río, to become the most important

[1] For an extreme statement of this view, see E. Suñer, *Los intellectuales y la tragedia española* (San Sebastian, 1938). By the paranoid style is meant that type of political thinking which sees the whole existence of a society threatened by an all-powerful and subtle 'foreign' conspiracy. Until Marxists and Jews appear, the conspiracy was always that of Protestant–atheist–Freemasons.

[2] The best treatments of Krausism are contained in J. López-Morillas, *El krausismo español*, and V. Cacho Viu, *La Institución Libre de Enseñanza* (1962).

and influential professor of the sixties, was a disciple of Krause whose doctrines he had absorbed on a visit to Europe in 1843.

This eccentric choice reflected Sanz del Río's concern for the moral regeneration of his country as well as his intellectual limitations. He found in Krausism an intellectualized version of the Protestant ethic of self-improvement; a mystical belief in a God-given natural harmony, connecting right thinking with good living. It was this strenuous tone which gave Krausism its force and allowed an outdated and, in many ways, preposterous system of thought to exercise great influence on a whole generation of Spanish intellectuals. It converted them into philosophic radicals, with Moral Purpose rather than Utility as the standard by which existing institutions should be judged. It was lack of moral purpose—supposedly characteristic of French thought—which led Sanz del Río and many of his disciples into the Gallophobia which sometimes characterizes Spanish intellectuals.[1]

Krausism left its profoundest mark on these men as educators. Sanz del Río, utterly devoid of intellectual originality but a teacher of genius, was the first professor to take his students seriously as individuals and to regard the university, not as a state-controlled purveyor of entrance certificates for the professions and the government service, but as the centre of the moral regeneration of the nation. Deeply influenced by his stay in Germany, he regarded the autonomous university as the central institution of German culture; it was his insistence on the 'freedom of the chair' which brought the quarrel between the Krausists and state catholicism to its crisis. One of the incidental achievements of conservative liberalism had been the rigid centralization of the university system; thus, as professors of the Central University at Madrid, the Krausists could become a powerful influence, flinging conservatives into a state of alarm. In 1867 the Krausists were deprived of their chairs in the Central University by a government under neo-catholic influence. Besides producing the first protest of European intel-

[1] 'Every day I regret more and more the influence which French philosophy and French learning have exercised amongst us, for more than half a century. What has it brought us except *laziness in working for ourselves*, false knowledge, and above all intellectual dishonesty and petulant egoism.' Sanz del Río, quoted Trend, op. cit. 33. The over-valuation of German thought, which is evident in later writers like Ortega y Gasset, was the positive side of this reaction.

lectuals against the intolerance of a reactionary Spanish catholic state, this action made the cause of intellectual freedom become part of the revolutionary movement.[1] The Krausist intellectuals moved towards Democrat politicians, since the professors had been dismissed for a political act—their refusal to sign a declaration of loyalty to Isabella II.[2] It was their philosophic radicalism which gave 1868 its transcendent significance by turning the well-tried procedures of discontented generals and politicians into what appeared to be a revolution of intellectuals.

The Krausists had no wish to offend the Church; indeed, many of them started from an attempt to revitalize and liberalize catholicism. The danger of Krausism lay precisely in that it was a quasi-religious movement with professors as its priests.[3] Whereas positivist materialism was an open foe, Krausism appeared as a modern version of older and more insidious heresies. Its curious blend of subjective mysticism and vague modernism was attacked by neo-catholics in the sixties as pantheism. Many of the Krausists would have been comfortable as liberal catholics. After the syllabus of 1864 and the attacks of the neo-catholics the movement was forced to defend itself, becoming in the process a synthetic or natural religion with a preference for the ethics of christianity but which could not remain catholic. It was this creed which was professed by many of the Republican intellectuals of 1868–73 and it was in its name that they fought the claims of the Church to impose religious unity by the sanctions of the state.

The neo-catholic attack on intellectual freedom had an unfortunate effect on Spanish intellectual life in that it forced intellectuals to defend a second-rate creed, to become a 'sect'. Exaggerations allowed the abler defenders of the Church some palpable hits while the lesser protagonists discredited freedom of inquiry as such. Menédez y Pelayo, the polymath who

[1] The protesters were German professors—including Bunsen and Helmholtz. J. B. Trend, *Origins of Modern Spain* (Cambridge, 1934), 46.

[2] The university question is discussed in V. Cacho Viu, *Institucion Libre*, 134–81. It is clear that the government would have avoided the issue by compromise, if compromise had been possible. Both the radical Krausists and the neo-catholics wished to fight the issue to victory.

[3] The religious side of Krausism is most sympathetically treated in P. Jobit, *Les Éducateurs de l'Espagne contemporaine* (Paris, 1936).

defended traditional Spain, recognized the Krausists' moral excellence as men and their function in getting philosophic discussion on its feet again; but he castigated them as insufferable pedagogues born to be disciples of one man and one book, as sectarian, dogmatic systematizers who retarded the intellectual progress of Spain by their rejection of all other modes of thought.[1] In fact their legacy was to be an open intellectual world: the Germanic exclusiveness and anti-scientific aspects of Krausism were sloughed off under attack. What was left was intellectual tolerance, a high moral concern for the cultural and educational regeneration of Spain as a premiss for her political and economic regeneration, and a permanent protest against the vulgarity and shallowness of the official culture of Spain.

[1] This most startling outburst is contained in his correspondence with Valera (letter of 2 Sept. 1886.)

VIII

THE REVOLUTION 1868–1874

FOR five years the statesmen of the September Revolution fought to stave off a relapse into anarchy which would turn men's loyalties back to the Bourbon monarchy as the only guarantee of political stability and social peace. Each government in turn sought to stabilize the revolution at a point which suited its own interests—a process Admiral Topete described, in naval metaphor, as keeping the revolution on course. The key to the failure of these repeated attempts must be sought in the composition of the revolutionary conspiracy and the rival claims of its constituent elements to power and patronage. Who had 'made' the revolution? Who deserved the rewards?

The Provisional Government of the Revolution, first under Serrano as regent and then with Prim as prime minister, struggled to create a constitutional monarchy which would command the loyalty of the September coalition of Unionists, Progressives, and Democrats. Almost immediately a monarchical settlement of any sort was rejected by those extreme Democrats who became Republicans. To them the generals and respectable politicians of the Provisional Government were revolutionaries after the fact: 'a few gentlemen' who demanded a fruit that others had shaken from the tree.[1] Provincial Republicans sought to bring the revolution back on course by rebellion in the summer of 1868. The Unionists and Progressives, who held together to defend the monarchical constitution of 1869 against those 'who when the fight was over toured towns and villages shouting *Viva la República*', then divided over the question of the person of the monarch.

By the time a king had been found to grace the monarchical constitution of 1869—Amadeo of Savoy telegraphed his acceptance of the throne on 30 October 1870—the September coalition

[1] J. Paul y Angulo, *Memorias íntimas de un pronunciamiento* (n.d.), 9–10.

was in ruins and the quarrels of its constituent elements for exclusive control of the monarchy drove Amadeo to abdication (11 February 1873). The Republican leaders of 1873 failed to establish the Federal Republic; their claims to embody the Revolution were contested by the revolt of the Cantonalist extremists. It was therefore destroyed by a general in the name of order (2 January 1874). Finally, General Serrano and his ministers succumbed in the task of creating a conservative republic and what the monarchists contemptuously called 'Spanish Macmahonism' was ended by the old-style pronunciamiento of an infantry brigade (29 December 1874). Alfonso XII, son of the queen dethroned by the Revolution of September, was accepted with relief.

1. *The Revolution and Cuba*

It was not merely party rivalry in Spain itself which destroyed the optimism of September. The cancer of the September Revolution, sapping its vitality, was the Cuban war, legacy of twenty years of liberal neglect. In 1868 the richest remnant of the colonial empire was still subject to the absolute power of the Captain General and his allies amongst the Spanish community on the island.

The creoles resented the presence of an administration staffed by *peninsulares* and their Cuban allies, while economically the Spanish connexion was an anachronism. The boom prosperity of mid-century Cuba depended on the North American market; hence it got its capital, thence it exported its sugar. It was to Saratoga Springs that the rich planters went for the 'dead season'; it was American merchants who supplied steam engines for the industrialization of plantations and cider for the Asturian immigrants.[1]

Why, apart from isolated conspiracies, was the independence movement delayed until the sixties? The answer lies partly in the political inertia engendered by prosperity. Only the creole *élite* could lead a successful movement against Spain in the mid-century. Why should a lazy society of absentee landlords risk imprisonment by challenging Spanish power? Moreover

[1] For a mass of detailed information on the Cuban sugar industry see Roland T. Ely, *Cuando reinaba su majestad el azúcar* (Buenos Aires, 1963), 87–105, 299–492.

such a challenge might upset the whole basis of their wealth; a war of independence might be the prelude to a slave rising such as had destroyed the French planters of Santo Domingo. Thus those creoles who hoped for greater control of their own affairs sought relief, not in independence, but in the prospect of annexation by the United States;[1] this combined a desire for greater political freedom under a democratic constitution with the dream of a great slave empire of the southern states, Cuba, and Puerto Rico—a strange aberration which collapsed finally with the defeat of the South in the American Civil War.[2]

In calculating the prospects of independence no one, at the time, could deny the power of the *peninsulares* in the complex society of the island. These immigrants were the middle class of urban Cuba, ranging from minor civil servants and sergeants through shopkeepers to the great merchant houses like the Pastors and the Zuluetas. All alike sought profit in exploiting the Spanish connexion. 'Complete Jews' who made a fortune in one generation, Spanish immigrants were prepared to work hard and consequently earned the dislike which a lazy establishment visits upon the industrious new-comer. Since they staffed the administration and since their loyalty to the Spanish connexion was undoubted, the *peninsulares* usually carried more weight with the Captains General than the creole landlords.

In the sixties the basic conditions of the struggle for reform in Cuba shifted in such a way that a significant section of the creole landowners backed the Reformist movement and, when this was defeated, the War of Independence which lasted for ten years (1868–78). Less certain of the prospects of a slave economy, the creole planters were willing to support the Reformist party in its demand that the Spanish government should live up to the 1837 promises of 'special laws' for Cuba, by granting local autonomy and a reduction of tariff barriers that impeded Cuban producers. In April 1867, Isabella's government ended negotia-

[1] It must be noted that parallel with a determination to retain the island at all costs there were elements in Spain ready to get rid of Cuba and its problems by sale to the United States. In general Spanish opinion, bitterly aroused by the filibustering expeditions of the fifties, was strongly opposed to any idea of purchase by the United States. Cf. A. A. Ettinger, *The Mission to Spain of Pierre Soulé 1853–55* (New Haven, 1932).

[2] For a Marxist outline of the social struggles of Cuba and their relation to independence see S. Aguirre, *Seis actitudes de la burguesia cubana en el siglo XIX* (Havana, 1961).

tions with the Reformists' committee: the sole result of its efforts in Madrid was even heavier taxation. Nothing, it appeared, could be expected from the monarchy and on the eve of the 1868 Revolution, the Reformists were in touch with the Septembrist conspirators in common alliance against 'what exists'. Serrano and Dulce, exiled by the Isabelline reaction, had both favoured concessions to Cuba. There was a hope that revolution in Spain might at long last bring reform in Cuba. This optimism was frustrated. Whilst the old course was still unmodified by Lersundi, as Captain General of Cuba and a declared enemy of Reformism, a separatist revolt broke out. Above all the liberalism of the Revolution—like the liberalism of 1812 and 1820—could not understand any political solution but that of equal rights for all within the empire. Thus Dulce, appointed Captain General by the Revolution, arrived offering elections, freedom of the press, and association. Such a programme might have satisfied the old Reformist party; it could not satisfy the secessionists.[1]

The secessionists distrusted Reformism and were given strength by its repeated rebuffs in Madrid. They were led by Céspedes, a cultured landowner; once he had declared for an independent Cuban Republic (10 October 1868) he needed the support of the poor planters of the Oriente and the slaves; thus the movement became democratic and the war itself escaped from the control of the creole aristocracy into the hands of the great *mestizo* guerrilla leaders of the Oriente.[2] Once the war had broken out Spanish policy was at the mercy of the Volunteers, the urban militia force of the *peninsulares*, financed by the rich Spanish families who dominated political life. Autonomy and free trade would have ended the privileged position of the Spanish community; it reacted to these threats with a violent reassertion of Spanish sovereignty in Cuba as a part of metropolitan Spain 'fertilized by the blood and

[1] For Lersundi's repression and Dulce's policy of concession see R. Guerra y Sánchez, *A History of the Cuban Nation* (Havana, 1958), v. 14–54.

[2] H. Portell Vila, *Céspedes* (1931), 103 ff. The secessionist rebellion was rooted in the two provinces of Oriente and Camagüey. In the Oriente the terrain was broken and the fighting was on foot; in Camagüey, which was a cattle province, the rebels used cavalry effectively. See R. Guerra y Sánchez, *Cuban Nation*, 4–5 and 7–20, for the social differences between Oriente and Camagüey which were to underly the splits in the revolutionary camp.

sweat of her sons'. The loyalist mob of the capital drove out Dulce, the Captain General, who had wished to negotiate a settlement to end the war. Dulce had to face two revolts: that of the creole secessionists of the countryside and that of the urban royalists. One demanded the old system in its entirety, the other the withdrawal of Spain from Cuba. Since neither side would accept any compromise Dulce's policy of conciliation was bankrupt after five weeks.

Prim as prime minister desperately wished for a settlement and the end of the Cuban war; he was willing to contemplate autonomy or even sale to the United States in order to free the revolutionary government from the waste of war. His statesmanship got no support from the governmental parties and was bitterly opposed by loyalists in Cuba; he was also under constant pressure from Catalan interests to maintain Spain's commercial advantages at all costs.[1] Opinion, infected with the rhetoric of the Volunteers, slid into patriotic obstinacy: no concession until the secessionist rebellion had been defeated. Since the Spanish army could not bring the war to an end, no settlement could be made. In 1895–8 the same disastrous logic was to have the same disastrous consequences. More troops were poured into Cuba (by 1870 there were 100,000) in an effort to terminate a savage guerrilla war of plantation raids and jungle operations, in which disease was the worst enemy.[2] Thus the Provisional government was forced to go back on the two most serious promises of the Revolution at home—the abolition of the *quintas*, as the Spanish form of conscription was called, and the reduction of taxation. Cuba brought against the Revolution both the Republicans who staged *quinta* riots and those conservative interests which distrusted Prim's conciliatory intentions; it was the organized conservative reaction to the abolition of slavery which was to play a large part in the fall of Amadeo's constitutional monarchy.

[1] In Barcelona a group of powerful interests (e.g. the agriculturists of the Institute of San Isidro and the industrialists of the Fomento) set up a 'Permanent Commission for the Defence of Spanish Interests in Cuba'. Catalan banks were willing to raise loans for the army in Cuba. Cf. J. Carrera Pujal, *Cataluña*, v. 347–71, for an account of Catalan interest in Cuba.

[2] General Martínez Campos considered battle casualties 'insignificant' compared with fever and the leg sores that came from a semi-jungle war.

2. *The Revolutionary Settlement, 1868–1870*

The task of the Provisional government under Serrano was the traditional task of all governments that issued from the combination of a pronunciamiento with a popular revolt: the substitution of a dualistic system, where local affairs were in the hands of 'revolutionary' Juntas, by the powers of a regular central government. In 1868 the situation was different only in that the Juntas in the larger towns included Democrats who were crypto-republicans. On 8 October the Provisional government, under pressure from the Madrid Junta, swallowed the Democrat programme—universal suffrage, religious freedom ('the most important of all freedoms'), the jury, and freedom of the press and association.[1] These were to be known as the 'liberal conquests' and represented the maximum concession which the 'grandees' of the Provisional government were willing to make to Democrat demands.

In return for the Provisional government's acceptance of all those Democratic demands which were compatible with a constitutional monarchy, the Democrats saw office go to their Progressive and Unionist rivals and the monarchy accepted as the form of government, even if it was to be a democratic monarchy which would be permanently closed to 'that impossible woman', Isabella, and to her heirs. Although the generals and the respectable Progressive politicians saw in the banishment of the dynasty a minimum precondition of constitutional government, they publicly declared their conviction that Spanish society was unfit for a republic on the French or American models and that the 'monarchical principle' was the only keystone of the social order. The Provisional government therefore positively encouraged the sovereign national will to vote for a monarchical constitution.

It was the recognition of the 'monarchical principle' which split the old Democrat party. The *cimbrios* were ready to accept the monarchy as a temporary form of government provided it was a true constitutional and democratic monarchy. Rivero, unable to force two Democrat ministers on Serrano, accepted

[1] The only modification of Democrat demands was that the voting age was fixed at 25 not 21. Universal suffrage applied to all elections and its immediate result was the capture of municipal government in twenty provincial capitals by Republicans.

popularity and patronage as mayor of Madrid. The hour of the Democrats would come when the Progressives tired of the conservative alliance with the Liberal Unionists. 'With Democratic principles assured, the Republic is only postponed.'[1] Democrats who opposed compromise and procrastination emerged as the first Republican party in Spain: a monarchy could not be accepted on any terms. It was condemned not merely by its record in Spain, a defect which Progressives could argue with reason ceased to count with a change of dynasty, but by its incompatibility with the truths of political philosophy. The strength of the new party was the unexpected feature which first threw the Revolution off course.

The idiosyncrasy of the Republican party was its extreme federalism. Its foremost theorist, Pi y Margall, regarded federalism as the *only* logical deduction in politics from the premiss of individual liberty and his translation of Proudhon's *Du principe fédératif* appeared a few months before the revolution. Hence federalism was fashionable in radical circles and one cannot avoid the conclusion that it was adopted by the nascent party because it represented what appeared to be one of the latest advances in European thought.[2] The effect of this decision on the fate of republicanism was decisive. On the one hand it gave the party a mass following of provincial enthusiasts: the intelligentsia of the urban lower middle and working classes, to whom committees, meetings, and militia duty represented a way of life. It could canalize Catalan provincialism, the resentment of the southern cities at the loss of revolutionary initiative, and a great deal of revolutionary infantilism and residual carbonarism. On the other hand it involved the Republican leadership in a series of conflicts with the provincial masses, and ultimately condemned the Republican party as a party of government to impotence and lasting discredit. With such doctrines the party could neither achieve nor tolerate a strong leadership.[3]

[1] Rivero in a letter quoted M. Fernández Almargo in *Historia política de la España contemporánea*, i. 158. This casts a light on Rivero's actions in February 1873 (see below, p. 325).

[2] The party seems to have adopted federalism, at least in part, through the absent-minded incompetence of the chairman at its founding meeting, Orense—according to M. Villalba Hervás, *De Alcolea a Sagunto* (1899), 21. The argument was clinched on the intellectual level by the publication of Salmerón's *La forma del gobierno* (1868).

[3] Cf. C. A. M. Hennessey, *Federal Republic*, 124 ff. The Republicans did not

Federalism apart, the new party's programme derived from popular grievances which had long been familiar themes in Democrat propaganda. One such grievance—the *quinta* system—was used by the Republicans in the first attempt by any Spanish party to recruit women: the mother weeping for her lost sons was the Democratic reply to the image of the wife attentive to the confessor. Dogmatic anti-clericalism, the mark of the Republican until 1936, did the party more harm than good, but could no longer be avoided by a radical party. Finally, the Republicans, resentful of the way the democratic revolution had been pushed aside by generals, were the first party that could afford to stress the threat of the army to civil liberty and to campaign for a small army. Civilianism was safe for a party which counted in its ranks only one deaf general. Azaña and the radical Republicans of 1931 were the ultimate inheritors of both its anti-clericalism and its civilianism.

The first threat to the monarchical compromise of the Revolution settlement came, not from the Madrid Republican leaders, but from provincial extremists who passed from a state of revolutionary euphoria to one of bitterness and disillusionment. Madrid, the intellectual centre of republicanism, never contained its fighting forces: the Volunteers of Liberty of the capital gave up their arms in return for doles and were organized by Rivero in labour battalions.[1] It was in the provinces that the Juntas had embodied the demands and the passions of the local zealots: hence the local abolition of the hated *consumos* and the anti-clericalism which resulted in church demolition, the closing of seminaries and convents. The Progressives, in accepting office and the dissolution of the Juntas, once more cut themselves off from their popular support—as the success of Republican candidates in the municipal elections of the provincial capitals showed.[2] With the Juntas dissolved (although these were by no

acquire a recognized leadership until Feb. 1870 at the very moment that they split between unitarians and federalists (M. Villalba Hervás, ibid. 99).

[1] I. A. Bermejo, *Historia de la interinidad y guerra civil de España desde 1868* (1875–7), i. 386–401. This was Rivero's greatest service to the government as mayor: the labour battalions kept 13,000 men out of demagogic temptation. Rivero was interested in Fernández de los Ríos's replanning of Madrid on Second Empire lines. 1868, like other revolutions, saw a demolition of monastic buildings, &c., in the interests of urban improvement.

[2] The Juntas were first appointed by acclamation and later elected. When the Provisional government excluded Democrats the Juntas were the only basis for

means exclusively Democratic concerns), the frustrated energy of the great southern towns was thrown into the channel of Federal Republicanism. Here was a creed which exactly represented the long-standing claim of the provincial radical to subject the democratic credentials and intentions of a central government to perpetual scrutiny by the sanction of renewed revolution. It was a systematic and imposing intellectual framework for the unique creation of Spanish radicalism—the *centralista* tradition. It rationalized an instinct.

This autochthonous federalism was fed by economic discontent. The moment of political disillusionment coincided with maximum seasonal unemployment (made acute by a bad harvest) in those very districts of the south with a violent revolutionary tradition, a tradition used by the conspirators of 1868 but now rejected by the Provisional government. Malaga was invaded by unemployed labourers; like Cadiz, its port was dead. Republican apostles had, perhaps carelessly, encouraged the indigenous socialism of the *reparto*. The government's attempt to reassert control by dissolving the Volunteers of Liberty (the strength of urban radicalism, as the Militia had been) and the stoppage of doles to the unemployed set off street fighting that lasted three days. It was a revolt of desperation, not a Republican conspiracy.

The second outburst, which came in the late autumn of 1869 after the voting of the monarchical constitution, was a political rebellion. By revolution the provincial leadership of federalism expressed its contempt for the party's 'official' leadership—now the Republic minority in the Cortes—and exploited the ambiguities of the leaders' attitude to the rights of rebellion. In May and June two great rallies at Tortosa and Cordoba, served by special trains, had attempted to realize Federal theory in a series of mutual pacts between the provinces. The pacts allowed a right of insurrection *if* the government made 'an attack of a general character' on individual rights. To the leaders this was not a vague definition: it embodied their consistent belief that attempts to force the dialectic of history with barricades were unfruitful, and justified only if the opportunities of legal existence and peaceful propaganda were

Democrat power (cf. J. Paul y Angulo, *Memorias*, 70–77). For the Madrid Junta see E. Rodríguez Solis, *Memorias de un revolucionario* (1880), 99–106.

denied. Nevertheless there was no organization to declare the correct moment for rebellion, while the leaders themselves, respectable legalists and bourgeois, could neither avoid oratorical flirtations with revolution nor disown the applause of activists. Thus the initiative in a loosely organized party with a revolutionary mystique came to lie in the intuitions of provincial zealots, amateurs of revolution experimenting for the first time with what professional anarchists were to call the revolutionary temper of the masses.

In September 1869 it appeared to the Federal enthusiasts of Catalonia, Aragon, and the Levante that the inescapable revolutionary moment had arrived. On 21 September the acting governor of Tarragona was brutally murdered by a Republican demonstration in honour of the sole republican general, Pierrad. The government's reaction was sharp. The Volunteers of the Catalan towns, spared in earlier disbandments, were 'reorganized' and Sagasta's circular of 25 September gave provincial governors powers which could kill any active Republican organization.[1] Relying on the mutual help of the Tortosa organization, the Catalan town of Reus set up a Federal Republic in the belief that Sagasta's 'clear and patent violation of our individual rights' would set off a general rebellion. In fact the movement fizzled out with a riot in Barcelona, a disorganized and hopeless three days' revolt in the Ampurdán, and sporadic fighting in Andalusia. The worst trouble occurred in Valencia and Saragossa. For nine days, waiting for a general rebellion which never came, Federal barricades held out against the desultory attacks of troops rushed from all over southern Spain by rail. Only in Valls was the movement 'socialistic':[2] in Valencia there was class co-operation rather than class war.

The government easily suppressed the revolt and trouble-making extremist leaders fled. Suñer, the atheist deputy who had led the Ampurdán revolt, repented in exile. 'Feverish agitation, barricades, shots and murder will always benefit the

[1] E. M. Villarasa and J. Gatell, *Revolución de Setiembre*, i. 808, for Sagasta's circular.

[2] In Valls, property registers were burnt and rich proprietors attacked. In Valencia property owners, more alarmed at the prospect of a government bombardment than by class war, interceded on behalf of the rebels. The best account of the Valencia rising is in I. A. Bermejo, *Interinidad*, i. 697–716.

government more than us.'[1] Republicans were cleared out of the municipal councils which they had captured in the 1868 elections and the Volunteers of Liberty finally dissolved. What Victor Balaguer, the Catalan Progressive and historian called 'the errors of the first moments' had been repaired and 'demagogy' suppressed. With the 'principle of authority strengthened' the country looked fit to receive a monarch.[2]

The maintenance of the principle of authority depended on one factor: the army. Only when the army deserted the government or was useless as a force against internal disorder would anarchy triumph. It was the army which had defeated the first two civilian revolutions in nineteenth-century Spain; General Caballero de Rodas, who had brought the south to order in 1869, disobeyed the government whenever it suited him and showed clearly the limitations of loyalty. 'Every town that rises is a town disarmed. If we don't devour them they will devour us. It looks as if the government is asleep. If we don't break with the Democrats we are ruined.' While Prim was the strongest influence in the government, the army was under the control of the only general—except O'Donnell before him—who showed gifts as a civilian statesman. Yet, like O'Donnell, Prim realized that his position as a statesman depended on his power as a general and Minister of War. Hence the essential conflict of Prim's civilian statesmanship: the Cuban question apart, he could not abolish conscription and reduce the army. Even if he looked like an undertaker, he was still a general. Moreover, as a general he knew the importance of generals in politics; his promotions gave him the loyalty of most officers from colonel down and he was popular with the sergeants. By 1870 it was apparent that he was losing the support of the Unionist generals at the very moment when it was essential to strengthen the principle of authority by the election of a king.

The Constituent Cortes, which was to make the monarchical settlement definitive, had met in February 1869. Sagasta's electoral management and the general temper of the country returned an assembly dominated by the revolutionary coalition—Progressives, *cimbrio* Democrats, and Liberal Unionists.

[1] *D.S.C.* 18, vii. 69, quoted in Sagasta's speech.

[2] R. Olivar Bertrand, *Asi cayó*, appendix 124. Letter of 11 June, prophesying that stability would come out of the successful suppression of revolution.

The Republicans and the Carlists were a minority, speaking violently only to be outvoted easily. The debates, which became classics of Spanish parliamentary oratory, gave rise to four-hour set pieces which read now like second-rate lectures. 'The country is being sacrificed for the sake of oratorical contests . . . it demands fewer speeches and more improvements.'[1] This complaint of sterility, inspired by the abuse of rhetorical traditions utterly foreign to English or French parliamentary life, misconceives the function of a Constituent Cortes in the tradition of Spanish revolutions: a Constituent Cortes was called for a specific political task—the drafting of a constitution which should embody the principles of a successful revolution. This the Cortes did with the constitution of 1869. The tragedy was that the delay in finding a king prolonged its life long after it had fulfilled its primary mission. The later sessions of the Cortes were ill-attended, short, and pointless.[2]

The revolutionary coalition of Progressives and Liberal Unionists had decided on a monarchical form of government. This was established in Article 33 of the constitution, a compromise between the Unionists' desire for the 'monarchy with all its attributes' and the democracy 'with all its consequences' of the Progressives and their *cimbrio* Democrat allies. The result was a constitutional monarchy on Belgian lines. The monarchical form, as such, was bitterly contested by the passionate but professor-like oratory of the Republican minority. A prefabricated monarchy was being foisted on a revolution given force by the Democratic–Republican ideas which inspired it. Practical criticism came from those conservative Unionists who had not accepted the revolutionary coalition. Universal suffrage applied to the Senate as well as the Lower Chamber would lead to socialism which could only be 'held' by the Church which the constitutional coalition had deserted; with a king stripped of power and a popular Senate there was no 'moderating power' capable of resisting the excesses of democracy. It was with this political philosophy that Cánovas staked his claim as leader of the conservative forces in Spain.[3]

[1] Quoted Villarasa and Gatell, *Revolución*, i. 860.

[2] In the October–December session of 1869 debates occupied only 184 hours. Some sessions lasted barely an hour.

[3] M. Fernández Almagro, *Cánovas*, 178–87.

One of the conquests of the revolution, embodied in the constitution, committed the Provisional government to a political theory that made the maintenance of order a legal impossibility and allowed Republicans to argue that the new order was another edition of sham constitutionalism. In the theory of the left, imprescriptible rights of assembly and free speech were 'superior and anterior to all laws'. Confronted with the revolution of the enthusiasts Sagasta, as Minister of the Interior, found these rights, guaranteed by the constitution, 'lead weights about the neck of government'. In October 1869 he used the powers granted under Article 31 of the constitution to suspend the constitutional guarantees. Such suspensions, as South American constitutional history abundantly proves, were an inevitable consequence of the impossibility of reconciling individualist premisses with the minimum claims of the state. Cánovas pointed to the dangers of granting extensive individual rights when there was no strong executive; the Republicans argued that by suspending these rights, even in the face of rebellion, the government had sacrificed the conquests of the revolution in order to make a country fit for monarchs to live in.

With the monarchical constitution voted and the Republican rising suppressed, the main task of the government became to find a king; to postpone this was to leave the constitution 'without the powerful sanction of fact'. The search for a monarch broke the September coalition on the exclusive ambitions of its constituent parties. Both the Liberal Unionists and the Progressive–Democrat group wanted to make their own candidate king in order to dominate his reign. Beneath this obstinacy lay genuine political difference. Montpensier as king meant a strong, catholic monarchy run by the Unionists as representatives of the conservative oligarchy. Against the duke of Montpensier the Progressives and Democrats proposed Fernando, the ex-king of Portugal and, when he withdrew, one of the princes of the new 'revolutionary' kingdom of Italy. This implied a democratic kingship, mildly anti-clerical, with power in the hands of the left wing of the September coalition.

The Progressives' and Prim's main difficulty lay in finding a willing alternative candidate to Montpensier who had put himself out of the running by killing his cousin in a duel.[1] A

[1] Prim's refusal to consider Montpensier was based on his knowledge of Napoleon

year after the vote of the constitution the government was still without a candidate for the throne and Prim took up the suggestion of a son of the Sigmaringen branch of the Hohenzollern family. This candidature brought on the Franco-Prussian war. In part a result of Prim's desperation—Ollivier called him a ruined gambler—the cause of the war lay in the contradiction between the methods by which a candidate had to be sought in order to avoid insulting Spanish dignity, and the French thesis that it was 'not permissible for a nation to exercise its sovereign rights in such a way as to threaten the security of its neighbours'. Prim's only chance was the *fait accompli* of a secret election by the Cortes; through an unexplained error of a decoding clerk the Cortes were dismissed (23 June 1870) before an election could be made and the secret of the Hohenzollern candidate leaked out via the Carlist press. Thus France was given an opportunity to object. 'My labour is lost, the candidate lost and God grant that is all.' Prim's gamble is understandable; its failure made it an error.[1]

In the end, Prim found his candidate in the house of Savoy. The duke of Aosta accepted the throne after Spain had allowed the Italian Foreign Office to sound European opinion.[2] Prim believed with a king he could stabilize the revolution. 'When the King comes all will be settled. There will be no cry but *Viva el Rey*. We will box up all those madmen who dream up "liberticide" plans and who confuse progress with disorder, liberty with licence.' Yet as Castelar pointed out, Amadeo was not the king of the September Revolution but the 'king of a fraction of a party', the candidate of Prim, the Progressives and their Democratic allies, accepted by the Liberal Unionists only with misgivings after their private hopes had been ruined. Without even the support of the totality of the September coalition, Amadeo was rejected out of hand by the Republicans, the

III's opposition to an Orleans candidate. 'Prim told me over and over again that the Emperor had placed a veto on Montpensier's election' (*F.O.*, Layard to Grenville, 3 Jan. 1873).

[1] Sagasta's circular tries to explain some of Prim's actions. Prim naïvely defended himself by saying he did not realize there would be European complications. This does not make sense, given his attitude to the Montpensier candidature. For a discussion of these issues see D. Steefel, *Bismarck, the Hohenzollern Candidacy and the Origins of the Franco-Prussian War* (Cambridge, Mass., 1962).

[2] The telegrams are printed Villarasa and Gatell, *Revolución*, i. 281–96. They reveal the terrible anxiety of the government to get a king.

Carlists, and the slowly growing band of Alfonsist aristocrats.[1] These latter (who pinned their hopes on a restoration of the old dynasty in the person of Isabella's son, Alfonso) still set the tone and attitudes of Madrid society from which the kingship had traditionally drawn its surest support. All these disparate forces were willing to co-operate against the new dynasty: Carlists formed a parliamentary alliance with Republicans; the Alfonsist and Carlist aristocracy, who for the first time came together in the capital, avoided painful reference to a past that separated them in order to campaign against 'what exists'.

3. *The Factitious Monarchy, 1870–1873*

On the day Amadeo arrived in his new kingdom he was greeted with the news that Prim had been shot in a Madrid street; his death was a catastrophe for the monarchy he had created.[2] The ablest of conspirators, he was a man of order: a soldier, who kept the War Office, he was capable of thinking as a civilian politician: a Progressive who could call in the Radicals, yet believed in continuing the revolutionary coalition with the Unionists as the only hope for a widely accepted régime. Tough—his opponents considered him a dictator—he was capable of the finesse and compromise of parliamentary politics. A stronger man than the dignified, ambitious Serrano or the bluff Topete, he was incontestably the greatest statesman of the Revolution. The proof is that his death meant the end of the coalition of 1868.

There was no enthusiasm for the new monarch. He was subject to insult in the theatres of Madrid and consistently cold-shouldered by the aristocracy. His court was a lugubrious, formal collection of revolutionary generals and politicians. Yet, if constitutional monarchy could be made to work in Spain, Amadeo was eminently fit for the role of constitutional king. His understanding of the system was perhaps unsophisticated: his conduct, he once said, was dictated by a Parliamentary

[1] The aristocracy had 'emigrated' to French spas in 1868; this represented its reflex action to political revolution rather than fear of social revolution.

[2] The most probable assassins were Federalist Republican extremists of Paúl y Angulos's stamp: his paper had made violent attacks on Prim whom he now hated, perhaps because Prim refused to consider him as an ambassador. Other candidates were: Cuban slave interests; Serrano (according to Paúl y Angulo); the *Montpenseristas* (according to Prim's widow).

majority of one. It is possible to subject the use of the personal prerogatives of the crown to such mechanical criteria only in a clearly defined two-party system. The king and his advisers worked hard to create a liberal and a conservative party out of the disintegration of the revolutionary bloc; Amadeo is thus one of many candidates for the title of inventor of the *turno pacífico*, the alternation in power of two parties created artificially by government influence exercised on an indifferent electorate. But the nature of his prerogative, and the exclusive ambitions of the parties, meant that the crown's granting of a dissolution gave such complete power to 'make' a Cortes that the defeated party must be driven to criticism of the crown itself. All the general elections of Amadeo's short reign returned majorities for the dissolving Minister of the Interior. The real issue of politics, as Ruiz Zorrilla admitted, was 'Which party is to be granted, by the high prerogative of the crown, a decree of dissolution?' The monarch, in these conditions, was not an impartial umpire but a player.[1]

Serrano, first prime minister of the new monarchy, formed a ministry of revolutionary conciliation—Unionists, Progressives, and Democrats. In the election of March (1871) a ministerial coalition of opposites fought an electoral coalition of incompatibles: Carlists and Republicans, who could only unite on a programme of 'Down with what exists' confronted, in the elections and in the Cortes, the revolutionary coalition, strong only in its possession of official influence.[2] The Democrat ministers were determined to drag their Progressive colleagues into open war with the Unionists and there were bitter disputes over patronage. The appointment of a batch of Unionist A.D.C.s was regarded by the Progressives and Democrats as a threat to liberty. Unable to unite his cabinet rather than 'morally' defeated by the opposition, Serrano resigned in July 1871. The revolutionary coalition of 1868 was dead.

[1] For Ruiz Zorrilla's views, see I. A. Bermejo, *Interinidad*, ii. 571, 824. Managed elections were inevitable in a country where, as Ruiz Zorrilla again admitted, twelve out of sixteen million people were totally indifferent to politics. As in every period, there were startling revelations about electoral corruption.

[2] The elections gave the Carlists and Republicans a decisive position in the Cortes when the coalition broke; Nocedal, the Carlist leader, could thus make and unmake ministers. This gave added tension and unreality to political life since Nocedal *a priori* could not be asked to enter a ministry.

For the first time in their long history the Progressives now assumed power under a civilian prime minister, Ruiz Zorrilla, peacefully and without the encumbrance of conservative fellow conspirators or *exaltado* Juntas. Yet, at this very moment, the party that Prim had held together, broke into Radicals, led by Ruiz Zorrilla, and conservative Progressives led by Sagasta. Both had been militia men in '54; both had served in the Provisional government. Now they were driven apart by their divergent political temperaments. Sagasta was a man of order and a manipulator of men; his rival saw politics as the expression of principles. Sagasta held that co-operation with the Liberal Unionists should continue and that, if it failed, the Progressives should slough off their Democrat allies forming a conservative party with the *fronterizos* (those of the frontier of the Progressive party) of the Union, shifting the balance of the party to the right. Ruiz Zorrilla held that conciliation was dead and that the Progressives must adopt the full Democratic programme. Both were concerned with the survival of the dynasty. Sagasta saw the danger of alienating the conservative interests; Ruiz Zorrilla believed that only by capturing Republican benevolence could the monarchy escape violent destruction.[1] These political differences were fought out with intense personal bitterness in the press and in the Progressive Club which excommunicated Sagasta as a traitor. This divergence could not become the basis of two alternating parties. Both Ruiz Zorrilla and Sagasta paid homage to the idea of a 'healthy' two-party system, but both wished to drive the other out of political life.

When Ruiz Zorrilla's ministry fell in October 1871, victim of Sagasta's parliamentary skill, ail hope of Progressive reunion was lost. Sagasta formed a ministry in which conservative Unionists increasingly predominated. It was to Sagasta that the king gave the decree of dissolution. This shook the royalism of the Radicals and Democrats.[2] Democrats like Martos and

[1] Ruiz Zorrilla's later programme is interesting in that it shows how purely political radicalism was: its main plan was a 'moral' administration as a way to economy. Apart from the abolition of the conscription and army reform, there was little to capture working-class support in an electorate of universal suffrage. Educational reform was a higher preference than irrigation or agricultural reform.

[2] Cf. I. A. Bermejo, *Interinidad*, ii. 545. They had already shown with their teeth by their attacks on the king's 'prolongation' of the short-lived ministry of

Rivero made it clear that their loyalty to the dynasty was conditional on the king behaving as a Radical party leader and abandoning any attempt to build up a conservative party within Amadeist liberalism.

Sagasta got his conservative majority by methods which caused its members to be called *lázaros*—politically dead men revived by the electoral artifices of the Ministry of the Interior. In face of Sagasta's ruthless use of his 'corrupt' majority the Radicals and Republicans revived the old threat of the *retraimiento*, a confession that the parties which abstained no longer believed in parliamentary government, a formal statement that they intended to appeal 'to other more decisive methods'. Before this threat Sagasta resigned and Serrano formed a frankly conservative ministry (May 1872).[1] It was short lived. Serrano believed that a prospective Republican rebellion could only be met with a suspension of the constitutional guarantees. This the king refused to grant although Serrano had a safe majority.

This decision made inevitable a Radical ministry and a Radical Cortes. It thus sealed the fate of the dynasty. When Ruiz Zorrilla at last got his dissolution the Liberal Unionists deserted a monarchy which they had only accepted when their own candidate for the throne had failed. Serrano announced his intention never to serve the king again; he himself, most of his fellow generals, and his political allies returned their decorations, refused to accept invitations to the court, and retired from politics, as the Radicals had done during the conservative essay. At the time when the Radicals were agitating violently against the king's prolongation of the life of the Malcampo

Malcampo, Ruiz Zorrilla's colourless successor. At a meeting at the Circo Price Rivero placed liberty above monarchy. One of the Radical's arguments is interesting as a prelude to the argument that forced Alfonso XIII's abdication after the Republican–Socialist victory in the municipal elections of April 1931: because the Radicals as a 'mass' party had gained the *municipal* elections it was the king's constitutional duty to appoint a Radical ministry.

[1] Sagasta resigned over his attempt to hush up the unauthorized transfer of two million pesetas from the Cuban budget. Sagasta claimed he had used the two million on a secret service which unearthed absurdities, e.g. reports that Castelar was about to seize the Bank of Spain and Ruiz Zorrilla to burn Catalan factories. Political enemies believed that he used the two million to fight his elections; in fact it was used to hush up a scandal in Amadeo's private life. M. Fernández Almagro, *Historia política*, i. 142.

ministry the king was clear that the Unionists were both more powerful—because they had the army—and less loyal than the Radicals. They must therefore be given power. Amadeo now reversed his political equation: it would be fatal to drive the Republicans and Radicals to revolt. Therefore Ruiz Zorrilla must be given power.

Ruiz Zorrilla's ministry and the Cortes it elected (August 1872) represented a pure 'Radical situation'; none of the great conservative figures of the Revolution were elected and the ministry's laws were an attack on established interests. The reduction of the ecclesiastical budget to the strict necessities of public worship made the clergy dependent for their wages on municipalities which might well be in the hands of anti-clerical Republicans. Throughout modern Spanish history the defence of a persecuted church was the rallying cry of conservative sentiment. The abolition of slavery in Puerto Rico produced 'a league of monied interests' against the government. A Republican rising in El Ferrol weakened the only conservative argument in favour of Radicalism—that it might contain republicanism.[1] The final and fatal onslaught of outraged conservatism came with the Hidalgo affair.

Hidalgo was believed to be responsible for the shooting of the artillery officers by the mutineers in the abortive San Gil rising of 1866. This was false. Nevertheless he did not disown the movement, and after the Revolution was promoted rapidly—by inference for his past services to the Progressives. In November 1872 he was made Captain General of the Basque Provinces. Rather than serve under him all the artillery officers went sick. He put them under arrest. Ruiz Zorrilla was determined to assert civilian control of the army and, like all Radicals, he disliked the 'aristocratic' *esprit de corps* of artillery officers. The result of the conflict was that the government accepted the resignation of the entire corps of artillery officers and handed over their commands to sergeants and infantry officers. In this extreme course the prime minister was backed up by his majority in the Cortes. The king disapproved of the attack on the artillery but he was powerless to resist it, since to call on the conservatives would drive the Radicals and the Democrats against the dynasty. After fulfilling his last duty as constitutional

[1] See below, p. 325, for the Republican rebellion.

king by signing the decree against the artillery officers he abdicated (February 1873).

It was neither his own general unpopularity nor the enemies of the dynasty (both the Carlist and the Republican threat was weak), but the domestic feuds of the September coalition which drove Amadeo to abdication. The constitutional parties made loyalty to the dynasty conditional on the political support of the king. Amadeo realized the full implications of the conservative withdrawal. It left the monarchy in the hands of a party with no natural monarchical sentiment. Ruiz Zorrilla was personally loyal to the dynasty, but his Democrat allies—Martos and Rivero—were prepared to usher in a republic if this would ensure their political power.

The weakness of the Republicans, on the eve of the declaration of the First Republic, must now be explained. The establishment of the monarchy had presented the Republicans with doctrinal and tactical issues which revealed once more the differences between the cautious responsible parliamentary leaders and the extremists of the provinces. For these latter the course of the party was clear; to a monarchy a Republican party could only offer absolute and intransigent opposition—hence they were known as 'intransigents'. The 'legal struggle' of electoral and parliamentary activity was both immoral and ineffective. The sacred duty of rebellion was imperative.

The resistance of the more responsible leaders to these intransigents was likewise based on principle and policy. It was a crime to revolt, provided the monarchy respected individual rights (i.e. the existence of Republicans as a legal party), and, even if these rights were denied, revolution should only be attempted if the party could hope for success. Moreover they believed the monarchy would falter and that the Radicals would have to accept the Republic as the only alternative to a conservative *revanche*. Hence they declared their 'benevolence' to Ruiz Zorrilla in his parliamentary battle against 'reaction'.[1] They were therefore known as *benévolos*.

Every time the Madrid leadership of *benévolos* tried to force through its policy of the legal struggle it was faced by the

[1] Castelar had close friends among the *cimbrio* Radicals, e.g. Martos. He probably dreamed of re-creating the old Democrat party of the sixties on a *unitary* republican basis.

prospect of an intransigent secession. This might well attract the mass of the party. The Republicans' papers consistently flattered the self-importance of local personalities—in the same way as did the later Anarchist press which printed the articles of a nationally known figure side by side with naïve utterances of the town's 'man with ideas'. Thus, with Ruiz Zorrilla's second ministry, most of the party press and its mass following had deserted the leaders of the Republican Directory as a protest against the 'benevolence' granted to Ruiz Zorrilla; by June 1871 the intransigents had created their own organization of central and local committees. They refused to accept Pi's contention that 'force is legitimate only when right fails' and in October backed the soldiers' revolt at Ferrol and exploited the widespread *quinta* riots. To their disgust, the party leaders condemned the insurrection and its total failure confirmed the Directory's estimate of revolutionary strength. The extremists' bluff was called. Nevertheless internal conflict had almost destroyed the party, as it was to destroy the Republic itself.

In this sorry condition the Republicans faced the crisis of the Hidalgo affair and the abdication of Amadeo. That this crisis was resolved in favour of a Republic was thus due less to the strength of republicanism than to the plans of Rivero and Figueras, the leader of the Republican parliamentary minority. Rivero resented his displacement as a political figure, probably intending to use his understanding with Figueras and the Hidalgo affair in order to drive out the king and bring in a republic, with himself as its first president. He would be the key figure in a crisis which he would dominate in the best traditions of revolutionary statesmanship.[1] His own parliamentary arrogance ruined his plans. But it was the Figueras–Rivero intrigue that finally secured the declaration of the republic in a joint session of the Senate and Congress.

Thus the Republican leaders got their bloodless 'legal' Republic. They sacrificed an immediate declaration of a *Federal* Republic on the grounds of democratic delicacy. This was a decision that only a Constituent Cortes could take. In

[1] What his real plans were are obscure: he seems to have been in touch with conservative generals like the marqués del Duero. His destruction by Martos's accusation of tyranny is a striking example of the sudden changes to which assemblies in revolutionary situations are subject.

fact it was the price paid for Radical support; Radicals could face a unitary but not a federal republic. No language about the historic inevitability of the Republic, so dear to Castelar, could hide the fact that it was not Republican conviction in the country but the exhaustion of alternative solutions and the exploitation of a propitious parliamentary situation that had created the Republic. Moreover, in the deal, the Republicans had postponed the issue of federalism—a decision that was to cost them dear. The Republican party entered the Republic with its own mass following disillusioned and restive, and with no support of any kind outside those masses.

The Republican leaders, like the Progressives before them, have been criticized for their failure to develop a class programme for a mass party. In 1869 this was unnecessary.[1] It was enough for the Republican party to support freedom of association and deliver the platitudes of French 'socialists' of 1848 on the harmony of capital and labour in order to get the Congress of Working Class Societies in Barcelona to declare unanimously for the Federal Republic (December 1868). Thus, to the alarm of Bakunin's apostles of total revolution, the only organized workers in Spain committed themselves to a bourgeois political alliance.[2]

By 1873 there are signs that this Republican alliance with working-class radicalism was dying if not dead. This was only in part the consequence of the activities of the International which, in its first Congress at Barcelona (June 1870) declared the Federal Republican programme 'insufficient' and political action a 'farce'—the beginning of the long anarchist tradition of apoliticism in Spain.[3] The International was not a powerful organization: in 1871 it could not meet its postage expenses. Yet its propaganda frightened the Republican leadership and

[1] See above, p. 289, and C. Martí, *Orígines*, 23–38.

[2] From October 1868 Fanelli, Bakunin's agent, preached that all political alliances were counter-revolutionary but could make no converts among the supporters of the Republican alliance (cf. M. Nettlau, *Bakunin y la Internacional en España* (Buenos Aires, 1925), 32 ff.

[3] The Republican defence of the International gave rise to the most famous debate of the Revolution. Of the interminable and unreadable speeches the most famous was that of Salmerón, which is full of his philosophy of reason immanent in human nature. No such speech could have been made in any other parliamentary assembly. It filled the Congress; it would have emptied the House of Commons or the Chamber of Deputies.

even more the extremist intransigents who feared its affects on their militants. By their defence of the International in the Cortes and by refurbishing their social programme, the Republicans no doubt hoped to recapture some working-class support; but their programme remained obstinately 'reformist and bourgeois'.[1] The intransigents hoped to capture the support the parliamentary leaders had lost by temporarily calling themselves socialists and using provocative language. Extremists made few converts among the respectable Catalan operatives; disheartened by the failures of 1869, they were not fitted to become the vanguard of social revolution. The explosive elements were the *bas fonds* of a great port who could be recruited by the agitators of the secret societies into a formidable mob. As Lerroux was later to see, this mob was susceptible, not to scientific socialism, but to the programmeless oratory of the revolution of destruction. Moreover, even in its origins, Spanish anarchism was as much a rural as an urban phenomenon. It was the desperate poverty of Andalusia which most readily provided enthusiastic converts to the Bakuninist vision of a new society.[2] It was to these urban *sans culottes* and to the primitive rebels of the countryside that the provincial Robespierres of 1873 were to appeal in the name of the Federal Republic denied by the 'hypocritical legality' of the Republican leaders.

4. *The Republic of 1873*

The four presidents of the First Republic, Figueras, Pi y Margall, Salmerón, and Castelar were respected and respectable lawyers or university professors—intellectuals who hated violence. Their task was to transform the unspecified Republic which had been granted them as a gift by political circumstance into a *Federal* Republic: this transformation must be sanctioned by the recognized machine for constitutional definition—the

[1] e.g. 'Opportunities for the workers' moral and intellectual improvement'; factory laws; reform of land tenure (the only sign that the Republicans believed there were potential voters embedded in agrarian discontent); the 'generalization of property' through Pi's panacea of cheap credit. The extreme limit of their social policy is presented in the programme of Feb. 1872 (printed, E. Vera y González, *Pi y Margall*, ii. 294–300); drawn up by Pi, it was never accepted by the party.

[2] For the splits in the International and the consequent predominance of Bakunin over Marx in Spain, see M. Nettlan, *La première Internationale en Espagne* (Dordrecht, 1969).

Constituent Cortes. Such a republic they would then defend against its enemies as the legal government of the Spanish people.

A republic, Prim had consistently maintained, was 'inconceivable' because Republicanism was a minority creed. Yet the whole policy of the Republican leadership was based on the assumption that a Federal Republic would be peacefully established by a freely elected Constituent Cortes reflecting the 'overwhelming force' of Federal Republican opinion which Pi sensed in the telegrams that came to the Home Office. Had they acted as the revolutionary dictators of an enlightened minority and declared for a Federal Republic, they could have confronted the cantonalist revolt with conviction and vigour because it could have no legitimate case. Instead, they posed as instruments of the majority voice of Spain. This respect for a democratically imposed Federal Republic and the firmness with which Pi and Figueras claimed to deal with the 'puerile impatience' of their co-religionaries contained a contradiction. It was not merely that sincere Federalists could not be shot for lack of a sense of timing or misconceptions about means to an end which the leaders recognized as legitimate. These same leaders might need what Martos euphemistically called 'the pressure of opinion' (that is, the strength of militant Federalism) against those who, between February and April, tried to block the legal birth of the Federal Republic. In the last resort, they might have to call the true believers into the streets.[1]

Figueras and Pi thus chose to regard themselves as the neutral supervisors of elections to a Constituent Cortes which could only give one verdict—the return of a Federalist majority.[2] They thus encountered a double-headed opposition: that of the Radicals who did not want a federal republic at all but a unitary republic which they could hope to dominate, and that of the Federalist extremists who wanted a federal republic *immediately*, not as an imposition from above (*arriba abajo*) but as the expression of revolutionary *élan* from below (*abajo arriba*).

[1] Cf. the judgements in E. Vera y González, *Pi y Margall*, ii. 442, *et passim*, on the difficulties presented by the leaders' 'fetish of legality'.

[2] Cf. Figueras's speech in Barcelona (12 Mar.). Though a Federalist by personal conviction, he believed that, as head of the state, to declare his views would be a 'violation of neutrality', M. González Sugrañes, *La república en Barcelona* (Barcelona, 1896), 114.

Unlike their leaders, most of the provincial Federalists were revolutionary anti-parliamentarians at heart.

The actions of the Radicals in the early months of the Republic have nearly always been described by Republicans in terms of treason and intrigue. Yet there was nothing politically immoral in their attempt to stave off a *Federal* Republic, which they regarded as a disaster, by the use of the parliamentary majority which had created the Republic itself. Martos, the Radical leader, wanted a conservative, unitary, lay Republic which would rally the September coalition round the Radical party; to secure this he must prevent the calling of the Constituent Cortes by a Federal Republican ministry. This meant the rupture of the Republican–Radical coalition. In Martos's own words the Radicals, in their determination to defeat Federalism and 're-establish the unity of the nation', were 'the enemies of the situation they had created'.

When Martos failed to stop the calling of the Constituent Cortes he planned a Conservative–Radical *coup*. Once more the politicians appealed to the generals to support their personal interpretation of majority rule. The generals could not but dislike the prospect of a Federal Republic since many Federalists had sought popular support by violent attacks on the 'privileged caste' of officers. They were on the look-out for a politician of order whom they could back.[1] On 23 April the conspirators planned to call the Ordinary Cortes, overthrow the government, and rally the conservative sections of the militia in the Madrid bull ring. The *coup* failed: Pi at the Home Office acted with vigour and, after hearing a confused speech from Admiral Topete, symbol of '68, the militia were disarmed and sent home. The chances for a Federal Republic had been saved at the price of driving the Radicals and their supporters outside the 'Republican orbit'. The September Coalition retired from politics when those implicated in the bull ring

[1] General Pavía suggested to Francisco Salmerón (the Radical brother of the Republican leader and president of the Radical-dominated Permanent Commission) that he should stage a military movement in support of the legal rights of the (Ordinary) Cortes and declare for a unitary, national Republican government. F. Salmerón refused and was lost. Serrano was not formally a leader of the April plot though his house was used for a series of non-committal and indecisive conversations. On the failure of the plot he shaved off his moustache and fled to Biarritz.

conspiracy emigrated; the Federals and a handful of Unitary Republicans were the only political parties in Spain. Thus the fierce political struggles of the summer of 1873 were fought out within the Federalist party itself. The rest of Spain was either in arms, as were the Carlists, or stupefied by the sudden turn the Revolution had taken. As in 1835, 1909, and 1931, the respectable classes shut themselves in their houses and left the streets to the revolution.

On the morning of 24 April Pi y Margall, now president, was the most powerful man in Spain.[1] Had he wished to set up the Federal Republic, no resistance would have been possible by discredited Radicals and hesitant generals. He did not declare it because he clung to the view that, given the certainty of the legal imposition of the Federation by the Constituent Cortes, a Federalist revolution was unnecessary and a crime. Federalists, who could not doubt Pi's convictions, believed him guilty of an immense political error. 'Did I act rightly? I doubt it in terms of political interest. I affirm that I did when I consult my conscience.'

When Pi consulted his conscience he read the forthcoming victory of the Federal Republic at the general election for the Constituent Cortes. '*Even before* the withdrawal of the other parties I expected the triumph of the Federals at the polling booths and therefore even more when, through malevolence and lack of confidence in their own strength, they decided on this course.'[2] Thus Pi conceived the Federal Republic as a genuine expression of the national will rather than as the imposition of a minority. Even granted his premisses, the 'legal' declaration of a Federal Republic by the duly elected Constituent Cortes could not stave off the Federalist revolt that had been brewing for months. The Cantonalist movement, as this provincial outburst is called, left legal federalism bankrupt: its bet on the temper of the provinces had failed and its hopes of creating a new Republican order were defeated by the collapse of the forces of order themselves.

The collapse of army discipline was inevitable when a party

[1] Pi y Margall, *La republica de 1873* (in *Opuscolos* 1914), 108. 'It is uncontestable that after 23 April I wielded immense power; as a result of the events of 23 April the government had become a revolutionary dictatorship.'

[2] Ibid. 109.

committed to the abolition of conscription came to power; soldiers left their units. The Provincial Deputation of Barcelona took matters into its own hands and turned the regular army into a volunteer force (9 March). Elsewhere the restoration of the Volunteers of Liberty, dissolved in 1869, and the encouragement of various free corps created large numbers of semi-military persons, ready to infect the troops with their own brand of military democracy. Worst of all, a handful of extremists regarded the destruction of discipline as a patriotic duty. Once a regiment had been stationed in a large town and exposed to subversive propaganda, it refused to move. By the early summer the Catalonian army was unusable.[1] 'No officer is a Republican at heart' declared Colonel Maza, an extremist of the secret societies. This excuse for mutiny was to be repeated in 1936. Officers tried to restore discipline, stick in hand, against soldiers shouting 'Down with Epaulettes', 'Dance'. Without the sanctions of the 'barbarous' military code the officers' position was intolerable; many gave up their commands while those who stuck to their posts got no help from the authorities. The Provincial Deputation of Barcelona was ready to petition for the pardon of soldiers who had murdered their colonel: 'One hair of a soldier is worth ten reactionary officers' heads.' Pi disliked militarism, Salmerón jibbed at the officers' one serious demand—the restoration of the death penalty. Until Castelar's presidency most of the officer corps was, therefore, staging its own revolution of withdrawal.

The agitated history of Barcelona, which remained at least formally loyal to the central government, reveals the appalling difficulties which confronted the Republican government, without an army, in its determination to await a legally established Federal Republic. At almost any moment between February and August 1873, extremists might have tipped the complicated balance of political forces in the city by a successful *journée* and forced the Provincial Deputation into a declaration of a Catalan federal state. Demonstrations were whipped up by the extremists of pure revolution organized in societies by Colonel Maza, by the International which, though it despised

[1] M. Gonzáles Sugrañes, *Barcelona*, 104, 257. The International was particularly active in garrison propaganda: the army existed to pay bourgeois officers at the expense of the people. On 6 June there was a full-scale mutiny at Igualada.

bourgeois politics, saw in their disorder the hope of another Paris Commune. The situation was saved, not by the telegrams and personal appearances of Republican leaders from Madrid, but by the local Republican committee, well organized in wards and faithful to Madrid, and by the relative prosperity of the cotton operatives.[1] The workers were indifferent to the Internationalists' pleas for revolutionary strikes and, after the failures of 1869, they had lost interest in the schemes of the artisan intellectuals of Catalanism.

What the propaganda of the International and the revolutionary ambitions of a group of extremists could not accomplish among the operatives of Barcelona, they accomplished with the Federalist energumens of the Levante and the south. The disintegration of forces of public order gave a minority of local extremists the opportunity to seize power and set up independent Cantonal republics. They were not resolute proletarian revolutionaries: in Cordoba the leaders included a feeble-minded law student and a professor of canon law, morbid and solitary, who had shocked his rich wife's friends by lectures on atheism. Roque Barcia, who became the leader of the Cartagena Cantonalists, was an amateur philosopher driven almost crazy by neglect of his works except in a small circle of extreme Federalists, to whom he was a lay saint.[2] Conservatives presented the Cantonalist rising as a social revolution; its weakness was that it was not.

Only the Alcoy rising (9 July 1873) and the sporadic outbreaks in Andalusia had overtones of social revolution. The Alcoy canton was the work of the members of the International's Federal Council, fortuitously concentrated in the town. Condemning the Republic as a mere political change, they succeeded in pushing a wage strike into a municipal revolution; the Federalist Republican mayor was murdered and the town taken over by workers. Even so the success was due less to the strength of the revolution—many of the workers were satisfied with high wages and loth to strike—than to the utter collapse of

[1] Thus the Volunteers followed their officers against church burners. The worst crises were on 21 Feb., 8–11 Mar., 23–24 Apr., 12–19 June. For the telegraphic exertions of Pi and Figueras, ibid. 81 ff. and appendix L.

[2] For Prieto and Cervantes see J. Díaz del Moral, *Agitaciones*, 93 ff. Roque Barcia was a revolutionary journalist whose hopes of high office had been frustrated. Cf. C. A. M. Hennessy, *Federal Republic*, 97.

the forces of order. The 'capitalists' and the army failed to back the mayor's resistance.[1] In rural Andalusia the endemic *jacquerie* appeared more sinister with the growing influence of Anarchist missionaries. Round Jerez the labourers were restive because all the promises of the Federals had not helped them in their traditional struggle over piece-work: the local Republican deputy sided with the employers. In Montilla a mob seized the town and burned some of the houses of the rich. This primitive revolution was characterized by the boast of one of its heroes. 'I have killed the richest man in Montilla.'[2]

Elsewhere the revolution was the *coup* of a minority of political activists. It represented the disappointed hopes of local intransigent Federalists who saw power slipping from them.[3] These violent men succeeded in discrediting republicanism for a generation. It was the intransigent deputy for Castellón who gave conservatives their case. 'The canton is the logical consequence of a federal republic.' Long after republicanism had ceased to be federalist, the Cantonalist revolt was held to prove that republicanism must result in anarchy.

In most of the towns of Andalusia and the Levante the Cantonalist revolt remained a minor affair of a few days, favoured by the collapse of the army and the drafting of reliable units to fight the Carlists. It was thus the Carlist rebellion that created the conditions of Cantonalist successes.[4] In Seville, Cadiz, and Granada the small garrisons withdrew; the few unreliable troops under Ripoll kept Cordoba in order but could not be used elsewhere.[5] The worst blow of all was the declaration of the Murcian canton at Cartagena, including the crews of the four best ships in the navy.[6] Cartagena had ample

[1] Cf. R. Coloma, *La revolución internacionalista en Alcoy* (Alicante, 1959), 28. The workers were getting wages 'inconceivable formerly'. The paper workers had to be forced to strike by armed pickets.

[2] For the Montilla revolt see J. Díaz del Moral, *Agitaciones*, 73. Montilla had a strong Federalist group, many of whom became Internationalists.

[3] In Cadiz, Salvochea (later an anarchist leader) who declared the canton, had failed to be re-elected as mayor. The role of the International, except in Alcoy, was small. The Cantonalists and the Internationalists failed to co-operate effectively and blamed each other for failure. For Salvochea see C. A. Hennessy, ibid. 225.

[4] For the Carlist rebellion see below, section 5.

[5] There were only 140 Civil Guards and *Carabineros* in Seville. The ease with which Ripoll held Cordoba shows that only the smallest show of resolution would have defeated the rebels.

[6] The declaration took place on 12 July. The movement was set off *locally*

supplies of food, and any government would hesitate before it blew up its own navy. The Cantonalists could hold out for a long time.

The Cantonalist revolt was to drive the republic to the right. It meant the immediate ruin of Pi's policy of persuasion and legalism: if he sought powers from the Cortes to deal with the rebellion, he was accused of liberticide by the left: if he used persuasion, he was accused of complicity by the right—a charge he bitterly resented. On 18 July he resigned and Salmerón was elected his successor; Salmerón saw that central government control must be re-established and the revolution that was terrorizing 'the conservative classes without whom no institution can root' must be crushed.[1]

To save the dignity of the Cortes and the unity of Spain, Salmerón called in the generals. 'If you can get one soldier to fire his rifle at a Cantonalist', he told Pavía, sent to pacify Andalusia, 'you have saved order.' Pavía was a remarkable soldier: he disciplined Ripoll's demoralized force at Cordoba and, with 3,000 indifferent soldiers and sixteen guns manned by cavalry officers, captured Seville after two days' fighting.[2] This broke the back of the Cantonalist movement: Cadiz and Granada gave in easily and on 7 August López Domínguez entered Valencia. The Cantonalist revolt had been crushed in a fortnight; it had failed through the lack of concerted effort and the intense localism inherent in Federalist attitudes, because the government managed to hold on to Catalonia, and because the extreme Federalists found little support outside their own enthusiasts.[3]

Only two cities held out: Malaga and Cartagena. Malaga was a special case; no government official or officer had been able to give orders in the city since February. It was the appanage of Solier and his *Voluntarios*, an acute case of localism

without instructions from the Central Committee. The representative of this committee, Roque Barcia and Contreras, took over after the movement was under way.

[1] Speech of 30 Aug.

[2] M. Pavía y Rodríguez, *La pacificación de Andalucía* (1878), gives an account of Pavía's conquest of his own army as well as of the Cantonalists.

[3] The most striking effects of localism were seen in the resistance of smaller towns to the attempts of Cartagena and Seville to 'absorb' the surrounding municipalities. Cartagena bombarded Almería when it refused to contribute funds to the Murcian canton.

rather than an element in a general revolution. In spite of Pava's pleas and resignations, the government dare not act until Solier had discredited himself since he was 'protected' by a deputy whose support was necessary to the ministry. The canton of Murcia at Cartagena was genuinely Cantonalist. Salmerón declared the rebel navy pirates and strove to concentrate a respectable besieging force. By December the town had only poor flour, though plentiful supplies of tunny and sardines, and the Cantonalist navy, after making piratical raids on the Levant, had vanished—two captured by a German captain, one sunk by bad seamanship, and one burnt. The rebels' only hope was the defeat of the forces of 'order' and the triumph of their extremist allies in the Cortes: when this failed on 3 January they had no hopes left.

Salmerón's treatment of the Cantonalists as criminals brought on his head the attacks of the left in the Cortes: like Pi, he resigned (6 September 1873). Castelar, his successor, was able to move more comfortably to the right and to renounce his Federal past with greater conviction. He now saw himself as a Lincoln to whom inconsistency was a political virtue. The Federal constitution had been 'burned at Cartagena'. If the Republicans were to survive they must become 'a party of government' that could win over the Radicals—he considered their rejection the cardinal error of the Republican politicians. He could talk of preserving 'national unity, that marvellous work of many centuries'. With such phrases and with more resolution than Salmerón, Castelar set out to regain the support of 'the conservative classes'. To carry out his governmentalization of republicanism, Castelar assumed a dictatorship. From 20 September to 2 January he ruled by decree, with the constitutional guarantees suspended. His most signal success was his recapture of the confidence of the army: the death penalty was restored; the artillery officers, suspended since the Hidalgo affair, were reinstated; a new batch of generals—politically suspect but commanding the confidence of an increasingly conservative officer corps—were sent to invigorate the war against Carlists and Cantonalists; the *Voluntarios* were disbanded. When the municipality of Madrid protested, it was dissolved in the old Sagastan manner. The extremists' papers were fined out of existence. The Republic looked conservative and the government got better terms from bankers than any government since 1868. Radicals returned from exile and professed Republican loyalty. On 4 December General Pavía, Captain General of Madrid, told Castelar, 'I will follow you anywhere'.[1]

The conduct which made Castelar the hope of conservatism condemned him in the eyes of left Republicans. Salmerón accused Castelar of 'abdication of principle'.[2] What Salmerón could not stomach was Castelar's attempt to create a republic which other than Republicans could enjoy: this was to go 'outside the Republican orbit'. As always political difference was envenomed by personal dislike and all attempts to patch up relations failed. As one of the mediators remarked, it was the destiny of the Spanish left to see its forces wasted on doctrinal obstinacy and the personal feuds of its leaders—Olózaga against Espartero, Ruiz Zorrilla against Sagasta, and now Castelar against Salmerón. During the whole of the First Republic's brief life, Republican politicians proved incapable of sinking their differences, personal and ideological, in order to form a strong Republican government.

The drift of Salmerón's centre party towards the left made Castelar's defeat in the Cortes and a return to a pure Federalist ministry a certainty. General Pavía, Captain General of Madrid, was determined to prevent a return to anarchy that might completely destroy the army and especially his own corps, the artillery. He would support Castelar loyally, but when Castelar made it plain that he would not be party to a pronunciamiento against a parliamentary majority, Pavía sounded Madrid politicians on the prospect of a 'national government'. Single-handed he laid his plans, and on hearing of Castelar's parliamentary defeat of 3 January, he decided that it was his officers' duty 'as soldiers and citizens to save society and the country' from a Federalist ministry. A few shots in the air ended the

[1] A. Houghton, *La Restauration des Bourbons en Espagne* (Paris, 1890), 86.

[2] Villarasa and Gatell, *Revolución*, ii. 832. To Salmerón Castelar's 'abdication of principle' (i.e. the Republican doctrine of separation of Church and state) was shown by the appointment of two bishops. Castelar believed that no government could survive the declared hostility of Spanish catholics and that it was better for the Spanish state to appoint than to allow its powers to lapse. The first point was sensible and only Salmerón's doctrinaire mind could reject it: the second looked suspicious when the separation of church and state was under debate in the Cortes.

Constituent Cortes of the Republic and the destiny of Spain fell into the hands of an artillery general. He called on all parties (except Federalists and Carlists) to form a national government 'in the name of the salvation of the army, of liberty and of the *patria*'. Though Pavía was no ordinary reactionary general, his *coup* presaged a return to the classic theory of military liberalism that, in times of social dissolution and perverted government, the army represented the national will. It was with this claim that General Franco killed another Spanish republic.

5. *The Carlist War and the Bourbon Restoration, 1873–1874*

Once the Alfonsists and Republicans of order refused to co-operate in Pavía's national government, power reverted to the only group willing to govern: the Radicals and Constitutionalists driven out of politics by the Federalist Republic. Under Serrano's presidency the unitary Republic took as its theme liberal conciliation. Increasingly conservative, this ultimate residue of the September coalition was in no danger from the Republicans condemned by their 'immense lack of foresight' on 3 January. The enemies to be feared were Carlism and Alfonsism—the movement to restore the constitutional monarchy with Isabella's son as king.

The difficulties of stabilizing the revolution gave Carlism its greatest chance since Vergara, and the greatest testimony to its inherent weakness was its failure to impose itself when Spain was an almost defenceless republic. To the conservative classes and to the mass of Catholics, Carlism remained a provincial rising committed to a hopeless civil war; the conservative classes and, most important of all, the higher officers sought their salvation in Alfonsism. Moreover Carlism was divided. Against an illegitimate system which, nevertheless, allowed political activity to its opponents, Carlists split, as did Republicans, into activists and legalists. The intransigents of Carlism counselled rising at all times and at all costs. The legalists prophesied that the September régime would collapse into anarchy of its own accord; then the legitimate throne would appeal 'even to the shop-keepers of Madrid'. Carlism would be voted to power as the last reserve of an ordered society.[1]

[1] Only in this sense could it be held that most Spaniards were Carlists at heart

The strategy of legalism appealed strongly to those new converts to whom Carlism appeared as the best hope for defeated clerical conservatism but who had no direct experience of the militant traditions of the old party. They supported Nocedal's plan for a party which would be swept to victory by the disintegration of the Revolution and its drift to the left—both of which were prophesied repeatedly in the abundant Carlist propaganda of the time. Their slogan was 'No Civil War'. Now that the government of Spain had deserted the Catholic faith, support would come of itself without any concessions to those who wished to liberalize the Carlist creed. In the elections of 1869 and 1871 the legalists could prove their point against those who backed a series of petty risings. In the first Cortes of Amadeo's reign it appeared as if a coalition of Republicans and Carlists might destroy the monarchy in its own parliament;[1] but in 1872, when the government used 'force' against Carlist candidates, the militants' arguments were irresistible. With the prospect of a large parliamentary party denied him, Nocedal was forced to consent to a military rising.

The militants were strongly represented among the survivors of the Carlist war in the north, training with sticks because they had no rifles, and in the entourage of the Pretender, the duke of Madrid, young and eager for action.[2] Cabrera, still the greatest name in militant Carlism, without whose support money could not be raised, resisted his monarch's impetuosity; an old man, long accustomed to a comfortable exile in England, he had lost faith in the simple creed of Carlism. He did not relish a guerrilla campaign against the regular army, nor could he bring himself to plunge Spain into a hopeless civil war.

and only thus, if at all, can one accept Butler Clarke's strange verdict, 'Most thinking Spaniards are Carlists in certain moods, at certain ages . . . its spirit disarms those who are sent against it. The Carlists had a definite cause, an object, and a plain way to reach it' (*Spain*, 370). No doubt many Spaniards admire the obstinacy of Carlism—but this is an aesthetic rather than a political reaction.

[1] See above, p. 320. Carlists and Republicans could combine in defence of those individual liberties which the government denied to its overt enemies. Thus Sagasta, as Minister of the Interior, was attacked for his failure to defend 'peaceful' demonstrations of loyalty to the pope.

[2] Montemolin, the Carlist pretender who had appeared at San Cárlos de la Rápita, died in 1861; his brother, Don Juan, was suspected of liberalism and the Carlist claim was therefore represented by his son, Don Cárlos María, who called himself the duke of Madrid.

Detesting the pretender's courtiers, he resigned.[1] In April 1872 Don Carlos declared for armed invasion, against the counsel of the most responsible local leader. The invasion was a complete fiasco and Don Carlos himself narrowly avoided capture at Oroquieta (May 1872). The polemics of defeat exhibited the 'personalism' which was to sap the strength of Carlism; it was only kept alive as a fighting creed by the raids of the undisciplined bands of Catalonia and Aragon.[2]

The Republic of 1873 gave Carlism its greatest opportunities. Whole units of the army were disaffected and in these conditions the Carlist armies scored their greatest successes: the battles of Eraul and Monte Jurra, the most splendid pitched battles ever won by Carlist forces, and the capture of Estella. One by one the small towns of the Basque Provinces and Navarre fell to the Carlists but, as in the Seven Years War, the large towns remained liberal islands in a Carlist countryside.

By 1874 Carlism was at its most powerful in terms of occupied territory. There was an organized Carlist state in the north with its own administration, postal system, electric telegraph, and newspapers. The capture of Eibar had given it a small arms factory and its agents abroad were buying surplus French arms and greatcoats to equip an army of 20,000 men, paid by levies on the countryside, customs duties, and payments by the railway companies whose lines went through Carlist territory.

Nevertheless Carlism in the 1870's still had the strength and shortcomings of the old inexpansible Carlism of the first Carlist war: an army of the faith, dedicated to the Virgin and with every battalion telling its rosary at sunset. Yet in spite of the apparent simplicity of this unifying creed, the movement was weakened by localism; it was confined to its historic strongholds in the north and lacked the artillery and cavalry needed to carry the war outside the hills. Even in the north the provincial regiments deserted outside their own borders.[3] In Catalonia,

[1] For the quarrels of Cabrera and Don Carlos, see I. A. Bermejo, *Revolución y la interinidad*, i. 595–610, and the correspondence in A. Pirala, *Historia contemporánea*, iii. 487–92.

[2] See the correspondence of Don Carlos with Rada after he had been dismissed for a failure he had prophesied. Villarasa and Gatell, *Revolución*, ii. 538–42. This shows that there were divisions amongst the militant Carlists as well as between militants and moderates.

[3] F. Hernando, *La campaña carlista 1872–1876* (Paris, 1877), 116–18.

Aragon, and Valencia the jealousies of local leaders prevented any concerted action: commanders made their names by individual raids and did not believe in a 'system'. Old-type leaders—Savalls with his medals and fancy clothes, Cucala an illiterate peasant—gained some striking local successes, but Eastern Carlism never looked like a national movement. Living on the country, holding third-rate towns to ransom, the more territory they occupied, the less popular they became; an erosion of local support kept it at the level of political brigandage.

Thus the chances of victory lay in the Basque Provinces and here the army remained anti-Carlist: once discipline was restored, as it was by the end of 1873, defeat was certain. It was an amateur war (the government troops could have occupied the Carlist lines around Bilbao any night, since the Carlists slept in villages) and fought by ill-equipped armies, without hatred; in the initial stages the troops fraternized between actions. Once again the compulsive attraction was Bilbao, and only Bilbao could make the Carlists fight as a unified force. In February 1874 a costly frontal attack on the Carlist lines failed, but in May the besieging Carlists retreated in face of General Manuel Concha's outflanking movement (May 1874). The culminating point of the Carlist advance was the defeat of Concha's plan to capture Estella; at the battle of Abárzuza, Concha was himself killed in an attempt to save the day. The turning-point was the Carlist failure to take Irun (November 1874).[1] Serrano, whose jealousy of other generals had been one of the minor irritants of the war, could now hope for the crowning victory that would establish his political position; but rain and snow stopped operations. Before they could be resumed, the Bourbon monarchy had been restored.

The greatest statesman of the Restoration, Cánovas del Castillo, has impressed on history his own conviction that the restoration of Alfonso was the work of organized civilian monarchism. In defeat and exile, Cánovas insisted that a restoration could only be successful if imposed by a great movement of opinion in favour of Alfonso XII, at the time a cadet at Sandhurst who would reach his majority (sixteen years of age) in November 1873. Alfonso, unlike his mother, could

[1] Irun was the main customs house on the frontier; its capture would have given the Carlists a steady income.

rally wide conservative support, from the faithful Moderates to repentant September conspirators now ready to work their passage as monarchist politicians. Cánovas sensed this growth of conservative support for the Alfonsine solution, especially in Catalonia where monarchist propaganda was carried on openly and backed by the rich. His achievement was less the organization of this opinion into an irresistible force than the elimination of those alternative monarchist solutions which would have been disastrous. It took him three years to convince Isabella that her hopes of restoration by military rebellion, favoured by the courtiers, by a 'fusion' with Montpensier or by intrigues with Serrano, were all alike doomed to failure.[1] By August 1873 Cánovas was the undisputed chief of Alfonsism: this cause he hoped to separate from what he called the 'miserable interests of militarism'.

Yet it was the 'gesture' of the young brigadier Martínez Campos at Sagunto (29 December 1874) and the 'negative pronunciamiento' of the northern army against Serrano which brought Alfonso XII to his throne. Alfonsism had spread rapidly amongst the younger officers. The more active monarchist conspirators among them (Martínez Campos was one of these) believed that a restoration was an immediate military possibility which postponement would weaken; rejecting Cánovas's 'wait and see' strategy, they warned the king of intellectuals who lacked faith and resolution. Others, like Concha, believed victory in the north must precede a restoration, which was to be forced on the government by pressure of a victorious officer corps rather than secured by rebellion against it. The death of Concha at Abárzuza, therefore, by disconcerting the plans of the senior generals, increased activist pressure. In December, Martínez Campos expressed his disbelief in the strategy of Cánovas by requesting the king's permission to act independently; before this permission could be granted and on the ground that the compromised colonels would be promoted out of the reach of sedition he declared, with his brigade, for Alfonso XII.[2] Thus the cry which was to

[1] These difficulties are described at length in the Marqués de Lema's *De la revolución á la restauración*.

[2] Letter of Martínez Campos to Alfonso of 21 Dec. 1874 (M. Izquierdo Hernández, *Historia clínica de la restauración*, 1946). Alfonso did not have time to reply to this letter before the Army of the Centre pronounced.

initiate the Restoration was the act of an impatient young commander.

It was successful because other commanders would not act against a brother officer whose political convictions they shared. In the north, Serrano was popular with his Alfonsist officers; embarrassed, they tried to spare his feelings, but it was clear they would not fight against the rebel Army of the Centre. Without reinforcements from the north, the government was powerless in Madrid, where Primo de Rivera, as Captain General, misled the government till the last moment about the loyalty of the garrison. At 5 a.m. on 30 December he woke the war minister to inform him the movement could not be resisted. Like all generals in similar situations, he argued that his first duty was to maintain order and that he must give in to military sedition when it was on the point of replacing the legal government. Sagasta rejected the appeal to street demagogy, and the government was handed over to Cánovas.

It was at this point that Cánovas's firm hold on the monarchist movement became a decisive factor. Although the army had restored the king, the government that issued from the pronunciamiento and which he dominated was determined to appear as a civilian concern. Thus he could argue 'that the Restoration came about as I had willed it: it came about when a large body of public opinion . . . was convinced of the absolute necessity of the proclamation of the King'. In forty-eight hours, two battalions, without firing a shot, could overthrow a rump which represented the September Revolution only because 'opinion' had been prepared. Thus Cánovas hid from himself the essential mechanism of revolution: either positively or negatively, the existence of any régime in Spain was a function of the loyalty of the army.

6. *The Legacy of the Revolution*

The ease with which a monarchist restoration was accomplished is, in some ways, surprising. Though it was amongst the Madrid aristocracy and the *haute bourgeoisie* of Barcelona that Alfonsism found its most active supporters and its financial and journalistic strength, the privileged classes no longer feared for social peace. By 1874 the social anarchy of 1873 was sternly controlled: Martínez Campos suppressed the revolutionary workers in Barcelona and the Cantonalist revolt was snuffed out leaving the urban poor with neither interest in defending the last remote representatives of the September Revolution nor strength to mount a new outburst. Perhaps more than any other factor it was the hope that Alfonso would end the Carlist war which created acceptance of change; if rain and snow had not impeded Serrano, a crowning victory in the north might have given his government confidence and energy. Counter-revolutions, like revolutions, depend for success on the weaknesses of legal governments rather than on their own strength.

The failure of all the governments that issued from the Revolution of 1868 had been a political failure; they could provide no guarantees for order and stability. It was a collapse of the forces of public order and not a collapse in economic prosperity which embarrassed government. One of the conquests of the revolution was free trade, since the strong free-trade element in Madrid had been engaged in the opposition to Isabella's conservative ministries. Figuerola's budget of 1869 abolished import prohibitions and its fifth base contemplated a further reduction of those protective duties which had been retained. Freer trade, there can be little doubt, helped to stimulate prosperity held back by 'absurd' regulations; Figuerola could proudly point to rising trade and production figures in order to refute the violent organized protests of the Catalan cotton interests.[1] The Catalan cork industry likewise protested against the reduction of export duties on raw cork. Foreign industry, equipped with modern machines and supplied with cheap Spanish cork, would destroy the livelihood of 6,000 artisans. Figuerola maintained machines were a 'divine blessing'. Liberal mining laws and currency reform encouraged foreign investment.[2] The first injection of British capital in iron and copper was the result. Agricultural exports boomed—and on these, Figuerola insisted, depended the solvency of Spain. Food prices were low after 1868. It is therefore hard to

[1] It is interesting that Suñer, the Republican deputy for Ampurdán, supported the protectionists, and took the 'reactionary' side in the polemic about machines. The whole issue shows how a highly protected industry had been able to cling to archaic methods of production (R. Medir Jofra, *Gremio corchero*, 91–93).

[2] Cf. J. Sardá, *Fluctuaciones*, 163.

believe that the bank and currency crisis of 1873 and a decline in mining exports created a favourable economic climate for the Cantonalist movement. No dramatic worsening of conditions gave the extremists strength; there was always enough urban misery to feed a rising. In so far as economic causes contributed to the Restoration, they are to be found in the hatred of the Catalan bourgeoisie for liberal free trade aided, perhaps, by the falling off of trade which was to become apparent in 1874, and which reflected a world depression. If the army had been usable in 1873 and loyal to Serrano in 1874, these economic difficulties would have been of little or no account.

The immediate political failure of the Revolution of 1868 obscures its fundamental importance in the history of the nineteenth century. The assumptions of a catholic monarchy, created and sustained by conservative liberalism, had been challenged by the assumptions of democracy and free thought. Later the liberal prime minister, Romanones, was to claim that the Revolution had transfigured Spanish society and that these changes could 'never, never' be reversed. By this he did not mean that the class balance of society had been shifted—a claim that would have been patently false—but that, in a significant section of the political nation, the nature of men's claims upon the state had been in some way modernized. As in every nineteenth-century Spanish revolution, the extent of this modernization was evident in the place of the Church in the constitution.

Thus it was in the realm of religion that the Revolution had its profoundest reverberations. Carlism apart, all the popular propaganda of royalism presented the Restoration as a return to a religion that had been systematically persecuted. Royalist historians wrote of convent-burning, the campaign against bells, the celebration of civil marriages, and the imprisonment of priests.[1] In the same way, to Republicans like Garrido, the September Revolution was a religious revolution, a freeing of the human spirit. It is the debate on the religious clauses of the constitution of 1869 which reveals, once more, those divisions in Spanish society which were to be disastrous to right and left alike.

[1] Cf. M. Menéndez y Pelayo, *Heterodoxos* (in *O.C.*, 1932), vii. 426 ff. Villarasa and Gatell's history of the revolution, written in 1874, catalogues the religious outrages of the revolution.

However much the governments of the Revolution of 1868 might in practice behave as heirs of the regalist tradition, they were committed, by the whole political philosophy of the revolution, to the freedom of religion embodied in the constitution of 1869. Though none of the arguments of the debates of 1869 were novel, they became classic statements—anthologized by Catholic and non-Catholic alike. Some like Pi and Castelar, denied dogmatic religion, and one Republican deputy, Sũner, denied God himself: 'the dead ideas are faith, heaven, God: the new science, the earth, man'. It was not surprising that the Church rejected such claims and erected strange counter-claims—for instance that the relatively obscure Thomist, Melchor Cano, was the greatest intellect of all time.

Most significant was the refusal of the Church to recognize at any point the claims of the 'neutral' state: thus the constitution of 1869, which still acknowledged Catholicism as the state religion but tolerated other religions, 'disinherited Catholicism'.[1] The error of the defenders of the Church was their persistent blindness to the advantages of freedom when the state was no longer willing to use its powers to maintain Catholic unity; with freedom, a Minister of Justice replied to Republican demands for separation of Church and state, Spain would be in the hands of the Jesuits within ten years. In vain Catholics appealed to the state to protect unity of belief and rejected the advantages of liberty for themselves because they were determined to circumscribe that liberty for others. Catholics could no longer hope to punish heresy as a civil crime, but they would not allow heresy a civil status. To allow freedom of conscience, a bishop argued, was to give to error the rights and privileges of truth. Thus revolution appeared once more as the persecutor of the faith. In the early days the Juntas destroyed convents to make way for new streets and renewed anti-clerical traditions of the Spanish left; governments suppressed Catholic organizations and Radicals revived the regalism of the liberal left.[2] Once more the defence of the Church appeared as the refuge of the right. Outraged Catholic sentiment had weakened loyalty

[1] Address of Barcelona clergy to Serrano (quoted Villarasa and Gatell, *Revolución*, i. 82–831). Many of the clergy refused to swear to the constitution.

[2] e.g. the reduction of the stipends of the clergy by a half, civil marriage, the removal of state education from Catholic influence. All these measures were repeated by the Republic of 1931, with similar consequences.

to Amadeo, member of an impious dynasty, and was the surest foundation of a movement for the restoration of the Bourbons.

For the Krausist professors, whose dismissal had connected political revolution and academic freedom, the experience of 1868–75 was a profound disillusionment. Fernando de Castro became Rector of the University of Madrid and installed a régime of complete liberty; by 1870 the students were using this freedom to neglect their classes and to riot against professors who supported Amadeo. In a small arena, this was the paradox of freedom which destroyed the principles of 1868 in practice. The individual rights enshrined in the constitution of 1869 could not be tolerated when they were turned against a government which regarded itself as the true heir of the Revolution. Hence Sagasta's suspension of the constitutional guarantees in 1869, his electoral management in 1872; hence Castelar's dictatorship and the press censorship of 1874—all of which offended the 'principles of September' by a reassertion of the authority of government. The disappointments of the Revolution made Giner, the disciple of Sanz del Río, a sceptic in politics. His verdict on the Revolution, written in 1870, was damning.

> It affirmed principles in legislation and violated them in practice; it proclaimed liberty and exercised tyranny . . . it professed to abominate the ancient iniquities and nourished itself on them alone. And as must happen with such conduct, it flung into insurrection all those parties which got no share of the booty; it disclaimed the proletarians and terrorized the rich; it humiliated rationalists and outraged the Church; it won the antipathy of liberals and conservatives alike, of the elite and of the vulgar.

Yet the principles of the Revolution, even if outraged by practice, were the principles of a liberal Spain. Until 1923, the 'liberal conquests' were never denied the status of public law with success—even if the laws which embodied them were suspended or circumvented, even when they appeared as the rhetoric of an oligarchy.

IX

THE RESTORATION AND THE DISASTER 1874–1898

THE Restoration monarchy was the most stable political structure erected by nineteenth-century Spanish liberalism, but its stability was based on a diminishing asset—the *ansia del vivir*, that desire for a peaceful life after anarchy which became, once more in 1939, a powerful force in Spanish politics. La Cierva, a future Minister of the Interior, in his old age, remembered the troops on the way to Cartagena, the Carlists murdering the local station-master, the flights in carts and carriages.[1] As long as the moral atmosphere was dominated by the fear of a relapse into political chaos and social revolution, the institutions of constitutional monarchy remained inviolable for all but Republicans and Carlists. These institutions were the expression of the political philosophy of one man, Cánovas del Castillo, and their aim was to comprehend within the monarchy those forces which sought to destroy it from without: 'to use whatever is usable in the movement which drove out Queen Isabella'. The Restoration would have neither conquerors nor conquered: it would be the most merciful and tolerant restoration in history. Cánovas, conscious perhaps of the threats of the past rather than the hopes of the future, over-estimated the political importance of the physical survival of a consumptive king as the centre of his system: the queen was kept from her husband's death-bed by enforced attendance at a theatre in order to discredit rumours of his illness. He believed that Alfonso's death would threaten his whole political achievement, a fear that the crisis of 1885 proved groundless. His system was no longer threatened by the historic enemies of the constitutional monarchy—Carlism and Republicanism—and it was only after defeat in Cuba in 1898 that its modern enemies—the proletarian parties and Catalanism—were to appear formidable.

[1] J. de La Cierva, *Notas de mi vida* (1955), 10.

1. *Cánovas and the Stabilization of Politics*

Like so many of the political oligarchs, Cánovas was a self-made provincial, a schoolmaster from Malaga who came to Madrid with nothing but a letter of recommendation to the banker Salamanca, a fellow townsman. Physically tough and a greater eater, he slept only six hours a night. His eminence was that of a hard worker in a lazy society. Unprepossessing in appearance—with his squint, nervous tic, and appalling clothes, he looked like 'a subaltern on half-pay'—he possessed intellectual powers that were an essential part of his political capital.[1] A serious historian in his own right (his work on Philip IV was finished in 1889), he was closely associated with the Ateneo and its activities as a conservative rallying-point during the revolution and he opened its new building in 1883 with a three-hour speech. In and out of office he influenced elections to the Royal Academy and he used this patronage and his friendships with men like Martos and Castelar to monarchize the intellectuals. As a speaker he was irresistible and his parliamentary prestige unchallenged. His opponents, half in admiration, called him 'the Monster'.

While he believed that 'Spain was going through the most miserable period of her long history', leaving him the mission of staving off total collapse, his political pessimism (which extended to the Latin race in general) was relieved by his sense of the greatness of the Spanish past. In the tumults of revolution, he retired to the archives at Simancas. His deepest political beliefs were akin to those of Burke: a distrust of abstract thinking in politics evident in his favourite word *lo hacedero*, which we may translate with Burke's 'expedient'. His aim was a monarchical constitution which should embrace 'all Spaniards without any distinction whatsoever', and in which sterile dogmatic conflict on the nature of the régime would be replaced by the peaceful coexistence of parties.[2]

[1] See, for his relations with intellectuals, A. M. Fabié, *Cánovas del Castillo* (Barcelona, 1928), 187, 200, 203, 228. His marriage in 1887, by cutting him off from his old circles and intellectual contacts, weakened his later career.

[2] *D.S.C.*, 27 Mar. 1876. Cánovas, it must be remembered, had served his political apprenticeship in the Liberal Union.

The constitutional monarchy was more than the political contrivance that divided Spain least; the king *and* the Cortes were 'the internal constitution of Spain' of the Moderates, a product of divine providence and history.[1] The sovereignty of history conditioned the sovereignty of the people by placing the monarchy itself outside political debate. What his political theory did not and could not embrace was any solution of conflicts between the twin sovereignties. He believed it was indecent to contemplate conflict between the king and the law, quoting Blackstone to prove his point: yet it was this conflict which was to destroy the constitution.

The constitution of 1876 was drawn up by a committee composed of all shades of monarchical opinion and it was to rule Spain until Primo de Rivera overthrew it in September 1923. Its centre was in Article 18: 'The legislative power lies in the Cortes with the king.' Its political foundation was the Moderate constitution of 1845; but its implications as they were developed in practice—and it was the practices of constitutionalism which were all important to Cánovas—were more in accord with the principles of '69 than those of '45. The king appointed ministers but these were responsible to the Cortes; he had a veto but never used it. He was made to read Bagehot and Erskine May and see himself as a constitutional king, obeying his prime minister as the representative of the power of the Cortes. Cánovas was harsher to his king than any other nineteenth-century statesman. Alfonso was forced to accept a minister who had driven the royal mistress from Madrid, and Cánovas was alleged to surround the Pardo Palace with troops to report the king's movements. Cánovas's constitution was a hybrid of the political theory of the mid-century Moderates and the practices of English parliamentarianism. He believed that with a constitution that ensured parliamentary control he could win back the liberals of the September Revolution into the political life of the monarchy and in this endeavour he counted on the strong support of Alfonso XII, determined to avoid the errors of 'exclusiveness' which had sent his mother on her travels.

[1] For the political ideas of Cánovas see L. Díez del Corral, *Liberalismo*, 529 ff.

Neither these ideas of comprehension nor the proposed constitution pleased old-fashioned conservatives. To Mañé, the doyen of conservative journalism in Barcelona, who advised Cánovas that the first act of the king should be the re-establishment of the conservative constitution of 1845, he replied: 'That means a restoration *a lo Ferdnando VII*. Can you possibly believe in that?'[1] The king could not act unilaterally: the constitution gave legislative power to the king *and* Cortes, and valid constitutional change could only be made by both. Thus, though Cánovas disliked the universal suffrage of 1869 and his political principles denied validity to the sovereign will of the people, he did not believe that the legislation of 1869, which had implanted universal suffrage, could be abrogated by royal decree. This seeming contradiction he resolved by resignation, allowing Jovellar to summon a Cortes based on universal suffrage in order to sanction a constitution which would abolish it. To die-hard conservatives this was to give a spurious validity to the revolutionary conquests of 1869. Flexibility, expediency, were the core of the Cánovite system. Once the parliamentary monarchy was accepted, its organic laws could be modified; however, as conservatives saw with alarm, modification could only be in a liberal direction.

Cánovas had already experienced the political disadvantages of the intolerance of old-fashioned Moderates. In February 1875 his minister Orovio had decided to end, by government supervision of textbooks and lecture courses, the freedom of the university which the right regarded as an encouragement to revolution; he grounded his action on the duty of the state to supervise morals and sound doctrine and on the democratic right of Catholic fathers to the education for their sons that corresponded with their own convictions.[2] By its attack on one of the most precious of the liberal conquests (press attacks on the monarchy were already prohibited) the decree caused the resignation of the luminaries of the Central University, the very class that Cánovas wished to reconcile with the constitution.

[1] J. Carrera Pujal, *Cataluña*, vi. 9.

[2] See V. Cacho Viu, *Institución de Libre Enseñanza*, 283 ff. 'When the majority . . . of Spaniards are Catholics and the state is Catholic . . . the Government cannot consent that a dogma which is the social truth (*la verdad social*) of our country should be attacked by professors supported by the state.'

This sudden revival of the conflict between faith and science embarrassed him and he worked for a compromise between the government and the 'martyr' professors without success.[1] His protection of the Ateneo as a stronghold of liberal thought, safe in its customary privileges from police action, showed his determination that the Restoration should not be associated with the suppression of free thought. Nevertheless he had to face another conflict with die-hard Catholic conservativism over the religious settlement of the constitution (Article 11).

Cánovas saw that the religious unity, which conservatives refused to sacrifice, would be totally unacceptable to those whose ideal was the religious freedom won in 1869. When the bishop of Avila offered to condemn Carlism in return for the imposition of religious unity, Cánovas's objections were so strong that he refused to sit at the same luncheon table as the bishop. Cánovas was a Catholic who believed that an irreligious society must fall victim to the omnipotent state, just as he believed that fashionable positivism meant the end, not merely of philosophy, but of freedom.[2] But Catholic unity, if desirable, was no longer expedient, for it was conceivable only in a society where the Inquisition was acceptable and efficacious.[3]

The debate in the Cortes on the religious clauses of the constitution of 1875 became a review of the place of religion in Spanish history. To conservatives, religious unity was synonymous with Spanish greatness; it was not her shame but her glory that she had remained isolated and immune from progressive but 'dissolvent' ideas from Luther to Voltaire. Tolerance was the demand of revolutionaries, who wanted to destroy the church in the name of progress and in the interests of a minute sect—the Protestants, consistently favoured by English and American money.[4] To Castelar, the denial of freedom of

[1] For the protests see A. Jiménez, *Ocaso y restauración* (Mexico, 1948), 143, 152. For Cánovas's attempts at compromise see V. Cacho Viu, op. cit. 292, 300.

[2] 'Individual rights are impossible in a nation without religious beliefs . . . for, the moment each man does not possess a conscience which protects the rights of others, that protection must inevitably be entrusted to the state.' *D.S.C.*, 3 Nov. 1871.

[3] Cánovas was sensitive to European pressure, especially that exercised from the German and British embassies in favour of the Protestants' rights. 'Are we to adopt this criterion . . . of opposing ourselves to the concert of European nations?'

[4] For a summary of the Catholic position see J. M. Antequera, *La unidad católica* (1875), esp. 30–60.

thought was the root cause of decline, making Spain 'an immense corpse in the laboratory of history teaching the nations the perils of handing over the constitution to an intolerant church.' Cánovas, though it cost him the support of the intransigent Moderates, forced through the recognition of catholicism as the religion of state together with tolerance of the private practice of all other faiths—in spite of the explicit condemnation of even this limited toleration by the pope and the archbishop of Toledo.[1] This *modus vivendi* was the maximum concession that Cánovas could force on his own majority.

Thus Article 11 of the constitution, though it represented a bad falling off from the ideals of 1869, produced the nearest approach to a tolerant society which Spain had known under a conservative government. The interpretation of Article 11 depended on the government and local authorities: hence Protestants suffered molestation over burial and the civil marriage of minors, and arrests for failure to take off their hats when the sacrament passed. Nevertheless, atheists and ultramontanes were professors, the Institute of Free Education, always considered a nest of heretics, was able to carry on the educational work of the Krausists. The Reformed Church, which had grown up in Seville after 1868, continued its Sunday schools and services, holding its first synod in 1880.[2] All that happened after 1875 was the suppression of its magazines and the prohibition of advertised services. Almost the last act of Cánovas was to resist the pressure of the Nuncio and the Catholic aristocracy against the building of a Protestant school in Madrid. From the Protestant community he earned a tribute granted to few Spanish conservative statesmen: 'He did justice.'[3]

[1] Cf. J. D. Hughes, *Religious Freedom in Spain* (London, 1955). Cánovas maintained a strict, mid-century, regalist position. Philip II, he pointed out, would have exiled the archbishop of Toledo for printing the papal condemnation.

[2] For curious information on this point see H. E. Noyes, *Church Reform in Spain and Portugal* (London, 1897).

[3] Cf. 'The Quest of Religious toleration in Spain in the nineteenth century', *Journal of Ecclesiastical History* (London, 1957), viii. 211 ff. In 1884 the Spanish representative of the British and Foreign Bible Society reported that 'the word of God had been scattered so widely over the land that it seemed impossible to him that it would ever again be uprooted'. Nevertheless, as Castelar once said, Spaniards found Protestantism 'too frigid' and they preferred either atheism or Krausist derivatives to Protestantism. In 1933 there were only 21,900 Protestants in the country.

Cánovas, and with him the king, resisted attempts to turn his own Liberal–Conservative party into a bleak authoritarian concern. The Isabelline die-hards and their queen had to be kept out of the way: Isabella's return 'would cause the irrevocable ruin of the king and the country' by driving out last-minute recruits like the former Septembrist revolutionary Romero Robledo. On the right Cánovas's recruitment drive was intended to capture more important forces than old-fashioned conservatism: it was his wooing of the 'honest Carlist masses' and their allies in the church which was to put the greatest strain on the liberal strand of Canovite conservatism.

Carlism, as a military threat, was ended by the victories, on the northern front, of a disciplined and well-supplied army which outnumbered the Carlists by four to one. The restored monarchy, by ending the Carlist war in February 1876 and the Cuban war a year later, avoided the drain of resources and prestige which had weakened, in turn, all the governments of the September Revolution. But Carlists remained unassimilated. Fortunately for liberal constitutionalism, they paralysed themselves by internal disputes and 'personalism'. When his father died, Ramón Nocedal expected the leadership of the movement but this Charles VII, as the duke of Madrid was called by his followers, refused him. Nocedal set up his own party of 'Integralists', accusing the Pretender of dangerous liberal deviations, and his paper *El Siglo Futuro* became the best-known organ of the extreme right. Nevertheless, Integralism was an impossible creed: by dropping the second person of the Carlist trinity, 'God, king, and country', it cut itself from the emotional roots of the party—loyalty to the true king. It was driven to the curious and possibly heretical step of proclaiming the Kingship of Christ.

Orthodox Carlism, under the leadership of the marqués de Cerralbo, an amateur student of pre-history and one of the few grandees who resisted the temptations of the court of Alfonso XII, organized itself in juntas of which there were over two thousand in the nineties.[1] In a young Galician orator,

[1] The programme of the nineties is best set out in the *Biblioteca popular carlista*, published in Barcelona. It was protectionist and regionalist—hence its strength in Catalonia—and hoped to gain working-class support by a revival of the guild system. But beneath this lay the old creed of 1833: a king who 'worked' and whose

Vázquez de Mella, Carlism found an impressive leader; a great talker, in his conversations and speeches the movement experienced the doctrinal overhaul it badly needed, turning from a bald dynastic fanaticism, which saw no distinction between Alfonso and revolutionary Republicans, to a doctrine of regional revival under a patriarchal, Catholic monarchy. The traditional monarchy was the *only* institution which could provide a home for regional aspirations and convert them into a regenerative force; outside it regionalism would degenerate into a number of separatist, sterile nationalisms which would destroy the monarchy's historic achievement—the unity of Spain.[1]

In their criticisms of the established order the Carlists became the first regenerationists: regeneration would come from a collapse of 'the system'.[2] They were ready, by arrangements with the extreme left, to precipitate this collapse. Nevertheless, in spite of an impressive paper organization, which sprang to life to commiserate or congratulate the family occasions of the true dynasty, Carlism was ineffective as a revolutionary force, a decline symbolized by Vázquez de Mella's futile prowlings about the streets of Madrid working out the tactics of a Carlist take-over. It survived on provincial loyalties, family traditions, and the adventure story of the Seven Years War.

The main activity of the Integralists was a continuous crusade against those of the Catholic right who came to join forces with the dynastic conservatives. The most considerable of these 'half-breeds' was the marqués de Pidal who, after hovering on the borderline between Carlism and Alfonsism, brought his Catholic Union party over to Cánovas by joining the ministry of 1883. Pidal was a Thomist scholar who regarded all modern thought as 'a total error' beside 'the unique total truth of Thomism'. By its alliance with the liberal conservatives the Catholic Union hoped to defend the last bastion, Catholic control of education. It denied the 'right to propagate error' and the propriety of state education.

ministers were secretaries: the idea of a national movement above party—considered a liberal device ('I am not the chief of a party').

[1] For Vázquez de Mella's views on regionalism and his attacks on Basque and Catalan 'separatist' nationalism see J. Vázquez Mella, *Regionalismo y monarquía* (1957).

[2] For regenerationism see below, Chap. XII.

The intellectual of the group was Marcelino Menéndez y Pelayo. A prodigious polymath, professor at twenty-three, he combined the erudition of the scholar with a passionately defended polemical version of history. Don Marcelino rejected Pidal's fierce medievalism, his imitations of French ultramontanes, and he could not stomach the bad scholarship of Catholic rhetoric—the appeal to Granada, Lepanto, Pavia. Nor could he, like Pidal, regard the Renaissance as a disaster and Vives as a heretic. There was, he held, a worthy and distinguished school of native Spanish Catholic philosophers, a view which, it must be confessed, resulted in his exaltation of second-rate figures to the stature of European geniuses. His attempt to modernize the functions of the Catholic intellectual makes him appear open-minded when compared with his political allies, but this should not obscure the biological racialism of his thought: the body of Spain had been poisoned by eighteenth-century philosophy, she must find again her true, Catholic, self. 'Spain evangelizer of half the planet: Spain the hammer of heretics, the light of Trent, the sword of the Pope, the cradle of St. Ignatius. This is our greatness and glory: we have no other.' It was this violent, intellectual nationalism which was to make him the lay saint of the Falange.[1]

To Cánovas the great advantage of the Catholic Union lay in its connexion with the episcopate and in its attacks on priests who clung to Carlism and Integralism against the true interests of the Church. With the bishops came the more recalcitrant of the Catholic aristocracy. Reading French right-wing tracts, cursing materialism and progress, they nevertheless accepted the court of Alfonso XII. These allies demanded their reward—religious education in state schools, the control of a Catholic state over university education—and to satisfy them Cánovas was prepared to imperil his policy of comprehension.

2. *The Political Life, 1875–1890*

Cánovas's difficulties with the clerical wing of his party derive from his determination to extend, as widely as possible, the area of acquiescence in constitutional monarchy. The

[1] For a modern *apologia* see P. Laín Entralgo, *Menéndez y Pelayo* (Buenos Aires, 1955).

instrument of this expansion was to be a two-party system: his own Liberal–Conservatives would extend to the right; a Liberal party would make conquests on the left.

In addition to widening the area of acquiescence, the *turno pacífico* allowed political evolution within the régime itself. Thus the liberal conquests of 1869, universal suffrage and the jury, were brought in by the Liberal party after 1885, the Conservative party saving its principles in opposition. Neither liberals nor conservatives needed the appeal to force: they could wait their turn of office within a constitution that was not the imposition of one-party dogmatism. The party system was thus a sufficient substitute for the old mechanisms of military rebellion. Cánovas was a civilian politician *par excellence*, and the generals became the representatives of an interest group that must be satisfied, the grandees but not the arbiters of political life. He constantly presented the Restoration as a civilian affair, to the mortification of Martínez Campos. He dimmed the fame of generals by the glamour of a soldier king, closely associated with victory over Carlism. The dangers of this course he did not appreciate: it made the king the representative of army interests and the security of its prestige within the state. This role was soon assumed by Alfonso XII: he was passionately interested in the details of army administration and had the Army Regulations by heart. Thus there was always a danger that any direct threat by civilians to military interests would bring the generals back into politics using the court as its instrument. Sagasta, the Liberal prime minister, bitterly remarked that abroad a general who did not respect the primacy of civilian government was not called a bad general but a Spanish general.[1]

Cánovas believed that the English party system was the *only* effective mechanism for a stable parliamentary monarchy. His peclared intention of anglicizing Spanish politics led his critics to accuse him of creating two artificial parties and then evolving a series of hypocritical conventions by which they should alternate in power. These conventions, supported by electoral management, constituted the *turno pacífico* which governed the political life and ministerial history of the Restoration.[2]

[1] Conde de Romanones, *O.C.* i. 104.

[2] The Liberals and Liberal–Conservatives alternated thus: Cánovas, Jan.–Sept.

Cánovas did not fabricate the two parties of the *turno*. The Fusionist Liberal grouping, as Sagasta's party was first christened, was the legitimate heir of the old Progressives and grew up independently of contrivance, while Cánovas's Liberal–Conservative party was descended from the Liberal Unionists and the sensible Moderates. Cánovas fought the Liberal–Fusionists as a party leader and detested their programme. But whereas conservatives before 1868 used the prerogatives of the crown to exclude the left from power, he was ready to use them to facilitate a 'liberal situation' when the conservatives were politically exhausted or when the vital interests of the monarchy, as in 1885, demanded a more liberal course. This is all there was in his 'system'. In a liberal monarchy, where no party could expect that opinion should endow it with political power by electoral triumph, the royal prerogative of dismissal and appointment must be used (in co-operation with the electoral influence of the Minister of the Interior) in order to 'make' a Cortes for a new government. In these conditions Cánovas saw that no party could be allowed to monopolize crown favour in what was still an oligarchy. The oligarchs must rotate in office, like Aristotle's citizens, in order to give the political nation the illusion of self-government. The artificiality lay not in the creation of parties, but in the creaking handle of ministerial crises by which the mechanism was turned.[1]

Desire for place and power by the old Progressives, Democrats, and left-wing Liberal Unionists created a party, once it was clear that Cánovas intended to play the parliamentary game according to English rules and that a Liberal party could expect office without a revolution. The leader of this party was Sagasta. A railway engineer who had been a militia officer in 1854–6, after serving Prim as a conspirator he had become the

1875, Dec. 1875–Mar. 1879, Dec. 1879–Feb. 1881; Sagasta, 1881–Oct. 1883; Cánovas, Jan. 1884–Nov. 1885; Sagasta, Nov. 1885–July 1890; Cánovas, July 1890–Dec. 1892; Sagasta, Dec. 1892–Mar 1895; Cánovas, Mar. 1895–Aug. 1896. The exceptional ministries, those of Jovellar, Sept.–Dec. 1875 (a tactical replacement to cover the unwillingness of Cánovas to use universal suffrage); Martínez Campos, Mar.–Dec. 1879; Posada Herrera, Oct. 1883–Jan. 1884. Martínez Campos began as a dissident conservative but joined Sagasta's Fusionists while Posada Herrera's ministry was a successful attempt to ruin the Dynastic Left—a potential liberal splinter group—by granting it a spell of power.

[1] For a further discussion of these issues see below, pp. 474–7.

strong man of the Progressives in office; he was the indispensable Minister of the Interior, an expert election-rigger with no compunctions about suspending the conquests of the September Revolution in the interests of strong government. In later life his techniques were less formidable. Whereas the characteristic weapon of Cánovas was the unanswerable speech, Sagasta relied on the slap on the back and the technique of 'personal conquest'. Devoid of intellectual culture—he never read a book, disliked society, and was considered by Cánovas to be an illiterate—the Liberal leader was a pure politician, an expert in the neutralization and absorption of dissident groupings. Constantly threatened, he held together his majorities by concession as he held together his cabinets by expert chairmanship. His political nickname was 'the Old Shepherd'.

From adherence to the constitution of 1869, Sagasta moved to acceptance of the constitution of 1876. The programme of his party became the embodiment, within it, of the liberal conquests—universal suffrage, the jury, liberal press laws, laws of association, and freedom of worship. His allotted task within the Restoration system was the absorption of radicalism, the neutralization of Republicanism, and the provision of a political home for those who fled the right-wing allies of Cánovas. The most serious threat to Cánovas would have been a party devoted to the constitution of 1869, and embracing the September coalition from generals like Serrano to respectable Republicans. In the late seventies such a radical–democratic coalition looked feasible; but once Sagasta had assumed power in 1881 the coalition crumbled and the radical *élite*—it included two future Liberal leaders, Moret and Montero Ríos—moved towards what was termed 'benevolence', i.e. acceptance of the régime as a means of attaining power. The first resting-place of these radicals within the régime was a group called the Dynastic Left under Serrano (1882) with a programme of immediate realization of the liberal conquests. A short interval of power (October 1883) ended the prospect of the Dynastic Left as a left-wing liberal party in competition with Sagasta. In his second ministry (1885) Sagasta established his leadership of a party stretching from the duke of Medina Celi and General Martínez Campos to former Democrats. Liberalism was respectable.

On 5 November the king finally died of consumption.[1] Cánovas believed that his death would provoke Republican and Carlist rebellion and that such dangers could be more easily contained by the Liberals than by his own party. With a curious throw-back to his early experience of dynastic wars, he wished to avoid the complications of declaring Alfonso's daughter heir, since the pregnant queen might give birth to a son. After privately consulting Sagasta, and on the legal grounds that his powers lapsed with the king's death, he advised the regent (María Cristina, the Habsburg wife of Alfonso) to appoint a Liberal ministry. Thus the Pact of the Pardo, as the negotiations for Sagasta's succession are known, was not a secret treaty between the leaders of two 'artificial' parties in order to set up in perpetuity a contrived rotation between them: the peaceful *turno* was already implicit in the king's appointment of Sagasta in 1881, when the conservatives could still command a majority. In 1885 the royal prerogative was used to effect a change of ministers against a parliamentary majority in order to surmount what Cánovas considered a desperate crisis for monarchical institutions. The Liberal–Conservative party, 'exhausted' and unpopular, would be unable to 'defend' the monarchy.[2] An English prime minister might well have tendered similar advice to the crown; the Pardo Pact cannot be advanced as the birth certificate of bastard constitutionalism.

Once called to power, Sagasta easily 'made' a working majority in the Cortes. With it and the confidence of the queen regent, who preferred his deference to the hectoring loyalism of Cánovas, he held office until 1890. Prodded by ex-democrats like Martos, who could still embarrass respectable liberals, Sagasta passed the liberal conquests of '69 into law. A law of association, trial by jury, and universal suffrage made Spain on paper 'the most democratic monarchy in Europe'. Religious freedom apart, the September revolutionaries could ask no

[1] The details of the king's illness and its political consequences are set out in M. Izquierdo Hernández, *Historia clínica*.

[2] It is a point, not often stressed by critics of the Pardo Pact, that Cánovas had been seriously weakened by the unpopularity attending the ministry's failures in the dispute with Germany over the Carolines. Thus *before* the king's death political journalists prophesied the fall of Cánovas and talked of the 'exhaustion of the situation'.

more. Thus it was that the Liberalism, which, in Castelar's phrase, had made Spain a full-blooded democracy, became the dominant political creed of the regency although the regent herself preferred Catholic conservatives both to Liberals and to the 'expediency' of Cánovite conservatism. Cánovas, unlike the monarch he had restored, never enjoyed popularity. Neither he nor his party appealed to the educated provincial who had begun to take an interest in politics. His party's paper, *La Epoca*, was dry and expensive, whereas the Liberal press probaly reached two-thirds of the reading public of Spain.

Sagasta's long ministry admirably fulfilled its function of strengthening the régime against the threat from the left. This task was made easier by the endemic division that afflicted those parties, Carlists and Republicans alike, which rejected in principle a régime that allowed its opponents a legal existence. In these conditions were benevolence and the legal struggle tactically preferable to intransigence and violence? Of the Republican leaders, Castelar, lionized by Restoration society, rejected any appeal to force; Salmerón hedged; Ruiz Zorrilla, a tight-faced Puritan with none of the intellectual pretensions which distinguished other Republican leaders, refused in exile to abandon the revolution and was willing to adopt a vague socialism to recruit mass support—a policy which Castelar detested.[1] Reliance on revolution alienated Democrats like Martos and Canalejas who had maintained themselves 'at an honest distance' from the monarchical parties but who felt that, with Sagasta in power and liberal laws of association, it was improper to appeal to force when appeal to the electorate was unimpeded. Ruiz Zorrilla held that these 'legal means' did not exist, reviving the old argument of false elections; to him the Republic was a mystique, the right government for Spain whether Spaniards wanted it or not, to be imposed by a revolutionary minority acting in advance of public opinion.

His chosen instrument of revolution was the army. Looking back it seemed that the Republic had failed because it had alienated army opinion; to succeed, it must revive the old Progressives' 'love for the army' by working on the discontents

[1] For Castelar's attitude to socialism see P. Gómez Chaix, *Ruiz Zorrilla* (1934), 105–6.

of the sergeants rather than on the ambitions of the officers. In his manifesto Ruiz Zorrilla offered more than the traditional promotions for successful rebels: he promised a modern army, purged of bureaucrats, based on conscription, good conditions, promotion for rankers, and widows' pensions.[1] A central committee in Madrid organized a conspiratorial nucleus in each military district. In August 1883 the garrison of Badajoz rose for the Republic with clockwork precision but the twenty-two other compromised garrisons failed to act. In September 1886 came the last serious Republican rising before 1930 with General Villacampa's attempt to stage a pronunciamiento in Madrid: only one regiment kept its 'compromise' when, as commonly happened, the rising was ill-advisedly pushed forward. For Republicans who could not forget Pavía and Martínez Campos, the appeal to generals was a strange contortion of Republican tradition. Nor were the generals eager to help. Apart from Villacampa, only junior officers were willing to gamble their careers on a Republican triumph.

These revolutionary activities embarrassed the legalist Republicans. They would have been as willing to *accept* a successful army rising as Cánovas had been to accept the sword of Martínez Campos but they were unwilling to encourage one. Sagasta tricked his cabinet into pardoning Villacampa in the knowledge that this would drive a wedge between Ruiz Zorrilla and Salmerón, still united for electoral purposes. For all his high-mindedness, Salmerón was an astute politician intriguing for leadership of the party by smudging the distinction between evolution and revolution. But he could not disown Zorrilla because he knew the appeal of his obstinate intransigence to the Republican masses who detested the political pessimism of the Castelarian *élite*.[2] Castelar openly disowned revolution, recognizing in public that the restored monarchy

[1] Gómez Chaix, *Ruiz Zorrilla*, 170 ff.; M. Tato y Amat, *Sol y Ortega y la política contemporánea* (1914), 69. Maura believed the whole army rotten (cf. letter of 15 Aug. 1883 in Duque de Maura and M. Fernández Almagro, *Por que cayó Alfonso XIII* (1948), 402). For a later description of the grievances of the sergeants who were effectively barred from promotion to commissioned rank see Muñoz de Quevedo in *El porvenir de los sargentos* (Madrid, 1895). The book was dedicated to Salmerón.

[2] Salmerón covered his alliance with Zorrillistas, to whose support he knew he owed his seat, by the formula 'no force for power, only for right', i.e. Republicans can rebel but any other rebellion would express a reprehensible desire for place and

had come to stay. The Spanish people judged governments by the fruits they yielded, not by the ideas they represented. The monarchy had given them what they wanted—social peace. It must be accepted. 'I regret it but I find it logical.' As an ex-president of the Republic he could not himself 'accept' a monarchy, however liberal, but in 1888 he advised his followers to do so.

With Castelar as the prize exhibit of the régime, Republicanism entered what Ruiz Zorrilla called the long night of defections and bitterness. Galdós, the great novelist who was given a safe seat in Puerto Rico by Sagasta, believed political liberty secure and the era of revolutionary politics closed. 'As a business the revolution is so depressed that it is impossible to gain a living by it.'[1] A Republican military rebellion would find no support in opinion. Castelar and Salmerón still professed to believe that the Republic, as a perfect form of government, was secure in the dialectic of history. Their faith must have been sorely tried.

The threat to the monarchy was to come not from the traditional enemies to the right and to the left. It lay in the political dangers implicit in the disintegration of the two monarchical parties, bereft of principle and purpose, into a conglomeration of groups. Repeatedly, Cánovas stated his belief that without two clearly defined parties the constitution would not work, a view entirely shared by Sagasta. Nothing is more surprising than the two leaders' determination to maintain each other's party as a going concern: the compromise by which the Minister of the Interior let in a substantial opposition must be respected, the primates of the opposing party must be favoured, its dissidents crushed. 'The first necessity is that the friendly relations of collaboration which should exist between the two parties be not interrupted' (Sagasta). 'Our duty is to maintain loyally our solidarity to the Liberal party avoiding all pretexts that could disturb it' (Cánovas).[2] The efforts of both statesmen

power. The comments of Galdós (*Obras ineditas*, i. 112, 119, 161, 174) are illuminating for this period of Salmerón's career.

[1] Galdós, op. cit. i.

[2] Both these statements come from 1890. Sagasta was afraid that Cánovas would give electoral encouragement to the dissident Democrats of Martos. Cánovas made it clear to Martos that he could not do so (cf. A. M. Fabié, *Cánovas*, 244, 255).

to maintain the unity of the two parties failed. After 1890 the simplicity of the early years seemed an artificial wonderland; as the leaders aged, a younger generation claimed and divided the heritage.

The leadership of Cánovas was unchallenged in the Liberal–Conservative party until 1885. In that year his peaceful donation of power to Sagasta appeared to Romero Robledo the gratuitous sacrifice of a sound conservative majority. A political buccaneer, Romero Robledo was the ideal Minister of the Interior who, from an office crowded with bull-fighters, clients, and provincial caciques, ran the electoral machinery of the conservative party. He was a dangerous dissident since his 'revolutionary' past allowed his 'hussars' the prospect of a relatively respectable alliance with dissident Liberals or even with discontented Catalans.[1]

Romero Robledo's departure left, as second-in-command to Cánovas, Francisco Silvela, a distinguished and high-minded lawyer who became Minister of the Interior in Cánovas's ministry of 1890. Yet Silvela himself was moving towards a rejection of the whole system of alternating parties based on electoral management and the leadership of 'the Monster' as a part of it. Dissidence, therefore, represented more than personal incompatibility. Silvela and Cánovas were both historians, but whereas to the latter the decline of Spain in the seventeenth century was the consequence of a failure of her statesmen to act within the limits of her resources (a conclusion from which he derived that necessity for caution which dominated his policies), to Silvela, decline was a consequence of a failure of personal morality in statesmen. Thus to the prime minister, Romero Robledo was an indispensable electoral manager, who worked within the limits of the parliamentary system, allowing Liberals a fair deal and Republicans and Carlists their strongholds in Navarre and the large cities. To Silvela such methods were an abomination in themselves; he was said to seek to conceal his distaste for the conversation of the provincial potentates of the party by feigning sleep. He could not tolerate what he called

[1] Romero Robledo (1838–1906) began as a Liberal Unionist and had served under Sagasta as Minister of the Interior (1872); after he had broken with Cánovas in 1885 he tried an electoral coalition with López Domínguez which became the short-lived Liberal Reformist party.

his leader's 'incurable penchant for rogues' and the party's nostalgic desire for the safe seats and the lively debating power of Romero Robledo.

Silvela's dissidence is of great significance because it represents the discontent of an intelligent high conservative with the Cánovite system as a protection for conservative interests in a régime of universal suffrage. Cánovas was 'worn out and unpopular—antiquated'; his role was exhausted now the monarchy had been safely established. Silvela's new conservatism rested on two propositions: first, the electoral techniques of party managers isolated and divorced from participation in government, a sound 'neutral' opinion; secondly, the function of party was to apply public opinion, through government, to the solution of the problems of a nation. Thus, where Cánovas saw in the mere mechanism of rotating parties the secret of the stability of English parliamentarianism, Silvela saw its strength in its sensitivity to public opinion, once that opinion was organized.[1] The new conservatism would, therefore, be a party based on organized opinion as opposed to organized patronage. Between 1894 and 1898 Silvela set forth the programme of this party. Its centre was a thorough reform of municipal government;[2] it was on the platform of municipal morality that he hoped to rally the honest opinion disgusted at the brutal use of municipal influence for electoral purposes which characterized Cánovas's system in decline. In spite of its novel puritanical air, Silvela's party was a true conservative party: its watchwords were religion, national grandeur, order, the organic society. It represented regeneration from above, by the 'superior classes'. Silvela's most enthusiastic admirers were young Catholic aristocrats.

In the cabinet, where Silvela sat silent in glum moral superiority, Cánovas could not conceal his contempt for him and his liking for Romero Robledo. In November 1891 Silvela resigned rather than tolerate the return of Romero Robledo. His friends made their opposition clear by pressing for an examination of the accounts of the Madrid municipality, a campaign which was primarily directed against Romero Robledo's seedier clientele. When the government refused to proceed against the

[1] F. Silvela, *Artículos, discursos, conferencias y cartas* (1933), ii. 131–3.

[2] For Silvela's reforms and their conservative implications see below, p. 477.

municipality in the law courts Villaverde, Silvela's representative in the government, resigned (December 1892). Silvela could neither keep his withdrawal a personal gesture nor patch up his relations with his leader, increasingly proud and inflexible in old age.[1] By 1895 his 'dissidence' had its press and its provincial enthusiasts; by 1897 he was appealing to the queen regent to dismiss Cánovas in order to give the new conservatism a chance.

The Liberals had their difficulties, less dramatic and personalized than those of the Liberal Conservatives; they had always been a loose federation of groups each of which owed primary allegiance to a chief. In the daily exchanges of his *tertulia*, he interpreted the implications of the day's debate to his 'unconditionals', i.e. those followers whose job prospects were bound up with the chief's political career. Sagasta's successors made the tasks of soliciting support from the groups and holding together a majority look like what it was, political trading. Sagasta was an artist in the grand manner, walking through the smoking-room with the air of a leader, not as an affable tout. Nevertheless, in the ministry of 1885–90 the ambitions of the groups taxed even his unrivalled political talents and made his tenure of power a succession of partial cabinet crises. To satisfy them, he bitterly remarked, he needed not a few sweets in his pocket but a confectionery business. On the left, Martos hoped to lever Sagasta out of office with universal suffrage. On the right, the duke of Tetuan and his group split off in disapproval of the manner in which Villacampa's pardon had been engineered. Ambitious remnants of the dynastic left hoped to form a reformist party by uniting with the conservative dissidents of Romero Robledo. These in turn hoped to capture Gamazo, an austere lawyer, who represented the wheat-growers of Valladolid and who was becoming increasingly hostile to Sagasta's sacrifice of policies to politics. General Cassola took into dissidence the small group which backed his unsuccessful attempt at military reform.[2]

These difficulties were a symptom of the exhaustion of the classical liberal programme. Once the liberal conquests were on

[1] For the attempts to reconcile Cánovas and Silvela see F. Silvela, *Artículos*, ii. 93, 103–6. This second volume is the best source for the history of the dissidence.

[2] Cf. Romero Robledo's letters to Gamazo in F. de Llanos y Torriglia, *Germán Gamazo* (1942), 142 ff.

the statute book, the old slogans were dead and the future lay with what were called 'material questions'—the modernization of the Spanish economy and social reform. It was the tragedy of Sagasta's leadership that he could not widen and revivify the liberal creed. He was content that his party should contain both free traders and protectionists at a time when the tariff issue was a burning question; army reformers and orthodox generals; believers in high taxation and public works and advocates of economy; moralists and managers. Forgetting his noble plea for religious freedom in 1876, he believed that the religious question was settled. The constitution was settled. Not merely the programme but the moral capital of liberalism was running out in Sagasta's hands. His allies were implicated in the municipal scandals of Madrid and in July 1890 Sagasta was forced to resign because his opponents had got hold of compromising papers connecting him with a dubious contract for the construction of a Cuban railway.[1]

3. *The System in Operation: Caciquismo and its Consequences*

We have examined the political superstructure of the *turno pacífico* and its disintegration after 1890. We must now examine its infrastructure, since it was this aspect of the system which was denounced as 'false' on the grounds that it had sacrificed the true interests of the country to the convenient working of a political apparatus. In order to provide a working majority of a hundred deputies, the political vitality of Spain had been sapped by reliance on 'orthopaedic appliances'. Yet these appliances were not invented by Cánovas. The *turno* was implicit in Isabelline parliamentarianism; the novel factor was the attitude of Alfonso XII which allowed the system to work as his mother had not. The king was capable of allowing his courtiers to slight Liberal ministers (they tossed one in a blanket on a royal shoot) but he recognized to the full his constitutional duty to appoint a liberal ministry. Nor was electoral manipulation a feature imported into politics by 'cynical' Restoration politi-

[1] For an account of this crisis, from Sagasta's point of view, see Conde de Romanones, *María Cristina* (1957), 68. The compromising papers were burnt by Sagasta's political heir Moret.

cians: since the 1840's the ministry chose its provincial governor and the latter—according to La Cierva, in the train journey to his capital—squared the local bosses or caciques. In return for the disposal of government patronage within their districts they brought out the vote for the government candidate—sometimes a Madrid politician—most usually the 'grand cacique' who controlled the party's network of influence in the constituency. The term cacique was one of those rare terminological discoveries which damn a whole régime: it concentrated criticism on one of the lower mechanisms of politics—falsification of the suffrage, and the system of influence which made this falsification possible.[1]

The main charge against caciquismo at the turn of the century was that it transformed what was legally and formally a democratic monarchy into an oligarchy. Thus was born a new feudalism, based on what eighteenth-century English politicians called obliging friends, ranged in hierarchy from the great oligarchy of Madrid to the petty tyrants of the municipalities. It was not a parliamentary régime with abuses: the abuses were the system itself. Yet caciquismo was a far more complex organization than its critics imagined. Nor can we accept literally the criticism of the parties outside the régime. They mythologized. The existence of a vast iron machine, crushing all independent opposition, conveniently concealed the numerical weakness of Republicanism outside the great towns. This myth allowed Ruiz Zorrilla to argue that revolution was the only realistic policy; what was the point of Castelar's 'benevolence' and 'possibilism' when no amount of Republican conversion could be reflected in the suffrage?

Such attacks failed to realize that caciquismo was only in part a system maintained by cynical politicians; it was also a natural growth. As a social institution by which local influences took political forms, it must be distinguished from illicit practices—the oversetting of voting urns, the resurrection of the dead for voting lists, bribery and intimidation. These abuses were discussed in the opening sessions of every

[1] Cacique is defined in the Academy Dictionary as 'a person who in a pueblo or district exercises excessive influence in political or administrative matters'. Imported from America the term is already used by Cervantes to denote a local bigwig. See P. Perissé, *Les Élections legislatives en Espagne* (Toulouse, 1909), for an outline of electoral machinery.

Cortes and were sharply dealt with by Maura's electoral law of 1907. Maura's law was a perfect electoral law on paper and probably did defeat the more spectacular devices, in spite of the boasts of old hands that they could drive coach and horses through it. These devices were on the decline, largely through the development of a climate of opinion hostile to them.

The grand cacique's power was based on his general services to, and interest in, his 'country'. Thus Gamazo, a liberal lawyer, who went into 'dissidence' against Sagasta precisely because liberal free trade was unacceptable to the wheat farmers of his constituency, never refused a local case or forgot a local worthy's face. He established a hold over Valladolid which was not challenged for thirty years, and then only because Sagasta was determined to break Gamazo's dissident liberals by every means at the government's disposal, not because Valladolid resented his 'dictatorship'.[1] A lawyer or landowner became, as a national politician, delegate for his province: Montero Ríos in Galicia and the Pidals and their aristocratic friends in the Asturias, La Cierva in Murcia. They served their constituents well. La Cierva, without whose permission, it was said, not a leaf fell in Murcia, got his district everything from secondary roads to a university. These great oligarchs represented permanent party interests and the more intrenched the party interests the less disastrous the effect on local government and justice. Thus in Murcia the Liberals, as the weaker party, were dependent on wholesale grants of patronage from the minister to compensate for their lack of 'roots in the countryside'.[2] As a machine for procuring a majority, the system depended on the caciques of the backward districts, such men as Natalio Rivas, who kept his local influence in the municipalities of the Alpujarras, south of Granada, until the Republic of 1931. Just as the magnates of eighteenth-century England agreed not to disturb the peace of the country by forcing costly elections, so amenable caciques worked for both parties.[3] Caciquismo thus depended on their mutual tolerance.

It was the result (and as such not confined to Spain) of the

[1] For a romanticized view of Gamazo as a good cacique see F. de Llanos y Torriglia, *Germán Gamazo*.

[2] J. de La Cierva, *Notas*, 21–24.

[3] These constituencies accounted for the *actas blancas* which escaped parliamentary scrutiny; after 1907, these constituencies were uncontested, left by Clause

application of a wide suffrage to a backward society with little interest in or comprehension of national issues. Like English sheep, English institutions degenerated in Spain. Clienteles, whether based on a brutal control of the local labour market or more subtle ties—the institution of god-parentage or the family connexions of the mayor—were the reality of local life; it was the boss who had always protected his village clientele from the laws, taxes, and conscription levies of the outside world of the state. These pre-existing systems were absorbed and given new form in the local politics of representative government. Maura, its most formidable conservative critic, defined it as the bastard feudalism of a decaying structure—'an inevitable scourge from the moment the historic society began to disappear'.

As a political device in a backward society, it could be defended. The neurologist Ramón y Cajal saw it as the necessary connexion between an indifferent electorate and the politicians: it was 'an indispensable organ of national life . . . the only link between the countryside and the city, the people and the state'.[1] There can be no doubt that caciquismo prolonged and intensified the conditions which made it necessary and possible—the political ignorance and apathy of the Spanish electorate. Politics ran, like an express train, through the desolate townships and villages of Spain, stopping only at election times.

It can be argued that caciquismo became an intolerable evil as the local ties on which it was based dissolved and the system could only maintain itself by violence, if at all. After 1887, in a régime of universal suffrage, it was openly recognized as a means of maintaining 'the legitimate interests of property'. While the influence of this interest was an uncontested social reality, improper electoral practices merged into the customary acceptance of the predominance of local families by a stable agrarian world. It was 'false' only when that world dissolved.

29 of Maura's law in the hands of local politicians. Their caciques were called *alternos*. The political correspondence of the time is full of information on deals in such constituencies. Clause 29 favoured candidates put up by local politicians. To stand, a candidate had to be supported by one-twentieth of the voters—a difficult requirement—*or* to be nominated on the recommendation of a provincial deputy or senator.

[1] J. Costa, *Oligarquía y caciquismo* (1902), 424 ff. In the *Ateneo* debates it was argued that caciquismo was a phenomenon of immature parliamentarianism *or* of a decaying society. It was both.

As the Asturias moved from fishing and farming to coal and iron so the 'Tsars of the Asturias', the Pidals, found their empire challenged by the university professors and socialists of Oviedo and Gijón. The system only worked in the large towns through the massive abstention of the politically indifferent; once the voters organized themselves they could break the hold of the electoral managers. The Catalan regionalists made great play of the 'exclusion' of genuine regional representatives by an electoral system rigged from Madrid; by 1893 the system was shaky and in 1901 it was destroyed once 'opinion' had been successfully organized by Catalan regionalists and Republicans against the traditional parties. The field in Catalonia was left to their organized votes.[1]

In the last resort the success of the Minister of the Interior's negotiations and safe constituencies for official candidates rested on the political indifference and apathy of most Spaniards as much as on the interest and the scepticism of the governing class. A people gets the electoral system it deserves. Perhaps the main charge against caciquismo is that it delayed a modern party organization, outside the great towns, by denying any opportunity for a gradual process of political education. The group of stalwarts who read their party papers in the casino and relied on the mayor could find no other way to organize their local influence when friends could no longer oblige them; thus, when the remnants of the old system had decayed away under Primo de Rivera, the monarchical parties were left defenceless in the elections of 1931.

All diagnoses of caciquismo found the roots of the disease in local government. The manipulation of municipal and provincial government for electoral purposes was made possible by the imitation of the highly centralized French system which left the municipalities 'slaves of the government'. The laws of 1877 and 1882 respected liberal centralization and the main charge was that the central government used the supervisory controls left it by the legislation in order to subordinate local government to the electoral interests of the parties. The governor,

[1] For the revolt of the *Silvelistas* and Regionalists against the Barcelona managers see pp. 548, 550. Cf. the revolt of Granada against its cacique (1917–19) who had supported a liberal cabinet minister in return for complete control of the municipal council, which embellished his estate and paid his bodyguard.

like the French prefect in the Second Empire, was not merely a provincial administrator but a party hack working for party ends in a régime of official candidates proposed by the government in power for the time being. An uncooperative municipality could be dismissed by abusive interpretation of the powers of supervision granted the governor by Article 189 of the municipal code: a failure to light the streets could be interpreted as a dereliction of statutory duties. *In extremis* the Minister of the Interior could suspend a municipality by decree.[1]

The aristocracy, in the seventeenth century, had maintained their urban clienteles by a combination of charity and jobbery. These techniques were inherited by the municipal counsellors of the nineteenth and twentieth centuries: the removal of customs guards to admit a friend's consignment tax free; the diversion of dustmen's pay into the pockets of political underlings; the unjustified dismissal of a local schoolmaster; the supply of poor oil for street lamps; the scheduling of a private drive as a public highway.[2] Public works provided electoral funds: road workers were taken on at election times. It is easy to see why these Dickensian practices were condemned by reformers but tolerated by the local poor: few families in a small town would not have a relation in the system. Spanish municipal politics are incomprehensible unless we realize that the understrappers of the politicians, like American Ward Secretaries, were distributors of doles, knowing the needs of each family and each voter, protecting the most favoured against the law and the tax collector.[3] The *tiranos chicos* were popular with their clientele but concealed charity and the diversion of municipal income for private ends did not make for progressive town government in an age of urban expansion. 'What municipalities of thieves and brutes there must have been and are to come in Malaga', wrote the novelist Valera in 1883. 'The roads and streets are horrifying. In a coach you're in risk of

[1] There are no statistics familiar to me on suspensions by governors. Between 1915 and 1923, when the system was in decline, 544 municipalities were suspended by the Minister of the Interior. Not all of these suspensions were political.

[2] These instances are drawn from the municipal histories of Madrid, Malaga, Barcelona, and Murcia.

[3] It is the Galician novelist Emilia Pardo Bazán who makes this observation on the popularity of the petty tyrants. In 1918 a curious situation was unearthed in Madrid: credits for road workers were eaten into by doles to 4,600 'unemployed'.

breaking your neck, on foot you sink into dust and garbage. The town is in darkness because the municipality won't pay the gas company. It has contracted a debt of fifty million pesetas.' All progress came from individual effort: the municipal counsellors thought only of private profit.[1]

The two major parties held to an implied truce in municipal politics. Thus the exposure of municipal corruption and the network of electoral patronage was left to parties outside the *turno pacífico* from Silvela's opposition conservatives to Republicans and socialists.[2] Silvela's friends ran a campaign against Romero Robledo's influence in the Madrid municipality; the Regionalist councillors of Barcelona, finding the municipality divided between 'robbers and non-robbers', exposed the robbers' scandalous gas and cement contracts.[3] Once in a majority on municipal councils the reformist zeal of the outs weakened. The Radical Republican party in Barcelona became as venal as the old gang it had criticized; while the Regionalists were honest, they were constantly accused of using municipal patronage for party ends. Thus it was the Socialists who were the ultimate heirs within the monarchy of the cry for honest municipal government: Largo Caballero confessed that his painstaking investigations, as a Madrid municipal counsellor into illicit contracts jobbery and false accounts were more demanding than his tasks as Minister of Labour in the republic.[4]

Thus the highest price Spain paid for her electoral system was inefficient local government and a legal system working through influence. If its most radical critic, Costa, is to be believed, it was impossible to gain a case against the cacique's judges, as this Aragonese radical found out to his own cost. Patronage had always conditioned justice; what enraged Costa was that this should go on in a country with 'modern' institutions and should so pervert these institutions that what looked, on paper, a civilized society should have its affairs run as if

[1] *Epistolario de Valera y Menéndez Pelayo* (1930), 187.

[2] Silvela's campaign demanded that the state should institute proceedings against the Madrid municipality which had been exposed by the efforts of a private individual, the marqués de Cabriñana. After an attempt to assassinate him, he became a popular hero. The campaign in his defence (Dec. 1895) was one of the few political issues that aroused 'opinion' in Restoration Spain.

[3] Cf. J. Pabón, *Cambó* (1951), 208–18.

[4] F. Largo Caballero, *Mis recuerdos* (Mexico, 1954), 68–79.

it were a Rif tribe. If Spain had possessed the independent judiciary of England or the enforceable code of administrative law of France, caciquismo could not have flourished.[1] Her lawyers lacked any tradition of resistance to the agents of the central government which, if it no longer dismissed judges could, by transferring them, involve them in exile to a poor district and expenses which their small salaries could not support. On paper the *droit administratif* of Spain was more liberal than that of France. In fact it was a totally unsatisfactory means of redress: the governor covered the mayor and his agents, the Minister of the Interior covered the governor.

Of necessity all those who wished to revivify political life became local government reformers. It was not merely that the existing structure of local government was the breeding ground of caciquismo: it was at the municipal level that the 'neutral masses' could be engaged in the political system and it was through a reformed system of local government that the energy of decent, uncorrupted Spaniards could be brought into political life. Silvela found that his campaign for municipal morality in the nineties was the first political issue which roused popular interest and the greatest of the municipal reformers was his successor as leader of the Conservative party, Antonio Maura.

How was local government to be made a vehicle for political regeneration? First, reform must weaken the connexion between central government and local authorities, secured by the dual functions of the governor and the mayor, who were both government servants, and the responsible executive organs of the elective Provincial Deputation and the municipality. Thus Maura, in 1907, wished to split the municipal functions of the mayor (for which he was to be responsible only to the courts and his own council) from his functions as a delegate of the state (only in this latter capacity would he be controlled by the governor). Rather optimistically Maura believed this would

[1] The methods of appeal against government officials are set out in Santamaría de Paredes, *Curso de derecho administrativo* (various editions). The municipal judges were appointed by the Audiencias and the colleges of lawyers, usually on the recommendation of the Deputy. The clause favouring qualified candidates seems to have been a dead letter (J. Chamberlain, *El atraso de España* (Valencia, 1919), 121.) Montero Ríos called the lower ranges of the judicial system 'an organism created for local passions and interests rather than a judicial institution' (*Gaceta*, 23. iv. 1893).

kill caciquismo by destroying the connexion between the Ministry of the Interior and municipal life. Secondly, reform must restore life to the 'natural unit' of the municipality by releasing local energies paralysed from the centre. The smallest alteration in the town budget, a sale of half an acre of municipal commons, the plans for a new village pump, had to be referred through the provincial governor to Madrid. There only political influence could secure a speedy resolution of the necessary *expediente*.[1] The aim of all reformers was to give the municipality a genuine and independent sphere of action such as had survived in the Basque Provinces and Navarre, where excellent roads and municipal services proved the efficacy of decentralization. Since the defeat of 1870, French models were at a discount and it was argued that the self-governing Anglo-Saxon town was both more efficient and more in the tradition of the autonomous Castilian municipality.

Concentrating on the evil effects of over-centralization and electoral corruption, reformers failed to appreciate the real defect of local government: its poverty. 'When the treasury is empty local liberties are a delusion.'[2] Neither the Provincial Deputations nor the municipalities had adequate incomes. The functions of the municipality were limited by its powerlessness to extend its budget in order to finance new needs. Up to 1912 the main source of municipal income was a fixed share of the *consumos*; the taxes which replaced it were clumsy and pegged down to a proportion of the state land taxes. With these incomes a small municipality could only keep the town hall from falling down and pay miserable salaries to the schoolmaster, doctor, vet, policeman, and night watchman. The great cities were rebuilt by private enterprise in the later nineteenth century, yet even these new cities lacked the services befitting their new European appearance and attempts to provide them resulted in the municipal debts that were a characteristic of the period. Madrid could only collect a third of the town's refuse in the

[1] H. Puget, *Le Gouvernement local en Espagne* (Paris, 1920), 188. Intervention went beyond the faculties conceded by the Municipal Law. By royal orders and decrees the Ministry of the Interior built up a formidable and uncontrolled body of jurisprudence. No municipality could undertake compulsory purchase without a government declaration as to public utility. The reforms of another conservative, Burgos y Mazo, transferred this essential power to the municipalities themselves.

[2] Ibid. 157.

1920's; the rest was left to private rag-pickers and scavengers.[1] In the outer suburbs the post-war building boom left a population of a hundred thousand without sewers and as a consequence the 'African death rate' of Madrid was twice that of London.

Between 1882 and 1923 there were twenty ministerial projects of local government reform of which the most serious was Maura's comprehensive law of 1907.[2] Conservative reform was sabotaged by the liberals because they sensed that, behind conservative enthusiasm for a system of local government that should be 'real' to those who participated in it, lay, not merely an anti-democratic philosophy, but party purpose. Like the Moderates in 1840, the Conservatives wished to substitute for the 'worst' elements given power with universal suffrage what were called the 'live forces' (*fuerzas vivas*) of the community. Both Silvela and Maura sought some acceptable form of corporate municipal suffrage which would bring the 'significant interests' into local life. These would be Conservative voters and might be relied on to use their electoral strength in order to exclude Radicals and Republicans. The Regionalist interests of Catalonia and the Basque Provinces (whose appeal to historic institutions of local government both Silvela and Maura professed to respect as an appeal to reality against the abstract formalism of liberal centralization) were originally largely conservative. Disliking caciquismo as much as Maura, Liberals feared that its eradication by disguised historical revivals and a corporative vote, by the substitution of a permanent committee for what Maura scornfully called 'municipal parliamentarianism', might lead to new and insidious forms of localism. The destruction of local liberties which had supported the Carlists had been the historic task of liberalism. Liberals now revived the cry of Cánovas against the *fueros* of the Carlists to resist the new course of his Conservative successors: centralization was 'not in order more nor less than civilization, nor more nor less than liberty'.[3] More than anything else this division

[1] 'They are the real group of dustmen in Madrid and without their help the streets of our city would soon be manure heaps.' *Heraldo de Madrid*, 19 May 1921.

[2] Most of Maura's ideas had been anticipated by Silvela in the nineties; cf. Silvela, *Discursos*, ii, passim.

[3] For an intelligent liberal criticism of Maura's 1907 proposals see the preface to A. Posada's *Regimen local.*

ruined the prospects of local government reform: what liberal parliamentarianism could not accomplish was achieved by Primo de Rivera's iron surgery.

The campaign against the evils of an over-centralized system of local government were only part of a more general campaign against the *turno*. Much of the criticism of the moral and mechanical defects of Restoration parliamentarianism represents the bile of those whom the system rejected or the justification of those who overthrew it *manu militari*. Thus it was constantly asserted by critics—especially in the nineties by dissident conservatives and Catalan regionalists—that parliamentarianism, by failing to represent or respond to the *fuerzas vivas* of the community, impeded the growth of a modern society. Sánchez de Toca, a dissident Conservative, believed that a modern capitalist economy was strangled by the persistence of old-fashioned interests in political life—for instance the strongly entrenched railway interest and foreign mineral and banking interests.[1] In fact these interests, and the 'conservative' agricultural interests, *were* the significant interests in Spanish society and there were truly reflected among the deputies. That they were not 'modern' interests is not a charge that can be legitimately levelled at the political system as such. Similarly, the constant charge of Catalans that caciquismo 'blanketed' Catalan aspirations should be restated: it was not that Catalan interests were 'neglected'—the whole history of protectionism exposes the myth—but that they clashed with other interests represented in the Cortes. No parliamentary system can reconcile interests which are exclusive: before a refusal to compromise liberalism must abdicate. Again the charge that the exigencies of party management precluded any 'national' policy was less a valid criticism of the specific evils of Spanish parliamentarianism than an attack on the inevitable consequences of parliamentary democracy as such.[2]

The most consistent criticism remained that stability was

[1] For these criticisms see his *Reconstitución de España* (n.d.).

[2] G. Maura, son of the great Maura, believes that the 'system' forced Sagasta to sacrifice a national policy to the necessity of keeping together discordant groups, each one of which possessed a *liberum veto* on beneficent legislation in any liberal ministry: hence the failure of Camacho's financial legislation and Cassola's army reform in Sagasta's Long Ministry. Yet both touched such a host of interests (debt-holders, protectionists, artillery officers) that even a strong government might

secured at the expense of connexion between government and the governed. To the general public the Congress of Deputies remained an area where professionals fought for the spoils of political life and political journalists lived by explaining the quarrels of this insulated world in the specialized jargon of 'crisology'.[1] Ministerial crises needed explanation because they were neither the result of an adverse election nor, in general, of an adverse vote in the Cortes: they obeyed conventions of the constitution derived from the fact that ministerial changes must *precede* an election if the political course was to be changed. Only a new ministry could 'make' a new majority. In the period between the 'exhaustion of a situation' and the new ministry's election the party battle was suspended 'in order to re-establish the free play of Parliamentary institutions'. This phrase of Cánovas decently concealed the truth that Sagasta must be allowed time to fabricate a Liberal majority to replace a Liberal Conservative majority.[2] Thus the liberty with which the Standing Orders of the Congress allowed to minorities and which enabled them to paralyse government legislation appears as a concession by a guilty majority. Elected by the Minister of the Interior rather than by its constituents it went in fear of an opposition *retraimiento* which would expose the falsity of the system. The Standing Orders were never reformed; when opposition blocked essential legislation the only course was to prorogue the Cortes and to rule by decree—a course increasingly followed after 1914. 'Majorities', wrote Maeztu, 'are at the mercy of minorities and as majority rule is the kernel of parliamentary government this means we do not understand parliamentary government.'

In the last analysis the discredit into which parliamentary government has fallen in Spain is explained less by its 'unreality'

have had to discard such reformers. For an exaggerated modern criticism see J. M[a] Garcia Escudero, *De Cánovas á la república* (1953).

[1] The phrase is an invention of Galdós. There were twenty-four 'crises' during the regency (1885–1902), many of which acquired a distinctive physiognomy and nomenclature which was, significantly, derived from proper names and not from issues, e.g. 'the crisis of the intuitions of General Martínez Campos', 'the Martos crisis'.

[2] It was always considered a proof of Silvela's determination to conduct honest elections—always called in political jargon 'sincere'—that he dissolved in 1899 *before* the necessary electoral arrangements could be made (G. Maura, in Lafuente, *Historia*, xvi. 293).

and its defects as a political arrangement than by the magnitude of the dual task it was called on to finance from a poor country: the conquest of economic and cultural 'backwardness' and the maintenance of Spain as an imperial power. To pose as an imperial power Spain must possess an expensive navy, whilst the unfulfilled programme of the generation of Charles III for a prosperous Spain demanded state intervention and investment in agriculture and public works on a scale which liberal parliamentarianism could neither contemplate nor afford. The orthodox finance ministers of the Restoration regarded a balanced budget as the only salvation for a falling peseta—hence the retrenchment and deflation of Gamazo and Villaverde since neither could face a stiff income tax to free the budget from its dependence on regressive taxes. In this they were no different from Gladstone or Giolitti. In central as in local government, poverty was as serious a bar to action as deficiencies in political structure or the vices of electoral management, though these defects, without doubt, impeded reform of abuses.

It was in the realms of imperial defence that the combination of national poverty and the incapacity to reform ancient abuse was decisive and where shortcomings were exposed to the test of war. For thirty years Maura campaigned in vain for the construction of a navy and naval reform as first necessities for Spain's existence as an imperial power. The Spanish navy nevertheless remained an archaic and expensive shore-based bureaucracy rather than a fighting force. Starved by the budget it could rarely put to sea with a ration of thirty-four tons of coal a day; with no port capable of refuelling under fourteen days and with a day's target practice a year it is scarcely surprising that the Spanish navy was without any sea experience when the crisis came in 1898.[1] The central administration apart, the three naval regions each employed more officers than the British Admiralty and most of these officers were engaged on registration of the merchant marine, fishing control, and other office chores. Naval education cost the state half as much as the

[1] In 1895 the pride of the navy, the *Reina Regente*, sank with all hands between Gibraltar and Tangier. For details see Sánchez de Toca, *Reconstitucion*, 354–5, and especially Maura's speeches of 13–14 May 1890, 8 July, 13 Dec. 1899, 5 Dec. 1901.

whole national educational system. Even after the shock of total disaster, which left Spain with over a hundred admirals and no capital ships to put them on, the naval budget remained, in Maura's phrase, an allowance for public employees, the conspicuous waste of a man who keeps his coachman but possesses no coach.

4. *The Cuban Disaster, 1895–1898*

It was Spain's weakness as a naval power which was to expose the Restoration to 'the Disaster' of 1898: total defeat at the hands of the United States and the loss of the remnants of her colonial empire—Cuba, Puerto Rico, and the Philippines. It was this catastrophe which cruelly discredited Cánovas's achievements as a political engineer. To his critics it proved beyond dispute that the pursuit of domestic stability had denied Spain the means to defend her status as a great power.

On Cuba—'the richest colony in the whole world'—were concentrated the strongest emotional ties and economic interests. 'Spaniards', said the foreign minister in 1848, 'sooner than see the island transferred to any power . . . would prefer seeing it sunk in the ocean.' Cuba had dragged the September Revolution into discredit; it was now to expose the failings of the Restoration. After successfully ending the Ten Years War and the first serious bid for Cuban independence with the peace of Zanjón (February 1878), the statesmen of the Restoration failed to find a settlement of the Cuban question which would save something of Spain's position in the Antilles. Once, in 1895, another separatist revolt got under way, it is hard to see how, even with consummate skill, Spain could have defeated the alliance of Cuban separatism with the power of the United States.

The Cuban problem, apart from the interests of the United States, presents a parallel of Britain's relations with Ireland in the nineteenth century: Cuba was represented in the Madrid parliament by a handful of deputies and ruled by a Captain General whose responsibility was diminished by distance and the fact that he was a soldier. After the failure of 'rational assimilation' the Cuban Autonomist party had urged, against overwhelming majorities in the Cortes, the case for moderate Home Rule—'the liberty of Cuba, acquired by legal means, within Spanish nationality'. Their argument was that the denial of their moderate demands would popularize the Separatists' demand for an independent republic.

The rich creoles of the Autonomist party had seen their leadership threatened in the long war of 1868–78. Their desire to save themselves by autonomy within Spanish sovereignty gave the Spanish government the opportunity to recover the alliance of a significant sector of Cuban opinion. This opportunity was wasted, partly by Spanish governments but above all by the 'Spanish party' in Cuba itself—the Constitutional Unionists, the Orangemen of Cuba. Composed of the Spanish bureaucratic and commercial classes and the tradesmen, shop-keepers, and artisans among the immigrants, they argued that, by political logic, autonomy must lead to separatism. Behind the debate on the nature and extent of Spanish sovereignty, the conflict between Unionists and Autonomists was a conflict for local power: the Unionists used 'Spanish sovereignty', as local representatives of the ascendancy, in order to monopolize the machinery of local government, a monopoly the Autonomists were determined to break. When, in 1890, the Liberals confined the vote to classes which supported the Unionists, the Autonomist position was intolerable and they withdrew from the Cortes.

Autonomy would not merely destroy the Unionists' control of local life; it might threaten their profits.[1] The Spanish colony, from wholesale merchants to shop-keepers, feared that effective self-government might allow the creole producers to abolish the protectionist customs union with Spain on which these profits were based and which had already been modified to suit Cuban demands. The Cuban economy, stagnant before 1884, was based on sales of tobacco and sugar to the United States, so that the 'Spanish' interest pulled against what Cubans called their natural market. Cuban producers argued that the true policy for Cuba, hopelessly at the mercy of an American tariff war, was free trade. Spanish merchants and economists argued that Cuba could become an integrated part of the metropolitan economy and that Cubans had no right 'without considering

[1] The Unionists wanted both a customs union with Spain (i.e. the *cabotaje* of 1882) *and* a commercial treaty with the U.S.A., i.e. the best of both worlds.

the interests of the metropolis . . . to be seduced by the lyricism of free trade'.[1] Spanish politicians argued that, even with existing customs revenues, Cuba was a net loss to the national exchequer. Cánovas held that the Cuban demand for tariff reductions meant the abandonment of Cuba, which would become an insupportable burden. The root problem was economic—as it had been for the empire lost after 1810. A poor metropolitan economy could not supply the colonial market and political control became intolerable for the colonists when it was exercised to keep out supplies of cheap goods or to distort 'natural' markets. By the 1890's the tariff advantages enjoyed by Spanish goods in Cuba were probably insufficient for the competitive power of Spanish industry.This doomed all hopes of imperial preference. We do not possess evidence to decide how far the shipping and textile interests of Catalonia or the flour millers of Santander could influence Spanish politicians: probably imperialism needed little support from the politics of interest. Romero Robledo would have been a Unionist without his marriage to a Cuban heiress.

As with Ireland, too little reform came to Cuba too late for Home Rule to stave off separatism. Maura, who was Sagasta's Minister of Colonies, was, like Gladstone, converted to Home Rule partly by the general arguments for liberal courses, and partly by the impossibility of ruling Cuba should the Autonomists continue to boycott the Spanish parliament. In 1893 he proposed that Cuba be granted a single assembly for domestic concerns. The Captain General would consider its advice with the help of a council composed of the 'live forces' of Cuba; the municipalities were to be removed from the control of the government. This reform would have weakened the electoral influence of the old parties in Cuba, and Sagasta was unwilling to take the political and party risks entailed.[2] A less drastic

[1] P. Alzola y Mindorro, *Relaciones comerciales entre la península y las Antillas* (1895), 16, 33, 107–10—an interesting example of Spanish special pleading against the facts of the U.S. connexion.

[2] Maura believed some degree of autonomy was 'safe' because racial conflict would keep creoles, without an army of their own, within the Spanish orbit. He did not believe the Cuban problem a problem *sui generis* but merely another indication of the evils of the suffocating centralization which paralysed Spanish energies; cf. his attitude to Catalonia (*D.S.C.*, 14 July 1896). Maura's reforms were supported in Cuba by the Autonomists and by the Reformists who split off from the Constitutional Unionists.

reform sponsored by Maura's successor, Abarzuza, was still being debated when the Separatist revolt broke out in the May of 1895. Even after the Separatist war had started, Maura believed that the continued refusal of reform would drive Autonomists and neutrals still loyal to Spain into the arms of the Separatists.

Against this enlightened liberalism Romero Robledo was the Chamberlain of Spain, and the political power of his group, in the confused political life of the late nineties, was sufficient to force Cánovas into the role of a reluctant Salisbury. Autonomy was 'shameful' and a Cuban chamber would pass from the hands of the Autonomists into those of the Separatists. 'Autonomy and Separatism are synonymous.' Glued to Spanish sovereignty by conviction and the interests of their political allies in Cuba, Romero Robledo's followers believed that, once revolt had broken out, Spanish sovereignty could be modified by administrative devolution only *after* the army had secured undisputed recognition of that sovereignty by Cuba. This argument, which precluded any reform, was reinforced when the Autonomist masses, as opposed to their leaders, showed their sympathies with separatism, and by the generals' belief that the honour of the army demanded unconditional surrender from the rebels. Cánovas, reflecting on Spanish history, probably concluded that Spain could not hold Cuba and that only a grant of autonomy would end the war. He seems to have viewed the Cuban question solely in terms of steering between the various pressure groups in Madrid in order to retain the leadership of his party, threatened on the one hand by Romero Robledo and the generals with their belief in 'salutary rigour' and on the other hand by the *Silvelista* conservatives who came to see in autonomy the only solution. It was the weakness of 'the Monster's' political position that denied him a Cuban policy.[1]

The consistent failure of the Autonomists to achieve any concession from Madrid strengthened those among the Separatists who had refused to accept the defeat of their ideal of an independent Cuban republic; rejecting the Peace of Zanjón they continued 'the little war' of guerrilla resistance. Their

[1] For an excellent discussion of Cánovas's Cuban policies see E. R. May, *Imperial Democracy* (New York, 1961), 94 ff.

declared programme was to oppose autonomy to the bitter end as a policy of 'radical and proven nullity'. The soul of the movement for a Cuban republic was Martí, whose hatred of Spanish rule dated from his college days—he had been jailed at the age of seventeen for laughing at Spanish soldiers. The most remarkable of the Latin-American liberators since the great generation of the early nineteenth century, he came from a poor family—his father was a sergeant; moved by a faith in the democratic capacities of 'the humble' he did not share the wealthy Autonomists' fears of a black Cuba. An able journalist, a tireless speaker and organizer, dogged by ill health and poverty, overcoming the jealousies and authoritarian tendencies of the exiled guerrilla chieftains, he built up in the United States the Cuban Revolutionary party and financed it by funds raised on speaking tours among the Cuban exiles.[1] In the end his ideal of a free, democratic republic was defeated. The liberation of Cuba was brought about by the intervention of the United States and Martí's revolution was 'frustrated'.[2] Cuba, freed from Spain, appeared subject to the rule of an oligarchy and to the dominance of American interests in a one-crop economy. The country which put its economic future at the mercy of a single crop, Martí always maintained, sold itself into slavery, a slavery emphasized by the Platt Amendmemt to the new Cuban constitution which gave the United States a right to intervene in the domestic affairs of the new republic. However necessary and salutary intervention was, it denied Cuba the status of a sovereign nation; thus the completion of Martí's 'frustrated revolution' by the redemption of the economic and political sovereignty of Cuba became the key concept of Fidel Castro's early thought.

In February 1895 Martí gave the orders which set off rebellion in Cuba. Arriving in Cuba with a pocket Cicero and a revolver, Martí himself was soon killed; but the Separatists kept the war in being until American intervention could

[1] The party was founded among the Florida tobacco workers in 1891. See R. Guerra y Sánchez, *Cuban Nation*, 123 ff. J. Manach's, *José Martí* (1933), though hagiographical in tone, gives an impression of Martí's tenacity as a revolutionary.

[2] For the concept of the 'frustrated revolution' see S. Aguirre, in *Cuba Socialista* (Havana, Feb. 1962, no. 6, 1–21). Martí's main fears were the emergence of a military *caudillo* and the subordination of David (Cuba) to Goliath (the U.S.A.); cf. his last letter, much quoted in Castro's Cuba.

secure independence. This they could do because of the nature of the war—a guerrilla war, of rural against urban Cuba. 'The few Spaniards who are on the island', declared Martínez Campos, 'only dare proclaim themselves such in the cities; the rest of the inhabitants hate Spain.' Led by experienced leaders like Gómez and Maceo, their ranks fed by poor whites and negroes who found taking to the hills a remedy for the ills of ancient hardship sharpened by economic depression, the guerrillas were armed by filibustering expeditions from America which the Spanish navy could not intercept. The aim of the Spanish command was to roll the rebel forces back from the west into the mountains of the east and there to destroy them. The strategy of Gómez was to deny this crowning victory; like all true guerrilla leaders he was convinced that by avoiding battle in a terrain made for partisan warfare he could win the war. Apart from the hostility of the inhabitants which gave all troop movements away, the Spanish army fought a lack of railways and roads, the jungle, rains, and disease rather than the enemy. Much has been blamed on the administrative deficiency of the Spanish army and its hospitals; yet even the American army, when it landed in Cuba, found that any military operation brought fifty per cent. sickness casualties in its train. After a month's campaign the American army was a ruin.[1]

Cánovas, who had succeeded Sagasta a month after the Cuban rebellion had started, appointed as commander-in-chief against the rebels Martínez Campos, whose liberal views on Cuba had long been known. Martínez Campos believed concessions were inevitable and should be attempted at the outset; Cánovas and the Unionists in Cuba, however, blocked any attempt at negotiated settlement which, in any case, the Separatists rejected out of hand. Unable to pursue his own policy of concession, Martínez Campos was unwilling to adopt the

[1] See the comments of Theodore Roosevelt, *The Rough Riders* (London, 1899), on the state of the Spanish army at Santiago. As in all colonial wars in the tropics, casualties from disease were vastly greater than battle casualties. In 1897 total Spanish casualties were 32,500, of which diphtheria and typhoid accounted for 14,500, yellow fever 6,000, malaria 7,000. For conditions in the American forces see H. H. Sargent, *The Campaign of Santiago de Cuba* (London, 1907), iii, esp. 45. On 3 Aug. the general officers reported 'this army must be proved at once or it will perish'.

drastic measures by which the war might have been ended while the rebels were at their weakest, and, by splitting his forces to defend isolated plantations, he destroyed his own army as a striking force. Late in 1895 Gómez marched across the island and made contact with Maceo in the west and by Christmas the rebels were making life uncomfortable in Havana itself. Confronted with military failure, Martínez Campos admitted that other methods, which he himself would not put into operation, might be more successful. His successor was Weyler, the military incarnation of the policy of resistance to the end (January 1896). Weyler, a non-smoker and a mild anti-clerical, was a military technician rather than the brute of American propaganda. He saw the war as a military operation which could be ended in two years by meeting rebel ruthlessness with concentration camps—a policy condemned as barbarous but which Great Britain was forced to adopt a few years later in South Africa as the only effective way to finish a commando war supported by the local population. 'How do they want me to wage war? With bishops' pastorals and presents of sweets and money?'[1] Weyler determined to cut off and destroy Maceo whom he regarded as the most dangerous of the Cuban leaders because of his influence over the negroes. In December 1896 Maceo was killed and the Spaniards regarded the war as finished; with the trains running on time and the tobacco harvest safely gathered, Weyler was preparing for a decisive campaign in the east. Cánovas, he held, could, in these conditions of near pacification, risk political concessions in order to disarm the mounting belligerency of the United States and hostile critics in Spain itself.[2]

Cánovas was acutely aware of the dangers of intervention by the United States. His government had missed an early chance of preventing it by the rejection of Olney's proposals for mediation; but, in the April of 1896, neither the army nor opinion would hear of anything else but *la política de la guerra*, a gamble on suppressing the revolt by military force before American opinion could veer from a sympathy with Cuba, which never-

[1] Cf. Valeriano Weyler, *Mi mando en Cuba* (1910–11), i. 165–6; iv. 533. This book is a long refutation of the charge of barbarity, from the purely military point of view.

[2] M. Fernández Almagro, *Historia política*, ii. 331–3.

theless respected Spanish sovereignty, to armed intervention against Spain in order to stop further destruction of life and property.[1] Such intervention both Presidents Cleveland and McKinley hoped to avoid by concessions which would placate the rebels and yet satisfy Spanish dignity—an impossible policy doomed to failure from the start. Cánovas's limited reforms of March 1897 recognizing the 'administrative personality' of Cuba neither altered the situation in Cuba nor eased relations with the United States and his policy was losing support in Spain itself. When in July 1897 the Liberals broke the party truce and Moret announced his conversion to autonomy, opinion swung to this talisman where previously it had seen no honourable salvation outside *la política de la guerra*. When Cánovas was assassinated by an Italian anarchist on his annual summer cure, his Cuban policy was bankrupt (8 August 1897). His last act, symbolically enough, was to telegraph the Minister of the Interior on the subject of a senatorial election in Cadiz.

After a number of caretaker ministries, Sagasta came to power (October 1897). He dismissed Weyler and gave Cuba autonomous government—a complete and hasty reversal of Spanish policy on which he did not even bother to consult the Cortes. Autonomy was bitterly opposed by the Unionists, and it was their riots which caused the United States to send the battleship *Maine* to protect American life and property. The *Maine* was blown up by an explosion which American experts attributed to a Spanish mine. Though this enraged American opinion it did not alter McKinley's policy. He disliked war, as did his business friends, and he did not believe in Cuban freedom; but he was incapable of resisting public opinion, now at the mercy of jingoists and idealists. By 1898 only the concession of complete independence could have pacified Cuba; Sagasta's autonomy, though satisfying every formal American demand, did not. With Cuba unpacified McKinley saw no alternative but to declare a war he did not want. The Cuban war, which

[1] The text of the Olney note is in O. Ferrera, *The Last Spanish War* (London, 1937). From 1896 on Spain constantly plotted to meet American intervention by an appeal to the concert of Europe: from the pope down sympathy took the form of counselling concession before opinion forced the president of the U.S.A. to declare war (op. cit. 120–1). Cf. Bülow's comment: 'I admire the courage Spain has shown but I would admire more a display of common sense.'

was the first satisfying display of national patriotism and unity after the Civil War, was 'a people's war, not an administration war'.[1]

The first blow fell on the Philippines where the army had been successful against a separatist revolt. The Spanish Pacific squadron was a fighting force on paper only; in May 1898, Admiral Dewey, in a battle which lasted an hour, blew the Spanish ships out of the sea from the safe range of two thousand yards, as if they had been practice targets.[2] In the Atlantic, Admiral Cervera knew he must be defeated should his squadron be ordered to the Antilles. His advice was rejected by the government and a board of admirals who could not face up to a confession of impotence and an immediate peace; Cervera's commanders later maintained 'in honour and conscience their conviction that the government in Madrid was determined that the fleet should be destroyed as soon as possible in order to find a means of arriving rapidly at peace'—an accusation which cannot be entirely dismissed. Once in the Antilles, Cervera, without coal to operate, shut himself in Santiago Bay, only to be ordered out of harbour and to certain destruction by the blockading American fleet. On 3 July 1898 the whole Spanish squadron was destroyed outside Santiago at the cost of one casualty to the Americans. Cervera had to swim from his flagship and the one modern ship with speed enough to escape ran out of coal. The two most complete naval disasters of modern times meant that Spain had to sign away, in the Treaty of Paris, Cuba, Puerto Rico, and the Philippines.

The loss of the greater part of the American empire in the twenties had left no psychological scar, for it was lost in a civil war of metropolitan against colonial Spaniards. Cuba was wrenched from Spain by defeat at the hands of a foreign power her press had taught her to despise as a nation of vulgar meat-vendors or to fear as a Colossus. It was the public destruction of the image of Spain as a great power which turned defeat into moral disaster. Defeat destroyed the confidence already eroded

[1] S. Flagg Bemis, *The Latin American Policy of the United States* (New York, 1943), 136.

[2] For the incredible story of the naval war see H. W. Wilson, *The Downfall of Spain* (London, 1900). Spanish experts had argued that the Spanish fleet was superior to the U.S. fleet; its greatest weaknesses, however, were that it had never been able to afford target practice or coal good enough to keep up speed.

by economic depression and political confusion and it was attributed to the political system which presided over the disaster. This attribution was unjust in that no political system could have saved the last remnants of the colonial empire of a second rate power.

X

THE FOUNDATIONS OF A MODERN ECONOMY

SINCE 1854 the vision of a 'modern' economy, growing towards prosperity, had haunted the imagination of progressive Spaniards. The gap between Spain and Europe was no longer seen as an intellectual problem, as a lag in culture, but as an economic fact. In the later years of the century the closing of this gap was conceived as a national necessity which would entail the destruction or modification of traditional attitudes. By 1900 the apologists of Europeanization were attacking 'hindrances' in the spirit of their eighteenth-century predecessors and preaching the Protestant ethic of hard work and the pursuit of wealth.

This chapter will attempt an analysis of the successes and failures of this pursuit in the later nineteenth and early twentieth century.[1] The main cycles are fairly clear. Between 1877 and 1886 there was a period of optimistic growth during an era of depression in Europe. When Europe recovered, Spain collapsed into the crisis of the 1890's. Recovery, punctuated by bad harvests and short-term crises in industry, was reasonably steady between 1900 and 1913 while the war of 1914–18 converted neutral Spain into a favoured nation. Primo de Rivera was fortunate in presiding over a period of prosperity which collapsed abruptly in 1929. Insulated to some extent from the effects of the world crisis, the economy was stagnant or declining under the Republic of 1931. The Civil War dealt it a terrible blow from which it could not easily recover after 1939. Thus 1929 may be seen as the apogee of the growth that had begun in the nineteenth century and it was not until the 1950's

[1] It does not examine in detail the years after 1913 except where such analysis follows naturally. For the effects of the war of 1914–18 see below, pp. 497–8. For developments after 1923 see pp. 577–81, 588–9, 613–15.

that agricultural production caught up with the levels of the last year of the Dictatorship.

It was in these difficult years that the imbalances and discontinuities of earlier growth were exposed. Spain was revealed as an underdeveloped economy where the growth of population exceeded that of production. Threatening since the turn of the century, this problem became acute after 1930. Infant mortality was halved in a country where agricultural improvement proved difficult and industrial growth slow.[1]

1. *Prosperity and Crisis: 1870–1898*

'Without being what you might call a rich country Spain has become comfortably off'; so an economist summed up the economic progress of the late seventies and early eighties, the boom years of the 'gold fever' when prosperity was unembarrassed by the claims of organized labour. In its early years, especially after 1877, the Restoration was fortunate: the Bessemer process and phylloxera created an unprecedented demand for iron-ore and wine; after 1882 the Cuban market was absorbing Catalan surpluses; railway construction picked up dramatically after it had practically ceased during the Revolution. A post-war boom seems to have eliminated the effects in Spain of depression in Europe;[2] however, in the late eighties expansion was halted by an agricultural crisis common to the continent. The 'gold fever' of the Restoration turned into the pessimism and literature of economic anxiety of the nineties, a phenomenon of depression sharpened and heightened by the loss of Cuba into the state of mind known as regenerationism.

The stimulus to prosperity came initially from the injection of foreign mining capital encouraged by the liberal mining laws of the September Revolution, just as the great inflow of French capital in the fifties had started with the Revolution of 1854. From the seventies the iron concerns of France, Germany, and England, as a result of the Bessemer process, were competitors for the low phosphorus 'red ore' of Biscay.

[1] Infant mortality 1900: 200 per 1,000; 1950: 90 per 1,000.

[2] Cf. the descriptions of the English consuls, e.g. *P.P.* 1877, lxxxiii. 1496, for the effects of the Carlist war on shipping and for the post-war recovery. 1877 was 'a quiet year and a prosperous year' and marked the beginning of the upward turn.

In 1899, the peak year, eight million tons were exported, England alone investing well over £7,000,000 in developing Basque iron.[1] The roots of Spanish economic nationalism lie in this hey-day of foreign control of mineral resources. Spain was imitating Esau to the detriment of a native iron industry; the great foreign concerns behaved as quasi-sovereign states governed in a foreign language, exploiting Spain as a colonial economy by corrupting her politicians. Yet Spanish capital had not and could not develop these resources unaided: ten years of British capital and British engineers quadrupled the output of the Rio Tinto mines, making Spain the greatest copper producer of Europe. It was the foreign capital injected by the export of ore which financed the modernization of the technically backward Basque iron industry. Even so it remained a high-cost industry, deprived of cheap supplies of good coking coal and technically backward—of the thirteen largest furnaces only five used coke and there was only one Bessemer converter in the industry by 1890. In the 1880's it could only absorb a tenth of the ore production.

Elsewhere, in industry and agriculture, the early years of the Restoration were years of relative prosperity and expansion. After the slump of 1866 cotton recovered and expanded once the cotton famine had passed; it survived the severe crisis of 1878, and the opening up of the Cuban market after 1882 brought what one historian has called 'the euphoria of cotton'.[2] Even more remarkable was the growth of the new large-scale wool industry, now the third largest in Europe. Again it is hard to accept the protectionist zealots' incessantly reiterated argument that freer trade had 'ruined' Catalan industry. If it destroyed anything, it destroyed, to the relative advantage of Catalan mills, the old semi-domestic wool industry spread throughout the towns and villages of Spain; once again peripheral Spain triumphed over the centre. Yet to Catalans this triumph seemed insecure; as in the mid-century, they hoped to

[1] The richest Biscayan deposits were the now exhausted Vena Campanil (*c.* 50 per cent. Fe). For British imports and investment see W. O. Henderson, *Britain and Industrial Europe* (Liverpool, 1954), 215 ff. The biggest concerns were Orconera Iron (owned by Guest, Keen & Baldwin) and the Consett Iron Co. Belgian, French, and German capital was also involved.

[2] Raw-cotton imports had nearly tripled 1875–89; exports of cotton goods expanded tenfold 1882–97. See J. Vicens Vives, *Els Catalans*, 60–61.

balance textiles by heavy industry. Although railways and the textile expansion brought good profits to the metallurgical and engineering industries, these had to struggle against failure to find Catalan coal: thus Catalonia was without a modern blast-furnace in 1900.

Confronted with this 'failure', Catalans continued to feel that the *Catalan* economy was 'lop-sided'; too much was invested in cotton when it absorbed half the industrial investment of Catalonia. This argument only makes sense in the framework of a Catalan economic nationalism which can, for example, call Asturian coal 'foreign'; for Spain as a whole, considered as an economic unit, it was reasonable that heavy industry should have concentrated where costs were lower. Catalan insecurity—which was at the roots of the drive for protection—came not merely from a desire to shore up a shipping and iron industry that was losing out to the Basques; it came also from a sense that in spite of rising production, the Catalan textile manufacturers had not succeeded in creating a truly competitive industry. Nothing is more remarkable, in Catalan protectionist literature, than the insistence on figures which showed Catalan 'inferiority': factories equipped with half the average number of spindles in the rest of Europe; output per man less than half that of the U.S.A. To modernize 'our poor and feeble' industry in order to make it competitive would fling half the cotton operatives out of work. However justifiable on humanitarian and social grounds this was scarcely the argument of a resolute entrepreneurial class.[1]

Industrial prosperity, as a permanent condition, was based on the purchasing power of the vast majority of Spaniards: that is on agricultural prosperity. In the seventies and eighties this was increased by a natural calamity—phylloxera in the French vineyards. From 1868 France began to import huge quantities of Spanish wine; between 1882 and 1892, with thirty steamers a week taking wine from Tarragona to French ports, Spain dominated the world wine market, a domination which was exploited with anarchic euphoria and little thought for the future.[2] The vine once more triumphed over wheat, spreading from the periphery inwards to the centre, establishing its

[1] *Memoria en defensa de los intereses moralesy materiales de Cataluña* (Barcelona, 1885), 127.

[2] *P.P.* 1880, lxxiv. 918.

primacy in La Mancha and Rioja. In 1885–6 the boom broke: prices fell by a half in some areas between 1885 and 1887.[1] The crisis was complete when phylloxera invaded Spain: the new vineyards were often simply abandoned.[2]

During the same years the other great traditional crop—wheat—was confronted by a collapse of prices which spread to other cereals like rice. Spain failed to hold the colonial market in flour and rice at the moment when native producers were undercut by imported grain and rice in the home market, a competition which made the extensions of recent years in the Valencian rice fields an unprofitable enterprise.[3] The wheat crisis was the consequence of cheap maritime transport combined with expensive internal transport: it was more costly to send wheat overland from the central regions to Barcelona than to import it by sea from Odessa or America. Thus these regions lost the peripheral market to the imported wheat which supplied the large-scale milling industry of Barcelona.[4] A spate of books and two government commissions investigated the agricultural crisis.

Thus by 1887 the 'gold fever' that had underwritten the political stability of the Restoration was turning into depression. Already in 1886 the metallurgical and engineering concerns in Barcelona were paying no dividends; in 1887 they began to lay off hands. Industrialists and agriculturists saw only one remedy: a return to protection.[5]

The Catalans could never accept the partial triumph of free trade in Figuerola's progressive tariff reductions of 1869. Their

[1] Cf. *La crisis agrícola y pecuaria* (1887), 350 ff. (1885: 45 pesetas per hectolitre; 1887: 22 pesetas). Thus in Aragon the great extensions of vineyards proved unprofitable.

[2] This is still apparent to the eye in coastal Catalonia. The tourist trade of the Costa Brava has set this region on its feet again and created an area of high prices and land values.

[3] For the loss of the Cuban rice market in the 1880's see the results of the government inquiry in *La crisis arrocera* (1887), 63. The Santander flour mills were losing the colonial market gradually after 1877 and there was a disastrous drop in 1891.

[4] Cf. J. Fontana i Lazaro, 'La gran crisi bladera', in *Serra d'or* (Nov. 1960). Cf. supplies to Barcelona by rail (in million kg.), 1884: 72; 1885: 54; 1886: 14. By sea: 1884: 55; 1885: 76; 1886: 111. For the conflict between the central wheat-growers and the large millers of the coast see J. M. Azara, *Apuntes sociales y agrarios* (Saragossa, 1919), 148.

[5] Cf. Martínez Maroto, op. cit. 320 ff.

organizations consistently campaigned for a return to protection and against any trade treaties which, by most-favoured-nation clauses, might hinder the abandonment of Figuerola's low duties.[1] Their arguments, powerfully stated though they were, could make little headway in a period of boom which contradicted their economic pessimism; powerful interests—the railway companies in particular—within the Liberal party still regarded freer trade as one of the conquests of September and were able to force through the commercial treaty with France (1882) in spite of bitter protectionist opposition.

With the crisis of the eighties the protectionist cause gathered strength and allies. As the 1887 Agricultural Commission revealed, the wheat interests now were strongly protectionist: textiles, shipping, and metallurgy had long clamoured for protection. Protectionism now began to make converts even among the Liberals: Gamazo, the best-known deputy for the corn interest, deserted the party on this issue. Romero Robledo announced his conversion, and it was the prospect of a protectionist coalition of dissident Liberals and Conservatives which led Cánovas (never an enthusiastic free trader since 1875, when he had restored protective tariffs for fiscal purposes) to make public his own conversion to protection. The conservative tariff of 1891 meant the triumph of protectionism. In 1892 Moret attempted to revert to free trade by a tariff treaty with Germany which would extend, through most-favoured-nation clauses, to the other countries with whom Spain had commercial treaties. Whereas the protectionists had failed against the French treaty of 1882, they were successful in 1892 when the Germany treaty was flung out of the Senate. In the National League of Producers Catalonia had at last succeeded, after forty years of propaganda, in creating a 'national' organization committed to protection, embracing the Basque steel interests and the Castilian wheat interests. From 1891 the Bilbao–Barcelona–Valladolid axis determines the economic decisions of Spain; tariffs move steadily upwards, until in 1906 Spain has the highest tariff walls in Europe.

Both the major parties had accepted protection, the Conservatives with enthusiasm, the Liberals as an electoral necessity and from fear of the social consequences of unemployment.

[1] This campaign is described in M. Pugès, *Proteccionismo*, 150 ff.

Rather than the application of an economic dogma, as the triumph of free trade had been, full protection came as the systematization of concessions to one interest group after another.[1] There was nothing peculiarly Spanish about the triumph of protectionism; it was triumphing throughout Europe. What was peculiar was the intensity with which the ideal of national self-sufficiency was pursued and the comparative ease with which 'interventionism' fitted into the traditions of the Spanish state. The liberal economy of Spain, incomplete as it was, always had an esoteric, foreign appearance. Now tariffs were not enough: there must be the effort to develop self-sufficiency, safeguarding national production by forcing up national consumption. 'Political economy must accept the concept of the *Patria* and subordinate itself to it. The *Patria* is an association of and for the mutual aid of consumers and producers in order to create a life of its own as an individual family is created.' The metaphysics of autarky were thus stated by Cánovas in the nineties: another conservative, Maura, gave it further extension by the legislation of 1907 which forced national products on all industries connected with the state—railways and public works in particular. Thus Spain preferred an expensive home-made navy to cheaper ships bought abroad.

High protection in the end compelled state regulation of production—the 'interventionism' that became a much criticized feature of Primo de Rivera's dictatorship. This was partly a consequence of protection as a device to establish 'missing' industries or, as in the case of the sugar industry, to regulate over-production of a protected crop. The traditional paternalism of the Castilian state had never been fully eroded. Thus the company law of the mid-century gave the state a representation in industry which would have been inconceivable in England. All these traditions were well advanced before 1923: nothing that Primo de Rivera did was not contained in the economic ideals of Cánovas del Castillo and little of his 'interventionism', as we shall see, could be abandoned by the Second Republic.

This trend towards protection and 'interventionism' was opposed by a handful of liberal economists, and the representa-

[1] Cf. in 1926 the concession of tariffs on imported maize was 'compensated' by an increase of meat and egg tariffs to the injured interests.

tives of the export trades and the railway interest. The consequences of the system, it was argued, were evident in high industrial costs which prevented exports, in high internal prices which kept consumption low, in the maintenance of crops —cereals and sugar for instance—in uneconomic conditions.[1] Dissident economists explained the slowness of economic progress in terms of this exaggerated autarky: the protected agriculture of Castile could never raise the purchasing power necessary to expand industrial demand; they argued that once this inelastic internal market was saturated, an increase in industrial production could only be absorbed by the periphery, where the export of Basque iron and the fruits of the Levante created profits. Thus a reduction of demand for these exports could have as important an effect as a crop failure in the great cereal areas.

Whatever the economic arguments against protection may have been, it is hard to see how Spanish politicians could have acted other than they did. If ill constructed tariffs are worse than no tariffs at all, freer trade was, nevertheless, a calculated risk as a recipe for the industrial take-off: in the end it staked all on the purchasing power brought by the increased export of the fruit and vegetable crops of the eastern coast. Yet, from wool to wine, all the agricultural export staples had been destroyed by developments outside Spain and in 1930 came the turn of the Levante: the Ottawa Agreements robbed rice and orange exporters of the London market. It was inconceivable that politicians should risk the social and political consequences of sacrificing Castilian agriculture and Catalan industry. Both agricultural protectionists and their critics based their arguments on the poverty of Spanish agriculture outside the periphery: free traders risked the reversion of the centre to scrub, protectionists demanded that the whole economy should be sacrificed to maintaining a huge marginal farm.[2]

[1] It can be maintained that protection kept valuable areas of irrigated land in sugar-beet that could have been better used for other crops, and that much cereal production was totally uneconomic. Anti-protectionists could always point to the very low consumption of sugar in Spain as a reflection of the high costs fostered by protection.

[2] The arguments against exaggerated protection, as well as the best bibliography of the subject, are contained in Román Perpiñá, *De estructura económica y economía hispana* (1952), esp. 283 ff. Of course it can be maintained that reversion to scrub

The demand for protection was only one aspect of the economic pessimism which followed the collapse of the Restoration boom. There was a spate of literature, largely devoted to budgetary problems, which emphasized the poverty of Spain, demanding a reduction in state expenditure and a consequent lessening of taxation on the 'productive classes'. Apart from protection, the measures suggested for economic regeneration (the phrase *hacer pais*—to 'make' a country—was already current) were scarcely distinguishable from the frivolous *arbitrismo* or projecting of seventeenth-century political economists. The remedies proposed were either worse than the disease they were to cure—for example the reduction of state expenditure on forest reclamation—or politically impossible. To demand in the name of economy, which was the watchword of the eighties, a reduction in the army and bureaucracy was to propose the alteration of the whole structure of Spanish society. It meant impoverishing a middle sector typical of an under-developed economy. To such a drastic step 'political considerations of the highest importance' were opposed.[1]

2. *Agriculture and Industry*

The loss of Cuba seemed to threaten economic disaster, particularly in Catalonia where by 1894 60 per cent. of the export trade was to Cuba, and had come to rest on manufactured goods.[2] This trade had become an important interest

was the 'correct' solution. A soil scientist might give the same answer as a radical free-trader, in that ruthless competition would have re-established better soil conditions by converting marginal wheat lands to other uses.

[1] Celedonio Rodrigañez (*El problema económica*, 1910) was one of the few writers in the flood of budgetary polemics who stood out against economy by insisting on the necessity of fostering increased production by increased investment. He proposed to raise the money for productive expenditure (then 12 per cent. of the budget) by raising 2,000 million by loan for railways, irrigation, agricultural and forestry improvements. These notions became the policy of Primo de Rivera. For a typical 'economy' pamphlet see M. de la Paliza, *La cuestión social y económica* (1892).

[2] The French consul concluded that 'les possessions d'outre-mer constituent les clients les plus serieux de la Catalogne', *Rapports consulaires: Barcelone* (Paris, 1894), 322. Cotton manufactures in the colonial trade (30 per cent.) now outdistanced shoes and leather goods (20 per cent.) and completely overshadowed soap (5 per cent.) and paper (10 per cent.). Total trade with Cuba was about equal to that with each of the two main European customers of Spain—England and France. Cotton exports, which had risen from 3,500 to 12,000 tons from 1892 to 1897 dropped by half in 1899–1900 and by 1900–4 to a third. English consuls prophesied disaster for ports like Coruña and Santander whose trade was with

with its financial centre in the Banco Hispano Colonial (1876), a combination of shipping, exporting, and textile interests. By 1900 the colonial trade had almost ceased to exist.

Yet after the disaster of 1898 foreign observers, over-estimating the importance of the Cuban trade to Spain as a whole and unconscious of the effects of changes in the terms of trade, were so impressed by 'recovery' that they frequently adopted the psychological theory—current amongst the post-disaster regenerationists—of a return to native vitality after a 'factitious' dependence on remnants of colonial greatness. The French consul at Barcelona noted *une grande poussée industrielle* in the years after the disaster; English consuls lyricized over 'truly wonderful growth' or reported 'a general forward movement'.[1] Others observed the erosion of traditional ways in a nation-wide railway economy, an acceleration in the rate of social change. Spaniards, on the whole, were less optimistic. Economic progress was a superficial ornament—Ortega y Gasset remarked that cars were symbols, to be kept highly polished by underpaid chauffeurs, not means of transport. Spain remained economically and socially invertebrate, a colonial economy exploited by foreign capital.[2] Rather than trust to the processes of development Spaniards hankered after a Messiah: a reputable economist could represent British prosperity as the unaided achievement of Adam Smith. They constantly appealed to the state and when the state could do nothing to induce prosperity they talked of 'the absence of the state'. This cast of mind lies at the root of the Spanish disillusionment with parliamentary liberalism.

What were the characteristics of the economy after 1900 that could justify pessimism or encourage optimism? There was an adverse balance of trade; hence the drive to create by protection a self-sufficient economy which would bolster up a depreciating currency which reflected the burden of import surpluses. There were promising new departures: the growth

the Antilles; cf. *P.P.* 1897, 539, 'the export trade of this district [the Coruña consular district] would certainly be almost entirely extinguished by the loss of Cuba'.

[1] *P.P.* 1905, xcii. 533 (Malaga); 1903, lxviii. 10113 (Barcelona). The consuls noted how new prosperity escaped certain regions, e.g. Cadiz with its 'lack of all activity'.

[2] It would be tedious to detail the host of pessimistic treatises, but J. Sendador Gómez, *Castilla en escombros* (Valladolid, 1915), will serve better than the literary laments of the 'generation of '98'.

of heavy industry in the north (in Biscay and to a lesser extent in Guipúzcoa) where the laws of industrial concentration and the availability of raw materials were working against the industrial primacy of Catalonia; later the beginnings of a light industry based on hydro-electric power redressed the balance in favour of the older industrial complex. But these developments, limited by an imperfect system of rail communication which was to collapse under the strains of the Great War, failed to stimulate the stagnant centre. In so far as Spain experienced a minor industrial and agricultural revolution it was confined, for the most part, to the periphery.

Throughout the nineteenth and twentieth centuries—except for the years of the First World War—the adverse balance of trade was financed by renewed foreign lending and the savings of *émigrés*. Thus was concealed the fundamental weakness of the economy—the incapacity of a producer of primary products to pay for the goods and industrial equipment it needed. This situation became even more precarious as, in the twentieth century, exports came to be dominated by agricultural products in uncertain markets.[1] It could not be cured by an unrelenting struggle to create a self-sufficient economy. Like all nineteenth-century statesmen, the rulers of Spain were obsessed with the maintenance of the exchange value of the national currency, and the 'defence of the peseta' links finance ministers as far removed as Villaverde and Calvo Sotelo. Since the adverse balance inevitably showed in the depreciation of the peseta and since to devalue would have brought 'national ignominy', there seemed only two remedies: the avoidance of government expenditure as a cause of internal inflation and depreciation—and this meant the avoidance of the public works Spain so desperately needed—or the attempt to cut down imports by protection.

Success was limited since certain imports—for example raw

[1] For the structure of the Spanish foreign trade see 'El desarollo del comercio exterior española' (*R. Ec. Pol.* vi. 2. 26 ff., Madrid, 1953); V. Andrés Álvárez 'Las balanzas estadísticas del nuestro comercio exterior' (ibid. l. 1), a critique of official statistics; J. L. Ezcurdia 'La estructura de la balanza comercial española' (*Boletín de estudios económicos*, viii (1953), 30 ff.). The main changes are: a shift in markets from France to Great Britain, and to a lesser extent, Germany; the replacement of wine exports (the leading export in 1877) by oranges; the 'golden year' of 1916; the reversal of the terms of trade in 1920.

cotton, until after the Civil War, and petrol could not be avoided. These efforts and, more important, the insignificance of her foreign trade—predominantly agricultural it constituted but a quarter of the foreign trade per inhabitant of France—may have insulated Spain, to some extent, from the violent fluctuations of the European economy. This insulation, it has been argued, saved her from the extreme consequences of the collapse of the thirties when prices remained stable although her main exports had been crippled by the world slump.[1] The price paid for stability, it may be argued, was high costs and low living standards. Before the Civil War bicycles were a rarity in rural Spain, motor-cycles nowhere to be seen; the Spaniard ate more frugally than anyone else in Europe outside the Balkans and southern Italy. It was necessity that had elevated sobriety to the rank of a national virtue.

Protectionists held that, since foreign trade played such a small part in the national economy, the trading deficit was of little importance compared with the creation of a domestic market. Here then lay the nub of the question. How can the purchasing power of an over-populated agricultural country, where agricultural improvement is difficult, be raised? It is relatively easy to stimulate growth in a backward agrarian economy where higher yields are an immediate possibility: not so in a long-standing traditional economy where production is often reasonably near the maximum permitted by natural conditions or restricted by the pattern of land-ownership, or where heavy over-population makes a more profitable use of land out of the question without a clearance of men. Since farming conditions in the *secano*, which prevailed over so much of central Spain, were capable of little immediate improvement and since there was no hope of an agrarian reform which might release productivity 'imprisoned' by the latifundia system—in any case a time-consuming process—the 'export provinces' of the periphery remained the dynamic factor in the economy—especially the provinces of Valencia and Barcelona which between them supplied 30 per cent. of Spanish exports.

Spectacular progress was limited to the traditional irrigated

[1] This immunity is studied in Lefaucheux, *La peseta et l'économie espagnole depuis 1923* (Paris, 1935). He concludes that isolation was as important a stabilizing factor as devaluation (131–5).

areas of the Levante, Catalonia, and those areas of Andalusia and Aragon where small-scale investment was richly productive; the greatest contribution towards curing the adverse trade balance which so alarmed the protectionists was made by the orange growers and market gardeners of the Levante and Catalonia. Orange groves grew up on the edge of the old *huertas* which had been intensively cultivated for centuries; they were watered, not by costly irrigation schemes, but by small pumps and wells.[1] The growth of the orange industry was prodigious (12·5 per cent. per year), quite unparalleled in other sectors of agricultural production; cereals, for instance, merely kept up with a growing population. As the single most important export it was probably as significant a factor in determining the national income as industry, while through its influence on the balance of payments it affected the process of industrial development itself. Until the depression of the thirties, apart from the war years when oranges suffered, demand increased as Great Britain displaced France as the main market. The record level of orange production was in 1930, but even the subsequent drying up of markets did not affect the extension of the orange area. The crisis was met by cutting costs without abandoning new plantation.[2]

Characterized by specialized crops the intensive small-scale farming of the Mediterranean coast was flexible, capable of crop changes in response to market demands, or to the ravages of disease such as that which destroyed silk in the fifties. The development of the Catalan *Maresme* is typical: with the electric pump the irrigated area rose from 10 per cent. (1920) to 90 per cent. (1940). When phylloxera reduced vineyards to a seventh of their former area, when the better Valencian oranges destroyed the prosperity of the groves which had replaced the vineyards, the *Maresme* turned to early potatoes and to flowers.[3] The price of this flexibility and specialization

[1] For this see E. Halpern, *La huerta de Valencia*, and A. Lopez Gomez, 'Evolución agraria de la plana de Castellón' (*E.G.* xviii (1957), 309 ff.). By 1933 there were 2,000 electric pumps, 384 steam pumps, and 742 petrol pumps.

[2] Cf. M. de Torres and H. Paris Eguilaz, *La naranja en la economía española* (Madrid, n.d.), 10–15, 25–36. By the 1930's oranges had assumed the role of wine in the nineties (21 per cent. of total exports; wine 8 per cent.). For the modern structure see M. Liniger Goumaz, *L'Orange d'Espagne* (Paris, 1962).

[3] The *Maresme* is the area round Mataró: it furnishes the most striking example of a shift from wheat, olives, and wine to export crops.

was dependence on foreign markets, above all London, which could dispense with Spanish imports.

Typical of the new forms of agricultural prosperity was the sugar-beet—again a crop that could not easily be introduced on the *secano*. Sugar-beet boomed after the cane sugar of the Antilles vanished. Behind the protective tariff of 1899 Spain was soon producing more sugar than the home market could absorb while its high price made export impossible. It was therefore the first field where protection demanded state regulation of production and prices and where it was practicable because of the concentration of the industry in a few factories. Cotton, which could be grown on rich land in Andalusia and Estremadura, was another crop which held out promise of a more complete autarky. Its encouragement was resisted by a powerful interest—the Catalan manufacturers who had no feelings for a national economy when it was financed by subsidies and import dues on raw cotton, that is by a reduction of their own profits. Characteristically, they argued that Cotton Boards would produce a new caciquisimo manipulated by Andalusian landlords, yielding yet another proof of the anti-economic bias of a state controlled by the 'traditional classes'.

The great crops of the *secano* remained wheat, wine, and olives. Supported by an 'orthopaedic appliance' (protective duties of 110 per cent.) cereals maintained their domination and production expanded sufficiently to feed the growing population in a good year. This expansion represented an increased yield from a smaller area sown and was a result of the use of chemical fertilizers, pushed hard by agronomists and salesmen.[1] Given the absence of fodder crops—the peasant used what animal manure there was with great skill—artificial fertilizers gave dry Spain its nearest approach to an agricultural revolution. The traditional concept of Spanish economic history as a 'struggle' between 'sterile' shepherds and 'productive' farmers put a psychological premium on cereal cultivation at the expense of grazing which was only challenged in the twentieth century; yet the primacy of cereals was a result of sun and soil. Where no grass grows no cows graze and desirable though the substi-

[1] Regional variation was still striking, e.g. 1901 Andalusian yields were halved while Castile and Léon were normal (*Rapports consulaires: Espagne*, 1901).

tution of the cow may have been for the sheep and the goat, the capacity of scrub pasture and corn stubble forbade it.[1] Wheat and long fallows were all the land would stand and represented good dry farming practice in the absence of alternative crops which permit more efficient rotations. There were some advances—the chemical treatment of lentils in storage allowed more profitable fallows—but in the poorer regions a triple yield on seed was the best that could be expected; average yields improved by about 10 per cent. but they were still under half French yields. This was scarcely surprising when perhaps a half of the total production as late as the 1950's still came from exploitations of under two hectares. Hence the primitive wheat cycle typically exhibited in the years 1929–34. A bad year meant high prices which set off new cultivations; over-production lowered prices and land went out of cultivation.

Many deplored this primitive cerealist monoculture. Without protection much ceral production would have become hopelessly uneconomic and large areas would have reverted to scrub grazing. Yet protection did not bring a reasonable living to the small farmers and peasants who struggled on small fields against drought and poor soil, although it allowed large cereal cultivators to make profits and the peasant with a medium farm to keep going. It was these two groups which furnished the recruits for Gamazo's protectionist brand of liberalism. Elsewhere the poor peasant, intermittently producing at a loss, was in bondage to village usurers and corn merchants, and it could be maintained that protection did little to help many of the two million who lived by wheat. Many peasants in Castile seem to have been reduced to the status of tenant farmers by foreclosures: until the advent of the U.G.T. in the countryside, these weaker classes had no voice.[2] Even

[1] There were twice as many sheep and goats as cows and oxen. Galicia (with a quarter of Spain's cows) and the Cantabrian coast were the only regions where dairy and stock farming were easy. One of the advocates of a return to grazing was the economist Flores de Lemus in 'Sobre un dirección fundamental de la producción rural española' (*Moneda y credito* (1951), 141–68).

[2] For the social struggle in Castile see below, p. 449. The figures of the Institute of Social Reform and the reports to the Agricultural Congresses reveal widespread peasant indebtedness: the interest was 10–15 per cent. (*Congreso agrícolo nacional de Valencia*, 22–23).

so the peasants of the wheat lands remained a conservative force, or at least a force that could be dominated by conservatives.

The peasants' most valuable cash crop, the vine, recovered slowly from the terrible blows of the loss of the French and colonial market and the invasion of Spanish vineyards by phylloxera; only the Jerez wines with their superb vintages, the reward of highly skilled methods of cultivation and blending, kept markets abroad with the aid of the new 'vulgar' brandies. For the ordinary wine, compensation for the loss of exports was sought once again in a home market which could never hope to absorb continuous over-production. Railways played an important part in creating this market. It took small producers a long time to realize that, in these new conditions, only co-operative production and marketing could save the small man from the growing power of the wine merchants.[1] The other classic staple, olive-oil, maintained and even improved its quality, though again a concern to maintain domestic price levels and a refusal to adopt modern methods weakened Spanish exports: thus Italy won the Argentine market.[2]

By 1900, in many other parts of the country, the railway had modified or was modifying the agricultural patterns of the *ancien régime*. The transhumant flocks had been on the decline throughout the century as permanent flocks took their place on the southern pastures; by the twentieth century merinos had ceased to eat their way across Spain and were taken to their winter pasture in three-tiered trucks.[3] Like the migrant sheep, the migrant labourers went by train. The Galician labourers with their sickles can still be observed in station booking-halls waiting for the trains to the south. While to

[1] An example of this process is the district of Cariñena. Rail developments centred the trade on Saragossa which supplied the northern markets; this led to the purchase of the crop by wholesalers in good years while in bad years the peasants made their own wine. Co-operation was tried and failed in the nineties and did not get under way till after 1939 when it produced a minor social revolution. Cf. F. Ferrer Regales, 'Las cooperativas del campo de Cariñena', *E.G.* xviii (1957), 429 ff.

[2] Olive yields are very dependent on weather (thus the drought of 1905 halved Spanish exports) but a bad olive crop, which might force oil imports, was not always accompanied by a bad wine harvest.

[3] See above, pp. 12–13. Cf. A. Fribourg, 'La transhumance en Espagne' (*Annales de Geographie*, xix (1909), 231 ff.). Excellent maps show how the old routes changed, e.g. the classic *Cañada Leonesa*. The new routes ran east–west not, as formerly, north–south. The first special rail tariff for sheep was established in 1899.

most areas the railway meant wider markets—thus Galicia supplied the markets of Madrid with fish and meat—to some it brought disaster. The wines of the Duero valley lost their monopoly of the adjacent wine-consuming areas of the northern coast because railways could bring cheap wine from La Mancha and Catalonia.[1] Some towns ceased to be enlarged agricultural villages (Venta de Baños, a quiet Castilian town, became an ugly junction with cheap hotels and restaurants). Others were ruined through lack of a station.[2] The lorry was to modify the traditional patterns even more radically.

It was on the purchasing power generated by this agricultural system of Spain that industry was dependent. Textiles, except for the 1914 war, were now confined to the Spanish market. There was no acute crisis but the continual malaise of over-production, small profit margins, periods of unemployment. Some saw in the cut-throat competition of small factories the 'atavistic individualism' of the Catalan artisan which so annoyed the prophets of big business and economies of scale. It was difficult for the larger cotton concerns to rationalize and modernize as they had done in the nineties. They met dwindling profits by firm resistance to wage demands and by laying off hands. The Catalan manufacturers were amongst the most rigid believers in the iron law of wages. Eusebio Bertrand Serra, the greatest figure in the cotton industry, was an enlightened employer who supplied his workers with homes and hospitals and deplored the first-generation, artisan hardness of the smaller employers. Yet he held that the dole could only demoralize the working class.[3]

In 1870 textiles were still the unique modern sector of the economy; by 1923 Spain had the beginnings of a heavy industry and of a remarkable expansion in the field of light industry. The dependence of heavy industry on iron and cheap coal (the return freight for the iron-ore sent to south Wales) brought the Basque Provinces to the fore.

It was near the iron and steel works of the north coast that a shipbuilding and metallurgical industry grew up. Catalan

[1] A. Huetz de Lemps, 'El viñedo de la tierra de Medina' in *E.G.* xx (1959), 122–3.

[2] J. B. Arranzn 'Venta de Baños' in *E.G.* xx (1959), 495 ff.

[3] R. Alberich, *Eusebio Bertrand Serra* (Barcelona, 1952), 110 ff.

metallurgy faced periods of diminishing orders (1902–7), and was saved by the Naval Programme of 1908 only to falter again in 1912. The 'Biscayan contribution' to the Spanish economy and the financial power of the Biscayan banks became decisive. It was in the two Basque Provinces of Guipúzcoa and Vizcaya that the new industries of cement and paper developed most rapidly as their rivers became polluted with the scum of industrial waste.[1] With few exceptions, except for the Catalans, the really rich men in Spain after 1900 were Basques; with Bilbao growing as a port in 1899–1901 her business men confidently embarked on shipbuilding on a scale which proved excessive when freight rates fell in 1904.[2] It was the naval programme of 1888 and 1908 which gave steel and shipbuilding their biggest boost. Initiated by the conservatives and continued, with less enthusiasm, by the liberals it represented a conscious effort to create a national industry as a corollary of Maura's law of 1907.

The growth of the steel and iron industry was of particular importance since the emergence of new iron fields elsewhere, the exhaustion of the richest mines, and new techniques in smelting diminished the importance of non-phosphoric ores and meant that the great days of Basque iron-ore were passing. By 1929 production was barely a half that of 1913. In the early twentieth century foreign investors were transferring their attention to the south. This investment seems to have taken the form of buying up small bankrupt Spanish concerns and developing them, a process which brought new prosperity to southern ports like Almería and Cartagena.[3] But mining activity contracted after 1920. With the gradual decay of her lead and copper exports Spain was ceasing to be one of the great mineral countries of the world, except for the wolfram which was to make her so important for European arms production.[4]

[1] In Biscay industry was concentrated round Bilbao; in Guipúzcoa it was more scattered, e.g. Tolosa was the paper capital of Spain while the biggest cement factory in Spain was near San Sebastian.

[2] *Rapports consulaires: Bilbao* (1905), 541.

[3] In 1904 there were 310 concerns and 2,750 unexploited concessions. For these activities see *Rapports consulaires: Almería* (1906, 551), *Málaga* (1907, 33), and 1904, 336.

[4] Lead declined first (after 1901), Spanish copper declined later, but it was being outstripped by the U.S.A. in the 1880's. For figures see N. Brown and C. C. Turnbull, *A Century of Copper* (London, 1906), 30 ff.

Native industry could now absorb some of the ore no longer exported. Spanish iron and steel became increasingly more significant and increasingly concentrated in the province of Biscay—by the 1930's it produced nearly three-quarters of the steel and a half of the iron of Spain—and in the few powerful firms built up in the eighties.[1] The war brought great profits and high wages and one of the most ambitious attempts at industrial expansion—the Basque capitalist, Soto y Llano's *Siderúrgica mediterránea*, which created a new steel centre at Sagunto on the Mediterranean. The post-war crisis was particularly severe and the Sagunto works went through a difficult period in the twenties. Strong labour organizations kept up wages in a period of falling world prices. Yet in 1929 iron and steel production was twice that of 1917.

Given the absence of cheap coal, the industrial future of Spain was linked with hydro-electric power once the transformer (1890) allowed the use of distant sources. It would free Catalonia from dependence on Welsh coal, give the Valencian orange-grower cheap power for his pumps, liberate the towns from dependence on the expensive gas of foreign-owned concerns. By 1910 Madrid was supplied with electricity by the longest high-tension line in Europe, and by 1914 there was enough electrical power to save Catalan industry from total breakdown as a result of the coal shortage.

As had been the case in railways, small native concerns were bought out by foreign capital.[2] Such a take-over bid was the foundation of the largest electrical power concern in Catalonia, the *Canadiense* (Barcelona Traction). It was the creation of Pearson, a former Massachusetts professor. He was first to see the future importance of electricity in Catalan industry and he could provide the capital which his Catalan rival Riu could not control. Thus Barcelona Traction (a holding company for Ebro Irrigation & Power Company) became part of a huge, foreign financial empire, the chief example of a shift in foreign

[1] Steel production expanded by 263 per cent. between 1900 and 1913, by 235 per cent. between 1920 and 1930: this was twice the rate of the expansion of world production 1900–50.

[2] See J. L. Martín Rodríguez, *Orígenes de la industria eléctrica en Barcelona* (Barcelona, 1961), 35, for the purchase of the Catalan *Sociedad Española* by A.E.G.

investment from railways and mining to public utilities which took place after 1900.[1]

The domination of foreign capital which had started with the French drive to capture the Spanish railway system and which remained characteristic of the early twentieth century was later reversed. Spanish banks made heavy investments in hydro-electric concerns, a process which reached its culmination in the 1940's and 1950's, when a large number of foreign interests were bought out. The Bank of Biscay (*Banco de Vizcaya*) was particularly active in this field and its activities, together with those of other banks, encouraged a process of concentration and absorption of small concerns so that the electrical industry became an oligopoly.[2] It was Primo de Rivera's technicians—Guadalahorce, the Minister of Public Works, was himself a distinguished engineer—who co-ordinated irrigation and hydro-electric power in the regional boards on which all interests—irrigation, power, and water supply—were represented. The most ambitious of these schemes, the Duero Board, was backed by Basque capital and the imaginative genius and tenacity of the greatest of the many engineers who had come from the School of Road Engineers, Orbegozo. After many set-backs, it began to operate in 1934. The social effects of electrification, especially in backward rural areas, have not been studied but are most important: thus the electrification of Madrid and the beginning of a light industry transformed the social functions of a suburb like Getafe.[3] In Catalonia abundant power began to draw back into the mountains the population which had escaped to the plains. Together with the lorry, electric power must alter the face of Spain.

Entering late in the race and with poor resources in coal, Spain had found it difficult to develop a classic heavy industry.

[1] Riu, an ardent mountain climber as were many Catalans at this period, hoped to break B.T. with French and German capital. By 1923 he was beaten. For the 'stock watering' and other financial techniques of holding companies, dominated by the great manufacturers of electrical equipment, see the very detailed work of J. L. Sureda, *El caso de 'Barcelona Traction'* (Barcelona, 1959).

[2] To take one example, the Banco de Vizcaya helped finance Hidroeléctrica Ibérica S.A. (later amalgamated with the Saltos de Duero), the Compañia Sevillana de Eletricidad (which absorbed Mengenor S.A.), and Eléctrica de Viesgo S.A. The large amalgamations were a relatively late development but the process started in the 1920's.

[3] For Getafe see F. Quirós Linares, 'Getafe' (*E.G.* xxi, 1960) 211 ff.

The most remarkable progress was made in light industry; cement and chemicals were the characteristic products of the twentieth century. Spain produced the greatest artist in reinforced concrete, Gaudí, some remarkable engineers, a concrete boat, and the highest cement chimney in Europe. Cement was an index of her progress, not merely in industry but in agriculture. Primo de Rivera's dictatorship was a cement age: his exhibitions, canals, dams, and municipal improvements outran national production. The abandonment of his ambitions by the Republic was a disaster for the factories that had expanded to meet the new demand.[1] Like cement, chemicals were financed by Spanish capital—Catalan and Basque—and satisfied a steady demand in agriculture and the textile industry, so that by the 1930's Spain was freeing herself from dependence on foreign manures and industrial chemicals.[2] Once again relatively expensive domestic production opened up debate between the proponents of autarky and those who saw prosperity in terms of the law of comparative costs.[3]

At the same time that the creations of the twentieth century—the hydro-electric and light industries—were showing growth and promise, the economic achievement of the nineteenth century—a national railway system—was entering a period of difficulties. New lines were laid, with peak years in 1878–80, 1882–4, 1893, 1896, and 1899. Yet by 1914 the system that had already been built was wearing out and could not find capital for modernization. The heavy war traffic (especially the transport of coal across Spain), the consequent delays and missed booked-crossings, dramatized the inadequacies of a system constructed on the cheap.[4]

[1] Cement, of course, needed relatively heavy capital investment. There were two surges in cement: the first in the years after 1898, the second from 1910 to 1914. One of the weaknesses of the industry was its dependence on cheap iron (for reinforced concrete) and cheap fuel and the sudden fluctuations of demand: in 1926 there was over-production, in 1928 considerable imports, and by 1932 over-production. The consumption of cement *per capita* passed that of iron in 1930. Cf. *La industria del cemento en España* (1933).

[2] For the chemical industry see *Banco de Bilbao*, 332–91.

[3] e.g. over the manufacture of synthetic nitrates as against the importation of cheaper nitrates: see Izaguirre, *La situacíon económica de la industria del nitrógeno sintético* (1933). The production of artificial manures quintupled 1920–30.

[4] Thus, during the 1914–18 war, the Catalan steel and cork manufacturers were, like many others, starved of raw materials coming from long distances. Delays

The difficulties confronting profitable exploitation were revealed by the fate of the narrow-gauge lines constructed after 1904 with state encouragement; these cheap lines were intended to fill the gaps between the great lines which struck out radially from Madrid and to serve those areas, particularly in northern Spain, which were outside the railway system altogether and which continued to rely, to a surprising extent, on coastal navigation. Much of the capital came from small investors who lost their money when narrow-gauge railways, serving the interstices of the national system, could not find enough freight.

The only period of optimism came with the boom of the twenties: under Primo de Rivera's Railway Council the companies succeeded in modernizing their locomotive and rolling stock.[1] With recession and slump, Berenguer's government and the Republic were landed, after 1930, with an insolvent railway system: their remedy was the cessation of construction on all new lines and the cancellation of all orders for new locomotives —a decision which affected adversely the whole metallurgical industry. Long before, Cambó had seen that the only remedy was nationalization: the Republic, largely concerned with recouping state loans to the companies, increased state control but jibbed at nationalization.[2] This was left for General Franco.

Many of the difficulties Spain shared with other countries: government-fixed rates which precluded profitable working, lines and marshalling yards which were kept in use after the great period of amalgamations had rendered them superfluous, and finally the competition of trucking. Others were symbolic of peculiar difficulties: steep gradients, lack of traffic

were perhaps increased by mild sabotage in 1917, faulty labelling, and re-routing by new staff. There were large claims for delay, pilfering, and damage.

[1] This modernization fitted in with the drive for national industry: thus locomotive orders kept *La Maquinista* going (M.Z.A. had a considerable holding in *La Maquinista*). Curiously enough, Catalonia and not the Biscay turned out most locomotives (687 out of 1,105).

[2] The case for nationalization had been argued for many years, e.g. in the 1907 Assembly of Production (*Ministerio de Fomento* (1907), 195 ff.). Debt charges made improvement impossible and state subventions to relieve companies, described as 'foreign states in our country', were inevitable but 'unpatriotic'. If they were to be supported by the state they must be nationalized. The state should buy out the companies and farm out the railways. Cambó's case for nationalization is argued in the preface to vol. 1 of *Elementos para el estudio del problema ferrovaria en España* (1918). This work contains a mass of technical information on rates, &c.

to keep the lines south and west of Madrid going concerns. All reflected the poverty of Spain: the railway system was, in extent and length, adequate for her needs—there was no need to build new lines or make double tracks. It was worn-out rails and wagons, old-fashioned equipment, that weakened the impulse which rapid transport gives to a whole economy.[1] The railways were in no position to challenge the lorry by competitive rates and express transport: commodities which in other countries were carried by rail, in Spain were carried by night lorries. Thus the railway, which had altered the working-class diet of Madrid in the 1860's by bringing fish from the north coast, had lost out to the lorry by 1935.[2]

Perhaps it was not till after the First World War that native banking institutions were capable of playing a full part in invigorating development by credit, as they had done in Italy. The profits of the war years were often frittered away in the construction of imposing edifices, or imperilled by ruinous competition for contracting business.[3] In spite of banking traditions, Catalan institutional credit was imperfectly developed and the manufacturer often forced to take on the double role of banker and producer.[4] Catalan bankers were conservative—banking, like other activities, was largely a family concern—and much capital was tied up in stable textiles and declining railways: only after 1915 did the Barcelona banks adopt modern methods from French rivals. Perhaps the Catalan banking system never recovered from the blows of 1866

[1] For a good description of the present system see I.B.R.D., *Economic Development*, 178–208, and the excellent maps of traffic density. Some railway engines in Spain are a hundred years old; the whole system is slowed down by worn-out light rails (ibid. 183).

[2] See A. López Gómez, 'El abastecimiento de pescado a Madrid' (*E.G.* xiv, 1953), 535 ff. By 1933 Madrid got 64 per cent. of its fish by lorry, Paris 4·5 per cent. Railways could only compete when the roads were bad. Cf. P. Vilar, 'Le rail et la route. Leur rôle dans le problème générale des transports en Espagne', *A.H.E.S.* (Paris, 1934), 571 ff.

[3] Cf. *Banking in Western Europe* (ed. K. S. Sayers, Oxford, 1962), 354. The Parliamentary Commission of 1915 dismissed the existing system as inadequate, antiquated, and insecure. The techniques of Spanish banking were backward: there was no central clearing system until 1923.

[4] Ventosa, a Catalan economist, observed that Catalan foreign trade was largely in the hands of English, French, and even Portuguese banks. J. Vicens Vives, *Els Catalans*, 85, for a description of activities in the seventies. Cf. *D. S. C. Senado* (7 Jan. 1901, Maluquer's speech) for a plea for better institutional credit for overseas trading.

and 1898. The ambitious Banco Hispano Colonial, with its huge interests in colonial trade, had lost three-quarters of its capital in 1898.[1] The industrial concentration which favoured the coal and iron districts of the northern coasts was matched by a corresponding concentration of financial power and Catalonia failed to create powerful mixed banks engaged in the financing of new enterprise.

This task fell to the Biscay mixed banks of which the Banco de Vizcaya, most successful of the new creations, was a symbol; the Basque financiers—like the Basque industrialists—proved capable of breaking beyond the family firm into the great modern corporation. Given the conservative habits of the Spanish rich and their preference for traditional forms of investment (especially urban real property) the supply of risk capital was narrowly limited; the mixed bank alone could pump savings into industrial growth. Thus in financing hydro-electric schemes, public utilities, and private industry, the large banks began the process of 'nationalization'—in the sense of establishing Spanish as against foreign financial control—which was to be such a feature of the economy after 1940. After the First World War they came to play a part in the Spanish economy resembling that of the German banks; hence their difficulties in the crisis of the thirties were due to their heavy holdings of falling industrial securities—a liability which had, in 1920, ruined the Bank of Barcelona, the most respected credit institution in Catalonia. Bank finance drove on a process of industrial and financial concentration which, as might be expected, was particularly marked in those concerns which produced the raw materials of industry: coal, iron, and electricity.

This process gave rise to sharp criticism from both socialists and economists. Socialists saw the whole Spanish economy in the hands of a few powerful bankers and industrialists, closely connected with each other and with the Treasury, which would pour public money into concerns from which they

[1] For an exaggerated picture of the small-back-room atmosphere of Catalan banking see J. Ma. Tallada, *Barcelona económica y financiera* (1944), 72–74. The most successful Catalan creation was the Banco Español de Credito (1901) especially created to finance foreign trade. In the twenties Catalan clearings were 38 per cent. with foreign banks, 32 per cent. non-Catalan banks.

indirectly profited as directors.[1] Economists argued that oligopolies and monopolistic competition starved secondary industries of cheap materials: coal and its successor, electricity, were alike in the hands of a few powerful concerns which had bought out the smaller companies. By 1930 there were representatives of 'modern' large-scale capitalism who maintained that Spanish industry was insufficiently concentrated—Cambó, the Catalan politician who had made a fortune out of financing concentration, was one of them—and pointed to textiles and cork as examples. Others maintained that the process of concentration had already gone too far and pointed to cement, paper, and hydro-electricity and, to a lesser extent, steel.

Most of this argument was either part of the political battle or a gloss on the fact that the conservative habits of the Spanish investor left only the mixed banks as suppliers of capital for industry. Nor was there anything 'unnatural' in a high degree of concentration in basic industry; after the Civil War the process of amalgamation and concentration of resources was to spread to banking itself.

3. *Population and the Land*

The late nineteenth century saw an intensification of the two interconnected processes which had been gradually altering the social structure and even the physical appearance of Spain since the second half of the eighteenth century: a growth in population and a movement of the excess rural population to the towns.

The year 1900 is significant in Spanish demography: the weight of an excessive death-rate—nearly twice that of the European average—began to lift significantly. Between the beginning of the century and 1930 the population rose from 18 to nearly 24 million—a process which was accelerated after that date by a dramatic decline in infant mortality. This increase could not be supported by an already over-populated countryside; it found its way either to America or to the cities. Starting in the seventies, the outward flow across the Atlantic reached its height in 1912 (134,000), and during these decades the loss of

[1] The socialist attack on the financial oligarchy is illustrated in A. Ramos Oliveira *El capitalismo español al desnudo*. Cf. the preface to C. Muñoz Linares, *El monopolio en la industria eléctrica* (1954). This excellent study is largely concerned with the situation after 1940. For the supposed paper monopoly see 'Consideraciores

population amounted to one-third of the national increase.[1] The sorrows of emigrants became a subject for sentimental realist painters and, indeed, abuses in the emigrant trade were startling: the *Heliopolis* transported four thousand Andalusian peasants to Hawaii.[2] Most of the emigrants went to the Argentine and to Brazil and their decision was clearly connected with pressures on the land at home. It was Galicia, with its pushing population and 'handkerchief plots', that became the prime exporter of men; from the arid regions of the Levante men sought new opportunities in north Africa and France.

The South American gates were closed by the 1914–18 war and never pushed open wide again. Thus the continued population increase, after a temporary sally into France, was forced to find some equilibrium within the frontiers of Spain. This took the form of a rush to the towns and it has been calculated that 40 per cent. of the rural increase found its way thither, especially to the great cities.[3] In broad terms, local advances towards the peripheral cities (Seville, Bilbao, San Sebastian, Valencia, and above all Barcelona) combined with the attraction of Madrid and of provincial capitals for their surrounding districts. Thus the province of Granada, like much of the Andalusian countryside, had a high rate of natural increase together with areas, like the Alpujarras, where land was limited and life poor; these conditions were met by seasonal migrations of whole families for the olive, sugar, and wheat

sobre algunas actividades monopolisticas en el mercado papelero español' (*R. Est. Ec.* vi. 3 (1955), 29–125). This is a highly polemical attack on *Papelera Española* which controlled one-third of the total production and was financed by the Bank of Bilbao: its rival (*Papeleras Reunidas*) was financed by the Bank of Biscay. This controversy attracted great attention in the twenties because of its effects on newspapers. *Papelera Española* supplied *El Sol* (a liberal daily owned by a right-wing proprietor) and was accused of seeking to raise tariffs in order to freeze out other papers.

1 See J. Vicens Vives, *Historia social*, v. 32. The significant impulse came from the crisis of the nineties.

2 See *D.S.C.* 1861, 14 Jan. La Cierva's law of 1907, based on suggestions of the Institute of Social Reforms, suppressed many of the recruiting abuses of shipping agents. One of the gardeners of Stanford University came from Malaga via Hawaii.

3 Between 1901 and 1910 the general increase was 7·22 per cent. provincial capitals 10·5 per cent. The influx into the great cities was even more marked. By the twentieth century, in some cases, half their population was composed of immigrants, of whom 70 per cent. had been agricultural labourers. The towns of the south and east, which remained reservoirs of agricultural labour, were described by Aznar as 'terrifying human slaughterhouses'.

harvests together with permanent immigration to the local capital, Granada, and to the more distant Seville.[1]

In Catalonia immigrants to the growing wool towns of Tarrasa and Sabadell came from the poorer mountain regions of Catalonia.[2] Barcelona itself, which absorbed the surplus labour of the surrounding countryside, was driven further afield to the distressed agricultural districts of Murcia and Aragon. Such immigrants were first attracted as casual labourers to meet some sudden demand—the Barcelona Exhibition of 1888, the improvements to the port of Bilbao, or, later, the needs of the building trades.

These population movements reflected the old contrasts between the periphery and the centre, between north and south. Old Castile, with a high natural rate of increase and little absorptive capacity, became a reservoir of labour for the periphery. In Andalusia the population grew but the increase remained to swell unemployment and to fill the agrarian towns; in some Andalusian towns over half the working population was redundant by 1936. Not until after the Civil War did the surplus population of the south seek opportunity on a massive scale elsewhere. At the same time the natural population growth of the periphery had slowed down; more and more of its inhabitants had come from the outside.[3]

It was in the twentieth century that the cities began to reflect the rural influx in terms of new suburbs and wider streets. Thus though Madrid and Barcelona had planned their development before 1868, it was only in the nineties that the projected new streets of the *ensanches* ceased to look like urban deserts as they filled out with uniform square blocks of flats divided by standard streets of two widths and adorned with impressive banks and public buildings. In the great cities, the congested area of the old town had to be broken through by wide streets—the Gran Via of Madrid, the Via Layetana of Barcelona (1910);

[1] A. Floristan, 'Movimientos migratorios de la provincia de Granada' in *E.G.* xviii (1957), 301 ff.

[2] 'Evolución del poblamiento del Vallés', *E.G.* iii (1942), 751 ff., and María de Bolos, ibid. (xx (1959), 209 ff.), 'La immigración en Barcelona'.

[3] Old Castile, between 1900 and 1950 lost annually perhaps 13,000 inhabitants by internal migration while Catalonia gained 23,000. These conclusions are based on an unpublished paper of J. M. Houston, *Population Changes in Spain 1900–1950* (presented to XVIII Geographical Congress, 1956).

it was the former which gave central Madrid the appearance of a modern capital city.

Later this wave of 'urbanism' struck provincial towns, some of which had remained cramped within walls with gates unsuitable for motor traffic.[1] Their demolition marked the end of an epoch of urban history and Cartagena celebrated its 'liberation' with a week of fiestas. The arrival of the railway and the destruction of its walls marked the conclusion of San Sebastian's history as a fortress and the beginning of its development as a great watering place; in the nineties the queen regent chose it as a summer residence, making it the diplomatic and political capital of Spain for two months every year. It was there that Isabella II was informed of the Revolution of 1868 and that her grandson received the news of the *coup d'état* of 1923.[2] San Sebastian was an early starter; even large cities like Saragossa only began to spread as late as 1908. The development of Albacete into an ugly modern city shows the effect of railway transport and the war boom on the provincial capital of an agricultural district; the decline of Igualda, the consequences of a mechanical invention (the self-acting mule), and lack of adequate railway connexion on an old Catalan industrial centre.[3]

Much modernization was superficial and the preference of Spanish small investors for urban property led to building development with which municipal services could not keep pace: thus although Leon had electric light in 1889 it had no adequate water supply until 1950.[4] All but the biggest towns kept their traditional functions as local markets, though some were acquiring new activities with chemical and light industries. The market-place was the centre of the old town, sur-

[1] e.g. walls were pulled down or circumvented in Cartagena (1890's), Jaca (1908), Pamplona (1920). Among the incentives to development were international exhibitions: thus the exhibitions of Barcelona (1888), Saragossa (1908), Seville (1924) were all reflected in new building round the exhibition sites.

[2] See L. Gordejuela Sanz, 'La geografía urbana de San Sebastián' (*Pireneos*, xi, Saragossa, 1955).

[3] For Albacete see F. del Campo Aguilar, *Albacete contemporánea* (Albacete, 1958); for Igualada, J. Mercader, *La ciutat d'Igualada* (Barcelona, 1953). Albacete rose from 25,000 inhabitants in 1916 to 64,000 in 1942; Igualada declined from 14,000 (1857) to 10,000 (1900). There was no water power in Igualada to work modern machinery and it had been served by excellent roads. Very frequently the water supply was the limiting factor on urban growth, e.g. Albacete until 1905 and again after 1925.

[4] J. L. Martín Galindo, 'La ciudad de León' (*E.G.* xviii, 1957), 95–169.

rounded by small shops; outside, a new society had grown up. Thus the tourist visiting one of Spain's historic towns is disheartened by the concrete and rubble of half-built housing estates which lie between him and his goal.

The rush to America and to the towns revealed the harshness of a rural life from which men sought only to escape. Whereas in the eighties and nineties interest was centred in the wheat regions and on the trials of the Castilian peasant, in the twentieth century it was absorbed by the violent social situation in the latifundia of the west, the centre, and the south. In the nineties politicians were bullied by the powerfully organized wheat interest; in the twentieth century they were alarmed by the threat of agrarian revolution on the great estates.

Inquiry after inquiry revealed wages which could not cover the day labourer's minimum expenditure on food: hence the assertion that he must expend his capital—his health—in order to balance his domestic budget. The curse of these areas of semi-starvation was seasonal unemployment. The traditional monocultures—olives, the vine, and wheat—gave permanent employment only for part of the labour force for part of the year: labourers moved from monoculture to monoculture and starved in the lean months.[1] Reformers, as in the eighteenth century, attributed these conditions less to the nature of the crop economy than to the pattern of landownership. The size of the large estates was considered in itself a sufficient explanation of agrarian distress: as Charles III's experts had argued it created 'superfluity of hands and lack of lands'. The breaking up of these latifundia was therefore seen as the solution of the agrarian problem in the south and west.

To a minority of reformers Andalusia and Estremadura were not merely regions of shame where conditions of life were comparable only to the worst areas of Sicily and eastern Europe; they were also regions of economic hope. Whereas little would be done to increase the productivity of the dry, stony farms of Avila or Soria, irrigation and family colonization might initiate a dramatic new prosperity in those areas of the south and west with good soil conditions. Reformers were correct in believing

[1] For a technical discussion of seasonal unemployment in areas of monocultures see *El paro estacional campesino* (*Sindicato Vertical de Olivo*, 1946). Typical monocultures are the vines of La Mancha and the olives of Jaen.

that it was on the better land that there was room for resettlement and it is on irrigated land that the small family farm has proved most successful; only varied crops could give employment all the year round: *vegas* were less stable than the intensive *huertas* because they tended towards monocultures, especially sugar beet.

'Internal colonization' was the remedy of Catholic reformers, who wished to avert the threat to social stability inherent in a flight to the towns, and of agronomists who realized the dangers of a mere redistribution of lands. Catholics were unwilling to allow this colonization to be undertaken by the state or at the cost of drastic expropriation: the landowners, by gentle prodding, must be made to realize the social nature of property rights and be mulcted of some of the unearned increment brought by irrigation.[1] To be successful resettlement policies needed an agency with extensive powers of expropriation and great capital resources for investment in irrigation. Private bodies would provide neither and radicals increasingly turned to the state. Its only response was a trickle of laws from 1907 onwards which neither gave adequate powers against landlords nor sufficient capital for resettlement. Yet some form of large-scale agricultural co-operation was the only solution to the social problems of the south which was economically sound. The objection that such solutions, by placing restrictions on the owner's right to do what he liked with his land, failed to satisfy the millenarian desire for a plot of one's own need not be taken too seriously. The *reparto* was a revolutionary demand; had the landless labourer been offered a family holding on a 'colonial' tenure he would have ceased to be a revolutionary.

It was on statistics of landownership rather than on the conditions of production that the emotional drive for radical agrarian reform fed in the 1920's and 1930's: the huge estates in the hands of a few grandees were contrasted with the miniscule plots of peasants; the natural solution seemed redistri-

[1] Severino Aznar, *Depoblación y colonización* (Barcelona, 1930), gives an outline of a Catholic colonization programme. For his attitude to property see 56 ff. For the unearned increment see P. Carrión, *La concentración de la propriedad y el regadio en Andalusia*. In the Guadalcain irrigated region of 8,959 hectares, 6,932 belonged to thirteen proprietors. Some Andalusian landowners had settled *colonos* but on hard terms for the settlers.

bution.[1] Convincing though these statistics were as propaganda devices of the U.G.T. and C.N.T., they tended to a misinterpretation of the conditions of production in the south.[2] Many of the huge latifundia consisted of poor pasture which could never flourish as peasant farms: others were *secano* only fit for extensive monocultures. Simply to redistribute such lands in a way that would have satisfied the land hunger of the peasants would have been to invite disaster. On the better land a *reparto* would have encouraged more intensive forms of cultivation—for instance a more profitable use of fallows. Yet there were no sound economic reasons for an agrarian reform which would immobilize rural unemployment in areas where a relatively small increase in investment would yield low returns—for example on the poorer *secano* of the great estates. The drift to the town was economically sound. The agrarian reform of the Second Republic inherited this traditional tendency to force employment where none could be gainfully found without a dramatic transformation of the agricultural system through heavy investment in irrigation projects. The famous *Ley de Términos Municipales*, whatever its foundation in social justice may have been, was economically indefensible except as an emergency measure.[3]

The fact that these arguments were overworked by the defenders of large property does not make them less valid: nor did statistics always reveal the nature of cultivation as opposed to the patterns of ownership; for instance they over-estimated direct farming by owners. In the twentieth century the large *cortijos* were rented by a single tenant forced to pay a high rent for an annual insecure tenancy and it was this exploitation of landless labour or the poorer tenant farmers that lay behind much of the social unrest that swept over Andalusia.[4]

[1] The first 'scientific' work on landownership was Pascual Carrion's *Los latifundios en España* (1932). It was based on statistics collected in the 1920's.

[2] In particular they paid no attention to those areas where reasonably satisfactory tenures were obtained.

[3] Cf. H. Paris Eguilaz, *El estado y la economía* (1939), 172–6. He estimates that close on a million labourers could have been released for more productive pursuits.

[4] For the problems of single lettings see vizconde de Eza, *El problema agrario andaluz* (1919), 6 ff. Of course there were exceptions, even within the areas of money rent. In areas of the south where small-scale production was agriculturally possible there were stable *aparcería* (crop-sharing) tenures—even on sections of the great estates. For the division of tenures, &c., in the province of Cordoba see J. Carandell, *Distribución y estructura de la propriedad rural en la provincia de Córdoba* (1934).

The new prosperity which came with the First World War to Andalusia as elsewhere (the growth of Seville is its symptom; in 1906 La Cierva could not find a typewriter in the town) escaped the agricultural proletariat. It was their poverty which absorbed the readjustments after the war, when the landlords endeavoured to maintain high war-time rents against falling agricultural prices and which supported the conspicuous waste of a landed aristocracy with little conception of any duty beyond that of collecting its rents. Illiterate, huddled together, workless in the towns, fed on the broadsheet legends of the brigands which fascinated the Andalusian poet García Lorca, they were easily won over by the apostles of anarchism who shared their dismal life and opened out to them a vision of social justice.[1]

Outside this classical home of agrarian violence there were regions where the steady growth of population precluded any increase in welfare or where some sudden alteration sharpened discontent and distress. Thus in the Catalan countryside, the sudden loss of the French market and the invasion of phylloxera (1890–2) brought social tension into what had been a stable economy by exposing a latent conflict of interest between the smaller tenants (the *rabassaires*) and their landlords. The Republic of 1873 had recognized the tenant's rights; the Restoration favoured the landlord. When phylloxera made tenancies based on the life of the old vine impracticable, the landlords calculated the duration of tenancies on the life of the phylloxera-resistant, shorter-lived American vine; the rabassaires protested violently; in the early nineties they organized strikes and boycotts. It was their plight, when the high prices of 1914–18 collapsed, which intensified the struggle in rural Catalonia between the Rabassaires' Union and the landlords' organization—the Institute of San Isidro.[2] By 1924 the conflict had cooled down but in the thirties, with yet another loss of markets, it was to reappear giving to Companys and the Catalan left their rural following.[3]

[1] For the brigand literature see J. Caro Baroja, *Los pueblos*, 406. For a famous description of an apostle working in the *cortijos* near Jerez see Ibañez's novel, *La bodega*.

[2] For a short description of the conflict see *Un segle de vida catalana* (Barcelona, 1961), 839 ff.

[3] For the struggle in the Panadés region see 'La rabassa morta y su reforma' (*I.R.S.* 1923), esp. 175 ff., for the effect of post-war conditions.

The Galician problem was more intractable: bitter agitation demanded a legal remedy which, when it came, could not cure rural misery.[1] As in the eighteenth century, at the centre of the land war in the north-west lay a confused notion of ownership: nothing could expunge from the peasant cultivator's mind the feeling that the land was his—after all, as in Ireland, he could cultivate it or subdivide it as he wished. Land values, and with them rents, soared until half an acre of middling land near Pontevedra was worth a plot in the *huerta* of Valencia. The *foristas*—the rural *bourgeoisie* of Galicia which had replaced the old aristocracy and the Church as landowners—sought to break rent strikes by taking their tenants to law: they were met by an Irish war of boycott, cattle maiming, and arson. Around Pontevedra and Orense anarchist influence embittered the struggle. Thus by the end of the nineteenth century the abolition or redemption of the *foros* was an absolute necessity for social peace and compulsory redemption was finally carried through in the 1920's. Yet the end of the *foros* did not mean the end of the Galician problem since the whole dispute had tended to hide the true roots of Galician misery. Minifundia were created, not by a peculiar form of tenure, but by the pressure of a rising population; with not enough land to go round, subdivision increased. As seasonal migration fell off and the American door was closed the situation deteriorated: tenurial reform could only ease a tragic situation. Galicia had no landless proletariat but a proletariat of miniscule proprietors.[2] Perhaps it was only the potato which averted a total failure of the land to feed its inhabitants.

Short of agrarian reform—a radical change of property relations in the countryside—what could be done to mitigate rural discontent and poverty?

'The countryside was thirsty for money.'[3] From Costa to

[1] See above, pp. 8–9. Bernaldo de Quirós, *El problema de los foros* (1923), esp. 33, 45 ff., and appendixes ii and iv. The anarchist *Unión Campesina* demanded abolition; the more moderate *Solidaridad Gallega* redemption. One of the difficulties of redemption was the legal obscurity of traditional tenures and the consequent difficulties of compensation.

[2] The problem was mitigated to some extent by the *Campiña Gallega* by which coheirs were bought out. Strangely enough the nutritive value of the potato never seems to have been exploited by the Gallegans as it was by the Irish.

[3] The phrase is J. M. Azara's, a leader of the Catholic Agrarian Syndicates. For his campaign against the banks and pleas for peasant credit see his *Apuntes sociales y agrarios* (Saragossa, 1919).

Father Vicent social reformers fought to provide the peasant with cheap credit. Land banks had been advocated ever since the 1830's, especially as the proper destination for the proceeds of the sales of 'national' property. Loans to the peasants from the large banks were difficult: the banks could not be bothered by a multitude of small long-term loans, especially when they could not be based on firm titles to land. Thus the crop-sharer or the peasant with a verbal tenancy was forced to the village money-lender. It was this situation which led the advocates of land registry to emphasize the connexion between insecure title and rural usury.

Catholic organizations saw in the plight of the indebted peasant an opportunity to compensate for urban losses by rural gains and conservatives the dangers of a radical peasant party. The early years of the twentieth century witnessed an earnest effort by a few socially conscious aristocrats and prelates, landowners, and agricultural engineers to set up agricultural syndicates. These syndicates, based on German and Belgian models, were instruments to provide cheap credit, manures, crop insurance, marketing facilities, and chemicals against phylloxera and mildew.[1] Loans were made on a personal basis, on the syndicate's view of a peasant's worth, not on his mortgageable assets. To Catholics the syndicates and cheap credit were a weapon against the attractions of socialism and 'Georgeism' (for Henry George's schemes had attracted regenerationists) and, at the same time, a declaration against the oligarchs of the banking world. Outside Navarre, and parts of Castile and of Aragon—regions of established peasant proprietors, already Catholic and in no need of redemption from the left—the movement made little headway: the religious spirit was in conflict with economic purpose and the benefits of syndicates were reserved for known Catholic homes.[2] Apart from cheap credit for the small farmer, the most simple remedy for his plight was the modification of abusive short-term leases; stable leases, together with loan facilities, would encourage improvement. The Civil Code remained a landlord's law and agricultural credit a local experiment.

[1] For Catholic Syndicates see below, p. 459.

[2] Nevertheless it was the advocacy of land banks—not only by Catholics—which led to Alba's proposed Agricultural Bank (1916) and to its diminutive

With such modest hopes unfulfilled reformers in the 1890's dreamt of a more radical redemption: the elimination of the semi-arid steppes by irrigation and the re-afforestation of the barren lands. In the end little was done, not least because propagandists advocated irrigation and afforestation as competing rather than complementary solutions.

'Water is all', Young had written. The premium on water is reflected both in poetry and land values: irrigated land (*regadío*) could be fifty times as valuable as *secano* land and only the poets of the late nineteenth century could reject the traditional images of fructifying streams and find inspiration in desolation and aridity.[1] But to bring water to dry lands demands immense capital investment. There were skilful irrigation systems where capital costs were low, but the great reservoirs and canals which could turn the *secano* into fertile land had remained, with the exception of the Imperial Canal of Aragon, projectors' schemes.

Haunted by statistics which revealed the huge differences between the value and productivity of irrigated land and *secano*, private speculators had undertaken irrigation works in the nineteenth century—thus Remisa and other Catalan capitalists had been interested in the Urgel Canal. The 'hydraulic' regenerationists, of the turn of the century, obsessed by the ambition to make the desert flourish, saw that the task was beyond private capital; in their appeal to the state they found an advocate in Gasset, owner of the most respected Madrid daily, *El Imparcial*. But their plans were over-ambitious and uncoordinated: only a fraction of the state-financed programme of 1902, embracing over a million acres, was accomplished; it was left to Primo de Rivera to plan for the future.[2] Moreover, as the first serious study of the problem revealed, a huge mass of masonry is not necessarily the cheapest recipe for higher production and there is a limit to the profitable creation of oases: *where resources are limited* it is better to concen-

successor set up by the vizconde de Eza, one of the most prominent Catholic land reformers.

[1] Cf. prices in the 1850's: *regadío* of Teruel 12,519 reales per fanega, *secano* 220. In the wheat districts of Salamanca reasonable land was rented at 500–700 reales per fanega: *regadío* in Alicante or Murcia varied between 18,000 and 44,000 reales.

[2] For an excellent survey see J. M. Houston, 'Irrigation as a solution to the agrarian problems of Spain' (*Geographical Journal*, cxv, 1950), 55 ff.

trate on tested types of small-scale irrigation. Before 1923 the motor pump and the water wheel had brought more land under intensive cultivation than the dam.

This is not to deny that only the building of great reservoirs can alter the conditions of the steppe; early enthusiasts, however, did not sufficiently realize that, to be a profitable investment, the value of the additional products which come from an irrigation project must show a reasonable return on the capital invested. If they do not, capital is better invested elsewhere. Large-scale irrigation now appears less of a universal panacea than was commonly held half a century ago; on arid soils the mere flooding of the land with water without adequate drainage can produce saline soil conditions within a relatively short time—and indeed this danger threatens some regions in Spain. It is a last resort rather than a preliminary treatment.[1] Nor did the early planners realize the social complexity of irrigation schemes. It was not enough for the state to build the main channels: without adequate subsidiary works, housing, and roads 'a sort of depression' sets in and produces a time-lag before the scheme can be fully utilized. Thus under the earlier legislation, the state erected what appeared to be the costly main works, but even greater expenditure, left to local private initiative, was usually needed for full development.[2] It was only in the 1920's that technicians in Spain came to realize how essential and expensive these secondary works were: they could exhaust the capital of a region.

The destruction of forests is the historic crime of agricultural Spain. In the past, sheep and the privileges of the *Mesta* may have been to blame: but the ravages continued into modern times, long after the great days of sheep. Sheep destroy trees less than goats or even donkeys and the main criminal is man.[3] Apart from the demands of the fleet, the building industry, and the kitchen, it was the constant extension of the plough that

[1] The 'last resort' argument is stated in *The Economic Development of Guatemala* (I.B.R.D., Washington, 1951), esp. 71 ff.

[2] Cf. L. Ridruejo Ruiz-Zorilla, *Función del estado en la transformación de secano en regadío* (1934).

[3] Should this be doubted, I had a hundred young beech trees ringed by one donkey in less than a month; sheep prefer grass seeds and dry pasture and I have watched sheep for days in Aragon without seeing them destroy saplings. Goats on the other hand, apart from ringing trees, will even climb stumpy trees to destroy foliage.

destroyed the forest cover.[1] The hatred of the peasant for trees is one of the most reliably attested and curious features of country life outside the north of Spain: trees harboured sparrows, weakened the corn, and 'wasted' land. Nowhere is the liberal optimism of the eighteenth century more evident than in Jovellanos's dogma that forests were better preserved by private interest than public legislation. In fact, only strict legislative control, a state forestry service, and large-scale state investment could begin the immense task of restoring the forests of Spain.

Without effective legislation the destruction of Spain's forest cover was continued in the late nineteenth century; between 1866 and 1932—largely to meet the increasing demands of the building industry—perhaps half of the woods left standing by the mid-century speculators were cut down, usually without replanting.[2] Critics pointed to the crime, to the mean grants for forest services, without realizing the immensity of the difficulties involved in replanting partially eroded scrub. In Murcia 5,000 trees were planted, protected by individual shields and hand-watered: after five years, twenty-five trees were still living.[3] Without adequate cover crops, the soil of Spain blew away or was washed away by the winter torrents, its balance and texture destroyed. In similar conditions in north Africa the cultivation of a slight slope meant total ruin within ten years.[4] Only scientific re-afforestation, combined with cutting on a sustained yield basis, could have re-established a permanent

[1] In some parts of Spain burning ground to improve grazing is a common, though illegal, practice. Sometimes fires do great damage in dry years and their origin is attributed to private feuds or to shepherd 'carelessness', a lingering relic of the great feud between graziers and agriculturists. The tourist may observe such fires on the Costa Brava between Puerto de la Selva and Cadaqués.

[2] A farmer in Aragon told me he had cut down all his trees in the lean years after 1939 and had assumed that they would replant naturally. In 1952 there were no signs of natural replacement.

[3] E. G. H. Dobby, 'The Agrarian Problem in Spain' (*Geographical Review*, New York, xxvi (1936), 187). For an examination of the budgetary allocations for re-afforestation see Celedonio Rodrigañez, *El problema económica*, 87. There was one forestry officer per 41,387 hectares as compared with 3,862 hectares in France. Half of the 'cultivable land' of Spain was classed as forest: of this 58 per cent. had no trees. Understandably the production of wood *per capita* was among the lowest in Europe (Portugal 1·59 cubic metres; France 0·63; Spain 0·10).

[4] It might be argued that latifundia scrub pasture (cf. J. Carandell, *Córdoba*, 14, for its extent in a typical latifundist area) respected the soil and prevented gully erosion. This is true *only* where the scrub is not heavily grazed.

stream flow by absorbing water in the higher reaches of the river system and reducing the enormous and devastating fluctuations characteristic of deforested watersheds: recurrent flood disasters were a consequence of heavy rains on a hard, baked soil. Useful rivers, which could form the basis of profitable irrigation and hydro-electric schemes, were thus a corollary of useful forests.[1]

Over against the inadequacies of men and the unsuitability of traditional institutions as a basis for economic growth, stood poverty of natural endowment, a factor which mid-century optimists overlooked and which *fin de siècle* pessimists were to stress. With regions of inadequate rainfall and poor soil, with an absence of cheap coal, Spain's economic growth was limited. Agricultural revolutions in the nineteenth century were confined to regions with rain all the year round. What could be done with a country, two-fifths of whose useable land could only support one sheep an acre and where a further quarter was devoted to badly cultivated cereals? There were regions where great progress was made, as remarkable as any in Europe. The result was the continuance of the eighteenth-century contrast between regions of movement and regions of stagnation, between a progressive periphery and a stagnant centre; that such imbalance between regions is a characteristic of development does not make it less distressing or diminish its social consequences. Beside the explosive growth of Bilbao, Barcelona, and Valencia and the rich black soil agriculture of the Guadalquivir must be set the 'true Spain, that chain of deserts without a bird, a tree, a drop of water or a flower, a heap of *pueblos* without roads, telegraphs, sewers, hospitals, slaughterhouses, lighting, police, fire-brigades, morals or hygiene'.[2] Moreover the prosperity of the periphery could not be easily transferred to the rest of Spain: there was still no true

[1] The flood flow of some Spanish rivers is 1,000 times that of the normal flow. Much Spanish replanting was of eucalypts, in itself a doubtful remedy (cf. South African experience).

[2] The exaggerated version of Sendador Gómez (see above, footnote 2, p. 398). Most villages had police and morals whatever else they lacked. As to birds, the bird life of Spain is enormously rich and even the Monegros is not without ornithological interest. With a few distinguished exceptions, Spaniards—especially rural Spaniards—have no knowledge of or interest in birds. It is part of their total indifference to their surroundings. A nation which cannot *observe* nature will never *manipulate* nature, i.e. be a pioneer in industrial and economic growth.

national economy.[1] This divergence of pace permitted two contrasting types of social tension: the clash between workers and capital in the advanced sectors and the age-old conflicts of the landlords, peasants, and labourers in the traditional sectors. One of the characteristics of the thirties was the combination of these discontents: by 1936 the U.G.T. was becoming an agricultural as well as an industrial union.

It was the unevenness of her economic growth that left the Spain of the twentieth century with those contrasts which had delighted the Romantic travellers. The Spain of small towns and the local fiesta persisted beside the Spain of the city and the modern mass-spectator sports. Bull-fighting itself, the fiesta *par excellence*, with the construction of great arenas (beginning in 1886 with the Murcia ring) became a business enterprise in the provincial capitals, once railways allowed the regular transport of both fighting bulls and spectators. In spite of the attempts of reformers to introduce bicycling and walking expeditions as part of Western ways, enthusiasts were confined to a relatively small class—Lerroux, for instance, was an ardent cyclist; the average Spanish worker could not hope to buy a bicycle. The only Western sport that became a national passion was football. Introduced in the late nineties, with the big stadia of the 1920's the city clubs had developed the economic consequences of professionalism by 1927.[2] The great centre-forwards replaced the great matadors in popular mythology, especially in those regions, such as the Basque Provinces and Galicia, where bull-fighting never became a popular mystique. Aguirre, the Basque politician and president of the Basque autonomous government in 1936, made his name as a centre-half. No doubt the Spain of

[1] Cf. H. Paris Eguilaz, *La expansion de la economía española* (1944). Cf. his calculation of real wages in Valencia and Spain as a whole (1914 = 100): 1920, Valencia 117 : Spain 79; 1925, 145 : 106; 1929, 163 : 103. The divergence between peripheral and central Spain can be seen in the taxation revenue of the various provinces (cf. *Estadística tributaria*, 1897, with excellent maps). The exceptions in central Spain are Valladolid and Saragossa; in peripheral Spain, Galicia as a whole, Castellón, and Valencia. The contrasts in tobacco consumption, which indicate the presence or absence of a certain degree of well-being, are particularly striking.

[2] Cf. the development of the Barcelona club. Football started as a recreation for Scottish engineers. The first winds of professionalism came from the *Español* club and by 1920 Barcelona had 20,000 *socios* who loaned money for the new stadium built in 1922. (Cf. A. Maluquer y Maluquer, *Historia del Club de Fútbol Barcelona*, Barcelona, 1949.)

the flamenco dancer still controlled the image of Spain in Europe. This was partly accidental—costume Spain made easy art; partly the image was deliberately encouraged by governments after 1920 when tourism became an important source of income.[1] Yet the tourists who came to observe 'typical Spain' were another of the agencies, if not of its destruction, at least of its isolation in those regions where tourist roads and tourist money could not penetrate.

It was the size of these stagnant areas which left Spain, as a whole, a semi-developed economy in 1936. Compared to France, a larger proportion of Spaniards were still dependent for their living on agriculture and a smaller proportion engaged in any productive occupation at all.[2] There were spectacular developments; as a neutral in the First World War her products were sought after by every European belligerent. Yet in spite of these opportunities and achievements Spain remained a poor country: she still remains a candidate for that sustained growth which characterizes the establishment of a modern economy.

The vicious circle of poverty had left Spain with neither the market, the capital, nor the institutionalized financial techniques to support great industry. Thus it was not the repeal of Navigation Acts by liberal free traders in 1869 which ruined the Catalan merchant marine but a lack of capital to finance the change from sail to steam. That Spain could not find the capital to build her own railway system is not surprising; her railway problem was the lack of domestic capital to repair it and of traffic to make it a profitable enterprise. Whatever standard is taken, Spanish industry was under-capitalized and thus its relative growth was far too slow for the elimination of *retraso*—that backwardness compared to western Europe which so dis-

[1] Cf. the frescoes by Sorolla (1863–1923) in the Hispanic Society of America's building in New York (they represent various regional scenes) or the 'Spanish' paintings of Manet or, earlier, Doré's illustrations. It was in the period of Primo de Rivera that folk-lore (e.g. regional dances except the Catalan *sardana*) flourished. Interest in the tourist possibilities of 'traditional' Spain and the preservation of historical monuments dates from the Royal Commission of 1911.

[2] The proportion in agriculture was still well over half. By 1956 it had fallen to 47 per cent. (cf. France 34 per cent). In 1913 Vandellós (reprinted in *Rev. de Ec. Pol.* vi. 2, Madrid, 1953) calculated that 66 per cent. of the national income derived from agriculture; in 1953 it was rated at 42 per cent. (J. Plaza Prieto, 'El producto national de España' (*De. Ec.* vi, 1953) with maps to illustrate distribution).

tressed the propagandists of regeneration.[1] In these conditions protection was not enough, and the free play of investment could only lend money to augment existing profits rather than to develop neglected factors of production in the depressed regions.[2]

Massive state investment on land resettlement schemes, agriculture, afforestation, and irrigation, as the polemics of the nineties made clear, entailed drastic reduction of expenditure on the army and the civil service—that is, the expropriation of the middle class. The only other remedies were to redistribute the national income in order to increase average purchasing power or to initiate an agrarian revolution—in itself a doubtful remedy for prosperity. Such heroic measures were beyond the liberal state: the army remained large and the gap between riches and poverty immense and disturbing. No Spanish government has seen fit to reduce it.

[1] Cf. E. de Figueroa, 'La escasez de capital' in *R. Ec.* vi. 24, 1953, esp. 766 ff. One proof lies in the relative size of the 'active' population: 46·9 per cent. in Great Britain; 37·5 per cent. in Spain.

[2] For the role of protection in underdeveloped economies see R. Nurkse, *Problems of Capital Formation in Underdeveloped Countries* (Oxford, 1960), 104–9.

XI

SOCIETY
1870–1930

It was frequently observed during the First World War, that Spain, as a collection of distinct societies, suffered from lack of a 'national conscience' capable of uniform reaction.[1] We must be wary of attributing this incoherence of structure, what Maura called the 'shapelessness' of Spanish society, to one of the supposed antipodean singularities of Spain: its traditionalism or its revolutionary individualism, its extremism or its static conformism. It was rather that the processes of economic modernization which have been described did not easily create a society with common concerns, a common centre of gravity. What we now recognize as a characteristic of developing or under-developed countries—separate societies evolving within a country at markedly different rates of change—was the common experience of Europe under the impulse of industrialization: everywhere development was uneven, a conjunction of changes and resistance to change. Spain was distinguished by the tardiness, the sporadic incidence of development. Railways, the great begetters of a progressive and unified economy, came late. The local market was broken down only by the lorry and the local society only by the bus.[2] On a larger scale, the persistence of regionalism and its development into separatist nationalisms was a function of insufficient prosperity: it was Salmerón who pointed out that if Spain had won in 1898, if she had become a prosperous and progressive community, no one would have turned to Catalan nationalism. All would

[1] e.g. Álvaro de Albornoz, *El temperamento español* (Barcelona, n.d.). 'The incomprehension which Spain, all Spain, displayed before this great event can only be explained by the lack of a national conscience' (op. cit. 95).

[2] Historians rightly emphasize the persistence of regional cultures in Spain, yet cf. the west Wales of the 1830's, a distinct, isolated society whose peculiar discontents could produce the Rebecca riots. Parallels to the Society of west Wales in the thirties could be discovered in the Spain of the 1890's. It was better communications which destroyed the separate societies of Wales.

have 'utilized' the Spanish state and found their interests in the general prosperity of the nation.

1. *Social Classes, 1870–1930*

The incoherence of Spanish society was evident in the survival of traditional structures and attitudes at a time when Maeztu was preaching the gospel of money and Anglo-Saxon self-help as the key to a regenerated Spain. In most of the small municipalities of Spain the old-fashioned *poderosos* were still the ruling group. Like the peasantry, who refused to recognize that the great days of wheat were over, the cacique class resisted change, clinging to the *mores* of the self-sufficing community and the satisfactions of acknowledged pre-eminence.

> It was incapable of understanding the organization of great capitalist exploitations in agricultural, commercial and industrial fields. It was very stupid, completely uneducated and with a sort of village egotism. . . . These men lived pretty well. There were not many who had motor-cars and very few of them took a bath. Their grandfathers saved up their gold pieces in a stocking or under a stone. They accumulated paper money in strong boxes and could never decide whether or not to take it to the bank, suspicious of being robbed by a failure or a suspension of payments.[1]

That these rural notables kept so tight a grasp on income above the minimum levels of consumption retarded economic progress and social change.

The economic behaviour of the aristocracy was often that of the village cacique writ large; yet it enjoyed social and, to a certain extent, political influence. Although its recreations were increasingly modelled on those of the more powerful English sporting nobility, it was conspicuous in its support of the traditional Catholic values.[2] Since its whole history in the nineteenth

[1] S. Casado, *The Last Days of Madrid*, 25–26 (London, 1939).

[2] English influence was salutary and needed. 'English' shooting became a passion with Alfonso XIII, as did polo. The lists of royal shooting guests are an indication of those forces in society which influenced the king's private mind: the parties were composed mostly of court aristocrats with a sprinkling of patrician professional politicians like Romanones—a bad shot but a frequent guest. The King shot with three loaders and three guns, killing two out of a possible six birds, missing on the left behind (*The Field*, 28 Sept. 1967). Proust observed the social importance of shooting to Alfonso XIII.

century had been one of accretion, through the incorporation of successful soldiers, *hauts bourgeois*, and politicians, it tended to impose these values on the upper ranges of society as it imposed its way of life.[1] Thus the court and aristocratic custom of the *veraneo* (summer retirement from the cities), a result of Isabella's precarious health, spread downwards once railways had made long journeys an economic possibility for others than the very rich. By the 1930's many middle-class Spaniards regarded a summer in the town as a social stigma.

Nevertheless, by then aristocratic influence was in sharp decline. The court and the old aristocracy failed to observe that its position was seriously threatened by the unpopularity of a king whose position it did little to defend, but whose existence was the *raison d'être* of an aristocracy. In the Republic of 1931 the aristocracy was a caste; isolated, useless, and alone.[2] This alienation had been apparent in the 1920's and was accentuated by the dictatorship of Primo de Rivera: thus, as one aristocrat noted, the response for volunteers for the Moroccan war was 'not great, at least not from the upper classes'.[3] Alfonso XIII did make occasional attempts to break down the aristocratic court barrier which cut him from his people and especially from the intellectuals: he forced himself on a dinner party in order to meet the famous neurologist Ramón y Cajal and made an expedition to the backward region of Las Hurdes with Dr. Marañón. His courtiers did not follow his example; their spiritual home was no longer Castile but Biarritz.

The strongest social force which emerged in the Restoration and the succeeding decades was that of the financiers and large-scale industrial entrepreneurs. They came to dominate the economic and social life of the industrial towns of Catalonia and the north coast, with extensions in Valencia, and finally, with the concentration of banking and the growth of light industry after electrification, of Madrid itself.[4] These were a more

[1] After 1875, 214 marquises, 167 counts, and 30 viscounts were created: these new creations swamped the old aristocracy.

[2] Cf. the portrait of the aristocracy in the conde de Foxá's historical novel, *Madrid de Corte á Cheka* (1938), 7–88.

[3] Marqués de Villavieja, *Life Has Been Good* (London, 1938), 303. The book is an extraordinary portrayal of the aristocracy's alienation from 'ordinary' society.

[4] Madrid developed little industry until the 1920's. Electric light came in 1915, but, as in Barcelona, it was used for industrial purposes before this. Electrification

respectable and solid class than the *nouveaux riches* of the mid-century. The career of Juan March, who became the richest man in modern Spain, represents the persistence of an earlier type of capitalism; like Salamanca his money was made out of a government monopoly (tobacco) or—according to his enemies—smuggling; like Salamanca he invested his gains in transport. Majorca became his private fief and Barcelona Traction the centre of his financial empire. Whereas most of the respectable industrialists and bankers became conservatives, Juan March was sympathetic to politicians like Santiago Alba and Lerroux; the conspirators of 1930–1 always hoped that he would finance a Republican rising. The *renversement des alliances* produced by the Republic, which regarded his conviction for fraud as a political duty, is shown by the fact that March, like all his fellow capitalists, supported Franco.

In Catalonia a class of great industrialists developed naturally out of the patriarchal family business; as in the old aristocracy inter-marriage concentrated their wealth and the spread of their interests was very large. Thus the second marqués de Comillas controlled the biggest Spanish shipping concern (the *Transatlántica*), mining interests, a bank, and large agricultural estates. With Comillas, a court chamberlain, the Catalan business magnates entered Spanish society in the narrow sense of that term, and shared its interests in the Catholic revival; he financed pilgrimages to Rome and laid down minute regulations to prevent opportunities for immorality on his ships.[1] In the north the great financial and industrial dynasties, sprung from humble origins like the Urquijos, followed a similar development somewhat later: thus the richest Basque industrialists

enterprises tended to be dominated by politicians (cf. the railways earlier) and, as an interest group, came into sharp conflict with the board of the Canal of Isabella II that supplied the water that had been the basis of Madrid's development as a great city. For this conflict within the conservative classes see *Memorias, informes y documentos relativos a la gestión de la Commisaria Regia . . . en el año 1907* (1908). The Santillana Electrical concern (with which the conservative leader Maura was connected) wished to sell water to the Canal of Isabella II (of which the conservative politician Sánchez de Toca was president); it therefore opposed the Canal board's plans for combining water supply with production of electrical power (op. cit., esp. 161 ff.).

[1] For a curious portrait of Comillas see E. F. Regatillo, *Un marqués modelo* (Santander, 1950). It is a curious quirk of history, and an indication of the economic importance of Comillas, that Huysman's hero, des Esseintes, had a *Transatlántica* poster in his room.

shunned Basque nationalism and preferred to pay court to the exiled Empress Zita at Lequerica.[1]

In Andalusia low wages encouraged local magnates to set up industrial enterprises. The role of these southern capitalists has not been studied. Next to the Basques and Catalans they were, with the Castilian wheat-growers, the most powerful economic grouping in Spain. They included the great sherry firms, cork, and later cotton interests. Seville and, to a lesser extent, Cordoba, were the centres of large semi-industrialized agrarian interests and the playgrounds of the typical product of the Andalusian rich—the *señorito*. Aristocratic by inclination and often by birth or marriage, these families were highly conservative and monarchist in sentiment but perhaps lacked what Maeztu called the 'sense of reverence for money'.[2] The Larios family, who controlled the life of Algeciras, set up a textile factory; after two generations it had acquired the dukedom of Lerma by marriage and sold out its textile interests to Catalans.

Even in Catalonia, the enterprise of the mid-century seems to have been weakened by the slump of 1866; only at the end of the century was there once more a marked drift away from small family concerns towards capitalist concentration, economies of scale and modernization—a process especially marked in new industries like chemicals and cement. Even so Cambó believed that Catalans remained a nation of shopkeepers whose horror of the limited liability company, whose fear of combination in order to win large markets, stemmed from the artisan's desire to be master in his own house.[3] It was in 1929 that Carlos Pi Sunyer maintained that the artisans' gospel of work, having created Catalonia as an industrial centre, now kept her as an economy without grandeur and without ambitions.

The newer recruits were less conservative in outlook. Cambó,

[1] One of the few Basque millionaires who was a Basque nationalist was Llano y Soto. He was not a true Basque by birth.

[2] They were often politically influential: thus Francisco Silvela married a Loring heiress. The brother of the Falangist leader José Antonio Primo de Rivera married a Larios.

[3] C. Pi Sunyer, *Aptitud*, ii. 246. J. Vicens y Vives (*Els Catalans*, 73–75) stresses the traumatic effects of the 1866 crash. Textile manufacturers did combine to meet the crisis of 1902–7 in the *Mutua de Fabricantes* but the war boom restored anarchy until the Regulatory Commission of 1926. Throughout the Catalan manufacturers worked by rule of thumb as far as export markets were concerned; their sense of common interest was created by the struggle for *domestic* protection.

sprung from middling farmer stock and first apprenticed to a chemist, was the greatest of the 'new promotion' in Catalonia; an industrial financier and banker, his greatest creation was the CHADE and his final *coup* was an attempt to corner the cork export.[1] With his art collection—it included the Botticellis now in the Prado—his yacht and his highly developed political interests he was the most prominent and successful self-made business man of Alfonsine Spain. In the Basque country the powerful capitalist dynasties fused in the early twentieth century.[2] Finally the company replaced the family because it could raise new capital more easily; because of their banking interests (30 per cent. of Spanish investment after 1908 was Basque) the Basque capitalists became the most important single financial interest in Spain. On the fringes of this class there were dramatic ascents and declines: the new rich of the Tarragona wine boom had been wiped out by 1895; the relatively large class of shipowners, a striking element in Barcelona society and throughout the Catalan littoral in the fifties and sixties, had gone by 1898. As was their habit, Catalan protectionists blamed its disappearance on the refusal of the Madrid government to protect 'national' shipping; in fact most Catalan shippers lacked the capital to finance the change from sail to steam.

Catalonia alone produced an autonomous middle-class civilization, vital and open to influences from abroad. Whereas 1898 brought a climate of pessimism in Castile the generation of 1901 in Catalonia was optimistic. The amazing architecture of the rich suburbs of Barcelona expressed the confidence of Catalan millionaires, whereas, in Madrid, the new rich built conventional palaces. Barcelona staged Ibsen plays and Wagner's operas as early as any other great city in Europe; it produced talented architects like Luis Domenech Montaner (1850–1923) and a truly great genius Gaudí, both of whom were closely connected with the urban expansion of the turn of the century and the building of new churches.[3] While Sert provided

[1] CHADE was the great hydro-electric combine created partly to accommodate German interests after the First World War.

[2] e.g. Chávarri, the Ybarras, and Echevarría merged their metallurgical interests around 1900 (*Banco de Bilbao*, 160–1).

[3] One of the most un-Castilian of Catalan cultural activities was the choral movement: starting with Clavé's working-class choirs (see above, p. 289) it became

large frescoes for the new rich, it was the Bohemian world of Barcelona, open to foreign influence, which nourished the early Picasso.[1] A serious middle-class culture did not develop in the Basque country—perhaps because there was no university or because Basque nationalism was a true peasant nationalism as Catalan nationalism never was. The Basque Provinces looked inward to *Euzkadi* or outwards to America and England.

Gradually technicians, especially engineers, appear beside lawyers as the intellectual aristocrats of bourgeois society. The early *técnicos* (for instance, Echegaray the engineer and dramatist who was foreign minister in 1868, and Sagasta) usually became straightforward politicians. Later arrivals were consultants. They quickly made their way on to the boards of the bigger companies—the Spanish Paper Company and the Madrid Metro for example—and their golden age was the dictatorship of Primo de Rivera when they appear in the cabinet with Guadalhorce, the engineer who had planned the dam from which he took his title, and in the government agencies which pullulated after 1923. Their ambitious plans could not be financed by Republican Spain and their political allegiance was suspect: hence they turned against the Republic. Within the professional classes the Republic was supported by doctors, journalists, and university professors rather than by engineers.

By 1936 the *clases medias* (a phrase which can best be translated as the 'intermediary classes') were even more complex in composition than those of the mid-century. The diversity and comparative weakness of the new middle classes in the post-war years is shown by the variety and short life of the periodicals which catered for their interests.[2] The revolutionary role of the urban middle classes in politics was taken from them as proletarian parties emerged which distrusted middle-class radicalism and its leaders; on the left only radical Catalan

a pride of Catalonia as a whole. Significantly enough the only other good choirs were in Bilbao and San Sebastian.

[1] Thus Picasso's early art was to some degree dependent on painters like Rusiñol who were acquainted with French painting. For Picasso's Barcelona life see J. Sabartés, *Picasso* (New York, 1948), and A. Cirici Pellicer, *Picasso avant Picasso* (Geneva, 1950). It is characteristic of the relative cultural influences that Picasso disliked Madrid and finally left Barcelona for Paris in 1904.

[2] Cf. the section called *Revistas varias* in the Madrid Hemeroteca for the years 1919–25.

nationalism remained a middle-class concern, and the revolution it sought was devoid of social content. The middle class had no organization, no party; by 1936 it had been pushed aside.[1]

Thus, at the outbreak of the Civil War, the middle classes were divided in their loyalties. The flower of middle-class civilization, the intellectuals, were uncertain in their allegiance: of the older generation, only the great poet Machado was a convinced Republican. The majority of them found the soil of Nationalist Spain inhospitable, tenanted as it was by the academic appointees of Primo de Rivera who had been pushed aside by the 'Masonic' appointments of the Republicans.[2] The Republic was overthrown in July 1936 by the army, prepared for its mission by its own discontents. Nevertheless the army could not have succeeded unless it had reflected those fissures in middle-class society which made rural caciques, small-town notables, and prosperous engineers alike seek salvation with the Nationalists against those sectors of the middle class who were prepared for an alliance with the working classes. This alliance, for middle-class Spaniards caught in Republican areas, was often an uncomfortable geographical necessity rather than a true union. As the Civil War went on, this alienation became more noticeable; it meant not merely the traumatic experience of anarchist patrols but the rejection of middle-class *mores*, a proletarianization of political forms that could not be abandoned even when, in 1937, middle-class politicians had, to some extent, recaptured political power. Long after the Anarchists had been domesticated and their social revolution dismantled, the Republic remained a Worker's Republic in its

[1] Cf. the curious *Heraldo de la clase media* published (one issue only) in 1918. The workers would force through their demands by strong organization and this meant that the 'middle classes' were 'neglected'. Their main demand was reasonable urban rents which reveals a conflict of interest with the property-owning *haute bourgeoisie*.

[2] Enrique Suñer, author of the most astonishing and violent polemic against the Republican *universitarios* as 'ignorant adventurers', had been passed over by the Republic (cf. his *Los intellectuales y la tragedia española*, San Sebastian, 1938). Suñer seems to have believed in a Jewish–Marxist–Masonic conspiracy for the capture of university patronage; the conspiracy was centred in the Institute for Free Education ('with its eyes on the ideal and its hands in the bread-basket') and led by successful and rich professors like Negrín against loyal and austere Catholic professors.

style; within it the middle classes felt cut off from the customary usages of their civilization.[1]

Lacking, as we do, reliable real wage statistics it is hard to examine the conditions of the lower classes. Given the marked regional variations in wages and standards of living, generalization about wages and prices mean little. It may be hazarded that skilled labour remained relatively well paid but that the conditions of semi-skilled and unskilled labour deteriorated in the late nineteenth and early twentieth century, except, perhaps, in regions of marked economic growth or marked stagnation. Marvaud, in 1905, calculated that the Paris worker was considerably better off than his Madrid counterpart since lower rents were counterbalanced by much more expensive food. Outside industry money wages seemed to have remained stable (perhaps because they were conventional) while prices rose: in the towns, a variety of trades (shoe-making, tailoring) demanded long hours for low wages while, in the country, the labourer's wages seemed to have risen little since the 1850's.[2] The deficit in the rural family budget was met by under-nourishment or emigration; thus Salamanca provided cheap labour for French farmers, the mountains of Cordoba the workers for the southern mines.[3] In the towns it was met by multi-employment —a daughter in one of the 'sweated' trades, a son as an errand boy, a wife as a washerwoman. Thus the poorer workers in the Catalan cork industry sought extra wages as part-time waiters.

What was characteristic of the labour world of Europe in the nineteenth century was the mass of suffering at the base of urban life: the new immigrants into the city before their absorption, the beggars and street pedlars, were its expression in Spain. Street selling became increasingly a marginal enterprise in

[1] Cf. the perceptive comments of J. Marías in *Los españoles* (1902), 15–17.

[2] Most calculations emphasize the stability of wages (e.g. the two pesetas a day wage in agriculture) in face of steep rises in food prices. For the extreme regional variation in agricultural wages and food prices, see 'Resumen de la informacíon acerca de los obreros agrícolas en las provincias de Andalusia y Estramadura' (*I.R.S.* 1905). For wages in 1895 see A. Barthe, *Le Salaire des ouvriers en Espagne* (1896). Barthe calculated that food prices had risen 60 per cent. since 1877 while the wages of most employees in artisan trades seemed to have remained at the 'standard' 2 pesetas per day: e.g. in dress-making, shoe-making. He calculated that an 'average' wage for a carpenter or mason would be 3·5 to 4 pesetas; the highest wages paid by foreign mining concerns (Huelva, 6·5).

[3] For emigration see C. Bernaldo de Quirós, 'La emigracíon obrera' (*I.R.S.* 1920).

central Madrid with the development of large shops just before the First World War, but it remained a necessary service for the urban poor, who could only buy in small quantities, and to the lazy.[1] The new poor lived in the *chozas* (shacks) that had begun to grow up at the edge of the great cities. Unlike the old urban poor these slum-dwellers largely escaped the influence of ecclesiastical charity. They also escaped municipal sanitation and were the victims of the high urban death rates from typhoid.

The true proletariat remained relatively small: the quarter of a million workers were still outnumbered by three-quarters of a million artisans (many on the descent towards wage labour) and the mass of agricultural labourers. There had long been a tradition of association in the established trades—coopers for instance—and among the Barcelona cotton operatives. After 1900 there was a tremendous upward surge in the number of workers' associations; though these unions were by no means all the work of Socialists or Anarchists, the proletarian parties were transforming the older associationist traditions into what were called 'societies of resistance'.[2] The new unionism of 'societies of resistance', first Socialist and later Anarchist, not only changed the nature of labour conflicts but spread that conflict to new areas and new industries.

2. *Labour Movements, 1868–1923: Anarchism and Socialism*

The fascination of the early history of Spanish labour movements has obscured their insignificance. Until the nineties Spanish politicians could regard labour troubles—the recurrent *jacquerie* of Andalusia, the terrorism of Barcelona—as questions of public order, as echoes of the time of troubles in 1873, rather than as portents for the future. In 1907 Spain was still the only major European country without a working-class deputy in parliament.

The strange implantation of the ideals of Bakunin's Alliance of Social Democracy by the Italian Fanelli in the seventies

[1] Cf. the present structure of street cigarette sales. There are excellent descriptions of the Dickensian world of the Madrid poor in the novels of Galdós and in Pio Baroja's *Aurora roja*.

[2] For the surge, see 'Estadística de la asociación obrera' (*I.R.S.* 1904). Unions classed as 'societies of resistance' numbered in 1898: 19; 1899: 80; 1900: 198; 1901: 129; 1902: 166; 1903: 224; 1904: 193.

lead to a bitter struggle between the disciples of Bakunin and the 'authoritarian' Marxists in the early seventies. In the early congresses a small group of Fanelli's disciples forced through the acceptance of a revolutionary programme of libertarian communism, sweeping aside Marxists and gradualists by tactical ruthlessness and congress rigging which shocked Anselmo Lorenzo, a simple dedicated man typical of the best in anarchism.[1] Though the libertarians had triumphed for the time being, this conflict was to have tragic results: it left the Spanish labour movement divided in its competition for the loyalty of the working classes between orthodox Socialists and Anarchists, a schism complicated by the division of the Anarchists themselves between syndicalists, professional revolutionaries, and terrorists, and by the personal and tactical divergencies within socialism. The division between Socialists and Anarchists was geographical (with Anarchist strongholds in Catalonia and Andalusia extending into the Levante, Aragon, and with outposts in the Asturias and Galicia) and temperamental. There was a type of Spanish revolutionary energumen, bred in the ferment of the seventies, to whom Marxist doctrine and gradualist tactics could make no appeal. To join the Socialists was 'to do the goose step in a Prussian Regiment'.[2] This image of a 'military' party limited Socialist recruitment in those revolutionary circles which were violently individualist.

The history of the anarchist movement was not one of a steady and continuous growth. The various federations, which proudly traced their origins to the Congresses of the First International in Spain, sprang up and died away. Outbursts of organization, when enrolled membership mounted, were followed by periods of persecution and of clandestine activity when the movement was reduced to a hard core of militants. Congress does not broaden down to congress: the movement takes sudden leaps forward and suffers disastrous defeats. This cyclical rhythm was set by contagious enthusiasms sweeping in from the anarchist movement of Europe and by the alternate periods of legal toleration and savage repression characteristic

[1] Anselmo Lorenzo, *El proletariado militante* (Mexico, n.d.), 292, 295, 342.

[2] The phrase was used by the young Catalanist, Nicolau d'Olwer, in order to describe his fellow students' reaction to Socialism. Pio Baroja's *Aurora roja* (published in 1904) contains a penetrating sketch of anarchist psychology: the disillusioned Republican idealist inevitably comes to rest with the Anarchists.

of weak government. In the early years the movement yawed from propaganda by words to propaganda by deed. After 1907 syndicalism brought the movement within the grasp of relatively moderate leaders; when these leaders tested their organization by a strike it was broken by massive imprisonments, leaving the movement in the hands of activist militants who used the revolutionary temper and resentments of the masses for courses which the moderates recognized as suicidal.

Sagasta's tolerance allowed the remnants of the First International to re-emerge at the Congress of Barcelona (June 1881) as the anarchist-dominated Regional Federation of Spanish Workers. Broken by repression after 1884, the terrorists of propaganda by deed set off a wave of bomb outrages and assassinations which reached their peak in the 1890's and included the *Liceo* bomb-throwing which killed twenty-one theatre-goers, that at the Corpus Christi procession which killed ten participants, and the assassination of Cánovas. These outrages, the work of isolated extremists, horrified opinion and exhibit the nature of anarchist terrorism: the *Liceo* and the Corpus Christi procession were symbols of corrupt bourgeois life. The horror the bomb-throwings provoked in bourgeois society provoked drastic police repression and this, in turn, set off the mechanisms of anarchist reprisal, which accounted for the assassination of three prime ministers. Police barbarity, in its turn, provoked a reaction of the European left: thus the protest of the left against the tortures of Montjuich (the prison-fortress of Barcelona) was an early example of the sensitivity of European liberal opinion on Spanish issues; it created a modern version of the Black Legend, of the Spain of the Inquisition.[1]

Terrorism was never more than a minority doctrine; parallel with it ran another anarchist tradition—that of self-improvement and rationalist education. Unsuccessful terrorism produces a feeling of profound lethargy, and it was in this trough of despair that Anarchists came to organize debates on themes like property, free love, or the city of the future, or to send their children to the rationalist Modern Schools of Ferrer.[2] Ferrer

[1] The police procedures were publicized in F. Tarrida del Marmol's *Les Inquisiteurs de l'Espagne* (published in 1897). The author contributed to the Black Legend in the pages of the *Nineteenth Century and After*.

[2] See below, p. 485.

was a free-thinker as well as an Anarchist, a Rousseauian idealist rather than a revolutionary, and it was as nurseries of atheism that attendance in his schools was castigated by the hierarchy. Nevertheless many of his ideas on property and the family were indistinguishable from Anarchists' beliefs. His activities corresponded with the period after the terrorist wave had weakened, when the anarchist classics became the property of the bolder spirits among the proletariat of Barcelona.

It is at this point that we must examine the geographical distribution of the *foci* of anarchist activity. The hold anarchism established over the minds and hearts of the day labourers of the Andalusian estates is understandable. What is more surprising is that Catalonia, an advanced industrial region, should have become the great anarchist homeland of Europe.

Until the 1890's the strength of anarchism lay in Andalusia. It spread rapidly on the Andalusian estates and in the villages, partly because Bakunin's gospel coincided with the messianic traditions of primitive society, but more importantly because anarchist apostles were prepared to adopt as their own the demands of the Andalusian labourers, even when these were theoretically in conflict with the principles of the movement. These demands had long included the abolition of piece-work, higher wages, and, behind these, the 'indigenous socialism' of the *reparto*—the 'magic word which has electrified the masses' with the cry for a division of the great estates. The strength of anarchism, as opposed to socialism, lay in the fact that its doctrines could contain and expand this primitive revolution and at the same time absorb the lees of the Federalist Republican ferment. Although the connexions between anarchism and Federal republicanism are often difficult to trace, it was in those areas with a long *exaltado* tradition, and where Federal republicanism had been strong, that anarchism took root. It was a proletarian edition of the *exaltado* extremism of the 1830's, and it was the Federalist, Pi y Margall, who became one of the few bourgeois deities in the anarchist pantheon.

At times this rural anarchism organized itself, or rather fell under the influence of small organized groups, and was carried into movements of social revolution or strike action. Then the great cyclical gusts of peasant violence, crop burnings, killings of watch dogs, assassinations of rural guards, swept over the south. The Regional Federation of Spain, set up in 1881, soon convinced the landlords that they were confronted with a vast revolutionary organization. It may well have been that the violent men of the Federation set up a secret revolutionary society, as was maintained by the prosecution in the Black Hand Trials (1883–4). These trials, which were publicized throughout the left in Europe, revealed police torture and the determination of judges to imprison leading Anarchists, whether guilty or not of the crimes attributed to them. Repression broke the movement though 'the idea' persisted. In 1892, driven by famine and unemployment, a peasant army, armed with sickles and shot guns, invaded Jerez, striking down 'those who wore good clothes'. An outburst of the compressed hatred of generations, it was the last of the andalusian *jacqueries* rather than an anarchist revolution although the anarchist militants participated in the movement. Gradually the propaganda tours of these militants and vague rumours of a new gospel—the general strike—changed the character of peasant revolt especially in the provinces of Cordoba and Cadiz. Spasmodic revolt was replaced by loosely organized strikes. These strikes culminated with a general strike in Cordoba in 1903. The movement was killed by hunger—1904 was almost a famine year—and for the next decade anarchism remained as a hope in the hearts of a few *fanáticos*; as an organized movement it almost ceased to exist in the rural south.[1]

Anarchism in Andalusia remained less an organization than a state of mind. When the federations were broken the movement kept its apostles—the village fanatic, 'the man who had ideas'—stranded by the ebb tide of revolution. The devotion inspired by these itinerant preachers and colporteurs was due to the simple fact that these apostles were the first educated men who spoke to the Andalusian day-labourer as to a human being.[2] They toured the *cortijos*, sharing the labourers' soup,

[1] There had been a strike in 1883 for the abolition of piece-work and some terrorist anarchist organization may have been behind it, see C. Bernaldo de Quiros, *El espartaquismo agrario andaluz* (Madrid, 1919), 30–33. It was broken by drafting soldiers to field work. After that there was no serious strike till the 1900's.

[2] The best-loved apostle was Salvochea, elevated by the Anarchists into the saint of the movement, the Christ of anarchism who gave his clothes to the poor. There is a splendid portrait of him in Blasco Ibáñez's novel *La bodega*, and a brilliant portrait of the *obrero consciente* in J. Díaz del Moral, *Agitaciones*, 226–7. At a later date Sánchez Rosa was the apostle of the province of Cordoba. *La*

reading extracts from the South American anarchist press, spelling out anarchist catechisms which the local *fanáticos* got by heart. Austere puritans, they sought to impose vegetarianism, sexual abstinence, and atheism on one of the most backward peasantries of Europe. A mania for self-improvement, which fed on anarchist classics like Kropotkin's *Conquest of Bread*, the *Ruins of Palmyra*, and popular science, is the most moving feature of the movement. This sudden injection of illumination could capture a whole village with the conviction that the day foretold by the apostles had come to pass. Thus strikes were moments of exaltation as well as demands for better conditions; spontaneous and often disconnected they would bring, not only the abolition of piece-work, but 'the day', so near at hand that sexual intercourse and alcohol were abandoned by enthusiasts till it should dawn.

Like all religious movements—and anarchism had many of the characteristics of a religious revival—it had an ultimate vision of the reign of justice when men would recapture a lost dignity and human relations move in perfect freedom and harmony. Whereas in a complex industrial society this utopia was an inconceivable anachronism, in the pueblo, once the rich and perverse had been eliminated, the anarchist dream could be translated into fact. Like Rousseau's citizens, in 1918–19 and 1936 the peasants ruled themselves with an unconcerned contempt for corrupt societies outside the regenerated village. 'Cut off the heads of the nobles and caballeros', seize the land, and the Andalusian labourer would find himself in the society that his economic instincts and his atavistic hatreds, as well as his dreams of justice and dignity, commended to him. Because the Andalusian *bracero* did not see the social war as a long struggle but as a sudden triumph of the truths learned from itinerant apostles and a primitive press, he failed to organize; this failure was accentuated by the fact that the movements which sought his support—anarchism and the later anarcho-syndicalism—themselves tended to deride organization as a Socialist vice.[1]

Voz del Campesino and other anarchist papers gave the Andalusian *bracero* a sense of his own dignity and, in the correspondence columns, contact with the South American *émigré* militants.

[1] The supposed distaste for 'organization' displayed by Anarchists needs qualification (see below, p. 453). As E. Hobsbawm remarks (*Primitive Rebels* (Manchester, 1959), 89) millenarianism may sometimes have been only the reflection of the village Anarchists' 'lack of organization, isolation and relative weakness'.

Once the prospect of land had vanished, millenarianism and religious fervour remained only in the hearts of *fanáticos*: thus is explained the cyclical nature of rural anarchism so brilliantly described by Díaz del Moral, the sudden relapse into 'Moorish' fatalism, apathy, and brute indifference. 'Quick to understand and enthuse,' wrote the militant Mella, 'quick to surrender and despair.'[1]

The conversion of the Catalan workers was a long and discontinuous process; moreover it was a conversion not to anarchism, though the purists of individual action remained, but to anarcho-syndicalism—the strong revolutionary union with the instrument of the general strike. It can therefore be seen as part of the general processes of 'Europeanization' characteristic of the years after 1898 with French syndicalist organization as its model.

The associationist tradition of Barcelona—as late as 1890 the old *Tres Clases de Vapor* was still the strongest union in Spain—seemed better suited to the socialist than to the anarchist alliance. Why, then, was this tradition swamped by anarcho-syndicalism? Immigration into the lower reaches of the working classes from the violent and backward areas of the south, the contagions of a great port, the persistence of small-scale industry which, as in the Juras, favoured anarchism, the existence of cramped working-class quarters within a rich city, all favoured revolutionary violence. To Catalan nationalists, believers in the *seny* (common sense) and 'in the analytic, positive spirit of the Catalan race', the Anarchist deviation is explained in terms of the immigration of 'foreign' elements from provinces with a tradition of primitive revolution—an explanation which is in the nature of an excuse. The port kept up contacts with foreign Anarchists, especially Italians, and no one who does not know the workers' quarters of central Barcelona can understand the premium narrow streets and crowded houses put on revolutionary violence. More important was the intransigence of the Barcelona employers and the brutality of police suppression. In these circumstances the old

[1] M. Buencasa, *El movimiento obrero español* (Barcelona, 1928), 151. E. Hobsbawm, op. cit. 79, talks of a ten-year cycle after 1860. Arid regions frequently exhibit phases of passivity and violent action; Euclides da Cunha shows how the struggle in the northern highlands of Brazil against appalling drought produces 'impulsive exaltation and an enervating pathy and inactivity' (*Rebellion in the Backlands* (Chicago, 1944, 112)).

associationist traditions were inadequate and futile. Employers get the working classes they deserve.

The history of the Catalan unions of these years—and they were numerous and already long established—has still to be written, and when written may alter our whole picture of the origins and efficiency of the great anarcho-syndicalist union the C.N.T. (*Confederacion Nacional del Trabajo*). Founded in 1911 as a national organization of Anarchists who had been converted to the tactics of syndicalism, it grew rapidly during the war.[1] The anarcho-syndicalism of the C.N.T. did two things: its doctrines afforded a bridge to the older unionism that anarchism itself had often lacked and, conversely, anarchist militants could now find a place in syndicalism. It was idle to expect that the Anarchists would reject their revolutionary utopianism for the 'daily revindicatory task' of syndicalism or that the older unions would forget their reformist traditions.[2] The precarious unity which the fighting strength of the C.N.T. demanded was forced on it from outside—by the intransigence of employers and the erratic governmental repression. Yet, once forged, unity vanished in post-mortem debates on strike tactics in which the profound conflicts between the revolutionist and more moderate syndicalist traditions welled to the surface. Thus the re-founded Federation of the Spanish Region found that the new doctrine of the general strike weakened rather than strengthened the movement. The wave of strikes in Barcelona from 1903 to 1904 was disastrous. The number of workers in the militant unions declined rapidly and the more powerful traditional unions remained on the margin of any single organized movement. Anarcho-syndicalism was still a minority movement, torn by doctrinal disputes and plagued by violent men. 'The strike became a scourge for the proletarians themselves and they ended by hating it.'[3]

[1] According to Angel Pestaña in 1915 the C.N.T. had only 15,000 members: in 1919, 600,000 (cf. *Leviatan*, no. 1, Madrid, 1934).

[2] This became clear in the objections of both elements to the *sindicato único* or local factory union (1918) which became the basis of the organizational strength of the C.N.T. Outside Catalonia reformism was weak; especially in towns like Seville and Saragossa, the pure anarchist tradition triumphed more easily.

[3] M. Sastre, *Las huelgas en Barcelona* (Barcelona, 1904), 5. Sastre is prejudiced in that he was a Catholic opponent of 'materialist' unionism. Yet his statistics are striking. Thus the 1903 strikes resulted in 264 imprisonments and left 2,000 unem-

Compared with the dramatic surges and recessions of anarchism the growth of the socialist party and its trades union (the *Union General de Trabajadores* or U.G.T., founded in 1882) was slow and painful. The socialist party was created in 1879 by those expelled from the Bakuninist Federation: it was a small party rooted in the aristocracy of the Madrid proletariat, the printers, who had always played a leading role in working-class radicalism. Pablo Iglesias, son of a poor washerwoman, turned their old-fashioned craft union, formed to negotiate with employers, into a militant organ to resist the employers: in 1882 the Union staged the first effective strike in Restoration Spain.

From its beginnings the socialist movement was deeply influenced by French Marxists through the channel of the party's first secretary Pablo Iglesias and of his friend Mesa, a Paris journalist. From the French leader Guesde, Iglesias derived his harsh but effective platform and journalistic style, his doctrinaire hostility to bourgeois politicians—especially Republicans—and his distaste for anarchist modes of thought and action.[1] The breach with the Republicans went back to memories of '73, of Castelar and Salmerón's excessively bourgeois republic. Though the Socialists preferred the republic to the monarchy they did not, until 1910, move from their declared 'indifference' to forms of government: thus Villacampa's rising was stigmatized as a bourgeois affair.[2] Pablo Iglesias's doctrinal inflexibility was coupled with superb qualities as an organizer. Single-handed, often a sick man, he ran the party from his home in the building of its paper *El Socialista*; his enormous network of correspondence, which made him known to every Spanish militant, provided him with the influence by which he could steer the party's congresses. This austere and ascetic invalid stamped the party with his concern for morality in political life, his rigidity and his exclusive proletarian brand of calvinism.

ployed: 7,000 left the militant unions. Of the 33 important strikes 16 were lost, 11 ended in compromise, and 6 were gained.

[1] For Guesde's influence see J. J. Morato, *Pablo Iglesias* (1931), 77–78. Not all Socialists were as orthodox as Iglesias's circle: cf. the reading of Balbontín in his Socialist days (*La España de mi experiencia*, Mexico, 1952), 142. He was attracted to Communism by the Marxist notion of 'the withering away of the state'. Pablo Iglesias, as an orthodox Socialist, was concerned to make a workers' state.

[2] See above, pp. 361 and 365.

Though it was founded in Barcelona, the U.G.T. failed to win over what would have seemed to be promising recruits—those workers familiar with the old associationist traditions and who were suspicious of revolutionary anarchism. Thus in Catalonia the U.G.T. remained inexpansible, and in 1899 its headquarters were removed to Madrid. Madrid, a non-industrial city, remained the capital of a socialism which has been seen as a typical movement of 'authoritarian' Castile: its discipline was, however, common to Marxist Socialists everywhere in Europe, although it may have appealed especially to the heartland of the old Spanish state. It was in Madrid that the party bought its most impressive *casa del pueblo* (People's house); there it printed its national daily. Its mass following came from the industrial regions in the north where the strikes of the 1890's in Bilbao gave the movement its first grip.

The strikes, which occurred in the Biscayan mining industry after 1890 and which were the first serious strikes in Spain, showed how socialist influence transformed the vague discontents of the past into 'societies of resistance'. This allowed the employers to dismiss the strikes as the work of agitators who represented only 10 per cent. of the men, and to reject the wage settlements negotiated by the Captain General—a curious illustration of the powers that reverted to the military on the declaration of a state of siege. Instead of 'giving in to socialism' what was needed were more Civil Guards. The demands of the strikers—the abolition of company shops and lodgings—reveal not only the archaic conditions of a mining industry set, isolated in the Basque countryside, but also the special grievances which divided the strikers and weakened the movement. The interests of the semi-migrant casual labourers, characteristic of the primitive stages of the industry, were quite distinct from those of the *fijos* or resident miners.[1] After 1900 the isolation of the mines (and therefore the necessity for shops and lodgings) diminished

[1] For a detailed examination of the grievances of the Basque miners see J. Pujol y Alonso, 'Informe referente a las minas de Vizcaya' (*I.R.S.* 1904). The division between *fijos* and others caused differences of opinion (e.g. over the desirability of weekly payment) which were exploited by the employers who also pointed to the 'unclean' alliance of Socialists and petty-bourgeois shopkeepers against the Company shops. These and the lodging houses were usually run by the *captaces*, i.e. foremen or butties. A man seeking work asked a foreman, 'Is there a bed in the house?' Thus the strikes were often directed against the foremen rather than the firms.

together with the numbers of casual labourers. This paved the way for a stronger form of unionism.

In the same years 'societies of resistance' were formed in the backward agrarian regions of Castile and the south. In Castile the movement reflected the chain effect of rising rents on a peculiar agrarian structure: the large farmers in Avila gave their labourers a miserable wage (1·75 pesetas for work 'from sun to sun'), some food, and a plot of land. This created a semi-peasant class among the poorest in Spain. As a result of the agricultural crisis of the 1880's even these miserable rewards were reduced. Suddenly, Castilian villages, after centuries of somnolence, saw the labourers gather together in a village 'Centre' in order to draft their demands, often under the influence of a socialist convert who had worked in the mines. Where the mayor was tactful trouble was avoided; more often he shared the view of the richer inhabitants—that association was an 'insult to the employing classes' scarcely to be distinguished from a servile revolt.

From Bilbao missionaries spread socialism in the Asturias—where over 80 per cent. of the workers could read and where the movement could count on the sympathy of the social reformists of Oviedo University. Conflict in Bilbao with the Catholic unions, and conflict in the Asturias with the Anarchists turned the northern Socialists into the *élite* of the U.G.T. Without a true peasant programme (this was an imposition of the party's intellectuals in the twentieth century) it made little progress in agrarian Spain outside the latifundia districts: both the C.N.T. and the Socialists concentrated on the under-employed agricultural labourer, and in this battle, after temporary successes 1900–12, the U.G.T. tended to lose out to the C.N.T.[1]

Like every other opposition party the Socialists had expanded with reaction to the defeat of 1898.[2] The Socialists had campaigned against the injustices of the recruiting system—as nineteenth-century radicalism showed, one of the shortest ways to a temporary increase of strength. Thus in 1898–1902

[1] The only Andalusian town where socialism remained a force was Granada (G. Brenan, *Labyrinth*, note A. 228).

[2] Between 1888 and 1896 the U.G.T. had risen from 3,355 to 6,154: in 1902 it was 34,778 and in 1904 43,665. For the subsequent collapse see Marvaud, *La Question sociale en Espagne* (Paris, 1910). The party got 3,101 votes in 1898 and 7,858 in 1901. By 1906 this had shrunk to 6,000.

the U.G.T. probably tripled its membership and the party's vote doubled. Yet by 1906 the party was shrinking and the U.G.T. in a state of crisis. A large proportion of its strikes were ill-organized and ill-timed and resulted in failure.[1] The employers' counter-offensive seemed to have triumphed: in the Asturias the Socialists had warned that an unsuccessful strike of 1905 would give the employers an excuse to break the movement. They were correct: dismissals reduced the union to a hundred militants, the circulation of *El Socialista* fell from 300 to 60 and the professors of the Oviedo University Extension found the workers afraid to attend lectures.[2] In the Castilian pueblos the sudden growth of Workers' Centres came to a stop.

This collapse the party attributed not to its own rigidity but to caciquismo. Unable to break through the corruptions of the electoral system it must become the protest of a minority against the immoralities which, it was maintained, destroyed the voting strength of socialism. It was in municipal politics after 1905 that the Socialists scored their first victories as moralizers. Iglesias was elected to the Madrid Municipality by a smart device which defeated the old gang and, once in municipal office, the Socialists made a corner in the exposure of minor electoral jobbery. This became the chief task of Largo Caballero, to whom Madrid municipal politics remained an all important field of the party's activities.[3]

The real increase in socialist strength, in the country as a whole, came with the political crisis of 1909 and the Republican alliance. Iglesias had been so hostile to bourgeois reformism that he refused to translate Jaurès, but in 1909 the Socialists accepted a 'Conjunction' with the Republicans in order to fight Maura.[4] This immediately gave the party a seat in the

[1] Cf. *Estadística de huelgas*, 1905–8, for lost strikes and the diminution of union activity.

[2] After the 1905 strike the employers set up a 'Black Cabinet' to exclude Socialists; even workers who lodged with Socialists were sacked. See J. Pujol y Alonso, 'Informe acerca de la fábrica y de los obreros de Mieres' (*I.R.S.* 1907), 16–17, 33.

[3] F. Largo Caballero, *Mis recuerdos* (Mexico, 1954), 74: cf. his efforts to expose faulty contracts, evasion of municipal taxation, &c., 68–70. On obtaining municipal office, the first act of the Socialists was a self-denying ordinance against their exercise of 'municipal' patronage which had rotated between the councillors and which had been an essential mechanism in electoral deals.

[4] See below, pp. 483–7.

Cortes, and when the Conjunction ended in 1919 the party's vote was halved.[1] Although never a true alliance (the Socialists refused a declaration of Republican principles until 1917) it nevertheless profoundly altered the character of the party. It came in contact with the new world of the intellectuals: Galdós, whose *Electra* had been dismissed as bourgeois, became a friend of Iglesias and admired the party's seriousness.[2] These intellectuals influenced the party towards participation in attempts to reform the whole political structure and in 1914 were largely responsible for its stand against the central powers.[3] At the same time its opposition to the expense in men and money of the Moroccan wars brought it the kind of working-class popularity which socialist doctrine alone could not: as in 1898 it capitalized the deep hatred of military service engrained in the Spanish worker.

Thus the party was involved in the 1917 movement for regeneration and reform led by 'bourgeois' politicians like Cambó and Alba; its strike failed, its relations with the bourgeois reformist movement soon cooled, but its numbers increased.[4] This enlarged party was no longer the simple structure of 'grandfather' Iglesias. Professors like Besteiro were Victorian social reformists rather than Marxist revolutionaries; Prieto, a new recruit from liberal Bilbao, was always fascinated by a liberal alliance. The heritage of Iglesias fell to Largo Caballero, a plasterer who increasingly saw the true strength of the party in the exclusively proletarian U.G.T. As in every other socialist party in Europe, there were divisions between politicians and trade unionists, between revolutionists and reformists, divisions which confused and threatened to break every alliance between bourgeois radical reformism and socialism. In 1921 the party was almost split by the question of joining the Third International; Iglesias's last assertion of his great influence on the party (typically exercised from his bed by

[1] The sudden increase of Iglesias's vote at Madrid makes the full importance of the Republican alliance evident: in 1907 he polled 6,000 votes, fewer than in 1901. In 1910 he polled 40,589; after 1919, when the Conjunction ended it sank from 36,469 (1919) to a mere 17,047.

[2] For Galdós's attitude see H. C. Berkowitz, *Pérez Galdós* (Madison, 1948), 402; cf. Díaz del Moral, *Agitaciones*, 163, n. B.

[3] Luis Araquistain, a journalist, was one of the intellectuals who joined the party and supported the allies.

[4] For the crisis of 1917 and its effect on the party see below, pp. 500–6.

correspondence) was to force through a rejection of the terms of the Third International. The dissidents founded the Spanish communist party, which was joined by two of the most intelligent Anarchists, Andrés Nin and Joaquín Maurín: the early years of the party were spent in internecine doctrinal brawls and, after 1923, it was not a serious threat either to the U.G.T. or to the socialist party.

As we have seen the greatest weakness of the proletarian protest was its division into two competing and often bitterly hostile camps—anarcho-syndicalism and socialism. It was this profound division, only occasionally and imperfectly bridged in the interests of common action, which was to play its part in giving Spain first to General Primo de Rivera and ultimately to General Franco.

Anarchists and Socialists were obviously divided by the aim set forth in the first article of the founding statute of the Spanish socialist party: 'the possession of political power by the working class'. To Anarchists a workers' state was no less evil than a bourgeois state. The apoliticism of anarchism was its fundamental doctrine and was strengthened by the deceptions of 1873, when Republican caciques turned out to be bad employers and feeble revolutionaries.[1] The ballot box was a trick to keep the workers in slavery. The desertion of the party's traditional apoliticism in the autumn of 1936 by the leaders of the C.N.T. therefore split the party.[2]

The most important divisions within the anarchist movement itself and, above all, between Anarchists and Socialists, centred on the function and nature of the revolution. Though bourgeois society was doomed, the C.N.T. had no belief in an ineluctable revolution the timing of which can be judged by experts in the 'study of objective conditions'. Revolution is the spontaneous act of the masses; it cannot be led from above; it can only be sensed and seized by the gifted leader and it was this which brought Anarchists into popular protests like the Tragic Week in Barcelona—a movement they had not organized but which they certainly exploited. Such views easily led to a mys-

[1] The bitterness felt by some Anarchists as a result of Republican deception comes out in the *Mano Negra* trial (cf. *El proceso de 'La mano negra'* (Toulouse, 1958), 25).

[2] See below, p. 665.

tique of violence and a worship of the revolutionary hero-superman (many Anarchists read Nietzsche). 'Nothing great has ever been achieved without violence. Violence is the natural mainspring of all action and reaction. The possession of revolvers and machine guns distinguishes the free man from the slave. . . . The sins of the old and corrupt system can only be washed away in blood. No social change has ever achieved any stable results without a great number of the representatives of the old order being annihilated.'[1] Hence the anarchist canonization of men like Durutti, bank robber on principle; hence the attraction exercised by anarchism on the most violent spirits of the Falange. Anarchism was a complex movement: it made lay saints of Salvoechea and the selfless intellectual federalist Pi y Margall but also of bandits. The attraction of violence was contradicted by a belief in the redemptive powers of love; hence its Dostoevskian concern for the redemption of the criminal—at the same time a useful revolutionary and a man who had been despised by a society indifferent to his sufferings.

The sober organizers of the socialist party and the U.G.T. despised this combination of sentimentality and infantile revolutionism. Anarchist pistol-firing at 'secret' meetings with the U.G.T. roused Largo Caballero's contempt.[2] What Pablo Iglesias called its 'fear of organization' and the opportunities its loose revolutionary enthusiasms gave to police spies made it an impossible ally in conspiracy.[3] The Anarchists made counter-accusations of bureaucratic timidity: Largo Caballero's alliance with Primo de Rivera revealed him as a revolutionary who put saving the organization above making the revolution.

It was not that the Anarchists were averse to organization; indeed they talked of little else at many congresses. Like the extreme Federalists of the seventies, they held revolution must come *abajo arriba*, from the bottom to the top; they sought, and failed, by a highly complex organizational structure, to

[1] E. Conze, *Spain Today* (London, 1936), 69.

[2] *Mis recuerdos*, 54. He also makes a jibe at Anarchist vegetarianism which always irritated non-Anarchists.

[3] J. Álvarez del Vayo's verdict in *The Last Optimist* (London, 1960), 196. The Republican conspirators of 1924–30 considered army officers more reliable allies than Anarchists because they did not become security risks after a revolutionary failure.

reconcile the contrary demands of effective joint action and individual liberty of choice. While Largo Caballero was giving the socialist main office paid secretaries and typewriters, the complicated anarchist organization was run by temporary, unpaid officials. Anarchist congresses remained sovereign bodies, without dictated agendas and managing committees; those of the U.G.T. were firmly controlled by the committees and topics which embarrassed the leadership kept off the agenda. To the end, every constituent union of the C.N.T. preserved its sacred right to individual direct action. It was this which made any effective joint strike action with the U.G.T. so difficult and which frequently, as in 1930–9, embarrassed the policies of the C.N.T. leadership itself.

It was the function of the union which divided the C.N.T. and the U.G.T. more than anything else. To the C.N.T. the union was both the blue-print of a new society, where the state should be replaced by the autonomous syndicate, and the revolutionary means by which it should be born. It was its insistence on the federation of autonomous groups, as well as its emotional revolutionism, which attracted to anarchism so many ex-federalists and made Pi y Margall into an honorary anarchist thinker. To use a syndicate in order to get better wages and conditions was to defeat its ends by weakening the basis of revolutionary solidarity; the most effective and bitter of the C.N.T.'s strikes were against imprisonment of its militants. The doctrine of 'direct action' dictated that the syndicate must *always* be, like Hobbes's sovereign states, in a state of war with the employers; it must not accept even a favourable settlement negotiated by a third party. While the Socialists were willing to accept the awards of Primo de Rivera's Tribunals and the Republic's wage arbitration, the C.N.T. rejected both on principle. Until 1934 socialist unionism was, on the whole, reformist in tone and the only effective union between the U.G.T. and the C.N.T. was based on common hatred of the police.[1]

Both parties played an important part in educating the Spanish proletariat: in the early twentieth century the socialist *Casas del Pueblo*, with their primitive libraries and lecture courses,

[1] It must be remembered that Socialist leaders as well as Anarchists were constantly under threat of imprisonment.

replaced the Republican casino as a centre of cultural diffusion. The Socialists were determined to give the workers immediate benefits: much of Largo Caballero's early work was devoted to setting up burial societies, sickness insurance, and co-operatives. The Anarchists gave the workers the vision of a heavenly city based on harmony and justice. In 1898 an anarchist congress portrayed the society which should issue from the great revolutionary destruction of the past: great apartment houses, lit by electricity, serviced by automatic lifts and rubbish disposers, would house workers who were to be the leisured supervisors of machines: a society where wood was replaced by steel and prisons by 'Houses of Medical Correction', money by tokens, and the state by a bureau of statistics co-ordinating 'harmonious labour'.[1] Some have seen anarchism as a sort of left-wing Carlism, looking back to a lost past. Anarchism was often nearer the world of science fiction and, indeed, such works did have a vogue in anarchist circles.

It is truly astonishing that on the verge of the Civil War, after twenty years of practical experience in working-class conflicts, the most powerful labour organization in Spain could still remain faithful to its principle that the self-supporting commune was the only feasible organization of human society, since it corresponded to the 'biological principle that the man who needs least from others is freest'.[2] The sympathy which liberal men must feel for the purity of their ideal of freedom should not hide the disastrous consequences of the Anarchists' rejection *in toto* of the democratic state. 'The Republic is not worth a drop of the workers' blood.'

3. *Social Reform after 1890*

The increasing violence of the social struggle after 1890 forced the attention of society to the problem of saving the working classes from revolutionary courses. This effort was to involve forces as disparate as Reformist Republicanism, Christian Democracy, and the co-operative movement.

Since the mid-century the *beati possidentes* were aware of the

[1] *Segundo certamen socialista* (Barcelona, 1903), *passim*, sep. 173–213.

[2] Cf. the *ponencia* of the Saragossa Congress (May 1936), printed in J. Peirats, *La C.N.T. en la revolución española* (Toulouse, 1951), i. 120 ff. The congress recommended free love and the medical treatment of crime.

uses of religion as a safeguard against 'the Revolution', and with the growth of the U.G.T. and C.N.T. it became a commonplace to argue that the working classes would either become Socialist or Catholic. After *Rerum Novarum* (1891) a small group of Spanish Catholics showed a serious interest in a positive social programme. Nevertheless Spanish conservatism, as a whole, was slow to appreciate the possibilities of an effort to win the working classes for the Church by an effective Catholic workers' movement; old-fashioned charity was preferred to a working-class organization. This rationalization of inertia accounts for the vogue, in Catholic aristocratic circles, of a harmless version of the ideas of Concepción Arenal, a Galician who made her name as a prison reformer. It also explains the early enthusiasm for, and ultimate failure of, the Catholic working-class movement started by Father Vicent. Both saw the solution to the social question in terms of the generalization of the traditional Catholic virtues. 'Restore charity and abnegation in the employer and patience and resignation in the worker.'[1]

Father Vicent was a Valencian Jesuit who had studied biology in France and Germany and his work represents yet another example of that infiltration of European ideas characteristic of the later years of the nineteenth century.[2] His *Socialism and Anarchism* does not contain a single original idea and is cast in a rigid medieval mould: poverty was the result of original sin, theology the basic social science. Thinkers like Balmes had already outlined his critique of liberalism:[3] *laissez-faire* capitalism had created a proletariat it could not feed and its ultimate solution of the social question must therefore be force—the suppression of discontent through the rule of the army. To the workers liberalism was a door whose superscription was 'Abandon Hope'; the alienated poor must become Socialists if they did not become true Catholics. At the same time liberalism was responsible for a decline in faith which made it less easy for the working classes to bear their lot. 'The poor man can suffer while he believes in Christ.'

[1] The slogan of Concepción Arenal. For a pretentious discussion of Concepción Arenal's ideas see J. Jobio Fernández, *Las ideas sociales de C. Arenal* (1960).

[2] For Father Vicent see M. Llorens, 'El P. Antonio Vicent, S.J.' (*E.H.M.* iv (1954), 399 ff.), and F. del Valle, S.J., *El P. Antonio Vicent* (1947).

[3] *Anarquismo y socialismo* (Valencia, 1895). Much of Father Vicent's work was a translation of Leo XIII's encyclicals via French Catholic Congresses.

Ergo re-catholicize the working classes and the social question is solved. The ultimate enemies are not Proudhon and Marx, but Voltaire and Luther.

Father Vicent's work took the form of Workers' Circles, financed mainly by the employers, and of Social Congresses to arouse and educate the social conscience of the Church and the Catholic laity. The Circles did not become Catholic trade unions, nor, as their founder seems to have wanted, a modern version of the medieval guild which would serve as the basis of a Catholic corporative state. They degenerated into friendly societies, clubs to keep the workers from the pernicious influences of the tavern and the Socialists, organizations of working-class piety more concerned with the suppression of blasphemy than with the improvement of working conditions. This was the result of the excessive participation of priests and the weight of the employers in the organization: to Pablo Iglesias, Father Vicent was 'a zealous servant of the bourgeoisie'. Yet despite his conservatism only a few employers—chief among them the marqués de Comillas—made any serious attempt to back the Circles, while the bishop of Salamanca regarded Father Vicent's work as an unnecessary perturbation of his flock.[1] In these conditions modest success (at their maximum the Circles held perhaps 80,000 members) was a tribute to Father Vicent's tireless energy.

By 1900 the imperfections of the Catholic Circles were evident. Christian Democrats, of whom the most notable were Severino Aznar and a Jesuit, Father Palau, saw the necessity of Catholic syndicates, independent of the employers and capable of being used against them; these must replace Father Vicent's 'mixed' syndicate of workers and employers with its emphasis on social peace. The attempt to create a National Federation of Catholic Workers' Syndicates from the old *Circulos* began in 1912 and was completed by 1919.[2] It was backed

[1] Cf. Vicent, *Socialismo*, preface, xxix: 'If the illustrious marqués de Comillas, model of Catholic capitalists, had found many imitators among the employers we should have gone a long way towards solving the social question' (Letter to the archbishop of Valladolid, Dec. 1895). For the extraordinary outburst of the bishop of Salamanca see F. del Valle, *Vicent*, 283.

[2] It is characteristic of Spanish unionism that the first *workers'* syndicate was the Typographers' Catholic Syndicate (1897). The first independent Catholic Workers' Syndicate in the north was founded in 1906. The Burgos Circle developed a syndicate in 1905 but it did not get beyond a modification of the old *mixto* type

by cardinals Aguirre and Guisasola and, though it came to accept the idea of independent workers' unions, the whole organization remained strictly confessional—one of its demands was that women and men should be separated in workshops—and subject to the influence of the church hierarchy. Nor did employers show any signs of favouring a truly independent Catholic Unionism, which they regarded as little better than the C.N.T. or the U.G.T. They refused to recognize the existence of workers' unions as distinct from 'mixed' syndicates, and only such unions could give the labourer anything beyond charity.[1] Many of the bishops were unsympathetic. The only region where Catholic Syndicates became a strong force was the Basque country: here *Solidaridad Vasco* (founded 1911) was relatively independent of the church authorities and its marked nationalism allowed it to attract some workers from Socialist unions hostile to Basque nationalism. Thus, in 1920–3 the Catholic unions were an important element in Basque proletarian struggles.[2]

Nevertheless, the strictly confessional nature of Catholic syndicates limited their effectiveness and their expansion in a field where U.G.T. and C.N.T. were already established.[3] At its height the Catholic Federation had perhaps 60,000 members, many of whom belonged to very conservative confessional unions. Thus in 1909 two Dominican Fathers Gafo and Gerard demanded the abolition of the confessional test for membership of a Catholic union: provided he respected the Church any worker was welcome. This 'free Catholic unionism', which represented an attempt not to impose a Catholic view of society on the working classes but to wean the workers away from Marxist materialism towards 'professional', non-revolu-

syndicate. One of the most surprising by-products of Catholic syndicalism was a pullulation of small papers and periodicals in the period 1919–23.

[1] For Catholic employers' objections to Catholic Workers' Unions as opposed to the conciliatory 'mixed' unions, see S. Aznar, *Impresiones de un democrata cristiana*, 71. There was always something naïve about Father Vicent: he believed that the honest accounting in co-operatives could be secured by the employment of nuns.

[2] The most important gains were made on the railways where the Catholics claimed 20,000 members; in the Asturias and Basque Provinces many small unions were Catholic and *Solidaridad Vasco* was a federation composed of such unions.

[3] For an interesting discussion of the problem of confessionalism in Catholic unions see Juan García Nieto, *El sindicalismo cristiano en España* (Bilbao, 1960), 196–206 *et passim*.

tionary unionism, came to nothing. The U.G.T.'s campaign against 'yellow' unionism—run, it maintained, by Jesuits whose universities were financed by the capitalist Comillas—kept the workers from trusting 'professional' unionism even when they disliked the militant 'political' unionism of the U.G.T. or the sterile revolutionism of the C.N.T. Frowned on by the hierarchy the unions were dissolved in 1922 and those who wanted purely 'professional' unionism went into the *Sindicatos Libres* of Ramón Sales. From 1923 on the history of Catholic unionism was one of decline: the dictatorship of Primo de Rivera and the Republic both favoured the socialist unionism of the U.G.T. Franco's Spain adoped a Falangist type of corporative state in which the Catholic unions could play no part.

Towards 1900 Father Vicent, and the Catholic social movement in general, began to turn to the countryside rather than the town: here was a vast field as yet unconquered by Socialists or Anarchists and which could be secured for the Church. Catholic Social Congresses constantly emphasized that urban workers were relatively unimportant numerically. The law of 1906, itself largely the achievement of a small Catholic pressure group, facilitated the setting up of rural co-operatives; the syndicates concentrated on practical remedies—joint marketing and purchase of seed, crop insurance, the provision of fertilizers. In 1916 the syndicates on a co-operative basis were organized in a National Confederation and by 1922 the movement covered over half a million families. This success, striking though it seemed, was limited to those regions in Castile and Navarre where there was a genuine peasantry which was already Catholic, and where the more intelligent landlords realized that the movement should be encouraged. In the south social Catholicism would entail an agrarian revolution: the movement, therefore, never penetrated those destitute regions, where, as Catholic Congresses recognized, the labourer must starve for half the year.[1]

[1] Cf. the *Semana Social* of Pamplona in 1912 for a particularly violent denunciation of the 'physiological deficit' implicit in wages of a peseta a day. For the relative failure of the efforts of Torres Cabrera and the Catholics in Cordoba see J. Díaz del Moral, *Agitaciones*, 233; cf. the geographical distribution of the syndicates: La Rioja (148), Palencia (106), Valladolid (125), Astorga (84), Navarre (99); at the other extreme were Murcia (25), Cuenca (15). There are no figures for Andalusia. For Yoldi's work in Navarre see A. Marvaud, *La Question sociale en Espagne* (Paris, 1910), 206.

There had always been a tradition of social action by the state within the conservative party. Cánovas had absorbed, in his early years, the ideas of Pastor Díaz, who saw socialism as a threat to be contained by ameliorative legislation since it could not be destroyed by resistance.[1] Liberalism was based on a materialistic individualism imported from France; it could not hope to resist the logical consequence of that individualism—socialism.[2] Cánovas was so absorbed by the problem of political stability that he had little time to devote to social legislation. It was with Dato, whose influence within the party grew after 1900, that a group of conservative politicians worked out a minimum programme of labour legislation; but by 1910 the social problem was no longer seen in terms of the either/or dilemma of the fifties—a dilemma rooted in the 'spectre' of 1848—or of the neo-Catholic view that only a Catholic society could resist revolution. Dato was a modest but modern social reformer, not a counter-revolutionary.

This change of climate is evident in the liberal party's abandonment of doctrinaire *laissez-faire* which precluded state action to improve social conditions. Moret, who became the leader of the liberal party in 1906, had made his name as a free-trader and his writings on industrial relations exhibit a concern to rebutt the fear that machines caused unemployment. His belief that high capitalism is best left alone is best illustrated in his activities as a company lawyer and director. On the other hand, he was influenced by Krause and the notion of the ethical state. Hence the interest in agrarian poverty which made him at one moment the hope of Costa and accounts for his inquiries into wages in Andalusia and Estramadura. Hence his work in the early years of the Commission of Social Reforms. His successor as prime minister in 1910, Canalejas, was influenced by the programme of English radical liberalism after 1906 and he appeared to his opponents as a dangerous social radical. Later still the Liberals were in electoral alliances with the Reformist Republicans, some of whom were indistinguishable from Fabian Socialists.

There was, therefore, a body of opinion running across party lines which favoured moderate social reform because it shared

[1] For Pastor Díaz see L. Legaz y Lacambra, 'El socialismo visto par P. Díaz' (*R.I.S.* 1955, iii. 125).

[2] Pastor Díaz, *O.C.* iv. 13 ff.

a belief in the ethical function of the state and which could derive equally from Catholic conservatism or the Krausist tradition that long inspired the best minds in the liberal party. Nevertheless the results in terms of modern labour legislation (which began with Dato's Workers' Compensation Act in 1900 and culminated in Romanones' eight-hour day in 1918) were meagre. The majority of what had been known as Sagasta's 'flock' and of the Conservative deputies had neither interest nor faith in social amelioration as a branch of political science. Moreover the poverty of the Institute, the indifference of the employers, and the persistence of large pockets of artisan and domestic industry made enforcement of labour legislation by a handful of inspectors aided by local committees almost impossible. As in all countries it was factory labour which first enjoyed protection; the sweated trades of Madrid, like those of London, escaped control.[1]

It was less the legislation itself than the body created to draft and enforce it which was the most striking contribution of the social reformers. The Institute of Social Reform, which grew out of a Commission set up by Moret in 1883, was a body unique in Europe. Of its twelve elected members six were chosen by the representatives of the workers, and were therefore Socialists until 1908, when the Catholics tried to break this monopoly. The Institute functioned as a government adviser on labour legislation. It published an impressive series of reports on strikes and labour conditions, largely based on the work of its inspectors.[2] Using the law of 1908, which set up arbitration machinery, it had some success in negotiating strike settlements —even though the U.G.T. was never satisfied with the law while the C.N.T. rejected it out of hand. It is conceivable that, without the C.N.T., labour relations might have taken on some of the placid tone which was to characterize the hey-day of Primo de Rivera's rule in the 1920's. The Institute was not destined to see this era of negotiated wages; in 1924 Primo de

[1] Cf. Praxedes Zancada, *El obrero en España* (Barcelona, 1902), 230–1. André Barthe (in 1896) calculated that the 'artisans' outnumbered the industrial population by four to one. For the inspectors' difficulties in forcing through the eight-hour day against the indifference of local committees of the Institute of Social Reform, see 'Aplicación de la jornada de ocho horas' (*I.R.S.* 1920), esp. 18 ff.

[2] Its reports, which I have used extensively, constitute the most valuable source for labour conditions 1900–24. Its library is now in the Ministry of Labour.

Rivera absorbed it into the Ministry of Labour. This ended its career as an independent institution, removed from the imperfections and delays of bureaucracy.

Most social reformers feared the dead hand of the administration which threatened to turn social reform, as it had turned education, into a party game. Thus, what was to be one of the most impressive achievements in the field of Spanish social legislation—the National Institute of Insurance (*Instituto Nacional de Previsión*—was intended by its founders to be an autonomous and independent body on the model of the Institute of Social Reform. Its task was to prepare, administer, and develop a modern system of social insurance.

In Spain, the notion of a welfare state based on workers' insurance was the creation of one obsessed man, José Maluquer, son of a Catalan lawyer. Maluquer was a Catholic who, through his work in an insurance company, had become a convert to social insurance as 'the mathematical formula of human solidarity'.[1] A muddled but tireless speaker, he gathered round him a small group of able assistants including Christian Democrats like Severino Aznar and insurance technicians like Shaw.[2] From this modest beginning and against every kind of resistance (70 per cent. of employers refused to register for their contributions to the retirement pensions begun in 1921) was to develop a structure of social insurance that was in many respects in advance of contemporary Europe. Yet Maluquer's fundamental Catholic hope—that society, with no more than encouragement from the state, would solve the social question—proved illusory. In the end the state took over social insurance as it had taken over labour relations.[3]

From the 1850's co-operation had been advocated as a solution to the social question, especially in Catalonia. At the turn of the century co-operation in various forms, from the Catholic Raffeisen schemes to the Rochdale system, re-

[1] For an outline of his ideas see M. Carbajosa Álvarez, *El ideario de Maluquer* (1934).

[2] The relative paucity of 'technicians' in Spain is shown by the fact that the chief administrator and actuary were, respectively, an Englishman and a Belgian. Cf. Severino Aznar, *Recuerdos del tiempo viejo* (1946), 11 ff. The connexion with social Catholicism was very close.

[3] Maluquer's fear of the all-pervading state can be seen in the stress he put on local initiative as opposed to central direction. As a Catalan and an admirer of Pi y Margall, he was a mild regionalist.

vived.[1] It encountered many obstacles. Governments inherited the suspicions that surrounded the word 'association' in the fifties, when co-operatives often camouflaged 'societies of resistance', and were connected with the Federal Republican movement. Nor were the proletarian parties sympathetic. The C.N.T. regarded co-operation as a dangerous irrelevance and the Socialists as an 'aristocratic' distraction unless it was geared to the class struggle by incorporation within the Socialist movement. Catholic co-operation, which found some sympathizers among conservatives, appeared as covert clericalism to liberals. Hence it was not until 1906 that co-operatives were given legal security as the result of a law proposed by Catholics in order to facilitate their agricultural co-operatives and credit schemes. The movement gathered strength only in Catalonia, where it could draw on the associationist traditions of the older unions, in Valencia, where it found convinced apostles, and in Valladolid and Navarre, where agrarian co-operatives were backed by the Catholics. Elsewhere most attempts came to grief.[2] It was, and is, often maintained that there was a native tradition of, and a national aptitude for, co-operation, exemplified by isolated examples of co-operative practices in fishing and agriculture, and that this native trait could form the basis of some modern co-operative system. This was not the experience of those who, like professor Piernas Hurtado, were advocates of consumers' co-operatives. 'Among us it is not merely that there is no spirit of association; it is rather that there is a spirit hostile to association.'[3]

Thus by 1923 none of these diverse efforts to solve the social question can be accounted successful. They had not weaned the working classes from the proletarian parties or conjured away the threat of violent revolution; nor, after the working-class revolution of 1936, did they provide the models for a new society.

4. *The Catholic Revival, Anti-clericalism, and Education*

No convincing description of Spanish society at the turn of the century can be drawn exclusively in terms of the social

[1] For the history of co-operation see J. Reventós Carner, *El movimiento cooperativo en España* (Barcelona, 1960).

[2] Cf. the failure of consumers' co-operatives in the Basque mining districts. When the members received no large profits they accused the administrators of pilfering and withdrew. J. Pujol y Alonso, *Minas de Vizcaya*, 17.

[3] Quoted, J. Reventós Carner, op. cit. 120.

conflicts common to western Europe. The survival, after a hundred years of liberalism, of an officially Catholic state and a Catholic society meant that religion was the prism through which all other conflict was refracted; more than this, it meant that the claims of the Church on society were a prime source of division in themselves.[1] Indifference or hostility to Catholicism cut off the *casa del pueblo* or the small-town republican club from the cultural world of the bourgeoisie. It was hostility to clericalism which marked the scission of the middle classes into a radical and a conservative wing. It was the Church settlement which provided the touchstone of political division in the Second Republic of 1931, and a minister of that republic could regard the Peace of Vergara as the greatest disaster of modern history. 'The embrace [of Vergara, between ultra-Catholic Carlists and Liberals] was a pact with the irreconcilable enemies of modern institutions, the recognition of the forces of the past as a directing element in Spanish society.'[2]

Such minds dismissed the Restoration as a spiritual waste of conventional religiosity and bad art, and the religious revival of these years as the protective reaction of a complacent bourgeoisie to the distant threat of socialism or to 'the revolution' which had thrown society into anarchy in 1873. This in part it was; but the evangelical spirit came from within the Church itself, alarmed by a change in the terms of the battle against infidelity. Here, at least, as the whole of Cánovas's policy revealed, liberalism had achieved results. In a society where the *esprit fort* was no longer, as in the eighteenth century, a marginal man, the state could no longer be relied on to enforce Catholic unity. The evangelical spirit revived by Father Claret was, in the last quarter of the century, devoted to the effective organization of existing piety in an attempt to preserve by social pressure, social power, and, above all, by a Catholic education the faith which the state could no longer be relied on to protect. Formal religion was no longer enough when the battle might be lost.

[1] This division was often concealed. Azcárate's father, a middle-class doctor and a radical, lost his faith but submitted to the 'obligatory hypocrisy' of his epoch. 'This frankness in political opinions and dissimulation in religious beliefs', the son noted in 1876, 'is a contrast, which, unfortunately, has existed in our country without interruption up to the present day.'

[2] Álvaro de Albornoz, *El temperamento español*, 139.

For this battle the Church did not present a united front. The Carlists and *integristas* remained a thorn in the side of the official church, yet their 'exclusivism' contained much of the fighting strength of Catholicism; the ultramontanism of Pidal's Catholic Union embarrassed moderate Catholics who believed that extreme assertions of Catholic claims would stir up battles which were best forgotten, and for which the Spanish clergy lacked adequate intellectual weapons. Most Catholics still read Balmes and Donoso Cortés, works directed against early nineteenth-century attacks on the Church. Neo-Thomism, at first a 'liberal' influence, became an excuse to reject the thought of the last three centuries as 'all or nearly all false'. Ultra-Catholics professed shock that Cánovas read Kant; they were therefore scarcely capable of meeting the attacks of positivists and Darwinians.[1] Abolished as a university course, theology in the seminaries was an antiquated instrument for modern controversy.

The most marked feature of the religious revival was a recatholicization of upper-class society in which the aristocracy took the lead. An evangelical rather than an intellectual process, its characteristic instrument was the devotional or charitable organization. These organizations were supported by the female piety of that 'elegant, sanctimonious swarm' of *beatas* who people the novels of Galdós, by the 'pompous and useless' aristocratic ladies who ran committees against white slavery or who organized protests, social boycotts, or social sieges of anti-clerical ministers.[2] It was the attempt to turn these organizations into instruments in a campaign to capture the masses for Catholicism which infuriated the Republicans and Socialists. It was the sheer economic and social power represented by Catholic organizations which made them formidable;

[1] For the state of Catholic philosophy see R. Ceñal, 'La filosofía en la segunda mitad del siglo XIX' (*Revista de Filosofía*, xv, 1956), 400 ff. One of the few Catholics who understood modern thought was Moreno Nieto, but he was an ineffective conversationalist with little influence outside the university and the *Ateneo*.

[2] A *beata* is a pious, narrow-minded female believer. Galdós was deeply depressed by the atmosphere of the early Restoration: his main theme (first advanced in *León Roch*) is the destructive effect of blindfold, conformist piety in private life, a theme which culminates in his most famous novel *Doña Perfecta*: H. C. Berkowitz, *Galdós* (Madison, 1958), 154. For a bitter attack on Catholic charitable organizations see M. Nelken, *La condición de la mujer en España* (Barcelona, n.d.), 147. Margarita Nelken was a Socialist and a feminist.

thus the marqués de Comillas, the Catalan multi-millionaire, financed and organized the Workers' Pilgrimage to Rome (1894) and was accused of using his influence as a railway director in order to further the aims of the Association of Catholic Fathers by censoring books on station bookstalls. It was Comillas too who backed the one large-scale attempt to win the masses for the Church—the Catholic Circles of Father Vincent.

Characteristic of the attempt to penetrate in depth was the work of Enrique de Ossó, a Catalan priest who became the organizer of the cult of St. Teresa of Avila.[1] After the destruction of his own seminary at Tortosa by the revolution in 1868 he became a declared enemy of the liberal state. Like many Catholics he saw his work as a crusade to gain the youth of Spain, especially its girls; his instrument was a teaching order dedicated to St. Teresa as a 'Falange' against 'laicism and indifference'. By 1881 the Order was teaching 1,000 girls; by 1925, 16,000; its training college in Barcelona was built by Gaudí, the greatest creative genius of modern Spain, whose mysticism cannot be conceived outside the Catalan religious revival.[2] Other priests, Poveda at Gaudix and Manjón, the founder of the Ave Maria schools for the poor of Granada, shared this concern with the redemption of youth by a Catholic education that would remove the child from the state schools—Jacobin, atheist, and copied from France—and reclaim for the Church the destitute who would otherwise get no education at all.

Orthodox liberals and anti-clericals reacted violently against a movement which held out the prospect that a whole generation might be captured for clericalism. This reaction was justified, sometimes by the low intellectual level of Catholic propaganda, always by its intent.[3] Manjón and de Ossó shared an extreme hostility to liberalism as such and to the tolera-

[1] For a description of de Ossó's work see M. González, *Don Enrique de Ossó* (Barcelona, 1953).

[2] J. M. Garrut, 'La dimensió humana d'Antoni Gaudí' in *La Renaixença, avui* (M. Arimay and others, Barcelona, 1960). Gaudí's greatest conception is, of course, the Sagrada Familia in Barcelona, a marvellous (uncompleted) building.

[3] Cf. the ecstatic sentimentality of de Ossó's devotional works (e.g. the 'Praises of St. Teresa', M. González, *de Ossó*, 249). This debased romanticism is a far cry from the truly great religious literature of St. Teresa herself or St. John of the Cross.

tion and the supposed laicism of the Restoration state. When the government proposed to organize a tribute to St. Teresa, de Ossó boycotted the proposal as impious; the state could not be allowed to treat 'his' saint 'as a Sappho or a George Sand'. To many pious Catholics the Restoration state was erected on vicious principles 'intrinsically evil and perverse, leading people to degradation and ruin'.[1] Popular catechisms proving the sin of liberalism were a constant source of liberal scandal up to 1936. All pose the question 'Can a Catholic be a liberal?' The answer is no. Liberalism, says Manjón, is an 'addition of negatives'. Liberalism came from Voltaire and the Masons; liberal Catholics were as 'rationalist' as free-thinkers; liberalism was a sin.[2] To such minds only the re-establishment of Catholic unity, that is the prohibition of any other religious faith on Spanish soil, could bring satisfaction: de Ossó's *Teresinas* prayed daily for its restoration 'in our time'.

The re-catholicization of Spanish upper-class society, especially evident in the control of secondary education by the Orders, and the attempt to regain the workers for the Church did not go unchallenged. Republicanism had always contained an anti-Catholic tradition from the mystical syntheses of the Castelarians to crude materialism; this was now reinforced by French positivism (which was influential not only in Spain but in Latin America) and by the anti-religious propaganda of the Anarchists.[3] Old fashioned anti-clericalism is represented in such productions as *The Empire of the Jesuits* (written in the nineties) which 'exposed' the high fees and bad food of the new Catholic university of Deusto, the hold of Jesuit confessors on upper-class youth, and the efforts of the marqués de Comillas and the Association of Catholic Fathers to clean up the book trade and the variety theatre as well as the university.[4] The production of Galdós's *Electra* crystallized and popularized the currents of anti-clericalism: 10,000 copies of the play were sold in two

[1] D. J. M. Orti y Lara, *El deber de los católicos con los poderes constituidos* (Madrid, n.d.), 74.

[2] Cf. Sarda's book '*El liberalismo es pecado*' and Manjón's worker's catechism (Y. Turin, *L'Éducation et l'école en Espagne de 1874 à 1902* (Paris, 1959), 336).

[3] Positivism was the official philosophy of Porfirio Díaz's dictatorship.

[4] The Association of Catholic Fathers instituted press prosecutions for obscenity and atheism and organized minor campaigns against known 'atheist' professors. It succeeded in banning the dancer Bella Chiquito from the Madrid stage.

days; there were 'Electra' watches, sweets, and cough-drops. Most significantly, the play was regarded—especially by Galdós himself—as an appeal to the youth of Spain to join battle against clericalism.[1]

The intensity of popular anti-religious sentiment in the capital and cities like Valencia and Barcelona was in sharp contrast to the popular piety of Navarre, parts of the Castiles, and the Basque country where deep Catholic sentiments found expression in the various lay *cofradias*—the societies responsible for religious ceremonies at the fiestas of the patron saint on the great festivals, and for pilgrimages to local shrines. It was only in Catalonia that the League of Free Thinkers succeeded, after 1900, in founding Modern Schools distinguished by an aggressive anti-clericalism.[2] The programme of these lay educators appealed to the Anarchists; both were influenced by French anti-clericals, by Comte and Spencer, both shared a belief in 'spontaneous' education as a cure for dogmatism. In 1909 the trial of Ferrer, the most active proponent of the Modern Schools, revealed the progress of professedly anti-religious education and the horror of the Church at an institution it regarded as more dangerous than the brothel.[3] After 1909 the movement seems to have petered out, and perhaps its most important legacy was the printing of cheap popular editions of works directed against religious faith from Voltaire to Nietzsche, Spencer, and Darwin.[4]

The anti-clericalism of the intellectuals and pseudo-intellectuals gave a crude ideological structure to those fixed popular beliefs about the Church's activities that have played such a role in working-class attitudes: abuse of the confessional by employers in order to obtain employees' secrets; the riches of the Jesuits who were reputed to own steamship companies, Moroccan mines—they were in fact owned by pious magnates like Comillas—and to compete with laundresses by employing orphan labour. Just as popular devotion was concentrated on

[1] Cf. H. C. Berkowitz, *Galdós*, 352–64. A young journalist called it 'a magnificent manifesto of the aspirations of the intellectual youth of Spain which, in its recent preparation for the battle against clericalism, has discovered in Peréz Galdós an indisputable leader'.

[2] Cf. Y. Turin, *Éducation*, 312 ff.

[3] Ibid. 320.

[4] Even the publications of an orthodox publishing house like España Moderna provided cheap editions (3 pesetas apiece) of Zola, Renan, Ibsen, Spencer, and Nietzsche (Catalogues of 1894 and 1914).

the Orders rather than on the secular clergy, so were popular hatreds: hence the belief that the Orders could make or break a tradesman according to his attendance at mass.[1] This resulted in indifference to official religion (which frequently extended to marriage but rarely baptism) and a confused conviction that the Orders and the Jesuits were responsible for every disaster. Hence the convent-burning of 1909 in Barcelona.

The attacks of the Anarchists, the Modern Schools, and Republican zealots were as crude as the religious dogmatism they sought to replace. Thus the clerical right in Spain has always regarded as its most potent enemy those intellectual and social forces which found expression in the Free Institute of Education.

The world of ideas from which the Institute sprang was the Krausism of the sixties and the radical-liberal beliefs of the Revolution of 1868. It was founded in Madrid by the professors who lost their chairs in 1875 and by their supporters in bourgeois liberal circles. It was to be a free university, dedicated to the ideal of a non-official, non-dogmatic education which should nurture the *élite* needed to modernize Spain. Only after its failure as a university did the Institute devote itself to primary and secondary education, fields where philosophical beliefs, antique and unfashionable to outside eyes, mattered less than their residue: the sense that the established ideas which underpinned traditional society were not final truths, that intellectual freedom and moral self-improvement were necessary conditions of progress in a backward society and that society itself was, in Krausist jargon, 'autonomous'. Until its bourgeois, optimistic reformism was swept aside by socialism, the Institute represented the most serious and consistent attempt to create the intellectual preconditions of a liberal democracy.[2]

From the beginning its presiding genius was Francisco Giner. The most devoted pupil of Sanz del Río, he possessed the prime

[1] Cf. Rafael Shaw, *Spain from Within* (London, 1910), for a collection of these popular beliefs. For the penetration of 'materialism' amongst working classes see P. A. Vicent, *Socialismo*, 42. Margarita Nelken seems to have considered that the regulation of domestic sweated labour was impossible because it would give an unfair advantage to convent seamstresses! (*Condición de la mujer*, 89–90.)

[2] This does not mean that the men of the Institute did not sympathize with social reform—on the contrary Azcárate was a life-long social reformer and president of the Institute of Social Reform.

gifts of the social reformer: the capacity to organize, to raise money (the Institute was always poor), to draft petitions and programmes while remaining himself in the background. His heir as director of the Institute was Cossío, the art historian who rediscovered El Greco. That Giner never abandoned his own Krausist dogmatism did not prevent him creating an educational system directed against learning traditional subjects by rote from professors without interest in the moral and intellectual personalities of their pupils. The school sought to establish personal contacts between teacher and taught, to embody every advance in European educational methods, to widen the syllabus by courses on art, folk-lore, and technical subjects; pupils were encouraged to play games and take excursions in the countryside. It was a first attempt (on the whole unsuccessful, because French influence was easily available and traditionally better understood in Spain) to turn the Europeanizing intellectuals away from French models towards Anglo-Saxon methods. In 1882 football was introduced.[1]

The Institute consistently aimed to avoid conflict either with the Church or the state.[2] Giner was apolitical to the point of fanaticism, as thoroughly disabused by the politics of the Revolution of 1868 as Sanz del Río had been by those of 1854. He believed in a gradual change of the spirit which would avoid polemical battle. His greatest insistence was that the child should not have his mind made up for him: religion was 'a permanent spiritual function which the school should educate' but 'by no means confessionally, that is to say, presenting no confession as the only one worthy of faith'. It was precisely to this neutralism that the Catholic right traced back the bifurcation of Spanish spiritual life which came to open war in 1936. Neutrality, respect for the conscience, hid an intention to destroy the Church's influence; however cautious in their public

[1] Cossío visited London and Oxford, where he called on Jowett. This English influence was strong in certain sectors of left-wing liberalism. Azcárate, one of the most prominent of the followers of Sanz del Río, married into a Scottish family and it was in Azcárate's home that Giner learned to admire Anglo-Saxon civilization. Moret, the future Liberal prime minister, was the grandson of an English general. He stayed in London from 1871 to 1875 and to the end of his life read *The Times*. Cf. V. Cacho Viu, *Institución libre*, 233–6. The first leather football does not seem to have arrived until 1889.

[2] This was a necessity for educational administrators like Castillejo concerned with obtaining funds to send students abroad from an officially Catholic state.

statements, Sanz del Río, Giner, Fernando de Castro, Azcárate had all rejected Catholicism as a personal faith and were protestant or humanist in temper.

It was not only the counter-attack of the Church and the indifference of a conformist society (the Institute found it increasingly difficult to raise loans from the liberal wing of a prosperous bourgeoisie which had accepted the Restoration) that limited the influence of the Institute. Giner was a sage who delighted in Socratic discussion with a small group of pupils, by which he created a family spirit such as might centre on a great house-master in an English public school. His message of tolerance, his puritan creed of self-reliance (which extended to punctuality and the encouragement of schoolboy saving), were, like his teaching methods, incapable of mass reproduction. Thus the influence of the Institute on the educational system *as a whole* was less than its founders had hoped.[1] Its congresses and publications inspired a minority of provincial schoolmasters.[2]

It had little effect on university teaching where it had hoped to accomplish so much. University education, to the student, remained a distant affair of textbooks and lectures, useful only for the acquisition of certificates needed for employment in the public services. Teachers and taught were bored.[3] The Institute's influence can be traced in later foundations: in the Junta for Further Studies, founded to send Spanish students abroad and of which the leading spirit was Castillejo; in the Residence of Madrid University, which (under Alberto Jiménez) continued the traditions of contact between professorate and pupils so central to Giner's message, and the ideas of autonomous and independent institutions derived from the Krausist tradition.[4] With all its excellences as a residential college on English lines,

[1] But cf. the verdict of J. B. Trend (*Origins*, 69) that the Institute 'has done more for the progress of Spanish education than all the reforms proposed or carried through by the state'.

[2] The Institute collected useful information on modern teaching methods which it publicized (see Y. Turin, *Éducation*, 262, for the list of six provincial and six Madrid 'little reviews' on pedagogic subjects). It is a curious commentary on the 'closed' nature of Krausism that Fröbel was received as the master largely because he admired Krause.

[3] There were exceptions. Unamuno must have been a challenging teacher. But cf. Pío Baroja's description of the lectures of the physiologist Letamendi—'juggler's tricks . . . without a single profound idea . . . only words and grand phrases' (*O.C.* ii. 467; vii. 587).

[4] For a description of Castillejo's work see his *War of Ideas in Spain*. Alberto

the *Residencia* could not become the model for a system of higher education; the halls of residence of the later University City, to the construction of which Alfonso XIII directed so much attention with so little reward, represented an 'American' concept of student welfare which seemed vulgar to the purists of the Giner tradition, who preferred quality to quantity. Yet they were needed to house a large student population.

As Francisco Giner confessed, society in Spain could not be relied on to supplement and ultimately replace the action of the state; everywhere in Europe education was increasingly a state concern. The problem in Spain was that the state, besides being a confessional state, was poor. The few educational reformers in the Ministry could do little. Compulsory primary education had been on the statute book since 1857 and some progress had been made in the battle against illiteracy.[1] Except for the Catholic schools of the larger towns, it was supported on a minimum scale by the municipalities and became involved in the tissues of minor electoral jobbery. State secondary education was miserably equipped and hence the education of the *élite* fell into the hands of those with the funds to support it: two-thirds of secondary education was in the hands of the teaching orders.[2] Most of the men who sat in the Constituent Cortes of the Second Republic had been educated in church schools—Azaña, its greatest political talent, had been educated by the monks of the Escorial. This may account for the violence of their attack on the educational privileges of the Church—a violence that had little to do with the spirit of Don Francisco. A heroic minority cannot hope to change an intolerant society by quiet persuasion.

Jiménez gives a moving account of the ideals and fortunes of the *Residencia* in *Ocaso y restauración* (Mexico, 1948).

[1] In 1901 perhaps 63 per cent. of the population of school age and over were illiterate—a reduction of perhaps 7 per cent. in twenty-four years.

[2] Barcelona, for instance, had one state 'Institute' tucked away in the university building.

XII

REGENERATION AND DISINTEGRATION

1898–1923

As with the Crimean war in Russia, the humiliation of defeat in 1898 forced Spaniards to self-examination. Was catastrophe explicable in terms of national original sin which perverted institutions imported from abroad, or had Spain, as the upholders of the Black Legend maintained, been held out of those currents of progress which swept other nations towards prosperity and power? This led to a debate on the problem of being a Spaniard which has continued to this day and changed the language of political life. Criticism of the Restoration system, now held responsible for the disaster, was not new; but those who were weary of it or sought to reform it now assumed the grandiloquent title of regenerators.[1]

At the turn of the century regeneration was a theme essayed by all, from the cardinal archbishop of Valladolid to Blasco Ibañez, the Republican novelist, from professors to poets, from heirs of the sober tradition of Jovellanos to political quacks, from Catalan nationalists to Castilian patriots. While Republicans held regenerationist meetings, the Catholic Congress debated on 'the participation of the clergy in the work of patriotic regeneration'. All were regenerationists of a kind. 'The Regenerator,' wrote a satirist, 'a tonic for weak nations. Recommended by the best doctors, apostles and saviours.' Only Sagasta, a sick man relying on patent medicines and oxygen, kept his head in the search for responsibilities and remedies. All Spain had wanted a war and courted inevitable defeat. 'We are a poor country, is it strange that we have been beaten?' Most politicians could not afford such realism; they subscribed to the regenerationist myth.

[1] The effects of the disaster of 1898 on the critics of the system are examined in Chapter XIII.

1. *Alfonso XIII and the Parties*

The political history of the period 1898–1923 may be seen as a prolonged attempt to redeem the parliamentary system, bequeathed by Cánovas, by making it a vehicle for the regeneration of Spain, thus saving it from its own failings and the attacks of its enemies. Dramatically punctuated by the two crises of 1909 and 1917, these repeated essays were defeated by the inertia of the system itself and by the difficulty of the external crises it was called on to face—the war of 1914–18 and the Moroccan War after 1920. In terms of political life this failure can be blamed on the disintegration of the historic party system; hence the repeated attempts to reconstruct a liberal and a conservative party out of a group system and to gather public opinion behind them. The two outstanding political talents of the early twentieth century, Maura and Canalejas—the one a conservative, the other a democratic radical—were both accused of substituting personality for party. Yet both repeatedly strove, not merely to discipline their own parties and provide them with a programme which should 'capture' opinion, but to encourage the emergence of strong opposition parties.[1]

It was this party system in decline which confronted Alfonso XIII when he came of age in May 1902. Despite the stuffy and constricted education given him by his mother, he was in many ways an open-minded, modern king whose enthusiasm for cars alarmed his ministers. Bored by the hieratic routine of a court ceremonial which to foreigners appeared the starchiest in Europe, he came to delight in the relative freedom of his political functions and to develop a taste and a talent for political intrigue. In so far as this was the result of a coherent political outlook rather than an expression of personal vanity, it derived

[1] 'The formation of a liberal party . . . is the main concern of Maura at this moment' (Ossorio y Gallardo in Oct. 1909, quoted J. Pabon, *Cambó*, 365). Maura repeatedly criticized the *mechanics* of the *turno* but not until the collapse of his own Conservative party did he abandon faith in a two-party system. All the 'corrupt' electoral deals (besides being directed at excluding Republicans and Socialists by a combination of Liberals and Conservatives) were designed to strengthen the fiction of an operating two-party system. In 1905 the Liberal Minister of the Interior respected 'the due preponderance' of conservatives in certain constituencies in order to produce an opposition party. Cf. the electoral correspondence in G. Maura, *Por qué cayó Alfonso XIII*, 110 (1903) and 1905 (appendix 19).

from a view of the history of his house: the *políticos*, the political oligarchs of the Restoration, had used his mother's regency in order to gather unto themselves the prerogatives left to the crown by the constitution, and had reduced to a fiction the power 'freely to dismiss and appoint ministers'. The parallel to George III is striking: Alfonso wanted to be a king, and a patriot king at that. He believed that only a monarchy that acted could ward off the threat of republicanism, always a nearer concern of the king than of his ministers. Like everyone else Alfonso was a regenerator of sorts; his pose was that of a go-ahead king surrounded by a clique of political fuddy-duddies. 'This year I took over the reins of the state, a transcendently important act as things are; *on me depends* whether Spain is to remain a Bourbon monarchy or become a Republic. . . . I can be a king who covers himself with glory regenerating his country . . . but I can be a king who does not govern and, being governed by his ministers, is put over the frontier.'[1]

His first act was to read a personal interpretation of the constitution to the cabinet. Ministers were to find the new tone adopted in interviews a time-wasting irritant. Decrees were held up in the palace and courtiers got to know their content. It was unfortunate that, isolated from ordinary life and often disabused with his ministers, his closest contacts were his earliest—his military adjutants: as with his father, his deepest feelings and interests came to centre on the army and as early as 1906 he showed an alarming sensitivity to army opinion. It was this sensitivity which was to lead him to share the army's concern with the Moroccan war and make him quite happy to see the back of all 'politicians' in 1923. The combination of his penchant for intrigues and his toleration of military dictatorship after 1923 was to produce a caste of monarchical politicians without much feeling of personal loyalty to the crown, as was amply proved by his moral isolation in 1931.

Alfonso's defenders are not entirely wrong when they argue that the system was as much to blame as the king's personal failings: he was not altogether the victim of his own political *folie de grandeur* when he saw the royal will as the only stable factor in a fluid system of competing parliamentary groups. Diplomats and generals looked to the king for continuity of

[1] Quoted M. Fernández Almagro, *Historia política*, ii. 716.

policy, rather than to the shifting combinations of a confused conglomeration of independent party leaders. Qualities which might have been mild irritants, or susceptibilities that might have been scotched at the start in a fully functioning parliamentary monarchy, were magnified by the mechanism of Spanish elections and the fragmentation of Spanish parties.

As in his grandmother's reign, this was illustrated by the troubles surrounding the prerogative of dissolution, or the demands for renewal of confidence which were at the origin of every 'Oriental Crisis'.[1] Given the extent of government electoral influence, the ministry which was granted a decree of dissolution *must* obtain an assured majority. Thus, if a ministry requested a decree of dissolution, it was for the king to judge whether that particular ministerial majority represented opinion. He could not, as in English practice, accept his minister's advice on a dissolution of the Cortes and leave the country to decide, nor was there any constitutional machinery to aid his decision. His only course was to consult politicians and palace officials in order to establish whether a 'situation' was 'exhausted'. In every case the king's decision must cause discontent either with the 'ins' who believed their situation still sound, or with the 'outs' who believed the 'country' demanded a change.[2] Moreover, a decree of dissolution granted to a leader of a parliamentary group within a divided party enabled that leader to establish his claims to the leadership of his party. Once the Liberals and Conservatives were divided into clans the most constitutional of kings must become the football of the factions.

The political fate of Alfonso XIII is strikingly illustrated in his relations with Moret, one of the Liberal politicians who hoped to establish his claim as leader of the party after Sagasta's death. In 1906 he asked the king for a decree of dissolution in order to consolidate his position as leader of the party on a radical programme. The king consulted the Liberal chiefs who advised against a dissolution. In 1910 Moret repeated his demand, and it was again refused after consultations with

[1] So called after the Palacio de Oriente, the Buckingham Palace of Madrid, built in the eighteenth century.

[2] This appeared in Sagasta's last ministry (Mar. 1901–Dec. 1902). Silvela attacked Sagasta as a 'king's friend' inherited from the regency and kept in power by royal favour against the wishes of the country.

other liberal Leaders.[1] Moret considered himself 'sacked' and discredited by royal intrigue; yet he was defeated, not by the king, but by the jealousies of rivals in his own party, none of whom would have accepted for a moment the English convention that the king must take the advice of his prime minister and of his prime minister only.

2. *The Conservative Regenerationists, Silvela and Maura, 1899–1909*

The conservative programme for the regeneration of Spain is associated with the ministries of Silvela and Maura.[2] Both were devout Catholics—Silvela took his cabinet to mass, Maura gave up smoking if his daily examination of his conscience revealed a fault. Both believed private and public morality were coincident; both possessed that combination of debating talent and moral austerity which is the mark of great statesmen in the nineteenth century. Both deplored caciquismo and its consequences—'insincere' elections and the indifference of a managed electorate. Both believed in a 'revolution from above' which, by effecting 'a ground clearance of caciquismo' would restore contact between the politicians and the people. Both were advocates of 'sincere' elections and the destruction of an electoral system which, in Maura's phrase, had maintained 'parasitic parties'. For both, therefore, the real centre of the revolution from above was a reform of local government as the best way to end the 'suicidal abstention' of the electorate. Both believed that a solution to the Catalan problem could be found in a vigorous system of local government which, by the destruction of 'Jacobin' centralization, would contain the 'energy of the regions'. Both failed in this endeavour.[3] It is an indication of the strength of the regenerationist myth that these High Tories have passed as proponents of a New Deal. Their social programme was modest: Silvela's most radical proposal was

[1] For this internal opposition see Romanones, *Notas*, ii. 245; La Cierva, *Notas*, 158; D. Sevilla Andrés, *Canalejas* (Barcelona, 1956), 319. Maura called Moret's demands 'inconceivably unconstitutional', yet he made a similar demand in 1909 (see below, p. 486).

[2] Silvela: Mar. 1899–Oct. 1900 and Dec. 1902–July 1903; Maura: Dec. 1903–Dec. 1904 and Jan. 1907–Oct. 1909.

[3] For a fuller treatment of the Conservative programme of local government reform see above, pp. 375–6; for the failure of Maura's Catalan policy see above, pp. 549–50.

accident insurance. They saw regeneration as the 'dignification of politics' not the modernizing of society.

Although Maura and Silvela's views on politics had come to coincide, their political personalities were, nevertheless, distinct. Cánovas had detected, behind Silvela's fine and fastidious face, a political hypochondria, a distaste for the unwholesome chores of politics, a pessimism which led him to dismiss Spain as 'without a pulse' when it failed to respond to his call for regeneration. Maura's confidence in his mission was as unbounded as his contempt for those who thwarted it; unable to forgive or forget, his injured pride destroyed his own party and blighted the prospects of parliamentary government in Spain. 'To govern is to have faith in oneself';[1] Maura's faith was unlimited. When he failed in his mission he would not admit that his own recipes were out-dated; it was that his enemies were blinded by party spirit.

The first essay in regeneration from the right took the form of 'Polaviejism'. The sudden popular vogue of General Polavieja, successful in the Philippines and known to have been an opponent of the government's Cuban policy, shows the persistence of the old belief in salvation from the army. Since it could no longer take the form of the pronunciamiento, it sought to make generals such as Polavieja, and his opponent Weyler, take on the role of political saviours by becoming party leaders. Popular at court, the Christian General was the ideal regenerationist candidate for the conservative bourgeoisie. His attack on civilian politicians who substituted 'the politics of abstraction for practical reform' and thus alienated the 'neutral masses' represented one of the commonplaces of regenerationism as well as a desire to shift responsibility for disaster from the army on to civilians. His promise of ample decentralization was a bid for support from Catalonia, where the demand for Home Rule was gaining strength.[2]

Polaviejism could not remain a movement above party; it entered politics via an alliance with Silvela, who became prime

[1] Cf. Speech of 12 Jan. 1892, quoted J. Ma. Escudero, 'El juego limpio en el liberalismo español' in '*España*' (*Arbor* publications, 1953), 622.

[2] A committee of Catalanists was set up in Barcelona to win adherents for Polavieja's programme; it gave money to Prat with which he founded *La Veu de Catalunya*, the most important Catalanist newspaper. For the growth of the Catalan demand for autonomy see below, Chap. XIII, sections 3 and 4.

minister in March 1899, with the general as his Minister of War. The failure of Silvela's ministry, after nineteen months, meant that the first wave of regenerationist politics had been broken on the still formidable rocks of the old system. Regenerationism was seen to be, not the realization of a state of mind, but a choice between conflicting ways of revival. Apart from Polavieja the strongest figure in the ministry was its finance minister, Villaverde. His recipe for regeneration—like all others he was a regenerationist of a kind—was a sound, conservative economy which would save the country from the humiliation of a depreciated currency or the repudiation of the National Debt. Taxation and rigid economy would 'liquidate the disaster' by paying off a debt which, after the war, ate up 60 per cent. of the budget. To Polavieja an efficient army was an essential feature of a revived Spain; when Villaverde insisted on cuts in the military budget, Polavieja resigned.

Thus the main legacy of conservative reform was a financial system which, by bringing Mon's principles up to date, ensured that the Spanish taxation system to this day has remained based on the ideas of mid-nineteenth-century conservatives. Villaverde's innovation, intended to correct the increasing reliance on indirect taxation which had distorted Mon's system, was the tax on *utilidades*, levied not on global income, but on certain specified sources (salaries, shares, net company profits) assessed separately.[1] Villaverde was indubitably successful in his immediate aims: the reduction of the debt and the fight against post-war inflation. By 1899 there was a budget surplus. Fierce disinflation saved the peseta and kept prices level, a policy based on the assumption that Spain was prosperous and that it was her taxation system which prevented these riches flowing into the Treasury.[2] He and his successors did not see that, though disinflation might be defended as an immediate remedy, it did not favour growth. His budgetary system became sacrosanct, and those like Primo de Rivera, who wanted to break it down in order to stimulate and modernize a sluggish economy by state investment, were forced to the expedient of an extraordinary budget.

[1] For an outline of Villaverde's plans see J. Ma. Tallada Pauli, *Finanzas españolas* (1946), 148 ff.

[2] For an appraisal of Villaverde's work see the preface by José Larraz to R. Mazo, *Villaverde* (1947).

The novelty of Silvela's failure lay in the large part played in it by Catalonia. It is almost incomprehensible how Catalanists believed that their minimum programme could be satisfied within the decentralization held out by Silvela, or how he hoped to bring his 'Castilian' supporters into an attempt to meet Catalan regionalism by some form of autonomy, however limited.[1] Villaverde's taxation, by breaking with 'bourgeois regenerationism' which saw revival in terms of productive enterprise released from penal taxation, completed the process of disillusionment in Catalonia and Madrid. Barcelona staged a tax-payers' strike. The atmosphere of hope vanished. Durán y Bas, the representative of Catalonia in the ministry, resigned and Catalan extremists embarrassed French naval officers with cries of *Catalogne française*—a reaction which seemed to justify the hostility of those who maintained that any concession to regionalism, however moderate, would strengthen separatism.[2] Durán y Bas wrote the epilogue of this first effort at conciliation, which, like so many in the future, ended in mutual recrimination: 'We shall never understand each other.'

In October 1903, after the failure of his second ministry, Silvela resigned from politics. 'You see before you a man who has lost faith and hope.' Once again he was defeated by the contradictions of regeneration: Villaverde's economies precluded a respectable navy, while to the prime minister a nation which preferred 'materialism' to dignity could not be saved; more significantly the political system could not survive the 'dignification of politics' as Silvela and Maura conceived it. Most politicians professed a belief in 'sincere' elections: Maura, as the Minister of Interior of Silvela's last government, acted on the belief. The result was Republican gains in the big cities—a side-effect of conservative regenerationism which did

[1] Silvela's maximum concession was the faculty to form *mancomunidades*, i.e. the association of Catalan provinces and municipalities for certain limited purposes. He was also prepared to favour regionalism in his appointments (e.g. Dr. Robert as mayor of Barcelona and the regionalist Torres y Bages as bishop of Barcelona) and by setting up a commission to examine Catalan civil law in order to save it from Castilian centralizers.

[2] Cf. *El Imparcial*, 25 July 1900. Romero Robledo opposed Torres y Bages (whose name he could not spell) as a theological ignoramus whose works consisted of 'two separatist pamphlets': J. de Camps i Arboix, *Durán y Bas* (Barcelona, 1961), 151 ff.

not endear its practitioners to the king, who preferred the more orthodox and pliant 'courtier' Villaverde.[1]

Silvela's heir, as a proponent of the revolution from above, and his successor as leader of the Conservative party, was Antonio Maura; sprung from a struggling Majorcan family, his local accent was mocked in his student days, and poverty would have kept him from qualifying as a lawyer but for the university legislation of the September Revolution. He entered politics as a Liberal under the patronage of Gamazo, in whose office he started work as a lawyer; Gamazo was increasingly uneasy in Sagasta's party and Maura left it altogether in order to join forces with Silvela. The similarity of their political ideals, increasingly evident in their speeches, triumphed over the embarrassments their alliance created for the party managers.

Maura's failure was even more resounding than that of his predecessor and it was to have more serious consequences in that it destroyed the 'fiction' of alternating parties, without substituting for it a method of government which made a genuine appeal to the electorate. The Liberals could not accept Maura's revolution from above and were prepared to ally with the revolution from below in order to defeat him. Once this had happened Maura refused to recognize the Liberals as a political party 'fit' to alternate with his own conservatives. Thus the conventional *turno* could no longer operate.

For this breakdown Maura's defenders blamed the Liberals' incomprehension of his patriotic intent. The Liberals saw the revolution from above, not as an honest attempt to produce a system responsive to opinion, but as a clericalist, authoritarian concern. His local government reform, based on a corporative franchise, seemed a modern version of the old Moderate attempt to write the predominance of the oligarchy into the law of the constitution. The alliance with 'reactionary' Catalanism was suspect. Maura professed to take public opinion as his political compass, yet what the Liberals regarded as opinion he rejected as the creation of street demagogues and a venal press—'the tinkle of a baby's rattle'. He never faced up to the problem of what would happen if the neutral mass *genuinely* voted for 'dissolvent' 'anti-patriotic' republicanism or socialism,

[1] Maura alarmed Alfonso for similar reasons in 1909; in the Bilbao municipal elections of that year twenty-nine seats went to anti-dynastic parties.

if the voters he sought to liberate from the shades of caciquismo turned against him. His contempt of 'false' opinion was rooted in his contempt for those who sought to destroy him by slander. Thus he made no serious attempt to keep 'opinion' on his side when the Liberal press 'trust' was organized for 'Maura, No!'[1]

In order to defeat this parliamentary dictator, who relied on 'a system of silence' when his policies were questioned, the Liberals were prepared to join with the parties hostile to the monarchy (the Republicans) in the cry of 'Maura, No!' A violent press campaign against his appointment of a monk to the see of Valencia (a Republican city) reduced Maura's first ministry to impotence. This was a prelude to the Block of the Left, formed in November 1908 during Maura's second ministry, in order to drive him from office by a campaign against his modification of the 'liberal conquests' in the interests of public order.[2] If the liberal conquests made government impossible, he proposed their 'honest' modification by law. The Liberals argued that liberties were sacred and should be 'saved' by suspension of the constitutional guarantees in times of danger, as they had done in Catalonia (1905–6). Thus to them Maura's 'honesty' covered an attempt to curtail liberty, and to him the Liberals' 'hypocrisy' covered pandering to a revolution which would destroy all liberty. Maura's bills were presented as an outrage, an 'attack on civilization . . . an attempt to Africanize Spain' which would imperil a monarchy which could only survive by 'attracting' its enemies on the left. That the Liberals' arguments for attraction were not entirely based on creating, at any cost, a combination that would defeat Maura is proved by those Republicans (for instance Lerroux and Costa) who spurned the Block of the Left on the grounds that it would strengthen the monarchy: die-hards preferred to prove that nothing good could come

[1] Maura's basic political beliefs are contained in his 1913 speech to the Royal Society of Jurisprudence (see *Treinta y cinco años de vida pública*, ed. J. Ruiz-Castillo Franco, 1957 ed., 59–65, a useful summary of Maura's views). The 'trust' figures in all *Maurista* apologetics; it was formed to cut printing costs as much as to defeat Maura by a monopoly of opinion.

[2] The Laws of Association hindered police action against terrorists; the parliamentary immunity of Republican deputies was held by Maura to cover seditious activities.

from the rebellion of Martínez Campos at Sagunto. It was the moderate Republicans who wished to re-establish the September coalition and force the Liberals to a genuine reform programme which would test the constitutional intentions of Alfonso and open up the prospect of a genuine parliamentary democracy.[1]

Maura regarded the alliance of dynastic liberals and the 'sewer' of street politics as little short of treason. If the Liberals went outside 'the monarchical orbit' they must be denied the use of the monarchical system: confronted with the 'revolution from below'—like the Carlists, he seems to have conceived it as a single, all-embracing threat—the Liberals allied with it; they must purge themselves of the French heresy of 'no enemies to the left' before they could be trusted as ministers of the crown. The king refused to adopt his prime minister's dramatic dilemmas: revolution or counter-revolution; resistance to the forces of disorder or the dissolution of political discipline—the only cohesive force in a nation which lacked 'social sinews'. This refusal, according to Maura's defenders, meant the end of the monarchy: the 'events of 1909', which caused the crown to reject Maura's counsels of resistance in favour of the attractionist argument of the Liberals, marked the first step in a process of concession to the revolution from below which would end, in April 1931, with the overthrow of the monarchy. Thus the crisis of 1909, to Maura and his supporters, became the watershed of political life.

Throughout the summer of that year Republicans and Socialists had built up an agitation against Maura's call-up of reservists for a minor campaign in Morocco. The monarchy was denounced as a monster full of pus, sending the poor of Spain to defend Moroccan mining concessions; gatherings of mothers at railway stations and counter demonstrations of Catholic ladies distributing crosses to the troops inflamed tempers. The government was particularly worried about Barcelona.[4] Yet

[1] They thus refrained from joining those who, like Sol y Ortega, wished to whip up mass agitation by accusing Maura of personal corruption. Tato y Amat, *Sol y Ortega*, 465. The aim of Sol's campaign was to charge Maura with putting his interests as a shareholder in the Santillana Electrical Co. above the public interest in cheap water and with making a corrupt contract with Vickers Armstrong. Sol's argument was that *even if* Maura was innocent, 'opinion' demanded his resignation; he then proceeded to create 'opinion' by a campaign of mass meetings.

[2] There had been a minor agitation against the governmental closure of brothels and gaming houses. J. La Cierva, *Notas*, 133–9.

in a city practically denuded of troops, and where the civilian police had long proved themselves inefficient, Ossorio, the civil governor and an admirer of Maura, was not on speaking terms with the Captain General. Not without reason the opposition accused the government of 'abandoning Barcelona'.[1]

On Monday, 26 July, a strike was called by the quasi-Anarchist organization *Solidaridad Obrera*. A hurried decision, it proved a disaster, for the Catalan workers were cut off from a strike movement planned for August throughout Spain in protest against the Moroccan war; with the turning over of trams (the tram drivers, the clientele of a conservative politician, refused to strike) it degenerated into uncontrolled violence and barricades. On 27 and 28 July, Barcelona, isolated from the rest of Spain, except for a telegraph line via the Balearics, was prey to a revival of the primitive anti-clerical violence of the 1830's, fed by Radical and Anarchist propaganda. Forty-two convents and churches were burnt or damaged: nuns were 'liberated' (a popular tradition more recently enshrined in Galdós' *Electra*); corpses were exhumed for signs of torture, and, as in 1936, enthusiasts masqueraded in pillaged vestments. Outside Barcelona, customs posts were burned and Juntas were set up, routine operations of popular revolution.[2]

The seriousness of a movement that cost only few fatal casualties in the government forces has been perhaps over-estimated. If the authorities had been united in dealing with the strike, the movement might never have become violent. Ossorio, at loggerheads with the military authorities, opposed the declaration of a state of siege and withdrew to the suburbs to watch the smoke produced by military bungling. From first to last he maintained that the revolution was a muddled protest, neither produced nor directed by professional revolutionaries: it sprang from 'morbid social conditions . . . in Barcelona there is no need to prepare a revolution; it is always ready made'.[3]

[1] *El Imparcial*, 8 July 1909.

[2] Some of the church-burning was what was later called 'administrative incendiarism', i.e. the work of agitators rather than of angry mobs. For a contemporary illustrated account see J. Brossa, *Revolución de julio en Barcelona* (Barcelona, 1910), esp. 172–96. None of the small-town revolutions were serious and they were all put down by local forces.

[3] Letter, 16 Sept. 1909, quoted J. Pabón, *Cambó*, 329. Anselmo Lorenzo similarly regarded the Tragic Week as a 'spontaneous', leaderless, social revolution

According to Maura, the revolution, repressed with ease in the streets, triumphed in the Cortes through the campaign against the execution of Ferrer. This view he maintained from his fall to his death, and it governed his political conduct for the rest of his life. Formerly a revolutionist under Ruiz Zorilla and Lerroux, Ferrer had concentrated since 1900 on the publication of rationalist literature and the propagation of crude anti-clericalism in the Modern Schools which he founded in Barcelona with funds provided by a woman admirer. These 'Godless' schools were sympathetic to Anarchist ideas, and though Ferrer denied any connexion with Anarchist conspiracy he financed Anarchist periodicals. He was tried, in public, by a military court as the leader of the troubles of July. This he certainly was not, even if he was not a complete innocent as his defenders maintained.[1] One of the few Spaniards known abroad, his execution (especially in Latin Europe were anti-clericalism needed martyrs) became the platform for a campaign of mass meetings from Budapest to Lisbon. Crowds stormed the Embassy in Paris and protested in Trafalgar Square. Maura was unperturbed: what others called the conscience of civilized Europe he regarded as another eruption of the Black Legend engineered by the European left.

The Liberal leader Moret decided to use the government's unpopularity in order to oust Maura, once it became evident that only 'war without quarter' in the Cortes would keep the Block of the Left in being. The core of Moret's case was that the state of opinion made Maura's rule impossible, while his refusal to distinguish between Liberal 'attraction' and an assault on the monarchy was a declaration of war against parliamentary government, since it denied the opposition a right to

which 'took' in the streets and was made worse by the use of troops. The 'conservative classes' refused to take any action; they simply withdrew (cf. *Diario de Barcelona*, 20 Aug. 1909).

[1] For a defence of Ferrer see W. Archer, *The Life, Trial and Death of Francisco Ferrer* (London, 1911). The charge against Ferrer was based on his presence and activities in Barcelona on 26 July, and on his connexion with feeble revolutionary attempts in two small towns. The evidence against him came from political enemies (Radical Republicans who had failed to lead the revolution and now wished to disown it), while those who might have cleared him were not allowed to appear. Ferrer's own evidence appears confused and unsatisfactory, perhaps because he wished to cover his associates. His own words probably represent his true position: 'Plutôt qu'un révolutionnaire, je suis un revolté.'

govern.[1] To Maura it was the Liberals who had made the continuation of parliamentary processes impossible by allying with the 'revolution from below' in order to discredit government itself. Confronted with Liberal obstruction in the Cortes the ministry decided to ask for a renewal of confidence from the king. To Maura's astonishment, Alfonso, who had changed his opinion in the previous twenty-four hours, treated the demand as a patriotic offer of resignation.

Although he covered the king's action so well that only his intimates knew of the interview which reduced that proud man to tears, he could never forgive or forget this 'desertion' in the face of his enemies. As to the Liberals, they had allied with revolutionaries and the slanderers of European Freemasonry. It was to these political pariahs that the king had chosen to listen and to give power.[2] Like his father, Alfonso saw the Liberal party had its uses: it was a safety valve 'to rescue the throne from Revolution', which Maura's intransigence threatened to produce rather than to prevent. Maura was hated as no other prime minister of the Restoration had been: 'The poor can't live under Maura.'[3] 'I subscribed to "Maura No!" then and since,' wrote the king in exile, 'because I was convinced he could not prevail against half Spain and all Europe.' Moreover Maura, though loyal, was no courtier; his austerity, his notions of his own indispensability did not endear him to a monarch who brushed aside criticism by the offer of a cigarette. Bonhomie was one of Alfonso's political assets; it held no appeal for Maura.

The Liberals had long been a collection of groups, a conglomeration of tribal chieftains. It was now the turn of the Conservatives to disintegrate, shattered by the political hubris of Maura and his obsession with the events of 1909. When the king chose Romanones and the Liberals once more in 1912 Maura's bitterness knew no bounds: the monarchy had deserted the defenders of public order for the defenders of

[1] Cf. Moret's speeches of 18 and 21 Oct. 1909 and the commentary of *El Imparcial* for those dates.

[2] For a discussion (sympathetic to Maura) of the crisis and its implications see G. Maura, *Por qué cayó Alfonso XIII*, 147–56. For a defence of the king's conduct see conde de Villares, *Estudios del reinado de Alfonso XIII* (1948), 60 ff. Villares regards Maura's attempts to 'bully' the king as a 'Frock-coat pronunciamiento'.

[3] See R. Shaw, *Spain from Within* (London, 1910), for an intelligent, if sometimes inaccurate and always biased, discussion of the political atmosphere after 1909, esp. 115 ff.

Ferrer.[1] Until the Liberals purged their sins and abandoned 'sordid collaboration' with the enemies of the dynasty, he would refuse to act in politics with them.[2] Against Alfonso's belief that the monarchy would only survive by following 'opinion' and by using the Liberal party to neutralize the Republican danger, Maura declared a conservative strike.

The Conservatives found it increasingly difficult to accept Maura's political abnegation. They wanted power. Maura's 'negativism . . . left the monarchy defenceless', with no alternative to the Liberals. Noble and impressive though he might be, Maura was now a political liability and his declaration of 'implacable hostility' against the Liberals indefensible. 'I stood aghast', wrote Sánchez de Toca, one of his Conservative critics, 'at the thought of the incalculable results that must spring from those furious voices invoking the whole Christian world to a Holy War against a ministry holding office under the crown, . . . shouting with anathemas that he was no true Conservative who held relations other than those of implacable hostility with men appointed by the king to office.'[3] Dato tried to modify Maura's proud intransigence: he failed, and in October 1913 the king called on him to form a government himself.

The Conservative party now split between the followers of Dato and those of Maura. With this final desertion by the crown Maura ceased to be a party leader and became the chief of a movement, Maurism, founded in October 1913. It attracted conservative youth, especially students, and was devoted to the denigration of the 'traitor' Dato and his accomplices as 'oligarchs' who sacrificed conservative principle to power. They had subscribed, by implication, to the cry of 'Maura No!'—the Maurist youth painted 'Maura Si!' on Dato's house. Since it

[1] The choice of Romanones reveals the curious mentality of the party leaders. Romanones saw that if his rival García Prieto were appointed prime minister this would give him a claim to the leadership of the party with Romanones as his inferior; '*as a defender of the parliamentary monarchy* I could not accept this'. Cf. his action on his own defeat in Oct. 1913. Romanones, knowing that Maura would support García Prieto in the elections, advised the king to call on Dato. Conde de Romanones, *Notas de una vida 1912–1931* (1947), 14.

[2] Note of 31 Dec. 1912.

[3] It is impossible to realize the importance of Maura's declaration of implacable hostility unless we remember that (owing to the lax nature of parliamentary discipline under the Standing Orders) the government could not get through essential financial legislation without a certain amount of help from the opposition, and was exposed to the obstruction of the Republicans.

professed to abstain, like its leader, from politics (without a party organization it made little impression on the electorate) it degenerated into 'Street Maurism', a dangerous deviation which had affinities with Maurras' movement in France.[1] It had what Falangists were later to call 'style', and with its parades and monster meetings it focused on a parliamentary statesman the discontents of violent men and youth; applauded by such enthusiasts, Maura sensed at last his 'reawakening of citizenship'. He began to appeal to the true Catholic Spain beyond politics, the 'essential Spain' which *must* be accepted by *all* who wished to participate in public life—an appeal to be made later by the United Patriotic Party of Primo de Rivera's dictatorship and the Falange. He dismissed both Republicans and the dynastic parties as 'bourgeois'.

Hence his appeal to Carlists as a Carlist *manqué*, who saw society threatened by a revolution which could only be resisted; otherwise government must result in a process of 'abandonment' to the left which would end only with a socialist republic.[2] Maura was to disappoint his followers: having failed to accomplish his revolution from above within the constitutional monarchy, he jibbed at the final stage of his political metamorphosis; he would neither become an anti-parliamentary dictator himself nor allow that position to anyone else. To the end he sought power in a way that would be consistent with his 'faith in parliamentarianism'. Thus he did not become, as the Carlist Vázquez de Mella hoped, 'a Mussolini before Mussolini'. His fate was to be prime minister in 'national' governments at moments of crisis, when the orthodox parties he had helped to destroy were in impotent confusion.

Beside Maurism orthodox conservatism, captained by Dato —'the man of vaseline'—appeared colourless. Yet Dato was an able politician who brought the party back to realities after the heady draughts of Maurism. From pure politics he turned to moderate social reforms. Dato had long been interested in the work of the Institute of Social Reform, and it was to him that

[1] Maura's main paper was significantly called *La Acción*: Maurism also had a weekly journal *Vida Cuidadana* and a satirical paper *El Mentidero*. The political cartoons of Maurism were as brilliant as its catechisms were banal and rhetorical. For both see J. Gutiérrez-Ravé, *Yo fuí un joven maurista* (n.d.).

[2] See Pradera, *O.C.* (1945), 58, for a Carlist view of the process of abandonment. Maeztu always stressed Maura's affinities with Carlism.

Spain owed her first labour legislation and the beginnings of social security.[1] It was Dato who finally gave Catalonia its Mancomunidad (18 December 1913). But all attempts to heal the breach between Maura's followers and the orthodox Conservatives of Dato failed, making it almost impossible for the king to form a homogeneous and strong conservative government. This mutual boycott, for which Maura rather than Dato must take the blame, did as much harm to the monarchy as Liberal co-operation with right-wing Republicans, denounced by Maura as the 'mediatizing of public power to the profit of those who need to be subject to the empire of law'. 'For years', wrote Lerroux, 'monarchists have torpedoed the King. We Republicans would have been satisfied with overthrowing the monarchy. The monarchists, when it does not serve them, dishonour it.' It was another Republican who saw that Maura had destroyed the 'compromise' of Cánovas which had at least allowed the monarchy to survive.[2] To Maura bare survival was not enough; using as his instrument a rejuvenated Conservative party, he wished to regenerate and popularize a system which he considered artificial and sterile. Neither the king nor the Liberals would give him any credit for these intentions. His bitterness at the success of 'Maura No!' is understandable; to boycott he replied with boycott. Unfortunately, even after his bitterness had lost its fury and he was more willing to co-operate with his fellow politicians, his personality was so overpowering that these politicians appeared second rate and lacking in vision. The impression persisted that a system which could not contain his brand of patriotism was an inadequate instrument for the governance of Spain.

3. *The Liberal Party and the Disintegration of the Conservatives, 1909–1917*

Maura's revolution from above has been treated with sympathy by modern Spanish historians while the Liberal party, in the period before 1923, has been dismissed as a characteristic

[1] This drew to him men like the vizconde de Eza and Burgos y Mazo. Cf. vizconde de Eza, *El sindicato obligatorio* (1919), for the interest this group of Conservatives felt for 'modern' social legislation. (See above, p. 461.)

[2] Álvaro de Albornoz, *El temperamento español* (Barcelona, n.d.), 142. Maura's attitudes of defiance fascinated the 'bullfight' mentality of Spaniards; this did not prevent them from being a political disaster.

phenomenon of decadent parliamentarianism, as a conglomeration of factions without a programme. It was one of the liberal group leaders, the conde de Romanones, who defined political life as 'an uninterrupted succession of trivial events', motivated by a lust for power comparable only to the sexual passions. Sagasta, with difficulty, had disciplined this lust in others; after his death (January 1903) competition between the chieftains of the Liberal clans for the leadership of the party went far in destroying its political effectiveness.

The main contenders for the leadership of the party after 1903 were Montero Ríos and Moret; after the assassination of Canalejas (November 1912) the leadership was in dispute between the conde de Romanones and García Prieto. Apart from Canalejas none were parliamentary *caudillos* like Maura. Moret and Montero Ríos were ageing party notables, distinguished lawyers whose intellects had been formed by the Revolution of 1868. In so far as their struggles concerned policy they reflected differences of opinion on the legitimacy of a policy of 'attraction'. How far should the party desert the comfortable world of Sagastian liberalism in order to attract advanced democratic opinion? It could be argued that attraction was both an electoral necessity and the *raison d'être* of the party in the constitutional monarchy. However, attraction proved to be a political gamble: thus, although Moret decided to bid for advanced liberal opinion by a radical programme in 1906, he could not maintain the Republican alliance except with the cry of 'Maura No!' Once Maura had fallen in 1909, the right-wing Republicans deserted the Block of the Left for the Republican–Socialist Conjunction. The Liberal party had failed as 'a Trojan horse' by which democrats could enter the dynastic orbit. What Maura called 'sordid collaboration' with the revolution had served no useful purpose; the so-called 'governmental' Republicans remained 'proud in their tents'.[1] Canalejas saw that Moret's tactics only discredited liberalism; the party must seek its recruits by a programme, not by 'accidental alliances'.

It was the difficulties of the radical alliance which led the Liberals to fall back on the classic programme of the nineteenth-century liberalism—resistance to clericalism. The right regarded this as yet another proof of the intellectual poverty of

[1] *La Época*, 12 Jan. 1913.

indigenous liberalism and its dependence on French example, as an artificial injection to revitalize a dying creed which, as Moret admitted, no longer attracted 'so large a portion of the vital forces of the country'. It was true that anti-clericalism was a well-tried demagogic device; it was also true that the clerical issue could no longer be avoided as it had been by Sagasta.

Anti-clericalism was forced on liberalism by the steady advances made by catholicism in Spanish society since 1876 and by the militant catholicism of the Conservatives. The Regular Orders had grown so alarmingly under favourable interpretations of the Concordat that Spain seemed threatened with 'a proletariat of soutanes' recruited from monks fleeing from the persecution of French radicals. The aim of liberal legislation was therefore to subject the church's activities to the control of the state: the 'unrecognized Orders' should be regulated by the application of the Law of Association of 1887. Once again the Liberals must not be seen as the allies of free-thinkers, but as the heirs of the eighteenth-century regalists who had expelled the Jesuits.

As in France, the real battle was over secondary and university education.[1] The extreme Catholics wanted obligatory religious instruction in state secondary schools and complete liberty from state control in their own schools. Liberals wanted 'respect for liberty of conscience' and at the same time state control over the private sector of secondary education by insistance on state qualifications for all teachers, and examining boards which should not favour Catholic schools. The Catholics maintained that there was no right to protect error and that the 'neutrality' of the state schools covered an attempt to introduce the positivist lay morals of the Third Republic; at the back of all their arguments lay the claim, never abandoned, to control the whole educational system in the interests of the church. Behind liberalism lay concern lest the governing *élite* of the future should be educated in the 'seminaries of a fanatic youth': since they could not afford an alternative system, their only remedy was to attempt control of Catholic education in the

[1] Y. Turin, *L'Éducation et l'école en Espagne de 1874 à 1902* (Paris, 1959,) esp. 374 ff. Primary education was in the hands of municipal committees; the demand of the Liberals for state payment of school-teachers was inspired less by a concern for miserably paid teachers than by a desire to break the hold of the priests and other conservative influences on local affairs.

cause of a more modern education. Thus the church defended Latin and Cervantes; Liberals advocated modern languages and science.

The battle certainly gave the appearance of a sharp division between liberalism and conservatism, but it neither saved the Liberal party from internal divisions nor gave it popular strength. From the beginning Sagasta disliked anti-clericalism as likely to do more harm than good, as an unnecessary imposition of young radicals which would divide the party.[1] As Romanones admitted, the Liberal party had misjudged the moment;[2] it had failed to realize that regalism was dead, that anti-clericalism would win radical support only at the expense of weakening the support of liberalism among the respectable classes; it was on this issue that the socially influential aristocracy of the Madrid salons and many of the army officers deserted the party. Finally the campaign failed: the Liberals did not even achieve their half-hearted Dreyfusard revolution.

The tragedy of the clerical issue, from the liberal point of view, was that it drove any other form of radical reform from the centre of the party's concern. Although Moret was interested in social questions—at one moment Costa regaredd him as a serious agrarian reformer—the main proponent of the radicalization and democratization of the party was Canalejas. His failure to become the Lloyd George of Spanish liberalism is therefore of great significance.

Canalejas was an academic who had become rich by entering his father's railway enterprises and famous through his platform oratory and journalism. Marked by the Cuban disaster he was a regenerationist patriot, proponent of a strong army and a forward foreign policy in the face of French advances in Morocco, and, in his student days, he had imbibed the Krausist notion of the state as an ethical 'form' with law as its instrument. This entailed 'intervention'—the use of state power in the interests of social justice. Canalejas wished to win the confidence of the working classes by a liberal party weaned from the

[1] Moret disliked the brutal regalism of Montero Ríos; Canalejas rejected Moret's hope of a settlement negotiated with the Vatican as vicious in principle—cf. his bitter attack of 2 Nov. 1902: 'I would not have raised the issue of anti-clericalism, if I had known that the liberal party would desert it after using it to capture power.'

[2] Cf. his remarks in *Notas de una vida* (1934), 148–9, 164.

extremes of bourgeois *laissez-faire*.[1] He thus favoured state-controlled wage arbitration, regulation of conditions and hours of labour, workers' insurance, and accident compensation. Like the reformist wing of the conservative party under Dato, he supported the Institute of Social Reform and its use by the government in the settlement of wage disputes and labour conditions.[2] One of the few politicians concerned with the lot of the agrarian poor, he wished to expand the legal notion of expropriation for public utility into expropriation for social utility, thus enabling agrarian reform to begin on under-cultivated latifundia. This programme he had popularized by the most extensive tour of speeches ever undertaken by a Spanish politician.

For this programme Canalejas had no party when he became prime minister in March 1910. Moret's hostility left him with a small following and a government beset with crises which he braved by a series of dramatic appearances as a parliamentary *caudillo*.[3] Hence his occasional appeals to Maura for support, as a kindred spirit, above the pettiness of party politics. Maura could not forgive him for his support of the Ferrer agitation; his supposed anti-clerical borrowings from Waldeck-Rousseau stamped him, in Maura's eyes, as a Mason, a Francophil radical, a 'delirious actor who mixed up odds and ends of his repertoire'. The king, less blinded by personal and party prejudice, saw in Canalejas's monarchist radicalism a useful instrument for the domestication of the left.

Canalejas appeared at his most radical, most unacceptable to the king and to the Conservatives, with his redemption of radical pledges to settle the church question. He immediately announced that the right of all to worship *in public* was part of modern civilization, and his later suspension of diplomatic relations with the Vatican (July 1910) released a torrent of Catholic indignation; the Basque Catholics threatened civil

[1] See *El partido liberal*, ed. Daniel López (1912). Based on conversations with Canalejas, this is an authoritative interpretation of his intentions.

[2] See pp. 461, 516.

[3] It seems to me that historians have over-emphasized Canalejas's difficulties with the Liberal party: though never free from intrigues, most Liberals recognized him as the greatest leader the party had known. Cf. Romanones's confession that there was no hope for his own leadership while Canalejas remained alive. 'The personality of Canalejas gave him such easy superiority that the hope of succeeding him was a dream' (*Notas*, ii. 320).

war and he was subjected to alternate campaigns of vilification and cajolery in aristocratic salons. This wave of feeling, which reached its height in the processions of the Eucharistic Congress, allowed Canalejas to retain his reputation for anti-clericalism while working for a moderate settlement behind the scenes. The Papal Nuncio and Conservatives like Dato and Cambó were aware that, if Canalejas could not settle the question while in office, he would be driven to press for a radical solution in opposition: they recognized that he would accept the terms negotiated by the Conservatives and that the formal issue—whether negotiations should precede or follow the state's law—was unimportant. Canalejas's famous *Ley del Candado* was thus a compromise settlement which gave little satisfaction to the left; recognizing the strength of Catholic feeling, he decided to swallow his radical past and listen to the advice of the marqués de Comillas.[1]

It was Canalejas's misfortune to deal with a series of violent strikes, part of the wave of labour violence which was to discredit liberalism in England. He strictly distinguished between permissible strikes for economic gains and revolutionary 'general' strikes aimed at paralysing the economy for political purposes. Thus in 1910 he negotiated wage settlements favourable to the Bilbao strikers. In 1911, however, when he believed that Pablo Iglesias, in collaboration with Republicans and Anarchists, was prepared to use a general strike for the 'overthrow of existing institutions', he suspended the constitutional guarantees, mildly censored the press, and closed the *casas del pueblo*. In 1912 he argued that railway strikes were an illegitimate threat by public servants to the whole country; like Briand, from whom his enemies maintained he copied his policies, he called up the reserves, putting 12,000 strikers under military discipline.

[1] See D. Sevilla Andrés, *Canalejas* (Barcelona, 1956), 354–72. The law (Dec. 1910) stopped the further growth of the Orders without government permission (which would not be granted to an Order with more than one-third of its members foreigners) until the passing of a new Law of Associations. The concession to the Conservatives lay in the clause that, if no such law was passed *within two years*, the *Ley del Candado* would lapse. For the king's pro-Catholic attitude see M. Fernández Almagro, *Historia del reinado de Don Alfonso XIII* (Barcelona, 1934), 184. He was only restrained with difficulty from presiding over the inaugural session of the Eucharistic Congress and thus making a public declaration against his own prime minister.

The Conservatives chose to regard his defence of order as a sham: his 'soft' treatment of misguided Republican naval mutineers and his reprieve of an Anarchist were sharply criticized in the conservative press.[1] To Socialists and Republicans he was a 'murderer', in the words of Pablo Iglesias 'the last cartridge of Liberalism'. The more 'governmental' Canalejas appeared, the more he lost prestige on the left. The Republican Reformist party, still in alliance with the Socialists, claimed to represent, outside the orbit of the monarchical parties, the practical democracy of which Canalejas had once been the apostle.[2] When he was assassinated (12 November 1912) by an Anarchist outside a Madrid bookshop, the repentant radical had already forfeited his *raison d'être* to monarchist politicians: he could not tame the revolution.

It was left for later right-wing historians to argue that, had he lived, Canalejas might have flung overboard every shred of the liberal parliamentary tradition in order to save Spain as a radical *caudillo*. Hence in polemics over what might have come to pass, historians have overlooked what he achieved. He was the only Liberal who got things done. He replaced the *consumos* (which he regarded as responsible for rising food prices) by taxes which fell on the wealthy, including a *progressive* tax on urban rents (the favourite form of upper middle-class investment in Spain and Latin America); he thus accomplished what fifty years of radical agitation had failed to do. He gave the clerical issue an interim solution. He overhauled local government finance. He abolished the odious practice by which the rich could buy themselves out of military service. But for his assassination he might have temporarily solved the Catalan question by the grant of a *Mancomunidad* now backed by the Lliga as the best settlement obtainable.[3] His attitude to Catalonia was remarkably unprejudiced and characteristically realist. The problem must be solved since 'it had been discussed to the point of exhaustion'.

[1] Canalejas was a convinced opponent of the death penalty but his cabinet agreed to execute Chato Cuqueta, an Anarchist who had murdered a judge. The king reprieved Chato Cuqueta and Canalejas formally 'resigned'. The reprieve brought the king popularity on the left at the expense of Canalejas.

[2] Cf. Melquíades Alvarez on 26 June 1912, in M. García Venero, *Melquíades Alvarez* (1954), 247.

[3] For details see below, pp. 551–2.

Quite apart from his resentment of Maura's hectoring tone, Alfonso XIII preferred to base his government on opinion rather than to trust Maura's interpretations of the supposed 'real will' of the dumb multitudes. This opinion he knew to be liberal: liberal newspapers had the largest circulations; the most prominent professors and intellectual writers were liberal. Thus he chose Romanones to succeed Canalejas, an action which Maura interpreted as a deliberate slight. Often a caricature of the worst features of parliamentary liberalism, Romanones nevertheless kept his party open for recruits from the left. It was the task of other Liberals to draft the modern programme that would attract the left for a joint effort in regenerationism: Santiago Alba, who became Romanones's Minister of the Interior in 1915, was a practical regenerationist of the Costa school. Entering politics with the Agrarian League of 1887, he saw in it a movement of the producers against the drones of political life. It was the 'proletariat of lawyers', the obsession for 'a career' (*tener carrera*—a key concept to the understanding of the psychology of insecurity which paralysed the energies of the middle class) which produced a Spain without technical education, with a monstrous, expensive, and semi-employed bureaucracy, and with a parliament where the lawyers outweighed every other interest. Spain could become a modern nation by productive investment in agriculture and education.[1] This would be financed by slashing expenditure on the civil service and the army and by reducing the interest on the National Debt—neither attractive policies for large sections of the middle class he hoped to woo.

Like Canalejas, Santiago Alba hoped to turn the liberal party into a party of 'realizations': this opened the prospect of weaning the newly formed Reformist Republicans from the real dangers of the Republican–Socialist Conjunction.[2] Encouragement to the intellectuals who formed the Reformist leadership—Romanones engineered interviews at the palace, and the king sent a telegram of condolence to Azcárate on the loss of his seat—split the Republican–Socialist Conjunction. The Reformists became 'governmental Republicans': if the

[1] For his ideas see his *Problemas de España* (Madrid, 1916). Santiago Alba believed that the Prussian schools had won in 1870 and the American schools in 1898.

[2] For the Reformist Republicans see below, pp. 536–8.

Liberals placed the monarchy on the road to practical reform, they would grant it benevolence and co-operate in its parliamentary life. If the monarchy defied 'opinion', it would face the permanent revolution of republicanism. The prelude to 1917 was the sensation that the old political system was doomed unless it could make room for a new 'collective ideal' of renovation before it was swept away by revolution. 'Our political society is giving birth to a movement of salvation. . . . It can develop in two ways: either by evolution, realizing the revolution from above . . . or by a radical revolution such as Russia or Portugal have experienced.'[1] The year 1917 was to give the answer.

4. *The Strains of War and the Crisis of 1917: the Reappearance of the Army in Politics*

In the crisis of 1917 Catalanism, the army, the Republican, and the proletarian parties combined in an attempt to force renovation and reform on the political establishment. The Assembly Movement, as this conglomeration of disparate forces is known, came to nothing; the system survived, not by its own strength, but by exploiting the conflicts between would-be regenerators. This failure was crucial: since the parliamentary monarchy could not be renovated by the processes of effective democratic government, it was destroyed in 1923 by a soldier who had lost faith in politics and politicians. It was the European war and its after-effects which undermined the constitutional monarchy in Spain; it was the Moroccan war which destroyed it.

Whereas the Second World War entailed privation that hid faults in the social structure in a common misery, the war of 1914–18 brought a prosperity that exposed them. As a neutral power, Spain, from 1915 to 1918, experienced boom profits and a spectacular rise in prices. Catalan mills supplied French soldiers, the disappearance of cheap Welsh coal stimulated

[1] *Renovación o revolución*, an account of 1917 published by the supporters of Marcelino Domingo, the Catalan Republican (Barcelona, 1917), 7–8.

feverish activity in the Asturian coalfields. European conditions stimulated an advance from the 'colonial' economy in which Spain was a supplier of primary products and a field for foreign investment.[1]

Certainly much of this activity represented quick profits rather than sound expansion. Cambó maintained that the 'hunger' for high dividends blinded industrialists to the opportunity of making up for the time-lag in the Spanish economy by the reinvestment of industrial and agricultural profits in growth. They took their profits with no thought for the future. It was agriculture rather than industry which kept the national production above the level of 1913; industrial production as opposed to industrial profits declined, lamed by transport difficulties and lack of cheap coal. Thus the real secret of Spain's war-time prosperity was the reversal of the terms of trade for primary products and the high prices her textiles could command, which, between them, brought about a dramatic and sudden elimination of the historic trade deficit; it was reflected, therefore, in the price of the peseta rather than in an industrial break-through. These conditions made possible a repatriation of the national and the railway debt and fostered the growth of the power of the great banks.[2]

The war boom and the dramatic price rise unsettled all labour relations. Wages rose rapidly, especially in the Asturian mines and among unskilled workers in Catalonia and the industrial north. In favoured sectors and regions they kept up with, and in many cases outstripped, prices; but some workers experienced no gain in real wages (in some occupations and areas there was a distinct fall) and this at a time when employers, it was assumed, were making vast 'speculative' profits.[3] These

[1] Thus the Asturian Royal Mine Company (a typical mid-century, foreign-financed creation for the exploitation of domestic ore in French zinc refineries) set up a refinery in Spain when its French factories were captured: most important, this venture was largely financed by Spanish capital. The most ambitious steel mill in Spain (Llano y Soto's works at Sagunto) was a war-time creation.

[2] Cf. F. Bernis, *Consequencias económicas de la guerra* (1923). The capital of the Bank of Spain doubled, that of private banks more than doubled. Bernis attributed the collapse of 1920 in part to the absence of an 'English' central banking tradition (op. cit. 320) which could influence internal prices by manipulation of the discount rate (cf. above, pp. 411–12).

[3] 'Estadística de huelgas' (*I.R.S.*), xxviii, xxxii.
Industrial wages: 1914, 100; 1920, 186. General wages: 1914, 100; 1920, 156.

conditions favoured a rapid growth of organized labour at a moment when the war was making Spain ungovernable by parliamentary methods.

The governments of Dato (October 1913 to December 1915) and Romanones (December 1915 to April 1916), struggling with inflation, labour troubles, and a breakdown of the railway system, found themselves caught up in the bitter polemics between supporters of Germany and the allies. This debate was largely artificial because the government was aware that active intervention was a military impossibility; as Basques and Catalans pointed out, the Spain of the *turno* had ceased to count in Europe and was doomed to become a neutral, a base for spies and profiteers.[1] The passionate supporters of intervention lay outside the government parties. It was the Carlists who regarded William II as a hero, while Lerroux wished Alfonso to lead his armies against Germany. The demand for intervention became, in the hands of those with no faith in the constitutional monarchy, a handy device to discredit the Spain of the political parties. 'A world conflagration in which principles as widely opposed as caesarism and democracy are fighting for survival has had no effect on our collective conscience.'

Most Spaniards recognized the limitations of impotence. Thus the historian Altamira was, like most liberals, pro-ally, while the majority of Spaniards were probably pro-German; he was therefore concerned to argue that liberals rejected intervention, not because they rejected the thesis that the

Prices: 1913, 100; 1915, 111; 1917, 149; 1920, 188; 1921, 182; 1922, 162 (F. G. Quijano, 'El nivel de precios en España', *Moneda y credito*, no. 65).

Barcelona wages:

	Electrical trades		*Textiles*		*Metallurgy*	
	Skilled	*Unskilled*	*Skilled*	*Unskilled*	*Skilled*	*Unskilled*
1914	100	100	100	100	100	100
1920	200	233	208	255	229	239
1925	262	250	220	295	290	297

[1] There is an abundant literature on these issues. A typical example is Luis Araquistain's *Dos ideales políticos*, esp. 103 ff. The atmosphere was impassioned by the propaganda efforts of the belligerents. Lord Northcliffe, for instance, claimed that Spain's policy was dictated by her German colony.

allies represented 'progress and humanity' but because 'we could not, and therefore ought not, to intervene'.[1] The issue was which side should benefit from a benevolent interpretation of neutrality. Maura regarded benevolence to the allies as anti-Spanish because Britain was the true enemy of Spain; Romanones and the left regarded the infraction of Spain's neutrality by German submarines as a crime against progress. Meanwhile, as the Reformist leaders and the Republican–Socialist opposition pointed out, parliamentary government had been dispensed with: Dato decided on neutrality without consulting the Cortes, while his successor, Romanones, ruled by decree and escaped any effective financial control by the Cortes. Romanones resigned (April 1917) on the submarine issue, after he had been bitterly attacked in the pro-German press.[2] He knew the army was about to re-enter politics.

The crisis of 1917 was initiated by the *Juntas de defensa*, the most curious and misunderstood of all the army's interventions in politics.[3] The Junta movement was a peaceful pronunciamiento 'within the concept of military discipline', a protest of officers below the rank of colonel against the generals and politicians, against low wages made even lower by inflation, and against 'political' promotions. The officers' Juntas were not, as is often assumed, imitations of trade unions but of the professional corporations which protected the interests of the specialized corps—the artillery and engineers.[4] Through these organizations the privileged corps had been able to circumvent 'political' promotions and enforce the rigid seniority of the 'closed scale' envied by the infantry. Thus, when Romanones attempted to force a proficiency test on officers, the artillery resisted successfully: when the government enforced these tests

[1] R. Altamira, *La Guerre actuelle et l'opinion espagnole* (Paris, 1919, but written in 1915).

[2] For Romanones's attitude see his *Notas* (1912–31), 106 ff. Romanones believed that Spain could not escape the French alliance, given both countries' joint interest in Morocco; he also felt strongly over the torpedoing of Spanish ships.

[3] See below, p. 562, for a further consideration of the Juntas as a military institution.

[4] If syndicalism did influence the officers it must have indeed been in 'a curious indirect way' (S. de Madariaga, *Spain*, 235). Cf. the remark of one of the *junteros*: 'The infantry looked up to the other arms, like the artillery, who have the *escala cerrada*' (i.e. promotion by strict seniority). In 1916 the Junta movement, starting in the IV Military District (Catalonia) and the cavalry, spread throughout the infantry.

in Catalonia, the infantry Juntas, which had been set up in 1916, organized an officers' strike. When the *junteros* were arrested they issued a declaration of their aims to the country: reasonable pay and conditions, recognition of their union as the proper body to negotiate over such matters with the state, 'moderation in rewards, justice in promotion, and respect for seniority'. These were the demands of a sedentary bureaucracy but they were made as part of a general plea for a modern, efficient, 'respected' army.[1]

The Juntas had included in their proclamations vague phrases about avoiding conflict between the army and the people, together with even vaguer promises about the necessity of reform. The army had been blamed by politicians for their own incapacity to make a strong *patria*; it was now the turn of the army to undertake the task in self-defence. The truly extraordinary result was that public opinion (i.e. those excluded from political life and the opposition) accepted these tetchy and self-interested soldiers as proper instruments to force national regeneration and renovation on the government and the politicians.[2] The chief *juntero*, Colonel Márquez, deaf, and a political simpleton, was treated as a saviour and was soon in touch with Cambó, Maura, and Lerroux; inconceivable praise was lavished on the army patriots by Republicans, Radicals, and Catalan conservatives: 'The ashes of Daoíz and Velarde ought to move in their sepulchres and the cross of Constantine, the sign of a new faith, shines out over the sky of the *patria*.'[3] Once more Spain suffered one of its periodic spasms of the military delusion, the conviction that the army could effect salutary change in the face of the impotence and indifference of the political establishment. The officers acted like gentlemen, not generals: they disclaimed any ambitions of power for themselves. When this new patriotic

[1] Cf. General E. Mola, *O.C.* iv, 65, 73–75. Mola later attacked the 'bureaucratic form-fillers' and called the Juntas 'a military trades union legalized by the weakness of the government . . . a stupid and tyrannical syndicalism, a refuge for evil passions'. Nevertheless the Juntas' manifesto embodied the general army view, i.e. that 1898 was the fault of politicians who starved the army and then expected it to win battles. The two key declarations of 1917 are printed in *Renovación y revolución*, 92–116.

[2] Thus the independent *El Sol*, one of the best papers in Spain, acclaimed the *junteros*.

[3] Daoíz and Velarde were the two military heroes of 2 May 1808. See above, p. 87.

pronunciamiento was met by the appointment of the orthodox conservative Dato (11 June 1917), the opposition and the renovationists were disillusioned: the army was not enough—even though it had 'anointed and sanctified itself with public opinion'.

The atmosphere of Catalonia was a sympathetic ambience for the Juntas; any protest was a potential vehicle for Catalan discontents. The economic consequences of the war to a neutral country re-created between Catalan industry and Castilian agriculture the politico-economic tensions of the free-trade struggle. Catalan business men wanted a free port and resented any attempt to tax war profits. Thus the Catalan bourgeoisie was in a militant, injured mood, and its instrument, the Lliga, since 1914 the political power in Catalonia, now supported a campaign for Catalan Home Rule with a Catalan parliament. In the Cortes its leader, Cambó, rejected all charges of separatism; but if he rejected secession from Spain he was ready to secede from the existing political system. 'Catalonia will save Spain or destroy her.' If the politicians refused to respond to the gospel of salvation via Catalonia then logic must lead Cambó to contemplate the overthrow of a system which he had always regarded as sterile and artificial.

That the working-class leaders were on the edge of violent protest at the rising cost of living had been evident since 1916. In the summer of 1916 the U.G.T. threatened a general strike for higher wages, which, if ineffective, would be followed by a revolutionary strike. This new tone made a *rapprochement* with the Anarchists possible, though the Socialist leaders felt both uneasy and contemptuous of the revolutionary infantilism of the C.N.T.[1] More surprising was the alliance (June 1917) of Socialist and Reformist Republicans to impose, by a revolutionary strike if necessary, a ministry under Melquíades Álvarez.[2] This ministry would summon a Constituent Cortes, a reversion to the doctrine of nineteenth-century revolutíonary radicalism. To deal with this revolutionary threat Dato closed the Cortes and suspended the constitutional guarantees.

It was Dato's action which united these divergent protests into the Assembly movement. The movement presented the possi-

[1] F. Largo Caballero, *Mis recuerdos*, 54.

[2] For Melquíades Álvarez and the Reformist Republicans see below, pp. 536–8.

bility of uniting Catalans, workers, and radicals into a national reform movement backed by an officers' *fronde*: on 10 July Cambó wrote to Colonel Márquez in the name of a 'joint effort at national regeneration'.[1] The Lliga, in face of Dato's obstinacy, summoned the Catalan deputies to Barcelona to demand the immediate opening of the Cortes 'as a constituent Cortes' in order to grant 'ample autonomy' to the regions. Should this demand be refused, a National Assembly would be summoned and the Cortes confronted with a revolutionary convention in the capital. Dato defied the movement and declared it seditious.

The Assembly, boycotted by the orthodox parties, met in Barcelona on 19 July, successfully eluding the police in taxis. After a show of Roman dignity the Assembly was dissolved by the police as a seditious meeting. Maura refused co-operation, as he had rejected the approaches of the *junteros*; in the eyes of his son, his friend Ossorio, and the mass of his following, this was a disastrous decision. After preaching a conservative revolution, Maura refused to back the 'almost legal revolution', of which the leader was a moderate politician who had always sought, as he had himself, to regenerate conservatism.[2] Maura's 'defection' left the movement too much a Catalan concern, isolated from Spain and open to the old accusations of Catalan selfishness; it also left Cambó dangerously dependent on allies to the left who were prepared to force through changes, much more radical than he himself desired, by a revolutionary strike.[3]

[1] The army, in spite of Cambó's repudiation of separatism, was chary of the Assembly movement: it saw its function as that of a political reserve, a last resort to force a national government on the king. Cf. B. Márquez, *Las juntas militares de defensa* (1923), 46. This the Juntas attempted to do by sending two delegations to Alfonso XIII (3 Aug. and 26 Dec. 1917); when the king supported his ministers, Márquez turned against the king for his 'contempt for popular opinion . . . he despised the army'. It was the king's attitude in December that split the *juntas de defensa* (ibid. 70 ff.).

[2] G. Maura, *Por qué*, 495–8, 505. Cambó's view was that the future of conservatism lay in a regionalist policy which would leave the Liberal party as the party of the working classes. Cf. *Discursos*, 204. The fact that the favourite candidates of the Juntas were La Cierva (*Notas*, 184) and Maura indicates how little there was in common between the officer corps and the left-wing renovators.

[3] Cambó was aware of the dangers: he sent Nadal to Madrid in order to get the support of the conservative right. This was refused. The king suggested a National government; this was refused by Cambó. See J. M. de Nadal, *Seis años con D. F. Cambó* (Barcelona, 1957), 13.

Moreover the strike might come as the result of pressure from beneath rather than of calculation from above, and thus defeat the desire of the Reformist and Socialist leaders to hold off any strike action until the Assembly movement had had its chance to alter the face of politics.

Cambó, by nature a conservative 'constructive' politician, had played for high stakes with dubious alliances. Márquez was quite capable of leading a Republican pronunciamiento; Marcelino Domingo, impressed by events in Russia, was appealing to soldier soviets against the king, whom he took care to remind of the fate of Louis XVI; Lerroux was an outright Republican, even if his revolutionary zeal was rapidly dwindling. Cambó's reward was the doubtful success of the Barcelona Assembly and the danger of social revolution. Clearly he hoped to ride the storm and, indeed, he claimed to be averting social revolution by appealing for profound political change. 'The most conservative thing is to be a revolutionary; if we do not act, the revolution will come from below'—a pronouncement for which the C.N.T. denounced him as the 'murderer of the revolution'.[1] To conservatives he seemed either a political innocent or a 'Girondin', ready to appeal to forces that would destroy his enemies and himself.[2]

With the general strike, which he denounced as a 'stupidity', the revolution he had planned to master and to mould escaped his hands; the railway strike of August was so convenient for the government that it was accused of stiffening the railway companies in order to produce the explosion which the leaders of the left were straining every nerve to prevent.[3] Pablo Iglesias, ill in bed, accepted the revolutionary strike 'through discipline and in order not to leave the working class without leadership'. The strike, as the leaders who knew the weakness of the U.G.T. foresaw, was a failure; though it was confined to certain regions its relative violence shows how much more serious was the revolutionary crisis of 1917 than the pseudo-revolutionary

[1] Cf. *Solidaridád Obrera*, 19 July 1917.

[2] See the bitter attack on Cambó by the Conservative M. de Burgos y Mazo in *Páginas históricas de 1917* (Madrid, n.d.), 106 ff., 139.

[3] For a complete rebuttal of these charges as far as the government was concerned, see M. de Burgos y Mazo, *Páginas históricas*, 167 ff. On the other hand the Norte company put every conceivable difficulty in the way of a settlement (ibid. 208 ff.).

crisis of 1909.[1] Moreover it had a profound effect on the socialist movement: on the one hand, by bringing into socialism intellectuals it created reformist socialism: on the other, it was the first attempt at political revolution by the party. Failed revolutions can create traditions as easily as successful revolutions.[2]

The Assembly finally met on 30 October in Madrid and committed itself to the creation, by a Constituent Cortes, of an English parliamentary system which should leave the elector as the final arbiter of political life. Such a change, as the Assembly movement had always maintained, could not be brought about by an orthodox party government but by a ministry which would embody 'the spirit of the Assembly'. After an agonizing crisis, García Prieto, leader of the left wing of the Liberal party, formed a coalition government that included La Cierva, a Maurista conservative who was the only politician trusted by the army, and two representatives of conservative Catalan regionalism. For this patchwork ministry Cambó and the right of the Assembly deserted revolutionary politics. When García Prieto refused a Constituent Cortes, which alone gave any guarantee of serious domestic reforms, Melquíades Álvarez and his Reformists went into opposition: they could not accept a watered-down version of the 'spirit of the Assembly', patronized by a ministry where La Cierva, directly responsible for the repression of 1909, was the key figure. Nor could the nationalist left accept Cambó as the representative of Catalan demands. Renovation was a slogan which had hidden the rifts in the Assembly movement. This now dissolved into its constituent parts, leaving in the newly elected Cortes as the most confused legislature that Spain had known.

It was now becoming apparent that the officers' revolt had paralysed civilian government: neither able to brave the army

[1] In Barcelona nearly all the fighting was caused by the army's attempts to keep the trams working; the tram drivers, under the influence of Foronda, a monarchist deputy, did not strike and were attacked by strikers. A state of siege was declared on 13 Aug.: for two days all shops, theatres, and cafés were closed. Rain on the 15th and arrests on the 16th broke the movement after 33 people had been killed. In Sabadell, where the relations between the workers and the police were notoriously bad, 10 people were killed.

[2] Cf. Largo Caballero's judgement. 'The progress in political activity of the workers is in the main attributable to that revolutionary movement' (*Mis Recuerdos*, 51).

without La Cierva, nor to tolerate La Cierva's condescensions to soldiers, García Prieto resigned (22 March 1918).[1] No government could be formed and for the second time the king threatened abdication if the politicians deserted him. The parliamentary monarchy was saved by a National Government under Maura. This cantankerous conservative visionary was the only politician whom the army respected.

The strength of the National Government lay not in its modest programme but in the ability of its individual ministers; its weakness lay in their conflicting ambitions for the country and for themselves. Maura had no great faith in his own government; Dato was infected with his followers' suspicions of his great rival; Alba was staking a claim for the leadership of a new liberal left. Only Cambó was enthusiastic and energetic: 'I have blind faith in Spain'; with care, Catalonia could gain her autonomy and infuse a new vitality into Spain which would carry him, her greatest political talent, to effective power. What he would have done with power he showed in the programme he developed in his eight months as Minister of Development: Cambó saw the possibilities of a ministry that was unique in Europe, in that it gave an opportunity for the rational planning of the whole economy.

Cambó was a great capitalist, but Catalan capitalism, in its struggle for protection, had long since deserted the doctrines of *laissez-faire*. It was the 'interventionist' tradition in Spanish political economy which equipped him for his declared aim: 'to harmonize public and private enterprise'. Hence his great plan was a systematization and rationalization of old remedies by new laws; agricultural credit, forestry control and replanting, irrigation and hydro-electric schemes; a new law of public works and increased public investment in them; a mining law that would reverse the economic liberalism of the September Revolution and dismantle foreign control. His most radical proposals concerned the railways, where private capitalism had failed to maintain efficiency and profitability. The companies could not raise new capital to carry out essential

[1] La Cierva's solution for military sedition was to satisfy the professional demands of the Juntas and to discredit Márquez and the political *junteros* with 'consideration and tolerance at other times inexplicable'. In fact, both the officers and La Cierva were alarmed at the spread of the Junta movement to sergeants and men: this true military syndicalism was sharply dealt with.

improvements. Cambó advocated nationalization by buying them out. Nowhere did he show concern for social problems: these would be solved with a high level of employment, the corollary of flourishing business.[1]

What distinguished Cambó from his predecessors was his energy, his determination to get his projects into laws, to complete existing projects rather than to engage in fantasy. He kept his civil servants working throughout the summer vacation of 1918; in a year he built a railway line calculated to take six years. It was this energy which gave the National Government its new look, but its political foundations were to collapse before much of Cambó's work had got beyond the stage of projects. Catalan capitalism was denied its chance to create a Spain in its own image through parliamentary liberalism. It was Primo de Rivera who implemented Cambó's plan.

The National Government differed from García Prieto's government in that it was fundamentally a conservative concern: it would not satisfy the left and it was this which led Santiago Alba to play against Maura and Cambó the role which Melquíades Álvarez had played against García Prieto. Both have been bitterly criticized as political Judases, destroying the prospects of regeneration; yet Alba's belief in reform from the left was just as genuine and proper as Cambó's belief in reform by the right. 'I am a partisan of a government resolutely orientated towards the left in which will co-operate all, absolutely all, the forces representative of the left': in his own words, of 'a Republic with a crown on it'.[2] Less creditably, his centralist prejudices led him to qualify as insincere Cambó's thesis of 'Great Spain'—a Spain in which the regions, led by Catalonia, could find their place. He chose to regard Cambó's programme as covert separatism. His resignation (2 October 1918) over the educational estimates ruined the prospects of the National Government. A month later, weakened by Dato's final resignation, Maura resigned. It was the end of a great illusion, the last illusion of the constitutional monarchy.[3]

Between 1919 and 1923 the remnants of the traditional

[1] Cambó's account of his plans is contained in his *Vuit meses al ministeri de Foment* (Barcelona, 1919), ix–lxxv, and of their implementation in ibid. 5–322.

[2] Quoted by J. Pabón, *Cambó*, 671.

[3] Cf. E. Aunós, *España en crisis* (Buenos Aires, 1942), 244.

parties could not, in the language of nineteenth-century politicians, offer the crown the instruments with which to govern. The Liberals, unacceptable to either the army or to Catalanism, were split between Romanones and his governmental Liberals, García Prieto's Democrats, and the Albistas. This opened the way, in the post-war years, for a series of conservative governments which proved only that the Conservatives were exhausted: they tried homogeneous governments (a cabinet composed of one group), conservatively tinged national governments, and 'governments of concentration' (a cabinet of all conservative groupings). None of these governments was stable or long-lived.

The split between Maura and Dato proved fatal: their mutual suspicions prevented either from governing and ruined the Conservative party as an instrument of government. Dato's followers wanted a reorganized party and a modern programme.[1] Maura had little interest in modern party organization and even less in giving the party any programme other than that of the defence of his political past. His personality was 'the Jordan that would wash away all political sins'. Thus the grant of a dissolution to Maura in July 1919 was a 'disaster' which Dato could force his group to accept only with difficulty. On Maura's fall his lieutenant, La Cierva, treated his conservative successor, Sánchez de Toca, as a relapsed heretic; to the cabinet, struggling with the social question in Barcelona, La Cierva appeared 'a right wing anarchist', sacrificing government itself to the satisfaction of his political hatreds.[2] All attempts to reunite the party failed: even Maura's distant relations with Dato set off a revolt of the Mauristas, while Dato's agreement to co-operate with Maura was rejected by his own party the day after his assassination (March 1921). The king was accused of fomenting these divisions according to the maxim of *divide et impera*: probably he was torn between the wearying task of driving the politicians to carry on the king's government and some ill-defined temptation to replace them.

[1] For the modernization of the party programme by the Datoists see *Revista Quincenal*, 25 Feb. 1918.

[2] Cf. M. de Burgos y Mazo, *El verano de 1919 en gobernación* (Cuenca, n.d.), 190 ff., for a bitter attack on La Cierva. La Cierva was consistently accused of 'domesticating' the *Juntas de Defensa* as a private political instrument.

5. *The Post-War Crisis, 1919–1923*

Between 1919 and 1923 the rickety structure of a constitutional government, operating without a firm party system, was subjected to two complementary stresses: post-war labour troubles and the return of the generals to politics. The system survived the rebellion of the masses. The significance of violent social struggle lay in the role it prepared for a resolute general as a saviour of society.

The post-war contraction of the European market brought crisis to Spain. The marginal Asturian mines closed down. The end of a war which had supported an enormous increase in shipbuilding brought correspondingly enormous losses when freight rates fell. Many companies found themselves crippled by the expense of ships built in the boom; the ships were laid up and the Bilbao yards lay idle; the new steel mills found no demand for their products. Landowners, who had brought marginal land into cultivation, allowed it to revert to scrub pasture. Thus agricultural under-employment aggravated unemployment in the towns.

Falling prices and unemployment, therefore, lay behind the revolutionary strikes of 1919–23. Dwindling profits produced in employers a determination to fight the unionism, which they had tolerated in the labour shortages of the war; at the same time the unions used their new strength in order to maintain employment and wages at war-time levels. Employers argued that unless they broke the unions, the unions would break them by demands which, if satisfied, would drive them out of business.[1] In what Largo Caballero called 'a general offensive' they were ready to use any weapons: the lock-out, refusal to employ union militants, and an attempt to patronize 'free' unions (the *Sindicatos Libres*) against the C.N.T. In this *guerre à l'outrance* they

[1] For Largo Caballero's views see 'Crisis de la edificación', *I.R.S.* 1922, 4 ff. There seems to be some justification for the attitude taken by employers in the case of *smaller* enterprises. In the Asturias, where the number of miners had doubled between 1913 and 1920, only the larger, well-equipped mines could hope to keep on war-time workers with the post-war slump and the invasion of British coal. In the Seron strike the employers' defiance of all government efforts at mediation seems understandable; at a time when production was falling fast the workers demanded doubled wages (cf. *I.R.S.* Report for 1923 and 'Crónica acerca de los conflictos en las minas de carbón' (*I.R.S.* 1922), esp. 24 ff.).

refused to recognize the legitimacy of the efforts of the government to impose settlements. When the Catalan employers could not bully ministries out of policies of concession, the Employers' Federation was willing to encourage the establishment of a parallel military government at Barcelona in defiance of Madrid. Thus in 1919 the Captain General of Catalonia, Milans del Bosch, acted as the ally of the Federation in its determination to break strikes, rather than as the agent of a central government which wished to negotiate wage settlements.[1]

All responsibility for the social war of 1919–23 in Catalonia cannot be placed on obdurate employers and feeble governments. Important as economic grievances were, they do not explain the sudden preponderance of what Spanish government statisticians called 'political' (i.e. revolutionary) strikes unconnected with wage issues. The C.N.T.'s tactical dogma of 'direct action' precluded any intervention by the government in the struggle between employers and workers. Even the most moderate leaders could not, and did not, conceal the ultimate revolutionary aim: the total and violent destruction of bourgeois society by the revolutionary general strike which would be declared as soon as the workers were strong enough to join battle. Seguí and Pestaña, the two outstanding leaders of the C.N.T., were men of organization and personally opposed to indiscriminate terrorism as a tactic, but they must not be considered as little removed from reformist socialism; strategically both were revolutionaries. An autodidact bred in anarchist cafés, Seguí was a devotee of Nietzsche: but he was also 'an instinctive of the streets' who knew the lassitude bred by defeat and the necessity of concrete gains; both he and, to a lesser extent, Pestaña preached moderate courses. It is a tribute to Seguí's powers as an orator that he could, at times, convince congresses that revolutionary courses were mistaken. The theoretical vulnerability of this position, in his struggle with extremism, was that anarchism, unlike socialism, had no comforting historicist vision of an inevitable collapse of capitalist society which could be used to palliate the postponement of

[1] His action in putting the civil governor on a train back to Madrid, though not quite as violent as has been sometimes supposed, nevertheless revealed the dualistic nature of Catalan government. See Romanones, *Notas*, iii. 164 ff., and *El Sol* (20 Mar. 1919) for Morote's account of his mission to Barcelona to settle the *Canadiense* strike and of his difficulties with the military authorities.

immediate revolutionary action. In practice 'moderation', which would turn the C.N.T. into a respectable union, had little chance of success when the employers could argue that the control of the moderates was insecure and that the only thing to do with the C.N.T. was to destroy it—a course which must ruin Seguí and Pestaña's position within their own union.

In the strikes of 1919, battle was joined between the Catalan employers, backed by the military authorities, and the C.N.T. In February a minor pay dispute of the clerical staff in the *Canadiense* (the hydro-electric concern that supplied Barcelona with light and power) set off what was to be an historic strike: it caught the imagination by plunging the city into darkness, closing its cafés and theatres, and, once it became general, by threatening food supplies.[1] The company refused to recognize the union and give securities for re-employment, while the C.N.T. committee refused to meet the company lest its members be recognized and arrested. Government efforts at mediation, which had brought about a settlement of the wage issue, collapsed when the Captain General declined to release imprisoned unionists; this allowed C.N.T. extremists to argue that any negotiated settlement would prove futile—a contention which was supported by the company's refusal to reinstall all workers.[2]

Thus a strike in which the strikers had gained their economic demands became a general strike of revolutionary solidarity, as Segui confessed, 'against our will'. It was broken by the declaration of a state of war and massive arrests. Later in the year the employers declared a lock-out. From the intransigent employers' point of view, the lock-out was a great success: it divided and weakened the C.N.T. Two civil governors, Amado and Bas, both admirers of Segui in his oratorical struggle with extremism, and determined enemies of the *pistoleros*, hoped to settle the conflict by the mediation of a Mixed Commission: 'sincere respect for the right of association', thought Bas, was better than imprisoning leaders and leaving the terrorists in command. To the employers the only solution was a strong civil governor. Such

[1] The earlier stages of the *Canadiense* strike are described in 'Estadística de huelgas' (*I.R.S.*, 1919).

[2] The refusal of immediate reinstallation was justified on the technical grounds that all machinery could not be immediately restarted after a strike: a similar excuse was alleged after the strike in the Royal Mine Company in the Asturias. To the workers this was victimization.

a governor they obtained in General Martínez Anido (November 1920), who for two years ruled Barcelona as he wished. The 'dualism' between Madrid and Barcelona was complete. 'Let them [the Madrid government] get rid of me if they can' was the general's customary reply to journalists.[1]

Martínez Anido favoured the 'yellow' *Sindicatos Libres* designed to break the monopoly of the C.N.T. and, as their later history shows, not entirely employers' unions of black-legs. Catholic social reformers had favoured the idea of free syndicates. They had founded a Federation of Catholic Free Syndicates in 1916 and some of their members joined the *Sindicatos Libres*. These were founded in 1920 as 'professional' trade unions and came to have some influence in the early years of the dictatorship of Primo de Rivera. Whatever hopes their leaders may have had of attracting the old conservative unionism away from the C.N.T. were defeated by the gunmen who infiltrated into the Free Syndicates. Hired by the employers as a private police force in order to safeguard the operations and recruitment of the Free Unions, the *pistoleros* operated a labour protection racket which took the form of an inter-union war waged by assassination.[2] Against the gunmen of the Free Unions the anarchist tradition of terrorism revived and plunged the labour world into the obscure vendettas of blood feud. None of the C.N.T. leaders wanted this warfare—Segui himself was one of its victims—but they were quite powerless to stop it once their techniques of organization had accomplished nothing and their cadres had been smashed by the employers' counter-offensive. Terrorism increased as syndicalism declined: in 1923, when the number of organized strikes was lower than at any time since 1919, the number of attempted assassinations increased tenfold.

Once more the organization of the *jacquerie* of the south in

[1] This period is described in F. Madrid, *Ocho meses y un dia en el gobierno civil de Barcelona* (Barcelona, 1932).

[2] The employers' private police force was organized by a former police chief, Bravo Portillo, who had probably been a German agent engaged in sabotage of factories, &c., supplying the allies. Reinstated as a special investigator by Milans del Bosch, he was assassinated and his 'gang' was inherited by a pure adventurer, 'Baron Koenig', who hired his services to individual employers. He thus became involved in obscure quarrels within the Employers' Federation where he was supported by the treasurer and had his flat raided by the president.

1918–19 proved the revolutionary connexion between Catalonia and the deep south. Vague rumours of a revolution in Russia—one Anarchist organizer changed his name from Cordón to Cordoniev—set off new waves of strikes in Andalusia where there had been a period of intense propaganda effort since 1910; militants had built up local agricultural unions with a paper, *La Voz del Campesino*, and a central congress. These strikes were therefore semi-organized as no previous agrarian protest had been: strikes for the concrete demands put forward at the Congress of Agricultural Workers held at Castro (October 1918). These demands were the abolition of piece-work, negotiated wages, and recognition of the workers' syndicates or centres. At first the strikes were remarkably successful, and employers—terrified by a revolutionary solidarity which included cooks, maids, and wet nurses—negotiated wage settlements.[1] Strike committees took over municipal government; the landowners lost their nerve and retired to the security of the provincial capitals. In the spring of 1919 the government sent troops to suppress the strike, and the rural anarchism of the south was left, once more, in the keeping of the 'men with ideas'. Yet this was one of the most active periods of anarchist propaganda, when over fifty pueblos had their papers and when the anarchists of the south were formally joined to the workers of Catalonia in the C.N.T. Above all, the Anarchists had penetrated the 'hard' regions of Valencia and Levante.

By mid-1923 revolutionary unionism was beginning to look a spent force. Its strength was sapped by disputes between the Syndicalists of the C.N.T. and the old Anarchist militants of Jerez and Cadiz. Sánchez Rosa, the greatest Anarchist apostle since Salvochea and founder of the Workers' Library, was actually expelled from the movement.[2] Prolonged revolutionary strikes left the unions 'tired' at the moment when the post-war slump was beginning to turn into a minor boom. This was particularly noticeable in Madrid which, for a time in 1921, had replaced Barcelona as the main battlefield of the social

[1] Cf. Vizconde de Eza, *El problema agrario andaluz* (1919). The smaller tenant farmers were too near ruin themselves to soften. It is often forgotten that these *labradores* were the immediate oppressors, since they rented the *cortijos*. In some cases the smaller farmers made common cause with the labourers, but this was rare. For a brilliant description of these strikes see Brenan *Labyrinth*, 179–182.

[2] M. Buencasa, *Movimiento obrero*, 167.

war.[1] Strikes of builders, carpenters, and bank employees were relative failures.[2] Above all the two great unions fell to fighting with each other.

At the Madrid Congress of December 1919 the C.N.T. looked a great force: in the pride of strength it declared the U.G.T. 'yellow' and clearly thought that it would absorb the Socialist unions. During 1920 the effects of the lock-out and Martínez Anido's drastic measures made the leaders feel that the movement was in danger; eight months after the declaration against the U.G.T. they sought its alliance. This alliance was rejected by a meeting at Barcelona as an unconstitutional reversal by the leadership of the decision of a sovereign congress. The feebleness and treason of the U.G.T. became favourite topics once more. The year 1921 was a catastrophic one; though the Congress of Saragossa (April 1922) seemed to mark a resurgence, failure left its legacy of bitter disputes over definitions and tactics, now made more intense by the problem of joining or rejecting the communism of the Third International. All over Spain Anarchists were expelling Syndicalists and vice versa, while 'Communists' (that is, C.N.T. militants who followed Nin and Maurín in their continued support of the Third International) were infiltrating to increase discord.

Outside Catalonia, in areas where the U.G.T. was strong, the main feature of the local history of these years is a bitter struggle of the C.N.T. against the Socialists: propaganda campaigns degenerated into street skirmishes and accusations of treason to the joint strike agreements of 1916 and 1917, even of betrayal of strike plans to the authorities. It was in these years that the C.N.T. established itself in towns like Gijón and La Felguera; this led to conflicts with the Socialist miners of the

[1] 'Estadística de huelgas' (*I.R.S.* 1920 and 1921) give the following proportion of total strikes. 1920: Madrid 5 per cent., Barcelona 11 per cent.; 1921: 21 per cent. and 7·7 per cent. respectively.

[2] Cf. the carpenters' strike of Aug. 1922. After a month the pressure of workers who wished for 'independent' (i.e. non-political) unions made it impossible to continue the strike; it therefore failed in its main demand—that the unions should control dismissals ('Huelga del ramo de la madera en Madrid', *I.R.S.* 1923). The bank strike was the only lower middle-class strike. Bank-clerks in Barcelona set up a Free Syndicate with some success; in Madrid the strike, after a period of sudden enthusiasm, was a fiasco because the U.G.T. refused support to a rival organization and the bank employees themselves were divided. Cf. 'Historia de las huelgas de empleados de banco y bolsa' (*I.R.S.* 1923), esp. 10 ff.

Asturias. The Rio Tinto strike, one of the toughest of the post-war years, was characterized by the refusal of the C.N.T. to admit any claim of the U.G.T. to be a workers' union.[1]

By these struggles the territorial division of the labour world was established. In Galicia there were strong Anarchist groups, strengthened by contacts with South American exiles.[2] Aragon was a pure Anarchist stronghold with its capital, Saragossa, the second great revolutionary centre in Spain. Aragonese strikes were characterized by their scorn for economic demands and the toughness of their revolutionary solidarity: strikes for comrades in prison were more popular than strikes for better conditions. In the Levante, though the C.N.T. picked up in 1922, it was deeply divided: the Metal Workers' Union proscribed the use of the word Anarchist and pressed for alliance with the Socialists, the very policy that was heresy in Saragossa. The general impression is the same as in Catalonia: the Russian revolution, the scandalous relation between large war profits and low wages, the general instability of 1919, combined to produce a great surge of enthusiasm which withered away with dissension and oppression. The gun-warfare of 1922–3 hid the fact that the C.N.T. was weakening; neither Martínez Anido nor Primo de Rivera saved Spain from an Anarcho-Syndicalist revolution. By 1923 the movement had almost destroyed itself.

The consequence of the labour war of 1919–23 was therefore to leave the U.G.T. less discredited, less torn by internal dissension than the C.N.T.; it survived the crisis of Communism which ultimately resulted in the foundation of a small Communist party; in its strongholds—the northern mining and industrial regions and Madrid—it was well organized. Socialists

[1] The Rio Tinto strike was perhaps the bitterest strike in Spanish labour history. Two-thirds of the workers emigrated to other towns after selling their beds and their clothes. The C.N.T. was fighting both the company and the U.G.T., whose participation in the direction of the strike it excluded by insisting that the union must 'clear itself of political interference', i.e. declare itself non-Socialist. The Socialist leaders professed to believe that the company was backing the C.N.T. in order to destroy the more 'serious' U.G.T. ('Huelgas 1920', *I.R.S.* 126–8).

[2] Vigo was the home of the most celebrated in Spanish anarchist writers, Mella, 'converted' from Federal Republicanism by the *Revista Social*. In Oct. 1920 there was a three-week general strike in Corunna and in Santiago strikers secured the dismissal of the mayor.

confessed scorn for a movement whose leaders were dragged along by *pistoleros*; as an instinctive reply to police repression, the infantile revolutionism of the C.N.T. lacked any understanding of the 'processes of historical evolution'. The dictatorship of Primo de Rivera was to increase the power of 'respectable' unionism; in 1931, therefore, the U.G.T., together with the Socialist party, represented the strongest organized body of opinion in Spain.[1]

The second consequence of the labour war, accompanied as it was by assassinations and violence—a prime minister, Dato, and an archbishop had been shot by C.N.T. gunmen in the war of reprisals—was that it scared the propertied classes, in particular the bourgeoisie of Barcelona and the landowners of the south. In the Barcelona Federation and in the clubs of the Andalusian capitals the employers felt that, not merely their living, but their lives were at stake. Successive governments refused to take this dramatic view: Conservatives like Dato and Sánchez de Toca, and Liberals like Romanones were prepared to use the Institute of Social Reform as an instrument for the settlement of strikes. The conservative classes dismissed governmental conciliation as weakness and bitterly attacked ministers who would not 'string up anarchists on lamp posts' and grant every request of the employers for armed force.[2] This lack of faith in civilian government accounts, in part, for the ready acceptance of a military dictatorship in 1923. The Barcelona employers had already appealed to the military government when civilian government refused to protect their interests. Just as in the Carlist wars, military rule began at the local level. The dictatorship of Primo de Rivera may be seen as the transposition of a local *condominium* into a national régime.

6. *The Moroccan Disasters: the Quest for Responsibilities, 1919–1923*

In July 1921, when the members of the government had followed the king to San Sebastian, terrible news of the most dis-

[1] Cf. E. Santiago, *La Union General de Trabajadores ante la revolución* (1932).

[2] For a bitter counter-attack on the employers and a defence of the conservative government of Sánchez de Toca in 1919 see M. de Burgos y Mazo, *El verano de 1919 en gobernacion*, esp. 171, 196, 306. Burgos y Mazo was Sánchez de Toca's Minister of the Interior: he was consistently insulted and bullied by the Barcelona Employers' Federation and even accused of smuggling arms to Syndicalists.

creditable defeat in the military annals of Spain fell on the cabinet 'like a bomb'.[1] The Spanish army in the eastern zone of Morocco, twenty thousand strong, had been driven in panic from its advanced positions around Annual into Melilla and the fruit of a decade of expensive and unpopular war had vanished before a few thousand tribesmen. Like the navy in 1898, the army could be tested and found wanting in a way that other governmental apparatus could not. The army cost Spain more than any other institution, yet the Melilla command had not a single tank or armoured car in 1921. 'Large doses of morphine'—the government's remedy for all difficulties—hid the prodromes of disaster from the country. Spaniards could only guess from their censored newspapers that thousands of their countrymen had been slaughtered by Moorish tribesmen.[2]

This defeat was, in part, the nemesis of a confused policy in Morocco. Up to 1904 Spain's interest in Morocco was satisfied by what politicians termed the *status quo*: this was the occupation of the garrison towns, Ceuta and Melilla, and the warding off of attacks on the surrounding country made by local tribesmen, who could not be effectively controlled by the Sultan as sovereign of Morocco. Even this limited action involved Spain in expeditions which revealed the weakness of the Spanish army and the hostility of public opinion to the expenditure of money and lives in Morocco. By 1909 Spanish commitments had widened. The local ruler, a tribal chief El Roghi, protected the iron mining operations of a Spanish–German firm which planned to export its ore through Melilla, but he could not hold off attacks on the company's railway.[3] Maura intervened to punish the tribes. It was the call up of reservists for these operations that set off the crisis of 1909.

Conflicting with the traditional limited policy of policing and the protection of Spanish nationals was the vague belief in Spain's historic destiny in north Africa. The expedition of 1859–60 had produced an extraordinary outburst of patriotism, and Costa, in the eighties, had preached Spain's African mis-

[1] According to La Cierva.

[2] Eduardo Ortega y Gasset's *Annual* (1922) gives a clear picture of the atmosphere of disaster, as does Arturo Barea's *The Track* (London, 1958).

[3] The Compañía Española de Minas del Rif was created in 1908: it did not export any ore until 1916.

sion.[1] This sense of mission could not, of itself, have produced military intervention. That rested on the belief of most Spanish politicians that Spain would be strategically vulnerable, and would cease to count as a great power, should any other nation install itself in northern Morocco: Cánovas, no rash expansionist, pronounced that Spain's frontier was the Atlas Mountains. After 1904, with the collapse of the Sultan's effective power and the termination of the Anglo-French rivalry that had maintained the *status quo* in Spain's favour, intervention in Morocco by France became a certainty. Spanish politicians now fought for a protectorate in north Morocco which would keep the coastline opposite Spain out of the hands of France. The dilemma was clear: if Spain did not appear as a north African power, she would cease to count in the councils of Europe.[2]

The Spanish zone of Morocco was a poor compensation prize, granted in order to buy off Spanish opposition to a French Morocco: held on lease from France, its international status derived from the Franco-Moroccan Treaty of 1912. With Tangier, its richest port, excluded, the Protectorate was an artificial zone, cut up into self-contained regions, which all the road building of the Spanish army could not make into a viable, self-sufficient economy. To the end of the Protectorate its imports of essential foodstuffs could be financed only by imports of capital from Spain.[3] Militarily, the zone presented every conceivable difficulty; it was indefensible and a drain on the metropolitan army.[4] Separated into two military zones, unconnected except by sea, the interior was a roadless, totally unexplored and unmapped mountain region, inhabited by the fiercely independent tribes which had never been subjected by

[1] M. Fernández Almagro, *Historia contemporánea*, i. 371 ff.

[2] Cf. Romanones's verdict: 'Morocco was for Spain her last chance to keep her position in the concert of Europe' (*Notas de una vida 1912–1931*, 34).

[3] Romanones called the delimitation of Spanish territory 'absurd' but the best that could be obtained from France. For the economic foundations see R. Perpiña, *De estructura económica* (1952), 209–17. As late as 1940 the Spanish tax-payer gave 86 million out of a total Moroccan budget of 113 million. The attraction of Spanish Morocco for business lay in the Rif iron mines; for them see J. A. Gutiérrez de la Paz, 'La explotación de mineral de hierro en el Rif' (in *De Ec.* iv (1951), 16 ff.) How far business interests backed military conquest is unclear: cf. the case of Romanones, who was a shareholder in the Rif mines.

[4] W. B. Harris, *France, Spain and the Rif* (London, 1927), 52.

the Sultan's government. Riddled with blood feuds, these tribes could nevertheless be brought into some temporary unity against the Spaniards by leaders like El Raisuli and Abd el Krim.

Confronted with the task of pacification, governments pursued conflicting policies: on the one hand, peaceful penetration by negotiation, bribery of the tribal chieftains, 'doctors, schools and medicine', and, on the other, the contrary policy of military subjugation and effective rule. It was the politicians who talked of peaceful penetration and the creation, through the independent Khalifate at Tetuan, of 'a Moslem power more accessible and more loved than the Sultanate'. They did not realize that penetration was impossible without subjugating the tribes, and that the line between backing the Khalif's power against tribal rebellion and military conquest was wholly artificial. The only logical policy was total withdrawal, yet few politicians—Cambó among them—could maintain that Spain had an 'option' and could leave Morocco. To take up the option was to confess that Spain was a minor power.

The soldiers, on the other hand, believed in conquest, the creation of block-houses, lines, military roads, and a native army. Morocco became their preserve, where dreary garrison life was exchanged for 'shooting and promotion'. To the generals the High Commissionership was the plum of the service, an irresponsible military proconsulate. For surrender to the army the politicians exacted their price: the army must satisfy its vanity on the cheap; it must not 'offend opinion'—in the words of the Minister of War in 1921—by heavy casualties amongst Spanish conscripts. Thus the parsimony of the politicians imposed a series of niggling advances, the dangers and futilities of which were resented by the soldiers.[1] Some, like General Primo de Rivera, hoping to cash in on the unpopularity of the war, became advocates of withdrawal from a costly and hopeless enterprise. The majority dreamed of a decisive operation which should join the two zones of the Ceuta and Melilla commands by the conquest of the Bay of Alhucemas.

During the 1914 war Spanish conquest had gone on unop-

[1] There was unending controversy as to how well the Melilla command was supplied at the time of Annual, i.e. how far the soldiers could blame 'niggardly' politicians for defeat. My opinion is that it was well enough supplied for the type of operation it undertook.

posed because German agents were turning the tribes against the French. In the Jibala these tribes were dominated by an aristocratic cattle thief of inconceivable cruelty, El Raisuli. During the war the Spanish High Commissioner had flattered El Raisuli: in 1920 a new commissioner, the energetic Berenguer, reversed this policy. He was determined to conquer Raisuli, pacify the eastern zone, and then join it to the western zone by methodical operations against Abd el Krim. Abd el Krim, from being a Spanish agent and client of the Iron Company, had turned into Spain's bitterest and ablest enemy; he showed a remarkable capacity for concentrating the fanatical enthusiasms of the Rif tribes on his own person. In the east Berenguer was successful, capturing Xauen, the beautiful mountain capital of El Raisuli, in 1920.[1] In the west the commander was Silvestre, whom Berenguer had dispatched to Melilla because he found his pretensions intolerable in the east. A difficult and ambitious man, alleged to be in confidential contact with the king who shared the army's pride and interest in Morocco, Silvestre planned to end the war by a decisive march on Alhucemas where he would found the city of Alfonso.[2]

As Silvestre advanced into the interior it was clear that there had been a serious miscalculation of the attitudes of the tribes; in desperation he thought advance would restore the situation, only hinting, in his dispatches, at the appalling morale of his troops. When he saw Abd el Krim attacking his camp at Annual in regular formation, after painful hesitation, he ordered the retreat that turned into a rout stopped only by exhaustion. Silvestre was killed and all discipline went. The war minister believed that the responsibility lay with the poor morale of the Spanish troops. 'Opinion' would not tolerate heavy conscript casualties and therefore native troops were generally used. The first time Spanish troops were exposed to heavy fire they broke.[3]

[1] D. Berenguer, *Campañas del Rif* (1923), 11–14, 50–54. This conquest was precarious because Berenguer had subdued none of the tribes between Xauen and Tetuan.

[2] The vizconde de Eza, war minister at the time, defends Silvestre from the charge of acting independently without informing either his immediate chief, Berenguer, or the government (*El desastre de Melilla* (1923), 28, 51). Both had agreed on minor operations and discussed an operation against Alhucemas. The disaster came as a total surprise (ibid. 56).

[3] Vizconde de Eza's *Mi responsibilidád ante el desastre de Melilla* (1923), 5, 12 ff. and *El desastre de Melilla* (1923), 66. Nearly all Spanish difficulties on campaign

In a few days five thousand square kilometres had been lost. What remained of the demoralized army was either cooped up with defeatist civilians in Melilla or shortly to be slaughtered in the surrounding posts like Monte Arruit; it had lost its guns and equipment, and only the arrival of troops from the western zone and the fortunate accident that Abd el Krim could not use his captured guns saved Melilla itself.

The immediate political consequence was general support for a new National Government under Maura. The troops were re-equipped with surplus equipment from the 1914–18 war and slowly and methodically Berenguer set about reconquest in the east, while in the west he reduced El Raisuli to his last stronghold. At this moment, the late summer of 1922, the mounting cry for 'responsibility' and a deepening distrust felt by politicians and journalists for the army undermined Berenguer's position. Troops were shipped home for political reasons against his advice; sick in mind and body, he threw in his hand.[1] His rival Burguete, a martinet, was sent out to liquidate the war by a policy of suborning the tribes, a confession of failure which culminated in the ransom treaty negotiated with Abd el Krim by a Basque millionaire who had bought up German interests in the Rif mines. This humiliation was bitterly opposed by a new interest, the warrior party of the Moroccan army, the devoted professional soldiers who had built up the Foreign Legion into the finest fighting force in the Spanish army. In these dark years Sanjurjo, Millán Astray, and a brave and fortunate young major, Franco, created a legend.

Rumours of army corruption seeped through the censorship and, in October 1921, the Cortes debates made these suspicions public property; officers spent over twice their incomes but never appeared at the front; captains grew rich while the men, whose catering they managed, starved; vermin infested the hospitals. From 1921 to 1923 the 'cry for responsibility' grew. Sánchez de Toca's conservative government of 1922 had no patience with the claims of the army—it dismissed Martínez

were rooted in the protection of water convoys to outlying posts. One tank or two armoured cars might have saved Monte Arruit. For a description of the horrors see A. Barea, *The Track*, esp. 90–92, and C. Martínez Campos, *Ayer*.

[1] Berenguer believed that El Raisuli held out only because he gambled on salvation by a change of system and the abandonment of 'military action' advocated by the opposition press.

Anido, resisted Moroccan *revanchisme*, and ended the Juntas—and it could not resist the demand for guilty men. General Picasso was sent out to Morocco to draw up a report. Yet it would be embarrassed by any real investigation of 'responsibilities': the army was its only instrument for a reconquest of lost territory, and to weaken its commanders would imperil reconquest by a further destruction of morale. Thus Berenguer was excepted from Picasso's inquiries while he was commander-in-chief. Moreover, the left was determined that responsibility should be pressed home against the Conservative politicians who presided over the disaster, and against the king, who they were convinced had encouraged Silvestre. The cry for responsibility seemed the best instrument to destroy 'reaction' which had reigned since 1917. It could be represented as the last attempt to reform the monarchy by democratizing and civilianizing it, as the inauguration of a 'new constitutional period' of 'serious government'. If the attempt failed this would mean the end of the monarchy. 'Either remedy or disaster.'[1] Socialists argued that it was too late for remedies. The army already weighed like lead on the country, 'imposing its mandate by a dictatorship in the shadows'; only 'the overthrow of the institutions' and the end of the monarchy could save Spain.[2]

The cry for responsibilities brought to power García Prieto as leader of a liberal concentration which represented more than the ambitions of an excluded party. Melquíades Álvarez had imported the Reformist programme into the Liberal party: reform of Article 11 of the Constitution (which established Catholicism as the state religion), radical social reform, and the democratization of the monarchy. The first step must be the assertion of responsibility against politicians and the army and the clear establishment of civilian control. The High Commissionership of Morocco was given to a civilian and on 11 July 1923 the Cortes set up a commission to examine and judge the Picasso Report. On 24 July the deputies left Madrid for the summer vacation.

When the Cortes reopened, the army and the king would be faced with a public tribunal. Ever since the Moroccan disaster the king had been suffering from fits of anti-parlia-

[1] Alcalá Zamora, *D.S.C.*, 24 Nov. 1922.

[2] Prieto, ibid., 16 Nov.

mentarianism. This was not surprising, for on three occasions, only the threat of his abdication had brought the politicians to their senses and enabled a ministry to be formed. He complained bitterly of 'desertion', which exposed the monarchy to the slanders of the left. He began to emerge as a political leader with policies of his own. Some of these were harmless—the encouragement of tourism and the building of the University City. Some were less innocuous. La Cierva was alarmed to hear, in an impromptu speech, a rousing royal appeal for reform 'with or without the constitution'. The idea of a royal dictatorship, backed by opinion disgusted at the ineptitudes of the politicians, was always at the back of his mind.[1]

On 23 September General Primo de Rivera pronounced in Barcelona. The government knew the army was unusable against generals and public opinion indifferent to the overthrow of the parliamentary system; it blamed its impotence on the king's acceptance of the old-fashioned device of the pronunciamiento as a legitimate instrument of political change. The politicians were never to forgive him for appointing Primo de Rivera as his prime minister while the success of the *coup* was still in doubt. Primo de Rivera, in turn, blamed them for lack of enough 'masculinity' to save Spain. He was successful because he caught parliamentary rule in its transition from oligarchy to democracy: the old political machine was broken, but the transition to the new political democracy envisaged by the advanced liberals had not conquered the indifference of the electorate. Not for the first nor for the last time, a general claimed that he was killing off a diseased body when he was, in fact, strangling a new birth.

[1] Alfonso consulted Maura in Aug. 1923. Though Maura thought the parties incapable of government, he believed that the crown could not risk dictatorship because there would be no way to return to normality (G. Maura, *Bosquejo histórico de la dictadura* (1925), 20–21). This was a remarkable prophecy.

XIII

THE PROTESTERS

1898–1923

'ALL is broken down in this wretched country: no government, no electors, no parties, no navy, no army. All is ruin, decadence.'[1] Written by an obscure secondary school teacher from Valladolid, this outburst of root-and-branch pessimism is typical of the flood of radical protest that the disaster of 1898 released. This protest was not *created* by the disaster. Discontent with the self-contained politics and the complacent social life of the Restoration was inveterate. There was no new birth, no new generation: the processes of criticism were merely accelerated and intensified. Ramón y Cajal was already a world-famous neurologist when, in the nineties, he made his plea for the opening up of Spain to foreign influences: Costa's vision of Spain 'wandering unburied amongst the tombs of extinct nationalities' went back to 1867; criticism of economic stagnation had long been a leitmotiv of protectionist propaganda and the literature of economic anxiety had flourished as a reaction to the agricultural crisis of the eighties.

The significance of 1898 lies less, therefore, in the creation of a specific protest than in the urgency and justification it gave to traditional protests. These protests came from those to whom the Restoration system was an evil in itself—the Republicans and the proletarian parties; from those who came to reject it once their efforts to make it respond to their purposes came to nothing—the Catalans; from those who regarded themselves, once their special interests were neglected, as a superior incorporation of the national will—the army; finally there were those who found official society and literature tasteless and degrad-

[1] R. Picavea Macias, *El problema nacional* (1899). This weak book, flawed by its insistence on the organic metaphor of a diseased body, acquired some notoriety. It is significant of the function of 1898, as a release of previously matured criticism, that Picavea confesses that he had contemplated writing his book for some time.

ing—the loose-knit group of intellectuals and artists known as the 'generation of '98'.

The aims of the protestors were often incompatible, and each protest was itself confused by differences within it of temperament and tactics. Thus the army was normally anti-Catalan and anti-Republican, the Catalan conservatives normally anti-Republican and always anti-Socialist. Republicanism could contain both an anti-militarist tradition, which was pro-Catalan, and men like Lerroux, the Radical Republican demagogue, who saw in the army a protector against 'reactionary' Catalanism and the final defence of the 'unity of the *patria*'. The Anarchists disowned all political alliances on principle, while the Socialists oscillated between a Republican alliance and the rejection of bourgeois politicians. The 'generation of '98' were intellectuals without fixed political alliances: they allied with all protests from Carlism to extreme Republicanism. Yet as we have seen, in the crisis of 1917 most of the protesters could sink their differences in a common action against 'what exists'. They failed because they lacked one of the traditional factors in the revolutionary equation: a general. When in 1923 a general, who believed in his star, was ready to stage a modernized edition of the pronunciamiento, the constitution could be overthrown without the alliance of the critics. They were presented with an authoritarian régime which, to most of them, was even more detestable than the 'old politics'. Generals remained the surest instrument of political change; as 1936 was to show, in the end it was officers who settled the political destinies of Spain.

Each of these protests had a long history by 1898 and all have entered into our account of the general history of Spain. In order to understand their action they must be analysed separately.[1]

1. *The Radical Protest: Joaquín Costa and the 'Generation of '98'*

We may take as the symbol of the radical regenerationism of the intellectuals its greatest figure, Joaquín Costa, the son of an Aragonese peasant. Embittered by years of hard struggle and a maimed physique, Costa was a social and legal historian

[1] The role of the proletarian parties is analysed on pp. 439–55 and 509–16.

of great distinction and even greater industry. He worked a seventeen-hour day and his works run into forty volumes. Intensely patriotic, he was obsessed by the quest for the historical roots of Spanish backwardness and it was the disaster of 1898 that gave to his harsh, long-meditated criticism, the note of urgency and an audience.

Costa's programme was noble but naïve. The existing system was bad; it was enough to destroy it and reverse all its assumptions. Spain must no longer be ruled by 'those who ought to be behind bars in Ceuta, in a lunatic asylum or on a school bench'. Who, then, should rule? The neutral masses whose qualification was that they had never exercised political power. Parliamentary government in the hands of the oligarchs—the term was popularized by Costa—had done nothing: a hundred and seventeen speeches on education in 1885 and no reform. Costa did not go as far as Picavea and abandon parliamentary government as the 'evil itself'; he contemplated its temporary replacement by a presidential régime, untrammelled by controls of a legislative, with a president who should combine the virtues of Gregory VII, Porfirio Díaz, the dictator of Mexico, and Hammurabi. An iron surgeon would operate on Spain to make her safe for parliamentary democracy, a task in which liberalism had lamentably failed. Indeed, its historic achievement, the sale of common lands—a half of the 'national' property of Spain squandered away at a tenth of its price—must be reversed; the municipalities must be empowered to set up a race of peasant proprietors by repurchasing the old common lands and setting up allotments.[1] This would be a return to the communal traditions of the Spanish past and to the work of the enlightened despotism of Charles III. The Caroline bureaucrats were Costa's heroes: patriotic men of vision, they had been defeated by petty local interests, just as his own campaigns for irrigation in Aragon had been defeated by the

[1] Cf. Costa's *La tierra y la cuestion social*, 53. His programme was a curious admixture of European remedies (e.g. the allotment system of England) and Spanish traditionalism. Costa collected every scrap of evidence for communal cultivation, every mention in the works of Vives, Mariana, &c., of the supposed 'traditional' view that large landowners could be expropriated if they did not fulfil a social function. Characteristically, when he was consulted by Dato on a modern system of social insurance, his reply was to give examples of medieval communal survivals which could serve as a basis for a system of old-age pensions.

local caciques whom he accused of perpetuating agrarian poverty in order to maintain their political influence over the poor.

Costa did not think a modern self-respecting state could be created by the mere aping of foreign techniques and ideologies, but rather that the patriotism of hard work must replace the rhetorical patriotism of lawyer politicians. In the February of 1899 the National League of Producers, under Costa's presidency, was formed with Paraiso, another reformer who represented the commercial bourgeoisie of the Chambers of Commerce.[1] The 'productive classes' were to be mobilized against the oligarchs in a crusade for the modernization of Spain. Money saved by cutting the navy, army, and civil service estimates should be spent on the encouragement of agriculture and industry; the abstractions of politicians must be replaced by a 'programme of realizations'—a modern, technical education, and agricultural reform.

Costa was doomed to failure because there was no new class to respond to his call. The neutral masses were no more than a powerful political myth: there were no reserves except those that were beginning to be mobilized by Socialists and Anarchists for very different purposes. Moreover, the regenerationist movement of Aragon dissolved into interest groups, each with its own remedy; thus Costa's farmers and Paraiso's Chambers of Commerce could only combine against high finance, the Bank of Spain, and the expense of the army. The National Union ended its career as the new middle-class party in a campaign against the new taxation of Villaverde's budget. What professed to be an independent, reformist, third party could be discredited as a selfish, shopkeepers' pressure group.

Costa remained a dark, brooding figure, a Goya of the economic and political world, reminding Spain that she 'lacks the aptitudes for modern life'. He could work successfully with no political party, once his plan of an independent third party had collapsed; he was 'the great failure', the man to whom politics in Spain had ceased to be an instrument for the betterment of society. Apart from his insistence on education his legacy has been one of inhibition as much as of stimulation, a criticism

[1] For its programme see M. Fernández Almagro, *Historia contemporánea*, ii, appendix no. 36.

that can be applied to many of the 'generation of '98'. By 1912 the 'incapacity' of Spaniards had attained the status of a topic in the conversations of youth, and like other 'topics'—Spanish extremism, individualism, and so on—substituted a generalized pessimism for constructive criticism.[1]

Unlike the Republican or the Catalan protests, that of the 'generation of '98' was without direct political significance, nor did it represent the grievances of a class or of an institution like the army. It was primarily the protest of a literary minority against the conformism, emptiness, rhetoric, and ignorance of the existing educational and literary establishment, which, in its turn, reflected the 'organized corruption' of the structure created by the Restoration statesmen.[2] The social and political overtones of the 'generation of '98' can easily be misunderstood: they were a group of individuals whose personal criticism cannot be subsumed in a movement with a programme; at their worst they were a 'rough, lazy, rebellious, ill-humoured group of bohemians', who resented the system which excluded them.[3] Without direct political influence, their importance lies in the tone they gave to the minds of a generation that came to the fore in the 1930's, and in their literary restatement of the problems of regeneration.

The difficulty with the much used concept of a 'generation of '98' is one of isolation and definition. Should it include the Catholic nationalist historian Menéndez y Pelayo, whose objections to the narrow-minded dogmatism of his predecessors may qualify him for membership? Should it contain Ramón y Cajal, whose accurate observation (he was an artist by training) mapped out the nervous system?[4] Should it extend back to

[1] 'La incapacidad de los españoles' (*España moderna*, xxiv (1912), 36).

[2] The phrase is Ortega y Gasset's (cf. *O.C.* i. 265 ff.). Spain, said Pío Baroja, gave itself to these men, not as a mistress to her lover, *sino como golfilla a su chulo*; cf. 'Azorín' in *Obras selectas*, 104–5. Unamuno was particularly violent in his criticism of his fellow professors; he regarded them as such 'asses' that they could not be trusted to run an autonomous university. Cf. Yvonne Turin, *Miguel de Unamuno, universitaire* (Paris, 1962), 29.

[3] Pío Baroja, *O.C.* v. 579.

[4] Ramón y Cajal's achievement was the greatest contribution made by a Spaniard to science and is the foundation of modern neurology. It is all the more astonishing in that Cajal worked in intellectual isolation and with limited scientific resources. In 1870, according to Cajal himself, no Spanish scientist could use a microscope. He would have been a bacteriologist but the necessary instruments were too expensive for Spanish laboratories.

Costa, an older man, and forward to Ortega y Gasset—both of whom exhibit ideas held to characterize the mental world of '98'? Perhaps it is most usefully confined to the group of creative writers born in the seventies, whose major works fall in the two decades after 1898.

In spite of the difficulties in defining the 'generation of '98' with exactitude, it remains true that the *concept* of such a generation has influenced subsequent thinking on the nature of the Spanish problem, that passionate process of self-examination that began as an intellectual pass-time with Angel Ganivet's essay on the nature of Spanishness.[1] The 'generation' subsumed a remarkable collection of strong, divergent personalities: Unamuno, violent, erratic, a professor of Greek who held that in Spain the true function of an academic was journalism rather than scholarship: a critic both of Spanish obscurantism and European progress, he was unable to resolve the conflicts between them; Valle Inclán, a Galician poet and writer, a fantastic bearded eccentric, and raconteur who flirted with Carlism; the novelist Pío Baroja, most talented writer of the group, but a natural intellectual anarchist who rejected all superiorities; Maeztu, an essayist, who, after preaching revival through imitation of the go-ahead money-making ethos of Basques and Anglo-Saxons, became an apologist of Primo de Rivera and a Catholic Fascist; the great poet of Castilian desolation, Machado; the painter of the uncorrupt 'people'—as opposed to the rotten governing class—Zuloaga. The often ill-digested influences to which this group was subject ranged from St. Teresa to Nietzsche and Shaw.[2] Any stick, from the thought of Europe to the example of Japan, was good enough to beat the values of the stuffy, decadent provincialism which so disgusted the young Pío Baroja in the cathedral city of Pamplona or the lecture halls of Madrid.

That the protest of '98 was not a purely literary movement is shown by its relations with modernism, which was. Both rejected the 'complacent' literature of the Restoration (indeed they neglected the cross currents of doubt it exhibited); but

[1] *Idearium español*, published in 1896.

[2] For the influence of Nietzsche see U. Rusher, *Nietzsche in der Hispania* (Bern, 1962). Nietzsche's 'aristocratic radicalism' influenced thinkers as distant from each other as Ortega and the C.N.T. leader Seguí.

whereas the modernists' protest was aesthetic (inspired by Rubén Darío, the Nicaraguan poet and closely linked to European literary movements), the protests of the men of '98 were ethical and social and derived from a contemplation of the Spanish past as well as of the European present.[1] The modernists created a minority, baroque language; the 'generation of '98' invented a clear, polemical style, stripped of adornment, which reached its culmination in the essays of Ortega y Gasset.

What, then, was the contribution of the 'generation of 1898' and of its immediate disciples? Like the men of the Enlightenment they were patriots distressed at the *atraso* (the backwardness) of Spain: the desolate poetry of Machado, the bitter criticism of Unamuno, Baroja, and the early Maeztu bear witness to their sombre concern for their country. Unlike the men of the Enlightenment they shared no common creed, no rational remedy for society. Hence their confusion when confronted by 'the inventory of all that was lacked'. Some, like Baroja, believed that the honest man in a corrupt society must be a hermit. In general the intellectuals—for by 1914 the men of '98 had become established reputations—proffered two contradictory solutions. Maeztu, in his early career, and Ortega y Gasset believed that only European influences could break down the inhibiting crust; Unamuno believed that to sacrifice Spanish values to 'japonization' would ruin all chance of a true revival. Few of them can be considered liberals in the ordinary sense of the term; their contempt for the society in which they lived was too violent.[2]

Indeed, their attitude to the liberal tradition in Spain was ambivalent. The cast of mind which was obsessed with *the* Spanish problem gave rise to a mode of analysis which was at the same time facile and inhibiting.[3] It was the pose of heroes

[1] For the relations of modernism to the 'generation of '98' see G. Díaz Plaja, *Modernismo frente a noventa y ocho* (1951). 'Clarín', the critic, opposed Rubén Darío's modernism as 'internal gallicism', while Maeztu and Baroja had little understanding of aesthetics—e.g. they 'neglected' Góngora (whose complicated poetry appealed to the modernists) while they made a hero of Larra because he was a social critic. Unamuno wrote in anarchist periodicals against 'art for art's sake'.

[2] Maeztu, in early life an enthusiastic Europeanizer, became a passionate defender of *hispanidad* and by 1936 was the only significant intellectual of the right. For his ideas see V. Marrero, *Maeztu* (1955).

[3] Cf. J. Marías, *Los españoles* (1962), 9. 'There was a sense, at the beginning of this century, in which the first problem for a Spaniard was none other than Spain itself.' What does this *mean*?

of the difficult, total solution for a diseased society. For this reason it is one of the psychological origins of the discredit of a parliamentary liberalism which could only offer piecemeal reforms, and of the popularity of 'iron surgery', of a radical operation on the body politic as the only salvation for Spain.

As was the case with their eighteenth-century prototypes, the patriotic intent of the intellectuals (which resulted, for instance, in a literary rediscovery of the Spanish landscape) was entirely disregarded by those to whom the only Spain was the Catholic Spain of the sixteenth century.[1] Thus the men of '98 were made to appear 'morbidly anti-Spanish', internationalists, and *afrancesados*.[2] To the right their inevitable progeny was Azaña, the prime minister who, having rebelled against the empty formality of a Catholic education, denied that Spain was Catholic.

Unamuno detested crude Catholicism just as he detested crude materialism and the philistinism of the upper classes.[3] Even the most enthusiastic Europeanizers always criticized the mere aping of foreign customs that had characterized the Progressives in the nineteenth century. The confident, imported positivism, which was the strongest current in the thought of the Restoration, repelled them.[4] European techniques must be fused with Spanish values. Bitter though their criticism of Spain was, they all held that there was some peculiar Spanish genius, still capable of great achievements, a genius embodied in the 'real' history of Spain and not in the 'surface' history of Restoration politics. Ortega, though he opposed Unamuno's 'Africanism', believed Spain must create, not merely absorb.

[1] The writers of '98 were the first Spaniards to experience the countryside as English writers have done, though it is significant that they always saw it as a symbol of Spain's problems, i.e. ethically rather than aesthetically. Thus they always saw the beauty of Spain against the ugly vulgarity of life in the official and artificial capital—Madrid.

[2] Unamuno was excepted from this judgement—although his religion was a highly personal affair, at times almost Protestant in feeling (cf. P. Laín Entralgo, *España*, ii. 110).

[3] Cf. his outburst in *La educación* (*Ensayos*, i. 334) and especially *Mi religión* (ibid. ii). He held the view that Spain was not truly Catholic (cf. Azaña), but that to 'get on' one had to pose as a Catholic.

[4] Cf. L. Alas, *Cuentos*, ed. J. Ma Martínez Cachero (1953). In *El cura de vericueto* (1896) he lampoons a medical student 'who thought himself a great positivist because he had read a translation of Spencer and French periodicals', and he denounced 'the great positivist wave, the swarm of *petits faits* according to Taine, predominating [in the University]' (*Un grabado* (1896), 105). The hero of this story is an eccentric widower who teaches that God the Father exists.

Partly because of internal schism, partly because of the indifference of Spain to intellectual issues, this intelligentsia had little influence on Spanish life until the dictatorship of Primo de Rivera.[1] When the dictator rejected the politicians he was led to attack the intellectuals; with all its faults, the liberalism they had decried as decadent at least allowed them to operate. Thus the opposition of the intellectuals—Unamuno and Ortega in particular—unexpectedly established them as the leaders of a political trend. The Republic of 1931 seemed born out of their protest. Yet the Republic itself revealed their incapacity to act in politics. Intellectuals could become civil servants in the eighteenth century; formed in the individualistic mould of '98 they could not become party men in the twentieth. By instinct and fastidiousness of mind, they rejected the politics of popular democracy and feared the rebellion of the masses. To Socialists they appeared as individualists, whose intellectual aestheticism removed them from practical politics.

2. *The Republicans*

The main stream of republicanism had always maintained that nothing but disaster would come from the constitutional monarchy of the Restoration: an absolute evil, it had been founded on force—the military rebellion of Sagunto. The year 1898 fulfilled this prophecy. For those who rejected *in toto* the régime which had brought national dishonour, there would be no other home but the Republic. Carlism was impossible, the workers' parties too weak.

Although the entry of independent regenerationists like Costa, and later Galdós, gave the party a new standing, the squabbles of Republican party politics prevented the exploitation of this opportunity. Intra-specific disputes weakened the species; the self-preservative instinct could produce only a series of electoral coalitions which fell apart once victory had been achieved. Doctrinal divergence and 'personalism' proved the law of bourgeois party life in Spain. The more to the left, the more fissiparous. As a party committed against 'what exists' it

[1] Ortega y Gasset complained of the smallness of the reading public and regarded the worship of Ramón y Cajal as a sacrifice to hide the general indifference to the intellect ('El poder social' in *O.C.* iii. 482 ff.; cf. the preface to the second edition of *España invertebrada*).

sought alliance with other enemies of the *turno pacífico*, some of whom, nevertheless, accepted the monarchy as such, but not its 'debased parliamentarianism'. Every such alliance, while it gave the party electoral strength, reinforced the tendency to divide: thus the two great political alliances of Republicanism, *Solidaridad Catalana* (1906) and the Republican–Socialist Conjunction of 1909, split the party. The first was regarded by the die-hards of the left as a coalition of the half-hearted with outright reactionaries; the second was regarded by the cautious as an imprudent and unprincipled tactical consortium with social revolutionaries. Republican newspapers, casinos, and centres changed hands between competing groups. The committee work behind these shifts of allegiance was the occupational disease of local Republican worthies.

The tripartite division of Republican forces in the nineties consecrated personal loyalty to the survivors of 1873 and was superimposed on the classic division between evolutionists and revolutionists.[1] In 1893, by means of blanket resolutions, the three groups formed a Republican front for electoral purposes, but this tenuous coalition of independent parties had collapsed by 1895, the year in which Ruiz Zorrilla returned to die in a Spain still ruled by a king. Ruiz Zorrilla was an eminent Victorian, austere and high-principled; though he never descended to the demagogic romanticism of Iberian revolutionaries he never succeeded in substituting for it a programme that would create a mass party. He offered to the worker the labour legislation of 'advanced capitalist countries', to the peasant the 'revolution' of cheap credit, French viticulture, German reafforestation, and English stock-rearing.[2]

The death of Pi in 1901 left Salmerón as the sole survivor of the great generation: an expert rigger of committees, congresses, and electoral deals, ambitious, but at heart a peaceful professor, he was ready to listen to the verbiage of revolution in order to gain the support of the violent men. Thus in 1903, backed by the revolutionary journalist Nakens, he emerged as leader of a unitary Republican party. The Republican Union scarcely survived the successes of the 1903 elections. With his

[1] For their division see above, pp. 360–1. Castelar's 'treason' left as competing groups Salmerón's Centralists, Ruiz Zorilla's Progressives, and Pi's Federalists.

[2] Gómez Chaix, *Ruiz Zorilla*, 168 ff.

leadership resting on the votes of obscure provincials, Salmerón thought to strengthen his position by the surprising step of joining *Solidaridad Catalana* in 1906.[1] This ended the unitary party. Lerroux, Sol y Ortega, the future reformists Azcárate and Melquíades Álvarez would not follow their leader into an 'unprincipled' alliance with conservative regionalism; neither the Block of the Left in 1908 nor the Republican–Socialist Conjunction of 1909, both formed on a negative platform of resistance to Maura's authoritarian conservatism, were the work of a united Republican party. The Republican strongholds of Barcelona, Madrid, and the Asturias were fiefs of local leaders, not constituent units of a national party. Hence the party's strength was evident in municipal rather than national politics.[2]

The electoral victory of 1903 alarmed the court into accepting Silvela's resignation and led Lerroux, one of the victors, to promise his followers that they would be eating their Christmas dinners in a Republic. Yet it came at a time when traditional republicanism, fed on the glories and disasters of 1873, was scarcely an attractive programme outside the traditional Republican urban strongholds. Salmerón's effortless ethical superiority belonged to the professors of '68 and, though it was a source of pride to his followers, it could make even fewer converts that Ruiz Zorilla's incorruptible revolutionary purpose. The future of republicanism was to lie in two diverging directions: on the one hand a revolutionary extremism, the vague social revolution of the *exaltado* tradition, and, on the other, the creation of an evolutionist party with a modern programme of social and political reform, a practical programme which would increasingly overshadow the formal question of the régime which was the heart of historic republicanism. The tradition of romantic revolution was exploited by men like Lerroux, son of an army veterinary surgeon who had made his name as a Republican journalist. The evolutionary tradition was represented by a group of university intellectuals in the Krausist traditions whose luminary was Azcárate.

[1] For the politics of *Solidaridad Catalana* see below, pp. 549–50.

[2] The Republicans' record was less impressive than the Socialists' as municipal reformers. Republicans tended to invent their own brand of caciquismo and there were constant accusations of pilfering, &c. Cf. E. Vaquero, *Del drama de Andalucía* (Córdoba, 1923), 129.

In spite of the Republican revival of the nineties, Lerroux realized that the old doctrines and leaders were exhausted and the party a collection of 'dry leaves at the mercy of circumstance'.[1] Without organization, without leadership, it could offer nothing to the masses except the incomprehensible polemics of political prima donnas. 'They [the old leadership] had compromised with every sort of social infamy. For this reason, the people, for so they call the wage earners without bread or education, have abandoned them.'[2] A demagogue, he offered the disappointed masses crude class-hatred and anti-clericalism, the permanent revolution of nihilism:

> Young barbarians of today, pillage the decadent civilization of this wretched country, destroy its temples, trample its gods under foot, tear aside the veils of novices and elevate them to the category of mothers . . . burst into the registries of property, make bonfires of their records so that the fires may purify an infamous society, enter the homes of the humble and raise legions of proletarians so that the world may tremble before its judges.

This revolution needed no programme, only recruits equipped with 'the daring of unreflecting youth, the virginity of adolescence, the cruelty of the child'. In 1936 this language was to resound once more in the streets of Spain. Like the Falange, Lerroux did not make a revolution; he bred a revolutionary atmosphere. The Tragic Week of 1909 is inexplicable unless we remember that the slum-dwellers of Barcelona had listened to this messiah for ten years.

The failure in Spanish politics of a man who, when caught drinking champagne, boasted that he was drinking today the drink the workers would drink tomorrow, was perhaps inevitable. Once his Radical Republicans controlled the municipality of Barcelona they became involved in a cement scandal. Since Republicans had protested against municipal corruption for a generation, this was particularly damaging. It led Galdós, titular head of the Republican–Socialist Conjunction, to prefer the 'sincerity' of the Socialists to large doses of bogus revolutionism. More fundamentally Lerroux and the Anarchist

[1] His rival for the leadership of what remained of Ruiz Zorilla's 'hosts' was Sol y Ortega, a respectable Barcelona lawyer who hoped to revive Republican spirits by a campaign of mass meetings.

[2] To Ferrer, 1 Dec. 1899, quoted S. Canals, *Los sucesos de 1909*, i. 46.

leaders were competing for the same public—the Barcelona proletariat. In this struggle the Anarchists, as a genuine revolutionary working-class party, presented Lerroux as a demagogue, who in 1909 spoke like a revolutionary but, when the revolution came, skipped the country, leaving his followers, who had waited in vain for his *mot d'ordre*, to prison and exile. 'I have never believed', wrote Pío Baroja, 'that the Republican party will make its revolution. I have never considered it an organ of progress and culture, nor have I been able to convince myself that its leaders are in any way superior to the monarchical caciques who are devouring Spain.'[1]

This brand of verbally violent republicanism found in Valencia a fitting figure-head in the novelist Blasco Ibañez, who once declared that the Browning automatic was the true security of individual rights.[2] It had a particular appeal in Andalusia, where memories of the Federal Republic fused with borrowings from Anarchists and Socialists. The vagueness of its programme allowed it to combine with the agrarian violence of 1902–4 and 1919–20, usually attributed solely to Anarchist influence. In 1919 the Republicans made remarkable gains in the Andalusian towns where militants, who were ready to play with a lunatic fringe of Andalusian separatists, planned for a Republic of the South.[3] The reading of the Republican militant presents the same hotch-potch as that of the *obrero consciente* of anarchism: Kropotkin, Marx, Henry George, popular science, Tolstoy, George Sand; the necessity of revolution was proved by examples from 'History, Geology, Astronomy and other sciences'.

What was best in historic republicanism scorned this primitive revolutionary rhetoric and followed the lead of Azcárate and Melquíades Álvarez into the Reformist Republican party, created as a separate grouping in 1912. The Reformist strength lay in the quality of its leadership; the party never gained

[1] Quoted D. Sevilla Andrés, *Canalejas*, 393. The article was written after the abortive mutiny in the coast-guard ship *Numancia*, the isolated act of deluded sailors.

[2] *D.S.C.*, 10 Feb. 1904, 3782. Blasco Ibañez's novels exposed social evils in Andalusia and Valencia. Of little importance in literature, his vigour gave him a large audience; he was the only modern Spanish novelist extensively read outside of Spain. He died in 1928.

[3] Vaquero, *Andalusia*, xvi. 95, 97.

more than twenty seats. It captured the allegiance of the new promotion of intellectuals: Ortega y Gasset—characteristically only for a short period—joined the party and the young Azaña stood as a Reformist candidate. The closest parallel in programme and temper to these reformers was the radical wing of the Liberal party which came to power in England in 1906. Their ideal, from first to last, was democratic parliamentary government *a la inglesa*—with or without a monarchy.[1]

The Reformist vision was a modernized Spain, tolerant, democratically ruled, with up-to-date educational and social legislation. The programme of 1912 and 1918 included agrarian reform and the setting up of homesteads on expropriated estates; in their educational policy the Reformists were as much concerned with modern technical education as with anti-clericalism.[2] Though Azcárate and Melquíades Álvarez rejected the class struggle as the basis of a political party, they were trusted by the Socialist leaders and their knowledge of working-class problems was profound. Azcárate had been a devoted president of the Institute of Social Reform, and the group was impressed by Bernstein's revisionism—again an indication of the predilection of the heirs of the Krausists for Anglo-Saxon practice rather than French theory. All their thinking ultimately derived from Krause's belief that ethics and politics were connected by law.

The Reformists were practical men in the tradition of Costa, and from the first 'they aspired to be a party of government'; their Fabian programme had little in common with the habitual catch-phrases of Republican revolutionism. Melquíades Álvarez believed that forms of government were less important than what governments did, though Azcárate remained until his death a Republican in the old sense. To Melquíades Álvárez republicanism became more a threat to force the monarchy along the paths of democracy and modernization than an end in itself. If the king recognized himself to be 'the slave of opinion', if he ruled through and by an honestly elected parlia-

[1] Azcárate was well informed on English politics and translated English works on Roman Law and Free Trade. For his ideas see J. B. Trend, *Modern Spain*, 169–91. His best book is a description of modern parliamentary government (*El Régimen parliamentario en la práctica*, ed. A. Posada, 1932).

[2] Nevertheless, revision of Article 11 was their main demand in the liberal alliance. See M. García Venero, *Melquíades Alvarez* (1954), 320–5.

ment, there was no harm in him. If he did not, then he would meet on his way the 'spectre of a Republic'. Like the reforming bureaucrats of the eighteenth century, they needed a Charles III, and perhaps they hoped to threaten Alfonso XIII into becoming 'the nerve of reform'. It was the unparliamentary rule of the war years that led them into the revolutionary coalition of 1917. In the 1920's they were ready to ally with monarchical Liberals in order to fight conservative reaction and militarism by pressing for 'responsibilities' and to preserve parliament itself as an instrument of reform and regeneration.[1] In the last government of parliamentary Spain they had a representative in the ministry, and Melquíades Álvarez was President of the Cortes. It was, perhaps, a slim hope, but it seemed the only alternative to the dictatorship of the army or, more remotely, of the proletariat.

Throughout its history republicanism constituted a threat to the monarchy neither through its strength as an organized party nor its danger as a revolutionary menace, but by its constant attacks on every failure, every defeat of the régime, from military disasters in Morocco to the peculations of a small-town mayor in Andalusia. Its political *raison d'être* was as a protest against the 'barbarities of the system'. Particularly in the towns, as the municipal elections of 1931 were to prove, the sustained propaganda of republicanism eroded the moral foundations of the monarchy. Azcárate's pessimism seemed justified.

> I believe that a kind of fatality prevents this dynasty from being able to solve the social and political problems which are arising at the present time; and as it is an illusion to think that any monarchy is possible in Spain except that of the Bourbons I consider that the only form of government likely to provide the solution is a Republic.[2]

3. *The Origins of the Catalan Protest*

The disaster of 1898 had its profoundest effects in Catalonia, where it turned Catalanism from a minority creed into the vehicle for a generalized protest. Catalanism, in the sense of

[1] M. García Venero, *Melquíades Alvarez*, 338, for a correction of the account Romanones gives of the Liberal–Reformist alliance.

[2] Quoted J. B. Trend, *Modern Spain*, 186–7, from Azcárate's *Minuta de un testamento*, published in 1876.

an explicit belief that Catalonia constituted a separate entity, either of race or of culture and tradition, demanding special treatment, rested on deeper foundations than linguistic revivalism; but, before 1898, it could be and was dismissed in Madrid as a fiction of Barcelona intellectuals or as the ideological superstructure of an industrial pressure group. In 1885 a *Memorial* presented by the industrial and professional classes of Catalonia raised no interest in Madrid; in 1901 Barcelona returned four Catalanist candidates against representatives of the national parties. Catalanism could no longer be neglected: it was to dominate and distort Spanish politics for the next half century.

To regard the growth of Catalanism as a process of conversion to a creed evolved by a minority of philologists, poets, and historians is to put the cart before the horse. If there was no force which reacted in unison—only gradually did the Carlism of the mountains come to terms with the liberalism of the cities of the plains—there was a recognizable complex of interests and emotions, discernible in every major political crisis since 1820, a complex which an earlier generation described with the colourless phrase 'the differential factor of Catalonia'. Its most obvious manifestation was the continued campaign for industrial protection.

Catalan industrialists had long been protectionists, but it was the revolutionary change to doctrinaire free trade in the budget of 1869—the handiwork of a Catalan, Figuerola—which brought them into a prolonged and bitter agitation. The demand for the restoration of protection became, in the seventies and eighties, the demand of all classes in Catalonia. Backed by the most powerful pressure group in modern Spain, the *Fomento del Trabajo Nacional*, the crusade was preached with all the moral overtones characteristic of the early free traders: Mañé, a conservative, saw free trade as a branch of the evil tree of liberal rationalism and political economy as a 'science divorced from God', while the bishop of Barcelona warned the Spanish Senate of the demoralizing effect which the unemployment that must accompany free trade would have on the workers.[1] Deputations were dispatched to argue with the economists of Madrid. The demand was so strong that it could not be neglected. In 1891 Cánovas abandoned free trade. From then

[1] J. Carrera Pujal, *Cataluña*, vi. 125–6, 140.

on it was the task of Catalan protectionists and their allies to maintain Cánovas's tariff against liberal after-thoughts and to press for tariff reform. In 1906 they triumphed with a tariff which even the militants considered 'little less than perfect'.[1]

This long struggle had created in Spanish minds the image of a Catalonia, egoistic and selfishly determined to press its case against every national interest. For Catalans 'neglect' turned a defence of interest into the awareness of a Catalan community that was attached, by the fortuitous processes of history, to 'something dead', and condemned to the calculated indifference of a 'Castilian' state as Catalans were wont to refer to the national government of Spain. This belief in the alien and uncomprehending hegemony of 'Castile', exercised at the expense of Catalan vitality, was and is the psychological root of Catalanism; to Catalans there was an element of pure contempt in Castilian attitudes which produced in Catalonia a sense of outraged virtue.[2]

To the end the culture of the Catalan language remained the living centre of Catalanism. Its heroes were poets, philologists, and historians.

A literary revival based on the Catalan language was possible because Catalan, unlike Basque, was flexible and could be used as the vehicle for modern life and culture. It was and is widely spoken in Catalonia. Its revival as a literary tongue, its elevation from popular speech to the status of a European language, is symbolically dated in Aribau's *Ode to the Fatherland*, written in Catalan (1833);[3] but the literary renaissance only got under way in the forties and its formal consecration came with the Floral Games, the annual poetic competitions in Catalan, inaugurated in 1859. By the 1870's it had produced in the priest Verdaguer a major poet, 'the Dante of Catalonia'. In Verdaguer the division between the stilted, archaic language of the *gai saber* of the revivalists and popular Catalan speech vanished; he was, to the poet

[1] M. Pugés, *Proteccionismo*, 305–6.

[2] It is probably true that a Catalan accent was less socially acceptable than an Andalusian lisp: the first represented the vulgarity of the merchant, the second was the careless speech the 'rural' aristocrat had picked up from his grooms and bailiffs.

[3] The arbitrary nature of this dating is shown by the fact that Aribau never wrote in Catalan again. He became an agent for Catalan business interests in Madrid.

Maragall, 'the master of us all . . . the poet who *created* our language'—a notable admission, for it was to this language that Catalanism owed its force.[1] Parallel with this literary renaissance went an historical revival dedicated to the reconstruction of the glories of the Catalan past; like the literary renaissance, it was part and parcel of European romanticism but inspired by Scott and the German Romantics, whereas Castilian romanticism flourished on imitation of French models. The scientific study of the archives of the Crown of Aragon portrayed institutions of medieval independence destroyed by Castile; scholarly erudition presented a version of Spanish history in which Catalonia and Castile represented distinct and competing national spirits.

The renaissance was the minority movement of a group of scholars and poets: the early generation had little faith in the viability of Catalan as a cultural instrument and wrote extensively in Spanish. These 'archaeologists' of the Floral Games were bitterly attacked in the sixties by those who were striving to create a popular vernacular theatre. It was this modest small-theatre movement and Clavé's working-class choirs which gave Catalanism its first real popularity in Democrat circles.[2] Nevertheless, the bourgeoisie, like the aristocracy and the working classes, was, for the most part, indifferent to the renaissance of Catalan culture and no Catalan daily attempted to support itself until 1879. It is, perhaps, a sign of this indifference that Catalonia left her greatest poet in poverty until consumption made his plight a public scandal. Later in the century so great a poet would have been secure in the patronage of prosperous Catalanist organizations.[3]

The literary revival in its early stages staked no claims that could not be reconciled with moderate regionalism and decentralization: it was supported in the seventies and eighties

[1] Cf. the verdict of Nicolau d'Olwer, 'with the verses of Verdaguer his generation *learnt* to read Catalan' (José Santaló, 'La vida política de Luis Nicolau d'Olwer, *C.A.* cxxvii (1963), 71).

[2] For a lively account of Soler and his friends and their connexion see C. Roure, *Vida larga*, ii. 47 ff. In a contemporary manuscript note in my copy of Roure is a statement that Soler's group became 'an association for mutual journalistic praise'. This was a tendency of many Catalanist groups, tending to limit their influence.

[3] Verdaguer was supported by the marqués de Comillas. He was a tortured personality and, as such, appallingly touchy in personal relations. For his history see J. Pabón, *El drama de mosén Jacinto* (Barcelona, 1954).

by conservatives like Mañé and Progressives like Balaguer. Lovers of Catalonia and her past, as influential politicians they nevertheless worked within the framework of the national parties for the special interests of Catalonia. Yet Catalanism could not remain the decorative appendage of moderate regionalism; it became the tool of radical nationalism. Hence moderate regionalism became treason to Catalonia; those who stuck to the old programmes were reviled as bad Catalans, as the allies of Madrid.[1] It is for this reason that the stubborn and consistent defence of Catalan interests and institutions by men like Mañé, the most influential journalist in Spain and a devoted local patriot, has been neglected as a factor in the growth of Catalanism.

The origins of political Catalanism have been tracked down by its historian, Rovira y Virgili, to the extreme poles of federal republicanism and Carlism.[2] This is misleading. Polar regions are unsuited to the support of large populations. If Catalanism had not spread to more temperate zones it would have remained a minority creed confronted with the task of re-awakening a people which had lost its sense of identity, a people which must be 're-catalanized'. What is true is that Catalanism always contained a right and a left. To the left, the spirit of Catalonia was one of progress and the positivism of a practical, forward-looking people; to the right, the piety and social stability of Catalonia was the last refuge against rationalistic, centralizing liberalism. It was the aim of Catalan politicians to combine these two traditions. This they never accomplished.

On the right, residual Carlism apart, there was always a sense in which Catalanism, like other forms of regionalism, was anti-liberal. The Liberals, as heirs of the Bourbon centralizers who had plunged Catalonia into 'the long winter' by destroying her peculiar political institutions, had divided historic Catalonia into four 'artificial' provinces; it was the electoral

[1] Thus Sala, the deputy for Tarrasa, was in from 1906 to 1910 bitterly attacked as a traitor to Catalonia. As early as 1888 Sala had seen that historical revivalism and sentimentality about lost provincial rights was irrelevant to the 'realistic' demands of moderate regionalism and must propel it past its target. 'I believe that the centuries have not passed in vain and that the social, economic and political condition of Catalonia has changed too radically to be treated by the application of the institutions of the fifteenth century.' A. Joaniqet, *Alfonso Sala Argemí* (1955), 90. This long-winded work must be read as a corrective to Catalan or Castilian views.

[2] A. Rovira y Virgili, *El nacionalismo catalan* (Barcelona, 1917), 123 ff.

machinery of 'liberal' parliamentarianism, as run by the national parties, which 'blanketed' Catalan demands; it was distaste for liberalism, as much as love of Catalonia, that flung the influence of the Church in Catalonia behind some of the Catalanist demands. The see of Vich became a centre of diffusion of Catalan culture; Morgades, restorer of Catalan monasteries and advocate of Catalan in the pulpit, was succeeded as bishop by Torres y Bages, one of the most widely read theorists of regionalism.[1] As a Thomist he defined Catalonia as a 'true entity, capable of its own life . . . *indivisum in se et divisum ab aliis*'; he posited a national school of thought, a national style evident in every activity from philosophy and poetry to architecture. Like many other early Catalanists, he recognized that this informing spirit must be re-awakened; but, once awake, it could not be denied a right to live. This spirit was conservative. Thus the region would be a vehicle to preserve social patterns and a religious spirit threatened by the urban civilization of sensual man. Christ was the Orpheus of the Catalan nation and only Christ could restore her.

On the left, federal republicanism undoubtedly gave Catalanism a possible structure. But, in the hands of theorists like Pi y Margall, it could not come to terms with the emotional content of an historically tinged regionalism. Though Pi himself, as an Catalan, felt the pull of local interests, Catalonia *as such* had no special place in Federalist theory: it was but one province in an all-federalist Spain, a logical deduction from the premisses of individualism, not from those of culture, language, or race.

The great figure of Catalanism was Pi's disciple, Almirall, as emotional and full-blooded a character as Pi was austere and reticent. In 1881 he finally broke his uneasy relations with the master. Federalism could not accommodate the 'fact' of Catalan particularism: a defined and self-sufficient body demanded specific treatment rather than a place in a general scheme. Moreover, federalism was 'prostituted' by its association with the violence and failures of '73: it would cut off Catalanism from any hope of bourgeois and peasant support.[2] 'We must

[1] In *La tradiciu catalana* published in 1893.

[2] Almirall's *Lo catalanisme* (1886) was the original bible of Catalanism. Almirall's realistic criticism of Catalan failings, his lack of sentimental idolatry for everything Catalan, cut him off from the pure literary nationalists.

have as our only banner love of Catalonia' and behind this banner all Catalans should rally whatever their political beliefs. In 1879 he founded the *Diari Catalá* in an attempt to popularize Catalanism against the literary exclusiveness of the 'Holy Brotherhood of the Floral Games'. In 1880 he organized the Catalan Congresses and in 1882 the Catalan Centre, in order to separate all Catalan parties from their connexions with the parties of Madrid. In 1885 he co-operated with every shade of Catalan opinion in the *Memorial* to the king. Almirall's great Catalan party was a failure and he was the first Catalan politician to experience the difficulties of running right and left in joint harness. Nevertheless he built the framework of Catalanism, endowing it with a doctrine, a tactic, and its characteristic anti-Castilian flavour: the positive and energetic Basque–Catalan–Iberian stock was held in slavery by Arab dreamers, the magnificent and ruthless system of the makers of Castile; the mark of their slavery was that they were governed in an alien tongue.

Conservative though it was in tone, the *Memorial to Alfonso XII* (1885) contained Almirall's doctrines still decently clothed in regionalist phraseology. It therefore constitutes an important step forward in the history of Catalanism. The vital forces (*fuerzas vivas*) of Catalonia—industrialists, agriculturists, and academics—spoke with one voice to defend Catalan demands in the name of a Catalan personality with moral as well as material interests. The intense local patriotism of regionalism, though many of its supporters failed to realize it, was moving towards a still diluted yet recognizable form of nationalism.

First, there is the assumption that Spain is a decadent state, run, under the appearance of parliamentary constitutionalism, by the professional politicians of Madrid in their own interests.[1] Secondly, Catalonia is a 'people', 'group', 'region', or 'race' (the radical word 'nation' is avoided), with its own language, culture, and institutions, its proper 'personality', the creation of a separate historical existence before union with Castile. This personality is 'positive and analytical, rooted in liberty', in contrast with the abstract genius of Castile with its 'mania for predominance'. Thirdly, the absorption of the various peoples of Spain by a centralizing monarchy and by liberals obsessed

[1] *Memoria*, 26–27, 64, 118.

with French precedent is responsible for the decline of Spanish vigour. It thus follows that the path of regeneration for Spain itself must be sought by reviving and protecting the remnants of a regionalist vitality.[1] Castile was the victim of her own violent courses which enervated her along with the regions she suppressed: the defence of protection was an argument derived from the economic weakness of Spain as a whole, for which the Castilian mania for uniformity was responsible. Catalan civil law, on the other hand, is defended simply because it is Catalan, 'the child of autonomy in the epochs when we were not dependent on Castile'. Its ethical basis was liberty: it was the testamentary freedom allowed by Catalan law which had produced an independent race of small farmers, the stable Catalan family, where the land was handed over to a single responsible head, the *hereu*.[2] With what right did liberal lawyers seek to subordinate this law to the norms of Castilian law which, like Catalan law, was the native law of but one of the peninsular peoples? Strength would come not from a 'dead unity' but from the competition of harmonious variety. In order to justify Catalan claims regionalists had invented the fiction of a Castilian 'nationalism', of a dominant master race. Yet all that existed was a unitary Spanish state. Who were Castilians other than those Spaniards who served it?

The ill-defined regionalism of the *Memorial* contained no claim for political autonomy.[3] It was the lowest common factor of political Catalanism; and it is the development of what the *Memorial* cautiously called 'the transcendental aims no longer contained in literary and artistic limits' which constitutes the next step forward. By 1888 the literary nationalists of the *Lliga de Catalunya* were demanding a Catalan parliament.[4]

The danger of this more radical nationalism was that it

[1] There is a strong streak of Francophobia in the *Memorial*. Centralizing uniformity on the French pattern had no future, as the defeat of 1870 and the prosperity of England under local self-government showed (op. cit. 93). The defence of Catalan law was deeply influenced by Savigny and the German historical school.

[2] Op. cit. 177, 179.

[3] Though the Memorialists did not claim political autonomy, their view that the future of Catalan law would depend on the existence of a body capable of changing it implied some sort of Catalan legislative or supreme court.

[4] This Lliga, to be distinguished from Prat's later organization, was a minority group of littérateurs who seceded from Almirall's Catalan Centre (see p. 544).

would convert Catalanism into a minority movement of intellectuals. It was to avoid this peril that a young man in his twenties, Prat de la Riba, revived Almirall's concept of an all-Catalan party; but this reconstruction was to come from the conservative right, which alone could hope to force from the politicians of Restoration Spain a fair deal for Catalonia; no sympathy for left-wing, quasi-Republican nationalism could be expected from the Cortes.

If Prat, as a social and political conservative, was convinced that the settlement of Catalan claims must be made with the consent of monarchical Spain and not imposed by separatist revolution against her, he nevertheless transposed the language of regionalism into that of nationalism. It was the 'strident tones', in Cambó's phrase, of this new nationalism set forth in his *Catechism* (1894) which made it increasingly difficult for Spaniards to believe that Catalan claims could be reconciled with the continued existence of Spain as a unitary nation state. To Prat, Catalonia was the natural unit, the *patria* which claimed the deepest loyalty of all Catalans; beside the *patria*, the Spanish state was an artificial structure—'one of the great mechanical units formed by violence'—holding Catalonia in a slavery which Prat and his followers were ready to equate with the dominion of the Turks over the Greeks. *Question*: 'What is the enemy of the Catalan *patria* which has perverted its growth?' *Answer*: 'The Spanish state.'[1] Prat repeatedly rejected any charge of separatism: 'age-old living together had created bonds with the larger unit of Spain which could not be broken'. Yet these bonds must be weak enough to allow 'a Catalan state in federative union with the other *nations* of Spain'. Catalonia's imperial mission (imperialism was the inevitable and legitimate activity of a superior culture) was to bring the other nations of Spain to self-realization within an Iberian federation.

His programme, shorn of its more obvious exaggerations, was set forth in the Bases of Manresa, which, with modifications and refinements, remained the essential programme of Catalanism until its triumph in the days of the Second Republic.[2]

[1] Prat's theoretical work *La nacionalitat catalana*, written in 1906, was translated by a critic of Catalan nationalism in 1917. The *Catechism* is alleged to have sold a hundred thousand copies in Catalonia.

[2] The Bases are printed in M. García Venero, *Historia del nacionalismo catalán, 1793–1936* (1944).

The Bases demanded Home Rule for Catalonia as an autonomous region within the Spanish state, its domestic concerns controlled by a Catalan parliament elected on a corporate franchise, with Catalan as its official language and with all posts reserved to born or naturalized Catalans. The Catalan parliament would control the police and would be the supreme legislative authority in civil and criminal law. Catalonia would have its own supreme tribunal and a fixed contingent of recruits to the Spanish army to be raised on a voluntary basis. Prat's aim was to unite all organizations in Catalonia behind the Manresa programme and, by taking the movement out of the hands of Barcelona intellectuals, to win over the conservative countryside. For this reason the congresses of Prat's organization, the Catalan Union, were held in provincial towns. In the congress of 1893 it was decided to enter the corrupt world of Spanish politics, to end the era of protests and memorials and start the organization of a political party to fight for Catalan rights.

4. *The Catalan Protest, 1898–1919, and Basque Nationalism*

Catalanism now had an organization and a creed. The disaster of 1898 gave it the first real opportunity for a mass following among the middle classes. The image of a moribund Castilian state which, after conscripting her youth had lost Catalonia her best market, allowed Catalanism to become part of the general forces of regeneration and an electorally effective force. It could therefore implement the tactical doctrine of Manresa; it could enter Spanish politics and, given the regionalist sympathies of conservative regenerationists, this entry could be effected via the Conservative party. In 1899 the Silvela–Polavieja ministry included a Catalan: the regionalist, Durán y Bas, defender of Catalan law; and Dr. Robert, a distinguished physician appointed by the government as mayor of Barcelona.

This alliance soon broke down.[1] As always, the attempt to settle the Catalan problem 'within Spain', by bidding for conservative support in Madrid, alienated the left wing groups in Catalonia. They boycotted any co-operation with Polavieja,

[1] For the collapse of Catalan co-operation and the resignation of Durán y Bas and Dr. Robert see above, pp. 478, 480.

whom they saw as a clericalist reactionary. It was the disillusioned right-wing supporters of Polavieja who, in 1901, drew together and, to their surprise, gained a striking electoral victory: the four Catalanist candidates defeated both Lerroux's Radical Republicans and the old parties. This victorious electoral combination was transformed into the *Lliga Regionalista*, the most effective political force Catalanism was to create before 1930–1. With the traditional parties out of the battle, the electoral politics of Barcelona were to be contained in the struggle between the Lliga and Lerroux's radical Republicans, a struggle which constantly reopened the fissure between the Catalanist right and left. If the Lliga remained an alliance dominated by the right, then Lerroux's diatribes would attract the left: if it became quasi-Republican in tone, it would lose the conservative regionalists.

It was an autocratic concern, run in Catalonia by Prat and his friends, with Cambó as their representative in national politics. Cambó, whose energy and ability was to make him a millionaire, was a born statesman who resented the fact that his career as 'a man of government' was thwarted by the indifference of Madrid politicians to the Catalan issue.[1] Both Prat and Cambó were pragmatists who wished to replace the extremism of nationalist nostalgia—the poets, Cambó said, exaggerated the exaggerations of historians—by a concrete, clearly defined programme of regional autonomy, which they could hope to achieve by the day-to-day task of propaganda and political activity. In their hands, the Lliga became a rich and highly organized pressure group with canvassers and card indexes. It organized propaganda tours in which its luminaries sought to establish relations with Basque nationalism and to win sympathy for the regionalist case throughout Spain. It became an organizing force of the cultural life of Catalonia. More than anything else, it was the splendid efforts of the Lliga and other private organizations, as patrons of the intellectual life of Catalonia, as founders of institutes, chairs, and libraries devoted to the Catalan language, which gave Catalans the sense of the renewed vitality of Catalonia in the 'desert' state where Catalan culture was cold-shouldered.

To the Catalan left the Lliga was doubly suspect: it was a

[1] For Cambó see pp. 434–5.

conservative affair run by millionaires unlikely to compete effectively against Lerroux, who could slate it as an 'Irish' clerical party; it was an organization of practical men, concerned with results. Its leaders were ready to sacrifice nationalist purity to the *realpolitik* of engineering autonomy by negotiation in Madrid.

The prospect of such a negotiated settlement was opened up in 1903 by the accession to power of Maura, a Conservative whose interest in local government reform might be expanded to satisfy the minimum demands of Catalonia. In the face of the total hostility of the Republican municipality, which refused to decorate the streets, and the icy indifference of the Lliga, Maura persuaded the king to visit Barcelona (April 1904). The visit was a popular success—in part through the efforts of the marqués de Comillas who lined the streets with a monarchist claque. Confronted with this enthusiasm, the Lliga changed course and petitioned the king for regionalist autonomy. But the action which opened up the prospect of an understanding between Barcelona and Madrid, between Maura and Cambó, split the Lliga; the implicit recognition of the monarchy drove the left of the Lliga to organize a separate party which was Republican and hostile to any compromise settlement engineered between Cambó and Maura.[1] Catalanism split into a practical right and a doctrinaire, nationalist left. Thus weakened, it was beaten badly by Lerroux in the elections of September. Nevertheless, in 1906, differences of right and left were glossed over once more in *Solidaridad Catalana*, the most powerful and all-embracing concentration of forces Catalonia had seen.

The experience of Solidaridad Catalana was to prove once more that Catalanism could only become politically effective as part of a generalized protest. In 1905 the weakness of Liberal governments provided such an opportunity: in the November of that year the officers of the Barcelona garrison, conceiving themselves to be insulted by a mild cartoon in a Catalan paper, assaulted its offices. The Liberal government not merely refrained from punishing the officers but gave in to the army's demand that press attacks on the honour of the army be tried by mili-

[1] The left-wing organization was called 'The Nationalist Republican Centre'. Its luminaries were Suñol and Jaime Carner. Cf. J. Pabón, *Cambó*, 240–53.

tary courts; the Law of Jurisdictions appeared to assuage the ruffled dignity of the army at the expense of liberty in general and Catalan liberty in particular. The response was a Catalan electoral coalition in defence of constitutional liberty, which extended from Salmerón's hitherto orthodox anti-Catalan Republicans to near-Carlists.[1] The organizing centre of Solidaridad was the Lliga, and it adopted as its programme a weakened version of the Manresa autonomy resolutions. With Lerroux's Radicals as the only considerable force in local political life outside it, and with the dynastic parties, as the Civil Governor confessed, 'a nullity', it carried 41 of the 44 Catalan seats in the elections of April 1907. The 'live forces' of Catalonia had triumphed over caciquismo in a contest which seemed to mark 'a step towards the political Europeanization of Spain'.[2] With a block of Catalan deputies in the Cortes, and with Maura in power, Cambó had high hopes of a settlement which would satisfy the minimum demands of Catalonia. As the organizer of Catalanism he could hope to keep Catalanism 'essentially conservative'.[3]

These hopes concealed a misunderstanding, both with Maura and with the left wing of Solidaridad. Maura believed that some form of administrative decentralization might purify and revive political life; consequently he approached the Catalan question as a problem in local government. Cambó, for all his 'realism' and his insistence on a solution 'within Spain', regarded some form of autonomy as the legitimate recognition of a 'personality', of a distinctive people whose claims stood outside and above the desirability of administrative devolution. Catalonia therefore found in Maura, not a Gladstone and emotional sympathy for a special case, but a Chamberlain and a very circumscribed Home Rule all round. For such small rewards Cambó could not hope to keep the Catalan left and its republican allies from

[1] Solidaridad was made possible by Salmerón's sudden and quite unexpected offer of an alliance to the Catalans in the debate on the suspension of the Constitutional Guarantees in Catalonia (Nov. 1905). Cambó immediately saw the possibilities of the offer for Catalanism: 'Accept immediately with your eyes closed.' J. Pla, *Cambó* (Barcelona, 1928), ii. 139 ff. Solidaridad was formed in Feb. 1906.

[2] The verdict of Adolfo Posada in *Régimen local*, preface, xxix.

[3] Ossorio y Gallardo, who as Civil Governor had observed Cambó's talents as the organizer of the victory of Solidaridad, had no doubts about Cambó's conservatism and was one of the first to encourage co-operation with Maura. J. Pabón, *Cambó*, 175–6.

attacking the conservative features of Maura's local government law—especially its corporative 'anti-democratic' franchise. Catalanism once more divided into a right and a left, into 'realists' and 'all or nothing' nationalists.[1] To the delight of the anti-Catalans, Solidaridad was proving to be a fortuitous and fragile electoral pact rather than the 'movement of a people in sacred unity', and so, with the breakdown of co-operation between Maura and Cambó in 1907, the second intervention of Catalanism in Spanish politics ended in disaster. In 1908 Solidaridad was defeated by the Radical Republicans of Lerroux at the polls and the whole of Cambó's and Maura's policy rejected by the Catalan electorate.[2]

It was now that left-wing Catalanism missed its opportunity, failing in its endeavour to build up a petty bourgeois nationalist party, strong against both Lerroux and the magnates of the Lliga. Its messiah, Corominas, whose vague violence and half-digested knowledge was considered a suitable weapon against Radical Republican demagogues, made what was to enthusiastic Catalanists an unpardonable tactical error in allying with Lerroux—the former arch-enemy of Catalonia.[3] Thus in 1911 the Lliga appeared once more as the only effective instrument of Catalanism.

It was under the Lliga, therefore, that Catalonia won its only substantial victory: the concession of the *Mancomunidad*. This was the culmination of the Lliga's modest endeavours to gain power in local government as a first step on the way to autonomy. Prat had become president of the Barcelona Pro-

[1] Suñol, the over-sensitive leader of the left, was ready to reject Maura's projected local government law out of hand. 'It was better to solve nothing at all than solve anything badly.' This would have meant the end of any possibility of getting advantages for Catalonia from Maura's project. Cambó hoped to amend it. 'If we reject the project we lose the opportunity of accomplishing part of our aspirations, and who knows when the opportunity will recur' (A. Rovira y Virgili, *Nacionalismo*, 164).

[2] See Tato y Amat, M., *Sol y Ortega la política contemporánea* (1914), 397–9. Many Republicans regarded Salmerón's alliance with Solidaridad as an incomprehensible disaster and could not understand co-operation with the 'historical survivals and the petty interests' which it had been the mission of liberalism to destroy.

[3] Corominas's party, the *Unió Federalista Nacionalista Republicana*, existed from 1910 to 1914. Its name indicates its divergence from the Lliga, which was never Republican and never called itself a nationalist party. The *U.F.N.R.* was succeeded by various collections of left-wing nationalists of Republican views, none of whom made any great impression on the electorate.

vincial Deputation in 1907, and he and his allies in municipal government had used their influence in local government affairs to further the cause of Catalan culture and the interests of Catalanists—so much so that Lerroux raised the alarm against a new brand of Catalanist caciquismo. The Lliga proposed to concentrate this strength by the creation of a Mancomunidad which should amalgamate the four Catalan Provincial Deputations for certain of their functions. This demand was successful, because, in creating a feeble reflection of the old historic province, it did not take any powers from the central state that had not already been granted to the Provincial Deputations; it therefore avoided oratorical debates on the principle of sovereignty and threats to national unity. It could be supported by Catalans like Sala, who could never accept the transformation of regionalism into nationalism, and by politicians like Canalejas and Dato who were anxious for any solution which would clear the Catalan question out of the way.[1]

The Mancomunidad devoted much of its energy to 'modernizing' Catalonia by technical education and an ambitious road and telephone system. Prat, as its first president, pushed its powers to the maximum. In 1917 he died, and his successor, a less energetic man, was Puig i Cadalfach, an art historian and archaeologist, who, like so many Catalanist politicians, had come into politics from the task of re-creating historic Catalonia. This task of cultural 'renationalization'—to use the phrase of Rovira y Virgili—was still central to Catalanism and the Mancomunidad was its greatest instrument.[2]

The Mancomunidad fell far short of autonomy; once the Lliga sought to expand its functions towards autonomy by claiming the delegation of powers hitherto belonging to the state, the old sterile discussions of sovereignty prevented any progress. Cambó's earnest endeavours to present his campaign for autonomy as part of the vision of a Great Spain, based on vigo-

[1] Even so the Mancomunidad was held up by the Senate: it was therefore granted, not as a law, but as a Royal Decree in Dec. 1913.

[2] For the work of the Mancomunidad see *L'obra realitzada Anys*, 1914–23 (Barcelona, 1923). It was the patron of the Institute of Catalan Studies, the centre of Catalanist philological and historical research. It financed museums, libraries, summer schools, lectures (the list on p. 61 indicates the cultural obsessions of Catalanists), agricultural, and technical schools. These activities, together with expensive public works, forced the Mancomunidad to raise loans, the existence of which were proof, to anti-Catalans, of the 'governmental incapacity' of Catalans.

rous regional governments, could not disarm suspicion. Mass meetings and plebiscites built up the demand in Catalonia, but no compromise could be found in Madrid between decentralization, which preserved the nation-state and autonomy which would 'tear the nation into tatters'. By 1919 the Lliga, which had promised autonomy by peaceful methods, was losing ground: the moderates' failure to achieve results always strengthened the radical nationalists of the left who accepted separatism as the logical result of defeat by the master race.[1]

The failure of the Lliga to find its solution 'within Spain' illustrates the fate of constitutional Home Rule movements, driven to revolutionary alliances in order to press their demands on an indifferent central government. Like Parnell, Cambó was a politician who faced two ways: a social conservative who played with revolutionary threats but detested revolution. In 1906 and 1917 he allied with a revolutionary atmosphere in the hopes of forcing concessions for Catalonia; in retrospect he realized that this alliance accomplished nothing beyond making him suspect in Madrid and Barcelona alike. The moment he dropped threats for co-operation he was accused of treason in Barcelona, while even sympathetic politicians in the Cortes resented the Catalan attitude of 'concession or else'. The language Catalan politicians would tolerate in Barcelona, when contrasted with their studied moderation in Madrid, gave rise to the classical accusation of double languages, one for the left and the other for the right bank of the Ebro.[2] Nor could Spanish politicians understand the extreme tactical nonchalance of Catalan politicians in their dealings with the party system and in their alliance with revolutionary threats to the monarchy. Catalanists did not care which party or combination of parties granted Catalan autonomy, nor, if the parliamentary monarchy refused to meet their demands, were they unwilling to seek allies outside it and against it.[3]

Hence the delight defenders of national unity found in exposing, as a political fraud, Prat and Cambó's campaign for harmonizing Catalan demands and Spanish interests within a

[1] Cf. A. Rovira y Virgili, *Nacionalismo*, 281.

[2] Cf. Joan Estelrich's remarks about sincerity in *Al servei dels ideals* (Barcelona, 1934), 14.

[3] It must be remembered that the autocratic permanent political committee of the Lliga could make any alliance it chose.

Great Spain revived by regionalism. Even Catalan politicians realized that, apart from the Basques and to a much smaller extent the Galicians, no region outside Catalonia possessed what they called 'personality'. Spanish politicians dismissed Great Spain at best as a stubborn defence of Catalan interests and Catalan profits, at worst as concealed separatism. No doubt Catalans did believe that inept 'Castilian' politicians were ruining their peculiar contribution to a prosperous, progressive *national* economy by demanding a profits tax on war industries, a demand which Cambó resisted. Yet, as in the protectionist struggle, the appeal to a national interest seemed to hide a demand that Spain should foot the bill for the continued prosperity of Catalonia. Cambó's argument, that the necessity of the Spanish market for Catalan products forbade separatism, was turned by anti-Catalans into the assertion that only economic interest kept Catalonia loyal to Spain, or into a belief that Home Rule could be killed by economic kindness. Unamuno could taunt a nation which, he held, was prepared to sell its soul for a tariff.

Nothing can hide the fact that moderate Catalanism failed because it never represented the masses in Catalonia: the emphasis on Catalan language and culture made its programme literally incomprehensible to large sections of the non-Catalan-speaking working classes. If the Bases of Manresa had triumphed, a large proportion of the population would not have been able to speak the language of state. This alienation drove moderate Catalanism into alliance with 'revolutionary' forces represented by the sedate republicanism of Salmerón; yet, as the collapse of Solidaridad proved, such an alliance could only be a temporary device for conservatives. Once the 'revolutionary' coalition of 1906 disintegrated, the voting strength of the Radical Republicans ruined the Lliga's programme of a settlement, relatively moderate, negotiated with Spain and functioning within the constitutional monarchy.

When it failed to produce any results from its solution 'within Spain' and without attacking the monarchy, Catalanists argued that the natural ally of Catalanism was republicanism and that the Lliga's conservatism was a disability not outweighed by its wealth and organizational strength. In 1917, with the Assembly Movement, it entered a 'revolutionary' alliance for the last time in order to secure Catalan autonomy.[1] Cambó then behaved as a bourgeois politician, deserted the alliance and allowed members of the Lliga to enter the government. Later, the violent social struggle in Barcelona convinced the *prohombres* of the Lliga that the police and army of the hated central state might have their uses against revolutionary syndicalism.

To Catalan nationalists the Lliga thus became 'an appendix of monarchical conservatism', and its insistence on a solution 'within Spain' seemed a permanent denial of the rights of Catalonia, while its business-men's conservatism held little appeal for the Barcelona middle classes or the tenant farmers of the countryside. Catalanism, therefore, turned to the left. The *rapprochement* of Catalanism and republicanism was the work of *Acció Catala* (1922), which laid the foundations for an understanding with republicanism that was to give Catalonia victory in 1931.[2] Cambó was still the most powerful man in Catalonia, but the emotional leader of Catalan nationalism was Maciá, who came to believe that Cambó's policy of winning 'practical' concessions would be barren and that Catalonia would have to fight for her recognition as a free Republic within a Federal Republican Spain.[3] He rejected the Lliga's monarchism, its moderation, and its ambivalent nationalism. For Maciá autonomy was not enough. He demanded separate representation for Catalonia at the Peace Conference of 1919.

An army officer who had sacrificed his career to Catalanism, resigning his seat in the Cortes in protest against the 'frivolous futility' of Spain where Catalonia was concerned, Maciá possessed the austerity and personal simplicity of a nationalist hero—a role which Cambó would have despised because he believed effective power lay with governments, not with ideals. Simplicity in politics means violence, and it was violence which this quiet man brought to Catalan youth and to Catalan intellectuals weary of the realism of the Lliga. It was the alarm inspired by the separatist violence of the younger Catalan

[1] For the Assembly Movement see above, pp. 503–5.

[2] One of the members of *Acció Catala* was to become a minister of the Second Republic—Nicolau d'Olwer. The Republican parties still kept their separate identities and many Catalanists never overcame their invincible repugnance to Lerroux.

[3] For the hagiography of Maciá see J. Aynami, *Maciá* (Barcelona, 1933).

nationalists that turned the older politicians of the Lliga into reluctant backers of an army *coup* in 1923. They paid for this folly with the electoral defeat of the Lliga in 1931. Catalanism had finally deserted its conservative origins and flowed into the rising torrents of the left.

This movement to the left was an impossibility for Basque nationalism, the second of the Home Rule movements of the later nineteenth century. Beside Catalan nationalism it appeared an archaic concern, 'savage' and primitive, while Catalan nationalism could attract the best in Catalan life.[1] As late as 1923 it had produced no literature even remotely comparable with that of the Catalan Renaissance; its cultural achievements remained at the level of ballads and folk-lore. The Basque tongue was rejected as a literary instrument by the greatest Basque writers—Maeztu, Baroja, and Unamuno. Moreover it was steadily on the retreat before Castilian, especially among the middle classes, and it was a sense of diminishing assets that drove Basque nationalism to the extremes of what Unamuno called 'absurd racial virginity'.[2]

Paradoxically it was the firmness of its institutional foundations which limited the scope of Basque nationalism. The Basques had lost what they called their 'medieval' political liberties as late as 1839, whereas Catalan liberties were a more obvious creation of historical scholarship. Thus whereas Catalan regionalism could become a form of nationalism, expansive and modern in tone, the Basques were committed to reclaiming the 'oldest liberties in the western world'—the antique foral institutions.

By siding with political reaction in the Carlist war of 1833–9 the Basques had prejudiced their claims to the *fueros*: centralization was not merely a dogma of victorious liberalism but a

[1] For an attack on Basque culture and linguistic claims see S. de Madariaga, *Spain* (1942), 176 ff. The language held its own only in Guipúzcoa (with the exception of San Sebastián). If Basque is a remnant of a language once common to all Iberia, surviving only in provinces which had not been Romanized, then Madariaga holds that it cannot provide a linguistic basis for Basque Home Rule. He sees the Basques as representatives, not of a distinctive and definable civilization, but of the 'dispersive tendency' characteristic of all Spaniards.

[2] For Unamuno's views see his *Ensayos*, iii. 104 ff. and vi. 142 ff. Unamuno's views on the inevitable decline of the Basque language made him unpopular with nationalists. If Basque declined, extremists maintained that the Basques should adopt French or English rather than Spanish!

punishment meted out to rebel provinces. For the next thirty years the foralists, with some success, struggled to save what could be saved from the centralizing policies of the Madrid liberals. The third Carlist rebellion in 1875 made a Liberal revenge certain and enabled Cánovas to carry out the aims of the Progressive liberals of 1839: the foral liberties were finally clipped so that they did not prejudice the 'constitutional union' of Spain.[1] Even so the provinces kept their *concierto económico* (a separate tax settlement negotiated with the government) and a large degree of administrative autonomy.

Foralism represented a sort of pre-nationalism based on the interests of the rural population; it did not become a sentiment until the ballads of Iparraguirre, which became popular in the sixties. It was transformed into nationalism under the direct influence of Catalanism. The prophet of this nationalism in the nineties was Sabino de Arana: like the Catalans, he stressed the distinction between the *patria* (his own province of Biscay and, by extension, Euzkadi, which included the Provinces, Navarre, and the French *Pays Basque*) and the Spanish state;[2] he insisted on the necessity of creating a Basque culture based on the Basque language; above all, with the Basque Nationalist party (the P.N.V. founded in 1894) he resolutely separated Basque nationalism from Carlism. Carlism, which had never truly cared for Basque liberties, had ended by destroying them in its own defeat.

Basque nationalism took from foralism its basic programme: the restoration of the liberty lost in 1839. It interpreted this liberty as complete independence (extending to the power to make foreign alliances) for a state based 'if not exclusively, principally on families of Basque race'. Thus it was more explicitly racial than Catalan nationalism: the P.N.V. in its early propaganda discouraged marriage to non-Basques. 'Let Euzkadi so restore its language to the point of exiling French and Spanish from its dominions; let it purify its race; let it isolate itself from the outside world in character and customs; let it recover its old religious fervour; let it long for its way of life before 1839.' It was also violently Catholic and supported

[1] This stage is described at length in F. de Lasala y Collado, *Última etapa de la unidad nacional. Los fueros vascongadas en 1876* (1924), 2 vols.

[2] Euzkadi as a political unit was an invention.

by priests who saw Basque culture and language as an insulation against liberalism. 'Don't teach your son Castilian, the language of liberalism.'[1]

This fierce programme would scarcely hope for widespread support in a region where the national language was on the decline and where the P.N.V. was confronted with powerful and established political enemies. The Carlists, strong in Navarre, detested its radical separatism; the Socialists, strong in Bilbao, denounced its reactionary Catholicism. Nevertheless it carried seven deputies to the Cortes of 1918. In the debates of the succeeding years its note of melancholic nostalgia gave added force to the protest of Catalonia. In spite of differences of temperament—Cambó recognized the Basques were more 'violent' than his own people—Catalans and Basques could ally against the unimaginative political egoism of a state run by Castilians. The emotional roots of separatism were less the conscious constructs of the nationalists than a sense of neglect—the indifference which the centre displayed for the concerns of the periphery. In fact the Spanish state neglected everyone, and the theory of the 'less favoured nations', adopted by the Basques, Catalans, and to a less radical degree by Galicians, was one of those myths on which nationalisms flourish.

5. *The Re-entry of the Army into Politics*

Up to and including the restoration of the monarchy itself in 1874, the effective instrument of political protest and political change had been the army; this role it appeared to have lost as a result of the civilianization of politics accomplished by Cánovas. Until 1923, except for Villacampa's Republican rising, no general staged a pronunciamiento.[2]

This civilian appearance of the political life of the Restoration

[1] Cf. the first draft of Sabino de Arana's political programme in 1894. 'Biscay will be established on a complete and unconditional subordination of the political to the religious, of the state to the church', quoted by M. García Venero, *Nacionalismo vasco*, 244.

[2] The idea, however, never sank far below the surface. In the late eighties some observers (e.g. P. Vasili, *La Société de Madrid* (Paris, 1886), 102) believed that the Liberals might force themselves on the king by means of a general, Salamanca, who had gained popularity in the army by providing cheap pharmaceutical supplies. Later, opposition Liberals hoped that General Weyler, whose Cuban campaign did not discredit him in Spanish opinion, might stage a pronunciamiento.

is deceiving: generals left politics to civilians only on condition that the civilians did not touch the army and that they themselves were always influential figures in political life. Lieutenant-General Martínez Campos, the most trusted and loyal adviser of the monarchy, was consulted in every major political crisis, and it was to a General Polavieja that conservative Spain had turned for salvation in 1898–9. Generals, sitting as Senators, could defend the interests of the army. The Minister of War was always a general, the military budget a 'sacrosanct preserve', before which civilian politicians felt 'a complete inhibition'.[1] Above all, in the king himself the army found a jealous defender of its cause. Alfonso XII was said to know the Army List by heart and his son confessed that, had he not been born a king, he would have been an infantry major. Neither the king nor his military courtiers fully accepted the constitutional relation between the monarchy and the armed forces and no politician had the courage to disillusion them.

The strange role of the army in the later nineteenth century cannot be understood without an examination of the peculiarities of its social and administrative structure. The Spanish army remained a bureaucratic machine, staffed by an underpaid officer corps recruited from the middle classes, with a sprinkling of aristocrats in the cavalry and the artillery; the generals of 1936—Varela, Moscardó, and even Franco himself—came from modest homes. Thus to many Spanish officers, their pay and their prospects of promotion were vital interests; both were prejudiced by the sheer size of the officer corps. To the officer, condemned to seek spare-time employment as a copyist or business agent in order to support himself, the attraction of the pronunciamiento had been the prospect it held out for promotion; the nemesis of recurrent military revolt was an army with no room at the top. In this crowded profession promotion still came from political influence.[2]

All attempts to reform a system which all recognized to be faulty failed. This failure was as much a result of the complexity of the military interests involved as of the cowardice of the

[1] Romanones, *D.S.C.*, 11 Nov. 1916. This inhibition was partly the consequence of the complication of military estimates. These were a deliberate fiction. Romanones confessed that in twenty years of political life he had never understood them.

[2] Cf. F. Navarro Muñoz, *Apuntes para un ensayo de organización militar* (Madrid, 1884), 70–76.

politicians. Thus the most powerful opponent of General Cassola's reforms was the artillery corps. The 'facultative corps' of the army (engineers and artillery) were the aristocrats of the army: they prided themselves on their professional attitudes, in an army where political influence outweighed professional competence, and all through the nineteenth century every artillery officer had refused promotion *within his regiment* except by a strict seniority.[1] This corporative power was envied by the other arms and they supported its reform by Cassola; the artillery brought powerful influence to bear and defeated reform.[2] In 1906 General Luque proposed a modern army, organized in divisions, with a reduced officer corps. In the Senate the generals argued that the way to cure the imbalance between officers and men was not to reduce the officers but to call more men to the colours.

All the best professional minds in the army realized the defects of an inflated officer corps, twice the size of that of the French army. From the 1880's there is an increasing interest in the creation of higher professional standards, reflected in the foundation of officers' clubs and military periodicals and in campaigns for a reform of conscription and military education.[3] But the large proportion of the military budget devoted to officers' salaries defeated professionalism and reform. All attacks on the inflated Spanish bureaucracy, which included the fighting services, were defeated by the same insoluble dilemma: only a reduction in size could finance efficiency, and reduction threatened the salaries of those who would find no place in a streamlined service. While the officer corps remained at strength, only half the men called up could be fed and trained. Thus when the Moroccan war came in 1909 the sudden call-up of reservists caused a minor revolution. In 1920 the

[1] The artillery officers accepted promotion *within the army* but not within the artillery corps; this resulted in a complicated 'double scale', i.e. a captain in the artillery might be a colonel on the Army List.

[2] For the artillery's views on reform see L. Vidart, *Las reformas militares* (1887), 13–30. The artillery officers were always reformers in the sense that they wished to make the army professional and take it out of politics. Their defence of 'closed-scale' promotion was precisely that it accomplished this, and that Cassola's reforms would mean a political army.

[3] Cf. Captain de Serignan, *L'Armée espagnole* (Paris, 1883), esp. 165, 195–6. Each branch of the army had its own periodical; cf. A. Blázquez, *La administración militar español* (Avila, 1886).

army went to Morocco without tanks, modern rifles, or decent hospitals. When the army broke down in the field, 'corrupt' officers were blamed by civilians for the defects of a military establishment which had never had the opportunity to train for war:[1] an army which could not afford manœuvres was condemned to paper work and barrack life. While the artillery and engineers maintained professional interest and standards, the enthusiasm of the infantry cadet turned to bitterness in the routine trivialities of provincial garrison life; his true military occupation gone, he became little better than a policeman, an apanage of public functions—in General Mola's bitter phrase, not a defender of the nation but a civil servant, a domestic ornament, a 'pair of pyjamas'.

As Galdós remarked in the eighties, 'soldiers considered themselves a class apart, a state within a state', dedicated to the defence of the material and moral interests of the army.[2] The chief moral interest in the army was the defence of its 'dignity' from attacks in the press; such attacks it wished to subject to the jurisdiction of military courts. In 1895 two papers 'insulted' the army by accusing officers of buying out of active service in Cuba, and young officers in uniform broke up the printing presses. Martínez Campos settled the army's discontents at the price of the resignation of the Minister of War. In November 1905 a caricature in a Catalanist paper set off a similar attack by the Barcelona garrison. The consequent crisis exposed the fragility of civilian control. General Weyler, as Minister of War, refused to obey the cabinet and the officers were only kept quiet by the king's personal assurance that he would guard their interests.[3] The prime minister, Montero Ríos, resigned rather than face a battle. Moret, his successor, gave the army a privileged court with the Law of Jurisdictions. The army, which had abandoned its old techniques of overt intervention as a political party, had scored a striking victory in its new role as a pressure group.

[1] Cf. a typical speech by the Republican Sol on corruption in the Cuban campaign. See Tato y Amat, *Sol y Ortega*, 240.

[2] B. Peréz Galdós, *Obras ined.* ii. 260.

[3] See above, p. 549. Once again the king could be said to be acting in the interests of the country if his assurances did postpone an army *coup*. General Weyler threatened 'invincible resistance' and Canalejas was told that the Civil Guard would not defend the Cortes against the army.

The years between 1917 and 1923 saw the army revert to its traditional function as the vehicle and expression of a national will subverted by the imperfect political institutions of a 'decadent' parliamentarianism. This intervention took two forms: the *Juntas de Defensa* movement of 1917 and the military take-over of September 1923.

The committee revolution of the Juntas in 1917 was, as we have seen, the culminating point of advance for underpaid military bureaucrats and at the same time an attempt to defend the 'moral' status of the army. In its essence an officers' strike for better conditions, the movement was accepted by public opinion as a legitimate means to force through a renovation of public life. Colonel Márquez, its figure-head, was later told: 'You held Spain in your hands. . . . You did much. You redeemed the middle class and taught it to hold its head high.'[1] The movement failed as an attempt to regenerate Spain: the king suspected it, the generals detested it, and the conservative politician, La Cierva, divided it by acceding to its 'technical' demands. In this way, rather than imposing terms on the parties, it became a movement of 'sordid' army interests—pay and promotions—manipulated by politicians for their own party purposes.

In the years after 1919 the Moroccan war once more modified the role of the army: the Moroccan officers, hardened in a difficult war, had no sympathy with the *junteros*' programme for peacetime soldiering, while the *junteros* abused the Moroccan officers as 'drunks' devoid of civil conscience. The military disasters of 1921 in Morocco made the army feel at the same time insecure and indignant: indignant in that it sensed that the politicians had starved it of the material basis of glory, insecure in that it feared that the same politicians would once more turn the cry of 'responsibility' against an army to which their parsimony had denied the sinews of victory. Since in 1923 it could be argued that the political system was 'decadent', the army could save itself by reverting to its traditional role as the embodiment of the national will. Primo de Rivera, in overthrowing the constitution and establishing a military dictatorship in September 1923, drew a sharp distinction be-

[1] Colonel Márquez and J. M. Capo, *Las juntas de defensa militares* (Barcelona, 1923), 156. For a further treatment see above, pp. 500–2.

tween military sedition and national salvation: 'in a state of decomposition [the army's action] was acclaimed by the people and sanctioned by the king, moved by the dictates of a wise patriotism.' The country which was prepared to accept colonels and majors in 1917 as novel interpreters of the general will felt a sense of relief when a general assumed the traditional role of his profession, vacant since 1875.

XIV

THE DICTATORSHIP OF PRIMO DE RIVERA AND THE FALL OF THE MONARCHY

1923–1931

WHEN Primo de Rivera seized power he had no aim beyond a purge of politicians, the re-establishment of 'social peace', and a solution of the Moroccan question. 'Our aim', ran his proclamation to the country on the eve of the *coup d'état*, 'is to open a brief parenthesis in the constitutional life of Spain and to re-establish it as soon as the country offers us men uncontaminated with the vices of political organization. We will then hasten to present these men to Your Majesty so that normality can be established as soon as possible.' The whole dilemma of the dictatorship was contained in this sentence: it was scarcely noticed at the time that Primo de Rivera was left to designate his successors at the moment he might think fit. This magic moment, like a fumbling conjurer, he could never find.

1. *The Dictatorship, Catalonia, the Labour Movement, and Morocco, 1923–1926*

Primo de Rivera's political thinking was primitive, personal, and naïve. The core of his political personality lay in an obsessional hatred of politics and politicians. From first to last his public utterances were sprinkled with attacks on the men who had, in his view, ruined and demoralized his country. A Spain with neither politicians nor parties in the old style was his ideal, and the clue to his actions lies in a conscious reversal of what had gone before.[1]

Unpatriotic professional politicians had destroyed Spain; a patriotic amateur would restore her. A political caste had,

[1] This does not fully apply to his social and economic policy; see below, pp. 570–2, 578–81.

through the farce of elections, isolated government from the people; he himself would enter once more into direct and personal touch with the people, restoring to government its democratic spirit. As ruler of Spain he 'talked' with the people, explaining his decrees and confessing his errors. This he did with a quite astonishing frankness, creating a picture of the benevolent despot, doing his best but not always succeeding, scribbling pencil notes to his subjects in the small hours of the morning after a hard day's work at his desk.[1] This style was elevated by his followers into the philosophy of 'intuitionism', which represented the triumph of the man of sense and feeling over the intellectual, the superiority of the Doctor of the Science of Life over the Doctor of Philosophy. False intuitions were subject to 'rectification', whereby the reactions of the man in the street were incorporated into policy. Thus the democratic spirit was safeguarded. 'Rectification is our homage to the sovereignty of the people when it is guided by reason.'

His paternalistic care for the nation bordered on eccentricity. Spaniards ate too much—they were counselled to take one large meal once a day between five and seven, with no lunch; he personally reinstalled a legally evicted butcher; his first budget surplus was devoted to redeeming the pawned sheets of the Madrid poor. This wide-ranging concern, which included an enthusiasm for women's rights, at first endeared him to the public, to whom the 'political tourism' of speeches and rallies made him familiar as no other Spanish ruler had been; ultimately it exasperated and humiliated. Familiarity with single-handed regenerationism bred contempt in the classes that had ruled, if not in the masses.

In the early stages his naïvety was a saving virtue. Primo de Rivera was an emotional patriot, and it is impossible, even now, not to be moved by the intensity of his feeling for Spain and by the embarrassing frankness in which it found expression. 'I have kissed a soldier, blackened and filthy. . . . Many times have I kissed with my heart on my lips: the crucifix, the flag, my mother, my sons and my beloved wife. To-day's kiss is also unforgettable.'[2] On his shoulders alone lay the responsibility for

[1] 'I speak now after a day of hard labour which I will have to resume in four hours.' *El pensamiento de Primo de Rivera*, ed. J. M. Pemán (1929), 169.

[2] Ibid. 146. Speech after an action in Morocco.

the regeneration of Spain. 'I know how little I am worth and I recognize Divine Guidance which allows one who could not govern himself to govern twenty million Spaniards.' Thus the Andalusian man of pleasure, devoted to women and wine, erected before himself the image of the dedicated and austere saviour under Providence. He came to talk of a divine mission, revealed by the gift of a sunny day for a speech. Thus guided, patriotism made political skill superfluous: 'I have no experience in government. Our methods are as simple as they are ingenuous. They are the methods which the good of the *patria* dictates and our resolutions are taken while we are kneeling at the shrine of the national spirit.'[1]

Nevertheless intuitions and divine guidance came to be contained in a more coherent ideology, which was worked out *a posteriori* by the dictator himself as he went from speech to speech, and more consistently by the journalistic theorists of his party, the Patriotic Union (U.P.). Hatred of the old gang was rationalized into an anti-parliamentary political theory which professed to be more truly democratic than parliamentary liberalism;[2] it attacked individualism and individual rights: men were born in society and must respect what, in that society, was 'real'. Doctrines of individual rights were not merely moral suicide for a nation but artificial inventions—'the arabesques of unemployed intellectuals'. The dictatorship would be pragmatic: it would respect the great existing social creations.

These great realities were the triad of the U.P.'s programme: Nation, Church, and King, *in that order*. The monarchy Primo de Rivera saw in a light not altogether satisfactory to convinced monarchists, for to him it was less a necessary institution than a *hecho*, a social fact. The dictator and his party accepted it because the vast majority of Spaniards did. As to the Church, the dictator, as repentant rakes so often are, was a devout Catholic, who thought all other Spaniards were too, or ought to be. Materialism was for oxen who had no history. Religion, like the

[1] Cf. J. Cortes Cavanillas, *La dictadura y el dictador* (1929), 313–23.

[2] Democracy was defined as a spirit, 'a level of civil culture' without institutional implications. Once it had become a political mechanism it could be manipulated: thus universal suffrage in Spain had become, in the hands of expert manipulators, anti-democratic.

monarchy, was a social fact, part of a natural order which conceived 'submission as a pleasure, because order is beauty'.[1] All this meant that the dictatorship was a less tolerant society than 'decadent' parliamentarianism.[2] If there was no persecution, the Protestant sects saw administrative hindrances multiplying about them. Even so, the régime's relations with the Church became uneasy: suppression of Catalan in church services awoke ghosts of eighteenth-century regalism, while support of socialist unions distressed *El Debate* and the Catholic trade unions. As it lost prestige and popularity, so the Church sought to separate its destinies from those of the dictator.

Primo de Riverism was not fascism. Its theory of sovereignty as the amalgamation of autonomous social entities, anterior to political society, was nearer to Aristotelian scholasticism than to totalitarianism. Mussolini was generally admired and fascist trappings and linguistic usages were imported, but the authors quoted by Primo de Rivera's apologists make strange, old-fashioned reading: Chesterton, Balmes, Maritain, Sturzo, Menéndez y Pelayo, Maura, Costa, Vázquez de Mella. Two conflicting strands in the ideology of the régime deserve emphasis: the criticism of parliamentary institutions deriving from Carlists on the one hand, and from the radical regenerationists from Costa to Ortega y Gasset on the other. Costa was the dictator's John the Baptist, prophesying the coming of an 'iron surgeon'. In Ortega he found an intellectual who had pleaded for an *élite*, rejecting the 'false assumption of the real equality of men'; Ortega was a disenchanted liberal and in Spain his famous attacks on the old political system became biblical texts, bandied about by the supporters of Primo de Rivera and of his son, José Antonio. Above all others loomed the great Maura, another heretical liberal. The dictator claimed that he was putting into effect Maura's revolution from above, which had been thwarted by parliamentary liberalism. Let Maura now recognize in the dictator his true heir.[3]

[1] J. M. Pemán, *El hecho y la idea de la Unión Patriótica* (1929), 301.

[2] In 1926 a woman was condemned to prison for maintaining that the B.V.M. bore other children after the birth of Jesus. Cf. J. D. Hughey, *Religious Freedom*, 112.

[3] Maura and his son Gabriel refused to advise *mauristas* to join the U.P. Maura

Inevitably, the dictatorship saw its greatest enemies in those forces which threatened the unity of the nation. More destructive than party politicians, who put party above the country, were regionalists whose aspirations had engendered separatism. It has been argued that Primo de Rivera's dramatic rectification of his supposed sympathies with Catalan regionalism was the result of pressure from the army; it was, in fact, consistent with his whole political outlook. His attack on Catalanism drove apologists of the régime into a remarkable series of historical contortions. Regionalists had argued that the region was, *par excellence*, the real historical unit: as the dictator's political theory rested on respect for realities, his theorists had to argue that the region, as a political unity, was neither socially nor historically 'real': it was the creation of a minority of separatist intellectuals who had exploited legitimate grievances against bad government and played on the excessive individualism which was the primal political sin of Spaniards. No claims to autonomy could be based on the existence of separate languages, because all these languages (except Basque, which was dismissed as a vestigial phenomenon) expressed an underlying 'national', that is, Spanish–Castilian spirit.[1] Catalanists were thus misguided in their attempts to substitute 'mechanistically fabricated archaisms, Gallicisms and Latinisms' for Castilian words. It was not Castilians who were attacking the Catalan language and literary heritage, but Catalans who were driving out Castilian, the language of Great Spain. 'Blind and perverse separatists' could only separate the Catalan soul from Spain by falsifying history. To the dictator, regionalism meant folk-lore, country-dancing, regional literature, and home crafts—politically safe, attractive to tourists, and a proof of diversity in un y.

Primo de Rivera's Catalan policy had no positive side: his mild regionalist sympathies, useful for creating a sympathetic *ambiance* for his *coup*, were rectified in March 1925, and on retirement he seems to have believed he had come to power to

wrongly diagnosed the dictatorship as 'creature and servant' of the *Juntas de Defensa*. Soldiers should govern if they would not allow others to do so, but he himself would remain resolutely civilian.

[1] The dictator's political theorists therefore argued that the *real* unit of Spanish history was the municipality not the region, which had been superseded by the civilizing march of the historical nation.

kill Catalanism.[1] Political Catalanism was suppressed and the official use of the Catalan language forbidden, even in church; the Mancomunidad was dismissed as a political and financial disaster. This was too much even for conservative Catalans, who had opposed the political pretensions of extreme Catalanism and who had supported Primo de Rivera as a saviour of society.[2]

In Catalonia the régime was a failure and by 1927 Cambó would write its epitaph.[3] The dictator could believe Catalanism was dead because, in a régime of silence, he could accept his desires as accomplished facts. Cambó argued that repression strengthened Catalanism; the immense expansion of Catalan literature in the twenties proved that Catalan could now 'satisfy all the necessities of the spirit'.[4] After the depression produced by the failure of the autonomy campaign, the suppression of the dictatorship accomplished a conversion in depth. Catalanism, Cambó argued, could not be assimilated by repression and the only future was a mutual 'emotional disarmament' of Castile and Catalonia: Catalonia would recognize the necessity of Spain, and Castile the existence of a Catalan territory and language. Cambó still hoped for a moderate solution on these lines, engineered by an alliance of Catalan and Spanish intellectuals *within* the framework of the monarchy. This solution was already impossible. Repression had made Catalan demands more radical and more sympathetic to Maciá's Republican separatism.[5] The grand bourgeoisie had lost control: Catalanism was now an affair of the radical middle classes who despaired of a solution within the monarchy.

[1] Cf. G. Maura, *Bosquejo*, 265. It seems to me that hostile critics, in order to prove that Primo de Rivera went back on his word, exaggerated his commitments in 1923 to the regionalists. He may have thought, according to Mola, that he was not bound to the Catalan industrialists because, in the event, he did not need the money they offered him.

[2] Thus Alfonso Sala Argemí supported Primo de Rivera and served as President of the Mancomunidad; but he fought attempts to reduce its powers as the dictator came under the influence of inflexible assimilationists. Like Girona and other Catalan capitalists he withdrew from politics in 1925 (cf. A. Joaniquet, *Sala*, 276–7, 296, 315). Primo de Rivera seems to have been determined to keep these moderate Catalanists from any contacts with the king.

[3] In *Por la concordia*, published in Oct. 1927.

[4] For the extension of Catalan see A. Peers, *Catalonia Infelix* (London, 1937), 181: at the Barcelona Book Fair of 1929, 40,000 Catalan and 5 Castilian books were sold (F. Cambó, *Concordia*, 36 ff.).

[5] Maciá built up a 'Catalan army' in Perpignan: in Oct. 1926 his 'invasion' of Spain was stopped by the French police.

Unlike his Catalan policy, Primo de Rivera's labour policy was a relative success; like Napoleon III, his political reputation was based on a liquidation of the red spectre combined with sympathy for virtuous labour. The state of siege, abolition of the jury, censorship of the press, and the revival of the *Somaten*, as a sort of special armed police reserve, broke the already shaken cadres of the C.N.T. Martínez Anido, as Minister of the Interior, was the government expert on the suppression of anarchism, and he renewed his old alliance with the *sindicatos libres*. Repression, as always, split the movement. Pestaña argued that the C.N.T. should accept the government's labour arbitration machinery, saving the organization at the expense of the principles of revolutionary syndicalism; at the other extreme, Anarchist purists revived the 'revolutionary and moral genius of Bakunin' by founding, in 1927, the F.A.I. (the Iberian anarchist Federation), a pure revolutionary organization of small groups of activists.[1] Although there was a clandestine organization of the C.N.T. and occasional conferences took place, with its militants scattered by jail and exile, 'the movement ceased to exist for seven years'.[2]

There was more in the dictator's labour policy than mere suppression: throughout, Primo de Rivera professed concern for the material well-being of the workers and for the claims of labour. If he stuffed down their throats the gospel of work, he also gave them cheap houses, a medical service, and above all machinery of labour arbitration which the Socialist leaders accepted and dominated. He had no objections to organized labour provided it did not use its strength for political ends, while the U.G.T. leaders did not mind if he cloaked his acceptance of trade unionism in the strange language of the corporative state or the medieval guilds. The régime's relation with unionism was formalized in the corporative labour code of Aunós (1926): its main feature was the *comités paritarios*—mixed

[1] Pestaña's line was rejected by most of his colleagues. The C.N.T. bitterly opposed the dictator's labour legislation in the name of direct action, a principle as fundamental as apoliticism. Anarchists held that the appointment of members of the mixed committees turned workers into bureaucrats—a hit at the U.G.T.—while the president's casting vote made the committees useless as a body for the settlement of strikes. Peiró, who opposed Pestaña, was as hostile as Pestaña himself to the revolutionary purism of the F.A.I.

[2] Cf. G. Moch Picard and J. Moch, *L'Espagne républicaine* (Paris, 1937).

committees, with equal representation for workers and employers and a government casting vote—which were entrusted with the settlement of wage disputes.[1] This device was not a fascist importation, for it had a long history in Spain, recommended alike by Pi y Margall, Catholic syndicalists, and the old Institute of Social Reform. As members of the committee, the U.G.T. officials became state-paid bureaucrats.

Most of the Socialist leaders were reformists and were unwilling to risk what they had already gained—a modern organization with typewriters, secretaries, burial insurance, the Madrid co-operative—by resistance. Alone strong enough for effective resistance, they refused to strike on the news of the *coup d'état*. Primo de Rivera immediately got into touch with Llaneza, the miners' leader, assuring him that the dictatorship would respect the U.G.T. 'There is nothing to fear', Llaneza announced in public.[2] Themselves recently shaken by the schism over the desirability of joining the Communist International and delighted at the discomfiture of the C.N.T., the U.G.T. leaders saw in co-operation the chance to build up their strength as the only effective workers' organization. In 1924 Largo Caballero even seems to have contemplated the unification of the U.G.T. and the Socialist party in a reformist labour party within the régime. He himself became a Councillor of State, saving his proletarian conscience by swearing his oath in a lounge suit, the sort of eccentricity that appealed to the dictator. The U.G.T. leaders could not share the politicians' horror at the rejection of the parliamentary system dear to bourgeois politicians, and they resisted attempts to bring them into conspiracies. 'Why should we fight him? To get Romanones again?' This quietism was opposed by the left wing of the Socialist party; with the intellectuals 'lackeys of the bourgeoisie' and the bourgeois parties morally ruined, Socialists must stake a claim as *the* party of the future by abandoning the dictator. This it could not do if it remained 'discreet', its congresses dominated by unimaginative bureaucrats and provincial worthies whose 'horror of a minority' prevented any real discussion. The Communist excision in 1922 not merely took away from the

[1] By 1929 the *Comités Paritarios* had made collective contracts involving over a million workers.

[2] A. Ramos Oliveira, *Politics, Economics and Men of Modern Spain* (London, 1946), 197.

party its ablest debaters; it left it dominated by conformism.[1] As Republicans and intellectuals warned, if the Socialists remained outside the fight against the dictatorship their successes would prove 'sterile', opening the way to 'frightful defeats'.

For its co-operation the U.G.T. earned the obloquy of the C.N.T. and the new, small Communist party: 1923 proved once more that 'the history of social democracy in Spain is a history of systematic treason'.[2] The defence of the leaders was that the tactics of the U.G.T. could not be those of the Socialist party; that the U.G.T. must remain an effective force in the fight against capitalism which it must not destroy lest the workers perish; that by 1929 Largo Caballero had, if belatedly, rejected not only the dictatorship but the monarchy as well, thus preparing the party for 'its historic mission'; that the strength of the U.G.T. in 1931 proved the correctness of limited collaboration. All that detractors could object was that growth and survival were not worth the moral stigma they brought with them; that in the industrial regions of Vizcaya, the Asturias, and Catalonia the party gained no recruits, leaving the new socialism a 'peasant party' of Andalusia, Estremadura, the Levant, and new Castile, dominated by the managers of Madrid.[3]

Socialism was thus the spoilt child of the régime, which at times took on the appearance of a two-party state of the U.P. and the Socialists. Hence the opposition of some employers and some Catholics. Catholic trade unionists disliked the 'unjust socialist monopoly' on the mixed committees and hoped to break it by a system of proportional representation. Those few regions where Catholic trade unionists were strong were the scene of struggles with the U.G.T.[4] Both the U.G.T. and the

[1] G. Morón, *El partido socialista ante la realidad política de España* (Madrid, 1929), 67, 75, 103, 116. Morón was an Andalusian *bracero* who became a Socialist. The Republicans were eager to support those who thought like Morón: Alvaro de Albornoz wrote a preface to the book and from it is taken the last quotation.

[2] J. Maurín, *Los hombres de la dictadura* (1930), 173 *et passim*. Most Socialist writers gave a much lower figure for agrarian gains than Maurín.

[3] E. Santiago, *La Unión General de Trabajadores ante la revolución* (Madrid, 1932), 27, 44, 45. One of the curious advantages of Largo Caballero's collaboration, his defenders argued, was the opportunity it gave for discovering government secrets, e.g. that Primo de Rivera was bribing *The Times*! (ibid. 42).

[4] The most bitter struggles took place in the Basque Provinces where the local alliance of Catholic unions (*Solidaridad Vasco*) could rival the U.G.T.; see J. N. García Nieto, S.J., *El sindicalismo cristiano en España* (Bilbao, 1960), 106–8.

National Confederation of Catholic Workers were fighting for the allegiance of the peasants and for the immense mass of unsyndicated workers and artisans. In this struggle the government favoured the ungodly: 'Catholic ideas are governing but not Catholic workers.'[1]

It was in Morocco, where the politicians had come to grief, and where he promised a 'dignified' solution, that Primo de Rivera was to find the success that consolidated his régime. By 1924 Abd El Krim's ruthless leadership and vague Berber nationalism had given the Rif tribes the appearance of an independent state which began to attract the sympathies of the left in Europe against 'colonial Spain'. Surprisingly enough, the dictator's first solution was to back the politicians' desire for withdrawal against the soldiers' desire for revenge; he maintained that the army's network of isolated, waterless posts in the interior was an indefensible liability and that to hold on to the mountain town of Xauen, the only considerable conquest of 1920, was to court another Annual.[2] At the risk of an officer rebellion he evacuated Xauen and concentrated behind the 'Primo de Rivera line'. This meant leaving El Raisuli, now so obese he could neither sit nor stand, at the mercy of Abd el Krim as undisputed master of the Jibala tribes.

In 1925 the possibility of Franco-Spanish joint military action against Abd el Krim altered the prospects of success in Morocco. France and Spain had never co-operated in Morocco and the frontier between the two protectorates was a no-man's-land whence friendly tribes supplied Abd el Krim's republic with grain. In the spring of 1925 French penetration into this no-man's-land forced Abd el Krim into an attack on the French lines; the French were disastrously defeated and their advance posts narrowly avoided disaster. Before we condemn the Spanish

[1] S. Nevares, S.J., *El porqué de la sindicación obrera católica* (1930), 95 ff. The clerical *El Debate*, which supported the régime in its struggle with students and intellectuals, strongly criticized Aunós's labour machinery as favouring 'the common enemy'.

[2] 'Abd el Krim has defeated us. He has the immense advantages of the terrain and a fanatical following. Our troops are sick of the war and have been for years.... I, personally, am in favour of withdrawing entirely from Africa and letting Abd el Krim have it.' Primo de Rivera maintained that Spain was forced to continue in Morocco because the English did not want the French to occupy Spanish Morocco; and that the English, via the queen (who was a daughter of Edward VII) had great influence over the king. Moroccan policy was perhaps one of the earliest occasions of friction between the dictator and his king.

army in Morocco for the defeats of 1921, it is well to remember the French disasters of 1925 which shook the whole fabric of the Protectorate and brought marauding parties within twenty miles of Fez.

Abd el Krim had never wished for war with France: the whole of his hatred, and that of Rif 'nationalism', were concentrated against Spain. Now he was faced with a war on two fronts. This was the basis of Primo de Rivera's second Moroccan rectification: from the defensive line he turned to the idea of the decisive defeat of Abd el Krim as the principal condition for the successful exercise of Spanish influence from the coast. The Spanish landing at Alhucemas Bay and the subsequent capture of Abd el Krim's capital were the crowning victories in Morocco: carefully planned, the landing achieved surprise in difficult conditions. As Spain broke in on the north, the French closed up from the south. Abd el Krim's defeats in the summer of 1926 turned the tribes against him: he surrendered to the French and the resistance of the Rif and Jibala tribes collapsed with the eclipse of their most remarkable and talented leader.

With Abd el Krim's defeat came Primo de Rivera's last rectification: from control and peaceful penetration he turned to military occupation. The wheel had come full circle with the triumph of the army's maximalist policy. This was not because Primo de Rivera had been weak and subject to military bullying but because events, above all the possibility of military co-operation between France and Spain, had made possible a policy he had rightly considered dangerous and beyond Spain's capacity in 1923. In 1924 he had been courageous enough to force his views on the African command. In 1925 he fearlessly assumed direct responsibility for a risky combined operation. In 1927 Xauen was reoccupied and the protectorate pacified. Primo de Rivera deserved the rewards of courage.

2. *The Iron Surgeon and the Regeneration of Spain, 1925–1928*

Repeatedly, through a variety of metaphors ranging from surgery to the science of pyrotechnics, Primo de Rivera declared his intention of handing over to 'normality'. There can be no grounds for doubting his sincerity, particularly when his health began to break down. Difficulties arose in his wildly differing judgements of the moments at which it would be prudent to withdraw, and of the nature of the régime which should be regarded as normal. Hence the perpetual 'rectifications' in his attempts to recross the Rubicon. From the Military Directory Primo de Rivera moved to the Civil Directory (1925); from the idea of the constitution of 1876, run by new men, he moved to the idea of a new constitution to be drawn up by a National Assembly, which might attract some of the old men. But by 1928 it was too late to establish any régime connected with the dictator. Primo de Rivera, in Calvo Sotelo's words, had an inveterate contempt for the notion of time; he had left the problem of the régime unsolved too long. Opposition had hardened and normality could now be conceived only in terms of the dictator's removal.

At first Primo de Rivera believed that a short, sharp period of military government and *ad hoc* decrees would cut out the vices from the constitution of 1876 which he considered 'suspended but not abrogated'. The central government was entrusted to a Directory of generals appointed according to seniority, thus excluding 'political' considerations: the provinces were ruled by brigadiers, while captains were appointed as delegates to the municipalities. This in itself would constitute a great economy in salaries. Primo de Rivera's favourite diagnosis of decline was the evil of a slack, over-staffed administration: this was now pruned and given a living wage in return for a full day's work. By the Decree of Incompatibilities no one who *had been* a minister or senior civil servant could sit on the board of companies involved in state contracts. This decree was a defiant threat to the old political classes.

By the end of 1924 the glow of optimism which had greeted the dictatorship had grown perceptibly dimmer. The Moroccan problem had not been given its promised solution, the press was restive, and continued military administration unacceptable even to the army. In these conditions a return to the 1876 constitution looked hazardous. The old politicians had been disgraced, but no new promotion had emerged to run the old constitution with 'clean hands'. This promotion Primo de Rivera set about to foster by government favour. The creation of the Patriotic Union (U.P.) in 1924 and the Municipal Statute of 1925 thus marked the first stages of demilitarization.

The dictatorship consistently denied that the U.P. was a political party. Conceived as an apolitical centre grouping of patriots, open to all, from Republicans to Carlists, it was a system of organized conduct, a form of moral regeneration, a league of citizenship; it represented the permanence of that 'daily plebiscite of public opinion expressed in streets and railway stations', that personally perceived approbation which had replaced the vote. It could be presented as a realization of Ortega's new politics of social regeneration in contradistinction to the old politics of place and power, as his dynamic *élite* in action.

The language of the dictator reflected profound political ignorance. He refused to see that the U.P. *was* a party in the old sense; that is, a group of men who shared a common conviction that a given political solution, the dictatorship, was in their interest. It was to this party, conceived as a communion of clean hands, a league of anti-caciques, that Primo de Rivera intended to hand over the task of governing Spain. Yet in spite of these prospects, the party refused to grow: great rallies, rousing speeches, and almost complete control of governmental patronage from civil governorships down, failed to bring in the men of goodwill. Its most sincere adherents were former Carlists and *Mauristas*, though Maura himself and his sons condemned its unnatural 'governmental' birth. Recruits came, so its opponents maintained, from local party bosses of the *ancien régime* and industrialists out for government contracts. 'Its ranks were filled', wrote Calvo Sotelo, 'with knights of the ideal and knights of industry, men of morals and soup and spoon men.' Far from encouraging Primo de Rivera in the democratization of the régime, its leaders, sensing their isolation, consistently opposed such a course—with disastrous results. The dictator had fallen victim to the regenerationist myth of a 'real', popular Spain buried under an artificial political class. There was no such reserve. The only group of men able enough to run the new Spain was the old political class. When the dictator suspected his error it was too late to rectify it and win back the outraged and rejected politicians.

The one structural reform of the Military Directory was the Municipal Statute: this was necessary because the *ad hoc* arrangements of 1923 had broken down into a chaos of independent authorities—as might have been foreseen when 500 officers were overnight turned into local government officials. The military delegates hung on till 1926, a vestigial remnant of purification by military rule. The Municipal Statute of March 1924 was meant, in the words of its creator Calvo Sotelo, to be the Magna Carta of Municipal Liberties and to provide a permanent framework of government. It gave municipalities, based on a mixed corporative and universal suffrage, autonomy and extensive powers to raise loans for local improvements. These loans, managed by the Bank of Local Credit, were the most consistently criticized feature of the régime. They were held to have encouraged an orgy of conspicuous waste: some municipalities engaged in building follies, but most devoted the 500 million to the modernization of water supply and sewage. The Municipal Statute, except for the loan clauses, was based entirely on projects which parliament had failed to turn into law: once more the inspiration of the régime was Maura. An excellent piece of legislation, it was still-born: the dictator dared not risk the elections that would have given it life. To the end, local life was run by government appointees.

The crowning victory of Alhucemas gave the dictator the opportunity and the prestige to change the emergency Military Directory for a civilian government, without at the same time facing the risks of a return to normality. The Civil Directory was a shift from *ad hoc* remedies to a planned economy run by young 'apolitical' technocrats at the centre and by the U.P. in the provinces. Most of Primo de Rivera's central achievements were the fruit of 'fifty months emotive cordiality' with a cabinet whose rallying cry was, 'We are not politicians'.

The achievements of the Civil Dictatorship lay in the field of financial reform and economic planning, and it was here that the technocrats encountered the opposition of orthodox bankers and capitalists who had no sympathy with mild social radicalism or a 'directed' economy. Primo de Rivera's financial views were those of a simple soldier: he wanted a tax on capital. In 1926 his finance minister, Calvo Sotelo, proposed to base the budget on an effective income tax (the so-called 'global' tax which would be a tax on total income instead of taxing independently certain sources of revenue). This he defended as modern, efficient, and socially just. 'True democracy is recognized to-day by the distribution of public taxation, not by a formal political constitution.' The government, nevertheless, dared not rally the masses against the classes; it gave in to a bitter press campaign led by the aristocracy of the banking world. However great his utility as the restorer of social peace, the conservatives had no time for the dictator's financial 'amateurism': the campaign against the income tax became a campaign against the government itself.[1]

Spain was thus denied a much-needed radical overhaul of her tax system and Calvo Sotelo's financial reforms were restricted to the largest consolidation of the Floating Debt in Spanish history, and to administrative and technical improvements.[2] But beyond this task of cleaning up (*saneamiento*) lay the greater task of reconstructing, modernizing, and expanding the Spanish economy according to a 'Ten-Year Plan'. The instruments of this policy were among the most criticized creations of the dictatorship: the Extraordinary Budget, the state monopolies, and special Regulatory Commissions.

The problem was to raise money for investment and public works without 'bolshevik' increases of taxation. The Extraordinary Budget (regarded by the enemies of the dictatorship as an immoral feat of financial prestidigitation, conceived in order to hide a real deficit beneath the apparent surpluses of the ordinary budget) was a scheme to finance public works out of loans, the interest of which was to be met out of the ordinary revenues. The gamble which was held to justify this departure was that ordinary income would increase with an expanding economy.

The Extraordinary Budget was flanked by new semi-state banks. The *Banco Exterior de España* (established in 1928) was to free Spanish foreign trade from dependence on foreign credit, and to open up the South American market—an attempt to convert into an economic reality the Pan-Hispanism which

[1] For a summary of the debate and documents see *De Ec.* viii (1955), 188 ff. The most bitter opponents were the conservative *El Debate* (now an opposition paper) and the *ABC*, where the vizconde de Eza (a consistent opponent of the dictatorship on political grounds) ran a long series of articles from Jan. to Mar. 1927. Calvo Sotelo defended himself against these 'aristocrats' and 'financiers' in *La Nación* (Dec. 1926 to Jan. 1927).

[2] They are described in Calvo Sotelo's apologia, *Mis servicios al Estado* (1931), 123–93.

was one of the showpieces of the dictatorship's ideology. A Mortgage Bank was set up to finance workers' housing; a Bank of Industrial Credit to finance new industry.[1] Much of this new activity was unwelcome in orthodox banking circles.

The creation of monopolies represented a desperate need for income as well as dogmatic economic nationalism. Though the aim of CAMPSA (the petrol monopoly granted to a consortium of Spanish banks) was to capture for the state the profits made in Spain by Standard Oil and Shell, it was presented as a defence of national interests against a private, foreign monopoly which threatened to 'Cubanize' Spain, an attempt to make the refining of petrol a national industry.[2] On 27 June 1927 a 'surprise' decree, nationalizing the distribution of petrol in the hands of a government-controlled company, set off a violent counter-campaign of the oil companies who found their installations illegally confiscated. Deterding arrived to threaten Primo de Rivera with a boycott, which would have ruined CAMPSA but for Russian supplies. Thus one of the most curious consequences of nationalization was to put the oil supplies of a nation, considered abroad as a clericalist dictatorship, at the mercy of the Soviet Union; one of the most dangerous consequences was that Spanish financial interests, which suffered in the new scheme, joined the grumbling opposition—among them the Majorcan multi-millionaire Juan March.[3] The government exaggerated the machinations of foreign capitalists, whom it accused of financing a slander campaign in order to cover the fact that the sudden confiscation had weakened the prospects of foreign investment in Spain.[4] This the economic

[1] For housing see *Que es una casa barata* (1928). Cheap workers' houses had long been advocated by the Institute of Social Reforms, now dissolved. Based on earlier legislation (modified in 1924) his housing projects reveal an essential feature of Primo de Rivera's rule: the fulfilment of earlier promises, on a modest scale, but with much publicity: cf. his extension of social insurance to pregnant women.

[2] For a violent attack on CAMPSA see J. Graudel, *Le Monopole du pétrole en Espagne* (Paris, 1935).

[3] One of the minor results was local discontent caused by the closing down of the old 'competing' company pumps. This was very typical of the opposition of local interest groups which plagued the dictator's government. Thus, in its attempt to cut distribution costs, CAMPSA left Spain only 2,703 pumps in 1933. France had 80,000. The unwary tourist still suffers.

[4] At the height of the campaign Calvo Sotelo's language became so violent that Primo de Rivera personally assured Rio Tinto, a British concern, that it was safe against nationalization.

technocrats of the régime, with their Ten-Year Plan for economic regeneration, could ill afford.

To these planners Spain was a poor economy because private enterprise had not been able to overcome the inherited time-lag, the 'backwardness' which had obsessed Spaniards since 1898. Recovery must be guided and helped by the state, which should grant weak industry monopoly conditions and invest heavily in basic public works.

Primo's public works, his roads and dams, are sometimes regarded as a piece of premature Keynsianism, or as an example of the economic exhibitionism of upstart, insecure régimes.[1] They were rather a reversion to the ideas of Costa and, behind him, to the ideals of the eighteenth-century reformers; like them, in his simplicity, the dictator was fascinated by the rationality of a single tax. In the same way his interventionism was an exaggeration of the nineteenth-century protectionists' faith in a national market. Haunted by dreams of autarky, he was pained by the French wines and American cars of the upper classes and the preference Spanish doctors showed for imported scalpels. Every article that could be produced or grown in Spain must be produced, regardless of production costs: hence 'intervention' to save domestic coal production, lead, and resin; hence the attempt to create a national car industry, to finance home-grown cotton by a levy on imported cotton, to intensify 'cerealist' policies. Thus the Spanish economy fell into the hands of committees regulating everything from hydro-electric power to the rabbit-skin industry.[2] Intervention and control were criticized by those groups that suffered or those that were not rewarded; for these, what the régime called a 'national' policy concealed support for 'interests' its members chose to favour by an inflated budget, and the new 'technical' bureaucracy opponents of the dictator's economic policies saw only as an attempt to create a pool of administrative patronage.

In spite of the defects of their policies the dictator's technocrats were responsible for a most remarkable and frequently under-estimated essay in modernization: the increase in road-

[1] There were constant criticisms that his roads were 'tourist' roads, not economic roads. This is nonsense: the roads were trunk roads; and, anyway, Spain needed the foreign exchange brought by tourism. Less successful and more exhibitionist was the Seville Exhibition, part of a campaign to 're-establish' Andalusia.

[2] For a list of these see R. Perpiñá, *De estructura económica*, 317–19.

building and rural electrification was spectacular by Spanish standards; iron and steel maintained something like their war-time growth; foreign trade increased 300 per cent.; the railways were re-equipped. Proudest creations of the dictatorship were the Hydraulic Confederations, which grouped together the various interests in an attempt to rationalize the uses of the great river systems of the Duero and the Ebro.[1] The dictatorship had an air of expansion and prosperity which in retrospect has turned it into a golden age. Not all this modernization and prosperity was, as the opposition maintained, 'false', nor was it merely a reflection of an international boom for which the régime could take no credit. It can be criticized for its failure to tackle agrarian reform—though Primo de Rivera's land schemes were more impressive than any previous achievement. Prosperity was partly the result of order, however achieved, and conscious effort. As long as the boom lasted the dictatorship benefited politically. It was not, however, the collapse of prosperity in 1929 that brought down the régime: the fundamental failure was a political failure. The régime could not be made acceptable to those forces that counted in Spanish society.

3. *Decline and Fall, 1928–1929*

The opposition of the politicians is understandable. They were the insulted and injured. At first many accepted Romanones's attitude of dignified abstention, but as the prospect of a return to the legality of 1876 faded their opposition stiffened; the 'constant plebiscite of public opinion' was no substitute for a constitution.[2] The opposition was led by conservatives who could not forgive the king the fact that it was royal appointment which gave the dictatorship its only semblance of legality. In June 1926 Sánchez Guerra, who became

[1] See M. Lorenzo Pardo, *La conquista del Ebro* (1931). Lorenzo Pardo was typical of the technocrats with ambitious schemes. He was obsessed by the potentialities of the Ebro. Between 1906 and 1926 the state spent 162 million pesetas for the irrigation of 16,000 hectares: between 1926 and 1931 it spent 160 million on schemes for the irrigation of 175,000 hectares. For a less rosy view of the Hydraulic Confederations see L. Ridruejo Ruiz-Zorilla, *Función del estado.*

[2] It is curious to note that this catch-phrase of the dictator is the basic concept of Fidel Castro's political thought; in both cases it is used to reject any form of representative mechanism which can change the government. Of course, in 1926 Primo de Rivera's philosophy was regarded as a heresy by the left.

the leader of the conservative opposition, made his views clear to Alfonso: he must dismiss Primo de Rivera on the grounds that his proposal for a National Assembly to draft a new constitution was an 'illegitimate and factious act—the official death sentence of parliamentary and constitutional government'. Alfonso refused, and there were good grounds for his refusal: few would have supported a return to the 'old gang', engineered by the exercise of the prerogative to dismiss ministers. It was impossible to defend a 'discredited' constitution; the proposed National Assembly, however faulty its composition, allowed some hope for an agreed return to normality.[1]

The most surprising feature of the opposition of the politicians was that it gained the support of the intellectuals; since Costa they had been critics of what Ortega, in a famous lecture, called the 'old politics'. Under the dictator both intellectuals and the politicians they had castigated suffered alike from an erratic censorship. To the mild criticism which was allowed to appear, the dictator replied personally, as if he were running the correspondence column of a broad-minded conservative magazine. 'I am a journalist by nature. I won my spurs on *El Guadalete* of Jerez in 1898. . . . I have written thousands of lines for *La Nación*. I am not, therefore, an enemy of the press, nor do I doubt its efficacy.' His Press Statute was not an instrument to persecute the press 'but to make it good'. This is typical of Primo de Rivera's *naïveté*; his sense of rectitude was so complete that he saw neither the complexity of problems dismissed in the notion of 'good' or 'patriotic', nor that there could be other definitions of these terms but his own.[2] Both politicians and intellectuals, many of whom were lawyers, were outraged by what they called the dictator's 'lack of juridical sense'. The dictator had an endearing propensity for Wild West justice and a soldier's contempt for lawyers: hence his intervention in the course of justice and his purges of the judiciary. Independent justice and the rule of law became the opposition's rallying cry: it was not merely that Primo de Rivera

[1] G. Maura, *Bosquejo*, 211. M. de Burgos y Mazo, *La dictadura y los constitucionales* (1934), 77–83.

[2] Although it was censored, the press could print criticisms of certain aspects of the régime (e.g. of economic policy) and at certain times (e.g. during the constitional debates). This criticism, especially in the form of cartoons—the cartoonist of *El Imparcial* was a genius—later dictators would have suppressed ruthlessly.

did not respect the old laws, he did not respect even his own decrees. Since he could make any law he saw fit, and since he regarded the rule of law as a process of 'suspending it and modifying it to suit concrete cases', the legal irresponsibility of the régime was its most outstanding feature.[1] It was a particularly scandalous suspension of the law in a concrete case which brought the intellectuals into declared and permanent opposition: Unamuno was dismissed from his chair and after a short term of confinement went into exile. Later, in alliance with Ortega and the Paris exiles, he savagely attacked the dictator.[2] Apart from Maeztu not a single intellectual of standing supported the régime, and the *Ateneo*, symbol of the worst and the best in Spanish intellectual life, was closed.

The opposition of the intellectuals merged with the opposition of the university students. Unamuno became a father figure to student rebels, addressing them letters in which he called the dictator a felon, a miserable robber, and a coward. Student opposition originated in the defence of student interests by the non-Catholic Students' Union, the F.U.E., against the attempt to allow Catholic private universities to confer degrees, which represented essential certificates for government jobs. On 8 April 1928 the protracted university dispute spread to all universities except Saragossa. The first overt opposition, Primo de Rivera struck it down with contempt, imprisoning the students, suspending the university courses, and putting Madrid University under Royal Commissioners; no one would regret the closing of universities, he remarked, as the professors were lazy and the students too numerous and frivolous. As in all the dictator's asides, there was truth in his attack on the shortcomings of the university. He had not what Spaniards call a 'university formation', and he believed that professors were exploiting their students and students wasting their time in politics.

[1] Note of 5 June 1926 (G. Maura, *Bosquejo*, 202). A series of decrees in 1926 put the government above any legal restraints: the only law was administrative law and the only judges government appointees. The decrees are conveniently summarized in R. Bec, *La Dictature espagnole* (Montpellier, 1935). These extensive powers were rarely used in 1926–7, but more frequently, as opposition increased, in 1928 and 1929.

[2] For a description of the Paris exile world see F. Madrid, *Els exilats de la dictadura* (Barcelona, 1930). Every conceivable shade of politics was represented, from the C.N.T. to Juan March, from General Millán Astray, who was to cry *Viva la muerte*, to Blasco Ibáñez.

Thus, throughout its decline, the dictatorship was subjected to a series of minor assaults which discredited the government and which spread even to South America, where the students set up sympathetic movements. Special squads of bicycle police were employed to remove seditious *graffiti*; the students' committee circulated clandestine leaflets; laudatory poems (written by 'a girl of fifteen'), of which the initial letters of each line spelled 'Primo is a Drunk', appeared in the press.[1] Primo de Rivera came to hate the students, and to the king the movement was particularly distressing. He had spent a great deal of energy on the new University City in order to conciliate the youth of Spain; his reward was the destruction of his bust by students, a clear indication of the dangers of continued support of the dictatorship. When Primo de Rivera fell it looked as if he had been defeated by a students' rag, to shouts of 'Efe! U! E! Efe! U! E! Allá va! Ra! Ra! Ra!'

But the grumblings of the old politicians and the sedition of the intellectuals he could have resisted; what he could not afford to lose was the loyalty of the army and the support of the king. The *coup* of September 1923 had received the unanimous support of the army and the constitutional blessing of the king. Here lies the lesson of 1923–30: once it was clear to the dictator that he could not count on the loyalty of the army he resigned. He was defeated, as he was made, by his fellow generals.

The discontents of the army originated in his 'lack of respect' for those conventions which had protected the military career from interfering civilians. The key promotion in the army was from colonel to general, and this had been regulated by an Army Board, under Weyler. Primo de Rivera made this body susceptible to his pressure in order to penalize officers whose political loyalty he suspected; Queipo de Llano was placed on reserve for a joke in poor taste—U.P., he observed, signified public urinal as well as Patriotic Union.[2] Such actions threatened the autonomy of the army and revived the old *juntero* spirit. 'If soldiers can do this, how on earth shall we defend ourselves against civilians?' Things had come to a pretty pass when a

[1] For these activities see J. López-Rey, *Los estudiantes frente a la dictadura* (1930), esp. 191 ff., 219, 294.

[2] See E. López de Ochoa, *De la dictadura á la república* (1930), 78–98. Queipo de Llano, *El General Queipo de Llano* (1930), 214–23.

policeman arrested a general on the order of an enthusiastic civil governor. Older generals, Berenguer and Weyler amongst them, believed that army rule in itself endangered the army by converting it into a political party.

These minor discontents were not dangerous: it was Primo de Rivera's onslaught on the artillery corps which, in Berenguer's words, 'broke the harmony of the military family' and made his fall inevitable. Too weak to push through the drastic reduction of officers which might have created a modern army, the dictator's reforming zeal concentrated on one glaring anomaly—the closed scale of artillery promotion by which artillery officers declined promotion which broke strict seniority. He had inherited the jealousy of the cavalry and infantry officer against the privileged corps; in June 1926 he took away the recompenses which compensated artillery officers' self-denial and, typically, made this retroactive to 1920. This latter injustice gave the artillery officers a case; in August an artillery assembly rejected any compromise and confined itself to barracks, i.e. struck.[1] The government's answer was to suspend the *whole* artillery officer corps and to relieve the sergeants and men of the duty of obeying their officers. Since no one supported their revolt, the artillery had to give in (December 1926). But the struggle had seriously weakened Primo de Rivera: the artillery officers were bitter against the dictator and lost faith in a king who did not defend their interests;[2] while some infantry and cavalry officers indulged in *schadenfreude*, the more responsible were distressed at treating brother officers as common criminals. The king himself disliked the way in which the dictator had dissolved the proudest corps in the army without consulting its Commander-in-Chief. Artillery officers, on the road from San Sebastian to Madrid, stopped the king's car and got a promise that he would revoke Primo de Rivera's orders. When he did not, a 'chasm opened between the king and the artillery corps', and it came to have republican leanings.

It is against this background of discontents that we must consider Primo de Rivera's major attempt to create a 'normality'

[1] There was a party of 'legalists' who wished to settle disputed promotions (i.e. after 1920) by special arrangements: but the moderates were out-voted in a decision 'to abandon judicial settlement and carry the conflict to the political field'.

[2] According to López Ochoa, *Dictadura*, 120 ff.

to which he could resign his mission: the constitution to be drafted by the National Assembly. The National Assembly was a non-elective, consultative body. The constitution which it drafted expressed the current, right-wing hostility to the practices of liberal, responsible parliamentary government: in the name of efficiency—'getting things done' was Primo's favourite motto—speeches were limited to thirty minutes; it instituted an extreme separation of powers, to the disadvantage of a legislature in which the corporative representatives sat beside elected deputies. Its main departures from classical parliamentarianism were the absence of any ministerial responsibility and the suppression of the royal prerogative of appointing and dismissing ministries, a power now shared with a body which was an imitation of the Fascist Grand Council. This constitution did not please the king and had been boycotted from the outset by the old politicians. Gabriel Maura and others nevertheless believed that, *if submitted* to an elected assembly, the new constitution might be an acceptable solution for the return to normality. The decree of July 1928 took away this last hope: the constitution was to be ratified by a plebiscite. This turned it into a *charte octroyée* which created a 'sterile and boring' caricature of parliamentary life.

Primo de Rivera chose to regard his constitution as an acceptable return to normality: he lifted the censorship and invited new members to the assembly. This olive branch is an indication of his political *naïveté*, and his reward was an outburst of criticism of the dictatorship as an emergency government whose task was now accomplished.[1] 'Slaves cannot co-operate with their masters.' This final denial of co-operation by every shade of opinion in the old political world hardened Primo de Rivera. His references to resignation became more elusive; physically exhausted, he could not see any way out, and fell increasingly into the hands of those who still professed to believe in his mission—the leadership of the U.P. To the last Primo de Rivera under-rated the forces against him and put his faith in the neutral mass. 'The greatest, perhaps the only support

[1] 'We advise General Primo de Rivera to abandon his post.' *El Sol*, 16 June 1928; cf. *El Sol*, 23 Feb. 1928 (censored), criticizing the proposed plebiscite; ibid., 12 July 1929 (pointing out that the legislative powers of the Cortes were totally subject to the Council of State); 16 July (the unlimited powers to suspend the constitutional guarantees).

of my government consists of women and workers.'[1] By the autumn of 1929 the problems of the return to normality had split the government itself.[2] Incapable of solving the political problem of the succession the régime had come to be based on the 'satisfaction of interests', the support of the army, the crown, and the 'neutral mass'. By 1929 the 'interests', the army, and the crown were looking elsewhere.

It was this withdrawal of support from the right, not the attacks of the left, which doomed the régime to destruction. The conservative classes chose to see themselves threatened by a corporative state run in the interests of the workers. The Church distrusted Primo de Rivera's mild regalism, the landowners of the south his equally mild agrarian reform, the bankers his high-handed interference with the autonomy of the large banks, and the non-favoured industrialists his interventionism. In view of later conditions it is astonishing how much of this criticism reached the public. Cambó, still the greatest representative of the grand bourgeoisie, published in 1929 an outspoken attack on the dictatorship as 'a syndicate of egoisms', without ideas and without a future, which threatened to produce the social revolution that burst forth in Mexico after the repression of the Porfirio Díaz régime.[3] Aunós, reflecting on the failure of Primo de Rivera's good intentions, saw them defeated by a 'coalition of selfish rightists', by 'the International of Gold'.[4]

By the July of 1929 these discontents had reached the point of conspiracy. The Valencian rebellion was an old-fashioned pronunciamiento of which the figure-head was the austere seventy-year-old conservative politician Sánchez Guerra, who had led the Datoist wing of the party since 1922. It represented

[1] N. Pazcazio, *La rivoluzione di Spagna*, 59.

[2] Yanguas and the U.P. leadership, to whom Primo de Rivera at one moment proposed to resign the task of transition to normality, regarded the Assembly constitution as viable if ratified only by a plebiscite, a prospect Calvo Sotelo regarded 'with horror'. Finally the ministry plumped for a single-chamber parliament to be called in September 1930. Calvo Sotello, *Seis años*, 336 ff.

[3] F. Cambó's *Las dictaduras* was an attempt to put the Spanish régime in a European setting. Dictatorships were inevitable in under-developed countries; they would prove impermanent and noxious *if prolonged*, unless, as in Russia and Italy, they embodied a true revolution.

[4] Aunós was Primo de Rivera's Minister of Labour. For his views see *España en crisis* (Buenos Aires, 1942), 267–333.

an alliance of politicians and army officers to save the monarchy from itself by forcing it to get rid of the dictator. But by 1929 not all conservatives were determined to defend the monarchy at all costs: the future Constitutionalists (Villanueva and Burgos y Mazo, both formerly Datoist Conservatives) held that, since the king had broken his contract in 1923, sovereignty reverted to the people, who could decide on the 'question of the régime' in a Constituent Cortes. This opened the conspiracy to declared Republicans. Although Sánchez Guerra himself wished to preserve the monarchy he was willing to join in a conspiracy with allies whose intention was to destroy it.

As usual, the problem was to get a general who would 'declare'. In Valencia General Castro Girona, whose wife could not resist the social prospects of a new command in Morocco offered her husband by the government, went back on his vague promises and arrested Sánchez Guerra; in Seville Burgos y Mazo found that the civilians waited on the soldiers and the soldiers on the civilians. The pronunciamiento was confined to a revolt of the artillery officers at Ciudad Real. The conspiracy was too narrowly based; few would risk their lives in an affair run by the old politicians.

The year 1929 was, in his son's phrase, the agony of Primo de Rivera's dictatorship. Its alternative to politics was prosperity, and in 1929 the whole bold front was crumbling with the fall of the peseta. The quotation of the peseta was regarded as the test of the régime by its supporters and its opponents alike; its collapse, which began in 1928, was a consequence of Spain's incurable trading deficit exacerbated by capital exports, a bad harvest, the falling off of South American immigrant payments, and the mild beginnings of the world slump. It was attributed by opponents of the régime *solely* to internal inflation caused by public works, the effects of which were concealed from the country by the fraudulent device of the Extraordinary Budget.[1]

The finance minister, Calvo Sotelo, hoped to stop further falls by state purchase of pesetas on the London Market. This failed, and Primo de Rivera (who persisted in the 'patriotic' delusion that the peseta could be stabilized at 40 to the pound

[1] Cf. *El Sol*, 27 Jan. 1928. The budget surplus had become 'a meaningless formality. The financial problem of the country passes from the Ordinary to the Extra-ordinary Budget.'

sterling when it was quoted at 32) was alarmed at the violent criticisms of Calvo Sotelo's policies by Cambó and an attack on the whole financial policy of the dictatorship contained in a report on the gold standard by Flores de Lemus, the most respected economist in Spain. Cambó blamed the government for its attempt to hide the effects of an inflation it had itself provoked; its monetary policies—in Calvo Sotelo's words, the maintenance 'with a soul full of faith' of the peseta as 'the index of the moral capacities of the Spanish race'—were in conflict with its inflationary economic policies; once internal and external price levels were out of joint only devaluation remained.[1]

Calvo Sotelo's reply to all criticism was that the economy was sound, and that the fall in the peseta had been engineered by speculators and blown up into a disaster by 'defeatists' and the 'obstructionism' of conservative financial circles and the Bank of Spain:[2] his most extreme supporters blamed the Jews. His resignation did not save the government, his two successors pursuing contradictory policies. The monetary debate was weakening confidence in a régime which appeared to be floundering in problems beyond its competence; the dictator himself confessed in one of his notes that he was 'too tired' to remember the arguments of his finance minister. Capital, argued Cambó, would never reflow into Spain 'while the present régime has not prepared its normal substitution'—i.e. until the dictator promised to resign.[3]

Economic difficulties made the conspiracy of the politicians and the soldiers appear more dangerous, as it gathered support in 'opinion'; the only result of the trial of the Valencia conspirators was to turn Sánchez Guerra into a national figure. In 1929 the conspiracy centred on the Andalusian garrisons, and in October the conspirators found the 'initiating general' in Goded: as in 1868 differences between Republicans and monarchists were blanketed by the formula of a Constituent

[1] Cambó's argument was that the peseta had risen as a result of speculative purchases in anticipation of stabilization at par or near it. In his view the government should have intervened *against* this speculation and not later sought to maintain a false, high rate by 'interventionism' on the exchange (*Valoración de la peseta*, chs. i and ii).

[2] The bank refused to co-operate with the ministry of finance by giving information to Rist, a French economist called in by Calvo Sotelo.

[3] F. Cambó, *Valoración*, 83.

Cortes.[1] When the conspiracy leaked out via a newspaper article, the Captain General of Andalusia warned the king that the widespread army discontent in the south made it advisable to get rid of the dictator.

Alfonso was well aware that Primo de Rivera's growing unpopularity was involving the monarchy: a pamphlet on 'Alfonso XIII as a dancing partner' appeared. Determined to escape its consequences, he saw that by dismissing the dictator he might appear as a liberator, and wash himself clean of the responsibilities of 1923. The king disliked the independence of a man who was technically a royal appointee; he objected to his determination that 'no one shall Bourbonize me', and his tendency to push his own party, the U.P., at the expense of monarchist groups. His new constitution eliminated the king's most precious prerogative, the dismissal of ministers.[2] In fact the personal prerogatives of the crown had been sequestrated in 1923 and the king was determined to recover them when a decent opportunity presented itself. In this determination he was encouraged by his court, which detested the dictator, and Madrid aristocratic society, which had never accepted him in the same way as the middle classes and the provincial aristocracy.[3]

The opportunity for which the king and court had been seeking was created by the last of the dictator's erratic intuitions. On 26 January, after a sleepless night and without consulting the king, he circularized the Captains General. The army had made him, did it still support him? If not, he would resign 'in five minutes'. It was not merely the unenthusiastic replies of his fellow generals, but the realization that the king wanted him to go, that forced Primo de Rivera's resignation.

[1] The Andalusian conspiracy has curious features: Goded insisted first on the co-operation of the Navy and, when this was impossible, of the Air Force. This was because he feared that the government would bring over the Moroccan Army to crush the revolt. This shows, for the first time, the importance of the 'uncontaminated' Moroccan Army in any calculation of forces. The Air Force conspirators included General Franco's brother, the aviator; by insisting on Republican demands, Franco drove Goded out of the conspiracy. Cf. M. de Burgos y Mazo, *Constitutionalistas*, ii. 173 ff.

[2] 'Can I appoint a socialist government under the new constitution?' he anxiously asked La Cierva. J. La Cierva, *Notas*, 306.

[3] For the hostility of the aristocrats see A. de Hoyos y Vinent, *El primer estado* (1931). 'The Madrid aristocracy had for the marqués de Estella (i.e. Primo de Rivera) the respect which the king commanded; the provincial aristocracy had for the king the respect which Primo de Rivera commanded' (op. cit. 225).

He retired to Paris and died a broken man within a few months. Very gently, he had been Bourbonized after all.

4. *The Collapse of the Monarchy, 1930*

The return to normality and the salvation of the monarchy were now entrusted to General Berenguer, who enjoyed a certain popularity from his known disapproval of the dictator's methods. He was an upright, old-fashioned, and ailing soldier, who was a talented musician; by April 1931 he was so ill that he was wheeled about in a chair belonging to the Empress Eugénie and allowed no photographs of himself to be taken. As Premier, his task was to engineer a return to constitutional government without imperilling the king. His formula was the constitution of 1876, to be re-established by free elections presided over by a neutral government, i.e. his own. This would avoid any discussion of the responsibilities of Alfonso for the dictatorship and eliminate the revolutionary appeal to a Constituent Cortes, which might reject the monarchy altogether. Berenguer's weakness was that his government, far from being a neutral election agency, was, as he himself confessed, 'frankly conservative'; its only supporters were those conservatives who had not been led against the dictatorship by Sánchez Guerra.[1] Santiago Alba, whom Cambó advised the king to approach, demanded constitutional revision, while monarchical liberals like Romanones were determined, if they helped the king at all, to help him on their own terms, which were control of the forthcoming elections. Hopelessly unaware of the rising current against the king, they were talking the antiquated language of 'conservative and liberal situations' in what an experienced politician of the 1850's would have recognized as a 'pre-revolutionary situation'. Immediately applied, Berenguer's solution might have stood a chance, but he delayed a year before summoning the Cortes for March 1931; by this time many politicians had lost confidence in the future of the monarchy, and the personal popularity of the king had been destroyed by a steady campaign against him.

[1] Cf. the letter of Fabié (30 Jan. 1930). 'The king's friends are radiant with joy' quoted M. de Burgos y Mazo, *Los constitucionales*, ii. 26.

The initial blow against the prestige of the monarchy was struck by Sánchez Guerra, whose conspiracy and trial had made him a popular hero: in a critical but ambiguous speech he refused to rally his conservatives to the defence of the monarchy. 'I am not a Republican, but I recognize that Spain has a right to be a Republic.' With this recommendation the man of the moment lost his moment: since he was a figure-head of the Constitutionalist party, it meant that party's eclipse. This grouping of unemployed politicians held a political significance beyond its numerical force. It represented the disillusionment of 'the monarchists without a king', the drying up of confidence, and the sympathy of monarchist politicians with those who wished to destroy the monarchy.[1]

How was the monarchy to be overthrown? The revolutionary tactics of 1930 are incomprehensible except on the assumption that the anti-monarchical coalition doubted whether the personal unpopularity of the king was great enough to drown residual monarchical conservatism in a general election. Although the monarchy lacked enthusiastic and committed support (the remnants of the U.P. were the only organized monarchist party, and they were fighting a private vendetta with the king over the dictator's dismissal) it might yet survive through inertia and the monarchism of the countryside. To hide this lack of faith in the general will Republicans could point to Berenguer's disastrous hesitations about an election, and revive the historic accusation that elections run by monarchical politicians would be 'insincere'. Hence a republic could legitimately be imposed by a *coup*. But for a republican rising to be successful it must be supported by the army in a pronunciamiento, by the workers in a general strike, and by rebellion in Catalonia.

In Catalonia the dictatorship had damaged the monarchy beyond repair. Republican Catalanist groups had grown at the expense of the conservative Lliga, committed by Cambó to the proposition that Catalan autonomy was attainable within

[1] The Constitutionalists represented an uneasy alliance of right-wing republicans and reformist monarchists. The formula of the Constitutionalist party was the acceptance of the decision of a Constituent Cortes—the standard formula to hide cracks in similar political alliances ever since 1868. To convinced monarchists this was little better than republicanism: hence defenders of the monarchy regarded the Constitutionalists as the initiators of an avalanche of treason.

the monarchy without revolution. Catalanist republicans were divided between the more cautious bourgeois and intellectual groupings and Maciá's *Estat catala*, which was frankly revolutionary and hoped for collaboration with the C.N.T. In July 1930 republican Catalanists of all shades agreed to co-operate with the Spanish republicans if they, in their turn, could present a united front: their price for co-operation was complete autonomy for Catalonia as the first claim on a victorious republic. In October 1930 a revolutionary committee was set up. But without money it could not stage a military rebellion (officers needed security in the case of failure) and without the army it must appeal to the C.N.T., a course which scared most of the conspirators. Thus the revolutionary initiative passed from Catalonia; though there was little monarchical feeling in Barcelona, there was no organized rebellion.[1]

As for the workers, Berenguer could no longer count on their passivity. He hoped that continued favour would retain the Socialists and the U.G.T. as a 'government force', but those who had always opposed co-operation with a dictatorship now swung into an alliance with revolutionary republicanism. It was Socialists like Prieto and Álvarez del Vayo who were most active in the purchase of arms for a rising. More important, in Barcelona the C.N.T. re-emerged. Mola, as chief of police, was convinced that here lay the most serious revolutionary threat to the régime.[2] What saved the government was the dogma of anarchism, which forbade co-operation with bourgeois revolutionaries. Nevertheless, in the revolutionary atmosphere of Catalonia it was hard for the C.N.T. Regional Committee to stick to purist tactics. Throughout the dictatorship the C.N.T. leaders had wooed Maciá's conspirators and had shared prison cells with them; smothering their principles in a distinction between illicit pacts and a licit intelligence, the C.N.T. leaders

[1] Catalonia was 'dragged along by Madrid and had lost the political hegemony of Spain': F. Sola Cañizares, *El moviment revolucionari* (Barcelona, 1932), esp. 46, 59, 87. So great were the fears of the C.N.T. and so uncertain its co-operation that the 'Maura plan' demanded revolution *outside* Barcelona.

[2] Mola's plan seems to have been to control the C.N.T. by using the government supervision allowed by the laws governing the right of association: he thus hoped to prevent the growth of revolutionary *sindicatos de ramo* which could paralyse a whole industry at a blow. Berenguer neither shared Mola's fears nor supported his policy. Thus the government tended to favour the *sindicatos libres* against the C.N.T., a policy which Mola considered a disastrous provocation.

signed *Intelligencia Republicana* (May 1930), a step for which they were subsequently to be bitterly criticized. In the event the C.N.T. contributed nothing to the rebellion of 1930, because the republican conspirators were frightened by its terms: arms for workers and a revolution in the streets. Bourgeois revolutionaries proved once again that they were not serious; the most they could extract from the revolutionary proletariat of Catalonia was a vague benevolence.[1]

The conspirators could, however, count on sympathy in the army, where the fruits of thirty years of royal flattery had turned rotten in the latter years of the dictatorship. The artillery, in spite of Berenguer's use of his prestige to restore the 'harmony of the military family', never fully recovered its loyalty to the king. The higher officers, personally loyal to Alfonso, would not denounce their juniors engaged in plots.[2] In this atmosphere unruly spirits were moving. Ramón Franco, the popular transatlantic aviator in whom Berenguer could see no evil, was a revolutionary exhibitionist with contacts in the Catalan left. Queipo de Llano, whom Berenguer rightly refused to reinstate, carried on his personal vendetta with a government that would not disown the dictator's acts. Captain Galán, passed over in promotion, saw himself as the Robespierre of the future republic.

Once more two theories of military obedience were in conflict. Mola maintained that it was the duty of soldiers to obey a legal government: to Queipo de Llano it was the duty of soldiers to examine the legality of the government before obeying it. Mechanical discipline was subject to the higher discipline of loyalty to the *patria*: a perjured king, who had broken his contract with the nation in 1923, could no longer command obedience.[3] A separate revolutionary committee controlled the military side of the rising. This military rising was never properly put to the test and it may be doubted whether the army would

[1] For these complicated negotiations see B. Pou, *Un año de conspiración* (Barcelona, 1933), esp. 160 ff. Peiró, the first editor of the revived *Solidaridad Obrera*, signed the *Intelligencia Republicana* (i.e. action for a Constituent Cortes and a federal republic); cf. J. Peirats, *La C.N.T. en la revolución española* (Toulouse, 1951) i. 22–25. The problems of co-operation in this period are set out in the debates in the *Memoria* of the 1931 June Congress (Barcelona, 1931).

[2] General E. Mola, *O.C.* 272–90.

[3] General Queipo de Llano, *El movimiento reivindicativo de Cuatro Vientos* (1933), 29 ff.

have risen against the king. What mattered was that in the crisis of April 1931 neither Berenguer nor Sanjurjo, commander of the Civil Guard, believed that the army could be used against a republican mob in the streets. In 1931 officers would not risk a civil war as they did so easily in 1936—hence they were responsible for what has been called a 'negative pronunciamiento', since their abstention left the monarchy defenceless. Their true loyalty lay to a conception of national order, which they saw imperilled in 1936, rather than to monarchical institutions as such. Then it was the turn of Mola to use the familiar arguments he rejected as treason in 1930.

In August of that year all the conspirators met in a San Sebastian hotel and signed a pact which committed the united Spanish republican groups and the Catalan left to joint action. The republican bloc accepted the terms of the Catalan left, and to get the Catalan alliance, Lerroux swallowed his political past. This reflected the discomfort of the Radical Republicans; they were treated as an old-fashioned, dwindling force because their inherited distaste for Socialists, the Church, and Catalans imperilled a broad 'modern' republican front—a miscalculation that hid the electoral strength of Radical Republicanism as the only anti-monarchical group with the remnants of an organization.[1] Thus Azaña, a littérateur without a party, was more useful, because his forward-looking republicanism reassured Socialists and Catalans and could appeal to the new recruits amongst the intellectuals as Lerroux's creed could not. On the other hand it was a figure from the past, Alcalá Zamora, a republican convert of a year's standing, who became the central figure of the conspiracy, because his promise of a conservative Catholic Republic would reassure the bourgeoisie on the right: it was symbolic that he was arrested for conspiracy coming from mass. Thus a liberal cacique from Andalusia, remembered for his emotional anti-Catalanism, became the chairman of the Revolutionary Committee set up at San Sebastian; this committee was to become the Provisional Government of the Second Republic.

The weakness of the revolutionary alliance set up by the Pact of San Sebastian was the uncertainty and tenuousness

[1] Lerroux's subsequent disgust with the San Sebastian arrangements is reflected in his *La pequeña historia* (Buenos Aires, n.d.), 53–59.

of its relations with the workers' parties. Prieto attended the conference in a personal capacity and the only security for revolutionary action by the C.N.T. was the series of loose understandings which the leaders, on their own initiative, had made with the extreme left elements in Catalonia. The Socialists agreed to support a non-socialist Republic—a compromise which, though it could be justified by Marxists, would only *work* if the bourgeois Republic legislated socialism into existence; as for the C.N.T., very soon the Socialists were accusing it of treason and 'vulgar delation' as an inevitable consequence of the leaders' incapacity to control their own militants.[1]

The rebellion was planned for 15 December, but at the last moment changes of plan confused the conspirators; on the 12th one of them, Captain Galán, rose at Jaca, an Aragonese garrison town. He was to become the martyr of republicanism; his action was that of a megalomaniac who dreamed of capturing the glory of a successful revolution for himself. His rising was ineptly directed and the rebels, without food or transport, were easily defeated by loyal troops. The Madrid conspirators, taken by surprise, were compelled to follow his action by issuing a mimeographed manifesto, signed by members of the Revolutionary Committee, who were promptly arrested by the government; the U.G.T. and the Socialist leaders were unable to call a general strike in the capital.[2] To Ramón Franco was left the last desperate gamble. With Queipo de Llano, who believed rebellion hopeless once he had seen the trams running in the early morning, he drove by taxi to the aerodrome of Cuatro Vientos and from there flew over Madrid, only to observe normal life going on in the streets.[3] A few bar pianos playing the 'Marseillaise', a few groups of undecided workmen,

[1] According to Enrique Santiago in *La Unión General de Trabajadores ante la revolución* (1932), the San Sebastian plans were 'revealed' in *Solidaridad Obrera*, 21–25 Oct. Cf. 76–77 for Peiró's and Pestaña's failure to control the militants: 'instead of resigning they went on with them.'

[2] Railway workers transported the troops who defeated Galán. Inaction reflected the fears inspired in reformist Socialists like Besteiro by the failure of the 1917 revolutionary strike. J. Álvarez del Vayo, *The Last Optimist* (New York, 1950), 204. Cf. M. Cordero, *Los socialistas y la revolución* (1932), 80–87.

[3] Both he and Queipo de Llano escaped by aeroplane to Portugal. The best account of Cuatro Vientos is in Queipo de Llano, *Cuatro Vientos*, esp. 92 ff. Franco believed his action failed because of minor dislocations: in fact there was no chance of success.

had been the only overt signs of rebellion. Neither the army nor the workers had moved and the only serious support was given by a series of peaceful general strikes in provincial capitals.[1]

To outside observers the government had mastered an unsupported rebellion and a mood of pessimism overwhelmed Republicans. Yet the failure of the December plot was the greatest blessing for the future Republic; had it succeeded, the Republic would have come, observed a Republican, as a result of yet another *militarada*. Its failure and the martyrdom of Galán and his fellow-conspirator García Hernández, whose execution was exploited as an example of Alfonso's cruelty, allowed a conversion of opinion to a republican solution which expressed itself in the vote against the monarchy in April 1931. Throughout the Republic portraits of Galán and Hernández were to be found pinned on working-class walls.

Active in this conversion were the intellectuals whom the dictatorship had brought into politics. In February the novelist Pérez de Ayala, Ortega y Gasset, and Doctor Marañón, all with considerable influence in upper middle-class society and none of whom was a professed Republican, publicly condemned the monarchy by originating a non-party grouping called 'In the Service of the Republic'. As soon as opinion could express itself it was critical of Alfonso. From this moment the greatest weakness of the monarchical cause was its lack of an influential press: apart from *A.B.C.* and the Catholic *El Debate*, it was undefended against a hostile campaign.[2] If the press was gingerly censored, books were free.[3] To monarchists the whole moral and social world that had supported the monarchy was in dissolution when Russian communism and sexual relations could be openly discussed. The monarchy had never taken the intellectuals seriously, and the blind and closed world of the court never suspected the growth of their influence. The king, after

[1] For these strikes, omitted by almost all Spanish sources, see *The Times*, 14–20 Dec.

[2] Cf. A. Alcalá Galiano, *La caída de un trono* (1933), 95–124.

[3] Cf. R. Llopis's book, *Como se forja un pueblo*, which praised the Soviet educational system with its 'faith in the future'. It is one of the first of a new genre of literature of enthusiasm for the 'Russian experiment'. Llopis could not publish the book as articles in *El Sol*. 'Whoever wishes to express his thoughts freely must necessarily resort to book form' (ibid. 10).

his famous approach to Azcárate, neglected them; like the politicians, they bored him; he was 'more interested in a turbine or a bridge than in a political debate'. The intellectuals and their allies among the politicians now took their revenge.[1]

At the same time that Berenguer's 'mild dictatorship' denied constitutional liberties, it was subject to a creeping paralysis in the face of disorder, a malignant disease described by Mola in his memoirs.[2] The Post Office and telegraph services were at the service of republican conspirators who had broken government codes. As chief of police, Mola found his office invaded by journalists, his forces riddled by jealousies, inefficient, corrupt, and ill-equipped—the Madrid police had to use taxis which were scarce in times of crisis. Officers and men alike sensed that a republic was coming and acted accordingly by failing to arrest their future masters. Tired out by student riots and strikes, the police voted republican, it was said, in order to get a good night's sleep.

It was Berenguer's long-postponed summons for a Cortes to meet in March 1931 which exposed the attrition that was working havoc in the monarchical forces. In February, to his surprise, his offer of an election was met by a wave of abstention; party leaders refused to accept his election as sincere while the old government-appointed municipalities were still in being. By February 1931 the bottom had dropped out of Berenguer's planned return to normality: he therefore resigned.

The king now did what he might have done with success a year before: he called on Sánchez Guerra to form a ministry, accepting his terms of a Constituent Cortes and the temporary suspension of his prerogatives. Sánchez Guerra visited the imprisoned revolutionary committee which rejected his offers. The king then turned to Melquíades Alvarez who insisted on the appointment of General Goded and Burgos y Mazo, two conspirators. This the king would not stand. 'With this man', commented Melquíades Alvarez, 'it is impossible to do anything.' The consultations had achieved nothing except to reveal that the monarchy was 'already in the ante-chambers of the revolution' and that the imprisoned revolutionary com-

[1] Cf. the remarks of Indalecio Prieto in 'La ideología de Marañón, *Cuadernos americanos*, xix (Mexico, 1960), 114 ff.

[2] His three volumes of memoirs are printed in *O.C.* (Valladolid, 1940).

mittee was more powerful than the king himself. This strangely old-fashioned crisis was resolved by the appointment of Admiral Aznar (a non-political figure, famed for his novel-reading in moments of acute crisis) as prime minister with a cabinet of old-fashioned monarchist politicians—both La Cierva and Romanones were ministers. The concession of municipal elections was the ministry's bid for popularity and acceptance by opinion.

The Aznar government rapidly lost what prestige surrounded its inception: from the outset it was divided between those like La Cierva, who believed the monarchy could and should resist to the point of civil war, and those like Romanones who put their faith in concession.[1] From the cells of the Model Prison the revolutionary committee saw its influence grow: when the government refused to satisfy all the railway workers' demands, the committee promised their satisfaction in a republic. The trial of the committee was turned by government weakness into a republican demonstration: the defendants were allowed to come from prison in private cars and were treated by the public as the future governors of Spain. On top of all came the worst of the student riots. Students barricaded themselves in the Medical Faculty and fired on the Civil Guards; the Minister of the Interior came to terms with the Dean and withdrew his forces. Afraid of creating martyrs by strong measures, the government trusted to a victory in the forthcoming elections as the only hope.

On the evening of 12 April the returns of municipal elections from provincial capitals came in: the Republican–Socialist bloc had triumphed everywhere. This result surprised the opposition as much as it did the government. The Republicans could turn what they would have been content to treat as administrative elections, if defeated, into a plebiscite against the monarchy; though the small towns voted monarchist and there was a majority of monarchist councillors in Spain as a whole, they were correct when they argued that 'numbers' (i.e. the large constituencies) and 'intellect' (i.e. the 'enlightened' urban

[1] La Cierva believed himself the obvious candidate for the Home Office: instead of a fighter, the neutral Hoyos was given this key post. Alfonso himself was nearer to Romanones than to La Cierva and was attracted by Cambó's latest project of a monarchical centre party. (Cf. J. de la Cierva, *Notas*, 342–3.)

voters) had rejected a king still acceptable to rural opinion. The cabinet was stupefied; it had scarcely discussed the elections and now ceased to act as a unified body. In the evening Berenguer, as Minister of War, without consulting the king or his colleagues, sent out a circular telegram to the army admitting defeat and counselling order and submission to the national will. Romanones, who had planned a cocktail party to celebrate victory, 'slept the sleep of he who knows all is lost'.

On the 13th Cambó, a sick man and distressed by the triumph of the Catalan left over the Lliga, summoned Romanones to the Ritz in Madrid: Romanones was to advise the king to come to terms with Alcalá Zamora's revolutionary committee. To this the king agreed, a decision which meant the end of the monarchy. In the evening, without revealing to the cabinet his morning's work, Romanones, against La Cierva's bitter opposition, persuaded the ministry to resign: each minister was to explain to the king his view of the significance of the elections and most agreed that the monarchy was now illegitimate. Even more decisive, Sanjurjo, as commander of the Civil Guard, made it clear that he could not bring out his forces against the revolution.

On the morning of the 14th, Romanones wrote a note to the king advising him to leave Spain, while Bugallal and La Cierva wrote counselling resistance with their aid. La Cierva, in full court dress, met Romanones leaving the king's study in a lounge suit: the king had clearly been convinced by Romanones's arguments.[1] Meanwhile, at noon, in Dr. Marañón's house, Romanones had negotiated with Alcalá Zamora the king's immediate removal from Spain and the revolutionary committee's assumption of power as a provisional government.[2] The committee was now supported by the streets and at three o'clock the republican flag was hoisted over the Telephone Building, for news had come through that a republic had been declared in Barcelona. At the evening audience La Cierva

[1] La Cierva was prepared to head a government of resistance. The king refused sharply. Only after his abdication did he recognize La Cierva's loyalty with the phrase, 'Don't bear a grudge against me, Juan'.

[2] Romanones tried to get a few days' truce and a government under the Constitutionalist Villaverde, in order 'to prepare for the future with serenity'. Alcalá Zamora pointed out that provincial governors were already communicating with him rather than with the government (I. Prieto, *Marañon*, 121).

realized that the king and Romanones had sold the pass. With the crowd already demonstrating outside the palace, the king's baggage was hastily packed and he left for Cartagena by car *en route* for Marseilles. It was all very sudden. 'The fall of the monarchy', wrote Alfonso's polo tutor, the marqués de Villavieja, 'gave me a greater shock than any fall from a polo pony.'

To militant monarchists, the ministers who supported Romanones had persuaded the king to make a shameful surrender in order to save himself from a mob controlled by the revolutionary committee.[1] Whatever the weaknesses of the government before the election results, its liberal wing was correct in believing that surrender was inevitable, once the results had come in, and that it was better for the country and the dignity of the monarchy that this surrender should be made in a formal manner rather than to a street revolution. It was true, as monarchists pointed out, then and since, that the countryside voted monarchist. Blinded by visions of traitors handing over in Madrid, they did not realize that whatever had happened in the capital, republics would have been declared in most large provincial cities. In Seville, without any knowledge of what was happening in Madrid, the Republicans and Socialists took over from a civil governor who had no mind to resist.[2] Barcelona had a Catalan Republic before the ministers had their last audience with the king. Only civil war could have imposed the monarchy on the large towns and Alfonso, to his credit, refused to face this prospect.

Thus it was not the last-minute defeatism of the ministry that brought down the monarchy but the personal unpopularity of the king himself, reflected in the municipal elections. 'We are out of fashion', Alfonso complained. It could not be forgotten that he had initiated the dictatorship in 1923. The monarchy's only chance would have been a change to civilian and parliamentary rule in January 1930; instead, the king appointed Berenguer's ministry, which continued for a year government by decree and censorship without the moral force to make authoritarian rule effective. Instead of being the engineer of political stability, Berenguer, in his own words, found himself

[1] The nature of the mob pressure on the 14th has been much disputed. It was a good-tempered mob but it would have turned nasty had the king not left by the evening.

[2] E. Vila, *Un año de república en Sevilla* (Seville, 1932), 18 ff.

the cork in a half-opened bottle of champagne. The conservative classes, during 1930, lost confidence in the monarchy as a bulwark against social revolution. Reassured by Alcalá Zamora's conservatism, overawed by students and strikers, they made no effort to organize a defence of the monarchy, cold-shouldering its defenders on the extreme right. From Berenguer down, conservatives resolutely disowned all connexion with the dictator's former supporters; this meant that the Monarchical Union (the U.P. with another name) defended the dictator's reputation rather than the monarchy which had rejected him. The conservative classes of Spain were not yet ready for an alliance with the extreme right. Rather than face resistance to a revolution, they let the king go. The aristocracy, which had never forgiven Alfonso for his co-operation with the dictator and his middle-class technicians, observed the fall of the monarchy as they might have watched a bad film.[1]

[1] A. de Hoyos y Vinent, *El primer estado*, 245. Cf. the king's observation to Lord Londonderry: 'Charlie, even the Navy turned against me'

XV

THE SECOND REPUBLIC
1931–1936

It was in the streets and plazas of Madrid that the constitutional kingship, which nineteenth-century Spanish liberalism had created and sustained, finally ceded victory to its historic enemy—republicanism. This chapter and its epilogue will briefly consider the failure, political and military, of the second Republic to maintain itself against those forces which had manipulated the constitutional monarchy—the army and the 'respectable' classes—and against the pressures of those who rejected the bourgeois Republic as they had rejected the constitutional monarchy before it—the extreme right and the revolutionary left.

To the left, in general, the task of republicanism was the liquidation of the institutional hindrances to a progressive, democratic society—notably an influential state church, a powerful army, *latifundismo*. The Republic must also solve the problems of Catalan and Basque nationalism. This programme would make the new régime more than a change in political nomenclature: its partial realization was the achievement of the Azaña coalition which dominated the constructive phase of the second Republic, after the elections to the Constituent Cortes (June 1931) had made the provisional government a parliamentary impossibility. The provisional government consisted of a mixture of converts from the *ancien régime* and a new generation of reformist Republicans and Socialists. It was presided over by Alcalá Zamora and included Miguel Maura; both were conservative Catholics and both last-minute converts to republicanism. Alcalá Zamora had served as Romanones's secretary and Maura was the son of the great conservative politician of the monarchy. They resigned in October 1931 in protest against a church settlement which was the consequence of the pressures of the left republican and socialist majority. Alcalá Zamora was elected President of the Republic and gave to the politics and ceremonial of the new régime in Madrid a somewhat old-fashioned look—a survival like those old influences in the countryside which distressed the optimists who believed that political *mores* could change overnight.[1]

The Azaña coalition had to offer a New Deal to the forces represented by the socialist strength in the Cortes. Azaña himself was consciously modern, an intellectual of the left and a student of French politics; he was not a Socialist but he could only survive as prime minister in the chamber with the aid of socialist votes. The resultant compromise made the Radical Socialists—largely modelled on the French party, without firm proletarian support, doctrinaire, and factious in its politics—a characteristic party of the coalition, and what was called 'humanist socialism' its ideology.[2] This was a deduction, not from the premiss of the class-struggle, but from the necessity of a modern society; it was Jacobin rather than Marxist in tone, middle class rather than proletarian. By 1933 Socialists were beginning to wonder if 'humanist socialism' was worth the socialist votes which kept the coalition in being. This disintegration of the electoral foundations of the Azaña coalition on the left was matched by its exposure to the disillusionment of those who would have accepted a conservative republic and to the hostility of those who could accept no republic at all. The electoral defeat of November 1933 was the consequence of this double process. To the socialist left, Azaña's government appeared old fashioned, already a relic from a side-track of the historical process. To the conservative right it appeared 'degraded' and its members, either from conviction or sheer incapacity, prepared to allow Spain to drift along the road towards social revolution.

[1] Cf. the compromises with the electoral influences of the *ancien régime* which were made by Republicans. In Corunna the Republicans were divided; Casares Quiroga made an alliance with one group of monarchical caciques, and his rival of the Republican Alliance with another. Cf. Quiroga Ríos, *Quien es y adonde va Santiago Casares* (Corunna, 1932), esp. 33 ff.

[2] For a discussion of 'humanist socialism' see *Cuadernos americanos*, lxxviii (Mexico, 1954), 83–113. The Radical Socialists represented some of the worst traditions of Spanish Republicanism, especially its small-town verbal violence. Some of the worst civil governors of the new régime were the party's hangers-on.

1. *The Republican New Deal*

The constitution enacted by the Constituent Cortes represented the ideals of humanist socialism before they had been soured. Its drafting was first entrusted to a juridical commission dominated by a conservative lawyer.[1] This was replaced by the parliamentary committee under Jiménez de Asúa, a socialist intellectual who was surprised by the ease with which drafts prepared by his party were accepted without modification. A compendium of those modern constitutions (beginning with the Mexican constitution of 1917) which went beyond the defence of individual liberties to the provision of a minimum of social well-being, it was to its opponents 'a jazz band of a constitution, without rhythm, without harmony'.

To its creators it seemed 'a daring constitution', left-wing but not socialist. It made property of all kinds 'the object of expropriation for social utility'—a compromise between the Radicals' distaste for all infringements of private property and the socialist draft declaring for gradual socialization. Thus it could be stretched to cover the enactment of extensive state socialism—or it could be limited to a mild control of the abuses of private property.[2]

The constitutional instrument of radical reform was present in the unrestricted power of a single chamber; bicameralism was rejected as a reminder of the Restoration Senate and the bastard constitutionalism of Primo de Rivera.[3] The revolutionary nature of the Republican New Deal would depend on how the government used the powers granted to it by the constitution, and there was little indication, in 1931, that it would go beyond humane labour laws and efficient machinery for the settlement of labour disputes.

[1] For the working of the juridical Committee, see A. Posada, *La Nouvelle Constitution Espagnole* (Paris, 1932), esp. 110–11.

[2] The closest parallel is Article 27 of the Mexican Constitution which is historically significant in that, while it was an attempt to make the social function of property part of constitutional law, it could be made to cover either a defence of the *status quo* or the radical reforms of Cárdenas (cf. F. Tannenbaum, *México* (New York, 1950), 102–12).

[3] For the virtues and dangers of unicameralism see H. Tremolet, *La Chambre unique dans la constitution espagnole* (Montpellier, 1935). Had the constitution possessed a second chamber it would have worked against radicalism in 1931–4, but might have sustained it in 1934–6.

It was not the democratic radicalism or social idealism of the constitution but its religious settlement, embodied in Article 26, that enraged the opposition, split the cabinet, and created the opportunity for a rally on the right to defend a persecuted church. A negotiated and peaceful separation of church and state, as recommended by the juridical committee, could be accepted neither by the intransigent right nor the anti-clerical left. To the former 'a neutral state is an idiot state'; if religious it must be Catholic. 'The Catholic Church is the Mother of Spain . . . the fount of all her glories.' To the left Republicans the classic mistake of nineteenth-century liberalism, which had destroyed its vitality, had been its desire to compound with a clerical past in order to avoid civil war.[1] There could be no compromise between those who praised monks and those who ridiculed martyrs. The accommodating attitude of the Vatican, based on the encyclicals of Leo XIII, and the patience of the Nuncio could achieve nothing.[2]

Article 26 separated church and state, turning the church into an association subject, like all other religious associations, to the law of the land. It cut state clerical salaries, prepared for the dissolution and confiscation of the property of the Jesuits, and made the continued existence of other Orders dependent on good behaviour. It forbade the Orders to teach and removed the crucifix from public schools.[3] The defence of the church, as in the Revolution of 1868, was that Catholics alone were denied rights (especially that of association which covered the Orders) which were guaranteed to all citizens by the constitution itself. Thus Alcalá Zamora quoted Castelar's defence of freedom of association as a foundation of democracy. The left maintained that the church was an institution incompatible with modern culture, politically reactionary, and so rich that it could well support itself by redistributing its vast income. The republican leaders combined the belief that the church was an outmoded institution—Azaña could maintain that Spain

[1] Álvaro de Albornoz, *La política religiosa de la República* (1934), 13 ff., 70, 153–7.

[2] Cf. A. Mori, *Crónica de las Cortes Constituyentes* (1932–3), iii. 159 ff., 187 ff. The extremity of argument is displayed in Leizaola's assertion that the suppression of Spanish friars would mean the replacement of the Spanish language by English in Latin America.

[3] This assault on the secondary schools, more than anything else, alienated those classes whose children had traditionally attended them.

had ceased to be a Catholic country—with the fear that, if given official recognition as a national religion, it would be strong enough to subordinate the state to the church. The Republic was not 'persecuting the church' but taking away the privileges that had made it the stronghold and nursery of political reaction.[1]

Once more the great themes of the nineteenth century were debated in public with a great deal of outworn rhetoric. Azaña saw the realities of the situation: no constitution which the Socialists would not accept was a political possibility. His fighting speech, therefore, marked him as the next prime minister when Alcalá Zamora was forced to resign as a result of his objections to the church settlement. He revealed for the first time the two axioms of his political creed: the Republic would perish if it did not make laws which respected the radical changes in contemporary society; and secondly, the duty of safeguarding such a Republic was superior to liberal principles or minority rights. An old and stable state could take risks for liberty. For a new state, the paramount duty was self-preservation. 'Dont tell me it is contrary to liberty; it is an issue of public safety.'[2]

To the 'respectable' middle classes, Catholic in sentiment and uneasy at the socialist tinge of the government, it appeared that by its church settlement the government had rejected their support in favour of an alliance between Jacobin doctrinaires and a dechristianized proletariat which 'burned the saints of the rich'. In May 1931 an outburst of church and convent-burning had spread from Madrid to Andalusia; this incendiarism was not the work of 'the people' but of small groups. The weakness of the authorities in the face of what Ortega called a reversion to the traditional fetishism of Mediterranean

[1] 'How can you deny that the most distinguished collaborators of the Dictatorship were formed, as to their ideas, in Deusto [the Jesuit University] and the Escorial?' Ibid. 49.

[2] Azaña's speech contains a fascinating examination of the position of the church after the disentailing laws. The suppression of the convents produced the revolutionary generation of 1868 and 1873 because it could be educated without undue clerical influence. When the church returned to influence after 1874, 'instead of seizing property, it seized the consciences of the propertied and thus made itself master of both conscience and property'. Thus the grandchildren of Mendizábal's collaborators were brought up to embrace dictatorship and despotism; 'in this evolution is comprised the whole political history of our country in the last century'.

democracy proved less that the Republic was in the hands of atheists and Masons—as the right was later to maintain—than that it was controlled by inexperienced, weak men.[1]

In the months before the 'persecution' of the church, the right was hesitant and confused; without Article 26 and the consequential legislation culminating in the Law of Religious Confessions and Congregations (10 May 1933) it may well be doubted if it would have gathered strength enough to defeat the Azaña coalition in the elections of November 1933. From the authoritative voice of *El Debate* to the sentimental defenders of a destitute priesthood—'condemned, with their female dependents, to die in hunger'—from monster meetings to theatre demonstrations, from the miraculous survival of images in burnt convents to the schoolboy martyrs carrying round their necks a replica of the crucifix torn down from the walls of their class-rooms, from this massive flood of emotional propaganda the right was drawing strength.[2] It would be necessary to 'sweep away the rot around us'.[2] The old paranoid charges of a revolution manned by an international conspiracy of Freemasons were revived. The Republicans of the left dismissed the Catholic reaction as rigged and 'insincere'; they could understand neither the pathos nor the violence. Their anti-clericalism was a reflex conditioned by history. 'Religion and the Church', maintained the Minister of Education, 'are the antithetical terms.'[4] This was an echo of the residual Krausism and French anti-clericalism that supplied much of the intellectual apparatus of 'humanist socialism'.

The Republic's greatest liquidation of the problems of the past was its solution of the Catalan question. At long last, in the Catalan Statute, Catalonia found a settlement that satisfied her and which turned her into the stronghold of the Republic.

[1] The church burnings took place whilst the Provisional Government was still in power. The one exception to the general weakness was Miguel Maura, Minister of the Interior. His pleas for prompt action by the Civil Guard went rejected by Azaña and his friends who must take the blame for this disaster. Cf. M. Maura, *Así cayó Alfonso XIII* (Mexico, 1962), 252–3. For a hostile account of the church burnings see J. Arrarás, *Historia de la Segunda República Española* (1956), i. 75–100.

[2] For a popular version of the sufferings of the church see Cipriano Nievas, *En torno a la República* (1933).

[3] Cf. J. Tusquets, *Orígenes de la revolución española* (Barcelona, 1932), 93 ff., 140, 200. It must be remembered that four members of the government were Masons.

[4] Marcelino Domingo, *La revolución de octubre* (1935), 157 ff.

Yet, at the outset, Catalan self-government came near to foundering. The Pact of San Sebastian had promised autonomy, to be voted and granted *by the Constituent Cortes*; Maciá, the charismatic leader of Catalan nationalism, tried to grasp the prize at once by declaring for a Catalan state; such a separatist solution would never be accepted by Spanish Republicans and a deputation from Madrid forced Maciá to withdraw.[1] The government of Catalonia would be handed over to a Generalidad (a name which reflected, on the day of triumph, the debt Catalanism owed to the medieval revivalists), which was to prepare a statute of autonomy. This would be presented to the Constituent Cortes after it had been submitted to the Catalan people in a plebiscite. Maciá could trust the Republic to give him back the autonomy he had seized for himself since to deny it would defy the dominant party in Catalonia—the Esquerra or Catalan left. This party was largely the creation of Companys, a lawyer whose contacts extended from pious *rabassaires* to the leaders of the C.N.T. In the short space of twenty-two days Companys destroyed the electoral strength of the conservative Catalanism of the Lliga, discredited by Cambó's last-minute appeals to the monarch. Catalanism now seemed resolutely a movement of the left. The crowds which chanted 'Long live Maciá' shouted 'Death to Cambó'.

The draft of the Catalan Statute was submitted to a referendum and overwhelmingly endorsed by Catalan opinion.[2] The evening of 2 August 1931 was the apotheosis of Maciá and all he had stood for. To a huge crowd 'Grandpa' announced, 'Ja som lliures. . . . At last we are free! No human power will be able to thwart the will of the Catalan people. . . . Let no bitterness, no hatred move you. . . . Catalonia will become great among the civilized nations.' Even as modified by the Cortes the Statute satisfied the reasonable demands of Catalonia. Its

[1] Apparently Prieto had to threaten the withdrawal of the army and the Civil Guard before Maciá would come to his senses. Cf. A. Ossorio, *Companys* (Buenos Aires, 1943), 81–88.

[2] For the elections see E. A. Peers, *Catalonia Infelix* (London, 1937), 200–2. The determination to Catalanize the educational system (e.g. professors lecturing in Catalan to Spanish-speaking students) represents the obsessive concern of Catalanism with the national language which found a harmless outlet in re-labelling museum exhibits. The educational settlement irritated non-Catalans attending schools and universities in Catalonia.

opponents (and these included those Socialists who wanted to keep labour legislation and overall economic planning out of the hands of the 'anachronistic and paternal' Generalidad) claimed that these demands were pitched unreasonably high; that the spheres of the central government and the Catalan government, particularly in the fields of finance, social legislation, and public order had been imperfectly defined.[1] Azaña's task was to remove objectionable features without 'mutilating' the expressed will of Catalonia; his firmness gave him the respect and support of the Catalan left.

The Republic declared itself to be a régime of social justice. By this not even the Socialists meant socialism but a welfare state with state-controlled labour relations, limited workers' participation in management, and a minimum wage. Reformist socialists were insistent that neither Spain nor the Socialist party were prepared for social revolution. 'Revolutions are successful when they bear a true relation to national capacities. . . . We know that a maximalist revolution would imperil the revolution itself.'[2] Rather than the distant prospect of a socialist government, the majority of the party preferred concessions obtained by pressure from within the Azaña coalition, while the leaders were attracted by the possibility of gaining a mass party by means of labour legislation frankly in favour of the worker and administered by Socialists in the government. Only in unguarded moments was the language of legalism abandoned for the threat of the proletarian revolution. In November 1931 Largo Caballero threatened that, if the Cortes were dissolved 'before they had completed their mandate', then the U.G.T. and the Socialists would interpret this as provocation 'which would oblige us to proceed to a civil war'. He later explained that he was 'speaking figuratively'. Such retractions did not reassure the bourgeois mind.[3]

The labour legislation was the work of Largo Caballero as an immensely experienced Trades Union leader. As Minister of Labour he produced a spate of decrees—sickness benefits, holidays with pay, the eight-hour day, minimum wages. Three

[1] Cf. J. Larraz. See A. Mori, *Cortes*, vi, for the debate on the statute.

[2] M. Cordero, *Los socialistas y la revolución* (Madrid, 1932), 308 ff. Cordero was a hard-working municipal councillor and a deputy in Constituent Cortes.

[3] Cf. *El Debate*, 24 and 26 Nov. 1931.

key laws created a machinery for the settlement of labour disputes, derived in part from the legislation of the dictatorship, which he had already worked to his own satisfaction.[1] Settlement was entrusted to mixed committees (where the representation of labour had been increased) under the supervision of Delegates of Labour appointed by the ministry. The Socialists and the U.G.T. were satisfied with this solution on two counts. The new bureaucracy was staffed by Socialists who thus became paid civil servants, as well as labour leaders; above all the imposition of a rigid, supervised system was a direct blow to the C.N.T., since syndicalist principles forbade its using the new machinery in order to gain advantages for its workers. Governmentally minded socialist leaders in 1931 were obsessed by distrust of the C.N.T.: 'There is a great deal of confusion in the minds of many comrades. They consider Anarchist Syndicalism as an ideal which runs parallel with our own, when it is its absolute antithesis, and that the Anarchists and Syndicalists are comrades when they are our greatest enemies.' With the only effective means of improving wages and conditions in their own hands, the Socialists were in a strong position against the C.N.T. with its lack of 'socialist sensibility'.[2]

The Socialists in the government were acutely aware that a decisive struggle was to be fought in the countryside. The rapid gains of the U.G.T. in the rural areas must be consolidated to the discomfiture of rural Anarchism; something must be done to remedy the creeping agrarian unemployment in the south and to fulfil the party's pledge of an agrarian reform. The Law of Municipal Labour, which forbade the employment of migrant labour in order to break wage strikes, and the new machinery of labour legislation, which gave the village Socialists of the *casa del pueblo* control of the local labour market, were mere palliatives, the former of doubtful utility.[3] To cure the immediate problem of rural unemployment, the Republic must take up again the interrupted programme of eighteenth-century

[1] The best account of this legislation is in G. Picard-Moch and J. Moch, *L'Espagne républicaine* (Paris, 1933), 254–76.

[2] M. Cordero, *Los socialistas*, 325, 336, 355.

[3] See above, p. 419, for the economic consequences of the *Ley de terminos municipales*. While it was justifiable to give local labour bargaining power, the boundaries of the municipalites bore little relation to the structure of employment. This made the law almost unworkable.

civil servants—the marriage of idle land with superfluous labour. Agrarian reform was inevitable.[1]

While revolutionary Marxists like Maurín believed the Republic condemned itself to destruction by its refusal to inaugurate a social revolution on the land, left Republicans and Socialists, for different reasons, were combined in the conviction that a truly socialist solution of the land problem would kill the Republic at once. Thus, while the extreme left dismissed the government's bill as not worthy of the name of agrarian reform, the sacrifices which Socialists were making for republican unity were painfully revealed in the speech of its socialist sponsor. 'This is not socialist, I know.' (Interruption: 'Yet a Socialist says this.') 'We respect the present situation and within it we want to solve a problem forced on us by reality: to settle those who are unemployed. . . . The Agrarian Reform is not directed against the régime of private property' (Interruption: 'There will be no land for the *campesinos*.')[2]

The Agrarian Statute of September 1932, together with the legislation of 1933, represented the characteristic compromise of 'humanist socialism' put forward by the Radical Socialists: private property was not an evil in itself but subject to legislative control in the interests of society. It tackled the classical problem of the latifundia where the evils were apparent—especially the lack of employment—and the statistics available.[3] Expropriated land was to be resettled, either collectively or in individual plots, by an Institute of Agrarian Reform. For political reasons, after Sanjurjo's revolt (August 1932), the land of the grandees was to be confiscated without compensation.[4] Other land could be confiscated with compensation, if it exceeded certain limits or

[1] Hence the spate of books on the subject—most of them ill-informed. For a respectable example see V. Rodríguez Revilla, *El agro español y sus moradores* (1931). The author recognizes the acute nature of the problem of *minifundia* but insists that land reform must satisfy 'the triumphant spirit in the countryside', i.e. the desire for 'individual possession'.

[2] A. Mori, *Cortes*, viii. 301 ff.

[3] Lack of adequate statistics nevertheless remained a difficulty: cf. the admission of the government that expropriation must be based on land held in each municipality because 'no public document exists from which we could tell [the totality of] the properties belonging to a single proprietor'. Ibid. viii. 32.

[4] The previous confiscation of the *señorios* was an almost meaningless piece of Jacobinism. Cf. vizconde de Eza, *La exhumación de los señorios* (1932). Eza supported moderate agrarian reform.

had been cultivated badly. The key to the reform lay, therefore, in the funds available for compensation, and these were initially fifty million pesetas: perhaps 10,000 of the agrarian poor were given plots. Agrarian reform, limited by the natural timidity of a coalition government, was whittled down by the 'technical' criticisms of the conservative opposition: the reform neglected any sound principles of land utilization; reforms copied from central Europe had no meaning for the Spanish 'bad lands'; 'general' remedies neglected regional idiosyncrasies; 'parcellization' would only increase rural unemployment.[1] As Eduardo Ortega y Gasset prophesied, limited reform would not capture the loyalty of the Andalusian rural poor: 'it is an old fashioned project of interior colonization, a little more generous and embellished with Socialist phrases'. Little was achieved and enthusiasm evaporated; by August 1933 legislation on leasehold lands, which affected the lives of thousands of rural families, could only muster a handful of deputies in the Cortes. On the whole, agrarian reform proved a disappointing muddle.

Agrarian reform bared the Republic's weakest sinew: 'the greatest of obstacles, that the state is poor, it does not possess a *céntimo*'. The Republic was unlucky in being born into a world depression, though it must be emphasized that Spain did not suffer that deep depression which paralysed the economies of most of Europe and the United States. The most remarkable feature was the relative steadiness of prices: this was due mainly to Spain's isolation from the economy of the rest of Europe, and the dependence of the whole economy on the prosperity of agriculture. Thus the bumper harvests of 1932 and 1934 provided enough purchasing power to support a minor textile boom and did something to compensate for the heavy losses of Valencian orange-growers and other exporters. Wages, protected by the new labour legislation, remained stable. The index of industrial production fell, but it fell less dramatically than in other countries. Spain's difficulties, however, were bad enough—especially in 1932 and 1933, which saw a sharp fall in iron and steel production, hard times for orange and olive-oil producers, and mounting unemployment. There was no national system of assistance to the half million unemployed; the municipalities were left to do what they could with limited resources.

[1] *El Debate*, 17 June 1932, and A. Mori, *Cortes*, viii. 240, 253, 317 ff.

Thus the great pool of agrarian unemployment in the stagnant south seemed to threaten to engulf the Republic itself.

Prieto, the socialist finance minister, reacted to depression in much the same fashion as his orthodox conservative colleagues in other countries: he strove for a balanced budget and a stable currency. This was a political as much as an economic decision. Prieto had been foremost in denouncing the lavish spending of the monarchy and the Extraordinary Budget of the dictatorship. He could scarcely embark on a mild inflation or deficitary budgeting in the interest of socialist planning; he and his successor, Carner, followed the conservative advice of the Gold Standard Inquiry which had insisted on the inflationary effects of lavish government spending. Republican finance was saved from straight deflationary policies only by its pledges to education—school building kept the building boom from breaking in Madrid—and by the fact that, as modernizers of backward Spain, the government could not but continue the more sound of Primo de Rivera's irrigation, hydraulic, and road-building projects.[1] Many of the autonomous 'development' bodies, dismantled in the first enthusiasm of April, reappeared with new members. The budget was not reduced but rearranged.

The weakness of republican legislation, both in the spheres of finance and of labour, was that it threatened fundamental change which the government lacked the will or the desire to implement. Like Blum's legislation in France, none of its provisions was incompatible with orthodox capitalism but altogether they caused capitalists to lose confidence. The railway legislation disrupted the old boards of directors, but stopped short of nationalization; the Banking Law, while it gave the government a control over the discount rate which Calvo Sotelo had sought in vain, left the banks almost as powerful as before. Savage control of foreign exchange operations was held to hamper the flow of trade. Income tax was raised—the top

[1] The Republic's concern for education as the premiss of democratic government was one of its noblest features. Its problem was to unite the subtleties of Giner's pupil–teacher relationship with a crash programme of mass education for an undeveloped country, to make education a 'shield against reaction' without abandoning the tolerant traditions of the Free Institute for militant secularism (cf. José Castillejo's comments in *War of Ideas in Spain*, London, 1937). Some of the educational fever of the Republic resulted in happy improvisation, some in administrative chaos (cf. S. de Madariaga, *Spain*, 316).

rate on fortunes over one million pesetas was 7·7 per cent.—but without any radical reform of a tax system which Primo de Rivera had stigmatized as 'undemocratic' and unjust. The capitalist classes were alarmed, but their power was untouched. Ventosa, a follower of Cambó, emerged as the mouthpiece of the outraged conservatism of the rich. It was not the Republic itself that created the crisis of confidence, but the demagogic excesses of its socialist-inspired government. State socialism would turn Spain into 'one immense latifundium, the State'.[1] If the régime aimed at Soviet collectivization, it should confess its intention and abandon its 'village notion of political economy'.

2. *The Defeat of the Azaña Coalition*

The constructive legislation which, to the supporters of the Azaña coalition was a proof that the Republic was 'serious', explains the defensive reaction of the conservative classes. Thus when the Catalan Statute was debated in the Cortes, 'Spanish' nationalism became a weapon in the hands of those who disliked a radical Republic. The right denounced the self-appointed revolutionaries who had bartered away national unity at San Sebastian. When Spain was seeking liberty, Catalonia thought of its own selfish interests and now demanded 'payment'. The Statute, forced on Spain as if she had been defeated, represented 'not the maximum demands of autonomists but the minimum demands of separatists'. Such attacks, as always, found proof in the unguarded utterances of Catalans. Azaña, who had hoped for a great joint work of Catalan and Spanish republicanism, had to meet the incomprehension engendered by fifty years of mutual misunderstanding.

The increasing hostility of the officer corps reflected in part the conservative reaction of the class it represented. In part it represented the resentment of those officers, whose pasts were monarchical and Catholic, as they observed the rise to influence of a new class of republican officer—the beneficiaries of Azaña's military reforms who were alleged to dominate his 'military cabinet' and monopolize promotions. The reforms themselves could be defended as necessary measures for the creation of a modern army—Azaña had no desire to destroy the army as

[1] J. Ventosa y Calvell, *La situación política y los problemas económicas de España* (Barcelona, 1932), esp. 47, 102–3, 130. Ventosa had been finance minister in Aznar's government.

such—and they embodied changes long advocated by professional soldiers: the pensioning of superfluous officers; the improvement of the conditions of non-commissioned officers, and the abolition of the privileges of the 'snob' corps. General Mola bitterly criticized Azaña's reforms, not so much for their content as for their 'vindictive spirit'.[1] Between 1932 and 1936 a concealed civil war divided the army between those who accepted the Republic loyally and those who believed that the Republic was determined to destroy the army 'morally' if not physically. By July 1936 the malcontents had won over the majority of officers in both the metropolitan and Moroccan armies. The army refurbished its traditional political theory: discipline (obedience to the civilian state) must not be confused with lack of dignity (*carencia de dignidad*). 'Indiscipline is justified', wrote Mola in 1933, 'when the abuses of power constitute an insult and a shame, or when they lead the nation into ruin.' In 1933 the critical moment had not arrived; by 1936 the officers were ready to put dignity above discipline.

In general, however, the forces of conservative resentment were initially weak, divided between those who hoped to canalize discontent into an electoral defeat of the Azaña coalition and those who saw no other course against 'the revolution' but revolt. The division between conspirators and legalists was vague; it was often hard to distinguish between those who would accept a clericalist or conservative Republic and those who would accept no Republic at all. Nevertheless, most parties of the extreme right had connexions with those army officers whose discontent was maturing into sedition.[2] General Orgaz, an Alfonsist, was concerned in vague plans for a military rising in 1931. Between 1931 and 1936 the monarchists occupied the position held by the majority of Republicans between 1874 and 1931. 'Legal' activity was a means of propaganda and it must be preserved at all costs: but it could not, in itself, destroy an illegitimate system.

[1] See his *O.C.* ii, esp. 65 ff.

[2] J. A. Ansaldo, *Mémoires d'un monarchiste espagnol* (Monaco, 1953), 18–21; J. A. Agiře, *Entre la libertad y la revolución* (Bilbao, n.d. but written in 1935), 151–5. Agiře regarded it as part of his duty to his party to learn Orgaz's plans but he did not regard it as part of his duty to the Republic to reveal these plans to the government. For Orgaz's refutation of Agiřes account see M. García Venero, *Nacionalismo Vasco*, 426–9.

Convinced monarchists could hope for little from the legal struggle. The exiled king refused to countenance violence, but he could scarcely hope to convince his followers.[1] *Acción Española*, set up in December 1931, was a remnant of the old U.P. organized as a propaganda centre rather than a party machine; its intellectual leader, Maeztu, saw in the Enlightenment of the eighteenth century and in his fellow *fin de siècle* intellectuals the origins of a monstrous revolution which must be fought to the bitter end in the name of the historic traditions of Spain. 'Let us fight our fathers with our fore-fathers.'

As always the fighting strength of the extreme right came from militant Carlism. For three generations it had denounced the revolution which Maeztu had just discovered. Already in 1931 the Carlists were running arms and building up a para-military organization in the remoter parts of Navarre. Ever since the schism, the *élite* of Carlism had been with the Integralists, the masses with the old dynastic cause. These two groups now fused in the Traditionalist Communion (January 1932) which rejected the Republic *in toto* though it participated as a legal party in the Cortes.[2] Fusion of the Traditionalists and the Alfonsine monarchists was more difficult—both personally and because the Traditionalist position implied that orthodox Alfonsine monarchists had been in a state of political sin since 1874. Nevertheless the Alfonsists were increasingly drawn towards the activist tradition in Carlism. It was to create a monarchical grouping which would attract Carlists that in February 1933 Goicoechea founded *Renovación Española*, a concentration of militant monarchism.

At first it looked as if the Catholic right would find its strongest *point d'appui* in the alliance of Basque nationalism and traditionalism which fought the elections of 1931 as the Basque–Navarrese Block. This alliance broke when the Basque Nationalist Party (P.N.V.) was prepared to recognize the lay Republic in return for the concession, by a statute similar to that proposed for Catalonia, of the autonomy which was their central demand. The Traditionalists were only interested in autonomy as long

[1] In the last days of April or the first days of May the editor of the *A.B.C.* interviewed Alfonso in London; he explicitly condemned military rebellion and insisted that the monarchy would only be re-established by universal suffrage (*A.B.C.*, 5 May 1931). *A.B.C.* was the main monarchist paper.

[2] For the Traditionalist programme see below, p. 645.

as it provided a means to undo the republican church settlement by the inclusion of a clause which would allow an autonomous government to sign a separate Concordat. Without this, the Autonomy Statute was represented by the Navarrese as 'atheist' and its press offered a 5,000 peseta prize to anyone who could find the name of God in the statute.[1] By rejecting the Basque Autonomy Statute as 'illegitimate, against History, against Tradition' they revealed the true meaning of Navarrese Carlism; its care for local liberties was less intense than its concern for the religious unity of Spain. On the eve of the Civil War, its leader was to tell Franco, 'You must impose unity on them. Unity above all.' The Basques who accepted the 'realist' line and the prospect of autonomy within a secular Republic were denounced as the allies of 'Jews, Masons, and Communists'.

The first attempt to force the Republic to the right by violence took the traditional form of a pronunciamiento and its failure provided complete proof of the weakness of the activist right. Its figure-head was General Sanjurjo, Lion of the Rif, the most popular general in Spain. Sanjurjo's incapacity to conceive of himself as a common rebel reflects the persistent strength of the political theory that had guided the political interventions of the army throughout the nineteenth century: his rebellion was not against the civil state but against a government which no longer reflected the general will. This will, as revealed to the general and his allies, rejected the drift to the left, the destruction of national unity with the Catalan Statute, and the *trituración* (grinding) of the army. In his own eyes, his moral, even his legal, fault lay not in rebellion itself but in risking rebellion without adequate preparation and secured support. Politically naïve, he did not realize the dangers of a patchwork conspiracy which ran from monarchists to old Constitutionalists. Compromises were broken in last-minute confusions. Sanjurjo's pronunciamiento suffered from those weaknesses of composition that had ruined so many of the political performances of the army in the past.[2]

In Madrid, where the conspirators attempted to seize the

[1] J. Agiřé, *Libertad*, 93 ff.

[2] Thus General Goded was in touch with Sanjurjo but the conspirators did not inform him of their plans; he was caught by police at the Escorial. Cf. M. Goded, *Un faccioso cien por cien* (Saragossa, 1939), 20. For Azaña's attitude and knowledge of the plans of the rebels see his *Memorias íntimas*, 186 ff.

War Office on the night of 10 August 1932, a *coup* in the hands of monarchists and officers pensioned off under Azaña's reform was a fiasco. In Seville, Sanjurjo declared for a moderate Republic, a solution he had in vain pressed upon Lerroux. Arriving with his uniform in an attaché case, he gave the *grito* 'Long Live Indivisible Spain'. The workers declared a general strike and the officers wavered. Sanjurjo, in a state of complete exhaustion, 'recognized defeat' and was captured escaping to Portugal. The army was not yet ready to support 'the nation' against the state. As his A.D.C. complained, the officers of Azaña's new army were not of sufficient moral stature to keep their compromises.[1] In 1936 the army of Africa was brought in as an insurance against domestic failure and there would be no question of recognizing defeat.

Sanjurjo's failure strengthened the government and republican enthusiasm. It allowed Azaña to point the lesson that too much talk of a Republic of the right had ended in an attempt at military dictatorship. It was not only monarchists but respectable politicians like Melquíades Álvarez who 'made these idiot generals believe that the country would support them'. The rebels were imprisoned or deported, the right-wing press was suspended for a period, and the remaining parts of the constitution, the Catalan Statute and Agrarian Reform (now supplemented by the confiscated land of the rebels and that of all grandees) were pushed through the Cortes. This was a temporary revival. All the indications prove a shift to the right throughout 1933: even in Catalonia the Esquerra, allies of the government coalition, lost in the municipal elections. From this conservative reaction two parties benefited, Lerroux's Radicals and the new Catholic party of Gil Robles—*Acción popular*.[2]

In San Sebastian Lerroux had felt passed over and in the cabinet he and his follower Martínez Barrio appeared as survivors of some lost era of politics. Yet he had topped the poll in Madrid and was the leader of the largest party, next to the Socialists, in the Chamber; but for his hostility to the Socialists he would have been prime minister in place of Azaña. The latter's accession to power had meant a shift of gravity to

[1] Cf. E. Esteban Infantes, *La sublevación del general Sanjurjo* (1933).

[2] Until the term *nacional* was forbidden Gil Robles's movement was known as *Acción nacional*.

the left and increasing dependence on the Socialists. Lerroux resigned and, out of power, it is scarcely surprising that he saw a new political future in rallying middle-class republicanism against socialist-dominated republican governments. Toning down his anti-clericalism, he announced himself as the saviour of civilization and the proponent of a 'Republic for all Spaniards'. In 1933 it is obvious that those who mistrusted Socialists and clericals alike voted Radical.

The mass movement of the right which could draw more directly on the reaction of Catholics to the religious settlement was *Acción popular*. Conceived by the editor of *El Debate*, Herrera, its leader was Gil Robles, son of a Salamanca professor interested in Catholic social reform. Young himself, the leader sought above all to attract youth to his party; most of its candidates were in their thirties and it had a strong Youth Movement. *Acción popular* was distinguished from the old right by its emphasis on a Catholic social policy which would win the masses from socialism by implementing the programme of Leo XIII's encyclicals.[1] It proposed 'a socio-ideological revolution which will coincide on many points with socialist solutions'. Its ideal was a corporative state based on 'free', professional unions; these would give the worker more control over his own destiny than socialist unions run by the caciques of the labour world in their own interests. The party's propagandists boasted of its single working-class deputy, but Gil Robles recognized that the conversion of the proletariat to Social Catholicism would be a long and difficult task. The movement's more immediate programme, and the precondition of social reform, was the recovery of the privileged position of the Spanish Church. This would be accomplished by beating the Azaña coalition at the polls on the platform of revising Article 26.

It was probably Gil Robles's intention that his group should become a parliamentary party functioning within the Republic and modelled on European Social Christian parties.[2] Thus he repudiated military rebellion and tried to get the Agrarian

[1] For an account of Gil Robles's early career see J. Arrabal, *Gil Robles* (Madrid, 1933).

[2] In the early days Angel Herrera talked of the 'Belgain model' and he was undoubtedly an orthodox Christian Democrat; later Gil Robles was influenced by Austria and by his Traditionalist upbringing. His most threatening language was used in the 1933 electoral campaign.

and Basque Deputies to refrain from a quasi-revolutionary *retraimiento*. His consistent embarrassment was his party's need for electoral support and funds from orthodox conservative groupings which shared neither his own preference for legal methods nor his programme of Social Catholicism. This weakness of structure he sought to conceal beneath the doctrine of 'accidentalism'. This assertion that, to Catholics, forms of government were indifferent was derived, like the movement's social policy, from the encyclicals of Leo XIII and the French liberal Catholics of the late nineteenth century. What mattered to Catholics was the position of the Church, not the republican form of the régime. But those conservatives whom Gil Robles wished to attract into broad 'anti-revolutionary' electoral coalitions would not have swallowed explicit loyalty to the Republic; as it was, his preference for legal revisionism disgusted monarchists. 'Accidentalism' did him more harm than good, because it confused his own intentions as a leader of an independent party with those of his allies among monarchist conspirators. Although he pleaded for legal courses the confusion remained. Against violence in politics by his own group, he was less clear about those conditions which might justify its use by others while his ultimate vision of the state, like that of his socialist enemies, was not that of orthodox liberal democrats: it contained current notions of a corporative legislative.

Thus Socialists and left-wing Republicans could present Gil Robles as a counter-revolutionary. They regarded his revisionist campaign, which gathered strength with the anticlerical legislation of 1932–3, as an illegal and improper attack on the Republic itself. Though Gil Robles claimed Windthorst as his hero and the *ralliement* as his model he was denounced by Socialists as a Fascist—a creed he dismissed as a branch of the post-Reformation heresy of 'stateolatry'. A monster meeting, to be held at Valladolid, was banned by the government under socialist threats of a strike, undoubtedly more illegal than the meeting itself. 'If the state crosses its arms before the provocative meeting of Valladolid, the workers will know how to take the place of the state.' This language played into Gil Robles's hands: the state was not a liberal state with a right of free speech and association. It was a socialist concern. By June

1932 the government had suspended sixty-one meetings and suspended the movement's paper, *El Debate*, for two months. Denying *Acción popular* the liberty to act as a constitutional party, the Socialists dismissed it as a conspiracy. 'The clericals, captained by a group of unemployed women, aim to overthrow the Republic created by the blood of the people. . . . Annihilate the enemy without hesitation or piety.'[1] Projected into 1934, when Gil Robles had shed his extremist allies, this attitude was a disaster.

To the republican government the dangers on the left appeared as serious as those on the right. From the first days of the Republic until the elections of 1933, it had to confront, with inexperienced civil governors and an inadequate police force, a series of strikes and revolutionary outbreaks comparable in violence and frequency only with those of 1920–3. The origins of these strikes, apart from the autochthonous agrarian unrest of the under-employed in Andalusia, lay only partly in worsening economic conditions.[2] Their causes are to be found in the implacable hostility displayed by the C.N.T. to a bourgeois Republic and often in the politics of the labour movement itself. Strikes were complicated and encouraged by the feuds of the C.N.T. and the U.G.T. and by a struggle for power within the C.N.T. itself between the 'moderate' syndicalist leaders and the acratic purists of the F.A.I. By 1932 the F.A.I. militants, whose task as a semi-secret pressure group was to permeate the C.N.T. with revolutionary activists, had not merely discredited the Republic: they had brought the C.N.T. itself to a serious crisis.

The socialist leaders had every reason to restrain their militants. Increases in the membership of the U.G.T., particularly in its Agricultural Workers' Federation, made trade union leaders feel that the mere organization of these masses stretched the resources of the U.G.T. to the utmost; the new members must be card-indexed, a *Casa del Pueblo* erected in each new conquest. As a result of the dismissal of monarchist councillors, they found

[1] *El Debate*, 2 Jan. 1932. These accusations were possible because the revisionist campaign (launched Oct. 1931) was waged by a 'union of the right' which included Traditionalists and Alfonsists as well as 'accidentalists'. Moreover, *Acción popular*'s youth movement used quasi-fascist language.

[2] 1933 was a bad year for trade and the number of days lost in strikes leapt from the three million mark to over twelve million. Textiles were booming, yet the textile industry reflects the general trend of strikes to an exaggerated extent (the number of days lost in strikes increased tenfold).

themselves in control of municipalities all over Spain. The new bureaucracy of labour negotiation had to be staffed by Socialists. These new tasks occupied leaders to the full and laid them open to charges of *enchufismo*, of seeking jobs instead of socialism.

The C.N.T. was perfectly aware that Largo Caballero's labour laws threatened their whole organization. As Minister of Labour he backed the U.G.T. in its attempt to wrest control of the Barcelona dockers from the C.N.T. In Madrid, Prieto put down a telephone strike organized by the C.N.T. and *El Socialista* called the strikers' leaders 'brutally ignorant' and their union 'a labour organization based on pistols'.[1] Thus C.N.T. extremists could paint Largo Caballero as a traitor and a collaborationist dog, as another Martínez Anido come to destroy the revolutionary proletariat.

In Catalonia any hopes of acceptance of the Republic by the C.N.T. vanished. In the first days of republican enthusiasm Companys had worked for an understanding with the C.N.T. leaders. 'My friends,' he told them, 'if you feel strong enough to bring off the social revolution, proceed. But if you understand that the only revolution possible is a radical, evolutionist policy that will give you ample freedom for your propaganda, help me.' Even 'moderate' syndicalists could not collaborate; much less was there any hope that they might control extremists. Catalan nationalists were blind enough to believe that the therapeutic powers of autonomy were enough to end strikes and tame anarchism. Maciá told strikers, 'When we have the Statute, conflicts like this will not arise.' Beyond easing the first few days, Companys's efforts at social peacemaking earned him a damaging reputation as a weak man who would betray the bourgeoisie for the sake of his political career.[2]

It was difficult for 'moderate' syndicalists like Pestaña to resist the drift towards revolutionary action. Though direct collaboration with a bourgeois régime was unthinkable they saw that consistent street action against it might strengthen the forces of counter-revolution. It was not the 'moderate' syndicalists' love for the Republic that separated them from the

[1] For an account of Prieto's attitude see *The Times*, 18 Dec. 1932.

[2] See F. Madrid, *Ocho meses*, 134 ff. Carlos Esplá, Companys's successor as Civil governor, proposed to the C.N.T. leaders that he should imprison the extremists in order to strengthen the forces of moderation within the C.N.T. Hardly surprisingly, this extraordinary suggestion was rejected.

activists: it was their conviction that the 'second revolution' must be a mass performance, not the work of a revolutionary *élite*. To the F.A.I. revolution was less a social phenomenon than the product of a resolute revolutionary will, a product not of organization but of the audacity which exploited 'the irresistible force in the hearts of the masses'.[1] To the moderates, this kind of talk and these tactics were 'infantile'. 'When you ask them [the F.A.I.], where shall we go after we have thrown ourselves in the street, they reply that when we are in the street we shall know where we must go.'[2] Relying on the autonomy of the individual unions, F.A.I. activists could propose revolutionary strikes against the will of the C.N.T. leadership. When the leaders refused to sanction such activity, they were denounced as traitors. By these tactics the F.A.I. gained control of the core of Catalan anarchism and its paper *Solidaridad Obrera*; in protest the moderates signed the 'Declaration of the Thirty' which denounced the F.A.I. infiltration and its disastrous effects. Expelled from the C.N.T. they sought to build up their strength by organizing *sindicatos de oposición*. Frank speaking and resistance to mindless revolutionism had cost Pestaña and his friends the leadership of the movement and divided it against itself.

The militancy of the C.N.T. meant the abstention of anarchist voters in the November elections, waves of strikes, and two revolutionary risings. It was not that Spain as a whole was in anarchy—many strikes were indistinguishable from bank holiday demonstrations and there were areas free from serious strikes—but that certain trouble spots stained the whole republican record.[3] Thus there were serious general strikes in Bilbao, where the Socialists were fighting the Basque Catholic Unions, and by the C.N.T. in Saragossa, Seville, and Barcelona. Few of the C.N.T. strikes arose out of economic grievances, though these existed; they were 'gymnastic strikes' to keep the workers' revolutionary muscles tensed, frequently organized by committees for the release of imprisoned militants and dominated by the F.A.I.

Barcelona apart, Seville was the most troublesome city.[4]

[1] A. G. Gilabert, *La C.N.T., la F.A.I. y la revolución española* (n.d.), 14.

[2] Diego Abad de Santillan in *Solidaridad Obrera*, 29 July 1931.

[3] See E. A. Peers, *The Spanish Tragedy* (London, 1936), 96.

[4] For the politics and unrest in Seville, as observed by a right-wing journalist, see

The police was weak, its nerves strained. The C.N.T. was strong, but it had lost the dockers to the Communists and was fighting the U.G.T. for the tramways; as always where there were strong C.N.T. elements, the Socialists were forced to pose as revolutionaries though they worked against any revolutionary outbreak. In July 1931 a minor revolt, aided by peasants from the surrounding districts and inspired by the C.N.T., was put down by the army—making a significant first appearance in its role as saviour of society from red revolution. In Catalonia the F.A.I. set off a more serious attempt at social revolution. In January 1932 a planless rising brought libertarian communism for five days to the Llobregat valley. In January 1933 the divided C.N.T. lurched into another rising in Barcelona.

It was in the abandoned countryside, where both the U.G.T. and the C.N.T. were making effective penetration, that the two most savage episodes took place.[1] The village of Castilblanco murdered and mutilated its Civil Guards; in January 1933, in Casas Viejas, a local enthusiast staged one of those declarations of village independence characteristic of the millenarian tradition of rural anarchism. The government forces suppressed this hopeless outbreak and twenty-five of the villagers were shot.

The damage had been done. It was the long-term effects of Casas Viejas which destroyed Azaña's government in September 1933. The cycle of disorder and repression not merely alienated the proletarian forces but put a weapon into the hands of malcontents on the right: the Republic was presented as other governments of the past—corrupt, incapable of preserving public order, yet violent. A campaign of calumny was opened. Joaquín del Moral, a lawyer who had played a part in the campaign against Primo de Rivera's 'lack of juridical sense', attacked the government for its high-handed interference with the judiciary. His book is contemptible in form and content, with its accusations of pluralism and the abuse of official cars. His exaggerations were taken up in an even lower key by Albiñana, the leader of the Nationalist Legionaries. 'When in the heights [of the

E. Vila, *Un año de república en Sevilla* (Seville, 1932). Unrest was worst in the port area; it was much exaggerated by the right wing press (e.g. *A.B.C.*)

[1] For a description of these events see G. Brenan, *Labyrinth*, 247–8, 255–6, and E. Hobsbawm, *Primitive Revels*, 84–86. The government acted with vigour because it could not afford to see the police forces alienated by 'softness'.

Republican government] dung is condensed only muck can fall.' Imprisoned for these attacks they posed as martyrs to a republican inquisition, more violent than the repression of the dictatorship and exercised by 'homincules' who did not wash their faces and who were protected by Jews and Masons.[1] These attacks were in themselves ridiculous, but they represented the lower regions of the 'desertion of the professional classes', the swing to the right which was to culminate in the electoral defeat of the Azaña coalition.[2]

The ministerial crises in the summer of 1933 showed that the republican unity forged at San Sebastian had degenerated into a party feud between its component parts; it was the Radical party of Lerroux which made the most bitter attacks on the government over the Casas Viejas affair. When Azaña resigned (June 1933), Alcalá Zamora tried to form a government which would exclude the prime minister but include both Radicals and Socialists. Prieto was willing to form such a government, but it was frowned on by Largo Caballero—an indication of their divergent attitude to participation in a bourgeois government which was to have grave consequences in 1936.[3] On Azaña's second resignation (September 1933) the President called on Lerroux. The Radicals could not govern without a new Cortes and the President refused Lerroux a dissolution; instead, it was granted to Martínez Barrio, who went to the country in November 1933. In his manipulation of the moderating power, Alcalá Zamora found the prerogative as short a way to unpopularity as had Alfonso XIII. Azaña believed he had been sacked. Lerroux maintained that he had been given power only to destroy him as leader of his party.[4]

[1] Albiñana, an embittered crank, was confined in Las Hurdes, a wild region. His lamentations are contained in *Confinado en las hurdes* (1933). The title of his earlier work was *Spain under the Republican Dictatorship. The chronicle of a petrified epoch* (Madrid, 1932). See also J. del Moral, *Oligarquía y enchufismo* (Madrid, 1933) —a play of words on the title of Costa's work.

[2] For comments on the 'desertion' of the intellectuals, see Carlos M. Rama, *La crisis española del siglo XX* (Mexico, 1960), esp. 105 ff. That the critical attitude towards the democracy of the Republic of such well-known thinkers as Ortega 'paralysed middle-class liberalism' seems to me an exaggeration.

[3] See below, p. 629.

[4] For these events, from Lerroux's point of view, see his attacks on Alcalá Zamora in *La pequeña historia* (Buenos Aires, n.d.), esp. 103, 123, 141, 151. His complaints are analogous to those made by Moret when he was refused a dissolution by Alfonso XIII in 1906 (see above, pp. 476–7).

More serious than the dissolution of the Republican parties—the Radical Socialists, for instance, were in complete confusion and thoroughly discredited—was the desertion of the Socialists. They refused to join Martínez Barrio's government and fought the elections as a separate party. This entailed a reduction in socialist strength and the annihilation of the Left Republicans (the group of which Azaña was the figurehead) who lost both socialist votes and the middle-class floating voters who now voted conservative, i.e. Radical. The Left Republicanscould not escape the charge of repressing the workers: the Radical Socialist Marcelino Domingo could not speak at election meetings against cries of 'Assassin', 'Casas Viejas'.[1] This was particularly disastrous in Catalonia, where the C.N.T. relations with the Esquerra had degenerated into bitter enmity as a result of police persecution, and in Aragon. The C.N.T., dominated by the F.A.I. purists, ran a campaign of 'Don't Vote' (*No votad*). The C.N.T. leaders realized that this would produce a right-wing victory in Catalonia; then, with a straight reactionary government in power, was the time to declare for the social revolution. As usual, C.N.T.–F.A.I. obsession with the revolutionary tactic was disastrous for a left-wing, progressive Republic.

Confronting the fragmented elements of the Azaña coalition stood an electorally more united right. Given the electoral law, any group which agreed on a list of candidates for the multi-member constituencies, must triumph over two disparate groups. The right found it exceedingly difficult to arrange co-operation between Gil Robles's C.E.D.A. (an electoral confederation of Catholic parties of which the most important group was *Acción popular*) and the counter-revolutionary monarchists, especially as in some constituencies the C.E.D.A. worked with Radicals in order to defeat Socialists.[2] Whereas to Gil Robles the election was to be welcomed as a test of whether a Catholic mass party was possible in Spain, monarchist activists partici-

[1] M. Domingo, *La revolución de octubre* (1935), 95–97. His meeting was so rowdy that he telephoned Azaña *and Prieto*, advising them to cancel their meetings in Aragon.

[2] The most valuable allies of the C.E.D.A. were the Agrarians whose strength lay in the rural constituencies of Castile. The Radical–C.E.D.A. alliance in Badajoz, Granada, Jaén, and Cárceres cut the socialist representation from thirty-eight seats to eleven.

pated in the election 'without faith, without illusion and without enthusiasm'. Gil Robles was convinced that his expensive propaganda would win votes, while the Carlists and *Acción Española* knew they had made few new converts. Nevertheless, in spite of difficulties, the right fought the elections on the same ticket: as a result they won 212 seats as against the 98 of the left (i.e. the Azaña coalition) and the 102 which were captured by the Radicals—many as a consequence of local electoral pacts.[1] It was this victory for anti-socialist republicanism, rather than the total defeat of the Azaña coalition, which was the most surprising feature of the elections; it meant that the next prime minister was that ageing figure from the past, Alejandro Lerroux.

3. *The* Bienio Negro *and the Revolution of October 1934*

The period from the November elections until the victory of the Popular Front in February 1936 is known to the Spanish left as *el bienio negro*—the two black years. Rather than a period of resolute reaction it represented a reversion to the negativism of 'pure politics' during which the construction of coalitions and frequent ministerial reshuffles revived the jargon of old-fashioned parliamentarianism. Some form of coalition government, either explicit or in the form of 'benevolence' granted by one group to another, there must be, since the elections of 1933 had given no party a clear majority. Thus Lerroux, called on to form a government, needed the support of the C.E.D.A., since his resolute anti-socialist platform made any *rapprochement* with the remnants of the Azaña coalition inconceivable. The key to the politics of the *bienio* is therefore to be sought in the relations of Lerroux and Gil Robles.

In the support of the C.E.D.A., conceded by Gil Robles, Lerroux saw not merely the necessary condition of a parliamentary majority but a triumph for the Republic. Gil Robles could have been a Spanish Parnell and reduced government to impotence; his support of Lerroux's ministry 'from the outside' proved his republican bona fides. The prime minister regarded it

[1] The final results of the election were: C.E.D.A., 110 seats; Traditionalists, 20; Agrarians, 36; Renovación Española, 15; Basque nationalists, 12; 'Spanish nationalist, 1; Independents, 18; Radicals, 102; Lliga, 26; Conservative Republicans, 18; Liberal Democrats, 9; Progressives, 3; Socialists, 60; Esquerra, 18; O.R.G.A. (Galician Republicans), 6; Republican Action, 5; Radical Socialists, 4; Communists, 1.

as his mission to turn the benevolence of parliamentary support into participation in a coalition government which would nail Gil Robles to the Republic and cut him off from the extreme right. Thus the admission of the C.E.D.A. ministers into the cabinet, an event which was to set off the October Revolution of 1934, represented the culmination of a policy of attraction. 'Who has evolved?' Lerroux could boast, 'They or we?' After a swing to the left there must be a swing to the right before the political pendulum settled in the centre, a region that Lerroux himself could hope to dominate. Gil Robles's own calculations were different: after the Radicals had failed, the C.E.D.A. could not be denied the right to govern, once he had declared his 'full loyalty to the régime which the people has willed'. The Republic, Gil Robles admitted, could be made to save Spain and he was well aware that his political future as a Christian Democrat *caudillo* was threatened by the conspiratorial plans of those whom even Alfonso dismissed as 'drawing-room monarchists'.[1]

Lerroux's hopes for domesticating the Catholic right in a Republic for all Spaniards alienated the left wing of his own party when his second-in-command, Martínez Barrio, rejected the rightward drift and went into 'dissidence' against his leader; they also struck on the rock of Alcalá Zamora's political obstinacy. In his legalistic, highly personal fashion, the president was a defender of republican dignity. He detested Lerroux and his seedier clients; he distrusted Gil Robles whose mass Catholic party with its dangerous monarchist allies imperilled the president's favourite dream of a respectably republican Catholic centre party. Thus he 'intrigued' against Lerroux (who resigned in April 1934 when the President made public his disagreement with the government's pardon of the rebels of 10 August 1932) and steadfastly refused to call on Gil Robles to form a ministry. His exclusion of the C.E.D.A., which opponents attributed to the influence of Socialists in the Presidential palace, not merely strengthened Gil Robles, enabling him 'to exact a kind of political blackmail from every cabinet'; it

[1] Cf. S. Galindo Herrero, *Partidos*, 130 ff.; for Alfonso's attitude to C.E.D.A. in 1935 see J. Cortes Cavanillas, *Confesiones y muerte de Alfonso XIII* (1951), 106. The monarchists were to avoid quarrels with the C.E.D.A. and Gil Robles 'would find, at the proper moment, the opportunity to escape his pledges to the régime'.

combined with his distrust of Lerroux to distort the whole history of the *bienio*.[1]

The Revolution of October 1934 was the direct consequence of the demand of the Socialists and anti-Radical Republicans that the largest elected party in the Cortes must be denied any participation in government. It was conditioned by the first acute conflict between Catalan autonomous government and the Spanish state, a conflict which coincided with a crisis in the Basque Provinces.

The latent constitutional conflict with Catalonia was hidden as long as Madrid and Barcelona were governed by political allies committed to making the Catalan Statute work; it arose inevitably when in Madrid right-wing governments, or governments dependent on right-wing majorities confronted a left-wing government in Catalonia.[2] The same polarization brought a dramatic *renversement des alliances* in the Basque country where the traditional conflict over the right of the central government to tax the 'exempted provinces' had reached an acute stage.[3] Fears of clericalism had made the left in the Constituent Cortes as lukewarm about Basque autonomy as they had been generous to Catalonia; hence the Basque Nationalists were an opposition party. Now the right, hostile to local autonomy, threatened Basque Nationalists as well as Socialists: Prieto appeared on the same platform as José Aguirre, singing 'The Tree of Guernika', and the fierce local quarrels of the U.G.T. and the Basque Catholic Unions ceased to trouble the meeting halls and the streets of Bilbao. Thus began the strange alliance between the anti-clerical left and the Catholic Basques which was to be consummated in the common defence of the Republic in the Civil War.[4] The Basque Nationalists found an even more surprising ally in the Communists who presented nationalism as part of the social revolution and published a paper in Basque.

The clash between autonomy and centralism, between the Catalan Statute and the constitution of Spain was revived by the

[1] S. de Madariaga's comments, *Spain*, 328. Madariaga calls the socialist pressure 'preposterous, unconstitutional and rebellious'.

[2] Catalonia had followed the national trend to the right in the general election of 1933, but in the elections for the Generalidad reverted to the Esquerra.

[3] For this quarrel see *The Times*, 15 Aug. 1934.

[4] La Pasionaria (Dolores Ibarruri) is a Basque. For 1933–4 in the Basque country see M. García Venero, *Nacionalismo vasco*, 443–57.

Ley de Cultivos. This agrarian reform was the reward given by Companys to his rural following—the *rabassaires* and the small tenant farmers; it offered them redemption of their tenures and regulated rents. The Catalan right maintained that the agitation for reform was 'artificial', whipped up by Companys for political purposes since distress was rooted, not in the iniquities of the landlord system, but in contracting foreign demand which hit owner and cultivator alike. Landowners combined to resist 'a vandalous and immoral avalanche which would destroy all property rights'.[1] Impotent to stop the passage of the law against the Esquerra majority in the Catalan parliament, the right achieved its purposes when the law was declared unconstitutional by the Tribunal of Constitutional Guarantees. The Radical government of Samper (leader of a Valencian autonomist grouping similar to the stronger Galician Republican party) which had replaced that of Lerroux in April 1934, upheld the Tribunal in what was probably a correct legal decision.

Though the question of the *Ley de Cultivos* sank into the background, it had, together with the Basque troubles, produced what Spaniards call a pre-revolutionary situation. Companys believed that the reversal of the law was tantamount to the deliberate destruction of Catalan autonomy by the right in the interests of the Catalan landlords. If the government behaved like the Bourbons, Catalonia would 'proceed to create a Catalan nationality'.[2] This linguistic violence infected even the non-socialist Spanish left which now began to evolve the theory of a Republic 'mutilated' out of recognition by the Radicals and their conservative-clerical supporters. Once the C.E.D.A. entered the government, such a Republic would have no claims to obedience. When Gil Robles announced that he would no longer support a Radical government, Samper, who had tried desperately to come to terms with the Basques and the Catalans, resigned (1 October 1934). Alcalá Zamora had two alternatives: he could either dissolve, as the left pressed him to do, or admit the C.E.D.A. to government. He chose the latter course. The

[1] J. de Camps y Arboix, *Historia del derecho catalán moderno* (Barcelona, 1958), 292–3.

[2] According to the testimony of Dencás, Companys talked of armed revolt in June; quoted C. Seco Serrano, *Historia de España* (Barcelona, 1962), vi. 91.

reply of the extreme left was the October Revolution, the great divide in the history of the Republic and the prelude to the Civil War.

The *Cedista* entry into the Lerroux cabinet was the signal for the October Revolution, not its cause.[1] Presented as 'an energetic protest against the hypocrisy of the reactionaries', the October Revolution was an attempt, half-hearted perhaps, to create a Workers' Republic in Spain as the only alternative to the destruction of the socialist party. It was conceived by socialist leaders obsessed by European parallels and pushed towards violent courses by the revolutionary temper of the masses, particularly evident in the youth organizations of the party. As Araquistáin confessed, 'the Revolution was the work of younger proletarians'; if the leaders had stood aside, 'the socialist proletariat would have broken through its trade union framework and become incorporated with the Anarchists and Syndicalists'. Confronted by a 'fascist' threat in Spain, Socialists like Araquistain, who had been in Germany, could argue that failure to revolt against a Spanish Hitler or Dolfuss would be 'the death certificate of the party'.

The militancy of the new left captured Largo Caballero, of all the labour leaders the most profoundly disillusioned by the experience of co-operation with bourgeois democracy between 1931 and 1933. He became the driving force behind the *Alianza Obrera*, designed as a revolutionary alliance of all working-class parties; he fought the obstructionist tactics of the reformist leaders and the hesitations of Prieto.[2] A committee was set up to organize the details of the revolutionary take-over and code telegrams were drafted to be sent off on 'the day'. If things went wrong, as they did, this organized movement was to be disguised as a 'spontaneous protest'. The risks were great. There would be no response in the countryside, exhausted by a strike in the spring and summer of 1934. The *Alianza Obrera* was new and untested, with most of the C.N.T. still outside it.

All that remained was to calculate the 'objective conditions' of successful revolution, and these were created when the appointment of the C.E.D.A. ministers split the bourgeoisie.

[1] Cf. A. Ramos Oliveira, *La revolución de octubre*, 19, 111. Written in prison after the revolution, this work makes clear the attitude of the militant Socialists.

[2] F. Largo Caballero, *Mis recuerdos*, 134 ff.

With the announcement of the ministry, Republican leaders from Martínez Barrio to Maura declared their incompatibility with a disfigured Republic. As Araquistáin remarked, the revolutionary sentiments of the Left Republicans remained 'platonic' and were contained in a new version of the well-tried device of the *retraimiento*—the declaration of a political boycott. As always the *retraimiento*, if it did not accept revolutionary action, implicitly sanctioned it. There could be little doubt that Azaña rejected revolutionary procedures, but his language in the summer was vague and threatening. He took no part whatever in the October Revolution; indeed he was trying to stop the Barcelona rising when he was arrested. It is nevertheless legitimate to ask what would have been his attitude had the revolution succeeded.

As a national movement the revolution was a fiasco. In Madrid, where a socialist ministry was waiting in an artist's flat for a revolutionary take-over, the leaders were hesitant. Neither the desultory shooting nor the half-hearted revolutionary strike shook the government. In Barcelona the revolution was damned from the start. It was made by the Esquerra leaders, with fear in their hearts and without adequate working-class support.

One of the consequences of the anti-Catalanism of the Radicals and the C.E.D.A. had been the increasing pressure of extreme nationalists. Their leaders, Dencás and Badiá, controlled the armed force of Catalan nationalism, and were prepared to use this force 'against Spain' in order to install a Catalan State when revolution in the rest of Spain made a separatist *coup* possible.[1] Companys, trapped by his own oratorical violence, saw that he must either use the army against such extreme supporters or 'guide' the movement by himself declaring a Catalan Republic. He knew that republican leaders like Azaña regarded the latter course as calamitous, but he had not the strength to resist it. 'It's done. . . . They won't he able to say I'm not a Catalanist.'[2] After appeals for moderation, and in the

[1] Dencás claimed that the slowness with which the governmental services, promised in the Statute, were transferred to Catalonia led to the idea of *Estat Catala* (i.e. separatism) and that, *with the knowledge* of the Generalidad, he organized a force of 4,000 para-military guards 'against Spain' (*A.B.C.*, 7 Mar. 1936).

[2] His words in Catalan were, 'Ja està fet! Ja veurem com acabarà i A veure si ara també direu que no soc catalanista!' Aymami i Baudina, *El 6 d'Octubre tal com jo l'he vist* (Barcelona, 1935), 103.

mistaken belief that the whole of Spain was in revolt, he declared for a Catalan Republic within the Federal Republic of Spain (6 October), thus reviving the old federal doctrine of Pi y Margall in order to save a connexion with Spain.[1] The army, in spite of appeals to the Catalanism of its commander, supported the Spanish government. Besieged by artillery, Companys surrendered on the morning of 7 October.

There was no force left to save a revolution for Catalan separatism. The *rabaissaires* failed to arrive from the surrounding countryside. The C.N.T., indifferent from the start to a revolution of bourgeois nationalists, was being shot down by Dencás's police. It rejected the *Alianza Obrera* as a socialist device and scorned a revolution based on the objective conditions of bourgeois politics rather than on the revolutionary temper of the masses.[2] Without the C.N.T. a revolution could not succeed in Barcelona. The *Alianza Obrera* acted out a rehearsal for the Civil War: it seized cars, set up committees, organized a militia, all without success; Dencás insisted on 'only one power here' and refused the workers arms. The failure of the October Revolution struck a blow at the *mystique* of Catalan nationalism from which it has never recovered. As Maurín was to point out, it once more illustrated the limitations of the revolutionary spirit of the Catalan petty bourgeoisie.

These failures left the Asturian rising in splendid isolation to terrorize the middle classes and establish the myth of a proletarian revolution. Here there were no complications over bourgeois collaboration. It was a workers' revolution, led by a respected militant, González Peña, in which the most educated and mature Spanish proletarians united in a single effort. In contrast to Barcelona, *Alianza Obrera* in Asturias included the C.N.T. The local leaders adopted Pestaña's thesis of the necessity of a common front against 'fascism' and, like the Socialists, were alarmed at communist inroads. Most surprisingly, the Communists themselves, after years of slanging all other workers' organizations, joined the *Alianza* on instructions from Moscow. Indeed, they were to claim that 'the workers of the Asturias fought for Soviet power under Com-

[1] Cf. Azaña, *Mi rebelión en Barcelona* (Bilbao, 1935), 106–12; Angel Ossorio, *Companys*, chap. xxiii.

[2] The Socialists, in spite of professions to the contrary, wished to keep socialist

munist leadership'[1]—an exaggeration of their role which was to supply the Nationalist propagandists of 1936 with the fiction of a 'red plot' directed by the Comintern. For the first time in Spanish history, all the working-class organizations were united in a common effort. Though union was not without its frictions, the battle cry of the Asturian miners, 'U.H.P.' (Unite Proletarian Brothers), was an emotional reality.

For a fortnight the mining area of Asturias was controlled by local workers' commitees of the Socialist Republic and the 'Red Army' militia with its famous dynamiters. With its brutal repression by the Moroccan Army, the Asturias rising reached the dimensions of a civil war with four thousand casualties and a great deal of physical destruction caused by the miner's attempt to take Oviedo. When it was over, the nation was morally divided between those who favoured repression and those who did not. Surrender of the vanquished did not reassure the victors, or discourage the defeated. 'We have been beaten only for the time being. . . . Our surrender is simply a halt on the road where we correct our mistakes, preparing for the next battle which must end in final victory of the exploited.'[2] The Asturias divided Europe as well as Spain: the charges of atrocities committed by both sides exercised the consciences of right and left, and were taken up in the European press. Like the revolution itself, this was a prelude to the greater resonances and divisions of July 1936. For those who had felt the power of Proletarian Brotherhood there was, however, a cloud on the heroic myth; the Socialists and the U.G.T. engaged in a post-mortem which was to embitter the divisions between Prieto and Largo Caballero and to discredit those reformist Socialists, like Besteiro, who had condemned the revolt.

From the October Rising to the elections of February 1936 the Republic was governed by a miscellaneous assortment of Radical–C.E.D.A. and Radical coalition ministries. It was a

domination of the *Alianza Obrera* and were 'timorous about joining too closely with the anarchist unions' of J. Álvarez del Vayo. *The Last Optimist*, 267. For the C.N.T. case see J. Peirats, *La C.N.T. en la revolución española* (Toulouse, 1951–3), i. 78–79.

[1] Quoted D. C. Catell, *Communism and the Spanish Civil War* (Berkeley, 1955), 39.

[2] M. Grossi, *La insurreción de Asturias* (Valencia, 1935), 218. Like Ramos Oliveira's book it was written in prison.

period of weak government rather than of determined reaction, and Gil Robles was bitterly denounced by the activist right as a political coward who failed to declare for an anti-Marxist dictatorship of order supported by the army on the morrow of an unsuccessful revolution.[1] The difficulties of governmental unity, combined with a desire to satisfy outraged conservatism, ensured the abandonment of what Marcelino Domingo called 'the peaceful revolution'—the constructive achievements of 1931–3. In so far as it represented a desire to destroy what the C.E.D.A. considered an aggressive lay state, this abandonment was deliberate. But, besides their conservatism, the governments of 1934–6 were swept along by those same currents of orthodox finance which had eroded some of the realities of socialist planning in 1931–3. Ministers were obsessed by the need for economy, a balanced budget, and a sound currency, and embarked on the economies characteristic of all European governments of the time. Schoolmasters saw their miserable stipends reduced—whereas it had been one of the glories of the Azaña régime that it had raised school-teachers' salaries when every other country was reducing them—and the reforming agencies found their budgets slashed. The Republic, as it had left Azaña's hands, was being 'mutilated': yet no real economy was effected by such measures as reducing the grant to the Prado and the wages of university charwomen because of 'anti-republican' expenditure on the armed forces.[2] The C.E.D.A.'s bid to win the working classes from the *caciquismo* of the U.G.T. or the violence of the C.N.T. to the Catholic corporate state had little chance of success. Given the atmosphere on the right after October it could not even be made; social policy went into reverse with the abandonment of wage regulation—wages dropped by a half in the agrarian south. Even the attempt to create a stable peasant class by agrarian reform (an old dream of social Catholicism supported by Gil Robles's Minister of Agriculture) was abandoned in face of the opposition of the right-wing of the governmental coalition.[3]

[1] To the left, the trials, the 30,000 political prisoners, and a press censorship which lasted until December 1935 justified the charge of fascism and brutality; fierce as it was, the repression was not the elimination of the left desired by right-wing *cedista*.

[2] These accusations are Azaña's, contained in *Discursos en campo abierto* (Bilbao, 1936).

[3] See A. Mendizábal, *The Martyrdom of Spain* (London, 1938), 231 ff.

Towards the end of 1935 Lerroux was involved in a series of financial scandals.[1] The consequences, less of personal corruption than of his Bohemian administrative incompetence, they killed the Radical–C.E.D.A. coalition government, discredited Lerroux in public opinion—Azaña could campaign against a government of 'jugglers and confidence men'—and destroyed his hold over his party. Since no stable radical compound could be formed to replace Lerroux and since President Alcalá Zamora would not allow the C.E.D.A. to replace the Radicals as the principal government party, no ministry could be formed at all and a general election was called for February 1936.

Against this background must be set the emergence of the Popular Front—the electoral coalition of Republicans and Socialists that was to triumph in February. For all its abuse of the election of November 1933 as a 'mixtification', the left knew it had been defeated by its own disunity. Unity must now be re-created on a programme of amnesty for the October rebels, a minimum agreed programme of social and educational reform, and freedom for working-class organizations—all to be carried out by a government of the republican left supported by socialist votes. Ruthless prosecution of the Asturian rebels and the attempt to prosecute Azaña created emotional solidarity with the socialist leaders,[2] while the socialist masses were feeling the pinch of the government's new course.

Azaña, with Prieto's help, set out to convert these discontents and the October solidarity into co-operation. During 1935, in a series of powerful and hard-hitting speeches, he proposed a Popular Front and made the first step towards it with the creation of a left republican *bloc*. The second stage, the socialist alliance, met with difficulties in his own grouping—Martínez Barrio disliked the idea—and even greater difficulties among the Socialists and the U.G.T., where Largo Caballero found it difficult to swallow a reconstruction of the alliance of 1931. Marcelino Domingo tried to turn the current obsession with

[1] The *estraperlo* scandal, which gave the Spanish language its term for black marketeering. *L'affaire Nombela* concerned compensation due for a rescinded contract in Spanish Guinea. See Martínez Barrio's *Orígines del Frente Popular* (Buenos Aires), 67 ff.

[2] For the attempts to secure favourable judges see Álvaro de Albornoz, *Al servicio de la República* (1936).

foreign example to the profit of union. The workers had failed in Austria and Germany, not because they revolted too little or too late, but because there was no alliance with bourgeois liberalism; *ergo*, as both had been defeated in discord, they could triumph in unison.

The one area where the Popular Front could confidently expect support was Catalonia. Companys had been turned by his prosecution into a popular figure, and the suspension and later revision of the Statute of Autonomy meant that the Republic of the left once again appeared as the only security for Catalan liberties. A similar situation had arisen in the Basque Provinces. In Catalonia the decisive factor was the anarchist vote. The C.N.T. could not bring itself to counsel voting for bourgeois democrats, but it now responded to Largo Caballero's appeal for working-class unity. In January it decided not to vote but to explore an alliance with the U.G.T. 'from an exclusively revolutionary point of view'.[1] No alliance could be formed, since Socialists were not 'exclusively' revolutionary. They could scarcely, however, avoid supporting a campaign for the amnesty of the 1934 rebels, the emotional foundation of the Popular Front, and it is a fair assumption that the *no votad* recommendation was disobeyed at the last moment and that many C.N.T. members voted for Popular Front candidates.

As the left united, the right-centre disintegrated as an electoral force. The extreme right, abusing Gil Robles as a collaborationist who had failed to become a *caudillo*, moved towards the 'dignfied gesture'. The violence of his denunciation of the men of 1931–3, his authoritarian talk of seizing power, although it allowed the left to charge him with counter-revolution, did little to redeem his credit on the right. To the pure right his 'accidentalism' was 'spiritually inelegant' and his alliance of Catholicism with 'atheistic positivism' sterile.

In May 1934 Calvo Sotelo returned from exile to lead the anti-Gil Robles right in the quest for 'a Spain authentic, faithful to its history . . . one and indivisible. Authority must be established by whatever means. Power must be conquered by whatever means.' Traditionalists were talking of the Third Reconquest for which it was training its youth movements. 'If the revolution wants war, it shall have war.' To reconcile

[1] J. Peirats, *C.N.T.* i. 102.

this sort of language with even the wildest of Gil Robles's threats was impossible. It was thus with the greatest difficulty that the right maintained the joint electoral action of 1933. It could not hope to gain much from an electoral deal with the Radicals: Lerroux's party was divided and discredited.[1]

The victory of the Popular Front at the polls was therefore the result of a reversal of the terms of battle as compared with the elections of November 1933. Once again, the electoral laws hid the strength of the defeated party and the fact that, politically, Spain was more equally divided than the 'triumph' of the Popular Front might lead one to believe. 4,838,449 voted for the left; 3,996,931 for the right. The right had *increased* in strength since 1933; its hold remained firm over Leon, Castile, and Navarre. These regions, where the middling peasant and landlord dominated, were to be the core of Nationalist Spain after 1936. The strongholds of the left were in the great cities to which were added, in 1936, the *latifundista* provinces and Galicia. Those regions where the explicit defence of national unity by the right must offend regionalists—Catalonia and the Basque Provinces—could not support the right.[2] Thus once more in Spanish history the periphery and the interior were out of step. In this process of polarization it was the centre parties which vanished: Lerroux and his Radicals were annihilated, Cambó, Melquíades Álvarez were unseated. The real strength of the Popular Front lay in the socialist vote. But, according to the terms of the Popular Front agreement, the Socialist party itself would not enter the government. The axis of the Republic after 1936 must therefore be Azaña's Republican Left and Martínez Barrio's Republican Union—parties whose representation reflected less electoral strength than the agreed distribution of seats made by the Popular Front leaders before the election.

Already, in this divided Spain, the attitudes which were to plunge Spain into civil war were apparent. Both right and left had based their electoral propaganda on their respective attitudes to the October Revolution. The appeal to violence had always been recognized in the language of the extreme right.

[1] Gil Robles clearly did not like the local electoral alliance with the Radicals which would last 'only till the elections'. See his speech of 11 Feb. (*A.B.C.*, 12 Feb.).

[2] Cf. C. M. Rama, *Ideología, regiones y clases sociales en la España contemporánea* (1958), 11 ff.

It was also in the logic of the extreme left since October 1934. The Left Republicans and the Radical Socialists had dreaded an appeal to force. Nevertheless, as the overtones of their speeches reveal, they could not recognize the democratic legitimacy of a Spain 'without books, without horizons, without battles of the spirit'. The Republic of 1931 was 'a work', a democratic content, not a democratic mechanism: the right would not respect that work, so the left denied it any claim to govern when it used the mechanism of democracy to its own advantage.[1] Influenced by the tensions of Europe the Socialists went even further. By their language they denied their opponents the right to consider themselves a legal party. 'An anti-Marxist Front is a Fascist Front.' By resuscitating the charge of caciquismo and adding to it that of the effect of well-financed right-wing electoral propaganda they hid from themselves the political truth: the right was as strong as the left.[2]

4. *The Descent into Violence, February–July 1936*

From the elections of February to the generals' revolt of July 1936 Spain was ruled by a pure republican government without socialist participation. Until he replaced President Alcalá Zamora, sacked for his use of the moderating power which had alienated all parties, Azaña was prime minister. His successor, in May 1936, was Casares Quiroga, a sick man who had made his reputation as a republican cacique in Galicia. It was during these months that the struggle for power shifted from the Chamber of the Cortes to the street, the club, and the officers' mess. The voices of the men of action on the right, those of the proponents of a proletarian revolution on the left, were isolating the legalists and gradualists. This descent into violence was neither universal nor always apparent to the eye;[3]

[1] A. Ramos Oliveira, *Octubre*, 19, 111; cf. Marcelino Domingo's opinion that those who reversed the 'peaceful revolution' of the Republic were the true authors 'responsible' for the October Revolution (*La revolución de octubre*, 17).

[2] There was foundation for the belief that the residual survival of caciquismo (of the right in the countryside) obscured the strength of the left, especially in the south and west. The 'defence' of the right was that the Socialists had created new forms of caciquismo in the cities.

[3] Cf. the testimony of the American ambassador Claude Bowers (*My Mission to Spain*, New York, 1954). For a short account of the pre-revolutionary atmosphere see B. Bolloten, *The Grand Camouflage* (London, 1961), 18–24.

whole regions were exempt from trouble—Catalonia, the habitual storm centre, was relatively quiet. Characteristic were street clashes between party militias in the great towns, monster meetings, an uncontrolled, lightning strike wave, and the emergence of the revolutionary peasant with the seizures of land in Estremadura. The government could do little but regularize squatting and attempt to hide the seriousness of the 'pre-revolutionary' atmosphere of the labour world by a clumsy press censorship.[1]

The government could no longer count on the steady support of the Socialist movement. During the whole period up to the outbreak of the Civil War it was divided on its attitude to the Republic. This division, though it took the public form of a bitter personal feud between Prieto and Largo Caballero, represented in Spain the dilemma that had faced all Socialists since Millerand and Briand had joined radical governments in France. Was it a licit policy for a socialist movement to participate in a bourgeois government?

Prieto believed in the Popular Front and in its logical corollary, co-operation with subsequent republican governments. The confusion of bourgeois parties would allow the Socialists to impose legislation that 'would make the power of the working classes indestructible'. He wanted a planned economy, not revolutionary euphoria. Rapid social change would drive the middle classes to fascism; strikes that went beyond the capacity of capitalism would mean the socialization of misery. He was ready, therefore, to enter a revived Left Republican–Socialist coalition government.

Largo Caballero, whom Prieto excluded from 'political' negotiations, considered this to be suicide: on 8 May the U.G.T. warned that Socialist participation would mean the end of the Popular Front: 'Wait till the Republicans have proved their inability to govern Spain and then take over the government.' Like Gil Robles, he couched this intention in the

[1] It may be true as F. E. Manuel remarks (*Politics of Modern Spain* (New York, 1938), 168) that the best source of *accurate* information as to strikes is the foreign press: *The Times* gives good coverage. Nevertheless, papers like *A.B.C.* devoted a whole page to labour troubles. Drastic censorship (apparent because the editors inserted 'Read *A.B.C.*' in replacement of the censored passages) heightened rather than damped down an atmosphere of social war (cf. issues of 9, 10 July). Almost every issue of *A.B.C.* in June was heavily censored.

language of the conquest of power and his language terrified the Spanish bourgeoisie. 'I want a Republic without a class war: but for this it is necessary that one class disappears.' Álvarez del Vayo and Araquistáin, the theoreticians of the new left, had seen the enthusiasm of the socialist masses in Europe evaporate and they wished to maintain what Anarchists called the revolutionary temper. The growing influence of the Communists, though it was directed at the maintenance of co-operation with the Republicans in accordance with the policy of the Third International, nevertheless brought a striking increase of interest in the Russian model, with Azaña cast as the Kerensky of the revolution. He would have to be pushed aside or threatened by revolutionary violence, since he would never appoint Largo Caballero as prime minister.

The influence of the new left and the Marxist reading of his prison days were not the only factors tempting Largo Caballero to assume the role of a revolutionary leader. All Socialists were fearful of the power of the C.N.T. Right-wing Socialists had sought to destroy it; now Largo Caballero began to think in terms of attracting it to the Workers' Alliance. This alliance would push Prieto and the Socialist party leaders out of the picture since the C.N.T. could never contemplate an alliance with a political party. *Caballeristas* began to emphasize the residual anarchism of Marxism: they emphasized the withering away of the state; planning could be left to bourgeois Socialists and Prieto; once liberated, the revolutionary masses would settle their own destinies. Nor was Largo Caballero only concerned with the counter-attractions of C.N.T. revolutionism. Since 1933 the Socialist Youth had become a power in the party. This concern for youth movements was common to all parties, except the Republicans, and the street clashes between the various semi-uniformed, semi-military organizations are among the most evident symptoms of growing violence. Largo Caballero now saw the increasingly militant Socialist Youth go over *en masse* to the Communists.

The struggle between Prieto and Largo Caballero filled the spring and early summer of 1936. Prieto was called a collaborationist and a traitor in the *caballerista* press which reprinted republican tributes to him as the Spanish Briand. In return, Largo Caballero was accused of personal ambition and infantile revolutionism. The two factions came to blows and broke up each other's meetings. By what were considered jesuitical practices Prieto retained his hold on the Socialist Party Executive while Largo Caballero's strength grew in the ranks of U.G.T. The issue between them and their policies was unresolved when the Civil War broke out.

Thus rather than firm revolutionary purpose the world of labour displayed, in July 1936, a chaotic incoherence. The C.N.T. and U.G.T. had failed to cement a revolutionary alliance: the C.N.T.'s terms at the Saragossa Conference were total revolution, which the U.G.T. could not bring itself to accept. Moreover, whatever the desires of the leaders, the rank and file of the two unions were bitterly hostile at the local level. In Malaga their militants were shooting each other; in Madrid the U.G.T. called off a building strike which C.N.T. wished to carry on; in Barcelona and Madrid C.N.T. waiters—striking for better wages and the prohibition of 'undignified' tipping—came to blows with those syndicated in the U.G.T. Largo Caballero's prestige was immense and he was treated as a monarch of the labour world, but it must be doubted whether he could have carried the U.G.T. to revolution or whether, indeed, he had any clear and immediate intention of so doing. To the serious revolutionist of the C.N.T. he still looked like 'the cushy job socialist of yester-year'.[1] Long experience had taught the C.N.T. that Socialists were unreliable revolutionists.

There is no evidence that there was any specific planned rising; the 'red plot' was a fabrication of the generals' propaganda. There was, however, a general revolutionary temper. For eight months Largo Caballero had harped on the coming revolution in every speech. 'All the militants,' wrote a sympathetic observer in May, 'both Anarchists and Socialists, believe that only an armed insurrection can give decisive victory to the workers.'[2] Yet it was not revolutionary purpose but resistance to the counter-revolution which was to unleash a social revolution in republican Spain. It cannot be doubted that the believers in a proletarian take-over saw that a counter-revolution would clear the air. As Frederica Montseny observed, the generals'

[1] *Solidaridad Obrera*, 2 June 1936.

[2] E. Conze, *Spain Today* (London, 1936), 118.

revolt 'hastened the revolution we all desire but which no one had expected so soon'.[1]

There was no ambiguity in the language of the extreme right about the violent nature of the coming struggle for power. The most strident of the new voices came from the Falange; the most sinister from Calvo Sotelo's Nationalist Block; to these were added the hundred year old protest of the Traditionalists. To all, the election result of February proved the fatuity of Gil Robles's legalist policy and the necessity for action against a government 'which rules against Spain'. It was this notion of an objectified historical Spain—disfigured and betrayed by the Masons of the Republic—which united the divergent political theories of generals, monarchists, Falangists, and Traditionalists. Yet none could agree on the lineaments of the true Spain to be restored by violence; as one of the conspirators observed, the ideology of the counter-revolution 'defined itself in negatives'.

Since Sanjurjo's rebellion, embarrassed by the deviations of Gil Robles and the hesitations of the army, the monarchist activists had been refurbishing their conspiratorial organization. In March 1934 a deputation representing the Alfonsist activists of *Renovación Española*, the Traditionalist Communion, and the army malcontents had visited Mussolini; the interview was not altogether a success but it prefigures (less the Falange and the C.E.D.A.) that alignment of forces which was to join the Nationalist Movement in the rebellion of July. *Renovación Española*, and the militant right in general, found in Calvo Sotelo a powerful and bitter leader. As an exile in France, under the influence of Maurras, he had evolved a semi-fascist brand of monarchism which aimed at the installation of a new order, not a mere restoration of monarchical forms; his declared aim was to 'intellectualize and activize' the right from 'mountaineers to art critics'. His Nationalist Block disowned old-fashioned conservatism and detested Gil Robles for his weakening of the *élan* of the right; it declared itself to be a radical, counter-revolutionary movement. Gil Robles himself was well informed of the plans of these rich monarchists; he could neither resist nor approve them, though he tried to dissociate his movement from their 'sterile' conservatism of resistance.

[1] Frederica Montsény was a member of the F.A.I.: her remarks are quoted by B. Bolloten, *Camouflage*, 26.

Throughout the Republican period, the most serious and consistent plotters were the Traditionalists. In Navarre their organization, which was helped by a junta of local priests, acquired a military appendage in the *requetés*, organized by General Varela as 'Father Pepe' and armed with rifles and machine-guns smuggled over the frontier. By 1934, well before the October revolution of the left, the extreme right had mustered 6,000 *requetés* in the villages and Navarre while, at the other end of Spain, in the provinces of Huelva and Cáceres, small Carlist groups were planning a *coup de main* in co-operation with Sanjurjo in exile in Portugal.[1]

The importance of the Traditionalist contribution meant that monarchism was moving away from constitutionalism as old-fashioned Alfonsists understood it. Victor Pradera, a follower of Vázquez de Mella, had worked in *Acción Española* and represented an endeavour to give Carlism a new look by modernizing its intellectual apparatus. Nevertheless, its negations remained the old negations: rejection of parliamentary monarchy as subjecting the nation to the 'despotism' of ministers responsible to a vote of 'a half plus one'; rejection of universal suffrage as a heresy derived from the anti-social individualism of Rousseau. Neither had its affirmations changed: the truly sovereign king, limited only by conscience and the 'objective norms' of tradition as embodied, for example, in the Justiciar of Aragon; organic suffrage; the 'canonical marriage' which indissolubly linked the regions to the nation. 'We have discovered', wrote Pradera, 'that the new state is nothing more than the old state of Ferdinand and Isabella.'

Falangism, on the other hand, was a consciously modern creed and its founding fathers were a collection of bizarre intellectuals. The synthesis of European fascism and Spanish nationalism was first propounded by Giménez Caballero, a wild prophet of Mazzinian cultural imperialism. He saw Mussolini as the saviour of 'Catholicity', Cervantes as an anti-Spanish chronicler of despair beside the true values represented in Don Juan and the bullfight.[2] Ledesma Ramos, a

[1] For the Carlist preparations see A. Lizarza Iribarren, *Memorias de la conspiración* (Pamplona, 1953), esp. 16 (priests), 25 ff. (the Mussolini interviews). Carlism was still divided, often bitterly (32 ff.).

[2] Giménez Caballero's ideas have the attraction of powerful fantasy. They can be best studied in his *Genio de España* (1932).

postal worker, had worked out in solitude what was to be the fundamental purpose of the Falange: the capture of the working classes for an authoritarian, socially radical nationalism. In October 1931, together with Onésimo Redondo, he founded the *Juntas de Ofensiva Nacional Sindicalista* (J.O.N.S.), a revolutionary syndicalist student movement. Onésimo Redondo was organizing a Catholic counter-revolutionary force in Valladolid. For him, the Castilian peasant would be the axis of a nationalist revolution, rallying the Castilian heart-lands for a revolutionary, national, corporative state against the class state of Jewish Marxism, against the separatism of peripheral Spain, and against the materialism of masonic liberalism. His call was to 'an austere and disciplined youth', shock troopers in a civil war that had already begun.[1] No significant politician of the conservative right was interested in these strange movements.

In October 1933 the Falange, which was to absorb with some difficulty the combined forces of Ledesma and Redondo, was founded by the son of the dictator, José Antonio Primo de Rivera. Driven to politics by the passionate defence of his father's memory, José Antonio was a complex character of great personal charm and with enough brains and authority to create a national movement. His main ideas were simple, derivative, and poetic.[2] His central theme was the definition of the nation as 'a unity of destiny', a position which led him into violent opposition to Catalan nationalism which he considered to be based on such 'false' criteria as race and language. His attack on parliamentary democracy was unoriginal but powerful. He saw both parliamentary liberalism and socialism as descended from Rousseau and the individualism of the eighteenth century—a revival of one of Menéndez y Pelayo's favourite theses. Individualism, as practised by liberal parliaments, led to the oppression of the workers; these, in turn, organized themselves on class lines. These conflicts, which put

[1] The best summary of Redondo's views is *O. Redondo, caudillo de Castilla* (1937). Neither Ledesma nor Redondo had any idea of the economics of National Syndicalism (cf. op. cit. 108), though Redondo had organized a syndicate of beet-growers.

[2] They are set out in his collected speeches and writings and from them is taken the summary which follows. Prieto took him seriously—a tribute he would not have paid to a mere student intellectual. His mystical and aesthetic streak caused him, nevertheless, to write much nonsense.

class interest above national destiny, must be resolved in the higher synthesis of the *patria*: liberalism destroyed this unity by a party system, socialism by the class war.

At first the few supporters of José Antonio's new party were the wilder and sometimes unscrupulous discontented spirits of the right, especially the old supporters of his father. In their weakness, therefore, Ledesma and José Antonio united in the 'Falange of the J.O.N.S.'[1] To José Antonio, and above all to Ledesma, the purpose of the Falange was to convert the workers to a nationalistic corporate state and to separate their modern, revolutionary authoritarian right from the 'materialism' of old-fashioned parties. While he respected the 'noble but absurd' Traditionalists, José Antonio scorned the C.E.D.A. as a party of terrified capitalists which covered its spiritual poverty by large expenditure on posters. 'Sterilized milk' could not hope to resist socialism. José Antonio worked to separate Falangism from the image of the *señorito* in a dinner jacket: his syndicalism, vague though his economic thought was, was meant to present a serious alternative to the workers.[2] Anarchists as efficient revolutionaries exercised a peculiar fascination for the Falangist intellectuals; to Giménez Caballero they were 'the most authentic refuge for popular Catholicism in Spain' and 'the repository of the heroic tradition of the *conquistadores*'.

Since rich monarchists cold-shouldered the movement when it refused to serve their purposes, and since the workers showed little inclination to join an attempt to capture the moral force of anarchism and the discontent of the proletariat for the Great Spain of history, the core of Falangism remained the university youth. Hence its romantic and rhetorical violence, the touch of wild poetry in its utterance: 'style' and 'austere' were the key words of its political vocabulary. Its adherents saw themselves as an *élite*, working on shoe-string budgets with a badly printed, bankrupt press, for national regeneration; as heroic missionaries in blue shirts preaching their vision of a Spain without wretched pueblos of mean houses, dirty streets, and sordid bars. 'I call you

[1] For the difficulties of the union of the 'anti-bourgeois, national syndicalist, and revolutionary J.O.N.S.' with the Falange of the *señoritos*, see F. Bravo Martínez, *Historia de la Falange Española de las J.O.N.S.* (1940), 13 ff.

[2] His proposals for agricultural reform were sensible and radical. Cf. the attitude of Giménez Caballero in Basaldúa, *En España sale el sol* (Buenos Aires, 1948), esp. 12–13.

to the ascetic labour of baring, beneath the rubble of a detestable Spain, the buried key of an exact and difficult Spain.' The speeches of José Antonio resound with the poetic patriotism of the generation of 1898.[1]

Student politics favoured the Falange and it grew fastest in university towns: Seville, with its violent labour world, Valladolid and Madrid itself, where law students, in particular, resented the Republican student oligarchs. In Barcelona it drew some strength from Castilian-speaking students' resentment at the Catalanization of the autonomous university. Both the tough elements of the right and the students pushed the movement towards the street warfare implicit in its mystique of violence. 'To concentrate on work was an impossible and reprehensible attitude. Always [in students' cases] wire clubs twisted to hold lead heads, or pistols lay beside books.'[2]

José Antonio disliked the gang-warfare of reprisals with Young Socialist militants as much as he disliked the alliance with the conservative right, but, as leader of an illegal and impoverished movement, he had little alternative but to accept both. Until the elections of February 1936, the right still had to accept Gil Robles's gamble on power; with the total failure of his 'legal' approach to power, his adherents drifted towards more violent courses and the Youth Movement of his party joined the Falange. Soldiers, who despised student antics and street parades, began to take the movement seriously. José Antonio, though he welcomed this interest, was chary of committing the purity of his revolution to conservative generals with no understanding of the necessity of winning the proletariat for the new Spain and with no desire to give the Falange power after their *coup*. Nevertheless, in May 1936, he was in direct contact with Mola, rather because he wished to exploit the generals' rebellion than because he had any sympathy with its aims. On 29 June he gave orders to join the generals. The Falange's main contribution to the Civil War may perhaps have been the maintenance of gang warfare; the streets in the summer of 1936 proved the generals' assertion that the govern-

[1] The leader of Spanish fascism derived two of his leading ideas—that of the function of an *élite* as a creative minority and of the nation as a destiny—from Ortega whom he admired greatly. F. Bravo Martínez, op. cit. 61.

[2] D. Jato, *La rebelión de los estudiantes* (1953), 69 ff.

ment was in the gutter. Had it not been for the ideological poverty of military leadership, the Falange might have remained little more than an interesting example of the transposition of right-wing irrationalist thought into the peculiar conditions of Spanish political life.

The counter-revolution of the extreme right and the grumblings of the conservative classes would have come to nothing without the generals, and the generals were divided as to the nature of the régime which they should implant as executants of the general will. Varela was a Carlist; failure in 1932 and prison had taught him the need for committed political support. Goded, Franco, and Mola—key figures because, unlike Sanjurjo, the nominal head of the conspiracy, they exercised commands—wanted a régime of order, republican or otherwise, that would respect the army and cease interfering with promotions. Like Gil Robles, Franco was an 'accidentalist'; he cared little for political forms provided they maintained 'order', which was threatened, in his view, by socialist violence. Other officers were old-fashioned monarchists and a handful were beginning to drift towards the Falange.[1]

Without the due hierarchical order from a general, the officers would not move. Thus the hesitations of Franco, whose authority was already remarkable, infuriated the activists. In February and March the generals decided to act. Franco's attempt to preserve a Republic of order had been rejected by the politicians after the February elections. The government, aware of the generals' declared hostility, transferred Goded to the Balearics, Franco to the Canaries, and Mola from Morocco, where he was 'working' on the African army, to Pamplona. This action has an exact parallel in the fate of the Unionist generals in 1868 and the result was the same: discontent was tightened into a plan of revolt by the government's defensive action against military malcontents. Before the transfer Franco—still strangely non-committal—Varela, and Mola met in Madrid and set out the grand strategy of revolt. In each provincial capital the military commander was to declare a state of siege and this take-over would be backed, in case of necessity, by the African army which

[1] Cf. F. Beltrán Güell, *Preparación y desarollo*. For the attitude of the professional 'soldiers of order' see Franco's letter to Casares Quiroga, 23 June (ibid. 47–49). There is a description of an army officer's relations with the Falange in Gironella's novel, *Los cipreses creen en Dios*.

could be counted on to obey its officers. The army in Spain itself was less reliable—new drafts of recruits were found to be 'contaminated'.[1] Details were left in the hands of Mola and a committee of generals. At this stage the military conspirators had still failed to establish formal commitments with either the Falange or the Carlists: the army would lead and these would follow and the question of the régime, as in 1868, would be left till after the rebellion.

The result of the redistribution of the triumvirate of serving generals was to shift the centre of conspiracy in Spain to the garrison town of Pamplona, capital of Navarre. It was a crass error to transfer Mola to Navarre for, in spite of liberal family traditions, he was an ambitious man and a declared and bitter opponent of military reform. Able and discreet, he became the most active of the conspirators, changing the strategy of revolt to a converging march on Madrid from Pamplona and Saragossa. As in the days of the radical conspiracies of the 1830's, conspirators must count the capital as a government stronghold to be swamped by a provincial rising. The junior officers trusted Mola and they had already been 'working' on local garrisons through the U.M.E., the right-wing counterpart to the organization which had sapped loyalty to the monarchy in 1930.

Mola's chief difficulty was with the Traditionalists, who sought to impose political conditions on co-operation by demanding a monarchical restoration. Mola, who represented the military tradition of order and the political theories of Primo de Rivera, did not want the army swamped by enthusiastic Traditionalist *tercios* and it was only the unreliability of his own troops, many of whom he considered 'Asturian socialists', which led him to accept the *tercios* as a political stiffener. He knew the army was taking a risk: Barcelona and Madrid might resist and escape the movement. In that case the leader of the new Spain would not be Mola with his levies, but Franco with the highly trained African army, which would pass from the role of a reserve force to that of the spearhead of the revolt. On 9 July the conspirators hired an English aeroplane which was to bring Franco to Morocco where the 'cry' would be given and the revolt set off.[2]

[1] Hence the necessity of rebellion before the 1936 draft arrived in barracks.

[2] For details see H. Thomas, *The Spanish Civil War* (London, 1961), 119 ff.

None of these preparations escaped notice but the war minister was lulled by the respectful attitude of his subordinates; neither he, the prime minister, nor Azaña thought a successful military revolt possible;[1] Largo Caballero, almost to the last minute, suspected Prieto's warnings as a move by his supporters to force him into the government. Obsessed with a proletarian revolution, Largo Caballero could not comprehend 'other violences than those of the working class.' Thus, when the army of Morocco pronounced, the government was caught napping. The signal for the rising was the murder, as a reprisal by government security forces, of Calvo Sotelo—the one civilian of the extreme right who might have dominated the counter-revolution and controlled the generals. His murder was the final proof that government was in the gutter, the final justification for placing dignity above discipline. To the despair of legalists, from Gil Robles to Prieto and Azaña, the men of violence had embarked on a course of which no one, least of all themselves, could predict the outcome.

[1] J. Zugazagoita in *Historia de la guerra en España* (Buenos Aires, 1940), 5 ff., gives a good picture of the government's nonchalance; but his account is directed at the justification of Prieto at the expense of Largo Caballero.

XVI

THE CIVIL WAR

THE generals' rebellion transformed the confused tensions of the early summer into simple issues and simple enthusiasms. Enthusiasm was the characteristic of life on both sides in the early days of the Civil War. 'On the evening of the 18th July, lorries hired by the mayors began to arrive from the villages far and near, crammed full with young and old of Navarre who responded to the call with indescribable enthusiasm. Each lorry, as it circled the main square of Pamplona received an ovation from the crowds which, at the sound of the bugles, appeared at balconies hung with flags. . . . Music and applause.'[1] In Republican Madrid 'there was a spirit of intoxication on the people, an infectious eagerness for sacrifice, a hot-blooded unreason and a fanatical belief in freedom, which could never lead to the construction of an orderly state on any earlier pattern'.[2] The history of the Civil War was the organization of this enthusiasm into military efficiency, a process accompanied by varying degrees of disillusionment as the conflicts, concealed by the initial euphoria, worked themselves to the surface of politics.

To the right, issues of the Civil War were Spanish issues decked out, for propaganda purposes, in the language of European politics. While the generals presented themselves as the defenders of Spain and Catholic Europe against a Red Plot of international Communism it was the political theory of the nineteenth-century army that inspired their rebellion. To the Traditionalists the 'Communist plot' was 'one of the various fashionable titles with which a very old enemy presented itself'.[3] From the beginning the left saw the Civil War more clearly as part of a wider struggle and as the course of the war became, though the politics of intervention, part of the power

[1] Lt.-General Carlos Martínez Campos (in *St. Antony's Seminars*), describing the arrival of Carlist volunteers.

[2] Gustav Regler, *The Owl of Minerva* (London, 1959), 273.

[3] R. Gambra, *La monarquía social y representativa* (1954), 8.

conflicts of Europe, so this involvement gave Spanish issues a universal significance. As in the 1830's the battlefields of Spain presented a contest between the ideologies that divided Europe—this time between democracy and fascism. To Hans Beimler, a German Communist, killed fighting with the International Brigade on the Madrid front, it seemed that 'the only way we can get back to Germany is through Madrid'. A process of identification with one or other of the two combatants transformed the war into a dividing line in domestic politics and intellectual discourse. In England the Spanish issue not merely cut Conservatives from the Labour and Liberal parties but divided parties among themselves. In the early months of the war Dalton and Bevin distrusted ardent Labour supporters of Republican Spain as enthusiasts ready to plunge Europe into war, as men in whom the revolutionary tradition of European Socialism was not altogether dead.[1] In Latin America the left-wing supporters of President Cárdenas saw the struggle of the Republic against 'old Spain' as part of their own struggle against old Mexico. 'General Cárdenas', ran the posters, 'defeated at Teruel.'[2]

This epilogue does not examine the larger context of the war. It attempts merely a brief explanation of the victory of General Franco.

1. *The Alignment of Forces, July 1936*

When the military revolt broke out in Morocco on the afternoon of 17 July and began to spread to the garrison towns of Spain on the afternoon of the following day, the reaction of the government was to resign. Its military advisers had been so confident that the prime minister, Casares Quiroga, was overwhelmed when catastrophe, so long prophesied, finally came about; his successor Martínez Barrio, refusing all socialist demands to arm the workers, sought to negotiate a settlement with General Mola, the chief of the rising in the north, and, at this moment, in charge of the military conspiracy. Mola refused to treat and the overthrow of Martínez

[1] For Bevin and Greenwood's attitudes see *Report of the 36th Conference of the Labour Party*, 170–1.

[2] L. E. Smith, *Mexico and the Spanish Republicans* (Berkeley, 1955), 166. The battle of Teruel was lost by the Republican armies in the winter of 1938 (see below, p. 690).

Barrio's right-wing Republican government by street pressure was the first act of a new revolution which was to condition the political and social life of Republican Spain. It is easy now to criticize the failure of orthodox Republicans 'to rise to their historic task'. Casares Quiroga, Martínez Barrio, and, behind them, President Azaña hesitated to arm a revolution in order to defeat a counter-revolution: to give arms to the people would have meant handing over the government to the workers' parties and a resurrection of the street power of early nineteenth-century radicalism. They therefore preferred a last-minute attempt at compromise in order to stave off the horrors of civil war. While the workers (who had got hold of five thousand rifles) were policing the capital and what authority there was lay in the Casa del Pueblo, a new Republican government was formed under Giral; under pressure, he armed the people.

During these critical days neither side acted with decision: if the army had been able to rise all over Spain on 18 July the old recipe of a pronunciamiento might have been once more effective as an instrument of political change and the Civil War might have been avoided. If the government had issued orders to arm the workers on the 17 July instead of two days later the rebellion might have been more effectively crushed. As it was, the hesitations of the Madrid government were repeated throughout Spain; each city acted independently in accordance with the local balance of loyalties. In Madrid itself, a city ringed by barracks, General Fanjul hesitated, waiting, shut up in the Montaña barracks, until he was attacked by revolutionary crowds in search of vengeance and rifle bolts.[1] General Goded's chances in Barcelona were prejudiced by last-minute changes of plan and minor mishaps. The troops from the barracks on the city perimeter were to march at dawn down the long straight streets to the centre of the city—an easy target from the side-streets. Goded's hydroplane failed; he arrived late from Mallorca to find a situation confused by the loyalty to the Republic of the commanding general and the Civil Guards. The undoubted heroism of the C.N.T. militants had less to do with the final issue (Goded was

[1] The seizure of the barracks was the first set piece of the Civil War. It is described in the early chapters of Malraux's *L'Espoir* (Paris, 1937).

captured and shot) than the number of troops involved: the rebels were outnumbered.[1]

All over Spain these desperate days were decided not only by the enthusiasm of the masses but by the determination of a few men in key posts and by the loyalties of the Civil Guard and the Republican Assault guards, who acted differently in different situations. Wherever the government authorities and the proletarian parties showed vigour it was difficult for the army officers to act daringly. Thus the rebels bungled their chances in the Levante. In Burgos and Carlist Navarre there was no effective opposition to the *coup*, while a combination of ruse and daring improvisation enabled Queipo de Llano and Aranda to seize Seville and Oviedo—both facing strong working-class organizations which lost their nerve. Varela succeeded in Cadiz with 600 troops and a Civil Guard colonel with fifty men held Avila for the rebels.

The confused struggles of 19–24 July settled the military frontier of the Civil War and ended the rebel plan of a rapid military take-over. Republican territory would have to be won by battle, by a war of reconquest which would turn a pronunciamiento into a crusade. The early days also divided Spain into political zones which did not always bear the exact relationship to previous political loyalties and social structure that has been imagined. Certain regions were committed: Navarre to the counter-revolution, Catalonia to the Republic. Others were engulfed by the fortunes of war: thus Estremadura and much of Andalusia had voted for the Popular Front but were soon brought within Nationalist territory. Certain classes must pin their faith on the victory of one side: thus the Falange attempt to create a Nationalist proletariat was unsuccessful. Yet for much of the population, political allegiance was the consequence of being 'caught' in one region or the other, and loyalty, to use a contemporary term, was geographical. Hence the problem of the Fifth Column in Republican areas and resistance behind the lines after Nationalist conquests. Gradually propaganda and the instinct of self-

[1] For a Nationalist description of the failure in Barcelona see F. Lacruz, *El alzamiento, la revolución y el terror en Barcelona* (Barcelona, 1943). The rebels had counted on the co-operation of the Civil Guard (ibid. 99); the Republican loyalty of General Llano de Encomienda 'confused' the rebel chances as did the negotiations of Martínez Barrio's government.

preservation hardened the geographical loyalty of the indifferent into a species of political conviction.

2. *The Politics of Republican Spain*

The weakness and indecision of the legal government and its local agencies reproduced the classic pattern of radical revolution in nineteenth-century Spain: the indigenous revolution of the town committee. In July 1936 the specific feature of this revolution was that the Juntas, which sprang up all over Republican territory, were dominated by the organized strength of the two great proletarian parties; it was to these parties that the militias owed their primary loyalty.[1] Committee and militia rule constituted what has been called the Bohemian stage of the revolution—the armleted patrols, the confiscated cars, the huge posters, and lorry loads of enthusiasts with clenched fists. To the outside world this repetition of a hundred years of revolutionary tradition was successfully presented as a great upsurge of the human spirit: to those who were fighting a war with limited resources it rapidly became a nightmare.

In 1936 the process of revolution went deeper than ever before because the state, which had to order the local revolution of provincial militants and master the defensive reaction of the masses, had lost most of its former servants while those who remained were under suspicion as 'geographically loyal'. 'The whole state apparatus was destroyed and state power lay in the streets.'[2]

It was for this reason that the revolutionary terror of the early days went unchecked; in spite of the efforts of responsible C.N.T. leaders it degenerated into indiscriminate killings by the 'uncontrollables'.[3] The destruction of churches all over the Levante and Catalonia, on the other hand, was not so much a result of mass hatred as of 'administrative' acts of local zealots. The church-burners revived all the techniques of

[1] The gift of arms to the population always tended to favour the extreme left, as the government had foreseen. Cf. G. L. Steer's comment on the course of events in San Sebastian: 'In spite of their arms everybody panicked: nobody except the extremists organized.' *Tree of Gernika* (London, 1938), 18.

[2] Dolores Ibarruri, *Speeches and Articles* (London, 1938), 214.

[3] These killings were criticized severely by the F.A.I. and strongly opposed by the government and the Socialist press (*Solidaridad Obrera*, 30 July).

mid-nineteenth-century revolutions—dressing up in vestments, parodying the mass.[1] It was this initial terror which confirmed the hostility of the upper middle classes. Revolutionary enthusiasm made Barcelona a city where it was injudicious to appear in a hat and decent clothes. In Madrid the rich crowded into Embassies, waiting an opportunity to slip into Nationalist territory. There they found a civilization where waiters and hotel porters existed. 'Now we are gentlemen again.'[2]

Behind the acute difficulties of the process of governmental concentration and the establishment of a strong war government lay a debate as to the very nature of the conflict in which the Republic was engaged. Was the Civil War part of a social revolution, set off prematurely by the generals' revolt which, *ex hypothesi*, could not be defeated by the sacrifice of that revolution and its spontaneous creations—committee rule, the militia columns, and collectivization? Or was it a war to defend an advanced form of democracy, a war whose successful prosecution was incompatible with radical social revolution which would alienate support abroad and drive out of the Republic those very classes whose skills and loyalty could best organize victory? On this latter assumption victory could not be won until the militia were replaced by a regular army and a collection of committees by regular government; that is, by a conscious repudiation of the spontaneous creations of the revolutionary *journées*, by the substitution of organization for enthusiasm, of regular municipal government for committee rule.

The chief proponents of the primacy of revolution and those who had most to lose by the establishment of 'social normality' and governmental control were the militants of the C.N.T. and F.A.I. Not merely interest—they knew that their fighting strength and political influence was in the militia columns—but philosophical principle forbade the demolition of revolutionary improvisation. The committee system was the legiti-

[1] Borkenau and others observed this phenomenon: most workers were perhaps indifferent to the Church rather than savagely hostile.

[2] The remark of A. Peña Boeuf. His *Memorias de un ingeniero político* (1954) gives a lively description of the feelings of an upper middle-class *técnico*. He escaped to become Franco's Minister of Public Works. It may be noted that the perils of bourgeois clothes in time of revolution were first remarked on in 1843.

mate successor of the police state, now in ruins; army discipline 'an assault on dignity and human personality'. The only discipline the militants understood was voluntary submission to the Nietzschean hero; saluting was unworthy of 'actors in a great epic'.[1]

To the Anarcho-Syndicalists the social revolution unleashed by war was contained in the word 'collectivization'. Collectivization (supported in many towns by the U.G.T. but in the main the work of the C.N.T.) represented a serious attempt to create a loose federation of free municipalities and workers' collectives; in this revolutionary society what central organization there was—and true Anarchists jibbed at the word 'state'—would merely co-ordinate production organized by the syndicates.

In Catalan industry, where most of the workers were members of the C.N.T., this revolution was feasible. The workers' syndicates took over textile factories, ran the trams and buses of Barcelona, set up collectives for fishing, shoemaking, even entertainment. In the centre and Valencia collectivization was less extensive, while it scarcely touched the north except for the Asturias. Collectivization extended even to small retail businesses; sometimes these were shut down and their owners converted into wage-earners on larger collectives.[2] The threat to collectivization lay less in the resistance of the collectivized than in the disruption of production; a partially collectivized economy would not work 'by spontaneous impulse from the bottom up'.

The Catalan textile industry, cut off from markets and from raw material through lack of foreign exchange, would have run down in any case. Of vital importance to the war effort

[1] *C.N.T.–F.A.I. Boletín de Información*, 5 Aug. 1936.

[2] These small collectives undoubtedly existed although compulsory legal collectivization included only firms with over fifty workers (H. E. Kaminski, *Ceux de Barcelone* (Paris, 1937), 222 ff.). The decrees regulating the various degrees of workers' control were immensely complicated: over 100 decrees preceded the General Decree on Collectivization of Oct. 1936 which tried to rationalize and legalize the workers' take-over. The main principle was the compulsory collectivization of large enterprises and the supervision of smaller enterprises by workers' committees. Co-ordination by the General Council of Industry was very imperfect: Fabregas, the C.N.T. minister, had no statistics and no record of stocks and sales. J. Peirats describes the formal structure of the collectives in *C.N.T.* i. 354 ff. There was active discussion about such issues as uniform pay, 'factory' control versus direction from Juntas representing a whole section of industry, &c.

was the improvisation of a war industry in Catalonia, since the northern industrial centres were isolated from the main territories of the Republic and, after 1937, were in enemy hands. Textile and light industry could not turn over to war production without careful and drastic planning which was impeded by the power of the syndicates and the sensitivity of the Catalan autonomist government. Catalonia now paid the price for her incomplete industrial revolution in a lack of machine tools; lipstick cases could be turned into cartridge cases, but such improvisations were limited. The whole process of collectivization and its effect on production was the centre of a long and still unresolved controversy—both in C.N.T. circles and between the C.N.T. and its enemies. Since no reliable statistics are available no conclusions are possible. In the end Prieto, as Minister of Defence, alleging that the system of direct contracts with Catalan factories had been sabotaged by the Generalidad and productivity subordinated to workers' control, put the war industry under his own ministry.[1] It was a solution that produced much hard feeling among Catalan Nationalists and was regarded by the C.N.T. as a Communist-directed attack on its syndical organization.

The revolution in the countryside was in part a legalization of the squatting which had swept over Estremadura and the south after the February elections. After July it came to represent an attempt to realize the ideals of libertarian communism in those rural areas under C.N.T. control. In principle the C.N.T., while it supported the compulsory collectivization and communal control of expropriated estates, respected the individual small owner's right to cultivate his own land provided this did not harm the interests of the collectives. Thus peasant holdings could only be collectivized by persuasion.[2] This policy could not be enforced in Catalonia where the *rabassaires* enjoyed the political support of the Esquerra and later of the Communist Minister of Agriculture, Uribe. Libertarian communism held only dangers for Catalan tenants (who were turned into true proprietors in February 1937), nor could collectivization make much progress in a

[1] The correspondence between Prieto and Companys is printed in A. Ossorio, *Companys*, 207–42.

[2] *C.N.T.-F.A.I. Boletín de Información, F.A.I.*, 6 Sept. 1936.

highly developed region like the *huerta* of Valencia. Thus the Aragon agrarian collectives, set up on large estates, remained the showpiece of the C.N.T., and some of the southern collectives the closest realization of Anarchist principle. On them money was 'abolished', retail trade suppressed, coffee, alcohol, and prostitution frowned on; at long last the heavenly city of anarchism was a reality.[1]

High idealism was sometimes combined with a degree of coercion: in some districts the small peasant had little alternative but to join his collective; without the committee he could get neither artificial manure nor the services of the doctor and the blacksmith. It was of little consolation to him that his working hours would be cut to enable him to read.[2] As an economic system it was producing a conglomeration of self-contained barter markets grinding slowly towards stagnation as the general economy ran down, though there is some evidence that, where collectives embraced a prosperous zone, production was maintained and, in some cases, increased. Collectivization by the U.G.T. of the larger estates seems to have merely substituted the local committee, and later the municipality, for the landowners; neither hours nor wages improved. The rural revolution offered nothing but an insecure future to the peasant proprietor, while the great areas of landless labourers who had something to gain were, in the main, outside Republican territory. Thus the enthusiasts of the C.N.T. and the F.A.I.—often urban revolutionaries by origin—found themselves forcing on areas, where peasant proprietors predominated, a vision of a new society which would have been welcomed by the *braceros* of the great estates.

In direct antithesis to the spontaneous social revolution of the C.N.T. militants stood the cautious policies of moderate Socialists like Besteiro or Prieto, the Republican parties, and the Communists. All were either on principle hostile to an advanced type of social revolution or believed it must take second place to the efficient organization of a conventional war effort. Thus the collectivization of barbers, bakers, and chemists reduced to the status of wage-earners the radical petty bourgeoisie of the towns from which Republicanism

[1] For a description see A. Souchy, *Entre los campesinos de Aragón* (Barcelona, 1937).

[2] Cf. B. Bolloten, *Camouflage*, 57 ff.

had drawn its strength. Yet the Republican parties were too weak to afford a refuge for this new distress: the withdrawal of Azaña to the monastery of Montserrat was a symbol of the defeat of his party by circumstances. The defence of injured interests, from those of the Valencian orange-growers seeking to recover lost profits from distributors' collectives to those of dentists and clerks, fell to the Communist party. The Jacobin paradox—that a party whose revolutionary credentials and ultimate revolutionary intentions are above reproach is best equipped to risk a policy of temporary social conservatism—brought the Communist party a flood of recruits. Its membership rose from perhaps 40,000 in July 1936 to 250,000 by March 1937 and in the process it almost ceased to be a workers' party; one of its most notable recruits was Constancia de la Mora, granddaughter of Maura. This accretion of strength, together with its control of the arms supply and its political skill, accounts for its predominance in the Popular Front governments.

The Communists appeared as loyal supporters of a broad-based democratic front supporting a strong national government, and as proponents of a studiously moderate social programme, defending the small proprietor and business man against forcible collectivization. Thus in October 1936 the Communist Minister of Agriculture, Uribe, halted the agrarian revolution of the C.N.T. and, where it had occurred, of the U.G.T. Social conservatism was part of a 'realistic' programme which gave the war primacy over the revolution. To the Communists 'the most revolutionary action is to win the war'; hence their support of government as such, their hostility to committees and improvised police, their mounting criticism of the militia system, and their campaign for military discipline, for a unified command, for the creation of a Popular Army. It was the drive to create and to control a disciplined army that characterized Communist policy throughout the Civil War. They had already demonstrated the virtues of political and military discipline in their own Fifth Regiment which distinguished itself in the battle for Madrid. This model it was now their aim to impose throughout the Republican armies.

'Objectively correct'—in Communist jargon—as their policies were in view of the necessities of the war, their pursuit of them was not disinterested. The domestic necessities of Republican Spain happened to correspond with the foreign necessities of the Soviet Union—the pursuit of a Western alliance which entailed disowning any immediate revolutionary intentions in Europe, and the support of democratic popular fronts against fascism. Moreover the Communists worked against the revolution in Spain itself because its initial stages belonged to the old establishments of the proletarian world: the C.N.T. and the U.G.T. They could hope for a greater measure of control in the regular organs of government and a new model army. Hence to most of their political opponents, whose power was based on the 'Bohemian' revolution of the militia committee, their common-sense policies either concealed a humiliating sacrifice of national policy to Russian pressure or an attempt by a small party to infiltrate the whole machinery of the state. This led the opponents of the Communists to the fatal blunder of opposing policies, some of which were indubitably sound, because they suspected the intentions behind them. It also makes it unnecessary to speak in terms of a Communist plot: what success the Communists attained—and it was more limited than it has become fashionable to believe—they attained not merely through a more ruthless police terror or superior conspiratorial techniques but through the advocacy of realistic policies, which were supported by non-Communists in the interests of an effective war effort.

Overwhelmed by Russian-trained advisers in daily radio contact with 'the house', it became apparent that the policy of the Spanish Communist party was subject not merely to the exigencies of Soviet foreign policy, but to the domestic feuds of Stalinism. In September 1936 Orlov was sent to set up a branch of the O.G.P.U. in Spain. The main victims of Communist terror—unlike Anarchist terror it was not mass terror aimed at the liquidation of an evil class but police terror aimed at political dissidents—were the P.O.U.M. The P.O.U.M. was a non-communist Marxist group, disowned by Trotsky; its members were nevertheless regarded by orthodox Communists as heretics to be eliminated. Its mere existence—its strength lay mainly in Catalonia—was intolerable to the Communists, if only because its paper *La Batalla* relentlessly exposed the brutalities of Stalinist Russia.[1] The P.O.U.M. was divided from

[1] Cf. *La Batalla*, 15 Nov. 1936.

the C.N.T. by its belief in the workers' state and in the necessity for *political* power;[1] from the Socialist and Republican parties it was distinguished by its refusal to accept the fiction of an 'Anti-Fascist Front' of workers and bourgeois parties. The Popular Front was not a proletarian government; it was a betrayal of the workers' revolution. The Communists could therefore present the P.O.U.M. as a discordant element which must be destroyed in order to save a united war effort directed by a democratic government.

The reappearance of old police methods, exercised by Communists against a dissident workers' party, alarmed the C.N.T. militants and a nervy atmosphere of arrests and *pistolerismo* developed in Barcelona where the Communist-controlled P.S.U.C. was driving against its opponents.[2] By the spring of 1937 Berzin, the chief Russian military adviser, was alarmed: 'our men are behaving to the Spaniards as if they were colonials.' Russian police methods, like Russian propaganda, were crude and offended patriotic susceptibilities; José Díaz, secretary of the Spanish party, saw his counsel scorned by advisers like Togliatti and Stepanov and their Spanish allies in the Political Bureau of the party. Díaz came to have a curious sympathy with those C.N.T. elements who wished for a 'revolution of an eminently nationalist flavour', which should have as its heroes the guerrillas of the War of Independence and the Cid rather than the sailors of the *Potemkin*.[3]

The Communists were ultimately defeated by their own brand of obstinacy. Capable of bold risks in preaching moderation in the midst of revolutionary euphoria, they were also capable of a ruthlessness in the pursuit of their objectives which was self-defeating. They were determined to control the new People's Army: hence their domination of the corps of commissars—a legitimate safeguard against doubtful officers—but which they turned into an instrument for proselytization and party control;

[1] For a P.O.U.M. denunciation of the failure of the C.N.T. and blindness to the issue of *political* power for the workers, see Julián Gorkín, *Canibales políticos* (Mexico, 1940), 67 ff.

[2] The P.S.U.C. was the Communist-dominated Unified Socialist Party of Catalonia; it was formed locally without consultation with the U.G.T. leaders and came to control the Catalan Socialist Unions.

[3] Cf. *Solidaridad Obrera*, 20, 24 Jan. 1937. Syndicalist poets were exalting the virtues of the Spanish race and seeking the roots of the revolution in Don Quixote and the *Romancero*.

hence their interference in promotions and their use of the press to destroy or popularize a commander.[1] This created a military opposition to Communist control that was to have fatal consequences.

It is in the light of these conflicts that we must examine the difficulties which surrounded the 'concentration of government' —the creation of a ministry capable of directing the war effort. Giral's government, a pure Republican affair, lacked all authority for such a task; Largo Caballero's government (September 1936) was a repetition of Mendizábal's tactic of absorbing the revolution in order to contain it. Apart from the C.N.T., the workers' committees were now represented in the central government; it could therefore attempt to re-establish the normal agencies of power—particularly the police—and begin the tasks of militarizing the militias, building up a regular army and slowing down the pace of spontaneous social change. Largo Caballero was not eminently suited for this undertaking; morose and secretive, he was conscious of the contradictions in his position as a working-class leader who had preached the revolution it was now his function to restrain. The cabinet was large and its long meetings exhausted the prime minister. Yet with all his faults he alone had enough prestige with the workers to attempt with success a policy of restraint.

The greatest remaining obstacle to the re-establishment of strong government was the C.N.T.—dominant in urban Catalonia, influential in Valencia, and an irritant in Madrid. In Catalonia Companys, as President of the Generalidad, had accepted that it was impossible to rule Barcelona against the C.N.T.; he was forced to gamble once more on what he called the 'common sense' of the C.N.T. leadership against the revolutionary instincts of the masses. The result was the rule of the Anti-Fascist Militia Committee (on which the C.N.T. was strongly represented) parallel to the regular governmental organs. This gave Barcelona, in the early months of the Civil War, a true proletarian flavour: C.N.T. syndicalism did not want higher wages but a wider life, the institutionalization of its

[1] Cf. their destruction of General Asensio, and their conversion of General Miaja, the defender of Madrid, into an international celebrity. The Russian ambassador, Rosenberg, constantly interfered in promotions.

religiosité prolétarienne. On 27 September the dual system ended with the entry of the C.N.T. into the Catalan government; on 4 November it joined Largo Caballero's government. These were important steps in the process of constructing a government out of the centrifugal forces of revolutionary enthusiasm; by November 1936 all the parties of Republican Spain, except for the P.O.U.M. and the purists of the C.N.T.–F.A.I., were represented in the central government. The coalition lasted until May 1937.

The entry of the C.N.T. into the governments of Catalonia and Republican Spain constitutes the most remarkable decision in the course of Spanish anarchism. It entailed the rejection of those root principles which had distinguished libertarian communism from orthodox Marxism: in anarchist theory the workers' state was as evil as any other state. Anarchist thought, therefore, furnished no *theoretical* permission for participation in a democratic government fighting for its life against military rebellion. Nevertheless, the C.N.T.–F.A.I. leadership realized that the Republic must be defended, since the triumph of the Nationalists would mean the end of all proletarian parties, and that anarchist improvisation must not be allowed to impede the war effort. 'There is no such thing as an Anarchist war; there is only one war and we must win it. We will win it but we must abandon many of our principles.'[1] The leaders were appalled at the militia defeats and the exploits of the uncontrollables. Moreover, since the committee–militia system was destined to be superseded by a regular government, the C.N.T. could only preserve its power and its revolutionary conquests in Aragon and elsewhere from *within* that government. Principles must be sacrificed to the preservation of the organized strength of the C.N.T.

The entry of the C.N.T. representatives into Largo Caballero's government caused a *crise de conscience* in the leadership itself and was never popular with the militant masses. In Frederica Montseny's words, once in the government, the C.N.T. could not be in the street; to the militants, in its eagerness to co-operate with the regularization of revolution, the leadership seemed to be turning against the street. The new language of

[1] Diego Adad de Santillán (Chief of the Militia Committee and a leading F.A.I. intellectual), quoted in H. E. Kaminski, *Barcelone*, 253.

moderation of C.N.T. ministers was concealing the destruction of the organization it professed to be saving. Under the slogan of 'a government which governs' political enemies of the C.N.T. in Catalonia (especially the Communist-dominated P.S.U.C.) were destroying the foundation of proletarian strength—the militia—by disarming it in favour of a regular army and an orthodox police force; to this danger the C.N.T. 'governmentalists' seemed blind. It was in this suspicious frame of mind that the 'revolutionary opposition' among the C.N.T. masses witnessed the Communist offensive against the P.O.U.M. Both the P.O.U.M. and 'the revolutionary opposition' saw themselves as victims of a new police state.[1] Under cover of the Anti-Fascist Front the revolution was being destroyed by a governmental counter-revolution.

In January the P.O.U.M. paper, *La Batalla*, began to print attacks on Communists and Catalan bureaucrats as the Mensheviks of the Revolution. The P.S.U.C. was identified as an instrument of a bourgeois counter-revolution: on it the P.O.U.M. declared 'implacable war'. When the P.O.U.M. warned that its militants would form pickets to shoot down 'reactionaries', it was not clear whether these were the P.S.U.C. or the Nationalists.[2] After a month of tension the crisis came on 3 May, when Rodríguez Salas of the P.S.U.C. and chief of the Catalan government police, raided the Telephone Building, held by the C.N.T.[3] His action precipitated four days of obscure, complex street and roof fighting. There was little sign of premeditation: both sides blazed away at buildings held by their opponents without plan, without any other logic than that your enemies were those who fire against you. The P.O.U.M. fought, and the C.N.T.–F.A.I. militants supported them, because there seemed

[1] The attitude reflected in *Solidaridad Obrera*, 2 May: 'The guarantee of the Revolution is the armed proletariat. Let no one give up his arms.' The P.O.U.M. (as opposed to the C.N.T. leadership) opposed the abolition of the Anti-Fascist Militia Committee. In December 1936 the P.O.U.M. representatives were excluded from the Catalan government.

[2] *La Batalla*, 2, 3, 6 Jan. 1937. *La Batalla* ran a campaign against Juan Comorera (leader of the P.S.U.C.) as responsible for the bread shortage—an inflammatory move.

[3] The C.N.T. had been intercepting government calls, according to Benavides of the P.S.U.C., *Guerra y revolución en Cataluña* (Mexico, 1946), 424. Salas's action was therefore presented as a non-provocative police action in order to end a vestige of 'double government' by re-establishing the overall control of the Generalidad government.

no escape from a counter-revolution within the Republic but by violent resistance to the encroachment of the police state. The C.N.T. leaders worked desperately for a truce by negotiations with the Generalidad in order to bring a compromise solution of the police question. Their failure to aid the P.O.U.M. was regarded by the latter as yet one more proof of the leadership's disastrous blindness to the necessity of seeking political power for the workers by replacing the 'hypocrisy of the Anti-Fascist Front' with a true proletarian government (i.e. of the C.N.T. and the P.O.U.M.). The fighting died down as food ran out and the arrival of government Assault Guards, commanded by a member of the C.N.T., restored complete order. The 'revolutionary opposition' was crushed and its prophet, Berneri, an Italian Anarchist distinguished for his anti-Stalinism, was assassinated on 6 May 1937.

The May troubles finally disrupted that concentration of forces within the Republic represented by the government of Largo Caballero. Already he had found it impossible to mediate between those who could not abandon the early conquests of the revolution and those who saw in their continued existence the premiss of certain defeat.[1] The May troubles forced a decision. They therefore constituted the watershed in the political life of the Republic.

The architect of the fall of Largo Caballero was the Communist party. The degeneration of the prime minister's relations with the Communists was striking. He felt deceived and bullied. The union of Socialist and Communist youth movements, which he had favoured, now appeared a move against himself; close advisers like Álvarez del Vayo were backing the communist line; the Russian ambassador badgered him over promotions and communist officers were withdrawing the army from his control as war minister. Who should control the army was the key issue: it was not as prime minister but as war minister that the Communists objected to Largo Caballero. In his pride he determined to break the Communists' growing power in the army before they broke him.

The crisis came on 13 May when Largo Caballero refused the communist demand to dissolve the P.O.U.M. on the

[1] For a summary of Largo Caballero's middle position see H. Rabasseire, *Espagne creuset politique* (Paris, 1938), 152.

grounds that its militants had provoked the May troubles as fascist *agents provocateurs*.[1] He would neither accept the ruthless repression of a working-class party nor accept the thesis that 'the Soviet People's justice is our justice'; in the subsequent cabinet manœuvres only the C.N.T. ministers sided with him.

If the fall of Largo Caballero was engineered by the Communists their 'plot' succeeded less because their influence was irresistible than because many others wanted the same result but had hitherto lacked enough political resolution to stage a cabinet crisis. Largo Caballero, now nearing seventy, had many faults as a war minister—'burnt out . . . a good Trade Union boss . . . no drive . . . not the slightest idea of military problems'[2] —and many critics in a cabinet he could no longer control. Most dangerous of these were Prieto and his followers. Scarcely on speaking terms with the prime minister, his moderate socialist views brought him close to the communist policy, while he shared the Communists' conviction that Largo Caballero was incompetent. Prieto's 'desertion' of Largo Caballero was decisive; he acted as he did, not as a servant of the Communists, but because his own aims coincided with those of the party.[3]

Behind the issue of effective war government lay one of the central problems of socialism: the relative role of the unions and the political party. The Communists, the moderate Socialists, and the Republicans wished the Republic to be based on political parties. They denied that the unions had 'real political capacity'; the syndicalist conception would narrow the Republic to the working classes and keep up pressures for social revolution which must be postponed until the war had been won with the alliance of the 'anti-fascist middle classes'.[4] Largo Caballero was above all a trade union leader. Thus the allies of the Communists, without whom they would have been powerless, were the socialist members voted into the cabinet by the Executive Committee of the party in September—amongst them Dr. Negrín, whom Largo Caballero had always mistrusted as a rich socialist intellectual without roots in the movement or understanding of the workers. The fall of Largo

[1] According to Juan Peiró (*Problemas y cintarazos*, Rennes, 1946) the demand for dissolution was backed only by the reading of passages from *La Batalla*, the P.O.U.M. daily.

[2] J. Martín Blazquez, *I Helped to Build an Army*, 201.

[3] For the relations of Prieto and the moderate Socialists with the Communists at this time see B. Bolloten, *Camouflage*, 301–6.

[4] *Mundo Obrero*, 5 May 1937.

Caballero is the last act in the long struggle between his own penchant for some form of revolutionary unionism and Prieto's preference for 'bourgeois' socialism.

The most important consequence of the May crisis was that it exposed the weakness of the main premiss of the Popular Front as conceived by Republicans and Communists: they argued that since the working classes *must* be anti-fascist, 'correct' policy was by 'moderation' to keep the middle classes at all costs within the 'new democracy'. The C.N.T. saw its social revolution dismantled: in August 1937 the independent C.N.T.–F.A.I. Council of Aragon was abolished and the collectives wound up by Lister, the most notable Communist commander, on the orders of Prieto;[1] in industry, collectivization and workers' control was replaced by nationalization and central planning. Thus the price that had to be paid for a government that was both unified and 'efficient' and that could appeal to what the nineteenth century would have called the 'respectable classes', was a loss of working-class enthusiasm and solidarity. Largo Caballero, against whom the Communist unleashed a frightful attack in the press and on the platform, took with him into opposition a section of the U.G.T. and of the Socialist party. The C.N.T. suffered for its support of Largo Caballero and its involvement in the fate of the P.O.U.M. Both the *Caballerista* unions and the C.N.T. were tempted by the vision of a merger to preserve their own strength and the integrity of what the C.N.T. called the Iberian Revolution. Even though they sensed their weakness, union once more proved impossible.

Largo Caballero's successor was Dr. Negrín and he remained prime minister until the end of the Civil War. Initially his government included neither the *Caballerista* section of the U.G.T. nor the C.N.T. It was not, however, 'dominated' by Communists. The party reflected the belief of the Soviet Union that 'the installation of a Communist régime is not the solution of the war problem'. If dependence on Russian arms deliveries precluded serious resistance to what Communists considered 'correct' policies there were limits to what governmental Socialists called 'our sense of self-denial'. Thus the cabinet would not back the Communists' private vendetta against the P.O.U.M. as 'demagogic Bukarinites' and fascist

[1] Some of the Aragon collectives were later refounded.

agents provocateurs. The Communists therefore had to 'eliminate' the P.O.U.M. leaders by their own police activities, a process the government was too weak to resist.[1]

Communists were less concerned with the capture of portfolios than with control of the army and the secret police. 'He who dominates the army dictates the orientation of the country', and to achieve this end the party set up a special agency—'agit-prop' designed to win recruits and to build up communist commanders. This infiltration was bitterly resisted by Prieto as Minister of Defence; he had long quarrelled with Russian technicians and communist leaders and it was against Prieto that the Communists mounted their last political offensive—a rigged campaign of telegrams, demonstrations, and newspaper articles demanding Prieto's resignation (April 1938). The elimination of Prieto was a risky move: he was a power in the Socialist party and in the anti-*Caballerista* trade unions. Once again the condition of success was that others besides the Communists wished to jettison Prieto on grounds of general policy: his 'defeatism' and sympathy for the idea of a negotiated peace appeared dangerous to his cabinet colleagues.[2]

These dissensions and feuds were unedifying at a time when the government was emphasizing the necessity of unity. 'The blame for defeat will not fall on the non-intervention policy of the British government which is equivalent to intervention against us. The principal culprits will be the Spaniards themselves. We suffer from an infirmity which I will call the moral misery of Spain—which will ruin Spain itself. This malady is internecine strife.'[3] The Communists did their best to repair the

[1] Cf. J. Gorkín, *Canibales*, 99 ff. The ferocity of this eliminatory process is proved by their murder of Andrés Nin and their assaults on all those who defended the P.O.U.M.—e.g. 'los Brockmay [*sic*], los Maxton, los Sam Baron' (*Mundo Obrero*, 2 Aug. 1937). The 'May line' can be detected in all subsequent Communist accounts, e.g. in Ludwig Renn and L. Longo. For the Nin murder see P. Broué and E. Témime, *La révolution et la guerre d'Espagne* (Paris, 1961), 275–80.

[2] For Prieto's differences with the Communists see L. Fischer, *Men and Politics* (London, 1941), 432. D. Sevilla Andrés, *Historia política de la zona roja*, 371. The Communists were so afraid a victory at Teruel (see below, p. 690) would strengthen Prieto's position that according to their bitterest enemies they 'set out to torpedo Prieto at the cost of losing Teruel'. 'It's not a question of liquidating the Popular Front but of making it do what we want. We've got to discredit the Socialists and the Anarcho-Syndicalists and show people that the Communists are the only people who can hold Teruel' (El Campesino, *Listen Comrades* (London, 1952), 22 ff.).

[3] *Claridad*, 5 May 1937.

damage their own ruthlessness had caused—on their own terms. They had always been more willing than the Republicans and moderate Socialists for an alliance with a repentant C.N.T. which accepted discipline and controlled the uncontrollables.[1] Once Largo Caballero had been ousted from control of the U.G.T. they proposed, once more, an alliance of the C.N.T. and the U.G.T. and pressed the C.N.T. to re-enter the government. This it did in March 1938. But the spirit of the C.N.T. had been broken when it accepted the view that syndicates were a contrivance to increase production. The governmental unity which the Republic finally achieved seemed, after the enthusiasm of July 1936, a peace of exhaustion.

This exhaustion was particularly evident in Catalonia when loyalty to the Republic had been an immediate response to a military rising which professed as its aim the re-creation of the unity of the nation—that is, the destruction of Catalan autonomy. The May crisis did not only disgust many C.N.T. militants, it also broke the balance of forces between an autonomous Catalonia and the central government, a balance symbolized by Companys. President of the Generalidad he was loyal to Republican Spain. Yet he was accused (by both Azaña and Prieto) of putting autonomy before the war effort, while to the Catalan bourgeoisie he appeared as little better than an Anarchist fellow-traveller. Sensing that the Catalan state could not risk a showdown with the C.N.T., he sought the co-operation of 'moderate' C.N.T. leaders. The May troubles exposed the contradictions in his policy: the 'moderates' could not hold their extremists and he was forced to rely on the central state to repress a workers' revolt. There was a connexion between Catalan autonomy and the power of the C.N.T.;[2] both declined together as the central government increased its control over Catalonia: thus both the Catalan bourgeoisie and, to a lesser extent, the Catalan proletariat opted out of the war.

[1] Individual Communists often felt a strange sympathy with the C.N.T.; to men like Kolzov the anti-Fascist front was something more than a device of Soviet foreign policy (cf. A. Garosci, *Gli intellettuali e la guerra di Spagna* (1959), 282 ff.).

[2] Of course this connexion was not explicit, as is revealed by Companys's telegrams to the Valencia government (printed in Ossorio, *Companys*, 178 ff.). He wished to settle the troubles by negotiation, but the C.N.T. terms (the resignation of the police chief) 'would make it [the C.N.T.] emerge stronger from the fight'.

Companys, in his despair, surrounded himself with Catalanist intellectuals. It was as if Catalan nationalism, in defeat, returned to the sources of its strength.

In the Basque country there was a more complex conflict between autonomy and the central direction of the war effort. Basque nationalism—satisfied late in the day (October 1936) by the Republic with the grant of a Statute of Autonomy—could hope for nothing from Franco's rigid insistence on national unity. The Nationalists never forgave the 'treason' of the Catholic Basques, especially of the priesthood, loyal to a Republic which had granted self-government. Yet the Catholic, conservative nationalism of the Basques, their ambition to expand autonomy into 'dominion status', made this loyalty suspect to the proletarian parties.

From the early days Basque Nationalist militia and police forces came into violent conflict with the C.N.T. The Basques, orderly and conservative, were appalled by C.N.T. arson and prison massacres; thus the Basque Militia fought the C.N.T. in their attempts at revolutionary terror after the fall of San Sebastian.[1] The Basque leaders fought nobly to save lives both in their own territory and through the Basque ministers in the central government. Irujo, the Basque Minister of Justice, worked for 'violence at the front and humanity at the rear', resisting the Communist onslaught on the P.O.U.M. Nevertheless, to sectors of the left, the Basques appeared lukewarm allies, uninterested in the triumph of the principles of the Popular Front, 'peasant reactionaries' to whom 'Red Spain and White Spain are the same thing', except that Red Spain guaranteed Basque self-government. These mutual suspicions were to play an important part in the collapse of the northern front where the C.N.T. distrust of Basque Nationalists was so great that militia units withdrew from the line at critical moments 'on political grounds'. They were to infect even the central government itself.[2]

[1] The worst prison massacres occurred after air raids (e.g. 4 Jan. 1937 when 124 were killed), and in resisting these outbursts of 'refugee' violence the U.G.T. sided with the Basque police.

[2] This was particularly the case in military aviation. The crushing superiority of the Nationalists was the result of the incapacity (the northern front was beyond fighter range) and perhaps the indifference of a hard-pressed central government. By Apr. 1937 the Basques had only three operational planes. Of food the Basques were deprived by British policy.

3. *Nationalist Spain and the Rise of Franco*

The Republicans had come near to destroying themselves in achieving a unified direction of the war. Their enemies were saved from this fate, not by any lack of competing cliques and ideologies, but by the primacy of the soldiers. The Nationalists met the challenge of political definition and governmental concentration by postponing the former and solving the latter *manu militari*. Until October 1936 (when Franco was declared Generalissimo and Head of the State) the leadership, as well as the political nature, of the rebellion was in abeyance, while its administrative machinery remained a primitive improvisation. The generals had no structure of government in the localities beyond the machinery of the state of siege, no political theory beyond the negative one of resistance to 'Communism', 'anti-Spain', and anarchy. Since they calculated on a short war there was no need to organize the competing conglomeration of parties on the Nationalist side into a state: the generals either used those parties which held power in the regions they commanded or neglected them entirely. With the resistance of Madrid and the prospects of a long war, the organization of a new state could not be deferred. If this were not done there was a danger that Nationalist Spain would disintegrate into military fiefs: Franco in the centre, Mola in the north, and Queipo de Llano in the south.

The supreme power of Franco as war-lord and charismatic leader could not have been foreseen in July 1936, even after the death of Sanjurjo in an aeroplane accident and Goded's execution had removed two rivals. His easy eminence was a result of military accident: Franco's Moroccan army was the core of Nationalist strength. Mola, his only surviving rival, with no triumphs behind him, could not effectively protest against Franco's leadership although it riled him.[1] Besides his technical competence (he was a general at thirty-two), his bravery, and his iron self-control, Franco's greatest strength lay in what Cromwell would have called 'waiting upon providences' and what his critics called excessive caution. In the

[1] Cf. Hitler's verdict: 'The real tragedy for Spain was the death of Mola [in an aeroplane accident]; there was the real brain, the real leader. . . . Franco came to the top like Pontius Pilate in the Creed.' Hitler's *Table Talk* (ed. H. R. Trevor-Roper, London, 1953), 608.

political in-fighting of Nationalist Spain this meant lack of political definition in terms of existing parties; his neutralism permitted him to use the conflicting opinions of others in order to ensure a leadership above party, a leadership he soon came to regard as bestowed by God. His political beliefs were the simple trilogy of the nineteenth-century soldier: the unity of the state (he regarded the war as a war against secessionists—Basques, Catalans, and Marxists), order, hierarchy. To these he added an intense Catholicism and even, initially, a vague social radicalism inherited perhaps from Gil Robles.[1]

Although Franco's leadership had been acknowledged it had not been institutionalized and until April 1937 the juridical and political nature of the Nationalist state remained ill-defined.[2] The need for a 'new state' and a unified party had been pressed on Franco by his brother-in-law, Ramón Serrano Suñer. Serrano Suñer, as a lawyer, was distressed by the lack of a public law which alone could 'transform an insurrection into a political enterprise' by giving it 'juridical form'. As an old friend of José Antonio he shared his conviction that democratic liberalism was unsuited to Spanish conditions and antithetic to Spanish values, a conclusion he derived from an enthusiasm for sixteenth-century history. The 'new state' was to be the legal expression of a single party and the instrument of a single man—Franco. Serrano's advice therefore fitted in with the distaste Franco and his military staff felt for the erratic courses of the Falangists and the Carlists.

Like the Falangists, the Carlists represented the Bohemian stage of revolution in Nationalist Spain; their militia (the Navarrese *requetés*) drew its strength from religious devotion and family tradition, frequently exhibiting an independence which irritated the generals. Moreover the Traditionalist leaders, as monarchists, had reservations about Franco's assumption of the headship of the state. Franco saw that a monarchical restoration, besides confining him to the role of

[1] Cf. the speech of 18 July 1937. 'We are making a deep revolution in a social sense, inspired by the teachings of the Catholic church. There will be fewer rich but also fewer poor.'

[2] Up to Franco's assumption of supreme power Nationalist Spain had been nominally ruled by a Junta of generals assisted by a skeleton civil service. The real administrators were, of course, soldiers. For a hostile description of these early lays at Burgos, see A. Ruiz Vilaplana, *Burgos Justice* (London, 1939).

a Monk, would stamp the 'movement' as old-fashioned and aristocratic. Independence, as conceived by the Carlist leader Fal Conde, bordered on treason.[1] When therefore there were rumours of a fusion of the Falange factions and Traditionalists, Franco was seriously alarmed.

The Falange was growing rapidly in numbers. Like the Communist party it was a refuge for those who wanted a party card in the dangerous early days; unlike the Communist party, it could not count on consistent support from foreign powers with a monopoly of essential arms supplies. Faupel, the German ambassador, was haunted by fears that Franco's movement would become a clericalist reactionary concern, but Germany was quite unwilling to back the Falange against Franco in order to create a National Socialist régime. Excessive growth, therefore, weakened rather than strengthened the party; the 'new shirts' had little sympathy for the social radicalism of José Antonio's visionary New Spain, while most of the generals disliked its anarchic violence and claims to power.[2] With José Antonio in prison (he was executed on 20 November 1936) the party, after disintegrating into autonomous regional groupings, fell into violent disputes about the leadership which came near to destroying it altogether. Hedilla, who became temporary chief, was an honest ex-ship's mechanic who symbolized the party's aspiration to become a working-class movement but his leadership was contested by the new arrivals. The 'personalism' of the feuds within the Falange matched in violence the intra-party struggles in Republican Spain.[3] It therefore failed to grasp political power commensurate with its inflated size and fell an easy victim to the will of Franco and his determination to create a single-party state in Nationalist Spain.

[1] Franco told Faupel on 11 Apr. he was on the 'point of deciding to have Fal Conde executed . . . but had refrained from doing so since that would have produced a bad impression among the Requetés at the front, who were fighting bravely there'. *Documents on German Foreign Policy*, Series D, iii, no. 243.

[2] According to A. Bahamonde y Sánchez de Castro (*Memoirs of a Spanish Nationalist* (London, 1939), 12), General Queipo de Llano in Seville was 'obsessed' by the Falange 'in which he placed not the slightest trust'. Only in those districts within his command where he could not exercise direct control (e.g. Badajoz) did the party become a powerful influence (ibid. 50).

[3] This stage of the Falange's history is excellently described in S. G. Payne, *Falange*, 117–31, 148–73.

The new unified party, to which all officers and government servants were automatically affiliated, professed to be a union of the two 'mass' parties—the Falange and the Traditionalists.[1] Doctrinally it was based on Falangist rather than Traditionalist principles. Franco saw that the main problem of the Nationalist movement was to regain the allegiance of the 'great unaffiliated neutral mass which has never wished to join any party', and that the Traditionalists lacked 'a certain modernity' necessary for this task.

Nevertheless it was Hedilla's group within the Falange that came out against the new party: Hedilla realized that union could mean the end of the Falange as an independent party, based on the social ideas of José Antonio, and prepared to resist what he had called the 'abysmal political mediocrity' of the generals. Hedilla's attempts at resistance were magnified by Franco into a movement against his leadership; he was imprisoned and the whole Falangist leadership disciplined.[2] This was the greatest political crisis in Nationalist Spain, and the ease with which it was mastered by the soldiers is in significant contrast to the contemporary crisis among the Republicans. Opposition groups of Falangists remained discontented with the supposed 'Vaticanist' tendencies of the progenitor of the new party, Serrano Suñer, and with the increasing influence of the conservative 'capitalist' right; but most of the membership subordinated resentment to the needs of the war, or, less nobly, to the rewards of power within the new party. All that was to survive of the old Falangist movement was the official cult of José Antonio and a debased version of his revolutionary rhetoric as the official language of the New Spain.

On the right the Traditionalists accepted fusion without enthusiasm. As monarchists they detested Serrano Suñer and the Falangist bias he had given the new state but they found their reward in the re-establishment of Catholic unity. The most serious opposition came from the generals: with the exception

[1] The clumsy name of the new party reflected its heterogeneous composition: *Falange Española Tradicionalista y de las J.O.N.S.*, known as the F.E.T.

[2] Serrano Suñer hints that Faupel sympathized with the dissidents (*Entre les Pyrénées et Gibraltar* (Geneva, 1947)). In fact he shared Serrano's own view that Franco dealt too severely with the rebels and accused Franco of acting in too brusque a fashion over unification, without giving Hedilla time to 'integrate' (*Documents on German Foreign Policy*, no. 248).

of Yagüe none of them had much time for the Falangists but many of them were old-fashioned Alfonsist monarchists.[1] Combined with military differences this was to produce an army opposition which never got beyond grumbling criticism. Franco came to have military favourites and his differences with Aranda, perhaps the ablest soldier on the Nationalist side, were notorious. He always suspected Queipo de Llano's independence. This independence Queipo de Llano could afford because his Andalusian fief was economically and militarily independent of Nationalist Spain; bombastic and erratic—he even exhibited in Franco's presence his claims as a rival Nationalist hero—he did not contemplate sedition. In contrast to civilians, the soldiers stuck together.

Perhaps the most remarkable phenomenon in Nationalist Spain was the political eclipse of C.E.D.A. and Gil Robles: both had too many attachments to some sort of parliamentary life to fit into an anti-parliamentary state. Some C.E.D.A. members became Falangists while others served loyally as bureaucrats, because they could not serve as politicians a régime without politics as the C.E.D.A. had understood them.

The new party reflected a balance of incompatible forces, managed by Serrano's political talents, and dominated by Franco as representative of the true power in the state—the army. Governments included old-fashioned Alfonsists, cynical Carlists, old and new Falangists, and, in Peña Boeuf as Minister of Public Works, a representative of the middle-class *técnicos* who were to become the *élite* of the new state. Although Franco professed to believe that Nationalist Spain must bid to attract the working classes, the balance of forces within it precluded such a bid. After a long struggle between the Falangist social radicals and what they called the 'Third Spain'—the Spain of conservative landed and business interests—the Labour Charter established a watered-down edition of Falangist 'vertical syndicalism': it aimed at 'an energetic revision, truly revolutionary, of the whole social structure without upsetting the respective situations of the different classes'. This entailed the paternalistic, disciplined labour world of Franco Spain.

The fundamental institutions of the Nationalists were not the

[1] It was Kindelán, Commander of the Air Force and a strong monarchist, who had engineered Franco's emergence as Head of State.

syndicates but the army and the church. It was the generals who elected Franco to supreme power in October 1936: they were rewarded with the lion's share in the new government. The militia was never a threat to the regular army: the Falangist militia did not succeed in establishing itself as an independent force and the Carlist *requetés*, after accepting the hierarchy of the army command throughout the war, at its end retired back to the hills whence they had come. It was the army rather than the civilians who were responsible for the political terror which liquidated working-class leadership and cowed any middle-class opposition. If Ambassador Stohrer's report is correct that 40 per cent. of the inhabitants of the Nationalist zone were initially 'politically unreliable', terror was remarkably efficient.[1]

In spite of some initial doctrinal difficulties over the legitimacy of armed revolt the Spanish Church—its priests murdered and its churches shut except in the Basque Provinces—backed the revolt. Subjected to a massive and brutal prosecution, its theologians worked out a defence of the rising as a just war; its bishops consecrated it as a crusade.[2] The Basque priests who sided with 'anti-Spain' were persecuted and disowned.[3] Thus the Nationalists could always appeal to monolithic Catholic emotion as a corrective to fissiparous tendencies. In return for its blessing the church recovered its privileges (the Jesuits were re-admitted in 1938) and, above all, its control of education and the mind. Much attention has been paid to Republican war-time education, less to the intensive re-catholicizing of Spain that began in the Nationalist zone in the Civil War. The church regained a position it had last enjoyed in the seventeenth century, with an official censorship dedicated to the resistance of 'pornography, Marxism, or dissolvent liberalism'.

Many of the Spanish middle classes had turned against the

[1] *Documents on German Foreign Policy*, no. 586. Early terror was more often the work of Falangists, &c.; the later executions were the work of military tribunals. The same shift from spontaneous to organized terror is evident on the Republican side.

[2] According to Nationalist calculations about 5,000 clerics were killed between July 1936 and January 1937; cf. A. Montero Moreno, *Historia de la persecución religiosa en España* (1961), 762.

[3] From the earliest days priests had blessed the troops, appeared with generals, &c. The famous letter of July 1937 therefore consecrated a position long adopted: it was for European, not domestic consumption.

church in the days of Primo de Rivera. Their return to it, starting under the Republic, was accelerated by the social revolution of July 1936 and its attendant priest killings. They found a fitting leader for their rightward evolution in a rigidly Catholic, middle-class general.

4. *The Course of the War*

Unity of government is a necessary but not a sufficient condition of victory. In the Spanish Civil War military success hinged on two factors: first, and most important, the degree and effectiveness of outside support in arms and, to a lesser extent, in trained personnel; secondly, the relative rapidity with which the two sides trained an efficient combat force. In both respects the Nationalists, by 1937, had come out on top.

The Western democracies failed Republican Spain. Fear of a general war, Chamberlain's desire for Italian friendship, and the Conservative government's distaste for 'Red' Spain committed England to non-intervention and brought pressure on Blum, sympathetic to Republican Spain, to adopt a similar course. In the early months the Labour leaders, on the supposition that they must support Blum, resisted pleas for the supply of arms to Spain. Like the Conservatives they were obsessed with the fear of a general war arising out of the supply of arms to a legal government not recognized as such by Germany and Italy. If non-intervention *worked* it must be supported; although they denounced it regularly after October 1937, they could not draw the logical conclusions from its failure. The reason is contained in Bevin's confession: 'Do the common people of this land want war? They do not.'[1] Blum was himself tortured by his impotence to help Spain, once it was apparent that non-intervention worked against the Republic. Thus French arms deliveries only took place in the early days and the French frontier was closed when the Nationalist blockade left the Pyrenean route the only safe passage for Russian arms.[2]

[1] Greenwood maintained that to reject non-intervention would be to run 'over the body of Léon Blum'. Dalton, who may have known better, adopted a similar attitude. See *36th Conference*, 171, and Bevin in *Tribune*, 19 Mar. 1937.

[2] For French deliveries of aircraft see P. Cot, *Le Procès de la République* (New York, 1944), ii. 332, in *Les Événements survenus en France. Rapport fait au nom de l'Assemblée*

After a period of hesitation which ended in September 1936, effective aid came only from Russia and this was to alter the domestic balance of power. Republican politicians, charged with being Russian dupes, would have welcomed the political independence arms deliveries from the West would have brought them; they did not come and all Republican efforts to destroy non-intervention by stressing ideological affinity, the legal rights of the Republican government, and the danger to British and French strategical interests in the Mediterranean failed. Finally Munich and the Anglo-Italian agreement, in Negrín's words, 'crushed beyond repair' the diplomatic hopes of the Republic; deserters told Nationalist interrogators that Munich meant the end of the war.

The Axis powers, though their Spanish policies were confused in execution by the operation of semi-private agencies, suffered none of the indecision of France and Great Britain, nor did they pull out like Russia. Their aims were clear even when their execution stumbled. Neither Italy nor Germany were *officially* committed to help the generals' revolt but the leaders of both countries saw its utility for their own purposes.[1] Ciano promised aeroplanes which arrived in Morocco on 30 July.[2] Hitler and Göring, against the wishes of both the Foreign Office and the Army Command, agreed to support the generals through special agencies. The first deliveries of Italian and German aeroplanes could therefore play a vital part in getting Franco's army into Spain.[3] Both Hitler and Mussolini, as opposed to their official advisers, calculated on an easy Nationalist triumph which, if supported, would provide an ally gained on the cheap. This

nationale. Temoinages (Paris 1951), 219. Blum states that contraband deliveries were allowed by his own and subsequent governments.

[1] There is frail documentary evidence for any *formal* promised help *before* the revolt. Mussolini's contacts with Goicoechea do not seem to have been followed up; Sanjurjo visited Germany in the spring of 1936. It is clear that both Germany and Italy had reliable information that a military rising was a *probability* in the summer of 1936: the arrival of Italian planes on 30 July would seem to indicate this.

[2] S. Mattiolo, *L'aviazione legionaria in Spagna* (Rome, 1940), 16–17. Franco told Mussolini that Axis planes came too late to be decisive and that a dozen bombers available in the first few days would have enabled him to win the war in a month.

[3] For the early negotiations see Manfred Merkes, *Die deutsche Politik gegenüber dem spanischen Bürgerkrieg* (Bonn, 1961), 17 ff., 68 ff. For the role of the Nazi party organizations and the consequent 'degradation' of the Foreign Office see E. von Weizäcker, *Memoirs* (London, 1951), 106–7.

calculation was proved wrong by the defence of Madrid and the prolongation of the war. Thus their over-optimistic recognition of Franco, by placing the prestige of the Axis powers publicly behind a Nationalist victory, involved them in the support of that cause until it triumphed.

Germany and Italy used the cumbrous machinery of the Non-Intervention Committee as a means to facilitate effective help to their friends and to block it from their enemies without running the risk of a general war; they enforced control when Franco was well supplied and at other times treated non-intervention as 'purely platonic', playing on the French and British desire to avoid war at all costs.[1] By November 1936 Germany and Italy began to fear Franco's defeat unless equipment and men were sent on a massive scale. The main initiative and the supply of combat troops was left to Italy and on 17 December 3,000 Blackshirt volunteers, later to be increased to 40,000 men, left for Spain. They were badly defeated at Guadalajara (March 1937); later they combined uneasily with Franco's army and the Italian generals' criticism and demands for strategical control produced 'certain undercurrents against foreigners'. The Italian contingent never became the *corps d'élite* that would bring victory at a stroke. By 1938 Franco was willing to dispense with the aid of Italian ground forces, though the Italian contribution to his air strength remained indispensable since the Nationalist Air Force fought with Italian planes. In disgust Mussolini declared 'there were no real men in Spain'. Ciano's gamble for an easy ally had resulted merely in a profitless depletion of Italian resources in arms and money that was to be felt when she entered the World War.[2]

The Germans did not see Spain as a field for glory and thus avoided the psychological blunders of the Italians. Intervention was to be primarily an Italian affair and even a prolonged civil war would have the advantage of distracting Mussolini's attention from German designs on Austria. Like Bismarck, Hitler saw strategical and economic advantages in a Spanish alliance

[1] *Documents on German Foreign Policy*, no. 73. Cf. no. 85: 'Now, however, when the Nationalist forces were well supplied . . . Germany and Italy were very much interested in having the embargo strictly enforced'; later the 'Russian stake' (no. 100) forced them to revise their attitude.

[2] Cf. F. W. D. Deakin, in *St. Antony's Seminars*.

and to gain these he was willing to send equipment (first-class communications material and anti-aircraft guns), tanks, infantry and tank instructors, and, above all, the best air group in Spain—the Condor Legion.[1] In return Germany expected a large share in Spanish raw materials; this was organized by the Rowak-Hisma concern, controlled by the Auslands-Deutsch organization. At first Bernhardt, a German-Moroccan business man known to the generals and who was the early agent for commercial transactions, appeared as the Santa Claus of Nationalist Spain. Short of foreign exchange, Germany could not afford philanthropy, however, and by 1938 relations had grown chilly as it became clear that Spain was to be a subsidiary colonial economy in the interests of Göring's Four-Year Plan. The Franco administration resisted German plans for monopolizing iron ore and Göring talked of holding a pistol to Franco's head, while Spain's delays in entering the anti-Comintern pact left 'a nasty taste'. Only with victory in Catalonia did relations ease. Franco's protracted and elusive defence of Spanish independence, continued to Hitler's fury after 1939, was remarkable. In the end Germany got little for her efforts: war-trained pilots had to be weighed against heavy losses. Perhaps the most substantial advantage was indirect: the welding of the two intervening powers firmly into the Axis.[2] Certainly Franco Spain was a profound disillusionment to Hitler; he prophesied that Falangists and Reds might make common cause 'to rid themselves of the clerico-monarchical muck' that had floated to the top.[3]

If Russia had not come to the aid of the Republic in the autumn of 1936 the Nationalists might have won the war in a few months. Russian supplies, especially aeroplanes and tanks, were vital. Russian agencies arranged the purchase of small arms. Russian advisers and the Comintern International Brigades helped to save Madrid; they put the new army on its feet and played a great part in the Jarama and Guadalajara

[1] The Condor Legion consisted of eight squadrons: in order to train as many men as possible the 'volunteers' spent a short spell only in Spain, never exceeding 5,600 men at one time.

[2] Cf. Cantalupo, the Italian ambassador's verdict, 'It was Spain that created the Axis', and Mussolini's remark to Göring in G. Ciano, *L'Europa verso la catastrofe* (1948), 133.

[3] *Hitler's Table Talk*, 520.

battles in the spring of 1937.[1] Thus it was a disaster when Russian supplies began to fall off in 1938. With Stalin's caution, the Mediterranean blockade, and finally Bonnet's closure of the French frontier, the Republican armies were so starved that in the final Catalan offensive there were only 37,000 miscellaneous rifles on the entire front. It is misleading to argue in terms of quantity of supply: there were periods (for instance in November–December 1936) when Russian aid was quantitatively more important than Axis aid to Franco. In the long run it was the *continuity* of German and Italian aid and the regularity with which Axis supplies met every crisis of Franco's armies which decided the war.

For the support of a war effort Republican territory enjoyed an initial advantage: the industry of the north (until 1937) and of Catalonia. This potential was ill-organized; the defence of local autonomy in the Basque Provinces and Catalonia, together with collectivizations of the C.N.T.–F.A.I., restricted the creation of a planned economy and hampered the war industry. The Nationalist war economy inherited defects from the local improvisations of the first months: thus Queipo de Llano, like Soult in the War of Independence, created a semi-independent fief based on the agricultural products of Andalusia. Yet, on the whole, the Nationalist war economy must be considered successful; by the end of 1936 it had solved its monetary problems and succeeded in financing the war without excessive taxation. The Nationalists avoided both the rationing and, by rigid price control, the inflation of the Republican zone.[2] Nationalist territory included the great food-producing zones and it was not until the semi-starving regions of the Republic were incorporated that food rationing became essential. The

[1] For Russian supplies see D. C. Cattell, *Communism and the Spanish Civil War* (Berkeley, 1955), 65, 69–83. For the early organization of supplies see General W. Krivitsky, *I was Stalin's Agent* (London, 1939); the arms bought by Krivitsky's companies on the international market (they therefore included German arms) began to reach Spain in October. According to an American report (Mar. 1937) only 8 out of a total of 400 aircraft were non-Russian. For some interesting side-lights on Russian aeroplanes and instructors see L. Tinker, *Some Must Die* (London, 1938), esp. 42, 140–1, 173. As late as Apr. 1937 Russian planes modelled on Boeing P. 12's were still giving the Republic air superiority on the Eastern Front.

[2] Cf. H. Paris Eguilaz, *Die Währungspolitik des spanischen Befreiungskrieges* (*Weltwirtschaftliches Archiv*, Jena, LXII, Sept. 1940, 330 ff. Prices rose faster than wages in both zones but less dramatically in Nationalist Spain.

knowledge that conditions of life were easier in Nationalist Spain told on loyalty in a Republican Spain of food queues and strict rationing; Bilbao was starved out and the war weariness of Madrid in 1938 was a consequence of a diet of lentils—'Dr. Negrín's Resistance Pills'. In the end supply of all kinds was the deciding factor: from the first the Nationalists received on credit the oil supplies without which their armies could not have moved; in the months that followed came military aid from Germany and Italy, available without immediate payment.

Both sides received help from their foreign allies in training their armies; but in the end the problems of organization had to be solved within Spain and in this task the Nationalists held a relative advantage from the beginning, an advantage which they increased as the war went on.

The problem, on the Republican side, was to replace the embarrassing inheritance of popular enthusiasm, the militia system, by a trained, disciplined army. Initially the improvised forces of the labour organizations captained by those who could seize arms and lorries and impose discipline by force of personality and party loyalty, the militia columns varied in quality: in battle ill armed columns broke before trained troops, and were seized, when bombed and shelled, by uncontrollable collective panics. With such forces the early disasters were inevitable: on the road to Madrid prepared positions were abandoned and the columns destroyed in the open. 'The militia', wrote an observer in 1937, 'has no conception that a position must never be left without express orders from the command. . . . If this is not changed, the insurgents will certainly win the war.' Even less did the militia prove capable of offensive operations: in Aragon a series of ineffective amateurish C.N.T.–P.O.U.M. militia offensives failed to break a thinly held front while, in spite of the publicity that surrounded the contest, the militia at Toledo failed to take a fortress that had been almost blown up.[1]

[1] F. Borkenau, *Spanish Cockpit* (London, 1937), 165; cf. ibid. 211–28, and H. Buckley, *Life and Death of the Spanish Republic* (London, 1940), 248–9. For Toledo, see L. Fischer, *Men and Politics* (London, 1941), 348–9, and his harsh judgement, 'I looked for this heroism at Toledo and the other fronts, but I never found it.' General Duval, who visited the Nationalist lines in 1938, called the Huesca–Saragossa line 'une position de surveillance plutôt que de résistance', *Les Espagnols et la guerre d'Espagne* (Paris, 1939), 2. Lack of artillery (there were three Republican batteries) tended to produce these stagnant situations.

These early catastrophes, hidden from the public by press reports of the imminent capture of Oviedo or Saragossa, were the despair of those regular officers loyal to the Republic. The political nature and consequent inbuilt competition of the militia columns made it impossible to distribute scarce supplies of transport and arms where they were most needed, or to send the militia columns themselves where they would be most effective on purely military considerations. A commander like Mangada, backed by the U.G.T. and the North Station Committee, could extort and keep what arms he wanted. Regular soldiers were distrusted as 'geographical loyalists' with no faith in the revolutionary mystique of the people in arms. Hence the resistance to elementary discipline and to the enforcement of truths 'valid in all times and in all armies' such as the wearing of distinctive uniform by officers.[1] In these conditions the emphasis of the Communists on discipline, the example of the International Brigades, and the advice of Russian technicians were of great importance.[2]

It was not until September that Largo Caballero could be persuaded to abandon the militia system and not until the following months that the organization of a Popular Army of mixed Brigades got under way. The fall of Malaga demonstrated how militia cannot be used by officers with no faith in a popular army and how the political connexions of militia columns precluded the primacy of military considerations. In the later stages of the Basque campaign regular officers made no attempt to understand the militia psychology; they therefore failed to discipline it. Yet, to a surprising extent, when organized by regular officers of imagination and sympathy, the new army fused military discipline and political enthusiasm. Nevertheless, to the end of the war, the Republicans never succeeded in breaking down the independence of the various fronts which had developed in the early months especially when, as in the

[1] J. Martín Blázquez, *I Helped to Build an Army* (London, 1939), 291.

[2] The Russian technicians were under the control of Berzin and Stashevsky—both later executed as were many of the Russians concerned in Spain. It is *very* difficult to estimate the influence of Russians on operations: cf. the extreme view of Krivitsky on the Madrid operations, 'General Berzin and his staff silently guided the fighting that General Miaja publicly commanded and Kleber, the Comintern General, dramatized before the world.' All Republican commanders known to me reject this claim *in toto*—perhaps naturally.

Basque country and Catalonia, it rested on independent regional governments. 'The single command' of the Communists was achieved on paper rather than in the field.

The difficulties of Franco and his generals, whilst never as terrible as those confronting the Republican General Staff, are often obscured by the assumption that 'the army' as an organized unit went over to the Nationalists. 'Aside from the troops in Morocco', wrote the German Ambassador, 'Franco did not have a single usable military unit available but only the wreck of an army.'[1] Mola's army of the north was a heterogeneous affair of regulars and Carlist militiamen; ill supplied, it was relatively easily brought to a halt in the sierras north of Madrid. Thus the decisive factor was the Moroccan army. Well disciplined and well equipped, its officers, trained in North Africa, felt at home in the difficult mountain terrain over which many of the actions were fought. Without it the Nationalists would have lost the Civil War. The Nationalists' problem was therefore to build up and train an army behind the screen of this *corps d'élite*. Helped by German officers, they succeeded in integrating the Falangist and Carlist militia within the regular army and in building up a new officer corps. By 1938 the Nationalist officer cadets were coming out of the academies at the rate of a thousand a month for an army which now counted perhaps 500,000 men. With plentiful Italian supplies, General Kindelán built up an efficient air force which, together with the Condor Legion, had driven the Republicans out of the skies by 1938. The final issue on the Ebro was decided by crushing superiority in the air.

Against this background we must briefly trace the course of the war. To the end, on European standards, it remained a minor war with significant, if small-scale, indications of things to come—the use of tanks in attack, dive-bombing, and the aerial bombardment of civilians among them. Neither side achieved total mobilization of its resources: there was unemployment in the Republican zone, no heavy taxation in Nationalist Spain. In material terms the war remained 'a pauper's war' to the end.[2]

[1] *Documents on German Foreign Policy*, no. 148.

[2] The phrase is Álvarez del Vayo's. The case for the importance of the 'Spanish laboratory' in German military thinking is made by F. O. Miksche, *Blitzkrieg* (London, 1941), 35–43. It must be remembered that the French and, it would seem, the Russians drew the wrong lessons from the tank battles of the war.

Franco's original aim was to bring the war to an end by the conquest of Madrid: his instrument was the Army of Morocco, ferried into Spain on German and Italian planes,[1] since the navy had remained loyal to the Republic and was now commanded by sailors' committees after the officers had been killed as 'unreliable'. The Moroccan army cut through militia columns without serious fighting, though its advance on Madrid had been slowed down when it turned aside to relieve the Alcázar of Toledo, a decision which put a symbolic gesture above military considerations. The capital was saved by a day; had Varela attacked on 6 November he could not have been stopped. Delay allowed Miaja and his Chief of Staff, Rojo, to improvise a brilliant defence, the central epic of the war.[2] Once the Republican line had been established and once this line had been stiffened by the International Brigades, Varela was committed to a slogging match in the suburbs and the lecture halls and laboratories of University City without enough troops to attempt a flanking operation. In the north Mola's offensive had ground to a standstill after his capture of Irun (4 September) and San Sebastian (13 September). By December the Nationalists had no striking victory to their credit; German and Italian advisers believed only large arms deliveries would save the situation.

The Nationalists made two attempts to end the resistance of Madrid by flanking attacks. The Jarama offensive was a muddled battle, costly to both sides, in which the best of the International Brigades were destroyed in pointless local counter-attacks.[3] The halting of the Italian advance on Madrid in the battle of Guadalajara was their great achievement: on 10 March 1937 the Brigades stabilized the front and two days later counter-attacked, the motorized Italian divisions piling up in chaos along a single road immobilized by mud and without air protection against bombing attacks. For the first time the Republican

[1] The airlift and sea convoys conveyed 20,248 seasoned troops to Spain, July–Sept. 1936. For the important convoy of 5 Aug. and its escort see M. Aznar, *Historia militar de la guerra española* (1940), 83–91. General Kindelán's orders give a total of nineteen planes, mostly Italian (*St. Antony's Seminars*). Later Junkers 52's played an important part.

[2] For the Madrid fighting see M. Aznar, op. cit. 280–94; R. G. Coldony, *The Struggle for Madrid* (New York, 1958), 37–91, and A. López Fernández, *Defensa de Madrid* (Mexico, 1954), which emphasizes the role of the Spanish forces as against the more usual stress on the role of the International Brigades.

[3] For the Jarama battle see T. Wintringham, *English Captain* (London, 1939).

armies behaved as a military machine, capable of manœuvre.[1] This success threw into relief the utter failure of the militia system in Malaga (8 February 1937); the simplest anti-tank defences would have held an attack before which the militia fled.

Though Franco did not abandon all idea of finishing the war by a decisive battle for Madrid until the battle of Teruel, the winter and spring battles of 1936–7 forced him to the strategy of *degaste*—the gradual conquest of Republican territory and the wearing down of the powers of resistance of a badly supplied army by a less badly supplied army. In this war of attrition Franco appeared to German and Italian experts as a slow and old-fashioned commander with no concept of the use in battle of tanks and aeroplanes.[2] This slowness, although sometimes the result of strategical error, rested on the belief that he could destroy the Republican armies without destroying the future resources of a Nationalist Spain. Convinced of final victory he resisted all talk of a compromise peace and a 'pink Spain' which his less confident foreign advisers believed might be the issue of 'an equilibrium of forces' produced by unimaginative generalship.[3] Thus the final victory in Catalonia astonished German and Italian military experts.

The Republican general staff sought to stave off a slow defeat by a series of surprise offensives intended to relieve the pressure of attrition elsewhere. The Brunete and Belchite offensives (summer 1937) were intended to save the Northern front from collapse; Teruel (winter 1937–8) to relieve the pressure on Madrid; the Ebro offensive to turn Franco from Valencia. This strategy was made possible by the existence of a straggling front of 2,000 kilometres. Provided surprise could be achieved a thinly held line could always be penetrated. Given the shortcomings of its army, the Republican command achieved truly astonishing successes: it broke three major movements against Madrid and twice seized the strategical

[1] For an Italian account of the battle see F. Belforte, *La guerra civile en Spagna* (Milan, 1938), ii. For a communist account see L. Renn, *Der Spanische Krieg* (Berlin, 1956), 196 ff.

[2] See the comments of von Thoma (who commanded the German contingent of 180 tanks) in B. H. Liddell Hart, *The Other Side of the Hill* (London, Panther Books, 1956), 88.

[3] For German fears see *Documents on German Foreign Policy*, no. 710 (1 July, on the bogging down of the Valencian offensive); nos. 743, 754–5, for their estimate of the situation Oct. 1938. For Catalonia, ibid. no. 828.

initiative. Nevertheless some difficulties proved insuperable: divisional commanders were improvised but it was difficult to create company commanders from men who had to be taught how to read and understand an order.[1] Thus in every Republican offensive forward troops lost contact with the command and the impetus was lost. All the major Republican offensives were well planned and all had ambitious plans for a follow-through; all achieved surprise but all were halted within a few days, and the great Republican battles took the form of a dogged defence of initial advances. Both the Teruel and Ebro offensives were followed by a period of weakness which proved disastrous and opened up chances for an army that could exploit and maintain an offensive after a break-through. This the Republican command never succeeded in doing and at the end of the war General Matallana told Negrín that, although the army 'had learned something of defensive tactics, they were incapable of retreat or counter attack'.[2]

The decisive campaign was the Nationalist conquest of the north in 1937. Total air superiority, exhibited to Europe in the bombing of Durango and Guernica, was on the Nationalist side.[3] The Republican armies of the north (where the regular officers were poor in quality and defeatist while the Basque Nationalist Militia were among the finest militia on the Republican side) showed many of their worst features—strong positions lightly held, sudden collapses of weak units which rendered useless the resistance of heroic units.[4] The 'Iron Ring' of fortifications

[1] For difficulties with the lower echelons of command, cf. L. Renn, *Spanische Krieg*, 344 ff. Renn was much concerned with the problems of military education.

[2] General Rojo in *España heroica* (Mexico, 1961) is more charitable than in his earlier work *Alerta los pueblos* (Buenos Aires, 1939). For an illustration of the weakening of an offensive (in the battle of Brunete) see Luigi Longo, *Le brigate internazionale in Spagna* (1956), 371 ff.

[3] See above, p. 686. From a military point of view Guernica and Durango were successful operations to cut off a retreating army and confuse the rearguard. When the Nationalists tried to camouflage the operation as an act of Anarchist incendiarism (such as had taken place at Irun) a German pilot commented, 'Of course it was bombed. We bombed it and bombed it and bombed it and *bueno*, why not?'

[4] There is a clear military account of the Northern campaign in General Duval, *Leçons militaires de la guerre d'Espagne* (Paris, 1937). For the artillery superiority from the early stages see G. L. Steer, *Gernika*, 49. Air superiority (100 to 15), ibid. 154–5, 161 ff. For the weakness of C.N.T. militia which ruined the plans of competent commanders, ibid. 219 ff.; for the final 'shameless and concerted rout', ibid. 339–41.

around Bilbao proved easily vulnerable, partly through treason, partly because it was ill-constructed. The government could do little to help the north while, after the fall of Bilbao, unprotected from the air and without food, the Basques had little interest in the contest. Three Basque divisions disappeared from the Santander front 'alleging that with Euzkadi lost they would not fight for those who had no aeroplanes'. The defences of Santander 'melted like a meringue dipped in water'. By October the whole northern coast, with its industrial potential undestroyed, was in Franco's hands. The tide of war had set in his favour; he could spare 150 battalions for a decisive battle. This battle he intended to fight for Madrid.

It was the Teruel offensive, in the winter of 1937, which disrupted this concentration against Madrid and altered the whole axis of the war. Franco abandoned Madrid and was forced to seek victory in the east. That such a daring operation as Teruel could be planned at all shows the remarkable progress made in professional training since the days when the militia columns had broken in confusion at Talavera on the road to Madrid. Rojo planned to bisect the Teruel salient (weakly held and with the town itself dominated from artillery positions on the surrounding heights) by a converging attack with 40,000 men. With the best of the Republic's guns and tanks the operation was completely successful. Franco was slow to react and his staff were throughout nervous of an attack to the north of the salient—an evident proof of their conviction that they were dealing with an army which could manœuvre—while Nationalist losses in counter-attacks, made in appalling weather, showed that frontal attack was too costly without surprise.[1] The attack was therefore shifted to the north of the salient where the collapse was symptomatic of those sudden reverses that upset all the careful Republican staff-work.[2] Under heavy dive-bombing the front broke in three days and Teruel was lost.

With his forces concentrated around Teruel, Franco took a strategic decision which was much criticized. Instead of turn-

[1] Lt.-Gen. R. García Valiño, *Guerra de liberación* (1949), esp. 187. For Rojo's account of Teruel see *España heroica*, 101–12.

[2] The Republicans had little artillery and no air support and the troops were in bad shape: the Commissar of the 117 Mixed Brigade wrote, 'besides being demoralized, its officers are all on sick leave', and characteristically suggested a wholesale sacking.

ing against Catalonia, where little serious resistance could have been mustered and where the war might have been ended quickly, he committed his armies to a painful advance across badly mapped mountain country to the sea and against Valencia.[1] This Aragon campaign was a vast operation, far removed from the relatively limited 'African' war of the north; it caught the Republican armies unprepared and exhausted after Teruel. Again and again sudden and inexplicable collapses made staff-work difficult and sometimes rendered tough resistance a waste of lives.[2] Even so it was a difficult campaign for the Nationalists and was not made easier by friction both between the local commanders and between them and Franco. Aranda came to a halt against a narrow, well-prepared front and García Valiño reached the Sierra de Espadón fought out.[3] The Germans once more prophesied a compromise peace.

In fact, with the increasing shortness of Russian deliveries and the steady supply to the Nationalists, the balance was tipped against the Republic. It was in the later stages of the Aragon campaign that the Nationalist air ace, Morato, complained he could not find a 'red' fighter to shoot down. It is against this mounting poverty that the last and greatest of the Republican surprise diversionary attacks must be seen. The battle of the Ebro was an attempt to halt the Nationalist advance on Valencia. It followed a familiar pattern: the breakdown of a brilliantly planned attack, which achieved complete surprise,[4] into a stubborn defence of four days' gains: with a maximum penetration of 20–25 kilometres Rojo's ambitious secondary objectives were abandoned.[5] Nationalist reinforce-

[1] Cf. General Kindelán (*St. Antony's Seminars*), 'I tried hard to dissuade him from this operation which seemed pointless to me.'

[2] In this thrust Italian motorized elements proved their worth in rapid advances. For the panic of the XII Corps and the contrasting resistance of the XXI Corps see General Rojo, *España heroica*, 113 ff.

[3] By August García Valiño (*Guerra de liberación*, 143) described his troops as 'in a very uncomfortable situation, worn out by fatigue . . . with an appreciable diminution of fighting spirit, a marked loss in efficiency . . . 2,528 casualties among which were irreparable losses in regimental and battalion commanders'.

[4] Yagüe, in command of the sector attacked, suspected an attack but had no clear idea of its direction or its seriousness (cf. his dispatch of 28 July, *Archivo Histórico Militar*).

[5] Rojo's operational order of 22 July to Modesto called for a strong bridgehead near Gandesa 'to serve as a basis for future operations'. Within two days the orders were 'dig in and hold at all costs'.

ments, which came up slowly, were at first fed into poorly planned frontal attacks which met with fierce and unexpected resistance;[1] not until October 1938, after the heaviest aerial and artillery bombardment of the war, did Franco master the heights which enabled him to drive the Republicans back over the Ebro. He had become the Haig of the Civil War; his repeated attacks on a narrow front had bled his enemy to death and destroyed material which could not be replaced. Short of shells and tanks, the decisive inferiority was in the air; it was this disproportion which allowed Franco to reverse the ratio between attack and defence casualties. Thus the result of the awful struggle on the Ebro was the collapse of the army of Catalonia. 'You could', observed Negrín, 'break our front with bicycles.'

Never, as in these last months, was the need for a unified direction of politics and war so desperate. The unification which had been achieved in the central government—there were even bitter complaints of Negrín's dictatorship—fell apart at the local level. Not only the physical but the moral balance of war had turned against the government. Negrín's government looked more solid than it was. The professional soldiers were irritated by the Communist drive to monopolize commands, the government obsessed by fears of an army *coup*. Political jealousies ruined the army spirit when the Communist censorship would not allow the Chief of Staff to congratulate non-Communist corps commanders in the press. Thus, in the words of General Rojo, it was with 'a state machine vitiated at its very roots, a low morale in the rearguard, a lack of co-operation in subordinate authorities so manifest that mayors covered up if they did not encourage desertion, and with an army worn out and with few material resources or reserves' that the Republican general staff tried to resist the greatest attack of the war—the final offensive against Catalonia. The XII Corps panicked after a light bombardment and the whole Catalan front was broken,

[1] Cf. García Valiño, *Guerra de liberación*, 231. The highly successful operation against the small Mequinenza–Fayón pocket to the north of the main bridgehead seems to have led the Nationalist command into undue optimism; the orders of 26 July and 17 Aug. both imply a general drive through to the Ebro (*Archivo Histórico Militar*). The difference between the Republican armies' conduct on the Ebro (cf. the resistance of the 27th and 11th Divisions on the Sierra de Pandols) and in some phases of the Aragon offensive is truly astonishing.

for there were no reserves to re-establish the situation. No desperate re-deployments could save an army where a battalion fled after ten shells. On 26 January 1939 the Nationalists entered Barcelona and all attempts to organize further resistance in the east broke in the atmosphere of collective rout.[1]

The final drama of the Civil War was tragic irony. It ended, as it had begun, with the pronunciamiento of a soldier who had convinced himself that the national will was contained in his own ambitions and resentments. Colonel Casado, commander of the Army of the Centre, the only army still in being, resented Communist monopoly of five of the eight operational commands and scorned Russian interference with staff-work. Once it was clear that the Communists intended to replace him, he set up a Defence Committee in Madrid, composed of anti-Communist groups from Besteiro's reformist Socialists to the C.N.T. The Committee rejected Negrín's authority and his declared intention of resisting to the bitter end as the best way to secure favourable terms.[2] Casado hoped to make his own terms with Franco and emerge as the soldier of the peace, an ambition which broke, as had all other attempts at negotiated peace, on Franco's insistence on unconditional surrender. Casado's language shows the continuity of the political theory of the army.[3] He revolted in order 'to pick up authority where Dr. Negrín's government had thrown it away'; the government was illegal and 'the legitimate power of the Republic' lay in its army, its sole defence against the buffoonery of the politicians; 'the putrefying corpse of government' did not respect the people's will for peace. As so many times in Spanish history, the army, through the voice of its commander, claimed to embody

[1] For the XII Corps collapse see General Rojo, *Alerta los pueblos*, 103. One of the brigades was the 179th Carabineers, one of the best-equipped units in the Republican armies; cf. the panic which opened the way to Cubèlls (ibid. 120) and at St. Coloma (141–3).

[2] Besteiro's and Casado's main concern was to obtain satisfactory guarantees for fair treatment of political prisoners. For a defence of Negrín's policy see Álvarez del Vayo, *Freedom's Battle* (277 *et passim*). Jesús Hernández maintains the unlikely view that the promotions which set off Casado's revolt were a deliberate provocation, because Togliatti and Stepanov wished to end the war. Thus the Communist slogans of resistance were the product of 'inertia' and covered a Russian desire to liquidate commitments in Spain; Jesús Hernández, *Yo fuí ministro de Stalin* (Mexico, 1953), 190 ff. esp. 222.

[3] Casado's own account of these events is contained in his apologia, *The Last Days of Madrid*, from which the quotations are taken.

'the movement of the people to free themselves from a hated government'. To make the parallel with Franco complete, Casado claimed to be saving Spain from Communism. The result of his revolt was a six days' civil war in the Republican capital between the Communists and the forces loyal to the Defence Committee. When it ended the last Republican army had melted away. The Civil War was over.

XVII

FRANCO AND FRANCOISM

1. *The Caudillo*

UNTIL his death in November 1975 General Franco remained, as his coins proclaimed, 'Caudillo of Spain by the Grace of God' responsible, as his apologists maintained, only to God and to history. As he aged he withdrew gradually from direct intervention in the day-to-day making of policy, but to the end without the 'green light from the Pardo'—Franco's palace outside Madrid—no major political decision could be taken. Until he died he retained, in what came to be called the Francoist Constitution, the power to appoint and dismiss ministers.

Iconography changed with time; the stern soldier became the grandfather among his grandchildren; the ultimate reality of power did not. 'All the cards are in his hands,' wrote a critic in 1967, 'he does not *make* politics, he *is* politics.'[1] In spite of age and the 'institutionalization' of what was in 1939 a personal dictatorship, the political personality of Franco remained a decisive element.

What was this political personality? Franco's image of society remained that of a patriotic professional soldier. Troops, well commanded, obey; if they do not they must be punished as mutineers. Subjects, well governed, obey; if they do not they must bear the consequences of sedition. On to this simple model was grafted a vision of Spanish history which rejected the liberal heritage of the nineteenth century responsible for the final eclipse of Spanish greatness. It was the selfish party politicans of liberalism who had starved a brave army in Cuba and brought Spain to its knees in 1898; it was the factious party politicans, who, in 1936, had brought Spain to anarchy and the brink of Communist take-over from which it was saved only by

[1] Juan Fernández Figueroa. 'La Izquierda: voto sin voz', *Indice* (1967), quoted by Ludovico Garrucco, *Spagna senza miti* (1968), 361.

the Rising of July 1936. Liberalism *must*, in modern conditions, open the gates to Communism. The party politics of 'inorganic democracy' had destroyed the unity of Spain. To the end of his life the word 'party' was not allowed to enter the political vocabulary of Spain.

Although Franco claimed the powers of the Weberian charismatic leader who had 'saved' society from chaos by his victory in the Civil War he did not possess the personality of a Hitler or a Mussolini. The pompous rhetoric was delivered in a squeaky voice. Nor was he, like Stalin, the boss of a monolithic party. He was a manipulator of men from a position of power. Though the 'legitimacy of victory' became the 'legitimacy of achievement', Franco never allowed the divisions of the Civil War to pass from the memory of his subjects. His vision remained Manichaean: Spain and anti-Spain, victors (*vencedores*) and vanquished (*vencidos*). Only the victors could inherit the spoils of victory. When it was suggested that Republican officers should receive pensions Franco opposed a project putting on an equal footing the 'glorious Nationalist army' with 'the scum of the Spanish people'.[1] It was the persistence of this Manichaean vision when the memory of the Civil War had faded from the minds of his subjects that doomed a policy of reconciliation or of any evolution towards democracy. This, as Laín Entralgo observed, could only come with the death of the dictator.[2]

His apologists invented the doctrine of *caudillismo* to describe what less resembled a modern dictatorship—its repressive mechanisms apart—than the monarchy of Philip II.[3] His dull and formal court revived the trappings of royalty and the austerity of the Escorial; he was a non-smoker, indifferent to food and drink. He himself found in the increasingly artificial and organized crowd ovations that same conviction of popular legitimacy which had supported Primo de Rivera. To the end his private world was haunted by the paranoia of the Civil War: 'Martyred Spain' was surrounded by 'a secret conspiracy' of Communists and Masons. Every domestic protest came from

[1] Francisco Franco Salgado, *Mis conversaciones privadas con Franco* (1976), 530. Franco Salgado was Franco's cousin and head of his military household.

[2] P. Laín Entralgo, *Descargo de conciencia* (1976), 418.

[3] *Caudillismo*, a Spanish edition of the *Führerprinzip*, was a product of the régime's ideological factory; the Institute of Political Studies. For *caudillismo* see F. J. Conde, *Contribución a la doctrina del Caudillaje* (1942).

their collaboration with 'traitors' within the gates. Every international protest was a revival by the eternal enemies of Spain of the Black Legend. 'All', he told Spaniards in his last public speech after a wave of protests—including that of the Vatican—against the execution of five terrorists, 'is part of a masonic leftist conspiracy.'[1] Perhaps it was this addiction to conspiracy theory that made him an easy prey to scientific charlatans with tales of huge gold deposits or recipes for making petrol from water—dreams of riches presented to console a starving population.[2]

His political nerve was unshakeable. Except to his intimates he was a remote and cold figure. He could dismiss a minister abruptly without a word of gratitude: Serrano Suñer, his brother-in-law and Foreign Minister, was sacked with the words: 'In view of the circumstances I am going to replace you.' 'Spain', he once asserted, 'is easy to govern' and, as if to prove it, left Madrid for long hunting trips—his one regular contact with businessmen and politicians outside his own circle.[3]

2. *The Political System*

The Francoist political system, though, from the outside, it appeared a monolith, was like many authoritarian régimes a Byzantine structure of political clans—Amando de Miguel calls them families—competing for ministerial power. *Within the régime*, amongst those who accepted Franco's title to rule—the legitimacy of 18 July 1936—there was a domesticated, limited pluralism.[4] Franco's selection of his ministers gave to each

[1] World Bank officials were astonished by a lecture on the evils of Freemasonry. Franco's paranoid suspicions extended even to the Lions Club. Cf. José Antonio Ferrer Benimeli, 'Franco contra la masonería, in *Historia 16*, no. 15, 37–51.

[2] R. Abella, *Por el imperio hacia Dios* (1978), 24, 36.

[3] Apart from his summer vacations in Galicia his hunting expeditions left him as few as ten working days a month (Francisco Franco Salgado, op. cit. 143). For his hunting see Luis Alonso Tejada, 'Las cacerías del franquismo', *Historia 16*, no. 37, 19–30.

[4] The location of Francoism in the taxonomy of dictatorial states has given rise to considerable controversy among political scientists. The failure of the Falangists (see p. 700) to install a totalitarian state based on a mass party and political *mobilization* led Juan Linz to define Francoism as a 'stabilized authoritarian régime' based on political *demobilization*: a 'political system with limited, non-responsible political pluralism; without elaborate and guiding ideology (but with a distinctive mentality); without intensive or extensive political mobilization (except for some points in their development) and in which a leader (or occasionally a small group) exercises power within formally ill-defined limits, but actually quite predictable limits'. This definition was

family a taste of power; none was allowed to create an independent base from which to challenge the power of the manipulator-in-chief. This political chemistry endowed the system with the flexibility to adjust to changes in international climate or to the necessities of economic policy with *minimum* changes in governmental personnel.

To understand the system these competing families must therefore be examined:[1] the army; the political groups representing the Church; the Falange Movement; the Francoist monarchists; the technocrats and the civil servants.

The loyalty of the officers of the armed forces was essential to the survival of the régime as 'the defence of the institutional order'. Those who had fought in the Civil War remained the most consistent bearers of the mystique of the Crusade. Until 1969 there were usually six service ministers in cabinets of eighteen or so; subsequent governments were increasingly manned by civilians. Moreover, the armed forces got an increasingly small share of the budget so that by 1970 that proportion was the lowest among the great Western powers. Franco left an army in which a Spanish soldier cost a tenth of his British counterpart. Pay and promotion prospects were poor in an overmanned officer corps; with 80 per cent of the army budget going on pay there was little room for modern equipment and the satisfactions of professional soldiering.[2] The armed forces as a whole were a prestigious rather than a pampered profession and by the 1960's even the prestige was dimmed: only the higher officers were favoured, their retirement eased by well-paid posts in business and in government agencies.

In the nineteenth century grievances over poor pay and promotion prospects had generated the classic pronunciamiento. In the 1970's a small group of young officers organized the *Unión*

unacceptable to those who defined Francoism as a 'Fascist' compromise between the different groups of a capitalist ruling élite determined to exclude the working class from power. For a perceptive account of Linz and his critics see J. M. Maravall, *Dictatorship and Dissent. Workers and Students in Franco's Spain* (1978), Chapter 1.

[1] The families of the régime are dissected in J. C. Amando de Miguel, *Sociología del Franquismo* (1975). The families, apart from the Carlists, had neither an autonomous political life nor a distinctive, definable ideology. They did acquire distinctive ways of thought.

[2] Franco was fully aware of the disadvantages of an over-officered army. Although the army reforms of 1952, 1953, and 1958 allowed increasing professionalization they did not end the problem.

Democrática Militar (U.D.M.): they wished to detach the army from its alliance with Francoism by playing on issues like bad pay, poor promotion, and 'lack of respect' in civilian society.[1] Their influence was minimal. Franco was troubled in the early years by monarchist military frondeurs and he was not always trusted by many of his old comrades in arms; they were summarily sacked or won over by emotional appeals.[2] Most generals and senior officers needed neither punishment nor blandishment. They shared Franco's simplistic vision of Spanish society. The armed forces—including the Civil Guard and the militarized police—remained essential preservers of public order; their jurisdiction over political offences was reduced but was still used to judge terrorists in the 1970's.[3] Ideological purity was carefully watched over by security agencies: to subscribe to a left-wing periodical meant a court martial. A largely self-recruiting officer corps was hermetically sealed against contact with the opposition.[4]

In these conditions few officers shared the U.D.M.'s belief that the only way to save the army in the eyes of the 'people' was to plan the overthrow of Francoism. By the 1970's, there was not the remotest prospect of an anti-Franco pronunciamiento or of a renewal of the drawing-room conspiracies of the forties. There was, nevertheless, a clear division between the 'immobilist' generals who regarded it as their constitutional duty to preserve the Francoist system *in toto* and those who were ready to accept political change. Without the support of these liberal-minded professionals loyal to the policies of their new Commander-in-Chief, King Juan Carlos, it is hard to see how Spain could have found a peaceful way to democracy.

[1] See Jesús Infantes, *El ejército de Franco y de Juan Carlos* (1976).

[2] Franco never trusted the older monarchist generals: Aranda and Kindelán were disgraced. Generals García Valiño and Martínez Campos were suspect. He was never at ease with Muñoz Grandes, Commander of the Blue Legion and a possible successor as Regent. Franco increasingly relied on younger officers like Barroso, head of his military household.

[3] The Burgos courts martial of 1970 indicated that some officers had, however, come to see the dangers of the use of the army as a police force. General García Valiño—the 'coffin maker' of the Aragon campaign—feared evidence of torture would discredit the army and Franco. 'The identification of the army with the régime only intensifies the alienation of the people.'

[4] For the sociological structure of the army see J. Brugulat Busquets, *El militar de carrera en España* (1967).

Besides the army, to foreign observers the Falange long appeared a fundamental pillar of the régime. With the defeat of the Axis the one-party, totalitarian, imperial state of Falangist dreams vanished. Its populist radicalism withered in the conservative atmosphere of post-war Spain. The poet Dionisio Ridruejo, as Delegate for Propaganda (1939–41) once the 'Goebbels of the party', retired into the political wilderness in 1942.[1] Arrese was the architect of the 'domesticated' Francoist Falange; but as an 'old shirt' in 1956 he made a belated attempt to reinvigorate the movement.[2] His plans were defeated by the monarchist clans. No Falangist held the key ministry of Finance on which the implementation of its social programme, with which it hoped to capture the loyalty of the working class, depended.[3] Girón, the 'old lion' of Falangism, lamented the betrayal of the Falangist revolution by the 'hidden forces of an unpatriotic, selfish oligarchy'.

With Solís, an ebullient but pragmatic Andalusian, National Delegate for the Syndicates from 1951 and Minister from 1957 to 1969, the Falange was subsumed as a separate *organization* in the wider Movement; the Movement was defined as a 'communion' of *all* Spaniards who accepted the legitimacy of 18 July, a movement whose structures were increasingly manned by ambitious bureaucrats mainly concerned with running the Official Syndicates which remained the Movement's power-base. Membership of the Movement became a ticket to office rather than a sign of commitment to an ideology (Fraga, Emilio Romero commented, was as much a Falangist as he was Bishop of Constantinople). Its function became negative. A revival of Falangism was a useful weapon against the ambitions of monarchists or technocrats. The enthusiasts of the Movement could always be called on to mobilize meetings to demonstrate 'mass support' against any liberal or monarchist deviation.[4] Its

[1] Juan Benet *et al.*, *Dionisio Ridruejo: de la Falange a la oposición* (1976), 31, 90.

[2] For Arrese's ideas see J. L. Arrese, *El Estado Totalitario en el pensamiento de José Antonio* (1945) and *Escritos y discursos* (1945). Arrese (b. 1905) had been a Falangist since 1933. He was made Secretary-General of the Movement in 1941. At this early period he was rejecting the notion that José Antonio was a totalitarian. Very early Franco wrote to Don Juan that the Falange 'is not a party it is a movement' ['no es un partido es un movimiento'] of which he was the 'conductor' ['soy yo su conductor'].

[3] Arrese was one of the few ministers who resigned—significantly because he was denied a budgetary allocation to carry out his housing programme.

[4] In 1964 the modesty of the Falange's claims was admitted by the 'old shirt' Fernández Cuesta. 'The State orders and executes. The Movement inspires and

National Council was the ideological watch-dog of the régime; but it accepted the installation of the monarchy. It was only the young *enragés* of the Movement who protested against what they regarded as a betrayal of all that the Founder, José Antonio, had stood for.

The true victors of the Civil War were not the enthusiasts of the Falange hankering after what came to be called 'the pending revolution' of which the residue was the labour and housing policies of Girón and Arrese, but the conservative elements: those monarchists who supported Franco and those groups which represented the Catholic Church. Both were determined to resist the advance of the Falange.

There can be no doubt but that the support of a traditional institution—the Church—rather than the new-fangled ideology and repulsive rhetoric of the Falange legitimized the rule of Franco in the post-war years. Explicable in terms of the persecutions of 1936 that support was, in the early years, enthusiastic and unconditional.[1] The most noticeable feature of post-war Spain was what the poet Carlos Barral called the return of the *curas* (priests) and the recatholicization of the educational system. The forties saw ambulant missions to reconvert Spain to a harsh brand of Tridentine Catholicism. The 1940's were the *blütezeit* of what was called 'National Catholicism', the modern edition of the old alliance of throne and altar.

It was not only that the Church was an integral part of the political system—bishops to whom Franco was *homo missu a Deo* sat in the Cortes—but also that two organizations were specifically concerned with penetrating and influencing it.

These were the A.C.N.P. and the Opus Dei. While their emphasis differed, both were conceived as élitist organizations concerned with the capture of *valores selectos*, an aim patently clear in the handbook of Opus Dei, written by the founder of this lay society, Father Escrivá, with its curious mixture of

collaborates.' To Franco the enduring function of the Falange was to provide reliable civil governors (see *Conversaciones*, 253). He criticized General Alonso Vega, as Minister of the Interior, for not listening to the Minister of the Movement 'who is responsible for the *política* of the government'.

[1] The opposition of Cardinal Segura of Seville, one of the finest exponents of the puritanical streak in Spanish Catholicism, was idiosyncratic; he detested the Falangists and refused to have José Antonio's name on the wall of his cathedral. A pastoral of the Cardinal Primate Gomá, advocating reconciliation was prohibited (8 August 1939). Gomá died conveniently in 1940 and was replaced by an admirer of Franco, Plà y Deniel.

traditional piety and the American creed of success through making friends and influencing people. The Opus with its secret statutes and hierarchy of members was a Catholic mirror image of Freemasonry; it was called by the opposition 'the Holy Mafia' and thoroughly distasteful to Falangists.[1] The *propagandistas* of A.C.N.P. were important in the early years when their connections with international Catholicism brought off the first diplomatic triumph of the régime, the Concordat of 1953; the men of the Opus, after an assault on the University, came to the fore in political life as the technocrats of development in the 1960's.

The early misgivings of those Catholics concerned with the spiritual revival of their faith as opposed to the recapture by the Church of a political pre-eminence it had lost in the nineteenth century, the hopes of liberal Catholics for a reconciliation suffered an early defeat in 1956.[2] Young priests, prepared in the sixties to protest against the persecution of Basque and Catalan nationalists or to transform the legally authorized Catholic workers organizations (the H.O.A.C. and the J.O.C.) into genuine instruments of protest in strikes, were rebuked by the hierarchy and vituperated as Marxists by their older colleagues.[3] But by 1970 the Catholicism of the Crusade was the property of a dwindling number of ageing bishops.[4] By then the 'church of confrontation' could count on the support of Rome and of a new generation of bishops, embarrassed by the legacy of unconditional support for a régime incompatible with the principles of Vatican II. This desertion was incomprehensible to the Caudillo; he attributed it to Communist penetration of the priesthood.

The integration of monarchists as the most socially imposing

[1] The early ideologue of the Opus was Calvo Serer whose 'Third Force'—an anti-parliamentary monarchy—was unpalatable to Franco. For Opus see Daniel Artigues, *El Opus Dei en España* (1968), esp. 71 ff.; for the A.C.N.P. (Asociación Católica de Propagandistas, founded in 1604) A. Saéz Alba, *La otra 'cosa nostra'. La Asociación Católica de Propagandistas* (1974). The 'Holy Mafia' line is pursued in J. Ynfante, *La prodigiosa aventura del Opus Dei* (1970).

[2] See p. 728.

[3] The hierarchy via Catholic Action nevertheless did protest against social injustices. Moreover, the jurisdictional conflicts—largely over the appointment of bishops—became increasingly acute in the later years of Francoism.

[4] The effects of this generational shift are examined in N. Cooper, 'The Church: from Crusade to Catholicism', in P. Preston (ed.), *Spain in Crisis* (1976), esp. 72 ff.

group among the victors—they included prestigious generals, landowners, and bankers—was a prime, even obsessive, concern of Franco in the early years. In 1947 he declared Spain a monarchy with himself as life Regent and with the selection and imposition of the successor monarch left in his hands. This split the monarchist camp. There were those who supported the claims of Don Juan, son of Alfonso XIII, as the legitimate heir, but who was unacceptable to Franco since Don Juan in 1945 had staked a claim for his own restoration as a constitutional monarch as an *alternative* to Franco. His supporters in Spain were given to minor conspiracies and enjoyed, in consequence, political ostracism.[1]

The pro-Franco monarchists were ready to accept the *installation*, not the restoration (*instauración* not *restauración*) of the monarchy as a *continuation* of Francoism, when and on what conditions the Caudillo should choose.

The Alfonsine monarchists remained economically powerful and socially infuential. The Carlists split on similar lines between compromisers and irreconcilable followers of the true king. They received a minimum compensation, in political terms, for their sacrifices in the Civil War. The main function of the monarchists was to resist the political preponderance of the Falange. To Pedro Saínz Rodriguez a single-party, totalitarian state was 'the worst of all political formulas'.[2] The family feuds between monarchists and Falangists were public property.

In its later years the governments were increasingly recruited from two related families: technocrats associated with Opus Dei who sought to combine authoritarianism, traditional Catholicism, and a 'modern' economy; and civil servants, the 'number ones' (*numeros unos*) of *oposiciones* (the competitive entrance examinations for the entrance into the civil service of which the University was a part). Competent and able administrators, they switched from chairs to the ministries and government agencies.

Both groups were modernizers after their fashion: Professor López Rodó of the Opus was the architect of the Development Plans of the sixties and of the administrative reforms necessary to put them into practice. Professor Fraga, who had sailed

[1] For a further discussion see p. 717.

[2] Quoted by Amando de Miguel, *Sociología del Franquismo* (1975), 180.

through his *oposiciones* as the perpetual *numero uno*, was the author of the Press law of 1966 which, whatever its limitations, altered the cultural climate of Spain. This governmental élite became the core of Francoism. Of Franco's last 21 ministers, 19 were civil servants, 18 of them professors. It was the career prospects and social mobility opened up to the ambitious among the middle classes that played its part in securing their loyalty.

Franco could always count on the support of his *incondicionales*—mostly service colleagues: Admiral Suances in the early years, General Alonso Vega as Minister of the Interior in a difficult period; above all on his political *alter ego*, Admiral Carrero Blanco. 'I am a man', the admiral confessed, 'a man totally identified with General Franco . . . my loyalty to his person and work is absolute.' He shared his master's obsession with Freemasonry and his aversion to pornography as a symptom of the democratic disease. Never out of political life after his appointment as Secretary to the Presidencia in 1941 he was, as the apostle of *continuismo* (the survival of Francoism as an institutional structure), chosen by the ageing Caudillo as his first Prime Minister (Presidente del Consejo) when, in 1973, Franco abandoned his twin supremacy as Head of State and head of the government. Franco's criterion was absolute loyalty to his person rather than efficiency. Whenever the more absurd measures of Arias Salgado (Minister of Information in control of press, radio, and cinema from 1951 to 1961) were criticized Franco replied, 'Yes, but he is faithful to me.'

3. *Cosmetic Constitutionalism*

If the system in its essentials depended on the mutation in ministries of the political familes from above by what was called 'the finger of Franco', an exercise in political chemistry in which the Caudillo excelled, its lawyers and political theorists sought to provide personal rule with a decent institutional clothing, to endow Francoism with a constitution which would convert Spain into a *rechtstaat*, an *estado de derecho*.[1]

The process of constitution-making via the Organic Laws

[1] Spanish constitutional lawyers were, in the early days, much influenced by the German concept of the *rechstaat*, a notion quite distinct from the English rule of law.

was a long one stretching from the Fuero de Trabajo in 1938 to the Law of the Principles of the National Movement in 1958 and the Organic Law of 1967.[1] The régime took pride in this slow process of 'perfecting itself'. Restraint was imposed by the 'prudence' of the Caudillo who believed society must settle down after the Civil War before it could be given a definitive political shape.

The informing principle of the constitution was 'organic democracy' as opposed to 'inorganic democracy' based on universal suffrage, the party system, and the parliamentary responsibility of governments. 'Organic Democracy', its apologists asserted, was a true democracy representing the great interests of society rather than the selfish interests of individual voters.[2] The organizations that represented these societal interests—the syndicates, the municipalities, the professional corporations—were the *cauces* (the channels) by which opinion would reach the government. In theory it was the '*contraste de pareceres*'—the clash of opinions—between the *cauces* in the Cortes which provided governments with the mechanism to test and adjust to opinion. In the Law of the Principles of the Movement (17 May 1958) Spain was defined as a traditional, Catholic, social, and *representative* monarchy.

The Cortes, set up in 1942, was supposed to satisfy this representative principle. It remained an advisory body. With most of its members indirectly elected or appointed, it was neither representative of opinion at large even after the admission of family representatives elected on a family franchise nor did it have any effective control over governments which could not be removed by its vote and which were strongly represented in the chamber both directly and indirectly—nearly half the Cortes membership belonged to the administration itself. Its

[1] For an English translation of the Spanish Constitution see José Amodia, *Franco's Political Legacy* (1977), 239–79.

[2] This Francoist view of the imperfections of democracy found support in Catholic thought. Democracy based on universal suffrage can have no base in morality or National Law. This is developed in Torcuato Fernández Miranda's *El Hombre y la sociedad* (1969 ed.). In democracies based on universal suffrage 'there can be no certainty about what is truth or error. . . . Everything is a matter of opinion. . . . Whatever the people want becomes legitimate. It is a doctrine of the absolute sovereignty of the popular will, characteristic of the extreme liberalism that has been expressly condemned by the Catholic Church' (ibid. 30 ff.).

debates were anodyne remaining a sounding-board rather than a formulator or critic of governmental policies.[1]

Two other bodies completed the structure: the Council of the Realm, composed of the dignitaries of the régime, had one important function: the drawing-up of the *terna*, the list of three from which the Head of State must select a president of the Council of Ministers. This was not a serious limitation on Franco's power although in 1973 he followed constitutional procedures. The National Council of the Movement was a substitute for a second chamber: its task was to 'perfect' the political institutions of Spain within the 'spirit of the Movement'.

The informing principle of the 'constitution' was 'unity of power'. The locus of that power was in the Council of Ministers (Consejo de Ministros) appointed by and presided over by Franco himself. It is one of the paradoxes of Francoism that governments composed of competing clans were weak in that they often lacked homogeneity and an agreed programme: old-style Falangists, for example, struggled for influence against monarchists. When such struggles became intolerable Franco dismissed those responsible by his famous 'judgements of Solomon' as in 1942, 1956, and 1969. Without parties to support them or a linkage to public opinion ministers were dependent on their civil servants—hence the frequent transfers from the civil service to a political ministry. As López Rudó was to discover, there was no administrative co-ordination in the vital area of economic planning: as a professor of administrative law he advised such a co-ordinating body in the 1960's; but it never succeeded in entirely eliminating the incoherence that derived from the power clashes between individual ministers and the contest for budgetary allocations which made the Minister of Finance the key figure.[2]

The mechanisms available to the individual citizen for challenging the power of the government, where they existed, were imperfect: the process of *contra fuero*, by which administra-

[1] It was the docility of the Cortes that made it unnecessary for Franco to exercise the personal legislative powers conferred in 1939 and confirmed by the Organic Law of 1967. It was pointless to have recourse to openly authoritarian measures. For a discussion of this issue see R. Fernández Carvajal, 'El gobierno entre el jefe del Estado y las Cortes', *R.E.P.*, nos. 183–4, May 1972, 5–21.

[2] K. N. Medhurst, *Government in Spain* (1973), 84 ff. See p. 746.

tive decisions could be contested, was largely controlled by the government itself. The *Fuero de los Españoles* drafted in 1945 as a Bill of Rights to present a respectable appearance to the victorious allies, provided no legal safeguards: they could be suspended. 'All Spaniards can freely express their opinions', ran Article 12, 'provided they do not attack the fundamental principles of the State.' The definition of such an attack was left to special jurisdictions: the military tribunals and the Tribunal of Public Order. Speculation whether the principles of the Movement were immutable or whether they were adaptable to new circumstances was the harmless pursuit of constitutional lawyers; it was wishful thinking to believe that by the exercise of what was called 'anticipatory constitutional law' the régime would be liberalized from within and the Cortes develop as a real centre of power.[1] The election of family representatives was intended to achieve this; after a brief show of independence the new member was described by the monarchist *ABC* as 'bald and chubby with shell-rimmed glasses and a small moustache rehearsing his speech in the Cortes by repeating "Yes . . . I agree . . . You are absolutely right".'

It was not merely that the ordinary Spaniard did not enjoy the right to vote; the basic democratic freedoms of expression and association were denied him. Public meetings were closely controlled by the Ministry of the Interior and its local agent the Civil Governor. Censorship remained a central feature of the régime until 1966 and after that attacks on the government or the principles of the Movement entailed fines and imprisonment.

In these conditions the organization of a public opposition remained impossible. This was partly a function of police repression; but authoritarian régimes, after a violent physical repression and elimination of the opposition such as occurred in Spain with the executions and long prison sentences of the early 1940's, tend to rely on less drastic methods, on what might be called administrative persecution—from the blighting of a

[1] Interpretations as to what the nature of the Constitution *would be* once it became fully effective (i.e. on Franco's death or surrender of his powers to a monarch) gave harmless employment to constitutional lawyers. Were the monarch's powers unlimited as M. Herrero de Mañon maintained in *El principio monárquico* (1972) J. de Esteban gives the arguments of the evolutionists in *Desarollo político y constitución española* (1973). For a general view see J. Zafra Valverde, *Régimen político español* (1973).

career to the withdrawal of a passport—procedures the efficacy of which those who have never lived under arbitrary régimes rarely comprehend. Control of all media—press, radio, and TV—allowed governments to smother the criticisms of the opposition or to present their activities as treason to the nation: thus the Munich meeting of the opposition in 1962 to protest against the admission of a dictatorship to the European Community of democracies[1] was presented as a *conturbio*, the 'dirty plot' of unpatriotic Spaniards 'without faith'.

The institutions of organic democracy were intended to replace for all time those of parliamentary liberalism. Franco's quarrel was with the *political* creations of nineteenth-century liberalism: the party system and responsible government. Its administrative achievements he respected. Liberals had seen in uniform centralization a weapon to destroy regional conservatism.[2] Rigid centralism fitted in with the Nationalist Crusade against separatism in the name of Spain One and Great and the 'unity of power'. This dogmatic pursuit of unity sought to suppress but could not destroy the nationalist sentiments of the regions. In the end repression proved ineffective; it intensified nationalist movements and broadened their base of support. This was the case with Basque and Catalan nationalism. By 1970 the revival of peripheral nationalism constituted a serious threat to a centralizing dictatorship.

The other creation of nineteenth-century liberalism was a civil service based on French models. The imitation was imperfect, flawed by political partisanship in jobs, insecure tenure, and the presence within the administration of powerful privileged corporations (*cuerpos*) which resisted standardization of promotion and pay. In the early years these vices persisted: enthusiastic Nationalists considered themselves possessed of a prescriptive right to office, just as had the victors of any nineteenth-century pronunciamiento. But by 1970 these passengers were vanishing. The bureaucrats who came to constitute the governing core of the Francoist élite were efficient young technocrats, well acquainted with modern management methods and post-Keynesian economics.[3] It was they who devised

1 Xavier Tusell, *La oposición democrática al franquismo* (1977), 388–520.

2 See p. 557.

3 The average age of Spanish senior civil servants in the 1970's was strikingly lower than that of their British—above all their Italian—counterparts. See Richard Gunther, *Public Policy in a No-Party State* (1980), 84. Gunther concludes, 'The Spanish state administration was surprisingly young and efficient.'

policies and executed them unencumbered by interference from elected representatives of the Spanish people. In what has been dubbed a 'no-party state' interests were represented, not by organized opinion in the form of parties, but in the persons of ministers representing the families of the régime. Their ministerial lives subject to the 'finger of Franco', they were, as one of them asserted, 'kings' in their own bailiwicks.

XVIII

THE WORLD WAR AND ITS AFTERMATH, 1939–1957

1. *Foreign Policy, 1939–1953: Ostracism to Acceptance*

ONLY five months after Franco entered Madrid as victor in the Civil War the ally of Nationalist Spain was at war with France and Britain in Europe. Thus the World War of 1939 appeared as a prolongation of the struggle between democracy and Fascism that had begun in Spain itself. For the first three years of the war totalitarianism was in the ascendant, and it seemed as if Franco's amalgam of reactionary Catholic conservatism and of Falangism might find a place in Hitler's New European Order. By 1945 Spain was surrounded by the victorious democracies.

Franco was forced to trim his policies—both domestic and foreign—to these dramatic shifts in the European balance of power. Until 1943 his 'prudence'—a quality which his apologists lauded as the supreme gift of his providential statesmanship—was at war with his convictions and prevented him from entering the war on the side of Hitler's Germany. Unable to adjust to the victory of the Allies, there was the prospect that the victors might actively support the opposition in the overthrow of a 'fascist' dictator. This proved to be the great illusion of the aftermath of war.

During the war, official policy, reflected in a controlled press that lauded every German victory and concealed, as long as possible, every defeat, openly supported the allies of the Civil War and repeatedly prophesied the defeat of degenerate democracies at the hands of a totalitarian New Order. Franco's support of Hitler was muted in the early months by his anti-Communism which could not accept German collaboration with the Soviet Union in the dismemberment of Catholic Poland and the Soviet attack on Finland. Franco therefore attempted mediation to end a war which Serrano Suñer confessed had come 'at a moment which suited us least'. With the German attack on Russia in June 1941 embarrassments of the Nazi Soviet Pact vanished.

While the régime's sympathy with the Axis was never in doubt, Spain did not intervene in the war in the West. Franco's supporters make much of his prudence in resisting what Ricardo de la Cierva calls 'the great temptation'—military support of a victorious Hitler. From the outset Franco made clear that 'the foreign policy of Spain will be determined by Spanish interests'.[1] These interests never dictated intervention: Hitler was never willing to pay a price high enough to justify the risks of military adventurism for a country exhausted by its own civil war. Faced with the painful task of post-war reconstruction and feeding a semi-starving population, imports of essential food supplies and petroleum were dependent on the benevolence of the United States and the 'navicerts' granted by the British. Franco did not waver in his belief in an Axis victory until early 1944 and never concealed his sympathies; but he made it clear to the British Ambassador, Sir Samuel Hoare, infuriated by the pro-German propaganda and attacks on his embassy, that sympathy did not imply action. Equally Churchill consistently opposed any sanctions which might drive Franco into the arms of Hitler.

The fall of Paris was hailed in the press as 'a mortal blow to democracy'. On 13 June 1940 Spain abandoned neutrality for non-belligerency. This allowed collaboration with Germany—for instance the use of the régime's propaganda services in Latin America and the provisioning of German submarines. On 14 June Franco offered to enter the war on Germany's side after a period of preparation—he consistently refused to pin himself to a precise date—in return for extensive concessions, at French expense, in North Africa. Hitler was unwilling to alienate France to gain Spain; his interest in Spain only revived with the failure of his plans to invade Britain. Operation Felix envisaged the possibility of cutting off Britain from the Mediterranean by the conquest of Gibraltar, an operation which made Spanish military co-operation essential. For Franco such a risk was unthinkable without German promises of adequate food supplies, the rearmament of the Spanish army, and a substantial empire in North Africa. On 15 October Serrano Suñer, whose

[1] Von Stohrer's (the German ambassador) summary of a conversation on 1 September 1939 with Beigbeder, the Spanish Foreign Minister. Quoted in Ricardo de la Cierva, *Historia del Franquismo. Orígnes y configuración 1939–45* (1975), 150.

declarations of sympathy with the Axis were a constant irritation to Sir Samuel Hoare, succeeded the cautious Beigbeder as Foreign Minister; but the aim of Serrano Suñer's diplomacy was to avoid *precise* commitment and the perils of a German invasion. In the famous interview between Hitler and Franco on 23 October at Hendaye railway station—an interview which Hitler likened to a visit to the dentist—Franco's attitude was cautious as to any date for intervention and his terms high.[1]

Nothing came of Operation Felix in spite of continued German pressure. In February 1941, in an interview with Mussolini, Franco repeated his faith in an Axis triumph; but he also repeated his cautionary tale of the poverty of an exhausted country and set his old conditions—wheat, petrol, an empire in North Africa.[2] The 'Latin Charlatans', as Hitler called the Spanish, in spite of their adulation of the Führer, had resisted his pressure at the very moment when commitment to his cause would have been most valuable.

The German attack on the Soviet Union made it possible for Franco to present his notion of two separate wars: the war in the West, in which Spain's interests might dictate non-belligerency, and the war in the East in which intervention was an ideological imperative. 'Russia is to blame for our Civil War', declared Serrano Suñer from the balcony of the headquarters of the Movement. 'The extermination of Russia is a demand of history.' In July 1941 the Blue Division of 18,694 men, largely Falangist volunteers including the poet Dionisio Ridruejo, disillusioned with the conservatism of the régime, left for the Russian front. There was a recrudescence of the martial spirit. In February 1942 Franco promised 'a million Spaniards' should the road to Berlin be open to the Russians. Britain, although it continued to maintain economic relations with Spain, could not accept Franco's concept of the two wars in one of which the Blue

[1] For Hendaye see besides the various statements of Serrano Suñer, Donald Detwiller, *Hitler Franco und Gibraltar. Die Frage dès Spanischen Eintritt in den Zweiten Weltkrieg* (1962), 55 ff.

[2] Throughout this period Admiral Canaris, an old Spanish hand who visited Spain officially in connection with Operation Felix, made clear to his friends including General Martínez Campos, Chief of the General Staff, the inadvisability of Spanish entry into the war. Cf. André Brissand, *Canaris: la guerra española y la II guerra mundial* (1972).

Division was not attacking Britain's ally but continuing the Civil War Crusade against Communism.[1]

With the entry of the United States into the war (December 1941), the Allied invasion of North Africa (November 1942), and the fall of Stalingrad (February 1943) the tide of war began to turn against the Axis. The prospect of defeat was not officially recognized: the war had reached a stalemate (*un punto muerto*). Franco revived, without success, his earlier plans of mediation. When these failed, rejected by both the Allies and the Germans, the days of pro-Axis non-belligerency were numbered. Even if Franco found it hard to abandon his faith in a German victory, the problem now became how to readjust Spanish diplomacy to the possibility of an Allied victory which might be utilized by Franco's domestic enemies to supplant him and his régime by a constitutional monarchy or a Republic backed by the anti-Fascist powers.[2] He had navigated between private arrangements with the Allies and public support of the Axis; he must change course.

On 17 November 1943 the Blue Division was withdrawn leaving 4,000 dead in Russia. By early 1944 the American Ambassador, Carleton Hayes, considered that Spain had entered into a period of benevolent neutrality.[3] Only supply of wolfram to Germany remained as the overt residuum of the régime's pro-Axis sympathies. American pressure ended this in May 1944. Hitler, exasperated with Franco in 1942, declared that Spain had sold herself to the Allies for food; Franco now sold Spain's neutrality for petrol. Yet it is an indication of his consistent balancing act that he continued to supply Germany with wolfram in secret.[4]

While the Spanish press still strove to hide the enormity of the German defeats—as late as May 1945 it reported victorious counter-attacks in Berlin—Franco's last attempt to square his convictions with the necessity of mending his bridges with a

[1] As if to demonstrate the artificiality of the concept of a divided war and implications for the West of the Crusade in the East, Serrano Suñer's speech was followed by a Falangist attack on the British Embassy.

[2] For the internal implications of an Allied victory see p. 716.

[3] J. H. Carlton Hayes, *Wartime Mission in Spain 1942–45* (1945).

[4] The foreign exchange earned by the supply of wolfram to *both* belligerents was a vital element in Spain's balance of payments and capacity to pay for imports of food and petrol; wolfram exports rose from 2·1 million gold pesetas in 1940 to 200 million by 1944.

victorious Britain and the United States was to revive his notion of 'two wars' and to seek to drive a wedge between the West and the East. Churchill, in spite of his expressions of gratitude to Franco in May 1944 for his helpful attitude over the invasion of North Africa and his even more comforting declaration that the internal affairs of Spain were the concern only of the Spaniards themselves, rejected *in toto* any idea of forming an anti-Soviet front. At Potsdam Stalin presented what were the views of the Spanish opposition; Churchill successfully resisted intervention against Franco; but it was agreed that Spain must be excluded from the United Nations.

Spain paid the penalty for its public support of the Axis and reaped no diplomatic benefits for Franco's double game. Spain was excluded from the United Nations because its government had come to power with the aid of the Axis and had collaborated with it during the war. Franco's balancing act, much praised by his latter-day apologists, between his convictions and what Beigbeder had called the 'interests of Spain' had skilfully resisted German pressure when Hitler's troops were the other side of the Pyrenees and averted the total disaster of an entry into the war on the side of Hitler. This was less a victory for prudence than a necessity given a prostrate economy, an ill-equipped army (German observers at Hendaye commented on the shabby appearance of the soldiers), and the Allies' stranglehold over vital imports. What Hitler chose to regard as excuses disguised in a 'Jewish' talent for hard bargaining, to Franco were harsh necessities which imposed a double policy.[1] Negative in its premisses, it could achieve no positive results. Spain ended the war isolated and alone, ostracized by the victors.

The late forties and early fifties were crisis years for the régime: the 'Black Night' of Francoism. In March 1946 the French government closed the frontier; in December 1946 the democracies withdrew their ambassadors from Madrid. These were symbolic gestures. Franco professed to be untroubled, pursuing his hobby as a painter while the U.N. was excluding him from the comity of nations. He turned international

[1] In June 1940 Beigbeder told Von Stohrer that only 'the difficult economic situation' kept Spain from joining the Nazi war effort. In his letter of 14 June Franco professed his eagerness to enter the war but that 'the terrible economic situation' forced him to be neutral.

ostracism into a monster demonstration of 'Numantian resistance' against a revival of the Black Legend by Communists.[1]

It was not only for domestic audiences that Franco beat the anti-Communist drum. With the coming of the Cold War the theory of the 'two wars', long an embarrassment, became a trump card. Before the age of inter-continental missiles, the importance of Spain was evident to American strategic planners: the concept of Spain as an anti-communist 'spiritual reservoir' was attractive to Congress. Only President Truman held off Congressional efforts to help Spain in 1950. In November 1952 the United Nations rescinded its 1946 resolution and the ambassadors returned to Spain. In 1953 came the agreement with the United States on the establishment of bases in Spain together with the grant of a substantial loan. In December 1955 Spain was admitted to U.N.O. Spain was becoming internationally respectable. 'Time', the monarchist newspaper *ABC* observed, 'works for General Franco'. With only cosmetic concessions to demands for the democratization of his personal dictatorship (the *Fuero de los Españoles* in 1945[2]) the Caudillo had been accepted by the greatest democracy in the world at his own valuation: the sentinel of the West. When, in 1959, Franco was embraced by General Eisenhower to the strains of 'The Yellow Rose of Texas' Franco could say, 'Now I have won the Civil War.'

2. *The Years of Crisis, 1939–1957*

After 1939 the ideology of the régime was coloured and the distribution of power amongst its families was conditioned by the World War and its aftermath. Nor was it only the politics of government that were affected by the war. The possibility that the victorious Allies would act in order to restore democracy shook the confidence of monarchist conservatives in Francoism, and gave the opposition of the defeated—Republicans and the working-class parties in exile or in clandestinity in the interior—the hope that their day had come. These hopes proved illusory; but these years nevertheless constituted a period when

[1] The fortress of Numantia, near Soria, was the scene of a desperate resistance of the Spanish indigenous tribes to the Roman conquerors.

[2] See pp. 707, 720.

the survival of Francoism, isolated in a hostile Europe, seemed in doubt.

Convinced monarchists, supporters of the restoration of Don Juan, had never accepted Franco's rule as a permanent solution; they disliked its concessions to 'vulgar' Falangism. The prospects of an Allied triumph in the war intensified their disquiet: a Fascist dictatorship would be unacceptable to the victors and would no longer guarantee 'social peace'. The disintegration of the dictatorship would open the road to the forces of the left. On 8 March 1943 Don Juan wrote to Franco stating his claim as a king acceptable in 'the reorganization of Europe'. A group of monarchist deputies in the new Cortes petitioned Franco. On 8 September monarchist generals—including Kindelán, who had engineered Franco's rise to supreme power, and Varela—wrote to Franco demanding a restoration 'without delay'. Franco dismissed these gestures with contempt. On 19 March 1945, when the Allies' victory seemed secure, Don Juan issued the Manifesto of Lausanne: it proposed a constitutional monarchy of reconciliation. This was a direct challenge: Franco now became obsessed with the intrigues of what he considered a clique of aristocratic courtier conspirators loyal to Don Juan.

While Franco's private conversations teem with irritated outbursts against Don Juan and his coterie, they make little mention of the opposition of the vanquished. They too set their hopes on the co-operation of the victorious Allies; equally they were to be disillusioned.

Monarchists could plot in Madrid; the leaders of Republican parties were in exile—either in Mexico or France—where they continued the feuds of the Civil War. Prieto's followers in the Socialist party struggled with Negrín and the Communists to control exile funds and organizations.

If the Republic was to be restored by the Allies, Prieto insisted, then it must create a credible government out of the warring factions and exclude the Communists who would never be acceptable to the West. Dr Giral's government (18 September 1945) excluded the Communists but included Republicans and moderate Socialists and later two representatives of the C.N.T., with the result that the movement split between *políticos* and those who remained loyal to the C.N.T.'s traditional apoliticism. Giral had no notion of a struggle in Spain itself; all his hopes were set on the overthrow of Franco with the active help of the Allies.

For Giral the only legitimate government was that of the Republic. Prieto was ready to co-operate with the monarchists if the question of the régime were submitted to a plebiscite. Gil Robles and Prieto met the British Foreign Secretary, Ernest Bevin.[1] Once it became clear that Don Juan was feeling his way to an understanding with the Caudillo over the education of his son, Prince Juan Carlos, any hope of collaboration between monarchists and Socialists was doomed. While the monarchists were negotiating with the P.S.O.E., Don Juan was meeting Franco on his yacht *Azor*. The sole result of Prieto's and Gil Robles's plans was to break up the semblance of Republican unity achieved by Giral (whose government had been joined by the Communists), embitter the monarchist hard-liners, and drive the conservative monarchists, scared by the Gil Robles's political audacity, back into the Francoist fold. Franco, Gil Robles confessed, was irremovable. 'Never has a nation been brought to such a state of collective madness.'[2] Prieto declared his 'total failure' in November 1950. His misguided faith in the democratic governments of the great powers had led him and his party to disaster.

The waverings of Don Juan between outright opposition in collaboration with the exiles aimed at a restoration backed by the democracies and a deal with Franco was, according to resolute opponents such as Gil Robles, to discredit the monarchist cause. The committed continued to plot: the 'cowards and the egotists', as Gil Robles called them, made their peace with Franco, becoming his enthusiastic supporters, much favoured for ambassadorial posts.

The illusions and chronic divisions of the exiles left the interior struggle to the persecuted remnants of the proletarian parties and unions. Three committees of the Socialist party were arrested in 1945, and six serious strikes in Catalonia and the Basque country, organized by the U.G.T. and the C.N.T., were broken by repression in 1947.

After the Civil War, the proletarian parties left in Spain groups of guerrilla fighters who could not return to civilian life. Thousands of exiles—the largest group in the XIV Corps of the

[1] For these negotiations see X. Tussell, *La oposición democrática al franquismo*, 170 ff.

[2] J. M. Gil Robles, *La monarquía por la que yo luché* (1976), 170.

French Forces of the Interior—had fought in the Maquis; Spanish tanks—their names reminiscent of former struggles 'Guernica' and 'Brunete'—arrived with Leclerc's army at the Hôtel de Ville on the liberation of Paris. The P.C.E now organized 4,000 volunteers (September 1945) for an invasion of Spain across the Pyrenees: it was defeated with relative ease but the party undertook the co-ordination and supply of the dispersed guerrilla groups in Galicia, Asturias, Andalusia, and Aragon. The only hope of success, as the P.C.E. recognized, was to trigger off a mass revolt in order to force the Spanish issue to the attention of the democracies—yet another example of the great post-war illusion. But there could be no mass response in a terrorized and apathetic population: the controlled press of the régime dismissed the guerrillas as bandits—and indeed, as in all guerrilla wars, they became bandits as their organizations weakened and they were forced to prey on the local population. In October 1948 the party, at Stalin's order, abandoned the guerrilla struggle for the policy of 'entrism'—penetration of the Francoist syndicates.[1]

Guerrilla activities—they reached their peak in 1946—and strikes did not shake the régime. The 1951 boycott of trams in Barcelona as a protest against a fare increase and the strikes that followed in Vizcaya, and even in 'ever loyal' Navarre, indicated a widespread malaise.[2] Dismissed as the work of 'reds' they were less 'political' strikes than generalized protests against the intolerable conditions of the 'years of hunger',[3] years of rising prices and stable wages, a warning to the régime that its economic policies had not produced a minimum of well-being. Subsequent governments would alter the policies. The immediate response was massive repression—sometimes as many as a thousand workers were arrested after a strike and the leaders condemned to long years of imprisonment.

[1] For accounts of the sufferings of the exiles and their contribution to the French war effort see D. Wingate Pyke *Vae Victis* (1969) and L. Stein, *Beyond Death and Exile* (1979), 124–81. The French consistently denied the importance of this contribution.

[2] For the Barcelona strike see F. Fanes, *La vaga de tramvies del 1951* (1977). The strike, which provided the first example of student–worker co-operation, is a significant landmark because the government conceded the strikers' demands. Immediately after the strike the National Congress of the Official Syndicates agreed, in the oblique language characteristic of the period, that the 'processes of transformation in the socio-economic system' should be studied.

[3] See p. 742.

Between 1939 and 1950 at least 22,000 Spaniards were executed—schoolmasters, trade-union leaders, mayors, Republican commanders, and politicans like Companys, handed over by Vichy to his executioners.[1] The victors in every village and town paid off old scores by 'denouncing' their enemies. What was called the 'pact of blood' bound the victors together and made reconciliation with the vanquished inconceivable. Those who did not accept the new Spain of Catholic unity were neither Spaniards nor Christians; the firing-squad and prison replaced the dungeons and fires of the Inquisition.

3. *The Governments of the Blue Era, 1939–1957*

In 1939 and the succeeding years the social and political life of every provincial capital was dominated by the 'authorities': the bishop, the military governor, and the Falangist mayor and governor; they were exhibited in endless parades and public functions and given reserved, roped-off seats in cinemas.[2] Mild sympathy with the vanquished meant unemployment: the burgeoning bureaucracy of the régime provided for the victors. The Youth Front and Feminine Section of the Falange indoctrinated the new generation in the ethics of service to the New State. The régime declared itself totalitarian.[3] School lessons began with the Fascist salute and the singing of the Falangist anthem: *Cara al sol*.[4]

In spite of the all-enveloping imperialist–Falangist rhetoric of the régime, the name of 'the absent one' José Antonio on church walls, the Yoke and Arrows at the entrance to every village, and a vast labour bureaucracy in the hands of Falangists, it became evident that the governance of the Francoist state would not be entrusted to the Falange.

The struggle between the families under Franco had begun; it came to the surface in 1942. The two contenders were General Varela, proponent of a conservative monarchist restoration and Serrano Suñer, the architect of the New State, still enamoured with Italian Fascism and the creation of a Falangist party that

[1] This *minimum* figure is based on the controversial researches of R. Salas Larrazabal.

[2] For a fictionalized portrait of post-war Gerona see J. M. Gironella, *Ha estallado la paz*.

[3] e.g. in the preamble to the Statute setting up the Instituto Nacional del Libro (May 1939).

[4] J. Caro Baroja, *Los Baroja* (1972), 360.

would be parallel to and control the apparatus of the state. Already the idea of a mass party as the instrument of the Falangist 'pending revolution' had suffered a blow with the fall, in July 1941, of its ideologue Gerardo Salvador Merino who hoped that with such a party the Falange could claim 'all power in our hands'.[1] On 16 August 1942 the tension between the ambitions of the monarchists and the Falangists erupted in the Basque sanctuary of Begoña. A group of Catholics shouted 'vivas' for the legitimate king after a mass at which General Varela had been present; a Falangist threw a bomb. Franco sacked both Serrano Suñer and Varela. This was a warning to monarchist generals and militant Falangists alike.[2]

Up till 1945 Franco's governments had been dominated by soldiers, Falangists, and monarchist elements including surviving servants of Primo de Rivera.[3] In the government of July 1945 the National Syndicalism of the Falange was diluted by the National Catholicism of the A.C.N.P. The central figure in the new government was the Foreign Minister, Martín Artajo, long a prominent figure in Catholic Action. Falangism had become an international embarrassment: in September 1945 the Nazi salute was discontinued.

It was not merely that the National Catholicism of the A.C.N.P. was overshadowing the National Syndicalism of the Falange. Martín Artajo's task as Foreign Minister was to win international respectability by dissipating the notion that Spain was 'fascist'. In July 1945 the *Fuero de los Españoles* with its illusory grant of 'liberties' was an essay in constitutional cosmetics for overseas consumption; it was blessed by the Cardinal Primate as marking 'the orientation of Christian liberty, opposed to statist totalitarianism' (*totalitarianismo estatista*). Spain's international critics saw not the emergence of Christian liberty but the evident survival of totalitarianism. Nor did what was intended as a step towards 'institutionalizing' a personal dictatorship carry more conviction: in 1947 Franco

[1] See his 'Aspectos políticos del sindicalismo español' in *Sistema*, no. 13 (1976).

[2] The fall of Serrano Suñer has been attributed, not to the tensions between the army and the Falange, but to the supposed rectification of his pro-Axis foreign policy. (*Entre el silencio y la propaganda, la Historia como fue* (1977), Chapter XVII.

[3] The dates of appointment and composition of Franco's eleven governments between 1939 and 1975 are given in E. de Blaye, *Franco and the Politics of Spain* (1976), Appendix 3, 520–5.

declared Spain a monarchy with himself as its perpetual Regent.[1] In July of that year Franco used for the first time the favoured instrument of authoritarian governments: a referendum on the new constitutional arrangements. The propaganda apparatus of the régime threatened a revival of civil war, 'Either Francoism or Communism'. The inevitable response was an 82 per cent 'Yes' vote.[2]

It was not these constitutional tinkerings that lifted Spain out of international Coventry. The first important power to grant diplomatic recognition to Franco was the Vatican—not because it believed in 'Christian liberty' but because the Concordat of 1953, which entailed formal recognition, established a confessional Catholic state where the public profession of other religions was prohibited and canon-law prohibitions were embedded in the Civil Code. The Base Agreement of September 1953 was a product of the strategic necessities of the United States.

These steps on the road to international respectability were the achievements of Martín Artajo who remained Foreign Minister in Franco's Fifth Government (July 1951–February 1957) which, with the historian's benefit of hindsight, can be seen to represent a transitional stage both in Francoism and in the character and tactics of the opposition. That government saw two departures: the cautious beginnings of a new economic policy and an even more cautious attempt at 'liberalization' from within. The first was to develop into a relatively consistent policy of faith in capitalism as the motor of economic growth; the second was to fall victim to a stop–go policy that was to characterize Francoism until its demise: once 'liberalization' threatened what was termed 'the essence of the state' the liberalizing ministers were summarily dismissed.

The state-fostered economic nationalism of autarky[3] was congruent with the introverted political nationalism of early Francoism and its paranoid fears of international plots.[4] The

[1] The Law of Succession was rejected by Don Juan because 'it converted a personal dictatorship into a life (*vitalicia*) dictatorship'.

[2] In spite of official pressure abstention reached 11·4 per cent. What is significant is that the rate of abstention in Barcelona was 20 per cent with 7·5 per cent of spoiled votes, i.e. double the national average.

[3] See pp. 739–743 for the economics of autarky.

[4] For autarky and its abandonment see p. 739. For the connection between autarky and foreign policy see Angel Viñas, 'Autarquía y política exterior en el primer franquismo', in *Revista de estudios internacionales*, Jan.–March 1980, esp. 71 ff.

first timid steps towards the abandonment of state interventionism were made by the new Minister of Commerce, Manuel Aburúa, notorious for his free-handed bestowal of import licences on chosen friends. Secondly the Minister of Education, Joaquín Ruíz Giménez, a liberal Catholic and a member of A.C.N.P., whom Franco regarded as one of his most docile ministers, moved cautiously towards what was to be later called '*aperturismo*'—a liberalization or 'opening' of the régime from within. This was enough to set off the first public exhibition of the hidden struggles for power within Francoism since 1942.

The mild, Catholic liberalism of Ruíz Giménez, evident in his support of his fellow liberal Catholics in the University, set off a violent counter-reaction in the Falange. In the freer atmosphere fostered by Ruíz Gimeńez and Laín Entralgo, Rector of Madrid University, students petitioned for a National Congress of Students, a protest against the Falange monopoly of the students union. Falange militia clashed with the students in the streets (9 February 1956). Franco summarily dismissed both Ruíz Giménez as patron of the students and the Minister Secretary, the Falange 'old shirt' Fernández Cuesta, who had failed to control his bully boys. Public protest the régime could not tolerate. The episode was followed by arrests and Franco, in his annual New Year speech, warned against 'the vices of liberalism'.

The episode illustrated not merely the limits of tolerance and the inbuilt resistance of the régime to a process of *apertura* and the recurrent fissures in Francoism. It also revealed an important transformation in the opposition: opposition would no longer be dismissed as an exile plot and it was no longer confined to the working class. University students came from respectable bourgeois families.

It was in response to these changes that the P.C.E. announced in 1956 its policy of national reconciliation—the creation of a broad front including the bourgeois opposition.[1] A tottering régime, Santiago Carrillo, the party's General Secretary insisted, could be overthrown by the 'pacific General Strike'. In 1959 this proved a complete fiasco. Yet the Communist party remained perhaps the most effective element in the opposition.

[1] P. Preston, 'The anti-Francoist opposition: the long march to unity', in P. Preston (ed.), *Spain in Crisis* (1976), 125–56.

Trained in clandestinity, recruiting and educating its militants in prison, it gained recruits less by its Marxism, than because its opposition was absolute and because of the primacy it put on the struggle *within* Spain. Official denunciations of the perils of Communism—the most consistent and strongest thread in the ideology of Francoism—became a self-fulfilling prophecy; they gave the party visibility.[1]

More significant still, the monolithic support of the Catholic Church was weakening at the base; the young militants of the H.O.A.C. sided with striking workers; strikes were beginning to be organized by *ad hoc* factory committees manned by Catholic and Communist militants.

Nevertheless the extent of disaffection must not be overemphasized; given Arias Salgado's censorship and the apathy of most Spaniards, the protest of intellectuals—many of whom joined the P.C.E.—, of Socialist and 'Christian Marxist' groups in the universities, of liberal monarchists, Christian Democrats, and disillusioned Falangists could have no national resonance. Moreover, the régime was about to embark on a policy that would lift the economy to a level of relative prosperity which would give Francoism a renewed lease of life. Already in 1962 a disillusioned Ridruejo observed that the régime enjoyed 'majority social support'.

The significance of this new era would not escape Claudín and Semprun, the most prominent intellectuals of the Communist party. Carrillo's 'subjectivism' and revolutionary optimism was based on a profound misunderstanding of the 'objective' social changes: by 1964 the régime could no longer be conceived as the creature of a reactionary clique dominating a poor economy. Well-being—limited as it might be—widened the area of support and the march to power would be a long one.[2]

[1] See Guy Hermet, *The Communists in Spain* (1971), 171 ff.

[2] Carrillo dismissed criticism as coming from frustrated intellectuals; the enthusiasm of militants could scarcely be maintained by laments that Francoism was there to stay. In 1964 Semprun and Claudín were expelled from the party; yet their heretical analysis became the basis of Carrillo's strategy, the first steps towards Eurocommunism. For the differences between Semprun, Claudín, and what they regarded as the Stalinist leadership of Santiago Carrillo see Jorge Semprun, *The Autobiography of Federico Sanchez* (1979), 50 ff., esp. 204–10 and F. Claudín, *Documents de una divergencia communista* (1978). For Carrillo's views, *¿Después de Franco, quie?* (1967).

XIX

FROM CONFORMISM TO CONFLICT, 1957–1975

1. *Neo-Conservatism, 1960–1970*

THE new resilience of the régime which the dissident Communists noted in 1964, the spread of conformist apathy which depressed the intellectual opposition, was perceived by both as a result of a rise in living standards coming after a world of shortages. The key to the so-called 'economic miracle' of the sixties and early seventies was the abandonment of the political economy of autarky for what has been called 'neo-capitalism': an economy open to the world and in which scarce resources were—in theory—allocated, not by the government, but by the mechanisms of the market. After a sharp dose of deflation and a wage freeze, productivity and living standards rose. Unemployment was relieved by the safety valve of emigration to the factories and farms of France and Germany; the balance of payments was fuelled by tourist revenues, emigrants' remittances, and foreign long-term investment in what now looked a promising economy.

The new economic policy was the work of the 'technocrats': university-trained ministers and a generation of civil servants distinct from the 'amateurs' who had occupied their positions 'by right of conquest' in the post-war years. The ministerial change came in February 1957: Navarro Rubio occupied the key post at the Treasury; Ullastres became Minister of Commerce; López Bravo became Director-General of Foreign Trade (1959) and López Rodó Minister of Planning in 1965. Almost all the new team were members of Opus Dei and closely connected with the financial world. Their advent to power was the final proof that the ruling élite had ceased to be an amalgam of generals, old-fashioned conservatives, and Falangists.

The achievements and shortcomings of the new faith in the market and its dramatic effects on society are discussed elsewhere.[1] Here one is concerned with its more immediate political implications, both for the régime and for the opposition.

In so far as it represented a coherent political attitude, the new deal was based on the premiss that prosperity would ease the social and political tensions already evident in the fifties. López Rodó stated that with a per capita income of $2,000 they would disappear; Franco himself believed that with 'decent clothes', football matches, and TV—he himself never missed Match of the Day on television—the working class would have no cause for complaint. Fernández de la Mora's *Twilight of Ideologies* (1965) was an apology for technocracy which elevated political apathy into a philosophy; apathy was the sign of a sound society.[2] The flaw in the argument was that, once satisfied with the consumer goods of the West, Spaniards became increasingly aware of the shortage of the political goods their neighbours enjoyed. When, after 1962, the government sought to join the E.E.C. it became evident that the lack of elementary democratic freedom was excluding Spain from the Europe of the Treaty of Rome and thus imperilling the future of the very prosperity which the régime claimed was the product of the 'peace of Franco'.

Stability—these years saw the 'perfection' of the Francoist 'constitution' according to the immutable Law of the Principles of the Movement (1958) and the Organic Law of 1966—could therefore, it was hoped, be achieved without any sacrifice of authority. A loosening of the economy was accompanied by a tightening of political controls; in the government of 1957 General Alonso Vega, friend of Franco and long head of the Civil Guard, became Minister of the Interior; he was a *duro*, a hard man, by whom the strikes and student protest were presented as a conspiracy engineered by international Communism. Even so the mass repression of the early years became increasingly difficult. The political police proved less capable of mastering an opposition with support in a public opinion no

[1] See Chap. XXI.

[2] This defence of technocratic remedies in a society where conflict had ceased has similarities with the early works of Daniel Bell and Seymour Lipset. Cf. Patrick Moynihan's *Coping: on the Practice of Government* (1973) for an American edition of the politics of stability.

longer terrorized. Individual labour leaders received long sentences from the Tribunal of Public Order (1963) which tried 4,317 cases in its first four years. But repression met with *public* protest at home as well as abroad.[1]

2. *Opposition, 1960–1969*

It was the economic progress on which the régime prided itself which engendered those contradictions between the new society and the old state which were to trouble Francoism till its demise. A flourishing capitalist economy demanded an expansion of higher education; the universities, particularly the Madrid Faculty of Political Science—produced not a race of docile technocrats but a generation of student radicals. The Official Syndicates—last remaining bastion of the conception of a hierarchically ordered society and economy—could not satisfy modernizing employers, heroes of the new age, who demanded effective collective bargaining for productivity deals and rationalization of the labour force. Collective bargaining had been legalized in 1958; but for wage settlements to stick at the factory floor they must be made by organizations in which the workers trusted, as they would not trust the Movement's 'vertical', bureaucratized syndicates in which they were not represented. Employers were, therefore, willing to negotiate with unofficial, illegal unions. The strike was an essential part of the negotiating mechanism. To Franco the strike was only 'licit' in liberal systems which had failed to end the class war; in Spain the class war had ended and strikes were therefore 'criminal' attacks on the welfare of the state and its citizens.[2] Yet, after 1967 strikes increasingly filled the newspapers.

As the intensity of its repression shows, the régime had most to fear from the workers' resistance. Solís, Minister Secretary of the Movement from 1957 until 1969, sought to refurbish the image of the Movement's Official Syndicates and to convert them into a more effective instrument for the settlement of wage

[1] Both the repression of the Asturian miners in 1962–3 and the execution after a military trial by firing-squad of the Communist militant Grimau on 20 April 1963 (which released a flood of international protest unknown since 1909 and the cancellation of a French loan) were 'justified' by the Minister of Information, Fraga.

[2] Speech to the IV Assembly of the Asamblea de Hermandades Sindicales de Agricultores y Ganaderos, 1951.

claims by conceding the right to strike (on labour issues only), by separating the employers' unions from the workers' unions, and by allowing democratic elections from the factory floor. The negotiation of collective agreements could take place within the Official Syndicates—a part of Solís's general plans for giving the régime a modern and democratic varnish by enlarging the area of participation.

The road to some form of democratic unionism within the Official Syndicates seemed open; the workers had begun to form their own organization outside the Official Syndicates. The rash of strikes of the sixties were organized by the independent Workers' Commissions (CC.OO): in their origins in 1956–60 they were *ad hoc* factory committees, manned by Communist militants and Catholic activists, effective because of their concentration on immediate demands. By the late sixties the CC.OO were approaching nation-wide organization and were falling under the control of the Communists.[1] The U.G.T. and the P.S.O.E. made a grave mistake in rejecting 'entrism' (i.e. the election of workers active in the CC.OO as shop stewards) on the grounds that entry into the Official Syndicates would be merely to fall in with the plans of Solís. When the government finally, in 1968–9, moved in to destroy the Commissions, it was too late. The ironical legacy of forty years of official syndicalism was a workers' movement dominated by the Communists. The strikes of the sixties were not political in origin: they represented the claim of a new working class in new industries, using the new bargaining methods, to get their share of the economic boom. In this sense the great Asturian strike of 1962 in a decaying mining industry confronted by an unacceptable productivity deal was a relic from the past. It was widely publicized. Repression politicized the working-class revival of the sixties; hence the increase in 'solidarity' strikes in support of dismissed elected shop stewards.

The student protest was a bourgeois affair. It began a decade before the European student revolution in 1968 and was to be an endemic disturbance in the political and social life of Madrid and Barcelona until the democratic elections of 1977.[2] It began

[1] F. Claudín, 'Le nouveau mouvement ouvrier', in *Les Temps modernes*, *Espagne 1964*, Dossier no. 357, 8–56; and N. Sartorius, *El resurgir del movimiento obrero* (1976), *passim*.

[2] J. M. Maravall, *Dictatorship and Political Dissent* (1978), 98–165; and A. Peña, 'Diez años de movimiento universitario', *Materiales* (March–April 1977).

as a protest against the 'vertical', Falangist student union, the S.E.U.: 'free assemblies', strikes, and the occupation of buildings ended in ritual street clashes with the police. Police repression politicized protest organized by Communists, radical Catholics, and the 'revolutionary socialists' of the Popular Liberation Front. In its origins an élitist concern recruited by personal contact from middle-class families with a Republican background, the student protest underwent a process of mass mobilization. Equipped with its own *Marxisant* subculture, it was fragmented by Byzantine feuds of the 'grupuscules' which were the origin of the new left of the seventies. By 1970 it was concerned less with specific political issues that an onslaught on the moral values of contemporary society and the transformation of the university from an instrument for the transmission of culture into a laboratory for social, sexual, and educational experiments. The legacy of the régime was a crisis-ridden mass university.

The student protest, rather than a direct threat to the régime, was a proof of its intellectual bankruptcy and its incapacity to capture the loyalty of a generation which had no direct experience of the Civil War, the memory of which weighed so heavily on older Spaniards and which was insistently exploited by Franco. The collapse of the S.E.U. like the decay of the Official Syndicates, demonstrated the erosion of the institutional foundations of the régime.

An even more alarming symptom of this process of erosion was the confrontation between the Catholic Church and the régime it had once legitimized. The days of National Catholicism were over, when the Vatican had bestowed international respectability on the Spain of the Crusade with the Concordat of 1953. John XXIII asked Ruíz Giménez to spread his message in Spain; its defence of ideological pluralism and human rights was completely incompatible with the role of the Church as Franco conceived it.[1]

Renewal from Rome corresponded with a longer process of spiritual renovation and self-criticism in Spain itself. Young priests and the Catholic workers' organizations which enjoyed a limited liberty of action denied to other groups, the H.O.A.C.

[1] On the influence of John XXIII see *Cuadernos para el diálogo* (July 1964) and S. Giner, 'Metamorfosis de la iglesia en diez años', ibid. (December 1973).

(Catholic Action Workers' Brotherhood) and its youth section J.O.C. (Catholic Workers' Youth) had played an important role in the labour struggles of the sixties.[1] The J.O.C. distributed pamphlets at factory gates; priests gave shelter to meetings of the Workers Commissions. In this attempt to create a rival organization to the Official Syndicates the activists enjoyed the occasional approval of the episcopate; but, in general, the young priests found no support among the older bishops still loyal to the Providential ruler. But by the late sixties the unreconstructed Crusaders were dying off. In 1969 Paul VI imposed Mgr Enrique y Tarancón as Primate, a liberal Catholic convinced that the old alliance of Church and state denied the Church control over its own affairs—particularly the appointment of bishops. The *franquista* bishops were increasingly isolated.[2] 'Red bishops' like Cirarda of Bilbao, who refused to say mass to celebrate the anniversary of Franco's capture of his see, were subject to hysterical outbursts of a new phenomenon: the right-wing anticlericalism of the Guerrillas of Christ the King. Cardinal Tarancón was given police protection.

Bishop Cirarda's actions in 1970 were in defence of imprisoned Basque nationalists; yet in 1960 the bishops had reprimanded the 339 priests who signed a letter demanding liberty for the Basques as being 'blinded by political passion'. While the Catalan bishops remained aloof from the protests of Catalan nationalists, the Abbot of Montserrat attacked the régime in *Le Monde* and parish priests defended imprisoned nationalists.

The suppression of the home rule granted by the Republic to Catalonia and the Basque Provinces represented the triumph of 'Spain One and Indivisible' over the disintegrating forces of 'separatism'. Rigid administrative centralism was accompanied by an attempt to enforce cultural uniformity: Catalans were to speak 'the language of Empire'. In the immediate post-war years, for the middle classes in both the Basque Country and Catalonia, the triumph of Nationalist Spain represented salvation from 'red hordes'; by the 1970's at least sections of the Catalan bourgeoisie were strongly anti-Francoist.[3]

[1] The H.O.A.C. was the Catholic Workers' organization opposed to the official 'vertical' syndicates.

[2] N. Cooper, 'The Church: from Crusade to Christianity', in P. Preston (ed.), *Spain in Crisis* (1976).

[3] J. A. Gonzalez Casanova, *La lucha por la democrácia en Catalunya* (1979), Chapter 4.

A renaissance of Catalan culture in the fifties became a surrogate for political nationalism and illustrated the limitations of authoritarian centralism. Some of its manifestations were the creations of an esoteric, Europeanized 'underground culture'; but by the 1960's the defence of that Catalan language and culture became a serious political threat because it commanded the support of wide sectors of the middle class, the sympathies of the clergy, and enthusiasm for it spread to youth with the emergence of a Catalan pop culture.[1] In 1960, in the presence of four ministers, the audience at the Palace of Music sang the prohibited Catalan anthem *Le Senyera*. One of those arrested was Jordi Pujol—a doctor who was to become a successful banker—a typical representative of the bourgeoisie that was to furnish Catalan nationalism with a flexible and intelligent leadership. Only in Catalonia did the opposition succeed in creating a unified movement: the Catalan Assembly of 1971. Opposition to Francoism had produced a profound change in the political landscape of Francoism; in the thirties the working-class parties had been hostile or indifferent to Catalanism; now *all* parties supported home rule for Catalonia.

Basque nationalism, while it had the support of the local clergy, lacked the secure cultural roots—only around 60,000 of the 2,300,000 inhabitants of the provinces could speak Basque—and the middle-class support characteristic of Catalan nationalism. Swamped by the flood of Castilian immigrants who came to the factories of Bilbao, Basque nationalism was in crisis; the moderation and legalism of the Basque Republican government in exile could provide no answer. The youth of the party founded ETA in 1959; it was soon influenced by Third World nationalism, Marxism, and the tactic of the 'armed struggle', all of which repeatedly divided what was, in its origins, a conventional nationalist protest.[2] Once it had embarked on the armed struggle—sabotage and assassination—its theorists were concerned that individual acts of terrorism should not be construed as contempt for the mass struggle.[3] Mass support of a kind, the

[1] A favourable account of the Catalan revival is presented in J. Rossinyol, *Le Problème national catalan* (1974), 412 ff.

[2] On ETA see 'Ortzi', *Historia de Euzkadi: el nacionalismo vasco y ETA* (1975) and Stanley Payne, *El nacionalismo vasco: de sus orígines a la ETA* (1974).

[3] For this concern to prove that individual acts of terrorism did not weaken strike activity see Julian Agirre, *Operation Ogro* (trans. B. Solomon, 1975), 18, 98, 176.

provision of what Mao Tse-tung called 'water for the fish to swim in' (i.e. that generalized sympathy without which terrorism cannot survive) was created by massive police repression which failed to distinguish between the guilty and the innocent. The military trial in Burgos of sixteen young ETA (nine death penalties and 518 years' imprisonment) moved Spanish and international opinion of an unprecedented scale. Franco commuted the death sentences—an action he would not have contemplated in the 1940's; the continued campaign of bank robberies and kidnappings, which was to culminate in the assassination of Admiral Carrero Blanco in December 1973, was a patent demonstration that 'the peace of Franco' was a thing of the past.

Finally, there is what has been called the 'democratic opposition' operating mostly in Spain itself, distinguished by its rejection of any co-operation with the Communists which would revive memories of the Civil War even though the party was now committed to a policy of 'national reconciliation' which would include bourgeois and Catholic elements. The democratic opposition ran from the liberal monarchists of Sartrustegui's Union Español and Gil Robles's right-wing Christian Democrats to Ruíz Giménez's left-wing Christian Democrats and Dionisio Ridruejo's Social Democrats. That this opposition was tolerated has led to the accusation that its existence strengthened the régime by allowing it to boast that liberty existed in Spain; this neglects its main function—the erosion of the moral credibility of a régime that it could not overthrow because it was denied any possibility of a mass following. An opposition of notables and its *actes de présence*—such as the Munich meeting of 1962—irritated rather than threatened.

It was the uncertain and arbitrary margins of tolerance that allowed the existence of a 'legal' tolerated opposition: that these margins shifted was a sign that Francoism was entering into the preliminaries of the stop–go struggle between *aperturismo* and immobilism.

Manuel Fraga, as Minister of Information from 1962 to 1969, saw that a 'modern' society could not be contained in the strait-jacket imposed in 1939. In 1966 censorship was abandoned. Fraga's Press Law of that year, while it allowed the government (by its notorious Article 2) a free hand to suspend and fine editors, was a genuine 'opening' of the régime.[1] The results were far from pleasing to hard-liners; Carrero Blanco and the Caudillo's wife were scandalized by the appearance of 'pornographic' films and literature.

Fraga's cultural opening was accompanied by an attempt at a 'political' opening by the Minister of the Movement, Solís. A 'contrast of opinions' based on 'associations' *within* the Movement and under the control of its National Council would, Solís hoped, enlarge the area of participation and present a semblance of pluralism. Such a narrow opening was rejected out of hand by the democratic opposition and yet alarmed the 'immobilists'. In July 1969 the opponents of Solís's modernization of the Movement and of Fraga's 'modernization' of cultural life secured their dismissal in yet another public eruption of family feuds.

In November of the same year Franco nominated Prince Juan Carlos as his heir. This was a triumph for López Rodó, whose modernization was limited to economic matters, and Admiral Carrero Blanco, the political embodiment of *continuismo*.[2] To most Spaniards Juan Carlos appeared a creature of the Caudillo to whom he had sworn loyalty and adherence as well as to the Movement. As Girón had reminded the faithful, the Caudillo was neither immortal nor a 'repeatable historical phenomenon'[3] and ever since a dangerous gun wound in 1961 the problem of the succession had preoccupied, even obsessed, the inner circles of Francoism. With Juan Carlos in the wings, all looked safe on stage.

3. *The Agony of Francoism, 1969–1975*

Franco continued confident that 'all is tied down, well tied down'. He was blinded by his long-standing obsessions and stereotypes. The troubles were due to Communist infiltration of

[1] *Cuadernos para el diàlogo*, edited by Ruíz Giménez, once a Francoist minister now a left-wing Christian Democrat, was open to all comers and published articles which could never have appeared before 1962. It suffered fines and suspensions, as did Calvo Serer's *Madrid* which was suppressed. For a critical view of Fraga's law see G. Cisquella, *Díez años de represión cultural. La censura de libros durante la Ley de Prensa 1966–1976* (1977).

[2] For the success of 'operation Juan Carlos' see L. López Rodó, *La larga marcha hacía la Monarquía* (1977).

[3] J. A. Girón de Velasco, *Reflexiones sobre España* (1975), 109.

the Church and the universities; Catalan nationalism was 'nonsense'. If his unconditional followers believed that, after the dictator's death, the institutional apparatus of Francoism would secure its survival, his more perceptive ministers were conscious of the gap between an authoritarian state and the European democracies of the E.E.C. which, since 1962, it was the official policy to join. Opposed by the 'immobilists' their attempts to secure democratic respectability by 'opening' the régime precipitated the crisis of identity which persisted until the Caudillo's death.

It was Carrero Blanco who formed and controlled the government of October 1969; in June 1973 he officially succeeded Franco as Head of the Government while the Caudillo remained Head of State. Carrero Blanco's ministry represented a return to authoritarianism and economic well-being as the recipe for stability—hence the presence of the technocrats of Opus Dei. With the appointment of the new government the stock market boomed; after the recession of 1969, in spite of inflation, real wages rose in 1971.

This could not conceal that the régime was entering into a process of decomposition that seemed to find a parallel in the physical decay of the Caudillo himself, stricken with Parkinson's disease. What gave these years of bleak authoritarianism their paradoxical character was the relative freedom of the press. With magazines like *Cambio 16* the press became, and remained, a fourth estate. Its criticism of the régime drove the extreme right into a frenzy. For the first time the general public gained some knowledge of the programme of the opposition and of the reformists within the régime—Fraga's *El Desarollo político* ('Political Development'), a plea for wider participation as the only recipe for stability was published in 1971. Above all it reported the erosion of the 'peace of Franco'. In March 1972 the Workers Commissions organized in the Caudillo's home province of Galicia a violent strike followed by a total stoppage in Pamplona—a conservative, quiet provincial town that had become an industrial city. These events were fully reported in the press.

Till the death of Franco the most intractable problem was the terrorism of ETA and of the left-wing revolutionaries modelled on the Bader Meinhof gang. In 1970 the Burgos Trials were a trial of the régime as much as of the terrorists themselves.[1] On 20 December 1973 ETA scored its greatest technical triumph: Carrero Blanco's car was blown clean over a church in an exclusive residential quarter of Madrid.[2]

For its perpetrators the purpose of this 'magnicide' was to force the government into the arms of the far right and reliance on the army, thus according to standard terrorist theory, releasing a revolution of the masses. In fact it ushered in the last attempt to 'open' the political system and the final struggle between the families of the régime engaged in a contest for the political succession to the moribund Caudillo. On the one side stood the *aperturistas*—the intra-régime reformists who believed that only an 'opening' of the régime could contain the demands and pressures of a society that had come to resemble the societies of the Europe they were so anxious to join.[3] On the other stood the 'immobilists' of the bunker.[4] To them, with their cry of 'After Franco the Institutions', any reform of part of the structure developed since 1939 imperilled the whole—Carrero Blanco had once said that to offer political change to a Spaniard was like offering a drink to a confirmed alcoholic. To allow the defeated of the Civil War back into political life, declared Girón, was to allow the memory of the Civil War to be 'devoured by pigs'. Both political strategies were recipes for the survival of sections of the governing élite.

Franco's choice as Carrero Blanco's successor, Carlos Arias Navarro, seemed to portend a return to the ice-age; he was called by the opposition the 'Butcher of Malaga' for his activities as a public prosecutor in the Civil War and had been Carrero's Minister of the Interior responsible for the security forces that had so signally failed to protect the Admiral. But on 12 February Arias's speech in the Cortes galvanized Spain: the 'way of adherence' must be replaced 'by the way of participation'; a

[1] For a presentation of the Burgos Trials as the grand crisis of Francoism see E. de Blaye, op. cit. 279–323.

[2] For a vivid account of the assassination—one of the most brilliantly planned in the history of terrorism—see J. Agirre, op. cit., *passim*. Carrero Blanco's security was poor—his address was in the telephone directory. The assassination was the first major operation of ETA outside the Basque Country.

[3] J. Meliá, *El largo camino de la apertura* (1975) is a good account by an *aperturista*.

[4] A. Alvarez Solís, *¿Qué es el Bunker?* (1976). The views of a typical representative, A. Girón de Velasco, are revealed in his *Reflexiones sobre España* (1975).

new Statute of Associations would allow the formation of *political* associations.

Arias, however, was becoming—and was to remain—a prisoner of the bunker. On 28 April the old lion of Falangism, Girón, published a denunciation of the freedom of the press; Blas Piñar, organizer of the forces of the bunker in his *Fuerza Nueva*, denounced the 'dwarfs' who had penetrated the régime in order to destroy it from within. In June Solís—once an *aperturista*, now a hard-liner—was brought into the government to strengthen immobilism. The liberal policies of Pío Cabanellas, as Minister of Information, had encouraged a rash of pornography: Spaniards rediscovered the female nude in magazines and films; Marxist tracts could be bought in any kiosk.[1] To the right, this exposed the moral and political consequences of liberalization. In October Pío Cabanellas was dismissed on Franco's demand. With Pío Cabanellas resigned Barrero de Irma, the Minister of Finance, and Ricardo de la Cierva, in charge of publications. This was a declaration that the financial bourgeoisie and the establishment intellectuals—de la Cierva was the Caudillo's official biographer—were deserting the régime.

By October it did not appear that Arias's 'opening', announced in February, would be a wide one. If it was to succeed it must embrace the *aperturistas*: they included Fraga, since 1973 Ambassador in London and at this time the most well-known, if not the most popular politician in Spain, with his plans for diluted democracy from above 'without a revision of existing institutions;' liberal monarchists like Areilza; the *Tacito* group of young Christian Democrats. By June 1974 Emilio Romero could reassure the right by announcing that the enthusiasts of the 'spirit of February 12' would need a candle to find it under their rocking-chairs.[2] When Arias's Law of Associations came in December 1974 it was clear that political

[1] The connexion by the right of democracy and the collapse of conventional moral standards goes back to 1868 and was common coinage under the Second Republic. Carrero Blanco and Franco's wife had protested against the moral consequences of an *apertura* as fostering commercial pornography since the first appearance on the screen of a woman in a bikini. See C. Alonso Tejada, *La represión sexual en la España de Franco* (1977), and his article in *El Viejo Topo*, special supplement no. 1 (1977), 43 ff.

[2] Romero was a hard-hitting old Falangist. See his article, 'Luz Verde', in *Pueblo*, 19 June 1974.

associations would be vetted by the National Council of the Movement and that the only associations formed under the new law would be manned by Francoists such as the government-backed U.D.P.E. (Union of the Spanish People), its president an ambitious bureaucrat Adolfo Suárez whose career had been made in the Movement. The new statute was contemptuously rejected by the opposition. Fraga's friends founded, not an association under the new law but a limited company ostensibly engaged in political research. Without Fraga, without Areilza and the *Tacito*, Arias's opening was doomed. 'Outdoors' (i.e. outside committed Francoists) 'the answer has been a resounding No.'

It was the persistence of labour unrest—in an attempt to contain it the government allowed elections of shop stewards in the Official Unions only to facilitate a victory of the opposition in the elections of 1975—and, above all, the continued activity of the terrorists that kept Arias a prisoner of the bunker. In August 1975 came the Anti-Terrorist Law which made the death penalty mandatory for terrorists; one month later the new law was applied to five militants of ETA and F.R.A.P.

The remote possibility that *aperturista* reformism might deprive the opposition of some of its arguments vanished: in 1973 Professor Aranguren had written, 'For the bourgeoisie, for the new middle and working classes, the opposition will increasingly become, not so much dangerous as without purpose.'[1] In fact political associationism—the recipe of the *aperturistas*—proved irreconcilable with the premisses of the Movement; to be effective these associations must become more than anodyne assemblies of the faithful; they must become parties extending beyond the confines of the Movement. These, Franco had warned, 'will never return'.[2]

It was not that opposition was concerned so much with the overthrow of Franco as with staking its claims for the inheritance that nature—the Caudillo was a frail eighty-one—would

[1] J. L. López Aranguren, 'Política Nacional', *España, Perspective 1973* (1973), 30.

[2] The incompatibility of *political* associations which would become parties and the Movement had been emphasized by Fernández Miranda in 1972. To say 'yes or no' to associations was to fall into what the Minister of the Movement mysteriously termed a 'Sadducean trap . . . the question is to see whether in saying yes or no to political association we also say yes, or no, or whether we do not say yes but no to political parties' (see 'El Ministro habla' in *Cuadernos para el diálogo*, March 1972).

soon place in its hands. They rejected a 'democracy with adjectives' granted piecemeal from above—the policy of the reformists—in the name of 'democracy without adjectives'. All opposition parties had adopted the Communist strategy: a modernized edition of a Popular Front running from Christian Democrats (Carrillo had explicitly rejected any return to the militant secularism of the Second Republic; from being the 'opium of the people' the Church had become 'the yeast of reform') to the non-revolutionary left. Remembering the Trojan Horse tactics of the thirties the democratic opposition could not accept the sincerity of Carrillo's Eurocommunist intentions and his acceptance of democratic pluralism. This was particularly true of the P.S.O.E., firmly in the hands of the 'interior' with the election of Felipe González as Secretary-General in 1974: Socialists were in competition with the Communists for the loyalty of the working class. Thus, although all opposition parties were committed to the *ruptura democratica*—a clean break with Francoism via a provisional government and a democratically elected Constituent Assembly—they formed two separate organizations. The Junta Democratica (July 1974) was regarded by the Socialists and Christian Democrats as a Communist concern; they therefore formed their own Platform of Democratic Convergence (July 1975).

Rebuffed by the reformists, rejected by the opposition, Arias in 1975 was struggling with the Vatican which rescued Bishop Añoveros of Bilbao from house arrest earned by his support of Basque nationalism; with a severe economic depression which threatened the prosperity on which the régime was based; with terrorism and strikes[1] which fuelled the hysteria of the extreme right. The repression the bunker demanded convinced the opposition that the régime could not grant even the most elementary of democratic freedoms. When Franco died on 20 November 1975 the alternatives were no longer—as when Carrero was assassinated—'immobilism' and the 'opening' of the reformists. The dilemma was now either reform or the breaking away (*ruptura*) of the opposition.

[1] 1974 saw the highest number of recorded strikes in Spanish history. Moreover, for the first time, these strikes and the ineptitudes of the government's economic policies in the face of inflation were fully reported in magazines like *Cambio 16* and *Actualidad económica*.

Reform from above could never satisfy the opposition. Yet the democratic break threatened incalculable political risks and the division of society between a new race of victors and vanquished. It was the political skills of President Suárez and the realism combined with the pressure of the opposition that substituted the 'negotiated break' for the perils of the 'democratic break'. Legitimized by the Caudillo's chosen heir—King Juan Carlos—democracy was peacefully and legally legislated into existence by the very institutions that were intended to perpetuate the political system that bore Franco's name.[1]

[1] This process is examined in detail in R. Carr and J. P. Fusi, *Spain: Dictatorship to Democracy* (1979), 207–52.

XX

FRANCOISM: FROM AUTARKY TO THE CONSUMER SOCIETY, 1939–1975

1. *The Rise and Fall of Autarky*

'In 1940', wrote París Eguilaz, one of the architects of the Nationalist war economy, 'the national income, at constant prices, had fallen back to that of 1914, but since the population had increased the per capita income fell to nineteenth-century levels; that is, the Civil War had provoked an unprecedented economic recession.'[1] From this poor economy Franco must find employment and, above all, food for the Spaniards he had, in his own terminology, 'liberated'.

The economy had not been destroyed—Republicans burnt churches, not factories; it was run down. Transport was, according to the American Ambassador, 'indescribably bad'—roads had degenerated, bridges been blown up, and half the rolling-stock of the railways lost.

Until the late 1950's Spain pursued reconstruction with the tools of a war economy based on Fascist models. These were the years of autarky: a self-sufficient, self-capitalizing economy, protected by tariffs created and regulated by state intervention, would embark on a massive programme of import substitution. 'Spain', as the Industrial Law of 1939 put it, 'must be redeemed from the importation of exotic products'; cut off from the outside world everything must be produced within Spain regardless of the cost.[2]

All the customary instruments of interventionism flourished in the forties: wages controlled by the Ministry of Labour; fixed multiple exchange rates; import quotas; government regulation of the setting-up of new industry. The penalties of exaggerated interventionism and direct, physical controls were bottle-necks

[1] *Evolución política y económica de España* (1969), 82.

[2] For a critical account of the economics of autarky see J. Clavera *et al.*, *Capitalismo español: de la autarquía a la estabilización* (1973), vol. i.

and corruption—for instance in the grant of import licences. The black market became a way of life, even a backhanded approach to the flexibility of the market.

In the forties self-sufficiency was not merely an ideological idiosyncrasy of the new state. In the post-war scarcities few European states could plunge into the risks and uncertainties of a market economy. What was unique about the Spanish economy was not that scarce supplies were rationed and prices controlled; it was the clumsiness of the apparatus that administered the controls and that *dirigisme* and autarky were seen, not as a temporary expedient, but as the proper and permanent policy for 'an imperial military state'. Thus autarky was not only a response to the post-war world of scarcities; it was also a philosophy of state, and its maintenance as a political economy that suited a totalitarian régime cut Spain off from the foreign loans it desperately needed to import the capital goods to re-equip its industry. Autarky was the reflection in economic policy of paranoia in politics; for Spain, surrounded by a conspiring hostile world, autarky was presented as a patriotic necessity.[1] It rested, too, on the belief that Spain was a country rich in mineral and other resources.[2] The consequences of this paranoia and pride were that throughout the forties Spain remained a poor economy in which there was neither production nor consumption. These were the 'years of hunger'. Franco made belt-tightening a proof of patriotism. 'We do not want an easy, comfortable life. . . . We want a hard life, the difficult life of a virile people.'[3]

Much of the early rhetoric of the régime was directed at the ennoblement of agriculture: this was partly because the problem of feeding Spaniards was paramount, partly because the régime regarded the peasant farmer as the true embodiment of the values of the Nationalist Crusade as against the urban worker corrupted by Marxism. Spain had gone through a process of reruralization (the percentage of the active population in agriculture had increased from 45 per cent in 1930 to 50 per cent by 1940) yet agriculture, starved of imported fertilizers, produced

[1] Cf. A. Viñas, op. cit., esp. 67–8. The American Ambassador rejected as 'plain misrepresentation of fact' the plea that Spain was *forced* to autarky, as were other nations after 1945.

[2] See p. 697.

[3] Speech of 18 July 1940.

less at higher costs—in 1950 wheat production, which occupied 40 per cent of all cultivated land, was still below the levels of the 1930's. The government's answer was regulation and guaranteed prices for wheat and marketing through the National Wheat Service. This benefited the large producer, kept agricultural prices well above industrial prices, fostered a flourishing black market, and failed to satisfy demand: Spain was only saved from starvation by massive imports and the 'gift' of Argentine wheat which converted Eva Perón into a national heroine. The situation was only remedied with the bumper wheat harvest of 1951. Agricultural stagnation which could provide no buoyant domestic market slowed industrial revival. 'A year of good harvests', ran the report of the Bank of Bilbao, 'is a year of prosperity for trade and industry.' This was the classic nineteenth-century pattern of underdevelopment.

The true locus of power in the forties was revealed by the régime's agrarian policy which put into reverse the distributive reforms of the Second Republic, substituting for them the colonizing schemes of the new, Italian-fashioned, Institute of National Colonization. Much publicized projects like the Badajoz Plan aimed to settle farmers on state-irrigated land; the plans benefited large landowners who got the lion's share rather than the needy settlers.[1] The one benefit that the small peasant gained was security of tenure at fixed rents; this was an aspect of Francoist policy at which large landowners never ceased to rail. Like security of employment in industry, it was the residual reflection of Falangist anti-capitalist rhetoric and the Catholic ideal of a just society.

While the immediate problem concerned food—bread above all—and while the rhetoric and the pricing policies of the régime seemed to favour agricultural interests, its basic aim was rapid, state-induced industrialization within the confines of autarky. Foreign investment was hamstrung while native entrepreneurs were granted minimum returns on new investments, their objectives closely controlled by government regulations for the establishment of new industries. The govern-

[1] In all, settlers constituted 0·56 per cent of the agricultural active population. They were responsible for the purchase on the instalment system of their mini-holdings. Pascual Carrion calculates that 80 per cent of the new irrigated land went to large proprietors in Seville, cf. his 'Transformación de las tierras de secano en regadío' in *Anales de economía*, December 1971, 30 ff.

ment holding company I.N.I. (Institute of National Industry), set up in 1941 under Franco's friend Admiral Suances on the model of the Italian I.R.I., was, by 'the creation of new industries and the multiplication of those that exist', to 'supply the new racial values with the indispensable support of a potent industry. This renaissance must be given an accelerated impetus if we are to realize the programmes that our historical destiny demands.' I.N.I. would supply the investment in basic industries (steel, energy, cars), supplementing and in some cases replacing private investment.[1]

The forties and the early fifties were years of intense suffering for the majority of the Spanish people: the 'long winter' of food queues, of patched-up clothes, of fountain pens bought on the instalment system, of reconditioned tooth-brushes.[2] Inadequate diet made tuberculosis a scourge; poverty turned prostitution into a respectable profession; in an attempt to discourage the horde of beggars the police fined those who *gave* alms. Even rural Spain, where conditions were better than in the towns, suffered terribly. 'The people ate anything they could find: thistles and weeds. . . . Our skin burst open with ulcers from not having enough to eat, from not washing. There wasn't any soap. . . . When they saw me giving the food to my dogs they began to cry. . . . A lot of others died like that, not directly of starvation but from eating only cabbage leaves and things.'[3] Political repression, combined with the apathy induced by a struggle to survive, left no time for protest. Ferocious legislation failed to eradicate a black market which embraced the total population but which enriched only the fortunate few.

It was the forced saving inflicted on the great mass of Spaniards, an inflation fuelled by a policy of cheap money,[4] that produced the beginnings of an industrial revival: between 1950 and 1957 industrial production almost doubled and the primacy of agriculture in the economy was broken as its contribution to the national income sank from 40 per cent in 1951 to 25 per cent in 1957; the national income itself was growing at a

[1] For a critical account of I.N.I's activities see J. Ma. López de Letona *et al.*, *La empresa pública industrial en España* (1973).

[2] For a vivid account see R. Abella, op. cit., esp. 90, 110. Some idea of the results of nutritional deficiencies can be gleaned from the issues of the *Revista de sanidad*.

[3] R. Fraser, *The Pueblo* (1973), 77, 83, and *passim*.

[4] The banks could literally coin money by rediscounting government loans.

rate of 6 per cent a year. Bread rationing ended in 1952. By 1954 the per capita income had at last climbed back to the levels of 1936.

As industry grew, so did its demand for capital goods and raw materials from abroad which could not be paid for by traditional agricultural exports or high-cost industrial exports. Spain's balance of payments steadily worsened. The situation had been eased for a time by the American loans that came with the 1953 agreement.[1] They came, in Sardá's words, like water in a desert; but by 1957 Spain was on the verge of bankruptcy and increasingly incapable of financing imports. Inflation was running at over 15 per cent worsened by a 30 per cent wage hike in 1956 pushed through by the Falangist minister Velasco de Girón. This was a response to working-class protest in Barcelona and in the Basque Provinces against one of the consequences of autarky: uncontrolled inflation combined with controlled wages.

2. *Neo-Capitalism*

By the late fifties the economy of autarky was in crisis: import substitution, as it always does, ran out of steam; the new industries demanded imports of capital goods which could not be purchased by the exports of a high-cost protected economy. Further growth was strangled. 'A moment arrived in which the desire for industrialization must be reconciled with the conditions industrialization demanded.' Autarky ceased to be a stimulus; it became a strait-jacket. The régime had only two choices. Either it had to turn in on itself and meet a drastic fall in living standards by a tightening of political control, or it had to abandon its 'fear of the market' and risk opening the economy to the outside world.

Although in the early fifties Aburúa, as Minister of Commerce, had made timid approaches to a market economy favoured by the most important industrial banks, it was the ministerial reshuffle of February 1957 that opened up the way to the second option—the 'liberalization' of the economy: the abandonment of the armoury of physical controls; the reliance on a more orthodox, tight monetary policy to meet inflation; and the adoption of a uniform rate of exchange to replace the

[1] See p. 715.

multiple discriminatory rates. In short, the abandonment of 'the fear of the market' and a reliance on prices, rather than on the state, to determine the allocation of scarce resources.

The apostles of the new style were Navarro Rubio at the Ministry of Finance and Ullastres as Minister of Commerce. They had to fight a rearguard action against the architects of autarky embedded in I.N.I. and the Ministry of Industry to whom a market economy risked, not only their own political careers, but also the whole social philosophy of the régime. It was the neo-capitalist liberalizers who were old-fashioned; and not only old-fashioned, but also indifferent to the sufferings that unrestrained capitalism inflicted on the less fortunate. In 1957 I.N.I. began its retrospective report with the words, 'The old theses of economic liberalism, of the pursuit of personal gain and economic dominance, of *tecnicismo* (a hit at the technocrats of Opus Dei) have been superseded by new and more generous ideals.'[1]

The liberalizers must convince Franco: the 'green light' from the Pardo was still the necessary condition for any change in policy.

Why did they succeed? Partly because something had to be done. Foreign exchange was rapidly running out; inflation had set off a wave of strikes, which, though attributed to 'Communism', were clearly the response of the working class to a sharp fall in real wages. The press did not conceal the effects of inflation from the public, though their remedy was still the old remedy of physical controls directed at the suppression of 'greed' and 'speculation'.

Undoubtedly the liberalizers[2] were influenced by a strange sea change in public opinion. The setting-up of the Common Market, the convertibility of European currencies, engendered an almost pathological fear of being left out of the new European economy. *Arriba*, hardly a mouthpiece of unrestrained capitalism, believed Spain must enter the new Europe or face collapse (22 January 1959). Navarro took the unprecedented step of consulting opinion by a questionnaire that set out the options: a

[1] Quoted in J. M. González, *La economía política del Franquismo* (1979), 31.

[2] They included economists like Sardá and Fuentes Quintana at the Bank of Spain who used *Información comercial* for the propagation of faith in private enterprise and a market economy.

liberal trade policy; the necessity of a painful process of stabilization (i.e. the driving down of inflation by a monetary policy) if the convertibility needed to bring Spain into line with Europe was to be a possibility. All the bodies consulted (with the notable and expected dissent of I.N.I.) accepted the principle that underlay Navarro's new policy: stable internal prices and a stable exchange rate were inseparable and what he himself confessed would be a 'bitter' remedy in the short run was inescapable.[1] Even the Sindicatos, which might have been expected to resist, counselled *immediate* entry into Europe and were prepared to pay the costs. As Navarro pointed out to his fellow ministers in his memorandum of January 1959, if something was not done to satisfy this generalized desire to escape *atraso*, the gap between Spain and Europe, then the political consequences would be dangerous: Spaniards would feel they languished in 'a prison subject to a series of controls which only exist on the other side of the Iron Curtain'.[2] This was a strong argument with the Caudillo. He did not like the taste of the new medicine; but he said, 'Que se haga' ('Let it be done').

There can be little doubt that the main propellants towards a new economic policy were the international agencies that must supply the loans to make stabilization work. In the two years before full implementation of the Stabilization Plan of 1959 much had been accomplished in the way of restoring monetary sanity and balancing the budget. As a result of meeting with the I.M.F. and the O.E.C.D. the final letter to those bodies made clear the liberalizers' acceptance of the agencies' criticism of the constrictions of the old system of splendid isolation. 'The government believes that the moment has arrived to adjust the political economy in order to place the Spanish economy on the same guide-lines as those of the countries of the Western world and to free it from interventions, inherited from the past, which are not adjusted to the present situation.' And what was the heritage of the past? The ideal set out in the Ley de Ordenación y Defensa de la Industria Nacional of November 1939: 'The creation of a great and prosperous Spanish economy, free from foreign dependence.'

[1] For Navarro's questionnaire see C. W. Anderson, *The Political Economy of Modern Spain* (1970).

[2] J. M. González, op. cit. 180 ff.

Once the green light from the Pardo was given, the recipes of orthodox Western capitalism were applied: a short, sharp deflation that would clear the decks for growth and integration into international capitalism; control of the money supply, cutting back on public expenditure, a realistic rate of exchange, a wage freeze, a partial liberation of foreign trade. Above all, the opening-up of Spain to foreign investment.

The results were as painful as Ullastres had predicted: a dramatic intensification of a recession that had begun in 1958 reflected in a sharp drop in investment, massive lay-offs, and unemployment.

But the medicine worked—even if the dose advised by the foreign advisers was stronger than the Spanish liberalizers could stomach. By 1961 recovery set in and Spain was to enter on a period of rapid growth: the 'miracle' of the sixties that was to continue unabated until 1966. When the S.E.A.T. factory was opened in 1952 its managers were concerned that the market might not absorb a hundred cars a month; by the 1970's the car industry was producing every year nearly a million cars for a car-hungry society. Industrial exports overtook agricultural products as the main earner of foreign exchange. The income of every employed Spaniard increased threefold between 1960 and 1972.

Governments claimed that these achievements were the consequence of the new policies and the technocrats' Development Plans from 1964 on, made possible only by the administrative reforms of López Rodó that aimed to turn an incoherent bureaucracy into an instrument for global planning. As with the French indicative planning (from which even the terminology of Spanish economists was derived), the Plans acted mainly as 'reducers of uncertainty'. This encouraged private foreign investment: standing at $100 million in 1960, by 1973 nearly $5,980 million were invested in Spain.

Even more important in fuelling the economy by supplying the foreign exchange for the inputs of the industrial take-off were tourist revenues and the remittances of emigrants. The first was the return on the natural capital of sun and beaches; by 1972 the million tourists had become an annual invasion of 34 million. The second was an indication of the failure of the new economy to absorb the rural poor into industry: by 1968 over a million Spaniards were working in the factories and farms of France, Germany, Switzerland, and Belgium.

These developments meant that the Spain of autarky and ration books had become a *relatively* affluent consumer society, a capitalist market economy—disfigured, it is true, by the entrenched remnants of the old apparatus of regulation of the forties—dependent for its continued health on the international economy of which it had become a part. To the Marxist Tamames, Spain was at the mercy of a financial and industrial oligarchy, allied with foreign capital, a 'neo autarky' in which the levers of state intervention were at the disposal of the interests of the strong.[1] To the resolute defenders of the free market this economy was a thing of bits and pieces held together by the 'sticking plaster' applied by paternalist bureaucracy.[2] The heady dose of liberalization of 1959–60 did not conquer the inertia of the system and its entrenched interests. Governments, by the 'privileged circuits' of preferential interest rates and the processes of *acción concertada*,[3] steered the flow of savings towards investment in favoured concerns.

The statistical triumphalism of what Franco himself called 'the new era' could not hide two failures. While real wages rose, income was not redistributed; the age-old gap between the 'two Spains', between the stagnant interior rural provinces and the industrialized regions of the north-eastern triangle and the prosperous Basque, Levante, and Catalan periphery widened. By 1970, 70 per cent of Madrid homes possessed a television set; only 11 per cent in the province of Soria. Ullastres was an unrepentant believer in unbalanced growth untroubled by regional imbalances which gave prosperous regions three times the disposable income of the poorer provinces;[4] 'progressive

[1] See his classic exposition in R. Tamames, *Los monopolios en España*. It is significant of the degree of overt criticism of the *economic* policies of Francoism that this book was published in 1967.

[2] See the *Informe económico* of the Banco de Bilbao for 1976, p. 237.

[3] *Acción concertada* was the supply of public funds to certain industries which modernized according to the 'indications' of the Development Plans. A particularly strong case of government control of investment was the channelling of the funds of the Savings Bank—whose increased reserves were nevertheless a sign of a new and generalized well-being—towards selected private firms.

[4] See the detailed figures of disposable family income in *Encuesta de equipamiento y nivel cultural de las familias* published by the *Presidencia del Gobierno* in 1975. The neglect of regional planning until the seventies and the concentration on aggregate growth is

priests' who criticized the sufferings of the working classes during deflation and the wage freeze of the Stabilization Plan did not understand the workings of the economy, advocating charity for the workers instead of trusting the well-being of the workers to the growth of the G.N.P. Excessive wage claims, Ullastres insisted, were the secret weapon of Communism to destroy the economies of the West by inflation.

The Church did not abandon its criticism or its concern for the workers. 'The only thing that has not developed as might have been hoped', observed Cardinal Herrera in 1968, 'is social justice.' Cardinal Pla y Deniel, politically a hard-liner, defended H.O.A.C. against the Falangist monopoly of labour. Its manifesto in 1961 was a frontal attack on the Stabilization Plan. As for the opposition, since criticism of the economic performance of governments was tolerated while attacks on the political system were suppressed, it concentrated its attacks on a regressive tax structure and the failure to provide adequate working-class housing or social services.[1]

The economy of neo-capitalism could thus be presented by the opposition as the preserve of an oligarchy. The private banks were the most conspicuous feature of the economic landscape. Where the stock exchange was weak they played a major role in the financing of industry, their directors sitting on the boards of the companies they supported; their connexions with government created a parallel network.[2] It has been argued that there was an increasing process of 'privatization' of the public sector. I.N.I. became, in López Rodó's scheme, a subsidiary (and subsidizer) of private enterprise; it financed lame ducks and lost control of its proudest creation—the car firm S.E.A.T. The processes of concentration, the increasing pre-

discussed in H. W. Richardson, *Regional Development Policy and Planning in Spain* (1975). Not least of the difficulties was the fear that the creation of rational planning units out of fifty provinces would encourage regionalist demands in Galicia, Catalonia, and the Basque Provinces. When the planners perceived that the 'spill over' effects of investment did not reach the poorer regions, the Third Plan set up Territorial planning Commissions. These Richardson regards as 'a typical method of developing pseudo-democratic institutions in an authoritarian society' (90).

[1] For a catalogue of these failures see Salustiano del Campo and M. Navarro, *Crítica de la planificación española 1964–1975* (1976).

[2] The construction of diagrams illustrating the interconnections between boards of directors was a favourite occupation of left-wing economists, e.g. S. Roldan and others. *¿Qué es el capitalismo español?* (1977), 39.

ponderance of capital-intensive industry, the connexions between the public and private sectors, the increasing penetration of multinational companies, were common features of Western capitalism; Spain was different only in that they were attributed to the peculiar nature of the political system.[1]

While the share of wages in the national income approached European levels,[2] while the worker in the industrial regions (and there alone as the agricultural worker enjoyed only 40 per cent of the average wage) could buy a wide range of the consumer goods provided by the new industries,[3] the main weakness of the political economy of Francoism was its incapacity to expand the tax basis on which the revenues of the state depended. This was again the consequence of a political structure that was closely integrated with the business world and dependent on middle-class support. Franco himself consistently resisted a tax reform that would penalize the higher income groups. The Spanish system was the most socially unjust in Europe; it was regressive with 65 per cent of total revenue coming from indirect taxes which lay heavy on the poorer classes. It was not only that it was socially unjust. The Spanish state, as in the nineteenth century, was poor.

This meant that governments were condemned to what is called 'revenue budgeting', characteristic of 'poor' American cities:[4] all expenditure had to be fitted into a tax base that expanded only with the growth of the economy. This was made worse by tax evasion which a Minister of Finance recognized as a 'generally and commonly accepted phenomenon of colossal proportions'. With over-all expenditure limited, only priorities could change—education for instance won over military expenditure.[5] The social services with which the Falange hoped to

[1] For a Socialist criticism of the role of multinational companies see F. Maravall, *Crecimiento, dimensión y concentración de las empresas industriales españolas* (1976), 64 ff.

[2] This is a controversial and complicated issue. For a critical view see J. Alcarde, 'Así se distribuye la riqueza y la renta en la sociedad española', *Revista sindical de estadística* (1974).

[3] When a worker's wife was asked what the Victoria strike of 1977 implied she replied, 'I have had to give up using sprays and detergents and have had to go back to soap and water.' This was the reply of a working-class wife in a consumer society of relative abundance.

[4] Richard Gunther, op. cit. 51.

[5] In 1953, 30·4 per cent of the total budget was allotted to military expenditure; by 1975 this had sunk to 13·8 per cent. The share of education had risen in the same period

win the loyalty of the working class were starved. Ministers, therefore, were engaged in a continuous battle for their share in a slowly expanding revenue, a battle in which the Minister of Finance became the ultimate arbiter. Those, like López Ródo, with a private line to Carrerro Blanco or the Caudillo won out.

3. *The Rural Exodus*

Rural Spain remained the poor relation of the new industrial Spain. The sixties saw the mass exodus from the impoverished countryside with its high birth-rate to the cities of Spain and the factories of Europe. In the seventies there was talk of the 'crisis of traditional agriculture'. Rural Spain, once considered 'the moral reserve of the nation', had become the Cinderella of an economy whose course was set on rapid industrial growth.

Without a vast transfer of human resources from the countryside to the cities—mainly to the old industrialized areas of Catalonia and the Basque Provinces—there could have been no industrial take-off.[1] By 1970 over a million Andalusians were living outside their native provinces, 712,000 in Barcelona alone. Madrid drained the surrounding regions, the metropolis of a deserted Castile. Emigration abroad was the response to the sharp and cruel recession of 1959; without that safety-valve there would have been massive unemployment.

In the 1950's emigration was an escape from unendurable poverty; in the sixties it became a search for social mobility.[2] The migrants at first settled in shanty towns; by the seventies in

from 8·2 per cent to 17·8 per cent. Even so, Spain's expenditure on education as a proportion of the national income was the lowest in Europe; and by 1973 only Luxemburg spent less on its military than Spain (U.K. 4.4 per cent of G.N.P.; Spain, 1.5 per cent).

[1] The concentration of population in pre-existing industrialized centres and the consequent increase in regional imbalances is characteristic of all industrializing countries. Increase in the per capita income of the poorer provinces reflected, not a levelling-off of living standards, but emigration which left a smaller population. The first economist to stress the concentration in industrialized 'core' areas was Román Perpiná (see his 'La problemática de la delimitación espacial a regional' in *Boletin de estudios económicos*, no. 83 (1971), 675 ff.). For population in general see J. Díez Nicolás, 'Tamaño, densidad y crecimiento de la población española', in *Revista internacional de la sociología*, no. 109 (1970), 87–123.

[2] Whereas internal migrants settled in the cities, those who migrate abroad often return to set up small businesses (e.g. as haulage contractors) or buy land (often only to fail once more). Some Galician old-time foreign emigrants have become prosperous; they return for the summer holidays to their native Galicia in smart cars.

the housing estates that revolutionized the urban landscape just as the modern houses built by returning emigrants have disfigured the countryside of Galicia. The process of reruralization of the immediate post-war years was reversed: the rural exodus left villages and small towns inhabited by the old and the children; their desolation was a favourite theme of the Castilian novelist Miguel Delibes. Agriculture as a way of life lost its attractions compared with the '*animación*' and opportunities of the cities. Sons deserted Basque homesteads, classic strongholds of peasant values, for the factories of Bilbao.[1] 'Nostalgia for country life', writes Amando de Miguel, 'is completely utopian.' Tastes and values are increasingly becoming those of the urban society.[2] In the rural townships Catalonian farmers adopted the 'bar culture' of the cities.[3]

At first the government had tried to stop the flow to the cities and abroad. Arrese in 1955 regarded 'every house built in the city' as 'a new temptation to the peasant', a drain on the 'moral reserve of the nation'. By the sixties the government bowed to the necessities of industrialization and rather than staunch the flow abroad set up government agencies to assist it. This was one of the most dramatic changes in the official vision of an ideal Spanish society.

The absorption of these quasi-literate village immigrants, arriving with wooden cases from crowded trains, put a severe strain on the social services and urban infrastructure of the cities of Barcelona, Madrid, Valencia, Bilbao, Seville, and Saragossa. In Catalonia the cultural absorption of non-Catalan-speaking immigrants posed a peculiar problem. At first they were cold-shouldered and complained of the Catalan 'racism' which kept them in low-paid jobs.[4] 'What I want', is the anguished cry of the 'Murcian' anti-hero of Marsé's novel on the life of an immigrant suburb, 'is that people should respect me.' He is treated as an illiterate delinquent by his

[1] For the effects of industrialization on the *caserio* see Miren Etxezarreta in R. Aracil and M. García Bonafé, *Lecturas de historia económica*, vol. ii, 357–79.

[2] Amando de Miguel, *Manual de estructura social de España* (1974), 102.

[3] For 'bar culture' see E. C. Hansen, *Rural Catalonia under the Franco Regime* (1977), 119. Its emergence is connected with the repression of the older associations and the social contacts necessitated by agricultural modernization (meeting salesmen representatives, government agents, etc.).

[4] For a vivid description of conditions and life in an immigrant suburb see F. Candel,

fiancée's upper-class Catalan mother. At first alarmed at the swamping of Catalan culture by *Xarnegros*, Catalan nationalists saw that only a patient policy of education could absorb and convert this foreign element.

The flight from the countryside was encouraged by the changing patterns of farming. Governments did not attack the great latifundia; but they did, by a policy of *concentración parcelaria*, mitigate the evils of farms split into minute fields by concentrating these plots in more rational units. But concentration tended to benefit the more substantial owners, leaving a rural proletariat of owners of a hectare or so for whom emigration was the only escape from unremitting and unrewarding toil.

Economic development created a race of kulaks and a proletariat of subsistence farmers. It was only the more substantial peasant who could modernize. The most obvious index of investment is the number of tractors: these increased by a factor of forty between 1960 and 1970. Mechanization transformed labour relations on the great latifundia: the gangs of day-labourers (*braceros*) hired in the local town plaza have been replaced by combine harvesters; modernization has thrown up a race of farm-managers. The rich *campiña* of Cordoba has been revolutionized by artificial fertilizers, mechanization, and market crops which require less labour.[1] Increasingly the *latifundista* saw himself, not as an absentee *rentier*, but as a modernizing, cost-benefit-conscious entrepreneur. Modernization and mechanization added to the pool of emigrant labour.[2]

Andalusia remained a depressed area where the highest rate of unemployment in the country was later to provide the social ground swell for a 'nationalist' movement, just as the plight of the Galician subsistence farmer would be the rallying-cry of Galician nationalism. The arid east, where a couple of bad years meant bankruptcy for the small peasant, supplied its quota of servants in the tourist hotels of the coast and labourers

Los otros catalanes (1964). Marsé's novel, published in 1966, is *Ultimas tardes con Teresa*.

[1] R. Tamames, *introducción a la economía espaõla* (1973), 84. For the effects of concentration in one pueblo see V. Pérez Díaz, *Pueblos y clases sociales en el campo español* (1974), 58–125.

[2] The early stages of these developments are described in J. Martínez Alier, *La estabilidad del latifundio en España* (1968). For the reluctance of landowners to rent out land at greater profit than they could make by direct cultivation lest they should lose their legitimization as 'useful' producers see 336 ff. For the transformations in the

in the French vineyards.[1] Even so Andalusia is a changing society. As elsewhere in rural Spain, the strict social control of the face-to-face society is vanishing; the Andalusian labourer is no longer a pariah in the society of grinding poverty and deference that was the basis of the power of the electoral managers—the *caciques* of the old parliamentary system. He no longer dreams of invading estates. He joins a trade union.[2]

Whole areas of Spain were untouched by the modernization of agriculture: eastern Andalusia, much of Galicia where tourists came to inspect a primitive society, whole areas of the Castilian heartland. The government had won the 'battle for wheat' of the forties; but the 'traditional' agriculture could not respond to the demands of changed dietary habits in the cities.[1] Overproduction of protected traditional crops generated surpluses; by the spring of 1977 Spanish farmers were imitating their French colleagues and bringing traffic to a halt by parades of tractors. Their demand was guaranteed prices—the very mechanism that had sustained the great Mediterranean monocultures. Farmers complained they had lost out to industrialists and urban workers. 'The massive protest of the farmers', commented the Banco de Bilbao's report for 1976, 'is more justified than that of any other sector of society.' In the early years of Francoism interest rates and the relative prices of agricultural and industrial goods favoured farmers; it was the transfer of their savings to industry that had helped to finance the modest beginnings of an industrialized economy.[2]

It was not only agriculture that was in trouble. The last two years of Francoism corresponded with the world recession, with its repercussions in Spain, now an industrialized society, linked to the international economy. Spain's energy imports constitute the highest proportion of export earnings in the world; workers returned to Spain from the contracting economies of Western Europe. 1975 was the worst year since 1959; growth, for the first

campiña see A. López Ontiveros, *Emigración propriedad y paisaje agrario en la campiña de Cordoba* (1974).

[1] For conditions in eastern Andalusia see M. Siguán, *El medio rural en Andalucía oriental* (1972) and the *Estudio socio-económico de Andalucía* published by Estudios de desarollo económico (1970), 195–224.

[2] These were not allowed under Francoism.

[3] This was especially true of meat. Between 1940 and 1980 consumption per capita increased by 30 ×, production 10 ×.

time, became negative. For the entrepreneur the golden age had become an age of iron; profits fell from 9·5 per cent of the national income to 5·8 per cent. With declining profits and the political uncertainties of a régime in crisis, investment languished. The middle-class investors who had rushed into the market in 1970 lost all their gains. To make up the deficit the government, as elsewhere in Europe, pumped money into lame ducks—steel and shipbuilding. The planners lapsed into stop–go policies.[1] The fall in investment the Bank of Bilbao attributed to 'a profound transformation': a sharp rise in wages that ate into profit margins. This revealed a new balance in Spanish society.

[4] For a detailed examination of the contribution of the agricultural sector to industrial development see J. L. Leal *et al.*, *La agricultura en el desarollo capitalista español* (1975).

[1] *Objectivos e instrumentos de la política económica de España* (Servicio de estudios, Banco Urquijo, 1973), 121–36.

XXI

SOCIETY, 1939–1975

1. *Conformity to Conflict*

In 1975 Madrid and Bilbao had the highest levels of atmospheric pollution of any European city. This was a measure of the rapid industrialization and urbanization of the sixties. From an agrarian society with an industrial appendage Spain had become an industrial society with an agrarian appendage. In other Western societies such a dramatic shift had taken place gradually over a long period: in Spain the final stage of the 'industrial revolution', cut short by the Civil War, and the advent of the consumer society took place in a country still—officially—committed to traditional Catholic values.[1] Hence the conflicts produced by what students of developing economies call 'superficial modernization'.

These changes were to modify the nature of the Francoist establishment. In its early stages—Falangists apart—it seemed as if the amalgam of landed proprietors and entrepreneurs, formed in the nineteenth century and threatened by the 'creeping socialism' of the Second Republic, had been restored to power: its more prominent members were Franco's chosen shooting-companions.[2] Like many modern dictators the Caudillo was given to admiration for technocrats and engineers—'doers' as opposed to 'thinkers'—and outbursts against the 'frivolous' aristocrats who were the courtiers of Don Juan. But the paraphernalia of his own rival, stuffy court sustained aristocratic values. The note of vulgarity in the new Spain was struck by the *nouveaux riches* of the Civil War and the black marketeers of the hungry forties.

Just as the success of industrialization doomed autarky, so it

[1] For the failure of an industrial revolution in Spain see J. Nadal, *El fracaso de la Revolución industrial en España, 1814–1913* (1975). I do not mean to deny that the forced industrialization of the forties laid the foundations for the breakthrough of the sixties or that the process of Spain 'catching up' from a low level was inevitable.

[2] L. Alonso Tejada, 'Las cacerías del franquismo', *Historia 16*, no. 37, 19–30.

modified the comfortable world of influence where 'everything in Spain . . . was obtained because you have a friend'.[1] The new slogans of the sixties were those of the impersonal, competitive world of the business corporations: efficiency, rationality. Emilio Romero complained, 'Dogma has gone out of the window. Now we have the solvers (*solucionadores*), the boys who have been to the university, especially in the Faculty of Economics'. If Falangist attacks on the rich became unfashionable, the change was not dramatic: the aim of Ullastres and López Rodó was to foster a new symbiosis between Catholic values, an authoritarian political system, and the American way of life.[2] Bureaucratization and rationalization did not so much change the essential composition of what the opposition called the 'oligarchy'; it merely absorbed new talent and became a managerial class.[3]

It was the expansion of the white-collar service sector that came with industrial expansion (as distinct from the inflated service sector characteristic of underdeveloped economies) that provided the recruits for what was called 'the new middle class'. There can be little doubt that its upper ranges were conformist, grateful for the limited social mobility and respectability provided by the 'peace of Franco'. The lower ranges underwent a gradual process of radicalization which would later enlarge the Socialist party. Bank clerks 'struck' by arriving at work unshaven and without ties and opening accounts of five pesetas.[4] Civil Servants once assured of a recognized place in 'decent' society—*decente* is a key word in middle-class vocabulary—saw their incomes and status eroded and sought to organize unions, opposed by the upper middle class and privileged members of the *cuerpos*. This presented a double threat from those supposed to be the docile executants of policies: not merely were civil servants 5 per cent of the active population; they also came from those middle classes which constituted the basic support of the

[1] Dionisio Ridruejo, *Escrito en España* (1962), 134.

[2] Carlos Moya, *El poder económico en España* (1975), 189 ff. Cf. the preamble to the Third Development Plan: 'The policy of development combines tradition and modernization at the same time.' L. López Rodó, *Política y desarollo* (1976), 59.

[3] The new entrepreneurs are analysed in A. de Miguel and Juan Linz, *Los empresarios ante el poder público* (1966).

[4] For the *cuerpos* see p. 708. For bank employees see J. F. Tezanos, *Estructura de clases en la España actual* (1975), 75 ff.

régime. To successive governments 'reform' meant efficiency and modernization, rather than negotiations and consultation. The civil service was a 'family', better off, Admiral Carrero Blanco told them, under a stable régime than in a democracy of 'fleeting collections of politicans' ready to interfere with promotion to reward party hacks.[1]

Bank clerks and civil servants were not resolute radicals; many of them were conformist, muddled victims of what sociologists call 'status inconsistency'. Bank clerks favoured 'socialism' and the nationalization of private banks; almost all supported compulsory religious education and only a minority favoured birth control. Yet since Spain's birth-rate was reaching European levels and was lowest of all in the middle classes, they must have practised in private what they condemned in public. This reveals, at the most intimate level of private life, the contradictions that were developing between private mores and the official ideology and it was typical of the processes of change and resistance to change that characterized latter-day Francoism among the Spanish urban middle class.

This was evident in the changing status of women. An expanding service sector gave new opportunities as accountants, typists—it is significant that the traditional occupation for women, domestic service, was contracting. While women's work outside the home—especially for married women—was still regarded as unnatural and while the proportion of women in the active work-force remained low, it was increased by a slow and silent revolution. Values were in conflict with the necessities and opportunities of economic life: even in villages where women's work outside the home is regarded as 'ugly' it is now a common practice.[2] The emancipation of women, increasingly equipped with a university education, was resisted by the Church while the Falange, which had mobilized women for welfare work in the war, trained them for their task as housewives (*amas de casa*) after it. 'In matters of morals', maintained José Antonio's sister, 'the Women's Sector [of the Falange Movement] has always upheld the position of the Church.[3] But

[1] For the attempts to unionize the civil service see the account by one of its organizers. Ciriaco de Vicente, *La lucha de los funcionarios públicos* (1977), 185 ff.

[2] M. García Ferrando, *Mujer y sociedad rural* (1977), 184 ff.

[3] *El País semanal*, 21 August 1977.

the Catholic view that woman's place is in the home, still preached in the seventies, could not be maintained in an industrialized, increasingly secularized society.[1]

These contradictions were a phenomenon of urban middle-class life; the old family patterns were maintained in the countryside by the upper classes and the rural petty bourgeoisie of small farmers. They alone continued to give some substance to the government's policy to encourage 'numerous families'—the 'Spain of 40 millions'. Yet even in rural Spain the birth-rate is declining. There is both knowledge of contraceptive methods and disapproval of their use. Practice and principle are once again at odds; rural Spain is accepting the values of urban Spain.[2]

With the decline of the agricultural sector the urban working class became the largest and potentially the most powerful class in Spain. But it was no longer the manual working class, isolated by dress and behaviour patterns: half the working class was composed of skilled and service-sector employees who increasingly enjoyed a lower middle-class standard of living even though they had to work longer and harder than their European equivalents to attain it; this 'working class in ties' falsified the Marxist prediction that industrialization would produce a homogeneous, class-conscious proletariat.

In the forties the workers were cowed. Political persecution apart, their life was an agonizing struggle to keep a job and feed a family. It was best to keep one's head down and run no risk of being sacked as a 'red' by making trouble over pay.[3] With the nascent consumer society of the early sixties it is scarcely surprising that workers thought of individual satisfactions—the TV set, education 'out of the working class' for children—rather than of collective action; only in those areas with a long tradition of unionization were there strikes. The Official Syndicates and the Labour Courts settled *individual* grievances.

With the legalization of collective bargaining which em-

[1] Cf. A. Ferrandiz and Vicente Verdu, *Noviazgo y matrimonio en la burguesía española* (1974), 131 ff. The authors also see genuine relationships between men and women as being impossible in bourgeois society because they have no 'market value'. Marxist critics attacked both the traditional and the new society.

[2] See Salustiano del Campo, *Análisis de la población de España* (1972), 81. M. García Fernandez (op. cit. 102) argues that there is no separate rural subculture where contraception is concerned.

[3] Some of the most illuminating, if amateur, studies of working-class attitudes are the works of F. Candel, *Ser Obrero es ninguna ganga* (1968) and *Los que nunca opinan* (1971).

braced an ever increasing number of workers, individual benefit was seen as a consequence of collective action. Changes in electoral procedures of the official bureaucratized syndicates opened up possibilities for the Communist policy of 'entrism'[1]: the election of factory committees and shop stewards became a meaningful activity. Solís hoped to revivify official syndicalism with a genuine working-class representation: 'Workers, your voice will be heard.'

When that voice was heard in the elections of 1975 it sounded the death-knell of official syndicalism. The prosecution of the Workers Commission in 1968 failed to stop the triumph of 'democratic' unionism; this 'democratic occupation of the unions', with the election of 'authentic' representatives responsible to the workers in their assemblies, was hailed by militants as a new dawn. To outraged syndicalist bureaucrats it was 'the officialization of reds'.

This did not mean—outside big concerns like S.E.A.T.—the emergence of working-class consciousness as the Marxists, obsessed with the dangers of *embourgeoisement* and the integration of the worker into a more resilient neo-capitalist society, defined it.[2] Face-to-face relationships persisted in a host of small concerns. There was a lumpenproletariat of marginal men, moving in and out of jobs and over half a million living on minimum legal wages that could not support a family. It was the new working class that supported the Workers Commissions. Even so strikes remained 'economic', a demand for a larger slice of what governments insisted was a growing cake, though solidarity strikes in support of dismissed elected officials increased. But there was a new militancy—especially in the younger workers who had not experienced the traumas of 1940 and 1959–60. In 1966 a C.N.T. veteran of the great pre-war struggles told his son, 'Don't think of those things. The first thing is to study. To get mixed up in political struggles could cost you your career.' By 1975 the son might tell his father it was time that he did get mixed up in political squabbles.[3]

[1] See p. 727.

[2] The problem of class-consciousness is discussed in A. C. Comin and J. N. García Nieto's study of a working-class suburb in Barcelona. *Juventud obrera y conciencia de clase* (1974).

[3] In spite of increasing labour militancy the working class did not radicalize its social habits. The workers were conservative in regard to the position of women. Their children—particularly those from rural backgrounds—did not join the ranks of student radicals.

'Spain is different' had been the slogan by which the government encouraged tourists. In 1975 it was no longer different; it was a Western European industrialized society. An environmentalist movement began its protests against the unacceptable faces of industrialism; motorways were the symbol of an attempt to 'Japanize' Spain, a ritual sacrifice 'to an economic and social philosophy that opts for the car as the symbol of Western industrial society'.[1] Once the growing pains of the Stabilization Plan of 1959 had passed, large sectors of the population enjoyed living standards inconceivable in the earlier years. Crowded beaches were not merely a result of the tourist invasion; they were, as Semprun noted in 1975, the 'unmistakable sign of the massive spread of economic well-being'.[2] Those who enjoyed the well-being Franco called the 'buenos', those who had benefited from 'the peace of Franco'.

If the coming of affluence, after the privations of the forties, induced what Aranguren denounced as 'apolitical consumerism'[3] and Emilio Romero could remind the opposition that the *ultimata ratio* of the 'present system' was the refusal of the Spaniards to sacrifice social peace and its material consequences, nevertheless a fissure was developing between Spanish society and the mentality that its governments continued to represent. López Rodó believed that prosperity would bring political peace, a crude calculation erected into a political philosophy by Fernández de la Mora: political apathy, he had written in the fifties, was the sign of a healthy society; by 1974 he defended the régime as the creator of an industrial society, a 'promising political instrument' which only madmen could reject.[4]

That the majority of Spaniards refrained from political

[1] These protests were derived from U.S. radicals: Baran, Sweezey, Nader, etc. For a general assault see *Triunfo* (22 December 1973). For motorways see M. Gaviria, *La autopista como ideología* (1973) and his *Libro negro sobre la autopista de la Costa Blanca* (1973). Gaviria also protested—as all must, though not for his reasons—against the rape of the Mediterranean coast, what he calls 'the colonial exploitation of beaches'. See his *Ecologismo y odenación del territorio en España* (1976). He proposed the nationalization of the tourist industry.

[2] Jorge Semprun, *The Autobiography of Federico Sanchez* (1979), 252.

[3] J. L. Aranguren, *La cruz de la monarquía española actual* (1974), 30. Romero quoted by X. Tussel, *La oposición democrática al Franquismo*, 47.

[4] G. Fernández de la Mora, 'El estado de obras', *ABC*, 1 April, 1973.

protest—as late as 1974 a poll found 53 per cent of Spaniards uninterested in politics—because they feared for their own well-being cannot be doubted.[1] How, then, is the total rejection of Francoism in the first free elections of 1977 to be explained?

Undoubtedly the constant attacks of the opposition had undermined the moral authority of the régime. That 'Organic Democracy' still kept Spain out of the E.E.C. was a powerful weapon in its hands. The desire for change was evident; it became a national choice when it was apparent that the advent of democracy would not imply, as Franco had constantly threatened, a return to social anarchy. Once political change was legitimized in July 1975 by Franco's chosen successor, King Juan Carlos, it was overwhelmingly accepted.

It was not only that Francoism increasingly appeared as an archaic and repressive political system isolated in Europe—its sister régime in Europe fell with the Portuguese revolution of 1974. The domestic economic changes over which Francoism had presided even if it had not induced them—opponents consistently maintained that Spanish prosperity was a mere reflection of the Western European boom of the sixties, distorted by an inept government—were also in conflict with the basic values on which the system still rested.

Rather than deriving from totalitarianism, these values were those of the traditional middle classes. A claustrophobic, conservative Catholicism, unrelieved by the creative cleavages fostered by religious dissent, provided the social orthodoxy of Franco's Spain. Nominal or sincere, it remained a promotional necessity of official life. Novels describing the sexual hypocrisies and personal conflicts this rigid ethic inflicted on adolescents, especially in the early years, became a literary genre.[2] While the Catholic values of austerity and abstinence 'fitted' an autarkic society of scarcity, they were eroded in an increasingly secular-

[1] The phenomenon of apathy is examined in A. López Piña and E. L. Aranguren, *La cultura política de la España de Franco* (1976), esp. 55 ff. It needs to be stated that opinion polls under Francoism diminished any expression of dissent.

[2] Carlos Barral's autobiography, *Años de penitencia* (1977), and Francisco Umbral's *Memorias de un niño de derechas* (1972) are key works for the understanding of the forties. The words 'sordid' and 'ugly' appear repeatedly in Barral. If literary evidence (and my ocular evidence in 1950) are to be trusted, adolescent recourse to prostitutes was a common feature of those years.

ized society of which the TV set and the motor car were the 'golden calves'.

As one might expect, this incongruence was first evident in the generation that had not known the Civil War as adults. The shift in values was first noticeable in clothes and musical taste—the *chicas topolinas* of the forties with their Camel cigarettes and painted toe-nails were in the novelist Umbral's phrase 'the frontierswomen of a new morality'. The formalized, supervised courtship of the *noviazgo* survived in rural Spain but was rejected by *progré* students for whom women were not 'boxes to put children in'. A seemingly immutable moral structure was challenged by those who had tasted an alternative culture in Paris bookshops. What had begun as the *aesthetic* repulsion felt by a minority of middle-class students in the face of what one of them (Carlos Barral, the Catalan poet) called the 'frighteningly ugly and vulgar' world of the post-war years with its tedious films, religious formalities, and empty rhetoric, became a total rejection of the régime: only the indifference of apathy or revolt were possible. It is tempting to exaggerate the extent of the revolt of the intellectuals beyond the confines of the bourgeois university world, soaked in its sub-Marxist culture, and to underestimate the areas of apathy and alienation. The alternative culture of protest found little resonance among rural and working-class youth.[1] Nevertheless the tourist invasion, against which bishops had thundered in vain once it became, for governments, a necessity of economic survival, brought cars, butane stoves, employment (a million jobs a season), and a glimmering of new sexual mores to the Mediterranean coast and its hinterland. The widening generation gap—an inevitable consequence of the weakening of parental authority in industrialized societies—remained largely a bourgeois phenomenon; but it revealed that the régime which had 'saved' the fathers had failed to attract the loyalty of the sons.

Franco, however, died in his bed as Caudillo of Spain. To the end Francoism enjoyed what Laín Entralgo called the 'distracted passivity of the great mass'.[2]

[1] For an examination of attitudes which reveals the widespread apathy, especially amongst young unskilled workers in rural Spain see J. R. Torregosa, *La juventud española* (1972), 131 ff., 143, 148.

[2] See P. Laín Entralgo, *Descargo de conciencia* (1975), 385 ff.

2. *Cultural Collapse, 1939–1975*

If Francoism was based on political demobilization, the early years saw an attempt to create a supportive culture. This was a difficult task: the poets, philosophers, and historians who had supported the Republic were the 'other Spain', the 'pilgrim Spain' in exile, leaving in Spain a handful of hacks who occupied posts in the cultural institutions of the régime and in the University 'by right of conquest'.[1] The official culture was a strange mixture of the 'virile', imperial enthusiasms of the Falangists, the exaltation of military virtues combined with an emotional religiosity which identified Spain with the defence of Tridentine Catholicism. Spaniards could believe that this curious amalgam of totalitarianism with its 'Doctrine of Caudillaje' (i.e. a Spanish version of the *Führerprinzip*), the imperial longings of the Falange (Gibraltar and a slice of French North Africa), and traditional Catholicism might find a place and an echo in Hitler's New Europe. By 1945 this was an absurdity. Though the régime's favoured physiologists might argue that psycho-analysis was a Jewish product of the degeneracy of democracies,[2] the idiosyncratic cultural constructs appeared specimens from an archaic age encapsulated in a democratic Europe. The *cordon sanitaire* of ferocious and ludicrous censorship was to prove ineffective against a slow but irreversible infection from abroad. By 1950 Freud was permitted reading and young sociologists were studying in America.

The National Catholicism which competed with the hold of the Falange in the commanding heights of the cultural institutions did not provide a viable, long-term alternative to the empty rhetoric of the Movement or an entry into the mainstream of European thought. Rather, it was a revival of the intellectual isolationism of Menéndez y Pelayo and the integrism of Donoso Cortés.[3]

The most important cultural institutions were the University and the government's Superior Council of Scientific Investigations (C.S.I.C.). The functions of the University in the New

[1] Franco himself was little concerned with cultural life; moreover, the state was too poor to embark on an ambitious programme.

[2] Carlos Castilla del Pino, 'La psiquiatria española', in *La Cultura bajo el franquismo* (1977), 79 ff.

[3] See pp. 233, 242–3, Balmes was considered heterodox.

State were set out in the University Law of 1943. The rectors must be Falangist militants; but the syllabus was to emphasize the identification of Spain and Catholicism excluding the whole corpus of the liberal heritage as 'heterodox'; the 'great imperial university' of Cisneros, 'creator of the theological army which gave battle to heresy in defence of Catholic unity', was to be revived and put 'at the service of the ideals of the Falange, which inspire the new state'.[1] As to the C.S.I.C., its aim was to re-establish the unity of Christianity and the sciences destroyed by the eighteenth-century Enlightenment. 'The C.S.I.C.', in the view of Ibañez Martín, the A.C.N.P. Minister of Education, 'was born, above all, to serve God . . . to inject theology into all our cultural activities.' Its periodical *Arbor* was the platform for the intellectuals of the Opus: its aim 'to rechristianize culture'.[2] Its leading spirit, Calvo Serer, employed the formulas of the integrists of the nineteenth century: Protestantism=the Enlightenment=liberalism=Marxism. The Catholic unity of Spain had been recreated by the victory of Franco. This endeavour to revive the Spain of Philip II—whom the Caudillo admired—was reflected in an architectural style based on that king's monastery–palace, the Escorial, and the vogue for colourless imitations of the soldier-poet Garcilaso de la Vega.[3] Historians, in their rejection of liberalism, reflected the vision of the Caudillo himself: 'the nineteenth century [i.e. the century of liberalism] which we should have liked to eliminate from our history is the negation of the Spanish spirit'. That spirit was to be found in sixteenth-century 'imperial Spain' of which the régime considered itself the heir: of the 54 theses in the University of Madrid in the forties, only 7 were devoted to contemporary history.[4]

Those who could not stomach the new style worked in silence, indifferent to the noise around them: the historian Carande who

[1] A. Fontán, *Los católicos en la universidad española* (1968), 90 ff.

[2] Cf. Franco's speech of 10 April 1940 to Acción Católica, 'We must rechristianize that section of the people who have been perverted and poisoned by corrupt doctrines.' For Arbor see D. Artigues, *L'Opus Dei en Espagne* (1968), 41–3.

[3] The most striking example of the Escorial style was the Air Ministry building; of the 'imperial grandeur' the Triumphal Arch across the road from the University City. (Cf. 'El Arco de Triunfo de la Ciudad Universitaria' in V. Palacio Atard, *Cinco Historias de la República y de la Guerra*, 121–40 (1973).

[4] J. M. Jover, 'Corrientes historiogáficas en la España contemporánea', in *Boletín informativo de la Fundación March* (March 1975).

exposed the economic consequences of imperial grandeur; the ethnologist Julio Caro Baroja; Vicens Vives, the great Catalan historian who restored nineteenth-century history to intellectual respectability.[1] The more sensitive spirits within the régime attempted to recover the intellectual tradition lost in 1939: Dionisio Ridruejo, the Falangist poet, in the periodical he edited, *Escorial*, was an admirer of Ortega y Gasset, whose élitism had always attracted young Falangists; Laín Entralgo, rector of Madrid University, whose *España como problema* (1948) was a minor assault on the ideological foundations of the régime in its admiration for the writers of the 'generation of 1898'. As Laín was later to confess, this timid opening was doomed to failure: for Calvo Serer there was no 'problem' (*España sin problema*, published in 1949); it had been solved by the restoration of national unity and the Catholic conception of life in 1939. The liberal Catholics favoured by Ruíz Giménez as Minister of Education were to Calvo Serer 'a hand outstretched' to heterodox liberals like Unamuno, a hand which would ultimately embrace the anti-Spain of the opposition intellectuals. Ruíz Giménez fell in 1956.

The government over-reacted. The gap between the intellectuals of the opposition, the Catholic *aperturistas*, and the general public was maintained by a régime that controlled the press and the journalistic profession, a control that showed no signs of relaxation until 1966. Censorship reached levels of comic absurdity in enforcing the puritanical Catholicism that had flourished in the Civil War:[2] boxers' torsos were concealed in press photographs by painted vests; the word 'thigh' was struck out of one of José María Peman's plays.[3]

In the forties the literary landscape was shaken by the 'tremendist' novels: Carmen Laforet's best seller *Nada* was a portrait of the pretensions and moral bankruptcy of the parasitic bourgeoisie of Barcelona 'saved' by Franco in 1939; the

[1] Vicens Vives replaced rhetoric by quantitative history and established the school of Catalan economic historians (Nadal, Reglá, and Fontana). The review he founded in 1951, *Estudios de historia moderna*, was the seed-bed from which grew a historical tradition that measures up to the best European standards. He was persecuted by the régime by being denied a chair.

[2] See R. Carr, *The Spanish Tragedy* (1977).

[3] Peman was one of the 'intellectuals' of the régime. His drama 'The Angel and the Beast' presented the Manichaean concept of Spain and anti-Spain central to the official vision.

violence of Camilo José Cela's *La familia de Pascual Duarte* (1942) revealed the social injustices of rural life. The Castile of the novels of Miguel Delibes—a sincere Catholic fond of hunting and who had fought in the Nationalist navy—was not the cradle of national glories but a desolate land of wretched villages and brutality.

It was Sánchez Ferlosio's masterpiece *Jarama* (1956) that revealed the true texture of the Spain of the forties and fifties. Here is a characteristic dialogue:

> 'Well, no politics for me . . . I can only read cinema posters'
> But you ought to be more aware of what's going on'
> 'More aware? Go on! Why?'

In spite of propaganda campaigns the majority of Spaniards, if they had no knowledge of or interest in the activities of dissident intellectuals, remained indifferent to the imposed culture of the régime. 'Intellectuals', wrote Ridruejo in 1952, 'have not known an epoch in which their social influence has been so restricted.' The mass of Spaniards were immersed in a culture of evasion[1] which was to become the mass culture of the consumer society of the 1970's. All societies have their culture of evasion—for instance the American commercial cinema of the thirties. It was the manipulation of this culture by Franco's governments that endowed it with its role in the system as a mask cast over the harsh realities of life.

One of its main instruments was professional football. In the pauperized Spain of the post-war years Real Madrid, the pride of the capital, built a stadium holding 100,000 spectators; Barcelona and the other capitals followed suit. It was a spectator sport that was deliberately furnished with nationalist overtones. Every victory—above all over 'perfidious Albion'—was lauded as an expression of 'the Spanish fury'. The leading radio commentator, who specialized in a brand of ecstatic nationalism, became an appointed member of the Cortes.[2]

It was the cinema that revealed the limitations and contra-

[1] For the culture of evasion see R. Carr and J. P. Fusi, *Spain: Dictatorship to Democray* (1979), 118–23. The *revista*—a light musical—was the earliest vehicle of the culture of evasion: its star was Conchita Picquer. For a splendid account see M. Vasquez Montalban, *Crónica sentimental de España* (1971).

[2] J. M. García, *El bisturí del futbol español* (1975).

dictions that beset the régime.[1] Governments were fully conscious of its influence in a country with the highest number of cinema seats per capita in Europe. It endeavoured to meet demand with 'heroic' films on the Civil War, with hyperbolic treatments of the great episodes in Castilian history, or with 'folkloric' trivialities.[2] But it could not satisfy popular demand; films were imported from the United States, Italy, and France, and with them values that compulsory official dubbing could not eliminate. 'The cinema', wrote Francisco Umbral of his youth in the forties, 'gave us the measure of our misery'. Betty Grable embodied values that could not be ingested into the morals of continence and austerity. Falangists flung paint at Rita Hayworth's *Gilda* on the screen. Bishops thundered at the film as the 'agent of the collective heresy of the West'.

By the mid-fifties it was apparent that intellectual autarky had died with economic autarky. While the repressive apparatus of the régime remained *in situ* to prevent the public emergence of an alternative culture, its efforts to impose its own culture had failed. The so-called social poets and novelists aimed to give the 'silent people' a voice in a nation 'idiotized' by the press. Until the mid-sixties they sustained a literary movement of overt social criticism; and many of them were committed Communists.[3] For the most gifted of them, the poet Gabriel Celaya, 'Poetry is a weapon loaded with the future.' Novels like López Pacheco's *Central Electrica* (1958), which describes the building of a hydro-electric station, has all the grey defects of social realism; but it exposed the injusticies and social conflicts that belied the announcement of the government spokesman in the novel that 'a new dawn, a splendid dawn is rising'. The dramatist Alfonso Sastre (b. 1926) openly sympathized with the striking Asturian miners in *Red Earth*; he was imprisoned and his plays mauled by the censor.

Apart from students and other intellectuals the social realists

[1] D. Font, *Del azul al verde. El cine español durante el franquismo* (1976).

[2] Franco himself was a football and film addict; he wrote the script for *La Raza*, a glorification of true Spanish values.

[3] P. Gil Casado, *La novela social española* (1973), 119 ff. The theorist of social literature was the critic J. M. Castellet. See his *Un cuarto de siglo de poesía española* (1978). Castellet later rejected social poetry and became a patron of the quasi-surrealist *novísimos*—an avant-garde movement whose practitioners were anti-Francoist in their personal views.

made little impression. The majority of Spaniards were satisfied with 'kiosk literature'—westerns, and sentimental 'photo novels'[1]—, foreign films, the trivial comedies of Alfonso Paso who had half a dozen plays running in Madrid simultaneously in the sixties. Above all television dominated Spanish social life as in no other country. 'Everybody is watching television serials with open mouths', wrote the Catalan Josep Pla in 1972. 'Such is today's culture.' Unlike the film, television was controlled by the government: Adolfo Suárez, future prime minister of a democratic Spain, put this most powerful of instruments at the service of the government and the moral prejudices of Admiral Carrero Blanco and Franco's wife.[2] This was enough to keep the Marx Brothers off the screen.

By the sixties, luminaries of Falangism and National Catholicism were neither read nor remembered. Their only legacy to Spanish culture was an inflated prose style. The régime, claimed Julián Marías, Ortega's disciple, had not succeeded in creating a 'single false prestige'; yet Spain was the scene of a 'flourishing intellectual life'.[3] The technocrats of the régime had opened the economy to Europe; Fraga's Press Law of 1966, with all its limitations, opened up cultural life. *Spanish* films described—often in subtle symbolism—Spanish reality;[4] Spanish sociologists and economists the failures of forty years of Francoism.[5] The forbidden writers of the forties could be bought in any bookshop. Three editions of Che Guevara's Bolivian diary were published in 1969. Magazines like *Triunfo* recovered the culture of exile. Buñuel's films, once banned, were shown to full houses in the seventies.

[1] One such—*Simplemente María*—sold 170,000 copies a week for two years. The novelist Benet considered 5,000 copies a year a success. On photo novels see M. J. Campo, *Simplemente María y su repurcusión entre la clase obrera* (1975), and A. Amorós, 'Fotonovelas', in *Insula* (June 1969).

[2] For the career of Suárez as director of Spanish TV see G. Morán, *Adolfo Suárez Historia de una ambición* (1979).

[3] See his *Los Españoles* (1963), 216.

[4] e.g. Saura's *La caza* (The Hunt) (1965); the first overtly political film was Patiños's *Nueve Cartas a Berta* (Nine letters to Bertha, 1965). The 'new cinema' declined after 1968. Cf. C. Santos Fontenela, *Cine español en la encrucijada* (1966). But in 1975 came Saura's *Cria Cuervos* and, the most subtle of all, Erice's *Espiritu de la colmena*. For a perceptive account of the 'new cinema' see V. Molina Foix, *New Cinema in Spain* (1977).

[5] One of the most remarkable and successful publications of 1973 was a sympathetic history of the Republic and a critical examination of Francoism written by the Communist economist Ramon Tamames.

In Catalonia, with Barcelona as the most Europeanized city in Spain, the Catalan renaissance and the avant-garde literature of the late sixties were proof—openly acknowledged by Fraga—of the failure to impose the 'language of Empire'. As early as 1959 universal protest in Barcelona had forced the government to dismiss the editor of *La Vanguardia* for his slights on Catalanism. For Miró, a painter like Tapiés with a world reputation, the years of Francoism were a scratch of the skin, impotent to uproot the deep-rooted, evergreen carob tree of 'Catalan identity'.[1]

By Franco's death, just as the Communists had captured the trade unions, so Marxism and a vague *mystique de gauche* was the dominant subculture of students and intellectuals; the liberal culture of the Republic had not been killed off. For Franco these were the twin 'corrupt' doctrines that had 'perverted' Spaniards and which he had regarded as his historic mission to burn out of the Spanish soul.

Franco's prolonged agony was a symbol of the Spain that he and his governments had created. The dying Caudillo was plugged into every modern medical device; on his bed was the mantle of the Virgin of Pilar and grasped in his hand the mummified arm of St. Teresa of Avila. His bequest was a schizophrenic governing class and a schizophrenic society. 'We have discovered', wrote a journalist enjoying the relative freedom of the spring of 1966, 'that Spanish society is a society of conflicts.' These conflicts Francoism could not contain; it was the task of the new democracy to resolve them.

That, after nearly forty years of Francoism, democracy came to Spain peacefully astounded Europe. This peaceful transition was the achievement of the negotiating skills of Adolfo Suárez and of the moderation of the democratic opposition. The demise of 'inorganic democracy' was legitimized with King Juan Carlos, in Areilza's words, as the 'motor of change'. In 1978 a constitution that turned Spain into a constitutional parliamentary monarchy based on universal suffrage and a party system was not, as had been the constitutions of the nineteenth century, the unilateral imposition of a party dogma. It was a settlement accepted by the vast majority of Spaniards.

[1] Interview in *El País* (19 February 1978). Miró refused to design posters with Castilian words for the Socialist party.

Apart from securing normal democratic freedoms it promised a solution of the regional problem that had haunted the history of modern Spain. In the first elections under the constitution the Spanish people voted for moderation.

In 1978, as in April 1931, there was a generalized feeling that democracy would, by offering solutions to every problem, usher in some new era of peace and prosperity. It did not and could not, above all in a period of economic recession which put new stresses on the political systems of the Western world as a whole. Euphoria evaporated; *desencanto* supervened, based on a false expectation. Democracy does not solve problems: it provides the machinery for their solution and the rules of the political game. It can only survive if those rules are accepted. Continued economic growth apart, the incorporation of peripheral nationalism within the constitution remains a problem not yet solved. Its exploitation by terrorists—particularly in the Basque Provinces—remains the most serious threat to the stability of the democratic system. While, in an authoritarian régime, a terrorist minority can argue that it represents a suppressed general will, in a functioning democracy terrorism becomes the claim of a self-appointed élite to override that general will by the use of violence. Its result, if not its purpose, in the jargon of our time, is to destabilize the democratic process.

The legacy of the last of the iron surgeons and the habits acquired under his rule still weigh on Spanish society. The reluctance of a democratic society to use force lends to the advocates of force a weapon to destroy it. Those who look back with nostalgia to the ordered society of authoritarianism which protected alike their interests and their values, appeal to the army to save them from what they regard as the dissolution of the political and social fabric, to an army whose officers are murdered by violent men and whose tradition tells them that, when public order collapses and the unity of the *patria* is threatened, then it is the function of the officer corps to 'save' the nation. The stand of a democratic monarch acting as Commander-in-Chief of the army thwarted the ambitions of a minority of military frondeurs on 23 February 1981. But one man cannot save democracy. Only the resolute determination of a nation can do that, and isolate the violent minority that yearns for the security that can always be secured by that sacrifice of liberty and human dignity which stunts societies.

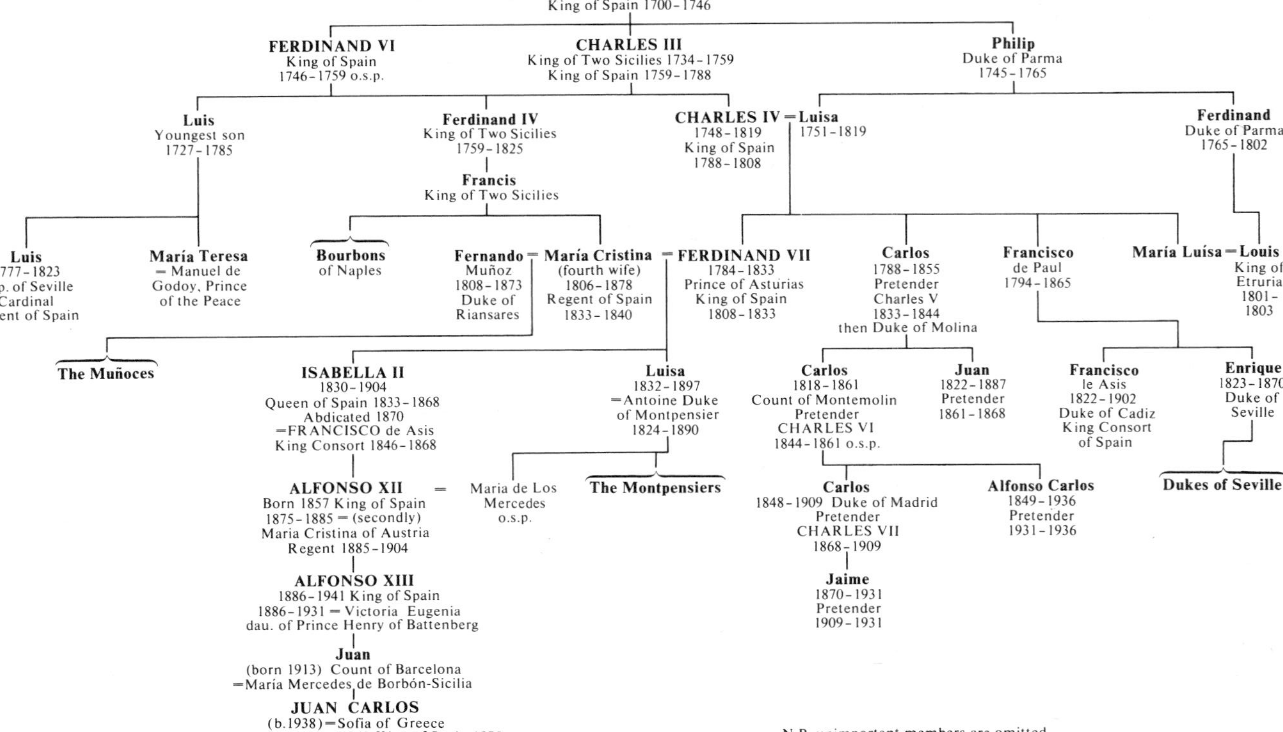
PHILIP V
King of Spain 1700–1746
FERDINAND VI
King of Spain
1746–1759 o.s.p.
CHARLES III
King of Two Sicilies 1734–1759
King of Spain 1759–1788
Philip
Duke of Parma
1745–1765
Luis
Youngest son
1727–1785
Ferdinand IV
King of Two Sicilies
1759–1825
CHARLES IV = Luisa
1748–1819
King of Spain
1788–1808
1751–1819
Ferdinand
Duke of Parma
1765–1802
Francis
King of Two Sicilies
Luis
1777–1823
Abp. of Seville
Cardinal
Regent of Spain
María Teresa
= Manuel de
Godoy, Prince
of the Peace
Bourbons
of Naples
Fernando = María Cristina = FERDINAND VII
Muñoz
1808–1873
Duke of
Riansares
(fourth wife)
1806–1878
Regent of Spain
1833–1840
1784–1833
Prince of Asturias
King of Spain
1808–1833
Carlos
1788–1855
Pretender
Charles V
1833–1844
then Duke of Molina
Francisco
de Paul
1794–1865
María Luísa = Louis
King of
Etruria
1801–
1803
The Muñoces
ISABELLA II
1830–1904
Queen of Spain 1833–1868
Abdicated 1870
=FRANCISCO de Asis
King Consort 1846–1868
Luisa
1832–1897
=Antoine Duke
of Montpensier
1824–1890
Carlos
1818–1861
Count of Montemolin
Pretender
CHARLES VI
1844–1861 o.s.p.
Juan
1822–1887
Pretender
1861–1868
Francisco
le Asis
1822–1902
Duke of Cadiz
King Consort
of Spain
Enrique
1823–1870
Duke of
Seville
ALFONSO XII =
Born 1857 King of Spain
1875–1885 = (secondly)
Maria Cristina of Austria
Regent 1885–1904
Maria de Los
Mercedes
o.s.p.
The Montpensiers
Carlos
1848–1909 Duke of Madrid
Pretender
CHARLES VII
1868–1909
Alfonso Carlos
1849–1936
Pretender
1931–1936
Dukes of Seville
ALFONSO XIII
1886–1941 King of Spain
1886–1931 = Victoria Eugenia
dau. of Prince Henry of Battenberg
Jaime
1870–1931
Pretender
1909–1931
Juan
(born 1913) Count of Barcelona
=María Mercedes de Borbón-Sicilia
JUAN CARLOS
(b.1938)=Sofía of Greece
Prince of Asturias 1969 King of Spain 1975–
N.B. unimportant members are omitted

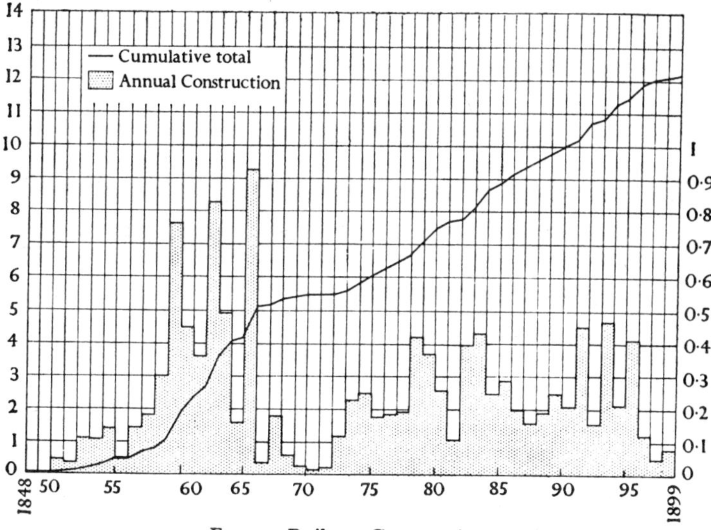

FIG. 2. Railway Construction
(Thousands of kilometres)
Read on left for cumulative total, on right for annual construction.

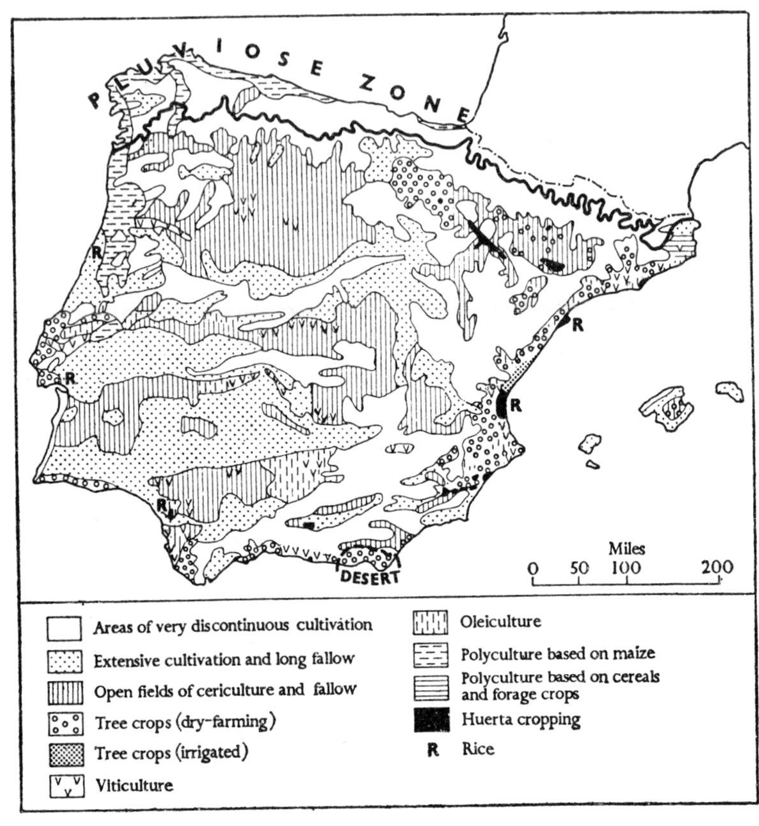
PLUVIOSE ZONE
R
R
R
R
R
DESERT
Miles
0 50 100 200
Areas of very discontinuous cultivation
Extensive cultivation and long fallow
Open fields of cericulture and fallow
Tree crops (dry-farming)
Tree crops (irrigated)
Viticulture
Oleiculture
Polyculture based on maize
Polyculture based on cereals and forage crops
Huerta cropping
R Rice

MAP I. LAND UTILIZATION (Present day)

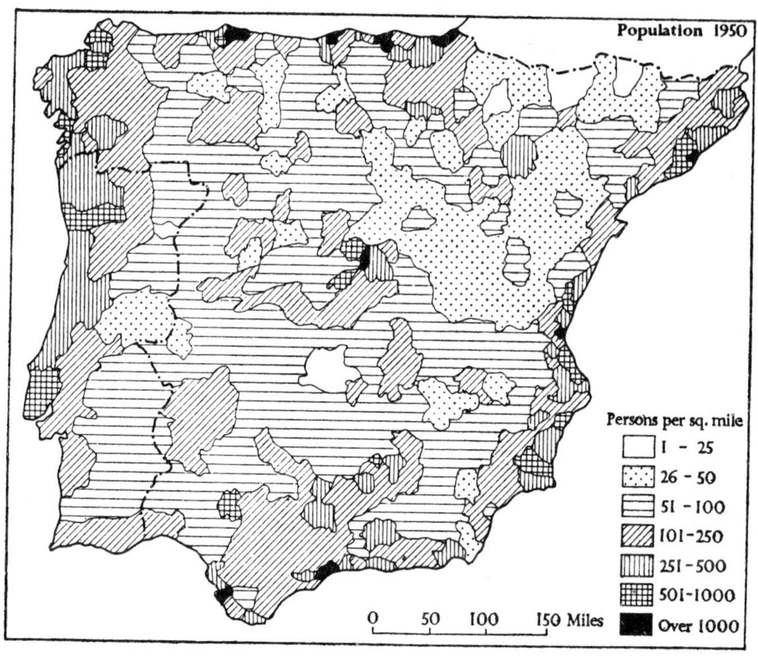
Population 1950
Persons per sq. mile
1 - 25
26 - 50
51 - 100
101-250
251-500
501-1000
Over 1000
0
50
100
150 Miles

MAP 2

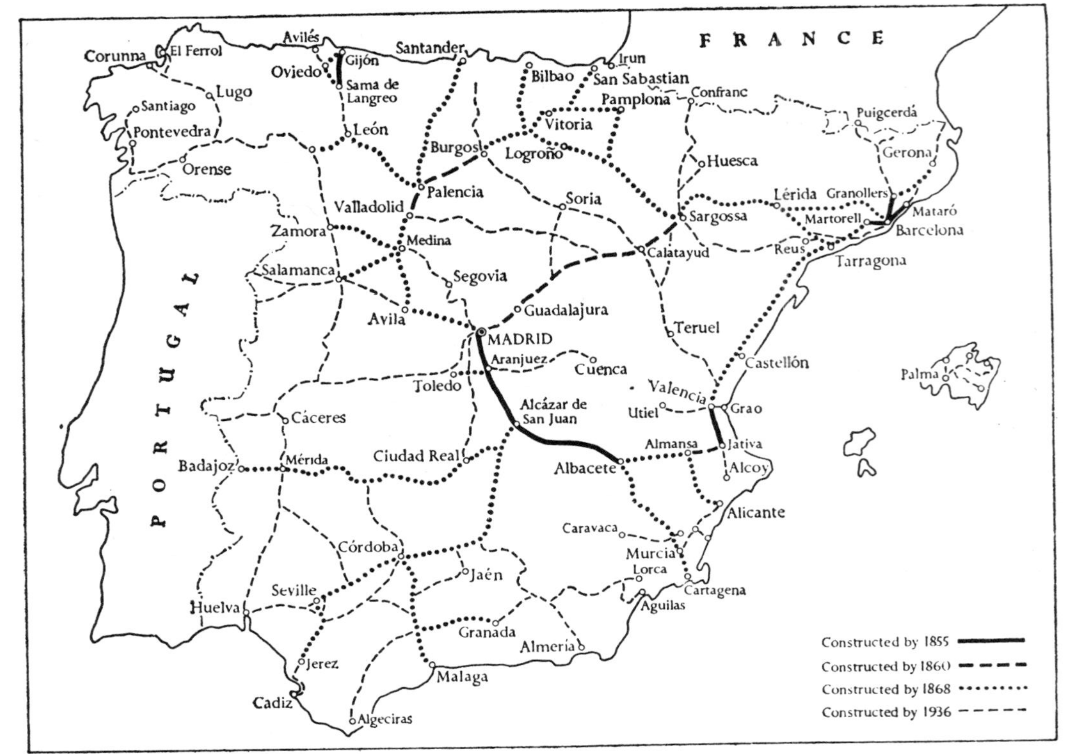

MAP 3. RAILWAY CONSTRUCTION

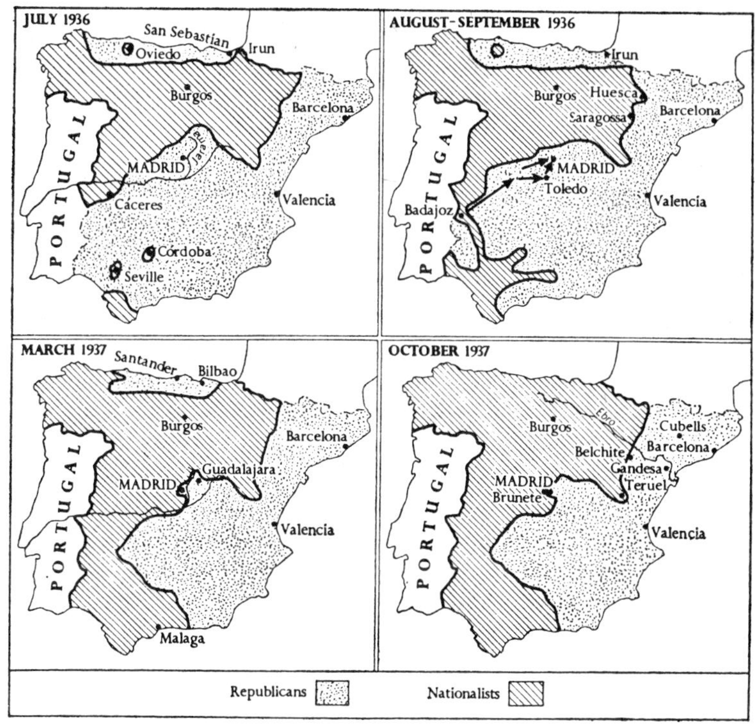

MAP 4. CIVIL WAR 1936–9

MAP 5. SPANISH AMERICA *c.* 1800

BIBLIOGRAPHICAL ESSAY

GIVEN that one of the declared aims of General Franco was to eliminate the nineteenth century from the collective mind of Spain except as a warning of the periods of liberalism, and while the Republic and the Civil War were delicate subjects, it is scarcely surprising that historians concentrated their attention on less sensitive areas. However, the sixties saw a renewal of interest. The impact of this renewed interest in the history of the nineteenth and twentieth centuries is discussed in J. Ma Jover Zamora, 'El siglo XIX en la historiografía contemporánea', in *El Siglo XIX en España*, ed. J. Ma Jover (1974). The popular vogue of modern history can be judged from the articles in *Historia 16*, many of which represent original and valuable contributions.

The new output on contemporary history threatens to overwhelm. This bibliography attempts to strike a balance between contemporary treatments, general works, and detailed studies which cast a concentrated light on significant topics. It is, therefore, highly selective.

For full references to works in Chapters I–XVI consult the Bibliographical Index; other words are given with date of publication.

I. BIBLIOGRAPHIES

The standard bibliography of Spanish history is B. Sánchez Alonso, *Fuentes de la historia española e hispano-americana* (3rd ed., Madrid, 1952). For all works published since 1953 the *Indice histórico español* (Barcelona, from 1953) is invaluable. Two useful specialized bibliographies are J. del Burgo, *Fuentes de la historia de España: Bibliografía de las luchas políticas y guerras carlistas en el siglo XIX* (Pamplona, 1953–5) and R. Lamberet, *Mouvements ouvriers et socialistes: chronologie et bibliographie* (Paris, 1953). A. Ballesteros Beretta, *Historia de España*, vols. vii, viii, and ix (Barcelona, 1934, 1936, 1941) contain extensive but unselective bibliographies for each chapter. For the Civil War see R. de la Cierva and collaborators, *Bibliografía sobre la guerra de España (1936–39) y sus antecedentes* (1968), and V. Palacio Atard, *Cuadernos Bibliográficos de la guerra de España* (1966). For the history of the labour movement in Catalonia see E. Giralt i Raventós, *Bibliografía dels moviments socials a*

Catalunya, País Valencià les Illes (1972), and in general R. Lamberet, *Mouvements ouvriers et socialistes (Chronologie et bibliographie 1750–1936)* (1953).

R. A. Humphreys, *Latin American History: a guide to the literature in English* (London, 1958) is excellent. For current literature the *Handbook of Latin American Studies* is indispensable.

2. GENERAL WORKS

The most stimulating and original introduction to Spanish history is still General Brenan's *The Spanish Labyrinth* (2nd ed., Cambridge, 1950). For the political history of the nineteenth century H. Butler Clarke's *Modern Spain* contains much information not easily obtainable elsewhere. F. Soldevila, *Historia de España*, vi and vii (Barcelona, 1957–9), is a modern history with very full bibliographical references, Salvador de Madariaga's *Spain* a 'liberal' commentary.

The contribution of Spanish scholars to the history of the nineteenth century is well represented in the series published by Alfaguara: M. Artola, *La burguesía revolucionaria, 1808–1869* (1973) and M. Martínez Cuadrado, *La burguesía conservadora, 1896–1931* (1973). For the later period see Xavier Tussell Gomez, *La España del siglo XX. Desde Alfonso XIII a la muerte de Carrero Blanco* (1975), and Ricardo de la Cierva, *Historia básica de la España actual 1800–1974* (1974), which concentrates on the period after 1875. Both have bibliographical references. A Marxist interpretation is N. Tuñon de Lara's two works: *La España del siglo XIX* (1968) and *La España del siglo XX* (1966). An indispensable aid is M. Artola, *Partidos y programas políticos*, 2 vols. (1975). Two general introductions by American scholars who have made major contributions are: Richard Herr, *Spain* (1971), pp. 51–288, and Stanley Payne, *A History of Spain and Portugal*, 2 vols (1973). P. Vilar's brief *Histoire de L'Espagne* (1955) is suggestive and much recent work is summarized in another French work, *Histoire de L'Espagne contemporaine* by E. Témime, A. Broder, and C. Chastagnaret (1979).

3. ECONOMICS AND SOCIETY

The economic and, to a lesser extent, the social history of the period is receiving increasing attention from Spanish historians. J. Vicens Vives, *An Economic History of Spain* (1969) is the work of a great pioneer; for Catalonia see his *Industrials i Politics* (1950). The Catalan school has continued to produce important studies.

The basic statistical information is weak compared with that of other Western European economies; but it is improving. The census of 1799 has been criticized by J. Fontana in 'El "Censo de frutos y manufacturas" de 1799' in *Moneda y crédito* (1967), pp. 54 ff. Two early compilations are Moreau de Jonnès's brief *Statistique de L'Espagne* (1934) and the vast encyclopedia of Pascual Madoz, *Diccionario estadístico histórico de España* (1845–50), in sixteen volumes. For the later periods the *Anuario estadístico* can be used and there is a useful collection in *Estadísticas básicas de España 1900–1970* (1975). For nineteenth-century agricultural prices there is a fine analysis in N. Sánchez Albornoz, *Materiales para la historia económica de España. Los precios agrícolas en la segunda mitad del siglo XIX*, vol I (1975). For the modern period the *Informes* of the Banco de Bilbao are invaluable, as are its reports on the national income and its provincial distribution.

G. Anes Alvarez's *Las crisis agrarias e la Espanña Moderna* (1970) and J. Fontana's *La quiebra de la monarquía absoluta* (1971) set the stage; Fontana's *Cambio económico y actitudes políticas en la Espagna del siglo XIX* (1973) examines the links between economics and politics. For the mid-century N. Sánchez Albornoz's contributions are outstanding, e.g. *España hace un siglo: una economía dual* (1968) and *Jalones en la modernización de España* (1975). J. Nadal, *El fracaso de la revolución industrial en España 1814–1913* (1975), and G. Tortella Casares, *Los orígenes del capitalismo en España* (1973), are concerned to explain Spain's failure to industrialize. S. Roldan *et al.*, *La consolidación del capitalismo en España* (1973) is a useful account of the economic effects of the 1914–18 war in the Basque country and Catalonia. See also J. A. Lacomba, *Introducción a la historia económica de la España contemporánea* (1969) and J. Sardá's fundamental work, *La política monetaria y las fluctuaciones de la economía española* (1949); J. Harrison, *An economic history of modern Spain* (1978) is a short survey with an excellent bibliography. For the demographic evolution, J. Nadal, *La población española. Siglos XVI al XX* (1971). José Luis García Delgado, *Orígenes y desarrollo del capitalismo en España. Notas criticas* (1975) includes chapters on the Dictatorship, the nineteenth century, and Francoism.

Agrarian history, in the past neglected, is now attracting scientific studies, e.g. by G. Anes for the eighteenth century (see above). M. Artola, *Los Latifundios* (1979) is the best study of the history of the great Andalusian estates and is complemented by A. Bernal, *La propriedad de la tierra y las luchas agrarias andaluzas* (1974); see also R. Herr's essay in D. Spring, *European Landed Élites in the Nineteenth Century* (1977), pp. 98–126. J. Martínez Alier's *La estabilidad del latifundismo* (1968) describes the changes in Andalusia in the 1960's; A. Balcells' *El Problema agrari a Catalunya* (1968) the fate of the Catalan *rabassaires*. Pascual Carrión's *Estudios sobre la agricultura española 1919–1971* (1974) and his *Los latifundios en España* (1931) remain classic works.

The history of industry is best studied in monographs and biographies. F. Sánchez Ramos, *La economía siderúrgica española* (1945) is detailed and sometimes unreliable. On textiles for the early period see J. C. La Force, *The Development of the Spanish Textile Industry 1750–1850* (1965); a short survey is L. Beltrán Flórez, *La industria algodonera española* (1943). Alberto del Castilla, *La maquinista terrestre y marítima, 1855–1955* provides an excellent history of an engineering firm; R. Medir Jofra, *Historia del gremio corchero* of a local industry. For the all-important orange, see M. Torres and H. Paris Eguilaz, *La naranja en la economía española. Historia del ferrocarril en España* (centenary volumes, 1948) has some valuable, some trivial, material on railways. More solid are A. Casares Alonso, *Estudio historico económico de las construcciones ferroriarias españolas en el siglo XIX* (1973) and F. Wais, *Historia general de los ferrocarilles españoles 1830–1941* (1967). *Un siglo en la vida del Banco de Bilbao* (1957) is a history of industry rather than of the bank. *El Banco de Vizcaya y su aportación a la economía española* (Bilbao, 1955) gives some impression of Biscayan investment generally.

For banking and finance generally there are important recent works. *La banca española en la Restauración*, ed. G. Tortella, 2 vols. (1974), and the two studies published by the Servicio de Estudios del Banco de España: *El Banco de España una historia económica* (1970) and *Ensayos sobre la economía española a mediados del siglo XIX* (1970).

For tariff policy there are two works which reflect the Catalan enthusiasm for protection: G. Graell, *Historia del Fomento Nacional de Trabajo* (1911) and M. Pugés, *Como triunfó el proteccionismo en España* (1931). More generally P. de Alzola, *La política económica mundial y nuestra reforma arancelaria* (1906) gives a picture of the interests and issues in tariff reform.

In 1966 I wrote, 'At the time this book was conceived, it was not feasible for me to establish satisfactory long-term series for production, etc.; hence the account of the economy is perforce descriptive. In the near future these gaps may be plugged and many of the assumptions of my work destroyed. As in economic development, so in the development of historical writing there are many false starts and much wastage.' The work of historians like Anes, Nadal, Sánchez Albornoz, Tortella, and Fontana supply the deficiences in my own version, and to their works I refer the reader.

Social history is less well served but there is a reliable introduction in J. Vicens Vives, *Historia social y económica de España y America* (1959), vol. v, pp. 21–469, and in J. M. Jover's *Política, diplomacia y humanismo popular* (1976), pp. 45–64 and 229–345. The collection published by Guadiana, *Historia social de España. El siglo XIX* (1972), has interesting individual essays but does not provide a continuous account.

The history of Spanish labour movements is a growth industry.

M. Tuñon de Lara, *El movimiento obrera en la historia de España* (1972) is a good introduction. A useful short summary of the Socialist movement (with some documents) is A. Padilla, *El movimiento socialista español* (1977); J. P. Fusi, *Política obrera en el País Vasco* (1975) is essential for an understanding of the P.S.O.E. Ignacio Olabarri Gortazar, *Relaciones laborales en Vizcaya 1890–1936* (1978) is a good study of the relations between labour and capital. G. H. Meaker, *The Revolutionary Left in Spain 1914–1923* (1974) is a detailed study of a critical period. J. Díaz del Moral, *Historia de las agitaciones campesinas andaluzas* (new edn, 1973) remains the classic study of rural anarchism. A modern study is Clara E. Lida, *Anarquismo y Revolución en la España del XIX* (1972). J. Termes, *Anarquismo y sindicalismo en España. La Primera Internacional 1864–1881* (1972) and C. Martí, *Orígenes del anarquismo en Barcelona* (1959) are both excellent scholarly accounts of the early history of anarchism in Catalonia. Anselmo Lorenzo's *El proletariado militante* (1905) is a moving (and prejudiced) account by a promiment militant. M. de Burgos, *El verano de 1919 en gobernación* and F. Madrid, *Ocho meses* are important for the undercurrents of anarcho-syndicalism. A general history of the labour movement in Catalonia is contained in E. Giralt and A. Balcells, *Els moviments socials en Catalunya* (1967), a more detailed study is A. Balcells, *Trabajo y organización obrera en la Cataluña contemporánea 1900–1936* (1974). For the C.N.T. see A. Balcells, *El Sindicalismo en Barcelona 1916–1923* (1965). For the non C.N.T. unions see M. Izard, *Revolució industrial i obrerisme: Les Tres Clases de Vapor* (1970).

For working-class conditions the reports of the Instituto de Reformes sociales are fundamental: the Informe of 1893 which gives details on working-class conditions has been edited by A. Elorza and María del Carmen Iglesias, *Burgueses y proletarios* (1973). The French journalist A. Marvaud wrote a workmanlike study, *La Question sociale*, in 1905 and it is a pity that he found no successors. The Reports of the I.R.S. on strikes are most important sources.

For the middle classes the essay of J. Ma Jover, *Conciencia burguesa* has interesting suggestions. For the upper classes much can be extracted from strange sources, e.g. biographies like the laudatory treatment given the second Marqués de Comillas, the pious industrialist, by his biographer E. Fernández Regatill. See also for the aristocracy Marques de Valdeiglesias, *1875–1949. La sociedad española vista por el marques de Valdeiglesias* (1957); A. Hoyos y Vinent, *El primer estado* (1931). J. Vivens Vives and Llorens Montserrat, *Industrials i politics* contains both Vicen's history of the Catalan economy and a number of short and useful biographies. Rural society is described in M. Kenny, *Spanish Tapestry* (for Castile), J. Pitt Rivers, *People of the Sierra* (for Andalusia), and Carmelo Lisón-Tolosana, *Belmonte de los*

Caballeros (1966) (for Aragon). Two modern studies of changes in eastern and western Andalusia respectively are M. Siguán, *El medio rural en Andalucía oriental* (1972), and A. López Ontiveros, *Emigración, propriedad y paisaje en la campiña de Córdoba* (1974).

For the Church there is R. García-Villoslada (ed.), *Historia de la Iglosia en España*, vols. iv and v (Madrid, 1979). Useful data are given in J. Saez Marín, *Datos Sobre la Iglesia Española Contemporánea 1768–1868* (Madrid, 1975), and there is a great deal of information in A. Martínez Albiach, *Religiosidad Hispana y Sociedad Borbónica* (1969). Of the works on the Church some of the most revealing are those of laborious piety or frank hagiography, e.g. A. Vinayo, *El seminario de Oviedo*, M. González, *Don Enrique de Ossó*, J. Calasanz Bau, *Historia de las Escuelas Pías de Cataluña*. The biography of Father Claret by Mariano Aguilar casts a great deal of light on the piety of the mid-century. The works of Father Lesmes Frías, *La provincia de España de la Compañia de Jesús* and *La provinica de Castilla de la Compañia de Jesús 1815–63* (1914), provide a history of the Jesuits. A. Peers gives a defence of the Orders in his *Spain, the Church and the Orders*. Almost any left-wing work will reveal the standard attack.

For the army see pp. 791 and 795.

4. THE EIGHTEENTH CENTURY AND THE WAR OF INDEPENDENCE

The indispensable work is G. Anes Alvarez, *El antiguo régimen. Los Borbones* (1975). R. Herr, *The Eighteenth Century Revolution in Spain*, A. Domínguez Ortiz, *La sociedad española en el siglo XVIII*, and Gonzalo Anes Alvarez, *Economía e Ilustración en la España del siglo XVIII* (1970), are all excellent. The brevity of my treatment of prices is excused by the existence of E. J. Hamilton's *War and Prices in Spain 1651–1800*. A great deal of information can be quarried out of J. Carrera Pujal's unreadable *Historia de la economía española* (3 vols., Barcelona, 1943–7). P. Vilar, *La Catalogne dans l'Espagne moderne* (3 vols., 1962) is a magnificent work. D. R. Ringrose, *Transportation and Economic Stagnation in Spain 1750–1850* (1970) is an important study. For the origins of conservative thought Javier Herrero, *Los orígenes del pensamiento reaccionario español* (1973).

For the enlightenment, in addition to Herr, see J. Sarrailh, *L'Espagne éclairée de la seconde moitié du XVIIIe siècle* (Paris, 1954). M. Defourneaux, *Pablo de Olavide* is a scholarly biography of a leading exponent of *las luces*; Laura Rodríguez, *Reforma e ilustracíon* (1975) is a study of a key civil servant, Pedro Campomanes; less revealing is G. Demerson's *Don Juan Meléndez Valdés*. J. Desdevizes de Dézert, *L'Espagne de l'Ancien Régime*, 3 vols. (1897–1904), contains much information but shows signs of age.

The domestic issues of the 'revolution' of 1808 are treated in Miguel Artola, *Los orígenes de la España contemporánea*; his *Antiguo régimen* is a thoughtful study of the origins of liberalism. H. Juretschke, *Vida, obra y pensamiento de Alberto Lista* (1951) and M. Artola's *Los afrancesados* (1953) deal respectively with the intellectual and political problems of the *afrancesados*. For a general study G. H. Lovett, *Napoleon and the birth of Modern Spain* (1965) is useful. For Joseph's reign J. Mercader Riba, *José Bonaparte, Rey de España 1808–1813* (1972) complements Artola. R. Solís, *El Cádiz de las Cortes* contains many interesting sidelights and C. Corona Baratech, *Revolución y reacción en el reinado de Carlos IV* many provocative ideas. A host of local histories of the War of Independence and the French Occupation exist; of these J. Mercader's *Barcelona durante la ocupacíon francesa* (1949) is outstanding. A. Fugier's study of the Asturian Junta and Desdevizes du Dezert's *La Junte supérieure de Catalogne* illustrate the local aspects of war government.

The war itself is studied in Charles Oman's *Peninsular War* and Gómez de Arteche's arid, strictly military *Guerra de la independencia*.

5. FERDINAND VII

The definitive study is M. Artola's *La España de Fernando VII* (vol. xxvi of *Historia de España*, ed. R. Ménéndez Pidal) (1968). There are many polemical works useful primarily as a corrective of liberal historiography, e.g. F. Suárez, *La crisis política del antiguo régimen de España* (1950) and M. del Carmen Pintos Vieites, *La política de Fernando VII*. The conservative school is responsible for the publication by the Seminario de Historia Moderna of source material in the series *Colección Historica de la Universidad de Navarra*. Although J. C. Comellas belongs to this school his *Los primeros pronunciamientos en España* is indispensable while J. Arzadún, *Fernando VII y su tiempo* has useful sidelights on the king's character. Of fundamental importance is J. Fontana, *La quiebra de la Monarquía absoluta* (Barcelona, 1971) and his *Hacienda y Estado en la crisis final del Antiguo régimen español: 1823–1833* (Madrid, 1973).

An early account of the Revolution of 1820–3 based on diplomatic sources is H. Baumgarten's *Geschichte Spaniens vom Ausbruch der französchen Revolution*. More recent works cast light on finances and the Church question: J. del Moral Ruiz, *Hacienda y sociedad en el Trienio Constitucional (1820–1823)* (Madrid, 1975); and M. Revuelta González *Política religiosa de los liberales. El Trienio Constitucional* (Madrid, 1973).

Alcalá Galiano's writings, collected conveniently in B.A.E. are most illuminating, in spite of special pleading. J. C. Comellas, *Los realistas en el trienio constutucional* describes the royalist reaction. J. Sarrailh, *Martínez de la Rosa* is useful for 'moderate' liberalism.

For the breakaway of the American colonies, as seen from the Spanish side, there is a useful treatment in M. J. van Akens, *Pan-Hispanism*. The best general account of the independence movement may still be W. S. Robertson's *Rise of the Latin American Republics* while R. A. Humphrey's *Liberation in Latin America* is a penetrating account of the movement in the Rio de la Plata. Perhaps most illumination is cast on Spanish attitudes by J. Delgado's *España y México en el siglo XIX*. For the Cuban question see below, pp. 793 and 794.

Besides Juretschke's *Lista*, Natalio Rivas Santiago's *Luís López Ballesteros* casts some light on royal policy between 1823 and 1830. For the final crisis of the reign see F. Suárez Verdaguer, *Los sucesos de La Granja* and R. Ortega Canadell, 'La crisis política española de 1832–1833' (E.H.M. v. 1955). For a view of the origins of Carlism critical of the Suárez school see *Estudios de Historia Contemporánea*, ed. V. Palacio Atard, vol. i (Madrid, 1976).

6. 1833–40

L. Díaz del Corral, *El doctrinarismo*, V. Llorens Castillos, *Liberales y románticos* (Mexico, 1954) are both excellent treatments of liberal thought in Spain and among the Spanish exiles; among accounts by contemporaries J. de Burgos, *Anales del reinado de Isabel II* is revealing for conservative liberal attitudes. A. García Tejero, *Historia político-administrativa de Mendizábal* is slight.

There is an outline history of the Carlist movement in Román Oyarzún's *Historia del carlismo* (2nd ed., 1944). More detailed are the works of Melchor Ferrer and his collaborators. All these works are polemical in tone. A. Pirala's long liberal history of the Carlist War is indispensable: it includes an account of Espartero's Regency. There are some excellent contemporary accounts of the Carlist War by foreigners, e.g. Henningsen and Lichnowsky. J. Múgica's study of San Sebastian conservative liberalism in *Carlistas, moderados y progresistas* and J. M. de Areilza's study of Bilbao in *Historia de una conspiración romántica*, by the illumination they cast on conventional interpretations, reveal the great need for further local studies. The historiography of the nineteenth century is cursed with an abundance of political histories which tend to derive from each other and from the more obvious sources, e.g. speeches in the Cortes, well-known newspaper articles.

Since the first edition of this book there has been considerable work on the liberal land settlement. Two summaries are F. Simón Segura, *La Desamortización española del siglo XIX* (Madrid, 1973) and F. Tomás y Valiente, 'Recientes investigaciones sobre Desamortización: intento de síntesis', in *Moneda y crédito*, no. 131, 1974; the *desamortización* is set in a wider context by Richard Herr in the same issue of *Moneda y crédito*, 'El significado de la desamortización en España'. A stimulating study of liberal finances is J. Fontana, *La revolución liberal. Política y Hacienda, 1833–1845* (Madrid, 1976). Some of its consequences for the Church are examined in M. Revuelta González, *La exclaustración, 1833–1840* (Madrid, 1976) and more generally in J. M. Cuenca, *La Iglesia española ante la revolución liberal* (Madrid, 1971). P. Janke, *Mendizábal y la instauración de la monarquía constutucional 1790–1830* (1974) gives details of liberal loans and political jockeying; for the first moderate liberal settlement see J. Tomás Villaroya, *El sistema político del Estatuto Real (1834–1836)* (1968).

7. 1840–68

No satisfactory account of military liberalism exists. R. Carr's 'Rule by generals' (in *Soldiers and Politics*, ed. M. Howard, London, 1957) is in many respects outmoded and only one general has an adequate biography in R. Olivar Bertrand's *Prim* (2 vols., Barcelona, 1951). E. Christiansen, *The Origin of Military Power in Spain 1800–1854* (1967) is a detailed scholarly study. Narváez was to be the subject of a full study by the late Jesús Pabón. An indication of his thought is contained in *La subversión contemporánea y otros estudios* (Madrid, 1971). Two general histories are M. Alonso Baquer, *El Ejército en la sociedad española* (Madrid, 1971) and José R. Alonso, *Historia política del Ejército español* (Madrid, 1974).

A Pirala's *Historia contemporánea* still remains the most detailed account and is especially revealing on the later history of Carlism. G. Hubbard, *Histoire contemporaine de l'Espagne* (Paris, 1869–85), 6 vols., contains much information as do the many works of Garrido and Vera y González's study of Pi y Margall. Fernández de los Ríos, *Luchas políticas* is useful for the politics of liberalism, 1837–54, as is M. de Marliani, *Histoire politique de l'Espagne moderne* (2 vols., Paris, 1840).

There is no adequate biography of O'Donnell: that of C. Navarro y Rodrigo (1969) is hagiographic and incomplete. The best study of the coming of the Revolution of 1868 is to be found in R. Olivar Bertrand's *Siglo de pasión política. Así cayó Isabel II*—much better than its title suggests. More recent works have illuminated the political struggles of the period: J. L. Comellas, *Los Moderados en el poder, 1844–1854* (1970); A. Eiras Roel, *El partido demócrata español, 1849–1868* (1961). For a short study see 'Qué fue la década moderada' in Tuñon de Lara's *Estudios sobre la España del siglo XIX* (1972). The Revolution of 1854 is treated fully in V. G. Kiernan, *The Revolution of 1854 in Spanish History* (1966). A useful work on the urban militia is J. Pérez Garzón, *Milicia nacional y revolución burguesa* (1978).

It is essential to study the few existing memoirs: the numerous productions if Miraflores (see Butler Clarke, p. 478) are tedious; the recollections of F. Fernández de Córdoba, though often trivial, contain invaluable information. Bravo Murillo's collected works are disappointing except on financial matters. The works of Borrego (especially *Organización de los partidos* (1855), *España y la Revolución* (1856)) are the most penetrating of contemporary political analyses; those of Balmes and Donoso Cortés, though interesting in themselves, have been overestimated through much partisan writing. There is a study of the former by J. Ma García Escudero and of the latter by E. Schramm, *Donoso Cortés* (1936).

For the intellectual background of the sixties Vicente Cacho Viu's *La Institución Libre de Enseñanza* is a splendid study but does not replace the earlier works of P. Jobit, *Les Éducateurs de l'Espagne contemporaine*, J. López Morillas, *El Krausismo español*, and J. B. Trend, *Origins of Modern Spain*. Carlos Seco's *Sociedad, literatura y política en la España del siglo XIX* (1973) provides an excellent introduction. S. Moxó's *La disolución del régimen senorial en España* (1969) remains an essential work on the aristocracy. On the civil service and the reforms of Bravo Murillo consult C. Carrasco Canals, *La burocracía en la España del siglo XIX* (1975). New work has appeared on the educational system: M. C. Simón Palmer, *La enseñanza privada soglar en Madrid 1820–1868* (Madrid, 1972), and M. and J. L. Peset, *La Universidad española (siglos XVIII y XIX). Despotismo ilustrado y revolución liberal* (Madrid, 1974); likewise on the food market and sanitary conditions of Madrid: A. Fernández García, *La alimentación de Madrid en el reinado de Isabel II* (Madrid, 1971) and M. and J. L. Peset, *Muerte en España. (Política y sociedad entre la peste y el cólera)* (Madrid, 1972).

8. THE REVOLUTION OF 1868 AND THE RESTORATION OF 1874–5

M. Tuñon de Lara, 'El problema del poder en el sexenio', in his *Estudios sobre el siglo XIX español* is a good introduction; there is a miscellaneous collection of essays in *La Revolución de 1868*, ed. Clara Lida and Iris Zavala (1970).

An outstanding and reliable guide to the politics of the left, 1868–74, is C. A. M. Hennessy's *The Federal Republic in Spain*. Of a host of biographies of Republican worthies the most illuminating is Gómez Chaix's *Ruiz Zorilla*. The near contemporary works of Bermejo and Villarasa and Gatell contain much prejudiced information. Pi y Margall's reflections on the Republic of 1873 have been edited by A. Jutlgar in 1970. M. Fernández Almagro's *Historia política de la España contemporánea*, vol. i (1956), is the best treatment in Spanish.

The interaction of European diplomacy and the 'search for the king' is discussed in A. Willard Smith, 'Napoleon III and the Spanish Revolution of 1868', *Journal of Modern History*, xxv (1953), and L. D. Steefel, *Bismarck, the Hohenzollern candidacy and the origins of the Franco-German War of 1870.*

For the Cuban question see R. Guerra y Sánchez, *Manual de historia de Cuba* (Havana, 1938) and *Guerra de los Diez Años*. The *Historia de la nación cubana* is uneven and the English translation appalling. G. Ely, *Cuando reinaba su majestad el azúcar* gives a lively picture of mid-century Cuba; P. de Alzola y Minondo, *Relaciones comerciales entre la Península y las Antillas* and *El problema cubano* (1898) reflect Spanish attitudes.

The monarchist politics of the period are studied in the Marqués de Lema's *De la Revolución a la Restauración* (1929) and in a much neglected work, A. Houghton, *Les Origines de la restauration des Bourbons en Espagne*. The best history of the Carlist campaign is F. Hernando's *La campaña carlista*.

9. THE POLITICS OF THE RESTORATION

M. Fernández Almagro's studies, *Cánovas* (1972), *Historia política de la España contemporánea* (2 vols., 1959), and his *Historia política del reinado de Alfonso XIII* (1934) describe the political vicissitudes of Restoration politics. Apart from the items on p. 784 J. Ma García Escudero, *Historia política de las dos Españas* (4 vols., 1975) is suggestive if idiosyncratic. Javier Tusell, *Oligarquía y caciquismo en Andalucía* (1976) and J. Varela Ortega, *Los amigos políticos* (1977) are essential for understanding the mechanics of electoral management. M. Martínez Cuadrado, *Elecciones y partidos políticos* (1969) contains all election results between 1868 and 1931 based on official figures. M. Artola, *Partidos y programas políticos 1808–1936* (2 vols., 1974) is a history of the parties together with their programmes. L. Aguiló Lúcia, *Sociología electoral valenciana 1903–1923* (1976) is useful as a local study of Levante politics. *La crisis del estado español 1898–1936* (VIII Coloquio de Pau, 1978) is a collection of studies particularly useful on the interaction of intellectuals and politics.

A defence of Maura and a 'monarchist' criticism of Alfonso XIII was written by Maura's son and M. Fernández Almagro in *Por qué cayó Alfonso XIII* (1948). The Maurista version is criticized in C. Seco Serrano, *Alfonso XIII y la crisis de la Restoración* (1969) and will be continued in his biography of Maura's rival for the leadership of the Conservative party, Dato. See his preliminary sketch in *Perfil político y humano de un estadista de la Restauración: Eduardo Dato* (Real Academia de la Historia, 1978).

M. García Venero's *Melquíades Alvarez* (1954) and *Santiago Alba*, *monárquico de Razón* (1963) cast some light on progressive politics. The biographies of Maura (1954) and Canalejas (1956) by D. Sevilla Andrés represent a modern reinterpretation, strongly favourable to Maura; Maura's views are collected in *Antonio Maura: treinta y cinco años de vida pública*, ed. J. Ruíz-Castillo.

The crises of 1909 and 1917 are studied in detail in J. Connelly Ullman, *The Tragic Week* (1968) and J. A. Lacomba, *La crisis española de 1917* (1970). J. Benet, *Maragall y la Semana Trágica* (1966) is a moving study on the reactions of a great poet to the repression of 1909. Márquez's apologia is contained in his *Las Juntas de Defensa*.

For the problem of 'regenerationism' J. Romero Maura, *La rosa de fuego* (1975) is excellent. Apart from a general background to the crisis of 1909, it contains a new interpretation of Lerroux whose later political career is described in O. Ruiz Manjón, *El partido Republicano Radical* (1976).

There is no satisfactory Spanish account of the Cuban disaster. Ernest May's *Imperial Democracy* is most illuminating, though primarily concerned with American issues. General Weyler's memoirs are extensive but mostly concerned with the problems of military administration (see also above, p. 000).

For the generation of 1898 see Laín Entralgo, *España como problema* (1956) and H. Ramsden, *The 1898 movement in Spain. Towards a Re-interpretation* (1974). Laín's book contains essays on the Catholic polymath Menéndez y Pelayo and on the neurologist Ramón y Cajal. J. B. Trend's essays are the best study in English. There are two interesting studies of individuals in Luis Granjel's *Retrato de Pío Baroja* (Barcelona, 1953) and V. Marrero's *Maeztu*. Enrique Suñer's *Los intelectuales y la tragedia española* is a pathological outburst against intellectuals. The educational issue is well dealt with by Y. Turin, *L'Éducation et l'école* in addition to the works in section 6. Ma. Dolores Gómez Molleda's *Los reformadores de la España contemporánea* (1963) is critical of the liberal interpretation of the Instituto Libre de Enseñanza sympathetically treated in V. Cacho Viu's excellent *La Institución de Libre Enseñanza* (1962). The position of the Protestant Church is described in J. D. Hughey, *Religious Freedom in Spain*.

J. Ferrater Mora discusses the development of Ortoga's thought in *Ortega y Gasset* (Barcelona, 1958) and Gabriel Jackson that of Costa in 'Costa et sa revolution par le haut' in E.H.M. iii (1953). Tierno Galván's *Costa* representsd a modern interpretation, differing from my own. A useful guide is J. Maurice and C. Serrano, *J. Costa: crisis de la Restauración y populismo 1875–1911* (1979). An intelligent Marxist survey of the cultural landscape is provided by M. Tuñon de Lara,

Medio siglo de cultura española 1885–1936 (1976). Javier F. Lalcona, *El idealismo político de Ortega y Gasset. Un análisis sintético de la evolución de su filosofía política* (1974) is a study of Ortega's political ideas.

The essential work on the clerical issue in politics between 1889 and 1913 is J. Andrés Gallego, *La política religiosa en España* (1975). There is an outline history of Catholic unionism: J. N. García Nieto, *El sindicalismo cristiano en España* (1960). O. Alzaga, *La primera democracia cristiana en España* (1973) studies the attempt to create a Christian Democratic party in 1922 to 1923 and provides an illuminating sidelight on the collapse of the Restoration system. J. Tusell continues the history of Christian Democracy until 1939 in *Historia de la democracia cristiana en España* (2 vols., 1974); see also Juan José Castillo, *Propietarios muy pobres. Sobre la subordinación política del pequeño campesino* (1979).

We now have two works by American scholars on the all-important role of the army in the politics of the Restoration: S. Payne, *Politics and the Military in Spain* (1967) and Carolyn Boyd, *Praetorian Politics in Liberal Spain* (1979).

Berenguer's *Campañas del Rif* is a general's account of the Moroccan War; Arturo Barea's *The Track* a soldier's impressions. There is an outline of earlier Spanish policy in Morocco in D. Andrés Sevilla, *Africa entre la política española*.

Catalanism has evoked an abundant literature. M. García Venero, *Historia del nacionalismo catalán* (1944) was written in the Franco period; the most useful modern history is A. Balcells, *Catalunya contemporánea* (2 vols., 1974); J. Rossinyol, *Le Problème national catalan* (1974) is enthusiastically pro-Catalan. Isidre Molas, *Lliga Catalana* (2 vols., 1972) provides a detailed description of the organization of the Lliga; J. Pabón, *Cambó* (3 vols., 1952–69), is essential reading, not merely on Catalan politics but on the Restoratation in general. The relationship between nationalism and the bourgeoisie is examined in A. Jutglar, *Historia crítica de la burguesía a Catalunya* (1972) and Borja de Riquer, *Lliga regionalista: la burguesía catalana i el nacionalisme* (1977).

The literature on Basque nationalism is growing fast. The best general histories are J. M. Azoala, *Vascunia y su destino* (1976) and Stanley Payne, *Basque Nationalism* (1975). The ideology of the founding father Sabino de Arana is dissected in J. J. Solozábal, *El primer nacionalismo vasco* (1975). A left-wing is given in 'Beltza', *El nacionalismo vasco 1876–1936* (1976). 'Valencianism' is studied in A. Cucó, *El valencianisme polític* (1971). For Galicia see M. R. Saurin de la Iglesia, *Apuntes y documentos para una historia de Galicia en el siglo XIX* (1977) and J. A. Durán, *Agrarismo y movilización campesina en el país gallego* (1977).

10. THE DICTATORSHIP AND THE FALL OF THE MONARCHY

G. Maura's *Bosquejo histórico de la Dictadura* describes the basic political issues of 1923–30; and Calvo Sotelo's revealing *Seis años* is especially valuable on local government reform and financial policy. The dictator's own philosophies can be studied in *El pensamiento de Primo de Rivera*, ed. J. M. Peman. Eduardo Aunós, *La política social de la Dictadura* (1944) is a study of labour legislation by one of its creators.

J. Velarde Fuentes, *Política económica de la Dictatura* (1970) is a sympathetic examination of the dictator's economic nostrums; there is a useful and uneven collection of essays on the economics and politics of the dictatorship in *Cuadernos Económicos del I.C.E.* (no. 12). Grandel's *Le Monopole du pétrole* casts light on a symptomatic crisis while Cambó's *Valoración de la peseta* exhibits the criticisms of the moneyed interests. The Report on the Gold Standard is a condemnation of the dictator's financial policies by an orthodox economist, Flores de Lemus.

There is an abundance of memoirs etc. on the period 1930–1. Of these the most important are those of General Mola (a revealing picture of an authoritarian régime in decline), of La Cierva, and of Ramonones (both of which contain details of the last days of the monarchy). General Berenguer's apologia is *De la Dictadura a la República*. The more neglected work of M. Burgos y Mazo gives a most interesting account of the conspiracies of the Constitutionalists; Generals A. López Ochoa and Queipo de Llano reveal the attitude of the military malcontents. Alcalá Galiano's *Caída de un trono* is the lament of an intelligent defeated monarchist. J. Andrés Gallogo, *El Socialismo durante la dictadura* (1977) has an intelligent introduction to a useful collection of documents. The definitive work is S. Ben-Ami, *The Origins of the Second Republic in Spain* (1978). For a dissection of the testimony on the last days of the monarchy see J. Pabón, *Dias de ayer* (1963), pp. 367–433; see also Rafael Sanchez Guerra, *Proceso de un cambio de régimen* (1932).

11. THE SECOND REPUBLIC

In the *blütezeit* of Francoism the Second Republic could only be treated with either outright hostility or extreme caution. The Nationalist version is presented in detail in J. Arrarás, *Historia de la Segunda República Española* (Madrid, 1968). Gabriel Jackson's *The Spanish Republic and the Civil War 1931–39* (1965) represents sound liberal scholarship. Carlos Seco Serrano's *Historia de España, época contemporánea* (1971) is the best modern account by a Spanish historian. S. Payne, *The Spanish Revolution* (1970) is a hard-hitting criticism of the left. Ricardo de la Cierva's *Historia de la Guerra Civil Española. Antecedentes 1898–1936* (1969) sees the Republic as doomed to failure.

Of the memoirs the two most important are J. ma Gil Robles, *No fue posible la paz* (1968), a defence of the C.E.D.A, and, in contrast, Joaquín Chapaprieta's *La paz fue posible* (1971). Alcalá Zamora's speeches have been collected in *Discursos* (1979) with an introduction by M. Tuñon de Lara.| Juan Marichal has edited Azaña's works, *O.C.*, 4 vols. (1968). Miguel Maura's *Así cayó Alfonso XIII* (1962) is useful for the history of the Provisional Government. Lerroux's *Pequeña Historia* exhibits the author's paranoia and the underside of political life. See also N. Alcalá-Zamora, *Memorias (segundo texto de mis memorias)* (1977).

The complications of a multi-party system are discussed in Santiago Varela Díaz, *Partidos y parlamento en la II República Española* (1978), an illuminating study; the elections of February 1963 in J. Tusell Gómez, *Las elecciones del frente popular en España* (1971). Differing views of the role of the C.E.D.A and the Socialists are presented in P. Preston, *The Coming of the Spanish Civil War* (1978) and R. A. H. Robinson, *The Origins of Franco's Spain* (1970). P. Preston's articles, 'Alfonsist Monarchism and the Coming of the Spanish Civil War', *Journal of Contemporary History*, vol. 7, nos. 3/4, 1972, and 'El accidentalismo de la C.E.D.A.: aceptación o sabotaje de la República?', *Revista internacional de sociología* (Madrid), 2ª Epoca, nos. 3/4, July–December 1972, contain material not included in his book. Carlism is well treated in M. Blinkhorn, *Carlism and Crisis in Spain 1931–36* (1975); the mind of the hard right is studied by R. Robinson, 'Calvo Sotelo's *Bloque Nacional* and its ideology', in *University of Birmingham Historical Journal* (vol. x, no. 2, 1966), pp. 160–84. For the formation of the Popular Front see Santos Juliá, *Orígenes del Frente Popular en España 1934–6* (1979).

The attitude of the Church is revealed in the correspondence of Vidal i Barraquer, *Esglesia i Estat durant a Segona República Espànyla* (2 vols., 1971) scrupulously edited by M. Batllori and V. M. Arbeloa; there is short account in José M. Sánchez, *Reform and Reaction* (1963).

The essential work on the agrarian question is Edward Malefakis, *Agrarian Reform and Peasant Revolution in Spain* (1970). There is no work on the general economic problems of the Republic. R. Tamames, *La República, la era de Franco* (1973) contains a brief treatment. For Catalonia A. Balcells *Crisis económica y agitación social en Cataluña* (1971) is an important contribution, as are the later sections of his *El Problema agrari a Catalunya 1890–1936* (1971) which helps to explain the social background of the 1934 October Revolution in Catalonia. For the revolution in Asturias see A. Ramos Olivera, *La revolución de Octubre* and M. Grossi, *La insurrección de Asturias*, both written in 1935; for modern accounts P. Preston, 'Spain's October Revolution and the Rightist Grasp for Power', in *Journal of Contemporary History*, vol. 10, no. 4, 1975, and J. A. Sánchez y García, *La revolución de 1934 en Asturias* (1974).

The conspiracy that led to the outbreak of the Civil War is revealed in J. del Burgo, *Conspiración y guerra civil* (1970); in A. Lizarza Iribarren, *Memorias de la Conspiración* (1952) and Felix Maïx, *Alzamiento en Espanña* (1952). Stanley Payne's *Falange, a History of Spanish Fascism* (1961) remains the standard work. J. A. Ansaldo *¿Para qué?* (1951) reveals the mind of the monarchist right.

For the history of labour movements see p. 787. In addition G. Mario de Coca, *Anti-Caballero* (1975) is what its title indicates. Largo Caballero's own 'memoirs' are disappointing: *Mis Recuerdos* (1953). Those of J. Maurín, especially *Hacía segunda revolución* (1935) represent an intelligent Marxist–Leninist analysis. For an exhaustive bibliography of contemporary accounts see P. Preston, *The Coming of the Spanish Civil War*, pp. 238–42. J. Brademas, *Anarco-sindicalismo y revolución en España* (1974) is useful for the C.N.T.; for the Socialists M. Cordero, *Los socialistas y la revolución* (1932) and G. Picard Moch and J. Moch, *L'Espagne republicaine* (1936) are still indispensable.

12. THE CIVIL WAR

The bibliography of the Civil War threatens to become unmanageable. Its extent can be sensed in Hugh Thomas's standard work *The Spanish Civil War* (Pelican ediction, 1965), pp. 992–1041. See also Ricardo de la Cierva and V. Palacio Atard on p. 783. For a view from the left see P. Broué and E. Temime, *The Revolution and the Civil War in Spain* (1972); from the right, the work of D. Sevilla Andrés, *Historia política de la zona roza* is still useful. Ricardo de la Cierva's *Historia ilustrado de la guerra civil española* (1971) reflects the more moderate tone of latter-day Francoism.

Here I give only those works which I found particularly illuminating. Ian Gibson's *The Death of García Lorca* (1973) gives the flavour of the early days in Granada, as does J. Ma Fontana's *Los catalanes en la guerra de España* (1951) for Barcelona.

The best guide to military operations is to be found in the campaign histories of J. M. Martínez Bande, published from 1968 onwards. Ramón Salas's huge four-volume *Historia del Ejercito Popular* (4 vols., 1973) contains a mass of information on the Republican armies. R. Carr, *The Spanish Tragedy* (1978) is analytical rather than chronological. Burnett Bolloten's earlier study on the role of the Communist party has been reissued as *The Spanish Revolution* (1979). D. Catell's *Communism and the Spanish Civil War* (1955) remains useful. Ronald Fraser's *The Blood of Spain* (1979) is an oral history of the war, concentrating on the proletarian parties. For the role of the C.N.T. see J. Peirats, *La C.N.T. y la revolución española* (1971), and for the P.O.U.M. the many works of V. Alba (a former P.O.U.M. militant), especially *El Marxismo en España* (1970) and *Historia del P.O.U.M.* (2 vols., 1974). V. Ramos, *La Guerra Civil en la provincia de Alicante* (3 vols., 1972) is an ill-ordered but revealing description of the war at the local level.

For the origins of German intervention see A. Viñas, *La Alemania nazi y el 18 Julio* (1974) and for the British attitude J. Edwards, *The British Government and the Spanish Civil War 1936–1939* (1979). Italian intervention is fully described in J. F. Coverdale, *Italian Intervention* in the Spanish Civil War (1975). For French policy see D. Wingate Pike, *Les Français et la guerre d'Espagne* (1975).

Collectivization is defended in N. Chomsky, *American Power and the New Mandarins* (1939), pp. 62–129. Alberto Pérez Baró, *Trenta meses de colectivisme a Catalunya* (1970), considers the legislation and its effects on reality; J. Bricall, *Política económica de la Generalidad* (1970) gives production figures. On agrarian collectives see R. Fraser, op. cit., pp. 347 ff. and H. Thomas in R. Carr, ed., *The Republic and the Civil War in Spain* (1971). For the dilemmas of the C.N.T. see C. M. Lorenzo, *Les Anarchistes espagnols et le pouvoir* (1961).

For the politics of Nationalist Spain, M. García Venero, *Falange en la Guerra de España* (1967) and M. Hedilla's *Testimonio* (1972) together give the Falangist version of unification. Stanley Payne, *Falange* (1961) is a history of the movement; both R. Serrano Suñer, *Entre el silencio y la propaganda* (1979) and Dionisio Ridruejo, *Casi unas memorias* (1976) are the memoirs of disillusioned enthusiasts. The general atmosphere is described in R. Abella, *La vida cotidiana durante la guerra civil*, i (1973), and J. del Burgo, *Conspiración y guerra civil* (1970).

For the fate of the exiles see L. Stein's moving *Beyond Death and Exile* (1979), P. W. Fagen, *Exiles and Citizens: Spanish Republicans in Mexico* (1973), and D. Wingate Pike, *Vae Victis* (1969).

Among the host of eye-witness accounts the best are H. E. Kaminski, *Ceux de Barcelone* (1937), George Orwell's classic *Homage to Catalonia* (1938), and F. Borkenau, *The Spanish Cockpit* (1937). For the Basque campaign there is a sympathetic account in G. L. Steer, *The Tree of Guernika* (1938). H. Southward's *The Day Guernica Died* (1977) is a definitive account of the bombing of Guernica.

For the Catalan collapse see V. Rojo, *Alerta los pueblos* (1939). For the Madrid rising S. Casado's own version is in his *The Last Days of Madrid* (1939) and there is a detailed account in J. M. Martínez Bande, *Los cien ultimos dias de la República* (1973). The Cartagena 'mutiny' is described in detail in L. Romero, *Desastre en Cartagena* (1971). The latest and best study of the International Brigades is A. Castells, *Las Brigadas Internacionales de la Guerra de España* (1974). For a Communist view see Luigi Longo, *Le Brigate Internationali in Spagna* (1956).

13. FRANCOISM

The Franco period with emphasis on the social and economic transformations is treated in R. Carr and J. P. Fusi, *Spain: Dictatorship to Democracy* (1979); R. de la Cierva's *Historia del Franquismo* (1975) provides a detailed history. R. Tamames, *La República: La era de Franco* (1973) is a remarkable instance of criticism of the régime while it still existed. J. A. Biescas and M. Tuñon de Lara, *España bajo la dictadura franquista 1939–1975* (1980) emphasizes the role of the opposition and the economic changes; Shlomo Ben-Ami, *La revolución desde arriba* (1980) provides a good general survey. The institutions of Francoism are dissected in K. N. Medhurst, *Government in Spain: The Executive at Work* (1973) and J. Amodia, *Franco's Political Legacy* (1977).

A prejudiced if vivid portrait of the Caudillo emerges from *Mis conversaciones privadas con Franco* (1976) by Lt.-Gen. Francisco Franco Salgado-Araujo; for the views of Spaniards on Franco and his régime see J. M. Gironella and R. Borràs, *100 Españoles y Franco* (1979). Franco's political utterances have been arranged thematically in *Pensamiento poplítico de Franco*, ed. A. del Río Cisneros (2 vols., 1975).

A. López Pina and E. Aranguren's *La cultura política de la España de Franco* (1970) is a penetrating summary of recent work. For the opposition see X. Tusell, *La oposición democrática al Franquismo* (1977), Guy Hermet, *The Communists in Spain* (1974), and P. Preston, ed., *Spain in Crisis* (1976). For a violent attack on the leadership by the dissident Jorge Semprun see his *Autobiografía de Federico Sánchez* (1977) and the articles of Claudin. For ETA, from the inside, see 'Ortzi', *Historia de Euzkadi: el nacionalismo vasco y ETA* (1975) and J. Aguirre, *Operation Ogro* (1975). For Catalonia see above p. 795.

J. M. Maravall has written two important works on student and working-class opposition, *El desarollo económico y la clase obrera* (1970) and *Dictatorship and Political Dissent* (1978). J. Amsden describes the working of the official trade unions in *Collective Bargaining and Class Struggle in Spain* (1972). C. W. Anderson, *The Political Economy of Modern Spain* (1970), and J. Clavera, J. M. Esteban, *et al.*, *Capitalismo español* (2 vols., 1973), discuss the changes in economic policy. R. Gunther, *Public Policy in a No-Party State* (1980) is an analysis of the budget to cast a light on the priorities of declining Francoism; M.-J. González, *La economía política del Franquismo 1940–70* (1979) is a good study of the changes in economic policy under Francoism. The post-war atmosphere is recreated in R. Abella, *Por el imperio hacia Dios* (1979).

For hostile accounts of Catholic attitudes to Franco see A. Sáez Alba, *La A.C.N.P. y el caso de 'El correo de Andalucia'* (1974) and Daniel Artigues, *El Opus Dei en España* (1968). For the cultural history of

Francoism see the works listed in Carr and Fusi, op. cit., pp. 263–6.

A first attempt to analyse the social composition of the army was made by Julio Busquets in his *El militar de carrera en España* (1971).

For the changes in Spanish society under Franco see A. de Miguel, *Manual de Estructura· social de España* (1974) and his *Sociología del Franquismo* (1975); Carlos Moya, *El poder económico en España* (n.d.) is a suggestive analysis of the economic élite and V. Pérez Díaz, *Pueblos y clases socialies en el campo español* (1974), of the rural scene. There is a great deal of raw information in *La España de los años 70*, ed. M. Fraga; in *Informe sociológico sobre la situación social de España*, published by the F.O.E.S.S.A. foundation in 1970, and in *Comentario sociológico. Estructura social de España*, published in 1978 by the Cajas de Ahorros. For an illuminating study of some aspects of modernization see Ronald Fraser, *The Pueblo* (1973).

14. NOVELS AND TRAVELS

When orthodox sources are mute, novels and travel books become of special value. In the case of travel books, this is particularly true of the late eighteenth century (see p. 000) and of the earlier nineteenth century (Widdrington, Ford, and, above all, George Borrow's strange masterpiece *The Bible in Spain*). Later in the century the tradition weakens until revived by Gerald Brenan and V. S. Pritchett.

The value of novels to the historian is frequently in inverse proportion to their literary merit: bad novels often make good sources. Historical novels as such are not to be trusted except in so far as they embody some traditional interpretation current at the time of their composition. Thus the *Episodios nacionales* of Galdós become more useful the later the period they describe; nevertheless, for the historian, his non-historical novels often give a fine picture of Spanish society, especially of middle-class life and of the strains and stresses produced by the challenge of 'modern' ideas in a traditional religious society. Clarín's *La Regenta* is superior as a description of Restoration provincial society. Of more recent novelists Pío Baroja is a most sensitive observer; his *Aurora roja* contains an excellent description of revolutionary attitudes. Many novels illuminate the crisis which began in 1931; beside the well-known works of Arturo Barea, André Malraux, Ramón Sender, and Georges Bernanos, Augustín Conde de Foxa's *Madrid de Corte a Cheka* (1938) is an impressionistic account of the atmosphere in the capital; J. M. Gironella's *Los cipreses creen en Dios* (1953) is a reconstruction of conflicts in a Catalan town.

Gironella's *Ha estallido la paz* continues the saga in the early years of Francoism. F. Umbral's *Memorias de un niño de derechas* (1972) and C. Barral's *Años de penitencia* (1975) are more sensitive descriptions of the same dismal period also revealed in Carmen Laforet's prize-winning *Nada* (1945). The classic novel of *tremendismo* is J. Ma Cela's *La familia de Pascual Duarte* (1942); Socialist realism can be sampled in López Pacheco's *Central Eléctrica.* Two fine novelists are Miguel Delibes and R. Sánchez-Ferlosio. J. Marsé's *Ultimas tardes con Teresa* (1966) is revealing of Catalan attitudes to Andalusian immigrants.

BIBLIOGRAPHICAL INDEX

References are to first citations, where the name of the author, full title, and place of publication will be found.

The Bibliography excludes archives, newspapers, and such sources as the Parliamentary Papers and the Cortes debates.

GENERAL INDEX

Centuries are represented by roman small capitals: XIX, & c.